W9-DCM-383

Born This Day

SECOND EDITION

ALSO BY ROBERT A. NOWLAN

A Dictionary of Quotations in Mathematics (2002)

ALSO BY ROBERT A. NOWLAN
AND GWENDOLYN NOWLAN

The Films of the Eighties: A Complete, Qualitative Filmography to Over 3400 Feature-Length English Language Films ... (1991, paperback 2006)

The Films of the Nineties: A Complete, Qualitative Filmography of Over 3000 Feature-Length English Language Films ... (2001)

A Dictionary of Quotations and Proverbs About Cats and Dogs (2001)

A Dictionary of Quotations About Communication (2000)

Cinema Sequels and Remakes, 1903–1987 (1989, paperback 2000)

Film Quotations: 11,000 Lines Spoken on Screen, Arranged by Subject, and Indexed (1994)

ALL FROM MCFARLAND

Born This Day

A Book of Birthdays and Quotations of Prominent People Through the Centuries

Second Edition

ROBERT A. NOWLAN

McFarland & Company, Inc., Publishers
Jefferson, North Carolina, and London

Library of Congress Cataloguing-in-Publication Data

Nowlan, Robert A.
Born this day : a book of birthdays and quotations of prominent people through the centuries / Robert A. Nowlan.— 2nd ed.
p. cm.
Includes index.

ISBN-13: 978-0-7864-2935-6
illustrated case binding : 50# alkaline paper ♾

1. Quotations, English. 2. Birthday books.
3. Literary calendars. I. Title.
PN6084.B5N69 2007 082—dc22 2007003809

British Library cataloguing data are available

Cover art: Todos a la plaza con Fidel, 28 de septiembre *(Library of Congress)*

Manufactured in the United States of America

McFarland & Company, Inc., Publishers
Box 611, Jefferson, North Carolina 28640
www.mcfarlandpub.com

To my wife, Wendy

"Grow old along with me!
The best is yet to be."
— Robert Browning, "Rabbi Ben Ezra" (1864)

Acknowledgments

Many thanks to all who read the first edition of *Born This Day* and made suggestions for additional individuals and quotations to include in the revised edition. Included in this number are my children and their spouses: Robert and Andy, Philip and Chrystal, Edward and Amy, Jennifer and Peter Golanski, Evan and Brenda, Andrew and Melanie. In addition, there is an ever growing number of grandchildren: Ally, Tommy, John, Cate, Lawson, Pierce, Owen, and Elliot. Also I thank my sister Mary, my brothers Michael, Steve, and Danny, and my brother-in-law Steve Johnson and their families. Special thanks goes to Isabella Anna for her understanding, loyalty and confidence.

Since the publication of the first edition, many people who have long been very important to me have been called to their eternal rest. Among them are Michael Adanti, Grace Kelly, Ray Lawson, Ed Schoonmaker, Pete Shields, my sister "Marty" Johnson — as ideal a human being as anyone could aspire to become — and my father, Robert A. Nowlan, Sr., a wise and gentle man, reunited at last with my beloved mother, Marian Shields Nowlan.

Contents

Preface to the Second Edition

Quotations help us remember the simple yet profound truths that give life perspective and meaning. When it comes to life's most important lessons, we can all use gentle reminders — Chriswell Freeman

Life is like quotations. Sometimes, it makes you laugh. Sometimes, it makes you cry. Most of the time, you don't get it. — Anonymous

It is a good thing for an uneducated man to read books of quotations. The quotations, when engraved upon the memory, give you good thoughts. They also make you anxious to read the authors and look for more. — Winston Churchill

Quotations (such as have point and lack triteness) from the great old authors are an act of reverence on the part of the quoter, and a blessing to a public grown superficial and external. — Louise Imogen Guiney

Numerous sources list people born on a particular day. Others provide capsule biographies of prominent people. There are also many books of quotations containing the wit and wisdom of individuals from across the centuries on innumerable topics.

Born This Day is a reference book that offers all three. It answers these three questions among others: Which prominent people share your birthday? What makes them prominent? What is some memorable thing they have said?

This second edition of *Born This Day* is revised and expanded. For each day of a 366-day year, the book lists twelve individuals who share the day as the anniversary of their birth. Capsule descriptions of the twelve individuals are provided along with a quotation from each that is meant not only to instruct and perhaps entertain readers but also to provide a bit of insight into the nature of the speaker.

In addition, for each day of the year, a section called *Others* provides another dozen or more people who share the birthday. The description of these individuals is limited to a few words, identifying their home country and their profession, and no quotations are provided.

The choice of individuals for each day of the year has been made with the intention of providing an interesting mix of people who share a particular birthday — representatives of both sexes from numerous centuries, from all the nations of the world, with assorted vocations and avocations, with conflicting social, political, religious and philosophical backgrounds, the good and the bad, the loved and the hated, the movers and shakers, the makers of beauty and the entertainers. In the final analysis those chosen for capsule descriptions are those who seem to be the most quotable.

Some of those chosen for a particular

day have had quite a lot to say, and choosing among their many memorable observations came down to a personal preference at the moment the quotation was chosen. There can be no formula for picking the ideal quotation when the goal is not to concentrate on particular topics but to have as many subjects as possible addressed somewhere in the work. I have been a collector of quotations for many years and my files contain tens of thousands of them on almost every conceivable topic. The quotations that mean the most to me are from men and women across the centuries who speak to me in a most profound way and demand that I think about what has been said and how it challenges or confirms my beliefs. I hope that readers will find thought provoking the choices I have made.

Many of the individuals who were chosen for the first edition remain in the revision. However, their capsule descriptions have been updated where necessary and in most cases a new quotation has been chosen. Some individuals have been "demoted" to the *Others* category or eliminated completely. The decision to do so is based on whether other individuals who share the birthday have something more interesting to say. Some of the quotations are outrageous and detestable, but are included despite their messages. Individuals who hold beliefs that most people despise cannot be ignored. Even observations with which we vehemently disagree can make us think and that is certainly one of the criteria for judging the worth of a quotation.

One caveat is that for certain individuals there is no common agreement as to the birthdays. Often this confusion can be traced to faulty record-keeping at the time of the birth. Other discrepancies are due to the conversion from the Julian calendar to the Gregorian calendar. The latter, now in general use, was introduced by Pope Gregory XIII in 1582. By Julian reckoning the solar year comprised 365¼ days. To deal with the fraction, a "Leap day" was introduced every fourth year to maintain correspondence between the calendar and the seasons. However, a slight miscalculation in the solar year caused the calendar dates to regress by about one day per century. By the time of Gregory, the Julian calendar was about 10 days out of sync with the seasons. To deal with this problem, ten days were dropped, making October 5 into October 15. The Gregorian calendar also tinkered with the leap year so that no century year is a leap year unless it is divisible by 4000, among other refinements. As a result someone like Sir Isaac Newton, who always believed he was born on December 25, 1642 (by the Julian calendar), is regarded as having been born on January 4, 1643 (by the Gregorian calendar). Some sources give Newton's birthday according to the old system and others according to the new system. In some cases, I have given the birthdays of individuals according to the Julian calendar, and in others according to the Gregorian calendar, depending upon how most respectable sources handle the situation.

The individuals chosen for each day of the year have influences on the world that range from great to minor. The authors of the quotations are meant to represent as much of the world and its history as possible given the restrictions of space. Unfortunately, some worthy individuals were born without record as to a specific date. On the other hand a number of prominent individuals who made important contributions to the progress of civilization seem to have had very little to say that could set us thinking. Readers may thus look in vain for some favorite people and quotations — and I acknowledge that those favorites have value as do the individuals and words listed here.

I hope readers will enjoy the entries and the quotations as much as I have in collecting them. It's been great fun. — R.A.N.

Birthdays

January 1

1449 **Lorenzo de Medici:** Statesman and autocratic ruler of Florence, known as "the Magnificent." A lyric poet, he was described by Macchiavelli as "the greatest patron of literature and art that any prince had ever been." Used the family wealth to patronize many artists, including Sandro Botticelli, Leonardo da Vinci and Michelangelo. His policies bankrupted the Medici bank, but the political power of the family endured. Grandson of Cosmo de Medici and the most brilliant of the family. His 13-year-old son Giovanni was created a cardinal by Pope Innocent VIII and later became pope as Leo X.

Whoever wants to be happy let him be so, about tomorrow there is no knowing.

1767 **Maria Edgeworth:** British-Irish children's writer of Irish life and moral tales. Her early stories, published in *The Parent's Assistant*, featured the first convincing child character since the work of Shakespeare. Author of the familiar saying: "Jack of all trades and master of none." Novels: *Castle Rackrent, Belinda, Tales of Fashionable Life,* and *The Absentee,* which focused attention on abuses of absent English landowners.

Some people talk of morality, and some of religion, but give me a little smug propriety.

1819 **Arthur Hugh Clough:** English poet who wrote pastoral works. Espoused progressive social views and disliked class distinctions. Especially remembered for his longer poems. His experimental techniques in his "long vacation" poem "The Bothie of Tober-na-Vuolich," the tale of a student reading party in Scotland, were received with both delight and outrage. "Amours de Voyage," an ironic narrative, concerning a traveler's spiritual crises in Rome, was published posthumously.

Thou shalt have one God only; who would be at the expense of two?

1839 **Ouida:** Pseudonym of **Maria Louise de la Rame:** English novelist whose pen-name is a childish mispronunciation of Louise. She wrote almost 50 books set in a fashionable world far removed from reality, including *Held in Bondage* and *Strathmore.* Her work showed a rebellion against moral ideals found in most fiction of the time. When her royalties dried up, she fell into debt and lived the last part of her life in destitution.

The longest absence is less perilous to love than the terrible trials of incessant proximity.

1863 Baron **Pierre de Coubertin:** French aristocrat and educator who conceived of an international competition to promote athletes. To this end he organized an international congress in Paris in 1894, where he proposed to reinstate the ancient Olympic Games. The first modern Olympic Games were held in Athens, Greece in 1896 with athletes from 12 nations participating in such events as gymnastics, cycling, fencing, lawn tennis, shooting, swimming, weightlifting and wrestling. His creed has become that of the Games.

The most important thing in the Olympic Games is not winning, but taking part; the essential thing in life is not conquering, but fighting well.

1864 **Alfred Stieglitz:** American photographer, critic and gallery director. With Edward Steichen founded the American Photo-Secession Group. Stieglitz influenced the development of photography, particularly pictorialist photography, as an art form in 20th century America. He established and edited the magazines *Camera Notes* (1897–1902) and *Camera Work* (1903–1917). Directed the Little Galleries of the Photo-Secession (1905–1917) in New York.

Photography is my passion, the search for truth my obsession.

1879 **E.M. [Edward Morgan] Forster:** English novelist and literary critic. Member of the Bloomsbury Group. Many of his novels have been adapted to very successful movies, including *A Passage to India, A Room with a View, Howards End. Maurice*, which dealt with homosexual themes, was published posthumously, although it was written in 1914. Also wrote volumes of essays, short stories and collaborated on the libretto of Benjamin Britten's opera *Billy Budd.*

Death destroys a man: the idea of Death saves him.

1895 **J. Edgar Hoover:** Became director of the FBI in 1924, which he remodeled into a more efficient crime fighting agency. Between the world wars he campaigned against gangster rackets and after World War II, he pursued Communist sympathizers. He was accused of abusing his position in his spying on liberal activists. When he died, President Nixon ordered a full state funeral. The *New York Times* wrote: "For nearly a half century, J. Edgar Hoover and the FBI were indistinguishable. That at once was his strength and its weakness...."

Justice is merely incidental to law and order.

1897 **Catherine Drinker Bowen:** U.S. historian, biographer and essayist. Among her works is *Miracle at Philadelphia*, a classic history of the Federal Convention at Philadelphia in 1787 that produced the Constitution of the United States. She also wrote the best-selling *John Adams and the American Revolution*.

Great artists treasure their time with a bitter and snarling miserliness.

1909 **Barry Goldwater:** Conservative U.S. senator from Arizona (1952–64, 1969–87). Unsuccessful Republican presidential candidate (1964) largely doomed because of charges that his call for a harsh diplomatic stance against the Soviet Union might lead to war. An architect of the conservative revival in the Republican Party. Author of *The Conscience of a Conservative*. Later his views moderated and he became the model of high-minded conservatism.

A government that is big enough to give you all you want is big enough to take it all away.

1912 **Harold "Kim" Philby (Harold Adrian Russell Philby):** Born in India, he became a Communist while studying at Cambridge. Recruited as a Soviet agent even before he took a position with the British Secret Intelligence Service. As a top liaison officer between England the U.S., he revealed top-secret information to the Soviets. In 1963 the most successful double agent during the Cold War fled to Russia, where he was granted citizenship.

To betray, you must first belong.

1919 **J.D. [Jerome David] Salinger:** U.S. novelist and short-story writer. His novel *The Catcher in the Rye*, the story of precocious Holden Caulfield, still sells some 250,000 copies annually. Other works: *Franny and Zooey* and *Raise High the Roof Beam, Carpenters*. Retreated into seclusion in New Hampshire. A 1998 memoir by a woman with whom he had a relationship when she was 19, brought him unwanted notoriety.

I keep picturing all these little kids in this big field of rye.... If they're running and they don't look where they're going I have to come out from somewhere and catch them.

OTHERS: 1484 Protestant reformer **Huldreich Zwingli**, 1735 American patriot **Paul Revere**, 1745 American Military Officer **Anthony Wayne**, 1854 Scottish anthropologist **Sir James Frazer**, 1873 Mexican novelist **Mariano Azuela**, 1879 U.S. film producer **William Fox**, 1900 Latin bandleader **Xavier Cugat**, 1911 American baseball Hall-of-Famer **Hank Greenberg**, 1913 U.S. economist **Eliot Janeway**, 1923 Senegalese filmmaker **Ousmane Sembeue**, 1925 Ugandan dictator **Idi Amin**, 1933 English playwright **Joe Orton**, 1942 U.S. singer **"Country" Joe McDonald**, 1961 U.S. actress **Marcia Cross**

January 2

1752 **Philip Morin Freneau:** American sailor, poet, journalist, and rebel. Known as the "poet of the American Revolution." When the revolution began, he wrote anti–British satire. Commanded a privateer in the Revolutionary War. Captured by the British. He wrote *The British Prison Ship*, while a prisoner. Edited the *National Gazette*. Often called the first American professional journalist.

Tobacco surely was designed/ To poison and destroy mankind.

1858 **Beatrice Potter Webb:** British social reformer, historian and economist. Sought to discover the root causes of poverty. With her husband Sidney James Webb, she spent a life devoted to Socialism and trade unionism. Together they established the London School of Economics and Political Science (1895). Their published works include the classics *History of Trade Unionism* and *English Local Governments*. Most of the reforms of the time were a result of their research and insight. After a visit to the Soviet Union, they were impressed enough to write *Soviet Communism: A New Civilization?*

Religion is love; in no case is it logic.

1857 **Martha Carey Thomas:** American educator and author, who helped create high standards in women's education. Organizer of Bryn Mawr College in 1884. Dean and professor of English (1885–94). President (1894–1922). Established summer schools for women working in industry. Dedicated suffragist, she was the first President of the National College Women's Equal Suffrage League (1908). Author of *The Higher Education of Women*.

Women are one-half of the world but until a century ago ... it was a man's world.... The man's world must become a man's and woman's world.

1865 **W. Lyon Phelps:** American educator and author. Taught 41 years at Yale and was instrumental in popularizing the teaching of contemporary literature. Introduced Russian novelists to American readers, with *Essays on Russian Novelists*. Also wrote *Way of All Flesh, The Advance of English Poetry in the 20th Century, Essays on Modern Novelists* and *Some Makers of American Literature*.

If happiness truly consisted in physical ease and freedom from care, the happiest individual would not be either a man or a woman; but an American cow.

1894 **Robert Nathan:** U.S. novelist and screenwriter. During the 1930s, his output and success grew exponentially, with a string of popular novels and anthologies of his poems. Wrote screenplays for MGM in the 1940s. His most popular books *Portrait of Jennie, One More Spring, The Enchanted Voyage* (filmed as *Wake Up and Dream*) and *The Bishop's Wife* were made into highly successful films.

There is no distance on this earth as far away as yesterday.

1895 Count **Folke Bernadotte:** Swedish humanitarian and diplomat. Nephew of King Gustav V.

Headed the Swedish Red Cross in World War II. Credited with saving some 20,000 concentration camp inmates. Acted as a mediator in both world wars. Representing the United Nations he drafted a partition plan in Palestine but was assassinated by Jewish terrorists when he proposed that Arab refugees be allowed to return to their homes in what had become Israel.

No settlement can be just and complete if recognition is not accorded to the Arab refugee to return to his home.

1903 **Sally Rand:** Originally **Helen Gould Beck**. American fan- and belly-dancer. Joined the circus as a teen as an acrobat, later moving to Hollywood where she appeared in a number of silent films. Gained notoriety as an exotic dancer at Chicago's World Fair (1933), performing nude dances to the melodies of Chopin and Debussy using only large ostrich fans. Her arrest for giving an "obscene performance" only made her more popular and in demand at fairs and expositions across the country. Plied her trade on stage and in clubs into her seventies.

I haven't been out of work since the day I took my pants off.

1915 **John Hope Franklin:** American historian, educator and author. First African-American president of the American Historical Association (1978–79). Wrote: *From Slavery to Freedom: A History of American Negroes* and *Land of the Free*. Helped design the legal brief that led to the landmark Brown vs. Board of Education decision. Awarded the Presidential Medal of Freedom in 1995.

One feels the excitement of hearing an untold story.

1920 **Isaac Asimov:** Prolific Russian-born U.S. writer of over 300 books. Taught for many years at Boston University. Called the "father of modern science fiction." His story "Nightfall" has often been called the "finest science fiction short story ever written." He was also a biochemist. Coined the term "robotics." Novels include *Foundation, The Caves of Steel, The Naked Sun* and *I, Robot*.

People who think they know everything are a great annoyance to those of us who do.

1932 **Jean Flora Little:** Canadian children's writer, who has always been severely visually impaired. She uses a special "talking" computer in her writing. Her books, which include *Anna, Hey World, Here I Am!* and *Mine for Keeps* are humorous and poignant descriptions of living with a disability. A recurring character in her books is eight-grader Kate Bloomfield, who offers her thoughts on life. Little has two seeing-eye dogs, Ritz and Pippa.

The only food he has ever stolen has been down on a coffee table. He claims that he genuinely believed it to be a table meant for dogs.

1939 **Jim Bakker:** American televangelist and Assemblies of God preacher. With his ex-wife Tammy Faye Bakker, he was the host of *The PTL Club* (acronym for "Praise the Lord"). He resigned in 1987 after a sex scandal and served an 8-year prison sentence for funneling $265,000 to church secretary Jessica Hahn to cover up their adulterous affair. It is estimated that the Bakker's squandering millions of their ministry's donations on luxury cars and six mansions. At the time of his arrest, there were 47 separate bank accounts in his name.

But when you come to Heritage USA, remember to bring your Bible and your Visa card— because the Bible is the Holy Truth, and God doesn't take American Express.

1956 **Lynda Barry:** Successful non-mainstream American cartoonist. Best known for her weekly comic *Ernie Pook's Comeek*. Her cartoons often reflect family life from the prospective of adolescent girls from the wrong side of the tracks. Her work depicts life as harsh but now and then joyful. They address themes of intolerance and psychic pain. One is as likely to cry as to laugh reading her works. Her musical play *The Good Times Are Killing Me* appeared off–Broadway.

Love is an exploding cigar we willingly smoke.

OTHERS: 1400 Venetian printer **Nicolas Jonson**, 1642 Sultan of Turkey **Mehmed IV**, 1647 American colonial leader **Nathaniel Bacon**, 1727 British general **James Wolfe**, 1822 German physicist **Rudolph Clausius**, 1831 U.S. Historian **Justin Windsor**, 1856 U.S. editor **Edward S. Morton**, 1857 U.S. cartoonist **Fredrick Opper**, 1866 Australian-born classical scholar, **Gilbert Murray**, 1901 Founding member of the Wilderness Society **Robert Marshall**, 1904 U.S. opera tenor **James Melton**, 1928 U.S. congressman **Daniel Rostenkowski**, 1930 American singer **Julius LaRosa**, 1936 U.S. songwriter and singer **Roger Miller**, 1969 U.S. model **Christie Turlington**, 1976 Spanish actress **Paz Vega**

January 3

106 BCE **Cicero [Marcus Tullius]:** Roman statesman, orator and philosopher. Sought a political career, attaining the consulship in 63 BCE. Great master of Latin prose and his letter writing provide a picture of contemporary Roman life. Sided with Pompey in the civil war (49–48 BCE) but was pardoned by Julius Caesar. After Caesar's assassination, he supported Octavian and violently attacked Mark Antony in speeches known as the "Philippics." On the reconciliation of Antony and Octavian he was murdered by Antony's soldiers.

Wise men are instructed by reason; men of low understanding, by experience; the most ignorant, by necessity; the beasts, by nature.

1698 **Pietro Metastassio:** Penname of **Pietro Trapassi**. Roman-born poet, who had a gift for versifying. Became the leading librettist of his day. Created 18th-century Italian *opera seria* (serious opera). Gained his reputation for his masque *The Garden of Hesperides*. Wrote the libretti for 27 operas, including Mozart's *Clemenza di Tito*. Became court poet in Vienna in 1729.

The bee and the serpent often sip from the selfsame flower.

1793 **Lucretia Coffin Mott:** American abolitionist, feminist, reformer and Quaker minister. Made her home a sanctuary for runaway slaves. With Elizabeth Stanton organized the first women's rights convention (1848), a major factor in the feminist movement in the U.S. Denied membership in the World Anti-Slavery Convention in London despite having organized and served as president of the Philadelphia women's group of the anti–Slavery movement in the U.S. In 1841, her husband James Mott published *Three Months in Great Britain* describing their ill-fated mission. After the Civil War she worked for voting rights for freedmen.

We too often bind ourselves by authorities rather than by the truth.

1803 **Douglas William Jerrold:** English wit, dramatist and journalist. An original contributor to *Punch*, using the pseudonym "Q." Editor of several magazines and newspapers. Novels: *The Story of a Feather* and *Mrs. Caudle's Curtain Lectures.* His topical and extremely popular play, *Black-Eyed Susan*, consisted of various extreme stereotypes representing the forces of good, evil, the innocent, the corrupt, the poor and the rich, woven into a serious plot with comic sub-plots.

Honest bread is very well— it's the butter that makes the temptation.

1883 **Earl Clement Attlee:** English political leader. Committed to social reform, he was elected to Parliament in 1922. Served in several Labor governments and in the wartime coalition government of Winston Churchill, whom he succeeded as prime minister in 1945. As Labor prime minister, he led England into welfare state (1945–51), introducing the National Health Service. Nationalized of major British industries and championed granting independence to India, a major step in converting the British Empire into the Commonwealth of Nations.

Democracy means government by discussion, but it is only effective if you can stop people talking.

1884 **E. Stanley Jones:** Eminent Methodist missionary and theologian. Concerned equally for social justice and spirituality. Chiefly remembered for his work in India, where he supported Indian aspirations for independence, and was sensitive to Indian religious traditions. Books: *The Christ of the Indian Road* and *A Song of Ascents: A Spiritual Autobiography*. Founder of the Christian Ashram movement.

We grow small trying to be great.

1886 **Josephine Hull:** Born **Josephine Sherwood**. Celebrated American stage character actress, who appeared in only a handful of films but made a lasting mark for her delightful performances in the comedies *Arsenic and Old Lace*, in which she is a dotty old poisoner of lonely old men and *Harvey*, as the sister of a man who has escaped reality through martinis and his friend, an invisible six-foot rabbit. She won and Academy Award for the latter.

Playing Shakespeare is so tiring. You never get to sit down unless you're a king.

1892 **J.R.R. [John Ronald Reuel] Tolkien:** English author and philologist. Professor of language and literature at Oxford. Scholarly works include studies of Chaucer and an edition of *Beowulf.* Best known for his fantasy stories *The Hobbit, The Lord of the Rings* and *The Silmarillion.* Honored by Tolkien societies and students groups, The Lord of the Rings was made into three tremendously successful films around the turn of the century.

It's the job that's never started as takes longest to finish.

1900 **Dorothy Arzner:** Former American film editor who became Hollywood's only woman director of the thirties. Also wrote a number of scripts, alone or in collaboration. Films directed: *Merrily We Go to Hell, Nana, Craig's Wife* and *Dance Girl Dance.* During World War II, she produced WAC training films. Taught film at the Pasadena Playhouse and UCLA, where among her students was Francis Ford Coppola. First woman member of the Director's Guild of America (1975).

It is my theory that if you have authority, know your business and know you have authority, you have the authority.

1909 **Victor Borge:** Originally **Borge Rosenbaum.** Witty Danish-born pianist, comedian and musical satirist. Made his concert debut in 1922, appeared in a musical revue and then began writing and directing shows, developing his style that combined humor with music. His philosophy is summed up in his observation, "Laughter is the shortest distance between two people." Emigrated to the U.S. in 1940, after Hitler put him on a list of enemies of the Fatherland for making anti–Nazi jokes. Became an American favorite through television appearances on "The Ed Sullivan Show." Famous for his "Phonetic Punctuation" routine, in which he recites a story, with full punctuation as onomatopoetic sounds.

I'd like to thank my parents for making this night possible. And my children for making it necessary.

1936 **Betty Rollin:** TV correspondent and author, formerly with NBC News. Now contributes reports for PBS. Among her six books is *First You Cry* about her breast cancer and mastectomy. It gave public awareness and encouragement to others facing the increasingly common disease. Her best-selling *Last Wish* deals with the suicide of her mother, terminally ill with ovarian cancer. Rollin assisted her mother in taking her life by obtaining pills from a doctor in Europe who supported voluntary euthanasia.

Scratch most feminists and underneath there is a woman who longs to be a sex object, the difference is that is not all she longs to be.

1945 **Stephen Stills:** American guitarist and singer/songwriter. Best known for his work with the groups "Buffalo Springfield" and "Crosby, Stills, Nash & Young." First person to be inducted into the Rock Hall of Fame twice in the same night for his work with the two groups. His biggest solo hits: "Love the One You're With," "Black Queen" and "Change Partners."

One thing the blues ain't is funny.

OTHERS: 1835 U.S. sculptor **Larkin Goldsmith Mead,** 1840 Belgian missionary on Molokai, **Father Damien,**

1870 Australian novelist **Henry Handel Richardson**, 1885 U.S. rare books collector **Harry Elkins Widener**, 1888 English playwright **James Bridie**, 1891 Polish/Russian poet/author **Osip E. Mandelshtam**, 1897 U.S. Movie actress **Marion Davies**, 1901 Dictator/1st president of the Republic of Vietnam **Ngo Dinh Diem**, 1911 U.S. film director **John Sturges**, 1916 American consumer advocate **Betty Furness**, 1921 Italian director of "Spaghetti" westerns **Sergio Leone**, 1923 Football coach **Hank Stram**, 1939 Canadian hockey star **Bobby Hull**, 1956 U.S. film actor and director **Mel Gibson**

January 4

1581 **James Ussher:** Irish Bishop and biblical scholar. Distinguished not only for his learning but also by his charity. Calvinistic in theology and moderate in his ideas of church government. Loyal to the monarchy, but honored by Oliver Cromwell. His major work was the *Annals of the Old and New Testament* in which he gave a long-accepted chronology of the Scriptures.

Which beginning of time according to our chronology [i.e., Creation] fell upon the entrance of the night preceding the twenty-third day of October in the year of the Julian calendar 710 [4004 BCE].

1785 **Jacob Grimm:** German folklorist, philologist and lexicographer. Librarian to Jérôme Bonaparte, king of Westphalia, and published a work on the Meistersingers. Famous for his work in comparative philology with his brother Wilhelm. They are best known for *Grimm's Fairy Tales*, published in 1812. Jacob did most of the work on the definitive *German Dictionary* and his German Grammar is perhaps the greatest philological work of the age. Also wrote on German mythology and German usages in the Middle Ages and the old Teutonic superstitions.

When we consider the richness, good sense and strict economy of English none of the other living languages can be put beside it.

1813 **Isaac Pitman:** English schoolmaster and inventor of a shorthand system. First proposed it in *Stenographic Soundboard* in 1837. Established a Phonetic Institute for teaching shorthand in Bath in 1839 and opened a similar institution in London six years later. Vice-president of the Vegetarian Society and grandfather of Sir James Pitman, developer of the Initial Teaching Alphabet.

Well-arranged time is the surest mark of a well-arranged mind.

1858 **Carter Glass:** American Democratic politician and government official. U.S. Representative from Virginia (1902–19). U.S. Secretary of the Treasury (1918–20). U.S. Senator (1920–46). Helped draft the Federal Reserve Bank Act of 1913.As Senator his most notable achievement was an act, which separated the activities of banks and securities brokers and created FDIC insurance. Determined opponent of New Deal legislation.

A liberal is a man who is willing to spend somebody else's money.

1883 **Max Eastman:** American editor, poet, critic and social analyst. Founder of the Marxist magazine, *The Masses*, which was closed in 1918 under the Espionage Act, due to its frequent explicit denunciation of U.S. participation in World War I. In 1919, he founded a similar publication titles *The Liberator*, which ultimately was taken over by the Communist Party, when Eastman quit working for it. During the 1930s he wrote critiques of contemporary literature, publishing several controversial works in which he criticized modernist writers, who, he claimed, had fostered "the cult of unintelligibility." Best known for *The Enjoyment of Poetry*. Other Works: *The Sense of Humor, Since Lenin Died, Artists in Uniform, Heroes, I Have Known*, and *Seven Kinds of Goodness*.

It is the ability to take a joke, not make one, that holds society together.

1896 **Everett Dirksen:** American politician, dubbed "the Wizard of Ooze" by his colleagues. Representative from Illinois (1933–51), Senator (1951–69). Republican minority leader (1959–69). Supported New Deal domestic programs while championing an isolationist foreign policy. Delivered key Republican support for Civil Rights Acts. Remembered for his canny political skill, rumpled appearance, elaborate manners, resonant bass voice and convincing, if somewhat overblown, oratory. A leading "hawk" on Vietnam. Most remembered for the quip: "A billion here, a billion there, pretty soon, you're talking real money." One of his pet projects was to make the marigold the national flower.

Life is not a static thing. The only people who do not change their minds are incompetents in asylums, who can't are those in cemeteries.

1914 **Jane Wyman:** Born **Sarah Jane Fulks**. American film actress who appeared in B movies as a wisecracking dame before studios discovered she had acting ability. Turning point in her career was *The Lost Weekend* (1945). Nominated for an Academy Award for her performance in *The Yearling*. Won the Best Actress Oscar for *Johnny Belinda* in the title role of a def-mute rate victim. Received two additional Oscar nominations for the tearjerkers *The Blue Veil* and *Magnificent Obsession*. Her second of four husbands was Ronald Reagan, whom she married in 1940 and divorced in 1948.

The opportunity for brotherhood presents itself every time you meet a human being.

1922 **Phyllis Battelle:** National syndicated columnist. From 1955 to 1988 she wrote the weekly column "Assignment: America. Wrote a book on Karen Ann Quinlan, who lapsed in a persistent vegetative state after swallowing alcohol and Valium, remaining in a coma for almost 10 years. Battelle also wrote a five piece series on the Beatles.

A broken heart is what makes life so wonderful five years later. When you see the guy in an elevator and he is fat and smoking a cigar and saying long-time-no-see. If he hadn't broken your

heart, you couldn't have that glorious feeling of relief!

1930 **Don Shula:** Football coach with the Baltimore Colts, whom he led to seven straight winning seasons and later the Miami Dolphins, where in 26 years he only experienced two losing seasons. He led his NFL teams to 347 victories. Won Super Bowls VII and VIII. His 1972 Dolphin, with a record of 17–0, are the only team in NFL history to go an entire season undefeated. Before becoming a coach at age 33, he spent seven seasons as a defensive back and halfback with the Browns, Colts and Redskins.

Sure, luck means a lot in football. Not having a good quarterback is bad luck.

1935 **Floyd Patterson:** American boxer. Youngest of eleven children born into a poor North Carolina family. Experienced a troubled childhood. Spent time in a reform school, which he credits for turning his life around. Began boxing at age 14 and at 17 he won the Middleweight gold medal at the 1952 Olympics in Helsinki. Turned pro, steadily rising through the ranks. When Rocky Marciano retired, Patterson defeated Archie Moor for the World heavyweight championship 1956. Lost title to Ingemar Johannson (1959). First to regain crown by beating Johannson in a rematch. In retirement the two men became close friends.

The fighter loses more than his pride in the fight; he loses part of his future. He's a step closer to the slums he came from.

1941 **Maureen Reagan:** American political activist, radio talk show host, commentator and health care advocate. Daughter of Ronald Reagan and Jane Wyman. Co-wrote with Dorothy Hermann, *First Father, First Daughter: A Memoir*. After her father was diagnosed with Alzheimer's disease in 1994, she became a member of the Alzheimer's Association board of directors and served as the group's spokesman. Died of melanoma (skin cancer) in 2001.

I will feel equality has arrived when we can elect to office women who are just as incompetent as some of the men who are already there.

1965 **Julia Ormond:** Classically beautiful English actress with many stage and screen credits. In 1989 she won the London Drama Critics' Award for her performance in *Faith, Hope and Charity* as best newcomer. Became a star in the U.S. with her appearance with Brad Pitt in *Legends of the Fall*, followed by the remake of *Sabrina*, and *Smilla's Sense of Snow*. In 2001 she was nominated for a Laurence Olivier Theatre Award for Best Actress for her performance in *My Zinc Bed* at the Royal Court Theatre.

If you do anything for too long, it starts to lack edge, to become easy. Easy is the kiss of death.

OTHERS: 1780 American lawyer, a leader of the bar in the U.S. **Horace Binney**, 1789 American abolitionist **Benjamin Lundy**, 1809 Developer of a reading system for the blind, **Louis Braille**, 1813 Napoleon I's youngest brother, the **King of Holland Louis Bonaparte**, 1822 Italian tragic actress **Adelaide Ristori**, 1838 P.T. Barnum's **General Tom Thumb** (Charles Stratton) 1878 Welsh artist **Augustus Edwin John**, 1890 German Chief of Staff **Alfred G. Jodl**, 1905 U.S. voice actor **Sterling Holloway**, 1937 American mezzo-soprano **Grace Bumbry**, 1939 U.S. actress and widow of Cary Grant, **Dyan Cannon**, 1966 Country singer **Deanna Carter**

January 5

1767 **Jean Baptiste Say:** French political economist best known for his law of markets. Professor of industrial economics and of political economy. Disciple of Adam Smith, Say expounded the Scottish economist's views in *La Decade*, which he edited. Author of *A Treatise on Political Economy*. Best remembered for *Say's law*, which expounds the idea of supply creating its own demand.

It is the aim of good government to stimulate production, of bad government to encourage consumption.

1779 **Stephen Decatur:** American Naval commodore in the War of 1812. Considered the most conspicuous naval figure in the history of the United States for the 100 years between John Paul Jones and David Farragut. Served against the French and the war with Tripoli. Forced Algerian pirates to declare the American flag inviolable. Remembered for his famous toast:

Our country! In her intercourse with foreign nations, may she always be in the right; but our country, right or wrong.

1864 **George Washington Carver:** African-American chemist, noted for his research into the industrial uses of vegetables. Born a slave, he revolutionized Southern agriculture by advocating planting peanuts and sweet potatoes, which enrich the soil, to replace cotton and tobacco, which impoverishes it. Developed some 400 byproducts of peanuts and sweet potatoes. Founded the Carver Foundation for Research at Tuskegee Institute. Awarded the Spingarn medal in 1923.

When I was young, I said to God, "God, tell me the mystery of the universe." But God answered, "that knowledge is for me alone." So I said, "God, tell me the mystery of the peanut." Then God said, "Well, George, that's more nearly your size."

1876 **Konrad Adenauer:** German statesman and first chancellor of the Federal Republic of Germany (1949–63). Led West Germany's amazing economic recovery after World War II, on the basis of a partnership with other European nations through NATO and the European Customs Union. Studied to become a lawyer, and was elected mayor of Cologne in 1917. After World War I as an official in the Weimar government, he was dismissed from all offices by the Nazis and imprisoned in 1934 and again in 1944. After the war, for the second time he became mayor of the city of Cologne and formed the Christian Democratic Union.

We all live under the same sky, but we don't have the same horizon.

1882 **Herbert Bayard Swope:** American journalist. After graduation for high school, spent a year in Europe before going to work as a reporter for the *St. Louis Post-Dispatch.* Also worked for the *Chicago Tribune,* the *New York Herald* and *New York Morning Telegraph* before becoming a war correspondent for *New York World.* Executive editor (1920–29). Originated the op-ed page. First recipient of a Pulitzer Prize for Reporting (1917). Noted crusader. Credited with coining the phrase "Cold War."

I cannot give you the formula for success, but I can give you the formula for failure — which is: Try to please everybody.

1918 **Jeanne Dixon:** American astrologer, clairvoyant, alleged psychic and writer. Proponent of extra sensory perception (ESP). Makes yearly predictions. Claims her visions are messages from God. Made the questionable claim that she predicted the assassination of President Kennedy prior to the 1960 election.

Respect is what we owe; love is what we give.

1921 **Friedrich Dürrenmatt:** Swiss painter and writer. Turned from painting to writing. His plays, which showed the influence of Bertolt Brecht and the theater of the absurd, were central to the post World War II revival of German theater. Plays include *The Marriage of Mr. Mississippi,* which established his international reputation, *The Physicists, The Visit,* and *The Appointed Time.* Also wrote novels, short stories, critical essays and works for radio. His works have been translated into more than 50 languages.

What was once thought can never be unthought.

1928 **Zulfikar Ali Bhutto:** Pakistani statesman, president and premier. Founded and headed the Pakistan People's Party, which won the army-supervised elections in West Pakistan. His social and economic reforms angered the right-wing Islamic parties. Ousted by the military, led by General Zia ul-Haq, he was convicted of conspiracy to murder and was executed in 1979 despite worldwide protests and appeals for clemency. Later his daughter Benazir Bhutto would become Pakistani prime minister.

Pakistan was once called the most allied of all of the United States. We are not the most nonallied.

1928 **Walter F. Mondale:** American politician, vice-president, and unsuccessful presidential candidate. Made his reputation as a local Democrat in his home state of Minnesota. Served in the U.S. Senate (1964–76). Jimmy Carter's running mate in the 1976 presidential election, but the two failed to be reelected four years later. After a crushing defeat to Ronald Reagan for the presidency in 1984 he retired from national politics to resume his law practice.

Political image is like mixing cement. When it's wet, you can move it around and shape it, but as some point it hardens and there's almost nothing you can do to reshape it.

1931 **Alvin Ailey:** African-American dancer and choreographer. Trained with Martha Graham. Formed the Alvin Ailey American Dance Theatre (1958), a popular multiracial modern dance ensemble. Most famous dance: "Revelations," a celebratory study of religious spirit set to black spirituals. From the 1960s to 80s, his company toured worldwide, marking him as one of the best known American choreographers. After his death of AIDs in 1989, dancer Judith Jamison assumed the title of artistic director of the company.

I think the people come to the theater to look at themselves. I try to hold up the mirror.

1932 **Umberto Eco:** Italian novelist, critic and semiotician. Explored the ideas of communication and semiotics in *The Open Work, A Theory of Semiotics, Semiotics and the Philosophy of Language* and *The Limits of Interpretation.* In his novels he has a "taste and passion for the Middle Ages." Best known work: *The Name of the Rose,* the story of an English Franciscan who solves a murder mystery in a medieval monastery. Others: *Foucault's Pendulum* and *The Island of the Day Before.*

The real hero is always a hero by mistake, he dreams of being an honest coward like everybody else.

1932 **Chuck Noll:** American football coach. Led the Pittsburgh Steelers (1969–1991) to Super Bowl victories in 1975, 1976, 1979, and 1980, the only coach in NFL history to achieve the feat. Took over a team that had never won any kind of title in 40 years of existence. His team's record the first year was 1–13. Though shrewd drafts and strong guidance, Noll's rebuilding program bore fruit in his fourth season, when his team finished with an 11–3 record and won the AFC Central Division. Besides the Super Bowls his teams won nine AFC titles.

Before you can win a game, you have to not lose it.

OTHERS: 1548 Spanish philosopher and theologian **Francisco Suárez**, 1660 Composer/leading figure in Italian opera **Alessandro Scarlatti**, 1787 Irish genealogist **John Burke**, 1811 U.S. missionary **Cyrus Hamlin**, 1909 American mathematician and logician **Stephen Cole Kleene**, 1923 U.S. record producer who made rock and roll a major form of popular music, **Sam Phillips**, 1931 Oscar-winning actor **Robert Duvall**, 1934 Wife of Mikhail Gorbachev, last General Secretary of the Communist Part of the Soviet Union, **Raisa M. Gorbachev**, 1938 King of Spain **Juan Carlos**, 1946 American actress **Diane Keaton**, 1969 U.S. singer **Marilyn (Brian Warner) Manson**

January 6

1412 Saint **Joan of Arc:** French saint and national heroine. "Maid of Orléans." Heard voices of Sts. Michael, Catherine and Margaret exhorting her to make the Dauphin king and drive the English from France. Dressed in men's clothes she visited the Dauphin and convinced him, his advisors and the church authorities to support her. Through inspired conviction, she rallied the French troops and raised the English siege at Orléans. The Dauphin was crowned king at Reims as Charles VII with Joan at his side. She had several other victories before being captured by the Burgundians who sold her to the English. Abandoned by Charles, she was turned over to the ecclesiastical court at Rouen, controlled by French clerics who supported the English. Tried for heresy and witchcraft she was burned at the stake when she would not recant her assertion that she had been divinely inspired. Not canonized until 1920.

The Lord will open a way for me through the midst of them.... For that was I born.

1811 **Charles Sumner:** American politician. Practiced law in Boston while crusading for abolition of slavery, prison reform, world peace and educational reform. U.S. Senator from Massachusetts (1852–74). His denunciation to the Kansas-Nebraska Act and its sponsors Senators Stephen A. Douglas and Andrew P. Butler resulted in an incensed relative of Butler invading the Senate and severely beat Sumner in 1856. He led radical Republicans in opposing President Andrew Johnson's moderate Reconstruction program for the South.

From the beginning of our history the country has been afflicted with compromise. It is by compromise that human rights have been abandoned.

1822 **Heinrich Schliemann:** Successful German businessman turned archeologist. Noted for his excavation of the ancient ruins of Troy at Hissarlik, Turkey in 1873, verifying the Trojan War as a historical event. He also discovered a treasure of gold jewelry, which he smuggled out of the country. Because the Ottoman government prevented his return, he began excavating Mycenae in Greece, where he found more invaluable remains and treasures. Later, working with Wilhelm Dörpfeld, he excavated the great fortified site as Tiryns.

I have looked upon the face of Agamemnon.

1850 **Eduard Bernstein:** Berlin-born Socialist leader. An associate of Friedrich Engels, he advocated revisionism, an evolutionary parliamentary form of Marxism. Joined the German Social Democratic Party and then spent a year in exile as an editor of socialists' journals. In London, he was influenced by the Fabian Society. Returning to Germany he became the political theorists of revisionist of Marxian tents, such as the imminent collapse of capitalism. As a member of the Reichstag in the first three decades of the 20th century, he inspired much of the reform programs of the Social Democrats.

Socialism is the legitimate heir of Liberalism, not only chronologically, but spiritually.

1878 **Carl Sandburg:** American journalist, poet and biographer. Fought in the Spanish-American War before moving to Chicago in 1913, where he worked as a journalist. Won recognition in 1914 for his poems, eulogizing American workers. Pulitzer Prize in history for the biography, *Abraham Lincoln: The War Years*. Poetry: "Chicago Poems" and "Good Morning, America." Awarded a Pulitzer for his *Collected Poems* (1950). Published *The American Songbook*.

A baby is God's opinion that the world should go on.

1882 **Sam Rayburn:** "Mr. Democrat." Taught school before becoming a lawyer, Democratic U.S. congressman from Texas (1913–61). Speaker of the House (1940–46, 1949–53, 1955–61). Southern populist and skilled tactician who sponsored New Deal legislation and supported Roosevelt and Truman's foreign power. Cowrote the legislation that enacted rural electrification.

A jackass can kick a barn down, but it takes a carpenter to build one.

1883 **Kahlil Gibran:** Originally **Jubran Kahlil Jubran**. Lebanese-born American writer, best known for his book of poetic essays, *The Prophet*, which gained near cult status with the young in the twenties. His works, written in both Arabic and English, are filled with lyrical outpourings and expressions of deeply religious and mystical nature. Other works: *The Madman*, *Sand and Foam* and *Jesus, the Son of Man*.

I have learned silence from the talkative, toleration from the intolerant, and kindness from the unkind; yet, strange, I am ungrateful to these teachers.

1892 **Stella Benson:** English feminist travel writer and novelist, who lived in the USA and China. Began keeping a diary at age ten and kept it up all her life. By age 14 she was writing poetry and later added novels to her repertoire. Many of her novels, such as *I Pose* and *This Is the End*, stories and travel sketches most are now long forgotten. *The Little World* (1925) describes her honeymoon with her husband that consisted with an automobile trip across America. They continued to travel throughout the rest of their lives, which ended for her just before her 41st birthday of pneumonia in Vietnam.

The artist has no mission in life except to tell the truth.

1900 **Kathryn Cavarly Hulme:** American author. Wrote *The Wild Place*, *The Nun's Story*, made into an award-winning novel, starring Audrey Hepburn, and *Undiscovered Country: A Spiritual Adventure*, a description of her years as a student of Greek-U.S. mystic and "teacher of dancing," Georges I. Gurdjieff.

Never forget that God tests his real friends more severely than the lukewarm ones.

1915 **Alan Watts:** American writer and lecturer on philosophy. An expert in comparative religion, for nearly 40 years, he interpreted Eastern thought to the West. His more than 25 books include *The Spirit of Zen* (1936) and *This Is It* (1960). Also wrote numerous articles on subjects such as personal identity, the true nature of reality, and consciousness and the pursuit of happiness. Often proclaimed that he wished to be a bridge between the ancient and the modern, between East and West, and between culture and nature.

History is the refusal to "let the dead bury the dead."

1920 **Early Wynn:** Known as "Gus." Hall of Fame right-handed baseball pitcher with Washington Senators, Cleveland Indians and Chicago White Sox. Burly, hard-nosed competitor won exactly 300 games, highlighted by five 20-win seasons, 49 shutouts and seven

All-Star selections. Cy Young winner (1959) at the age of 39. Elected to the Hall of Fame in 1972.

That space between the white lines — that's my office. That's where I conduct my business.

1931 **E.L. [Edward Lawrence] Doctorow:** American novelist. Editor of the *New American Library* (1960–64) and chief editor at Dial Press (1964–69). His best-known work *Ragtime* combines historical figures with fiction. Received the National Book Critics Circle Award for fiction and was made into a film in 1980 and a musical in 1996. Also wrote *The Book of Daniel*, nominated for a National Book Award, a fictionalized account based on the story of Julius and Ethel Rosenberg who were executed for spying. Also wrote *Billy Bathgate*, which was nominated for a Pulitzer Prize and was made into a movie that the author disowned.

Writing is an exploration. You start from nothing and learn as you go.

1937 **Lou Holtz:** U.S. football coach with William & Mary, North Carolina University, a year with the pro New York Jets, University of Arkansas, University of Minnesota, University of Notre Dame, with whom he won a national title (1988), and the University of South Carolina. Known for lesson-filled one-liners. His career has been plagued by controversy. Minnesota, Notre Dame and South Carolina were placed on probation by the NCAA shortly after he left, although he was never found culpable.

The man who complains about the way the ball bounces is likely the one who dropped it.

OTHERS: 1367 French King of England **Richard II**, 1579 English colonist **Captain John Smith**, 1745 French hit air balloon co-inventor **Jacques-Étienne Montgolfier**, 1859 English philosopher **Samuel Alexander**, 1872 Russian composer **Alexander Scriabin**, 1880 Cowboy movie star **Tom Mix**, 1906 Dutch sculptor **Jaap Wagemaker**, 1911 U.S. comedian **Joey Adams**, 1913 U.S. movie actress **Loretta Young**, 1920 Founder of the Unification Movement **Sun Myung Moon**, 1921 U.S. pollster **Lou Harris**, 1921 U.S. golfer **Cary Middlecoff**, 1924 U.S. bluegrass musician **Earl Scruggs**, 1933 French actress **Capucine**, 1955 English actor **Rowan Atkinson**, 1957 American golfer **Nancy Lopez**

January 7

1611 **James Harrington:** English political philosopher, best known for his controversial work *Commonwealth of Oceana*, in which he pictured a utopian society in which political authority rested entirely in the hands of the landed gentry. He advocated a written constitution, vote by ballot and rotation of magistrates and legislators. In his society, there would be agrarian reform and primogeniture would be abolished. There would be a limit to the amount of land an individual could own. William Penn's Pennsylvania government is said to owe much to Harrington's ideas, and also found their way into the doctrines of the American and French Revolutions.

Every man, either to his terror or consolation, has some sense of religion.

1718 **Israel Putnam:** American Revolutionary soldier. Fought in the French and Indian War, rescued at the last minute from being burned at a stake by Indians. By the eve of the American Revolution he had become a prosperous farmer and tavern owner. Outspoken against British taxation and at about the time of the Stamp Act crisis in 1766, he was elected to the Connecticut General Assembly and was one of the founders of the Connecticut Sons of Liberty. Shortly after the Battle of Lexington, he was given command of Connecticut forces. He planned the fortifications at the Battle of Bunker Hill, which proved to be the greatest achievement of his life.

Men, you are all marksmen — don't one of you fire until you see the whites of their eyes.

1768 **Joseph Bonaparte:** Born **Giuseppe Napoleone Buonaparte**. Corsican-born king of Naples and Sicily and of Spain. Eldest surviving brother of Napoleon I. Despite his efforts to win popularity, his foreign birth and his membership in a Masonic lodge, meant he would never be accepted as legitimate by the majority of Spaniards. His army was defeated by Wellington at Victoria. Spent much of his life in exile in New Jersey but died in Florence, Italy.

Gold is, in the last analysis, the sweat of the poor, and the blood of the brave.

1820 **Austin Phelps:** American Congregational minister and educator. A brilliant preacher, his *Theory of Preaching* and *English Style in Public Discourse* became standard textbooks. Pastor of the Pine Street Church in Boston (1842–48), professor of sacred rhetoric and homiletics at Andover Theological Seminar (1848–79) of which he was president from 1869 to his resignation due to poor health.

Wear the old coat and buy the new book.

1861 **Louise Imogen Guiney:** Poet and writer, born in Massachusetts, she was part of Boston's "aesthetic revival in the 1890s. Her Roman Catholicism and literary conservatism is reflected in her sentimental style. She is best known today for "discovering" Khalil Gibran. Her books*: Songs at the Start*, *The White Sail and Other Poems*, and *Goose Quill Papers*. A walking tour of England with her friend Alice Brown led to their collaboration on *Robert Louis Stevenson — A Study*.

Character demonstrates itself in trifles.

1871 **Émil Borel:** French mathematician and politician. Along with René-Louis Barre and Henri Lebesque he pioneered measure theory and its application to probability theory. Among the entities named for him are Borel algebra, Borel's lemma, Borel measure, Borel's paradox, Borel space and Borel summation. He served for many years in the French parliament and during World War II he was a member of the French Resistance.

Events with a sufficiently small probability never occur, or at least we must act, in all circumstances, as if they were impossible.

1873 **Charles Pierre Peguy:** French nationalist, poet, philosopher and Christian socialist. In 1900, he founded *Cahiers de la quinzaine* in which he published his own work and that of other writers. Throughout his life he worked for justice, truth, and the good of the common man in the world. Staunch supporter of Alfred Dreyfus in the infamous Dreyfus Affair. Works: *Le Mystère de la charité de Jeanne d'Arc* and *L'Argent*. Killed in the Battle of the Marne in World War I.

Short of a genius a rich man cannot even imagine poverty.

1873 **Adolph Zukor:** Hungarian-born film pioneer and executive. Immigrated to America at age 16 and worked his way up to being a prosperous furrier. When his cousin Max Goldstein approached him in 1903 for a loan for opening an arcade that would feature Edison's phonographs, electric lights, and moving pictures, Zukor not only provided the money, he became a partner. Formed Famous Players (1912) to bring popular plays to the screen. Merged his company with Jesse Lasky's productions, changing its name to Paramount. Revolutionized the industry by organizing production, distribution and exhibition within a single company. The centenarian's autobiography is *The Public Is Never Wrong*.

Fish stinks from the head.

1901 **Zora Neale Hurston:** African-American dramatist, novelist, folklorist and cultural anthropologist. Wrote of rural black life. Prominent in the Harlem renaissance and in the establishment of black literature as a genre. Novels: *Jonah's Gourd Wine, Their Eyes Were Watching God* and *Seraph on the Suwanee*. In the 1950s she withdrew from public life, distanced from many of her contemporaries for her controversial attack on the Supreme Court's ruling on school desegregation. She claimed that pressure for integration denied the value of black institutions.

Research is formalized curiosity. It is poking and prying with a purpose.

1919 **Robert Edwards Duncan:** American poet. His essay "The Homosexual in Society" identified the plight of the homosexual with that of the Negro and Jew in contemporary society. His reputation as a major poet was established in the 1960s with the publication of three collections of poems.

Responsibility is to keep the ability to respond.

1920 **Albert Meltzer:** English anarchist activist and writer. As the Spanish Revolution turned into the Spanish Civil War, he became active in organizing solidarity appeals and became involved in smuggling arms from Hamburg to Spain. Also acted as a contact for the Spanish anarchist intelligence services in Britain. Cofounded the anarchist newspaper *Black Flag*. Among his books were *Anarchism, Arguments For and Against* and *The Floodgate of Anarchy*.

Optimism is inevitably the last hope of the defeated.

1948 **Kenny Loggins:** American singer and songwriter. Teamed with singer-songwriter Jim Messina from 1970 to 1976.Some of there songs: "Danny's Song," "Your Mama Don't Dance," "House at Pooh Corner" and" Lately My Love." His songs as a solo artist include: "I Believe in Love," "Footloose," and "Conviction of the Heart," which Former Vice-President Al Gore billed as "the unofficial anthem of the environmental movement." On Earth Day, 1995, Loggins performed the song at the National Mall in Washington, D.C. to a crowd of 500,000.

Sure, sadness can spark creativity. But so can happiness and love.

OTHERS: 1528 Queen of Navarre **Jeanne d'Albret**, 1800 Thirteenth U.S. president **Millard Fillmore**, 1845 Last king of Bavaria, **Louis III**, 1879 Visionary who claimed to have received several apparitions of the Blessed Virgin, **St. Bernadette of Lourdes**, 1911 African-American actress, **Butterfly McQueen**, 1912 Macabre U.S. cartoonist, **Charles Addams**, 1922 Renown French flutist, **Jean-Pierre Rampal**, 1925 India-born English zoologist/writer, **Gerald Durrell**, 1928 U.S. novelist **William Peter Blatty**, 1929 Hollywood actress **Terry Moore**, 1956 U.S. track star **Rosalyn Bryant**, 1957 U.S. Telejournalist **Katie Couric**, 1958 U.S. model **Donna Rice**, 1964 American actor **Nicolas Cage**

January 8

1572 **Thomas Dekker:** English dramatist and writer of prose pamphlets. Memorable for lively depictions of London life. His pamphlets included: *The Wonderfull Yeare*, about the plague, *The Belman of London*, about roguery and crime, and *The Guls Horen-Booke*, an account of behavior in London theaters. Best known and most popular play, *The Shoemaker's Holiday, or the Gentle Craft*, which is about the daily lives of ordinary Londoners.

Were there no women, men might live like gods.

1601 **Baltasar Gracián y Morales:** Spanish Jesuit prose writer. Rector of the Jesuit College of Tarragona. Acquired fame as a preacher, including reading a letter from Hell. Published collection of 300 maxims, offering a distillation of wisdom. Best known for allegorical novel *The Criticón* (Faultfinder), in which civilization and society are seen through the eyes of a savage. Critilo, the "critical man," is shipwrecked where he meets Andrenio, a natural man who has grown up ignorant of civilization. Together they take a long voyage to the Isle of Immorality, traveling the long road of life.

Truth always lags behind, limping along on the arm of Time.

1821 **James Longstreet:** Confederate Army general during the American Civil War. Held important commands at the first and second battles of Bull Run, Peninsular campaign, Antietam, Fredericksburg, Gettysburg, Chickamauga and the Wilderness campaign. After the war he befriended U.S. Grant and became a Republican. Served as Grant's minister to Turkey. Served as commissioner of Pacific Railroads under presidents William McKinley and Theodore Roosevelt.

Why do men fight who were born to be brothers?

1824 **Wilkie Collins:** English novelist, playwright, and writer of short stories. Studied law and was a painter. Wrote 27 novels, more than 50 short stories, at least 15 plays and more than 100 pieces of non-fiction. Suffering from "rheumatic gout" he became addicted to opium, the effects of which he features in his most famous novel *Moonstone*. Other works: *The Woman in White*, *Armadale*, and *No Name*.

I have always maintained that the one important phenomenon presented by modern society is — the enormous prosperity of fools.

1830 Baron **Hans von Bülow:** German conductor and composer of the Romantic era. First modern virtuoso pianist and first to conduct from memory. A student of Liszt, whose daughter he married. Notoriously tactless, he alienated many musicians with whom he worked. Critical to establishing the success of Richard Wagner. Conducted the first performances of *Meistersinger* and *Tristan und Isolde* at the Munich Court Opera. Besides championing the music of Wagner, he was a supporter of the music of both Brahms and Tchaikovsky.

I believe in Bach, the Father, Beethoven, the Son, and Brahms, the Holy Ghost of music.

1881 **William Thomas Piper:** American aircraft manufacturer of the first successful mass-produced inexpensive planes. Designer of the Piper Cub airplane. Founder and first president of Piper Aircraft Corporation (1929–1970). Became known as "the Henry Ford of Aviation." Fought in the Spanish-American War and World War I.

A speech is like an airplane engine. It may sound like hell but you've got to go on.

1891 **W. M. Kiplinger:** American journalist and publisher. Founder of Kiplinger, a Washington, DC publishing company. Editor of *Kiplinger Washington Letters*. Author of *Washington Is Like That*. The Kiplinger Distinguished Contributions to Journalism is an award given by the National Press Foundation in his honor.

Investment is like seed corn; a little makes a lot next year and much more a few years later.

1902 **Carl R. Rogers:** American psychologist. With Abraham Maslow, he founded the humanist approach to psychology. Instrumental in the development of non-directive psychotherapy. His theories is based on nineteen propositions, including: All individuals exist in a continually changing world of experience of which they are the center and Behavior is basically the goal directed attempt of the organism to satisfy its needs as experienced, in the field as perceived. Major works *Counseling and Psychotherapy and Client-Centered Therapy*.

The good life is a process, not a state of being. It is a direction not a destination.

1908 **Pamela Frankau:** Popular English author. Daughter of the novelist Gilbert Frankau and satirist Julia Davis. Had success as a writer from an early age. Her affair with married Humbert Wolfe ended with his death in 1940. Converted to Catholicism and spent much time in the U.S., where she had a brief marriage. Maintained a long-time relationship with theater director Margaret Webster. Novels: *Jezebel*, *The Willow Cabin* and *A Wreath of the Enemy*. Wrote *The Offshore Light* using the pseudonym Eliot Naylor.

The English find ill-health not only interesting but respectable and often experience death in the effort to avoid a fuss.

1914 **Thomas Watson, Jr.:** American business executive. Son of Thomas J. Watson, the founder of IBM. The younger Watson served as a pilot in the Army Air Force in World War I. He became president of IBM in 1952.Unlike his father, who had repeatedly rejected electronic computers, he took the company in a new direction, and hiring electrical engineers put to work designing mainframe computers. His new products were well-received and IBM was the first computer giant. Received the Presidential Medal of Freedom in 1964. Appointed U.S. ambassador to U.S.S.R. (1979–81) by President Carter.

In the next 40 years we will accomplish so much more than in the past 40 years that people will wonder why we didn't do more in the first 40.

1935 **Elvis Presley:** "The King." American singer and actor. Most popular rock 'n' roll singer of 1950s and 1960s. An icon of modern American pop culture, representing a rise from rags to riches through talent and hard work. When he first burst onto the music scene and made appearances on TV shows such as The Ed Sullivan Show, his sexuality, body gyrations, sideburns, and a hint of delinquency delighted young fans, especially the girls, and outraged adults. Hits: "Don't Be Cruel," "Hound Dog," "Love Me Tender" and "Are You Lonesome Tonight?" Made more than thirty films, unexceptional for plots or acting, but as a showcase for Elvis' singing. Died at age 42, presumably from a heart attack combined with an abuse of prescription drugs. His popularity and legend survives till today.

Music should be something that makes you gotta move, inside or outside.

1942 **Stephen Hawking:** British physicist and mathematician. Most brilliant theoretical physicist since Einstein. Established link between black holes and thermodynamics. Currently the Lucasian Professor of Mathematics at Cambridge, a chair once held by Isaac Newton. His body, but not his mind, is afflicted with amyotrophic lateral sclerosis (Lou Gehrigs' disease). Diagnosed with the disease at age 21, shortly before his first marriage, physicians said he would not survive more than two or three years. He became increasingly disabled; gradually losing the use of his arms, legs and voice, and now is almost completely paralyzed. He communicates with the aid of a computer. Wrote the popular *A Brief History of Time*, *The Universe in a Nutshell*, *Black Holes and Baby Universes*, and *A Briefer History of Time*.

The goal is simple. It is complete understanding of the universe.

OTHERS: 1587 Danish entomologist **Johannes Fabricius**, 1791 U.S. politician **Jacob Collamer**, 1792 U.S. music educator **Lowell Mason**, 1885 Australian politician **John Curtin**, 1891 German subatomic particle physicist **Walter Bothe**, 1891 English writer **Storm**

Jameson, 1888 German-born mathematician **Richard Courant**, 1900 **Queen Mary of Yugoslavia**, 1902 Successor to Stalin as prime minister, **Georgiy Malenkov**, 1904 Satirical U.S. cartoonist **Peter Arno**, 1909 U.S. reading teacher **Evelyn Wood**, 1912 Puerto Rican actor/director **José Ferrer**, 1923 U.S. basso **Giorgio Tozzi**, 1928 U.S. news anchor/host **Sander Vanocur**, 1931 U.S. rock producer **Bill Graham**, 1937 Welsh singer **Shirley Bassey**

January 9

1854 **Jennie Jerome Churchill:** Brooklyn-born wife of Lord Randolph Churchill and mother of future Prime Minister Winston Churchill. Long considered to be one of the most beautiful women of her time, an admirer said of her, there was "more of the panther than the woman in her look." Influential in the uppermost British social and political circles. She had numerous lovers during her marriage, including King Edward VII, with the full knowledge of her husband. Founded and edited the *Anglo-Saxon Review*. Wrote *The Reminiscences of Lady Randolph Churchill* and a play starring Mrs. Patrick Campbell. She married two more times and later in life became extremely eccentric.

One is forever throwing away substance for shadows.

1856 **Lizette Woodworth Reese:** American poet. Taught school for 45 years. Her poetry has been likened to that of Emily Dickinson, remarkable for its intensity and concision. Probably best remembered for the sonnet "Years," a sonnet in which the conventional theme of regret is energized by a series of fresh and arresting images. Her volumes of poetry include *A Branch of May*, *A Handful of Lavender* and *Spicewood*.

The old faiths light their candles all about, but burly Truth comes by and puts them out.

1859 **Carrie Chapman Catt:** American leader of women's rights movement and inflamed the country with her oratory. Reorganized National Woman Suffrage Association, transforming it into the League of Women Voters, which was organized to educate American women in the intelligent use of their newly won right to vote. Spent her latter years of her life campaigning for world peace. Organized the National Conference on the Cause and Cure of War.

When a just cause reaches its flood-tide, as ours has done ... whatever stands in the way must fall before its overwhelming power.

1890 **Karel Čapek:** Czech writer, playwright, novelist and essayist. Best remembered for play *R.U.R.* (Rossum's Universal Robots), first use of the word "robot" from the Czech *robota*. Widely read between the world wars but never won the Nobel Prize for Literature allegedly because the Swedes were fearful of offending Hitler to honor such a well-know anti-fascist. Other works: *War with the Newts*, *Apocryphal Tales*, *The Gardener's Year* and *Talks with T.G. Masaryk*.

A short life is better for mankind, for a long life would deprive man of his optimism.

1881 **Lascelles Abercrombie:** British poet and literary critic, known as the *Georgian Laureate*. Taught at Leeds University, the University of London, and Oxford. Wrote several books of poetry criticism, as well as his *Gregorian Poetry*. His poetry is characterized by its rugged forms and complex philosophy. Works: plays *Deborah* and *The End of the World, Interludes and Poems*, *The Theory of Poetry* and *Principles of Literary Criticism*.

The poet's business is not to describe things to us, or to tell us about them, but to create in our minds the very things themselves.

1894 **Lester Markel:** Autonomous czar who ran the *New York Times*' Sunday sections with its powerful Book Review section for 40 years. One of three founders of the International Press Institute. The citation of the 1953 Pulitzer Prize for Journalism awarded to the *New York Times*, read "For the section of its Sunday newspaper edited by Lester Markel and headed, "Review of the Week," which for seventeen years has brought enlightenment and intelligent commentary to its readers."

What you see is news, what you know is background, what you feel is opinion.

1902 Sir **Rudolph Bing:** Anglo-Austrian impresario. In 1927 he joined a theatrical agency in Berlin and later served as general manager of opera houses in Darmstadt and Berlin. Moved to England in 1934 and helped found the Glyndebourne Festival, where he was named general manager the next year. Cofounder and director of the Edinburgh Festival (1935–49). Came to the U.S. in 1949 and was named general manager of Metropolitan Opera (1950–72). During his long tenure the number of subscribers to the opera increased from 5,000 to 17,000. Remembered for his feud with soprano Maria Callas and opening the house to African-American Leontyne Price.

We are similar to a museum. My function is to present old masterpieces in modern frames.

1904 **George Balanchine:** Russian-born choreographer. Named ballet-master and choreographer for the Russian Ballet in Paris (1925). Founded School of American Ballet (1934). Cofounder Ballet Society which emerged as the New York City Ballet in 1948. Artistic director (1948–83). Among his ballets: *The Prodigal Son*, *Serenade*, *Balustrade*, *Orpheus*, *Stars and Stripes*, and Meditation.

Old people don't get tired — it's only the young who tire. Confusion exhausts them.

1908 **Simone de Beauvoir:** French philosopher, novelist, essayist, and influential feminist. Articulate exponent of Sartre's philosophy of existentialism. Wrote *The Second Sex*, a pioneering feminist text and one of the most widely read. In it she argued "One is not born a woman, one becomes one." Women are "the other," the sex defined by men and patriarchy as not male, and consequently are less than fully human. Other works: *The Blood of Others*, *All Men Are Mortal*, *The Mandarins*, *Letters to Sartre*, *Memoirs of a Dutiful Daughter* and *A Very Easy Death*. During the last period of her life, dependence on alcohol hastened her physical and mental collapse.

When we abolish the slavery of half of humanity, together with the whole system of hypocrisy that it implies, then the "division" of humanity will reveal its genuine significance and the human couple will find its true form.

1913 **Richard M. Nixon:** Thirty-seventh president of the United States. Red-baiting California congressman and senator. Dwight Eisenhower's running-mate, serving two terms as vice-president. Gained notoriety on a visit to Moscow in 1959 by his outspoken exchanges with Nikita Khrushchev. Lost close election for president to John F. Kennedy (1960) and failed to become governor of California in 1962. In a remarkable comeback from the politically dead, he was elected president in 1968. Resigned 1974 under threat of impeachment, after several members of his government were found guilty of being involved in the Watergate scandal. The following month he was given a full pardon by President Gerald Ford.

When the President does it that means that it is not illegal.

1922 **Ahmed Sékou Touré:** African political leader and first President of Guinea. Began as a labor union activist and became General Secretary of the Postal Worker's Union. Led Guinea out of the French Community and was the nation's effective dictator for twenty-six years. Believed to have killed upwards of 200,000 people, delivering slavery and poverty to his people and riches for himself.

We prefer the poverty in freedom to riches in slavery.

1941 **Joan Baez:** American folksinger, songwriter and civil rights activist. Her soprano voice is of remarkable purity and clarity. Subjected to racial slurs and discrimination as a child because of her Mexican heritage and features, she became involved in a number of social causes from early in her career. Imprisoned briefly for refusing to pay taxes to protest Vietnam War. In 1968, the Daughters of the American Revolution denied her permission to perform at Constitution Hall, just as they had done earlier to Marian Anderson. Among her albums: *Joan, David's Album, Diamonds and Rust, Brothers in Arms,* and *No Woman No Cry.*

Hypothetical questions get hypothetical answers.

OTHERS: 1554 Italian pope **Gregory XV**, 1729 English poet **Thomas Wharton**, 1790 Swedish poet **Per Daniel Amadeus Atterbom**, 1829 German explorer **Adolf von Schlagintweit**, 1878 U.S. psychologist **John Broadus Watson**, 1894 Polish painter **Henryk Stazweski**, 1898 English singer **Gracie Fields**, 1901 U.S. comic strip creator **Chic Young**, 1915 Argentine actor **Fernando Lamas**, 1928 U.S. romance novelist **Judith Krantz**, 1934 U.S. quarterback, **Bart Starr**, 1935 U.S. comic actor **Bob Denver**, 1935 American sportscaster **Dick Enberg**, 1942 British actress **Susannah York**, 1951 U.S. country singer **Crystal Gayle**, 1967 U.S. singer **Dave Matthews**

January 10

1592 **Henry King:** English bishop and poet. Friend of John Donne, Samuel Johnson and Isaak Walton Wrote the solemn and moving *Exequy* for his young wife, one of the greatest English elegies. His works illustrated the manners and tastes of the time. Because of his reluctance to publish his poetry and his habit of freely sharing his pieces, many were pirated and found their way into print under different names. Published *Poems, Elegies, Paradoxes, and Sonnets.*

Nature's true-born child, who sums his years/ (Like me) with no arithmetic but tears.

1750 **Thomas Erskine:** Scottish born barrister and writer. Defender of personal liberties. Studied law and became famous for his successful defenses of Thomas Baillie accused of criminal libel, Admiral Lord Keppel on a charge of incompetence in the face of the enemy and Lord George Gordon, charged with high treason. In 1792, he undertook the defense of Tom Paine on a charge of seditious libel with his "Rights of Man."

Every man, not intending to mislead, but seeking to enlighten others with what his own reason and conscience, however erroneously, have dictated to him as truth, may address himself to the universal reason of a whole nation, either upon the subject of governments in general, or upon that of our own particular country.

1814 **Aubrey de Vere:** Irish poet, critic, and essayist. His work is in part historical and in part literary. His aim was to illustrate supernatural truth by recording the conversion to Christianity of Ireland and England. His most popular works include *The Sisters, The Infant Bridal, Irish Odes, Legends of St. Patrick* and the verse dramas *Alexander the Great* and *St. Thomas of Canterbury.*

Man should be ever better than he seems.

1822 **Theodore Ledyard Cuyler:** American Presbyterian minister and writer for the religious press, to which he contributed nearly 3,000 articles. Remarkably influential preacher. He wrote many tracts on temperance. His books include *Stray Arrows* and *God's Light on Dark Clouds.*

God never built a Christian strong enough to carry today's duties and tomorrow's anxieties piled on the top of them.

1834 Lord **Acton [John E.E. Dalberg]:** Naples-born English historian, Christian liberal, who developed and extraordinary knowledge of European political history. Editor of *The Rambler,* a Roman Catholic monthly. Founder-editor of the *Cambridge Modern History.* Famous for his epic warning that "power corrupts, and absolute power corrupts absolutely." He transmitted to the English-speaking world the rigor of studying history as much as possible from original sources.

The danger is not that a particular class is unfit to govern; every class is unfit to govern.

1869 **Grigori Rasputin:** Russian monk born in Siberia. Gained favor with Emperor Nicholas II and Empress Alexandra by being able to control the bleeding of the hemophiliac heir to the throne Tsarvich Alexey by hypnosis. A number of influential churchman were taken in by the "holy man" early in his career, but later they turned on him and attempted to have him banished from St. Petersburg, but it was the bishops and monks who opposed him who found themselves exiled or in disgrace. He was notorious lecher and drunkard. A group of aristocrats murdered him, but he didn't die easily.

God has seen your tears and heard your prayers. Fear not, the child will not die.

1887 **Robinson Jeffers:** American poet, who claimed that without originality, a poet was "only a verse-writer." He affirmed that to make an advance, to contribute to poetry, would require "emotions or ideas, or a point of view, or even mere rhythms that had not occurred to his contemporaries." Poems include: "Roan Stallion," "The Woman at Point Sur" and "At the Fall of an Age." Collections: *Tamar and Other Poems*, *Descent to the Dead*, and *Give Your Heart to the Hawks*.

Pleasure is the carrot dangled to lead the ass to market; or the precipice.

1903 **Barbara Hepworth:** English abstract sculptor. One of the foremost nonfigurative sculptors of her time. Her works drew on geometric as well as organic shapes. She introduced into England the idea of piercing the solid mass of a sculpture with a "hole," making the object more transparent. Made Dame of the British Empire. Works: "Reclining Figure," "Winged Figure" and "Four-Square."

I rarely draw what I see. I draw what I feel in my body.

1904 **Ray Bolger:** American rubber-legged dancer, singer, and actor. Notable roles include the Scarecrow in *The Wizard of Oz* and as Charley in the Broadway musical *Where's Charley?* In the latter his singing "Once in love with Amy" stopped the show every night. Bolger sang it a second time with the audience lending their voices to the rendition. It earned him a Tony Award. His reaction when he learned of the death of Judy Garland, who played Dorothy, was:

How lonely is it going to be now on the Yellow Brick Road.

1939 **Linda Lovelace:** Born **Linda Susan Boreman.** Reformed porn star, most infamous for the film *Deep Throat*. The production cost $22,000 supplied by the mob and has probably grossed at least $600 million. In 1980 Lovelace published an autobiography in which she portrayed herself as a victim. The adult film industry considered her a traitor and anti-porn crusaders used her as their poster child. She died in 2002.

I would like to see all the people who read pornography or have anything to do with it put in a mental hospital for observation so we could find out what we have done to them.

1945 **Rod Stewart:** British singer and guitarist. Was the original lead singer of the Jeff Beck Group, but quit it on the eve that the band was scheduled to appear at Woodstock. Hits: "Maggie May," "Tonight's the Night" and "Do Ya Think I'm Sexy?" Inducted into the Rock and Roll Hall of Fame in 1994.

Instead of getting married again, I'm going to find a woman I don't like and just give her a house.

1949 **George Foreman:** American boxer. Olympic heavyweight champion in 1968. World heavyweight champ (1973–74), after beating Joe Frazier. Lost title to Muhammad Ali in an epic bout in Zaire called the "Rumble in the Jungle." Regained it at 46 in 1994, becoming the oldest champion of all time. Has become famous as a pitchman for the George Foreman Grill and Big & Tall Men's Clothing products. Has five daughters and five sons, each of the boys given the name George and a Roman numeral to distinguish them.

Boxing is like jazz. The better it is, the less people appreciate it.

OTHERS: 1638 Dutch astronomer **Niels Stensen**, 1769 French marshal **Michel Ney**, 1870 Chief engineer of the Golden Gate Bridge, **Joseph B. Strauss**, 1880 Swiss clown **Grock** [**Adrien Wettach**]. 1908 Italian-born actor **Paul Henreid**, 1913 Slovakian Communist leader **Gustav Husák**, 1921 U.S. race car driver **Roger Ward**, 1927 U.S. singer **Johnnie Ray**, 1931 Paparazzo stalker **Ron Galella**, 1935 American baritone **Sherrill Milnes**, 1938 U.S. baseball player **Willie McCovey**, 1939 American actor **Sal Mineo**, 1939 U.S. decathlon champion **William Tooney**, 1943 U.S. singer-songwriter **Jim Croce**, 1953 U.S. singer **Pat Benetar**

January 11

1757 **Alexander Hamilton:** American statesman, lawyer and author. Born on the island of Nevis, British West Indies. Immigrated to New Jersey and New York in 1772 to received educational training. Entered the Continental Army, becoming General Washington's aide-de-camp. Member of the Philadelphia Constitutional Convention that adopted the constitution, Became Federalist Party leader and first U.S. secretary of treasury. Killed in duel with Aaron Burr.

Man is a reasoning rather than a reasonable animal.

1842 **William James:** U.S. philosopher, physiologist and teacher. Brother of writer Henry James. Struggled throughout life with such severe bouts of hypochondria, melancholy and depression that he regarded himself as persisting only by means of a deliberate effort of will. Works include: *Pragmatism*, which offered significant expansions of Charles Saunders Peirce's philosophy of pragmatism, and *Principles of Psychology*, the classic exposition of a discipline in translation towards a natural science. Helped found the American Society for Psychical Research.

Thinking is what a great many people think they are doing, when they are merely rearranging their prejudices.

1859 **George Nathaniel Curzon:** Conservative British statesman who served as Viceroy of India. His first wife was the daughter of a Chicago millionaire and cofounder of the department store now named Marshall

Field. When she died he had a long affair with novelist Elinor Glyn, before marrying the daughter of the U.S. Minister to Brazil.

The U.S. is having the same trouble as Rome in its search for "definable frontiers."

1864 **H. George Selfridge:** British merchant. Founded Selfridge and Co., Ltd., a major British department store. Coined the maxim, "the customer is always right," which had long and lasting effects. Consumer infallibility changed the face of commerce because instead of producing goods and trying to pass them off on customers, merchants began appraising customer's needs and sought to provide products and services that met them.

Remember always that the recollection of quality remains long after the price is forgotten.

1870 **Alice Hegan Rice:** American humorist and children's writer. Best known for the sometime humorous, sometime heart-wrenching Mrs. *Wiggs of the Cabbage Patch,* which was a thinly veiled social commentary on a Shantytown near Louisville. Also wrote *Sandy, Calvary Alley. A Romance of Billy Goat Hill* and *The Lark Legacy.* Also had a life-long philanthropic career advocating the rights of the underprivileged.

It ain't no use putting up your umbrella till it rains.

1873 **Dwight Morrow:** U.S. lawyer, financier and statesman. Father of author Anne Morrow Lindbergh. President Calvin Coolidge appointed him ambassador to Mexico (1927–30), where his work set a strong precedent for the Good Neighbor policy. Elected to the U.S. Senate as a Republican from New Jersey, serving until his death in 1931.

We judge ourselves by our motives and others by their actions.

1885 **Alice Paul:** American suffragist leader. Working with others, she led a successful campaign for women's suffrage that gained women the right to vote in the U.S. federal election of 1920. While spending three years working in the settlement house movement, she took part in radical protests for woman suffrage, including participating in the hunger stripes. Back in the USA, she earned a PhD from the University of Pennsylvania. After the 1920 victory for the federal amendment, she became involved in the struggle to introduce and pass an Equal Rights Amendment, which finally passed Congress in 1970.

There will never be a new world order until women are a part of it.

1897 **Bernard De Voto:** American editor, critic, historian and novelist. While teaching English at Northwestern University, he contributed articles for the *American Mercury* and wrote three novels two of which were published. Wrote "Easy Chair" column for *Harpers.* Editor of *The Saturday Review of Literature* (1936–38). Published Mark *Twain's America's, Mark Twain at Work and Mark Twain's Eruption,* and produced an edition of the journals of Lewis and Clark.

The mind has its own logic but does not often let others in on it.

1899 **Eva Le Gallienne:** English-born actress, producer, and director. Although primarily known for her work on the stage, she earned an Oscar nomination for her performance in the 1980 film *Resurrection.* She won an Emmy Award for a televised version of *The Royal Family.* The National Endowment of the Arts recognized her with the National Medal of Arts in 1986.

Innovators are inevitably controversial.

1903 **Alan Paton:** South African novelist and humanitarian. A founder of Liberal Association of South Africa, which opposed apartheid and offered a nonracial alternative to government policy. The party was banned in 1968 and Paton was harassed by the racist government. His political consciousness was formed during the 3 years he was the head of a reformatory for young offenders. His first and best-known novel, *Cry, the Beloved Country,* depicted the collective guilt and friendship across racial prejudices in the story of a black South African. Also wrote: *Too Late the Phalarope* and *Ah, But Your Land Is Beautiful.*

When a deep injury is done us, we never recover until we forgive.

1934 **Jean Chrétien:** 20th Prime Minister of Canada. One of his main focuses was to prevent the separation of the province of Quebec. In 1955 a referendum on Quebec sovereignty was narrowly defeated. His government then passed what became known as the *Clarity Act,* which stated that no Canadian government would acknowledge an independent Quebec nation unless a "clear majority" supported sovereignty in a referendum based on a clear question.

A proof is a proof. What kind of proof? It's a proof. A proof is a proof. And when you have a good proof, it's because it is proven.

1946 **Naomi Judd:** American country music singer. Formed a highly successful singing duo known as *The Judds* with her daughter Wynonna Judd. There biggest hits included "Why Not Me" and "Have Mercy." Her second daughter is actress Ashley Judd.

A dead end street is a good place to turn around.

Others: 1746 English botanist/publisher **William Curtis**, 1807 U.S. industrialist/philanthropist **Ezra Cornell**, 1815 Canadian prime minister **John A. Macdonald**, 1848 International philatelist **Philipp la Renotiere von Ferrary**, 1849 German dermatologist **Oskar Lassar**, 1860 Russian/French painter/author **Marie Bashkirtseff**, 1873 Spanish playwright **Joaquin Álvarez Quintero**, 1878 Greek general/dictator **Theodorus Pangalos**, 1887 U.S. conservationist **Aldo Leopold**, 1896 American football coach **Paddy Driscoll**, 1907 French prime minister **Pierre Mendès-France**, 1924 U.S. singer **Don Cherry**, 1963 U.S. swimmer **Tracy Caulkins**

January 12

1729 **Edmund Burke:** British politician, writer, orator and statesman. Played a prominent role in the major political issues of for some 30 years. Worked for a more conciliatory policy towards American colonies.

His powerful parliamentary orations on the subjects; "On American Taxation" and "On Moving His Resolutions for Conciliation with America" were ignored. Author of *A Vindication of Natural Society*, *A Philosophical Inquiry into the Origin of Ideas of the Sublime and Beautiful* and *Reflections on the French Revolution*.

The only thing necessary for the triumph of evil is for good men to do nothing.

1746 **Johann Heinrich Pestalozzi:** Swiss educational reformer. Put Rousseau's theories into practice thus becoming the first applied educational psychologist. Pioneer in providing mass education for poor children. His method of education consisted of a gradual unfolding, prompted by observation, of children's innate facilities. His principles: "Begin with the concrete before the abstract; begin with the intermediate environment before dealing with the distant and remote; begin with easy exercises before introducing complex ones, and always proceed gradually, cumulatively, and slowly."

Sense-impression of Nature is the only true foundation of human instruction, because it is the only true foundation of human knowledge.

1856 **John Singer Sargent:** American portrait and genre painter. A master of composition and surface effects, he was the most sought-after portrait painter in both Europe and the U.S. Early, he painted exotic beauties, but most scholars conclude that he was not interested in them sexually, as he was a homosexual. His portraits subtly capture the individuality and personality of his subjects. They include *The Daughters of Edward Darley Boit*, *Portrait of Madame X*, *Claude Monet Painting at the Edge of a Wood* and *Portrait of Robert Louis Stevenson and His Wife*. He also did decorative murals for the Boston Public Library.

Portrait painting is a pimp's profession.

1863 **Swami Vivekananada:** Hindu spiritual leader, who suddenly left to fame at the Parliament of Regions held in Chicago in 1893. He attempted to infuse vigor into Hinduism by stressing the universal and humanistic aspects of the *Veda*, a group of sacred hymns and verses composed in archaic Sanskrit. Emphasized service over dogma. In his homeland, he is considered the patron saint of modern India and an inspirer of her national consciousness.

All search is vain, until we begin to perceive that wisdom is within ourselves ... then we may know the sun is rising, that the morning is breaking for us.

1876 **Jack London:** Born **John Griffith Chaney.** Most successful American novelist in the early 20th Century. At 17 he ventured to sea on a sailing ship. Turning point of his life was a 30-day imprisonment that he found degrading and made him vow to get an education and pursue a career in writing. Many of his 50 books of fiction and non-fiction are romantic depictions of struggles for survival as well as socialist tracts. His books include *The Son of the Wolf*, *The Call of the Wild*, *White Fang*, and *The Sea-Wolf*. Retired to his ranch near Sonoma, where he died at age 40.

Everything is good ... as long as it is unpossessed.

Satiety and possession are Death's horses; they run in span.

1878 **Ferenc Molnár:** Pseudonym of **Ferenc Neumann.** Hungarian playwright, director, journalist, novelist and short-story writer. He gained fame in 1907 with the novel *The Paul Street Boys*, about two rival boy's gangs on the streets of Budapest. His play *Liliom* is the basis for the musical *Carousel* by Rogers and Hammerstein. Earlier Puccini had considered setting it to music. Also wrote: *The Devil* and *The Good Fairy*. During World War I, he served as a war correspondent with his reports published as *The Diary of a War Correspondent* in 1916. Asked how he became a writer, he replied:

In the same way that a woman becomes a prostitute. First I did it to please myself, then I did it to please my friends, and finally I did it for the money.

1884 **(Mary Louise Cecilia) "Texas" Guinan:** American actress and saloon keeper. Began her career as a singer, touring the vaudeville circuit. Became known less for her singing and more for her "wild-west" patter. In 1917, she became the first movie cowgirl, the gun-toting "Queen of the West." During Prohibition, she opened a speakeasy in New York City called the "300 Club," which soon became famous for its troupe of 40 scantily clad dancers and the notorious personality and outspoken views of Guinan, who greeted customers with "Hello suckers!"

A politician is a fellow who will lay down your life for his country.

1893 **Hermann Göring:** German Nazi leader. In World War I he became a flying ace and commanded the famous "Death Squad." Joined the Nazi Party in 1922 but the failed Munich Pusch sent him into exile for five years. A Nazi deputy in the Reichstag, he became its president in 1932. When Hitler came to power, Göring became the Fuhrer's chief lieutenant. He founded the Gestapo, set up concentration camps for political, racial and religious suspects, and built Germany's air force. By the end of the war, he was in disgrace and was condemned to death by Hitler, but escaped and captured by U.S. troops. Main defendant at the Nuremberg War Crimes, he committed suicide shortly before he was to be hung for war crimes.

Would you rather have butter or guns? Preparedness makes us powerful. Butter only makes us fat.

1908 **José Limón:** Mexican-born premiere modern dancer, choreographer and teacher of the 20th century. Ranks with Martha Graham as a creator of modern dance. His José Limón Company became the first American modern dance company to tour Europe. His works are considered masterpieces and are still performed today by his company and others. Some of his most famous dances are: There Is a Time and A Choreographic Offering. Died of prostate cancer in 1972.

Dancers aren't pompous; they're too tired.

1920 **James Farmer:** American civil rights activist. Helped found Congress of Racial Equality (1942).

Served as its first director. Leader of 1961 freedom rides. Disciple of Mohandas Gandhi, Farmer used the strategy of nonviolent direct action against discrimination. Always believing that blacks should participate in government, he accepted an invitation for President Nixon in 1969 to become an Assistant Secretary in the Department of Health, Education and Welfare, for which he was severely criticized by some militant civil rights advocates.

We, who are living, possess the past. Tomorrow is for our martyrs.

1944 **Joe Frazier:** "Smokin' Joe." American boxer, famous for his lethal "left hook." 1964 Olympic heavyweight champ. World heavyweight champ (1970–73). Lost the heavyweight championship to George Foreman. Fought Muhammad Ali three times, winning once. The most famous meeting was held in the suffocating heat of Quezon City in the Philippines in January, 1974, where the two aging fighters dueled for 14 rounds in a bout billed by Ali as "The Thrilla in Manila."

I don't want to knock out my opponent. I want to hit him, step away and watch him hurt. I want his heart.

1951 **Russ Limbaugh:** American radio talk show host and writer. Known for sarcastic right-wing political commentary and his combative responses to listeners' call-in comments. Wrote the best selling book *The Way Things Ought to Be* in 1992, followed by *See, I Told You.* Won the Marconi Radio Award for Syndicated Radio Personality of the Year four times. In 2003 he admitted to his listeners that he had abused prescription painkillers and would enter inpatient treatment for 30 days. In 2006 accused of "doctor shopping" to get the painkillers he says he needs for long term back problem and a botched surgery.

If Thomas Jefferson thought taxation without representation was bad, he should see how it is with representation.

OTHERS: 1588 1st Governor of Massachusetts **John Winthrop**, 1628 French scholar/author **Charles Perrault**, 1737 President of the Constitutional Congress **John Hancock**, 1852 French general **Joseph Joffre**, 1902 Nightclub comedian **Joe E. Lewis**, 1906 U.S. country singer **Tex Ritter**, 1906 U.S. comedian, **Henny Youngman**, 1910 Austrian actress **Luise Rainer**, 1916 South African prime minister **P.W. Botha**, 1921 U.S. detective fiction writer **Patricia Highsmith**, 1935 U.S. Psychic/magician **The Amazing Kreskin [George Kresge]** 1942 U.S. revolutionary **Bernardine Dohrn**, 1954 Shock radio personality **Howard Stern**, 1955 U.S. actress **Kirstie Alley**

January 13

1616 **Antoinette Bourignon:** Flemish Christian mystic and adherent of quietism. Believed herself divinely directed to restore the pure spirit of the Gospel, she gather a fanatical following in Amsterdam. Her views and disregard of all religious sects gained her both followers and critics. According to her revelations, religion was a matter of internal emotion, not of faith and practice. As a child she noticed the great dissimilarity between the lives around her to what she found in the Gospels. She asked her parents:

Where are the Christians? Let us go to the country where the Christians live!

1785 **Samuel Woodworth:** American journalist, verse writer and editor of the *New York Mirror.* Pen name "Selim." Best known as the author of "The Old Oaken Bucket," described by some critics as one of the most beautiful works in the English Language. The poem was set to music in 1826 by G.F. Kiallmark, and memorized or sung by generations of American schoolchildren.

How dear to this heart are the scenes of my childhood,/ When fond reflection recalls them to view!

1808 **Samuel P. Chase:** American jurist, lawyer, and teacher. Federalist-partisan and signer of the Declaration of Independence as a representative from Maryland. U.S. Treasury Secretary (1861–64). Originated national banking system. Associate Justice of Supreme Court (1864–73). In 1805 the House of Representatives brought impeachment charges against him, alleging political bias in dealing with court cases Thus far, he is the only Supreme Court Justice to be impeached, but he was acquitted by the Senate.

I would rather that people should wonder why I wasn't president than why I was.

1810 **Ernestine Rose:** Polish-born feminist, abolitionist, free thinker, atheist, socialist and crusader against bigotry and prejudice. A leading intellectual force in the women' right movement in America she was the target of much scorn.

It is an interesting and demonstrable fact, that all children are atheists and were religion not inculcated into their minds, they would remain so.

1832 **Horatio Alger, Jr.:** American author of popular boys' books such as *Ragged Dick* and *Tattered Tom.* They pointed out a moral and their heroes triumphed over adversity. His books illustrated how down-and-out boys were able to achieve the American dream of wealth and success through hard work, courage, determination, and concern for others. In Alger's lifetime, his books rival the success and popularity of those of Mark Twain. Despite his great literary output, Alger didn't become rich. He game most of his money to homeless boys.

I wrote my name upon the sand,/ And trusted it would stand for age;/ But, soon, alas! the refluent sea/ Had washed my feeble lines away.

1879 **Melvin Jones:** American insurance executive. Founder of the Lions Club International, whose civic-minded members, successful men due to their drive, intelligence and ambition, put their talents to work to improve their communities. His personal code:

You can't get very far until you start doing something for somebody else.

1884 **Sophie Tucker:** Born **Sophia Kalish**. "The Last of the Red Hot Mamas." American singer, comedienne, and vaudeville star, whose fame lasted for fifty years. Appeared on stage, in films, on television, and in nightclubs. Her stage image emphasized her "fat girl" image with humorous suggestiveness in songs like "I Don't Want to Be Thin" and "Nobody Loves a Fat Girl, But Oh How a Fat Girl Can Love." Signature song: "Some of These Days." She never retired. She played the Latin Quarter in New York just months before her death at 82.

I have been poor, and I have been rich. Rich is better.

1890 **Elmer Davis:** American broadcast newsman. Rhodes Scholar before taking an editorial position with *Adventure* magazine, before becoming a reporter for the *New York Times*. Left the paper in 1923 to become a free-lance writer. In 1939 he became a radio correspondent in Europe for CBS and during the war years radio listeners tuned in regularly to hear his analysis of the day's events. President Roosevelt appointed Davis director of the Office of War Information. Joined ABC after the war, conducting a nightly newscast until 1953.

This will remain the land of the free only so long as it is the home of the brave.

1925 **Gwen Verdon:** Born **Gwyneth Evelyn Verdon**. American Broadway dancer and actress. Took up dancing to strengthen her legs badly bent and misshapen because a childhood disease. Besides flaming red hair, her trademark was her throaty, grainy, yet girlish voice. Nicknamed "The Superior Posterior." Best known for her role of Lola in Bob Fosse's *Damn Yankees*, both on Broadway and film. Married to Fosse, from 1960 until his death in 1987. Four-time Tony winner for *Can Can*, *Damn Yankees*, *New Girl in Town* and *Redhead*. Also nominated as Best Actress in a Musical for *Sweet Charity* and *Chicago*.

Sex in a dance is in the eyes of the beholder. I never thought my dances sexy. I suppose that's because I see myself with my face washed, and to me I look like a rabbit.

1926 **Caroline Heilbrun:** American academic and feminist author. She wrote mystery novels under the pen name of Amanda Cross. Her heroine Kate Fansler, like Heilbrun, was an English professor. Heilbrun was the first woman to be awarded tenure in the English department of Columbia University.

Ideas move rapidly when their time comes.

1961 **Julia Louis-Dreyfus:** U.S. actress, best known for her role as Elaine Benes on TV's *Seinfeld*. A distant relative of Captain Alfred Dreyfus, her father is a French billionaire. The 5'2½" Dreyfus was chosen as one of *People* magazine's 50 most beautiful people in the world in 1998. Her series *Watching Ellie* was quickly canceled. Currently she stars in the sitcom *The New Adventures of Old Christine*.

It is, I think, harder for women. I haven't quite figured it out ... how the hell do you do this? How do you work and have families?

1977 **Orlando Bloom:** English-born actor, best known for his roles as the elf Legolas in the *The Lord of the Rings* trilogy and The Pirates of the Caribbean films with Johnny Depp and Keira Knightley. Also appeared in the critically acclaimed movie *Wilde*. Currently ranks as the number one heartthrob for young girls. Replaced Britney Spears as the top celebrity download in 2004.

People come into your life and people leave it ... you just trust that life has a road mapped out for you.

OTHERS: 1381 Founder Poor Clares **Saint Colette**, 1804 French caricaturist **Paul Gavarni**, 1827 U.S. poet **Ethel Lynn Beers**, 1885 Fuller Brush Co President **Alfred Fuller**, 1892 U.S. Olympic gold-medal winning yachtsman **Paul Smart**, 1895 Spanish opera singer **Fortunio Bonanova**, 1913 TV host **Ralph Edwards**, 1919 Gossip columnist **Army Archerd**, 1918 Pioneer music publisher **Lester Sill**, 1919 U.S. actor **Robert Stack**, 1924 French choreographer Roland Petit, 1925 U.S. writer **Ernestine Ulmer**, 1933 U.S. artist **Frank Gallo**, 1934 U.S. comedian **Rip Taylor**, 1940 U.S. novelist **Edmund White**, 1949 Indian cosmonaut **Rakesh Sharma**, 1957 U.S. professional golfer **Mark O'Meara**

January 14

1730 **William Whipple:** American Revolutionary leader, legislator and soldier. Signer of the Declaration of Independence. Member of Continental Congress (1776–79). Brigadier general in the Revolutionary Army.

Human passion is the hallucination of a distempered mind.

1875 Dr. **Albert Schweitzer:** French theologian, musician, medical missionary. Based his personal philosophy of a "reverence for life" and a deep commitment to serve humanity through thought and action. At 21 he set the course of his life. For nine years he would study science, music and theology, thereafter, he would devote his life to the service of humanity. Set up a native hospital in French Equatorial Africa in 1913, now in Gabon. A renowned organist, he wrote a biography of Johann S. Bach. Awarded the Nobel Peace Prize in 1952 for his work for the brotherhood of nations. Writings: *The Quest for the Historical Jesus* and *Out of My Life and Thought*.

As we acquire more knowledge, things do not become more comprehensible, but more mysterious.

1882 **Hendrik Willem Van Loon:** Dutch-American journalist and historian. An engaging, energetic interpreter of the arts and humanities. As an avowed skeptic he did not shy away from controversies In *The Story of Mankind*,, he gave an extended treatment of evolution but chose not to mention the biblical account of creation and was accused of heresies Also wrote *The Story of the Bible* and *The Story of the Pacific*. To Van Loon, human achievement mattered among all things and that Man is the center of the universe.

The history of the world is the record of a man in quest of his daily bread and butter.

1892 **Martin Niemoller:** German Lutheran pastor who opposed Hitler's policies. A submarine commander in World War I, he initially welcomed the Führer's rise to power, but by 1934 his faith in Hitler collapsed, Formed the "Confessing Church," a Protestant group that opposed Nazi policies. Arrested in 1937 he was interned in concentration camps, from which he was released in 1945.

First they came for the Communists, and I didn't speak up, because I wasn't a Communist. Then they came for the Jews, and I didn't speak up, because I wasn't a Jew. Then they came for the Catholics, and I didn't speak up, because I was a Protestant. Then they came for me, and by that time there was no one left to speak up for me.

1896 **John Dos Passos:** American novelist and war correspondent. Served as an ambulance driver in France and Italy during World War I. Supported the Republicans during the Spanish Civil War, but gradually became disillusioned with left-wing politics. Wrote the anti-war novel, *Three Soldiers*. Best known work is the experimental trilogy *U.S.A.* (*The 49th Parallel, 1919* and *The Big Money*) as a vast portrait of American society. Other novels *Chosen Country* and *Midcentury*, and a biography *The Head and Heart of Thomas Jefferson*.

Individuality is freedom lived.

1901 **Carlos Romulo:** Philippines general, statesman, and writer. Served with Douglas MacArthur in the Pacific during World War II. Ambassador to the U.S. First Asian to win the Pulitzer Prize in journalism (1942). President of the Fourth Session of UN General Assembly (1949–50) and chairman of the Security Council. Books: *I Saw the Fall of the Philippines, I See the Philippines Rise, Crusade in Asia*, and *I Walk with Heroes*.

Brotherhood is the very price and condition of man's survival.

1902 **Alfred Tarski:** Born **Alfred Teitelbaum**. Polish logician and mathematician. Invited to address a Congress to be held at Harvard University, he Left Poland in 1939 on the last ship to leave his homeland for the USA before the German invasion and the outbreak of World War II. So oblivious to the Nazi threat he left his wife and children behind in Warsaw and did not see them again until 1946. One of the four greatest logicians of all time. (The OTHERS: Aristotle, Gottlob Frege, and Kurt Gödel). Introduced the concept of truth in formalized languages.

You will not find in semantics any remedy for decayed teeth or illusions of grandeur or class conflict.

1904 Sir **Cecil Beaton:** Noted photographer of British royalty and entertainment celebrities. Often photographed the Royal family for official publication. Queen Elizabeth, the Queen Mother was his favorite sitter. During World War II, he worked for the British Ministry of Information, as a documentary photographer. Worked as staff photographer for *Vanity Fair* and *Vogue*. Most lauded achievement for stage was the sets and costumes for Lerner and Loewe's *My Fair Lady*, the film version and *Gigi*, both of which earned him Academy Awards for Costume Design. Speaking of mini skirts:

Never in the history of fashion has so little material been raised so high to reveal so much that needs to be covered so badly.

1919 **Andy Rooney:** American humorist, author and television personality. Began his career in newspapers, writing for *Stars and Stripes* in the European Theater during World War II. One of the first American journalists to visit the Nazi death camps and one of the first to write about them. In the early 1950s he was a writer for Arthur Godfrey. Shares his varied and sometimes controversial views on television's "60 Minutes." Has won three Emmys for his essays and also received a lifetime Achievement Emmy.

We're all proud of making little mistakes. It gives us the feeling we don't make any big ones.

1925 **Yukio Mishima:** Japanese novelist, playwright, essayist, famous for his nihilistic post-war writing. His first novel was *Thieves*, followed by *Confession of a Mask*, an autobiographical work about a latent homosexual who must hide behind a mask to fit into society. It mad him a celebrity at age 24. Other works: *The Sailor Who Fell from Grace with the Sea, The Temple of the Golden Pavilion* and *Sea of Fertility*. He committed ritual suicide in traditional Samurai manner as a protest of the Westernization of Japan.

If we value so highly the dignity of life, how can we not also value the dignity of death? No death may be called futile.

1940 **Julian Bond:** Leader of the Civil rights movement and member of both Georgia legislative bodies, As a student, help found SNCC, the Student Nonviolent Coordinating Committee. In 1968 his name was put into nomination for the vice-president of the U.S. but redrew his name because at 28 he was too young to serve. Currently is chairman of the NAAC, working to educate the public about the history of the civil rights movement and the injustices that African Americans and the poor still endure.

Many are attracted to social service — the rewards are immediate, the gratification quick. But if we have social justice, we won't need social service.

1952 **Sydney Biddle Barrow:** The "Mayflower Madam." A woman of impeccable style, she created an escort service of choice among rich, powerful and prominent men. She adapted business management methods to the oldest profession. The bestselling book *Mayflower Madam* tells the story of her career.

I was naughty, I wasn't bad. Bad is hurting people, doing evil. Naughty is not hurting anyone. Naughty is being amusing.

OTHERS: 1741 American traitor **Benedict Arnold**, 1806 Confederate Naval Commander **Matthew Fontaine Maury**, 1841 French painter **Bethe M.P. Morisot**, 1821 German dramatist **Salomon von Mosenthal**, 1863 Dutch educator **Pieter Oosterlee**, 1866 English writer **Hugh Lofting**, 1892 U.S. filmmaker **Hal Roach**, 1906

U.S. actor **William Bendix**, 1914 Oscar winning handicapped actor **Harold Russell**, 1919 Italian prime minister **Giulio Andreotti**, 1929 U.S. C&W singer **Billy Walker**, 1938 U.S. singer **Jack Jones**, 1941 U.S. actress **Faye Dunaway**, 1952 U.S. journalist **Maureen Dowd**, 1963 U.S. filmmaker **Steven Soderbergh**, 1967 English actress **Emily Watson**, 1968 U.S. rapper **LL Cool J**

January 15

1622 **Molière:** Stage name of **Jean Baptiste Poquelin**. French comic dramatist. Wrote 12 of the most durable and penetratingly satirical full-length comedies of all time. Ranks with Aristophanes, Plautius and George Bernard Shaw. Also the leading French comic actor, stage director and dramatic theoretician of the 17th century. Attacked hypocrisy and vice in French society. Among his most famous comic masterpieces are *Le Misanthrope* and *Le Tartuffe*.

The true touchstone of wit is the impromptu.

1809 **Pierre-Joseph Proudhon:** French socialist, working man and printer, who was the first one to identify himself as an "anarchist." He rejected Capitalism, and used the term Mutualism for his brand of anarchism. Called for a complete reorganization of modern society and abolishing most of its trappings, including money and the state itself. He envisioned workers controlling the means of production and factories run by "labor associations."

What is property? Property is theft.

1850 **Sonja Sophia Kovalevsky:** Russian-born mathematician. She convinced Karl Weierstrass, the most renowned German mathematician of the period, to take her as a student. Since the university did not accept women students, he could only give her private lessons. Despite numerous obstacles put in her path, she obtained a PhD in 1874. Invited to teach at Stockholm, her lectures proved a huge success. By the end of the first year she gained a tenured position at the university, was appointed an editor for a mathematics journal. The next year, she was appointed as a full professor, becoming the first woman since the physicist Laura Bassi and the mathematician Maria Gaetana Agnesi to hold a chair at a European university.

Say what you know, do what you must, come what may.

1897 **Stringfellow Barr:** American educator, historian and author. As president of St. John's College, Annapolis, Maryland, together with Scott Buchanan instituted the Great Books curriculum, requiring students to know 120 classics of world literature. In 1959, he became one of a number of signatories to a petition asking the U.S. Congress to abolish the House Committee on Un-American Activities. His 1958 warning:

Today, colleges have come to think of students as customers, and as long as they do, we'll have the higher illiterates we see on campuses today.

1899 **Goodman Ace:** Born **Goodman Aiskowitz:** American humorist, writer, critic and actor. His humor was low-keyed, literate drollery. A gentle curmudgeon, he had a softly tart way of tweaking trends, acts or deeds he disliked. Famous for a long radio run of *Easy Aces*, a domestic comedy, which featured his wry wit and the delightfully delivered malapropos of his wife Jane, such as "I am his awfully wedded wife." In his later years, Ace became a regular columnist for *Saturday Review*.

I keep reading between the lies.

1906 **Aristotle Onassis:** Greek shipping executive. Started oil tanker business (1935) that grew to become a large fleet of cargo and passenger ships. Dumped mistress Maria Callas, who reportedly he really loved, to marry Jackie Kennedy, who would not agree to an affair, so as not to scandalize her children. When he died in 1975, his fortune went to his daughter Christina, which has since passed to her only child, Athina Roussel.

The secret of business is to know something that nobody else knows.

1908 **Edward Teller:** Hungarian-born American physicist. "Father of the H-bomb." Emigrated to the U.S. in the 1930s and was an early member of the Manhattan Project, charged with developing the first atomic bombs. His controversial testimony in the security clearance hearing of his former colleague at Los Alamos, Robert Oppenheimer, caused him to be ostracized by much of the scientific community. Became known for his advocacy of controversial technological solutions to both military and civilian problems. Considered as one of the models for the title character in the 1964 movie *Dr. Strangelove*. As a scientist, he repudiated any moral implications of his work.

The main purpose of science is simplicity and as we understand more things, everything is becoming simpler.

1914 **H.R. [Hugh Redwald] Trevor-Roper:** Notable English historian, author, Cambridge University professor. An amusing and abrasive lecturer and essayist. Won international fame for *The Last Days of Hitler*, followed by *Hitler's Table Talk* and *The Goebbels Diaries*. As a historian of early modern Britain, he was famous for his disputes with fellow historians, whose explanations of the English Civil War he vigorously attacked. Late in his career he was embarrassed when it was proven that the *Hitler Diaries*, which he had endorsed as authentic, were fakes.

The function of genius is not to give new answers, but to pose new questions which time and mediocrity can solve.

1918 **Gamal Abdul Nasser:** Egyptian leader. One of the most important Arab politicians in modern times, especially well-known for his Arab nationalist and anti-colonial foreign policy. Led the coup d'état against King Farouk. First president of Egypt and of United Arab Republic. Unsuccessful in his ambition to build an Arab empire stretching across North Africa. In 1956 he nationalized the Suez Canal in order to raise funds to build the Aswan High Dam, which would create the largest man-made lake in the world and generate electric power for most of Egypt.

I have been a conspirator for so long that I mistrust all around me.

1919 **Etty Hillesum:** Dutch-born young Jewish woman who kept a diary during World War II. She was executed in Auschwitz concentration camp on November 30, 1943. Her diary and letters were saved and published after the war. They dealt with her personal development and how she experienced God.

We are always in search of the redeeming formula, the crystallizing thought.

1929 **Martin Luther King, Jr.:** American clergyman, who led a mass struggle for racial equality that helped end segregation and changed America forever. His successes, which benefited both blacks and whites, were the culmination of two centuries of agitation hundreds of thousands of courageous men and women. First came to prominence leading the black boycott against segregated buses in Montgomery, Alabama (1955). Advocated non-violent resistance. Organized massive civil rights march on Washington, D.C. (1963). Awarded Nobel Peace Prize (1964). Assassinated on a motel balcony in Memphis, Tennessee (1968).

Nothing in all the world is more dangerous than sincere ignorance and conscientious stupidity.

1937 **Margaret O'Brien:** Born **Angela Maxine O'Brien.** Considered one of the most accomplished child actors in film history. Her most famous role was as "Tootie" in *Meet Me in St. Louis.* Received a special Academy Award as "Outstanding Child Actress" of her day. Other films: *Our Vines Have Tender Grapes* and *Little Women.* She was not able to maintain her stardom as an adult actress.

When I cry, do you want the tears to run all the way or shall I stop them halfway?

OTHERS: 1432 King of Portugal **Alfonso V "The African,"** 1716 New York merchant/patriot **Philip Livingston,** 1779 Austrian tragic dramatist **Franz Gillparzer**, 1798 Irish antiquary **Thomas Croton Croker**, 1812 Norwegian fairy tale writer **Peter C. Asbjønsen**, 1873 Austrian social theorist **Max Adler**, 1909 U.S. big band drummer **Gene Krupa**, 1909 American composer/conductor **Elie Siegmeister**, 1913 U.S. actor **Lloyd Bridges**, 1920 Eleventh bishop of New York **John Cardinal O'Connor**, 1926 U.S. guitarist/singer/songwriter **Chuck Berry**, 1926 Austrian actress **Maria Schell**, 1933 American author **Ernest J. Gaines**, 1975 Canadian-born French tennis star **Mary Pierce**

January 16

1603 **Roger Williams:** Anglo-American theologian. Notable proponent of separation of Church and State. Advocate of fair dealings with Native Americans. Banned from the Massachusetts Bay Colony for his operation to civil authority. Founder of the city of Providence, Rhode Island and co-founder of Rhode Island, which became a haven for Quakers and others, seeking religious freedom.

This conscience is found in all mankind, more or less, in Jews, Turks, Papists, Protestants, pagans, etc.

1749 Count **Vittorio Alfieri:** Greatest Italian tragic poet. Spent his early life in extensive travel and dissipation. Turned his attention to literature; made a methodical study of the classics. Tragedies almost always pit a champion of liberty with a tyrant. Wrote: *Flippo, Antigone, Oreste, Mirra,* and his masterpiece, *Saul*, considered the most powerful Italian drama.

Often the test of courage is not to die but to live.

1872 **Edward G. Craig:** English actor, stage designer and drama theorist. Son of Ellen Terry and William Godwin. His aim was to simplify scenes and emphasize actors in his stage designs. Published the quarterly, *The Mask* (1908–29). Books: *On the Art of the Theatre* and *Scene.*

That is what the title of artist means: one who perceives more than his fellows, and who records more than he has seen.

1874 **Robert W. Service:** English-born Canadian poet and journalist. Wrote popular ballads about frontier life in the Yukon*: Songs of Sourdough* and *Ballads of a Cheedhako.* Known as the "Canadian Kipling." Best known for "Rhymes of a Rolling Stone" and "The Shooting of Dangerous Dan McGrew."

Ah! The clock is always slow;/ It is later than you think.

1901 **Fulgencio Batista y Zaldívar:** Poor Cuban mulatto who worked his way up through the army, coming to power as a strongman. Led an army coup against President Machado. President (1940–44). Lost the 1944 elections but returned by way of army revolt overthrowing President Pio (1952). Ruled as dictator until overthrown by the forces of Fidel Castro (1959).

A government needs one hundred soldiers for every guerrilla it faces.

1903 **Eric Liddell:** "Flying Scotsman." Scottish runner and missionary in China. Winner of the Men's 400 meters in the 1924 Olympic Games held in Paris. Also excelled in cricket and rugby. Portrayed by Ian Charleston in *Chariots of Fire*, which won an Academy Award for Best Picture of 1981.

God made me for a purpose. When I run I feel his pleasure.

1909 **Ethel Merman:** Born **Ethel Zimmerman.** American singer, actress. "Queen of Broadway." Exuberant stage personality. Her booming powerful untrained voice brought down the house in musicals such as *Girl Crazy, Annie Get Your Gun, Call Me Madam,* and *Gypsy.* Films: *Alexander's Ragtime Band* and *There's No Business Like Show Business.*

Always give them the old fire, even when you feel like a squashed cake of ice.

1911 **Jay Hanna "Dizzy" Dean:** Colorful, bragging hall-of-fame right-handed baseball pitcher with St. Louis Cardinals and Chicago Cubs. Last NL pitcher to win 30 games in a season, 30–7 (1934). Teamed with his brother Paul (nicknamed "Daffy") to lead the Cards to a World Series victory in 1937. As a baseball announcer, he was criticized for his grammar.

It ain't braggin' if you kin do it.

1928 **William Kennedy:** American writer and journalist. His novels were based in local New York history and the supernatural. Won 1984 Pulitzer Price for Fiction for his novel *Ironwood.* Also wrote the screenplay for *Ironwood* and *The Cotton Club.*

There's only a short walk from the hallelujah to the hoot.

1934 **Marilyn Horne:** American mezzo-soprano, particularly associated with the music of Rossini and Handel. Her first professional work was dubbing the voice of Dorothy Dandridge for the film *Carmen Jones.* Her distinctive voice had a remarkably wide range. Had virtuoso control of breath and pitch.

You have to know exactly what you want out of your career. If you want to be a star, you don't bother with the other things.

1935 **A.J. [Anthony Joseph] Foyt:** American automobile racing driver. Seven-time USAC/CART national champion. First four-time Indianapolis 500 winner. Only driver to win Indy 500, Daytona 500 and 24 hours of Le Mans. Also amassed numerous wins in sports- and midget-car racing.

Every car has a lot of speed in it. The trick is getting the speed out of it.

1947 **Laura Schlesinger:** Host of a popular nationally syndicated radio call-in-show. An outspoken critic of abortion, euthanasia, no-fault divorce, and same-sex marriages. Her show features short monologues on these and other social and political topics, followed by direct, no-nonsense responses to callers' comments, questions, and problems.

When you're the victim of the behavior, it's black and white; when you are the perpetrator, there are a million shades of gray.

OTHERS: 1697 English poet **Richard Savage**, 1728 Italian classical composer **Niccolò Piccinni**, 1757 UA architect **Samuel McIntire**, 1847 Hungarian writer **Kálmán Mikszáth,** 1853 French industrialist **André Michelin**, 1873 English explorer **Boyd Alexander**, 1893 Dutch psychiatrist **Henry C. Rümke**, 1908 English actress **Diana Wynyard**, 1910 U.S. World War II ace pilot **David Campbell**, 1909 American art critic **Clement Greenberg**, 1929 U.S. political strategist **Allard Lowenstein**, 1932 U.S. cartoonist **Jim Berry**, 1932 American ethologist interested in gorillas **Dian Fossey**, 1944 American singer **Ronnie Milsap**, 1944 U.S. singer **Jim Stafford**, 1974 U.S. supermodel **Kate Moss**

January 17

1600 **Pedro Calderón de la Barca:** Spanish poet and dramatist. Wrote plays for the court of Philip IV including: *The Surgeon of His Honor, Life Is a Dream* and his masterpiece *The Daughter of the Air.* Took part in the hostilities in Catalonia in 1640. Created 76 one-act religious dramas, notably *The Great Theater of the World* and *The Faithful Shepherd.*

Absence is the death of love.

1706 **Benjamin Franklin:** American statesman, diplomat, inventor, scientist and publisher. Considered one of the most extraordinary and brilliant public servants in U.S. history. Founded the Pennsylvania Gazette (1730–48) and wrote *Poor Richard's Almanack* (1732–57). Experiences with electricity led to the invention of the lightning rod. Also invented the Franklin stove, and bifocal spectacles Became prosperous and promoted public services in Philadelphia, including a library, fire department, hospital and insurance company. Helped draft and signed the Declaration of Independence. Minister to France, where he negotiated a treaty providing loans and military support for the American Revolution.

Experience keeps a dear school, but fools will learn in no other.

1853 **Alva Ertskin Belmont:** née **Smith**. Multi-millionaire socialite and major funder of the women's suffrage movement. One time married to William Henry Vanderbilt. Became a wealthy widow after the death of her second husband Oliver Hazard Parry Belmont. Developed an interest in women's rights and donated huge sums of money to the cause and also to children's hospitals. Her pieces of advice to women:

Just pray to God. She will help you and first marry for money, then marry for love.

1860 **Anton Chekhov:** Russian playwright and master short-story writer. Supported his family by writing popular comedy sketches while studying to be a physician. Plays include: *The Seagull, Uncle Vanya, Three Sisters* and *The Cherry Orchard.* Married actress Olga Knipper who appeared as the female lead in many of his plays. Short stories include: "The Steppe," "A Dreary Story" and "The Black Monk."

If you are afraid of loneliness, do not marry.

1863 **David Lloyd George:** British statesman and last Liberal to serve as Prime Minister of the UK. Gained national attention for his opposition to the Boer War. Devised the National Insurance Act of 1911, which laid the foundation for the British Welfare State. As Minister of Munitions (1915–16), used unorthodox methods to ensure that war supplies were where they were needed. Succeeded H.H. Asquith as PM in December 1916 and served in that capacity until October, 1922.

Liberty has restraints but no frontiers.

1863 **Konstantin Stanislavsky:** Russian actor, director, producer and acting teacher. Won praise for his first production, *The Fruits of Enlightment* (1891). Developed the theory of acting he called the "method," most successful in the works of Chekhov, Gorky and Andreyev. Cofounder and director of Moscow Art Theatre. Books that influenced the later development of the Group Theatre and the Actors Studio in the USA: *My Life in Art* and *An Actor Prepares.*

Remember, there are no small parts, only small actors.

1886 **Ronald Firbank:** British novelist, known for witty phrases. His masterpiece *Valmouth* (1918) is based on the activities of various people at a health resort on the West Coast of England, most of who are centenarians. Wrote witty, inconsequential dialogue in novels *Vainglory*, *Prancing Nigger* and *Concerning the Eccentricities of Cardinal Pirelli*, in which the hero meets his end while in ardent pursuit of a choir boy.

The world is disgracefully managed, one hardly knows to whom to complain.

1899 **Al Capone:** U.S. mobster. "Scarface Al." Most powerful crime boss of his day. Achieved worldwide notoriety as a prohibition racketeer. Ran most of Chicago and the surrounding area (1925–31). Ruthless and cruel in protecting his business, he ordered what would come to be known as the St. Valentine's Day Massacre. Imprisoned for federal income tax evasion.

You can get much further with a kind word and a gun than you can with a kind word alone.

1899 **Robert Maynard Hutchins:** U.S. educational reformer. Dean of Yale Law School. President of University of Chicago at 30. Chancellor (1945–51). Critic of overspecialization and failure of American universities to maintain and enlarge intellectual traditions of the Western world. Deplored any tendency toward vocationalism and dismantled the intercollegiate athletic program. Headed many foundations including the Ford Foundation. His views on education are contained in *Higher Learning in America*.

A civilization in which there is not a continuous controversy about important issues is on the way to totalitarianism and death.

1927 **Thomas Anthony "Tom" Dooley:** American author, lecturer and medical missionary. "Jungle doctor." Made a career of providing medical aid in underdeveloped countries in South East Asia. Founded Medico, an international welfare organization and medical clinics in Cambodia, Laos and Vietnam. Made Gallup's list as Ten Most Admired men in America. Died at age 34.

I have spent six years of my life among different men, and always I find that the similarities outweigh the differences. Each life is infinitely precious as a life, everywhere.

1928 **Vidal Sassoon:** One of the world's most influential hair stylists. Father of modernistic style. Founded a network of schools and salons in New York, London and San Francisco. Sold his name to a franchise of hair salons and manufactures of hair care products. Wrote*: A Year of Health and Beauty*.

Hair is another name for sex.

1942 **Muhammad Ali [Cassius Clay]:** American boxer, known for his aggressive charm, invincible attitude and colorful boasts. Won the Olympic light heavyweight crown (1960). Only three-time heavyweight champion (1964–67), 1974–78, 1978–79). Stripped on his title for refusing induction into the armed forces following conversion to Islam. Career record, 56-5, 37 KOs, 19 successful title defenses. Diagnosed with Parkinson's disease (1984).

It's just a job. Grass grows, birds fly, waves pound the sand. I just beat people up.

OTHERS: 1342 Duke of Burgundy **Philip the Bold**, 1463 Elector of Saxony/protector of Luther, **Frederick III**, 1732 Last King of Poland **Stanislaw II**, 1771 Father of American novel **Charles Brockden Brown**, 1820 English novelist **Anne Brontë**, 1851 U.S. illustrator/humorist **Arthur Burdett Frost**, 1871 British admiral **David Beatty**, 1880 Pioneer U.S. comedy filmmaker **Mack Sennett**, 1883 English writer **Sir Compton Mackenzie**, 1892 U.S. manufacturer **J.D. Zellerbach**, 1917 New Jersey political boss **Frank Hague**, 1925 American actor **Rock Hudson**, 1927 U.S. singer and actress **Eartha Kitt**, 1931 American actor **James Earl Jones**, 1931 Baseball player/coach/manager **Don Zimmer**

January 18

1689 **Charles-Louis de Secondat Montesquieu:** French lawyer, philosopher and man of letters. Wrote *Persian Letters*, a series of 160 fictional letters satirizing religious intolerance, individuals, institutions and royal power. His magnum opus, *The Spirit of the Laws* profoundly influenced European and American political thought. He advocated the separation of the legislative, judicial and executive powers of government.

If triangles created a God, they would give him three sides.

1782 **Daniel Webster:** U.S. lawyer, politician and orator. Congressman from New Hampshire (1813–17 and 1823–27). Massachusetts senator (1827–41 and 1845–50). Secretary of state (1841–43 and 1850–52). A Whig, he refused his party's nomination for president (1844). Famous orator in support of the Union and in opposition of the nullification movement forwarded by his chief adversary John C. Calhoun.

The past, at least, is secure

1840 **Henry Austin Dobson:** English writer of light verse. Published monographs of Fielding, Steele, Hogarth, Goldsmith and others. Poetry collections: *Vignettes in Rhyme*, Proverbs *in Porcelain*, *Old World Idylls* and *The Story of Rosina*.

Time goes, you say? Ah no!/ Alas, Time stays, we go.

1882 **A.A. [Alan Alexander] Milne:** English dramatist, novelist and humorous journalist. Wrote light essays and comedies. Best known for his children's books, written for his own son, Christopher Robin, particularly: *Winnie the Pooh* and *The House at Pooh Corner*.

I am a Bear of Very Little Brain, and long words bother me.

1892 **Oliver Hardy:** The heavyset member of the comedy team of Laurel and Hardy. The two made more than 200 shorts and full length films, which continue to delight audiences. Fat, pretentious and blustering, constantly fiddling with his tie, Hardy was no brighter than his bullied and confused partner. No one ever grew tired of the line Ollie first said to Stanley in the classic comedy *Sons of the Desert* (1933):

Well, here's another nice mess you've gotten me into.

1904 **Cary Grant:** Originally **Archibald Leach.** Handsome, suave and debonair English-born actor, equally at home in adventure, romantic or comedy films such as: *The Awful Truth, The Philadelphia Story, Arsenic and Old Lace, Notorious, To Catch a Thief* and *North By Northwest.* A master of timing, he could do a double-take with the best comedians. Received a special Academy Award (1970) for his "unique mastery of the art of screen acting."

I think that making love is the best exercise.

1908 **Jacob Bronowski:** English scientist, philosopher, poet, literary critic, dramatist, physicist and mathematician. Wrote *The Common Sense of Science* and *The Origins of Knowledge and Imagination.*

Knowledge is an unending adventure at the edge of uncertainty.

1913 **Danny Kaye:** U.S. actor, comedian and humanitarian. Special Oscar (1954) for service to industry and American people. Well known for fund-raising activities in behalf of UNICEF. Films: *Up in Arms, The Secret Life of Walter Mitty* and *Wonder Man.*

Life is a great big canvas; throw all the paint on it you can.

1932 **Joe Schmidt:** Hall-of-Fame football player. One of the toughest middle linebacker in the NFL. Played for the Detroit Lions from 1953 to 1965 and coached the club from 1967 to 1972.

Life is a shit sandwich, and every day you take another bite.

1933 **John Boorman:** English film director of documentaries such as *The Newcomers.* His feature films include *Point Blank, Deliverance,* and *Hope and Glory.* Nominated for Academy Awards for the last two.

Movies are the repository of myth. Therein lies their power. An alternate history, that of the human psyche, is contained and unfolded in the old stories and tales. Films carry on the tradition.

1938 **Curt Flood:** Baseball outfielder with the St. Louis Cardinals who challenged the constitutionality of the rules that bound him to one club, which could without his permission trade him to another club. Free agency came too late for him.

I am a man, not a consignment of goods to be bought and sold.

1944 **Paul Keating:** Australian politician and 24th Prime Minister of Australia. Briefly was Minister for Northern Australia, becoming one of the youngest ministers in the country's history. First came to prominence as the reforming Treasurer in the Bob Hawke government. Served two terms as Prime Minister but the public's concern for economic issues led to his defeat in 1996.

I try to use the Australian idiom to its maximum advantage.

OTHERS: 1752 Neapolitan admiral **Francesco Caracciolo**, 1779 British physician who created the 1st thesaurus, **Peter Mark Roget**, 1813 Inventor of usable barbed wire **Joseph F. Glidden**, 1849 First Australian prime minister/judge **Edmund Barton**, 1857 English architect **W.R. Lethaby**, 1867 Nicaraguan poet/short story writer **Rubén Dario**, 1880 Austrian-born physicist **Paul Ehrenfest**, 1896 U.S. Umpire **Bill McGowan**, 1910 English-born economist **Kenneth Boulding**, 1933 U.S. inventor of the Dolby Sound system **Ray Dolby**, 1941 American singer/guitarist **Bobby Goldsboro**, 1950 U.S. film director **John Hughes**, 1955 Movie star **Kevin Costner**, 1961 Canadian hockey star **Mark Messier**

January 19

1200 **Dōgen Zenji:** Japanese Zen Buddhist teacher. Founded the Soto school of Zen in Japan. Leading religious figure and important philosopher. "Zenji" means "Zen master," and Dōgen means "Source of the Way."

A flower falls, even though we love it; and a weed grows, even though we do not love it.

1686 **Hakuin Ekaku:** One of the most influential figures in Japanese Zen Buddhism. Transformed the Rinzai school into a tradition that focused on meditation and koan practice. A *koan* is a nonsense question asked of a student to force him, through contemplation of it, to a greater awareness of reality.

Those who testify to the truth of the nature of the Self, have found it by reflecting within themselves.

1798 **Auguste Comte:** French philosopher and founder of positivism. Applied methods of observation and experimentation used in sciences to philosophy, social science and religion. Gave the science of sociology its name and established the new subject on a conceptual basis. Believed that social phenomena could be reduced to laws just as natural phenomena could.

Love, our principle; order, our foundation; progress, our goal.

1807 **Robert E. Lee:** American military leader. In 1859 he led U.S. troops to suppress John Brown's insurgents at Harper's Ferry, Virginia. Offered command of U.S. troops to force the seceded Southern states back into the Union. Although opposed to succession, he resigned U.S. commission to become commander-in-chief of Confederate forces. Victorious at Fredericksburg and Chancellorsville. Defeated at Gettysburg. Surrendered at Appomattox Courthouse.

Duty is the most sublime word in our language. Do your duty in all things. You cannot do more. You should never wish to do less.

1809 **Edgar Allan Poe:** U.S. Poet, short-story writer. Invented modern detective story with "The Murders in the Rue Morgue." Other stories: "The Black Cat," "The Pit and the Pendulum," "The Tell Tale Heart," and "The Fall of the House of Usher." Poems: "The Raven," and "Annabel Lee." Alcohol addiction took his irregular and eccentric life at age 40.

Those who dream by day are cognizant of many things that escape those who dream only at night.

1839 **Paul Cézanne:** French post–Impressionist painter. Considered by many as the greatest figure in modern French painting. His style dynamically assembles simple masses of color and shapes in contrasting planes of still lifes, landscapes and figure studies. Paintings: *Card Players, Mont Sainte-Victoire with Large Pine Trees* and *L'Oeuvre.*

Nature must be treated through the cylinder, the sphere, the cone.

1851 **David Starr Jordan:** American eugenicist and a leading ichthyologist, educator, and peace activist. President of Indiana University and Stanford University. His extensive field trips led to his naming over a thousand genera and more than 2500 species of fish. Prolific writer of more than 2000 books and articles.

Wisdom is knowing what to do next, skill is knowing how to do it, and virtue is doing it.

1887 **Alexander Woollcott:** American journalist, writer and drama critic. Hosted radio show, "The Town Crier" (1929–42). Wrote for *New Yorker* magazine. Known for his acerbic wit, he became a leading member of the Algonquin Round Table of writers, musicians and artists. The inspiration for the play and movie *The Man Who Came to Dinner.*

All the things I like to do are either immoral, illegal, or fattening.

1904 **Roger Blough:** American corporation lawyer, steel executive and philanthropist. Chairman of the board and CEO of U.S. Steel (1955–69). Member of corporation's executive committee (1956–76).

Steel prices cause inflation like wet sidewalks cause rain.

1918 **John H. Johnson:** Founder of the Johnson Publishing Company, an international media and cosmetics empire, which includes *Ebony,* which he modeled after *Life* magazine and *Jet* magazines. Also published black-oriented books, moved into radio and TV broadcasting, insurance and cosmetics manufacturing.

Every day I run scared. That's the only way I can stay ahead.

1943 **Janis Joplin:** "Pearl." Hard-drinking, hard-living American white blues-rock singer. Joined the band Big Brother and the Holding Company in San Francisco in 1996. Soon became famous for her raw, whiskey-powered emotional voice. Died of heroin overdose (1970). Biggest hit: "Me and Bobby McGee."

I'd trade all my tomorrows for a single yesterday.

1946 **Dolly Parton:** American country singer, songwriter, author and actress, known for her enormously busty, blonde-wigged appearance. Performed with Porter Waggoner's band and spent seven years on the Grand Ole Opry. Hit songs include "I Will Always Love You," "Here You Come Again," and "Islands in the Stream. Movies include *9 to 5, The Best Little Whorehouse in Texas,* and *Steel Magnolias.*

Leave something good in every day.

OTHERS: 1736 Scottish industrialist/inventor **James Watt**, 1813 English inventor and engineer **Henry Bessemer**, 1850 English politician and scholar **Augustine Birrell**, 1858 French playwright **Eugene Brieux**, 1859 Canadian botanist **Alice Eastwood**, 1905 Newspaper publisher **Oveta Culp Hobby**, 1916 U.S. actor **Victor Mature**, 1917 American Broadway singer **John Raitt**, 1923 American film/TV actress **Jean Stapleton**, 1931 Canadian newsman **Robert MacNeil**, 1932 U.S. film director **Richard Lester**, 1935 Blonde U.S. actress **Tippi Hedren**, 1938 U.S. singer **Phil Everly**, 1944 English stage actor and singer **Michael Crawford**

January 20

1732 **Richard Henry Lee:** American Revolutionary patriot. Signer of the Declaration of Independence. Opposed ratification of the U.S. Constitution because it lacked a Bill of Rights. U.S. senator from Virginia (1789–92). Made the resolution in the Continental Congress, June 1776:

That these United Colonies are, and of right ought to be, free and independent states.

1806 **Nathaniel Parker Willis:** U.S. poet, editor, journalist and playwright. Founded *The American Monthly Magazine* and *The New York Mirror.* Works: *Inklings of Adventure* and *Letters from Under a Bridge.*

The innocence that feels no risk and is taught no caution, is more vulnerable than guilt, and oftener assailed.

1866 **Richard Le Gallienne:** English man of letters. Wrote for various papers over the signature of *Logroller.* His works include *My Ladies' Sonnets* and *Quest of the Golden* Girl. Father of actress Eve La Gallienne.

A woman's beauty is one of her great missions.

1880 **Ruth Saint Denis:** Originally Ruth Dennis. American dancer and choreographer. First to incorporate the traditions and practices of the vaudeville stage into the world of serious concert dance. She and her husband, Ted Shawn, established the Denishawn dance company and school to provide a new choreographic style of abstract "music visualization."

I see dance used as communication between body and soul, to express what is too deep to find for words.

1889 **Huddie "Leadbelly" Ledbetter:** African-American folk and blues musician. Imprisoned for murder in 1918, pardoned in six years, then imprisoned again in 1930 for attempted murder. Released in 1934 through the efforts of folklorists John and Alan Lomax. Songs highlight the plight of blacks during the Great Depression. Composed the song, "Good Night, Irene."

We all in the same boat brother. You rock it too far to the right you fall in the water, rock it too far to the left you fall in the same water, and its just as wet on both sides.

1896 **George Burns:** Originally **Nathan Birnbaum**. American vaudeville comedian. Married partner Gracie Allen. Then had successful radio and television shows until Gracie's death. At eighty, he found a new career in movies, clubs and television. Academy Award for *The Sunshine Boys*. Famous for his wry humor, attempts at singing, cigars and attraction to pretty young dates.

Acting is all about honesty. If you can fake that, you've got it made.

1904 **Renato Caccioppoli:** Italian mathematician. Grandson of Russian anarchist Mikhail Bakunin. During a visit of Hitler with Mussolini to Naples, Caccioppoli convinced an orchestra to play *La Marseillaise* while he spoke against Italian and German dictators. Arrested, he was able to get himself declared insane and sent to an asylum, where he continued to write mathematical papers, published in a Vatican scientific review.

If you are afraid of something, measure it, and you will realize it is a mere trifle.

1910 **Joy Adamson:** Originally **Joy-Friederike Victoria Gessner**. Austrian-born British author, naturalist. Lived in Kenya. Won international fame by writing *Born Free*, the story of lioness Elsa, who she and her husband raised from a cub and returned her to her natural habitat. It was followed by *Living Free* and *Forever Free*.

Since we humans have the better brain, isn't it our responsibility to protect our fellow creatures from, oddly enough, ourselves?"

1920 **Federico Fellini:** Italian director, actor and screenwriter of films such as *I Vitelloni, a Strada* (which won an Academy Award), *La Dolce Vita, Eight and a Half* and *Satyricon 69*. The best of his later films were *Amarcord* (Academy Award) and *Ginger and Fred*. Awarded a special Oscar for lifetime achievement in 1992.

All art is autobiographical; the pearl is the oyster's autobiography.

1926 **Patricia Neal:** American actress. Made her Broadway debut in *The Voice of the Turtle* (1946). Oscar winner for *Hud*. Other films: *The Fountainhead, The Hasty Heart* and *A Face in the Crowd*. Suffered a series of massive strokes that damaged her nervous system and left her confined to a wheelchair and in a state of semi paralysis and severely impaired speech. With the help of her husband British writer Roald Dahl, she courageously fought back, resumed her career and won an Oscar nomination for *The Subject Is Roses*.

A master can tell you what he expects of you. A teacher, though, awakens your own expectations.

1930 **Edwin "Buzz" Aldrin, Jr.:** NASA astronaut. Flew 66 combat missions in the Korean War. Received a PhD from MIT. 2nd Man to step on the lunar surface following Neil Armstrong during the Apollo 11, the first manned lunar landing mission. Altogether Aldrin logged 289 hours, 53 minutes in space.

Mars is there, waiting to be reached.

1956 **Bill Maher:** Talk show host, comedian, and author. On *Politically Incorrect*, he and celebrity guests discussed political issues of the day, but with humor and few constraints. This was followed by a similar show, *Real Time*, aired live.

Remember, guns don't kill people — unless you practice real hard.

OTHERS: 1586 German composer **Johann Hermann Schein**, 1763 Irish nationalist **Theobald Wolfe Tone**, 1775 French mathematician/physicist **André-Marie Ampére**, 1820 English proponent of women's higher education **Anne Jemina Clough**, 1873 U.S. sociologist/psychologist **Charles A. Ellwood**, 1876 Polish-U.S. pianist **Josef Hofmann**, 1891 Hungarian-U.S. violinist **Mischa Elman**, 1894 Creator of "Little Orphan Annie," **Harold Gray**, 1904 Russian ballerina **Alexandra Danilova**, 1910 U.S. writer **Josephine Johnson**, 1922 U.S. bandleader **Ray Anthony**, 1934 American comedian **Arte Johnson**, 1940 U.S. figure skater **Carol Heiss Jenkins**, 1949 Celebrity ex-wife **Ivana Trump**

January 21

1737 **Ethan Allen:** American Revolutionary commander of the Vermont "Green Mountain Boys," who captured Ft. Ticonderoga, 1775. As a volunteer with General Philip Schuyler's troop, he attempted to take Montreal but was taken prisoner by the British. Held in captivity (1775–78).

Virtue and vice are the only things in this world, which with our soul, are capable of surviving death.

1824 **Thomas "Stonewall" Jackson:** Confederate Army general. Served with distinction in the Mexican War. At the start of the Civil War, he organized a brigade of Virginia volunteers. Won acclaim and his nickname for standing fast in the face of the enemy at the first Battle of Bull Run. Victorious in the Shenandoah Valley campaign. Accidentally killed by his own men during the Confederate victory at Chancellorsville.

Always mystify, mislead and surprise the enemy if possible.

1829 **Oscar II:** King of Sweden (1872–1907) and of Norway (1872–1905). An outstanding orator who loved music and literature. Published books of verse and wrote on historical subjects. A domestic conservative who sought Scandinavian cooperation.

I would rather have my people laugh at my economics than weep for my extravagance.

1895 **Cristóbal Balenciaga:** Spanish-French fashion designer. Inspired to become a couturier by a visit to Paris and by age 20 had his own firm in San Sebastián. Spanish Civil War led him to relocate to Paris, where his business flourished for 30 years. Helped popularize capes and flowing clothes without waistlines in the 1950s.

If you want publicity — add a touch of vulgarity.

1904 **Richard Palmer Blackmur:** American critic and poet. Resident fellow and professor at Princeton University. His appraisals of literature include *The Art of the Novel* and *Primer of Ignorance*.

Myths ... gossip grown old!

1905 **Christian Dior:** French fashion designer. After World War II, introduced "new look" of small shoulders, long hemlines and full skirts as a reaction to the padded shoulders and short skirts, a consequence of scarce material. In the 1950s, introduced the "sack" or "H" line, which became the characteristic silhouette of his designs.

My dream is to save women from nature.

1905 **Karl Wallenda:** Patriarch of *The Flying Wallendas,* the most famous high-wire act of the 20th century. Worked without a safety net. Famous for such dangerous stunts as the seven-person human pyramid. The family has endured various tragedies including Karl falling to his death at age 73.

Being on the tightrope is living, everything else is waiting.

1925 **Benny Hill:** English comedian. Worked his way up through men's clubs, revues and end-of-pier shows to become television personality of the year (1954). Best known for his bawdy and slapstick-filled television comedy show.

Just because nobody complains doesn't mean all parachutes are perfect.

1938 **Wolfman Jack (Bob Smith):** Radio legend in the early 1960's. Known for his gravelly voice and howling. The *Guess Who* recorded a hit song, *Clap for the Wolfman.*

We are put on this earth to have a good time. This makes other people feel good. And the cycle continues.

1940 **Jack Nicklaus:** Dominant American world golf figure. The "Golden Bear." All-time leader in major tournament wins, 20; including 6 Masters, 5 PGAs, 4 U.S. Opens, and 3 British Opens. Named Golfer of Century by PGA (1988). Had the ability to combine skill and power with remarkable concentration and composure. Regarded as the greatest golfer in the game's history, but Tiger Woods may eventually earn that designation.

Golf is a game of precision, not strength

1941 **Placido Domingo:** Spanish opera tenor and conductor. Among the world's leading lyric-dramatic tenors. Acclaimed for his musicality and impressive voice. His repertoire consists of more than 80 roles, most notably in *Tosca, Otello, Carmen* and *Tales of Hoffman.*

When it becomes clear that no one else shares your level of passion, you are where you belong.

1957 **Geena Davis [Virginia Elizabeth Davis]:** U.S. actress. Former Victoria's secret model. Mensa member. Won Oscar for Best Supporting Actress for *Accidental Tourist.* Nominated for Best Actress for *Thelma and Louise.* Currently appearing as the president of the U.S. in TV's *Commander in Chief.*

I can't be feminist and sexy? Oh please, that's so '80s.

OTHERS: 1338 King of France **Charles V**, 1743 Built first U.S. steamboat, **John Fitch**, 1813 American explorer and surveyor **John C. Frémont**, 1815 American dentist who pioneered the use to anesthesia **Horace Wells**, 1855 U.S. inventor **John Moses Browning**, 1883 Irish-born U.S. novelist, historian and editor **Francis Hackett**, 1921 First person to receive a permanent artificial heart **Barney Clark**, 1922 English actor **Paul Scofield**, 1924 American baldpate actor **Telly Savalas**, 1941 U.S. singer/guitarist **Richie Havens**, 1956 U.S. actor **Robbie Benson**, 1963 Nigerian-born NBA star **Akeem "The Dream" Olajuwon**, 1976 British singer with the "Spice Girls" **Emma Bunton ("Baby Spice")**

January 22

1263 **Ibn Taymiyah:** Islamic scholar who sought to return Islam to its sources: the Qur'an and the prophetic tradition of Muhammad. Imprisoned several times for his outspokenness, puritanical views and literalism in conflicts with the prominent jurists and theologians of his day. Known for his prodigious memory and encyclopedic knowledge. Skeptical of giving any undue religious honors to shrines to rival in any way the two most holy mosques within Islam, Mecca, and Medina.

What can my enemies possibly do to me? My paradise is in my heart; wherever I got it goes with me, inseparable from em. For me, prison is a place of (religious) retreat; execution is my opportunity for martyrdom; and exile from my town is but a chance to travel.

1561 Sir **Francis Bacon:** English philosopher, statesman, and essayist. Lord Chancellor of England (1618). Published works on philosophy of science. He was the practical creator of scientific induction. Works: *The Advancement of Learning, Novum Organum* and *New Atlantis.*

A prudent question is one-half of wisdom.

1592 **Pierre Gassendi:** French physicist and philosopher. Described and named the aurora borealis. First to describe the transit of Mercury. Studied velocity of sound. Strong advocate of the experimental approach to science. Tried to reconcile an atomic theory of matter with Christian doctrine. Early critic of René Descartes' philosophical views as found in his *Meditations.*

What is clearer than man is not furnished for hunting, much less for eating other animals?

1654 **Richard Blackmore:** English poet and physician. Primarily remembered as the object of satire and as an example of a dull poet. However, he was a respected physician and religious writer. Had a passion for writing epics, most notably, Prince Arthur, a thinly veiled celebration of the achievements of King William III. Blackmore intentionally offended the wits of the day, when he denounced the degeneracy of their poems. John Dryden called Blackmore a "Pedant, Canting Preacher, and a Quack."

Betting is the manure to which the enormous crop of race-horses and racehorse breeding in this and other countries is to a large extent due.

1729 **Gotthold Ephram Lessing:** German critic, dramatist, writer on aesthetics, physician and epigrammatist. Defender of independent thinkers. Works: *Miss Sara Sampson, Emilia Galotti* and his novel plea for tolerance, *Nathan der Weise.*

A heretic is a man who sees with his own eyes.

1788 **George Gordon, Lord Byron:** English poet. Profligate life-style. Created the "Byronic hero"—a defiant, melancholy young man, brooding on some past, mysterious sin. Works: "Childe Harold's Pilgrimage," "Lara," "Siege of Cornith" and "Don Juan." Lame from birth, his mother's violent temper produced a repression in him, which perhaps explains some of his later actions, when he dramatized himself as a man of mystery and a gloomy romantic figure.

Opinions are made to be changed—or how is truth to be got at?

1849 **August Strindberg:** Swedish playwright, novelist, short-story writer. Later works are the first example of Swedish realism. His plays *The Father, Miss Julie* and *The Creditors* make him a forerunner of expressionism and a major influence on modern theater.

Family ... the home of all social evil, a charitable institution for comfortable women, an anchorage for house-fathers, and a hell for children.

1874 **D.W. [David Wark] Griffith:** U.S. director. Most influential figure in early history of American film. A founder of United Artists. Films: *The Birth of a Nation, Intolerance, Broken Blossoms,* and *Orphans of the Storm.*

Taken as drama, war is, in some ways, unsatisfactory.

1890 **Frederick M. Vinson:** U.S. politician, jurist. Secretary of the Treasury under President Truman. Helped establish the International Bank for Reconstruction and Development. Chief justice of the Supreme Court (1946–53). Upheld powers of federal government versus individual rights.

Wars are not "acts of God." They are caused by man, by man-made institutions, by the way in which man has organized his society. What man has made, man can change.

1893 **Conrad Veidt:** German Jewish actor. Famed for his roles as the somnambulist in the silent classic *The Cabinet of Dr. Caligari,* the evil Jaffar in *The Thief of Bagdad, and* the detestable Nazi Major Strasser in *Casablanca.*

No matter what roles I play. I can't get Caligari out of my system.

1909 **U Thant:** Burmese teacher, journalist, independence agitator. Third Secretary General of United Nations General Assembly (1962–72). Played a major diplomatic role during the Cuban crisis, devised a plan to end the Congolese Civil War and sent peacekeeping forces to Cyprus.

In modern war there is no such thing as victor and vanquished ... there is only a loser, and that loser is mankind.

1934 **Graham Kerr:** English–born Cooking personality who gained fame through his TV show "The Galloping Gourmet," filmed in Canada. Previously he had been a catering advisor to the British Army and General Manager of England's Royal Ascot Hotel.

I prefer to regard a dessert as I would imagine the perfect woman: subtle, a little bittersweet, not blowsy and extrovert. Delicately made up, not highly roughed. Holding back, not exposing everything and, of course, with a flavor that lasts.

Others: 1802 U.S. gothic architect **Richard Upjohn,** 1874 U.S. number theorist **Leonard E. Dickson,** 1894 English writer **Charles Morgan,** 1892 French airplane builder **Marcel Dassault,** 1894 U.S. opera singer **Rosa Ponselle,** 1899 Finish linguist/poet **Martii Haavio,** 1928 Former U.S. senator from Indiana, **Birch Bayh,** 1932 Petite American actress **Piper Laurie,** 1934 U.S. actor **Bill Bixby,** 1935 American singer **Sam Cooke,** 1937 Former policeman/author **Joseph Wambaugh,** 1938 American photographer **Peter Beard,** 1940 British actor **John Hurt,** 1952 U.S. musician **Teddy Gentry,** 1957 Canadian hockey player **Mike Bossy,** 1959 U.S. actress **Linda Blair,** 1963 American actress **Diane Lane**

January 23

1783 **Stendahl:** Pseudonym of **Marie Henri Beyle.** French novelist and critic, he wrote biographies and critical works on art, literature and music. Best known for novels: *The Red and the Black,* a powerful study of an ambitious young man that also offers an astute picture of Restoration France and *The Charterhouse of Parma,* a remarkable study of human psychology.

The shepherd always tries to persuade the sheep that their interests and his own are the same.

1832 **Édouard Manet:** French painter and printmaker. Forerunner of impressionists. Paintings: *Luncheon on the Grass* and *Bar at the Folies-Bergère.* Broke new ground by choosing subjects from his own time. His genius was only recognized after his death.

The country only has charms for those not obliged to stay there.

1862 **David Hilbert:** German mathematician. For a large part of two centuries this giant dominated the world's mathematical development. In 1900, he presented a lecture before the Second International Congress of Mathematicians in Paris. He proposed 23 problems, which crystallized mathematical thinking throughout the 20th century. It was not merely his reputation as the outstanding mathematician of his age that made these problems significant. They were types of questions mathematicians wanted to answer. Each problem in its own way is important enough and difficult enough to be of interest, and each led to the development of a large body of new mathematics.

The infinite! No other question has ever moved so profoundly the spirit of man.

1898 **Sergei Eisenstein:** Soviet film director and theorist. Introduced startling and often discordant images to the main action to create the maximum impact. Major influence on world cinema with films *The Battleship Potemkin,* often called the greatest film ever made, and the historical biographies *Alexander Nevsky,* and *Ivan the Terrible* I and II.

The profession of film director can and should be such a high and precious one; that no aspiring

to it can disregard any knowledge that will make him a better film director or human being.

1899 **Humphrey Bogart:** American actor with cult status. Best in roles as average guys reluctantly thrust into demanding situations, who somehow rise to the occasion. Oscar winner for *The African Queen*. Nominated for *Casablanca* and *The Caine Mutiny*. Memorable in *The Petrified Forest, The Maltese Falcon, High Sierra* and *The Big Sleep*. Starred in four films with his fourth wife Lauren Bacall, beginning with *To Have and Have Not*.

The whole world is three drinks behind.

1910 **Katharine Tyson Hinkson:** Prolific Irish writer. In addition to her 105 novels, she wrote two anthologies, sixteen other collections of poetry, five plays, seven books of devotion one book about dogs, twelve collections of short stories and numerous newspaper articles.

Against stupidity the gods fight in vain.

1915 **Potter Stewart:** American jurist and lawyer. Judge of U.S. Court of Appeals, Sixth Circuit (1954–58). Independent and moderate associate justice of the Supreme Court, appointed 1959 by President Eisenhower, serving until 1981.

Swift justice demands more than just swiftness.

1919 **Ernie Kovacs:** Brilliant creative U.S. comedian. Offbeat humor best featured in his irreverent and imaginative TV show "The Ernie Kovacs Show" (1955–56). Movies: *Operation Mad Ball, Bell, Book and Candle* and *Our Man in Havana*. Killed in a car crash (1962).

Television, a medium. So called because it is neither rare nor well done.

1928 **Jeanne Moreau:** French actress of the Comédie-Française and Théâtre National Populaire. Noted for her sensuality and sophistication. Respected film star in *The Lovers, Jules and Jim, Diary of a Chambermaid, The Bride Wore Black* and more recently, *The Summer House*. Directed *Lumière* and *L'adaolescente*.

Acting deals with very delicate emotions. It is not putting up a mask. Each time an actor acts he does not hide; he exposes himself.

1930 **William Pogue:** American astronaut. Air Force Colonel and instructor at the Air Force Aerospace Research Pilot School. Gained proficiency in more than 50 types of aircraft. Logged 7,200 hours flight time, including 2,017 hours in space flight.

As I looked out into space, I was overwhelmed by the darkness. I felt the flesh crawl on my back and hair rise on my neck.

1934 **Frank Lautenberg:** United States senator from New Jersey. Known as one of the Senate's most liberal members, Pro-choice, supported gun control, and authored the Ryan White Act which provides services to AIDS patients.

One thing I have learned in my time in politics is that if one of the parties is shameless, the other party cannot afford to be spineless.

1946 **Susan L. Taylor:** Editor-in-Chief of the African-American magazine *Essence* and senior vice-president of Essence Communications, Inc. Author of *In the Spirit* and *Lessons in Living*.

Use missteps as stepping stones to deeper understanding and greater achievement.

OTHERS: 1582 Scottish satirist **John Barclay**, 1752 Italian composer **Muzio Clementi**, 1816 German stage magician **Carl Hermann**, 1830 Dutch-U.S. missionary **Guido Verbeck**, 1840 German physicist **Ernst Abbe**, 1841 French actor **Benoit-Constant Coquelin**, 1887 Premier of Hungary **Miklós Kállay**, 1888 British sculptor **Gilbert Ledward**, 1897 Indian politician **Subhas Chandra Bose**, 1898, U.S. film actor **Randolph Scott**, 1904 U.S. historian **Benjamin A. Quarles**, 1930 St. Lucian Nobel Prize winning poet and playwright **Derek Walcott**, 1933 U.S. actress and dancer **Chita Rivera**, 1948 U.S. singer **Anita Pointer**, 1957 Princess of Monaco, **Caroline**, 1964 TV actress **Mariska Hargitay**

January 24

76 CE **Publius Hadrianus (Hadrian):** Roman emperor. Executed his opponents, abandoned some of his predecessor Trajan's conquests and traveled widely. The empire reached its height during his reign. Strengthened fortifications did extensive building, and reorganized law and civil service. Began the continuous Roman defensive barrier, know as Hadrian's Wall that guarded the northwest frontier of the empire from barbarian invaders. Brutally crushed a Jewish rebellion.

Little soul, wandering, gentle guest and companion of my body, you who will now go off to places pale, stiff, and barren, nor will you make jokes as has been your wont.

1664 Sir **John Vanbrugh:** English playwright and Baroque architect. Wrote successful Restoration comedies of manners: *The Relapse* and *The Provok'd Wife*. Designed Castle Howard, Yorkshire and his masterpiece Blenheim Palace, which brought the English baroque style to its culmination.

He laughs best that laughs last.

1670 **William Congreve:** English dramatist. Protégé of John Dryden. Considered master of Restoration comedies with his brilliant comic dialogue, satirical portrayal of fashionable society and uproarious bawdiness. Wrote *The Old Bachelor, Love for Love* and his masterpiece *The Way of the World*. Also wrote many poems, translations and two opera librettos.

Courtship is to marriage, as a very witty prologue to a very dull play.

1712 **Frederick the Great:** Prussian king, military leader (1740–86). Noted for social reforms. Led Prussia in the Seven Years' War. A writer and composer as well as a great military commander. Under his rule Prussia became a major European power.

God is always with the strongest battalions.

1732 **Pierre de Beaumarchais:** French author, courtier and dramatist. Best know for his satirical plays *Barber of Seville* and *Marriage of Figaro*, which criticized the aristocracy. The plays, which sometimes were said to have sparked the French Revolution, became famous operas by Rossini and Mozart, respectively. Founded the Société des Auteurs.

It is not necessary to understand things in order to argue about them.

1832 **Joseph H. Choate:** Brilliant American lawyer, diplomat, and orator. Distinguished for over 50 years of public service. Works: *American Addresses* and *Arguments and Addresses.*

Do not make long prayers; always remember that the Lord knows something.

1850 **Hermann Ebbinghaus:** German experimental psychologist. Best remembered for *On Memory*, which first applied experimental methods to memory research. Demonstrated that memory is based on associations. Introduced the "forgetting curve," which relates forgetting to the passage of time.

Psychology has a long past, but only a short history.

1862 **Edith Wharton:** American novelist and short-story writer. Wrote of life among the middle-class and aristocratic New York society of the 19th and early 20th centuries. Her close friendship with Henry James helped to support and shape her work. Works: *The House of Mirth, Ethan Frome, The Age of Innocence* and *The Old Maid.*

There are two ways of spreading light; to be the candle or the mirror that reflects it.

1888 **Vicki Baum [Vicki Hedvig]:** Austrian-born novelist. Focused on independent women caught up in the turmoil of society. Made her name with *Grand Hotel*, which became a best seller and a popular film. Also wrote *Falling Star* and *The Mustard Seed.*

Marriage always demands the greatest understanding of the art of insincerity possible between two human beings.

1915 **Robert Motherwell:** American artist. One of the founders of Abstract Expressionism in New York City in the 1940. Interest in Freud and psychoanalysis led to spontaneous paintings and huge images. His *Elegy to the Spanish Republic* series began in 1949 and continued over three decades.

Wherever art appears, life disappears. Art is much less important than life, but what a poor life without it.

1920 **Jerry Maren:** U.S. actor who stands just four foot three. Appeared as the Munchkin who hands Dorothy a welcoming lollipop. Appeared as Buster Brown on TV and radio during the 1950s and 1960s. Has made many commercials for McDonald's as Mayor McCheese.

I'm Buster Brown and I live in a shoe. This is my dog Tige, and he lives there too.

1928 **Desmond Morris:** British zoologist and writer. Curator of mammals at the Zoological Society of London. Wrote best-selling *The Naked Ape*, a study of human behavior, followed by *The Human* Zoo and *Manwatching*. Hosted many television programs on animal and social behavior.

I viewed my fellow man not as a fallen angel, but as a risen ape.

OTHERS: 1705 Italian castrato **Farinelli [Carlo Broschi]**, 1798 German mathematician **Karl von Staudt**, 1829 U.S. pianist **William Mason**, 1865 U.S. sculptor **Paul Wayland Bartlett**, 1902 German/U.S. economist **Oskar Morgenstern**, 1911 U.S. sci-fi author **C.L. Moore**, 1915 Oscar winning actor **Ernest Borgnine**, 1916 U.S. sports broadcaster **Jack Brickhouse**, 1918 U.S. televangelist/ faith healer **Oral Roberts**, 1925 U.S. ballerina **Maria Tallchief**, 1936 Cajun singer/guitarist **Doug Kershaw**, 1941 U.S. singer/songwriter **Neil Diamond**, 1943 Murdered U.S. actress **Sharon Tate**, 1949 U.S. comic actor **John Belushi**, 1968 American gymnast **Mary Lou Retton**

January 25

1736 **Joseph-Louis Lagrange:** Italian-born French mathematician. Called "The Lofty Pyramid of the Mathematical Sciences" by Napoleon, who made him a Count of the Empire. A great analyst, his attack on mechanics marked the first complete break with Greek tradition. First to develop today's familiar methods of finding *maximum* and *minimum* values of functions, which he regarded as his best mathematical work. Put his mathematical discoveries and inventions to use in solving the great problems of his day in mechanics and astronomy.

As long as algebra and geometry have been separated, their progress has been slow and their uses limited; but when these two sciences have been united, they have lent each mutual force, and have marcher together towards perfection.

1759 **Robert Burns:** Scotland's greatest poet. His humble origin as the son of a farmer and his identification with the Scottish folk tradition, which he rescued, refurbished and embellished, are factors in his unwavering popularity in his homeland. Best known for his lyrics written in the Scottish vernacular, praising lowland life. Poems: "Epistle to Davie," "The Holy Fair," "The Address to a Mouse" and "Tam o' Shanter." Most widely famous for: "Auld Lang Syne" and "Comin' Thru the Rye."

The best laid schemes o' mice and men/ Gang aft a-gley.

1874 **Hewlett Johnson:** Bishop of Canterbury nicknamed the "Red Dean," a sobriquet self-bestowed title when during the Spanish Civil War he said, "I saw red — you can call me red." Visited Russia and with the publication of The Socialist Sixth of the World began his years praising Sovietism. Champion of the Communist state and Marxist policies. Received the Stalin Peace Prize. Wrote *Christians and Communists.*

Noble words ... find echoes down the ages.

1874 **W. Somerset Maugham:** English novelist, playwright and master of the short-story. Served with a Red Cross unit in France in 1914, then as a secret agent in Geneva and finally in Petrograd, where he was to attempt to prevent the outbreak of the Russian Revolution. Works include: *Of Human Bondage*, *The Moon and Sixpence* and *The Razor's Edge*. Best known for short stories including "Rain." Several were filmed under the titles *Quartet, Trio* and *Encore*.

It is bad enough to know the past; it would be intolerable to know the future.

1881 **Emil Ludwig [Colin Ludwig]:** German-born Swiss biographer, internationally known for his many popular biographies, including those of Goethe, Napoleon, Wilhelm II, Bismark, Christ and Lincoln. First wrote plays and novella, and worked as a journalist. His biographies were very popular outside of Germany and were considered particularly dangerous by Joseph Goebbels. At the end of World War II, he retrieved the coffins of Goethe and Schiller that had disappeared from Weimar in 1943.

Just make sure your intentions are not pretensions.

1882 **Virginia Woolf:** English novelist, critic, and essayist. Used techniques of interior monologue and stream of consciousness. Had a tremendous influence on the form of the English novel. Novels: *Mrs. Dalloway, Orlando, To the Lighthouse* and *The Years*. Suffering from poor health and depression she committed suicide by drowning.

On the outskirts of every agony sits some observant fellow who points.

1918 **Edvard Shevardnadze:** Soviet-Georgian politician and diplomat. Replaced Andrei Gromyko as Minister of Foreign Affairs in 1985. Implemented the Soviet withdrawal from Afghanistan in 1988, new arms treaties with the USA, while promoting the policies of Glasnost and Perestroika. After the collapse of the Soviet Union he returned to the newly formed independent republic of Georgia as the elected head of state.

I think it would be fair to say that my role in ending the Cold War was crucial.

1919 **Edwin Newman:** American news commentator, author. Defender of clear use of English language. Books: *Strictly Speaking* and *A Civil Tongue*.

The prevalence of "Y'know" is one of the most far-reaching and depressing developments of our time.

1924 **Lou Groza:** U.S. football player called "The Toe." Defensive lineman and placekicker with the Cleveland Browns, Scored 1,608 points during his NFL career.

Old placekickers never die; they just go on missing the point.

1933 **Corazon C. Aquino:** née **Cojuango.** Filipino political leader. Widow of assassinated Benigno Aquino. Defeated Ferdinand Marcos in 1986 for presidency by leading nonviolent "people's power" campaign. Did not run for the presidency in 1992, instead supported the successful candidacy of General Fidel Ramos.

One must be frank to be relevant.

1950 **Gloria Naylor:** African-American novelist. Oprah Winfrey's Harpo Productions adapted Naylor's best-known novel *The Women of Brewster Place*, which consists of seven stories, each focusing on a different African-American woman, to a film in 1989. Other works: *Linden Hills* and *Mama Day*.

One should be able to return to the first sentence of a novel and find the resonances of the entire work.

1951 **Steve Roland Prefontaine:** American Olympic runner. Primarily a long distance runner. Once held the American record in every running event from the 2000 meters to 10,000 meters. Killed at age 24 in an auto accident.

I don't just go out there and run. I like to give people watching something exciting.

OTHERS: 749 Byzantine emperor **Leo IV [The Khazar]**, 1540 First of the English Jesuit martyrs **Edmund Campion**, 1626 Dutch landscape painter **John van de Cappelle**, 1627 Anglo-Irish physicist and chemist **Robert Boyle**, 1813 U.S. surgeon/inventor **James Marion Sims**, 1825 Confederate General **George E. Pickett**, 1860 U.S. inventor and engineer **Charles Curtis**, 1863 U.S. Quaker preacher **Rufus Matthew Jones**, 1899 Belgian Socialist politician **Paul-Henri Spaak**, 1900 Russian-born U.S. geneticist **Theodosius Dobzhausky**, 1901 American actress **Mildred Dunnock**, 1913 Polish composer **Witold Lutoslawski**, 1934 U.S. poet and journalist **Elizabeth Akers**, 1938 U.S. singer **Etta James**

January 26

1715 **Claude-Adrien Helvétius:** French philosopher, remembered for his hedonism, his attack on the religious foundations of ethics and his educational theory. His controversial "De l'ésprit" advanced the view that sensation is the source of all intellectual activity and self-interest is the motivating force of all human action.

To limit the press is to insult a nation; to prohibit reading of certain books is to declare the inhabitants to be either fools or slaves.

1871 **Samuel Hopkins Adams:** American journalist and editor. Exposed quack patent medicine in "The Great American Fraud," which spurred the passage of the Pure Food and Drug Act of 1906.

It is better that a marriage end by a clear severance than be slowly stifled to death through years of intolerable contact.

1880 **Douglas MacArthur:** American general. Military adviser to the Philippines prior to World War II. Ordered to withdraw from Corregidor (1941) pledging "I shall return." Supreme Commander of Allied Forces in the Southeast Pacific. Liberated Philippines (1944–45). Commander of occupation forces Japan (1945–50). Commander-in-chief U.N. forces Korea (1950–51). Dismissed by Truman over disagreement about who was in command, the general or the president.

It is a fatal error to enter any war without the will to win it.

1884 **Roy Chapman Andrews:** American explorer and director of the American Museum of Natural History. Made a complete scientific survey of the vast area of Outer Mongolia, greatly increasing the knowledge of prehistoric life. Famous for finding dinosaur eggs, new geological formations and the remains of the largest mammal known to have existed. It seems likely that he was the model for fictional adventurer/archaeologist Indiana Jones.

Man is an ape with possibilities.

1907 Sir **Henry Cotton:** One of Britain's greatest golfer of the 20th century. Won British Open three times, almost single-handedly fighting off the American challenge. Played in four Ryder Cup tournaments. In retirement was a journalist and course designer. Much in demand as a teacher and consultant.

The big trick in putting is not method; the secret of putting is domination of the nerves.

1925 **Paul Newman:** U.S. actor, director. Famous for his piercing blue eyes and anti-heroic roles. Survived a disastrous film debut in *The Silver Chalice*. Became on of the key stars of his generation and later as a distinguished character actor and director. Nominated for Oscars for *Cat on a Hot Tin Roof, The Hustler, Hud, Cool Hand Luke, Absence of Malice, The Verdict* and *Nobody's Fool*. Received Oscar for *The Color of Money*. Married to actress Joanne Woodward since 1958.

Acting isn't a creative profession. It's an interpretative one. Acting is a question of absorbing other people's personalities and adding some of your own experience.

1929 **Jules Feiffer:** American cartoonist, screenwriter and dramatist. Satirist for *The Village Voice, Playboy, London Observer*. Awarded Pulitzer Prize (1986). Screenplay for *Carnal Knowledge*. Plays include *Little Murders*, which blend farce and social criticism. Also wrote children's books.

Jesus died to forgive our sins. Dare we make his martyrdom meaningless by not committing them?

1935 **Bob Uecker:** American baseball catcher, sportscaster and self-depreciating humorist. Long-time Hall-of-fame telecaster of Milwaukee Brewers games. Wrote a very funny autobiography *Catcher in the Wry*. Gave himself the nickname "Mr. Baseball."

The way to catch a knuckleball is to wait until it stops rolling and then pick it up.

1944 **Angela Davis:** American revolutionary, black militant, communist activist, author. Doctoral candidate at the University of California, studying with Herbert Marcuse. Champion of the cause of black prisoners. Acquitted of charges of kidnapping, murder and conspiracy in connection with shootout at Marin County courthouse. Ran for president in 1980 on the Communist Party ticket.

Radical simply means grasping things at the root.

1945 **Jacqueline du Pré:** Arguably the greatest talent ever to play the cello. Played with precision, fullness, and purity of tone. Left a legacy of recordings. Married pianist Daniel Barenboim. Diagnosed with multiple sclerosis 1n 1973. Pursued a teaching career, including master classes. Died at age 42.

Playing lifts you out of yourself into a delirious place.

1958 **Ellen DeGeneres:** Stand-up comedian, actress, and writer. Voted "Funniest Person in America" in 1982. Came out as a lesbian on her show *Ellen* in April 1997. Birminghams' ABC affiliate refused to air the show, and some of her sponsors withdrew their advertisements. On hosting the Emmys in 2001, she said:

What would bug a guy from the Taliban more than seeing a gay woman in a suit surrounded by Jews?

1961 **Wayne Gretzky:** "The Great One." Hockey player with Edmonton, Los Angeles and St. Louis. Holds many records in the sport. All-time scoring champion with more than 800 goals. Leads in career points and assists. His modesty and courtesy brought him respect as a model of sportsmanship.

You miss 100 percent of the shots you don't take.

OTHERS: 1786 English historical painter/writer **B.R. Haydon**, 1804 French novelist **Eugène Sue**, 1831 American writer/editor **Mabel Dodge**, 1884 German-born educator **Arnold Brecht**, 1884 German-born linguist/anthropologist **Edward Sapir**, 1905 Austrian-born singer **Maria von Trapp**, 1907 Canadian endocrinologist **Hans Selye**, 1913 U.S. composer **Jimmy Van Heusen**, 1925 Canadian Liberal Party leader **Claude Ryan**, 1928 French film director **Roger Vadim**, 1934 U.S. musician **Huey "Piano" Smith**, 1942 U.S. actor **Scott Glenn**, 1946 British playwright **Christopher Hampton**, 1946 Movie critic **Gene Siskel**, 1957 U.S. guitarist **Eddie Van Halen**, 1958 U.S. singer **Anita Baker**

January 27

1720 **Samuel Foote:** English dramatist and actor. Studied law and lawyers, whom he satirized in *The Lame Lovers*. Ran through two fortunes, passing into severe straights, which led him to appear on the stage. His brilliant mimicry of prominent people led to legal proceedings against him on several occasions. Other plays: *Taste*, and *The Minor*.

Death and dice level all distinctions.

1756 **Wolfgang Amadeus Mozart:** Austrian musical genius, pianist and world-renowned composer. Son of violinist, composer and theorist Leopold Mozart who was eager to showcase his son's exceptional talents and those of his pianist daughter Maria-Anna. Child prodigy. Began playing at age 3, composing at 5 and by age 13 had written concertos, sonatas, symphonies, and a German operetta. His more than 600 works in every genre are unsurpassed in lyric beauty, rhythmic variety and melodic invention. Works: *The Marriage of Figaro, Don Giovanni* and *The Magic Flute*. Also prolific in writing sacred vocal pieces and instrumental works. The annual Salzburg Festival is held in his honor.

Melody is the very essence of music. When I think of a good melodist I think of a fine race horse. A contrapuntist is only a post-horse.

1775 **Friedrich von Schelling:** German writer, idealist, critic and philosopher. Examined the relation of the self to the objective world and argued that consciousness is the only immediate object of knowledge. An important influence on Romanticism, stressing that only in art can the mind become full aware of itself. Works: *Thoughts on Poetry*, *Of the World-Soul*, and *System of Transcendental Idealism*.

Architecture in general is frozen music.

1805 **Samuel Palmer:** British landscape painter and etcher. Produced mainly watercolors displayed in a mystical but precise depiction of nature. His work had an overflowing religious intensity. Member of a group including John Linnell and George Richmond that called themselves, the *Ancients*. Palmer's work was almost forgotten until rediscovered by Neo-Romantics during World War II.

Wise men make proverbs, but fools repeat them.

1832 **Lewis Carroll:** Pseudonym of **Charles Lutwidge Dodgson**, English minister, mathematician and author. As a child, invented many board games, acrostics and other puzzles. Best known for classic fantasies *Alice in Wonderland* and *Through the Looking Glass*, written for Alice Liddell, daughter of the head of Oxford College. His books were famously illustrated by John Tenniel. Other Works: *The Hunting of the Snark and Rhyme? And Reason*. Dodgson also made contributions to symbolic logic and wrote *Euclid and His Modern Rivals*.

When I use a word it means just what I choose it to mean — neither more nor less.

1836 **Leopold von Sacher-Masoch:** Austrian lawyer and writer of many short stories and novels. The term *masochism* was coined for the form of eroticism he describes in his later works. His *novel Der Don Juan von Kolmea* depicts the life of small-town Polish Jews.

Man is the one who desires, woman the one who is desired. This is woman's entire but decisive advantage. Through man's passions, nature has given man into woman's hands, and the woman who does not know how to make him her subject, her toy, and how to betray him with a smile in the end is not wise.

1850 **Samuel Gompers:** English-born American labor leader. A cigar maker by trade, in 1886 he helped found the American Federation of Labor (AFL). Served as its first president (1886–1924). Known for his opposition to radicalism. Argued that unions should avoid political involvement and focus on economic goals, brought about by strikes and boycotts.

The worst crime against working people is a company which fails to operate at a profit.

1859 **Wilhelm II:** Last German Emperor (Kaiser) and last King (König) of Prussia. He was the grandson of England's Queen Victoria. A traumatic breech birth left him with a withered arm. Dismissed Otto von Bismark to begin a long period of personal bellicose rule. Had a nervous breakdown in 1908 and had less influence on the destiny and policies of Germany than generally believed. During World War I became a mere figurehead and after it, he abdicated and settled in The Netherlands.

If I rest, I rust.

1872 **[Billings] Learned Hand:** American jurist whose more than 2000 opinions ranged through all fields of law. Chief justice of the federal court of appeals, serving on the court for 52 years. His opinions so influenced the U.S. Supreme Court that he was known as its "10th man."

There is no surer way to misread any document than to read it literally.

1885 **Jerome Kern:** American composer. Composed almost exclusively for the theater. Wrote the score for the musical version of Edna Ferber's novel *Show Boat*. Other Broadway shows: *Sally*, *Roberta* and *Very Warm for May*. Songs include the standards "Smoke Gets in Your Eyes" and "The Last Time I Saw Paris."

Nothing is wrong when done to music.

1900 **Hyman Rickover:** Russian-born American admiral and educator. Known as "Father of the Atomic Submarine" and outspoken views and single-minded advocacy of nuclear power. Supervised construction of the first nuclear submarine, U.S.S. *Nautilus* (1947–54). Headed research on reactor development for the Atomic Energy Commission.

If you're going to sin, sin against God, not the bureaucracy. God will forgive you, but the bureaucracy won't.

1948 **Mikhail Baryshnikov:** Russian-born American dancer, choreographer, director, and actor. Defected from the Soviet Union (1974). He has a gravity-defying style. Has worked with the American Theater Ballet and New York City Ballet as well as appearing in films such as *The Turning Point*.

The essence of all art is to have pleasure in giving pleasure.

OTHERS: 1662 English theologian and classical scholar **Richard Bentley**, 1723 German judge, legal scholar and philosopher **Johann Cramer**, 1814 French architect/archaeologist **Eugene Viollet-le-Duc**, 1834 Russian chemist **Dmitri Mendeleev**, 1891 Soviet Jewish writer/journalist **Ilya Ehrenburg**, 1918 Orchestra leader **Skitch Henderson**, 1919 Creator of the musical "Chipmunks" **David Seville**, 1921 Oscar winning actress **Donna Reed**, 1924 Indian actor **Sabu**, 1931 Canadian writer **Mordecai Richler**, 1945 British musician **Nick Mason**, 1948 Singer with the "Ronettes" **Nedra Talley**, 1951 U.S. keyboardist **Seth Justman**, 1974 Iranian conjoined twins **Laden and Laleh Bijani**

January 28

1833 **Charles George Gordon:** British general and national hero for his exploits in China. Known affectionately as "Chinese Gordon," "Gordon Pasha" and

"Gordon of Khartoum." Distinguished himself as a young officer in the Crimean War and helped defend Shanghai during the Taiping. Appointed governor of the providence of Equatoria in Southern Sudan. Later governor-general of the Sudan. Sent to evacuate Anglo-Egyptian forces in Khartoum, he was killed in the siege of the city by Madhist movement insurgents.

If you tell the truth, you have infinite power supporting you; but if not, you have an infinite power against you.

1841 Sir **Henry Morton Stanley:** English-U.S. journalist. The *New York Herald* commissioned him to find British missionary, physician and explorer David Livingstone, who had not been heard from in Africa for many years. When Stanley located Livingstone, he greeted him with:

Dr. Livingstone, I presume?

1851 **José Martí:** Cuban poet, patriot. Leader of Cuban struggle for independence. Deported for political activities in 1868. Died leading an invasion of Cuba (1895). As a writer, noted for his personal prose and verse on themes of a free and United America. Essays: *Our America.*

Charm is a product of the unexpected.

1873 **[Sidonie-Gabrielle] Colette:** French novelist. Music-hall dancer and mime. Her early books were written in collaboration with her first husband Henri Gauthier-Villars. Her best known later works include the *Claudine* series and *Gigi.*

Look for a long time at what pleases you, and for a longer time at what pains you.

1887 **Artur Rubinstein:** Polish-born American concert pianist. Child prodigy. Became U.S. citizen in 1946. Made over 200 recordings. Famed for interpretations of Chopin. Active through his eighties, his repertoire also included Johann Sebastian Bach and Johannes Brahms.

A concert is like a bullfight — the moment of truth.

1892 **Ernst Lubitsch:** German-born actor and director. Acted with Max Reinhardt's German stage company before turning to directing costume dramas. Moved to Hollywood to direct films of sophisticated wit. Focused attention on two main themes — sex and money. Examples of films with the "Lubitsch Touch": *The Love Parade, Trouble in Paradise, Ninotchka* and *To Be or Not to Be.*

Nobody should try to play comedy unless he has a circus going on inside.

1912 **Jackson Pollock:** American painter. Studied with Thomas Hart Benton and was employed by the WPA Federal Art Project. Leader of abstract expressionist movement in the U.S. Initiated the Op art movement of fifties and sixties. His "drip" painting *One* is 17 feet long. Other works: *No. 32* and *Echo and Blue Poles.* Died in a car crash at 44.

Painting is self-discovery.

1929 **Claes Oldenburg:** Swedish-U.S. sculptor. Moved to New York City where he became one of the artists who created Pop Art. Chose banal subjects from consumer culture to sculpt. Introduced soft sculptures of usually hard objects such as *Giant Clothespin* and *Giant Soft Shuttlecock.* Use of soft, yielding vinyl often gave his sculptors sexual overtones.

I am for art that is political-erotical-mystical that does something other than sit on its ass in a museum.

1933 **Susan Sontag:** American essayist, philosopher, novelist, short-story writer and filmmaker. Best known for essays on avant-garde culture. Books: *The Style of Radical Will, On Photography* and *Illness as a Metaphor.* Coined word "camp."

What is most beautiful in virile men is something feminine; what is most beautiful in feminine women is something masculine.

1935 **David Lodge:** English novelist and critic. Novels include *Changing Places* and *Nice Work.* Critical works include *Language of Fiction* and *The Novelist at the Crossroads.*

Literature is mostly about having sex and not much about having children; life is the other way around.

1936 **Alan Alda:** Originally **Alphonse Joseph d'Abruzzo.** American actor, director and writer. Son of actor Robert Alda. Earned his greatest popularity for his extensive involvement in the long-running TV series *M*A*S*H,* for which he won four Emmys. Notable films include *The Four Seasons, Same Time, Next Year* and *Flirting with Disaster.* Academy Award nomination for *The Aviator.*

I don't want to go into politics. I want to do some good in the world.

1981 **Elijah Wood:** Short actor with limited facial expressions. Best remembered for his role as Frodo in box-office smash *The Lord of the Rings* trilogy in which he had only one expression no matter what emotion he was supposedly feeling.

So much time is wasted on trying to be better than others.

OTHERS: 1540 British admiral/explorer **Sir Francis Drake,** 1608 Italian Renaissance physicist/chemist **Giovanni Borelli,** 1706 English printer **John Baskerville,** 1807 British artic explorer **Robert McClure,** 1823 German physiologist **Moritz Schiff,** 1834 English Victorian hagiographer/antiquarian/novelist **Sabine Baring-Gould,** 1879 French-born painter and poet **Frances Picabia,** 1884 Swiss inventors/balloonists **Auguste Piccard** and his twin brother **Jean Felix Piccard,** 1912 Wall Street financier **Louis Wolfson,** 1929 Leading jazz clarinetist **Acker Bilk,** 1932 U.S. shot-put champion **Parry O'Brien,** 1946 U.S. organist **Rick Allen,** 1985 One of the richest young women in the world **Athina Onassis**

January 29

1628 **Emanuel Swedenborg:** Swedish mystic, poet and scientist. "Sweden's Greatest Son." Wrote books on algebra, navigation, astronomy and chemistry. Published his monumental *Philosophical and Logical Works* in 1734. Pioneer in the modern approach to science. Devoted himself to the spiritual universe.

True charity is the desire to be useful to others without thought of recompense.

1737 **Thomas Paine:** English-American colonial political philosopher and crusader for freedom. Wrote *Common Sense*, which advocated immediate independence from England and helped spark the revolutionary movement in America. Other works: *The Rights of Man*, in support of the French Revolution and *The Age of Reason*, favoring deism.

My country is the world and my religion is to do good.

1843 **William McKinley:** Twenty-fifth U.S. president (1897–1901). Governor and congressman from Ohio. Advocated protectionism. In his first term, U.S. went to war with Spain. Assassinated by anarchist Leon Czolgosz at beginning of second term, succeeded by Theodore Roosevelt.

Our differences are politics. Our agreements, principles.

1862 **Frederick Delius:** English composer of German-Scandinavian descent. After 1890 he lived in France, where he composed six opera including *A Village Romeo and Juliet* and works such as *Appalachia*.

It is only that which cannot be expressed otherwise that is worth expressing in music.

1866 **Romain Rolland:** French essayist, novelist, biographer, musicologist and polemical writer. Author of ten-volume epic novel *Jean Christophe* based on the life of Beethoven. Took an active role in the Alfred Dreyfus affair in France. Outstanding pacifist. Nobel Prize in Literature winner (1915).

A hero is a man who does what he can.

1874 **John D. Rockefeller, Jr.:** American capitalist and philanthropist. Used vast family fortune to fund Rockefeller Institute for Medical Research, and Rockefeller Center in New York City. Major supporter of Admiral Byrd's polar expeditions, restoration of Colonial Williamsburg and Lincoln Center for the Performing Arts.

A friendship formed on business is better than a business found on friendship.

1880 **W.C. Fields:** U.S. vaudeville, stage, radio and screen performer. Eccentric comedian and master juggler. Noted for large red nose, gravel voice and dislike of children. Films: *David Copperfield, My Little Chickadee*, and *The Bank Dick*.

Anyone who hates children and dogs can't be all bad.

1911 Professor **Irwin Corey:** U.S. comedian, a product of night clubs, bistros, and radio. He is billed as "The World's Foremost Authority." His brand of comedy is surrealistic, an acquired taste, but brilliant.

If we don't change direction soon, we'll end up where we're going.

1939 **Germaine Greer:** Australian author, educator and lecturer. Author of *The Female Eunuch*, one of the most successful feminist books. It portrayed marriage as a legalized form of slavery for women. Later works include *Sex and Destiny: the Politics of Human Fertility* and *The Change*, dealing with the menopausal transformation in women.

Loneliness is never more cruel than when it is felt in close propinquity with someone who has ceased to communicate.

1941 **Robin Morgan:** U.S. poet, writer, and feminist activist. As a youngster, she played Dagmar on TV's *I Remember Mama*. Worked in civil-rights, antiwar and feminist movements. Came out as a lesbian in the 60s. Helped revive *Ms.* Magazine.

Don't accept rides from strange men, and remember that all men are strange.

1953 **Hwang Woo-Suk:** South Korean biomedical scientist. Rose to prominence after claiming a series of breakthroughs by his research team at Seoul National University in the field of stem cell research. Major claim was that he had successfully cloned a human embryo and produced stem cells from it, a technique that could one day provide cures for a range of diseases. Allegations that he used unacceptable practices to acquire eggs from human donors, and then faked two landmark pieces of research into cloning human cells, destroyed his reputation and his career. He was forced to resign key posts and was stripped of his status as a "top scientist."

We were crazy, crazy about our work. But I was blinded. All I could see was whether I could make Korea stand in the center of the world through this research.... I feel so crushed and humiliated that I hardly have the energy to say I am sorry. I seek your forgiveness.

1954 **Oprah Winfrey:** African-American television personality and actress. Known for her quick wit, genuine compassion and her weight control efforts. Highest paid entertainer on television. Hosts a nationally syndicated talk show. First woman to own and produce her own talk show. Oscar nomination for *The Color Purple*. Also appeared in the made-for-TV movie *The Women of Brewster Place*, which she also produced.

You cannot hate other people without hating yourself.

OTHERS: 1700 Swiss physicist and mathematician **Daniel Bernoulli**, 1761 U.S. statesman **Albert Gallatin**, 1867 Spanish writer **Vicente Blasco Ibáñez**, 1878 American race driver and daredevil **Barney Oldfield**, 1882 U.S. poet **Berton Braley**, 1895 U.S. lawyer, diplomat and author **Adolf Berle**, 1911 Composer of film music **Bernard Herrmann**, 1923 U.S. dramatist **Paddy Chayevsky**, 1927 American author **Edward Abbey**, 1931 English/U.S. composer **Leslie Bricuse**, 1945 U.S. pro golfer **Donna Caponi**, 1945 U.S. actor **Tom Selleck**, 1960 U.S. Olympic gold medal diver **Greg Louganis**, 1968 American actor and director **Edward Burns**

January 30

1628 **George Villiers, 2nd Duke of Buckingham:** English politician, born only eight months before his father the 1st Duke of Buckingham was assassinated. Brought up with the family of Charles I. Fought for Charles II in the English Civil War. After the Restoration, Villiers was a leading member of Charles' inner circle of ministers, known as the Cabal. Dismissed from his posts by Parliament for alleged Catholic sympathies.

Men's fame is like their hair, which grows after they are dead, and with just as little use to them.

1775 **Walter Savage Landor:** English poet, literary critic and essayist. Outstanding classicist. Originally wrote many of his works in Latin. Best known work: the many-volume prose dialogue *Imaginary Conversations.*

States, like men, have their growth, their manhood, their decrepitude, their decay.

1846 **Francis H. Bradley:** British idealist philosopher. Considered mind to be more fundamental than matter. Most important person in the Absolute Idealist movement of his period. Works: *Ethical Studies, Principles of Logic,* in which he denounced the psychology of the empiricists, and his most ambitious work, *Appearance and Reality,* in which he maintained that reality is spiritual, but the notion cannot be demonstrated because of the abstract nature of thought.

Metaphysics is the finding of bad reasons for what we believe upon instinct.

1862 **Walter Damrosch:** German-born American conductor, composer and educator. Leader of the Weimar court orchestra under Franz Liszt. Emigrated to New York, where he became conductor at the Metropolitan Opera House, where he popularized Wagner. Music adviser to NBC radio. Pioneered weekly music appreciation broadcasts. Speaking of Aaron Copland:

If a young man of twenty-three can write a symphony like that, in five years he will be ready to commit murder.

1866 **Frank Gelett Burgess:** U.S. poet and cartoonist. Worked in magazines and books. Invented the word "blurb." He also penned the immortal lines:

I never saw a purple cow, I never hope to see one; But I can tell you, anyhow, I'd rather see than be one.

1871 **Seymour Hicks:** English actor, prolific author of commercial stage hits, often written in conjunction with his partner, Harry Nichols. Performed with his wife Ellaline Terriss, who was his leading lady in productions such as *Bluebell in Fairyland* and *The Beauty of Bath.* Gave P.G. Wodehouse his first employment as a writer.

A man does not buy his wife a fur coat to keep her warm, but to keep her pleasant.

1882 **Franklin Delano Roosevelt:** American Democratic politician and thirty-second U.S. president. Cousin of Theodore Roosevelt. Served three full terms and part of a fourth (1933–45). Led the United States out of the Depression by initiating many reforms. Expanded government power through New Deal programs. Played a major role in the Allied alliance in World War II with Great Britain and the U.S.S.R. Stricken with polio (1921), he feared his political career was over, but although he would never regain his ability to walk he remained active in politics, becoming Governor of New York in 1929, before defeating Herbert Hoover in the 1932 presidential election.

We cannot accept the doctrine that war must be forever a part of man's destiny.

1909 **Saul Alinsky:** U.S. social activist. Self-proclaimed "professional radical." Taught the use of picketing, sit-downs, strikes and boycotts to exert pressure on businesses and governments.

In any fight with the Establishment, you can count on it for at least one glorious gaffe that will bring renewed life to your languishing cause.

1912 **Barbara Tuchman:** Originally **Barbara Wertheim.** American historian. Wrote for *The Nation* and other publications before setting out on a career that made her the leading popular historian. Had a masterfully literary style and grasp of complex issues. Pulitzers for her best-selling historical books *The Guns of August* and *Stilwell and the American Experience in China.*

Books are the carriers of civilization. Without books, history is silent, literature dumb, science crippled, thought and speculation at a standstill.

1928 **Ruth Brown:** Legendary singer nicknamed "Miss Rhythm." Her recordings of songs such as "Teardrops in My Eyes" and "(Mama) He Treats Your Daughter Mean" with Atlantic Records made it the preeminent label in Rhythm and Blues. Later the business forgot her, forcing her to work as a domestic. She rebuilt her career in the mid 1970s. Won a Tony Award as Best Actress in a Musical for *Black and Blue.*

Unfortunately, I'm a little concerned where the legends are coming from nowadays.

1933 **Richard Brautigan:** American novelist, short story writer and poet. *Lay the Marble Tea* was his first published collection of poems. His most popular works include *Trout Fishing in America* and *In Watermelon Sugar.* His body was found several weeks after he committed suicide.

Language does not leave fossils, at least not until it has become written.

1941 **Richard Bruce "Dick" Cheney:** As an archconservative congressman from Wyoming opposed abortion, gun control, Clean Water Act, Head Start and the Department of Education. Supported citizen's rights to own armor-piercing weapons and corporations' rights to keep quiet about what toxins were dumped in streams. Served as Secretary of Defense under President George H. W. Bush at the time of the First Gulf War. Formerly CEO of Halliburton Corp. As Vice-President of the United States, supported the belief that Saddam Hussein had connections with Osama bin Laden, and had weapons of mass destruction to justify the second war with Iraq. Classified as 1-A during the Vietnam war but did not serve.

I had other priorities in the 60's than military service.

OTHERS: 1839 U.S. educator **Samuel Chapman Armstrong**, 1841 Civil War Journalist **Alfred Townsend George**, 1885 U.S. naval officer **John Henry Towers**, 1894 Tsar of Bulgaria **Boris III**, 1911 U.S. Jazz trumpeter **Roy Eldridge**, 1915 Disgraced English politician **John D. Profumo**, 1922 "Laugh-In" comedian **Dick Martin**, 1928 U.S. producer/director **Harold Prince**, 1931 Oscar winning actor **Gene Hackman**, 1933 U.S. financial whiz and advisor **Louis Rukeyser**, 1937 British actress **Vanessa Redgrave**, 1937 Russian chess champion **Boris Spassky**, 1951 English singer/drummer **Phil Collins**, 1957 American professional golfer **Payne Stewart**, 1974 Welsh actor **Christian Bale**

January 31

1797 **Franz Schubert:** Austrian composer. Whose songs have placed him among the immortals, but during his life he was unrecognized and lived a penniless existence. Sir Arthur Sullivan discovered a large number of his unpublished and forgotten manuscripts in 1867 in the house of a music publisher Combined classical and romantic styles. Major works: *Trout Piano Quintet*, *C Major Symphony* and *B minor Symphony*, known as the *Unfinished Symphony*. Greatest exponent of German Lieder. Wrote "Ave Maria."

No one really understands the grief or joy of another.

1860 **James Gibbons Huneker:** American essayist and music critic. Music, art, and drama critic for the *New York Sun*, then preeminent music critic for the *Times* and later for the *World*. His impressionistic criticism made him one of the most influential critics of his day.

All men of action are dreamers.

1892 **Eddie Cantor:** American comedian, actor and song-and-dance man. Known for his rolling "banjo eyes" and unique speech pattern. Tremendously popular in vaudeville and burlesque. Got his first big break in "The Midnight Follies." Appeared in several *Ziegfeld Follies*, musicals and films. Repeated his Broadway hits *Kid Boots* and *Whoopee* in films. Brought his act first to radio and then TV.

The two most common causes of divorce: Men and women.

1893 Dame **Freya Stark:** Paris-born English writer, who through her extensive travels became an expert in Arab affairs. Lived to the age of 100. Devoted her life to the art of solo travel. Wrote two dozen highly personal books about her exploits. Notable among these is *The Valley of the Assassins*, which described her traveling through the home of a heretical sect of Muslims, infamous for committing political and religious murders. Other works: *The Southern Gates of Arabia* and *The Journey's Echo*.

To awaken quite alone in a strange town is one of the pleasantest sensations in the world.

1903 **Tallulah Bankhead:** Legendary American theater actress. Lauded equally for her stage performances and tempestuous, quick-witted personality and uninhibited behavior. Known for a deep, raspy voice and explosive laugh. Starred in *The Skin of Our Teeth*, *The Little Foxes* and *Private Lives*. Film work was intermittent, including *Tarnished Lady* and *Lifeboat*.

We're all paid off in the end, and the fools first.

1905 **John O'Hara:** American short story writer and novelist. His *Pal Joey* collection of stories was made into a successful Broadway musical and then a film. *Butterfield 8, Ten North Frederick and From the Terrace* were also made into films.

America may be unique in being a country which has leapt from barbarianism to decadence without touching civilization.

1915 **Thomas Merton:** Later **Father M. Lewis**. French-born U.S. clergyman and author. Joined the Trappist order. Wrote the best-selling autobiography *The Seven Storey Mountain*, prompting many to become monks. He maintained voluminous correspondences. Wrote on poetry and social criticism. Other titles: *Mass Persuasion*, *Social Theory and Social Structure* and *On the Shoulder of Giants*.

The biggest human temptation is ... to settle for too little.

1919 **Jackie Robinson:** First African-American of the modern era to play major league baseball with Brooklyn (1947). Rookie-of-the-year (1947), MVP (1949), four-sport athlete at UCLA. Civil rights activist. Winner of the Spingarn Medal in 1956. Elected to Baseball's Hall of Fame in 1962.

Life is not a spectator sport. If you're going to spend your whole life in the grandstand just watching what goes on, in my opinion you're wasting your life.

1923 **Carol Channing:** American comic actress. Exuberant saucer-eyed entertainer of U.S. stage, nightclubs, television and movies. Smash hit as "Lorelei Lee" in Broadway's *Gentlemen Prefer Blondes* in which she sang what became her theme song "Diamonds Are a Girl's Best Friend," and as Dolly Levi in *Hello, Dolly*. Nominated for a Best supporting Actress Oscar for *Thoroughly Modern Millie*.

Laughter is much more important than applause. Applause is almost a duty. Laughter is a reward. Laughter means they trust you.

1923 **Norman Mailer:** American novelist and journalist. Known for iconoclast writings. His first novel *The Naked and the Dead*, which drew on his wartime service in the Pacific, established him as a major post war writer. Other novels: *An American Dream* and *Why Are We in Vietnam?* Turned to writing journalistic works that convey actual events: *Armies of the Night* (Pulitzer) and *The Executioner's Song* (Pulitzer).

Sentimentality is the emotional promiscuity of those who have no sentiment.

1925 **Benjamin L. Hooks:** American jurist, minister, and government official. Was executive director of the National Association for the Advancement of Colored People, succeeding Roy Wilkins. Stressed the need for affirmative action.

The most enduring contributions made to civilization have not been made by brawn; they have been made by brain.

1931 **Ernie Banks:** American baseball player. "Mr. Cub." Hall of fame shortstop–first baseman for Cubs (1953–71). Hit 514 HRs. MVP (1958, 1959). Voted "Greatest Cub Ever" (1969). A fine power hitter with 512 lifetime home runs. Elected to the Hall of Fame in his first year of eligibility.

It's a great day for a ball game; let's play two.

OTHERS: 1804 Hungarian author/poet/critic **Jósef Bajza**, 1866 German writer **Emil Strauss**, 1872 American western writer **Zane Grey**, 1877 German philosopher **Max Ettinger**, 1881 U.S. chemist **Irving Langmuir**, 1882 Russian ballerina/choreographer **Anna Pavlova**, 1886 Columbian President of UN security council **Alfonso Lopez**, 1902 Swedish diplomat/Nobel Peace Prizewinner **Alva Myrdal**, 1914 Heavyweight boxing champ **Jersey Joe Walcott**, 1915 TV host **Garry Moore**, 1920 U.S. Secretary of the Interior **Stewart L. Udall**, 1921 U.S. actor and first husband of Shirley Temple **John Agar**, 1921 Italian-American operatic tenor **Mario Lanza**, 1947 U.S. baseball pitcher **Nolan Ryan**

February 1

1552 Sir **Edward Coke:** Eminent English legal specialist on the supremacy of common law and jurist. His defense of common law against claims of royal prerogative was a profound influence on the development of English law and the constitution. Famous for his book *Coke upon Littleton*, still read in the study of English law.

The home to everyone is to him his castle and fortress.

1763 **Thomas Campbell:** Irish religious leader who founded, with his son, the Church of the Disciples of Christ in America. Pioneer in the theology of spiritual maturity. His "Declaration and Address" set forth his ideas for unifying not only Christian sects, but all spiritual movements around the world. He and his son were influential in forming the Restoration Movement.

The patriot's blood is the seed of Freedom's tree.

1787 **Richard Whatley:** English scholar, logician, theological writer. Anglican archbishop of Dublin. Supported Catholic emancipation and worked for unsectarian religious instruction. Unpopular because of his caustic wit and outspokenness.

To know your ruling passion, examine your castles in the air.

1874 **Hugo von Hofmannsthal:** Austrian poet, dramatist, and essayist. Famed for his collaboration with German composer Richard Strauss. With Max Reinhardt founded the Salzburg Festival. His most famous essay was *Ein Brief.*

To grow mature is to separate more distinctly, to connect more closely.

1895 **John Ford:** Born **Sean Aloysius O'Feeney. American** actor and director of over 125 films. Master storyteller and poet of the moving image. Won Four Academy Awards for directing *The Informer, The Grapes of Wrath, How Green Was My Valley*, and *The Quiet Man*. Nominated for *Stagecoach*. His films express a deep aesthetic sensibility for the American frontier.

You can speak well if your tongue can deliver the message of your heart.

1900 **Stephen Potter:** English author, biographer, reviewer, diarist and producer of radio programs. Published *Gamesmanship — the Art of Winning Games without Actually Cheating, Lifemanship, One-Upmanship*, and *Supermanship*.

A good general rule is to state that the bouquet is better than the taste, and vice versa.

1901 **Clark Gable:** U.S. movie star. "The King." His charmingly naughty smile and self-confidence represented the ultimate in masculinity for millions. Nominated for Oscars for *Mutiny on the Bounty* and *Gone with the Wind*, won for *It Happened One Night*. Among his 70-odd films: *Red Dust, San Francisco* and *The Misfits*. After the death of his third wife, actress Carole Lombard, he joined the Army Air Forces. Received the Distinguished Flying Cross for his bombing missions.

It's an extra dividend when you like the girl you're in love with.

1902 **Langston Hughes:** African-American poet, author, and journalist. Expressed black view of America with *Shakespeare in Harlem* (1942). Wrote in dialect, using blues and jazz rhythms. Other works: *The Poetry of the Negro, Famous Negro Heroes of America* and *First Book of Africa.*

What happens to a dream deferred? Does it dry up like a raisin in the sun?

1904 **S.J. [Sidney Joseph] Perlman:** U.S. author. Noted for humorous short stories and screenplays for the Marx brothers. Oscar for screenplay of *Around the World in Eighty Days*. Books: *Strictly from Hunger, One Touch of Venus* and *Acres and Pain.*

Hollywood is a dreary industrial town controlled by hoodlums of enormous wealth with the ethical sense of a pack of jackals.

1918 Dame **Muriel Spark:** née **Camberg**. Scottish novelist, short-story writer, biographer, poet and satirist. Editor of *Poetry Review* (1947–49). Published critical biographies on Wordsworth, Mary Shelley and Emily Brontë. Best known for her novel, *The Prime of Miss Jean Brodie*, a portrait of an English schoolteacher in a girl's school who planned to make her the students the "crème de la crème" with her advanced educational ideas.

It is impossible to repent of love. The sin of love does not exist.

1931 **Boris Yeltsin:** President of the Republic of Russia and prime minister of the Russian Federation from 1990 to 1999. Tried to institute economic reform in the largest country of the former U.S.S.R., employing both parliamentary and military means to push his programs. When Chechnya unilaterally declared independence he sent troops to fight the rebels. During his second term as president he suffered a heart attack, but rejected suggestions that he step down, even when his public and private behavior became erratic. Finally resigned in 1999, replaced by Vladimir Putin.

You can build a throne out of bayonets, but you can't sit on them long.

1933 **Richard Schickel:** One of the U.S.' most influential film critics. Film critic for *Life* magazine and from 1972, *Time* magazine. Producer-writer-director of TV programs, such as the eight part PBS series *The Men Who Made the Movies.*

Memory is the personal journalism of the soul.

OTHERS: 1757 English actor/ director at Drury Lane, **John Phillip Kemble**, 1791 Belgian musical instrument builder **Charles J. Sax**, 1801 Romantic landscape painter **Thomas Cole**, 1844 U.S. psychologist **Granville Stanley Hall**, 1859 Irish/U.S. conductor/composer **Victor Herbert**, 1896 President of Nicaragua **Anastasio Somoza**, 1906 Night club singer **Hildegarde Adell**, 1908 Collegiate Hall of Fame football star **Albie Booth**, 1910 U.S. movie director and writer **Michael Kanin**, 1922 Italian soprano **Renata Tebaldi**, 1934 Singer with the Kingston Trio **Bob Shane**, 1937 Musician/actor **Ray Sawyer [Dr. Hook]**, 1942 British comedian with Monty Python **Terry Jones**, 1948 LPGA golfer **Debbie Austin**

February 2

1651 **Nell Gwyn:** Originally **Eleanor.** English actress. Was selling oranges at Drury Theatre when she became mistress of the leading actor, Charles Hart, who trained her for the stage. Leading comedienne of the King's company. "Pretty, witty Nell" was in demand as speaker of impudent prologues and epilogues. As Mistress of Charles II, she was popular with the public. When accosted by an anti-Catholic mob she implored:

Pray, good people, be civil. I am the Protestant whore.

1745 **Hannah More:** English playwright and religious writer. Best known for her philanthropic works written for the benefit of the poor. Publications: "Sacred Dramas," "Estimate on the Religion of the Fashionable World" and "Cheap Repository Tracts."

Going to the opera, like getting drunk, is a sin that carries its own punishment with it. We do not so much want books for good people, as books which will make bad ones better.

1754 **Charles-Maurice de Talleyrand-Périgord:** French statesman and diplomat. Leading politician of his time. Minister of Foreign Affairs for Napoleon I. Helped restore the Bourbons. Negotiated Treaty of Paris. Brilliantly represented France at the Congress of Vienna. Had a brilliant knack for surviving many changes in government.

Speech was given to man to disguise his thoughts.

1859 **Henry Havelock Ellis:** English scientist. Pioneer author on psychology of sex. Conducted first study of homosexuality. Advocated sex education. Author of the seven-volume *Studies in the Psychology of Sex,* the first detached treatment of the subject free of guilt feelings. It caused considerable controversy and was banned in Britain. A brilliant literary expositor, writing about Elizabethan and Jacobian dramatis.

The Promised Land always lies on the other side of a Wilderness.

1864 Dame **Margot Tennant Asquith:** British socialite, author, and politician. She and her sister Laura grew up wild and uninhibited. They became the central figures of an aristocratic group of intellectuals known as the "Souls." Margot was known for her acerbic wit. Allegedly when she met actress Jean Harlow she corrected the platinum blonde's mispronunciation of her name by saying:

No, no; the "t" is silent, as in Harlow.

1882 **James Joyce:** Irish novelist and poet. Took seven years to write *Ulysses* (1922), considered to be a masterpiece of world literature. Noted for complex design and combination of realism and stream of consciousness. *Ulysses* was banned in the United States as obscene until 1933. Other writings: *Portrait of the Artist as a Young Man* and *Finnegans Wake.* Life was difficult, marked by financial troubles, chronic eye diseases that occasionally left him totally blind and censorship problems.

Mistakes are the portals of discovery.

1895 **George Halas:** "Papa Bear." American football player, and coach and owner of the Chicago Bears. Most Valuable Player in the 1919 Rose Bowl. One of the founders of professional football. Retired as coach in 1968 with 8 NFL championships. During his four coaching stints with the Bears, he compiled a record of 326–151–31.

Nothing is work unless you'd rather be doing something else.

1901 **Jascha Heifetz:** Russian-Polish-born American violinist. Child prodigy. Noted for silken tone, careful regard for composer's markings. Settled in the United States after the Russian Revolution. Became a citizen in 1924. Among works he commissioned from leading composers was William Walton's violin concerto. Last played in public in 1974.

No matter what side of an argument you're on, you always find some people on your side that you wish were on the other side.

1905 **Ayn Rand:** U.S. novelist and philosopher. Began her career as a playwright and screenwriter. Created superior characters to illustrate philosophy of rational self-interest, which she called objectivism, best illustrated in her novels *The Fountainhead* and *Atlas Shrugged.*

The truth is not for all men, but only for those who seek it.

1915 **Abba Eban:** Originally **Aubrey Solomon**. Israeli diplomat and politician, born in Cape Town, South Africa and educated in England. Taught oriental languages at Cambridge before serving as a liaison officer in the Middle East Arab Center in Jerusalem. Israeli U.N. representative (1949–59). Ambassador to U.S. (1950–59). Foreign Minister (1966–74). Author of *Israel in the World.*

History teaches us that men and nations behave wisely once they have exhausted all other alternatives.

1923 **Liz Smith:** U.S. journalist and gossip columnist with the *New York Daily News*. Dubbed "the Grande Dame of Dish: wrote her memoir *Natural Blonde* and *Dishing: Great Dish—and Dishes—From America's Most Beloved Gossip Columnists*, both best-sellers.

Gossip is just news running ahead of itself in a red satin dress.

1937 **Tommy Smothers:** U.S. singer/comedian. Starred with his brother Dick in a controversial TV show, which was always testing the censors with their political comedy, skits and songs. Network cancelled the show despite high ratings, because of their anti-war and anti-administration songs, skits and humor.

The only valid censorship of ideas is the right of people not to listen.

Others: 1600 French librarian **Gabriel Naudé**, 1861 U.S. philanthropist **Solomon R. Guggenheim**, 1875 Austrian violinist **Fritz Kreisler**, 1878 U.S. educator **Christian Gauss**, 1882 Irish poet **James Stephens**, 1884 Hungarian-born actor **S.Z. "Cuddles" Sakall**, 1886 U.S. poet **William Rose Benet**, 1890 Andy of radio's "Amos & Andy **Charles Correll**, 1912 Broadway composer **Burton Lane**, 1923 U.S. author **James Dickey**, 1926 President of France **Valéry Giscard d'Estaing**, 1927 Jazz tenor saxophonist **Stan Getz**, 1931 U.S. writer **Judith Viorst**, 1937 Opera diva **Martina Arroyo**, 1942 Guitarist **Graham Nash**, 1947 U.S. actress **Farrah Fawcett**, 1954 U.S. model **Christie Brinkley**

February 3

1809 **Felix Mendelssohn:** Properly **Mendelssohn-Bartholdy**. German composer, famous for piano and violin concertos, oratorios and chamber music. Made his first public appearance at age nine. Prolific composer even as a child. His works include *A Midsummer Night's Dream*, the *Hebrides Overture* and the *Scottish Symphony*. Founded an Academy of Arts in Berlin. Devoted admirer of J.S. Bach's music, he revived public interest in that composer, whose popularity had declined after his death.

Though everything else may appear shallow and repulsive, even the smallest task in music is absorbing, and carries us so far away from town, country, earth, and all worldly things, that it's truly a blessed gift of God.

1811 **Horace Greeley:** Pioneer American newspaper journalist. Founder and editor of *New York Tribune* (1841–72). Crusader against slavery. Liberal Republican presidential candidate (1872). Through his vigorous editorials on questions of the day, his paper became the greatest single journalistic influence in the country at the time. However, he did not coin the phrase "Go west, young man." It was first said by John Soule, editor of an Indiana newspaper.

The illusion that times that were are better than those that are, has probably pervaded all ages.

1816 **Frederick William Robertson:** English divine, exceptional preacher and a scientific theologian. Moderate Calvinist and an enthusiastic evangelist. Committed to memory the entire New Testament in both English and Greek.

The true aim of everyone who aspires to be a teacher should be, not to impart his own opinions, but to kindle minds.

1821 **Elizabeth Blackwell:** English-American physician. First American woman to earn a M.D. degree (1849). Founded New York Infirmary for Women and Children (1849) and London School of Medicine for Women (1875). Lectured on hygiene and preventive medicine. Pioneer in furthering medical education of women. An American Women's Medical Association Award is named in her honor.

For what is done or learned by one class of women becomes, by virtue of their common womanhood, the property of all women.

1826 **Walter Bagehot:** English economist, political analysis and literary critic. Editor of *Economist* (1860–77). Applied concept of evolution to political societies. Wrote the classic *English Constitution*, which describes how the British system of government really operates. Other works: *Physics and Politics* and *Literary Studies*. One of the first to attempt to apply the concept of evolution to societies.

Poverty is an anomaly to rich people; it is very difficult to make out why people who want dinner do not ring the bell.

1842 **Sidney Lanier:** American poet, musician and lecturer in English Literature at Johns Hopkins University. One of the most distinguished minor poets and an accomplished musician. Illustrated his belief in a scientific approach to poetry-writing in poems such as "Corn" and "The Symphony."

If you want to be found stand where the seeker seeks.

1872 **Alexander Meiklejohn:** American philosopher, university administrator, and free-speech advocate. Served as Dean of Brown University and President of Amherst College. The AAUP established a freedom award in his name. Received the Presidential Medal of Freedom.

Democracy is the art of thinking independently together.

1874 **Gertrude Stein:** American-born writer and patron of the arts in the 1920s. Her *Making of Americans* led to a heated literary controversy over style and meaning. Conducted a celebrated salon for writers in her Paris home between the two world wars. Named the members "The Lost Generation." Famous for her line, "rose, is a rose, is a rose." Wrote *Three Lives, Tender Buttons* and *The Autobiography of Alice B. Toklas*, which was actually Stein's autobiography.

What is the answer? ... In that case, what is the question?

1894 **Norman Rockwell:** American illustrator. Using oils, he developed a realistic style, idealizing small-town America. Best known for his homey magazine cover art His works appeared in magazines including *St. Nicholas, Colliers, Look* and most especially *The Saturday Evening Post.* His favorite subjects were children and animals.

I say that if you can tell a story in a picture, and if a reasonable number of people like your work, it is art.

1907 **James A. Michener:** America writer of best-selling epic, detailed and extensively researched novels with exotic settings: The Pulitzer Prize winning *Tales of the South Pacific* was adapted into the Broadway musical, *South Pacific,* in 1947 and filmed in 1958. Others: *Hawaii,* and *Centennial.*

There are no insoluble problems, only time-consuming ones.

1909 **Simone Weil:** French mystic and social philosopher. Born Jewish, she converted to Roman Catholicism in the 1940s. As a pacifist he served as a cook with Republican forces in the Spanish Civil War. Worked for Free French in London during World War II. Died of voluntary starvation in an attempt to identify with the Resistance fighters in France. Posthumously published books: *Waiting for God* and *Gravity and Grace.* At her best in her notebooks.

Evil, when we are in power, is not felt as an evil, but as a necessity, even a duty. Evil being the root of mystery, pain is the root of knowledge.

1940 **Fran [Francis] Tarkington:** Football quarterback, All-American at Georgia, 18 seasons for Vikings and Giants. Player of the year (1975). NFL records: threw for 47,003 yards and 342 TDs. His records were later broken by Dan Marino.

It's a lonesome walk to the sidelines, especially when thousands of people are cheering your replacement.

OTHERS: 1368 King of France known as the "Foolish," **Charles VI**, 1820 Artic explorer **Elisha Kent Kane**, 1830 British prime minister **Robert Cecil**, 1889 Danish director **Carl Dryer**, 1890 Swiss philosopher **Heinrich Barth**, 1900 U.S. cabaret singer **Mabel Mercer**, 1904 FBI most wanted criminal **Pretty Boy Floyd**, 1918 Comedian actor **Joey Bishop**, 1920 Inventor of the Heimlich maneuver **Dr. Henry Heimlich**, 1926 U.S. comedian **Shelley Berman**, 1932 U.S. actress **Peggy Ann Garner**, 1945 NFL quarterback **Bob Griese**, 1952 Baseball player **Fred Lynn**, 1956 American comic actor **Nathan Lane**

February 4

1802 **Mark Hopkins:** American educator and theologian. Connected with Williams College in Massachusetts for 57 years. President (1836–72). Symbol of a great teacher. Famous for his ability to arouse students to express their thoughts and natures. U.S. president James A. Garfield saluted him with "A pine bench, with Mark Hopkins at one end of it and me at the other, is a good enough college for me!"

Language is the picture and counterpart of thought.

1842 **Georg Brandes:** Danish critic and scholar. Believed it was his mission to bring Denmark out of cultural isolation. Catalyst of the breakthrough from Romanticism to realism. Best known for his monumental *Main Currents in 19th Century Literature* (6 volumes, 1871–87).

The stream of time sweeps away errors and leaves the truth for the inheritance of humanity.

1876 **Sarah N. Cleghorn:** American author, poet, suffragist, civil rights worker, pacifist and antivivisectionist. Published *A Turnpike Lady, The Spinster* and *Portraits and Protests.*

The golf links lie so near the mill/ That almost any day/ The laboring children can look out/ And see the men at play.

1892 **Ugo Betti:** Italian poet, playwright and jurist. Served as judge and librarian of the Ministry of Justice in Rome. Wrote three volumes of poetry, three collections of short stories and 26 plays. Works: *Landslide, Corruption in the Palace of Justice* and *The Fugitive.*

Memories are like stones, time and distance erode them like acid.

1897 **Ludwig Erhard:** German statesman and economist. Economics minister, West Germany (1949–63). Chief architect of the nation's post World War II miraculous economic recovery, through his "social market system," based on a free market capitalism, but included special provisions for housing, farming and social programs. Chancellor (1963–66).

A compromise is the art of dividing a cake in such a way that everyone believes he has the biggest piece.

1900 **Jacques Prévert:** French poet involved with the surrealism movement, writing songs, cabaret pieces, scenarios for Pierre Auguste Renoir, and the screenplay for the acclaimed *Les Enfants du Paradis* (*The Children of Paradise*).

Even if happiness forgets you a little bit, never completely forget about it.

1902 **Charles Lindbergh:** "The Lone Eagle." American aviator. Made first nonstop solo trans–Atlantic flight from New York to Paris (1927) in 33 1/2 hours. In the next decade more than 250 songs were written in his honor, the best-known being "Lucky Lindy." First American private citizen to become a public hero. Championed isolationism (1939–41). Flew Pacific combat missions during World War II.

I owned the world that hour as I rode over it, free of the earth, free of the mountains, free of the clouds, but how inseparably I was bound to them.

1906 **Dietrich Bonhoeffer:** German Lutheran pastor and theologian. Protested against anti–Jewish legislation. Part of German Resistance movement which planned Hitler's overthrow. Arrested in 1943 and hanged a month before the end of World War II. One of the most insightful theologians of the 20th century. Books: *The Cost of Discipleship*, *Ethics*, and *Letters and Papers from Prison.*

Action springs not from thought, but from a readiness for responsibility.

1913 **Rosa Lee Parks:** Sparked the Civil Rights Movement by refusing to give her seat on a bus to a white man. Her action triggered a year-long Montgomery Alabama bus boycott led by Martin Luther King, Jr. Resulted in desegregation of the bus system. She moved to Detroit in 1957 and dedicated the rest of her life to work in civil rights.

My only concern was to get home after a hard day's work.

1921 **Betty Friedan:** Born **Betty Naomi Goldstein**. American feminist and author. Wrote the highly influential and best-selling feminist classic *The Feminine Mystique* (1963), which analyzed the role of women in American society and articulated their frustrations. Founded National Organization of Women (NOW) in 1966; president until 1970. Autobiographies: *It Changed My Life* and *The Second Stage.*

The feminine mystique has succeeded in burying millions of American women alive. Man is not the enemy here, but the fellow victim. The real enemy is women's denigration of themselves.

1925 **Russell Hoban:** One of the most original writers of the 20th century. American author of fantasy, science fiction, mainstream fiction, poetry, and children's books. His works include *The Mouse and His Child, Turtle Diary,* and *The Medusa Frequency.*

An idea is an eye given by God for the seeing of God. Some of these ideas we cannot bear to look out of; we blind them as quickly as possible.

1948 **Alice Cooper:** Born **Vincent Daman Furnier.** American Rock star. Songs often had violent themes and were performed with violent staging. Biggest hits were "Eighteen," "Killer" and "School's Out."

If you're listening to a rock star in order to get your information on whom to vote for, you're a bigger moron than they are.

OTHERS: 1688 French writer **Pierre de Marivaux**, 1693 English dramatist **George Lillo**, 1747 Polish patriot **Tadeusz Kosciusko**, 1819 First emperor of the U.S.A. **Joshua Norton**, 1869 President/founder of the Industrial Workers of the World **"Big Bill" Haywood**, 1878 New Zealand Prime Minister **Joseph Gordon Coates**, 1881 French cubist painter **Fernand Léger**, 1895 Columnist/songwriter **Nick Kenny**, 1904 U.S. novelist **MacKinlay Kantor**, 1906 Italian heavyweight boxer **Primo Carnera**, 1912 Austrian conductor **Erich Leinsdorf**, 1912 Won 19 golf event in 1945 **Byron Nelson**, 1914 English actress/director **Ida Lupino**, 1931 President of Argentina **Isabel Perón**

February 5

1626 Marquise **Marie de Sévigné:** née **Marie de Rabutin-Chantal**. Member of French court society and Europe's most famous letter-writer. Over a period of 25 years wrote more than 1500 letters and received about the same number from others, which provide a portrait of the age of King Louis XIV in wonderful detail.

In love affairs it is only the beginnings that are amusing. Therefore, you should start over again as soon as possible.

1723 **John Witherspoon:** Scottish-American clergyman. President of College of New Jersey (now Princeton University). Advocate of colonists rights. Delegate to the Continental Congress. Only clergyman to sign the Declaration of Independence. Helped organize the American Presbyterian Church into a National Body.

Never rise to speak till you have something to say; and when you have said it, cease.

1788 Sir **Robert Peel:** English political leader and able speaker in parliamentary debate. Major founder of the Conservative Party. As Home Secretary founded the London Police Force (1829), whose constables are known as "bobbies." Prime minister (1834–35, 1841–46). Advocated many liberal reforms.

Agitation is the marshaling of the conscience of a nation to mold its laws.

1837 **Dwight Lyman Moody:** American shoe salesman, evangelist and urban revivalist. Built the first YMCA building in America. Conducted revivals all over the world. Founded the Moody Church and the Moody Bible Institute of Chicago.

The Bible will keep you from sin, or sin will keep you from the Bible.

1838 **Abram Joseph Ryan:** American Roman Catholic priest, poet. Poet of the Confederacy. Poems: "The Conquered Banner," "The Lost Cause," "The Sword of Robert E. Lee" and "The March of the Deathless Dead."

A land without ruins is a land without memories — a land without memories is a land without history.

1866 Sir **Arthur Keith:** Scottish physical anthropologist. Held doctorates in medicine, science and law. Best known for his work on fossilized humanoid forms. Wrote *Introduction to the Study of Anthropoid Apes, Concerning Man's Origin* and *New Theory of Human Evolution.*

No two human beings have made, or ever will make, exactly the same journey in life.

1900 **Adlai E. Stevenson II:** American grandson of a U.S. Vice President, politician and diplomat, noted for his eloquence and wit. Participant at the foundation of U.N., San Francisco (1946). Illinois governor (1948–52). Twice Democratic candidate for presidency. Defeated each time by Eisenhower. U.S. delegate to U.N. (1961–65).

All progress has resulted from people who took unpopular positions.

1906 **John Carradine:** Born **Richmond Reed Carradine. American** character actor in hundreds of films including *Stagecoach, The Grapes of Wrath* and *Of Human Bondage*. His three sons David, Keith and Robert also became actors.

Never do anything you wouldn't want to be caught dead doing.

1914 **William Seward Burroughs:** American author. Chief speaker for "Beat movement." Wrote experimental novels in deliberately erratic prose, depicting a nightmarish sometimes hilarious world. His novel *Naked Lunch* graphically deals with the surreal world of the drug addict. Also wrote *The Soft Machine, Nova Express, The Wild Boys* and *Cities of the Red Night*. Grandson of the U.S. inventor and founder of the Burroughs Adding Machine Company.

Sometimes paranoia's just having all the facts.

1934 **Henry "Hank" Aaron:** Hall of fame outfielder with the Braves and Brewers. All-time leader in HRs (755). Had 2297 RBIs, 6,856 total bases, played in 24 All-Star Games, a record he shares with Stan Musial and Willie Mays. Most Valuable Player in 1957. Elected to Baseball Hall of Fame in 1982.

Guessing what the pitcher is going to throw is eighty percent of being a successful hitter. The other twenty percent is execution.

1939 **Jane Bryant Quinn:** American writer and television correspondent. Financial business columnist for *Newsweek*. Wrote *Everyone's Money Book*.

Lawyers are operators of the toll bridge across which anyone in search of justice has to pass.

1942 **Roger Staubach:** All-American quarterback at the Naval Academy and Heisman Trophy winner. After serving his stint on active duty, joined the Dallas Cowboys, which he helped make into a dominant team. Five-times leading passer in the NFL.

Winning isn't getting ahead of others. It's getting ahead of yourself.

OTHERS: 1725 Colonial lawyer **James Otis**, 1840 Inventor of the automatic rifle **Hiram S. Maxim**, 1848 U.S. female western outlaw **Belle Starr**, 1878 French automobile maker **André-Gustave Citroën**, 1898 U.S. newspaperman/editor **Ralph McGill**, 1903 U.S. sportswoman **Joan Whitney Payson**, 1919 U.S. comedian/actor **Red Buttons**, 1926 U.S. publisher **Arthur Ochs Sulzberger**, 1945 English actress **Charlotte Rampling**, 1948 U.S. writer/comic **Christopher Guest**, 1948 U.S. actress **Barbara Hershey**, 1966 Spanish golfer **José Maria Olazabal**, 1968 Puerto Rican baseball player **Roberto Alomar**, 1969 U.S. singer **Bobby Brown**

February 6

1612 **Antoine Arnauld:** French Roman Catholic theologian, philosopher, and mathematician. His contemporaries called him *le grand* to distinguish him form his father. Produced numerous Jansenism pamphlets that were very critical of the Jesuit methods. Also wrote against Calvinists and heretics of all kinds.

Rest, rest, shall I have not all eternity to rest?

1866 **Philander C. Johnson:** American journalist, humorist, and dramatic editor. Wrote for the Washington Evening Star and Everybody's Magazine. Advised everyone: *Cheer up, the worst is yet to come.* Books include *Senator Sorghum's Primer of Politics: Or Helpful Hints on the Science of Not Getting the Worst of It.*

It is fortunate that for society that the courts do not get the same chance at the Ten Commandments as they do at the Constitution of the United States.

1878 **Walter B. Pitkin:** American psychologist, journalist and editor. Wrote the pop psychology book *Life Begins at Forty*. Other books: *How to Write Short Stories, The Art of Rapid Reading, The Art of Learning* and *The Best Years*.

[Politicians] are the semi-failures in business and the professions, men of mediocre mentality, dubious morals, and magnificent commonplaceness.

1895 **George Herman "Babe" Ruth:** Baseball's most dominant player. A successful pitcher-outfielder with the Red Sox. Became home run king when traded to Yankees. Led the American League in home runs 11 times. Had 714 career HRs, which has since been surpassed by Hank Aaron and Barry Bonds. Hit 60 in 1927, since surpassed by Bonds. Sammy Sosa and Mark McGuire. Dominated the game like no other player before or since. Played in 10 World Series with his team winning 7 championships.

Never let the fear of striking out get in your way.

1902 **Eva Braun:** German woman. Secretary to Hitler's staff photographer. Became Hitler's mistress in the 1930s. Thought to have provided him with companionship rather than sexual gratification. Married him before they both committed suicide in the bunker under the Chancellery during the fall of Berlin. She was often unhappy because he didn't appear with her in public.

Why doesn't that Devil take me with him? It would be much better with him than it is here.

1902 **Louis Nizer:** Celebrated London-born American lawyer and writer. Specialized in cases in the entertainment field. Authority on contracts, copyright and plagiarism law. Books: *What to Do with Germany, My Life in Court* and *The Jury Returns*.

A speaker who does not strike oil in ten minutes should stop boring.

1911 **Ronald Reagan:** Fortieth president of the United States. Excellent swimmer saved over 70 lives while a lifeguard when he was a teen. Led a student strike against the administration of Eureka College in 1928. The University of Southern California's Division of Fine Arts selected him as having "the most nearly perfect male figure." Known for conservative policies and appointments. Oldest and the first divorced president. Governor of California. Film and television actor. Best film role in *King's Row*. Married to actresses Jane Wyman and then to Nancy Davis.

Politics is just like show business. You have a hell of an opening, coast for a while, and then have a hell of a close.

1913 **Mary Leakey:** née **Nicol**. English anthropologist and anthropologist whose evacuations and discoveries of fossils in East Africa helped push back the dates of the first true man to almost four million years ago. Discovered *Proconsul Africanus, Zinjanthropus* and *Homo habilis*. Discovered certain evidence that our ancestors already walked upright 3.6 million years ago. Wrote: *Olduvai Gorge: My Search for Early Man*.

In archaeology you almost never find what you set out to find.

1919 **Zsa Zsa Gabor:** Born **Sari Bagor**. Hungarian actress and celebrity. "Miss Hungary" in 1936. She and her sisters made marrying wealthy men an art form. A congressman called her "the most expensive courtesan since Madame de Pompadour." Movies include *Moulin Rouge*.

I want a man who's kind and understanding. Is that too much to ask of a millionaire?

1932 **François Truffaut:** French filmmaker. Producer, director, screenwriter and actor. Greatly influenced by directors Jean Renoir and Alfred Hitchcock. Quickly gained a reputation as the most ferocious and caustic among the young film critics, who would soon become the core of the French New Wave. Films include *The 400 Blows, Jules et Jim, Fahrenheit 451* and *The Story of Adelle H.*

In love, women are professionals, men are amateurs.

1940 **Tom Brokaw:** U.S. newscaster. NBC's White House correspondent. Host of the morning "Today Show" (1976). NBC anchorman from 1981 to his retirement in 2005.

It's all storytelling, you know. That's what journalism is all about.

1945 **Bob Marley:** Originally **Robert Nesta**. Jamaican musician with his group *The Wailers*. His music reflected his Rastafarian beliefs in universal peace, love, equality and empowerment for the black race. Leading exponent of reggae music. Songs include "Catch a Fire," "Exodus," "Uprising," and "I Can See Clearly Now." Wrote "I Shot the Sheriff," a big hit for Eric Clapton. Since his death from cancer at 36, he has attained near-legendary stature.

Open your eyes look within. Are you satisfied with the life you are living?

OTHERS: 1665 Queen of England **Anne Stuart**, 1756 U.S. vice-president **Aaron Burr**, 1788 Hungarian poet/dramatist **Károly Kisfaludy**, 1833 Confederate General **Jeb Stuart**, 1874 U.S. architect **Milton Bennett Medary**, 1897 Brazilian film director **Alberto Cavalcanti**, 1899 Silent screen star **Ramon Novarro**, 1905 Polish Premier **Wladislaw Gomulka**, 1907 Industrialist/inventor **Sam Green**, 1922 English actor **Patrick MacNee**, 1929 English writer **Keith Waterhouse**, 1931 U.S. actress **Mamie Van Doren**, 1943 U.S. singer **Fabian Forte**, 1950 U.S. singer **Natalie Cole**, 1961 Russian cosmonaut **Yuri I. Onufriyenko**, 1962 U.S. singer **Axl Rose**

February 7

1477 Sir **Thomas More:** English statesman, lawyer, poet, humanist, and author. Wrote *Utopia* (1516) of an ideal state based on reason. Appointed Lord Chancellor, 1529. Executed 1535 for refusing to accept Henry VIII as head of the Church. "In public and private life the ideal Christian." Canonized 1935.

If evils come not, then our fears arevain; /And if they do, fear but augments the pain.

1812 **Charles Dickens:** Pseudonym, **Boz**. English novelist and social critic. Most loved writer of the English language. Novels include *Oliver Twist, A Christmas Carol, David Copperfield, A Tale of Two Cities* and *Great Expectations*. Made public readings, private theatricals, speeches, wrote innumerable letters, pamphlets, and plays and ran a successful magazine.

In the little world in which children have their existence ... there is nothing so finely perceived and as finely felt, as injustice.

1817 **Frederick Douglass:** African-American abolitionist, orator and journalist. Born into slavery. Escaped to Massachusetts. British admirers bought his freedom. Founded an abolitionist weekly *North Star*. Helped recruit blacks for service in the Civil War. First black citizen to hold a high rank in the U.S. government as a consultant to President Lincoln and U.S. minister to Haiti.

Without a struggle, there can be no progress.

1863 **Laura Ingalls Wilder:** American author of *Little House in the Big Woods* books, basis of the television series "Little House on the Prairie." Lived on a farm all her life and it wasn't until she was in her sixties that she took her daughter's suggestion that she write down her childhood memories.

I am beginning to learn that it is the sweet, simple things of life which are the real ones after all.

1870 **Alfred Adler:** Pioneer Austrian psychiatrist, author and major proponent of the "inferiority complex." Prominent member of the psychoanalytical group formed about Sigmund Freud. Broke with Freud to investigate the psychology of the individual considered to be different from others.

The truth is often a terrible weapon of aggression. It is possible to lie, and even murder with truth.

1877 **Godfrey Harold Hardy:** English mathematician. Patron saint for those who consider themselves pure mathematicians. Among the purest of pure and was quite proud of the fact. Considered mathematics an art, insisting that practicality be divorced from his mathematics. Described applied mathematics as "repulsive, ugly and interminably dull." Wrote his mathematical philosophy in laymen's terms in *A Mathematician's Apology*. Introduced the mathematical world the self-taught Indian genius Srinivasa Ramanujan.

A mathematician, like a painter or a poet, is a maker of patterns. If his patterns are more permanent than theirs, it is because they are made with ideas.

1883 **Eubie Blake:** U.S. jazz pianist, composer. Son of former slaves. Played piano in a "sporting house." Appeared in vaudeville with Noble Sissle. Wrote: "I'm Just Wild About Harry" (1927). The ragtime revival brought him out of retirement in his eighties. Received Presidential Medal of Honor (1982).

Be grateful for luck. Pay the thunder no mind—listen to the birds. And don't hate nobody. The world goes on no matter what you do.

1885 **Sinclair Lewis:** American novelist. His best works are characterized by satire of contemporary life and realism: *Main Street*, *Babbitt*, *Arrowsmith* (Cited for a Pulitzer Prize, but declined it), *Elmer Gantry* and *Dodsworth*. Nobel Prize in Literature in 1930, becoming the first American to receive the award.

There are two insults no human being will endure: that he has no sense of humor, and that he has never known trouble.

1920 **An Wang:** Chinese-born U.S. business executive. Invented the magnetic core memory for computers. Founded the Wang Laboratories, one of the world's largest automation systems companies.

Success is more a function of consistent common sense than it is of genius.

1923 **George Lascelles, Earl of Harewood:** Eldest son of Princess Mary. Cousin of Elizabeth II. Involved in the direction of operatic and art institutions, such as at Covent Gardens.

There is an old proverb...: If you want the flowers in your garden to be glorious and to smell good, you must risk an occasional stink.

1932 **Gay Talese:** U.S. journalist. Reporter for *New York Times* and wrote short-story fiction for *Esquire* magazine. Spent several years immersed in the sex and porn world researching for his best-selling nonfiction "Novel," *Thy Neighbor's Wife*.

The real problem is what to do with the problem-solvers after the problem is solved.

1966 **Chris Rock:** U.S. stand-up comedian and actor. Was a cast member of the TV comedy series *Saturday Night Live*. Hosted the 77th Academy Awards Show. Has had three HBO comedy specials and a talk show.

Gun control? We need bullet control! I think every bullet should cost 5,000 dollars. Because if it cost five thousand dollars, we wouldn't have any innocent bystander.

OTHERS: 1612 English humorist/playwright **Thomas Killigrew**, 1693 Russian Empress **Anna Ivanova Romanova**, 1804 Manufacturer of farm equipment **John Deere**, 1837 Scottish creator of Oxford Dictionary **Sir James Murray**, 1906 Last emperor of China **Henry P'u-i**, 1908 Olympic gold medal swimmer/actor **Buster Crabbe**, 1920 U.S. comic actor **Eddie Bracken**, 1920 U.S. folk singer **Oscar Brand**, 1934 U.S. blues singer/guitarist **Earl King**, 1946 Argentine-born Brazilian film director **Hector Babenco**, 1950 Baseball pitcher **Dan Quisenberry**, 1962 U.S. country singer **Garth Brooks**, 1964 U.S. swimmer **Cynthia Woodhead**

February 8

1577 **Robert Burton:** English philosopher and humorist. His great work was *The Anatomy of Melancholy*, a learned miscellany on the ideas of his time. It describes in a sometimes humorous style, the kinds, causes, symptoms and cures of melancholy. His Latin comedy *Philosophaster* is an exposure of charlatanism.

A blow with a word strikes deeper than any blow with a sword.

1819 **John Ruskin:** English writer, art critic and social reformer. Believed faith, morality, education and good social conditions were prerequisites of creating good art. Critic of the new Industrialism. Works: *Modern Painters*, *The Seven Lamps of Architecture* and *The Stones of Venice*.

If a book is worth reading, it is worth buying.

1820 **William Tecumseh Sherman:** American Union army general. Second only to U.S. Grant in his contribution to the Union cause. Led the "March to the Sea" through Georgia and the burning of Atlanta. Ended Republican Party's attempts to draft him as their presidential candidate by saying: "I will not accept if nominated and will not serve if elected."

War is cruelty. There is no use trying to reform it, the crueler it is the sooner it will be over.

1825 **Harriet J.H. Robinson:** American suffragist, mill worker, and writer. Best known for *Massachusetts in the Woman Suffrage Movement*. Other books: *The New Pandora* and *Loom and Spindle, or, Life Among the Early Mill Girls*.

Skilled labor teaches something not to be found in books or colleges.

1825 **Jules Verne:** French novelist. His writings stimulated the development of science fiction. Wrote some 50 romantic-adventure and science-fiction stories. Anticipated many scientific achievements of the 20th century, including the submarine, television and space-travel. Works: *Five Weeks in a Balloon*, *A Journey to the Center of Earth*, and *Twenty Thousand Leagues Under the Sea*.

Whatever one man is capable of conceiving, other men will be able to achieve.

1851 **Kate O'Flaherty Chopin:** American author of novels of Cajun and Creole life, including *Bayou Folk, A Night in Acadie* and *Désirée's Baby*. Her realistic novel *The Awakening* was severely criticized because it dealt with female sexuality. Interest in her work was revived by the critic Edmund Wilson.

There are some people who leave impressions not so lasting as the imprint of an oar upon the water.

1876 **Joseph A. Schumpter:** Moravian–U.S. economist. Known for his theories of capitalist development and the business cycle. Believed that capitalism would eventually perish as a result of its own success. Books: *Capitalism, Socialism and Democracy* and *History of Economic Analysis.*

There is inherent in the capitalist system a tendency toward self-destruction.

1884 Lord **Brabazon:** British statesman and aviator. Served with the Royal Flying Corps during World War I. Responsible for several innovations in aerial photography. Minister of Transport and Aircraft Production during World War II. Resigned because of displeasure with his criticism of Britain's ally, U.S.S.R.

If you cannot say what you have to say in 20 minutes, you should go away and write a book about it.

1911 **Elizabeth Bishop:** American poet and short story writer raised in Nova Scotia. Noted for the elegance and imaginative power of her verse. In the 50s and '60s lived in Brazil with her female lover. Her *north & South: A Cold Spring* was awarded a Pulitzer Prize in 1956.

The iceberg cuts its facets from within/Like jewelry from a grave.

1878 **Martin Buber:** German Jewish philosopher, theologian and Zionist thinker. Saw Israel an ideal place for fulfillment of nationalist and humanist aspirations. Believed that the Bible developed from the encounter between God and the people. Rejected many Talmud's laws as emerging from a relationship in which God was objectified rather than addressed. Author of *Tales of Rabbi Nachman* and *Kingship of God.*

Solitude is the place of purification... Play is the exultation of the possible.

1931 **James Dean:** Charismatic U.S. actor, died in a car crash at age 24 before his last film was released. Personified "cool" for young people of fifties. Still is regarded a cult figure. Films: *Rebel Without a Cause, East of Eden* and *Giant.*

Death is the only thing left to respect. Everything else can be questioned. But death is true. In it lies the only nobility for man and beyond it the only hope.

1940 **Ted Koppel:** British-born American television broadcaster. Emigrated to the U.S. in 1953 and worked as a correspondent for ABC from 1963. Won several Emmys for his work as anchor of the late-night interview show *Nightline.*

History is a tool used by politicians to justify their intentions.

OTHERS: 412 Patriarch of Constantinople **St. Proculus**, 1712 French general in America **Joseph de Montcalm**, 1795 German chemist **Friedlieb F. Runge**, 1876 German "entartet" painter **Paula Modersohn-Becker**, 1880 German painter **Franz Marc**, 1885 English actress Dame **Edith Evans**, 1890 Filipino Nationalist **Claro Mayo Recto**, 1895 U.S. movie director **King Vidor**, 1906 Polish/U.S. pianist **Artur Balsam**, 1906 U.S. writer **Henry Roth**, 1919 Orchestra leader **Buddy Morrow**, 1920 U.S. movie star **Lana Turner**, 1925 U.S. actor **Jack Lemmon**, 1942 U.S. comedian/actor **Robert Klein**, 1942 U.S. actor **Nick Nolte**, 1950 U.S. singer **Dan Seals**, 1955 U.S. novelist **John Grisham**

February 9

1773 **William Henry Harrison:** Major general in the War of 1812. U.S. senator from Ohio. Elected 9th President of the United States. Died of pneumonia, contracted at his inauguration, after only one month in office, succeeded by Vice-President John Tyler. Grandfather of Benjamin Harrison 23rd President of U.S.

I contend that the strongest of all governments is that which is most free.

1854 Lord **Edward Carson:** Irish lawyer and politician. Led the Irish Unionist Party. Known as the "uncrowned king of Ulster." Elected to the British House of Commons. Served as First Lord of the Admiralty.

My only qualification for being put at the head of the Navy is that I am very much at sea.

1863 **Anthony Hope:** Pseudonym of **Anthony Hope Hawkins**. English novelist and lawyer. Chiefly remembered for his "Ruritanian" romances *The Prisoner of Zenda* and the sequel *Rupert of Hentzau*. Knighted in 1918.

Boys will be boys. And even that wouldn't matter if only we could prevent girls from being girls.

1865 **Mrs. Patrick Campbell:** née **Beatrice Stella Tanner**. Leading English actress of turn of the century London stage. Possessed outstanding talent and charm as well as a mercurial temper. First came to prominence with *The Second Mrs. Tanqueray*. George Bernard Shaw wrote Eliza Doolittle role in *Pygmalion* especially for her.

It doesn't matter what you do in the bedroom as long as you don't do it in the street and frighten the horses.

1866 **George Ade:** American humorist and playwright. Famous for his *Fables in Slang*. Wrote popular column for Chicago *Record*, and the plays, *The Sultan of Sulu, The Country Chairman* and *The College Widow*. Humorous books: *Artie, Pink Marsh* and *Doc' Horne.*

Anybody can win, unless there happens to be a second entry.

1874 **Amy Lowell:** American poet, critic, and biographer. Leader of imagist movement. Wrote numerous poems in free verse and polyphonic prose. Author of a monumental life of John Keats. Other works: *A Dome of Many-colored Glass* and *Sword Blades and Poppy Seeds.*

Won a posthumous Pulitzer Prize in 1956 for *What's O'Clock?*

All books are either dreams or swords;/ You can cut, or you can drug, with words.

1909 **Dean Rusk:** American statesman. President of the Rockefeller Foundation (1952–61). Secretary of State (1961–69) under Presidents John F. Kennedy and Lyndon Johnson. Played a major role in the Cuban crisis of 1962. Defended U.S. involvement in Vietnam.

The United States is not just an old cow that gives more milk the more it's kicked in the flanks.

1911 **Gypsy Rose Lee:** Born **Rose Louise Hovick.** American entertainer. Considered to be the Queen of Burlesque in the 1940s. Famed for her gimmick, the intellectual striptease act, with more emphasis on tease than stripping. First of her profession to receive widespread fame and entry to Broadway revues. Musical *Gypsy* is based on her life, her sister and mother.

God is love, but get it in writing.

1914 **Bill Veeck: William Louis Veeck, Jr.** Zany American baseball owner of St. Louis Browns, Cleveland Indians and Chicago White Sox. Enlivened games with a midget batter, exploding scoreboards and giveaways. During World War II, he offered some morning games to accommodate the war workers on night shifts. Signed Larry Doby, the first African-American baseball player in the American League.

It isn't the high price of stars that is so expensive; it's the high price of mediocrity.

1923 **Brendan Behan:** Irish playwright with exuberant wit, his work spiced with bawdy caricature. His three years in an English reform school for the possession of explosives for the IRA led him to write the autobiographical *Borstal Boy*. His plays, *The Quare Fellow* and *The Hostage* are based on two other prison terms.

An author's first duty is to let down his country.

1944 **Alice Walker:** African American novelist and poet. Instrumental in the development of black feminist literature. Best known for her third and most popular novel *The Color Purple*, winner of the 1983 Pulitzer Prize for fiction and made into a major film starring Whoopi Goldberg and Oprah Winfrey. Other works: *In Search of Our Mothers' Gardens, The Temple of My Familiar* and *Living by the Word.*

Womanism is to feminism as purple is to lavender...

1945 **Mia Farrow: Maria de Lourdes Villiers.** American actress of winsome and frail appearance. Daughter of actress Maureen O'Sullivan and director John Farrow. Appeared on the cover of the first issue of *People* magazine. TV series: *Peyton Place*. Films include *Rosemary's Baby, The Great Gatsby* and *Hannah and Her Sisters.* Married to Frank Sinatra and André Previn. Long relationship with Woody Allen, which ended badly. He married her adopted daughter.

I can match bottoms with anyone in Hollywood.

OTHERS: 1404 Last Byzantine emperor **Constantine XI**, 1775 Hungarian mathematician **Farkas Wolfgang Bolyai**, 1814 U.S. philanthropist **Samuel Jones Tilden**, 1853 South African statesman **Sir Leander Starr Jameson**, 1867 Japanese author **Natsume Sôseki**, 1890 Dutch architect **Jacobus J P Oud**, 1891 English-born actor **Ronald Colman**, 1892 American actress **Peggy Wood**, 1906 British soprano **Gwen Catley**, 1909 South American singer/dancer **Carmen Miranda**, 1914 U.S. guitarist/singer **Ernest Tubb**, 1923 Pioneer Cardiac transplant surgeon **Norman E. Shumway**, 1928 U.S. news anchor **Roger Mudd**, 1942 U.S. singer/pianist **Carole King**, 1979 Chinese actress **Ziyi Zhang**

February 10

1609 Sir **John Suckling:** English Cavalier poet, dramatist and courtier. Famed for his wit, extravagance and love of gaming. Best known for his lyrics. His masterpiece is "Ballad Upon a Wedding." Also wrote "A Session of Poets" and "The Goblins." Wrote the play *Brennoralt, or The Discontented Colonel.*

'Tis expectation makes a blessing dear,/ Heaven were not heaven, if we knew what it were.

1685 **Aaron Hill:** English dramatist and miscellaneous writer. Author of 17 plays, including *Zaire* and *Mérope* (adapted from Voltaire). Wrote the scenario for Handel's opera *Rinaldo*. One of Alexander Pope's targets in the *Dunciad*, which he answered in *Progress of Wit*. Also involved in many successful commercial schemes.

Youth is ever apt to judge in haste, and lose the medium in the wild extreme.

1775 **Charles Lamb:** Penname **Elia**. English essayist of the romantic period. Best known for *Essays of Elia*, which included "A Dissertation on Roast Pig," "A Chapter on Ears" and "The Praise of Chimney Sweepers." Collaborated with his sister Mary on a popular children's book *Tales from Shakespeare*. He took lifelong care of his sister, who in a fit of madness killed their mother.

The greatest pleasure I know is to do good by stealth, and to have it found out by accident.

1865 **Frank Moore Colby:** American educator and writer Member of the editorial staff of *Johnson's Cyclopedia*. Editor of the *International Year Book*. One of the editors of the first and second edition of the new *International Encyclopedia*.

Tolerance is composed of nine parts of apathy to one of brotherly love.

1868 **William Allen White:** "The Sage of Emporia." U.S. journalist, editor and owner of *The Emporia* [Kansas] *Gazette* (1895–1944). Pulitzer Prize for editorial writing (1923). Pulitzer Prize for his autobiography (1947). The William Allen White Children's Book Award is given annually for a children's book chosen by Kansas school children.

Consistency is a paste jewel that only cheap men cherish.

1890 **Boris Pasternak:** Russian lyric poet, novelist and translator. His novel *Doctor Zhivago* was rejected for publication in the U.S.S.R., but an Italian edition appeared, earning the author a Nobel Prize he was forced to reject. In addition to his novel, his prose work includes an autobiographical sketch, *Safe Conduct*, and several short stories, including the memorable, *Aerial Ways*. Collections of poems: *My Sister Life* and *Themes and Variations*.

In every generation there has to be some fool who will speak the truth as he sees it.

1893 **Jimmy Durante:** American long-nosed comedian, singer, and actor. Nicknamed "the Schnoz." Teamed with Eddie Jackson and Lou Clayton in a Vaudeville act. Appeared on radio, films and TV. Songs: "Ink-a-Dink-a-Doo" and "You Got to Start Off Each Day with a Song." Always closed his act with *Good night, Mrs. Calabash, wherever you are*, a salute to his wife.

Be nice to people on your way up because you'll meet them on your way down.

1894 **Harold Macmillan:** English statesman. Conservative prime minister (1957–63). His perseverance made possible the unprecedented nuclear test–ban treaty (1963), signed in Moscow, by Great Britain, the U.S. and the Soviet Union. Making a speech at the U.N. when Nikita Khrushchev began pounding his desk with his shoe. Dryly said, "I'd like that translated if I may." Hurt by the Profumo Scandal.

A Foreign Secretary is forever poised between a cliché and an indiscretion.

1898 **Bertolt Brecht:** German poet and dramatist. Collaborated with Kurt Weill on his major work *The Three Penny Opera*, a scathing satire on the modern bourgeoisie. Ardent Marxist, he was driven from Germany by the Nazis and began a 14 year exile in Denmark, Sweden and Finland. His plays of this period were direct attacks on Nazism: *The Private Life of the Master Race* and *Schweyk in the Second World War*. Other plays: *The Life of Galileo*, *Mother Courage and Her Children* and *The Good Woman of Setzuan*.

Those who don't share the good fortune of the mighty often share in their misfortune.

1920 **Alex Comfort:** English writer, biochemist, and director of research in gerontology at the University of London. As well as numerous academic texts, he wrote best-selling *The Joy of Sex: A Gourmet's Guide to Love Making*. Also wrote books of poems and novels.

Male sexual response is far brisker and more automatic: it is easily triggered by things, like putting a quarter in a vending machine.

1927 **Leontyne Price:** African-American operatic lyric soprano. Early in her career she had a success appearing as Bess in the folk opera *Porgy and Bess* (1952–54). Famous for her role as Aïda. Much associated with the work of Samuel Barber, who created the role of Cleopatra for her. Won more than twenty Grammy awards. Received Presidential Medal of Freedom award (1964).

I have never given all of myself, even vocal, to anyone. I was taught to sing on your interest, not your capital.

11955 **Greg Norman:** Australian profession golfer. Nicknamed "The Great White Shark" for his aggressive style and light blond hair. Although he has won many tournaments, his only major victories are the 1986 and 1993 British Opens, although he has been runner-up on eight occasions in major tournaments. Infamous for losing leads in the final round, most notably in the 1996 Masters. In 1995 he became the PGA's leading money winner. His advice for average players:

Attack this game in a bold, confident, and determined way, and you'll make a giant leap toward realizing your full potential as a player.

OTHERS: 1686 Dutch physician/botanist **Johann F. Gronovius**, 1728 German/Russian Czar of Russia, **Peter III**, 1844 U.S. magician **Alexander Herrmann**, 1846 English admiral **Lord Beresford**, 1880 Designer of fist V-12 engine **Jesse G. Vincent**, 1893 U.S. tennis champion **Bill Tilden**, 1898 Australian-born actress **Dame Judith Anderson**, 1906 The wolf man **Lon Chaney Jr.**, 1914 U.S. harmonica player **Larry Adler**, 1929 U.S. pianist/composer **Jerry Goldsmith**, 1930 U.S. children's writer **E.L. Konigsburg** 1930 U.S. actor **Robert Wagner**, 1939 American vocalist **Roberta Flack**, 1950 U.S. Olympic swimmer, **Mark Spitz**, 1961 Presidential advisor/journalist **George Stephanopoulos**

February 11

1657 **Bernard De Fontenelle:** French scientist and man of letters. Won a great literary reputation in Paris, writing idylls, satires, dialogues, critical essays, histories and tragedies. Wrote conversations between historical figures in order to circulate new philosophical ideas. Best works: *A Plurality of Worlds* and *History of the Oracles*.

It isn't very intelligent to find answers to questions which are unanswerable.

1802 **Lydia M. Child:** American abolitionist, suffragist, writer, journalist and editor. Editor of the National Anti-Slavery Standard and published many essays on political and social issues. Founded and edited first U.S. children's monthly, *Juvenile Miscellany* (1826–34). Other works: *The History of the Conditions of Women in Various Ages and Nations* and *An Appeal in Favor of That Class of Americans Called Africans*. Also wrote the novel *Philothea*.

We first crush people to the earth, and then claim the right of trampling on them forever because they are prostrate.

1838 **J. Willard Gibbs:** America's first true physicist, mathematician and one of its greatest scientists. Recipient of the first PhD (from Yale University) in engineering. Worked out most of the details of chemical thermodynamics and statistical mechanics. Founder of physical chemistry.

A mathematician may say anything he pleases, but a physicist must be at least partially sane.

1847 **Thomas Alva Edison:** "Wizard of Menlo Park." Told by teachers when he was a boy that he was too stupid to learn anything. American inventor of first electric bulb and nearly 1300 other items, including the phonograph, dictating machine, first practical typewriter and the motion picture projector. Pioneer in the field of electric power distribution and in the motion picture industry. Discovered "Edison effect," basis of modern electronics. Approached invention in a rational and business-like way. Tried to remove ancient elements of magic and mystery from the art of invention.

To invent, you need a good imagination and a pile of junk.

1898 **Leo Szilard:** Hungarian-born American physicist. Fled Germany in 1933 and emigrated to the U.S. in 1938. Ghost-wrote the letter from Einstein to President Roosevelt advocating the development of an atomic bomb. Central figure in the Manhattan Project. After the war became a proponent of peaceful uses of atomic energy. Worked with Enrico Fermi to build the first nuclear reactor.

A scientist's aim in a discussion with his colleagues is not to persuade, but to clarify.

1900 **Tommy Hitchcock, Jr.:** American-born polo player. Generally regarded as the world's greatest during the two decades just prior to World War II. Received his ten-goal rating (1922). Serving in World War II, he was killed in an airplane crash when he was unable to pull out of a dive while doing tests.

Lose as if you like it; win as if you were used to it.

1916 **Florynce Kennedy:** Flamboyant lawyer, feminist and political activist. Partial to wearing a cowboy hat and pink sunglasses, and making outrageous comments. Deeply committed to liberal causes, including civil, human, and women's rights. Founding member of the National Women's Political Caucus and the national Feminist Party.

Sweetie, if you're not living on the edge, then you're just taking up space.

1917 **Sidney Sheldon:** American novelist, playwright and screenwriter. Won a Tony Award for Broadway's *Redhead* and an Academy Award for *The Bachelor and the Bobby Soxer*. Best-selling books: *Windmills of the Gods*, *Rage of Angels*, and *The Other Side of Midnight*.

What I do is put my characters into situations that are so precarious there is no way to get out. And then I figure how to get them out.

1920 King **Farouk:** Became King of Egypt when his father died. Since he was underage, a regency council was formed to run the country until his constitutional powers were handed over to him in 1937. During his reign, Egypt suffered from chaos and corruption. With the revolution in 1952 he was forced to abdicate, noting that:

There will soon be only five kings left: the Kings of England, Diamonds, Hearts, Spades, and Clubs.

1921 **Lloyd Bentsen, Jr.:** U.S. senator from Texas (1971–93), also served in the House of Representatives (1949–55). Vice-presidential running mate of Michael Dukakis. U.S. Treasury Secretary during the early years of the Clinton administration. During a debate between vice presidential candidates he commented on Dan Quayle comparing himself to John F. Kennedy:

Senator, I served with Jack Kennedy. I knew Jack Kennedy. Jack Kennedy was a friend. Senator, you're no Jack Kennedy.

1925 **Virginia E. Johnson:** American psychologist and sexologist. With colleague and one-time husband William H. Masters did work in sex therapy and wrote *Human Sexual Response*, *Human Sexual Inadequacy*, *Homosexuality in Perspective* and *On Sex and Human Loving*.

We were born man, woman and sexual beings... Your sexuality is a dimension of your personality, and whenever you are sexually active, you are expressing yourself— the self that you are at that moment, the mood that you're in, the needs that you have.

1934 **Mary Quant:** English fashion designer, who helped make London a fashion center. Developed "Chelsea Look," sixties. High priestess of the Mod cult and mother of the mini-skirt. First fashion designer named officer of the Order of the British Empire. Her description of a fashionable woman:

Having money is rather like being a blonde, it is more fun but not vital.

OTHERS: 1380 Italian humanist **Gianfrancesco Poggio Bracciolini**, 1535 Roman Catholic pope **Gregory XIV**, 1800 English photographic pioneer **William Henry Fox Talbot**, 1821 French Egyptologist **Auguste Édouard Mariette**, 1833 8th Chief Justice of Supreme Court **Melville Weston Fuller**, 1907 U.S. businessman/community planner **William J. Levitt**, 1908 U.S. folk singer **Josh White**, 1909 Heavyweight boxing champion **Max Baer**, 1909 U.S. film director **Joseph L, Mankewicz**, 1922 U.S. actor **Leslie Nielsen**, 1926 Great French chef **Paul Bocuse**, 1935 U.S. singer **Gene Vincent**, 1940 U.S. singer **Bobby Pickett**, 1941 Brazilian musician **Sergio Mendes**, 1965 Country singer **Sheryl Crow**

February 12

1567 **Thomas Campion:** English composer, poet and physician. His book on poetry, *Observations in the Art of English Poesie* as critical of the practice of rhyming in poetry. Wrote over 100 songs with lute accompaniment in the *Book of Arts*.

Follow thy fair sun, unhappy shadow.

1663 **Cotton Mather:** American Colonial clergyman, man of letters and author of the most important literary work produced in the colonies, the *Magnalia Christi Americana*, an "ecclesiastical history of New England." Son of Increase Mather. Pastor, Second Church of Boston. Helped establish Boston as a culture center. Advocated use of scientific evidence in witchcraft trials.

Charity ... is kind, it is not easily provok'd, it thinks no evil; it believes all things, hopes all things.

1791 **Peter Cooper:** American inventor, industrialist, philanthropist and pioneer civic reformer. Designed and constructed first U.S. steam locomotive, the "Tom Thumb." Founded and endowed the Cooper Union for the Advancement of Science and Art for workers.

The Dealers in money have always, since the days of Moses, been the dangerous class.

1809 **Charles Robert Darwin:** English naturalist. After five-year voyage on the H.M.S. *Beagle* to South America and the Galapagos Islands developed a theory of evolution through natural selection, which came to be called Darwinism. His most-noted books are *On the Origin of Species by Means of Natural Selection, or the Preservation of Favored Races in the Struggle for Life* and *The Descent of Man.*

A man who dares to waste one hour of time has not discovered the value of life.

1809 **Abraham Lincoln:** American lawyer and debater from Illinois and Sixteenth U.S. president Great humanist and spokesman for the common man. Preserved the Union through the Civil War. Published the Emancipation Proclamation, freeing slaves. Named "The Great Emancipator." Delivered famous address at dedication of Gettysburg memorial cemetery, a prose classic. Assassinated by actor John Wilkes Booth at Ford's theater in Washington, D.C. Permanent memorials to the man have been established in Kentucky, Illinois, Washington D.C., and elsewhere.

As I would not be a slave, so I would not be a master. This expresses my idea of democracy. Whatever differs from this, to the extent of the difference, is no democracy.

1813 **James Dwight Dana:** Foremost American geologist, scientific explorer, editor and teacher. Celebrated for his *System of Mineralogy*, written when he was only 24, for his report on the geology of the U.S., exploring expedition, monographs on crustaceans and corals, and for a seminal text on volcanoes he wrote during his 70s. His *Manuel of Geology* was in the library of almost every American geologist. A devout Christian, Dana viewed the growth and change of Earth's history as plan, not chance, the work of a benevolent creator, whom he termed the "Power Above Nature."

The grand old Book of God still stands; and this old earth, the more its leaves are turned over and pondered, the more it will sustain and illustrate the Sacred Word.

1828 **George Meredith:** English novelist and poet. A disastrous marriage gave him insights into relations between the sexes, which appear in his work. He also had a great interest with natural selection as Nature's way of perfecting man. Achieved distinction with his novel *The Ordeal of Richard Feveral.* Other Works: *Beauchamp's Career, The Egotist,* and *The Amazing Marriage.* Credited with helping Thomas Hardy begin his literary career.

A witty woman is a treasure; a witty beauty is a power.

1880 **John L. Lewis:** American labor leader. Left school in the 7th grade to work in the coal mines. President of United Mine Workers of America (1920–60), most powerful union in country at the time. Formed a combination of unions, the Congress of Industrial Organizations (CIO), of which he was president until 1940. Later Broke with the CIO to form the American Federation of Labor (AFL).

He that tooteth not his own horn, the same shall not be tooted.

1884 **Alice Roosevelt Longworth:** Only daughter of President Theodore Roosevelt, who once said *I can either run the country or I can control Alice, but I cannot possibly do both.* Beautiful, aloof, self-confident and calculating, she was known as a rule-breaker. Became a fashion icon, with the song *Alice Blue Gown* written to commemorate her signature color. Much in demand in society, her father claimed: "She is the bride at every wedding and the corpse at every funeral."

I have a simple philosophy. Fill what is empty. Empty what is full. And scratch where it itches.

1893 **Omar Bradley:** American army general. Known as the "GI's General." Led U.S. ground troops at the Normandy invasion. First permanent chairman of the U.S. Joint Chiefs of Staff (1949–53). Promoted to five-star general (1950). Published his wartime memoirs in *A Soldier's Story* and his autobiography, *General's Life.*

Ours is a world of nuclear giants and ethical infants. We have grasped the mystery of the atom and rejected the sermon of the Mount.

1934 **Bill Russell:** U.S. basketball player who played an important role in the Boston Celtics dynasty that won 11 championships in the 13 years he played. Raised defensive play to a new level. Played college ball at the University of San Francisco, which he led to two NCAA championships. Coached the Celtics as the first African-American head coach in a major team sport history.

Durability is part of what makes a great athlete.

1938 **Judy Blume:** American author of frank and controversial books for adolescents. *Are You There God? It's Me Margaret* is her candid approach to the onset of puberty, such as menstruation and sex, written in a natural style. Efforts were made to suppress the work and to keep it out of schools and libraries. Other books: *Then Again, Maybe I Won't, It's Not the End of the World,* and books for adults, including *Wifey* and *Smart Women,* both about women trapped in traditional marriages.

My own adolescent rebellion came late. Somewhat around the age of 35. I don't recommend waiting till then. Better to drag your parents through it than your kids.

OTHERS: 1211 Roman Catholic German King **Henry VII**, 1585 Physician and writer on anatomy **Caspar Bartholin**, 1768 Holy Roman Emperor **Francis II**, 1850 Flemish missionary **Amaat Vyncke**, 1885 Nazi district leader **Julius Streicher**, 1894 German conductor **Hans Guido Bülow**, 1904 TV host **Ted Mack**, 1914 U.S. singer/ bandleader **Tex Beneke**, 1915 Canadian actor **Lorne Greene**, 1918 Outfield with Boston Red Sox **Dom DiMaggio**, 1923 Italian director **Franco Zeffirelli**, 1926 Baseball player/sportscaster **Joe Garagiola**, 1930 U.S. senator **Arlen Specter**, 1944 U.S. C&W musician **Moe Bandy**, 1945 Swedish actress **Maud Adams**

February 13

1825 **Julia Ripley Dorr:** American poet, novelist and essayist. Poems: "Afternoon Songs," "November," "A Red Rose," "A Cathedral Pilgrimage," "Silence," "Darkness" and "Grass-Grown." A novel, *Farmingdale*, published under the pen name Caroline Thomas. Also wrote a series of essays on marriage.

A new beatitude I write for thee, "Blessed are they who are not sure of things."

1877 **Sidney Smith:** American cartoonist with *Chicago Tribune* (1911–35). Created "The Gumps" comic strip (1917). After signing a new million dollar contract for three years with the *Tribune* in 1930, his car collided with another auto and he was killed instantly. The Gumps survived, taken over by Gus Edson.

One evil in old age is that, as your time is come; you think every little illness the beginning of the end. When a man expects to be arrested, every knock at the door is an alarm.

1879 **Sarojini Naidu:** Indian feminist and poet. Campaigned for the abolition of purdah, a curtain or veil to hide women from strangers. Imprisoned many times for civil disobedience. Participated in the negotiations leading to independence. First Indian woman to be president of the Indian National Congress.

Sense of justice is one of the most wonderful ideals of Islam, because as I read the Qur'an I find those dynamic principles of life, not mystic nut practical ethics for the daily conduct of life suited to the world.

1881 **Eleanor Farjeon:** English writer of fantasies and children's stories. Collaborated with her brother Herbert on *Kings and Queens*. The Farjeon Award is given for outstanding work in children's literature. Works: her first novel *Martin Pippins in the Apple Orchard*, the play *The Glass Slipper*, a selection of short stories *The Little Bookworm* and her autobiographical *A Nursery in the Nineties*.

The events of childhood do not pass, but repeat themselves like seasons of the year.

1892 **Robert H. Jackson:** American jurist, lawyer and Associate Justice of the Supreme Court. Opposed monopolies. Supported civil liberties. Believed in judicial restraint. Did groundbreaking work on international law. Member of the War Crimes Commission. Chief American prosecutor at the International Military Tribunal at Nuremberg (1945–46).

The validity of a doctrine does not depend on whose ox it gores.

1892 **Grant Wood:** American philosopher-artist, teacher of the graphic and plastic arts and painter, who depicted rural Midwestern life. Meticulous craftsman and ardent promoter of humble, hometown vales. Best known for *American Gothic*. That same year he painted his first major landscape *Stone City, Iowa*, a boom town gone bust.

All the good ideas I ever had came to me while I was milking a cow.

1902 **Harold D. Lasswell:** Leading American psychologist, political scientist and communication theorist. Researched politics, personality and social sciences. Argued that democracies needed propaganda to keep the uninformed citizens in agreement with what the specialized class had determined was in their best interests. One of his most famous works was "Propaganda Techniques in World War," in which he defined propaganda and discussed its major objectives. Most famous and widely read book is *Politics: Who Gets What, When, How*.

We must put aside democratic dogmatisms about men being the best judges of their own interests since men are poor judges of their own interests, flitting from one alternative to the next without solid reason.

1903 **Georges Simenon:** Belgian-born French novelist. Master of the crime novel. Began a journalist, and then moved to Paris, where he wrote psychological novels as well as detective stories. Created tough, morbidly psychological Inspector Maigret. Wrote over three hundred books, including autobiographical works and diaries.

Writing is not a profession but a vocation of unhappiness.

1910 **Margaret Halsey:** American author wrote travel memoirs. Best remembered for her witty novels that lampooned the English and their customs/ Her books include: *With Malice Towards Some, Color Blind: a White Woman Looks at the Negro, No Laughing Matter: The Autobiography of a WASP, Some of My Best Friends Are Soldiers* and *Folks at Home*.

Every time I think I've touched bottom as far as boredom is concerned, new vistas of ennui open up.

1918 **Patricia Jane "Patty" Berg:** American Hall of fame golfer. Won the U.S. amateur title in 10 of the 13 tournaments she entered. Named Outstanding Female Athlete of the Year in 1938, 43 and 55 by the Associated Press. Co-founded t he LPGA. Served as its first president (1949–52). Won more than eighty pro tournaments, the all-time women's leader in major championships.

If I were a man I wouldn't have a half dozen Tom Collinses before going out to play golf, then let profanity substitute for proficiency on the golf course.

1920 **Eileen Farrell:** American operatic soprano. Made her concert debut at the Columbia Broadcasting studios where she soon had her own radio show. Sang with San Francisco and Chicago operas before making her Met debut. Made her rather late debut on stage in 1956 where she was tremendously successful, but she preferred the concert hall. Never reconciled herself to the life of a diva. Best known for roles in Wagnerian operas.

You create a role on stage — when you're off it should stop already.

1923 **Charles "Chuck" Yeager:** American most famous test pilot. Trained as a fighter pilot, flying many European missions in World War II. First to break the sound barrier in 1953, flying the Bell X-1A two and a half times the speed of sound.

Rules are made for people who aren't willing to make up their own.

OTHERS: 1805 Lawyer/law codifier **David Dudley Field**, 1805 German number theorist **Peter G.L. Dirichlet**, 1849 English politician **Lord Randolph Churchill**, 1861 Japanese religious writer **Uchimura Kanzo**, 1885 U.S. First Lady **Bess Truman**, 1888 Greek premier **Georgios Papandreou**, 1908 U.S. journalist **Pauline Frederick**, 1910 U.S. Nobel winning physicist **William B. Shockley**, 1919 Long-time Grambling football coach **Eddie Robinson**, 1919 U.S. country singer **Tennessee Ernie Ford**, 1934 U.S. actor **George Segal**, 1946 German director/actor **Ranier Werner Fassbinder**, 1933 American blonde actress **Kim Novak**

February 14

1401 **Leon Battista Alberti:** Florentine architect, poet, art theorist, moral philosopher and mathematician. One of the most brilliant figures of the Renaissance. His architectural works are among the best examples of the pure Classical style. His treatise on architecture, *De re aedificatoria*, had a considerable influence on the style of Renaissance architecture. Equally influential was his work on painting, *De picture*. His masterpiece, *On the Family*, uses dialogue to discuss his social philosophy.

Men can do all things if they will.

1760 **Richard Allen:** African-American Methodist preacher. A former slave he bought his freedom. He was the first ordained African-American minister. Helped form the "Free African Society" and founded the African Methodist Episcopal Church in Philadelphia and was elected its first bishop.

The only place Blacks felt that they could maintain an element of self-expression was the church.

1766 **Thomas Robert Malthus:** English political economist, sociologist and clergyman. Pioneer in modern population theory. Anonymously published his "Essay on the Principle of Population." It formulated the Malthusian theory that "there is an ever present tendency for the population to outrun the food supply." Darwin was influenced by the essay in formulating his theory of "survival of the fittest."

Population, when unchecked, increases in a geometric ratio. Subsistence only increases in an arithmetical ratio.

1845 **Quintin Hogg:** English philanthropist. Moved by the plight of poor children he and his wife opened a "ragged school" for destitute children, then a Youths' Christian Institute and Regent Street Polytechnic where various trades were taught.

Don't confuse biology and religion — one is a science to be proved or disproved, the other is a life to be lived.

1856 **Frank Harris:** Irish-born American editor, journalist, biographer, and novelist. Edited some of America's leading journals: *Fortnightly Review*, *Saturday Review* and *Vanity Fair*. Detailed his debauched life in a scandalous quasi-autobiography, the three-volume, *My Life and Loves*, which was banned in England and the U.S. Also wrote a malicious biography of Oscar Wilde.

Memoirs are a well-known form of fiction.

1858 **Joseph Thomson:** Scottish geologist and naturalist. Conducted explorations in Africa that yielded important data on the flora and fauna of the African continent. Thomson's gazelle, an East African species, was named for him. His motto was "He who goes gently goes safely; he who goes safely goes far." Books: *To the Central African Lakes and Back* and *Travels in the Atlas and Southern Morocco.*

The Most hazardous part of our expedition to Africa was crossing Piccadilly Circus.

1864 **Israel Zangwill:** English novelist and playwright. A leading Zionist. Widely known for his novels on Jewish themes including *Children of the Ghetto: A Study of a Peculiar People* and *The Melting Pot.*

A man likes his wife to be just clever enough to appreciate his cleverness, and just stupid enough to admire it.

1882 **George Jean Nathan:** American editor, essayist and drama critic. Co-founded *The American Mercury* and *American Spectator*. Devoted most of his career to the interpretation of the theater. Noted for his wit, cynicism, sophistication and erudition. Mentor of such playwrights as Eugene O'Neill, Arthur Miller and William Saroyan.

The test of a real comedian is whether you laugh at him before he opens his mouth.

1894 **Jack Benny:** Born **Benjamin Kubelsky**. American entertainer, comedian, violinist in vaudeville, films, radio and television. Had a weekly series on CBS-TV from 1950 through 1965. Played a wisecracking miser, but was actually generous and modest. Master of timing, who could milk a laugh by merely pausing. Eternally 39. His car, often mentioned on his shows was a 1924 Maxwell. His movies included: *Charley's Aunt*, *To Be or Not to Be*, *George Washington Slept Here* and *The Horn Blows at Midnight.*

It's not so much knowing when to speak, rather when to pause.

1913 **Jimmy Hoffa:** U.S. union leader. President, International Teamster Union (1957–71). Imprisoned for jury-tampering and fraud (1967–71). Pardoned by President Nixon. Disappeared from a Detroit restaurant

July 30, 1975 and was declared dead in 1982. Body was never found.

I do unto others what they do unto me, only worse.

1913 **James A. Pike:** American Episcopalian priest and lawyer. Dean of St. John the Divine in New York City. Later bishop of California. Spoke out against McCarthyism. Advocated civil rights and planned parenthood. Died on an expedition in the Judean desert.

A man needs self-acceptance or he can't live with himself; he needs self-criticism or others can't live with him.

1944 **Carl Bernstein:** U.S. journalist and author. As a reporter for the Washington Post, he and Robert Woodward played a major role in uncovering and publicizing the Watergate Scandal and cover-up. With Woodward wrote *All the President's Men.*

For the first time, the weird and the stupid and the coarse are becoming our cultural norms, even our cultural ideal.

OTHERS: 1483 Founder of India's Mughal dynasty **Zahir al-Din Mohammed Babur Shah**, 1819 U.S. inventor **Christopher Latham Sholes**, 1824 Union Civil War general **Winfield Scott Hancock**, 1847 U.S. suffragette **Anna Howard Shaw**, 1859 Engineer/inventor of the Ferris Wheel, **George Washington Gale Ferris**, 1864 U.S. sociologist **Robert E. Park**, 1905 U.S. actress **Thelma Ritter**, 1907 Jockey/trainer **Johnny Longdon**, 1913 U.S. sportscaster **Mel Allen**, 1921 U.S. TV journalist **Hugh Downs**, 1931 U.S. singer **Phyllis McGuire**, 1931 Canadian hockey player **Bernie "Boom Boom" Geoffrion**, 1935 LPGA champion golfer **Mickey Wright**, 1941 U.S. senator **Paul Tsongas**

February 15

1368 **Sigismund:** Holy Roman Emperor. Third and last German Emperor and fourth Bohemian king of the Luxembourg dynasty. Burned the Czech religious reformer Jan Hus at the stake for heresy. Instrumental in helping convene the Council of Constance, which ended the Papal schism. When a Cardinal at the Council tried to correct the emperor's Latin, he roared:

I am the king of the Romans, and am superior to the rules of grammar.

1564 **Galileo Galilei:** Italian astronomer, physicist, and philosopher. A founder of experimental science. Improved the refracting telescope and was the first to use if for astronomy. Ran afoul of the Catholic Church for defending the Copernican system, which maintains the earth revolves around the sun and not the other way around. Tried by the Inquisition, he was forced to recant. The validity of his scientific work was finally recognized by the Vatican in 1993. Although totally blind, he continued his research while under house arrest. Among his other discoveries: law of uniformly accelerated motion towards the Earth, the parabolic path of a projectile, and the law that all bodies have weight.

In questions of science, the authority of a thousand is not worth the humble reasoning of a single individual.

1748 **Jeremy Bentham:** English philosopher, jurist, economist and social reformer. Founder of utilitarianism, first systematic effort to describe and evaluate all human acts. Argued that the proper objective of all conduct and legislation is "the greatest happiness of the greatest number." Pioneering works: *A Fragment of Government* and *Introduction to the Principles of Morals and Legislation.* Founded University College, London, where his clothed skeleton is preserved on public view.

Every law is an infraction of liberty.

1820 **Susan Brownell Anthony:** Militant American social reformer. Crusader for women's suffrage. Organized International Council of Women (1888) and International Woman Suffrage Alliance (1904) with Elizabeth Stanton. Besides the right of the ballot, she fought for the right of women to control their own property and children, and for opportunities for higher education. Also a crusader for temperance and Negro suffrage. First woman to have her likeness on a U.S. coinage, the dollar coin.

I always distrust people who know so much about what God wants them to do to their fellows.

1845 **Elihu Root:** American lawyer and statesman, Served as U.S. Secretary of War under William McKinley and Theodore Roosevelt. Named Secretary of State by Roosevelt, Root maintained the Open Door Policy and supported arbitration in solving international disputes. Received the Nobel Peace Prize (1912) for his efforts to improve relations with Latin America.

Men do not fail; they give up trying.

1861 **Alfred North Whitehead:** English mathematician and idealist philosopher. Made major contributions to mathematics, logic, philosophy of science and meta-mathematics. His *Treatise on Universal Algebra* extended Boolean symbolic logic. Coauthored the epochal *Principia Mathematica* with his former student Bertrand Russell. Popular writings: *An Introduction to Mathematics, Science and the Modern World, Process and Reality, Adventures of Ideas* and *Modes of Thought.*

Civilization advances by extending the number of important operations which we can perform without thinking about them.

1882 **John Barrymore:** Born **John Sidney Blythe.** "The Great Profile." Admired stage matinee idol and movie star. Brother of Lionel and Ethel Barrymore, grandfather of Drew Barrymore. His silent films were mainly romantic dramas, comedies and swashbuckling adventures. With the coming of sound his wonderful voice and handsome appearance made him a box-office smash. Heavy drinker, he led a reckless lifestyle, filled with countless romantic scandals and four unsuccessful marriages. Films: *Dr. Jekyll and Mr. Hyde, Don Juan, Grand Hotel* and *Dinner at Eight.*

The trouble with life is that there are so many beautiful women and so little time.

1883 **Sax Rohmer:** Pseudonym of **Arthur Sarsfield Ward.** English mystery writer. Creator of the sinister, sardonic, Chinese criminal genius Dr. Fu Manchu featured in many spine-chilling tales, including *Dr. Fu Manchu, The Yellow Claw* and *Re-enter Fu Manchu.*

There is no incidental music to the dramas of real life.

1935 **Susan Brownmiller:** American author, radical feminist and journalist. Wrote best-selling, provocative and influential *Against Our Will: Men, Women and Rape,* a comprehensive study of rape. Argued that rape had hitherto been defined by men, rather than women, that it was not a sexual act but an expression of power and control. Her study of the history, cultural significance and psychology of sexual assault helped alter conceptions of rape.

My purpose in this book has been to give rape its history. Now we must deny it a future.

1874 Sir **Ernest Henry Shackleton:** Anglo-Irish explorer chiefly remembered for his Antarctic expedition of 1914–1916 in the ship *Endurance,* which was caught in an icepack and drifted for 10 months before being crushed. He and his crew drifted on ice floes for another five months, before reaching Elephant Island. He and five others sailed 800 miles to South Georgia Island to get help, and then led four rescue expeditions to get his men. Shackleton placed the following ad in the Times of London:

Men wanted for hazardous journey. Small wages. Bitter cold. Long months of complete darkness. Constant danger. Safe return doubtful. Honor and recognition in case of success.

1910 **Millicent Fenwick:** American fashion editor, politician and diplomat. Long time moderate Republican member of the U.S. House of Representatives. Walter Cronkite called her "the conscience of Congress." Outspoken in favor of civil rights and the women's movement. Affectionately remembered as the pipe-smoking grandmother who served as the model for Garry Trudeau's "Doonesbury" character Lacey Davenport.

Never feel self-pity, the most destructive emotion there is. How awful to be caught up in the terrible squirrel cage of self.

1912 **George Mikes:** Hungarian-born British author. His books were commentaries on various countries. England: *How to Be an Alien,* Japan: *The Land of the Rising Yen,* Israel: *Milk and Honey, The Prophet Motive* and U.S.A.: *How to Scrape Skies.*

English humor resembles the Loch Ness Monster in that both are famous but there is a strong suspicion that neither exists.

OTHERS: 1519 Spanish explorer **Pedro Menéndez de Aviles,** 1571 German composer/music theorist **Michael Praetorius,** 1797 Piano maker **Henry E. Steinway,** 1800 Dutch hydraulic engineer/railroad pioneer **Frederick W. Conrad,** 1803 Initiated California Gold Rush **John Augustus Sutter,** 1809 U.S. inventor **Cyrus Hall McCormick,** 1812 U.S. jeweler **Charles L. Tiffany,** 1823 Chinese rebel leader **Li Hung-Tshang,** 1894 Brazilian statesman **Oswaldo Aranha,** 1905 U.S. composer **Harold Arlen,** 1914 U.S. actor **Kevin McCarthy,** 1929 English auto racer **Graham Hill,** 1929 U.S. Secretary of Defense **James Schlesinger,** 1945 U.S. author **Douglas Hofstadter**

February 16

1497 **Philipp Melanchthon:** Born **Philipp Schwartzerd** German religious leader. *Loci Communes* is the first great Protestant work on dogmatic theology. Succeeded to the leadership of the German Reformation after Luther's death. Wrote guidelines leading to first modern school system in Saxony.

In necessary things, unity; in doubtful things, liberty; in all things, charity.

1514 **Georg Joachim Rheticus:** Austrian-born cartographer, instrument maker, medical practitioner and teacher. Spent two years with Copernicus. Rheticus arranged for the first publication of Copernicus' *De Revolutionibus.*

The planets show again and again all the phenomena which God desired to be seen from the earth.

1822 Sir **Francis Galton:** English anthropologist who studied the inheritance of physical and mental attributes in humans, with the aim of improving the human species. Coined word "eugenics, of which he is considered the founder. Developed the modern technique of weather mapping. Devised the system of fingerprint identification.

Well-washed and well-combed domestic pets grow dull; they need the stimulus of fleas.

1834 **Ernst Heinrich Haeckel:** German naturalist, biologist and philosopher. Leading exponent of the biological theory of evolution. Made basic studies of the eyes and ears. Contributed to the formulation of the law of conservation of energy.

The voluntary death by which a man puts an end to intolerable suffering is really an act of redemption.

1838 **Henry Adams:** American historian and philosopher. Son and grandson of presidents, John Quincy Adams and John Adams, he chose scholarship over politics. Editor and journalist for the *North American Review.* Harvard history professor. Author of *Mont-Saint-Michel and Chartres* and of one of the most famous autobiographies in the English language, the Pulitzer Prize winning (1919) *The Education of Henry Adams.*

There is no such thing as an underestimate of average intelligence.

1876 **George Macaulay Trevelyan:** English historian. Regius professor of history at Cambridge (1927–40). Pioneered the study of social history. Works include *Garibaldi and the Thousand* and *British History of the Nineteenth Century English Social History.*

Education has provided a vast population able to read but unable to distinguish what is worth reading.

1884 **Robert Flaherty:** American filmmaker and explorer. Considered the father of documentary filmmaking. Lived with the Eskimos in remote northern Canada for 16 months. His film *Nanook of the North*, depicting the Eskimos' way of living was an international critical and commercial success. Other documentaries: *Moana*, a South Seas documentary, *Tabu*, *Elephant Boy*, *Man of Aran*, and the Standard Oil sponsored *Louisiana Story*.

There's a saying among prospectors: "Go out looking for one thing, and that's all you'll ever find."

1886 **Van Wyck Brooks:** American author, critic and scholar. "Master of the art of interpretative biography and literary history." Associated with magazine *The Seven Arts*. Wrote *America's Coming of Age*, *Makers and Finders: A History of the Writer in America, 1800–1915* and *The Flowering of New England: 1815–1865* (Pulitzer Prize in history, 1937).

Earnest people are often people who habitually look on the serious side of things that have no serious side.

1904 **George Kennan:** American diplomat and historian. Served in the U.S. embassies in Moscow, Vienna, Prague, Berlin and Lisbon. In an anonymous article, he proposed policy of "Containment" in dealing with the Soviet Union after World War II, which became the basis of U.S. policy toward the Soviet Union. Pulitzer prizes for *Russia Leaves the War* (1956) and *Memoirs 1925–50* (1967).

A war regarded as inevitable or even probable and therefore much prepared for, has a very good chance of eventually being fought.

1926 **John Schlesinger:** British film and theater director and actor. British films: *Billy Liar* and *Darling*. His first American movie *Midnight Cowboy* was a major commercial success, followed by *Sunday Bloody Sunday* and *Marathon Man*.

Hollywood is an extraordinary kind of temporary place.

1932 **Aharon Appelfeld:** Rumanian-born Jewish poet, novelist, short story writer and essayist. Sent to a concentration camp at age eight. Escaped and spent three years hiding in the Ukraine. Joined the Russian army. After the war he made his way to Israel. Professor of Hebrew Literature at Ben Gurion University of Negev.

The Holocaust is a central event in many people's lives, but it also has become a metaphor for our century. There cannot be an end to speaking and writing about it. Besides, in Israel, everyone carries a biography deep inside him.

1959 **John McEnroe:** German-born American professional tennis player. Four times number one tennis player in world (1981–84). Nine grand slam titles. Noted for his displays of temper and invective on the court. First player ejected from a Grand Slam event in 30 years. Once married to actress Tatum O'Neal.

I think it's the mark of a great player to be confident in tough situations.

OTHERS: 1519 French Huguenot leader **Gaspard de Coligny**, 1740 Italian printer **Giambattista Bodoni**, 1746 German novelist/ art critic **Johann Heinse**, 1821 German explorer **Heinrich Barth**, 1822 Chinese diplomat **Li Hung Chang**, 1848 Dutch botanist **Hugo de Vries**, 1850 French writer **Octave Mirbeau**, 1866 Austrian composer **Johann Strauss**, 1898 U.S. stage actress **Katharine Cornell**, 1901 U.S. bandleader **Wayne King**, 1903 U.S. ventriloquist **Edgar Bergen**, 1914 Country singer **Jimmy Wakely**, 1920 U.S. singer with her sisters **Patty Andrews**, 1926 U.S. actress/dancer **Vera-Ellen**, 1934 U.S. LPGA golfer **Marlene Bauer Hagge**, 1935 Singer/comedian/congressman **Sonny Bono**

February 17

1864 **Andrew Barton "Banjo" Paterson:** Australian journalist and folk poet. Became a literary celebrity following the publication of *The Man from Snow River* (1895). Regarded as the premier Australian poet. Wrote words of "Waltzing Matilda," adapted from a traditional ditty which became Australia's national song.

Once a jolly swagman camped by a billabong,/ Under the shade of a coolibar tree,/ And he sang as he sat and waited for his billy-boil,/ You'll come a-waltzing, Matilda, with me.

1874 **Thomas J. Watson:** U.S. industrialist. Converted a financially ailing manufacturer of business machines into the international giant IBM, the largest manufacturer of electric typewriters and data processing equipment. President and director (1914–49). CEO and chairman of the board (1949–56). Backed an aggressive research and development program, forming a highly-motivated, well-trained and handsomely-paid staff. Active in civic affairs, he was noted for his efforts on behalf of the arts and world peace.

Think... Think about Appearance, Association, Action, Ambition, Accomplishment.

1879 **Dorothy Canfield Fisher:** American novelist of stories dealing with Vermont life. Wrote *The Montessori Mother*, *The Brimming Cup* and *Something Old, Something New*. Member of the Book-of-the-Month Club selection committee (1926–51). A Dorothy Canfield Fisher Library Award was established by the Book-of-the-Month Club as a memorial, with funs to be used by small libraries for the purchase of books.

A mother is not a person to lean on, but a person to make leaning unnecessary.

1881 **Bess Streeter Aldrich:** American author of about 200 short stories and thirteen novels, including *Miss Bishop*, which was made into a motion picture. Her works commemorated small town values and morality through vivid portrayals of pioneer life. She hoped that the young people who read her books would gain a sense of history.

Thoughts are acrobats, agile and quite often untrustworthy.

1888 **Ronald Knox:** English theologian and crime writer. Converted to Roman Catholicism. Translated the St. Jerome Vulgate Bible into English. Noted for his *Essays in Satire* and in particular his mock-serious critical writings on Sherlock Holmes. In 1926, he broadcast a pretended live report of a revolution across London on his regular BBC program. As Orson Welles' "War of the Worlds" sometime later, the broadcast resulted in a minor panic.

A good sermon should be like a woman's skirt: short enough to arouse interest but long enough to cover the essentials.

1890 Sir **Ronald Fisher:** British statistician and geneticist. Working for an agricultural research institute, he investigated the linkage of genes for different traits. To avoid unintentional bias in selection of materials used in experiments, he introduced the principle of randomness. Developed the concept of analysis of variance, used to design experiments that answered several questions at once.

To call in the statistician after the experiment is done may be no more than asking him to perform a post-mortem examination: he may be able to say what the experiment died of.

1908 **Walter Lanier "Red" Barber:** American sportscaster. Began as play-by-play announcer for the Cincinnati Reds. Covered Brooklyn Dodgers and New York Yankees baseball games for almost four decades Fired by the Yankees for mentioning the small crowd at a game. Signature exclamation: "Oh-ho, Doctor!"

When I'm talking to a large audience, I imagine that I'm talking to a single person.

1930 **Ruth Rendell:** Critically acclaimed British modern crime writer. Began writing novels in 1964. Created the character Chief Inspector Wexford, featured in many of more than sixty crime novels. Also published novels under the name of Barbara Vine. Won three Edgar Awards from the Mystery Writers of America. Books that have been translated into twenty-two languages include From *Doon with Death, The Lake of Darkness, A Judgment in Stone. A Dark-Adapted Eye* and *A Demon in My View.*

While most of the things you've worried about have never happened, it's a different story with the things you haven't worried about. They are the ones that happen.

1934 **Barry Humphries:** Australian comedian, best known for his appearances as Melbourne housewife Dame Edna Everage, which has made her and her creator international famous. Her greeting to her adoring fans is "Hello Possums!" Humphries had developed many other characters, none as famous as Edna. He is also regarded as one of his country's best landscape artists.

Australia is an outdoor country. People only go inside to use the toilet. And that's only a recent development.

1938 **Mary Frances Berry:** U.S. historian and public servant. Author of seven books including *Episodes of Racism and Sexism in the Courts from 1865 to the Present* and *Long Memory: The Black Experience in America,* with John Blassingame. Member of the U.S. Commission on Civil Rights. One of 75 women featured in *I Dream a World: Portraits of Black Women Who Changed America.*

When it comes to the cause of justice, I take no prisoners and I don't believe in compromise.

1942 **Huey P. Newton:** African-American political activist and civil rights leader. Co-founder of Black Panther Party with Bobby Seale. Spent time as a fugitive in Cuba. Accused of murder. Freed after two trials. Found gunned down on a street in Oakland, California.

If you stop struggling, then you stop life.

1963 **Michael Jordan:** African-America basketball superstar. Nicknamed "Air Jordan" or "His Airness" for his apparent ability to hang in the air when taking a shot. Led North Carolina to NCAA title (1984). Has two Olympic gold medals (1984, 1992). His records and basketball accomplishments would take dozens of pages to list. Led Chicago Bulls to three consecutive NBA titles (1991–93). Left the game to try baseball, then returned to basketball in 1995 and three more championships. Arguably the best basketball player ever. Came out of retirement of play for the Washington Wizards at the time he was its President of Basketball Operations. Currently part-owner of the Charlotte Bobcats.

When I'm on my game, I don't think there's anybody that can stop me.

OTHERS: 1444 Dutch humanist/organist **Rudolf Agricola**, 1653 Italian violinist/composer **Arcangelo Correlli**, 1774 U.S. painter **Raphaelle Peale**, 1781 French physician/inventor **René Laennec**, 1844 Founder of mail-order business **A. Montgomery Ward**, 1867 English chocolate manufacturer **William Cadbury**, 1888 German/U.S. physicist **Otto Stern**, 1889 U.S. Billionaire oilman **H.L. Hunt**, 1909 Australian soprano **Marjorie Lawrence**, 1922 U.S. singer **Tommy Edwards**, 1924 President's daughter **Margaret Truman**, 1925 U.S. actor **Hal Holbrook**, 1929 U.S. novelist **Chaim Potok**, 1936 U.S. football player/actor **Jim Brown**, 1981 U.S. heiress/ model/ celebrity **Paris Hilton**

February 18

1795 **George Peabody:** American merchant, financier and philanthropist. Earned a fortune in the wholesale dry-goods business and as president of the Eastern Railroad. Moved to London permanently and founded a merchant banking house that specialized in foreign exchange. Spent most of his fortune to promote education and the arts.

Education: a debt due from present to future generations.

1836 **Ramakrishna [Gadadhar Chattopadghyaya]:** Indian mystic. Worked as a priest in a temple of Kali, where he had a vision, which led him to hold that all religions are essentially the same and that are all true. Denounced sexual desire and money. Rejected the caste system.

The world is indeed a mixture of truth and make-believe. Discard the make-believe and take the truth.

1838 **Ernst Mach:** Austrian philosopher and physicist. An empiricist believed that science is a record of facts perceived by the senses, and that acceptance of a scientific law depends solely on its standing the practical test of use. His study of airflows revealed a sudden change of airflow over an object moving close to the speed of sound. Unit for speed of sound is named after him.

Physics is experience, arranged in economical order.

1859 **Sholom Aleichem:** Penname of **Solomon Rabinowitz.** Russian writer. Master of the short story. Served as a government rabbi. Published more than 40 volumes of novels, stories and plays in Yiddish, which were widely translated. Known as the "Yiddish Mark Twain." His short stories about Tevye the dairyman formed the basis for the musical *Fiddler on the Roof.*

Life is a dream for the wise, a game for the fool, a comedy for the rich, a tragedy for the poor.

1862 **Charles M. Schwab:** American manufacturer. "Boy Wonder" of the steel industry. President of U.S. Steel (1901–3). President of Bethlehem Steel (1903–13). Chairman of the Board (1913–39). Although he became a multimillionaire he died bankrupt due to the Stock Market Crash of 1929.

When a man has put a limit on what he will do, he has put a limit on what he can do.

1894 **Andrés Segovia:** Spanish classical guitarist, teacher. In 1985, awarded the Gold Medal of the Royal Philharmonic Society of London. Reinstated the guitar as a concert instrument. Made many transcriptions for the guitar. One of the few classical guitarists to have earned a gold record. Explaining why he maintained such a heavy concert schedule at so an advanced an age:

The guitar is a small orchestra. It is polyphonic. Every string is a different color, a different voice.

1898 **Luis Muñoz Marín:** Puerto Rican politician and poet. Elected to Puerto Rica's Senate, he fought hard for the interests of the poor. And for Puerto Rica's independence from the U.S. Founder of the Commonwealth of Puerto Rico. During World War II, he started a program called *Operation Bootstrap*, which was a program for enhancing farming methods, education and in creating new industry. First elected governor of Puerto Rico (1948–64).

There is an old saying on the island, that a man must do three things during his lifetime: plant trees, write books and have sons. I wish they would plant more trees and write more books.

1919 **Clifford Truesdell:** American mathematician and physicist. Refounded Continuum Mechanics and was an outstanding historian of science. Published 26 monographs, 268 papers, and a countless number of essays and reviews. His shortest review follows:

This paper gives wrong solutions to trivial problems. The basic error, however, is not new.

1922 **Helen Gurley Brown:** American author, publisher and businesswoman. Commentator on gender affairs. Outspoken advocate of women's sexual freedom. Wrote best-selling *Sex and the Single Girl* (1962). Editor *Cosmopolitan* magazine for 32 years, which she transformed into an international success. Other works: *Outrageous Opinions, Sex and the New Single Girl* and *Having It All.*

Good girls go to heaven, bad girls go everywhere.

1928 **Len Deighton:** Leading English author of spy novels. Best sellers: *The Ipcress File, Funeral in Berlin* and *The Billion Dollar Brain.* Developed a keen interest in cookery—a subject he featured in an animated strip for the *Observor.* Also wrote two cook books.

In Mexico an air conditioner is called a politician, because it makes a lot of noise but doesn't work very well.

1931 **Toni Morrison:** née **Chloe Anthony Wofford.** African-American novelist. Taught at Howard University before becoming a senior editor at Random House. Explores the stories of rural African Americans in novels *Song of Solomon, Tar Baby* and *Beloved,* for which she won a Pulitzer Prize in 1988. Nobel Prize for Literature winner (1993).

The loneliest woman in the world is the woman without a close woman friend.

1934 **Audre Lorde:** African-American poet and feminist. Self-described as "Black lesbian, mother, warrior, poet." Graduated from Columbia University and Hunter College, where she later held the Thomas Hunter Chair of Literature. Published over a dozen books of poetry and six books of prose. Founded the Sisterhood in Support of Sisters in South Africa.

It is not our differences that divide us. It is our inability to recognize, accept, and celebrate those differences.

OTHERS: 1516 First reigning Queen of Great Britain **Mary I Tudor**, 1677 French astronomer **Jacques Cassini**, 1745 Physicist and inventor **Count Alessandro Volta**, 1781 English missionary **Henry Martyn**, 1848 Glassmaker **Louis Comfort Tiffany**, 1857 German graphic artist/painter/sculptor **Max Klinger**, 1860 Swedish painter **Anders Leon Zorn**, 1890 U.S. actor **Adolphe Menjou**, 1892 Republican presidential candidate **Wendell Wilkie**, 1895 Notre Dame football star **George Gipp**, 1896 French founder of surrealism **André Breton**, 1914 Country singer **Pee Wee King**, 1927 U.S. senator **John W. Warner**, 1933 Japanese artist **Yoko Ono Lennon**, 1945 U.S. LPGA golfer **Judy Rankin**

February 19

1473 **Nicolaus Copernicus:** Latin version of the astronomer's Polish name **Mikolaj Köpenick** in the German-Prussian dialect. Laid the foundation for modern astronomy by asserting that the earth and the other planets revolved around the sun in individual orbits while spinning on their axes. Wrote a short manuscript "A Commentary on the Theories of the Motions of Heavenly Objects from Their Arrangements" (1510–1514), summarizing his new ideas, which he privately circulated among friends. His findings were met with hostility, as they challenged ancient teachings of Earth as the center of the universe. A perfectionist, even after thirty years he didn't feel his novel theory was a complete work. Legend has it that he was on his deathbed when the first printed copy of his *De Revolutionibus Orbium Coelestium* (*On the Revolutions of the Heavenly Spheres*) was placed in his shaking hands.

Finally we shall place the Sun himself at the center of the Universe.

1717 **David Garrick:** English actor and theater manager. Regarded as one of the greatest actors of the British theater. Attended a school ran by British lexicographer Dr. Samuel Johnson. The good doctor claimed Garrick's distinguishing characteristic was his "universality." Dominated the English stage for 30 years in the 18th century. Joint manager of Drury Lane (1747–76), changing the face of theatrical performance. Actors' Garrick Club established in his honor (1831).

You are indebted to your imagination for three-fourths of your importance.

1893 Sir **Cedric Hardwicke:** English stage and screen actor. Trained for the stage at the Royal Academy of Dramatic Art. Made his name in Shaw's plays and *The Barretts of Wimpole Street*. Films: *Les Misérables*, *Stanley and Livingstone*, *Tom Brown's School Days* and *The Winslow Boy*. His autobiography: *A Victorian in Orbit*.

Actors must practice restraint, else think what might happen in a love scene.

1903 **Kay Boyle:** Award-winning American writer, educator, and political activist. Published more than forty books, including novels, volumes of poetry, collections of short fiction, children's books, and essays. Her 1936 novel *Death of a Man* was an attack on the growing threat of Nazism. Active supporter of Amnesty International and the NAACP.

Ah, trouble, trouble, there are the two different kinds ... there's the one you give and the other you take.

1911 **Merle Oberon:** Originally **Estelle Merle O'Brien Thompson.** Tasmanian-born (or perhaps in Bombay) British actress. Groomed for stardom by her first husband Alexander Korda. Lent her sultry and regal beauty to films Including *The Private Life of Henry VIII* as Anne Boleyn, *Wuthering Heights* memorable as Cathy, and *A Song to Remember* as French novelist George Sand [Armandine Aurore Lucile Dupin.]. Nominated for an Academy Award for her performance in *The Dark Angel*.

Without security it is difficult for a woman to look or feel beautiful.

1912 **Stan Kenton:** American bandleader, arranger, and composer. Bands featured precise reed sections and cutting brass sound. Success was enhanced by vocalists Anita O'Day and June Christy. Hits: "Tampico," "Artistry in Rhythm," "Eager Beaver" and "And Her Tears Flowed Like Wine." Third person named to the Jazz Hall of Fame. His horn charts were used by the rock group *Chicago*.

I don't think you can replace great themes. But I think people do want to hear fresh arrangements of them. They don't want to hear them played the same way all the time.

1916 **Eddie Arcaro:** American jockey. Nicknamed "The Master." Won 4,779 races including five Kentucky Derbies, six Preaknesses, and six Belmont Stakes. Only jockey to win the Triple Crown twice, with Whirlaway in 1941 and Citation in 1948. After 24,000 career mounts and total earnings of more than thirty million dollars, he retired to become a network TV racing analyst.

When a jockey retires, he just becomes another little man.

1917 **Carson McCullers:** née **Smith**. American novelist and short-story writer. Works reflect the sadness of lonely and frequently grotesque people. Together with William Faulkner, Tennessee Williams and Truman Capote she is credited with creating a type of fictions critics called Southern Gothic. Wrote *The Heart Is a Lonely Hunter*, about a deaf mute, *Reflections in a Golden Eye*, *The Member of the Wedding*, and *The Ballad of the Sad Cafe*.

I live with the people I create and it has always made my essential loneliness less keen.

1924 **Lee Marvin:** American film actor, known for his early roles as "heavies." Later played mostly good guys but tough ones. Won an Academy Award for Best Actor for his comedic performance in the offbeat western *Cat Ballou*, showing his talent for robust comedy. Sang (not particularly well) "I Was Born Under a Wandering Star" in the movie *Paint Your Wagon*. Made headlines in a landmark legal case that established the California courts "palimony doctrine." Sued by a woman who lived with him for six years but who he never married. Claim was rejected, but he was required to pay her a nominal sum for rehabilitation.

I'll know my career's going bad when they start quoting me correctly.

1930 **John Frankenheimer: American** director for the stage, TV and films. Directed more than 125 TV plays for shows such as *Studio One* and *Playhouse 90*. Films: *Birdman of Alcatraz*, *The Manchurian Candidate*, *Seven Days in May* and *The French Connection II*.

There doesn't seem to be room for the qualified success.

1940 **William "Smokey" Robinson:** African-American singer, songwriter and producer. Formed "The Miracles," while attending Detroit's Northern High School. Bert Gordy took him under his wing. Left the group in 1972 to do a solo act. Hits: "Tears of a Clown," "The Tracks of My Tears" and "Being with You." Produced songs by The Supremes, The Temptations, Mary Wells and Marvin Gaye.

Weed does nothing but cloud your mind and make you think you are something you are not.

1962 **Hana Mandliková:** Professional tennis player and coach from the Czech Republic. Known for her lethal serves, backhand topspin lobs, and flat forehands. Three-times Wimbledon singles champion John Newcombe called her "one of the most natural athletes" in women's tennis. Won 4 Grand Slam single titles. Defeated Martina Navrátilová ending the latter's winning streak of 58 matches.

It's difficult to play against a man ... I mean against Martina Navrátilová. She scares you with her muscles.

OTHERS: 3 CE Persian writer **Sadiq Hidajat**, 1532 French poet **Jean-Antoine de Baïf**, 1683 French-born King of Spain **Philip V**, 1817 Last male monarch of The Netherlands **Willem III**, 1833 Swiss pacifist/writer **Élie Ducommun**, 1843 Spanish operatic coloratura **Adelina Patti**, 1859 Swedish chemist/physicist **Svante August Arrhenius**, 1865 Swedish scientist/explorer **Sven Hedin**, 1877 French composer **Louis Aubert**, 1894 Hall of Fame pitcher **Herb Pennock**, 1902 U.S. rhythm tap dancer **John Bubbles**, 1927 French cognac manufacturer **René Firino-Martell**, 1943 U.S. singer **"Mama" Cass Elliot**, 1956 U.S. astronaut **George D. Low**, 1960 Duke of York **Prince Andrew**

February 20

1794 **William Carleton:** Irish novelist. Outstanding observer of peasant life. Most famous work was two series, both entitled, *Traits and Stories of Irish Peasantry* (1830 and 1833). His unsparing criticism and occasional exaggeration of the darker sides of Irish character alienated many Irishmen. In his own words he was the "historian of their habits and manners, their feelings, their prejudices and superstitions, and their crimes."

We arg'ed the thing at breakfast, we arg'ed the thing at tea,/ And the more we arg'ed the question the more we didn't agree.

1805 **Angelina Grimké:** American abolitionist and feminist. Born to a major slaving owning family. Rejected this life to join the Quakers. Published a letter in the anti-slavery newspaper *The Liberator*. Became a public figure during an unprecedented speaking tour against slavery. Resisted efforts to silence her. Wrote *Appeal to the Christian Women of the Nominally Free States* and *Appeal to the Christian Women of the South*.

Thou are blind to the danger of marrying a woman who feels and acts out the principle of equal rights.

1829 **Joseph Jefferson:** American stage actor, third actor of this name in a family of actors and managers. One of the most famous American comedians. Identified with the role of Rip Van Winkle and as Bob Acres in Sheridan's *The Rivals*. Appeared on the stage for 72 years.

We are but tenants, and ... shortly the great Landlord will give notice that our lease has expired.

1874 **Mary Garden:** Scottish-born U.S. opera soprano. Considered the greatest singing actress in history. Created the role of Mélisande in Debussy's *Pelléas et Mélisande* at the composer's request. Associated with the Chicago Grand Opera (1910–30). Asked the secret of her youthfulness:

I have never been married.

1887 **Vincent Massey:** Canadian statesman, diplomat and University chancellor. Ambassador to the United States (1927–30). High Commissioner of Canada. Eighteenth Governor-General of Canada (1952–59), the first to be born in Canada. Believed the Crown belonged to Canadians and it was the Sovereign's representative responsibly to strengthen the bond. Brother of actor Raymond Massey.

What we should have is a Canadian character. Nobody looks his best in somebody else's clothes.

1887 **Hesketh Pearson:** English biographer, actor and director. Known mainly for writing racy biographies including *Gilbert and Sullivan*, *Oscar Wilde* and *Charles II*. In 1926, the anonymously-published *Whispering Gallery*, purporting to be diary pages from leading political figures led to his prosecution for attempted fraud, but won the case.

When people are old enough to know better they are old enough to do worse.

1888 **Georges Bernanos:** French novelist, political writer and Catholic polemicist. Preoccupied with problems of sin and grace. His novels deal with the conflicting forces of God and Satan. Most memorable novels are *The Star of Satan* and *The Diary of a Country Priest*. Dedicated Royalist until he witnessed firsthand the atrocities of the Spanish Civil War, prompting him to write an angry polemic against Franco in *A Diary of My Times*. His anti–Vichy government writings were collected in *A Plea for Liberty*.

The first sign of corruption in a society that is still alive is that the end justifies the means.

1901 **René Dubos:** French-born American bacteriologist, experimental pathologist and environmentalist. Pulitzer Prize winning author, credited with the Maxim, "Think globally, act locally." Discovered tyrothricin, the first commercially produced antibiotic. Had a great concern for the need to protect the environment. Believed there need be a creation of a World Order in which "natural and social units maintain or recapture their identity, yet interplay with each other through a rich system of communications." Books: *The Unseen World* and *Only One Earth: The Care and Maintenance of a Small Planet*.

The most important pathological effects of pollution are extremely delayed and indirect.

1902 **Ansel Adams:** American landscape photographer, notable for his technical and artistic innovations in depicting Western wilderness and mountain panoramas, especially this black and white photographs of the Yosemite in the 1930s. Author of numerous books on photography, including technical instruction manuals: *The Camera*, *The Negative* and *The Print*. Mount Ansel

Adams, an 11,760 peak in the Sierra Nevada, was named for him in 1985.

A picture is usually looked at, seldom looked into.

1924 **Sidney Poitier:** Bahamian-African-American actor and director. Generally acknowledged as Hollywood's first black movie superstar. Nominated for Oscar for: *The Defiant Ones*; Oscar winner for *Lilies of the Field.* Received the Life Achievement Award from the Academy of Motion Picture Arts and Sciences in 2002. Also appeared in *The Blackboard Jungle, Porgy and Bess, To Sir with Love* and *In the Heat of the Night.* Knighted by Queen Elizabeth II in 1974.

We all suffer from the preoccupation that there exists ... in the loved one, perfection.

1941 **(Beverly) Buffy Sainte-Marie:** Canadian-born Cree Indian folksinger and writer of songs about her heritage and the cause of peace. Her song "It's Time for You to Go" was a love song that became a hit for Elvis Presley. Co-wrote "Up Where We Belong," which was a number one hit for Joe Cocker and Jennifer Warnes in 1982. Also wrote "Universal Soldier" and "Until It's Time for You to Go." Founded Native Creative to help increase cultural awareness of American children. Writes of North American Indian life for periodicals.

Here the melting-pot stands open — if you're willing to get bleached first

1963 **Charles Barkley:** African-American basketball player. Nicknamed "Sir Charles" or "The Round Mound of Rebound." Voted one of the 50 greatest basketball players of all time. Six-time NBA all-star with the Philadelphia 76ers and the Phoenix Sun. MVP in 1993. Member of the 1992 U.S. Olympic Dream Team. Now an outspoken sports commentator, who is considering making a run for the governorship of Alabama. Book: *I May Be Wrong, But I Doubt It.*

We don't need refs, but I guess white guys need something to do.

OTHERS: 1507 Italian artist **Gentile Bellini**, 1791 Austrian pianist/composer **Carl Czerny**, 1808 French painter **Honoré Daumier**, 1834 British graphic humorist **George Du Maurier**, 1844 Austrian physicist **Ludwig Boltzmann**, 1883 Japanese novelist **Shiga Naoya**, 1893 U.S. journalist/ playwright **Russel Crouse**, 1898 Italian racing car manufacturer **Enzo Ferrari**, 1899 U.S. railroad tycoon **Cornelius Vanderbilt Whitney**, 1904 Soviet premier **Aleksei Kosygin**, 1907 U.S. soprano **Nadine Conner**, 1914 Game show host **John Daly**, 1925 U.S. director **Robert Altman**, 1927 U.S. lawyer **Roy Cohn**, 1934 Auto racer **Bobby Unser**, 1954 Kidnapping victim **Patty Hearst**, 1966 U.S. model **Cindy Crawford**

February 21

1801 **John Henry Cardinal Newman:** English churchman. Leader of the Oxford Movement. Resigned as Protestant vicar of St. Mary's. Converted to Catholicism. Became a cardinal (1879). Author of "Lead kindly light" and *Apologia pro sua sita*, a "masterpiece of religious autobiography." Also wrote *Catholicism in England* and *The Idea of a University.* Honored by Newman Societies at colleges and universities all over the United States and Europe.

To live is to change, and to be perfect is to have changed often.

1821 **Charles Scribner, Jr.:** American publisher. Founder with Isaac Baker (1846) the New York publishing firm which became Charles Scribner's Sons in 1878. Founder and publisher of *Scribner's Monthly* magazine.

Reading is a means of thinking with another person's mind; it forces you to stretch your own.

1852 **Brander Matthews:** American writer and professor of dramatic literature at Columbia University. Worked as an editor, essayist, drama critic, and novelist. Well-known figure in theatrical and literary circles in Paris and London as well as New York City. Works: *Development of the Drama, Principles of Playmaking* and *Playwrights on Playmaking.*

A gentleman need not know Latin, but he should at least have forgotten it.

1865 **Arthur Symons:** English critic and poet. Contributed to *The Yellowbook*, an avant-garde journal and edited *The Savoy*. Familiarized the British with the literature of France and Italy. Published the influential *The Symbolist Movement in Literature*, the first English work championing the French Symbolist movement in poetry.

Without charm there can be no fine literature, as there can be no perfect flower without fragrance.

1876 **Constantin Brancusi:** Romanian sculptor who spent most of his working life in France. Pioneered work with abstract figures. Stressed form over detail. Reduced the essence of form to their ultimate, almost abstract, simplicity, which can be seen in his series of 28 "bird" sculptures. Also famed for the sculpture *The Kiss.*

Architecture is inhabited sculpture.

1885 **Sacha Guitry:** Born **Alexandre-Pierre Georges Guitry.** Russian/French actor and playwright. Wrote more than 120 plays, mostly light comedies that were performed in English. Also wrote and directed several films. In 1944, he was arrested and charged with having collaborated with the Nazi occupiers of France, but was vindicated.

You can pretend to be serious; you can't pretend to be witty.

1895 **Joseph Fields:** American playwright and screenwriter. Son of comedian Lew Fields and brother of songwriter Dorothy Fields and playwright Herbert Fields. Collaborated with Jerome Chodorov on successful Broadway musicals, *My Sister Eileen, Junior Miss* and *Anniversary Waltz* and with Anita Loos on *Gentlemen Prefer Blondes*. Films: *The Tunnel of Love* and *Flower Drum Song.*

My advice to writers who are trying to write

comedy is to try to have the comedy come from the characters and the situation and not try to work their jokes in.

1903 **Anaïs Nin:** French-born American novelist and diarist. Best known for *The Diary of Anaïs Nin*, journals spanning the years 1931–74, detailing the avant-garde life of Paris and New York and coming to terms with her feminine identity. Novels: *House of Incest* and *A Spy in the House of Love*. Seminal figure in the new feminism of the 1970s.

The only abnormality is the incapacity to love.

1907 **W.H. [Wystan Hugh] Auden:** Anglo-American poet and dramatist. Regarded one of the major poets of the 20th century. Best known as a "Poet's Poet." Called the "Poet of the Thirties" for his prodigious production of poems and literary criticism. Works: *The Age of Anxiety* (Pulitzer Prize, 1948), *The Dance of Death* and *Look, Stranger!* Also worked on several opera libretti, including Stravinsky's *The Rake's Progress.*

Death is the sound of distant thunder at a picnic.

1915 **Ann Sheridan:** Born **Clara Lou Sheridan**. American actress whose pin-up picture was one of the most popular with GIs during World War II. Films: *Angels with Dirty Faces, King's Row* and *The Man Who Came to Dinner.* Her last was performing in the dreadful TV series *Pistols 'n' Petticoats.* Died at the age of only 52.

They labeled me "the oomph girl." To me oomph is the sound that a fat man makes when he bends over to tie his shoelaces in a phone booth.

1927 **Erma Bombeck:** U.S. columnist, author. Syndicated column "At Wit's End" humorously dealt with life of a suburban housewife and mother. Books: *Motherhood, The Second Oldest Profession, If Life is a Bowl of Cherries, What Am I doing in the Pits, When You Look Like Your Passport Picture, It's Time to Go Home* and *Eat Less Cottage Cheese and More Ice Cream.*

Guilt: the gift that keeps on giving.

1936 **Barbara Jordan:** African-American politician, educator and lawyer. First black woman to serve in Texas legislature in 20th century. U.S. representative (1972–78), at the time the only woman and only black in the Congress. Impressed the nation with her eloquence and firm faith in the U.S. Constitution during the Watergate Impeachment hearings concerning President Nixon. Ignited 1976 Democratic National Convention with her keynote speech.

If you're going to play the game properly, you'd better know every rule.

OTHERS: 1494 Danish chancellor who helped establish Lutheranism **Johann Friis**, 1794 President of Mexico **Antonio López de Santa Anna**, 1815 French painter/sculptor **Ernest Meissonier**, 1836 French ballet composer **Léo Delibes**, 1855 U.S. educator **Alice Freeman Palmer**, 1867 U.S. banker **Otto H. Kahn**, 1888 U.S. actress **Florence Bates**, 1890 Lithuanian born restaurateur **Michael Romanoff**, 1903 U.S. baseball owner **Tom Yawkey**, 1924 President of Zimbabwe **Robert G. Mugabe**, 1925 U.S. director **Sam Peckinpah**, 1927 French fashion designer **Hubert de Givenchy**, 1933 U.S. singer/pianist **Nina Simone**, 1947 U.S. actress **Tyne Daly**

February 22

1732 **George Washington:** First United States president, giving the shortest inauguration speech — 90 seconds. Virginia planter and early scientific farmer at Mount Vernon; surveyor; colonel of the Virginia militia and member of the House of Burgess. Commander-in-chief of Continental forces during American Revolution. As president he attempted to enlist the ablest men in the country to serve in the government. Warned against the dangers of party politics and foreign entanglements.

Few men have virtue to withstand the highest bidder.

1778 **Rembrandt Peale:** American neoclassical painter and lithographer. Son of painter and inventor Charles Wilson Peale, with whom he studied at the Royal Academy in London. Painted a strong but idealized likeness of George Washington which enjoyed great popularity. His masterpiece is a painting of Thomas Jefferson.

O don't be so sorrowful, darling!/ And don't be sorrowful, pray;/ Taking the year together, my dear,/ There isn't more night than day.

1788 **Arthur Schopenhauer:** German philosopher and author of extreme pessimism. His greatest work is *The World as Will and Idea* emphasizes the central role of human will as the creative, primary factor in understanding. Claimed that life consists of suffering and only by controlling the will through the intellect can suffering be diminished. His views influenced existentialism and scores of writers and artists, including Wagner, Tolstoy, Proust and Mann.

Fate shuffles the cards and we play.

1819 **James Russell Lowell:** American poet, editor, critic, and diplomat. Foremost man of letters of his time. Long poem: "The Vision of Sir Launfal." Chairman of modern languages at Harvard, succeeding Longfellow and first editor of *The Atlantic Monthly.* Leader of what is now called the popular, conservative school of American letters. Also served as minister to both Spain and England.

A compromise is a good umbrella but a poor roof.

1864 **Jules Renard:** French author and member of the Académie Goncourt. Notable works: *Carrot Hair* and *Natural Histories/Stories*. Some of his works are inspired by the countryside he loved in the Nièvre region. His journal (1897–1910) is a masterpiece of introspection, irony, humor and nostalgia.

Writing is an occupation in which you have to keep proving your talent to people who have none.

1892 **Edna St. Vincent Millay:** American poet. After Vassar she lived in Greenwich Village. Made her reputation with the publication *of Renascence* in 1917. Poetry volumes: *A Few Figs from Thistles* and the Pulitzer Prize–winning *The Harp Weaver and Other Poems.*

My candle burns at both ends,/ It will not last the night,/ But ah, my foes and oh my friends —/ It gives a lovely light.

1900 **Luis Buñuel:** Spanish-born director. With Salvador Dali scripted surrealistic film, *An Andalusian Dog.* His surrealistic masterpiece *The Golden Age* assaulted Church, Establishment and middle-class morality. Other films: *The Young and the Damned, The Brute, Viridiana,* and the Academy Award winning *The Discreet Charm of the Bourgeoisie.*

Mystery is the essential element in every work of art.

1900 **Sean O'Faolin [John Francis Whelan]:** Irish writer, involved in anti–British activities during Irish "troubles" (1918–21). Wrote lyrical short stories about Ireland's lower and middle classes. Argued against the oppressive provincialism of Irish Catholicism. Novels: *A Nest of Simple Folk, Bird Alone* and *Come Back to Erin.* Short story collections: *Midsummer Night Madness, The Man Who Invented Sin* and *The Talking Tree.*

Love lives in sealed bottles of regret.

1901 **Charles Evans Whittaker:** American Supreme Court justice and lawyer. Swing vote on a sharply divided Supreme. Retired from the court to become chief counsel for General Motors. Became a critic of the Warren Court and the Civil Rights Movement. Labeled the civil disobedience as practiced by Martin Luther King Jr. to be lawless.

Justice cannot be produced through any system of procedures alone, In the main it is, and must always be, the product of long hours of hard, diligent, painstaking labor by highly competent, experienced, careful and practical lawyers

1917 **Jane Bowles:** Originally **Sydney Auer**. American writer and playwright. After attending boarding school in Switzerland she gravitated to the intellectual bohemia of Greenwich Village in New York, where she sexually experiments with people of both sexes. Moved to Tangier with her husband and remained an expatriate for the rest of her life. Novel: *Two Serious Ladies.* Short-story collection: *Plain Pleasures.* Play: *In the Summer House.* Works frequently describe conflicts between repression and uncontrolled passion.

The face of victory often resembles the face of defeat.

1926 **Nelson Bunker Hunt:** U.S. heir of the Hunt Oil Company fortune. Supporter of radical right activism. Donated millions to Campus Crusade for Christ, Moral Majority, and Strategies to Eliminate Poverty. Declared bankruptcy in 1988 and convicted for trying to corner the silver market.

People who know how much they're worth aren't usually worth that much.

1938 **Ishmael Reed:** American poet, essayist and novelist. One of the most controversial and politically left-wing American writers of his generation. Consistently satirizes the American right-wing. Professor at the University of California, Berkeley. Works: *The Free-Lance Pallbearers* and *Mumbo-Jumbo.*

It's the little hurts that build up.

OTHERS: 1403 King of France **Charles VII**, 1796 Belgium mathematician /statistician **Adolphe Quetelet**, 1857 German physicist **Heinrich Hertz**, 1857 Boy scouts founder **Lord Robert Baden-Powell**, 1874 U.S. baseball umpire **Bill Klem**, 1882 English sculptor/engraver **Eric Gill**, 1883 Voice of Disney's "Snow White" **Marguerite Clark**, 1892 U.S. labor leader **David Dubinsky**, 1896 U.S. composer **Nacio Herb Brown**, 1908 English actor **John Mills**, 1918 Canadian hockey player **Sid Abel**, 1918 U.S. baseball owner **Charles O. Finley**, 1927 U.S. singer **Guy Mitchell**, 1932 U.S. senator **Edward "Ted" Kennedy**, 1945 U.S. singer **Oliver**

February 23

1633 **Samuel Pepys:** English public official, best know for his *Diary*, the most frequently quoted work of its kind in the English language. He met the outstanding personalities of his day. Diary written in shorthand between 1660 and 1669 was deciphered and published in 1825.

Strange to see how a good dinner and feasting reconciles everybody.

1685 **George Frideric Handel:** German-born English composer. Gained a reputation as a keyboard virtuoso and as an operatic composer. Wrote "Water Music." Experimented with oratorios. Best known for the *Messiah*. He believed the "Hallelujah" chorus was divinely inspired. At the first London performance of the work, King George II and his court, moved by the grandeur of the chorus, rose to their feet in reverence, a tradition that has carried on from that time.

Whether I was in my body or out of my body as I wrote it I know not. God knows ... I did think I did see all Heaven before me — and the great God Himself.

1743 **Mayer Rothschild:** German moneylender whose business would be expanded by his five sons into the House of Rothschild financial dynasty, first among banking houses of the world. His surname derived from the red shield on the house in the Jewish ghetto where his ancestors lived. The family's financial transactions during the Napoleonic Wars were the basis of its fortune.

Give me control of a nation's money and I care not who makes her laws.

1787 **Emma Hart Willard:** Pioneer American leader in education for girls. Denied admission to Middlebury College, she borrowed books to teach herself non-traditional subjects, which she then taught to her students of the Middlebury Female Seminary located in her home. Opened the Troy Female Seminary, which was comparable to a college preparatory school for boys. Generations of teachers she trained carried forth the message of intellectual and educational rights for women.

Rocked in the cradle of the deep, I lay me down in peace to sleep.

1840 **Carl Menger:** Austrian economist, who eschewed the mathematical scaffolding for economics favored by William Stanley Jevons and Léon Walras. His work, *Principles*, set out the principles of marginalist value theory, using the concept of subjective value to underpin all economics.

Money is not an invention of the state. It is not the product of a legislative act. The sanction of political authority is not necessary for its existence.

1857 **Margaret Deland:** American novelist short-story writer and poet. Works include: *Old Chester Tales, The Awakening of Helena Ritchie, Partners,* and *Small Things.* Also wrote a two volume autobiography *If This Be I.*

As soon as you feel too old to do a thing, do it.

1868 **W.E.B. [William Edward Burghardt] Du Bois:** African-American historian, sociologist and civil rights leader of French Huguenot descent. Founder of National Negro Committee which became National Association for the Advancement of Colored People (1909). Awarded the 1920 Spingarn Medal for leadership in securing opportunities for blacks. Joined Communist Party (1961), moved to Ghana, renouncing U.S. citizenship.

The cost of liberty is less than the price of repression.

1883 **Karl Theodor Jaspers:** German psychologist and philosopher. A founder of modern existentialism. Stripped of teaching position at Heidelberg by the Nazis, who banned his works. He stayed in Germany. Awarded Goethe Prize (1947) for his uncompromising stand. Wrote *The Great Philosophers* and *The Future of Mankind* in which he explores the possibility of a world political union in which everyone could live and communicate in peace and freedom.

The beginning of modern science is also the beginning of calamity.

1901 **Alan Valentine:** U.S. Gold Medal winning Olympian rugby player, Rhodes Scholar, writer and educator. Dean of Admissions at Yale University and at age 34 became the youngest president in the history of Rochester University. Books: *1913: America Between Two Worlds* and *Trial Balance: The Education of an American.*

Whenever science makes a discovery, the devil grabs it while the angels are debating the best way to use it.

1904 **William L. Shirer:** American author, journalist. CBS broadcaster of momentous events in Europe (1937–40). Wrote a column for *New York Herald.* Blacklisted during the McCarthy era. Wrote the monumental *The Rise and Fall of the Third Reich,* winner of the National Book Award.

Perhaps America will one day go fascist democratically by popular vote.

1929 **Leslie Halliwell:** British journalist, cinema manager, television program buyer, author of much admired and highly opinionated *Halliwell's Filmgoers Companion* and *Halliwell's Movie Guide.* His personal tastes were for the films of the 1920 and 30s. Also wrote: *Seats in All Parts: Half a Lifetime in the Movies* and *Halliwell's Harvest.*

Cynics have claimed there are only six basic plots.* Frankenstein *and* My Fair Lady *are really the same story.

1942 **Haki Madhubuti:** African-American poet, publisher, editor and educator. Pivotal figure in the development of a strong Black literary tradition. Books: *Black Men: Obsolete, Single, Dangerous?* and *The African American Family in Transition.*

Reality is not the same to the doer as it is to the sayer.

OTHERS: 1417 Italian pope **Paul II**, 1680 French explorer **Jean Baptiste Le Moyne**, 1817 British painter **George Watts**, 1832 U.S. bishop/preacher **John Heyl Vincent**, 1874 Estonian dictator **Konstantin Päts**, 1883 U.S. film director **Victor Fleming**, 1911 U.S. governor/ Supreme Court justice **G. Mennan Williams**, 1911 U.S. writer **Walter Ernest Allen**, 1926 U.S. congressman **Louis Stokes**, 1929 First African-American New York Yankee **Elston Howard**, 1937 U.S. football coach **Tom Osborne**, 1938 U.S. newscaster **Sylvia Chase**, 1940 U.S. actor **Peter Fonda**, 1944 U.S. guitarist **Johnny Winter**, 1950 Irish novelist **Neil Jordan**, 1951 NFL football player **Ed "Too Tall" Jones**, 1994 U.S. actress **Dakota Fanning**

February 24

1304 **Muhammad Ibn Battutah:** Arab travel writer. After making a pilgrimage to Mecca, he decided to visit as many parts of the world as possible. 27 years later after traveling 75,000 miles through Africa, Asia and Europe he returned to his home in Tangier, Morocco, where he dictated his reminiscences, which became the world's most famous travel book. At the start of his epic journey he vowed:

Never to travel any road a second time.

1500 **Charles V:** King of Spain (1516–50). Holy Roman emperor (1519–56). Last emperor to pursue the medieval ideal of universal empire and the last to be crowned by the pope. Struggled to hold his vast Spanish and Hapsburg Empire against the growing forces of Protestantism, Turkish and French pressure. In 1555–6 abdicated his claims to the Netherlands and Spain to his son Philip II and the title of emperor to his brother Ferdinand I, and retired to a monastery.

To God I speak Spanish, to women Italian, to men French and to my horse — German.

1776 **Samuel Wesley:** English organist and composer. Nephew of John Wesley and son of Charles Wesley, the cofounders of Methodism. Many of Samuel's best-known compositions were written for the church, including the motet *In Exitu Israel.*

Style is the dress of thought; a modest dress. Neat, but not gaudy, will true critics please.

1797 **Samuel Lover:** Irish singer, songwriter, novelist and portrait painter, mostly of miniatures. One of his best known portraits was of Paganini, which he exhibited at the Royal Academy. Songs: "Molly Bawn" and "The Four-leaved Shamrock. Novels: *Rory O'More* and *Handy Andy*.

My advice to you concerning applause is this: enjoy it but never quite believe it.

1824 **George William Curtis:** American essayist, orator and editor. Lived among some of American's leading literary figures, such as Emerson, Hawthorne and Thoreau at Concord, Massachusetts. Began the "Editor's Easy Chair" papers in *Harper's Monthly*. Principal lead writer for *Harper's Weekly*. From these positions the independent-minded Republican sought to influence public opinion in support of a number of politicians.

My advice to a young man seeking deathless fame would be to espouse an unpopular cause and devote his life to it.

1836 **Winslow Homer:** American landscape and seascape painter. Began his career as lithographer and an illustrator for magazines such as *Harper's Weekly*. Moved to Protus Neck, an isolated fishing village on the U.S. eastern seaboard where he painted maritime scenes for the rest of his life.

Never put more than two waves in a picture, it's fussy.

1837 **Rosalia de Castro:** Spanish Writer and poet. Most outstanding modern writer in the Galician language. One of the greatest protagonists of regionalism in Spanish literature. Publication date of her first collection of poetry, *Galician Songs*, is an official holiday in Galicia. Novels: *The Daughter of the Sea* and *Ruins*.

I see my path, but I don't know where it leads. Not knowing where I'm going is what inspires me to travel it.

1852 **George Moore:** Irish novelist, playwright, poet and critic. Introduced naturalism to the Victorian novel. Wrote *A Modern Lover*, *Spring Days*, *Minerva*, *Esther Waters* and an autobiographical trilogy *Hail and Farewell*.

A man travels the world in search of what he needs and returns home to find it.

1885 **Chester W. Nimitz:** American admiral. After the Japanese attack on Pearl Harbor, named Commander of U.S. naval forces in Pacific, World War II. Directed battles of Coral Sea and Midway. Directed landings on the Solomons, Gilberts, Marshalls, Marianas, Philippines, Iwo Jima and Okinawa. The Japanese surrender was signed aboard his ship, the U.S.S Missouri. Speaking of the marines at Iwo Jima:

Uncommon valor was a common virtue.

1928 **Michael Harrington:** American social scientist, democratic socialist, political activist and writer. Best known for landmark study, *The Other America: Poverty in the United States*, in which he showed that growing affluence, creates a growing subculture of poverty. The work had an impact on the Kennedy administration and on Lyndon Johnson's subsequent War on Poverty.

Poverty is expensive to maintain.

1943 **George Harrison:** Known as the "quiet Beatle" and the youngest of the Fab Four, His songs include: "Hey Jude," "Here Comes the Sun," "Something," and "My Sweet Lord." Devoted to Oriental mysticism. Appeared in films *A Hard Day's Night* and *Help!* Organized the first large-scale charity concert, *The Concert for Bangladesh*. Died of throat cancer in 2001.

As long as you hate, there will be people to hate.

1955 **Steven Jobs:** American businessman. Dropped out of college to design video games for Atari Corporation. Co-founded Apple Computer Inc. (with Steve Wozniak) in 1976. Popularized the concept of a home computer with the Apple II. Left Apple in 1985 but returned in 1996 to become CEO of Apple Computer. Also Chairman and CEO of Pixar Animation Studios, which produces computer-animated films.

By a yardstick of quality, some people aren't used to an environment where excellence is expected.

OTHERS: 1536 Last Counter-Reformation pope **Clement VIII**, 1684 Empress of Russia **Catherine I**, 1786 Collector of fairy tales **Wilhelm Karl Grimm**, 1840 U.S. inventor **John Phillip Holland**, 1860 U.S. printer **Daniel Berkeley Updike**, 1874 Hall-of-fame shortstop **Honus Wagner**, 1890 U.S. character actress **Marjorie Main**, 1914 U.S. actor **Zachary Scott**, 1927 U.S. lawyer/ conspiracy theorist **Mark Lane**, 1909 Dutch/ British/U.S. philosopher **Max Black**, 1932 French composer **Michel Legrand**, 1934 Italian soprano **Renata Scotto**, 1940 British soccer player **Denis Low**, 1942 U.S. senator/VP candidate **Joseph Lieberman**, 1947 U.S. singer **Rupert Holmes**, 1973 Prizefighter **Oscar de la Hoya**

February 25

1707 **Carlo Goldoni:** Italian playwright and lawyer. Wrote some 150 comedies. Creator of the modern Italian comedy in the style of Molière. He led a dramatic revolution of Italian comedy by replacing its masked stock figures with realistic characters. *The Fan* was one of his greatest successes. As a writer for the Italian theater in Paris, he was impoverished as a result of the French Revolution.

The world is a beautiful book but of little use to him who cannot read it.

1841 **Pierre Auguste Renoir:** French painter. Formed a close friendship with Claude Monet and became leader and founder of the French Impressionist movement. Excelled in color and light effects. Used reds, orange and gold to portray nudes in sunlight. Among his masterpieces are: *The Luncheon on of the Boating Party* and *Bathers*. French film director Jean Renoir was his son.

The pain passes, but the beauty remains.

1842 **Camille Flammarion:** French astronomer. Founder and first president of the *Société Astronomique de France*. Maintained a private observatory. Prolific writer, including popular science works about astronomy and science fiction, including *Real and Imaginary Worlds* and *The End of the World.*

Men have had the vanity to pretend that the whole creation was made for them; while in reality the whole creation does not suspect their existence.

1848 **Edward H. Harriman:** Wealthy American railroad executive and land owner. Bought bankrupted railroads, rebuilt them and sold them at tremendous profits. Chairman and President of both the Union Pacific system and the Southern Pacific railroad. The railroad trust he formed with J.P. Morgan was dissolved by the U.S. Supreme Court in 1904.

Much good work is lost for the lack of a little more.

1866 **Benedetto Croce:** Italian humanist, statesman, patriot, critic and historian. Foremost Italian philosopher of the first half of the 20th century. Made major contributions to idealistic aesthetics. Minister of Education (1920–21). Passionate anti–Fascist, he opposed the totalitarianism of Mussolini. Forced to resign his professorship at Naples. After World War II, he helped revive liberal institutions including the Liberal Party which he led (1943–52).

Art is ruled uniquely by the imagination.

1873 **Enrico Caruso:** Italian operatic lyric tenor. Singer of universal popularity. Regarded by many as the greatest tenor the world has known. For dramatic effect, he often resorted to the "coup de glotte," which became known as the "Caruso sob." Excelled in realistic Italian operas such as *Tosca* and *Pagliacci.*

[A great singer should have] a big chest, a big mouth, ninety per cent memory, ten per cent intelligence, lot of hard work and something in the heart.

1888 **John Foster Dulles:** American government official and diplomat. Counsel to the American Peace Commission in Versailles after World War I. Helped prepare the U.N. charter. U.S. delegate to U.N.'s General Assembly (1946–50). Negotiated the complex Japanese peace treaty. U.S. Secretary of State (1953–59). Advocated active opposition to Soviet actions and developed the Eisenhower Doctrine. Practiced "brinkmanship" in checking Communist expansion.

If you are scared to go to the brink you are lost.

1904 **Adelle Davis:** American nutritionist expert, author. Crusader for the use of natural foods. Wrote *Let's Cook It Right, Let's Have Healthy Children, Let's Get Well* and *Let's Eat to Keep Fit.* Promoted many controversial theories that have been labeled unfounded and dangerous by the medical community.

Eat breakfast like a king, lunch like a prince, and dinner like a pauper.

1917 **Anthony Burgess:** Pen name of **John Anthony Burgess Wilson**. English novelist, critic and composer. Major characters are often comic victims. He has a mordant wit and violent view of the future. Novels: *The Long Day Wanes, A Clockwork Orange* and *Earthly Powers.* In addition to extensive literary criticism, biographies and works of music and linguistics, he composed more than 65 musical works.

Readers are plentiful; thinkers are rare.

1918 **Bobby Riggs:** American tennis champion and hustler, who gained greater fame in his 50s as a result of challenge matches with the top female players in the world. Played the male chauvinist role to perfection, gaining him greater notoriety. Finally met his match with Billie Jean King in what was billed as the "Battle of the Sexes."

If I am to be a chauvinist pig, I want to be the number one pig.

1925 **Edward Gorey:** American writer, artist, and cartoonist. Noted for his wry, macabre illustrated books. Known for arch nonsense verse and mock-Victorian prose. Books: *The Doubtful Guest* and *The Hapless Child.* Won a Tony Award for designing the Best Costume Design for Broadways' *Dracula.* Noted for his fondness for ballet and cats.

I realize that homosexuality is a serious problem for anyone who is — but the, of course, heterosexuality is a serious problem for anyone who is, too. And being a man is a serious problem and being a woman is, too. Lots of things are problems.

1925 **Lisa Kirk:** Beautiful photogenic American supper club and Broadway stage actress and singer. Famed for renditions of "Why Can't You Behave" and "I'm Always True to You, Darling, in My Fashion" from *Kiss Me Kate.* Also starred on Broadway in the musical *Allegro.* Although she didn't smoke, she died of lung cancer in 1987.

A gossip is one who talks to you about others; a bore is one who talks to you about himself; and a brilliant conversationalist is one who talks to you about yourself.

OTHERS: 1725 French composer **Armand-Louis Couperin**, 1778 Liberator of Argentina/Chile/ Peru **José Francesco de San Martin**, 1814 Ukrainian poet **Taras Shevchenko**, 1842 German writer **Karl May**, 1890 English concert pianist **Myra Hess**, 1895 NFL commissioner **Bert Bell**, 1906 Spanish bullfighter **Domingo Ortega**, 1913 U.S. actor **Jim Backus**, 1916 Champion harness driver **Roger Baldwin**, 1919 Baseball hall-of-famer **Monty Irvin**, 1928 U.S. writer/producer **Larry Gelbart**, 1937 Newscaster **Bob Schieffer**, 1938 Australian runner **Herb Elliott**, 1940 Chicago Cub player/broadcaster **Ron Santo**, 1961 U.S. race car driver **Davey Allison**

February 26

1564 **Christopher Marlowe:** English novelist, dramatist, and romantic poet. Contemporary of William Shakespeare. Established blank verse in drama. Wrote *Tamburlaine the Great, Dido, the Queen of Carthage* (co-written with Thomas Nashe), *The Tragical History of Dr. Faustus* and *The Famous Tragedy of the Rich Jew of Malta*. Led a disreputable life and died in a violent tavern brawl at age 29.

While money doesn't buy love, it puts you in a great bargaining position.

1671 **Anthony Ashley Cooper, Lord Shaftesbury:** English politician. Joined Oliver Cromwell's Council of State, but resigned in protest of the Grand Protector's dictatorial policies. Worked for the Restoration of Charles II and served on the commission that tried the Regicides, who had participated in the execution of Charles I. Became Lord Chancellor and First Lord of Trade.

When men are easy in themselves, they let others remain so.

1802 **Victor Hugo:** French poet, novelist, and dramatist. An accomplished poet before he was 20. Leader of Romantic Movement in France. Elected to the Constituent Assembly (1848). Exiled by Napoleon III for his republican views. Works: *Les Contemplations*, *The Hunchback of Notre Dame* and known universally for his greatest novel *Les Misérables*, the story of the redemption of the convict Jean Valjean.

When a woman is talking to you, listen to what she says with her eyes.

1839 Sir **John Pentland Mahaffy:** Irish classical scholar, Considered to be one of Dublin's greatest curmudgeons. Notable works: *History of Classical Greek Literature*, *The Empire of the Ptolemies*, and *Greek Life and Thought from Alexander to the Roman Conquest*.

In Ireland the inevitable never happens and the unexpected constantly happens.

1852 **J. H. [John Harvey] Kellogg:** American surgeon. Ran a sanitarium in Battle Creek, Michigan. Developed a process of making a nourishing breakfast of corn flakes, inadvertently found the principle of "tempering grains." Founder of the health food industry with his industrialist brother W.K. (Will Keith) Kellogg.

A dead cow or sheep lying in the pasture is recognized as carrion. The same sort of carcass dressed and hung up in a butcher's stall still passes for meat.

1857 **Émile Coué:** French pharmacist and psychotherapist. Studied hypnosis, opening a free clinic in Nancy in 1910, developing his own method of psychotherapy based on "auto-suggestion." His system became world famous as "Couéism," expressed in his famous formula, which was to be constantly repeated by the patient:

Every day, in every way, I'm getting better and better.

1897 **Elizabeth Asquith Bibesco:** English writer. Daughter of British Prime Minister Herbert Asquith. Wrote three collections of short stories, four novels, two plays and a book of poetry. A final posthumous collection of her stories, poems and aphorisms were published under the title *Haven*.

Blessed are those who can give without remembering and take without forgetting.

1916 **Jackie Gleason:** American actor and comedian. Found his niche in television's "The Honeymooners" and "The Jackie Gleason Show," where he created the characters the Poor Soul, Reggie van Gleason and Joe the Bartender, Tony Award for Broadway's *Take Me Along*. Oscar nominated for *The Hustler*. Other films: *Requiem for a Heavyweight* and *Soldier in the Rain*. Smoked six packs of cigarettes a day and died of cancer in 1987.

Modesty is the artifice of actors, similar to passion in call girls.

1921 **Betty Hutton:** Born *Elizabeth Thornburg*. "The Blonde Bombshell." American actress and singer. Song hits: "Murder, He Said" and "Doctor, Lawyer, Indian Chief" from the 1945 movie *Stork Club*. Got her film break as a replacement for ailing Judy Garland in *Annie Get Your Gun*. Other films: *The Miracle of Morgan's Creek* and *The Greatest Show on Earth*.

Nobody loved me unless I bought them, so I bought everybody.

1928 **Fats Domino:** Rhythm and blues piano-playing singer, influenced by Fats Waller. Biggest hits: "Ain't That a Shame" and "Blueberry Hill." Rock and Roll Hall of Fame (1986). Grammy's Lifetime Achievement Award (1987). Got his nickname from the first song he recorded (1949), "The Fat Man," which some consider the first rock and roll song.

A lot of fellows nowadays have a B.A., M.A. or Ph.D. Unfortunately they don't have a J.O.B.

1932 **Johnny Cash:** "The Man in Black." American country singer, guitarist, and songwriter. Noted for his distinctive voice. Began each concert with the announcement, "Hello, I'm Johnny Cash." Hit songs: "I Walk the Line," "Folsom Prison Blues," "Ring of Fire," and the humorous "A Boy Named Sue." Second wife was singer and songwriter June Cash. They both died within months of each other.

Success is having to worry about every damn thing in the world, except money.

1933 Sir **James Michael Goldsmith:** Millionaire British businessman. Powerful and dynamic personality, fiercely loyal to causes he espoused. Founded the Eurosceptic Referendum Party and financial backer of the think-tank The European Foundation. Vehemently opposed further European integration and the monetary union. Poured millions of his fortune to campaign against them in the general elections.

When a man marries his mistress it creates a job opportunity.

OTHERS: 1361 King of the Romans **Wenceslas of Bohemia,** 1832 Abe Lincoln's biographer **John George Nicolay**, 1845 Russian Tsar **Alexander III**, 1846 U.S. scout/buffalo hunter/showman **Wild Bill Cody**, 1866 Pioneer in chemical industry **Herbert Henry Dow**, 1868 British pianist **Leonard Borwick**, 1887 Baseball pitcher **Grover Cleveland Alexander**, 1893 U.S. actor **William Frawley**, 1900 Romanian film director **Jean Negulesco**, 1908 U.S. cartoonist **Tex Avery**, 1920 U.S.

actor **Tony Randall**, 1932 U.S. reporter **Robert D. Novak**, 1933 U.S. comedian **Godfrey Cambridge**, 1958 U.S. astronaut **Susan J. Helms**

February 27

280 **Constantine the Great:** First Roman emperor to profess Christianity. Issued the Edict of Milan, granting tolerance to Christians. Gave the Christians land for their churches and granted the church special privileges. Convoked the Council of Nicae, the first ecumenical Christian Council, which drew us the Nicene Creed. Moved his capital from Rome to the site of Byzantium, which he renamed Constantinople. It is now Istanbul.

Under God's watch, we shall conquer and never fall!

1807 **Henry Wadsworth Longfellow:** American poet, translator, and college professor at Harvard. Distinctively the poet of America. However, he was among the few American writers abroad. Before 1900 his poems had been translated into 12 languages and his translations made the poetry of other countries available to Americans. Poems: "The Wreck of the Hesperus," "The Village Blacksmith," "The Children's Hour," "Evangeline," "Hiawatha" and "The Courtship of Miles Standish."

It takes less time to do a thing right than it does to explain why you did it wrong.

1847 Dame **Ellen Terry:** English Shakespearean actress born into a theatrical family. Formed a notable partnership with Henry Irving in performing a number of Shakespearean roles, notably Portia, Cordelia and Viola. Most popular actress in England and U.S. King George V conferred upon her the honor of Dame of the British Empire in 1925.

Eulogy is nice, but one does not leant anything from it.

1886 **Hugo L. Black:** U.S. senator from Alabama (1927–37). Supreme Court associate justice (1937–71). Strong supporter of New Deal legislation. Wrote majority opinion forbidding prayers in schools. Best known for his absolutist belief in the Bill of Rights as a guarantee of civil liberties. Last major opinion was to support the right of the *New York Times* to publish the Pentagon Papers.

The layman's constitutional view is that what he likes is constitutional and that which he doesn't like is unconstitutional.

1891 **David Sarnoff:** Russian-born American communications executive. At age 21 gained fame by remaining at his Marconi radio for 72 hours relaying news of the sinking of the Titanic. Chief executive of RCA. Proposed the first commercially marketed radio. Formed the radio network NBC, followed by NBC television network.

Let us not paralyze our capacity for good by brooding on man's capacity for evil.

1896 **Arthur William Radford:** American admiral. Engaged in the Gilbert and Marshall Islands campaigns during World War II. Commander-in-Chief of the U.S. Pacific Command. At the height of the Cold War, he became the third Chairman of the Joint Chiefs of Staff (1953–57). Considered the most politically powerful and influential Admiral in U.S. history.

A decision is the action an executive must take when he has information so incomplete that the answer does not suggest itself.

1902 **Marian Anderson:** American contralto and concert artist, who triumphed over racial prejudice to become the first African American to perform a major role at the Metropolitan Opera (1955). In 1939 she was prevented from performing at Constitution Hall in Washington D.C. First Lady Eleanor Roosevelt and others arranged for her to perform in concert at the Lincoln Memorial, before an audience of 75,000. U.S. delegate to U.N. (1955). Awarded the Spingarn Medal in 1938. U.S. Congressional Medal (1977). Her autobiography: *My Lord, What a Morning*. Speaking of racial prejudice:

Sometimes, it's like a hair across your cheek. You can't see it, you can't find it with your fingers, but you keep brushing at it because the feel of it is irritating.

1902 **John Steinbeck:** U.S. novelist, short-story writer. Pulitzer Prize (1940), Nobel Prize (1962). His major work, *The Grapes of Wrath*, made an eloquent plea for human values and common justice. However, some churchmen attacked it as being obscene. Also wrote *Tortilla Flat*, *Of Mice and Men*, *East of Eden* and *The Wayward Bus*.

I have come to believe that a great teacher is a great artist and that there are as few as there are any other great artists. Teaching might even be the greatest of arts since the medium is the human mind and spirit.

1910 **Peter De Vries:** American novelist and short story writer. Known for his satiric wit. Worked for the *New Yorker* (1944–67). Developed a comic manner displayed in novels such as *The Tunnel of Love*, *Comfort Me with Apples*, *The Tents of Wickedness* and *I Hear America Swinging*.

The difficulty with marriage is that we fall in love with a personality, but must live with a character.

1912 **Lawrence Durrell:** Indian-born Anglo-Irish novelist, poet, and playwright. His reputation was made with the publication of *Justine*, the first novel of *The Alexandra Quartet*, which also included: *Balthazar*, *Mountolive* and *Clea*. The tetralogy explores the erotic lives of a group of exotic characters in Alexandria, Egypt.

Music is only love looking for words.

1932 **Elizabeth Taylor:** Very beautiful English-born actress. As a child star she was in numerous films, including two "Lassie" stories, *National Velvet* and *Little Women*. First seen in a film as an adult in *Father of the*

Bride, about the time she married Nick Hilton of the hotelier family. Nominated for Oscars for *Raintree County*, *Cat on a Hot Tin Roof* and *Suddenly Last Summer*. Won for *Butterfield 8* and *Who's Afraid of Virginia Woolf?* Married eight times, including actor Michael Wilding, producer Michael Todd, singer Eddie Fisher, U.S. Senator John Warner and twice to actor Richard Burton, with whom she had a torrid affair during the making of *Cleopatra*. Her perfumes are "Passion" and "White Diamonds."

You find out who your real friends are when you're involved in a scandal.

1934 **Ralph Nader:** American attorney consumer advocate and political activist, writer. Founder of consumer rights movement in the United States. Wrote *Unsafe at Any Speed*, about GM cars (1965). His entry into the 2000 presidential race probably gave the election to George W. Bush.

This country has far more problems than it deserves and far more solutions than it applies.

OTHERS: 1622 Dutch painter **Rembrandt C. Fabritius**, 1835 English author **Richard Garnett**, 1850 U.S. railroad executive **Henry E. Huntington**, 1863 Spanish artist **Joaquín Sorolla y Bastida**, 1867 U.S. economist **Irving Fisher**, 1881 Dutch mathematician/ logician **L. E.J. Brouwer**, 1888 German soprano **Lotte Lehmann**, 1893 U.S. cultural anthropologist **Ralph Linden**, 1899 Co-discoverer of the Insulin treatment for diabetes **Charles H. Best**, 1902 U.S. golfer **Gene Sarazen**, 1904 U.S. author **James T. Farrell**, 1910 U.S. actress **Joan Bennett**, 1917 U.S. politician **John B. Connally**, 1920 Cuban orchestra leader **José Melius**, 1930 U.S. actress **Joanne Woodward**, 1961 U.S. comic **Wendy Liebman**

February 28

1533 **Michel de Montaigne:** French philosopher, moralist and author. First to use the term *essay* to describe the literary form he so successfully executed, short prose reflections on many subjects. Wrote three volumes of essays, 1580, 1588, 1595. They form one of the most intimate self-portraits ever written. Advocated humanistic morality.

If there is such a thing as a good marriage, it is because it resembles friendship rather than love.

1797 **Mary Lyon:** American educator. Studied at various academies, supporting herself by teaching. Pioneer advocate of education for women. Founded and first principal of Mount. Holyoke Seminary, now Mount Holyoke College, in South Hadley, Massachusetts, the first women's college in the United States (1837).

When you choose your fields of labor go where nobody else is willing to go.

1812 **Berthold Auerbach:** Germany novelist with a special interest with Benedict de Spinoza, on whose life he based a novel. Revealed an unrivalled insight into the soul of the Southern German country folk, in particular the peasants of the Black Forest and Bavarian Alps. Fame rests mainly on *Black Forest Village Stories*.

An idea not capable of realization is an empty soap-bubble.

1823 **Joseph Ernest Renan:** French skeptical writer, philosopher, historian and scholar of religion. Abandoned traditional Catholic faith after studying Greek and Hebrew biblical criticism. Author of the five-volume *History of the Origins of Christianity*, which included the controversial *The Life of Jesus*. In it, he tried to reconstruct the mind of Jesus as a wholly human person. Later work: *History of the People of Israel*.

The agnostic's prayer: O Lord, if there is a Lord, save my soul, if I have a soul.

1865 Sir **Wilfred Grenfell:** Renown English physician and medical missionary, Fitted out the first hospital ship for North Sea fisheries. Founded hospitals, orphanages and other social services in Labrador, where he established a record of service with religion evenly blended with adventure.

The service we render to others is really the rent we pay for our room on this earth.

1890 **Vaslav Nijinsky:** Internationally famous Russian dancer and choreographer. Joined Sergei Diaghilev's *Ballets Russes*. Danced leading roles in *Giselle*, *Swan Lake*, and *Sleeping Beauty*, often with Anna Pavlova and Tamara Karsavina. Noted for his athleticism, characterization and interpretative powers. In 1909, he joined the new Ballets Russes. Innovative choreographer of *The Afternoon of a Faun*, *Jeux*, and *The Rite of Spring*, all of which caused scandals. Mental illness ended his career prematurely.

People like eccentrics. Therefore they will leave me alone, saying that I am a "mad clown."

1893 **Ben Hecht:** American newspaperman, novelist and playwright. Perfected a type of human-interest sketch that was widely emulated. Often collaborated with Charles MacArthur. Wrote the plays *The Front Page*, *Twentieth Century* and *Ladies and Gentlemen*. Film scripts include *Gunga Din*, *Spellbound* and *Notorious*.

Prejudice is a raft onto which the shipwrecked mind clambers and paddles to safety.

1895 **Marcel Pagnol:** French playwright, screenwriter, film director. Widely known for his witty trilogy about life in Marseilles —*Marius*, *Fanny* and *César*. Established his own studio and entered the world of sound films, producing and directing adaptations of some of his plays.

The most difficult secret for a man to keep is his own opinion of himself.

1901 **Linus Pauling:** Outstanding American chemist of the 20th century. His scientific work is exceptional in its range, covering inorganic and organic chemistry, theoretical chemistry and practical devices, work on minerals and biology. Major advocate of nuclear disarmament and end to nuclear testing. Won two Nobel Prizes, for chemistry in 1954 and for peace in 1962. Advocated major doses of vitamin C to maintain health.

The way to get good ideas is to get a lot of ideas, and throw the bad ones away.

1915 **P.B. [Peter Brian] Medawar:** Brazil-born British immunologist and biologist. Co-winner of the 1960 Nobel Prize for medicine with Sir MacFarlane Burnet for the discovery of acquired immunological tolerance. Limited by several strokes to writing seven popular science books during his last 18 years.

The human mind treats a new idea the way the body treats a strange protein; it rejects it.

1915 **Zero Mostel:** Exuberant American comic actor, singer and artist of stage and screen. Established a successful theater career, particularly comedy roles as in *Rhinoceros*, *A Funny Thing Happened on the Way to the Forum* and as a memorable Tevya in *Fiddler on the Roof.* Films included: *Panic in the Streets*, *The Producers* and *The Front*.

The freedom of any society varies proportionately with the volume of its laughter.

1941 **Alice May Brock:** American writer and restaurateur. She and her husband lived in a former church in Great Barrington, Massachusetts. She operated a restaurant formally known as the "Back Rest Room," named for its location down an alley behind a grocery store. "Alice's Restaurant" was made famous in a song by Arlo Guthrie and a movie of the same name.

Tomatoes and oregano make it Italian, wine and tarragon make it French. Sour cream makes it Russian; lemon and cinnamon make it Greek. Soy sauce makes it Chinese; garlic makes it good.

OTHERS: 1552 Swiss/German mathematician **Jobst Bürgi**, 1663 English co-invented the steam engine **Thomas Newcomen**, 1820 English cartoonist/illustrator **John Tenniel**, 1824 French acrobat/aerialist **Charles Blondin**, 1882 U.S. soprano **Geraldine Farrar**, 1906 Mobster founder of Las Vegas casino **Ben "Bugsy" Siegel**, 1910 Movie director **Vicente Minnelli**, 1923 U.S. actor **Charles Durning**, 1927 British actor **Stanley Baker**, 1934 Jazz drummer **Willie Bobo**, 1939 Dancer/choreographer **Tommy Tune**, 1940 Racecar driver **Mario Andretti**, 1942 British guitarist **Brian Jones**, 1945 Football player/actor **Bubba Smith**, 1948 U.S. actress **Bernadette Peters**, 1973 hockey star **Eric Lindos**

February 29

1468 Pope **Paul III:** Originally **Alessandro Farnese**. Son of a noble Tuscan family. Member of the circle of Lorenzo de Medici. Named a cardinal-deacon in 1493. Served as bishop of Parma and Ostia before being named dean of the College of Cardinals by Pope Leo X. Pope from 1534 to 1549. Summoned the Council of Trent to reform the Church, initiating the Counter-Revolution. Guilty of lax personal morality (had three sons and a daughter) and gross nepotism. Threatened an uncooperative Michelangelo, who reluctantly agreed to paint the ceiling of the Sistine Chapel:

There is no redemption from hell!

1731 **Charles Churchill:** English poet, wit and satirist. Noted for his savage onslaughts of his critics. Wrote lampoons and polemical satires in heroic couplets, "The Rosciad," "The Apology," "The Ghost" and "The Prophecy of Famine."

Few have reason, most have eyes.

1736 **Ann Lee:** Known as "Mother Lee." English-born American mystic and religious leader. Founder of American sect of Shakers at Niskayuna, now Watervilet, near Albany, New York. The Shakers were a radical branch of Quakers, sometimes called the "Shaking Quakers." While in prison for street preaching she had a vision that convinced her it was essential for people to remain celibate if they wanted to succeed in doing Christ's work. Her followers embraced her as the embodiment of the missing female half of the divine dual nature.

Do your work as though you had a thousand years to live, and as if you were to die tomorrow.

1792 **Gioacchino Antonio Rossini:** Italian opera composer. Wrote 39 operas, including: *The Barber of Seville* and *William Tell* and the sacred composition *Stabat Mater*. A superb craftsman who created atmospheres of excitement for his audiences.

Give me a laundry list and I will set it to music.

1900 **George Seferis:** Penname of **Giorgos Seferiadis.** Greek poet and Foreign Service officer. One of the most important Greek poets of the 20th century. Poetic works imbued with references to ancient Greek history and classical mythology. Supporter of the demotic Greek language over the formal, official language. Book of Poems: *Imerologio Katastromatos III*, inspired by the island of Cyprus.

Don't ask me who influenced me. A lion is made up of the lambs he's digested, and I've been reading all my life.

1904 **John "Pepper" Martin:** American baseball player. One of the leaders of the *Gas House Gang* of St. Louis Cardinals in the thirties. Lee Allen described him in The National League Story (1961): "A chunky, unshaven hobo, who ran the bases like a berserk locomotive, slept in the raw and swore at pitchers in his sleep.

You can take an ol' mule and run him and feed him and train him and get him in the best shape of his life, but you ain't going to win the Kentucky Derby.

1908 **Balthus [Comte Balthazar Klossowski De Rola]:** French artist of Polish descent. Self-taught painter, who supported himself through commissions for stage sets and portraits. Noted for doll-like portraits and interiors with adolescent girls. In his work, females endlessly appear gracing an artistic landscape that is at the same time alluring and repulsive. His disturbing and erotic images, including the scandalous *The Guitar Lesson*, made him an international cult figure.

Painting is a language which cannot be replaced by another language. I don't know what to say about what I paint, really.

1917 **Dinah Shore:** Born **Frances Rose Shore**. American singer and actress. Films include: *Thank Your Lucky Stars* and *Up in Arms*. Hit songs: "I'll Walk Alone" and "Buttons and Bows." Television's "Dinah Shore Show" won five Emmys in fifties.

Trouble is part of your life — if you don't share it, you don't give the person who loves you a chance to love you enough.

1920 **Howard Nemerov:** American poet laureate on two separate occasions. *The Collected Poems of Howard Nemerov* won the National Book Award and a Pulitzer Prize. His work has a reputation for being witty and playful. Brother of photographer Diane Nemerov Arbus.

The secrets of success are a good wife and a steady job. My wife told me.

1948 **Patricia McKillip:** American writer, Won the Fantasy Award for *The Forgotten Beasts of Eld*, the Locus Award for *Harpist in the Wind* and the Ballrog award in the short fiction category for "A Troll and Two Roses."

Imagination must be visited constantly, or else it begins to become restless and emit strange bellows at embarrassing moments, ignoring it only makes it grow larger and noisier.

1956 **Aileen Carol Wuornos:** "American first female serial killer." Working as a highway prostitute she killed six men. Claimed she shot them in self-defense after they attempted to sexually assault her. Sentenced to death by lethal injection. Last words:

I'd just like to say I'm sailing with the rock, and I'll be back like Independence Day, with Jesus June 6. Like the movie, big mother ship and all, I'll be back.

1960 **Anthony Robbins:** American motivational speaker and writer. Inventor of what he calls neuroassociative condition, based on Neuro-linguistic programming. Offers four day seminars *Unleash the Power Within*.

More than anything else, I believe it's our decisions, not the conditions of our lives that determine our destiny.

OTHERS: 1692 English printer **Edward Cave**, 1784 German architect for St. Petersburg's Hermitage **Franz von Klenze**, 1860 U.S. inventor of 1st electronic tabulating machine **Herman Hollerith**, 1896 Premier of India **Morarji Desai**, 1896 U.S. movie director **William Wellman**, 1904 U.S. bandleader **Jimmy Dorsey**, 1908 U.S. writer/historian **Dee Brown**, 1928 English actor **Joss Ackland**, 1928 U.S. stripper **Tempest Storm**, 1936 Canadian hockey player **Henri Richard**, 1936 U.S. astronaut **Jack Lousma**, 1944 U.S. cop/actor **Dennis Farina**, 1952 Russian cross-country skier **Raisa Smetanina**, 1976 U.S. rapper **Ja Rule**

March 1

40 CE **Martial [Marcus Valerius Martialis]:** Latin epigrammatist and poet from Hispania. Renowned for correctness of diction, versification and form. Best work is his 12 books of bawdy *Epigrams*. With these he joyfully satirizes the scandalous activities of his acquaintances.

Conceal a flaw and the world will imagine the worse.

1810 **Frédéric Chopin:** Polish pianist and composer. Creator of a unique romantic style. As a pianist, he revolutionized the technique of pianoforte-playing, concentrating on solo piano pieces. Moved to Paris where he lived with novelist George Sand (Madame Dudevant) and wrote concertos for piano and orchestra, sonatas, nocturnes, etudes, mazurkas, polonaises, waltzes and a funeral march. His life was cut short at age 39 from tuberculosis.

Simplicity is the final achievement. After one has played a vast quantity of notes and more notes, it is simplicity that emerges as the crowning reward of art.

1837 **William Dean Howells:** American printer, novelist, editor, critic and poet. His association with Harper's magazine (1886–91) made him king of critics in America, writing an "Easy Chair" column (1900–20). Author of *Criticism and Fiction*, *Years of My Youth*, and *My Mark Twain*.

Some people can stay longer in an hour than others can in a week.

1848 **Augustus Saint-Gaudens:** Outstanding Irish-born American sculptor. Influenced by the Italian Renaissance. Foremost sculptor of his time. Established a new standard for public monuments. Major works: Lincoln in Lincoln Park, Chicago, the equestrian statue of General Sherman in New York's Central Park, "The Puritan" in Springfield, Massachusetts, the Shaw memorial in Boston and the Adams Memorial in Washington, D.C.

What garlic is to salad, insanity is to art.

1858 **George Simmel:** German philosopher and sociologist. Wrote essays on sociological methodology, metaphysics and aesthetics. He is instrumental in establishing sociology as a social science. Books: *Philosophy of Money* and *On Women, Sexuality and Love*.

He is educated who knows how to find out what he doesn't know.

1880 **Lytton Strachey:** English biographer. Began writing career as a critic with *Landmarks in French Literature*. Member of the Bloomsbury Group. Biographies: *Eminent Victorians*, *Queen Victoria*, and *Elizabeth and Essex: A Tragic History*. Last words:

If this is dying, then I don't think much of it.

1904 **Glenn Miller:** American bandleader and trombonist. A major force in the Big Band era of the 1930s and 40s. Produced the "Glenn Miller" sound, which blended clarinets and saxophones to create a mellow tone. Hits include "Moonlight Serenade." "String of Pearls" and "In the Mood." Formed the U.S. Army Air Force band to entertain the troops during World War II. Disappeared in December, 1944 over the English Channel on a flight to Paris for a show.

By giving the public a rich and full melody,

distinctly arranged and well played, all the time creating new tone colors and pattern, I feel we have a better chance of being successful. I want a kick to my band, but I don't want the rhythm to hog the spotlight.

1914 **Ralph Waldo Ellison:** African-American writer. Inspired by Richard Wright to turn to writing. Works show a major concern with identity. His literary reputation rests on first, and only, novel, *Invisible Man*, which won National Book Award (1953); Presidential Medal of Freedom (1969).

History has no vacuum. There are transformations, there are lesions, there are metamorphoses, and there are mysteries that cloak the clashing of individual wills and private interests.

1917 **Robert Traill Spence Lowell:** American leader of the Confessional school of poetry in the 1950s. His work stressed the importance of individualism, especially in times of war. Awarded Pulitzer Prizes for *Lord Weary's Castle* and *The Dolphin*. War protester and civil rights activist in the 1960s.

The light at the end of the tunnel is just the light of an oncoming train.

1922 **Yitzhak Rabin:** First native-born Prime Minister of Israel. His strategies helped with the Six-Day War in 1967, Secured a cease-fire with Syria in the Golden Heights. Ordered the raid on Entebbe to rescue Jewish airline passengers high jacked by the PLO and held captives in Uganda.

You don't make peace with friends; you make it with very unsavory enemies.

1927 **Robert Bork:** American legal scholar, former Solicitor General, acting Attorney General and circuit judge for the U.S. Court of Appeals. His nomination to the Supreme Court by Ronald Reagan was rejected by the Senate because of his conservative views. Bork bases his understanding of law on that of the Framer's of the U.S. Constitution.

Those who made and endorses our Constitution knew man's nature, and it is to their ideas, rather than the temptations of utopia, that we must ask that our judges adhere.

1935 **Judith Rossner:** American novelist. Best known for her best-selling novel *Looking for Mr. Goodbar*, based on the murder of a young New York woman. Made into a movie, starring Diane Keaton. Also wrote *Attachments*.

The past isn't useful until its place in the present is found.

OTHERS: 72 CE Chinese poet **Po Tjiu-i**, 1610 German poet/historian **Johann B. Schup**, 1828 Italian playwright **Vittorio Bersezio [Carlo Nugelli]**, 1852 French statesman **Theophile Delcassé**, 1885 English actor **Lionel Atwill**, 1886 Russian-born painter **Oskar Kokoschka**, 1895 U.S. civic leader **Edmund Fitzgerald**, 1896 Greek conductor/composer **Dimitri Mitropoulos**, 1905 Flemish author **Pol le Roy**, 1909 British actor **David Niven**, 1911 Chess grandmaster **Harry Golombek**, 1914 Baseball broadcaster **Harry Carey**, 1927 U.S. singer/actor **Harry Belafonte**, 1954 UA producer/director **Ron Howard**

March 2

1760 **Camille Desmoulins:** French revolutionary and journalist. An effective orator who played a dramatic part in storming the Bastille. Elected to the National Convention and voted for the execution of the king. Angered Robespierre by arguing for moderation. Arrested and guillotined.

Clemency is also a revolutionary measure.

1769 **De Witt Clinton:** American politician and lawyer. U.S. senator from New York and Mayor of New York City. Defeated by James Madison for the presidency in 1812. Sponsor of the Erie Canal Scheme, which opened in 1825. A founder of the New York Historical Society.

Pleasure is a shadow, wealth is vanity, and power a pageant, but knowledge is ecstatic in enjoyment, perennial in frame, unlimited in space and indefinite in duration.

1793 **Sam Houston:** American politician, soldier, and lawyer. Virginia-born leader of fight with Mexico for control of Texas. Avenged the Alamo massacre by defeating Santa Anna's troops. President of Republic of Texas (1836–38, 1841–44). Democrat Texas senator (1846–59) and governor (1959–61). Only person to have been elected governor of two different states, having previously served in Tennessee. The city of Houston is named for him.

A leader is someone who helps improve the lives of other people or improve the system they live under.

1810 Pope **Leo XIII [Vincenzo Giocchino Pecci]:** Italian papal nuncio in Belgium, Archbishop of Perugia and Cardinal. Elected Pope (1878–1903). Patron of literature and education. Potent force in religion and morals. Restored the hierarchy in Scotland, Denounced the Irish Plan of Campaign. Opened the Vatican archives to scholars. Issued an encyclical pronouncing Anglican orders invalid.

It is quite unlawful to demand, defend, or to grant unconditional freedom of thought, or speech, of writing or worship, as if these were so many rights given by nature to man

1829 **Carl Schurz:** German-born American statesman, journalist and orator. Political reformer who led the Liberal Republicans and the Mugwumps. U.S. senator from Missouri (1869–75). As U.S. Secretary of the Interior (1877–81), he introduced competitive examinations for positions in the civil service. Editor, New York Evening Post (1881–84).

Our country, right or wrong! When right to be kept right; when wrong, to be put right.

1862 **John Jay Chapman:** U.S. lawyer and writer. *Causes and Consequences* and *Practical Agitation* expressed his views on the need for political change. Argued that politicians tended to be influenced by the power of big business. He wrote about the failure to prosecute the parties known to be responsible for a lynching in Coatesville, Pennsylvania, which appeared in *Harper's Weekly* in September 1912.

People who love soft methods and hate iniquity forget this,— that reform consists in taking a bone from a dog. Philosophy will not do it.

1876 Pope **Pius XII [Eugenio Pacelli]:** Italian Roman Catholic pope (1939–58). Remained neutral during World War II. Vigorously opposed communism. Has been criticized for not condemning Hitler and the persecution of the Jews. Announced that there was no opposition between the theory of evolution and the teachings of the Church, he observed:

One Galileo in two thousand years is enough.

1880 **Ivar Kreuger:** Swedish industrialist and financier. One of the most powerful businessmen in Europe. Called the "Match King." Cornered world's match trade through irregular practices. Other ventures were to acquire majority interests in the telephone company Ericsson, the mining company Boliden and major interests in the ball bearing manufacturer SKF. Bankrupted by the Great Crash of 1929, he committed suicide 1932 rather than face his creditors.

But what certainty is there about money, which after all, holds all the world together? It depends on the good will of a few capitalists to keep to the agreement that one metal is worth more than another.

1904 **Theodor Seuss Geisel:** Dr. Seuss. American author and illustrator of immensely popular humorous children's books including *The Cat in the Hat, Green Eggs and Ham* and *The Grinch Who Stole Christmas.* Created the "Beginner Books" industry starting with *Horton Hears a Who* in 1954. Became synonymous with learning to read.

Adults are obsolete children and the hell with them.

1931 **Mikhail Gorbachev:** U.S.S.R. political leader. Secretary General of U.S.S.R. from 1985 until December 25, 1991, when it was dismantled. Initiated policies of perestroika (restructuring Soviet economy) and glasnost (openness of information). Awarded Nobel Peace Prize (1990).

What the 21st century will be like depends on whether we learn the lessons of the 20th century and avoid repeating its worst mistakes.

1931 **Tom Wolfe:** Popular name of journalist, pop-critic and novelist Thomas Kennerley Wolfe. Proponent of the New Journalism. Much of his work first appeared in Rolling Stone magazine. Coined phrase "radical chic." Wrote *The Right Stuff, The Electric Kool-Aid Acid Test* and *The Bonfire of the Vanities.*

A cult is a religion with no political power.

1943 **John Irving:** U.S. novelist. Taught English at Mount Holyoke College. His works that were noted for colorful characters, macabre humor and examinations of contemporary issues include *The World According to Garp, The Hotel New Hampshire, The Cider House Rules* and *Until I Find You.*

Your memory is a monster; you forget— it doesn't. It simply files things away. It keeps things for you, or hides things from you— and summons them to your recall with a will of its own. You think you have a memory; but it has you.

OTHERS: 1316 King of Scotland **Robert II**, 1545 English diplomat/scholar **Sir Thomas Bodley**, 1817 Hungarian epic poet **János Arany**, 1824 Bohemian composer **Bedřich Smetana**, 1876 Swedish radiologist **Gösta Forsell**, 1878 Dutch physicist **Wander J. de Haas**, 1900 German composer **Kurt Weill**, 1905 U.S. composer **Marc Blitzstein**, Dutch playwright **Jan Fabricius**, 1909 Hall-of-Fame baseball player **Mel Ott**, 1917 Cuban-born bandleader, singer, actor **Desi Arnaz**, 1919 U.S. actress **Jennifer Jones**, 1920 U.S. movie director **Martin Ritt**, 1942 American singer **Lou Reed**, 1943 U.S. congresswoman **Rosa DeLauro**, 1950 Vocalist/drummer **Karen Carpenter**, 1962 U.S. singer **Jon Bon Jovi**

March 3

1606 **Edmund Waller:** English poet and Member of Parliament. Arrested for his part in a plot to establish London as a stronghold of the king. Avoided execution by betraying his colleagues and paying lavish bribes. Know for the smoothness and harmony of his verse. Two of his best known poems are "On a Girdle" and "Go, Lovely Rose." Later wrote poetic tributes to Oliver Cromwell and after the Restoration to King Charles II.

Vexed sailors cursed the rain, for which poor shepherds prayed in vain.

1652 **Thomas Otway:** English dramatist and poet. After failing as an actor he turned to writing. Translated Racine and Molière. Wrote Restoration comedies. His masterpiece is *Venice Preserved,* one of the finest tragedies of the Restoration. Also wrote *The Orphan, or The Unhappy Marriage,* about twin brothers in love with the same woman.

There are rogues that pretend to be of religion now! Well, all I say is, honest atheism for my money.

1756 **William Godwin:** English novelist and political theorist. Leading radical of 18th century. Influenced by the ideas of Rousseau and the French Encyclopedists. In turn he was a great influence on the likes of Wordsworth, Coleridge, Shelley and Byron. Husband of Mary Wollstonecraft and father of Mary Shelley. His masterpiece, the novel *The Adventures of Caleb Williams,* or *Things As They Are.*

The ... source of crime is ... one man's possessing in abundance that of which another man is destitute.

1847 **Alexander Graham Bell:** Scottish born American/Canadian inventor. By profession a teacher of the deaf. His mother was deaf and both his father and grandfather dedicated their lives to teaching deaf people to speak. Bell's wife was also deaf. First to patent and commercially exploit the telephone. Founded *Science* journal. Also invented the photophone and the graphophone. Pioneer in aeronautics.

Great discoveries and improvements invariably involve the cooperation of many minds. I may be given credit for having blazed the trail but when I look at the subsequent developments I feel the credit is due to others rather than myself.

1868 **Alain:** Pen name of **Émile-Auguste Chartier**. French philosopher, essayist and teacher. Like Socrates, he tried to provoke thought by stimulating and shocking men's minds. Best known for thousands of aphoristic essays like fables or parables, called "propos." Many of these express his commitment to pacifism and distrust of official power.

When we speak, in gestures or signs, we fashion a real object in the world; the gesture is seen, the words and the songs are heard. The arts are simply a kind of writing, which, in one way or another, fixes words or gestures, and gives body to the invisible.

1872 **Wee Willie Keeler:** American baseball player, mostly with Baltimore, Brooklyn and New York in the National League. At 5'4" and 140 pounds, one of the smallest men to ever play Major League Baseball. Used the smallest bat in the game, only 30 inches long and weighing 29 ounces, and choked up on that. Had eight straight seasons of having 200 or more hits. Hall-of-famer with a lifetime batting average of .341. Claimed the secret of his success was:

I keep my eyes clear and I hit 'em where they ain't.

1895 **Matthew Ridgeway:** American army general. Commanded the Army's first major airborne campaign. Directed airborne assaults on Europe (1943–45). Succeeded General MacArthur as Commander of U.N. forces in Korea (1951–52). Supreme commander Allied Forces in Europe (1952–53).

The more you sweat in peace, the less you bleed in war.

1911 **Jean Harlow:** Born **Harlean Carpentier**. Most sensational American film star of the 1930s. First came to public acclaim for her role in *Hell's Angels*. The platinum blonde beauty proved to be a deft comedienne in *Red-Headed Woman* and *Dinner at Eight*. In private life the sex symbol was unhappy, her husband Paul Bern committed suicide several months after they married. The original blonde bombshell died at 26 of uremic poisoning.

Men like me because I don't wear a brassiere. Women like me because I don't look like a girl who would steal a husband. At least not for long.

1920 **Julius Boros:** American golfer, whose slogan was "Swing easy, hit it hard." U.S. Open champion in 1952 and 1963. PGA champion in 1968, at age 48, the oldest player to win a major tournament. Won the 1971 and 1977 National Senior PGA titles. Helped launch the Senior Tour. Elected to the World Golf Hall of Fame (1982).

By the time you get to your ball, if you don't know what to do with it, try another sport.

1926 **James Merrill:** American poet. Widely known as "The Ouija poet," for his poems that record the Ouija board sessions he conducted with "spirits from another world." First volume of poems, *First Poems*, established his reputation as a poet. His more personal and passionate collections *Nights and Day* and *Mirabell: Books of Numbers* both received the National Book Award. Has also written plays and novels.

In life, there are no perfect affections.

1958 **Miranda Richardson:** Gifted, versatile English actress, who from an early age showed talent for turning herself into other people. Studied at the Old Vic Theatre School. Appeared on the London stage and British TV before making films that include her debut *Dance with a Stranger*, in a superlative portrayal of the last woman to be hanged in England, *Enchanted April*, and *The Crying Game*. Nominated for a Supporting Role Academy Award for *Damage* and a Best actress nomination for *Tom and Viv*.

Insecurity, commonly regarded as a weakness in normal people, is the basic tool of the actor's trade.

1962 **Jackie Joyner-Kersee:** Track and field two-time world champion in both long jump and heptathlon. First heptathlon competitor ever to score 7,000 points, breaking the barrier six times. Won Olympic gold in 1988 and 1992. Sullivan Award winner. Only woman to be named *Sporting News* "Man" of the Year. *Sports Illustrated* named her the greatest female athlete of the 20th century. Married woman's track coach Bob Kersee.

I always had something to shoot for each year; to jump one inch further.

OTHERS: 1500 English heretical Cardinal **Reginald Pole**, 1589 Dutch reformed theologist **Gilbertus Voetius**, 1747 Polish Revolutionary War General **Kasamir Pulaski**, 1820 Dutch writer **Eduard Douwes Dekker**, 1831 Inventor of railroad sleeping car **George Pullman**, 1838 U.S. astronomer **George W. Hill**, 1841 Canadian oceanographer **John Murray**, 1845 German mathematician **Georg Cantor**, 1873 President of American Federation of Labor **William Green**, 1895 Norwegian economist **Ragnar Frisch**, 1903 Costume designer **Gilbert Adrian,** 1928 Singer/songwriter **Don Gibson**, 1933 U.S. socialite **Lee Radziwill**, 1968 NHL defenseman **Brian Leetch**

March 4

1745 **Charles Dibdin:** British composer, actor, theatrical manager and writer. First attracted notice as a singer and began a stage career in 1762. Appeared in a popular series of one-man musical entertainments. Known for his seas songs. Wrote over 1,000 songs, including "Snug Little Island," "Poor Jack" and "Tom Bowling."

In every mess I finds a friend,/ In every port a wife.

1782 **Johann Rudolf Wyss:** Swiss folklorist and Professor of philosophy at Bern from 1806. Editor of his father Johann David Wyss's *Swiss Family Robinson*, which has been translated into many languages.

I want to see my sons strong, both morally and physically... That means ... brave to do what is good and right, and to hate evil, and strong to work, hunt, and provide for themselves and others, and to fight if necessary.

1880 **Channing Pollock:** American drama critic, editor, lecturer, broadcaster and dramatist. Dramatic critic for the *Washington Post, Washington Times, The Smart Set* and *The Green Book*. Wrote 30 plays, including *Such a Little Queen, Roads to Destin, The Fool* and *Mr. Moneypenny*. Also wrote the song, "My Man," made famous by Fanny Brice.

A critic is a legless man who teaches running.

1888 **Knute Rockne:** Legendary Norwegian-born American football player and coach. Changed the emphasis of football on sheer physical brawn to one of pace, elusiveness and ball handling. Dominated College football with a career record at Notre Dame of 105–12–5 in 13 years. His teams won three consensus national championships (1924, 1929, and 1930). Famed for the development of the "Fighting Irish" and the "Four Horsemen." Killed in plane crash (1931).

Show me a good and gracious loser and I'll show you a failure.

1889 **Pearl White:** Extremely popular American silent film actress, best known for her roles in long running serialized melodramas, such as *The Perils of Pauline, The Exploits of Elaine, and The Black Secret.* Gained a tremendous reputation in these "cliffhangers," in which each chapter of the serial ended with our heroine in deadly danger — a successful ploy to get audiences to come back the next week to learn the outcome.

But you know, work that interests us and that we thoroughly enjoy is never drudgery.

1901 **Charles Goren:** American bridge master, writer and advocate. Published *Winning Bridge Made Easy*, the first of his many books on playing bridge in 1936. Developed a high card count system as an improvement over the existing system of counting *honor tricks*. First professional card player to be featured on the cover of *Time* magazine.

I remember so many people who all but live for bridge. Who would almost have curled up and withered away if they hadn't been able to play. Most of them found it difficult to even express themselves in non-bridge terms away from the table.

1904 **George Gamow:** Russian/U.S. physicist and cosmologist. Developed the first successful explanation of the behavior of radioactive elements. Working with Edward Teller, he developed a theory of the internal structure of red giant stars. Proposed theories of genetic-code structure that were later found to be correct. Wrote popularizations of science, including *One, Two, Three ... Infinity*.

Which is more useful, the Sun or the Moon? The Moon is more useful since it gives us light during the night, when it is dark; whereas the Sun shines only in the daytime, when it is light anyway.

1913 **John Garfield:** Born **Julius Garfinkle**. Intense American stage and film actor. His characters were most often what he was, a cynical, defiant young man from the wrong side of the tracks. Forerunner of James Dean, Marlon Brando and Paul Newman. Oscar nominated for *Four Daughters* and *Body and Soul*. His career abruptly came to an end in the early 1950s as the result of the House Un-American Activities Committee investigation. Not accused of any crimes, merely being suspected of left-wing sympathies was enough to get him blackballed for refusing to name friends as Communists. Friends said this was the cause of the heart attack that took his life in 1952.

Hollywood dangles a fortune at you and you get softened. Money seeps through. You begin to step up the pace for more money. Before you know it, you're rich and a failure.

1927 **Robert Orben:** American comedy writer. Author of 47 books of humor: *Encyclopedia of Patter, Laugh Package, Screamline Comedy* and *Speaker's Handbook of Humor*. Wrote monologues for the *Jack Parr Show* and the *Red Skelton Show* and gags for Dick Gregory. Became a speechwriter for President Gerald Ford and Director of the White House Speechwriting Department.

A vacation is having nothing to do and all day to do it in.

1928 **Alan Sillitoe:** English writer and novelist. Wrote angry accounts of working-class life, which he had experienced as a factory worker from the time he was 14. His first volume of verse: *Without Beer or Bread.* Novels: *Saturday Night and Sunday Morning* and *The Loneliness of the Long-Distance Runner*.

He felt a lack of security. No place existed in all the world that could be called safe, and he knew for the first time in his life that there had never been any such thing as safety, and never would be, the difference being that now he knew it as a fact, whereas before it was a natural unconscious state.

1932 **Miriam Makeba:** South African-born American singer. Leading singer of African-jazz music. Hit: "Pata Pata." Developed an internationally following and played a vital role in introducing the sounds and rhythms of traditional African music to the West. Among her five husbands were South African trumpeter Hugh Masekela and Black Nationalist Stokely Carmichael.

There are three things I was born with in this world, and there are three things I will have until the day I die: hope, determination and song.

1936 **Jim Clark:** Gentlemanly Scottish auto racer. Scottish National Speed Champion (1958–9). Two-time Formula One world champion (1963, 1965). Won

Indy 500 (1965). In all he won 25 Grand Prix. Killed in a car crash (1968) during a Formula 2 race in Germany.

When you are a racer, there isn't time to worry about the dangers.

OTHERS: 1394 Sponsor of Portuguese voyages of discovery **Prince Henry the Navigator**, 1678 Venetian violin virtuoso/composer **Antonio Vivaldi**, 1754 Smallpox vaccine pioneer physician **Benjamin Waterhouse**, 1835 Italian astronomer **Giovanni Schiaparelli**, 1909 Built Empire State Building **Harry B. Helmsley**, 1918 U.S. tennis pro **Margaret Osborne DuPont**, 1934 U.S. singer/actress **Barbara McNair**, 1937 Jazz bassist **Ron Carter**, 1941 U.S. film director **Adrian Lynn**, 1942 U.S. baseball player **Willie Stargell**, 1944 R&B singer/guitarist **Bobby Womack**, 1945 Swiss singer/children book writer **Dieter Meier**, 1951 U.S. violinist **Eugene Fodor**, 1961 U.S. boxer **Ray "Boom Boom" Mancini**

March 5

1133 **Henry II:** Known as **Henry of Anjou.** Duke of Normandy. Gained vast territories in France by marrying **Eleanor of Aquitaine**. Invaded England and to settle the war he was named heir to the throne. King of England (1154–89). One of the most powerful and respected monarchs. Driven from the throne by his son Richard the Lionheart, who allied with Philip II of France. Had a falling out with his close friend Thomas à Becket whom he had appointed his chancellor archbishop. They clashed over clerical privileges. In a rage Henry uttered the words that four knights used as a pretext to murder Becket in his cathedral.

Who will free me from this turbulent priest?

1512 **Gerardus Mercator [Gerhard Kremer]:** Flemish cartographer, skilled engraver, calligrapher, and scientific-instrument maker. Perfected what is known as the Mercator projection, in which parallels and meridians on a globe are represented by straight lines on a map spaced so as to produce at any point an accurate ratio of latitude to longitude. Coined the term "atlas."

I began to have doubts about the truth of all philosophers

1639 **Charles Sedley:** English poet, dramatist, courtier, wit, and Member of Parliament. Prominent member of the group of court wits called "the merry gang." Best known works: *Bellamira*, *The Grumbler* and *The Mulberry Garden*.

She deceiving, I believing; what need lovers wish for more?

1870 **Frank Norris:** American novelist and journalist. Known for his naturalistic depictions of life in the U.S. On the staff of "The Wave," San Francisco, for whom he covered the Spanish-American War, *McClure's Magazine* and *Doubleday Page*. Wrote *Moran of the Lady Letty*, *McTeague*, The *Octopus* and *The Pit*.

The People have a right to the Truth as they have a right to life, liberty and the pursuit of happiness.

1879 **William Henry Beveridge:** Indian-born English economist and social reformer. Had a lifelong interest in the problem of unemployment. Helped shape Great Britain's post–World War II Welfare State policies and institutions through Social Insurance and Allied Services. Books: *Full Employment in a Free Society* and *Pillars of Security*.

Scratch a pessimist and you find often a defender of privilege.

1887 **Heitor Villa-Lobos:** Brazilian composer and music educator. Proponent of Brazilian folk music. Wrote more than 1400 works including: "Bachianas Brasileiras" and "Choros." Founded the Ministry of Education Conservatory and Brazilian Academy of Music.

A truly creative musician is capable of producing from his own imagination, melodies that are more authentic than folklore itself.

1891 **Chic Johnson: Harold Ogden Johnson.** American comic. Former ragtime pianist. In 1914 teamed with Ole Olson in a popular vaudeville comedy act. Their biggest success was *Hellzapoppin*, a mad, nearly surrealistic film version of their Broadway hit.

And may you laugh as long as you live.

1897 **Soong Mei-Ling [Madame Chiang Kai-Shek]:** Wife of Chiang Kai-Shek, Sister-in-law of Sun Yat-Sen. She accompanied her husband to Taiwan and publicized his cause in the West. She was very popular in the U.S.

We write our own destiny; we become what we do.

1908 Sir **Rex Harrison:** Born **Reginald Carey Harrison**. English stage and film actor. Nicknamed "Sexy Rexy." An adroit master of "black-tie" comedy. Marvelous both on stage and screen as Prof. Henry Higgins in *My Fair Lady*, for which he won both a Tony and an Oscar. Other films: *Blithe Spirit*, *The Rake's Progress*, *The Ghost and Mrs. Muir* and *Doctor Doolittle*. Married six times, including actresses Lilli Palmer, Kay Kendall and Rachel Roberts.

Tomorrow is just a fiction of today.

1922 **Pier Paolo Pasolini:** Italian director, screenwriter, and novelist. His films and novels reveal a compassion for the proletariat of the slums motivated by a combination of influences, a commitment to Marxism and a deeply felt religiosity. Clashed with the Italian authorities and the church over the sexual, violent and anti-establishment content of his works. Films: *Teroma*, *The Gospel According to St. Matthew*, *Mama Roma*, *Accatone!* (from his own novel), *The Canterbury Tales* and *Salo—The 120 Days of Sodom*. In 1975 he was bludgeoned to death by a 17-year-old youth who claimed he had made homosexual advances.

It is through the spirit of television that the essence of the new power clearly shows itself.

1931 **Barry Tuckwell:** Australian French horn player. Joined the Melbourne Symphony Orchestra at age 15. Settled in England. Played successively with The Scottish Symphony, the Halle and Bournemouth Symphony and principal horn player with the London Symphony for 13 years. Resigned to pursue a solo career. Most recorded horn player in history, winning three Grammy awards.

The (French) horn is perhaps the least efficient instrument of the brass family, but it produces the most beautiful sound of all.

1955 **Penn Jillette:** U.S. comic magician and showman. He and his partner Teller present magic as an openly acknowledged trick rather than the result of some mysterious power. Standing 6'6" Penn towers over Teller who is 5'9". Penn does all the talking, Teller never speaks.

My favorite thing about the Internet is that you get to go into the private world of real creeps without having to smell them.

OTHERS: 1324 King of Scotland **David II (David Bruce)**, 1326 King of Hungary **Louis I the Great**, 1575 English inventor of the slide rule **William Oughtred**, 1637 Dutch painter/invented the fire extinguisher **John van der Heyden**, 1658 French colonial governor of America **Antoine de la Mothe Cadillac**, 1733 Italian dancer/choreographer **Vincenzo Galeotti**, 1824 U.S. founder of American Public Health Association **Elisha Harris**, 1824 U.S. lithographer, worked with Nathaniel Currier **James Merritt Ives**, 1852 Irish playwright **Lady Isabella Gregory**, 1853 U.S. painter/illustrator **Howard Pyle**, 1893 U.S. Water Treatment businessman **Emmett J. Culligan**, 1958 English singer **Andy Gibb**, 1975 U.S. model **Niki Taylor**

March 6

1475 **Michelangelo:** Born **Michelangelo di Ludovico Buonarroti-Simoni.** Tuscany-born sculptor, painter, architect and poet. Greatest figure of the Renaissance and one of the most influential artists of all time. Sculpting: *Pietà*, *David* and *Moses*. Appointed architect to continue the building of St. Peter's after Donato Bramante, who died in 1514. Took 4½ years to single-handily paint his masterpiece on ceiling of Sistine Chapel (1508–12), and *Last Judgment* on end wall (1542). His statues for the tomb of the Medici family in Florence reveal a powerful imagination and superb technical skill.

The more the marble wastes, the more the statue grows.

1483 **Francesco Guicciardini:** Italian historian and diplomat. Wrote *Storia d'Italia*, a dispassionate monument of Italian historiography.

Advice is less necessary to the wise than to fools; but the wise derive most advantage from it.

1619 **Savinien Cyrano de Bergerac:** French soldier, satirist and dramatist. Studied with the philosopher Pierre Gassendi. Wrote plays and fantastical works combining science-fantasy with political satire. He became the basis of many romantic legends, including Edmond Rostand's play *Cyrano de Bergerac*, in which he was portrayed as a gallant and brilliant but shy and ugly lover with a remarkably large nose. He did in fact have a remarkably large nose.

A large nose is the mark of a witty, courteous, affable, generous and liberal man.

1806 **Elizabeth Barrett Browning:** English poet. Wife of Robert Browning. Her father was opposed to his children marrying so she eloped when she was 40 and he was 33. Addicted to opium because of a chronic spinal ailment. Works: *Sonnets from the Portuguese*, *The Seraphim and Other Poems* and *Poems Before Congress.*

Let no one till his death/ Be called unhappy. Measure not the work,/ Until the day's out and the labor done.

1831 **Philip Sheridan:** Union army general. Known as "Little Phil" because of his size. Commanded Army of the Shenandoah (1864–65). Made the famous ride to Cedar Creek, turning a Union defeat into a great victory. Cut off Robert E. Lee's line of retreat at Appomattox. Grant said he ranked Sheridan with Napoleon, Frederick and the great commanders of history. Sheridan's assessment of his assignment as a young officer:

If I owned Texas and Hell, I would rent out Texas and live in Hell.

1885 **Ring Lardner:** American reporter, sportswriter, and columnist prior to publishing fiction. Wrote popular comic stories about a baseball player, collected in *You Know Me, Al.* A master of the narrative style and the use of memorable lines such as: *"Are you lost, daddy?" I asked tenderly, "Shut up," he explained* and *They gave each other a smile with a future in it.*

A good many young writers make the mistake of enclosing a stamped, self-addressed envelope, big enough for the manuscript to come back in. This is too much of a temptation to the editor.

1906 **Stanisław Jerzy Lec:** Polish writer, poet, satirist, and aphorist. Imprisoned in a Nazi concentration camp during World War II, he escaped in 1943 wearing a German uniform. Reached Warsaw, where he joined the resistance movement. Works: *Barwy*, *Spacer Cynika*, and *List Gonczy.*

The only fool bigger than a person who knows it all is the person who argues with him.

1917 **Will Eisner:** Acclaimed American comics writer, artist, and entrepreneur. Created a highly influential series *The Spirit.* Founded a cartoon studio which developed comics to serve and educational purpose. Established the graphic novel as a form of literature with his book *A Contract with God, and Other Tenement Stories.*

I've spent my whole life working in a medium that was regarded with contempt largely because of historical reasons.

1920 **Roger Price:** American publisher and comedy writer. Creator of "Doodles," which became a craze and launched the 1954 TV show of the same name. Price collaborated with Leonard Stern on the creation of Mad Libs. Together they founded Price-Stern-Sloan Publishers. Price also wrote about his plans to form a new and revolutionary political party, called the "I'm for Me First"–party.

Democracy demands that all of its citizens begin the race even. Egalitarianism insists that they all finish first.

1921 **Gabriel García Márquez:** Major Latin-American novelist and short-story writer. Born in Columbia, he worked many years as a journalist in Latin American and European cities. Also was a screenwriter and publicist, before settling in Mexico. His writing style is known as *Magic Realism*. Novels: *One Hundred Years of Solitude*, *Chronicle of a Death Foretold* and *The General in His Labyrinth*. His collections of short stories include *No One Writes to the Colonel* and *Leaf Storm*. Nobel Prize for literature in 1982.

It is not true that people stop pursuing dreams because they grow old, they grow old because they stop pursuing dreams.

1924 **Sarah Caldwell:** American opera conductor and opera company director. Headed Boston University's opera workshop. Established the Opera Company of Boston, specializing in contemporary music. Became the first female conductor of the Metropolitan Opera. Received the National Medal of Arts in 1996.

If you can sell green toothpaste in this country, you can sell opera.

1926 **Alan Greenspan:** American economist and government official. Served as chairman of the president's Council of Economic Affairs under President Ford. Long-time chairman of the Federal Reserve System, having been appointed to the post by President Reagan. Controller of the nation's money. Saw it as his obligation to control inflation by controlling the discount rate.

If I seem unduly clear to you, you must have misunderstood what I said.

OTHERS: 1459 German banker/merchant **Jacob Fugger**, 1698 Dutch theologist/philologist **John Alberti**, 1765 Dutch agronomist **Jan Kops**, 1870 Austrian composer **Oscar Strauss**, 1898 NFL coach/team owner **Jimmy Conzelman**, 1898 Dutch soprano **Jo Vincent**, 1900 300 game winner baseball pitcher **Robert "Lefty" Grove**, 1903 U.S. platform diver **Elizabeth Pinkston Becker**, 1906 U.S. comedian/actor **Lou Costello**, 1909 President of Nigeria **Obafemi Awolowo**, 1923 TV host/actor **Ed McMahon**, 1927 U.S. astronaut **Gordon Cooper**, 1935 Irish 1500 meter runner **Ronnie Delaney**, 1937 U.S. Multimillionaire **Ivan Boesky**, 1937 Soviet cosmonaut **Valentina Tereshkova**

March 7

1671 **Robert Roy MacGregor:** Usually known simply as **Rob Roy**. His doomed attempts to drive the British troops out of Highland Scotland made him a legendary Scottish hero, seen as an outlaw and terrorist by the British. On the run for years with a price on his head for High Treason, he was eventually pardoned by King George I, and died in his bed at age 63. As he lay dying, he was informed that an old enemy had come to see him. Rob Roy armed himself, saying:

Never let it be said that any enemy of MacGregor ever saw him defenseless and unarmed.

1792 Sir **John Frederick William Herschel:** British astronomer and chemist from a family of astronomers. His father William discovered Uranus and his aunt Caroline carried out many of her brother's calculations and discovered three nebulae and eight comets. John journeyed to the Southern Hemisphere to survey the stars there and recorded 68,948 stars. Also a contributor to the development of photography.

Self-respect is the cornerstone of all virtue.

1844 **Anthony Comstock:** American reformer. Agitated against abortion and pornography. Founded the Society for the Prevention of Vice. As an agent for the U.S. Post Office, he led spectacular raids on publishers and vendors.

I believe that there is a devil. Those who disagree with me in this may translate my language. All I ask is that they admit the vital truth on which I insist. Let my language be considered symbolical, provided the evils I denounce are regarded as diabolical.

1849 **Luther Burbank:** American botanist, naturalist and horticulturist. Pioneer in improving food plants through grafting and hybridization. Introduced over six hundred varieties of plants to America, many of which form the basis of the fruit industries. Developed new potato, new varieties of plums and berries, and new flowers.

Men should stop fighting among themselves and start fighting insects.

1850 **Tomáš Masaryk:** Czech statesman, philosopher, teacher and patriot. Taught philosophy at the Czech University of Prague and wrote on the Czech Reformation. At the Versailles Peace Conference after World War I, he negotiated the inclusion of the liberation of the future Czechoslovakia as one of Wilson's "14 points." Called "the Father of Czechoslovakia." Chief founder and first president of Czechoslovak Republic (1918–35). Instituted extensive land reform and tried to reconcile church and state.

Dictators always look good until the last minute.

1872 **Piet Mondrian:** Dutch painter. Broke away form the prevailing Dutch tradition of painting landscapes and still-lifes. His mature style resulted in "Neoplasticism," a purely objective vision of reality, based on simplest harmonies of straight line, right angle, and the primary colors. Example: *Composition in Yellow and Blue*.

The position of the artist is humble. He is essentially a channel.

1875 **Maurice Ravel:** French composer for the piano and ballet. Master of orchestral composition. Known for Impressionist style. Composed scintillating and dynamic music. Made exquisite use of wind instruments and unusual percussion effects. Works include "Daphnis et Chloe," "La Valse" and "Bolero." The latter played an important role in the movie *10*.

Music, I feel must be emotional first and intellectual second.

1888 **William L. Laurence:** Lithuanian-born American journalist. Science writer for New York Times. Books: *Dawn Over Zero: The Story of the Atomic Bomb* and *New Frontiers of Science*. Pulitzer Prize for reporting (1937, 1946). Translator and adapter of Maxim Gorky's *At the Bottom* and Leonid Andreyev's *Devil in the Mind.*

And just at that instance there rose from the bowels of the earth a light not of this world, the light of many suns in one.

1904 **Richard Heydrich:** German Nazi official. Heinrich Himmler's chief deputy. Noted for his ruthlessness against "enemies of the state." Organized mass executions in German-occupied territories. Known as "the Hangman." While serving as Deputy Administrator of Bohemia and Moravia he was assassinated by Czech patriots. In retaliation the Nazis demolished the village of Lidice and executed its male population and send its women and children to concentration camps.

Women and children are Jews too.

1909 **Anna Magnani:** Earthy Italian actress of international films. Considered the greatest Italian star of her time. After playing a number of minor roles, she made her mark in Roberto Rossellini's *Rome, Open City.* Academy Award for Best Actress for *The Rose Tattoo*. Nominated for *Wild Is the Wind*. Later did much of her work on the Italian stage and TV.

Great passions don't exist; they are liar's fantasies. What do exist are little loves that may last for a short or longer while.

1930 **Anthony Armstrong-Jones:** Earl of Snowden. English photographer, known for his celebrity photographs. Ex-husband of Britain's Princess Margaret.

I have learned only two things are necessary to keep one's wife happy. First, let her think she is having her own way. Second, let her have it.

1938 **Janet Guthrie:** American motor racing driver. In 1976 she became the first woman to race in a NASCAR Winston Cub event. First woman to qualify and race at the Indianapolis 500 (1977). Placed ninth at Indy (1978). Member of the International Women's Sports Hall of Fame. When her strength for the sport was questioned, she observed:

You drive the car, you don't carry it.

OTHERS: 1602 Japanese painter **Kano Tanju**, 1659 English composer **Henry Purcell**, 1693 Italian Pope **Clement XIII**, 1715 German lyric poet **Ewald Christian von Kleist**, 1762 Director-general of the East Indies Company **Sebastiaan C. Nederburgh**, 1799 Czech poet, writer of national anthem **Frantisek L. Celakovsky**, 1841 U.S. newspaper publisher **William Rockhill Nelson**, 1904 Norwegian speed skater **Ivar Ballangrud**, 1934 Weather forecaster **Willard Scott**, 1940 German student leader **Rudi Dutschke**, 1942 TV evangelist **Tammy Faye Bakker**, 1942 CEO Walt Disney Studios **Michael Eisner**, 1950 NFL running back **Franco Harris,** 1960 Czech tennis player **Ivan Lendl**

March 8

1788 **William Hamilton:** Scottish metaphysician and teacher. Exerted a remarkable influence over the thought of the younger generation in Scotland. Main work, *Lectures on Metaphysics and Logic*, was published posthumously. Not to be confused with Irish mathematician William Rowan Hamilton.

Truth, like a torch, the more it's shook it shines.

1799 **Simon Cameron:** American newspaper owner, editor, and political boss. U.S. Senator from Pennsylvania. (1845–49, 1857–61, 1867–77) Helped secure the nomination of Abraham Lincoln. President Lincoln appointed him Secretary of War in 1861 but he was dismissed for showing favoritism in awarding army contracts. Made Minister plenipotentiary to Russia in 1862.

An honest politician is one who, when he is bought, stays bought.

1841 **Oliver Wendell Holmes, Jr.**: Foremost American jurist of his time. Son of the celebrated author of the same name. Served in the Civil War and took his law degree from Harvard, admitted to the bar in 1867. Appointed to U.S. Supreme Court (1902–32) by President Theodore Roosevelt. Noted for the elegance of his written opinions. Known as "The Great Dissenter" because of his dissents on anti-trust, labor law, and First and Fourth Amendment cases.

Any two philosophers can tell each other all they know in two hours.

1859 **Kenneth Grahame:** Scottish banker, essayist, and author. Fame rests on the children's classic *The Wind in the Willow*, with its quaint riverside characters, *Rat, Mole, Badger* and *Toad*. The book was dramatized by A.A. Milne as *Toad of Toad Hall*, which became a popular play for Christmas-tide presentations.

As a rule, indeed, grown-up people are fairly correct on matters of fact; it is in the higher gift of imagination that they are so sadly to seek.

1888 **Stuart Chase:** American author, economist and engineer trained at MIT. Originator of the expression "New Deal," which became identified with Franklin D. Roosevelt's economic programs. Wrote *The Economy of Abundance, The Tragedy of Waste, A New Deal, The Tyranny of Words* and *The Proper Study of Mankind.*

Democracy ... is a condition where people believe that other people are as good as they are.

1890 **Gene Fowler:** American journalist, biographer and playwright. Started writing for the Denver Republican in 1912 but soon moved to the Rocky Mountain News where as city editor, he kept a pistol loaded with blanks on his desk to keep sleepy reporters alert. In 1918, Fowler was induced to try his luck in New York by Damon Runyan, who was impressed with his writing. Fowler wrote several works that were later filmed, including *The Great Mouthpiece, Father Goose,* and *Beau James* and an outstanding biography of one of his drinking buddies, John Barrymore, *Goodnight Sweet Prince.*

The best way to become a successful writer is to read good writing, remember it, and then forget where you remembered it from.

1890 **George M. Humphrey:** American lawyer, industrialist and statesman. General Counsel and then partner of the steel manufacturer M.A. Hanna and Company, an association that lasted 35 years. President Eisenhower appointed him U.S. Secretary of the Treasury (1953–57). He was instrumental in writing and presenting to the Congress an overall revision of the tax structure. Board chairman of the National Steel Corporation. Believed in the trickle-down theory of economics.

It's a terribly hard job to spend a billion dollars and get your money's worth.

1899 **Eric Linklater:** Scottish historical writer of 20 novels, short stories, autobiography, travel writing, and military history. Gained world fame with his cosmopolitan *Juan in America*, which was criticized in the U.S. for not showing enough respect for the country and its institutions and the comedy *Private Angelo*. Other works: *A Dragon Laughed and Other Poems, A Spell for Old Bones, A Year of Space*, and *The Campaign in Italy*.

All I've got against golf is it takes you so far from the clubhouse.

1900 **Howard Aiken:** American computer engineer who designed the Mark I computer, built to his specifications by IBM. In January 1944, the machine was transferred to the Cruft Laboratory at Harvard. It stood 8 feet high, 51 feet long and 2 feet wide. It weighed five tons and consisted of some 760,000 parts, including 2,000 counter wheels, 3,300 relay components, and 530 miles of wire. It made three calculations per second, a snails pace compared to today's simplest digital calculators, but amazing speed at the time.

Don't worry about people stealing your ideas. If you're ideas are any good, you'll have to ram them down people's throats.

1909 **Claire Trevor:** American. stage and screen actress. Not a classical beauty, she often played cynical, tough girls with hearts-of-gold. Oscar nominated for Best Supporting Actress for *Dead End* and for *The High and the Mighty*, winning the award for *Key Largo*. Other films: *Stagecoach, Murder, My Sweet*, and *Marjorie Morningstar*.

What a holler would ensue if people had to pay the minister as much to marry them as they have to pay a lawyer to get them a divorce.

1939 **Jim Bouton:** American baseball player, sportscaster and author. As a pitcher with the New York Yankees. Wrote a controversial best-selling book *Ball Four* about his and his teammates experiences and activities, upsetting the players and their wives.

Baseball players are smarter than football players. How often do you see a baseball team penalized for too many men on the field?

1943 **Lynn Redgrave:** Tall (5'10") brash English actress. Daughter of Sir Michael Redgrave and sister of Vanessa Redgrave. Oscar nominee for best actress in *Georgy Girl*, playing a plump ugly duckling. Having shed dozens of pounds in the 1980s she became a spokeswoman for a weight-loss program. Co-hosted NBC's syndicated talk show "Not for Women Only." Fired from the TV series "House Calls" for breastfeeding her baby on the set. Appeared on Broadway in a one-woman show, *Shakespeare for My Father*.

God always has another custard pie up his sleeve.

OTHERS: 1495 Portuguese saint/founder of the Brothers of Mercy **Juan de Dios**, 1714 German composer **Carl Philipp Emanuel Bach**, 1828 Helped create modern plastic surgery **Karl Ferdinand von Gräfe**, 1862 U.S. Recreational pioneer **Joseph Lee**, 1865 U.S. printer/type designer **Frederick William Goudy**, 1886 Nobel Prize winning chemist **Edward Kendall**, 1902 U.S. actress **Louise Beavers**, 1920 Scottish-born actress **Eileen Herlie**, 1921 U.S. dancer **Cyd Charisse**, 1934 Australian cinematographer **Ron Taylor**, 1936 Hungarian jazz pianist **Gabor Szabo**, 1938 U.S. country singer **George DeWitt**, 1939 Welsh Opera tenor **Robert Tear**, 1945 Pianist **Keith Jarrett**, 1946 U.S. lyricist **Carol Bayer Sager**

March 9

1454 **Amerigo Vespucci [Americus Vespucius]:** Italian-Spanish navigator and explorer of the new world. Helped outfit the ships for Christopher Columbus' expeditions. Took part in as navigator in expeditions that probably discovered the mouth of the Amazon River. The terms America and New World were first used to describe the lands he visited.

Those new regions which we found and explored with the fleet ... we may rightly call a New World ... a continent more densely people and abounding in animals than our Europe or Asia or Africa; and in addition, a climate milder than in any other region known to us.

1763 **William Cobbett:** English essayist, journalist, radical politician and agriculturist. Champion of the poor. His writings embody the history of the common people between the 18th century revolutions and the dawn of the Victorian era. Works: "Rural Rides" and "History of the Reformation."

To be poor and independent is very nearly an impossibility.

1824 **A. Leland Stanford:** U.S. financier, entrepreneur, and philanthropist. President and director, Central Pacific railroad (1863–93). California governor (1861–63). U.S. senator (1885–93). Played a major role in California railroad development. One of the builders of the first transcontinental railroad in the U.S. He and his wife Jane founded Stanford University (1885) in memory of his son.

The advantages of wealth are greatly exaggerated.

1881 **Ernest Bevin:** English union leader and politician. Became head of the Dockers' union, which he merged with other unions to create the largest trade union in the world, the Transport and General Worker's Union. As minister of labor (1940–45), mobilized manpower for World War II. Foreign minister (1945–51). Helped lay the basis for NATO.

There has never been a war yet which if the facts had been put calmly before the ordinary folks, could not have been prevented. The common man is the great protection against war.

1890 **Vyacheslav Molotov:** Soviet political leader. Staunch supporter of Stalin. Served as Prime Minister, and Foreign Minister. Negotiated the German-Soviet non–Aggression Pact. During World War II ordered the production of crude bottle bombs later called "Molotov cocktails." Dismissed by Nikita Khrushchev, Molotov joined an unsuccessful effort to overthrow the Soviet leader. Stripped of his party offices, he was expelled from the Communist Party. Speaking of Khrushchev, Molotov noted:

Khrushchev was no accident. We are primarily a peasant country.

1892 **Victoria "Vita" Sackville-West:** English poet and novelist. Maintained her marriage to diplomat Harold Nicolson despite both their homosexual affairs. Wrote *The Land, The Edwardians. All Passion Spent,* and *No Signposts in the Sea*. Passionate gardener, she wrote a weekly gardening column for the *Observor* for many years.

I have come to the conclusion, after many years of sometimes sad experience that you cannot come to any conclusion at all.

1906 **David Smith:** American sculptor and painter. His sculptures grew out of his abstract paintings. First U.S. artist to make welded metal sculpture. Made large yet seemingly weightless metal structures of abstract biomorphic and geometric forms. Killed in a car crash in 1965.

It's the season to scam, gate, bash and amokize every noun around Washington.

1910 **Samuel Barber:** U.S. composer, Had a lifelong association with Gian-Carlo Menotti. Barber's lyrical and neo-Romantic style appealed to the public. Works: "Adagio for Strings," "Hermit Songs" and the Pulitzer Prize winning opera "Vanessa" and another for a piano concerto.

I was meant to be a composer and will be I'm sure. Don't ask me to try to forget this unpleasant thing and go play football—please.

1918 **Mickey Spillane:** Originally **Frank Morrison**. American writer. His Mike Hammer, private-eye novels *I, the Jury* and *My Gun Is Quick*, emphasized sex and violence. At one time he was the best-selling author in the world. Earlier, he was a comic book writer who helped create *Captain Marvel and Captain America*.

A writer is someone who always sells. An author is one who writes a book that makes a big splash.

1923 **James Buckley:** U.S. Senator form the Conservative Party of New York State. Older brother of conservative writer William F. Buckley, Jr. Formerly vice president and director of the Catawba Corporation and afterwards a federal judge. Ran for re-election to the Senate as a Republican but was defeated by Daniel Patrick Moynihan. Also lost the election for Senator from Connecticut to Christopher Dodd.

We had to fight the connotations that come with hip-hop, like gangs, shootings and drugs... People don't see what a vibrant force there is in hip-hop.

1934 **Yuri Gagarin:** Soviet cosmonaut. Aboard Vostok I in April 1961, at age 27, became the first human to travel in space in a rocket-propelled five-ton space capsule, 187 miles above the Earth's surface. The flight, which took 1 hour and 29 minutes. made only one orbit. Killed at age 34 when his jet crashed during a routine training flight.

I could have gone on flying through space forever.

1943 **Bobby Fischer:** U.S. chess master. First American to hold world chess title, defeating Boris Spassky, 1972. Derived on his world title in 1975 after refusing to meet the Soviet challenger, Anatoly Karpov. Temperamental, controversial and immodest. Has often expressed his hatred for the U.S. and has remained abroad since violating U.S. sanctions against Yugoslavia in 1992.

I like the moment when I break a man's ego.

OTHERS: 1564 German astronomer **David Fabricius**, 1568 Italian prince/Jesuit saint **Aloysius "Luigi" van Gonzaga**, 1777 Polish painter/graphic artist **Alexander Orlowski**, 1791 1st surgeon to use ether **George Hayward**, 1905 English biographer/critic **Peter C. Quennell**, 1905 English poet/writer **Rex Warner**, 1910 Dutch writer/poet **Edward Hoornik**, 1915 One-armed major league outfielder **Pete Gray**, 1923 French fashion designer **André Courrèges**, 1926 Greek actress **Irene Papas**, 1933 Country singer **Lloyd Price**, 1935 Singer with Louie Prima band **Keely Smith**, 1943 U.S. singer **Mark Lindsay**, 1958 U.S. ballet dancer **Fernando Bujones,** 1959 OJ Simpson houseguest/witness **Kato Kaelin**

March 10

1503 **Ferdinand I:** Holy Roman Emperor (1558–64). Faced the threat of the encroachment into Europe of the Ottoman Empire led by Syleyman II, the Magnificent. As Emperor he separated the Habsburg domains into Spanish and Austrian parts. He also sought to revive Catholicism in Eastern Europe.

Let justice be done, though the world perish.

1772 **Friedrich von Schlegel:** German romantic poet and critic. With brother August Wilhelm von Schlegel founded the quarterly, *Athenäum*. Defined romantic poetry as "progressive universal poetry." Advocated free love in novel *Lucinde*. Published pioneering work on

Sanskrit and Indo-Germanic linguistics. Books: *Philosophy of History* and *History of Literature*.

The beginning and end of history are prophetic; they are no longer the object of pure history... The historian is a prophet in reverse.

1858 **Henry Watson Fowler:** English lexicographer and philologist. With brother F.G. Fowler wrote *The King's English* and *The Concise Oxford Dictionary of Current English*. H.W.'s major work was *A Dictionary of Modern English Usage*, an alphabetical listening of points of grammar, syntax, style, pronunciation and punctuation.

Prefer geniality to grammar.

1892 **Arthur Honegger:** French-born Swiss composer. Advocate of polytonality. Member of *Les Six*, a group of Parisian composers (the others, Milhaud, Poulenc, Auric, Durey and Tailleferre). Best known works: *Pacific 231, King David* and *Joan of Arc at the Stake*. Married the pianist-composer Andrée Vaurabourg, who often played piano parts in his works.

There is no doubt that the first requirement for a composer is to be dead.

1916 **James Herriot:** Pen name of **James Alfred Wight** a Scottish veterinarian and writer. At age 50, his wife convinced him to write down his collection of anecdotes. Best known for a series of books about his life as a vet, including *All Creatures Great and Small*, which were adapted for two films and a long-running TV series.

If having a soul means being able to feel love and loyalty and gratitude, then animals are better off than a lot of humans.

1918 **Heywood Hale Broun:** American sportswriter, television commentator and son of U.S. journalist Heywood Broun. Well-recognized figure on CBS, with a rust-colored droopy mustache and multicolored sports jackets. Covered the Masters Golf tournament wearing a Sherlock Holmes deerstalker hat and a cape. Once said her was content to tell of "those athletes who exist merely for the sun that shines on them." Speaking of his many callings, he said:

I'm either a Little League Renaissance man or simply a person who can't make up his mind.

1940 **Wayne Dyer:** Popular American psychologist and self-help guru. Author of *Your Erroneous Zones* and *Pulling Your Own Strings*. Affectionately called the "father of motivation" by his fans.

If you change the way you look at things, the things you look at change.

1940 **David Rabe:** American playwright. Made his reputation with *Sticks and Bones* and *The Basic Training of Pavlo Hummel*. Based on his experiences in Vietnam they deal with the horrors and absurdities of the military mind, as well as the tragic results of unquestioning adherence to dubious values. Other plays: In the *Boom Boom Room, Streamers* and *Hurlyburly*.

Nothing, not even writing, is as completely fulfilling as being successful in athletics.... Like a writer, an athlete knows what real pain is.

1946 **Jim Valvano:** American basketball coach Nicknamed "Jimmy V." Led North Carolina State University to an unexpected NCAA National Championship in 1983. Resigned from NCSU in 1990 because of NCAA rules violations. Became a broadcaster for ESPN and ABC. Before he died after a yearlong struggle with cancer, Valvano announced the formation of the "V Foundation," dedicated to finding a cure for cancer.

My father gave me the greatest gift anyone could give another person, he believed in me.

1947 **Avril Phaedra Douglas "Kim" Campbell:** Canadian politician. Earned a doctorate in Soviet Government at the London School of Economics. Practiced law in Vancouver. Member of Brian Mulroney's Cabinet as Justice Minister (1990–93) and then Defence Minister (1993). Nineteenth Prime Minister of Canada and the only woman to have led a national government in North America. Her tenure was brief as in the national elections, she and all but two of her Party's candidate lost their seats and the Liberal Party under Jean Chrétien took over.

A comparison between Madonna and me is a comparison between a strapless evening gown and a gownless evening strap.

1958 **Sharon Stone:** Sexy blonde American model, film actress and producer. Her fame primarily rests on her role in *Basic Instinct* as an underwearless writer and ice-pick murderer. Its sequel was made in 2005, with a similar plot and the lady still looking great. Other films: *Total Recall, Silver, Intersection* and *The Muse*.

Women might be able to fake orgasms. But men can fake whole relationships.

1983 **Carrie Underwood:** American country music singer. Winning artist on the fourth season of TV's *American Idol*. Multi-platinum selling recording artist. Voted the "World's Sexiest Vegetarian" by the animal-rights organization PETA.

Sometimes a girl's gotta have some chocolate

OTHERS: 1538 Duke of Norfolk, executed by Elizabeth I **Thomas Howard**, 1748 Scottish clergyman/mathematician **John Playfair**, 1771 German historian **George F. Creuzer**, 1787 English painter **William Etty**, 1839 U.S. concert organist **Dudley Buck**, 1867 U.S. sociologist/founder of Visiting Nurses **Lillian D. Wald**, 1873 German novelist **Jakob Wassermann**, 1888 Irish-born actor, **Barry Fitzgerald**, 1900 Talk show host **Sherman Billingsley**, 1903 Jazz cornet player **Bix Beiderbecke**, 1923 Football coach **Ara Parseghian**, 1928 Assassin of Martin Luther King Jr. **James Earl Ray**, 1940 U.S. actor **Chuck Norris**

March 11

1544 **Torquato Tasso:** Italian epic poet and dramatist. Last of the four eminent Italian poets of the Renaissance, including Petrarch, Aristo and Dante. Wrote romantic epic "Rinaldo" at 18. His masterpiece, "Gerusalemme Liberta" (*Jerusalem Delivered*), is the epic tale of the capture of Jerusalem during the first crusade. His work had great influence on English literature, notably that of Spenser, Milton, Dryden and Gray. Byron and Goethe both wrote works on his tragic life.

Any time that is not spent on love is wasted.

1730 **Robert Treat Paine:** American lawyer and merchant. Gained recognition as a prosecuting attorney in the murder trial of British soldiers involved in the Boston Massacre. A signer of the Declaration of Independence as a representative of Massachusetts. Served as speaker of the Massachusetts House of Representatives and as Attorney General. Ancestor of actor Treat Williams.

And ne'er shall the sons of Columbia be slaves,/ While the earth bears a plant or the sea rolls its waves.

1885 Sir **Malcolm Campbell:** At various times held the world's speed record on both land and water. At Bonneville Salt Flats in Utah he became the first person to drive an automobile in excess of 300 mph. His son, Donald Campbell was killed 30 years later trying to repeat his father's achievements.

The tires are scorching hot; in fact I burned my fingers on one.

1890 **Vannevar Bush:** American electrical engineer and administrator. In the late 1920s and 30s he and his students at MIT built the world's first analog computer (1925). It took up an entire 20 × 30 ft room. Helped found Raytheon Co. and served as president of the Carnegie Institute. Director of the U.S. Office of Scientific Research and Development, in which capacity, he helped organize the Manhattan Project, which developed fission bomb. As an advisor to President Franklin D. Roosevelt, he laid the groundwork for establishing the National Science Foundation.

It is a man's mission to learn to understand

1903 **Dorothy Schiff:** American publisher. First woman publisher in the U.S. Wealthy socialite who in 1939 used family money to purchase majority control of the *New York Post.* As owner, president and publisher for nearly 40 years, the Post became a crusading liberal newspaper, supporting unions and social welfare legislation. She sold the *Post* to Rupert Murdoch in 1976 for $31 million.

Taxes seem to me to be far less demoralizing than private charities. I am glad to be taxed because it is the least devastating way to meet social needs both for the underprivileged and the overprivileged.

1903 **Lawrence Welk:** American musician, bandleader, accordion player and TV impresario. Although many called his "Champagne Music" square and corny, he found great success and large audiences with his nationally televised *The Lawrence Welk Show* (1951–82), which featured talented clean-cut musicians, singers and dancers. His trademark was the count-off before each number, "A one, and a two..."

There are good days and there are bad days, and this is one of them.

1916 **Harold Wilson:** English Labor politician, statesman and economist. Prime minister (1964–70 and 1974–76). His government's economic plans were undermined by the balance-of-payments crisis. His government introduced a number of social reforms, including lowering the voting age to 18, liberalizing the laws on divorce, homosexuality and abortion and introducing comprehensive schooling. Abroad he was unsuccessful in an attempt to impose sanctions against supremacist Rhodesia.

A week is a long time in politics.

1926 **Ralph Abernathy:** African-American civil rights leader and clergyman. Succeeded Martin Luther King as president of the Southern Christian Leadership Conference, which they had founded. Together they organized the nonviolent 1955 Montgomery, Alabama bus boycott.

I'm sick and tired of black and white people of good intent giving aspirin to a society that is dying of a cancerous disease.

1931 **Rupert Murdoch:** Controversial Australian publisher and media entrepreneur. Founder and head of the News International Communications empire. Owned British and American newspapers, including *The Times* of London, *New York Post* and *Boston Herald.* Also owns film and TV companies and the publishing firm HarperCollins.

Newspapers don't change tastes. They reflect taste.

1934 **Sam Donaldson:** ABC news correspondent. Appears on "Prime Time Live since 1989." In 1977 he was assigned to cover the Carter administration a as ABC's Chief White House Correspondent. He became famous for shouting difficult questions in a booming voice over those of the rest of the White House Press Corps, even to passing presidents as they hurried to the Presidential helicopter.

The questions don't do the damage. Only the answers do.

1936 **Antonin Scalia:** American Supreme Court justice appointed by President Reagan. A prominent conservative and one of the most outspoken defenders of textualism in statutory interpretation and original intent in constitutional interpretation. Opposes judicial activism. Applies narrow interpretations of Acts of Congress while granting some leniency to state and local laws.

Mere factual innocence is no reason not to carry out a death sentence properly reached.

1952 **Douglas Adams:** Cult British comic radio dramatist, musician and author. A self-described "radical atheist." Best known work was *The Hitchhiker's Guide to the Galaxy*, which was a radio series, a book, a television series, a computer game, and a feature film.

He was a dreamer, a thinker, a speculative philosopher ... or, as his wife would have it, and idiot.

OTHERS: 1596 Book publisher **Isaac Elsevier**, 1726 French writer **Madame Louise-Florence d'Épinay**,

1796 U.S. clergyman/educator **Francis Wayland**, 1811 Co-discover of Neptune **Urbain Jean Joseph le Verrier**, 1819 English sugar producer **Henry Tate**, 1860 Architect New York Public Library **Thomas Hastings**, 1898 Stage and screen actress **Dorothy Gish**, 1907 German politician **Helmuth J. von Moltke**, 1910 German chemist **Robert H.G. Havermann**, 1921 U.S. radio commentator **Earl Nightingale**, 1926 English architect **Patricia Tindaole**, 1934 Greek medical genetics researcher **George Stamatoyannopoulos**, 1945 Vocalist/organist **Mark Stein**, 1950 U.S. director **Jerry Zucker**

March 12

1554 **Richard Hooker:** English theologian. Author of the eight volumes *Laws of Ecclesiastical Polity* (1593–97), which anticipates the common consent grounds for government of Locke and Rousseau. It is mainly due to his work that Anglican theology owes its tone and direction.

Change is not made without inconvenience, even from worse to better.

1672 Sir **Richard Steele:** Irish-born British essayist, dramatist and politician. Known for his writings in the periodicals *The Tatler* and *The Spectator*. His works are the beginning of the domestic novel. At his best in scenes of domestic felicity. Works: *The Christian Hero*, *The Tender Husband*, and *The Lying Lover*.

Reading is to the mind what exercise is to the body.

1685 Bishop **George Berkeley:** Influential Irish philosopher. Advanced the principle of subjective idealism. Published works included *Treatise Concerning the Principles of Human Knowledge*, *Three Dialogues between Hylas and Philonous*, and *The Analyst*, a critique of the foundations of science, which was very influential in the subsequent development of mathematics.

We have first raised a dust and then complain we cannot see.

1835 **Simon Newcomb:** Canadian-born American mathematician and one of the most distinguished astronomers of his time. Born in Nova Scotia. Moved to the U.S. for his schooling at Harvard University. Professor at the United States Naval Observatory. Measured the positions of the planets as an aid to navigation. Recalculated all the major astronomical constants.

Aerial flight is one of that class of problems with which men will never have to cope.

1858 **Adolph Simon Ochs:** American journalist and publisher of the *New York Times* (1896–1935). Through his policies and public spirit he brought it to a position of eminence among newspapers. In 1904, he moved the newspaper to a newly-built building on Longacre Square in Manhattan that the city renamed Times Square. On New Year's Eve 1904, Ochs had pyrotechnics illuminate his new building with a fireworks show.

If a newspaper prints a sex crime, it's smut, but when the* New York Times *prints it, it's a sociological study.

1860 **Gabriele D'Annunzio:** Italian poet, novelist, dramatist, daredevil and war hero. Had a controversial role in politics as a precursor of the fascist movement. Wrote articles and criticism for newspapers. Short stories collected under the general title *San Pantaleone*. Considered by some as a perverter of public morals, while to others he brought a new vitality to his work.

Limit to courage? There is no limit to courage.

1912 **Irving Layton:** Rumanian-born Canadian poet originally named **Israel Pincu Lazarovitch**. Known for his poems of protest against the social inequities he saw throughout the country. Shocked readers with his harsh, "un-poetic" images. Works: *The Bull Calf and Other Poems* and *The Darkening Fire: Selected Poems*. Nominated for the Nobel Prize for Literature.

Idealist: a cynic in the making.

1922 **Jack Kerouac:** American novelist and poet. Called himself a "jolly storyteller." His works *On the Road* and The *Subterraneans* epitomized what he named the "Beat Generation," a label he later regretted and repudiated. He said, "Beat means beatific, not beat up." His favorite means of writing was to wind a roll of paper in his typewriter and "write about 10 feet in a good day," without editing, because "Whatever you try to delete from a manuscript, that's what's most interesting to a doctor."

I don't know. I don't care. And it doesn't make any difference.

1922 **Lane Kirkland:** American labor union leader. Served as President of the AFL-CIO for over 16 years. Supported the Solidarity movement in Poland, which contributed to the decline of communism. Posthumously giver Poland's highest award, the Order of the White Eagle.

The only way to convert the heathen is to travel into the jungle.

1928 **Edward Albee:** American playwright. Leading exponent of the "Theater of the Absurd." Best known for *A Delicate Balance*, *The Zoo Story*, *The American Dream* and *Who's Afraid of Virginia Woolf?* The latter was filmed as an exhausting movie starring Elizabeth Taylor, Richard Burton, George Seagal and Sandy Dennis.

Sometimes it's necessary to go a long distance out of the way in order to come back a short distance correctly.

1932 **Andrew Young:** African-American political leader. Active in the civil rights movement, working with Martin Luther King and Ralph Abernethy in the Southern Christian Leadership Conference (1961–70). U.S. House of Representatives (1972–77) Ambassador to U.N. (1977–79), the first black to hold the post. Mayor of Atlanta (1982–92). Awarded French Legion of Honor (1982).

Influence is like a savings account. The less you use it, the more you've got.

1948 **James Taylor:** American singer, songwriter and guitarist. Singer of sensitive and gentle acoustic songs, many of which were contained in his popular album

Sweet Baby James. Was married to singer Carly Simon. Six-time Grammy winner. Song hits: "You've Got a Friend," "Handy Man," and "Don't Let Me Be Lonely Tonight."

Time will take your money, but money won't buy time.

OTHERS: 1479 Monarch of Florence **Giuliano de' Medici**, 1710 English composer of "Rule Britannia" **Thomas Augustine Arne**, 1788 French sculptor **Pierre J. David**, 1824 Prussian physicist **Gustav R. Kirchoff**, 1831 Automobile pioneer **Clement Studebaker**, 1832 Irish estate manager **Charles Boycott**, 1862 Us founder of Red Cross **Jane Delano**, 1889 English historian **Philip Guedalla**, 1910 Boxer **Tony "Two-Ton" Galento**, 1912 U.S. orchestra leader **Paul Weston**, 1923 U.S. astronaut **Wally Schirra**, 1931 "Little Rascals" actor **William "Buckwheat" Thomas**, 1946 U.S. singer/actress **Liza Minnelli**, 1949 TV reporter **Mary Alice Williams**, 1962 U.S. baseball player **Darryl Strawberry**

March 13

1733 **Joseph Priestley:** English chemist, philosopher and nonconformist clergyman. He and his family narrowly escaped an angry mob attacking their home because of their religious convictions and political views. Became the first great chemist in Great Britain. Study of gases resulted in discovery of ammonia, sulfur dioxide and oxygen. Wrote on theology, education, history, philosophy, politics, physics and physiology as well as chemistry.

In completing one discovery we never fail to get an imperfect knowledge of others of which we could have no idea before, so that we cannot solve one doubt without creating several new ones.

1855 **Percival Lowell:** Wealthy amateur American astronomer. Laid the groundwork for the discovery of the "planet" Pluto, 14 years after his death. Convinced that there were canals on Mars. Founded the Lowell Observatory in Flagstaff, Arizona. Published his findings of his 15 year study of Mars in three books: *Mars*, *Mars and Its Canals* and *Mars as the Abode of Life*.

Imagination is as vital to any advance in science as learning and precision are essential for starting points. Let me warn you to beware of two opposite errors: of letting your imagination soar unballasted by facts, but on the other hand, of shackling it so solidly that it loses all incentive to rise.

1884 Sir **Hugh Walpole:** New Zealand–born English novelist. Wrote short stories, criticisms, essays, travel books and plays. Novels: *Mr. Perrin and Mr. Traill*, *Jeremy*, *The Secret City*, *The Cathedral* and *The Herries Chronicle*.

The whole secret of life is to be interested in one thing profoundly and in a thousand other things well.

1886 **Jean Starr Untermeyer:** American poet and widely known for producing over fifty-six anthologies, including *Modern American Poetry*, *The Book of Living Verse*, *A Treasury of Great Humor* and *Fifty Modern American and British Poets*. His poems include "Growing Pains," "Dreams Out of Darkness" and "Job's Daughter." Also wrote or edited numerous books for children.

In bad times poets prophesy. They are dedicated to courage and their function, for one thing, is to relate the material world and the moral world, interpreted in no narrow sense.

1892 **Janet Flanner:** American journalist. *The New Yorker* correspondent for 50 years. Wrote "Letter from Paris," published under the name "Genêt," a pseudonym given her by Harold Ross. Her first political profile was of Hitler. Provided a vast record of French social, political and cultural events. Books: *Pétain, Men and Monuments* and *Paris Was Yesterday*.

The stench of human wreckage in which the Nazi regime finally sank down to defeat has been the most shocking fact of modern times.

1908 **Walter Annenberg:** Billionaire publisher and philanthropist. His biggest success and fortune came from the creation of *TV Guide*. His *The Philadelphia Inquirer* attacked Senator Joseph McCarthy at time most publications were afraid to do so. Named Ambassador to England in 1970.

I want to remind you that success in life is based on hard slogging. There will be periods when discouragement is great and upsetting, and the antidote for this is calmness and fortitude and a modest yet firm belief in your competence. Be sure that your priorities are in order so that you can proceed in a logical manner, and be ever mindful that nothing will take the place of persistence.

1911 **L. Ron Hubbard:** Originally **Lafayette Ronald Hubbard**. American religious leader and science fiction writer of books: *Slaves of Sleep*, *Fear*, *Final Blackout* and *Death's Deputy*. In 1950, formulated dianetics, a method of achieving mental and physical health, the basis of his religion Scientology. Related books: *Dianetics: The Modern Science of Mental Health* and *Science of Survival*.

A society in which women are taught anything but the management of a family and the creation of the future generation is a society which is on the way out.

1917 **Ina Ray Hutton:** U.S. singer, dancer, and bandleader. Although she could play no musical instrument, she led a very successful all-girl orchestra. She didn't "lead" her band; she sensuously weaved around the stage dressed in a form-fitting silver-lame gown. Tagged the "Blonde Bombshell of Rhythm."

I guess I saw all the men in America out front. Some of them tried to get backstage — some sent mash notes. But I kept the sex in saxophones.

1924 **Igor Youskevitch:** Ukrainian-born ballet dancer. Starred in American Ballet Theatre and the Ballet Russe de Monte Carlo. Master of classical style. Artistic director of the New York International Ballet Competition in 1990.

Dance, one of the oldest forms of artistic expression, requires only the human body for its realization.

1936 **Clarence "Ducky" Nash:** American voice actor, best known as the voice of Donald Duck for the Disney Studios. Also provided the voice of Daisy Duck and Donald's three nephews Huey, Dewey and Louie.

Words were written out for me phonetically. I learned to quack in French, Spanish, Portuguese, Japanese, Chinese and German.

1950 **William H. Macy:** American actor, director and teacher in theater, film and TV. Nominated for an Academy Award for his role in *Fargo*. Emmy winner both for the lead role and as co-writer of the made for TV film *Door to Door*. Married to *Desperate Housewives* Felicity Huffman.

Nobody became an actor because he had a good childhood.

1960 **Adam Clayton:** British bass player for the Irish rock band U2. Winner of the Best Bassist award in the Orville H. Gibson Guitar Award in both 2001 and 2002. Hits include: "Desire" and "With or Without You." Along with Bono, Clayton contributed to the 1984 African famine charity single "Do They Know It's Christmas?"

If you believe in a cause, you must be willing to put yourself on the line for that cause.

OTHERS: 1599 Dutch Jesuit **St. Johannes Berchmans**, 1696 French marshal **Louis, Duke de Richelieu**, 1741 Roman Catholic German emperor **Josef II**, 1770 English giant (weighed 739 lbs.) **Daniel Lambert**, 1781 German architect/painter **Karl F. Schinkel**, 1813 U.S. restaurateur **Lorenzo Delmonico**, 1872 American journalist **Oswald Garrison Villard**, 1886 Baseball Hall-of-famer **John "Home Run" Baker**, 1907 Pretender to the Portuguese throne **Dona Maria Pia de Bragança**, 1910 U.S. bandleader **Sammy Kaye**, 1913 British actress/singer **Tessie O'Shea**, 1916 Democratic congresswoman **Lindy Boggs**, 1955 U.S.S.R. pentathlete **Olga Rukavishnikova**, 1956 U.S. actress **Dana Delany**

March 14

1854 **Paul Ehrlich:** German bacteriologist. Famous for his experiments on the effects of various chemicals upon living tissue. Pioneer in haematology and chemotherapy. Developed a treatment for syphilis. Discovered "silver bullets," chemicals that act primarily on disease-causing organisms without harming healthy cells. Shared Nobel Prize for Physiology or Medicine (1908) with Ilya Mechnikov.

The first rule of intelligent tinkering is to save all the parts.

1854 **Thomas Riley Marshall:** American lawyer and politician. Served as popular Democratic Governor of Indiana (1909–13). Sponsored a broad program of social legislation. Served two terms as Woodrow Wilson's Vice-President (1913–21). Nationally known wit, he achieved fame for his remark as an aside during a U.S. Senate debate: "What this country needs is a really good five-cent cigar." Apparently the president didn't give him much to do.

Once there were two brothers: one ran away to sea, the other was elected Vice-President — and nothing was ever heard from either of them again.

1868 **Maksim Gorky [Aleksey Maksimovich Peshkov]:** Russian novelist, short-story writer and revolutionist. For his Bolshevik activities in the revolution of 1905 he was arrested, but public indignation forced his release. First great Russian proletarian author. Master of the short story. Depicted wretched lives of the lowest levels of Russian society. Helped develop the literary doctrine of Socialist Realism. Wrote *Chelkash, Foma Gordeyev, Mother,* and *The Lower Depths*.

You must write for children just as you do for adults, only better.

1877 **Edna Woolman Chase:** American editor-in-chief of Vogue magazine (1914–55). Organized first U.S. fashion show (1944). Hard-to-please autocrat, who noted, "My wastebasket is my strongest ally." Frankly snobbish she said, "We are reflecting the way of life of people with wealth and taste and social position." Mother of actress Ilka Chase.

Fashion can be bought. Style one must possess.

1879 **Albert Einstein:** Eminent German-born Swiss-American theoretical physicist. Formulated the general theory of relativity (1916), stemming from his attempt to reconcile the laws of mechanics with the laws of the electromagnetic field. Aware of the inadequacies of Newtonian mechanics, Einstein wrote several papers applying the special theory of relativity to mass and energy. In September 1905 he reported a remarkable consequence of his theory, namely that if a body emits a certain amount of energy, then the mass of that body must decrease by a proportionate amount. The relationship is expressed as the famous equation $E = MC^2$ (The energy content of a body is equal to the mass of the body times the speed of light squared.). He had developed an explanation of the fundamental problems about the nature of energy, matter, motion, time, and space. Awarded Nobel Prize for Physics (1921). Although a Pacifist, he was among a group of scientists to suggest that energy of split atoms could be used in bombs.

Science without religion is lame, religion without science is blind.

1899 **James Laver:** English writer and critic. Won the Newdigate Prize for Verse while at Oxford. Books of verse: *His Last Sebastian and Ladies' Mistakes*. Critical books of art: *French Painting and the 19th Century and Fragonard*. Also wrote on the history of English costume in works such as *Taste and Fashion*.

The same dress is indecent ten years before its time; daring one year before its time; chic (contemporarily seductive) in its time; dowdy five years after its time; hideous twenty years after its time; amusing thirty years after its time; romantic one hundred years after its time; beautiful one hundred and fifty years after its time.

1923 **Diane Arbus:** American photographer who rebelled against her work in conventional fashion photography. Sought to portray people "without masks." Achieved fame in the sixties with her studies of deprived classes, studies of social poses and "freaks." Depressed over a number of years, she took her own life in 1971.

A photograph is a secret about a secret. The more it tells you the less you know.

1925 **John Barrington Wain:** English novelist, poet and critic. His first four novels debunk the virtues of the postwar British. Works include: *Hurry on Down*, *Living in the Present*, *Weep Before God* and *The Pardoner's Tale*. *Professing Poetry* is a collection of lectures on contemporary poetry. *Edited Everyman's Book of English Verse*. Wrote biographies of Gerard Manley Hopkins and Samuel Johnson.

Poetry is to prose as dancing is to walking.

1928 **Frank Borman:** U.S. astronaut on Gemini 7 flight (1965), highlighted by the first rendezvous with Gemini 6A. Commander of the Apollo 8 flight, the first manned flight around moon (1968). Retired from NASA and the Air Force in 1970 to join Eastern Airlines. Became President and CEO (1975–76) and elected chairman of board (1976).

Exploration is really the essence of the human spirit.

1933 **Quincy Jones:** African-American composer, bandleader and music producer. Played trumpet with Lionel Hampton and became an arranger or Dizzy Gillespie and others. Has written film scores, including those for *The Pawnbroker*, *In Cold Blood*, *In the Heat of the Night* and *The Color Purple*. Founded Quest Productions and has produced enormously successful albums for many musicians. Among many others, he produced Michael Jackson's *Thriller* album, which sold 51 million copies. Jones used his influence to draw many major recording artists of the day into a studio to record "We Are the World," to raise money for the victim's of Ethiopia's famine. He taped a simple sign on the entrance to the studio that read, "Check Your Ego at the Door."

Jazz has always been a man telling the truth about himself.

1942 **Edward Tufte:** Professor emeritus of statistics, graphic design, and political economy at Yale University. Expert in the presentation of informational graphics, important to fields such as information design and visual literacy. Books: *The Visual Display of Quantitative Information*, *PowerPoint Is Evil* and *Beautiful Evidence*.

The commonality between science and art is in trying to see profoundly — to develop strategies of seeing and showing.

1947 **Billy Crystal:** American comedian and actor. Portrayed one of the first openly gay characters on U.S. TV in *Soap*. Member of *Saturday Night Live* cast. Famous for his tagline "You look marvelous!" Nominated for a Golden Globe for the romantic comedy *When Harry Met Sally*. With Robin Williams and Whoopi Goldberg hosts *Comedy Relief*, which raises money for the homeless. Hosted the Academy Awards broadcast 8 times. Other films: *Throw Momma From the Train* and *City Slickers*.

Women need a reason to have sex. Men just need a place.

OTHERS: 1681 German baroque composer **George Philipp Telemann**, 1755 French composer **Pierre-Louis Couperin**, 1782 U.S. congressman **Thomas Hart Benton**, 1804 Viennese violinist/composer **Johann Strauss the Elder**, 1820 Italian king **Victor Emmanuel II**, 1837 U.S. Library pioneer **Charles Ammi Cutter**, 1862 Norwegian physicist **Vilhelm F.K. Bjerknes**, 1864 U.S. railroad engineer **Casey Jones**, 1884 Dutch archaeologist **Albert Egges van Giffen**, 1903 Iranian Kurd leader **Molla Mustafa Barzani**, 1905 French sociologist **Raymond Aron**, 1919 U.S. novelist **Max Schulman**, 1922 U.S. orchestra leader **Les Baxter**, 1933 English actor **Michael Caine**, 1943 English actress **Rita Tushingham**

March 15

1767 **Andrew Jackson:** "Old Hickory." American Soldier, self-taught lawyer and planter. Seventh U.S. president (1829–37). First to be elected by a mass base of voters and to come from the West. Rewarded supporters by establishing the "Spoils System." Military hero at the Battle of New Orleans (1815). Accused of marrying an adulteress because at the time of their marriage his wife Rachel's first marriage had not yet been dissolved. He was wounded in a duel in 1805, in which his adversary was killed. As the bullet in Jackson's chest was too close to his heart to remove safely, he carried it for the rest of his life.

Any man worth his salt will stick up for what he believes is right, but it takes a slightly better man to acknowledge instantly and without reservation that he is in error.

1779 **William Lamb Melbourne:** Second Viscount. English statesman and prime minister (1834–41). Queen Victoria's friend and political advisor during the early years of her reign. Husband of novelist Lady Caroline Lamb. He was involved in a scandal that almost brought down his government when a Tory MP tried to extort money from him. When Melbourne refused, the MP went public with his accusation that the PM had an affair with his wife, a charge he was unable to substantiate.

Never disregard a book because the author of it is a foolish fellow.

1849 Dame **Madge Kendal:** Stage name of **Margaret Brunton Grimston**, née **Margaret Shafto Robertson**. English actress popular on the stage and screen, usually in roles as lovable English eccentrics. Made her debut as Ophelia and *Hamlet* and continued to be acclaimed for her Shakespearean roles as the leading actress of the Haymarket Theatre. Speaking of her rival Sarah Bernhardt:

A great actress, from the waist down.

1874 **Harold L. Ickes:** U.S. social activist and public official. A liberal Republican, who helped swing progressive votes to the Democrats in 1932. Appointed Secretary of the Interior, where he fought for preservation of natural resources. Headed the Public Works Administration, which built highways, public buildings and dams. Speaking of Huey Long of Louisiana:

The trouble with Senator Long is that he is suffering from halitosis of the intellect. That's presuming Senator Long has an intellect.

1875 **Wallace Irwin:** American journalist, editor and humorist. In his letters as a Japanese schoolboy Hashimira Togo, which appeared in *Collier's Weekly*, he created a new form of humorous literature. Books: *The Love Sonnets of a Car Conductor*, *The Love Songs of a Hoodlum*, and *The Rubaiyat of Omar Khayyam Jr.*

Statistics show that of those who contact the habit of eating, very few survive.

1902 **Wolcott Gibbs:** American humorist, parodist, drama critic, and short story writer for *The New Yorker* magazine. Delighted readers with playful language and an acerbic wit. Member of the famed Algonquin Round Table group. Made a famous parody of *Time* magazine in 1938. Wrote the play *Season in the Sun*, a comedy of errors.

It is my indignant opinion that 90 percent of the moving pictures exhibited in America are so vulgar, witless and dull that it is preposterous to write about them in any publication not intended to be read while chewing gum.

1915 **David Schoenbrun:** Energetic and much traveled American journalist, who aimed to be "the world's greatest expert on France." Foreign correspondent France (1946–62). Chief of CBS Washington bureau (1962–63). ABC news (1963–79). Books: *The Three Lives of Charles de Gaulle, Close to Events,* and *Vietnam: How We Got In, How to Get Out.*

Being a great power is no longer much fun.

1916 **Harry James:** American trumpet virtuoso and bandleader. Hits: "You Made Me Love You," "I Don't Want to Walk Without You," "I'm Begging to See the Light" and "I've Heard That Song Before." Appeared in many Hollywood movies. Was married to Betty Grable.

... When you're worried and upset, you don't feel like playing and you certainly can't relax enough to play anything like good jazz.

1926 **Norman Mack "Norm" Van Brocklin:** "The Dutchman." Hall-of-Fame American football quarterback and coach. Led NFL in passing three times, punting twice, and the L.A. Rams and Philadelphia Eagles to NFL titles. MVP (1960). As coach of the expansion Minnesota Vikings, had a contentious relationship with quarterback Fran Tarkington that led to his resignation after six years and an unimpressive 29–51–4 record. Also coached the Atlanta Falcons, from which he was fired after seven seasons.

If you don't discipline them [his players], they won't know you love them. There's no love on third down and one. You need discipline then.

1933 **Ruth Bader Ginsberg:** Associate justice of the U.S. Supreme Court, appointed by Bill Clinton to replace retiring Justice Byron "Whizzer" White (1993). Second woman, after Sandra Day O'Connor, to be appointed to the Supreme Court. She's also the first Jewish justice.

The state controlling a woman would mean denying her full autonomy and full equality... The emphasis must be not on the right to abortion but on the right to privacy and reproductive control.

1935 **Jimmy Swaggart:** American preacher and pioneer TV evangelist. Established a lucrative ministry under the Assembly of God, which made over $150 million per year. He tearfully confessed to his documented meetings with prostitutes, and temporarily left preaching, losing much of his audience, which once numbered in the millions.

If I do not return to the pulpit this weekend, millions of people will go to hell.

1944 **Sly Stone:** Born Sylvester Stewart African-American singer with Sly & The Family Stone, which played a critical role in the development of soul, funk and psychedelia in the 1960s and 70s. Biggest hit: "Everyday People." A Sly & The Family Stone tribute album was released in 2005.

Different strokes, for different folks.

OTHERS: 1713 Astronomer who mapped the Southern Hemisphere **Nicolas Louis de Lacaille**, 1801 Dutch cocoa manufacturer **Coenraad J. van Houten**, 1809 President of Liberia **Joseph Jenkins Roberts**,1838 Ethnologist **Alice Cunningham Fletcher**, 1852 Irish playwright **Lady Augusta Gregory**, 1858 U.S. botanist **Liberty Hyde Bailey**, 1875 U.S. Theater producer **Lee Schubert**, 1905 Attempted assassin of Hitler **Berthold Schrenck von Stauffenberg**, 1907 Jazz trumpeter **Jimmy McPartland**, 1912 Blues stylist **Sam "Lightnin'" Hopkins**, 1918 U.S. literary scholar/writer **Richard Ellmann**, 1933 Country singer **Roy Clark**, 1935 U.S. actor **Judd Hirsch**, 1941 Saxophonist/vocalist **Mike Love**

March 16

1751 **James Madison:** Virginia lawyer, known as "the Father of the Constitution." U.S. Secretary of State under Thomas Jefferson. Political theorist and fourth president of the U.S. (1809–17). At 5'4" and 100 pounds, the smallest U.S. president. Author with Alexander Hamilton and John Jay of the Federalist Papers. Sponsored the first ten amendments (Bill of Rights) to Constitution. His wife, Dolley Madison, was an able, witty and tactful hostess, who during the burning of Washington D.C. by the British during the War of 1812, saved some of the young nation's most precious documents.

If Tyranny and Oppression come to this land, it will be in the guise of fighting a foreign enemy.

1774 **Matthew Flinders:** British navigator and chart maker. Sailed with Captain Bligh, circumnavigated Australia and encouraged the use of the continent's name. Survived a shipwreck, imprisoned as a spy and identified and corrected the effect of iron ships upon compass readings. Wrote the widely read *A Voyage to Terra Australis* in which he gave the name "Australia" general currency.

The name Terra Australis will remain descriptive of the geographical importance of the country... [But] had I permitted myself any innovation upon the original term, it would have been to convert it into Australia; as being more agreeable to the ear, and an assimilation to the names of other great portions of the earth.

1903 **Michael Joseph "Mike" Mansfield:** American Democratic politician, diplomat, and engineer. Montana U.S representative (1943–53) and senator (1953–76). Senate majority leader (1961–76). Outspoken critic of U.S. involvement in the Vietnam War and sponsored a bill calling for a cease-fire and phased withdrawal. Persistently criticized President Nixon, especially during the Watergate investigation. Ambassador to Japan (1977–88).

I was not able to stop or slow down the Vietnam War.

1906 **Henny Youngman:** English-born radio, TV and stand-up comedian. Famous for his one-liners and his never quite playing his violin. Dubbed the "King of the One-Liners" by columnist Walter Winchell. His most oft-repeated line was "Take my wife — please." He never retired, performing until his final days, dying of pneumonia at age 91.

Getting on a plane, I told the ticket lady, "Send one of my bags to New York, send one to Los Angles, and send one to Miami." She said, "We can't do that!" I told her, "You did it last week!"

1908 **Robert Rossen:** U.S. screenwriter, director and producer. Won an Academy Award for writing, directing and producing *All the Kings Men*. Other films: *The Sea Wolf, Body and Soul, A Walk in the Sun, The Strange Love of Martha Ivers*, and *The Hustler*.

It works. It plays. Don't improve it into a disaster.

1912 **Patricia Nixon:** Born **Thelma Ryan**. American First Lady. Wife of Richard M. Nixon, thirty-seventh U.S. president. Her husband nicknamed her Pat because she was born the day before St. Patrick's Day. Sacrificed her life in order to advance the career of her husband.

Being first lady is the hardest unpaid job in the world.

1926 **Jerry Lewis:** Zany American comedian and actor. Once teamed with Dean Martin on television, in nightclubs and films. After the split, he became a cult hero, crowned by serious French critics as "Le Roi du Crazy." Hosts annual telethon for muscular dystrophy, raising hundreds of millions of dollars. Had a hit record in 1956: "Rock-a-Bye Your Baby with a Dixie Melody." Films alone: *The Nutty Professor, The Family Jewels* and *Hardly Working*.

I've had great success being a total idiot

1927 **Daniel Patrick Moynihan:** American scholar and politician. Professor of Education and Urban Politics at Harvard. U.S. Ambassador to India (1973–74) and U.N. (1975–76). Democratic U.S. Senator from New York. Liberal advocate for social reform. Book: *Maximum Feasible Misunderstanding*.

To strip our past of glory is no great loss, but to deny it honor is devastating.

1940 **Bernardo Bertolucci:** Italian director, screenwriter of films: *Once Upon a Time in the West, The Conformist, Last Tango in Paris, The Sheltering Sky* and *The Last Emperor* for which he received an Oscar for directing and screenwriting. Charged with obscenity in Rome for *Last Tango*, he was eventually cleared because of "changing morals."

Pornography is not in the hands of the child who discovers his sexuality by masturbating, but in the hands of the adult who slaps him.

1954 **Hollis Stacy:** American professional golfer. Joined the LPGA tour in 1974. Rookie of the Year (1974–75). Won four major championships. Only golfer to win the U.S. Girls Junior Amateur Golf Association three times, consecutively (1969–71). Designed Blackhawk Golf Course in Austin, Texas. Recognized in 2000 as one of the LPGA's top 50 players and teachers.

Why do we work so hard to feel so terrible?

1955 **Isabelle Huppert:** Versatile French leading lady. Interpreter of a wide range of roles from a delicate innocent to a hardened mystery woman. Cannes Film Award for Best Actress (1977). Films: *César and Rosalie, Violette, Entre Nous*, and *Madame Bovary*.

Acting is a way of living out one's insanity.

1956 **Ozzie Newsome, Jr.:** Former American football tight end for the University of Alabama followed by an outstanding pro career with the Cleveland Browns. He retired as the NFL's all-time leading tight-end receiver and fourth among all receivers. Elected to the Pro Football Hall of Fame. First African-American to become a general manager in the league. Currently general manager of the Baltimore Ravens. Speaking of "Bear" Bryant:

Martin Luther King Jr. preached equality. Coach Bryant practiced it.

OTHERS: 1609 Composer **Michael Franck**, 1729 German vicar/librarian **George W. "Franz" Panzer**, 1750 First modern woman astronomer **Caroline Herschel**, 1787 German physicist **George Simon Ohm**, 1822 French landscape painter **Rosa Bonheur**, 1839 First Nobel prize winner **René François Sully Prudhomme**, 1918 Dutch architect **Aldo E. van Eyck**, 1920 Australian actor **Leo McKern**, 1932 American astronaut **Ronnie Walter Cunningham**, 1936 U.S. high jumper **Thelma Hopkins**, 1942 TV game host **Chuck Woolery**, 1949 Welfare & Tenement rights advocate **Bertha Knox Gilkey**, 1951 Country singer **Ray Benson**, 1951 Canadian actress **Kate Nelligan**, 1954 U.S. singer **Nancy Wilson**

March 17

1777 **Roger Brooke Taney:** American lawyer and jurist. As U.S. Attorney General fought against the federal bank. As fifth Chief Justice of the Supreme Court (1936–64) upheld federal supremacy over state authorities. In the Dred Scott case held that slaves were not citizens. Although opposed to slavery, he believed that its elimination should be brought about by the states where it existed.

They [the blacks] have no rights which the white man was bound to respect.

1781 **Ebenezer Elliott:** English industrialist and poet. Born in an iron foundry and 24 years later he was owner of the facility. A steel maker with a conscience, he was interested in poetry and politics. Dared to challenge the government, he denounced social evils, especially the "bread tax" in his "Corn Law Rhymes," which brought him national fame. Described as "a red son of the furnace he was dubbed "the Yorkshire Burns."

What is a communist? One who hath yearnings/ For equal division of unequal earnings.

1820 **Jean Ingelow:** English poet and novelist, she wrote devotional poetry, lyrics and ballads. Remembered for her narrative poem "High Tide on the Coast of Lincolnshire." Tales for children include *Mopsa the Fairy* and among her novels is *Off the Skellings.*

Man is the miracle in nature. God is the one miracle to man.

1866 **Pierce Butler**: American jurist and Associate Justice of the U.S. Supreme Court (1923–39). While serving on the Board of Regents of the University of Minnesota He railed against "radical" and "disloyal" professors. He was the first justice from the state of Minnesota and the first Democrat to be appointed by a Republican. While on the court he vigorously opposed regulation of business and the handing out of welfare by the government. Voted against Franklin D. Roosevelt's "New Deal" laws that came before the court.

The two great evils to be avoided are cabal at home and influence from abroad.

1899 **Arthur E. Summerfield:** American businessman and government official. Ran unsuccessfully for governor of Michigan in 1946. Served as chairman of the Republican National Committee (1952–3).GOP strategist and money-raiser. Postmaster General in the Eisenhower administration (1953–61). Oversaw a brief experiment with rocket-delivered mail. On his banning of D.H. Lawrence's *Lady Chatterley's Lover* in 1959:

I make no claim of being a literary critic ... but I feel I have some sense for what is decent and what is filthy ... and filth is filth.

1902 **Robert Tyre "Bobby" Jones:** American golfer. Won U.S. Open and British Open plus U.S. and British Amateurs (1930), becoming the first Grand Slam winner. He then retired from competitive golf at age 28, having never become a professional. Helped establish the Masters Tournament (1934).

Some people think they are concentrating when they're merely worrying.

1910 **Bayard Rustin:** African-American civil rights activist. Organized the New York branch of the Congress on Racial Equality in 1941. Worked for the Fellowship or Reconciliation (1941–53). Special assistant to Martin Luther King Jr. Organized March on Washington for Jobs and Freedom. President of the A. Philip Randolph Institute.

[Bigotry's] birthplace is the sinister back room of the mind where plots and schemes are hatched for the persecution and oppression of other human beings.

1914 **Sammy Baugh:** Outstanding football quarterback and defensive back with the Washington Redskins. Held numerous passing and punting records at the time of his retirement. Elected to the Pro Football Hall of Fame. Referring to a very religious linebacker:

He knocks the hell out of people, but in a Christian way.

1915 **Gale McGee:** American historian, politician and statesman. U.S. Democratic Senator from Wyoming (1959–77). Chairman Senate Post Office and Civil Service Committee (1969–77).U.S. Ambassador to the Organization of American States. On learning that Arthur E. Summerfield was banning books:

I'm going to introduce a resolution to have the Postmaster General stop reading dirty books and deliver the mail.

1919 **Nat King Cole:** African-American jazz pianist and singer. The most popular black recording artist of the postwar era and the first black performer to have his own TV show. Had 78 hit singles between 1944 and 1964, including: "Nature Boy," "Mona Lisa," "Ramblin' Rose" and "Unforgettable." Father of singer Natalie Cole. Died of lung cancer in 1965.

I'm a musician at heart. I know I'm not really a singer. I couldn't compete with real singers. But I sing because the public buys it.

1920 Sheikh **Mujibur Rahman:** Bengali political leader in East Pakistan and the liberator of Bangladesh. President and prime minister. Struggled to address the challenges of intense poverty and unemployment. Banned other political parties and declared himself "president for life" in 1975 He and his family were assassinated in a military coup that same year.

In the war between falsehood and truth, falsehood wins the first battle and truth the last.

1938 **Rudolph Nureyev:** Soviet-British ballet dancer. Defected from U.S.S.R. and the Leningrad Kirov Ballet. Became permanent guest artist at Royal Ballet, London. Partner of Margot Fonteyn (1962–79). Noted for suspended leaps and fast turns. Roles: *Swan Lake*, *Don Quixote* and *Romeo and Juliet.*

A pas de deux is a dialogue of love. How can there be conversation if one partner is dumb?

OTHERS: 1473 King of Scotland **James IV**, 1789 English tragic actor **Edmund Kean**, 1834 German engineer/inventor **Gottlieb Daimler**, 1846 English artist/illustrator **Kate Greenaway**, 1874 President of Zionist Organization of America **Stephen Samuel Wise**, 1888 American adventurer/actor/filmmaker **Frank Buck**, 1901 Premier of Japan **Eisaku Sato**, 1919 U.S. baseball player **Hank Sauer**, 1925 British zoologist **G.M. Hughes**, 1927 Folklorist/enthomusicologist **Kenneth S. Goldstein**, 1929 U.S. astronaut **James Irwin**, 1930 U.S. flutist **Paul Horn**, 1941 U.S. singer **Gene Pitney**, 1942 U.S. serial killer **John Wayne Gacy**, 1944 U.S. singer with the Loving Spoonful **John Sebastian**

March 18

1782 **John Caldwell Calhoun:** American South Carolinian Democratic politician. Brilliant exponent of states rights and champion of slavery. Opposed prohibition of slavery in newly admitted states. U.S. Secretary of War (1817–25), U.S. Vice president (1824–32). First vice-president to resign when he was elected to the U.S. Senate.

The surrender of life is nothing to sinking down into acknowledgment of inferiority.

1837 **Grover Cleveland:** American Democratic politician. Mayor of Buffalo, New York and governor of the state. Twenty-second and twenty-fourth U.S. president (1885–89 and 1893–97). Attempted to lower the tariff. Supported creation of Civil Service Commission. These policies provoked opposition and he was defeated by Republican Benjamin Harrison in 1888, but returned to office in 1892, becoming the only president to serve two non-consecutive terms. Married in the White House. His daughter, Esther, was the first child to be born in the White House.

The ship of democracy, which has weathered all storms, may sink through the mutiny of those on board.

1840 **William Cosmo Monkhouse:** English poet and critic. Poetry collections: *A Dream of Idleness and Other Poems*, *Corn and Poppies*, and *Pasiteles the Elder and Other Poems*. After publishing a novel *A Question of Honor*, he devoted himself almost exclusively to art criticism.

There once was an old man of Lyme/ who married three wives at a time/ when asked, "Why a third?"/ he replied "One's absurd!/ and bigamy, sir, is a crime!"

1842 **Stéphane Mallarmé:** French poet. An originator with Paul Verlaine and leader of the Symbolist Movement. Most of his verse expresses a longing to transcend reality and find an ideal world. His "Afternoon of a Faun" inspired Claude Debussy's famous prelude. Other works: *Complete Poems*, *Verse and Prose*, and *Digressions*.

Dreams have as much influence as actions.

1844 **Nikolai A. Rimsky-Korsakov:** Russian composer of Romantic music. Used Russian folk idiom and rhythms in his compositions. His work is representative of the Russian nationalist school. "Past master of the modern art of orchestration." Operas: *The Snow Maiden*, *Le Coq d'or* and *Scheherazade*. Known for brilliant instrumentation. He also completed works by other composers, for example, Modest Mussorgsky's *Boris Godunov*. Teacher of Igor Stravinsky.

God does not bless the tears of sorrow,/ God blesses the tears of celestial joy.

1869 **Neville Chamberlain:** British Conservative politician. English prime minister (1937–40). Ever associated with appeasement for signing the Munich Pact, which granted most of Hitler's demands, abandoning Czechoslovakia. He claimed the agreement brought "peace in our time," but it failed to prevent the outbreak of World War II. Resigned in 1940 following the defeat of British forces in Norway.

In war, whichever side may call itself the victor, there are no winners, but all are losers.

1877 **Edgar Cayce:** American psychic and faith healer. Known as "the sleeping prophet" because he would close his eyes and appear to go into a trance when he did his readings. His followers maintained that he was able to make connection with a higher consciousness, such as God, to get his "psychic knowledge." Established a hospital and the Association for Research and Enlightenment in Virginia Beach, Virginia. Made prophecies of the destruction of New York City and California.

Dreams are today's answers to tomorrow's questions.

1901 **Manly Hall:** Canadian-born U.S. philosopher, minister, author and founder of the Philosophical Research Society, modeled on the ancient school of Pythagoras. Interested in occult matters. As leader of the Church of the People, he started a magazine called the *All Seeing Eye*. Said to have delivered over 7,000 lectures on mystical topics.

It is only a step from boredom to disillusionment, which leads naturally to self-pity, which in turn ends in chaos.

1915 **Richard Condon:** American satirical novelist, playwright, and crime writer. Best known for the best-selling thrillers *The Manchurian Candidate* and *Prizzi's Honor*, both of which have been adapted to acclaimed films. Other works: the play *Men of Distinction*, *Winter Kills* and *The Star-Spangled Crunch*.

It is the rule, not the exception that otherwise unemployable public figures inevitably take to writing for publication.

1921 **Edgar Z. Friedenberg:** American educator and author. Professor of education, Dalhouse University, Canada. His educational theories were in opposition to the John Dewey–inspired view that education's purpose was to prepare citizens that would benefit society. Instead, he promoted the virtues of competency, of facts as opposed to dogma, and a mastery of subjects. Books: *The Vanishing Adolescent*, *Coming of Age in America* and *The Dignity of Youth and Other Atavisms*.

Part of the American dream is to live long and die young.

1932 **John Updike:** American novelist, short-story writer, critic and poet. Associated with *The New Yorker* magazine from 1955. Explores human relationships in contemporary society. Deals with the tensions and frustrations of middle-class life and their effects on love and marriage. Books: *The Witches of Eastwick, The Centaur, Rabbit, Run* and *Rabbit Is Rich* (Pulitzer Prize). Short story collections: *The Same Door* and *Museums and Women.*

Life is like an overlong drama through which we sit being nagged by the vague memories of having read the reviews.

1952 **Will Durst:** American political satirist, sometimes referred to as an "equal opportunity offender" for his quiver full of barbs, transcending political party lines. Heir to Mort Sahl and Dick Gregory. Five-time Emmy nominee is a regular commentator on NPR and CNN. Former contributing editor to *National Lampoon* and *George.*

Comedy is defiance. It's a snort of contempt in the face of fear and anxiety. And it's the laughter that allows hope to creep back on the inhale.

OTHERS: 1483 Painter of the Sistine Madonna **Raphael**, 1657 Italian composer **Giuseppe Ottavio Pitoni**, 1690 German mathematician **Christian Goldbach**, 1809 Cuban poet **Gabriel de la Concepción Valdés**, 1858 German engineer **Rudolph C.K. Diesel**, 1886 U.S. actor **Edward Everett Horton**, 1890 Dutch religion historian **Gerardus van der Leeuw**, 1893 English anti-war poet **Wilfred Owen**, 1899 Russian chief of Soviet Secret Police **Lavrenti Beria**, 1905 New York fashion designer **Mollie Parnis**,1905 English actor **Robert Donat**, 1911 U.S. actor **Smiley Burnette**, 1927 U.S. composer **John Kander**, 1927 U.S. sportswriter **George Plimpton**, 1941 Rhythm & Blues singer **Wilson Pickett**

March 19

1721 **Tobias George Smollett:** Scottish novelist. Studied medicine and settled in London as a surgeon. Wrote realistic satires on the folly, selfishness and cruelty of mankind. Spent several years in journal editing, translating and writing historical and travel works. Books: *The Adventures of Roderick Random* and his masterpiece *Humphrey Clinker.*

Some folks are wise and some are otherwise.

1813 Dr. **David Livingstone:** Scottish-born British medical missionary and African explorer. Taught the church to develop an overall Christian culture in foreign lands. Discovered Lake Ngami, the Zambesi River, the Victoria Falls and Lake Nyasa. Found in Ujiji by journalist Henry Stanley, who was sent to look for him by the *New York Herald.*

I am prepared to go anywhere, provided it is forward.

1821 Sir **Richard Burton:** English explorer, author. Set out with John Speke on the journey that led to the discovery of Lake Tanganyika. Traveled in West Africa, Brazil, Damascus and Trieste, holding numerous consular posts. Made a literal translation of the *Arabian Nights.* His wife Isabel Arundell Burton, who shared in much of his traveling, burned her husband's journals after his death.

The more I study religions the more I am convinced that man never worshipped anything but himself.

1824 **William Allingham:** Irish man of letters and poet. Editor of *Fraser's Magazine.* Produced much lyrical and descriptive poetry, thoroughly national in spirit and local coloring. Works: *Day and Night Songs*, illustrated by Rossetti and Millais and *Irish Songs and Poems.*

Writing is learning to say nothing, more cleverly each day.

1860 **William Jennings Bryan:** "The Great Commoner." American lawyer and political leader, also known as the "Silver-Tongued Orator." Elected to Congress for Nebraska in 1890. Three-time unsuccessful U.S. presidential candidate. Made the famous "Cross of Gold" speech. Provided powerful support to woman suffrage. Appointed Secretary of State by President Wilson, but as a pacifist he resigned in 1915. Prosecutor in the famous Scopes or "monkey trial," a test case on the banning of teaching evolution in Tennessee schools.

The humblest citizen of all the land, when clad in the armor of a righteous cause is stronger than all the hosts of Error.

1883 **Joseph W. Stilwell:** Four-star American general noted for his service in China as Chief of Staff to General Chiang Kai-shek. Known as "Vinegar Joe," because of his lack of tact and a capacity for conventional diplomacy. Hated and was hated by Chiang because of Stilwell's insistence on a united front of the Generalissimo's troops and those of the communists.

Illegitimus non carborundum. Latin: Don't let the bastards grind you down.

1891 **Earl Warren:** American Republican politician and jurist. Governor of California (1943–53) and 14th Chief Justice of the U.S. Supreme Court (1953–69). Presided over period of rapid change in civil rights, guaranteeing the rights to counsel in criminal cases and protecting accused persons from police brutality. Wrote decision in school desegregation case, Brown vs. Board of Education. Headed official investigation of assassination of President John F. Kennedy.

The only thing we learn from history is that we do not learn.

1905 **Albert Speer:** German architect and Nazi government official. Called "the first architect of Germany's Third Reich. Also served as minister of armaments in Hitler's cabinet. Streamlined Germany's war production. Openly opposed Hitler in the final months of the war. Tried at Nuremberg, he expressed repentance and his life was spared. Sentenced to 20 years in prison. Upon his release, became a successful author.

One seldom recognizes the devil when he has his hand on your shoulder.

1906 **Adolph Eichmann:** High-ranking German Nazi official. Largely responsible for the logistics of the extermination of millions during the Holocaust, particularly Jews. Often referred to as the "Chief Executioner" of the Third Reich. After the war escaped to South America, where he was apprehended by Israeli agents, tried in Israel, convicted of war crimes and hanged.

To sum it all up, I must say that I regret nothing.

1928 **Hans Kung:** Roman Catholic priest, eminent Swiss theologian and prolific writer. First major modern theologian to reject the doctrine of papal infallibility in his book *Infallible? An Inquiry*. Stripped of his license to teach as a Roman Catholic theologian, he continued to teach ecumenical theology at the University of Tübingen. He was not excommunicated and remains a priest. President of the Foundation for Global Ethic.

The election of Cardinal Joseph Ratzinger as pope is an enormous disappointment for all those who hoped for a reformist and pastoral pope.... But we must wait and see, for experience shows that the papacy in the Catholic Church today is such a challenge that it can change anyone.

1930 **Ornette Coleman:** American jazz alto saxophonist, trumpeter, violinist and composer. Musician who stirred equal amounts of interest and controversy. Experimented with free-form jazz and atonality. Writer of jazz works in unconventional forms; he also composed several classical pieces. Toured Europe as part of a trio. Composed "Skies in America."

Jazz is the only music in which the same note can be played night after night but differently each time.

1933 **Phillip Roth:** American novelist, short-story writer. Concentrates mostly on Jewish-American life and modern society in comedies of manners. Won National Book award for *Goodbye, Columbus*. Also wrote the best-selling *Portnoy's Complaint*, *My Life as a Man*, *The Ghost Writer*, and *Zuckerman Unbound*.

The Jewish man with parents alive is a fifteen-year-old boy and will remain a fifteen-year-old boy until they die.

OTHERS: 1589 Governor of Plymouth Colony **William Bradford**, 1610 Japanese painter **Hasegawa Tohaku**, 1716 French sculptor **Guillaume Coustou**, 1845 Dutch historian **Willem H. de Beaufort**,1847 U.S. painter **Albert Pinkham Ryder**, 1848 Western Marshall **Wyatt Earp**, 1872 Russian ballet director **Sergei Diaghilev**, 1888 German/U.S. graphic artist/painter **Josef Albers**, 1894 U.S. comedienne **Jackie "Moms" Mabley**, 1901 Set designer **Jo Mielziner**, 1914 First Heisman Trophy winner **Jay Berwanger**, 1916 U.S. author **Irving Wallace**, 1925 Air Force general **Brent Scowcroft**, 1927 Baseball outfielder **Richie Ashburn**, 1928 British Actor **Patrick McGoohan**, 1936 Swiss actress **Ursula Andress**

March 20

43 BCE **Ovid [Publius Ovidius Naso]:** Latin poet. Roman writer of love elegies experimented with the imaginary letter, and mock didactic verse. Related disconnected stories inside a large historical or chronological frame. First major writer of the Roman Empire. In Middle Ages, Ovid's poetry was one of the major sources of Western man's knowledge of antiquity. Works: *Medea*, *Heriodes*, *Ars amatoria* and *Metamorphoses*.

Fortune and love favor the brave.

1828 **Henrik Ibsen:** Norwegian dramatist, poet and critic. Father of modern prose social drama. Wrote realistic plays emphasizing social problems and psychological conflicts: *Brand*, *Peer Gynt*, *A Doll's House*, *The Master Builder*, *Ghosts*, *The Wild Duck* and *Hedda Gabler*. Near the end of his life he commented that he was "more of a poet and less of a social philosopher than people ... suppose." Also declared that his interest was not so much in women's right, but in human rights.

A man should never put on his best trousers when he goes out to battle for freedom and truth.

1856 **Frederick Taylor:** American engineer and inventor. Chief engineer of Midvale steelworks in Pennsylvania. Introduced *time-and-motion study* as an aid to efficient management. It had an immediate impact on mass production techniques. Influenced the development of nearly every modern industrial company. Wrote *The Principles of Scientific Management*.

In the past the man has been first; in the future the system must be first... The first object of any good system must be that of developing first class men.

1882 **René Coty:** French statesman. Last president of the French Fourth Republic (1953–9). After the constitutional crisis precipitated by generals in Algeria, he assisted the return to power of Charles de Gaulle and the birth of the Fifth Republic.

It's taken me all my life to understand that it is not necessary to understand everything.

1883 **Wilfred Funk:** American publisher and author. President of Funk and Wagnall's (1925–40). Books: *30 Days to a More Powerful Vocabulary* (with N. Lewis) and *Word Origins and Their Romantic Stories*.

I wish the reader might be encouraged to walk among words as I do, like Alice in Wonderland, amazed at the marvels they hold.

1904 **B.F. [Burrhus Frederic] Skinner:** American psychologist. A leading proponent of behaviorism, of the belief that man is controlled by external factors and free will does not exist. Invented "Skinner's Box" for observing animals' stimulus-response behavior. Presented his "Air Crib," a soundproof germ-free, air-conditioned box meant to serve as an optimal environment for the first two years of childhood. Works: *The Behavior of Organisms*, *Walden Two*, *Science and Human Behavior*, and *Beyond Freedom and Dignity*.

Education is what survives when what has been learnt has been forgotten.

1922 **Carl Reiner:** U.S. actor, film director, producer, writer and comedian. Performed in several Broadway musicals before joining Sid Caesar's comedy shows as one of the best second bananas around. Created, wrote and appeared in *The Dick Van Dyke Show*. Recorded the LP "The 2000-Year-Old-Man" with Mel Brooks. Films directed: *Where's Papa, The Jerk*, and *All of Me*.

I think that comedy tells you how it is. The other thing about comedy is that—you don't even know if you're failing in drama, but you do know when you're failing in comedy. When you go to a comedy and you don't hear anybody laughing, you know that you've failed.

1928 **Fred Rogers:** American television host and producer. An ordained Presbyterian minister, he became admired by millions of viewers for his internationally acclaimed children's PBS TV series *Mister Rogers' Neighborhood* from 1967. Known for his gentleness and desire to educate. Used puppets, music and guests to teach his young viewers about various subjects and emotions.

Play is often talked about as if it were a relief from serious learning. But for children play is serious learning. Play is really the work of childhood.

1945 **Pat Riley:** Two-sport college player at Kentucky, he was drafted both by the NBA and the NFL. Chose basketball and later helped the Lakers win a NBA championship in 1972. After retirement, began a long run as a successful coach, winning championships with the Lakers. Also coached the New York Knicks and currently coaches the Miami Heat. Led then to the NBA championship in the 2005–06 season.

A champion needs motivation above and beyond winning.

1948 **Bobby Orr:** Canadian hockey star. Ranked along side of Wayne Gretzky as the greatest hockey player of all time. At age 18, playing for the Boston Bruins, won the Calder Memorial Trophy for outstanding rookie. An outstanding defenseman who revolutionized the game with his offensive play. Won the Norris Cup 8 times and led the NHL in scoring twice and assists 5 times. Led Boston to their first Stanley Cup in 29 years.

Forget about style; worry about results.

1957 **Spike Lee:** Originally **Shelton Jackson**. African-American director and actor. His films have won praise for presentations of black themes and stories. Condemned by some as racist, by others as advocating violence. Films: *She's Gotta Have It, Do the Right Thing, Mo' Better Blues, Malcolm X* and *She Hate Me*.

I ain't Martin Luther King, I don't need a dream. I have a plan.

1958 **Holly Hunter:** American actress began her film career with *Raising Arizona*, followed by *Broadcast News* which earned her an Oscar nomination. Won the Academy Award for Best Performance by an Actress for *The Piano*, the same year she was nominated for best supporting role in *The Firm*. Also nominated for an Oscar for *Thirteen*. Earned two Emmy awards for TV films.

To me, being creative is a very fragile thing, and somehow I've always felt the need to very protective of that.

OTHERS: 1634 Frisian theologist **Balthasar Bekker**, 1750 Dutch chemist **Martinus van Marum**, 1811 King of Rome **Napoleon Bonaparte II**, 1813 German hymn writer **Mathias Keller**, 1834 Harvard President **Charles William Elliot**, 1890 Danish baritone **Lauritz Melchoir**, 1906 1st Jewish mayor of New York **Abraham Beame**, 1906 U.S. bandleader **Ozzie Nelson**, 1908 CBS broadcasting executive **Frank Stanton**, 1908 English actor **Sir Michael Redgrave**, 1917 English singer **Dame Vera Lynn**, 1918 Game show host **Jack Barry**, 1920 magazine editor **Lenore Hershey**, 1920 Jazz pianist **Marian McPartland**, 1922 U.S. bandleader **Larry Elgart**, 1925 Nixon aide **John Erlichman**

March 21

1685 **Johann Sebastian Bach:** German composer, especially of church music, and instrumentalist of the late Baroque Period. Master of counterpoint. Perhaps the greatest organist and harpsichordist of his era. Cantor at the great church of St. Thomas in Leipzig. Wrote vast numbers of cantatas, sonatas, preludes, fugues and chorale preludes for organ. Works: *Brandenburg Concertos, Well-Tempered Clavier* and *Goldberg Variations*. After his death, his work went relatively unnoticed until the early 19th century when they were revived by Felix Mendelssohn. Later Bach was described as "the most stupendous miracle in all music." Fathered 20 children in two marriages.

Music is an agreeable harmony for the honor of God and the permissible delights of the soul

1763 **Johann Paul Friedrich Richter:** German novelist and humorist. Studied theology before turning to literature. Combined idealism with "Sturm und Drang." Works: *Extract's from the Devil's Papers, The Invisible Lodge, Hesperus, Leyana* and the four-volume *Titan*.

Criticism is a practice which strips the tree of both caterpillars and blossoms.

1768 **Jean Baptiste-Joseph Fourier:** French mathematician and Egyptologist. While an engineer with Napoleon in Egypt he made anthropological investigations. Primarily known for his work in heat conduction, Fourier series to solve differential equations and the concept of Fourier transform.

The profound study of nature is the most fruitful source of mathematical discoveries.

1806 **Benito Juárez:** Mexican leader and national revolutionary hero. Born of Zapotec Indian parents. As president of the Mexican republic, fought the French and their puppet emperor Maximilian. Juarez prevailed and Maximilian was executed. Juarez died in office. Sometimes called "the Mexican Washington."

Among individuals as among nations, the respect to other people's rights is peace.

1839 **Modest Mussorgsky:** Russian composer and song writer. Inspired by folktales. Founder of realistic national music. Called "the most truly and thoroughly national of all Russians." Works: *Pictures from an Exhibition*, *Night on Bald Mountain* and his masterpiece, the opera *Boris Godunov*. Died of alcohol-related illnesses at age 42.

Art is not an end in itself, but a means of addressing humanity.

1905 **Phyllis McGinley:** Pulitzer Prize–winning American poet for *Times Three: Selected Verse from Three Decades*, and author of children's books. Also wrote prose essays. Other Works: *Pocketful of Wry*, *The Horse Who Lived Upstairs*, and *A Little Girl's Room*.

Sticks and stones are hard on bones./ Aimed with angry art,/ Words can sting like anything,/ But silence breaks the heart.

1918 **Howard Cosell:** U.S. lawyer turned sports journalist. Self-proclaimed intellectual among riff-raff. His abrasive personality and tendency to speak his mind no matter whose ox was gored earned him the distinction of being named both the most-liked and most-hated TV reporter, according to one poll. Was a commentator for *Monday Night Football* and hosted a variety show *Saturday Night Live with Howard Cosell*.

Sports is the toy department of human life.

1922 **Julius K. Nyerere:** African politician and statesman. Prime minister and president of Tanganyika (1962–64). Negotiated the union of Tanganyika and Zanzibar as Tanzania (1964). As president led the new nation on a path of Socialism. When his policies failed, he resigned in 1985.

Small nations are like indecently dressed women. They tempt the evil minded.

1930 **John Malcolm Fraser:** Australian statesman and farmer. Liberal prime minister (1975–83). In 1955, became the youngest MP in the House of Representatives. A member of the Commonwealth Group of Eminent Persons which worked to replace apartheid in South Africa.

Self-criticism is luxury all politicians should indulge in, but it is best done in private.

1946 **Russ Meyer:** U.S. film director. Specialized in nudie films that featured women with very large breasts. Titles include: *Beyond the Valley of the Dolls* and *Beneath the Valley of the Ultravixens*. During a panel discussion at Yale, he was confronted by an angry woman who accused him of being "nothing but a breast man." His reply:

That's only half of it.

1962 **Matthew Broderick:** American film and stage actor. Most widely known for the film *Ferris Bueller's Day Off*, giving voice to the adult Simba in *The Lion King*, and starring with Nathan Lane in Mel Brooks' stage musical *The Producers*, as well as the film version.

You have to fight the green monster with your mind not your fists.

1962 **Rosie O'Donnell:** U.S. comedian, actress and former TV talk show host. Appeared to good notice in a string of film comedies, including *Sleepless in Seattle* and *A League of Their Own*. On her daytime talk show, *The Rosie O'Donnell Show*, she highlighted various charitable projects. She adopted four children and ultimately announced she was gay. Married Kelli Carpenter in San Francisco in 2004.

I always think: Go big or go home.

OTHERS: 1474 Italian monastery founder/saint **Angela Merici**, 1609 Cardinal/King of Poland **Jan II Kasimierz**, 1869 Architect **Albert Kahn**, 1869 Broadway producer **Florenz Ziegfeld**, 1880 German/U.S. painter **Hans Hoffmann**, 1880 German sociologist **Wilhelm Pessler**, 1884 U.S. mathematician **George D. Birkhoff**, 1900 Russian actress **Eugenie Leontovitch**, 1902 Folk blues musician **Eddie "Son" House**, 1910 U.S. choreographer **Nick Castle**, 1916 American novelist **Harold Robbins**, 1927 U.S. science reporter **Jules Bergman**, 1927 German Minister of Foreign Affairs **Hans-Dietrich Genscher**, 1929 U.S. actor **James Coco**, 1934 U.S. actor **Al Freeman Jr.**, 1945 Gospel singer **Vernon Guy**

March 22

1808 **Caroline Norton:** née **Sheridan.** Irish poet and novelist. Campaigned for improvements in the laws of marriage and divorce. Charges of adultery with her friend Lord Melbourne by her husband from whom she was separated made her a notorious figure. Her countersuit greatly influenced the Marriage and Divorce Act of 1857, abolishing some injustices against women. Works included an attack on child labor in *Voice from the Factories*, *The Dream* and *The Lady of Garaye*. Published a successful book of verses, *The Sorrows of Rosalie*.

They serve God well/ Who serve his creatures.

1868 **Robert A. Millikan:** American physicist, teacher and writer. Proved that electricity consists of particles. Determined the charge on the electron, for which he was awarded the Nobel Prize for Physics (1923). Invented term cosmic rays which he showed came from space. Received the Presidential Medal of Honor for his work on rockets and jet propulsion during World War II.

My idea of an educated person is one who can converse on one subject for more than two minutes.

1884 **Arthur H. Vandenberg:** American public official. Editor of the Grand Rapids Herald, from 1906 to 1928. Republican U.S. Senator from Michigan (1928–51). One time isolationist played an important role in the formation of the U.N. Led Republican congressional support for legislative measures introduced by President Truman, including the Marshall Plan, the Truman Doctrine and NATO.

It is less important to redistribute wealth than it is to redistribute opportunity.

1907 **James M. Gavin:** American Army paratrooper general and diplomat. Served at the Battle of the Bulge and Normandy, World War II. Won the Distinguished Service Cross with oak leaf cluster, the Purple Heart and the Silver Star. Resigned from his post as head of Army Research and Development in 1958, blasting Defense Secretary Wilson, who according to Gavin, dealt with his Chiefs of Staff as thought they were recalcitrant Union bosses." U.S. ambassador to France (1960–62). Critic of American military strategy in Vietnam.

If you want a decision, go to the point of danger.

1908 **Louis L'Amour:** Originally **Louis Dearborn LaMoore**. American writer of over 100 books, mostly formula Western novels, which have sold more than 200 million copies in 20 languages. *Hondo* is his best known. It was made in a successful film starring John Wayne and Geraldine Page. More than 30 other of his novels were the basis of films. Awarded the Presidential Medal of Freedom in 1984.

A man ought to do what he thinks is right.

1910 **Nicholas Monsarrat:** British diplomat and novelist best known for his sea stories, particularly *The Cruel Sea*. A pacifist, he served in World War II as an ambulance driver and a member of the Royal Navy Volunteer Reserve. Later works included *The Story of Esther Costello* and *Smith and Jones*.

The marvelous maturity of London! I would rather be dead in this town than preening my feathers in heaven.

1923 **Marcel Marceau:** French pantomimist. Studied with pantomimist Étienne Decroux and had his first success in the role of Arlequin in *Baptiste*. World famous mime; formed a mime company (1948–64) and earned world-wide acclaim in the 1950s with his production of the "mimodrama" of Gorky's *Overcoat*. Most famous for his celebrated white-faced character "Bip." Devised the mime-drama *Don Juan*, the ballet *Candide* and about 100 pantomimes, including *The Creation of the World*.

To communicate through silence is a link between the thoughts of man.

1924 **Allen Neuharth:** American businessman, author and columnist. Headed Gannett, which he helped build into the largest newspaper company in the U.S. Founded *USA Today*, the most widely read newspaper in the U.S. Sparked a controversy when he wrote a column calling for bringing home American troops from the "ill-advised adventures" in Iraq, which he compared to the immorality of the Vietnam War.

When the voices of democracy are silenced, freedom becomes a hollow concept. No man or woman should be sentenced to the shadows of silence for something he or she has said or written.

1930 **Derek Bok:** American lawyer and educator. Taught law at Harvard, where he served as dean of the law school. Harvard's president for 20 years. His wife Sissela Mydral Bok is the daughter of two Nobel laureates, Swedish economist Gunnar Mydral and politician and diplomat Alva Mydral.

If you think education is expensive, try ignorance.

1930 **Pat Robertson:** American Southern Baptist minister, Christian televangelist, entrepreneur and Christian right political activist. Founded the Christian Broadcasting Network with $70 in 1960. Hosts the TV program *The 700 Club*. Strongly conservative views always provoked controversy. Advocates abolishing separation of church and state. Condemns groups he considers living in sin. Denounces perceived communists. Sought the Republican nomination for president in 1988.

Feminism is a socialist, anti-family, political movement that encourages women to leave their husbands, kill their children, practice witchcraft, destroy capitalism and become lesbians.

1930 **Stephen Sondheim:** American composer, lyricist. Lyric-writer for Leonard Bernstein's *West Side Story*. Composed the very popular: "Maria," "Tonight" and "Send in the Clowns." Shows as lyricist and composer: Tony Award–winning *A Funny Thing Happened on the Way to the Forum, Company, A Little Night Music, Sweeney Todd*, and Pulitzer Prize–winning *Sunday in the Park with George, Follies* and *Into the Woods*. Received the Kennedy Center Honor (1993) and the National Medal of Arts (1997).

One difference between poetry and lyrics is that lyrics sort of fade into the background. They fade on the page and live on the stage when set to music.

1934 **Orrin Hatch:** American lawyer and politician. Republican United States Senator from Utah. Committees: Judiciary, Finance, International Trade, Taxation, Health Care, and Intelligence.

The First Amendment is not an altar on which we must sacrifice our children, families, and community standards. Obscene material that is not protected by the First Amendment can and must be prohibited.

OTHERS: 1459 German Emperor **Maximilian I of Habsburg**, 1599 Flemish painter **Sir Anthony Van Dyck**,1797 King of Prussia **William I**, 1846 English artist **Randolph Caldecott**, 1887 American comedian **Chico Marx**, 1905 U.S. ballet director/choreographer **Ruth Page**, 1913 German soprano **Martha Mödl**, 1920 Concert pianist **Fanny Waterman**, 1931 Canadian actor **William Shatner**, 1936 Teamster's president **Ron Carey**, 1936 Singer **Roger Whittaker**, 1943 Guitarist **George Benson**, 1948 English composer **Andrew Lloyd Webber**, 1952 Sportscaster **Bob Costas**, 1957 Rhythm & Blues singer **Stephanie Mills**, 1976 U.S. actress **Reese Witherspoon**

March 23

1749 **Pierre-Simon Laplace:** French mathematician, astronomer and mathematical physicist. Applied his mathematical knowledge to the study of the stability of orbits in the solar system. Developed celestial mechanics, suggesting a hypothesis for the origin of the solar system. His masterpiece is *Mécanique celeste*, a five volume opus. Modernized theory of probability. Developed the concept of "potential," and its description by the Laplace equation.

All the effects of nature are only the

mathematical consequences of a small number of immutable laws.

1857 **Fannie Farmer:** "Mother of Level Measurements." American cookery expert. Suffered a stroke at age 16, making it impossible for her to attend college, so she turned to cooking, first at home then at the Boston Cooking School. Established Miss Farmer's School of Cookery (1902). One of the first to stress importance of following recipes. Author of *The Boston Cooking School Cook Book.*

Progress in civilization has been accompanied by progress in cooking.

1858 **Ludwig Quidde:** German historian, politician and pacifist who made acerbic criticisms of Kaiser Wilhelm II. Published a 17-page pamphlet *Caligula: A Study of Imperial Insanity* in which he compared Roman Emperor Caligula and Wilhelm. After World War I, Quidde warned that the sanctions and reparations demanded by the Allies in the Treaty of Versailles would backfire. With Hitler's rise to power, his prediction came true. Quidde escaped to Switzerland.

A humiliated and torn German nation condemned to economic misery would be a constant danger to world peace, just as a protected German nation whose inalienable rights and subsistence are safeguarded would be a strong pillar of world peace.

1887 **Juan Gris:** Spanish painter, who worked in Paris. Produced drawings in the Art Nouveau style for newspapers. Became involved with the Cubist artists. Developed his own version of Synthetic Cubism. Also produced sculpture, book illustrations and ballet costumes.

I always pet a dog with my left hand because if he bit me I'd still have my right hand to paint with.

1887 **Sidney Hillman:** Lithuanian-born American labor leader. First president of the Amalgamated Clothing Workers of America (1914–46). A founder of the Congress of Industrial Organizations. The Sidney Hillman Foundation presents an annual award for a book dealing with race relations, civil liberties, trade-union development, or world understanding.

Labor also wants shorter hours and a say in how work shall be done.

1900 **Erich Fromm:** German-born psychologist and social philosopher. Developed a humanist psychology. Sought to identify the sources of man's estrangement from himself in an industrial society. Explored man's paradoxical fear of freedom, his need for authority, particularly as applied in the extreme represented by Nazism. Books: *Escape from Freedom, Man for Himself* and *The Sane Society.*

Immature love says, "I love you because I need you." Mature love says "I need you because I love you."

1908 **Joan Crawford:** Born **Lucille LeSueur**. American actress in films for over five decades. Played leading ladies well into her fifties. Best as a bitch-goddess. Oscar nominated for *Possessed* and *Sudden Fear*. Won for *Mildred Pierce*. Other movies: *Our Dancing Daughters, The Women* and *Whatever Happened to Baby Jane?* Married to actors Douglas Fairbanks, Jr., Franchot Tone and Philip Terry. Her fourth husband, Alfred Steele, was chairman of the board of Pepsi-Cola. After her death, her daughter, Christina Crawford, wrote a best-selling book about how she mistreated her adopted children, *Mommie Dearest*, which was made into a movie, starring Faye Dunaway.

I love playing bitches. There's a lot of bitch in every woman — a lot in every man.

1910 **Akira Kurosawa:** First Japanese film director to win international acclaim. Studied painting before turning to films. During World War II, the films he directed had to conform to themes prescribed by official state propaganda policy. A Man of all genres, all periods, and all places, he combined Japanese aesthetic and cultural elements with a Western sense of action and drama. Films: *Rashomon*, which won an Oscar for Best Foreign Film, *Seven Samurai, Throne of Blood, Kagemusha* and *Ran.*

In a mad world, only the mad are sane.

1912 **Wernher Von Braun:** German-born American engineer. Early rocketry pioneer. After World War II, he turned all his research over to the U.S. Developed Germany's V-2 missiles, World War II and U.S. rocket engine program, designed the Saturn rocket, culminating in manned moon flight.

There is just one thing I can promise you about the outer-space program — your tax dollar will go further.

1929 Sir **Roger Bannister:** British athlete and physician. First person to run a mile race in under four minutes (3:59.4, May 6, 1954). Within months of his triumph a new sub four minute mile was run by John Landry of Australia (3:58). In one of the most famous races ever, Bannister (3:58.8) beat Landry (3:59.6), but failed to break the record. Since that time the record has been lower many times by many different runners.

The earth seemed to move with me. I found a new source of power and beauty, a source I never knew existed.

1937 **Craig Breedlove:** American high speed car driver. Five-time world land speed record holder. First to reach 400mph, 500mph, and 600mph using turbojet-powered vehicles named "Spirit of America." He believes his vehicle is capable of exceeding 800 mph. His wife, Lee, became the fastest woman on wheels in 1965 when she ran his car at 335 mph.

There's only one thing that can guarantee our failure, and that's if we quit.

1942 **Christina Ama Ata Aidoo:** Ghanaian author, poet and playwright. Her fiction deals with the tension between Western and African world views. Also has written children's books. Works: *The Dilemma of a Ghost, Birds and Other Poems,* and *The Girl Who Can and other Stories.*

For us Africans, literature must serve a purpose:

to expose, embarrass, and fight corruption and authoritarianism... It is understandable why the African artist is utilitarian.

OTHERS: 1699 Father American botany **John Bartram**, 1801 Dutch industrialist **Peterus D. Regout**, 1823 17th U.S. Vice President **Schuyler Colfax**, 1883 First king of Iraq/Syria **Faisal I**, 1887 Dutch musicologist **Anthony van Hoboken**, 1887 Russian assassin of Rasputin **Felix Felixovitch Yussupov**, 1901 Dutch resistance fighter **Jan H. de Groot**, 1911 British amateur golf champion **Richard Chapman**, 1921 English boat racer **Donald M. Campbell**, 1922 Italian actor/director **Ugo Tognazzi**, 1933 British bass-baritone **Norman Bailey**, 1953 American singer **Chaka Khan**, 1955 U.S. basketball player **Moses Malone**, 1956 U.S. chef **Laura Thorne**

March 24

1693 **John Harrison:** English clockmaker and mechanical genius. Pioneered the science of portable precision timekeeping. Invented a clock that would carry the true time from the home port allowing for the calculation a ship's precise longitude, which had been one of humankind's most epic quests. Harrison designed and built the world's first successful chronometer (maritime clock).

I think I may make bold to say that there is neither any other Mechanism or Mathematical thing in the World that is more beautiful or curious in texture that this my [longitude] Timekeeper.

1834 **William Morris:** English poet, artist, manufacturer and socialist. Designed fine furniture, wallpapers and tapestries. His firm revolutionized the art of house decoration and furniture in England. Founded a Society for the Protection of Ancient Buildings in 1877. Owner of the famous Kelm-scott Press. He translated Icelandic sagas.

Have nothing in your house that you do not know to be useful or believe to be beautiful.

1855 **Andrew Mellon:** American industrialist, financier, art collector, bibliophile, philanthropist. Developed extensive interests in coal, railroads, steel and water power. Secretary of Treasury (1921–32) under Presidents Harding, Coolidge and Hoover, ambassador to Great Britain (1932–33). Donated his art collection and the building to house it, the National Gallery of Art (1937).

Give tax breaks to large corporations, so that money can trickle down to the general public, in the form of extra jobs.

1855 **Olive Schreiner:** Pseudonym, **Ralph Iron**. South African novelist, feminist, social critic. Worker for human rights. Her novel *The Story of an African Farm* was the first imaginative work to come from her country. It describes life on the African veld.

There was never a great man who had not a great mother.

1874 **Harry Houdini [Erik Weisz]:** Hungarian-born escape artist and conjurer raised in Wisconsin. Earned an international reputation for his daring feats of escape from locked boxes while shackled with chains, handcuffed and underwater. Later took to debunking spiritualists and mind readers.

The greatest escape I ever made was when I left Appleton, Wisconsin.

1890 **John Rock:** American physician and scientist. Roman Catholic developer of the birth control pill. He believed that the church would approve of the birth control pill for the same reason it approved the Rhythm Method of birth control, in that it did not kill sperm, mutilate organs, or involve a physical barrier in the reproductive tract. He was profoundly disappointed when in 1968 with the release of the encyclical Humanae Vitae, which condemned oral as immoral along with all other artificial methods of birth control contraceptives.

A society which practices death control must at the same time practice birth control.

1897 **William Reich:** Austrian-American psychologist. In *The Function of the Orgasm* he argued that failure to achieve orgasm could produce neurosis. Advocate of sex education and radical left-wing politics. Conceived of mental illness and certain physical illnesses as deficiency of cosmic energy, which he treated by placing the patient in an orgone box, a cabinet with reflective inner surfaces.

Most intelligent people do not believe in God, but they fear him just the same.

1902 **Thomas E. Dewey:** American politician. "Racket-busting" prosecuting attorney for New York City (1935–37). Successful prosecution of organized crime led to three terms as New York governor. Twice unsuccessful Republican candidate for president (to Roosevelt in 1944 and Truman in 1948). The latter race is considered one of the greatest electoral upsets in U.S. history.

No man should be in public office who can't make more money in private life

1903 **Malcolm Muggeridge:** British writer, journalist and social critic. Served in British Intelligence during World War II. Editor of *Punch*. Outspoken critic of liberalism. Controversial iconoclast. Avowed atheist who gradually embraced Roman Catholicism. Wrote some 30 books. Popular interviewer and TV panelist. *Chronicles of Wasted Time* is his autobiography.

People do not believe lies because they have to, but because they want to.

1919 **Lawrence Ferlinghetti:** American poet, best known as the co-owner with Peter D. Martin of the City Lights Bookhouse and publishing house in San Francisco that published the early works of the Beat Generation, including Jack Kerouac and Allen Ginsberg.

Southern California, where the American Dream came too true.

1919 **Robert L. Heilbroner:** American economist, social philosopher and critic of capitalism, who describes himself as a radical conservative. Best known for *The Worldly Philosophers*, a survey of the lives and contributions of famous economists, most notably Adam Smith, Karl Marx and John Maynard Keynes. The book sold nearly four million copies. Classified economies, as either Traditional (primarily agriculturally-based), Command (centrally planned economy by the state), Market (free market capitalism) or Mixed (a combination of the other three).

The cure for capitalism's failing would require that a government would have to rise above the interests of one class alone.

1951 **Pat Bradley:** American golfer. Member of the LPGA Hall-of-Fame. Won thirty-one tournaments, including six major championships. Played for the U.S. in the Solheim Cup four times and twice served as captain of the team. First woman golfer to pass $3 million in career earnings.

When I would play badly, Mom would give me a shoulder to cry on, but Daddy would tell me to pick myself up and dig in.

OTHERS: 1494 German mineralogist **Georgius Agricola**, 1755 Framer of the U.S. Constitution **Rufus King**, 1834 U.S. geologist/explorer **John Wesley Powell**, 1835 Austrian physicist **Josef Stefan**, 1869 French director of Comédie Française **Émile Fabre**, 1887 Silent screen comedian **Roscoe "Fatty" Arbuckle**, 1893 Baseball first baseman **George Sisler**, 1895 U.S. dancer/dance teacher **Arthur Murray**, 1909 American bank robber **Clyde Barrow**, 1911 U.S. animator **Joseph Barbera**, 1920 U.S. actor/dancer **Gene Nelson**, 1928 U.S. concert pianist **Byron Janis** 1930 American actor **Steve McQueen**, 1940 Fashion designer **Bob Mackie**, 1944 Last 30-game winning pitcher **Dennis McClain**

March 25

1862 **George Sutherland:** English-born American politician and jurist. Congressman from Utah (1901–3). U.S. Senator (1905–17). Pushed passage of the 19th (woman suffrage) Amendment to the U.S. Constitution. Justice of the Supreme Court (1922–37).

For the saddest epitaph which can be carved in memory of a vanished liberty is that it was lost because its possessor s failed to stretch forth a saving hand while yet there was time.

1867 **Arturo Toscanini:** Italian musician. Considered by critics to be the greatest virtuoso conductor of the first half of the 20th century. Began his professional life as a cellist. Conducted in various Italian opera houses. Premiered *I Pagliacci* and *La Bohème*. Served as music director of La Scala and at the Metropolitan Opera. Stopped performing in Germany to protest Nazi policies. Led the NBC Orchestra for 27 years. The maestro of rebuke, he would throw his baton during rehearsals. He was sued by one musician that he hit with the baton.

I kissed my first woman and smoked my first cigarette on the same day; I have never had time for tobacco since.

1881 **Béla Bartók:** Hungarian composer and pianist. Noted for employing Hungarian folk themes in his opera, *Bluebeard's Castle*, ballets, *The Wooden Prince* and *The Wonderful Mandarin* and piano collection, *Mikrokosmos*. Professor of piano at the Budapest Academy. Left Hungry to settle in the U.S.A. in 1939.

I cannot conceive of music that expresses absolutely nothing.

1881 **Mary Webb:** née **Meredith.** English novelist and poet. In her novels including *The Golden Arrow* and *Precious Bone* she conveyed rich and intense impressions of the Shropshire countryside and its people, doing for her home what Thomas Hardy did for Dorset. Other works: *Gone to Earth, Seven for a Secret* and her nature essays, *The Spring of Joy*.

If you stop to be kind, you must swerve often from your path.

1908 Sir **David Lean:** British director. Early on, he was known for intimate drama, but later turned to super productions with which he came to be identified. Oscar winner for *The Bridge on the River Kwai* and *Lawrence of Arabia*. Others: *Blithe Spirit, Brief Encounter, Great Expectations, Oliver Twist, Doctor Zhivago, Ryan's Daughter* and *A Passage to India*. Married six times, his first wife was actress Kay Walsh and the second, actress Ann Todd.

I'm first and foremost interested in the story, the characters.

1921 **Simone Signoret:** Born **Simone Henriette Kaminker**. German-born French actress. An intelligent, sensuous woman, who projected strength and vulnerability at the same time. Oscar winner for *Room at the Top*. Nominated for her role in *Ship of Fools*; one of the finest performances ever when she and Oskar Werner were together. She aged gracefully and ended her brilliant career with a series of superb portrayals, most notably, *Mama Rosa*. Others: *La Ronde, Casque d'Or*, and *The Sea Gull*.

Chains do not hold a marriage together. It is threads, hundreds of threads, which sew people together through the years.

1925 **Flannery O'Connor:** American short-story writer and novelist. Most of her fiction is set in the South, homing in on the Protestant fundamentalists who dominated the region. Stories blend a strong religious faith with the grotesque. Novels, *Wise Blood* and *The Violent Bear It Away*. Short story collections: *A Good Man Is Hard to Find and other stories* and *Everything that Rises Must Converge*.

The truth does not change according to our ability to stomach it.

1934 **Gloria Steinem:** American feminist, journalist, and editor. Activist for women's rights and in protesting the Vietnam War, and racism. Cofounded *Ms.* magazine (1971). Founded *Coalition of Labor Union Women* and *Women USA*. Cofounded the *National Organization for Women*. Books include: *Outrageous Acts* *and Everyday Rebellion, Revolution from Within* and *A Book of Self Esteem.*

Self-esteem isn't everything; it's just that there's nothing without it.

1939 **Toni Cade Bambara:** African-American author, social activist, and college professor. Studied theater in New York City and mime in France. Taught at Rutgers University and Spelman College. She classified her writing as upbeat fiction. The narrator in many of her stories is a tough, brave, caring and sassy young girl. First collection of Stories was *Gorilla, My Love.* Other works: *Tales and Stories for Black Folks* and *If Blessings Come.*

My mother, religious-negro, proud of having waded through a storm, is, very obviously a sturdy bridge that I have crossed over on.

1940 **Anita Bryant:** American singer, who had three pop hits: "'Til There Was You," "Paper Roses," and "In My Little Corner of the World." Became a spokesperson for the Florida Citrus Commission in 1969. Most remembered for her successful campaign in the 1970s to repeal a local Miami ordinance that prohibited discrimination on the basis of sexual orientation. Her political activism all but ended her entertainment career.

In victory, we shall not be vindictive. We shall continue to seek help and change for homosexuals, whose sick and sad values belie the word "gay," which they pathetically use to cover their unhappy lives.

1942 **Aretha Franklin:** American singer of soul music. Known as "Queen of Soul" and "Lady Soul" Made her first recording at age 12. First woman inducted into the Rock and Roll Hall of Fame. Hit songs: "I Never Loved a Man," "Rose in Spanish Harlem," "Respect," "Chain of Fools," "Think," and "Natural Woman." Albums: *I Never Loved a Man the Way I Love You* and *Love All the Hurt Away.*

If a song's about something I've experienced or that could've happened to me it's good. But if it is alien to me, I couldn't lend anything to it. Because that's what soul is all about.

1947 **Elton John:** Born **Reginald Kenneth Dwight**. British singer, composer and pianist. Very successful partnership with lyricist Bernie Taupin. Hit album: *Goodbye Yellow Brick Rose.* Hit songs: "Rocket Man," "Bennie and the Jets," and "Don't Go Breaking My Heart," recorded with Kiki Dee. His version of "Candle in the Wind" performed at the funeral of Diana, Princess of Wales, immediately became the best selling record of all time.

There is nothing wrong with going to bed with someone of your own sex. People should be very free with sex; they should draw the line at goats.

OTHERS: 1594 Dutch writer **Maria Tesselschade Roemers Visscher**, 1653 French physicist **Joseph Sauveur**, 1702 Dutch merchant **Pieter Teyler Van der Hulst**, 1782 Napoleon's sister **Caroline Bonaparte**, 1784 Belgian/composer **François-Joseph Fétis**, 1797 Founder of Church of God **John Winebrenner**, 1839 U.S. educator **William Bell Wait**, 1867 Mount Rushmore sculptor **Gutzon Borglum**, 1877 French writer **Alphonse de Châteaubriant**, 1887 Czech painter/critic **Josef Capek**, 1899 Hungarian playwright **Bella Spewack**, 1903 Orchestra leader **Frankie Carle**, 1921 U.S. actress **Nancy Kelly**, 1922 U.S. Modeling agency head **Eileen Ford**, 1937 U.S. Pizza tycoon **Tom Monaghan**

March 26

1850 **Edward Bellamy:** American author and journalist. Achieved immense popularity with his Utopian romance, *Looking Backward,* which predicted a new social order. It influenced economic thinking both in the U.S. and Europe.

Looking Backward ***was written in the belief that the Golden Age lies before us and not behind us.***

1859 **A.E. [Alfred Edward] Housman:** English scholar and lyric poet. Taught first at University College, London, then at Cambridge. His spare and simple styled poetry expressed a Romantic pessimism. Works: *A Shropshire Lad, Last Poems* and posthumously, *More Poems.* Published critical editions of Manlius, Juvenal and Lucan.

The house of delusions is cheap to build but drafty to live in.

1874 **Robert Frost:** American poet especially known for his lyric poem "A Boy's Will" and the narrative poem "North of Boston." Best known for his verse dealing with New England life written in traditional verse forms. Poems: "The Road Not Taken," "Birches," "Stopping by Woods on a Snowy Evening" and "The Gift Outright." Pulitzer prizes for *New Hampshire* (1923), *Collected Poems* (1930) and *A Further Range* (1936). Poetry consultant at the Library of Congress. Read one of his poems at the inauguration of President Kennedy.

In three words I can sum up everything I've learned about life. It goes on.

1893 **James Bryant Conant:** American chemist, educator and diplomat. President of Harvard (1933–53). Chaired Defense Research Committee (1941–46), which developed atomic bomb. Ambassador to West Germany (1955–57). Headed a Carnegie Corporation study of U.S. high schools.

There is only one proved way of assisting the advancement of pure science — that of picking men of genius, backing them heavily, and leaving them to direct themselves.

1904 **Joseph Campbell:** American mythologist. As a child he became fascinated with Native American culture, which led him to his lifelong passion with myth and its similar, cohesive threads among all human cultures. Studied with Carl Jung. Professor at Sarah Lawrence College for 38 years. One of his best-known books is *The Hero with a Thousand Faces,* which discusses the myth of the hero's journey. Collaborated with Bill Moyers on the PBS series *The Power of Myth.*

The function of an artist is the mythologization of the environment and the world.

1905 **Viktor Frankl:** Austrian psychiatrist, neurologist and psychotherapist. One of the key figures in existential therapy. In his world famous book *Man's Search for Meaning*, he objectively described the life of an ordinary concentration camp inmate (which he had been for 3 years) from the perspective of a psychiatrist. He describes his psychotherapeutic method for finding a reason to live.

When we are no longer able to change a situation — we are challenged to change ourselves.

1911 **Tennessee Williams:** Born **Thomas Lanier Williams**. His professional name comes from an ancestor who was the first senator of Tennessee. American playwright. Often considered the foremost dramatist of the post–World War II era. Plays: New York. Drama Critics' Circle Award winner *The Glass Menagerie*, Pulitzer Prize winners *A Streetcar Named Desire*, and *Cat on a Hot Tin Roof.* Others: *Sweet Bird of Youth* and *The Night of the Iguana*.

Life is all memory, except for the present moment that goes by you so quickly you hardly catch it going.

1913 **Paul Erdős:** Hungarian born mathematician. A mathematical gypsy; he belonged to no country, had no wife, no children, no permanent address, nor an employer. Instead he moved about the world to talk to other mathematicians about his one true love, mathematics, and produce papers for publication. The total number of papers published in his lifetime, with or without collaborators, is approximately 1,500. When he showed up, often unannounced, at the home of a mathematician with whom he planned to stay for some unspecified time, he would announce, "My mind is open," meaning he was ready to do mathematics.

Why are numbers beautiful? It's like asking why is Beethoven's Ninth Symphony beautiful. If you don't see why, someone can't tell you. I know numbers are beautiful. If they aren't beautiful, nothing is.

1913 **Cyril O. Houle:** American educator and author. Internationally recognized scholar of adult and continuing education. Professor of Education at the University of Chicago (1939–78). Books: *The Inquiring Mind* and *Continuing Learning in the Professions*.

Adults can learn most things better than children, though it may take them longer.

1930 **Sandra Day O'Connor:** American lawyer and jurist. Assistant Attorney-General (1965–9) in Arizona, then a state senator. Superior court judge (1974–79) and judge of the Arizona Court of Appeals (1979–81). First woman appointed to the U.S. Supreme Court where she was considered a moderate. Was the swing vote on many important 5 to 4 decisions, including the one that guaranteed George W. Bush the presidency. She retired in 2005.

The more education a woman has, the wider the gap between men's and women's earnings for the same work.

1942 **Erica Jong:** Born **Erica Mann**. American novelist and poet. Her first novel, *Fear of Flying*, detailed the sexual misadventures of a young woman named Isadora Wing. It became a runaway best-seller. Isadora reappeared in *How to Save Your Own Life* and *Parachutes and Kisses*. Jong's poetry collections: *Fruits and Vegetables* and *Half-Lives*.

Show me a woman who doesn't feel guilty and I'll show you a man.

1944 **Diana Ross:** Originally **Diane Earle**. African-American actress and singer with the Motown trio "The Supremes." Their classic hits: "Baby Love" and "Stop! In the Name of Love." Left the group for a solo career. Notable film roles as Billie Holiday in *Lady Sings the Blues*, *Mahogany* and *The Wiz*.

I know my fans want to know who I'm sleeping with, but it's really none of their business.

OTHERS: 1516 Swiss naturalist **Konrad von Gesner**, 1753 English physicist **Benjamin Thompson**, 1773 Mathematician/astronomer **Nathaniel Bowditch**, 1819 German author/feminist **Louise Otto**, 1863 British founder of Rolls Royce **Henry Royce**, 1868 King of Egypt **Faud I**, 1875 President of South Korea **Syngman Rhee**, 1880 U.S. restaurant guide writer **Duncan Hines**, 1888 Swedish ethnologist **Sigurd Erixon**, 1893 Founder of Italian Communist Party **Palmiro Togliatti**, 1908 U.S. writer **Betty MacDonald**, 1914 U.S. general **William Westmoreland**, 1916 U.S. actor **Sterling Hayden**, 1925 French composer/conductor **Pierre Boulez**, 1948 U.S. drummer/vocalist **Steven Tyler**

March 27

1797 **Alfred de Vigny:** French poet, dramatist and novelist. Wrote of his experiences as a captain in the Royal Guards, in *Servitude et grandeur militaires*. His masterpiece is the romantic drama *Chatterton*, written for his lover, actress Marie Dorval.

The existence of the soldier, next to capital punishment, is the most grievous vestige of barbarism which survives among men.

1857 **Karl Pearson:** English mathematician and scientist. Published *The Grammar of Science*, and works on eugenics, mathematics and biometrics. Motivated by the study of evolution and heredity. Founder of modern statistical analysis.

Statistics is the grammar of science.

1879 **Edward Steichen:** World-famous Luxembourg-born American photographer and artist. Noted for pioneering efforts to establish photography as a fine art and his studies of nudes. Associated for many years with the Museum of Modern Art. Organized the world-famous exhibition "The Family of Man" (1955).

Photography records the gamut of feeling written on the human face, the beauty of the earth and skies that man has inherited, and the wealth and confusion man has created. It is a major force in explaining man to man.

1886 **Ludwig Mies van der Rohe:** German-born American architect. Leading practitioner of 20th century functionalist architecture. A pioneer of glass skyscrapers. Buildings: Seagram Building, New York City, and the Public Library, Washington, D.C.

Less is more.

1892 **Thorne Smith:** U.S. writer of fantasy fiction. Once one of America's best known humor authors, now nearly forgotten. His endearing comedies, filled with naughty double entendres, included: *Topper, The Night Life of the Gods, The Bishop's Jaegers* and posthumously *I Married a Witch.*

Steven's mind was so tolerant that he could have attended a lynching everyday without being critical.

1899 **Gloria Swanson:** American silent screen actress in films such as *Male and Female, The Great Moment, Queen Kelly.* Had an affair with Joseph P. Kennedy, father of President Kennedy, who backed her in producing her own films through United Artists. Oscar nominated for *The Trespasser, Sadie Thompson* and *Sunset Boulevard.* Married 6 times, the first briefly to actor Wallace Beery when she was 17. Autobiography: *Swanson on Swanson.*

I've given my memoirs far more thought than any of my marriages. You can't divorce a book.

1912 **James Callaghan:** Leader of Britain's Labor Party. Chancellor of the Exchequer in the Harold Wilson government, introducing some of the most controversial taxation measures in British history. Prime Minister (1976–79).

A lie can be half way around the world before the truth has got its boots on.

1914 **Budd Schulberg:** American novelist, screenwriter. Wrote *What Makes Sammy Run?* a best-selling novel about film industry people, Oscar winner for the screenplay of *On the Waterfront.* Also wrote screenplays for *The Harder They Fall* and *A Face in the Crowd.*

Living with a conscience is like driving a car with the brakes on.

1917 **Cyrus R. Vance:** American public official. Active supporter of the Vietnam War as deputy secretary of defense. Later urged Lyndon Johnson to cease bombing North Vietnam. Negotiated a peace with the Vietnamese. Secretary of State under Jimmy Carter but resigned in a disagreement about the management of the Iran hostage crisis.

You have to listen to adversaries and keep looking for that point beyond which it's against their interests to keep on disagreeing or fighting.

1923 **Louis Simpson:** Jamaican-born American poet. Received a Ph.D. from Columbia University and taught there as well as the University of California, Berkeley. Pulitzer Price winner for poetry for *At the End of the Open Road.* Other works: *The Arrivistes* and *A Revolution in Taste: Studies of Dylan Thomas, Allen Ginsberg, Sylvia Plath, and Robert Lowell.*

Health care in this country is in a rut... The system doesn't care, politicians don't listen and insurance companies are looking only at the bottom line.

1924 **Sarah Vaughan:** "Sassy." African-American singer and pianist. Got her start on the "Dave Garroway Show." First be-bop singer. Sometimes forgot the lyrics because she was concentrating so hard on the notes and phrases. Noted for her pure yet sophisticated styling. One of the great jazz singers, ranking alongside Billie Holliday and Ella Fitzgerald. Hits: "Make Yourself Comfortable" and "Broken Hearted Melody."

When I sing, trouble can sit right on my shoulder and I don't even notice.

1963 **Quentin Tarantino:** U.S. screenwriter, film director and actor. Makes bold use of nonlinear storylines, bloody violence, and memorable dialogue in films such as *Reservoir Dogs, True Romance, Natural Born Killers, Pulp Fiction* and *Kill Bill I* and *II.*

I don't believe in elitism. I don't think the audience is this dumb person lower than me. I am the audience.

OTHERS: 1760 French ballet dancer **Auguste Vestrius,** 1780 German publisher **August L. Crelle,** 1785 Pretender to the French throne during the revolution **Louis XVII,** 1844 U.S. Arctic explorer **Adolphus Washington Greely,** 1845 Discovered X-rays **Wilhelm Conrad Röntgen,** 1868 U.S. songwriter **Patty Smith Hill,** 1871 German novelist **Heinrich Mann,** 1892 U.S. composer **Ferde Grofé,** 1893 Yugoslavian general/Nazi collaborator **Dragoljub "Dragon" Mihailović,** 1893 Hungarian socialist **Karl Mannheim,** 1920 U.S. musician **Richard Hayman,** 1920 U.S. singer **Snooky Lanson,** 1927 Newspaper columnist **Anthony Lewis,** 1927 U.S.S.R. cellist/conductor **Mstislav L. Rostropovich**

March 28

1515 Saint **Teresa of Avila:** Spanish religious reformer, mystic, author and saint. Returned Carmelite order to its original austerity of total withdrawal. Her doctrines have been accepted as the classical exposition of contemplative life. Experienced ecstasies and the fame of her sanctity spread. Wrote beautiful mystical and spiritual pieces, including *The Interior Castle, Way of Perfection* and *The Book of Foundations.* First woman to be elevated to Doctor of the Church.

It is true that we cannot be free from sin, but at least let our sins not always be the same.

1592 **Johann Amos Comenius:** Bohemian educational reformer, theologian and religious leader. Author of the first illustrated textbook, *Orbus pictus.* It was used for 200 years. Pioneer of new language teaching methods. Emphasized learning about things rather than about grammar per se.

Man differs from animals in his capacity as the living image of God, that is, his creative power.

1862 **Aristide Briand:** French statesman, lawyer and journalist. Eleven times French premier. Foreign minister (1925–32). Worked for the renunciation of war. Achievements included the Pact of Locarno and the Kellogg-Briand Pact. Shared the Nobel Peace Prize with Gustav Stresemann, advocating a United States of Europe.

A country grows in history not only because of the heroism of its troops on the field of battle; it grows also when it turns to justice and to right for the conservation of its interests.

1891 **Paul Whiteman:** "The King of Jazz." American musician and bandleader. Pioneer of "sweet style." Popularized a musical style that helped to introduce jazz to mainstream audiences during the 1920s and 1930s. Responsible for George Gershwin's experimentations with symphonic jazz. Introduced the composer's *Rhapsody in Blue* in concert.

Jazz came to America 300 years ago in chains... Jazz is the folk music of the machine age... Jazz tickles your muscles, symphonies stretch your soul.

1909 **Nelson Algren:** American author. Leading member of the "Chicago school of realism." Wrote brutally realistic novels about life in Chicago slums, skillfully capturing the mood of the city's poor. Greatest successes: *The Man with the Golden Arm* and *A Walk on the Wild Side*. Had a transatlantic affair with Simone de Beauvoir.

Never eat at a place called Mom's. Never play cards with a man called Doc. And never lie down with a woman who's got more trouble than you.

1914 **Edmund Muskie:** American politician and lawyer. Governor of Maine. U.S. senator. Democrat candidate for the vice-presidency in 1968. Secretary of State during Carter administration.

In Maine we have a saying that there's no point in speaking unless you can improve on silence.

1921 **Dirk Bogarde:** British actor. Early in his career he mainly appeared in enjoyable light comedies such as *Doctor in the House*. In his mature roles he demonstrated his acting range in films such as *Victim, The Servant, Darling, The Damned* and *Death in Venice*.

The camera can photograph thought.

1928 **Zbigniew Brzezinski:** Polish-born American government official and political scientist. Assistant to President Carter for national security affairs (1977–81). Chief architect of a tough human rights policy directed against the Soviet Union.

Doing it all by ourselves on our terms, ignoring the rest of the world, shouting loudly that if you're not with us, you are against us, is not going to be a very successful policy.

1931 **Jane Vincent Rule:** American-born Canadian novelist and critic. Outspoken advocate of both free speech and gay rights. Her novels include *Desert of the Heart, This Is Not for You, Against the Season, Contact with the World* and *Lesbian Images*.

Mortality is a test of our conformity rather than our integrity.

1936 **Mario Vargas Llosa:** Peruvian journalist, broadcaster, novelist and essayist. Committed to social change before turning increasingly conservative. Ran for Peruvian president. Works: *The Time of the Hero, The Green House* and *The War of the End of the World*.

If you are killed because you are a writer, that's the maximum expression of respect, you know.

1942 **Neil Kinnock:** Welch politician. Rose through the Labor Party ranks. Member of the Party's National Executive Committee. Elected party leader in 1983. Persuaded the party to abandon its radical policies on disarmament and large-scale nationalization.

Loyalty is a fine quality, but in excess it fills political graveyards.

1955 **Reba McEntire:** One of the best selling American country singers of all times. Won the Female Vocalist of the Year award from the Country Music Association four years in a row. Songs: "I'd Really Love to See You Tonight," "(You Lift Me) Up to Heaven," "Can't Even Get the Blues No More," and "Love Needs a Holiday."

For me, singing sad songs often has a way of healing a situation. It gets the hurt out in the open into the light, out of the darkness.

OTHERS: 1472 Florentine Renaissance painter **Fra Bartolomeo**, 1660 King of England **George I (Ludwig)**, 1731 Spanish playwright **Rámon de la Cruz**, 1760 English abolitionist **Thomas Clarkson**, 1859 Founder of French Rosicrucians **Joséphin Péladan**, 1887 Curaçao composer **Rudolf F.W. Boskaljon**, 1895 12th prophet of Mormon Church **Spencer W. Kimball**, 1903 Bohemian pianist **Rudolf Serkin**, 1905 Host of *Wild Kingdom* **Marlin Perkins**, 1905 Film producer **Pandro S. Berman**, 1924 Child actor **Freddie Bartholomew**, 1944 Basketball star **Rick Barry**, 1948 U.S. keyboardist **John Evans**, 1948 U.S. actress **Dianne Wiest**

March 29

1790 **John Tyler:** American lawyer and tenth U.S. president. First vice president to attain presidency upon the death of a president, William Henry Harrison. States-rights supporter. As president he vetoed a national bank bill supported by his party, the Whigs, causing most of the members of his cabinet to resign.

Popularity, I have always thought may aptly be compared to a coquette — the more you woo her, the more apt is she to elude your embrace.

1819 **Isaac Mayer Wise:** Bohemian-born American rabbi and religious leader. Founded Reformed Judaism in the United States. Principal founder of American Hebrew Congregations. President of Hebrew Union College. Compiled a standard Reform prayer book. Worked to establish Palestine as a home for the Jews.

The Greek grasped the present moment, and was the artist; the Jew worshipped the timeless spirit, and was the prophet.

1831 **Amelia Barr:** English-born American writer and journalist. Author of more than 70 books. Wrote historical fiction such as *Remember the Alamo*. Her remarkable life story was told in her autobiography *All the Days of My Life*.

There are no little events in life, those we think of no consequence may be full of fate, and it is at our own risk if we neglect the acquaintance and opportunities that seem to be casually offered, and of small importance.

1869 **Edwin Lutyens:** British architect. Working with designer Gertrude Jekyll, he built the house at Munstead Wood, Godlaming, Surrey, which established his reputation. Adapted pass styles to contemporary structures in original ways. Combined aspects of Classical architect with Indian motifs for his buildings in the new capital of India, New Delhi.

There will never be great architects or great architecture without great patrons.

1889 **Howard Lindsay:** American dramatist, producer, and actor. Wrote librettos for Cole Porter musicals *Anything Goes* and *Red, Hot and Blue*. Co-wrote with Russel Crouse, *Life with Father*, which he starred in on Broadway (1939–46).

An optimist in the atomic age is a person who thinks the future is uncertain.

1892 **Joseph Cardinal Mindszenty:** Hungarian religious leader, who opposed fascism and communism. Refused to permit Hungary's Catholic schools to be secularized by the communists. Became internationally known in 1948 when he was arrested by the Communist government and charged with treason. He sought asylum in the U.S. embassy and lived there for 15 years.

The most important person on Earth is a mother ... she has built something more magnificent than any cathedral— a dwelling for an immortal soul, the tiny perfection of her baby's body.

1916 **Eugene McCarthy:** "Clean Gene." College professor and U.S. politician, First congressman to challenge red-baiting Senator Joe McCarthy. Liberal democrat, and outspoken critic of the Vietnam War. Minnesota congressman (1949–59), Senator (1959–70). Sought Democratic presidential nomination three times. In 1968, as the peace candidate, his early success in the primaries convinced Lyndon Johnson not to seek reelection. The following are lines from his poem "Vietnam Message."

We will take our napalm and flame throwers/ out of the land that scarcely knows the use of matches.../ We will leave you small joys/ and smaller troubles.

1918 **Pearl Mae Bailey:** African-American singer with the Count Basie band. Known for her lively and earthy style. Starred in Broadway productions *St. Louis Woman* and received a Tony Award with the all-black cast of *Hello Dolly*. Films: *Carmen Jones* and *Porgy and Bess*.

Hungry people cannot be good at learning or producing anything except perhaps violence.

1918 **Sam Walton:** American retail magnate and founder of Wal-Mart stores Inc., the largest retail sales chain in the U.S. Opened his first store in Rogers, Arkansas in 1962. At his death there were more than 1700 Wal-Marts, making his family the wealthiest in the U.S.

There's only one boss. The customer. And he can fire everybody in the company from the chairman on down, simply by spending his money somewhere else.

1925 **Emlen Tunnell:** "Offense on Defense." One of best defensive backs ever. New York Giants and Green Bay Packers (1948–61). Had 79 career interceptions. Football Hall of Fame (1967).

Tackling is football. Running is track.

1936 **Judith Guest:** American novelist. The great-niece of writer Edgar A. Guest. Best known for *Ordinary People*, which was made in a movie in 1976, winning the Academy Award for Best Picture.

Depression is not sobbing and crying and giving vent; it is plain and simple reduction of feeling.

1964 **Elle Macpherson [Elanor Nancy Gow]:** Australian supermodel and actress. Nicknamed "The Body." Most financially successful of all the world's supermodels. First living Australian entertainer to be put on a postage stamp. Made her movie debut as an artist's model in *Sirens*. Appeared in five episodes of the TV sitcom *Friends*.

If your wearing lingerie that makes you feel glamorous, you're halfway to turning heads.

OTHERS: 1819 Drilled first productive U.S. oil well **Edwin Drake**, 1867 Winningest baseball pitcher **Cy Young**, 1869 Bohemian–U.S. anthropologist **Aleš Hrdlička**, 1875 Composer **Paul Rubens**, 1888 Founder United Parcel Post **James E. Casey**, 1905 Orchestra leader **Mantovani**, 1906 English organist/composer **E. Power Biggs**, 1917 Racehorse winner of 20 of 21 races **Man o' War**, 1939 Hong Kong actress **Nancy Kwan**, 1943 English comedian/actor **Eric Idle**, 1943 British Prime Minister **John Major**, 1943 Greek composer/ keyboardist **Vangelis**, 1944 Pitcher with 31 wins in 1968 **Denny McLain**, 1954 Comatose patient **Karen Anne Quinlan**, 1956 Gymnast **Kurt Thomas**

March 30

1135 **Moses Maimonides:** Jewish philosopher, jurist, and physician born in Córdoba, Spain. Obliged to practice his faith in secrecy under Islamic rule. Organized and clarified Torah, the Jewish oral law. Attempted to reconcile the Bible, Jewish tradition and Aristotle. Moved to Egypt where she became court physician to the sultan Saladin. Wrote a classic work of religious philosophy, *The Guide of the Perplexed*.

Do not consider it proof just because it is written in books, for a liar who will deceive with his tongue will not hesitate to do the same with his pen.

1568 Sir **Henry Wotton:** English poet, traveler, connoisseur and diplomat. Wrote poems "You meaner beauties of the night" and "Character of a Happy Life." Also wrote *The Elements of Architecture*. Ambassador to Venice.

An ambassador is an honest man sent to lie abroad for the good of his country.

1746 **Francisco de Goya y Lucientes:** Spanish painter and etcher. The three phases of his career: portraits and genre works, powerful romantic depictions of heroes of war, and macabre renderings of nightmare subjects. Famous for his portraits. Works include: *The Family of Charles IV, The Naked Maja* and an 82-etching series *The Disasters of War.*

Fantasy, abandoned by reason, produces impossible monsters; united with it, she is the mother of the arts and the origin of marvels.

1820 **Anna Sewell:** English novelist. An invalid most of her life, she wrote the children's classic *Black Beauty,* the story of a horse, as a plea for the more humane treatment of animals. Perhaps the most famous book ever written about a horse.

We call them dumb animals, and so they are, for they cannot tell us how they feel, but they do not suffer less because they have no words.

1844 **Paul Verlaine:** French poet. Among the first symbolists. Prominent in the bohemian literary life of Paris. His marriage was destroyed by his fascination with Arthur Rimbaud. Verlaine shot Rimbaud when the latter threatened to leave him. While in prison he converted to Catholicism. Described his religious faith and his emotional odyssey in *Sagesse.* Spent his later years in poverty. Wrote *Songs Without Words* and *The Accursed Poets.*

Take eloquence and wring its neck.

1853 **Vincent Van Gogh:** Dutch post–Impressionist painter, lithographer and etcher. Leader of the post–Impressionist school. Noted for brilliant colors and swirling brush strokes. Committed suicide (1890). Produced more than 800 paintings and 700 drawings in a ten year period, only one of which was sold in his lifetime. His work became popular 50 years after his death. Paintings: *The Potato Eaters, Starry Night, Sunflowers* and *Cornfields with Flight of Birds.*

For my part I know nothing with any certainty, but the sight of the stars make me dream.

1880 **Sean O'Casey:** Irish dramatist. Embraced the Irish nationalist cause and was active in the labor movement and its paramilitary Irish citizens Army. His writings were noted for his rigid social conscience and his vitality of language. Plays: *Juno and the Paycock* and *The Plough and the Stars,* an anti-war drama which provoked a full-scale riot, and caused him to leave Ireland for good.

The world's a stage and most of us are desperately unrehearsed.

1919 **McGeorge Bundy:** U.S. government official and administrator. Dean of Arts and Sciences at Harvard. Played a major role in foreign policy decisions during the Kennedy and Johnson administrations, notably in the Vietnam War. President of the Ford Foundation.

Although war is evil; it is occasionally the lesser of two evils.

1928 **Tom Sharpe:** English satirical author. Moved to South Africa, doing social work and teaching. His novels *Riotous Assembly* and *Indecent Exposure* were bitter and outrageous satires of the apartheid regime. His other works took on dumbed-down education, British class snobbery, the literary world, all political extremists, political correctedness, bureaucracy and stupidity in general.

We must not only strike the iron while it is hot; we must strike if until it is hot.

1937 **Warren Beatty:** U.S. actor, producer, director and writer. Brother of Shirley MacLaine. Nominated for Oscars for *Bonnie and Clyde, Heaven Can Wait, Reds* (also nominated for writing, won for directing) and *Bugsy.* After having affairs with many of the most beautiful women in films, he married Annette Bening.

Marriage requires a special talent, like acting. Monogamy requires genius.

1968 **Céline Dion:** Canadian singer, who first came to show business prominence with her recording of the theme song from the film *Beauty and the Beast,* which earned a Grammy and an Oscar. This has been followed by a string of hit albums, including *Falling Into You.*

I'm not trying to be a nice girl, but it's me. I'm not afraid to be nice.

1970 **Secretariat:** "Big Red." Arguably the greatest race horse in history. Won the first Triple Crown in 25 years in 1973, becoming the only horse to break the 2-minute mark in the Kentucky Derby and won the Belmont Stakes by 31 lengths. Appeared on the covers of *Time, Newsweek* and *Sports Illustrated* the same week. Won 16 of 21 races. Died October 4, 1989. On ESPN's Classic's Sports Century series, author George Plimpton said of Secretariat:

He was the only honest thing in this country at the time. This huge magnificent animal who wasn't tied up in scandal, wasn't ties up in money, he just ran because he loved running.

OTHERS: 1432 Sultan of Turkey **Mehmed II**, 1672 Russian tsar **Peter the Great**, 1674 Agricultural writer **Jethro Tull**, 1719 Author of 1st music history **Sir John Hawkins**, 1842 U.S. historian/philosopher **John Fiske**, 1864 German sociologist **Franz Oppenheimer**, 1876 U.S. mental hygienist **Clifford Whittingham Beers**, 1883 U.S. sculptor **Jo Davidson**, 1888 Swedish actress **Anna Q. Nilsson**, 1894 Russian airplane builder **Sergei Ilyushin**, 1903 U.S. film producer **Sol Siegel**, 1913 CIA head **Richard Helms**, 1913 U.S. singer **Frankie Laine**, 1930 TV game host **Peter Marshall**, 1940 Brazilian singer **Astrud Gilberto**, 1945 Guitarist **Eric Clapton**, 1962 Rap artist **M.C. Hammer**

March 31

1596 **René Descartes:** French mathematician and philosopher. Considered the father of modern philosophy. He developed a dualistic system in which he distinguished radically between the mind and matter. His philosophical theories formed the basis for 17th century rationalism. Originated modern scientific method. As a mathematician, he founded analytic geometry, the marriage of algebra and geometry, reformed algebraic notation and ushered in the era of modern mathematics.

In order to reach the Truth, it is necessary, once

in one's life, to put everything in doubt — so far as possible.

1621 **Andrew Marvell:** English poet, satirist and public official. Assistant to John Milton in the foreign affairs office. Considered one of the finest Metaphysical poets. Poems: "The Garden," "To His Coy Mistress," and "A Dialogue Between the Soul and Body."
The grave's a fine and private place,/ But none, I think do there embrace.

1809 **Edward Fitzgerald:** English translator, man of letters. His most famous work was his interpretation of the *Rubaiyat* of Omar Khayyam. It was not merely a translation; it was essentially a completely new work.
The Moving Finger writes; and having writ/ Moves on; nor all your Piety nor Wit/ Shall lure it back to cancel half a Line/ Nor all your Tears wash out a Word of it.

1835 **John La Farge:** American painter, stained glass window maker, decorator and writer. Among his masterpieces are the "Battle Window" at Harvard and two of his largest windows, the "Angel of Help" and "Figure of Wisdom, both in Unity Church in Easton, Massachusetts. Illustrated Alfred, Lord Tennyson's *Enoch Arnold* and Robert Browning's *Men and Women.*
The past though it cannot be relived, can always be repaired.

1844 **Andrew Lang:** Scottish man of letters, poet, novelist, and literary critic. Fellow of Merton College, Oxford, where he studied myth, ritual and totemism. He also made contributions to anthropology. Best known as the collector of folk and fairy tales. Books: *Custom and Myth, Ritual and Religion, The Making of Religion* and a *History of English Literature.*
An unsophisticated forecaster uses statistics as a drunken man uses lamp-posts — for support rather than for illumination.

1878 **Jack Johnson:** American boxer nicknamed the "Galveston Giant." First black heavyweight champion, which he won when he battered the World Heavyweight Champ Canadian Tommy Burns and later did the same to American champ John Jeffries. At age 37, he lost the title — some say, he threw the fight — to Jess Willard, "the Great White Hope." Johnson was sent to prison for a year for violating the Mann Act, when he sent a railroad ticket to his white girlfriend to travel from Pittsburgh to Chicago.
I made a lot of mistakes out of the ring, but I never made any in it.

1914 **Octavio Paz:** Mexican poet, essayist, social philosopher and critic. Poetry is lyrical, expressing the deep loneliness of man which can be transcended through sexual love, compassion and faith. First book of poetry: *Savage Moon.* Prose works include an influential essay on Mexican history. Nobel Prize winner.
Solitude is the profoundest fact of the human condition. Man is the only being who knows he is alone.

1924 **Leo Buscaglia:** Born **Felice Leonardo Buscaglia.** American guru, educator, lecturer on interpersonal relationships. Advocate of the power of love. Worked to overcome social and mental barriers that inhibited the expression of love between people. Books: *The Fall of Freddie the Leaf, Bus 9 to Paradise, Living, Loving and Learning,* and *Love.* Claimed, "I got the copyright for love!"
Love is life. And if you miss love, you miss life.

1926 **John Fowles:** British novelist and essayist. Novels: *The Collector, The Magnus,* and *The French Lieutenant's Woman.* Also wrote *The Aristos,* a collection of philosophical reflections. Many critics consider him the forefather of British postmodernism.
That is the great distinction between the sexes. Men see objects, women see the relationships between objects.

1927 **Cesar Chavez:** American farm worker, activist and labor-union organizer. Founder and first president of National Farm Workers Association, AFL-CIO, which later became the United Farm Workers. Employed nonviolent tactics, including fasts, marches, strikes and boycotts. Led a strike of California grape-pickers, which lasted five years. The UFW urged all Americans to boycott table grapes in a show of support. He later led a boycott to protest the use of toxic pesticides on grapes.
In some cases non-violence requires more militancy than violence.

1936 **Marge Piercy:** American novelist, essayist and poet. The author of at least seventeen volumes of poems, including the feminist classic *The Art of Blessing the Day.* Also has written fifteen novels, one play and a collection of essays. Employs vernacular language and speech rhythms to good effect.
It is not sex that gives pleasure, but the lover.

1948 **Al Gore, Jr.:** American political leader. Democratic senator from Tennessee (1958–92). Vice president of the U.S. Lost the presidency to George W. Bush in 2000 despite winning the popular vote. The outcome wasn't resolved until a ruling by the Supreme Court in a split vote effectively ended a statewide recount of votes in Florida, which gave Bush a narrow majority in the Electoral College. He has remained busy traveling the world speaking on global warning awareness and prevention. Starred in the Oscar-winning movie about global warming, *An Inconvenient Truth* (2006). His book, *Earth in the Balance.*
When you have the facts on your side, argue the facts. When you have the law on your side, argue the law. When you have neither, holler.

OTHERS: 1732 Austrian composer **Franz Joseph Haydn**, 1809 Russian novelist **Nikolai Gogol**, 1811 German chemist **Robert W.E. von Bunsen**, 1855 U.S. mining engineer **John Hays Hammond**, 1872 Irish journalist/founder of Sinn Féin **Arthur Griffith**, 1922 U.S. actor/singer **Richard Kiley**, 1928 Canadian hockey player **Gordie Howe**, 1929 U.S. fashion designer **Liz Claiborne**, 1931 U.S. golfer **Miller Barber**,

1933 U.S. actress/singer **Shirley Jones**, 1935 Bandleader/trumpeter **Herb Alpert**, 1940 U.S. congressman **Barney Frank**, 1940 U.S. Democrat **Senator Patrick J. Leahy**, 1955 Scottish rock guitarist **Angus Young**

April 1

1578 **William Harvey:** English physician, physiologist, and anatomist. Physician to James I and Charles I. Discoverer of circulation of blood (1628), which he described in his celebrated treatise *On the Motion of the Heart and Blood in Animals.* To reach his conclusions he depended upon his own observations and reasoning, numerous animal dissections, autopsies and clinical observations.

All we know is still infinitely less than all that still remains unknown.

1647 **John Wilmot [2nd Earl of Rochester]:** English poet and wit. A patron of the arts, he was considered the most notorious debauchee in the Restoration court. Wrote excellent letters, satires and amatory songs and verses. Poems include *Verses to Lord Mulgrave* and *Verses Upon Nothing.*

Before I got married I had six theories about bringing up children; now I have six children and no theories.

1753 **Joseph Marie de Maistre:** French lawyer, diplomat, philosopher and politician. Following the French Revolution, he argued for the restoration of hereditary monarch, which he regarded as a divinely sanction institution, Also advanced the case for the supreme authority of the Pope in both religious and political matters.

Every country has the government it deserves.

1815 Prince **Otto von Bismarck:** "The Iron Chancellor." Prussian statesman. Advocate of German unity. Founder and first chancellor of Unified German states into one empire under Prussian leadership (1871).Made alliances against France. Deliberately provoked the Franco-Prussian War (1870–71), which helped him achieve his goal of political unification. Presided over the Congress of Berlin (1878).

When you want to fool the world, tell the truth.

1858 **Agnes Repplier:** American essayist and biographer. Essays esteemed for their scholarship and wit. Wrote *Books and Men, Counter-Current, Points of Fiction* and a historical study of types of humor, *In Pursuit of Laughter.* Biographer of Père Marquette, Junipero Serra and Agnes Irwin.

People who cannot recognize a palpable absurdity are very much in the way of civilization.

1868 **Edmond Rostand:** French playwright of poetic, romantic drama. Wrote plays for Puppet Theater before his first stage play, *The Red Glove.* Achieved international and enduring fame with his play *Cyrano de Bergerac,* the story of the poetic, long-nosed soldier, who despairs of winning the love of the beautiful Roxanne. Other verse-plays: *The Eaglet* and *Chanticleer.*

A pessimist is a man who tells the truth prematurely.

1897 **Alberta Hunter:** American blues singer who wrote her own songs, which flowed from the powerful and complex experiences she had as a young black woman. Sang with bands of King Oliver and Louis Armstrong. Compositions: "Down-Hearted Blues," "You Shall Reap What You Sow," and "Chirping the Blues." Left her career and spent 20 years working as a nurse. Made a remarkable comeback at age 82, writing the sound track for the film *Remember My Name,* recorded an album of new and old blues, supervised reissues of her earlier work and maintained an engagement at a New York club.

Blues means what milk does to a baby. Blues is what the spirit is to the minister. We sing the blues because our hearts have been hurt, our souls have been disturbed.

1908 **Abraham Maslow:** American philosopher and psychologist. Regarded as the founder of humanistic psychology, explored in his seminal work, *Motivation and Personality.* Maintained that each person has a hierarchy of needs that must be satisfied. As each need is satisfied, the next higher level in the emotional hierarchy dominates conscious functioning, until one reaches self-actualization.

If the only tool you have is a hammer, you tend to see every problem as a nail.

1922 **William Manchester:** U.S. novelist, foreign correspondent, contemporary historian and biographer. Commissioned by Jacqueline Kennedy to write *Death of a President.* She changed her mind, unsuccessfully suing to prevent its publication. Other works: *The Arms of Krupp* and *American Caesar.*

Men do not fight for flag or country, for the Marine Corps or any other abstraction. They fight for one another. [And] if you come through this ordeal, you would age with dignity.

1929 **Milan Kundera:** Czech-French novelist, playwright and poet. Works combine erotic comedy with political criticism. His first novel, *The Joke,* was a satire on Czechoslovakian-style Stalinism. Fled to Paris and took French nationality. Other works: *The Book of Laughter and Forgetting* and *The Unbearable Lightness of Being,* filmed in 1987.

Dogs are our link to paradise. They don't know evil or jealousy or discontent. To sit with a dog on a hillside on a glorious afternoon is to be back in Eden, where doing nothing was not boring— it was peace.

1931 **Rolf Hochhuth:** German playwright. Known for the controversial subject of his plays. *The Deputy: A Christian Tragedy* accuses Pope Pius XII of not intervening to stop Nazi persecution of Jews. His second play *Soldiers* accused Winston Churchill of involvement in the assassination of a Polish wartime leader General Sikorski and was banned in England. Others: *Guerillas, The Midwife,* and *The Survivor.*

Truth is with the victor — who, as you know, also controls the historians.

1950 **Samuel A. Alito, Jr.:** Conservative American federal appeals judge, nominated by George H. W. Bush to take Sandra Day O'Connor's place on the Supreme Court. Jurist in the mold of his colleague Justice Antonin Scalia, he has been referred to as "Scalito," or "little Scalia."

I am particularly proud of my contributions in recent cases in which the government has argued in the Supreme Court that racial and ethnic quotas should not be allowed and the Constitution does not protect a right to an abortion.

OTHERS: 1283 Roman Catholic Bavarian Emperor **Ludwig IV**, 1697 French novelist/journalist **Abbé Prévost**, 1755 French politician/author **Jean Anthelme Brillat-Savarin**, 1847 French explorer **Jules-Nicolas Crevaux**, 1852 U.S. painter **Edward Austin Abbey**, 1864 Dutch fairy tale writer **Marie Jungius**, 1873 Russian composer **Sergei Rachmaninov**, 1883 Man of 1000 faces **Lon Chaney**, 1884 Broadway actress **Laurette Taylor**, 1886 U.S. actor **Wallace Beery**, 1905Social worker/founder of Hale House **"Mother" Clara Hale**, 1928 U.S. singer/actress **Jane Powell**, 1932 U.S. singer/actress **Debbie Reynolds**, 1939 U.S. singer **Rudolph Isley**, 1938 U.S. actress **Ali MacGraw**

April 2

742 **Charlemagne:** French soldier, emperor. Patron of learning and King of the Franks. Founder and ruler of the Holy Roman Empire (742–814) Conqueror of almost all Christian lands in Europe (768–814). Developed a high degree of statesmanship. His goal was to consolidate order and Christian culture among the nations under his control, but his empire didn't survive long after his death. Gave France the germs of modern democratic institutions that survived his realm.

To have another language is to possess a second soul.

1725 **Giovanni Jacopo Casanova:** Italian clergyman, soldier, violinist, author and adventurer. Wandered throughout Europe for 20 years, meeting all the greatest men and women of the day. His memoir, *History of My Life*, was a bawdy account of his many loves. After preaching a sermon, the collection plate was filled with propositions from women. Once when a woman turned him down, he said he began to die.

I have always loved truth so passionately that I have often resorted to lying as a way of introducing it into the minds which were ignorant of its charms.

1805 **Hans Christian Andersen:** Danish writer of fairy tales, poet, novelist, and dramatist. Wrote 168 fairy and folk tales that mix mature wisdom and gay whimsy. Stories: "The Red Shoes," "The Ugly Duckling" and "The Emperor's Clothes." A literary award, the Hans Christian Andersen Prize, is presented biennially at each Congress of the International Board of Books for Young People.

Every man's life is a fairy tale, written by God's fingers.

1840 **Émile Zola:** French novelist and critic. Leader of the naturalism fiction school in France. Defined naturalism as "Nature seen through a temperament." His passion for social reform was translated into action in his famous *J'Accuse* letter, in defense of Captain Alfred Dreyfus. Novels: *The Bell of Paris, Nana,* dealing with prostitution, *Earth* and *The Beast in Man.* He died under peculiar circumstances of carbon monoxide poisoning. At his funeral, Anatole France declared, "He was a moment of the human conscience."

Civilization will not attain to its perfection until the last stone from the last church falls on the last priest.

1862 **Nicholas Murray Butler:** American educator and statesman. Student of international affairs. President Columbia University (1901–45). Helped found Teacher's College at Columbia and establish Carnegie Endowment for International Peace (1925–45). Shared the Nobel Peace Prize (1931) with Jane Addams.

Many people's tombstones should read "died at 30, buried at 60."

1875 **Walter Chrysler:** U.S. automobile pioneer. In 1919 was paid the astonishing sum of a million dollars a year to run Willys-Overland Motor Company. When he failed in a takeover of the company, he acquired controlling interest in the ailing Maxwell Motor Company which he renamed the Chrysler Corporation, which today is the third largest North American automaker.

The timid hang back. But those with courage will march on.

1891 **Max Ernst:** French painter and sculptor. Worked in expressionistic mode of surrealism, later a convert to Dadaism. In 1939 he was interned in France as an enemy alien. Two years later he fled to the U.S. with Peggy Guggenheim, whom he married early in 1942. Received the Grand Prize for painting at the Venice *Biennale* in 1954. Works: *Oedipus Rex* and *Polish Rider.*

I have never seen a beautiful painting of a beautiful woman. But you can take an ugly woman and make a beautiful painting of her. It is the paint itself that should be beautiful.

1905 **Kurt Herbert Adler:** American conductor born in Austria. Assistant to Arturo Toscanini at the Salzburg Festival (1936). Following the Nazi occupation of Austria in 1938, as a Jew he was forced to leave the country. Assistant chorus director at the Lyric Opera of Chicago. Spent ten years as chorus director at the San Francisco Opera, before succeeding Gaetano Merola as General Director. Originated the Merola Opera Program and "Opera in the Park," from 1971, an annual free concert in Golden Gate Park.

Tradition is what you often resort to when you don't have the will, time or money to do it right.

1927 **Kenneth Tynan:** Influential and controversial English drama critic and author. Supported the raw new drama of the *Angry Young Men*. Fiercely opposed to censorship and was determined to break taboos that he considered arbitrary. By the late 1960s, his career was in decline, leading him to leave London for California, where in his last years he wrote articles, notably for *The New Yorker*.

Show me a congenital eavesdropper with the instincts of a Peeping Tom and I will show you the makings of a dramatist.

1928 **Serge Gainsbourg:** French poet, actor, director, musician, singer, songwriter, pianist and character. Wished to explore new musical ground. His most famous song was "Je t'aime ... moi non plus," which featured simulated sounds of female orgasm. The "ultimate love song" was censored in various countries. Other works include the album *Rock Around the Bunker*, entirely on the subject of Nazis, and a reggae version of the French national anthem "La Marseillaise."

Ugliness is in a way superior to beauty because it lasts.

1935 **Georgie Anne Geyer:** U.S. journalist, syndicated columnist and foreign correspondent. Speaks Spanish, Portuguese, German and Russian. First Westerner to interview Saddam Hussein. Jailed in Angola for her articles about that country's civil war. Guatemala's White Hand death squad threatened to kill her. Wrote *Guerilla Prince*, an acclaimed biography of Fidel Castro.

It was when reporters became journalists and when objectivity gave way to searching for truth that an aura of distrust and fear arose around the New Journalist.

1947 **Camille Paglia:** U.S. social critic, author and professor of Humanities and Media Studies at the University of Arts in Philadelphia. First book: *Sexual Personae: Art and Decadence from Nefertiti to Emily Dickinson.* Writes about popular culture and feminism. A believer in Amazon Feminism, a reaction to the rigid, doctrinaire "feminism" that many found stifling.

There is no female Mozart because there is no female Jack the Ripper.

OTHERS: 1618 Mathematician/physicist **Francesco Grimaldi**, 1827 English painter **William Holdman Hunt**, 1834 French sculptor of Statue of Liberty **Frédéric-Auguste Bartholdi**, 1891 U.S. garden developer **John Grimke Drayton**, 1894 Swiss aviation pioneer **Walter Mittelholzer**, 1907 Hollywood producer **Irene Mayer Selznick**, 1908 U.S. actor **Buddy Ebsen**, 1911 Tap dancer **Charles "Honi" Coles**, 1914 English actor **Sir Alec Guinness**, 1920 "Dragnet" Creator **Jack Webb**, 1928 Cardinal of Chicago **Joseph Bernardin**, 1939 U.S. singer **Marvin Gaye**, 1945 300-game winning pitcher **Don Sutton**, 1947 Country singer **Emmylou Harris**, 1959 Comedian **Victoria Jackson**

April 3

1593 **George Herbert:** English clergyman and devotional poet of the metaphysical school of John Donne. Public orator and Member of Parliament before entering the church. His verse is collected in *The Temple.* His chief prose work A *Priest in the Temple*, containing guidance for the country parson, was published in *Remains.*

Living well is the best revenge.

1764 **John Abernethy:** English surgeon. Famous for his eccentric lectures, which attracted large crowds. His practice increased with his celebrity, which the rudeness of his manners helped to heighten. Works: *Constitutional Origin and Treatment of Local Diseases.*

Why, Madam, do you know there are upward of thirty yards of bowels squeezed underneath that girdle of your daughter's? Go home and cut it; let Nature have fair play, and you will have no need of my advice.

1783 **Washington Irving:** American essayist, biographer, and historian. Wrote humorous and satirical pieces using the name of Diedrich Knickerbocker, a quaint and humorous Dutchman. The classics *Rip Van Winkle* and *The Legend of Sleepy Hollow* were contained in The Sketch Book, written under the pseudonym "Geoffrey Crayon." Also wrote biographies of American naval heroes.

Great minds have purposes; little minds have wishes. Little minds are subdued by misfortunes; great minds rise above them

1822 **Edward Everett Hale:** American clergyman, humanitarian and writer. Produced numerous essays, short stories, pamphlets and novels. Helped found Unitarian Church of America. Best known for *The Man Without a Country*, which encouraged patriotism during the Civil War. Edward Everett was his uncle and Nathan Hale was his great-uncle.

Education is a better safeguard of liberty than a standing army.

1823 **William Marcy Tweed:** "Boss Tweed." American corrupt politician and criminal. Notorious "boss" of the Tammany Society. As commissioner of public works for New York City he controlled the city's finances. Gigantic frauds were exposed by the *New York Times* (1871). He escaped to Cuba and Spain but died in a New York jail while suits were pending against him to recover $6,000,000.

As long as I count the votes, what are you going to do about it?

1837 **John Burroughs:** American essayist, naturalist and nature writer. Wrote *Wake-Robin, Birds and Poets* and *The Breath of Life.*—The John Burroughs Memorial Association was established in his memory to encourage writing in natural history. A Burroughs Medal is awarded each year for the best book in the field of natural history. The first recipient was William Beebe.

I go to nature to be soothed and healed, and to have my senses put in order.

1898 **Henry R. Luce:** American publisher born in Shantung, China. With Briton Hadden founded weekly news magazine *Time* (1923), followed by *Fortune, Life, Sports Illustrated, Architectural Forum* and *House and Home.* Also inaugurated the radio program "March of Time," which later became a film feature. Married socialite and writer Claire Boothe Luce in 1935.

Show me a man who claims he is objective and I'll show you a man with illusions.

1909 **Stanislaw Ulam:** Polish-born American mathematician. In 1943 he joined a team of the world's leading physicists, chemists and mathematicians at Los Alamos, New Mexico to work on the Manhattan Project that ushered the world into the atomic age. His major contribution to the project was testing the theories and designs of physicists and other mathematicians. He employed mathematics to develop the means for simulating the nuclear reaction that would take place in the atomic bomb.

It is still an unending source of surprise for me how a few scribbles on a blackboard or on a piece of paper can change the course of human affairs.

1916 **Herb Caen:** Pulitzer Prize winning San Francisco columnist. Known for his dry wit and intricate knowledge of his beloved city. Had a considerable influence on pop culture and its language. Coined the terms "beatnik" and "hippie." Many books include: *Don't Call it Frisco* and *Baghdad-by-the Bay.*

The trouble with born again Christians is that they are an even bigger pain the second time around.

1924 **Doris Day:** Originally **Doris Kappelhoff.** American singer and actress. Took her name from a song she made popular "Day by Day." Song hits: "It's Magic" and "Secret Love." Proved her dramatic worth in films including *Love Me Or Leave Me.* Played wholesome, happy girl-next-door types, and came to embody the idealized American woman of the 1950s. Perennial virgin in a series of frothy sex comedies, often pursued by Rock Hudson. Oscar nomination for *Pillow Talk.* After movie career went on to television success. Works for animal rights and AIDs awareness. Beneath her public carefree vivacity was a woman who suffered much personal heartbreak and turmoil.

If it's true that men are such beasts, this must account for the fact that most women are animal lovers.

1926 **Virgil "Gus" Grissom:** One of the seven original U.S. Mercury astronauts. Third man to enter space; first man to return to space. Died along with astronauts Ed White and Roland B. Chaffee from a flash fire aboard Apollo I Spacecraft.

If we die, we want people to accept it. We are in a risky business, and we hope that if anything happens to us it will not delay the program. The conquest of space is worth the risk of life.

1934 **Jane Goodall:** British primatologist and anthropologist. Known for her forty-year study of chimpanzee social and family life, as director of the Jane Goodall Institute in Gombe Stream National Park in Tanzania. Her observations established that chimpanzees are omnivorous rather than vegetarian and can make use of tools, and have highly developed social behavior. Books: *In the Shadow of Man* and *The Chimpanzees of Gombe.*

The male [chimp] has no part in family life, but the bond between a mother and her offspring is strong until the young are mature. If the mother is killed, an older sister will often "baby-sit" with her orphaned younger siblings.

OTHERS: 1367 English king **Henry IV**, 1715 1st president under Articles of Confederation **John Hanson**, 1871 Mexican poet **José Juan Tablada**, 1894 U.S. singer/actor **Dooley Wilson**, 1898 Toastmaster general/entertainer **George Jessel**, 1923 U.S. actress **Jan Sterling**, 1924 U.S. actor **Marlon Brando**, 1925 British Minister of Technology **Tony Benn**, 1930 U.S. Senator/Governor **Lawton Childs**, 1930 German chancellor **Helmut Kohl**, 1938 U.S. soul singer **Philippe Wynne**, 1942 U.S. singer **Wayne Newton**, 1944 U.S. singer **Tony Orlando**, 1949 Football player/actor **Lyle Alzado**, 1961 U.S. comic actor **Eddie Murphy**

April 4

1802 **Dorothea Lynde Dix:** American social reformer, philanthropist and author. Opened a school for girls in Boston and taught Sunday school in a jail. Pioneer in movement for specialized treatment of the mentally ill and the establishment of state hospitals for the insane. Pioneer in the reform of prisons.

In a world where there is so much to be done I felt strongly impressed that there must be something for me to do.

1809 **Benjamin Peirce:** American mathematician who taught at Harvard University for 40 years. Instrumental in developing the institutions first science curriculum and served as the school's librarian. Made contributions to celestial mechanics, number theory, algebra and philosophy of mathematics. Father of scientist and scholar Charles Sanders Peirce.

Mathematics is the science which draws necessary conclusions.

1810 **James Freeman Clarke:** American Unitarian clergyman, reformer, theologian and author. Founded the Unitarian Church of the Disciples at Boston (1841). Held a chair of natural theology at Harvard University. Wrote: *Ten Great Religions, Memorial and Biographical Sketches* and *Self-Culture.*

Seek to do good, and you will find that happiness will run after you.

1828 **Margaret Oliphant:** née **Wilson.** Scottish novelist. Widowed at 31, she began a prolific writing career to support herself and her children. Wrote more than 100 books and more than 200 contributions to magazines. Major works: *The Rector and the Doctor's Family, The Minister's Wife, Salem Chapel* and *Miss Mar-*

joribanks. Also wrote biographies, translations, tales of the supernatural, literary histories and an autobiography.

Temptations come, as a general rule, when they are sought.

1843 **Hans Richter:** Hungarian conductor. An authority on the music of Richard Wagner with whom he was closely associated at the Bayreuth festivals. Gave a series of annual concerts in London (1879–97). Conductor of the Hallé orchestra (1897–1911).

To create a vision of harmony of the unreal, balance the infinite variety, the chaotic, the contradictions — in a unity.

1858 **Remy de Gourmont:** French critic, essayist, philosopher and novelist. Most contemporary critic of symbolism. Played a major role in disseminating its aesthetic doctrines. Co-found the journal *Mercure de France*. Wrote 50 volumes, mainly collections of articles, and novels *Very Woman*, *The Dream of a Woman* and *A Virgin Heart*.

Women still remember the first kiss after men have forgotten the last.

1896 **Robert Sherwood:** American playwright and editor of a New York magazine. Member of the Algonquin Round Table. Plays: *Idiot's Delight* (Pulitzer Prize), *The Petrified Forest*, *Abe Lincoln in Illinois*, and *There Shall Be No Night* (Pulitzer Prize). Many of his plays were adapted for film. Won an Academy Award for his screenplay for *The Best Years of Our Lives*.

To be able to write a play ... a man must be sensitive, imaginative, naive, gullible, passionate; he must be something of an imbecile, something of a poet, something of a damn fool.

1914 **Marguerite Duras:** Pseudonym of **Marguerite Donnadiue.** French novelist, screenwriter, playwright and director. Reputation made with her novels such as *The Sailor from Gibraltar*. Wrote the screenplay for Alain Resnais' film *Hiroshima Mon Amour*. Her autobiographical novel *The Lover* was made into a successful film. Began directing her own highly atmospheric movies.

You have to be very fond of men. Very, very fond. You have to be very fond of them to love them. Otherwise they're simply unbearable.

1915 **Muddy Waters [McKinley Morganfield]:** African-American blues singer, composer and guitarist. First recorded by Alan Lomax, the folk music researcher. Had a moan-and-shout vocal style and his lyrics were usually mournful, boastful or sexual. Gained his first national success with "Rollin' Stone." One of his best known singles is "I've Got My Mojo Working."

I rambled all the time. I was just like that, like a rollin' stone.

1924 **Gil Hodges:** American baseball player and manager. Hit 370 homeruns as a first baseman for the Dodgers and the Mets. After his playing days, he became the manager of the expansion Washington Senators. Managed the "Miracle Mets" to a World Series win in 1969.His career was prematurely cut short when he suffered a fatal heart attack while playing golf in Florida at age 48.

There are only two kinds of managers, winning managers and ex-managers.

1928 **Maya Angelou:** Originally **Marguerite Jonson**. African-American writer, singer, dancer and black activist. Raped at age eight, went through a period of muteness. Before becoming a writer she worked as a waitress, prostitute, cook, dancer and actress. Toured Europe and Africa in *Porgy and Bess*. Poetry collections: *And Still I Rise* and *I Shall Not Be Moved*. Autobiographical books chronicle her experiences growing up in Arkansas, *I Know Why the Caged Bird Sings* and *All God's Children Need Traveling Shoes*. Read a poem she wrote at President Clinton's inauguration, bringing her world-wide fame.

There is no greater agony than bearing an untold story inside you.

1938 **A. Bartlett Giamatti:** American scholar, president of Yale (1978–86),lifelong fan of the Boston Red Sox, National Baseball League president and commissioner of baseball. Declared no one was above the game and banished Pete Rose from baseball for gambling on games. Father of actor Paul Giamatti.

Teachers believe they have a gift for giving; it drives them with the same irrepressible drive that drives others to create a work of art or a market or a building.

OTHERS: 188 Roman Emperor **Marcus Aurelius Antoniius**, 1792 Radical congressional leader **Thaddeus Stevens**, 1821 Invented the Yale lock **Linus Yale**, 1843 U.S. photography pioneer **William Henry Jackson**, 1875 French conductor **Pierre Monteux**, 1881 U.S. encylopediest **Charles Funk**, 1884 Admiral of Japanese fleet **Isoroku Yamamoto**, 1888 Hall-of-Fame outfielder **Tris Speaker**, 1907 U.S. educator **Nathan M. Pusey**, 1913 U.S. singer **Francis Langford**, 1920 French director **Eric Rohmer**, 1922 Movie music composer **Elmer Bernstein,** 1924 U.S. actress **Eva Marie Saint**, 1932 American actor **Anthony Perkins,** 1939 South African trumpeter **Hugh Masekela**

April 5

1588 **Thomas Hobbes:** English philosopher and political theorist. Father of materialism and leader of modern rationalism. Held a pessimistic view of human nature. His masterpiece, *Leviathan*, expresses his political philosophy. In it he reasserted his absolutist position and argued against separation of church and state. Pioneer in Utilitarianism, justifying obedience to moral rules as the means to peaceful and comfortable living.

Laughter is nothing else but sudden glory arising from some sudden conception of some eminency in ourselves, by comparison with the infirmity of others, or with our own formerly.

1784 **Louis Spohr:** Originally **Ludwig.** German composer and violinist. Kapellmeister in Kassel throughout his life. Wrote 15 violin concertos, four clarinet concertos, many operas, nine symphonies, and chamber music. Considered a giant as a performer and composer during his lifetime, he has since been largely neglected. Speaking of Beethoven's Fifth Symphony:

An orgy of vulgar noise.

1827 Baron **Joseph Lister:** English surgeon and medical scientist. Regarded as the founder of antiseptic medicine. Noticed that 45–50% of amputation patients died from infection. Initially he theorized that airborne dust might cause sepsis, but learning of Louis Pasteur's theory that infection was caused by microorganisms, he introduced the use of antiseptic practices in surgery and hospitals. Using phenol as an antiseptic, he reduced mortality in his ward to 15% within four years.

Next to the promulgation of new truth the best thing I can see that a man can do, is the recantation of a published error.

1837 **Algernon Swinburne:** English poet, critic and man of letters. Known for his rebellion against Victorian social conventions and religion. His verse drama *Atalanta in Calydon* first showed his lyric powers. Famous for elegies and monographs on Shakespeare. Suffered from epilepsy, alcoholism and masochism. Works: *Poems and Ballads, Songs Before Sunrise* and *Essays and Studies.*

And the best and worst of this is/ That neither is most to blame/ if you have forgotten my kisses/ And I have forgotten your name.

1856 **Booker Taliaferro Washington:** Distinguished African-American educator and social reformer. His mother was a slave. Established Tuskegee Institute (1881), which he headed until his death. Founded self-help organization for blacks. Principal spokesman of black people. First African-American to be features on a U.S. postage stamp. Elected to the American Hall of Fame. Wrote *Up from Slavery.*

Excellence is to do a common thing in an uncommon way.

1871 **Glenn "Pop" Warner:** Originally **Glenn Scobey**. Legendary American football coach and innovator for over 49 years. His seven college teams had a total of 313 victories. He produced 47 All-Americans, most notably Jim Thorpe at Carlisle Indian School. Perfected the single- and double-wing formations, which now are rarely used, but at the time helped redefine the modern game of football.

You play the way you practice.

1873 **Mistinguett:** Stage name of **Jeanne-Marie Bourgeois.** French dancer, singer and actress, a symbol of Parisian gaiety. Most famous comedienne of her time. Her shapely legs were allegedly insured for one million francs. Reached the height of her career with Maurice Chevalier at the *Folies Bergère.* Also successful in serious productions, *Madame Sans-Gene* and *Les Misérables.* Memoirs: *Mistinguett, Queen of Paris Night.*

A kiss can be a comma, a question mark or an exclamation point. That's basic spelling that every woman ought to know.

1900 **Spencer Tracy:** American actor. Leading man in more than 60 movies, frequently with his lover Katharine Hepburn. Nominated for an Academy Award seven times, winning for *Captains Courageous* and *Boy's Town* in consecutive years. Other films: *Adam's Rib, Father of the Bride, Bad Day at Black Rock, Inherit the Wind* and his last *Guess who's Coming to Dinner.* Had no use for method actors. Preached a simple philosophy of acting:

Learn your lines and don't trip over the furniture.

1908 **Bette Davis:** American actress. "First Lady of the American Screen." As independent in real life as her characters on screen. Oscar winner for *Dangerous* and *Jezebel.* Nominated for *Dark Victory, The Letter, The Little Foxes, Now, Voyager, Mr. Skeffington, All About Eve, The Star* and *What Ever Happened to Baby Jane?* Received American Film Institute Life Achievement Award.

Sex is God's joke on human beings.

1916 **Gregory Peck:** Distinguished American actor, mainly in roles of men of sterling integrity. Academy Award winner for *To Kill a Mockingbird.* Other notable films: *The Keys of the Kingdom, Spellbound, Duel in the Sun, Gentlemen's Agreement, Twelve O'clock High, The Man in the Gray Flannel Suit* and *The Omen.*

Tough times don't last, tough people do.

1917 **Robert Bloch:** Prolific American writer and scriptwriter. Author of hundreds of short stories and more than twenty novels, mostly crime fiction, science fiction and horror fiction, including his most famous work *Psycho.* Penned several scripts for the original *Star Trek* series.

The man who can smile when things go wrong has thought of someone else he can blame it on.

1937 **Colin L. Powell:** American Army general. Youngest and first African-American chairman of the Joint Chiefs of Staff. Advised George Bush on deployment of U.S. troops in "Operation Desert Storm," against Iraq. U.S. Secretary of State in George H. W. Bush's first term.

Great leaders are almost always great simplifiers, who can cut through argument, debate and doubt, to offer a solution everybody can understand.

OTHERS: 1732 French painter **Jean-Honoré Fragonard,** 1752 Piano/harp manufacturer **Sébastien Erard,** 1795 English general **Sir Henry Havelock,** 1820 French painter/balloonist **Nadar [Félix Tournachon],** 1823 English physicist **Sir William Siemens,** 1893 Finnish speed skater **Clas Thunberg,** 1901 Ambassador/writer **Chester Bowles,** 1901 U.S. actor **Melvyn Douglas,** 1909 Film producer **"Cubby" Broccoli,** 1920 English author **Arthur Hailey,** 1921 U.S. TV host **Robert Q. Lewis,** 1923 President of South Vietnam **Nguyen Van**

Thieu, 1923 Belgian philosopher/economist **Ernest Mandel**, 1926 U.S. producer/director **Roger Corman**, 1934 Impressionist **Frank Gorshin**, 1941 Musician **Eric Burdon**

April 6

1741 **Sébastien-Roch Nicolas de Chamfort:** French writer. Most famous for his *Maximes et Pensées*. Possessor of good looks, wit and immense physical strength. Wrote the successful comedy, *La Jeune Indienne*, followed by a series of epistles in verse, essays and odes. His literary reputation was established with his *Eloge* on Moliére, which won the prize of the Académie Française.

When a man and a woman have an overwhelming passion for each other, it seems to me, in spite of such obstacles dividing them as parents or husband, that they belong to each other in the name of Nature, and are lovers by Divine right, in spite of human convention or the laws.

1773 **James Mill:** Scottish philosopher, historian and economist. A major promulgator of Jeremy Bentham's utilitarianism. Wrote the 3-volume *History of British India*. His criticism of British rule brought about changes in the government of India. His *Elements of Political Economy* summarized the views of David Ricardo. Father of British philosopher and economist John Stuart Mill.

It cannot be precisely known how any thing is good or bad, till it is precisely known what it is.

1866 **[Joseph] Lincoln Steffens:** American journalist and reformer. Managing editor *McClure's Magazine* (1902–6). One of the first muckrakers, who publicized the political and business corruption in the U.S. One of the first to expose the corruption of state and municipal governments. Saw the villain not as boss corruption but public apathy. Supported revolutionary activities in Mexico and Russia. In 1919 he visited post-Revolutionary Russia and announced:

I have been over into the future and it works.

1884 **Walter Huston:** Started out as an engineer before following his passion for the stage. Made his Broadway debut in 1924 and moved to Hollywood in 1929. Although not a singer, he introduced the classic "September Song" in the Broadway production of *Knickerbocker Holiday*. Notable films: *The Virginian, Dodsworth, All That Money Can Buy, Yankee Doodle Dandy* and won an Oscar for his performance in *The Treasure of the Sierra Madre*, directed by his son John Huston, whom he advised:

Son, always give 'em a good show, and travel first class.

1888 **Emmanuel Celler:** American politician and lawyer. Democratic U.S. congressman from New York (1922–72). Supported New Deal programs and fought Joe McCarthy. Served as the chair or ranking minority member of the House Judiciary Committee (1949–72). Co-authored numerous civil right bills. His recipe for success in Congress:

... The brashness of a sophomore ... the perseverance of a bill collector.

1890 **Anton Herman Gerard Fokker:** Dutch Aviation pioneer. Went to Germany where he learned how to build an airplane. Made a living by taking passengers into the skies. During World War I his airplane manufacturing produced the feared Fokker fighter. After the war he opened a second factory in the U.S. and became the largest civil aircraft manufacturer of the 20s. Died in America in 1939.

I have always understood aeroplanes a lot better than women.

1892 **Lowell Thomas:** American author and radio news commentator. War correspondent in Europe and the Middle East during his 20s. One of the first news people to broadcast from an airplane. Radio broadcaster with CBS for nearly twenty years. Voice of *Movietone News* for years. During his globetrotting, he filmed and narrated travelogues and wrote books about his travels. Wrote *The Seven Wonders of the World* and helped make T.E. Lawrence famous with his book *With Lawrence in Arabia*.

He [T.E. Lawrence] had a genius for backing into the limelight.

1895 **Dudley Nichols:** American screenwriter and director. Highly regarded for his collaborations with John Ford on *The Lost Patrol, The Plough and the Stars* and *Stagecoach*. His screenplay for *The Informer* won an Oscar (1935). Also nominated for Academy Awards for the screenplays of *The Long Voyage Home, Air Force* and *The Tin Star*.

A script is only a blueprint— the director is the one who makes the picture.

1926 **Ian Paisley:** Protestant leader in Northern Ireland. Cofounded a new sect, the Free Presbyterian Church of Ulster. Voice of an extreme Protestant opinion in the sectarian strife of Northern Ireland. Opposed all concessions to the Catholics. Organized a paramilitary group of fighters called the Third Force.

You can't build the bridge of trust with the scaffolding of lies and underhand deals.

1928 **James D. Watson:** American geneticist and biophysicist. With F.H.C. Crick worked out the structure of DNA. In 1953 he suddenly saw that the essential DNA components, four organic bases, must be linked in definite pairs, which allowed the two scientists to formulate a double-helix molecular model for DNA. Shared the Nobel Prize (1962) with Crick and Maurice Wilkins. Wrote *The Double Helix*, a best-selling account of the DNA discovery.

One could not be a successful scientist without realizing that, in contrast to the popular conception supported by newspapers and mothers of scientists, a goodly number of scientists are not only narrow-minded and dull, but also just stupid.

1929 **André Previn:** German-born U.S. composer, conductor, arranger, musical director, and pianist. Fled Nazi persecution with his family, settling in L.A. in 1939. Won Academy Awards for the scores of *Gigi, Porgy and Bess, Irma La Douce*, and *My Fair Lady*. Served as principal conductor of the Houston Symphony, Pittsburgh Symphony, Los Angles Philharmonic and Royal Philharmonic orchestras. Received Kennedy Center Honor in 1998. His five wives included Dory Previn, Mia Farrow and until recently, Anne-Sophie Mutter.

The conductor is there ... first of all for the oversimplified reason of just being the traffic cop, making sure everyone is playing at the same speed and the same volume.

1937 **Merle Haggard:** U.S. country and western singer. At age 21, paroled from San Quentin Prison, where he did a lot of rethinking while in solitary. Has had 38 number one singles. Entertainer of the Year (1970). Biggest hit, "If We Can Make It Through December." Other Hits: "Sing a Sad Song," "Okie from Muskogee," "The Fightin' Side of Me" and "That's the Way Love Goes."

In 1960, when I came out of prison as an ex-convict, I had more freedom under parolee supervision than there's available ... in America right now.

OTHERS: 1671 French playwright/poet **Jean-Baptiste Rousseau**, 1785 U.S. Unitarian clergyman **John Pierpont**, 1823 Canadian-born U.S. newspaper editor **Joseph Medill**, 1852 U.S. wood engraver **Timothy Cole**, 1866 U.S. Criminal leader of the Wild Bunch **Butch Cassidy**, 1869 Dutch painter **Louis Raemaekers**, 1892 U.S. aircraft pioneer **Donald Wills Douglas**, 1903 Baseball hall-of-fame catcher **Mickey Cochrane**, 1922 U.S. film director **Barry Levinson**, 1927 Saxophonist **Gerry Mulligan**, 1929 Mobster **"Crazy" Joe Gallo**, 1943 Investigative journalist **Roger Cook**, 1953 Ice skater **Janet Lynn**

April 7

1506 Saint **Francis Xavier:** Navarrese priest and missionary. Born into a noble Basque family. Met Ignatius of Loyola at the University of Paris and became one of the original members of the Jesuits, ordained in 1537. "Apostle of the Indies." Began his missionary work in Goa, India, 1534. Traveled to the Malay and Japan, where he was the first to systematically introduce Christianity. Died while trying to enter China. Said to have baptized some 30,000 converts, successful in part because of his adaptation to local cultures. Canonized (1622).

Give me the children until they are seven and anyone may have them after.

1725 **Francis Cabot Lowell:** American businessman. Member of the prominent Massachusetts Lowells. His Boston Manufacturing Co. was apparently the world's first textile mill in which all operations were performed that turned raw cotton into finished cloth. His example stimulated the growth of New England industry. Lowell, Massachusetts is named for him.

Gardeners instinctively know that the flowers and plants are a continuum and that the wheel of garden history will always be coming full circle.

1770 **William Wordsworth:** English Lake poet and philosopher "Moral interpreter of nature." Greatest poet of the English Romantic movement. Known for his worship of nature, his humanitarianism and his interest in common people. English poet laureate. Poetry: "Lyrical Ballads," "Tintern Abbey," "The Solitary Reaper," and the unfinished "The Recluse."

Poetry is the spontaneous overflow of powerful feelings; it takes its origin from emotion recollected in tranquility.

1780 **William Ellery Channing:** American moralist, Unitarian clergyman and author. Known as the "apostle of Unitarianism." Pastor of Boston's Federal Street Church for 40 years. Played an integral role in the intellectual life of New England. Lectures on slavery, war and poverty made him one of the most influential clergymen of his day.

We look forward to the time when the power to love will replace the love of power. Then will our world know the blessings of peace.

1837 **John Pierpont Morgan:** American financier and philanthropist. J.P. Morgan and Co. became world's most influential banking firm. Financed companies that became U.S. Steel and International Harvester. Formed a syndicate to supply the U.S. government's depleted gold reserves. Helped avert a general financial collapse following the stock-market panic of 1907. Donated art collection to New York's Metropolitan Museum of Art.

Well, I don't know as if I want a lawyer to tell me what I cannot do. I hire him to tell me how to do what I want to do.

1889 **Gabriela Mistral:** Pseudonym of Chilean poet and educator **Lucila Godoy de Alcayaga**. Her pen-name combines the names of the poets Gabriele D'Annunzio of Italy and Frédéric Mistral of France. Rose to important posts in the Chilean educational system and helped to reorganize the rural schools in Mexico. All her poetry is a variation on the theme of love and sorrow. Poetry: "Sonnets of Death" and "Desolation." Nobel Prize for Literature (1945), first woman poet and first Latin American so honored.

Love beauty; it is the shadow of God on the universe.

1891 Sir **David Low:** New Zealander political cartoonist, historian and psychologist. Began his career at age 15 publishing drawings in magazines and newspapers in New Zealand. Moved to London to accept a position with the *Star*. Later joined Lord Beaverbrook's *Evening Standard*. Famous during World War I for his pictorial satires, which he resumed during World War II. His work criticizing Hitler, Mussolini and British appeasement resulted in his work being banned in German and Italy.

I have learned from experience that, in the bluff and counterbluff of world politics, to draw a hostile war lord as a horrible monster is to play his game. What he doesn't like is being shown as a silly ass.

1897 **Walter Winchell:** Controversial American journalist. Wrote an internationally famous syndicated gossip column. Hosted a long-running and very popular highly opinioned radio gossip program. Noted for his very slangy idiom. Roused the ire of many prominent public figures. Founded the Damon Runyan Cancer Fund in 1946.

Gossip is the art of saying nothing in a way that leaves practically nothing unsaid.

1915 **Billie Holiday:** Originally **Eleanora Fagan**. "Lady Day." African-American jazz singer. Toured with Count Basie and Artie Shaw. Recorded with Benny Goodman and Paul Whiteman, among others. Considered the finest interpreter of torch songs, jazz and ballads of her era. Hits: "Them There Eyes," "God Bless the Child" and "Don't Explain." Personal crises and drug and alcohol addition plagued her life. Died of a heroin overdose in 1976.

If I'm going to sing like someone else, then I don't need to sing at all.

1935 **Hodding Carter:** American journalist and news publisher. Started his own paper the Hammond, Louisiana *Dailey Courier*, which opposed the activities of Huey Long. Moved to Greenville, Mississippi, where he started the *Delta Democrat-Times*. After World War II, he wrote a series of articles on racial, religious, and economic tolerance that won his a Pulitzer Prize for editorials. Books: *Mississippi, The Angry Scar* and *Doomed Road of Empire*.

There are two lasting bequests we can give our children: One is roots, the other is wings.

1938 **Edmund G. "Jerry" Brown, Jr.:** American politician. Governor of California (1975–82). Sought the Democratic nomination for president several times, refusing to accept political contributions of more than $100.

The insatiable appetite for campaign dollars has turned the government into a Stop and Shop for every greed and special interest in the country.

1951 **Janis Ian:** U.S. singer and songwriter. Began writing songs at age 12 and recorded "Society's Child" at age 15, a social comment on interracial romance, which rose to the top of the charts and made her an overnight sensation. Nominated for a Grammy for her recording with Mel Torme of her song "Silly Habits." For many her most recognizable song is the plaintive song "At Seventeen."

I learned the truth at seventeen,/ That love was meant for beauty queens,/ ... We all play the game and when we dare,/To cheat ourselves at solitaire,/ Inventing lovers on the phone/ ... That call and say, come dance with me,/ And murmur vague obscenities,/ At ugly girls like me,/ At seventeen.

OTHERS: 1772 French socialist **Charles Fourier**, 1859 Father of American football **Walter Camp**, 1860 U.S. Manufacturer **W.K. Kellogg**, 1869 U.S. botanist **David Grandison Fairchild**, 1873 U.S. baseball manager **John McGraw**, 1893 U.S. diplomat **Allen Dulles**, 1893 U.S. dancer **Irene Castle**, 1896 Lightweight boxing champ **Benny Leonard**, 1894 English writer **Gerald Brennan**, 1908 Musical conductor **Percy Faith**, 1920 Indian sitar player **Ravi Shankar**, 1928 U.S. actor **James Garner**, 1931 U.S. whistleblower **Daniel Ellsberg**, 1939 TV host **David Frost**, 1939 Film maker **Francis Ford Coppola**, 1954 Martial arts actor **Jackie Chan**, 1954 Heisman winner **Tony Dorsett**

April 8

563 BCE **Buddha [Gautama Siddhartha]:** Indian spiritual leader. Hindu prince of the Sakyas, on the Indian-Nepal border, who founded Buddhism. Renounced his life and spent seven years seeking enlightenment. Finally while meditating under the Bodhi tree, he realized the Four Noble Truths. The term "Buddha" is Sanskrit for "Enlightened One," a title rather than a name. Buddhists believe that there are an infinite number of past and future Buddhas.

To understand everything is to forgive everything.

1582 **Phineas Fletcher:** English poet, best known for his religious and scientific poem, "The Purple Island, or The Isle of Man." Brother of poet Giles the Younger Fletcher. *The Locusts of Apollyonists*, two parallel poems in Latina and English furiously attacked the Jesuits, and allegedly is one of the sources of John Milton's conception of Satan.

Beauty when most unclothed is clothed best.

1894 **Mary Pickford:** "America's Sweetheart." Canadian-born American silent screen star. One of the first and most popular movie stars. Typical role was a sweet, innocent, loveable girl as in *Tess of the Storm Country, Rebecca of Sunnybrook Farm* and *Pollyanna*. Won an Oscar for *Coquette*. One of the founders of the United Artists Film Corporation in 1919 with Charlie Chaplin and her second of three Douglas Fairbanks, Sr. Long married to actor Buddy Rogers.

It would have been more logical if silent pictures had grown out of the talkies instead of the other way around.

1898 **E.Y. "Yip" Harburg:** American lyricist. Collaborated with composers Vernon Duke, Arthur Schwartz, Jerome Kern and most often, Harold Arlen. Songs: "Brother Can You Spare a Dime?" "It's Only a Paper Moon" and "Over the Rainbow." Also wrote the lyrics for the Broadway musical comedy *Finian's Rainbow*.

Words make you think a thought. Music makes you feel a feeling. A song makes you feel a thought.

1912 **Sonja Henie:** Norwegian-born ice skater. Won gold medals in the 1928, 1932 and 1936 Olympics. Toured with an ice show before moving to a Hollywood career in films: *One in a Million, Sun Valley Ser-*

enade and *The Countess of Monte Cristo.* First to popularize shorter skirts for women skaters and first female athlete to earn $1 million.

Jewelry takes people's minds off your wrinkles.

1918 **Betty Ford:** Originally **Elizabeth Bloomer**. American first lady. Wife of Gerald R. Ford, 38th president of the U.S. Her early career was as a dancer, including touring with the Martha Graham Concert Group. Her public battle with breast cancer created awareness of women's health problems. Her problems with substance abuse led to her founding the Betty Ford Center for Drug Rehabilitation. Autobiographies: *The Times of My Life* and *Betty: A Glad Awakening.*

My makeup wasn't smeared, I wasn't disheveled, I behaved politely, and I never finished off a bottle, so how could I be an alcoholic?

1919 **Ian Smith:** Rhodesian politician. First native born Prime minister (1964–79). Ardent advocate of white rule. A founder of the Rhodesian Front, dedicated to immediate independence without African majority rule. Unilaterally declared independence (1965), which resulted in severe sanctions by the U.N. at Britain's request. In 1977 he was finally compelled to negotiate a transfer of power to the black majority.

I would say colonialism is a wonderful thing. It spread civilization to Africa. Before it they had no written language, no wheel as we know it, no schools, no hospitals, not even normal clothing.

1922 **Carmen McRae:** African-American singer and pianist. Worked with bands of Benny Carter, Count Basie and Mercer Ellington. Not only handled the rhythmic and harmonic challenge of bebop but mastered it. One of the most accomplished scat singers and ballad interpreters of jazz. Voted *Down Beat*'s Best New Female Artist in 1954. Honored as a "master of jazz" by the National Endowment for the Arts.

Blues is to jazz what yeast is to bread — without it, it's flat.

1929 **Jacques Brel:** Belgian-French singer and songwriter. Songs were sharply satirical and often implicitly religious. Acted and directed a number of films. Reputation spread to the U.S. with the revue *Jacques Brel Is Alive and Well and Living in Paris.*

To be bourgeois is to have a certain type of materialism. You have to think of what that means. It means everything that destroys dreams, everything that destroys anything attractive. That's what being bourgeois means for me. It means security. It is a type of mediocrity of the spirit. It's everything I dislike.

1937 **Seymour Hersh:** American journalist, beginning his career as a police reporter in Chicago. Later worked for UPI and the New York Times, and as a national correspondent for the *Atlantic Monthly.* Won a Pulitzer Prize for his coverage of the Mai Lai incident. Has been a critic of both President Bushes and the wars in the Persian Gulf.

Its shades of Vietnam again, folks: body counts.

1947 **Tom Delay:** Prominent Republican congressman from Texas. Known as "The Hammer" for his enforcement of party discipline in close votes and his reputation for exacting political retribution on opponents. Elected House Majority Leader in 2002, which he resigned when he was indicted on criminal charges of conspiracy to violate election laws. He describes the charge as a "sham" and "political retaliation."

A woman can take care of her family. It takes a man to provide structure, to provide stability.

1955 **Barbara Kingsolver:** American fiction writer and activist. Active in organizations that advocate social change and humanitarian goals. Social justice and Native Americans figure prominently in her novels *The Bean Trees, The Poisonwood Bible* and *Pigs in Heaven.*

Pain reaches the heart with electrical speed, but truth moves to the heart as slowly as a glacier.

OTHERS: 1460 Spanish conqueror/explorer **Ponce de León**, 1605 King of Spain and Portugal **Philip IV**, 1614 Greek painter **El Greco [Domenikos Theotopoulos]**, 1783 English horticulturalist **John Claudius**, 1850 U.S. pathologist/founded Johns Hopkins **William Henry Welch**, 1859 German philosopher **Edmund Husserl**, 1869 U.S. physician/surgeon **Harvey Williams Cushing**, 1889 English conductor **Sir Adrian Boult**, 1898 British classics expert **Cecil Bowra**, 1904 British economist **John R. Hicks**, 1905 Anti-apartheid writer **Helen Fennell Joseph**, 1911 U.S. chemist **Melvin Calvin**, 1921 Deadpan singer **Virginia O'Brien**, 1943 AIDs victim/choreographer **Michael Bennett**

April 9

1758 **Fischer Ames:** American statesman, publicist, essayist and orator. Son of almanac maker Nathaniel Ames. Initially worked as a teacher and lawyer. Defeated Samuel Adams for a seat in the first session of the House of Representatives. As a Federalist, opposed Jeffersonian democracy.

A monarchy is a merchantman which sails well, but will sometimes strike on a rock and go to the bottom; a republic is a raft which will never sink, but then your feet are always in the water.

1821 **Charles Pierre Baudelaire:** French poet. As a law student he became addicted to opium and hashish, and contracted syphilis. Important figure among the French symbolists and modern poets. His single volume of poetry, *Les Fleurs du Mal* (*The Flowers of Evil*) dealt with erotic, aesthetic and social themes. He was convicted of obscenity and blasphemy. The work became one of the most influential collections of lyrics published in Europe.

Nature is a temple in which living columns sometimes emit confused words. Man approaches it through forests of symbols, which observe him with familiar glances.

1865 **Charles P. Steinmetz:** German-born American electrical engineer, inventor and physicist. Forced to leave Germany because of his socialist activities. In the U.S. he worked for General Electric, beginning in 1893 and taught at Union College from 1902. Worked out the mathematics necessary to predict the efficiency of electrical motors and alternating current circuits. Patented over 200 inventions.

There are no foolish questions and no man becomes a fool until he stops asking questions.

1872 **Léon Blum:** French politician and writer. A brilliant literary and drama critic. First Socialist and first Jewish Premier of France. Introduced reforms including a 40-hour work week and collective bargaining. Arrested by the Vichy government in 1940, he was imprisoned until the end of World War II.

The free man is he who does not fear to go to the end of his thought.

1888 **Sol Hurok:** Russian-American impresario. Came to the U.S. in 1905 and in 1913 inaugurated the concert series *Music for the Masses*. Represented several Eastern European artists including Feodor Chaliapin, Mischa Elman, Arthur Rubinstein, and Anna Pavlova. Made a significant contribution to world peace at the height of the Cold War by arranging visits the U.S. of Soviet opera and ballet companies.

When people don't want to come, nothing will stop them.

1894 **Tommy Manville:** Manhattan socialite, heir to the Johns-Manville asbestos fortune. Married 13 times to 11 different women. Considered something of a clown, but maybe he wasn't so dumb. His father left the family money in a trust to which his son was only entitled to the interest. However, Tommy was able to draw a million dollars when he married. The will did not specify that this codicil only applied to the first marriage.

She cried, and the judge wiped her tears with my checkbook.

1898 **Paul Robeson:** African American actor singer and athlete. Son of former slaves. Phi Beta Kappa and All-American football player at Rutgers University. Admitted to New York bar. Chose not to practice law. Starred on Broadway in *The Emperor Jones*. His vibrant bass voice is identified with the song "Ole Man River." Increasingly controversial, arguing that the Soviet Union was superior to the United States in the treatment of blacks.

As an artist I come to sing, but as a citizen, I will always speak for peace, and no one can silence me in this.

1905 **J. William Fulbright:** American Democratic politician, lawyer, and teacher. President of the University of Arkansas (1939–42). Elected to the U.S. House of Representatives in 1943, where he introduced a resolution favoring U.S. participation in what would become the U.N. U.S. Senator from Arkansas (1945–74). As chairman of Senate Foreign Relations Committee, major critic of the Vietnam War. Initiated the Fulbright scholarship program (1946), an international student exchange program.

We must dare to think about "unthinkable things" because when things become "unthinkable" thinking stops and action becomes mindless.

1910 **Abraham Ribicoff:** American politician who served as Governor of Connecticut, in the U.S. Congress and as Secretary of Health, Education and Welfare during the Kennedy administration. During the contentious 1968 Democratic Convention inside and outside the hall, he was nominating George McGovern while Mayor Richard J. Daley was heckling him. Ribicoff deviated from his speech to respond:

If George McGovern were president, we wouldn't have these Gestapo tactics in the streets of Chicago.

1926 **Hugh Hefner:** U.S. founder, editor and publisher of *Playboy* magazine. Used his magazine as a forum for his philosophy on sex, hedonism and sexual freedom. The magazine was a seminal influence on the sexual revolution of the 1960s. His playmates of the month usually are buxom girl-next-door types.

The interesting thing is how one guy, through living out his own fantasies, is living out the fantasies of so many other people.

1928 **Tom Lehrer:** U.S. singer, songwriter and mathematician. As an undergraduate at Harvard he entertained his friends with satirical tunes, such as "Fight Fiercely, Harvard." He paid to record an album *Songs of Tom Lehrer*, which he sold by mail order. It included the macabre "I Hold Your Hand in Mind," the lewd "Be Prepared" and the mathematical "Lobachevsky." The album was a cult sensation. Lehrer embarked on a series of concert tours and release a second album. He gave up his touring in the early 60s and concentrated on teaching mathematics and work in musical theater.

If a person feels he can't communicate, the least he can do is shut up about it.

1966 **Cynthia Nixon:** American actress best known for her role as Miranda in TV's *Sex and the City*. Before and since this series, she has made many appearances on and off Broadway, including *Little Darlings*, when she was 14, *The Real Thing*, *The Heidi Chronicles*, *Angels in America*, *The Women* and *Who's Afraid of Virginia Woolf?*

I have low self-esteem, but I express it the healthy way ... by eating a box of Double-Stuff Oreos.

OTHERS: 1785 Dutch physician/chemist **Sibrand Acker Stratingh**, 1830 Pioneered study of motion photography **Eadweard Muybridge**, 1835 King of the Belgians **Leopold II**, 1889 Concert violinist/composer **Efrem Zimbalist**, 1898 Football coach of the Green Bay Packers **"Curly" Lambeau**, 1930 U.S. medical researcher **Gregory Pincus**, 1906 Hungarian conductor **Antal Dorati**, 1919 Co-inventor of ENIAC **John Presper Eckert**, 1920 Jazz accordionist **Art Van Damme**, 1932 Comic strip cartoonist for *Mad* magazine **Paul Krassner**, 1932 U.S. singer/songwriter **Carl Perkins**, 1933 French stage and screen actor **Jean-Paul Belmondo**, 1957 Spanish golfer **Seve Ballesteros**

April 10

1583 **Hugo Grotius:** Also known as **Huig de Groot**. Dutch jurist, statesman and theologian. In 1618 religious and political conflicts led to his imprisonment but he escaped to Paris. His "De Jure Belli et Pacis" in which he appealed to "natural law" and the social contract as a basis for rational principles on which a system of laws could be formulated is regarded as the beginning of the science of international law.

A man cannot govern a nation if he cannot govern a city; he cannot govern a city if he cannot govern a family; he cannot govern a family unless he can govern himself; and he cannot govern himself unless his passions are subject to reason.

1778 **William Hazlitt:** British writer, best known for his humanistic essays. Encouraged by Samuel Taylor Coleridge to write *Principles of Human Action*. Master of epigram, invective and irony, many of his most brilliant essays appeared in his two most famous books *Table Talk* and *The Plain Speaker*.

Though familiarity may not breed contempt, it takes off the edge of admiration.

1827 **Lew Wallace:** American military officer who served in the Mexican War and author. Major general of union volunteers during Civil War. Headed Andersonville court of inquiry. Governor of New Mexico (1878–81) and Minister to Turkey (1881–85). Best known as author of the remarkably successful religious novel *Ben Hur*, twice filmed as a spectacular movie.

One is never more on trial than in the moment of good fortune.

1829 **William Booth:** English spiritual leader and social reformer. Underwent a religious conversion at age 15. Became a revivalist preacher. In 1864 with his wife Catherine Mumford Booth, also a preacher and social worker, he found the Christian Mission, which evolved into the Salvation Army with Booth as first general. Vachel Lindsay wrote the very popular poem, "General William Booth enters into heaven."

I consider that the chief dangers which confront the coming century will be religion without the Holy Ghost, Christianity without Christ, forgiveness without repentance, salvation without regeneration, politics without God, and heaven without hell.

1847 **Joseph Pulitzer:** Hungarian-born American publisher. Bought the *St. Louis Post-Dispatch* and the *New York World*. Founded the *Evening World*. Pulitzer prizes, annual awards in journalism, letters, and music, were endowed by his will as was the Columbia University Graduate School of Journalism.

Publicity, publicity, publicity, is the greatest moral factor and force in our public life.

1867 **George William Russell:** Pseudonym Æ. Irish poet and mystic. While working as draper's clerk published his first book *Homeward: Songs by the Way*, which earned him a recognized place in the Irish literary renaissance. Best known book is *The Candle of Vision*, an expression of his religious philosophy. Other works: volumes of verse *The Divine Vision* and *Midsummer Eve*.

Nations hate other nations for the evil that is in themselves.

1880 **Frances Perkins:** American social reformer and government official. As U.S. Secretary of Labor (1933–45), the first woman to serve in a presidential cabinet. Made major strides in women's rights, child labor and factor legislation. Supervised President Roosevelt's New Deal Labor regulations, including the Social Security Act and the Wages and Hours Act. Chairwoman, U.S. Civil Service Commission (1946–53).

But with the slow menace of a glacier, depression came on. No one had any measure of its progress; no one had any plan for stopping it. Everyone tried to get out of its way.

1903 **Clare Boothe Luce:** American editor, playwright, politician and diplomat. Editor for *Vogue* and *Vanity Fair*. Married publisher Henry Luce. Best known for theatrical success *The Women*. U.S. Congress woman from Connecticut (1943–47). Ambassador to Italy (1953–57). Unable to accept the appointment of Ambassador to Brazil in 1959 due to poor health.

A man has only one escape from his old self; to see a different self in the mirror of some woman's eyes.

1929 **Max von Sydow:** Swedish actor who established his early reputation in Ingmar Bergman films *The Seventh Seal* and *The Virgin Spring*. Portrayed Christ in *The Greatest Story Ever Told*. Other films: *Hawaii, The Exorcist, Needful Things* and *The Immigrants*.

If Jesus came back today, and saw what was going on in his name, he'd never stop throwing up.

1930 **Dolores Huerta:** American labor leader. Recruited in the 1950s to work with Cesar Chavez to unionize farm workers. Registered Chicano workers in order that they might vote for policies and politicians to influence farm labor reform and immigration. Served as Vice-President and chief negotiator of the United Farmworkers Union. Fought union takeover by the Teamsters.

Walk the street with us into history. Get off the sidewalk.

1936 **John Madden:** U.S. football coach. Won 112 games and a Super Bowl (1976) with Oakland Raiders. Has won 9 Emmy awards as football analyst with CBS and Fox. Admits to be afraid of the dark and hates elevators, planes and trains. Familiar face in Ace Hardware commercials.

The only yardstick for success our society has is being a champion. No one remembers anything else.

1941 **Paul Theroux:** American travel writer and novelist. Lectured in Uganda and Singapore. His novels include *Waldo, Saint Jack, The Mosquito Coast* and *Chicago Loop*. Travel books include *The Great Railway Bazaar* and *Traveling the World*.

Travel is glamorous only in retrospect.

OTHERS: 1512 King of Scotland **James I**, 1755 German physician/originator of homeopathy **Samuel Hahnemann**, 1794 Commodore opened Japan **Matthew C. Perry**, 1862 Connecticut Governor **Wilbur Cross**, 1868 Stage and screen actor **George Arliss**, 1885 Department store magnate **Bernard Gimbel**, 1885 Musicologist **Sigmund Spaeth**, 1909 U.S. columnist/sportswriter **Jimmy Cannon**, 1910 Society pianist/bandleader **Eddy Duchin**, 1915 U.S. actor **Harry Morgan**, 1921 U.S. singer **Shelby "Sheb" Wooley**, 1932 Egyptian actor/bridge master **Omar Sharif**, 1934 U.S. journalist **David Halberstam**, 1938 Football quarterback/sportscaster **Don Meredith**

April 11

1770 **George Canning:** English statesman. Known for his liberal policies as foreign secretary (1822–27). Earnestly contended for Catholic Emancipation and repeal of the Corn Laws. Became prime minister in 1827, but died the same year.

I can prove anything by statistics except the truth.

1794 **Edward Everett:** American Unitarian minister, masterful orator, educator and statesman. President of Harvard (1846–49). Governor of Massachusetts (1835–39). Ambassador to Great Britain (1841–45). Noted for his oration at the dedication of the Gettysburg National Cemetery where Lincoln gave his famous address. On admitting the first black student to Harvard:

If this boy passes the examination he will be admitted; and if the white students choose to withdraw, all the income of the college will be devoted to his education.

1825 **Ferdinand Lassalle:** German socialist. Founder of the German labor movement. Helped form the General German Worker's Association. Established contact with Karl Marx and Friedrich Engels. His advocacy of an evolutionary rather than revolutionary approach to socialism through a democratic constitutional state based on universal suffrage led to estrangement from Marx.

There is nothing more dangerous than a principle which appears in a false and perverted form.

1862 **Charles Evans Hughes:** American jurist, lawyer and "judicial statesman." Republican presidential nominee (1916). Secretary of State under presidents Harding and Coolidge. Eleventh Chief Justice, Supreme Court (1930–41). Resisted attempts of Franklin D. Roosevelt to "pack" the court with justices favorable to his New Deal programs.

When we lose the right to be different, we lose the privilege to be free.

1864 **Robert Loveman:** American poet. Works: *The Gate of Silence* and *On the Way to Williamdale*. The following are some lines from his most famous poem "April Rain."

It is not raining rain to me,/ It's raining daffodils./ In every dimpled drop I see/ Wild flowers on the hill.../ It's not raining rain to me,/ It's raising roses down,/ It's not raining rain to me,/ But fields of clover bloom.../ A health unto the happy,/ A fig for those who fret!/ It is not raining rain to me/ It's raining violets.

1893 **Dean Acheson:** American lawyer and statesman. U.S. Secretary of State (1949–53). Formulated the Truman Doctrine. Chief architect of the containment policy of communism expansion. Helped create NATO. Pulitzer Prize in history for *Present at the Creation.* Also wrote: *Power and Diplomacy* and *Morning and Noon.*

A memorandum is written not to inform the reader but to protect the writer.

1902 **Quentin Reynolds:** One of the most famous World War II correspondents. Covered Hitler's rise to power and reported from Europe, the Pacific, Russia, North Africa and the Middle East. During the German blitz on London, Reynolds and Edward R. Murrow were the only American correspondents in the city. Published 25 books including *London Diary, Dress Rehearsal* and *Courtroom.* He began *The Wounded Don't Cry* with the lines:

Hitler marched into Belgium just as I marched into the Ritz bar. The first thing I did was to order a drink. I don't know what Hitler did first.

1908 **Leo Rosten:** Polish-born American humorist, political scientist, and teacher. Author of scholarly works, film scripts, novels, stories and essays. Best known for *The Education of H*y*m*a*n* K*a*p*l*a*n,* a series of humorous sketches of a night school for immigrants.

Humor is the affectionate communication of insight.

1914 **Norman McLaren:** Scottish-born animator. Joined the GPO Film Unit in London (1936). Put in charge of the National Film Board in Ottawa (1943). Oscar for cartoon *Neighbors* in which he animated live actors.

Animation is not the art of drawings that move, but the art of movements that are drawn.

1923 **Theodore Isaac Rubin:** American psychoanalyst. Columnist with *Ladies' Home Journal.* Author of more than 20 books. Fiction deals with the lives of schizophrenics, catatonics and autistic children as in *Lisa and David* and *The Angry Book.*

Have you considered that if you "don't make waves," nobody including yourself will know that you are alive?

1938 **Michael Deaver:** American politician. One of the most prominent image-makers. Close advisor to Ronald Reagan, both as governor and president. In the White House, he was deputy chief-of-staff. After his political life, he provided strategic counsel for the clients of the public relations firm *Edleman.*

The media I've had a lot to do with is lazy. We fed them and they ate it every day.

1941 **Ellen Goodman:** American journalist. Pulitzer Prize winner for commentary (1980). Her syndicated column *At Large* appears in more than 450 newspapers. Widely acclaimed as a voice of sanity, helping her readers make sense of the many complicated issues that concern them. Her books include: *Turning Points, Paper Trail: Common Sense in Uncommon Times,* and *Value Judgments.*

In journalism, there has always been a tension between getting it first and getting it right.

OTHERS: 1722 English poet/journalist **Christopher Smart**, 1772 Spanish author/poet **Manuel José Quintana**, 1862 U.S. astronomer **William W. Campbell**, 1901 Italian typewriter manufacturer **Adriano Olivetti**, 1907 American actor **Paul Douglas**, 1908 Japanese industrialist **Masura Ibuka**, 1913 Fashion designer **Oleg Cassini**, 1916 Film producer/director **Howard Koch**, 1919 Governor of New York **Hugh Carey**, 1928 Widow of Bobby Kennedy, **Ethel Kennedy**, 1930 Scriptwriter/playwright **Clive Exton**, 1932 U.S. actor/singer **Joel Grey**, 1931 "Boy" in Tarzan movies **Johnny Sheffield**, 1934 photographer **Richard A. Garland**, 1944 U.S. writer **John Milius**, 1950 U.S. choreographer **Bill Irwin**

April 12

1777 **Henry Clay:** "Great Pacificator." American politician, lawyer, U.S. congressman (1811–31) and senator from Kentucky (1831–42). Unsuccessful candidate for the presidency (1824, 1831 and 1844). U.S. Secretary of State (1825–29). Drafted Missouri Compromise, which prohibited slavery from territories north of Missouri's southern border. In effect the compromise highlighted the sectional division in the country.

Let him who elevates himself above humanity say, if he pleases, "I will never compromise"; but let no one who is not above the frailties of our common nature distain compromise.

1822 **Donald Grant Mitchell:** American essayist and novelist. Produced books of travel, volumes of essays, sketches of English monarchs, and a novel entitled *Doctor Johns.* Best known as the author of sentimental essays contained in *Reveries of a Bachelor* and *Dream Life.*

There is no genius in life like the genius of energy and industry.

1823 **Aleksandr Ostrovsky:** Russian dramatist. Greatest representative of the Russian realistic period. His 47 plays include *The Bankrupt, Poverty Is No Crime, The Diary of a Scoundrel* and *The Storm.* Also wrote a fairy tale in verse, *The Snow Maiden,* which became the basis for Rimsky-Korsakov's opera.

The entire civil service is like a fortress made of papers, forms and red tape.

1900 **Claire Leighton:** English-born American illustrator and author. Created unique wood-engravings for classics and children's books, including *Four Hedges.* Her engravings consist of large areas of dark, defined by finely engraved lines often depicting scenes of workers or fishermen.

Does one think the world wicked, or foolish, or falling to bits, then half an hour with a bulb catalogue will cure that nonsense. It is a greater act of faith to plant a bulb than to plant a tree.

1904 **Lily Pons:** French-born U.S. coloratura soprano with Metropolitan Opera (1931–56). During World War II, toured battle fronts in North Africa, India, China and Burma. Repertoire included. *Lakmé* and *Lucia di Lammermoor.* Her motto:

Earn a lot and give gloriously.

1909 **Lionel Hampton:** American jazz vibraphonist, pianist, drummer and bandleader. First to exploit the vibraphone in jazz. Played with Benny Goodman quartets and quintets (1936–40). Formed his bands in the forties. Compositions: "Vibraphone Blues," "Flyin' Home" and "Hey-baba-re-bop." Speaking of his collaborative work with Goodman:

That was a big deal at the time, because no blacks were integrated with whites in anything—not in sports, basketball, football, nothing.

1919 **Ann Miller:** American dancer, actress. A zestful dancer with about the best legs in Hollywood. Appeared as the second female lead in MGM musicals *Easter Parade, On the Town,* and as a marvelous Bianca in *Kiss Me Kate.*

At MGM, I always played the second feminine lead; I was never the star in films, I was the brassy, good-natures showgirl. I never really had my big moment on the screen.

1933 **Montserrat Caballé:** Spanish soprano opera singer. Born **Maria de Montserrat Concepción Caballé i Folch** in Barcelona. Made her professional debut with the Basel Opera in 1956 as Mimi in *La Bohème.* International breakthrough occurred when she substituted for an indisposed Marilyn Horne in a performance of Donizetti's *Lucrezia Borgia* at New York's Carnegie Hall. Best known for her bel canto roles. Sang for over eighty operatic roles. Also a noted recitalist, patricianly songs of her native Spain. Since retiring from the stage she has become a UNESCO Goodwill Ambassador.

I have always made impresarios a lot of money across my career and have never, so far as I am aware, given any of them heart attacks.

1939 **Alan Ayckbourn:** British playwright and actor. Wrote his early plays under the pseudonym Roland Allen. Has written more than 50 plays, mostly farces and comedies dealing with marital and class struggles including *Relatively Speaking, Absurd Person Singular, The Norman Conquests* and *Communicating Doors.*

Comedy is tragedy interrupted.

1940 **Herbie Hancock:** African-American pianist, composer, and bandleader. Part of the superb rhythm section of Miles Davis' group. In the 1970s became involved in funk music and later disco. Acted in and scored *Round Midnight.*

Jazz is music that is open enough to borrow from any other form of music, and has the strength to influence any form of music.

1947 **Tom Clancy:** American novelist. Master of a series of military thrillers, creating the "technothriller" with *The Hunt for Red October* and *Patriot Games*. Worked as an insurance agent before beginning his writing career. Other novels: *Clear and Present Danger* and *Sum of All Fears*.

There are two kinds of people: the ones who need to be told and the ones who figure it out all by themselves.

1947 **David Letterman:** American comedian and late-night talk show host. Star of NBC's "Late Night with David Letterman" which followed "The Tonight Show" (1982–93), before moving to CBS as a competitor with Jay Leno (1993). Noted for humorous lists of ten.

The White House is giving George W. Bush intelligence briefings. You know, some of these jokes just write themselves.

OTHERS: 1550 Earl of Oxford **Edward De Vere**, 1721 Revolutionary political leader **John Hanson**, 1724 Physician/signed Declaration of Independence **Lyman Hall**, 1791 U.S. newspaper editor **Francis Preston Blair**, 1838 U.S. librarian/army physician **John Shaw Billings**, 1852 German mathematician **Ferdinand von Lindemann**, 1869 French sex murderer **Henri-Desiré Landru**, 1879 German–U.S. zoologist **Richard B. Goldschmidt**, 1883 Photographer **Imogen Cunningham**, 1884 German psychologist/biochemist **Otto Meyerhof**, 1903 Dutch economist **Jan Tinbergen**, 1916 Children's writer **Beverly Cleary**, 1932 Singer **Tiny Tim [Herbert Khaury]**

April 13

1519 **Catherine de Medici:** Daughter of Lorenzo de Medici of Florence, Italy. Married Henry II of France. Regent (1560–74). Mother of Francis II and Charles IX. Nursed dynastic ambitions. Drawn into political and religious intrigues. Her authorization of the assassination of Huguenot Gaspard II De Cougny and his principal followers led to the infamous Massacre of St. Bartholomew.

Ah, sentiments of mercy are in union with a woman's heart.

1618 **Roger de Bussy-Rabutin:** Or **Roger de Rabutin, Comte de Bussy**. French courtier, soldier, and satirist. Member of the Académie Française. Chiefly known for his urbane and malicious "Histoire amoureuse des Gaules," a partially fictitious tale of court scandals.

Absence is to love what wind is to fire; it puts out the little, it kindles the great.

1648 **Jeanne-Marie Bouvier de la Mothe-Guyon:** French mystic. Key advocate of Quietism, a Christian philosophy which insists on intellectual stillness and interior passivity as essential conditions of perfection. The doctrine was considered heretical by the Catholic Church. Madame Guyon was imprisoned in a convent for 8 years.

I wish that he would not judge by his reason but by his heart.

1743 **Thomas Jefferson:** American statesman. Man of genius and learning: a classical scholar, architect, scientist, farmer, and lover of books. At a dinner whose guests included many of the country's top scholars and Nobel Prize winners, President Kennedy observed "There has not been so much brilliance in the White House since Jefferson dined alone." Third president of the U.S. (1801–9). As a delegate to the Continental Congress (1775–76), drafted the Declaration of Independence. Governor of Virginia and minister to France. John Adams' vice-president in 1800 election tied with Aaron Burr in electoral votes. Chosen president by House of Representatives. Established the University of Virginia.

I have the consolation of having added nothing to my private fortune during my public service, and of retiring with hands clean as they are empty.

1875 **Ray L. Wilbur:** American educator, cabinet official and author. U.S. Secretary of Interior (1929–33) in the Hoover administration. President of Stanford University (1916–43). University's chancellor (1943–49).

The potential possibilities of any child are the most intriguing and stimulating in all creation.

1906 **Samuel Beckett:** Irish-born French novelist, dramatist, and poet. Wrote most of his plays in French, and then translated them to English. Best known for his literature of the absurd. Plays: *Waiting for Godot* and *Endgame*. Nobel Prize (1969).

We are all born mad. Some remain so.

1907 **Harold E. Stassen:** American liberal politician. The "Boy Wonder" was at age 33 the youngest person to serve as Governor of Minnesota. A delegate to the San Francisco convention that established the United Nations. Sought to become the Republican Party's' presidential candidate nine times, but never was nominated. By releasing his delegates at the 1952 convention to Dwight Eisenhower gave the nomination to Ike. Stassen led the movement to "dump Nixon" prior to the 1956 convention.

Government is like fire. If it is kept within bounds and under the control of the people, it contributes to the welfare of all. But if it gets out of place, if it gets too big and out of control, it destroys the happiness and even the lives of the people.

1909 **Eudora Welty:** Pulitzer Prize–winning American novelist and short-story writer. Noted for her historical works about Southern families. Author of The *Ponder Heart* and *The Optimist's Daughter* (Pulitzer Prize). Received two Guggenheim fellowships, three O. Henry awards and the National Medal for Literature.

Integrity can be neither lost nor concealed nor faked nor quenched nor artificially come by nor outlived, nor, I believe, in the long run, denied.

1919 **Madalyn Murray O'Hair:** American social activist, atheist and avowed anarchist. Led the fight to ban prayer in public schools. Her suit reached the United States Supreme Court, which voted 8 to 1 in her favor. At the time she was labeled *the most hated woman in America*. Founded American Atheists, which defends the civil rights of non-believers. In 1995, she disappeared under unusual circumstances leading to much speculation. In 2001, her killer, informed police of the location of her body, buried on a ranch in Texas cut into dozens of pieces with a saw.

An Atheist believes that a hospital should be built instead of a church. An atheist believes that deed must be done instead of prayer said. An atheist strives for involvement in life and not escape into death. He wants disease conquered, poverty vanished, war eliminated.

1922 **John Braine:** One of the "angry young men" of English literature. Best-selling author of *Room at the Top*, *Life at the Top*, *One and Last Love* and *Stay with Me Till Morning*. Published a biography of the writer J.B. Priestley.

Solitude and quiet are highly desirable, but the lack of them is no barrier to writing ... The will to work builds all the seclusion that one needs.

1939 **Seamus Heaney:** Irish poet, writer, lecturer from County Londonderry, Northern Island. Awarded the Nobel Prize for Literature in 1995. Collections of Poetry: *Death of a Naturalist*, *Wintering Out* and *The Haw Lantern*. Essays: *Preoccupations: Selected Prose 1968–1978* and *The Place of Writing*. Plays: *The Cure at Troy* and *The Burial at Thebes*.

Even if the hopes you started out with are dashed, hope has to be maintained.

1963 **Garry Kasparov:** Russian chess grandmaster. Won the world title by defeating reigning champ Anatoly Karpov, becoming the youngest champion in the history of the game. In 1996 he defeated the powerful IBM–built chess-playing computer Deep Blue. Was defeated in a rematch the next year by an upgraded Deep Blue.

Women, by their nature, are not exceptional chess players: they are not great fighters.

OTHERS: 1732 British Prime Minister **Frederick Lord North**, 1772 U.S. clockmaker **Eli Terry**, 1810 French composer **Félicien C. David**, 1849 Cuban sociologist/psychologist **Enrique José Varona**, 1852 Founder of 5¢ and 10¢ stores **Frank W. Woolworth**, 1854 U.S. economist **Richard T. Ely**, 1885 Hungarian philosopher **György Lukács**, 1892 English physicist **Robert A. Watson-Watt**, 1899 Inventor of Scrabble **Alfred Moser Butts**, 1906 Jazz saxophonist **Budd Freeman**, 1909 Wildlife conservationist **Mervyn Hugh Cowie**, 1919 U.S. actor/singer **Howard Keel**, 1924 U.S. film director **Stanley Donan**, 1937 U.S. playwright **Lanford Wilson**, 1939 U.S. stage/screen actor **Paul Sorvino**

April 14

1629 **Christiaan Huygens:** Dutch mathematician, astronomer and physicist. First to use a pendulum to regulate a clock. Used the telescopes, the lens of which he grinded and polished, to discover the true shape of Saturn's rings. Developed explanations of reflection and refraction. Developed wave theory of light and was the first to determine acceleration due to gravity.

What a wonderful and amazing scheme have we here of the magnificent vastness of the Universe! So many Suns, so many Earths.

1866 **Anne Sullivan Macy:** American educator. Nearly blind from a childhood fever, she was educated at the Perkins Institution. Returned there in 1887 to teach seven-year-old Helen Keller. Sullivan became able to communicate with Helen by spelling out words on her hand.

My heart is singing for joy this morning! A miracle has happened! The light of understanding has shone upon my little pupil's mind, and behold, all things are changed.

1879 **James Branch Cabell:** American novelist, essayist and poet. Wrote: a sequence of 18 novels, collectively called *Biography of Michael* of which *Jurgen* is the best known. They are set in an imaginary mediaeval kingdom.

The optimist proclaims that we live in the best of all possible worlds; and the pessimist fears this is true.

1889 **Arnold J. Toynbee:** English historian and student of international affairs. Often confused with his uncle, economic historian Arnold Toynbee. His greatest work, the 12-volume *A Study of History*, offered a philosophy of history based on the analysis of the development and decline of 26 civilizations. Believed that societies thrive best in response to challenge and that society's most important task is to create a religion. Other works: *Civilization on Trial*, *East to West* and *Hellenism*.

Civilizations die by suicide, not by murder.

1891 **Bhimrao Ramji Ambedkar:** Called the most prominent Indian Untouchable leader of the 20th century. His first published book was a paper *Castes in India: Their Mechanism, Genesis and Development*. Awarded a Ph.D. from Columbia University in New York for a thesis eventually published as the book *The Evolution of Provincial Finance in British India*. Led the Untouchables in a series of nonviolent campaigns for the right to enter Hindu places of worship and to draw water from public tanks and wells. In his words, he became "the most hated man in India." Clashed with Gandhi on the subject of separate electorates for the depressed classes, which he insisted on, and the Mahatma opposed.

Despotism does not cease to be despotism because it is elective. Nor does despotism become agreeable because the Despots belong to our own kindred. To make it subject to election is no guarantee against despotism. The real guarantee against despotism is to confront it with the possibility of its dethronement, of it being laid low, of its being superseded by a rival party.

1904 Sir **John Gielgud:** British actor of stage and screen. One of the most eminent interpreters of Shakespeare, notably Hamlet and Richard II. Nominated for an Oscar for *Becket*, won one for *Arthur*.

Acting is half shame, half glory. Shame at exhibiting yourself, glory when you can forget yourself.

1914 **Richard Salant:** American television executive and lawyer. President of CBS news division. Lifetime commitment to freedom of the press, ethics in news production, and the relationship of government, corporate broadcast management, and news production.

If newsmen do not tell the truth as they see it because it might make waves, or if their bosses decide something should or should not be broadcast because of Washington or Main Street consequences, we have dishonored ourselves and we have lost the First Amendment by default.

1923 **John Caldwell Holt:** American educator, writer, proponent of home schooling, and pioneer in youth rights theory. Author of *How Children Fail*, *How Children Learn*, *The Underachieving School*, and *Escape from Childhood: The Rights and Needs of Children*. Concluded that reform of the school system was not possible because it was fundamentally flawed.

Since we can't know what knowledge will be most needed in the future, it is senseless to try to teach it in advance. Instead, we should try to turn out people who love learning so much and learn so well that they will be able to learn whatever needs to be learned.

1935 **Loretta Lynn:** U.S. country singer. Married at 14. Had 6 children, grandmother at 32. "Coal Miner's Daughter" is her nickname, one of her biggest hits, the title of her best-selling autobiography, and also a film based on her life. Youngest person elected to the Country Hall of Fame (1988). Her sister is popular Country star Crystal Gayle.

[I am] a spokesperson for every woman who had gotten married too early, gotten pregnant too often, and felt trapped by the tedium and drudgery of her life.

1941 **Pete Rose:** American baseball player and manager. "Charlie Hustle" was noted for his all-around ability and enthusiasm. His 4,256 career hits and 3,562 games played both all-time records. Holds the National League for consecutive games with a hit, 44. Suspended from baseball for life for betting on his own team while its manager, which has made him ineligible to be elected to the Hall-of-Fame.

Somebody's got to win and somebody's got to lose and I believe in letting the other guy lose.

1945 **Steve Martin:** American comedian, writer, producer, actor and musician. Appeared on TV's *Saturday Night Live*. Noted for absurd and slapstick comedy. Films include: *The Jerk*, *Dirty Rotten Scoundrels*, *L.A. Story*, *Father of the Bride* and *Cheaper by the Dozen*.

Don't have sex, man. It leads to kissing and pretty soon you have to start talking to them.

1954 **Bruce Sterling:** American science-fiction writer. Proponent of cyberpunk, sci-fi dealing with harsh urban societies dominated by computer technology. Novels: *Islands in the Net* and *Distraction*.

I used to think that cyberspace was fifty years away. What I thought was fifty years away, was only ten years away. And what I thought was ten years away ... It was already here. I just wasn't aware of it yet.

OTHERS: 1578 King of Spain **Philip III**, 1592 Book publisher **Abraham Elsevier**, 1710 Spanish/Italian dancer **Marie de Camargo**, 1802 U.S. Congregational preacher **Horace Bushnell**, 1813 U.S. merchant/philanthropist **Junius S. Morgan**, 1819 Pianist/conductor **Charles Halle**, 1886 U.S. psychologist **Edward C. Tolman**, 1904 Russian choreographer **Sonia Gaskell**, 1906 King of Saudi-Arabia **Faisal ibn Abd al-Aziz**, 1907 Dictator of Haiti **François "Papa Doc" Duvalier**, 1913 Dutch flautist **Everhard van Royen**, 1925 U.S. actor **Rod Steiger**, 1941 English actress **Julie Christie**, 1966 U.S. baseball pitcher **Greg Maddux**

April 15

1452 **Leonardo da Vinci:** Italian painter, sculptor, architect, engineer, and scientist. Archetypal Renaissance man. Universal genius. One of the greatest intellects in the history of mankind. Wrote treatise on the "science of painting," architecture, mechanics, and anatomy. His *Notebooks* are a treasure of art criticism, scientific investigation and inventions centuries ahead of their time. As military architect and engineer for Cesare Borgia, he helped lay the groundwork for modern cartography. His numerous surviving manuscripts re noted for being written in backward script that requires a mirror to read. Paintings: *The Adoration of the Magi*, *The Last Supper* and *Mona Lisa*.

There are three classes of people: those who see, those who see when they are shown, and those who do not see.

1707 **Leonhard Euler:** Swiss mathematician and universal man. Freed geometry from that of ancient Greece and made it an independent branch of mathematical analysis. Summarized everything that was known in his day about the calculus. His over 900 publications fill more than 70 large volumes. Euler revised almost every branch of pure mathematics then known, filling in the details, adding proofs, and arranging everything in a cohesive and consistent whole. Continued to be productive when he became totally blind.

For since the fabric of the universe is most perfect and the work of the most wise Creator, nothing at all takes place in the universe in which some rule of maximum or minimum does not appear.

1814 **John Lothrop Motley:** American diplomat and historian. Best remembered for the three-volume *The Rise of the Dutch Empire*. Minister to Austria (1861–67) and to Great Britain (1869–70). Appointed U.S. minister to Austria and later was sent to represent his country in London.

Deeds, not statues, are the true monuments of the great.

1832 **Wilhelm Busch:** German cartoonist and poet. Best known for wise, satiric drawings, accompanied by his short rhymes, chastising human weaknesses. His "Max und Moritz" were the prototypes for Rudolph Dirks' "Katzenjammer Kids."

Becoming a father is easy enough/ But being one can be rough.

1837 **Horace Porter:** American brigadier general in the Union Army during the Civil War. Afterwards he served as personal secretary to President U.S. Grant. Appointed U.S. ambassador to France. Paid to have John Paul Jones' body shipped back to the U.S. for reburial. Wrote *Campaigning with Grant* and *West Point Life*.

A mugwump is a person educated beyond his intellect.

1843 **Henry James:** American expatriate novelist, short-story writer, essayist and critic. Brother of philosopher and psychologist William James. Major figure in the history of the psychological novel. Master of characterization and of the technique of fiction. His early novels, *Portrait of a Lady* and *The Bostonians,* explored the relationship between innocence and experience, with Americans representing innocence and Europeans, experience. Placed special emphasis on the individual consciousness of his central characters. Other works: *The Turn of the Screw* and *The Ambassadors.*

I've always been interested in people, but I've never liked them.

1889 **A. Philip Randolph:** American black labor leader. Organized the Brotherhood of Sleeping Car Porters (1925). Co-founded the journal *The Messenger* (later called *Black* Worker). Influenced Harry S Truman to ban segregation if the armed forces. Found the Negro American Labor Council to fight discrimination in the AFL–CIO. Directed the massive 1963 civil-rights march on Washington, D.C.

Equality is the heart and essence of democracy, freedom and justice.

1892 **Corrie Ten Boom:** Dutch evangelist who with her family saved many Jews from certain death at the hands of the Nazis. The entire family was sent to Ravensbrück concentration camp from which she was released due to a clerical error. After World War II, she began a career of preaching the Christian Gospel, with emphasis on forgiveness in over 60 countries. Wrote many books, including *Tramp for the Lord.*

Worry is a cycle of inefficient thoughts whirling around a center of fear.

1894 **Bessie Smith:** African-American blues and jazz singer. The most successful black entertainer of her time. She possessed a powerful voice with precise diction. Became known as the "Empress of Blues." Died of injuries in a car crash, having been denied medical treatment because of her color.

When my bed is empty,/ Makes me feel awful mean and blue./ My springs are getting rusty,/ Living single like I do.

1920 **Thomas Szasz:** Hungarian-born American psychiatrist and author. Professor of psychiatry emeritus at State University of New York Health Science Center in Syracuse. Wrote: *Pain and Pleasure, The Myth of Mental Illness* and *The Ethics of Psychoanalysis.*

If you talk to God, you are praying. If God talks to you, you have schizophrenia.

1938 **Claudia Cardinale:** Italian actress who combined a dark beauty, flashing eyes, explosive sexuality and genuine acting talent. Got her movies break after winning a Tunisian beauty contest. Italian films: *The Leopard, Once Upon a Time in the West* and *Sandra/Of a Thousand Delights.* Hollywood films include: *The Pink Panther* and *To Hell With Heroes.* Involved in pro-women and pro-gay issues, as well as many humanitarian causes.

I never felt scandal and confessions were necessary to be an actress. I've never revealed myself or even my body in films. Mystery is very important.

1951 **Heloise Cruse Evans:** American writer and columnist, who specializes in lifestyle hints including consumer issues, food, travel, home improvement, health and do forth. Contributing editor of *Good Housekeeping.* Her mother, Heloise Bowles Cruse began the nationally syndicated column, which would become "Hints from Heloise" in 1959. Heloise Evans took over the column in 1977 when her mother died.

No matter our wonderful new technology is, we still have to clean it.

1990 **Emma Watson:** English actress utterly delightful as Hermione Granger in the *Harry Potter* movies. Her prior experience had been limited to leading roles in school plays at the renown preparatory school The Dragon School in Oxford.

Oh my God, no, no chance, no chance. That [kissing her co-stars]'s not in my contract.

OTHERS: 1469 First guru of Sikhs **Nanak**, 1741 U.S. painter **Charles Wilson Peale**, 1800 British explorer Sir **James Clark Ross**, 1829 First American female surgeon **Mary Harris Thompson**, 1858 French Socialist **Émile Durkheim**, 1874 German physicist **Johannes Stark**, 1882 Italian anti-fascist/newspaper editor **Giovanni Amendola**, 1889 U.S. painter/muralist **Thomas Hart Benton**, 1891 Actor/director/screenwriter **Wallace Reid**, 1912 President of North Korea **Kim Il Sung**, 1922 1st African-American mayor of Chicago **Harold Washington**, 1931 Violinist **Florian Zabach**, 1957 100 meter runner **Evelyn Ashford**

April 16

1844 **Anatole France:** Pseudonym of **Jacques Anatole François Thibault**. French poet, novelist and critic. Member of the French Academy. Reached peak of his fame at the turn of the century. Dreyfus case stirred him to become a champion of internationalism.

Nobel Prize for Literature (1921). Novels: *The Crime of Sylvester Bonnard*, and the tetralogy *L'histoire contemporaine*, whose final volume *Monsieur Bergeret in Paris*, reflects his support of Alfred Dreyfus.

If a million people say a foolish thing, it is still a foolish thing.

1867 **Wilbur Wright:** U.S. inventor and aviation pioneer. With his brother Orville made the first powered, controlled and sustained airplane flight, December 17, 1903.Orville flew the airplane for 12 seconds and later Wilbur flew it for 59 seconds. Their Flyer III, built in 1905, could turn, bank, circle and stay airborne for 35 minutes.

The desire to fly is an idea handed down to us by our ancestors who ... looked enviously on the birds soaring freely through space ... on the infinite highway of the air.

1871 **John Millington Synge:** Foremost dramatist of Irish Renaissance. Claimed his works amounted to literal transcriptions of the language of Western Ireland's peasants. Plays: *Riders to the Sea* and *Playboy of the Western World.*

There is no language like the Irish for soothing and quieting.

1881 **Edward F. L. Wood, Earl of Halifax:** English statesman, Viceroy to India, where he worked out terms of understanding with Mohandas Gandhi and accelerated constitutional advances. Foreign Secretary in Neville Chamberlain's government and ambassador to the U.S. during World War II.

Pride is as loud a beggar as want and a great deal more saucy.

1889 Sir **Charles Chaplin:** London-born actor, director, producer, screenwriter, and composer. Widely regarded as the greatest comic artist of the screen. Considered one of the most important figures in motion picture history. Chaplin developed the character of the "Little Tramp." Chaplin's genius was with pantomime. Cofounder of United Artists. Refused to cooperate with HUAC, causing him to be absent from U.S. for 20 years. Films: *The Tramp*, *The Kid*, *The Gold Rush*, *City Lights*, *Modern Times*, *The Great Dictator* and *Monsieur Verdoux.*

Life is a tragedy when seen close-up, but a comedy in long-shot.

1900 **Polly Adler:** America's most famous madam. Began her career in 1920. Operated very successful Broadway bordellos. Wrote a best-selling autobiography, *A House Is Not a Home.*

The women who take husbands not out of love but out of greed, to get their bills paid, to get a fine house and clothes and jewels; the women who marry to get out of a tiresome job, or to get away from disagreeable relatives, or to avoid being called an old maid— these are whores in everything but name. The only difference between them and my girls is that my girls gave a man his money's worth.

1906 **Wendell Johnson:** American psychologist, speech pathologist, and author. Proponent of General Semantics. One of his main interests was the cause of stuttering, but his experiments with orphan children led half of them suffering lifelong psychological damage in the form of speech defects.

Always and never are two words you should always remember never to use.

1915 **Robert Paul Smith:** American writer. Worked for CBS radio and wrote four novels. Wrote the battle-of-the-sexes play *The Tender Trap* with Max Shulman. Best known for the classic evocation of childhood, *Where Did You Go? Out. What Did You Do? Nothing.*

B is for Breasts of which ladies have two; Once prized for the function, now for the view.

1918 **Spike Milligan:** Comedian, novelist, playwright, poet, and jazz musician. Born in India, he lived most of his life in England with Irish citizenship. Best remembered as the creator, principal writer, and performing member of *The Goon Show*. Considered the father of modern British comedy.

All I ask is a chance to prove that money can't make me happy.

1921 Sir **Peter Ustinov:** British actor, director, playwright, novelist, raconteur. Possessed a wonderfully mellifluous voice. Winner of a Tony, two Oscars, three Emmys and a Grammy. Directed an opera at Covent Garden (1962). Wrote best-selling memoir, *Dear Me.* His films include his Oscar winning *Spartacus* and *Topkapi*. Plays: *The Love of Four Colonels* and *Romanoff and Juliet.*

The point of living and of being an optimist is to be foolish enough to believe that the best is yet to come.

1922 Sir **Kingsley Amis:** English novelist, poet, critic and teacher. His comic figure creation, *Lucky Jim*, became a household word in Great Britain in the 1950s. His more than 40 books include four volumes of poetry. Novels: *That Uncertain Feeling*, *The Green Man* and *The Old Devils*. Father of writer Martin Amis.

No pleasure is worth giving up for the sake of two more years in a geriatric home at Weston-super-Mare.

1947 **Kareem Abdul-Jabbar:** African-American basketball player, Born Ferdinand **Lewis Alcindor, Jr.**, 7'2" Kareem led UCLA to an 88–2 record and three national championships. Had his greatest pro success with L.A. Lakers, winning 5 NBA championships in 9 years. Dominant center of his time. Voted Most Valuable Player a record six times.

One man can be a crucial ingredient on a team, but one man cannot make a team.

OTHERS: 1652 Italian pope **Clement XII**, 1660 Founder of the British Museum **Hans Sloane**, 1682 Inventor of 1st reflecting telescope **John Hadley**, 1703 Italian castra singer **Caffarelli [Gaetano Majorano]**, 1786 British navigator/explorer **Sir John Franklin**, 1823 U.S. religious leader **Mother Joseph [Esther Pariseau]**, 1898 Radio comedienne **Marion "Molly McGee" Jordan**, 1904 U.S. Senator **Clifford Case**, 1922 British sci-fi writer **Christopher Samuel Youd**,

1924 Composer/conductor **Henry Mancini**, 1929 U.S. singer **Roy Hamilton**, 1930 Jazz musician **Herbie Mann**, 1931 U.S. actress **Edie Adams**, 1935 U.S. singer **Bobby Vinton**, 1940 Queen of Denmark **Margrethe II**

April 17

1586 **John Ford:** English dramatist, known for his portrayal of passion and concentration on sexual abnormalities in works such as *The Lady's Trial, The Broken Heart, The Lover's Melancholy, Perkin Warbeck*, and his best known work, *Tis a Pity She's a Whore*, a sympathetic story of incestuous lovers.

There are the silent griefs which cut the heart-strings.

1622 **Henry Vaughan:** Anglo-Welch poet, physician and mystic. Studied law but practiced medicine. Chiefly remembered for the spiritual vision or imagination evident in his religious verse. Considered one of the major practitioners of metaphysical poetry. Wrote *The Vanity of Human Wishes* and *Mount of Olives*.

Man is the shuttle, to whose winding quest/ And passage through these looms/ God order'd motion, but ordain'd no rest.

1699 **Robert Blair:** Scottish poet and clergyman. His family's wealth game him leisure for his favorite pursuits gardening and the study of English poets. His literary reputation rests solely on his extremely popular didactic blank-verse poem on death, "The Grave," which ran to 767 lines.

How blunt are all the arrows in thy quiver in comparison with those of guilt.

1806 **William Gillmore Simms:** American editor, novelist and poet. Editor and partial owner of the *Charleston City Gazette*, which when failed, he was reduced to poverty. Determined to devote himself to literature he produced many novels about the South, particularly South Carolina, and marked with local color. *The Yemassee* is considered his finest novel.

Tact is one of the first mental virtues, the absence of which is often fatal to the best of talents; it supplies the place of many talents.

1842 **Charles H. Parkhurst:** American Presbyterian clergyman, reformer and author. Best known for his efforts in exposing political corruption in New York City. Books: *Our Fight with Tammany, A Little Lower Than the Angels* and *The Pulpit and the Pew*.

All great discoveries are made by men whose feelings run ahead of their thinking.

1870 **David Grayson:** Penname of **Ray Stannard Baker**. U.S. author, journalist and historian. Dreamed of writing the "Great American Novel," but he soon gained a reputation as one of the leading muckrakers," the title Theodore Roosevelt applied to crusading journalists. Helped found the *American Magazine*. Served as Woodrow Wilson's press secretary at Versailles. Earned a Pulitzer Prize for his eight-volume biography of Wilson.

Most of us, Anglo-Saxons, tremble before a tsar when we might fearlessly beard a tiger.

1882 **Artur Schnabel:** Austrian pianist and composer. Gave legendary performances of the complete sonatas of Ludwig van Beethoven and Franz Schubert. During World War II, he moved to London and then to the U.S. Though he mostly played the works of past masters, such as Beethoven and Schubert, his own compositions were ultramodern.

Applause is a receipt, not a bill.

1885 **Isak Dinesen:** Pseudonym of **Baroness Karen Blixen**. Danish novelist and short-story writer. From 1914 to 1931 lived on a coffee plantation in what is now Kenya. Wrote *Seven Gothic Tales, Out of Africa* and *Winter's Tales*.

What is man, when you come to think upon him, but a minutely set, ingenious machine for turning, with infinite artfulness, the red wine of Shiraz into urine?

1894 **Nikita Khrushchev:** Soviet communist leader. Born in the Ukraine. As first secretary of the Soviet Communist Party and premier started a program of de–Stalinization. Enunciated a policy of peaceful coexistence with Western powers, strained by the Cuban missile crisis and his showdown with President Kennedy. Ideological differences and the signing of the Nuclear Test-Ban Treaty let to a split with the Chinese. This and agricultural failures that necessitated the importing of wheat from the West led to his forced retirement in 1964.

Revolutions are the locomotives of history.

1897 **Thornton Wilder:** American novelist, playwright. Pulitzer Prize for *The Bridge of San Luis Rey. The Eighth Day* won the National Book Award (1968). Plays: *Our Town* (Pulitzer Prize), which became one of the most enduringly popular and performed plays, and *The Skin of Our Teeth* also were Pulitzer Prizewinners and *The Matchmaker*, which was adapted into the musical *Hello, Dolly!*

Life is an unbroken succession of false situations.

1923 **Harry Reasoner:** U.S. journalist. Principal anchorman for ABC (1970–78). His tenure as co-anchor with Barbara Walters was not a good match and so he left ABC to return to CBS. Regular and three time Emmy winner on television's "60 Minutes" (1968–70, 1978–91).

Journalism is a kind of profession, or craft, or racket, for people who never wanted to grow up and go out in the real world. If you're a good journalist, what you do is live a lot of things vicariously, and report for other people who want to live vicariously.

1928 **Cynthia Ozick:** American novelist and short-story writer. Jewish themes and that artistic creation can be considered an arrogant attempt to rival God the Creator. Her works include *Trust, Leviathan, The Shawl* and collections of her essays, *Metaphor and Memory* and *Fame and Folly*.

I'm not afraid of facts. I welcome facts but a congeries of facts is not equivalent to an idea. This is the essential fallacy of the so-called "scientific" mind. People who mistake facts for ideas are incomplete thinkers; they are gossips.

OTHERS: 1676 King of Sweden **Frederick I**, 1741 American judge **Samuel Chase**, 1827 Flemish architect **French C. Baeckelmans**, 1845 U.S. editor **Isabel Barrows**, 1876 Scottish novelist **Ian Hay**, 1896 Ventriloquist **Señor Wences**, 1899 Entomologist **Vincent Wigglesworth**, 1916 1st Prime Minister Sri Lanka **Sirimavo Bandaranaike**, 1918 U.S. actor **William Holden**, 1923 British director **Lindsay Anderson**, 1923 Cabinetmaker **Norman Potter**, 1929 Orchestra leader **James Last**, 1932 Italian opera singer **Graziella Sciutti**, 1934 Rock & Roll producer **Don Kirschner**, 1948 Czech composer **Jan Hammer**, 1961 U.S. football quarterback **"Boomer" Esiason**, 1972 U.S. actress **Jennifer Garner**

April 18

1480 **Lucrezia Borgia:** Roman-born noblewoman. Illegitimate daughter of Cardinal Borgia (later Pope Alexander VI). Sister of Cesare Borgia. Three times married to further her father's political ambitions. Patroness of art and education. Her reputation as a wanton and poisoner is probably unwarranted. Her child may have been the result of an incestuous relation with her father. After her father's death, she turned to religion and died at age 39.

The more I try to do God's will the more he visits me with misfortune.

1570 **Thomas Middleton:** English dramatist. One of the most popular playwrights of his period. His talents were in comedy and satire. Often collaborated with Thomas Dekker or William Rowley. His masterpieces are *The Changeling* and *A Trick to Catch the Old One.*

All is not gold that glisteneth.

1797 **Louis Adolphe Thiers:** French historian, journalist and statesman. Outstanding figure in French politics for nearly 40 years. Twice Premier under King Louis Philippe. As first President of the Third Republic he negotiated the end of the Franco-Prussian War and restored domestic order by crushing the Paris Commune. Books: *History of the French Revolution* (ten volumes) and *History of the Consulate and the Empire* (20 volumes).

In politics it is necessary that everything be taken seriously, nothing tragically.

1817 **George Henry Lewes:** English philosophical writer and literary critic. Chiefly remembered for his theory of metaphysical development of positivism and his liaison with novelist George Eliot (Mary Ann Evans), whom he lived with from 1854 until his death in 1878. Publications: *Actors and Acting, The Spanish Drama, The Biographical History of Philosophy*, and *Life of Goethe*, probably the best known of his writings.

We must never assume that which is incapable of proof.

1837 **Henri Becque:** French dramatist and critic. Wrote the book of the opera *Sardanapale* for the music of Victorin Joncières (1867). Broke with the tradition of the convention of the well-made play. Plays *Michel Pauper, Les Corbeaux* and *La Parisienne.*

The defect of equality is that we only desire it with our superiors.

1857 **Clarence Darrow:** American lawyer, lecturer, and writer. Categorically opposed to capital punishment. Saved the lives of thrill killers Leopold and Loeb. Lost the battle in the famous "Scopes Monkey Trail," but won the war by destroying his opponent William Jennings Bryan, when Bryan took the stand as an expert Bible witness. His career is the subject of *The Story of My Life.*

I do not consider it an insult, but rather a compliment to be called an agnostic. I do not pretend to know where many ignorant men are sure — that is all that agnosticism means.

1864 **Richard Harding Davis:** American journalist, novelist, short-story writer, and one of the first roving correspondents. War correspondent in six wars. Managing editor of *Harper's Weekly*. Author of *Soldiers of Fortune* and *The Bar Sinister.*

No civilized person goes to bed the same day he gets up.

1882 **Leopold Stokowski:** Originally **Antoni Stanislaw Baleslawowich**. English-American Music conductor and organist. Director, Philadelphia Orchestra (1912–36), making it a world class ensemble, creating the lush "Philadelphia sound." Organized All-American Youth Orchestra (1940–41). Helped popularize classics. Widely known for his transcriptions of Bach. Starred as himself in Walt Disney's *Fantasia (*1940). Lecturing a talkative audience:

A painter paints his pictures on canvas. But musicians paint their pictures on silence. We provide the music and you provide the silence.

1915 **Joy Desham:** Born **Helen Joy Davidman**. American Jewish writer, radical communist and atheist until her conversion to Christianity in the late 1940s. Author of *Smoke on the Mountain.* First husband was writer Douglas Gresham. Moved to England where she met and married writer and Oxford don, C.S. Lewis. Succumbed to cancer at the age of 45. Their relationship was the basis of the romanticized film *Shadowlands* in 1993. In it, Joy stoically addresses her cancer:

We can't have the happiness of yesterday without the pain of today. That's the deal.

1917 **Frederika Louise:** German-born Princess of Hanover, Duchess of Brunswick and Lunenburg and Queen Consort of King Paul I of the Hellenes (1947–64) as Queen Frideriki. Went into self-imposed exile when the monarchy was overthrown in 1973.Her daughter Sophia, became Queen of Spain and their son and heir Constantine, King of Greece. When she married, she told the Greek people:

I was born a barbarian. I came to Greece to be civilized.

1947 **James Woods:** Intelligent intense American actor. Nominated for An Academy Award for Best Actor in *El Salvador* and for Best Supporting Actor for *Ghosts of Mississippi*. He was superb as a gangster in *Once Upon a Time in America*. Emmy Award for *My Name is Bill W.* and *Promise*.

Celebrity — I don't even know that that means. Obviously it's the same basic word as celebration, but I don't know what's being celebrated.

1963 **Conan O'Brien:** American comedian and writer. Writer for *Saturday Night Live* for 3½ years. Also worked as a writer and producer for the series *The Simpsons*. Best known as host of television talk and variety show *Late Night with Conan O'Brien*. Slated to replace Jay Leno as host of *The Tonight Show* in 2009.

Apparently Arnold [Schwarzenegger] was inspired by President Bush, who proved you can be a successful politician in this country even if English is your second language.

OTHERS: 1521 French General **François de Coligny**, 1764 Pianist/conductor **Bernhard Anselm Weber**, 1881 Polish **Max Weber**, 1896 Swiss geologist **C. Eugène Wegmann**, 1903 Russian/U.S. actor **Leonid Kinskey**, 1906 Dutch poet **Clara Eggink**, 1907 Hungarian movie composer **Miklós Rózsa**, 1911 A&P heir **George Huntington Hartford**, 1912 British actress **Wendy Barrie**, 1924 Blues singer **Clarence "Gatemouth" Brown**, 1937 U.S. actor **Robert Hooks**, 1937 U.S.S.R. long jumper **Tatyana Shchelkanova**, 1940 U.S. union official **Ed Garvey**, 1946 English actress **Hayley Mills**, 1948 NBA basketball player **Nate "Tiny" Archibald**, 1961 British Member MP/prostitute **Pamela Bordes**

April 19

1721 **Roger Sherman:** American statesman, lawyer, and surveyor. Helped draft and signed the Declaration of Independence. Also signed the Articles of Association, Articles of Confederation and the Constitution, the only person to sign all four documents. U.S. Senator from Connecticut (1791–93).

Let us live no more to ourselves, but to Him who loved us, and gave Himself to die for us.

1772 **David Ricardo:** English political economist. Proposed an iron law of wages, stating that wages tend to stabilize around the subsistence level. Much of modern conceptions of currency, taxation, and international trade have been influenced by his analysis. Most known for *Principles of Political Economy and Taxation*.

There is no way of keeping profits up but by keeping wages down.

1900 **Richard Hughes:** British playwright, short story writer and novelist. Vice President of the Welsh National Theatre (1924–1936). His play *Danger* broadcast of BBC was the first written especially for radio. Best known for *A High Wind in Jamaica*, which was chosen as one of the 100 best novels of the 20th century.

All that non-fiction can do is answer questions. It's fiction's business to ask them.

1901 Baroness **Edith Clara Summerskill:** English politician, gynecologist, Member of Parliament and writer. Fought for women's welfare on all issues, often provoking hostility. Wrote *A Woman's World*. Under-Secretary to the Minister of Food and chairman of the Labor Party (1954–5).

I learned that economics was not an exact science and that the most erudite men would analyze the economic ills of the world and derive a totally different conclusion.

1932 **Jayne Mansfield:** née **Vera Jayne Palmer**. American actress. Buxom sexpot of films in the fifties and sixties. Break came in Broadway production of *Will Success Spoil Rock Hunter?* in which she appeared clad only in a Turkish towel. Much brighter than the women she played, who were always the same breathless, dizzy blonde. Killed in a car accident. Mother of actress Mariska Hargitay.

I do bathe in pink champagne. I do it, I definitely do it. I've got a champagne man. It takes bottles and bottles. I do it all the time ... because I think it is terribly exciting. I do all sorts of weird things. I sun bathe in the nude outsides. I just feel I have to. I don't know why.

1935 **Dudley Moore:** English-born actor, musician, and composer. The 5'2" Moore was recognized as a fine jazz pianist and composer of music scores. Teamed with Cambridge undergraduates Jonathan Miller, Peter Cook and Alan Bennett to form the popular student satire "Beyond the Fringe." Became a film star with *10*. Oscar nominated for *Arthur*. Married a number of times, his wives included British actress Suzy Kendall, American actress Tuesday Weld and former Miss America Susan Anton.

I'm always looking for meaningful one-night stands.

1938 **Stanley Fish:** American literary theorist. After earning his Ph.D. from Yale, he has had a long and distinguished academic career in a number of prestigious universities. Leading scholar of John Milton. Books: *Surprised by Sin: The Reader in Paradise Lost* and How Milton Works. Known for examining how the interpretation of a text is dependent upon each reader's own subjective experience in one or more communities.

It is always incorrect to assume you can know what's someone's moral convictions are based on their philosophical theories.

1946 **Tim Curry:** English-born actor, composer and singer. First professional success was in the London production of *Hair*. Created the role of Frank N. Furter in *The Rocky Horror Picture Show*, appearing in stage productions both in England and Broadway and in the movie, which has become a cult classic. Earned three Tony Award nominations, for his performances as the title character in *Amadeus*, his role in *My Favorite Year* and as King Arthur in *Spamalot*.

It's so comforting to know that there are so many people in the world sicker than I am.

1962 **Al Unser, Jr.:** American race car driver nicknamed "Little Al." The son of race car driver Al Unser

Sr. and nephew of Bobby Unser. Won the Indianapolis 500 twice. By the age of 11, he was racing sprint cars. Continued to improve on the CART circuit, finishing fourth in the points standings in 1986, third in 1987, second in 1988 and finally first in 1990.

Winning is my business is everything.

1968 **Ashley Judd:** Born **Ashley Tyler Ciminella.** American actress. Her mother and step-sister are the country music singers Naomi Judd and Wynonna Judd. Ashley has become an accomplished actress to go along with her great beauty. Films include *Heat, Double Jeopardy* and *Someone Like You*. Self-proclaimed feminist, vegetarian, and an etymologist.

Tough girls come from New York. Sweet girls, they're from Georgia. But us Virginia girls, we have fire and ice in our blood. We can ride horses, be a debutante, throw left hooks, and drink with the boys, all the while making sweet teas, darlin'. And if we have an opinion, you know you're gonna hear it.

1979 **Kate Hudson:** American actress with a winning smile. Daughter of Actress Goldie Hawn and musician Bill Hudson. Raised by Kurt Russell, Hawn's longtime partner. Made a major splash in *Almost Famous. Other films: Raising Helen, Le Divorce*, and *How to Lose a Guy in 10 Days.* Named one of the "50 Most Beautiful People in the World" by *People* Magazine (2000).

I have zero problems when people say, "God, you look like your mother." I go, "Well, great! Thanks!"

1987 **Maria Sharapova:** Russian professional tennis player. In 2004, she became the second youngest Wimbledon's women's champion in the Open Era. The 6'2" blonde has done some modeling and has been compared with another Russian tennis beauty and model Anna Kournikova. Sharapova's fame rests on both her beauty and her tennis ability, while Kournikova has not had a successful pro career. Maria's on-court presence reminds tennis fans of Monica Seles, with her powerful groundstrokes, intensity, focus and determination.

I'm not the next anyone, I'm the first Maria Sharapova.

OTHERS: 1728 Italian playwright **Francisco Albergati Capacelli**, 1795 German zoologist **Christian Gottfried Ehrenburg**, 1835 Spanish dramatist **José Echegaray y Eizaguirre**, 1858 Australian-born actress **May Robson**, 1866 Dutch oil magnate **Henri Deterding**, 1885 U.S. novelist **Philip Curtiss**, 1891 Italian writer/poet **Ricardo Bacchelli**, 1897 Sculptor/art benefactor **Gertrude Vanderbilt Whitney**, 1900 American silent screen star **Constance Talmadge**, 1903 Prohibition Agent of Treasury Department **Eliot Ness**, 1910 Historian/diplomat **Andrew Gilchrist**, 1922 German World War II pilot/ace **Erich Hartmann**, 1936 U.S. singer **Ruby Johnson**, 1940 U.S. singer/songwriter **Bobby Russell**

April 20

121 **Marcus Aurelius [Antoninus]:** Roman emperor and Stoic philosopher. Renowned for the nobility of his principles. Chose to dress plainly, live frugally, and work from early morning to midnight. Philosophical reflections contained in *The Meditations of Marcus Aurelius*, one of the great books of wisdoms. Opposed Christianity and supported the persecution of its followers. His reign is often thought to mark the Golden Age of Rome.

To the wise, life is a problem; to the fool, a solution.

1492 **Pietro Aretino:** Italian poet, prose writer and dramatist. Distinguished himself by his wit, impudence and literary talents. Celebrated for his bold and insolent literary attacks on the powerful, penned in fiery letters and dialogues. His play *Orazia* is often described as the best Italian tragedy of the 16th century. Allegedly while sitting on a stool listening to a droll story told by his sister, he laughed so heartedly that he fell and died on the spot.

I am indeed a king, because I know how to rule myself.

1813 **Henry Theodore Tuckerman:** American essayist and critic. Published American *Artist Life*, an account of American art. Not particularly discriminating, he praised all good artists and honored the rest mostly for being American. Lived much in Italy, where he produced *The Italian Sketchbook, Thoughts on Poets*, and *Leaves from the Diary of a Dreamer.*

There is a strength of quiet endurance as significant of courage as the most daring feats of prowess.

1826 **Dinah Mulock Craik:** English poet and novelist. Author of Victorian best seller *John Halifax, Gentleman.* First published at age 20 with *The Ogilvies.* Encouraged Victorian women to examine their role. Also wrote essays, children stories and fairy tales.

There are no judgments so harsh as those of the erring, the inexperienced, and the young.

1871 **William Henry Davies:** Welsh poet. Emigrated to the U.S. at age 22. Most of his poetry is on the subject of nature or life on the road. Also known for two novels and autobiographical works. Best known for *Autobiography of a Super-Tramp.* Other works: *A Soul's Destroyer* and *Adventures of Johnny Walker.*

As long as I love Beauty I am young.

1889 **Adolf Hitler:** Austrian-born German politician and dictator. "Der Führer." Leader of National Socialist Party (Nazis) (1921–45). Dictator of Germany (1933–45). Wrote of his intentions in his virulent autobiography *Mein Kampf* while imprisoned. Instituted policies of anti–Semitism and German territorial expansion, seeking world domination, leading to World War II. Allied with Italy's Benito Mussolini in the Rome-Berlin Axis. Responsible for the Holocaust that cost the lives of 6 million Jews. Committed suicide in a Berlin bunker (1945) after marrying his mistress Eva Braun.

How fortunate for leaders that men do not think.

1893 **Joan Miró:** Spanish (Catalan) artist. Became a member of the French school of surrealist painters. His works are predominantly abstract using curvilinear, fantastical forms in dreamlike settings. They are a mix of frivolous humor and nightmares. Worked extensively in lithography and produced numerous murals, tapestries and sculptures.

The works must be conceived with fire in the soul but executed with clinical coolness. Painting is made as we make love, a total embrace, prudence thrown to the wind, nothing held back.

1906 **Stanley Marcus:** U.S. merchant. President of Texas' Neiman-Marcus. Started the international fashion expositions and the Neiman-Marcus awards. Wrote "America is in Fashion," an article appearing in Fortune magazine in 1939, establishing him as a national fashion authority. Lived to be 96.

Any fine store can dress a few women beautifully. Our idea is to dress a whole community of women that way.

1920 **John Paul Stevens:** American jurist. Judge of U.S. Court of Appeals for the Seventh District (Chicago) (1970–75). Appointed associate justice of the U.S. Supreme Court (1975), replacing Justice William O. Douglas. Nominated by President Nixon he was confirmed by the Senate by a vote of 99–0. Considered a legal centrist. Oldest and longest serving incumbent member of the court; the only Associate Justice to have served under three Chief Justices.

It is not our job to apply laws that have not yet been written.

1924 **Nina Foch:** Dutch-born American film actress. Tall blonde leading lady of the 1940s and 50s, who played cool, aloof, women of distinction. Films include *Spartacus* and *An American in Paris*. Since the 1960s she has been an acting teacher for USC and the American Film Institute.

When I'm cleaning the house I wear an apron, but nothing else. It makes my activities—dusting, washing—more interesting for my husband.

1949 **Jessica Lange:** U.S. actress. Made her debut as a toothsome foil in 1976 remake of *King Kong*. Developed into one of the screen's finest actresses. Oscar for her supporting role in *Tootsie*; the same year she was nominated in the Best Actress category for *Frances*. Best Actress Oscar winner for *Blue Sky*. Also nominated for *Country*, *Sweet Dreams* and *Music Box*.

When you learn not to want things so badly, life comes to you.

1961 **Don Mattingly:** American major league baseball first baseman with the New York Yankees (1982–95). Nicknamed "Donnie Baseball: and "The Hit Man." American League MVP in 1985, Gold Glove Award (1985–89 and 91–94). In 1987, he tied a major leaguer record by hitting a home run in eight straight games and set a major league record of six grand slam home runs in a single season, since tied by Cleveland Indians Travis Hafner in 2006.

Honestly, at one time I thought Babe Ruth was a cartoon character. I really did, I mean I wasn't born until 1961 and I grew up in Indiana.

OTHERS: 1442 King of England **Edward IV**, 1808 French Emperor **Louis-Napoleon [Napoleon III]**, 1839 King of Romania **Carol I**, 1850 American sculptor **Daniel Chester French**, 1893 Silent film comic **Harold Lloyd**, 1897 Russian actor/director **Gregory Ratoff**, 1901 French anthropologist **Michel Leiris**, 1923 Puerto Rican bandleader **Tito Puente**, 1927 Swiss physicist **Karl Müller**, 1939 U.S. singer **Johnny Tillotson**, 1941 U.S. actor **Ryan O'Neal**, 1943 Sci-fi author **Ian Watson**, 1948 U.S. keyboardist **Craig Frost**, 1950 South Africa President **Itumeleng J. Mosala**, 1951 U.S. singer **Luther Vandross**, 1952 Russian cosmonaut **Tamara S. Zakharova**, 1972 U.S. model/actress **Carmen Electra**

April 21

1729 **Catherine the Great:** German-born **Sophia Frederike von Anhalt-Zerbst**. Russian empress (1762–96). Overthrew neurotic husband Czar Peter III with help of the palace guard. Annexed Crimea. Divided Poland among Russia, Austria and Prussia (1795). Turkish War vastly increased the empire, as did the war with Sweden. One of Europe's most successful rulers. Notorious for her love affairs with Gregory Orlov, Augustus Poniatowski and Grigori Potemkin, among many others.

I shall be an autocrat: that's my trade. And the good Lord will forgive me: that's his.

1782 **Friedrich Froebel:** German educator and founder of the kindergarten, which means "garden of children." Saw the teacher's role as not to drill or indoctrinate but rather to encourage self-expression, "self-activity" and play as essential factors in a child's education through play. Aim was to help the child's mind grow naturally and spontaneously.

Play is the highest expression of human development in childhood, for it alone is the free expression of what is in the child's soul.

1816 **Charlotte Brontë:** Pseudonym **Currier Bell**. English novelist. Her novel *Jane Eyre*, a classic of romantic literature, was in part based on her unhappy experiences at the dreadful Clergy Daughters' School where her two eldest sisters died. Other novels: *The Professor*, *Shirley* and *Villette*. Masterfully depicted women in conflict with their individual needs and social conditions.

Conventionality is not morality. Self-righteousness is not a religion. To attack the first is not to assail the last. To pluck the mask from the face of the Pharisee is not to lift an impious hand to the Crown of Thorns.

1818 **Josh Billings:** Pseudonym of **Henry Wheeler Shaw**. American auctioneer, real-estate agent, lecturer, humorist and homespun philosopher. Studied techniques of Artemus Ward. Turned his hand to writing humorous essays: *Josh Billings: His Book of Sayings* and annual volumes *Josh Billings' Farmer Allminax* (1870–90). His brief one liners display considerable humorous good sense.

A dog is the only thing on earth that loves you more than you love yourself.

1828 **Hippolyte A. Taine:** French literary and art critic, historian and intellectual leader. Known for emphasis on role of scientific determinism in literature. Taught at the École des Beaux-Arts in Paris for 20 years, where he became one of the most esteemed exponents of 19th century French positivism. Greatest work: *The Origins of Contemporary France.*

I have studied many philosophers and many cats. The wisdom of cats is infinitely superior.

1838 **John Muir:** Scottish-born American naturalist, explorer and conservationist. Began efforts to establish a federal forest conservation policy. His writings on the matter swayed public opinion, which led to the conservation policies of Grover Cleveland and Theodore Roosevelt. Muir was largely responsible for establishing Sequoia and Yosemite National Parks. Founder and first president of the Sierra Club. The only stand of redwoods in the U.S. National Park System is named the Muir Woods National Monument.

I never saw a discontented tree. They grip the ground as thought they liked it, and though fast rooted they travel about as far as we do.

1882 **Percy Williams Bridgeman:** American physicist. Nobel Prize winner (1946) pioneering for work in the development of high-pressure chambers for the study of matter at extreme pressures. Obtained a new form of phosphorus and proved experimentally that viscosity increases with high pressure.

It is the nature of knowledge to be subject to uncertainty.

1896 **Henri de Montherlant:** French novelist and playwright. Advocated the overcoming of conflicts of life by vigorous action. Major work is a four-novel cycle, beginning with *Pity for Women.* Wrote several plays, including *Don Juan.*

Throughout history the world has been laid waste to ensure the triumph of conceptions that are now as dead as the men that died for them.

1909 **Rollo May:** American existential psychologist, profoundly affected by Paul Tillich, the existential theologian and the writings of Soren Kierkegaard, the Danish religious writer, who inspired much of the existential movement. May was also influenced by American humanism. Interested in reconciling existential psychology with other approaches, in particular that of Sigmund Freud. Many of May's unique ideas can be found in his book *Love and Will.*

The relationship between commitment and doubt is by no means an antagonistic one. Commitment is healthiest when it's not without doubt but in spite of doubt.

1913 **Norman Parkinson:** Originally **Ronald William Parkinson Smith.** English photographer. Became one of Britain's most popular portrait and fashion artists. Work was widely used in quality magazines. Style was essentially elegant and romantic.

The camera can be the most deadly weapon since the assassin's bullet. Or it can be the lotion of the heart.

1923 **John Mortimer:** British playwright, novelist and barrister. Participate in several celebrated civil cases. Constant defender of liberal values. His series of novels featuring barrister Horace Rumpole were adapted for TV as *Rumpole of the Bailey.* Wrote the TV screenplays for *I, Claudius* and *Brideshead Revisited.* Plays include: *The Dock Brief, The Wrong Side of the Park* and *Two Stars for Comfort.*

No brilliance is needed in the law. Nothing but common sense and relatively clean finger nails.

1927 **Robert Brustein:** American drama critic, teacher, and director. As Dean of the School of Drama at Yale University, he founded the Yale Repertory Theater. He was also director of the American Repertory Theater at Harvard University. Author of a collection of essays, published under the title *Who Needs Theater.*

The love that previously dared not speak its name has now grown hoarse from screaming it.

OTHERS: 1546 Composer **Arcangelo Crivelli**, 1774 French physicist/astronomer **Jean-Baptiste Biot**, 1775 U.S. engraver/illustrator **Alexander Anderson**, 1837 Danish politician/pacifist **Fredrik Bajer**, 1840 German priest/musicologist **Franz Xaver Haberl**, 1878 German painter **Albert Weisgerber**, 1898 Football coach New York Giants **Steve Owen**, 1905 California Governor **Edmund "Pat" Brown**, 1911 U.S. operatic baritone **Leonard Warren**, 1915 Mexican-born actor **Anthony Quinn**, 1919 U.S. singer **Don Cornell**, 1926 British monarch **Queen Elizabeth II**, 1930 Italian actress **Silvano Mangano**, 1958 U.S. actress **Andie Macdowell**

April 22

1451 **Isabella of Spain:** Queen of Castile (1474–1505). Married King Ferdinand II of Aragon, jointly ruling both kingdoms. Brought Spain "from the debasement and degradation of the preceding reign and raised it to being the nursery of virtue and generous ambition." Patron of Christopher Columbus, financing his voyages to the New World.

Although I have never doubted it ... the distance is great from the firm belief to the realization from concrete experience.

1707 **Henry Fielding:** English novelist, playwright and magistrate. Best known for picaresque novels. A satirist of political corruption. Organized the detective force that became Scotland Yard. Had a weakness for women which he wrote about in his most popular work *The History of Tom Jones, a Foundling*, noted for its great comic gusto and *Joseph Andrews*, a parody of the work of Samuel Richardson.

Public schools **[i.e. private English schools]** ***are the nurseries of all vice and immorality.***

1724 **Immanuel Kant:** German philosopher and metaphysician. Taught at the University of Königsberg, where had had been a student, for more than 40 years. One of the foremost thinkers of the Enlightenment, Maintained that there are basic concepts, like cause and effect, which are not learned from experience but constitute the basic conceptual apparatus by which we make sense of experience and the world. Major works: *Critique of Pure Reason*, *Critique of Practical Reason* and *Critique of Judgment*.

In law, a man is guilty when he violates the rights of another. In ethics he is guilty if he only thinks of doing so.

1766 Madame **Germaine de Staël [-Holstein]:** Swiss-French novelist, political propagandist, conversationalist and woman of letters. Known for her salons which were attended by the leading literary and political figures of her day. Had a reputation as a lively wit. Works: *The Influence of Literature Upon Society*, the novel *Delphine* and her unfinished masterpiece published after her death, *Considerations on the Principal Events of the French Revolution*.

The desire of the man is for the woman, but the desire of the woman is for the desire of the man.

1840 **Odilon Redon:** French Symbolist painter, lithographer and etcher. Came to be associated with the Symbolist painters. His oils and pastels where chiefly still lifes. His prints explored fantasies and often had macabre themes.

A painter is not intellectual when, having painted a nude woman; he leaves in our minds the idea that she is going to get dressed again right away.

1870 **Vladimir Ilyich Lenin:** Originally **Vladimir Ilyich Ulyanov**. Russian revolutionary leader and writer. Spent many years in Western exile. After the overthrow of the Czar, led the Bolsheviks to power (1917). Became head of Soviet state, establishing the "dictatorship of the proletariat." Retained post until his death in 1924. Loved music but would not listen to it, claiming it made him too mellow and nice.

The substitution of the proletarian for the bourgeois state is impossible without a violent revolution.

1873 **Ellen Glasgow:** Pulitzer Prize winning American novelist. Wrote 20 novels, mostly about Virginia. Credited with being the first to write honestly about the South. Novels: *The Descendant*, *The Deliverance*, *Virginia*, and *In This Our Life*.

The only difference between a rut and a grave are the dimensions.

1891 **Nicola Sacco:** Italian anarchist and shoemaker. With Bartolomeo Vanzetti arrested and convicted of the murder of a paymaster and a guard during a robbery at a shoe factory. Despite protests that the two were innocent, they were executed. Their trial was flawed and they deserved a retrial. Many are convinced that they were convicted for their beliefs and had nothing to do with the crime. In a final letter to his son, Sacco wrote:

So, Son, instead of crying, be strong, so as to be able to comfort your mother ... take her for a long walk in the quiet country, gathering wild flowers here and there... But remember always, Dante, don't you use all for yourself only ... help the persecuted and the victim because they are the comrades that fight and fall ... for the conquest of the joy of freedom for all the poor workers. In this struggle for life you will find more love and you will be loved.

1899 **Vladimir Nabokov:** Russian-born American novelist and poet. Became U.S. citizen in 1945. Taught at Wellesley College and Cornell University. His novel *Lolita* brought him international fame and allowed him to abandon teaching to spend full time writing. Other novels: *Invitation to a Beheading*, *Laughter in the Dark*, *Pale Fire*. *Ada* and *The Gift*. Regarded for his linguistic ingenuity and dazzling intellect. From 1959, lived in Montreux in Switzerland. Also translated Pushkin's *Eugene Onegin*.

Our existence is but a brief crack of light between two eternities of darkness.

1904 **J. Robert Oppenheimer:** Enrico Fermi Award winning American theoretical physicist. Trained a generation of American physicists at Caltech. In World War II he headed the Army's Manhattan Project in laboratories at Los Alamos, New Mexico, which developed the atomic bomb. Directed the Institute for Advanced Study at Princeton. Proclaimed a security risk and suspended from secret nuclear work for his reluctance to proceed with the development of the hydrogen bomb.

Now I am become death, the destroyer of worlds.

1916 **Yehudi Menuhin:** American-British violinist and conductor. Made his debut at age 7 with the San Francisco Symphony. Performed in concerts to tremendous acclaim throughout the world. Founded a chamber orchestra. His interest in forgotten music has led to his discovery and revival of the original and complete works of Paganini, Bach and Schumann. Later in his life he devoted considerable time and effort to the cause of international cooperation and world peace.

The violinist must possess the poet's gift of piercing the protective hide that grows on propagandists, stockbrokers, and slave traders, to penetrate the deeper truth which lies within.

1923 **Paula Fox:** American author. Noted for her books intended for children and autobiographical novels. Awarded the Hans Christian Anderson Medal, a biennial award for an author's entire body of work. Two of her most famous books for children are *The Slave Dancer* (a Newberry Medal Winner) and *One-Eyed Cat* (a Newberry Honor Book). Her books for adults include *Desperate Characters: A Novel* and *Borrowed Finery: A Memoir*.

A lie hides the truth. A story tries to find it.

OTHERS: 1775 German philosopher/theologist **Georg Hermes**, 1799 French physician/physiologist **Jean**

Poiseuille, 1816 English poet **Philip James Bailey**, 1832 U.S. politician **Julius Sterling Morton**, 1839 German botanist **August W. Eichler**, 1853 French anthropologist **Alphonse Bertillon**, 1854 Belgian jurist **Henri Lafontaine**, 1876 Norwegian novelist **Ole Rőlvaag**, 1884 Austrian psychoanalyst **Otto Rank**, 1908 U.S. actor **Eddie Albert**, 1914 Dutch/English writer **Jan de Hartog**, 1917 French ballerina **Yvette Chauviré**, 1922 Jazz musician **Charles Mingus**, 1923 Pinup model **Bettie Page**, 1929 English mathematician **Michael Atiyah**, 1937 U.S. actor **Jack Nicholson**

April 23

1584 **William Shakespeare:** English poet, dramatist of the Elizabethan and early Jacobian period, born at Stratford-upon-Avon. Most widely known author in English literature. Universally acknowledged to be the greatest dramatist and poet of all time. His plays have been performed almost continuously to this day. Many actors and actresses believe playing a Shakespearean role to be the crowning achievement of professional success. Wrote comedies, histories and tragedies, as well as 154 sonnets. Plays include: *Henry IV, Henry I,* and *Henry II, Richard III, A Midsummer Night's Dream, Romeo and Juliet, The Merchant of Venice, Henry V, Julius Caesar, Hamlet, Othello, King Lear, Macbeth* and *Antony and Cleopatra.* Died on his 52nd birthday.

What a piece of work is man! How noble in reason! How infinite in faculty! In form, in moving, how express and admirable! In action how like an angel! In apprehension how like a god! The beauty of the world! The paragon of animals! And yet, to me, what is this quintessence of dust? Man delights not me — no, nor woman neither, though by your smiling you seem to say so.

1813 **Stephen A. Douglas:** American Democratic politician and lawyer. "Little Giant." Congressman from Illinois (1843–47), Senator (1847–61). A great orator known for debates with Abraham Lincoln during 1858 Senate campaign on questions of slavery. Defeated for presidency by Lincoln (1860). Speaking of himself:

Between the Negro and the crocodile, he took the side of the Negro. But between the Negro and the white man, he would go for the white man.

1818 **James A. Froude:** English historian and biographer. His historical works, which displayed an anti-Catholic bias, were criticized by reviewers for carelessness, but proved very popular with the public. Best known work is *History of England from the Fall of Wolsey to the Defeat of the Spanish Armada.* Produced a biography of his friend Thomas Carlyle.

No person is ever good for much, that hasn't been swept off their feet by enthusiasm between ages twenty and thirty.

1852 **Edwin Markham:** American poet and lecturer. Called the Dean of American poets. Best known for his poem, "The Man with a Hoe." Other works: *Lincoln and other Poems, The Ballad of Gallows Bird, Gates of Paradise* and *Field Folk: Interpretations of Millet.*

We have committed the Golden Rule to memory; let us now commit it to life.

1858 **Max Planck:** German physicist. Modern physics began with his proposal of quantum theory, which states that electromagnetic radiation consists of quanta (particles of energy). 1918 Nobel Prize in physics. Championed Albert Einstein's special theory of relativity, but opposed the statistical worldview introduced by Niels Bohr, Max Born and Werner Heisenberg. Appealed to Adolf Hitler to no avail to reverse his racial policies. His son was implicated in the plot to kill Hitler and was executed.

We have no right to assume that any physical laws exist, or if they have existed up until now, that they will continue to exist in a similar manner in the future.

1897 **Lester Bowles Pearson:** Canadian statesman, diplomat, and educator. Taught at the University of Toronto. Ambassador to the U.S. (1945–46) Headed Canadian delegation to U.N. (1948–57), and served as president of the General Assembly. Awarded 1957 Nobel Peace Prize for his help in resolving the Suez crisis of 1956. Prime minister (1963–68).

We are all descendants of Adam, and we are all products of racial miscegenation.

1916 **Charles W. "Bud" Wilkinson:** U.S. football player and coach. As a quarterback led the University of Minnesota to three national championships in the 1930s. As coach led Oklahoma to thirteen consecutive conference tittles three national titles. His teams had a 47-game winning streak snapped by the University of Notre Dame. After retiring from coaching, he became a color commentator on college football telecasts.

We compete, not so much against an opponent, but against ourselves. The real test is this: Did I make my best effort on every play.

1925 **Art Hoppe:** American columnist with the *San Francisco Chronicle* for more than 40 years. Skewered political target on both the left and right with satirical humor and eloquence. His column gave birth to a cast of whimsical characters including a confused redneck, a Harvard-educated gorilla, and a presidential candidate named "Nobody." On his 60th birthday, he expressed his gratitude in print to one of his favorite readers, God.

We all worry about the population explosion, but we don't worry about it at the right time.

1926 **J.P. Donleavy (James Patrick):** American-Irish dramatist, novelist, and short story writer. His first novel, *The Ginger Man,* was hailed as a comic masterpiece, but did not appear in the U.S. as an unexpurgated edition until ten years after its initial publication in Paris. Other works: *A Singular Man, The Onion Eaters* and *Are You Listening, Rabbi Low?*

But Jesus, when you don't have money, the problem is food. When you have money, it's sex. When you have both, it's health, you worry about getting ruptured or something. If everything is simply jake then you're frightened of death.

1928 **Shirley Temple Black:** American child actress. Precocious performer known for her dimples and golden curls. The country's most popular star during the Depression. Received a special Academy Award in 1934. Films included *Little Miss Marker*, *Bright Eyes*, and *The Little Princess*. Did not find the same success when she became an adult. Later served as U.S. ambassador first to Ghana and then Czechoslovakia.

I stopped believing in Santa Claus when I was six. Mother took me to see him in a department store and he asked for my autograph.

1929 **George Steiner:** French-born American-Swiss critic, scholar and fiction writer. Works range from political commentary to criticism in all areas of the humanities. Studied the relationship between literature and society. Writings on language and the Holocaust have found a large audience beyond academic circles. Works include: *Language and Silence, After Babel* and *Fields of Force*.

We know that a man can read Goethe or Rilke in the evening, that he can play Bach and Schubert, and go to his day's work at Auschwitz in the morning.

1947 **Bernadette Devlin:** Now known as **Bernadette McAliskey**. Irish political activist. At 21, became the youngest woman ever elected to British Parliament, where she served 1969–74. Her book *The Price of My Soul* publicized the claims of the Roman Catholics about discrimination in Northern Ireland. Helped found the Irish Republican Socialist Party. She and her husband were shot many times and seriously wounded, apparently by Loyalists, who broke into their home, but both survived.

Among the best traitors Ireland has ever had, Mother Church ranks at the very top, a massive obstacle in the path to equality and freedom. She has been a force for conservatism ... to ward off threats to her own security and influence.

OTHERS: 1551 Tsar of Muscovy **Boris Godunov**, 1697 British explorer **George Baron Anson**, 1775 English landscape painter **Joseph Mallord Turner**, 1791 15th U.S. President **James Buchanan**, 1857 Italian composer **Ruggerio Leoncavallo**, 1861 British field marshal **Edmund Allenby**, 1897 U.S. General **Lucius D. Clay**, 1899 Kiwi mystery writer **Dame Edith Ngaio Marsh**, 1902 Icelandic novelist **Halldór Laxness**, 1914 French actress **Simone Simone**, 1921 300 game winning pitcher **Warren Spahn**, 1923 U.S. Senator **Chauncey Depew**, 1932 Fashion designer **Halston**, 1936 U.S. singer **Roy Orbison**, 1942 U.S. actress **Sandra Dee**, 1954 Filmmaker **Michael Moore**, 1955 Australian actress **Judy Davis**

April 24

1815 **Anthony Trollope:** Prolific English writer of novels of Victorian life. Produced 47 novels. Best known works are the two series, *Chronicles of Barsetshire* and the *Palliser* novels. Wrote *The Way We Live Now*, a view of the Victorian upper classes. Began each day by writing 2,500 words before breakfast. Credited for inventing the mailbox.

No man thinks there is much ado about nothing when the ado is about himself.

1856 **Henri Pétain:** French Army marshal. Defense of Verdun made him a national hero. Minister of War in 1934. His sponsorship of the useless Maginot Line defense system reflected the defeatist spirit of France. French premier in 1940, at age 84, negotiated armistice with Germany. Headed Vichy government of unoccupied France until 1944. Tried as a collaborator after war, his death sentence was commuted to life in prison. Died in captivity in 1951. His promise at Verdun in World War I:

They shall not pass.

1889 Sir **Stafford Cripps:** British statesman, economist, chemist and patent lawyer. Made a fortune in patent and compensation cases. Member of the Labor Party. Chancellor of the Exchequer. Ambassador to the U.S.S.R. Helped found the left-wing Socialist League. Conducted the Cripps Mission in 1942, an unsuccessful attempt to rally Indian support against the Japanese. Believed that politics was a proper sphere for the practice of Christianity.

Productive power is the foundation of a country's economic strength.

1893 **Leslie Howard:** British stage and screen actor. Won acclaim for plays *Her Cardboard Lover*, *The Petrified Forest*, and *Hamlet*. U.S. films included: *Of Human Bondage*, *Pygmalion*, *Intermezzo*, and *Gone with the Wind*. Killed when his plane was shot down by the Germans en route from Lisbon to London.

I haven't the slightest intention of playing another weak, watery character such as Ashley Wilkes. I've played enough ineffectual characters already.

1900 **Elizabeth Goudge:** English author of novels, short stories, and children's books. Her *Island Magic* is based on Channel Island stories. Awarded the Carnegie Medal for *The Little White Horse*. *Green Dolphin Company* was made into a successful Hollywood movie *Green Dolphin Street*.

The Communist is a Socialist in a violent hurry.

1904 **Willem De Kooning:** Dutch-born American artist. His work had a strong influence on American Abstract Expressionism. Supported himself by working for the WPA Federal Art Project. Awarded Andrew W. Mellon Prize (1979). Noted for his controversial series "Woman" (1950–53).

The attitude that nature is chaotic and that the artist puts order into it is a very absurd point of view, I think. All that we can hope for is to put some order into ourselves.

1905 **Robert Penn Warren:** American poet and novelist. Belonged to the Fugitives, a group of poets who advocated the agrarian way of life in the South. Coeditor of two anthologies of Southern writing. *Poetry: Promises* and *Now and Then Poems* both of which were awarded Pulitzer prizes. Became internationally famous for his political novel *All the King's Men*, loosely based on the life of Louisiana's Huey Long. First U.S. poet laureate.

Storytelling and copulation are the two chief forms of amusement in the South. They're inexpensive and easy to procure.

1914 **William Castle:** American film director, producer and actor. Famous for directing low budget B-movies, extensively promoted. Famous for his gimmicks, which included electrified theater seats, fright insurance policies, duo-colored glasses that revealed ghosts and seat belts. Films included *Project X*, *The Tingler*, *House on Haunted Hill*, *I Saw What You Did* and *Mr. Sardonicus*.

I suppose you could say I've devoted my career to scaring the hell out of people.

1930 **Dorothy Uhnak:** American mystery novelist and policewoman. New York City cop for 14 years. Received department's highest award for heroism. Wrote best-selling novels *The Investigation* and *Law and Order*. Her shoot-from-the hip memoir *Police Woman*, recounting her decade as one of New York City's first female detectives.

He maintained that the case was lost or won by the time the final juror had been sworn in; his summation was set in his mind before the first witness was called.

1934 **Shirley MacLaine:** U.S. actress, at home in comedies and dramas. Worked as a dancer on Broadway. Made her film debut in *The Trouble with Harry*. Equally adept in comic or dramatic roles. Oscar for *Terms of Endearment*. Nominated for *Some Came Running*, *The Apartment*, *Irma La Douce* and *Madame Sousatzka*. Wrote best selling books about her out-of-body experiences. Sister of actor Warren Beatty.

It's useless to hold a person to anything he says when he's in love, drunk, or running for office.

1940 **Sue Grafton:** American writer. Created the character Kinsey Milhone, a female private investigator. Her first book in the series was *"A" is for Alibi*, followed by *"B" is for Burglar*, *"C" is for Corpse*, and so forth through the alphabet. A recent book, published in 2005, is *"S" is for Silence*.

People talk about "dysfunctional" families; I've never seen any other kind.

1942 **Barbra Streisand:** U.S. singer, actress, producer, director, and songwriter. Conquered Broadway with *Funny Girl*. Has a richly beautiful voice. One of the world's most popular singers in the 70s and 80s. Song hits: "People," "The Way We Were," "Evergreen," and "Woman in Love." Superb in both comic and dramatic roles. Oscar winner for *Funny Girl*. Nominated for *The Way We Were*. Directed and starred in *Yentl* and *The Prince of Tides*.

The principal difference between a dog and a man is if you pick up a starving dog and make him prosperous, he will not bite you.

OTHERS: 1620 English founder of science of demography **John Graunt**, 1743 English inventor of power loom **Edmund Cartwright**, 1814 Argentine historian **Vincente F. López**, 1837 German diplomat **Friedrich von Holstein**, 1841 U.S. dendrologist **Charles Sprague Sargent**, 1851 Uruguayan writer **Eduardo Acevedo Diaz**, 1874 Architect Jefferson Memorial **John Russell Pope**, 1882 Guatemalan–U.S. artist **Tony Sarg**, 1883 Czech writer **Jaroslav Hašek**, 1916 U.S. playwright **Stanley Kaufmann**, 1942 Chicago mayor **Richard Daley Jr.**, 1953 U.S. actor **Eric Bogosian**, 1958 Spanish tennis player **Fernando Luna**, 1971 Australian swimmer **Phil Rogers**, 1972 Baseball player **Chipper Jones**

April 25

1533 **William I:** "The Silent." Prince of Orange. First stadtholder (governor) of the United Provinces of the Netherlands. Great leader in the struggle for the independence of the Netherlands from Spanish rule. King Philip II of Spain offered a reward for his assassin. Last words as he fell under a fanatical Catholic's bullets:

May God have mercy on my soul and on my poor people.

1599 **Oliver Cromwell:** English Puritan leader and military genius. Lord Protector of the Realm (1653–58). Commanded famous cavalry regiment Ironsides, parliamentary forces that defeated the Royalists, leading to the execution of King Charles I, making Cromwell virtually a dictator as Lord Protector. He refused Parliament's offer of the title king. Though a devout Calvinist, he championed religious tolerance.

Do not trust to the cheering, for those persons would shout as much if ... I were going to be hanged.

1849 **Felix Klein:** German mathematician. Worked on geometry, function theory and elliptic modular functions. His *Erlanger Programm* showed how different geometries could be classified in terms of groups of transformations. Also wrote on the history of mathematics. Promoted general mathematics education.

Everyone knows what a curve is, until he has studied enough mathematics to become confused through the countless number of possible exceptions.

1873 **Walter de La Mare:** English poet, novelist, anthropologist. Romantic writer with interests in childhood, nature, dreams and the uncanny. Works: *Songs of Childhood*, *The Return* and *The Veil*.

A lost and happy dream may shed its light upon our waking hours, and the whole day may be infected with the gloom of a dreary or sorrowful one; yet of neither may we be able to recover a trace.

1874 **Guglielmo Marconi:** Italian physicist and electrical engineer. Experimented with a device to convert electromagnetic waves into electricity. Made the first successful experiment in wireless telegraphy, now known as radio. In 1898 he transmitted signals across the English Channel and in 1901 across the Atlantic. Later developed short-wave radio equipment. Greatest achievement may have been in putting laboratory science to practical use in the world of science. Shared the 1909 Nobel Prize for physics.

Have I done the world good; or have I added a menace?

1883 **Elsa Maxwell:** American socialite, songwriter, radio host, gossip columnist, special events planner and hostess. "The Hostess with the Mostest "appeared in vaudeville and South African music halls. Published some eighty songs. Her lavish parties were attended by many famous guests who enjoyed the amusements she devised to keep them entertained. Hosted the radio program *Elsa Maxwell's Party Line* and had a syndicated gossip column.

Seeing unhappiness in the marriage of friends, I was content to have chosen music and laughter as a substitute for a husband.

1900 **Wolfgang Pauli:** Austrian-born theoretical physicist. Moved to the Institute for Advanced Study at Princeton in 1940. Postulated the existence of an electrically neutral particle, the neutrino, later confirmed by Enrico Fermi. Nobel Prize winner for physics in 1945. Became an American citizen in 1946. Commenting on a paper submitted by a physicist colleague:

This isn't right. This isn't even wrong.

1906 **William J. Brennan, Jr.:** American jurist. Associate justice of Supreme Court (1956–1990), nominated by President Eisenhower. Wrote many majority decisions dealing with areas of obscenity and antitrust. From the Little Rock (Arkansas) School desegregation battle to upholding flag burning as free speech, he supported civil rights. His judgments reflected his concern with the balance of individual rights and the interests of the community as a whole.

The Framers of the Bill of Rights did not purport to "create" rights. Rather, they designed the Bill of Rights to prohibit our Government from infringing rights and liberties presumed to be preexisting.

1908 **Edward R. Murrow:** Born **Egbert Roscoe Murrow**. Legendary journalist fondly recalled for his inspirational reports from London before the U.S. entered World War II, always begun with a slow precise "This — is London." Regular on television's *See It Now* (1951–58), *Person to Person* (1953–59), *Small World* (1958–60), and *CBS Reports* (1959–61). First newsman to challenge Senator Joseph McCarthy's "witch hunting tactics. His questioning of McCarthy led to the latter's downfall.

We cannot defend freedom abroad by deserting it at home.

1918 **Ella Fitzgerald:** African-American singer, composer. Began singing at 16 with Chick Webb band. Became a star with "A-tisket, a-tasket," which she cowrote. It remained number one for ten weeks. Her wide-ranging and rare sweet voice and superb phrasing made her perhaps the greatest jazz ballad and scat singer. Won 12 Grammy Awards.

I stole everything I ever heard, but mostly I stole from the horns.

1940 **Al Pacino:** Intense, brooding American actor. Oscar winner for *Scent of a Woman*. Nominated for *The Godfather, The Godfather Part II, Serpico, Dog Day Afternoon, ...And Justice for All, Dick Tracy* and *Glengarry Glen Ross*. Won two Golden Globes, the first the Cecil B. DeMille Award for lifetime achievement and the second for his role in *Angels in America*.

It is easy to fool the eye but it's hard to fool the heart.

1976 **Timothy Theodore Duncan:** African-American NBA basketball power forward for the San Antonio Spurs. Born in St. Croix, Virgin Islands. Nicknamed "The Big Fundamental." All-American at Wake Forest University, who graduated with honors and a degree in psychology. NBA Rookie of the Year (1998) MVP in 2002 and 2003. Helped the Spurs win three NBA championships.

Good, better, best. Never let it rest. Until your good is better and your better is best.

OTHERS: 1214 King of France **Louis IX**, 1284 King of England **Edward II**, 1792 Anglican priest/founder Oxford Movement **John Keble**, 1825 Standardized time zones **Charles Ferdinand Dowd**, 1862 English liberal politician **Sir Edward Grey**, 1914 Dictator of Venezuela **Marcos Pérez Jiménez**, 1918 Swedish soprano **Astrid Varnay**, 1921 Painter **Karel Appel**, 1923 Blues singer/guitarist **Albert King**, 1930 Writer/director **Paul Mazursky**, 1932 Basketball player **Meadowlark Lemon**, 1933 Songwriter **Jerry Leiber**, 1945 U.S. guitarist **Stu Cook**, 1946 U.S. actress **Talia Shire**, 1946 Russian ultranationalist **Vladimir V. Zhirinovsky**, 1969 U.S. actress **Renée Zellweger**

April 26

1661 **Daniel Defoe:** English author, pamphleteer, journalist, political agent and adventurer. Celebrated for his frank and dramatic realism in fiction. Won King William II's favor with his satirical poem "The Trueborn Englishman," an attack on xenophobic prejudice. Greatest fame is reserved for his best-known work *Robinson Crusoe*. Other works: *Moll Flanders* and *Roxana*.

The best of men cannot suspend their fate: the good die early, and the bad die late.

1711 **David Hume:** Scottish philosopher and historian. Restricted all knowledge to the experience of ideas or impressions. Maintained the mind consists only of accumulated perceptions. Wrote *A Treatise of Human Nature*, but his views only became widely known after the publication of two volumes of *Essays Moral and Political*. Also published a six volume *History of England*.

Nothing is more surprising than the easiness with which the many are governed by the few.

1798 **Eugène Delacroix:** French painter. One of the great colorists of the Romantic Movement. Used literary and historical subjects for his paintings, *Dante and*

Vergil in Hell, Massacre at Chios and *Liberty Guiding the People.*

What makes men of genius, or rather, what they make, is not new ideas, it is that idea — possessing them — that what has been said has still not been said enough.

1834 **Artemus Ward:** Pen name of **Charles Farrar Browne**. Droll American humorist, editor, newspaperman, and lecturer from Maine. Works: *Artemus Ward: His Book* and *Artemus Ward: His Travels.* Editor of *Vanity Fair* magazine. Said to have inspired Samuel Clemens, better known as Mark Twain. Ward's most familiar techniques, what he called "ingrammaticisms," were humorous misspellings. Loved puns and plays on words. In 1866 he departed for England to become an editor of *Punch*, and where he died of tuberculosis the next year.

I'm not a politician and my other habits are good.

1886 **Ma Rainey:** Born **Gertrude Pridgett**. African-American blues singer and composer. One of the first to sing the blues on a stage. Began making recordings in 1923. Toured with her company in vaudeville. Bessie Smith, a member of the troupe, became her pupil and protégée.

White folks hear the blues come out, but they don't know how it got there. They don't understand that's life's way of talking. You don't sing to feel better. You sings 'cause that's a way of understanding life.

1889 **Ludwig Wittgenstein:** Austrian-born philosopher. His work was central to the development of Logical Positivism. Studied mathematical logic with Bertrand Russell. During World War I service in the Austrian army, Wittgenstein wrote the *Tractus logico-philosophicus*, which he submitted as his doctoral thesis at Cambridge. In it he argued that any sentence is a picture of the fact it represents, and any thought is a sentence. He rejected his own doctrines in *Philosophical Investigations*, insisting that linguistic meaning is a function of the use to which expressions are put.

What can be said at all can be said clearly; and whereof we cannot speak thereof one must be silent.

1893 **Anita Loos:** American novelist and scriptwriter. Wrote scripts for D.W. Griffith at 15. Plays: *Happy Birthday* and *Gigi*. Her novel *Gentlemen Prefer Blondes*. A huge best-seller, translated into 12 languages, has been filmed twice and staged as a Broadway musical. Wrote a sequel, *But Gentlemen Marry Brunettes.*

I'm furious about the women's liberationists. They keep getting up on soapboxes and proclaiming that women are brighter than men. That's true, but it should be kept very quiet or it ruins the whole racket.

1898 **Vicente Aleixandre:** Spanish poet. As a young man he began to have serious problems with his health, being forced to retire to his father's house in the countryside as a semi-invalid. He devoted himself exclusively to writing. Later he moved into a small villa on the outskirts of Madrid, where he spent the rest of his life. Refusing to submit to Franco's regime, he was not allowed to publish his works for quite some time. Works: *Destruction of Love, Shadow of Paradise, Poems of Consummation, Dialogues of Insight* and *A Longing for the Light*. Awarded the Nobel Prize for Literature in 1977.

Solitude and meditation gave me an awareness, a perspective which I have never lost: that of solidarity with the rest of mankind.

1902 **Jonathan Worth Daniels:** American writer and editor. Published dozens of books and articles: biographies, historical studies and social and political commentaries. Assumed the editorship of the Raleigh *News and Observer*, which had been held by his father. Strong supporter of Franklin D Roosevelt's New Deal, advocated equal rights for African-Americans and championed the cause of organized labor.

The man who reads only for improvement is beyond the hope of much improvement before he begins.

1914 **Bernard Malamud:** American short-story writer and novelist. Novels often made parables out of Jewish immigrant life. Works include *The Natural*, which later became a successful baseball film starring Robert Redford, *The Assistant* and the Pulitzer Prize winning *The Fixer*. Collections of short stories include: *Magic Barrel, Idiots First*, and *Rembrandt Hat.*

I work with language. I love the flower of afterthought.

1917 **I.M. Pei:** American architect known for innovative modernist structures. Buildings: National Airlines Terminal, Kennedy Airport; Herbert F. Johnson Museum of Art, Cornell University; National Gallery of Art, East Building, Washington, D.C. and a controversial glass pyramid for a courtyard of the Louvre Museum.

There are endless mysteries within discipline. Infinite possibilities exist with a set of rules.

1936 **Carol Burnett:** American comedian, actress and singer. Came to prominence in the mid–1950s singing "I Made a Fool of Myself Over John Foster Dulles." Made her Broadway debut in *Once Upon a Mattress*. Regular on TV's *The Garry Moore Show*. Landed her own weekly show *Carol Burnett Show*, one of TV's most popular musical comedy variety shows, for which she earned five Emmys. Later returned to TV with "Carol and Company." Acted in several films, including *Four Seasons* and *Annie*.

Comedy is tragedy plus time.

OTHERS: 1573 Queen of France **Marie de'Medici**, 1718 Fist commander-in-chief U.S. Navy **Esek Hopkins**, 1785 Bird watcher/painter **John James Audubon**, 1808 Children's book author **Martha Finley**, 1822 Architect/designed NY Central Park **Frederick Law Olmsted**, 1836 U.S. ethnologist **Erminnie Adelle Platt**, 1880 Russian choreographer **Mikhail Fokine**, 1895 Hitler's Deputy Führer **Rudolf Hess**, 1898 Documentary filmmaker **John Grierson**, 1900 Earthquakes seismologist **Charles Richter**, 1910 Dutch journalist/resistance fighter **Johan Doorn**, 1942 Rock 'n' Roll singer/actor **Bobby Rydell**

April 27

1737 **Edward Gibbon:** English historian. Entered Parliament (1774). Became commissioner of trade and plantations. Member of Dr. Samuel Johnson's literary circle. His masterpiece is *The History of the Decline and Fall of the Roman Empire*, which he was inspired to write during a tour of Italy. It remains a model of literature and history.

History is indeed little more than the register of the crimes, follies and misfortunes of mankind.

1759 **Mary Wollstonecraft Godwin:** Anglo-Irish feminist and writer. Best know for the first great feminist manifesto, *Vindication of the Rights of Man*, in response to Edmund Burke's *Reflections on the French Revolution*. Her controversial *Vindication of the Rights of Women* advocated equality of the sexes and equal opportunities in education. Also wrote *Thoughts on the Education of Daughters*. Died shortly after her daughter Mary, later Mary Wollstonecraft Shelley, was born.

I do not wish [women] to have power over men, but over themselves.

1820 **Herbert Spencer:** Evolutionary English philosopher, psychologist, journalist and social scientist. Applied the scientific principles of evolution to philosophy and ethics. A firm pre–Darwin believer in evolution and a leading advocate of "Social Darwinism." Works: *Principles of Psychology* and *System of Synthetic Philosophy* (ten volumes).

The wise man must remember that while he is a descendant of the past, he is a parent of the future.

1822 **U.S. (Ulysses Simpson) Grant:** Eighteenth President of the United States. As Union Army general captured Vicksburg (1863). Made Commander-in-chief of Union Army (1864). Forced and accepted Robert E. Lee's surrender. Presidential administration beset by corruption and partisan politics. Presided over the reconstruction of the South. Wrote two volumes of memoirs, which were highly praised for their contribution to military history.

In every battle there comes a time when both sides consider themselves beaten, then he who continues the attack wins.

1840 **Edward Whymper:** British climber and explorer. Claimed to have made the first ascent of Mount Chimborazo in the Andes. Best known for making the first ascent of the Matterhorn. However, on the descent four members of his party were killed. Speculation is that the accident led to his alcoholism.

Every night, do you understand, I see my comrades of the Matterhorn slipping on their backs; their arms outstretched one after the other, in perfect order at equal distances ... Yes I shall always see them.

1874 **Maurice Baring:** English man of letters, dramatist, poet, novelist, translator, essayist, travel writer and war correspondent. Reported on the Russo-Japanese War for the London *Morning Post*. Works include novels *Passing By* and *Cat's Cradle*. His autobiography is *The Puppet Show of Memory*.

If you want to know what the Lord God thinks of money, you have only to look at those to whom he gives it.

1896 **Rogers Hornsby:** American professional baseball player and hall-of-famer. Generally considered the game's greatest right-hand hitter. Nicknamed the "Rajah." Lifetime batting average of .358. Hit over .400 three times with .424 being the highest ever in modern major league baseball. Managed the Cardinals, Cubs, Braves, and Browns.

People ask me what I do in winter when there's no baseball. I'll tell you what I do. I stare out the window and wait for spring. I don't want to play golf. When I hit a ball, I want someone else to go chase it.

1898 **Ludwig Bemelmans:** Austrian-born American writer and painter. Often illustrated his books with his own watercolors and drawings. His experiences in the hotel and restaurant business furnished him with ample material for his many entertaining stories. Wrote books for children, most notably, *Madeleine*. Others: *My War with the United States*, *Hotel Splendide*, and *Now I Lay Me Down to Sleep*.

If painting goes well, then it goes that way like a happy little train running through a landscape, whistling.

1904 **Cecil Day-Lewis:** Irish-born British poet, critic, and author. Wrote detective stories under pen name **Nicholas Blake**. Wrote many didactic verses and used the imagery of the industrial society. Named Poet Laureate (1968). Father of actor Daniel Day Lewis. Collections: *From Feathers to Iron*, *The Magnetic Mountain* and *The Gate*. Made verse translations of Virgil's *Georgics* and *Aeneid*.

No good poem, however confessional it may be, is just a self-expression. Who on earth would claim that the pearl expresses the oyster?

1927 **Coretta Scott King:** African-American civil rights leader, lecturer, and author. Trained in music, she made her concert debut in 1948. Widow of Martin Luther King, Jr. President Martin Luther King Center for Nonviolent Social Change. She successfully led the fight to establish a national holiday honoring her husband.

Struggle is a never ending process. Freedom is never really won; you earn and win it in every generation.

1932 **Gian-Carlo Rota:** Italian-born American mathematician. Transforming combinatorics, from an under explored field to one of the most important in mathematics today. He described combinatorics as "putting different colored marbles in different colored boxes, seeing how many ways you can divide them."

Co-author of a book of essays on mathematics, science and philosophy called *Discrete Thoughts* followed by *Indiscrete Thoughts*. Enjoyed creating lists of tens, such as "Ten rules for the survival of a mathematics department."

A mathematician's work is mostly a tangle of guesswork, analogy, wishful thinking, and proof, far from being the core of discovery, is more often than not a way of making sure that our minds are not playing tricks.

1945 **August Wilson:** African-American playwright and poet, largely self-educated. Participated in the Black Aesthetic Movement. Cofounded and directed Pittsburgh's Black Horizon Theater. His plays were inspired by the colloquial language, music, folklore, and storytelling tradition of black Americans. His cycle of plays, each set in a different decade of the 20th century include the Pulitzer Prize winning *Fences* and *The Piano Lesson*.

Confront the dark parts of yourself, and work to banish them with illumination and forgiveness. Your willingness to wrestle with your demons will cause your angels to sing. Use the pain as fuel, as a reminder of your strength.

OTHERS: 1707 Dutch botanist **John Burman**, 1791 Inventor of the telegraph **Samuel F. Morse**, 1865 Dutch hagiographer **Emile Erens**, 1875 Belgian/French author **André Baillon**, 1891 Russian composer **Sergei Prokofiev**, 1893 Theatrical designer **Norman Bel Geddes**, 1894 Pinup artist **George Petty**, 1900 U.S. animator **Walter Lantz**, 1904 Chairman Federal Reserve Board **Arthur F. Burns**, 1912 Philanthropist **Frederick Rand Weissman**, 1916 U.S. baseball player **Enos Slaughter**, 1918 U.S. news correspondent **John Scali**, 1918 Jazz combo leader **Kirby Stone**, 1922 U.S. actor **Jack Klugman**, 1932 Radio personality **Casey Kasem**, 1937 U.S. actress **Sandy Dennis**, 1938 Bowler **Earl Anthony**

April 28

1758 **James Monroe:** Fifth American president (1817–25). Won his second term by an overwhelming majority. Secured all but one vote in the Electoral College. As minister to France, participated in the negotiations for the Louisiana Purchase. Secretary of State (1811–17). Established the Monroe Doctrine, warning Europe not to interfere in the Western Hemisphere. Monrovia, the capital of the African nation Liberia, is named for him. Last of three presidents to die on the 4th of July, the others being Thomas Jefferson and John Adams.

National honor is national property of the highest value.

1780 **Charles Caleb Colton:** English cleric, collector and writer. Well known for his eccentricities. Settled in Paris where he invested in an art gallery. Had a large private collection of valuable paintings. Also collected wine and frequented gambling salons, which eventually cost him his fortune. His books included collections of epigrams and short essays on conduct. His *Lacon, or Many Things in Few Words, addressed to those who think*, went through six editions and was followed by *Lacon Volume II.*

Examinations are formidable even to the best prepared, for the greatest fool may ask more than the wisest can answer.

1874 **Karl Kraus:** Austrian journalist, critic, playwright and poet. Satirist compared to Juvenal and Jonathan Swift. Publisher and sole writer of the radical satirical magazine *The Torch* (1899–1936). Believed that language was of great moral and aesthetic importance. Attacked the misuse of language, especially by the press, which he viewed as both a symptom and a cause of a sick society. Plays: *The Last Days of Mankind* and *The Unconquerable One*.

Corruption is worse than prostitution. The latter might endanger the morals of an individual; the former invariably endangers the morals of the entire country.

1878 **Lionel Barrymore:** American stage, screen and radio actor. First of the three Broadway Barrymore star siblings to appear on screen. Oscar winner for *A Free Soul*. Others: *Young Dr. Kildare* (14 more films in series) and *Key Largo*. Annually played Ebenezer Scrooge in *A Christmas Carol* on radio for many years. After twice breaking his hip, he was confined to a wheelchair, but continued his career.

Half the people in Hollywood are dying to be discovered and the other half are afraid they will be.

1896 **Joseph Dunninger:** American magician and mentalist. Offered $10,000 to anyone who could prove that he used confederates or assistants in his mind reading act. The most popular parts of his act were challenges to his powers. Took his act first to radio and later to television, and was a great success in both forums. In a 1940 poll it was shown that his voice was more recognizable than the presidents. Dunninger's dictum was the statement:

For those who believe, no explanation is necessary. For those who do not, none will suffice.

1901 **George Crane:** American psychologist. Author of *Radio Talks*, *Psychology Applied* and a syndicated column "The Worry Clinic." Suggested that criticism was best given as part of a sandwich, it being the meat between two pieces of bread of praise.

You can have such an open mind that it is too porous to hold a conviction.

1906 **Kurt Gödel:** Czech-U.S. logician and mathematician. In 1931 made one of the major mathematical discoveries of the 20th century. With his "Incompleteness Theorem" he showed that it is impossible to define a complete system of axioms, which is also consistent, that is, has no contradictions. As a result, any formal system that can generate meaningful statements is powerful enough to generate true statements that cannot be proved within the system. Ended a hundred years of attempts to derive logically the whole of mathematics from a logical axiom system. It demonstrated the impossibility of ever having a computer programmed to answer all mathematical questions.

I would rather be an optimist and a fool that a pessimist and right.

1924 **Kenneth Kaunda:** Zambian politician. Founded the Zambian African National Congress (1958). Played a leading role in country's independence negotiations. Became first president (1964) when independence was obtained.

The power which establishes a state is violence; the power which maintains it is violence; the power which eventually overthrows it is violence.

1926 **Harper Lee:** Born **Nellie Harper**. American lawyer and novelist. Her only novel *To Kill a Mockingbird* won unanimous critical acclaim and a Pulitzer Prize (1961). It was made into an Academy Award winning film starring Gregory Peck.

You never really understand a person until you consider things from his point of view.

1930 **James A. Baker III:** U.S. corporate lawyer and politician. White House Chief-of-Staff during both the Ronald Reagan and George H. Bush presidencies. U.S. Treasury Secretary (1985) and Secretary of State (1989).Resigned as Secretary of State to manage Bush's troubled reelection campaign.

Never let the other fellow set the agenda.

1948 **Terry Pratchett:** English fantasy writer and journalist. Best known for his *Discworld Series*, now containing over 30 books, which parodies everything. Has sold over 40 million books worldwide.

In ancient times cats were worshipped as gods; they have not forgotten this.

1950 **Jay Leno:** American Television host and comedian. Began his career as a standup comedian in night clubs and on TV. Succeeded Johnny Carson as host of *The Tonight Show* in 1992. He was rejected by Carson when he first auditioned for the show.

If God had wanted us to vote, he would have given us candidates.

OTHERS: 1774 Astronomer **Francis Baily**, 1831 Scottish physicist **Peter Guthrie Tait**, 1838 Dutch jurist **Tobias Michael Carel**, 1869 U.S. architect **Bertram Grosveonor Goodhue**, 1876 U.S. football coach **Frank Cavanaugh**, 1882 Italian industrialist **Alberto Pirelli**, 1889 Dictator of Portugal **António de Oliviera Salazar**, 1906 Novelist **Pierre Boileau**, 1915 U.S. economist **George L. Bach**, 1917 U.S. writer **Robert Anderson**, 1937 Iraqi dictator **Saddam Hussein**, 1941 Swedish/U.S. actress **Ann-Margret**, 1964 Baseball shortstop **Barry Larkin**, 1966 American pro golfer **John Daly**, 1967 NFL placekicker **Pete Stoyanovich**, 1974 Spanish actress **Penelope Cruz**

April 29

1667 **John Arbuthnot:** Scottish satirist, mathematician and physician. Wrote the political allegory *The History of John Bull*. Founding member of the famous Scriblerus Club, whose aim was to ridicule bad literature and false learning. Other members included Jonathan Swift, Alexander Pope and John Gay.

All political parties die at last of swallowing their own lies.

1745 **Oliver Ellsworth:** American politician, statesman and jurist. Member of the Continental Congress. Coauthored the Connecticut Compromise, which resolved the issue of representation in Congress. One of Connecticut's first U.S. senators. Chief author of the Judiciary Act that established the federal court system. Third Chief Justice of the United States Supreme Court.

Legislatures have no right to set up an inquisition and examine into the private opinions of men. Test-laws are useless and ineffectual, unjust and tyrannical.

1833 **Julia Louise Woodruff:** American author and compiler. Used pen name W.M.L. Jay. Wrote, *Shiloh or, Without and Within*, *My Winter in Cuba* and *The Daisy Seekers*.

Excellence in any pursuit is the late, ripe fruit of toil.

1854 **Henri Poincaré:** French mathematician, theoretical astronomer and philosopher of science. Made major contributions in most areas of mathematics, especially the three-body problem and tidal forces, opening up new directions in celestial mechanics. Independent of Albert Einstein, he obtained many of the results relating to the special theory of relativity.

If nature were not beautiful, it would not be worth knowing, and if nature were not worth knowing, life would not be worth living.

1863 **William Randolph Hearst:** American newspaper publisher. His family made their fortune when his father struck it rich in gold mining. Built a vast newspaper and magazine empire. Name became synonymous with "yellow journalism." Helped launch the Spanish-American War. Served in Congress (1903–7), but ran unsuccessfully for other offices. Built a grandiose estate at San Simeon, California. Spent the last part of his life in virtual seclusion.

News is something somebody doesn't want printed; all else is advertising.

1875 **Rafael Sabatini:** Italian-born novelist who wrote in English. Settled in England where he wrote many swashbucklers including *The Sea Hawk*, *Scaramouche*, and *Captain Blood*. Also wrote historical biographies.

He was born with a gift of laughter and a sense that the world was mad.

1879 Sir **Thomas Beecham:** British conductor. Devoted to broadening British musical tastes. Founded British National Opera Company, the London Philharmonic and Royal Philharmonic. Artistic director of Covent Garden. Championed the works of Richard Strauss and Frederick Delius.

A musicologist is a man who can read music but can't hear it.

1899 **Duke [Edward Kennedy] Ellington:** African-American jazz composer, bandleader, and pianist. Major jazz influence. Performed regularly at Harlem's Cotton Club. Known for his distinctive "jungle" sound and the integration of blues elements in his music. Led his orchestra (1923–74). Compositions: "Take the A Train," "Mood Indigo," "Satin Doll" and "Sophisticated Lady."

By and large, jazz has always been like the kind of a man you wouldn't want your daughter to associate with.

1922 **George Allen:** American football coach of the Rams, leading the team to 9 divisional titles, and Redskins which he took to the Super Bowl. Noted for his hard-driving work ethic and his preference for experienced players as Redskins general manager, saying "the future is now."

Winning is the science of being totally prepared.

1936 **Zubin Mehta:** Indian orchestral conductor, pianist and violinist. His father Mehli Mehta was a violinist and founding conductor of the Bombay Symphony Orchestra. Zubin Mehta has been Musical Director of the Montreal Symphony Orchestra, the Los Angeles Philharmonic Orchestra, and the New York Philharmonic Orchestra. He was made the musical director for life of the Israel Philharmonic Orchestra.

Although I am flexible and ready to take advice, I can't carry an umbrella of thoughts over my head that would distract me and affect my music making.

1951 **Dale Earnhardt:** American stock-car race driver. Dominate driver for NASCAR in the 1980s and 1990s. Earned a reputation as an aggressive driver and was nicknamed "the Intimidator." Died from injuries in a crash during the final lap of the 2001 Daytona 500 race.

You win some, lose some, and wreck some.

1970 **Andre Agassi:** American tennis player. Known for his aggressive style and demeanor on and off the court. Won the Grand Slam tennis tile in 1992. Won many tournaments with his popular style, but then dropped far in the world's rankings. Made a comeback to become the number-one ranked player in the world in 2000. Retired in 2006.

Being number two sucks.

OTHERS: 1818 Russian Tsar **Alexander II**, 1860 U.S. sculptor **Lorado Taft**, 1893 Bulgarian poet **Elisaveta Bagrjana**, 1893 U.S. physicist **Harold C. Urey**, 1895 English conductor **Malcolm Sargent**, 1901 Emperor of Japan **Hirohito**, 1904 Orchestra leader **Russ Morgan**, 1907 Austrian-born film director **Fred Zinnemann**, 1908 U.S. sci-fi author **Jack Williamson**, 1909 U.S. actor **Tom Ewell**, 1915 U.S. singer **Donald Mills**, 1919 U.S. actress **Celeste Holm**, 1924 French dancer **Renée Jeanmarie**, 1927 Physicist/auto company executive **Betsy Ancker-Johnson**, 1933 U.S. poet/songwriter **Rod McKuen**, 1947 U.S. runner **Jim Ryun**, 1955 Comedian **Jerry Seinfeld**, 1958 U.S. actress **Michelle Pfeiffer**

April 30

1771 **Hoseau Ballou:** American preacher. Originally a Baptist, he was the chief founder of Universalism. Editor of *The Universalist Magazine* (1819–28). His book, *A Treatise on Atonement*, radically altered the thinking of his colleagues in the ministry and their congregations.

Education commences at the mother's knee, and every word spoken within the hearsay of little children tends toward the formation of character.

1777 **Karl Friedrich Gauss:** German mathematician. Usually ranked with Archimedes and Newton as one of the three greatest mathematicians of all time. Often called the founder of modern mathematics. Did research in infinitesimal calculus, algebra and astronomy. His book on theory of numbers is generally considered his greatest accomplishment. Applied rigorous mathematical analysis to such subjects as geometry, geodesy, electrostatics, and electromagnetism. Involved in the first worldwide survey of the Earth's magnetic field. Not one to rush to publish, he did not consider that hasty spreading of the news of breakthroughs in mathematics was as necessary as it might be in the various sciences. Saw no excuse for publication of "slovenly or ill-digested work." His intention was to publish "Few, but ripe."

Mathematics is the queen of the sciences and arithmetic [number theory] is the queen of mathematics.

1870 **Franz Lehár:** Hungarian composer and conductor. Was a military bandmaster like his father. Popular composers of marches and waltzes. Wrote popular operettas *The Merry Widow*, *The Count of Luxembourg* and *The Land of Smiles*. Last words:

Now I have finished with all earthly business and high time too. Yes, yes, my dear child now comes death.

1877 **Alice B. Toklas:** Expatriate American. Longtime secretary, cook, confidante and companion of author Gertrude Stein in the latter's Paris literary salon. Stein wrote *The Autobiography of Alice B. Toklas*, which was really her autobiography. Toklas published *The Alice B. Toklas Cookbook*. Stein called Toklas "Pussy" and Alice addressed Gertrude as "Lovey."

This has been a most wonderful evening. Gertrude has said things tonight it will take her 10 years to understand.

1898 **Cornelius Vanderbilt, Jr.:** Great grandson of American railroad magnate Cornelius Vanderbilt and grandson of Cornelius Vanderbilt the Younger, who established the Vanderbilt Clinic and the Cathedral of St. John the Divine. Our subject became a well-known writer, traveler, newspaper publisher and movie producer. Wrote *Man of the World: My Life on Five Continents*.

Until the age of 12 I sincerely believed that

everybody had a house on Fifth Avenue, a villa in Newport, and a steam driven ocean going yacht.

1909 **Juliana:** Queen of the Netherlands (1948–80). On the German invasion of Holland, she escaped to Britain and from there to Canada. Returned to Holland (1945). Became queen on the abdication of her mother Wilhelmina. Later abdicated in favor of her daughter Beatrix.

I can't understand it. I can't even understand the people who can understand it.

1914 **Vermont Royster:** American journalist. Joined the *Wall Street Journal* as Washington correspondent. After serving in the Navy in World War II, returned to the *Journal* as editor and senior vice-president of the publishing company Dow Jones & Co. After retiring wrote a weekly column "Thinking Things Over." Award two Pulitzer Prizes and the Presidential Medal of Honor.

War itself is a terrible thing, but we find more terrible the fact that there are men walking about who talk of peace as if it was terrible.

1916 **Claude Ellwood Shannon:** American electrical engineer. Research mathematician with Bell Laboratories and professor at MIT. Considered the founder of communication theory for his seminal 1948 paper "The Mathematical Theory of Communication." Awarded the National Medal of Science in 1966 and the Kyoto Prize in 1985.

Information is the resolution of uncertainty.

1933 **Willie Nelson:** American country and western singer, songwriter, and guitarist. Winner of three Grammies and eight Country Music Association Awards. His first hit was "Crazy," recorded by Patsy Cline, followed by "Hello Walls" sung by Faron Young. In 1961 he wrote the classic "Funny How Time Slips Away," eventually recorded by more than 80 artists. Came to National attention when President Carter named him his favorite singer. Hits singing: "My Heroes Have Always Been Cowboys," "On the Road Again" and "Always on My Mind." Recorded "To All the Girls I've Loved" with Julio Iglesias.

We create our own unhappiness. The purpose of suffering is to help us understand we are the ones who cause it.

1945 **Annie Dillard:** American writer-in-residence at Wesleyan University in Connecticut. Best known for her nature-themes writing. Has explored the past and present dealings with nature through poetry, essays and novels. Her best known work, *Pilgrim at Tinker Creek,* has been described as a "book of theology." 1975 Pulitzer Prize for general non-fiction.

The dedicated life is worth living. You must give with your whole heart.

1961 **Isiah Thomas:** American basketball player, coach and executive. Considered one of the greatest point guards of all team, having a career 9,061 assists. All-American with University of Indiana. Led Detroit Pistons to two championships (1989, 1990).General manager and part-owner of the Toronto Raptors. Coached Indiana Pacers. Became general manger of the New York Knicks and is currently the team's coach.

When I was in high school and college, I thought the guys in the NBA always cooled it out until the fourth quarter. It was almost as if they didn't care. Well, it's true.

1982 **Kirsten Dunst:** American actress. Started in show business at age three, when she began filming TV commercials. Made her film debut in a segment of Woody Allen's *New York Stories.* Her breakthrough performance was in *Interview with the Vampire: The Vampire Chronicles,* earning her a Golden Globe Award. Named one of *People* magazine's *50 Most Beautiful People.* Other films: *Little Women, The Virgin Suicides* and *Spider-Man.*

Boys frustrate me. I hate all their indirect messages. I hate game playing. Do you like me or don't you? Just tell me so I can get over you.

OTHERS: 1374 Italian mystic/social worker **Saint Catherine of Sienna**, 1651 French priest/saint **Jean-Baptiste de la Salle**, 1770 English/Canadian explorer **David Thompson**, 1851 Icelandic playwright **Indriò Einarsson**, 1888 American poet/critic **John Crowe Ransom**, 1893 German foreign minister **Joachim von Ribbentrop**, 1896 Blues/folk guitarist Reverend **Gary Davis**, 1912 U.S. actress **Eve Arden**, 1913 Folklorist **Edith Fowke**, 1916 U.S. choral director **Robert Shaw**, 1917 U.S. singer **Bea Wain**, 1924 Broadway lyricist **Sheldon Harnick**, 1926 U.S. actress **Cloris Leachman**, 1927 U.S. singer **Johnny Horton**, 1944 U.S. actress **Jill Clayburgh**, 1945 U.S. astronaut **Michael J. Smith**

May 1

1602 **William Lilly:** English astrologer and occultist. Published astrological almanacs. Particularly adept at interpreting astrological charts. Predicted the Great Fire of London 14 years before it happened. Immortalized as Sidrophel in Samuel Butler's "Hudibras."

Ambition has one heel nailed in well, though she stretch her finger to touch the heavens.

1672 **Joseph Addison:** English poet, essayist, dramatist, and critic. With Richard Steele, he was a leading contributor to and guiding spirit of the periodicals *The Tatler* and *The Spectator.* Helped perfect the essay as a literary form with his contributions to *The Tatler* and *The Spectator.* Works: "The Campaign" and "Cato."

Man is distinguished from all other creatures by the faculty of laughter.

1769 **Arthur Wellesley, Duke of Wellington:** British general nicknamed "The Iron Duke." Served in the Irish Parliament. His victories against the French in Portugal and Spain and invaded France to win the war in 1814 led to his being made field marshal. Represented England at the Congress of Vienna (1814–15). Commanded the Allied armies to victory over Napoleon at Waterloo. Briefly served as English Prime Minister.

The battle of Waterloo was won on the playing fields of Eton.

1830 Mother **Mary Jones:** Irish-born U.S. labor leader. Gained fame as agitator for Appalachian coal miners. Traveled across the country organizing for the United Mine Workers and supporting strikes wherever they were held. Led children's march from Kensington, Pennsylvania, to the Sagamore Hill, New York, home of President Theodore Roosevelt to dramatize the evils of child labor.

I belong to a class, which has been robbed, exploited, and plundered down through many long centuries. And because I belong to that class, I have an impulse to go and help break the chains.

1852 **Santiago Ramón y Cajal:** Spanish histologist and physician. His basic study revealed the connection between the cells in the brain and the spinal cord. Nobel Prize for Physiology or Medicine 1906.

The brain is a world consisting of a number of unexplored continents and great stretches of unknown territory. That which enters the mind through reason can be corrected.

1881 **Pierre Teilhard de Chardin:** French Jesuit priest, theologian, and paleontologist. Spent his life attempting to reconcile Christian beliefs with scientific knowledge. Directed the evacuations of the Peking Man site at Zhoukoudian. The Jesuit order would not allow the publication of his major philosophical works *The Divine Milieu* and *The Phenomenon of Man* until after his death.

Growing old is like being increasingly penalized for a crime you haven't committed.

1900 **Ignazio Silone:** Italian author, political leader, and journalist whose novels reflect his belief in the need for social reform. A founder of the Italian Communist Party, but became disillusioned and began to write antifascist works, including *Fontamara*, Bread *and Wine* and *The Seed Beneath the Snow*.

Liberty is the possibility of doubting, the possibility of making a mistake, the possibility of searching and experimenting, the possibility of saying No to any authority — literary, artistic, political, philosophic, religious, social and even political.

1909 **Kate Smith:** American singer, known as the "First Lady of Radio." Won a Broadway role as an overweight girl who was the butt of jokes. In 1931 she began her immensely popular radio show "Kate Smith Sings." Famous for her theme song, "When the Moon Comes Over the Mountain" and in introducing Irving Berlin's "God Bless America." Awarded the U.S. Medal of Freedom in 1982.

The best we can do is to go through life trying to be happy and helping those we meet along the way.

1918 **Jack Parr:** American radio and television talk show host. Became the host of *The Tonight Show*, and was so popular its title was changed to *The Jack Parr Show*. Emotional and unpredictable, he reacted to the censoring of a joke in February 1960 that the next night he walked off the show saying he was quitting. It wasn't too long after that he and NBC made up and he returned to the show after a vacation.

Poor people have more fun than rich people, they say; and I notice it's the rich people who keep saying it.

1923 **Joseph Heller:** American novelist. Used his experiences as a World War II bombardier as the backdrop for his first and best known novel, *Catch-22*. Based on the simple premise that a fighter pilot who wants to be excused duty need only ask, but by asking proves that he is sane and fit to fly. Heller maintained he wrote it only to make money. Other novels: *Something Happened* and *Good as Gold*.

Success and failure are both difficult to endure. Along with success come drugs, divorce, fornication, bullying, travel, meditation, depression, neurosis and suicide. With failure comes failure.

1926 **Terry Southern:** American novelist, short-story writer, and screen-writer. Best known for his black comedy *Candy*, a parody of pornographic books. Screenplays: *Dr. Strangelove*, *The Loved One* and *Easy Rider*.

The important thing in writing is the capacity to astonish. Not shock — shock is a worn-out word — but astonish.

1939 **Judy Collins:** American folk and standards singer. Inspired by the music of Woody Guthrie and Pete Seeger. Released her first album, *A Maid of Constant Sorrow*, at age 22. At first she recorded the songs written by social poets of the time including Tom Paxton, Phil Ochs, Bob Dylan, and newcomers Leonard Cohen and Joni Mitchell. Notable singles: "Both Sides Now," "Amazing Grace," "Send in the Clowns" and her own compositions such as "My Father" and "Born to the Breed."

Irish Alzheimer's: you forget everything except the grudges.

OTHERS: 1238 King of Norway **Magnus VI**, 1545 French Calvinist theologist **Franciscus Junius**, 1764 Engineer/architect **Benjamin Henry Latrobe**, 1818 Spanish historian/poet **José M. de Alencar**, 1825 U.S. landscape painter **George Inness**, 1852 Frontier adventurer **Calamity [Martha] Jane [Burke]**, 1862 French publisher/writer **Marcel Prévost**, 1863 U.S. portrait painter **Cecilia Beaux**, 1892 Conductor Voice of Firestone **Howard Barlow**, 1896 U.S. general **Mark Clark**, 1898 U.S. President of World Bank **Eugene R. Black**, 1908 Italian writer **Giovanni Guareschi**, 1922 Comedian **Louis Nye**, 1924 TV Game Show host **Art Fleming**, 1960 U.S. jockey **Steve Cauthen**

May 2

1551 **William Camden:** English antiquary and historian. Headmaster of Westminster School. Compiled a pioneering topographical survey of the British Isles, "Britannia." Published a list of the epitaphs in Westminster Abbey. Also wrote *Annals of the Reign of Elizabeth to 1588*.

Better a bad excuse, than none at all.

1772 **Novalis:** Influential German author and philosopher of early German Romanticism. Real name was **Friedrich von Hardenberg**. Developed a unique personal faith in the mystical unity of all things. His writings expressed a mystical yearning for death, probably as the result of the death at an early age of his beloved fiancée. Tuberculosis gave him his release at age 29. Works: the prose-poems *Hymns to the Night* and his unfinished novel *Heinrich von Ofterdingen*.

Poetry heals the wounds inflicted by reason.

1859 **Jerome K. Jerome:** English humorist, novelist and playwright. Wrote the magnificently ridiculous *Three Men in a Boat* and his morality play *The Passing of the Third-Floor Back*.

Ambition is only vanity ennobled.

1860 **Theodor Herzl:** Hungarian-born journalist. Founder of modern Zionism. Established the Zionist newspaper *Die Welt*. Negotiated with Turkey and Britain for a Jewish settlement in Palestine. Wrote *The Jewish State*. Honored in Israel and in Jewish communities throughout the world.

Whoever would change men must change the conditions of their lives.

1860 Sir **D'Arcy W. Thompson:** Scottish biologist and classical scholar. Wrote the classic *On Growth and Form* and *A Glossary of Greek Birds*, written in rich literary style, exemplifying his great erudition in physical and natural sciences.

Sagging wrinkles, hanging breasts and many other signs of age are part of gravitation's slow relentless handiwork.

1870 **Lewis J. Selznick:** Russian-born impoverished Jew who first made his way to England and then to the U.S., where he worked as a jeweler. Saw the potential in motion pictures and in 1914 founded the World Pictures Corporation to distribute movies. Moved to Hollywood in 1920 where he teamed up with Adolph Zukor and Jesse L. Lasky to produce films. Went bankrupt in 1925 and retired from the movie business. Father of Producer and studio heard David O. Selznick. Lewis Selznick once cabled the deposed Czar of Russia:

When I was a boy in Russia your police treated my people very badly. However, no hard feelings. Hear you are now out of work. If you will come to New York, can give you a fine position acting in pictures. Salary no object. Reply my expense. Regards you and your family.

1879 **James S. Byrnes:** American politician, lawyer, and editor. Democratic U.S. Senator from South Carolina. Associate justice of the Supreme Court (1941–2).During World War II, served as director of economics stabilization and director of war mobilization. U.S. Secretary of State (1945–7). Governor of South Carolina.

Power intoxicates men. When a man is intoxicated by alcohol, he can recover, but when intoxicated by power, he seldom recovers. It is never voluntarily surrendered. It must be taken from them.

1882 **Sigrid Undset:** Norwegian novelist who won the Nobel Prize in Literature in 1928.Fled Norway with the German occupation and made it to the U.S., but returned home after the war. Best known work is *Kristin Lavransdatter*, a modernist trilogy portraying the life of a woman from birth to death in Scandinavia in the Middle Ages.

Nobody has tried to wrest a living from this country except us — and it is ours, ours. We will not give up our right to it, if we must wait a hundred years to get it.

1892 **Manfred Freiherr von Richthofen:** "The Red Baron." World War I German flying ace with 80 aerial victories. Began his military career as a cavalry officer, but transferred to the air force. Commander of the 11th Chasing Squadron, more popularly known as "Richthofen's Flying Circus," because of their decorated, scarlet aircraft. Shot down beyond British lines and perished at the age of 25.

I honored the fallen enemy by placing a stone on his beautiful grave.

1903 Dr. **Benjamin Spock:** U.S. pediatrician and author. Major influence on modern American child-rearing practices and health care. *Common Sense Book of Baby and Child Care*, published in 1946, has sold over 30 million copies. Vigorously opposed the United States role in the War in Vietnam.

I am not a pacifist. I was very much for the war against Hitler and I also supported the intervention in Korea, but in this war we went in there to steal Vietnam.

1921 **Satyajit Ray:** Indian film director. His film *Pather Panchali*, a human documentary dealing with a Bengali village, was a smash hit at the 1956 Cannes Film Festival. Ray made two sequels *Aparajito* and *World of Apu*. The trilogy was one of the most beautiful film series in screen history. Although he maintained a high artistic level, his subsequent films could not match his masterpieces for authenticity, sincerity, beauty and magic.

I do not seek to compete with Doris Day.

1945 **Bianca Pérez Morena de Macais Jagger:** Nicaraguan model and ex-wife of Mick Jagger of the Rolling Stones. During a visit to Nicaragua after the Sandinista victory over the brutal and oppressive regime of the Somoza family, what she saw persuaded her to commit her life to the issues of justice and human rights. Champions the rights of women and indigenous people in Latin America, opposes capital punishment, works on behalf of saving the rain forests and is a member of a task force whose purpose is to bring war criminals to justice.

We do not want war for oil, which will leave a trail of blood of innocent lives in Iraq and of American and British soldiers. We want to live in a world where peace, democracy and security are enshrined in the United Nations charter.

OTHERS: 1601 German inventor **Athanasius Kircher**, 1740 American patriot **Elias Boudinot**, 1768 French dermatologist **Jean-Louis Alibert**, 1837 U.S. parliamentarian **Henry Martyn Robert**, 1844 African-American inventor, "The Real McCoy," **Elijah McCoy**, 1884 Dutch economist **François de Vries**, 1887 Baseball Hall-of-Famer **Eddie Collins**, 1907 Children's show host **Pinky Lee**, 1912 German newspaper magnate **Axel Springer**, 1924 Austrian/U.S. actor/folk singer **Theodore Bikel**, 1935 King of Iraq **Faisal II**, 1946 U.S. singer **Lesley Gore**, 1952 U.S. actress **Christine Baranski**, 1962 LPGA golfer **Nancy Harvey**, 1963 Dutch soccer player **Jos van Eck**

May 3

1469 **Niccolò Machiavelli:** Florentine statesman, political philosopher and author. His masterpiece *The Prince* is regarded as a pioneer of political science. During his lifetime he had the reputation of being a teacher of treachery, intrigue and immortality. The term "Machiavellian" came to describe cynical and ruthless politics. Fame also rests on *The Discourses*.

It is better to be feared than loved, if you cannot be both.

1748 **Emmanuel Joseph Sieyes:** French Abbé and statesman. Won considerable popularity with his pre-Revolution pamphlet "What Is the Third Estate?" One of the chief theorists of the French Revolution. An architect of the coup that replaced the Directory by the Consulate. After the monarch's restoration he lived in exile in Belgium.

They want to be free and they do not know how to be just.

1849 **Jacob Riis:** Danish-born American newspaper reporter, photographer and social reformer. Shocked the nation's conscience in 1890 by his factual description of slum conditions of New York's Lower East Side in the book *How the Other Half Lives*. It spurred the state's first significant legislation to improve tenements.

The slum is the measure of civilization.

1853 **Edgar Watson Howe:** "Sage of Potato Hill." American editor *Atchison Daily Globe* (1877–1911). Publisher, *E.W. Howe's Monthly* (1911–33). Author of novel *The Story of a Country Town* and *The Anthology of Another Town*. Autobiography: *Plain People*.

If you don't learn to laugh at trouble, you won't have anything to laugh at when you're old.

1874 **Josephine Preston Peabody:** American poet and playwright. Author of: *The Wayfarers, Fortune and Men's Eyes, The Singing Leaves* and *Harvest Moon*.

One never learns by success. Success is the plateau that one rests upon to take breath and look down from upon the straight and difficult path, but one does not climb upon a plateau.

1896 **Dorothy Gladys "Dodie" Smith:** English writer, dramatist and theater producer. She started her career as an actress, but turned to writing and producing such successful plays as *Dear Octopus* and the novel *I Capture the Castle*. Also known for her children's books, such as *The Hundred and One Dalmatians*.

The family, that dear octopus from whose tentacles we never quite escape, nor in our innermost hearts never quite wish to.

1898 **Golda Meir:** Born **Goldie Mabovitch** in Kiev, Russia. Israeli stateswoman. Came to America in 1906 and became a school teacher in Milwaukee, Wisconsin. She and her husband moved to Israel in 1921. First woman premier of Israeli (1969–74). A leader in the fight for a state of Israel. Worked to achieve peace with Arab neighbors through diplomacy, but the fourth Arab-Israeli war interfered. Autobiography*: My Life*.

Whether women are better than men I cannot say — but I can say they are certainly no worse.

1903 **Bing [Harry Lillis] Crosby:** American singer and actor. His mellow "crooning" style and casual stage manner made him extremely popular with Paul Whiteman's orchestra, on records, radio, in movies and on television. His film career included seven "road" pictures with Bob Hope and Dorothy Lamour. Earned an Academy Award for his performance in *Going My Way*. His recording of "White Christmas" was among the most popular songs of all time.

I think popular music is one of the few things in the twentieth century that have made giant strides in reverse.

1912 **May Sarton:** Belgian-born American poet, novelist and memoirist. Wrote 53 books, 19 novels, 17 books of poetry, 15 nonfiction works included her journals, 2 children's books, a play and some screenplays. Many of her poems and novels deal with lesbian experiences, in particular her most openly lesbian work *Mrs. Stevens Hears the Mermaids Singing*.

No partner in a love relationship ... should feel that he has to give up an essential part of himself to make it viable.

1913 **William Inge:** American dramatist. One of the first to explore small-time life in the Midwest as subjects for plays. Earned the nickname "playwright of the Midwest." Transformed the lives or ordinary people living in drab surroundings into significant human experiences. Wrote *Come Back Little Sheba, Bus Stop, The Dark at the Top of the Stairs* and *Picnic* (Pulitzer Prize). Won an Academy Award for writing the original screenplay for *Splendor in the Grass*.

People with emotional problems are just as unable to cope with good news as with bad.

1919 **Pete Seeger:** American folksinger, composer. Ranks with Woody Guthrie as the all-time great protest singer. Formed the Weavers with bass Lee Hays. Group's best-sellers: "Irene, Goodnight," "On Top of Old Smoky" and "Wimoweh." Hits as a soloist: "If I Had a Hammer," "Where Have All the Flowers Gone" and "Guantanamera." A prominent supporter of anti-war, civil rights and environmental causes.

Throughout history, the leaders of countries have been very particular of what songs should be sung. We know the power of songs... Songs won't

save the planet, but neither will books or speeches. Songs are sneaky things; they can slip across borders.

1920 **Sugar Ray Robinson: Born Walter Smith.** African-American boxer. Won all 89 of his amateur fights. As a professional he was six-times a world champion, once as a welterweight (147 lbs.) and five times as a middleweight (160 lbs.), Had 109 knockouts and only 19 defeats in 207 professional bouts.

Fighting to me seems barbaric. I don't really like it. I enjoy out-thinking another man and out-maneuvering him, but I still don't like to fight.

OTHERS: 1455 King of Portugal **Joâo II**, 1844 French anti–Semitic journalist **Édouard A. Drumont**, 1844 English opera impresario **Richard D'Oyly Carte**, 1859 Writer of cowboy stories **Andy Adams**, 1874 French perfumer **François Coty**, 1886 French recital organist **Marcel Dupré**, 1892 U.S. actress **Beulah Bondi**, 1897 Indian statesman **V.K. Krishna Menon**, 1904 Baseball pitcher **Red Ruffing**, 1906 U.S. actress **Mary Astor**, 1907 U.S. columnist **Earl Wilson**, 1919 U.S. songwriter **Betty Comden**, 1921 U.S. basketball player **Goose Tatum**, 1922 Ballerina/choreographer **Martina Svetlova**, 1936 Singer **Engelbert Humperdinck**, 1937 U.S. singer **Frankie Valli**, 1946 Sportscaster **Greg Gumbel**

May 4

1796 **Horace Mann:** "Father of American Public Education." American lawyer, educator, and legislator. Entire life was dedicated to building a system of universal free public education. As secretary of Massachusetts state board of education, labored to improve the public schools, increase teacher salaries and establish teacher training institutions. First president of experimental Antioch College.

A house without books is like a room without windows. No man has a right to bring up his children without surrounding them with books, if he has the means to buy them... In a republic, ignorance is a crime.

1825 **Thomas H. Huxley:** English biologist, educator and writer. In the 1850s he established his reputation for several important papers on animal individuality, certain mollusks, the methods of paleontology, the methods and principles of science and science education and the structure and function of nerves. Best known for his defense of Charles Darwin's theory of evolution. His lectures and writings helped popularize science. Writings: *Evidence as to Man's Place in Nature* and *Evolution and Ethics*.

Every great advance in natural knowledge has involved the absolute rejection of authority.

1864 **Richard Hovey:** American poet who in his 36 years of life won the enthusiasm of both the conventional school of poetry and the modernists. His best work is probably *Lancelot and Guinevere: A Poem in Dramas*.

Many a man has fought because he feared to run away.

1889 **Francis Cardinal Spellman:** Roman Catholic clergyman. Auxiliary Bishop of Boston and Archbishop of New York (1939–64). Made a cardinal in 1946. Strong administrator. Religious conservative and ardent anti–Communist. Interests lay in education and charities. Advocate of state aid to parochial schools.

You've heard of the three ages of man — youth, age, and you are looking wonderful.

1896 Dr. **Frank Baxter:** American educator who hosted television series "Now and Then" and "Gateways to the Mind" on such diverse subjects as Shakespeare, the sun, time and the human senses. His shows won 10 major awards, including an Emmy.

No one is supposed to tell others what is good. I tell you what is good, you can't live, you can't mesh with this world, unless you read.

1907 **Lincoln Kirstein:** American dance authority, impresario and writer. Focused his artistic interests on ballet. Persuaded George Balanchine to come to the U.S. to found The School of American Ballet in 1934. Kirstein was general director of the New York City Ballet, which he helped establish. Of his seven books on ballet, *Dance* remains a classic history.

In liberal democracy and anxious anarchy, the traditional classic dance, compact of aristocratic authority and absolute freedom in a necessity of order, has never been so promising as an independent expression as it is today.

1916 **Jane Jacobs:** American-Canadian urbanologist and writer. For ten years she was an editor at *Architectural Forum*. She wrote of the multiple needs of modern urban areas in *Death and Life of Great American Cities*. Her book, *The Economies of Cities*, stressed the importance of diversity to a city's prospects.

There is a quality even meaner than outright ugliness or disorder, and this meaner quality is the dishonest mask of pretended order, achieved by ignoring or suppressing the real order that is struggling to exist and to be served.

1929 **Audrey Hepburn:** Belgium-born stylish actress. The radiant model-thin beauty won an Oscar for *Roman Holiday*. Nominated for *Sabrina*, *The Nun's Story*, *Breakfast at Tiffany's* and *Wait Until Dark*. Special Ambassador for UNICEF, devoting much of her free time to charity. Led a mission of mercy to famine- and war-torn Somalia. Died of colon cancer.

People, even more than things, have to be restored, renewed, revived, reclaimed, and redeemed; never throw out anyone.

1935 **Jane Howard:** American journalist and writer. In *Families*, she tells the stories of dozens of families in an effort to discover what makes the best ones work so well. Her other books included: *A Different Woman*, *Please Touch: A Guided Tour of the Human Potential Movement*, and *Margaret Mead: A Life*.

Parents, however old they and we may grow to be, serve among other things to shield us from a sense of our doom. As long as they are around, we can avoid the fact of our mortality; we can still be innocent children.

1936 **El Cordobés:** Professional name of **Manuel Benítez Pérez.** Also: **Manolo.** Spanish matador. Purists were shocked by his athleticism, but his theatrical style and disregard for danger made him an idol of the crowds and the highest paid matador in history. Gored 20 times. Became a multimillionaire in 1965 when he fought 111 corridas. In 1970, he received $1,800,000 for 121 fights. Once made a promise to his mother.

If I become popular I will buy you a house ... or I will dress you in mourning.

1941 **George F. Will:** American journalist, columnist and author. Conservative syndicated columnist. Served as an editor for the magazine *National Review* from 1973 to 1976. Became a contributing editor for *Newsweek.* Won 1977 Pulitzer Prize for editorial journalism. Political analyst for ABC. Wrote two best selling books on baseball and three books on political philosophy.

The nicest thing about being a pessimist is that you are constantly being either proven right or pleasantly surprised.

1958 **Keith Haring:** American pop artist and social activist. He first gained attention for his art for his drawings in New York subways. He also painted a mural on the Berlin Wall. A tireless AIDs activist. The disease took his life at age 31.

Drawing is still basically the same as it has been since prehistoric times. It brings together man and the world. It lives through magic.

OTHERS: 1006 Persian mystic poet **Abd-Allah Ansari**, 1631 Queen of England **Mary I**, 1655 Italian harpsichord maker **Bartolommeo Cristofori**, 1776 German philosopher **Johann F. Herbart**, 1820 English publisher **Joseph Whittaker**, 1881 Russian Premier **Aleksandr F. Kerenski**, 1909 U.S. actor **Howard Da Silva**, 1918 Japanese Prime Minister **Kakuei Tanaka**, 1926 NASA test pilot **Milt Thompson**, 1928 Egyptian president **Hosni Mubarak,** 1930 Operatic soprano **Roberta Peters**, 1942 British drummer **Ronnie Bond**, 1948 Harness race driver **Billy O'Donnell**, 1956 German high jumper **Ulrike Meyfarth**, 1959 Country singer **Randy Travis**, 1973 Miss America **Michelle Martinez**

May 5

1813 **Søren Kierkegaard:** Danish philosopher, whose writings influenced such modern schools of thought as existentialism. Survived a gloomy early life which no doubt affected his thoughts on faith, knowledge, reality, free will and God. He believed that man's relation with God must be a lonely, agonizing experience. Books: *The Concept of Irony*, *Either-Or* and *Fear and Trembling.*

Life can only be understood backwards, but it must be lived forward.

1818 **Karl Marx:** German socialist, who as a youth was greatly influenced by G.W.F. Hegel. With Friedrich Engels, Marx formulated principles of Dialectical Materialism, or economic determinism. Maintained that economic structure is the basis of all history and determines all social, political and intellectual aspects of life. Works: *The Communist Manifesto* and *Das Kapital.* Fled to England after the Revolutionary upheaval of 1848 and spent most of the rest of his life in the poor section of London.

The oppressed are allowed once every few years to decide which particular representatives of the oppressing class are to represent and repress them.

1882 **Sylvia Pankhurst:** Socialist feminist and campaigner for women's suffrage. Daughter of suffragist Emmeline Pankhurst and sister of evangelist Christabel Pankhurst. Produced a weekly paper for working class woman called *The Women's Dreadnought.* Supported the republicans in Spain, helped Jewish refugees from Nazi Germany, and led a campaign against Italy's occupation of Ethiopia.

I am going to fight capitalism even if it kills me. It is wrong that people like you should be comfortable and well fed while all around you people are starving.

1883 **Archibald Wavell:** British Field Marshall. Commander of British Army forces in the Middle East during World War II. Let British troops to victory over the Italians, but was later defeated by the German army. Wounded at the Battle of Ypres in 1915, he lost his left eye. In 1939, given the task of creating the Middle East Command and protecting the Suez Canal. Viceroy of Burma in 1943. Books: *The Palestine Campaigns*, *Allenby*, and *Generals and Generalship.* Commenting on the treaties to end World War I:

After the "war to end war" they seem to have been pretty successful in Paris at making a "Peace to end Peace."

1887 Lord **Geoffrey Fisher:** English clergyman. Ordained in 1912. Served as headmaster of Repton School from 1914 to 1932. One hundredth archbishop of Canterbury. Crowned Queen Elizabeth II in Westminster Abbey. Made a life peer in 1961.

Until you know that life is interesting — and find it so — you haven't found your soul.

1888 **Paul Eldridge:** American educator, novelist, and poet. Wrote *My First Two Thousand Years*, *Men and Women*, *The Crown of Empire,* and *The Tree of Ignorance.*

Man is ready to die for an idea, provided that idea is not quite clear to him.

1890 **Christopher Morley:** American novelist, essayist and editor. A Rhodes Scholar at Oxford. Founder with William Rose Benet of the *Saturday Review* and editor (1924–41). Founder of dozens of clubs including the "Baker Street Irregulars." Wrote: *Tales from a Rolltop Desk* and *Kitty Foyle.*

Read, every day, something no one else is reading. Think, every day, something no one else is thinking. Do, every day, something no one else would be silly enough to do. It is bad for the mind to be always part of unanimity.

1895 **Charles MacArthur:** American newspaperman, playwright and screenwriter. With Ben Hecht wrote plays *The Front Page* and *Twentieth Century*, noted for their crisp, witty dialogue. They collaborated on the screenplays for these two as well as for *Wuthering Heights* and *Crime Without Passion*. His other collaborators included Edward Sheldon and Sidney Howard. Husband of Helen Hayes.

Complaints are only a sign you've been hurt. Keep the wounds out of sight.

1903 **James A. Beard:** American chef and cookbook author. Through his Greenwich Village cooking school he influenced such future chefs as Julia Child and Craig Claiborne. Popularized American cooking. *Beard on Bread* is considered to be the definitive work on baking. Championed simple American and English dishes. Among his 20 cookbooks was one of the first serious cookbooks for outdoor cooking.

A gourmet who thinks of calories is like a tart who looks at her watch.

1903 **Sally Stanford:** Born **Marsha Owen**. The last grand madam of San Francisco. For thirty years she was the queen of the Bay's city high-toned bordellos, reportedly with the prettiest and most elegantly gowned girls, before retiring tin 1950 to open the plush Sausalito waterfront restaurant, the Valhalla. A quarrel over installing an electric sign at the restaurant caused her to seek public office. Won a seat of Sausalito's City Council on her sixth try. In 1976 she became the city's mayor.

Well, there's a Book that says we're all sinners and I at least chose a sin that's made quite a few people happier than they were before they met me.

1912 **Alice Faye:** Born **Ann Leppert**. Appealing blond American actress and throaty contralto singer. Began her career as a singer with Rudy Vallee's band. Usually appeared in musicals and introduced many popular standards, including the Academy Award winning "You'll Never Know." Films included: *In Old Chicago*, *Alexander's Ragtime Band*, *Lillian Russell* and *State Fair*. Married to comedian Phil Harris for 54 years until his death.

What did I have? I don't know. Maybe it was the girl-next-door, the one you left behind. It was wartime.

1923 **Richard Arthur Wolheim:** British philosopher whose best known work concentrated on the relationship between art and psychology. His *Art and Objects* was one of the most influential texts on aesthetics of the 20th century. Other publications: *Ethical Studies*, *Hume on Religion*, and *On Pictorial Organization*.

[The artist's] intentions must be taken to include desires, beliefs, emotions, commitments, wishes.

1942 **Tammy Wynette:** Born **Virginia Wynette Pugh.** American country music singer. Recorded 20 number one songs and 50 albums. Some of her biggest hits were: "Your Good Girl's Gonna Go Bad," D_I_V_O_R_C_E" and her anthem "Stand by Your Man." Was married to her idol, country star George Jones, with whom she recorded many duet hits. Ultimately his alcohol problems made him impossible to stand by.

Stand by your man. Give him two arms to cling to and something warm to come to.

OTHERS: 1819 Polish composer **Stanislaw Moniuszko**, 1830 U.S. hatter tycoon **John Stetson**, 1832 Historian/publisher **Hubert Howe Bancroft**, 1846 Polish-born author **Henrik Sienkiewicz**, 1867 Famous journalist **Nellie Bly**, 1883 Native-American major league baseball pitcher **Chief Bender**, 1895 Co-creator of *Amos 'n' Andy* **Freeman Gosden**, 1904 British jockey **Sir Gordon Richards**, 1909 Presidential press secretary **James C. Hagerty**, 1914 U.S. actor **Tyrone Power**, 1926 U.S. actress **Ann B. Davis**, 1937 U.S. C&W singer **Johnnie Taylor**, 1943 Monty Python's **Michael Palin**

May 6

1754 **Joseph Joubert:** French thinker and essayist on philosophical, moral and literary topics. Wrote private diaries of original insights, remarkable for their cool and disciplined idealism. Found fame with his *Pensées*.

Genius is the ability to see things invisible, to manipulate things intangible, to paint things that have no features.

1758 **Maximilien Robespierre:** Radical Jacobin leader and one of the main figures of the French revolution. Dominated the Committee of Public Safety which instituted the Reign of Terror (1793–94). Overthrown by the Convention of 1794 and was sent to the guillotine without a trial as he had sent so many others.

The revolution ate its children.

1856 **Sigmund Freud:** Austrian neurologist and founder of psychoanalysis. A neurotic, constantly depressed, deathly afraid of open spaces and lived in terror of dying at 51. Spent a half-hour each day analyzing himself. Postulated the existence of three internal forces governing a person's psychic life: the *id*, the instinctual force of life; the *ego*, the executive force that has contact with the real world; and the *superego*, or moral conscience.

The contribution of psychoanalysis to science consists precisely in having extended research to the region of the mind.

1861 Sir **Rabindranath Tagore:** Bengali poet, philosopher, novelist, painter, essayist and composer. Collected legends and tales which he included in *The Tragedy of Rudachandra*, *Binodini* and *Chitra*. Founded an experimental school where he sought to blend Eastern and Western philosophies. Nobel Prize for Literature (1913), the first Asiatic so honored. Spoke ardently in favor of Indian independence for India. In protest against the Massacre of Amritsar, he renounced the knighthood he had been awarded in 1915.

I slept and dreamt that life was joy. I awoke and saw that life was service. I acted and behold, service was joy.

1895 **Rudolph Valentino:** Born **Rodolfo Pietro Alfonzo Filiberto Raeffella Guglielemi di Valentina d'Antonguolla.** Italian-born silent screen star, the leading heartthrob of his time. His first job in the U.S. was as a gardener in Central Park, New York. Became an overnight sensation with the film *The Four Horsemen of the Apocalypse*. Consider the screen lover of his day. At his untimely death at 31, there was a wave of mass hysteria among female fans. Other films: *The Sheik*, *Blood and Sand*, and *Monsieur Beaucaire*.

Women are not in love with me but with the picture of me on the screen. I am merely the canvas on which women paint their dreams.

1902 **Harry Golden:** American nonfiction writer, editor and publisher of *The Carolina Israelite* in Charlotte, North Carolina. Author of *Only in America*, *For 2 Cents Plain*, *Mr. Kennedy and the Negroes*, and *The Greatest Jewish City in the World.*

Talk is the greatest of all Jewish sports.

1906 **Andre Weil:** French mathematician. Brother of French mystic Simone Weil. He made notable advances in the areas of algebra, number theory, algebraic geometry, differential geometry, topology, Lie groups and Lie algebras, analysis, and history of mathematics. Together with Henri Cartan, Weil co-founded a group of young French mathematicians, working under the name "Nicolas Bourbaki." The group was dedicated to the production of a collective work, providing up-to-date foundations for the whole of modern mathematical science.

God exists since mathematics is consistent, and the Devil exists since we cannot prove it.

1914 **Randall Jarrell:** U.S. poet, critic and novelist. His criticism is collected in *Poetry and the Age*. He revitalized the reputations of Robert Frost, Walt Whitman and William Carlos Williams in the 1950s. His poems appeared in *Little Friend, Little Friend* and *Losses*. Author of *Blood for a Stranger* and *The Gingerbread Rabbit*.

A poet is a man who manages, in a lifetime of standing out in thunderstorms, to be struck by lightning five or six times.

1915 **Orson Welles:** American actor, director and producer, screenwriter. His Mercury Theater radio production "The War of the Worlds," scared thousands one Halloween, who believed it a newscast. Collaborated with Herman Mankiewicz to create perhaps the greatest American film, *Citizen Kane*, shortly followed by another masterpiece, *The Magnificent Ambersons*. Spent his life trying to earn enough money to make movies the way he wished.

If you want a happy ending that depends, of course, on where you stop the story.

1920 **Ross Hunter:** Hollywood film producer of more than sixty films. Most were either light and bright confections starring Debbie Reynolds, Doris Day and Julie Andrews or melodrama weepers such as *Imitation of Life*, staring Lana Turner. His biggest success was *Airport*, for which he received an Academy Award nomination.

The way life looks in my pictures is the way I want life to be. I don't hold a mirror up to life as it is. I just want to show the part which is attractive.

1931 **Willie Mays:** African-American baseball player, who began his professional career with the Birmingham Black Barons in the National Negro League when he was only 16. The "Say Hey Kid" played in the major leagues fro the Giants, first in New York and then in San Francisco. One of the greatest centerfielders ever to play the game and one of the finest right-hand hitters of all time. Considered one of the greatest all-round players in the history of the game, so his comment below is not conceit, but fact:

I think I was the best baseball player I ever saw.

1961 **George Clooney:** American actor, director and producer. Son of TV host Nick Clooney and nephew of singer Rosemary Clooney. Made his fist big splash for his role in TV's long-running medical show ER. Films include: *One Fine Day*, *The Perfect Storm*, *O Brother, Where Art Thou?*, *Ocean's Eleven*, *Good Night, Good Luck* and *Syriana*.

I don't like to share my personal life ... it wouldn't be personal if I shared it.

OTHERS: 973 German emperor **Henry II**, 1785 Swedish story teller **Arvir A. Afzelius**, 1806 U.S. dentist **Chapin Aaron Harris**, 1812 U.S. physician **Martin Robinson**, 1829 First Female ordained minister in New England **Phoebe Ann Coffin**, 1856 U.S. artic explorer **Robert E. Peary**, 1870 Cartoonist **John McClutcheon**, 1875 Five sat U.S. admiral **William D. Leahy**, 1898 Baby food manufacturer **Daniel Gerber**, 1902 Film director/writer **Max Ophüls**, 1905 U.S. restaurateur **Toots Shor**, 1907 Colts & Jets football coach **Weeb Ewbank**, 1913 U.S. pianist **Carmen Cavallaro**, 1913 British actor **Stewart Granger**, 1926 Operatic soprano **Marguerite Piazza**, 1947 U.S. high jumper **Dick Fosby**

May 7

1812 **Robert Browning:** Major English poet of the Victorian age. Noted for his mastery of dramatic monologue and psychological portraiture. Married poet Elizabeth Barrett and moved with her to Italy where they remained until her death in 1861. The story of their love was dramatized by Rudolf Beiser in *The Barretts of Wimpole Street*. Poems: "My Last Duchess," "The Pied Piper of Hamelin," and climaxed his career with *The Ring and the Book*.

Grow old with me! The best is yet to be, the last of life, for which the first was made.

1833 **Johannes Brahms:** German romantic composer and concert pianist. One of the world's great composers. Long time resident of Venice. Wrote symphonies, chamber music, piano works, concerts, choral works, songs, and lieder. Works: *Hungarian Dances*, *Violin Concerto in D Major* and *Lullaby* and *A German Requiem*.

It is not hard to compose, but what if fabulously

hard is to leave the superfluous notes under the table.

1836 **Joseph G. Cannon:** "Uncle Joe." Staunchly conservative Illinois Republican congressman. Despotically ruled House of Representatives from his positions as chairman of the House Rules Committee and as Speaker of the House (1903–11). In 1910 a coalition of Democrats and insurgent Republicans were able to get a resolution passed, making the Speaker ineligible to serve on the Rules Committee, the source of Cannon's power.

Sometimes in politics one must duel with skunks, but no one should be fool enough to allow skunks to choose the weapons.

1840 **Peter Ilyich Tchaikovsky:** Russian composer of the Romantic era, conductor and professor of composition. Although his music is loved for its distinctly Russian character, it much more western than those of his Russian contemporaries. His works include: *Piano Concerto No. I*, the ballets *Swan Lake*, *Sleeping Beauty* and *The Nutcracker Suite*, his opera *Eugene Onegrin* and his "*Pathétique" Symphony*, which premiered only four days before his death due to a cholera epidemic raging through the city.

Truly there would be no reason to go mad were it not for music.

1882 **Smiley Blanton:** American psychologist and writer. Among the earliest in the United States to work in the field of speech pathology. Offered counseling and family therapies to children and adults who stuttered and had voice and articulation problems. Director of the first university speech clinic, located at the University of Wisconsin. Later in his life, he directed a famous free counseling clinic in New York City, connected with the church of Norman Vincent Peale.

A sense of curiosity is nature's original school of education.

1892 **Archibald MacLeish:** American poet, critic and Librarian of Congress. Graduated from Harvard Law School and practiced law for three years. Moved to Paris to join the community of literary expatriates including Gertrude Stein and Ernest Hemingway. Pulitzer Prize (1932) for narrative poem "Conquistador." His verse plays were political messages. *Panic* was about the Depression and *The Fall of the City*, was written during Hitler's rise to power. Won two more Pulitzers, one for his play *J.B.*

Love becomes the ultimate human answer to the ultimate human question... What love does is affirm. It affirms the worth of life in spite of life... It answers life with life.

1892 Marshal **Tito [Josip Broz]:** Led Yugoslav partisans against Nazis in World War II. Prime minister of Yugoslavia (1943–53). First communist leader to defy Soviet control. Worked for conciliation of country's diverse nationalities, which only postponed the bloody civil war until the manufactured nation came apart, followed by military conflicts, brutality and ethnic cleansing.

Any movement in history which attempts to perpetuate itself becomes reactionary.

1901 **Gary Cooper:** American film actor, who was at his best in roles that required understated, stoic, and emotionally restrained performances, best seen in his many Westerns. Poet Carl Sandburg said of "Coop," *He is one of the most beloved illiterates this country has ever known.* Won two Academy Awards, the first for *Sergeant York* and for *High Noon*, probably his best performance. Only married to Veronica Balfe, he had numerous affairs before and after his marriage, including those with Clara Bow, Lupe Vélex, Grace Kelly and Patricia Neal.

The general consensus seems to be that I don't act at all.

1909 **Edwin H. Land:** American scientist, inventor and college dropout. Founder of the Polaroid Corporation in 1937, which among other things produced the Polaroid camera in 1947 and the optics for Lockheed's U-2 spy plane. He had over 500 patents, second in number only to Thomas Edison. Awarded the Medal of Freedom.

Creativity is the sudden cessation of stupidity.

1919 **Eva "Evita" Perón:** Argentine political figure. Active in the campaign to elect her husband Juan Perón president (1946). All but co-governed with him. Developed an adoring following among the poor whose enthusiasm for her did not end with her death of cancer at 33. The Broadway and movie musical *Evita* based on her life showed her anything but saintly.

Keeping books on social aid is capitalistic nonsense. I just use the money for the poor. I can't stop to count it.

1930 **Totie Fields:** American comedian, who got her biggest laughs by making fun of her weight problems. Got her first big break appearing on the *Ed Sullivan Show*, making 39 additional appearances on the show. Wrote a humorous diet book, *I Think I'll Start on Monday: The Official 8½ oz. Mashed Potato Diet.* Despite having a leg amputated above the knee, two heart attacks, and breast cancer, she continued to perform, until she suffered a fatal heart attack.

I've been on a diet for two weeks and all I've lost is fourteen days.

1932 **Jenny Joseph:** English poet, educator, and journalist. Best known for her poem "Warning," a witty piece about growing old, which inspired the formation of the Red Hat Society. A BBC poll found it to be the most popular 20th century poem.

When I am an old woman, I shall wear purple/ With a red hat which doesn't suit me,/ And I shall spend my pension on brandy and summer gloves/ And satin sandals, and say we've no money for butter.

OTHERS: 1769 Italian composer **Giuseppe Farinelli**, 1847 British Prime Minister **Archibald Primrose**, 1870 Movie theater chain owner **Marcus Lowe**, 1885 U.S. actor **"Gabby" Hayes**, 1917 Bomb disposal expert **William Geoffrey Biddle**, 1920 Etiquette columnist

Elizabeth Post, 1923 U.S. actress **Anne Baxter**, 1927 Indian screenwriter **Ruth Prawer Jhabvala**, 1927 U.S. singer **Jim Lowe**, 1931 U.S. sci-fi writer **Gene Wolfe**, 1931 U.S. pop-singer **Teresa Brewer**, 1933 Great NFL quarterback **Johnny Unitas**, 1940 English novelist **Angela Carter**, 1953 U.S. film director **Amy Heckerling**, 1968 U.S. actress/former porn star **Traci Lords**

May 8

1592 **Francis Quarles:** English religious poet. A churchman and royalist. Many of his books were destroyed during the Civil War. Best known works are *Emblems*, a series of symbolic pictures with verse commentary and a prose book of aphorisms, *Epigrams*.

Meditation is the life of the soul: Action, the soul of meditation, and honor the reward of action.

1668 **Alain René Lesage:** French novelist and prolific satirist dramatist. Early works are translations of Spanish authors. Celebrated for an animated style and dramatic presentations of human weaknesses. Best known works are *The Adventures of Gil Blas of Santillane*, one of the earliest realistic novels, and *Turcaret*.

Justice is such a fine thing that we cannot pay too dearly for it.

1884 **Harry S Truman:** Thirty-third president of the United States (1945–53), succeeding Franklin D. Roosevelt at the latter's death. A haberdasher, he was the last of eight U.S. presidents who did not attend college. Democratic U.S. Senator from Missouri (1933–45). Made decision to drop atom bomb on Japan to speed end of World War II. Decided to send troops to Korea. Announced policy of containment of communist influence in the world. The "S" in his name is not an abbreviation for anything. It was common practice in the U.S. and England to use a letter as a middle name in the period prior to World War I. If written properly the "S" is not followed by a period.

I never give them hell. I just tell the truth and they think it's hell.

1886 **Horatio Smith:** American educator and writer. Professor of French Literature at Amherst, Brown and Columbia. Editor *Romantic Review* and *Columbia Dictionary of Modern European Literature*. Books: *The Literary Criticism of Pierre Bayle* and *Masters of French Literature*.

Inconsistency is the only thing in which we are consistent.

1895 **Fulton J. Sheen:** Roman Catholic bishop and broadcaster. National director of the Society for the Propagation of the Faith. Internationally famous for his radio program *Catholic Hour* (1930–52) and the television show, "Life Is Worth Living" (1952–65). It was followed by two more series. One of the best known clerics in the U.S.

There are 200 million poor in the world who would gladly take the vow of poverty if they could eat, dress and have a home like I do.

1895 **Edmund Wilson:** American critic, journalist, editor, novelist, short-story writer, poet. Editor and writer for *Vanity Fair*, *The New Republic* and *The New Yorker*. Books: *Axel's Castle, Patriotic Gore, Memoirs of Hecate County,* and *The Scrolls from the Dead Sea.*

At 60 the sexual preoccupation, when it hits you, seems sometimes sharper, as if it were an elderly malady, like gout.

1899 **Friedrich August von Hayek:** Austrian-British economist. Opposed the theories of John Maynard Keynes. Criticized government intervention in the free market. Books include: *The Road to Serfdom, The Constitution of Liberty* and *The Political Order of a Free People*. Views were very popular among conservatives, including Prime Minister Margaret Thatcher.

Competition means decentralized planning by many separate persons.

1906 **Roberto Rossellini:** Italian film director. During World War II, he made Fascist propaganda films, but also made secretly filmed antifascist activities. After the war, he burst onto the international scene as a leading neorealist director. Had a scandalous adulterous affair with Ingrid Bergman which produced a son and twin girls. Films: *Open City*, *Paisan*, *Stromboli*, *General Della Rovere* and *The Rise of Louis XIV*.

Don't get married to an actress because they're also actresses in bed.

1911 **Rudolf Flesch:** Critic of the American education system. Proponent of the phonics approach to reading. His controversial bestsellers were *Why Johnny Can't Read*, *Teaching Johnny to Read* and *Johnny Still Can't Read* prompted a widespread debate in educational circles. His books identified the cause of reading problems: the look-say method.

Johnny couldn't read for the simple reason is that nobody ever showed him how.

1914 **Romain Gary:** Lithuanian-born Polish-French novelist, World War II pilot and diplomat. One of France's most popular and prolific writers. Authored more than 30 novels, essays, and memoirs, some of which he wrote under the pseudonym Émile Ajar. Secretary of the French Delegation to the United Nations. Became General Consul of France in Los Angles in 1956.Only person to win the Prix Goncourt twice, once for *Les raciness du ciel* and then for *La vie devant soi*.

Humor is an affirmation of man's dignity, a declaration of man's superiority to all that befalls him.

1920 **Sloan Wilson:** American novelist. His characters are usually middle-aged, upper-to-middle class New Englanders, whose lives seem to be passing them by. His best-selling novels *The Man in the Gray Flannel Suit* and *A Summer Place* both were made into successful Hollywood films.

Success in almost any field depends more on energy and drive than it does on intelligence. This explains why we have so many stupid leaders.

1937 **Thomas Pynchon:** American novelist. Began as a technical writer before turning to fiction. His pessimistic works have included black humor and fantasy to illustrate human alienation in the modern chaotic society. Novels: *V*, *The Crying of Lot 49*, *Gravity's Rainbow* and *Mason & Dixon*. His works are chock full of information about physics, electronics, history, cybernetics and information theory.

If they can get you asking the wrong questions, they don't have to worry about the answers.

OTHERS: 1753 Father of Mexican independence **Miguel Hidaglo y Castilla**, 1810 Union general **James Cooper**, 1814 Russian anarchist **Mikhail Bakunin**, 1828 Swiss founder of Red Cross **Jean Henri Dunant**, 1829 First internationally recognized pianist **Louis Moreau Gottschalk**, 1846 German playwright **Oscar Hammerstein**, 1855 U.S. barbed wire tycoon **John Wayne Gates**, 1871 French historian **Louis Madelin**, 1892 Italian basso **Ezio Pinza**, 1893 U.S. golf great **Francis Quimet**, 1926 U.S. comedian **Don Rickles**, 1928 JFK advisor **Theodore Sorensen**, 1934 U.S. boxer **Sonny Liston**, 1940 Novelist **Peter Benchley**, 1940 Singer **Rick Nelson**, 1924 Puerto Rican jockey **Angel Cordero**

May 9

1738 **John Wolcot:** English physician, clergyman and verse satirist. Wrote under the pseudonym **Peter Pindar**. His satires were first directed towards members of the Royal Academy, but later set his sights higher to including the King and Queen, stinging them to the quick. As long as one was not the target of his remarkable wit and humor, his verses were intensely comic.

Learn what you are, and be such.

1800 **John Brown:** "Old Brown of Osawatomie." Connecticut-born U.S. abolitionist. Obsessed with fleeing slaves by force, with his five sons slaughtered settlers at Potwatomi Creek. Withstood an attack by proslavery forces at Osawatomie in bloody Kansas. Led a raid on the U.S. arsenal at Harper's Ferry, Virginia. His insurrection was opposed by federal forces led by Colonel Robert E. Lee. Captured, convicted and hanged, he became a martyr to abolitionists. He was immortalized in the song "John Brown's Body," which was popular with Union troops during the Civil War. His last words before his execution were:

I, John Brown, and now quite certain that the crimes of this guilty land will never be purged away but with blood.

1860 Sir **James Barrie:** Scottish dramatist and novelist. Known for whimsy and sentimental fantasy in his novel *The Little Minister* and plays *The Admirable Crichton* and *Peter Pan*, which has provided a celebrated role for generations of famous actress, beginning with Maud Adams. The Peter Pan stories were created to entertain a friend's son. Barrie financed the expedition of his friend Robert Scott to explore the Antarctica. He memorialized Scott in his famous address on "Courage."

When the first baby laughed for the first time, the laugh broke into a thousand pieces and they all skipped about, and that was the beginning of fairies.

1870 **Harry Vardon:** Amateur British golfing champion. He turned professional at age 20. Won the British Open six times and the U.S. Open once. A technical innovator, he was one of the first golfers to have a product tie-in, his "Vardon Flyer" guttie golf ball for A.G. Spalding. The Vardon Trophy is awarded annually to the pro player with the best scoring average.

Golfers find it a very trying matter to turn at the waist, more particularly if they have a lot of waist to turn.

1874 **Howard Carter:** English archaeologist and Egyptologist. Famous for the discovery of the tomb of Tutankhamen in the Valley of the Kings at Luxor, Egypt. Carter's search for the tomb of a previously unknown Pharaoh was financed by Lord Carnavaron, an eager amateur archaeologist. Carter is also known for finding the remains of the tomb of Queen Hatshepsut in Deir el Babri.

Those were the great days of excavating ... anything to which a fancy was taken, from a scarab to an obelisk, was just appropriated, and if there was a difference with a brother excavator, one laid for him with a gun.

1882 **Henry J. Kaiser:** American industrialist. He organized combinations of construction companies that built the San Francisco Bay Bridge, levees along the Mississippi, the Hoover, Bonneville and Grand Coulee Dams. Turned his attention to shipbuilding, constructing some 1,460 ships during World War II in record time of less than five days each. Established the first Health Maintenance Organization, the Kaiser Plan, for his employees. After the war, he dealt primarily in aluminum, steel, and automobiles.

You can't sit on the lid of progress. If you do, you will be blown to pieces.

1883 **José Ortega y Gasset:** Spanish philosopher, existentialist humanist and politician. Considered individual life to be the fundamental reality. His critical writings on modern authors made him an influential figure. Works included *Adam in Paradise*, *Quixote's Meditations* and *Modern Theme*. His *The Revolt of the Masses*, which advocated rule by the creative minority, foreshadowed the Spanish Civil War, after which he lived in voluntary exile in South America and Portugal.

Life is a series of collisions with the future; it is not the sum of what we have been, but what we yearn to be.

1918 **Mike Wallace:** U.S. television interviewer and reporter. Early in his career he hosted several television quiz shows. Joined CBS as a reporter in 1963. Was coeditor of the long-running *60 Minutes* from its inception in 1968. Won numerous Emmy Awards. Famed for his aggressive, take-no-prisoners interviewing style.

I determined that if I was to carve out a piece of reportorial territory for myself it would be [doing] the hard interview, irreverent if necessary, the façade-piercing interview.

1921 **Daniel J. Berrigan:** U.S. Roman Catholic priest, political activist, and poet. Convicted of destroying draft records in 1968 when he and his brother and fellow priest Philip protested the Vietnam War.

A revolution is interesting insofar as it avoids like the plague the plague it promised to heal.

1934 **Alan Bennett:** English stage and film actor, dramatist and screenwriter. First gained attention for the brilliant satirical work *Beyond the Fringe*, which he cowrote and performed with Dudley Moore. His stage plays include *Forty Years On*, *Habeas Corpus*, *The Old Country* and *The Madness of King George*. Wrote the screenplay for *Prick Up Your Ears*.

Children always assume the sexual lives of their parents come to a grinding halt at their conception.

1936 **Glenda Jackson:** British actress and politician. Appeared on the British stage as the mad Charlotte Corday in Peter Brook's production of *Marat/Sade*. Famous for her tense portrayals of complex women, Won Academy Awards for Best Actress for her performances in *Women In Love* and *A Touch of Class*. In 1992 she won a seat in the House of Commons.

When I have to cry, I think about my love life. When I have to laugh, I think about my love life.

1949 **Billy Joel:** American pianist, singer, and songwriter. Struggled for years, working in small bands and cocktail lounges. Wrote "Piano Man" about his experiences playing piano in a sleazy L.A. lounge, which became an "over night" success. Other Hits: "It's Still Rock and Roll to Me," "Tell Her About It," "Uptown Girl" and "We Didn't Start the Fire." Won Grammy's Legends Award.

If you are not doing what you love, you are wasting your time.

OTHERS: 1783 Canadian fur trader **Alexander Ross**, 1785 U.S. meteorologist **James Pollard Espy**, 1837 German car manufacturer **Adam Opel**, 1843 Confederate spy **Belle Boyd**, 1873 Manager of Old Vic & Sadler's Wells Theater **Lillian M. Baylis**, 1910 Dog training expert **Barbara Woodhouse**, 1911 U.S. choral director **Harry Simeone**, 1914 Canadian-born country singer **Hank Snow**, 1918 U.S. Secretary of Agriculture **Orville Freeman**, 1927 German physicist **Manfred Eigen**, 1928 U.S. tennis player **"Pancho" Gonzalez**, 1928 Canadian figure skater **Barbara Ann Scott**, 1936 British actor **Albert Finney**, 1942 U.S. Senator/Attorney General **John Ashcroft**, 1946 U.S. actress **Candice Bergen**

May 10

1727 **Anne-Robert-Jacques Turgot:** French economist and minister of finance, trade and public works. Attempted to reform the most stifling of government economic policies. His most important work, *Reflections on the Production and Distribution of Wealth*, predated Adam Smith's *The Wealth of Nations* by six years. Turgot recognized the function of the division of labor. Pointed out that capital was necessary to economic growth and the only way to accumulate capital was not to consume all that had been produced.

The expenses of government, having for their objective the interest of all, should be borne by everyone, and the more a man enjoys the advantages of society, the more he ought to hold himself honored in contributing to those expenses.

1760 **Claude Joseph Rouget de Lisle:** French army officer. Wrote words and music of French national anthem "La Marseillaise" while stationed as captain of engineers at Strasbourg in 1792. The piece was originally named "Chant de guerre de l'armée du Rhin" (War Song of the Rhine Army). Became known by its more familiar title when it was sung by volunteers from Marseilles during the French Revolution.

Allons, enfants de la patrie,/ Le jour, de gloire est arrivé! ... / Aux armes, citoyens!/ Formez vos bataillons!/ Marchons! Marchons! Qu'un sang impur/ abreuve nos sillons!

1838 **John Wilkes Booth:** American actor and presidential assassin. A member of a notable theatrical family. Achieved success in Shakespearean roles but resented the greater fame of his brother Edwin Booth. A fanatical believer in slavery and the Southern cause, John Wilkes Booth shot Abraham Lincoln as he was watching a performance at Ford's Theater. During his escape, he broke his leg. Tracked down by federal troops, he refused to surrender and was either shot and killed by a soldier's bullet or his own.

I have too great a soul to die like a criminal.

1838 **James Bryce:** British jurist, politician, diplomat and historian. Irish secretary (1905–7). Ambassador to U.S. (1907–13). Took an active interest in university reform. Wrote the prize essay "The Holy Roman Empire."

No wonder that, when a political career is so precarious, men of worth and capacity hesitate to embrace it. They cannot afford to be thrown out of their life's course by a mere accident.

1850 Sir **Thomas Lipton:** British merchant who built the Lipton tea empire. A small Glasgow grocery owner started the Thomas J. Lipton Co. Ran his own tea, coffee and cocoa plantations in Ceylon, as well as fruit farms, jam factories and bakeries, to produce inexpensive products for his shops. A multimillionaire by age 40. A keen yachtsman, he made five unsuccessful attempts to win yachting's America's Cup, earning the title of "the world's best loser." As he had no heirs, he left most of his fortune to the city of Glasgow to aid the poor and build hospitals.

The man who on his trade relies/ Must either bust or advertise.

1886 **Karl Barth:** Swiss theologian. One of the most influential theologians of the 20th century. Developed a "theology of the word of God." Led church opposition against Hitler and the Third Reich. Works include *Knowledge of God and the Service of God* and *Church Dogmatics*.

Men have never been good, they are not good and they never will be good.

1878 **Gustav Stresemann:** German chancellor and 1926 Nobel Peace Prize winner. The most exceptional political figure of his time. Held values of liberalism and nationalism, which enabled him to adjust to defeat and revolution. Believed that the Weimar Republic was the only basis on which Germans could unite and European cooperation was the only way to avoid a new war. His early death in 1929 was the beginning of the end of the Republic. As the only clear alternative to the Nazis, Hitler was the beneficiary of his death.

Sometimes you think you hear the voice of Almighty God, and it is only that of a Privy Councellor.

1899 **Fred Astaire:** Premiere American film dancer. Danced with his sister Adele on Broadway before becoming a movie star when RKO teamed him with Ginger Rogers for a series of thirties' delights. Films: *The Gay Divorcee, Top Hat, Swing Time, Easter Parade, The Band Wagon* and *Funny Face*. Received an Oscar nomination for a non-dancing role in *The Towering Inferno*.

The search for what you want is like tracking something that doesn't want to be tracked. It takes time to get a dance right, to create something memorable.

1902 **David O. Selznick:** American independent Hollywood producer. Founded his own company, Selznick International which produced quality films including: *Gone with the Wind, Rebecca, Since You Went Away, Duel in the Sun* and *Portrait of Jennie*.

There are only two classes—first class and no class.

1910 **Eric Berne:** Canadian-born U.S. psychiatrist and author. Best known as the creator of Transactional analysis. Interpreted relationships to three ego-states of the individuals involved in the parent, adult and child states. Berne called the interpersonal interactions of individuals, *transactions,* and certain patterns of transactions that occurred repeatedly in everyday life, *games.* His most successful work was the best-selling *Games People Play: the Psychology of Human Relations.*

Games are a compromise between intimacy and keeping intimacy away.

1919 **Ella T. Grasso:** American politician. Won her first election in 1952 to the General Assembly of the state of Connecticut and never lost an election thereafter. Served as Secretary of State, two terms in the U.S. Congress and was elected Governor of Connecticut in 1974, becoming the first woman elected governor in the U.S. in her own right. Resigned in 1980 because of poor health and died the next year.

It is not enough to profess faith in the democratic process; we must do something about it.

1960 **Bono:** Stage name of **Paul David Hewson,** lead singer of the Irish rock band, U2. Having appeared in Band Aid and Live Aid concerts, Bono increasingly campaigned for third-world debt relief and the plight of Africa. Formed an organization named "DATA," which stands for Debt, AIDS, Trade in Africa. In 2005, Bono was named as one of *Time* magazines' Persons of the Year, along with Bill and Melinda Gates.

It's an amazing thing to think that ours is the first generation in history that really can end extreme poverty, the kind that means a child dies for lack of food in its belly. That should be seen as the most incredible, historic opportunity but instead it's become a millstone around our necks. We let our pathetic excuses about how it's "difficulty" justifies our own inaction. Be honest. We have the science, the technology, and the wealth. What we don't have is the will, and that's not a reason that history will accept.

OTHERS: 1788 French optics pioneer **Augustin-Jean Fresnel**, 1830 French physicist **François M. Raoult**, 1843 Spanish novelist **Benito Pérez Galdós**, 1885 American actress **Mae Murray**, 1886 British religious sci-fi writer **Olaf Stapledon**, 1888 Austrian-born composer **Max Steiner**, 1899 Russian-born U.S. composer **Dmitri Tiomkin**, 1908 U.S. Speaker of the House **Carl Albert**, 1909 British union leader **Lord Harold Collison**, 1910 U.S. pro golfer **Jimmy Demaret**, 1916 U.S. mathematician/composer **Milton Babbitt**, 1921 U.S. comedian **Nancy Walker**, 1930 U.S. football player/sportscaster **Pat Summerall**, 1933 Romance writer **Barbara Taylor Bradford**, 1955 Murderer of John Lennon **Mark David Chapman**

May 11

1766 **Isaac D'Israeli:** English man of letters. Father of British statesman Benjamin Disraeli. Forte was literary illustrations of persons and history. Works: *Curiosities of Literature* and *Calamities of Authors.*

Education, however indispensable in a cultivated age, produces nothing on the side of genius. When education ends, genius often begins.

1888 **Irving Berlin:** Born **Israel Baline**. Russian-born American composer, lyricist. Could only play the piano in one key, but found a way to write more than 1000 songs and scores of Broadway musicals, including, "Alexander's Ragtime Band," "What'll I Do," "All Alone," "White Christmas," "God Bless America," "Easter Parade" and "Blue Skies." Died at the age of 101.

We depend largely on tricks, we writers of songs. There is no such thing as a new melody.

1894 **Martha Graham:** American dancer, teacher, choreographer of modern dance. Primary influence on the development of the modern dance in the U.S. Founder and artistic director of Martha Graham School of Contemporary Dance (1927). Choreographed more than 150 works.

Dance is the hidden language of the body of the soul. The body never lies.

1891 **Henry "Hans" Morgenthau, Jr.:** American public official. Editor of *American Agriculturist.* Served as Secretary of the Treasury in his close friend Franklin D. Roosevelt's cabinet. As such he was responsible for financing the New Deal programs and the expenditures of World War II. After Roosevelt's death, he retired to his farm.

Man is a political animal by nature; he is a scientist by chance or choice; he is a moralist because he is a man.

1892 Dame **Margaret Rutherford:** Delightful British character actress. Began her long thespian career as a student at London's Old Vic, debuting on stage in 1925. Appeared in more than 40 films, usually charmingly as scene-stealing audacious spinsters and slightly daft dowagers, she is most remembered for two roles created for her, Agatha Christie's indomitable sleuth, Jane Marple, and Madame Arcati, the fake psychic in Noel Coward's *Blithe Spirit*. Won an Academy Award for her supporting role in *The V.I.P.s*.

You never have a comedian who hasn't got a very deep strain of sadness within him or her. One thing is incidental on the other. Every great clown has been very near to tragedy.

1895 **Jiddu Krishnamurti:** Indian spiritual leader and theosophist. Raised and educated within the world-wide organization of Theosophical Society by Annie Besant, who believed him to be the prophesied "World Teacher," a messiah-like figure who was to bring about world enlightenment. He disavowed this destiny and dissolved the Order established to support it. Spent his life traveling throughout the world giving lectures on the subject of peace and awareness. His desire, he avowed was to set people free, a goal that could only be achieved through unflinching self-awareness.

The description is not the described. I can describe the mountain, but the description is not the mountain, and if you are caught up in the description, as most people are, then you will never see the mountain.

1895 **William Grant Still:** African-American musician and composer. Studied medicine at Wilberforce University but eventually dropped out. By this time his primary instrument was the oboe. His musical works included African American themes and spanned jazz, popular, opera, and classical genres. He wrote five operas, four symphonies, three ballets, chamber and choral music and orchestral pieces.

I knew I wanted to write a symphony; I knew that it had to be an American work; and I wanted to demonstrate how the blues, so often considered a lowly expression, could be elevated to the highest musical level.

1904 **Salvador Dalí:** Spanish painter, etcher. Disciple of surrealism. Experimented with pointillism, scientific cubism, futurism and constructivism. Most famous painting: *The Persistence of Memory*, limp, melting watches sagging over cliffs and leafless trees. Speaking of himself:

Dali was a Renaissance man converted to psychoanalysis.

1911 **Phil Silvers:** Born **Philip Silverman**. American vaudeville, movie and television fast-talking comic actor. Joined Gus Edwards' famous children's vaudeville troupe as a boy soprano when he was 12. Star of Broadway's *Top Banana*, repeating his success in film version. Enormously popular in television series, "You'll Never Get Rich" (1955–59) as Sgt. Bilko.

Sunday brunch at Mr. Mayer's beach house was like an audience in the Vatican. Of course, it wasn't His Highness' ring you kissed.

1918 **Richard Feynman:** American physicist. Helped develop the atomic bomb. Greatly expanded the theory of quantum electrodynamics. Received the Nobel Prize in Physics for 1965. An influential popularizer of physics through his books and his lectures, which included *There's Plenty of Room at the Bottom* and *Surely You're Joking Mr. Feynman*. A member of the commission investigating the 1986 Challenger Space Shuttle disaster conducted an experiment before a nationally televised audience, dunking a piece of the rocket booster's rubber O-ring gasket into a cup of ice water. As a result he quickly showed that it lost all resiliencies at low temperatures, thus demonstrating the physics of the disaster that allowed rocket exhaust to burn a hole in the shuttle.

What does it mean, to understand? ... I don't know. What I can't create, I do not understand.

1927 **Mort Sahl:** Canadian comedian, satirist, and iconoclast. Popular in fifties with the liberals by making fun of the conservatives. His fans were less amused when John F. Kennedy became president and Sahl continued to fire his zingers at those in power.

Liberals feel unworthy of their possessions. Conservatives feel they deserve everything they've stolen.

1933 **Louis Farrakhan:** Originally named **Louis Eugene Walcott**. African-American religious leader. Joined the Black Muslims in 1955 and became an assistant of Malcolm X. When Farrakhan converted to Sunni Islam, the two became enemies. Farrakhan formed the Nation of Islam in 1978. Known for his forceful speeches calling for racial separatism, his anti-Semitism and conspiracy theories. Was the main organizer of the Million Man March in Washington in 1995.

Without an advocate for the poor, without a new state of mind in America, the country lies on the brink of anarchy.

OTHERS: 1654 Dutch historian **Cornelis van Alkemade**, 1811 Chinese Siamese twins **Chang & Eng Bunker**, 1854 U.S. inventor **Ottmar Mergenthaler**, 1855 Russian composer **Anatol K. Lyadov**, 1894 Dutch Nazi leader **Anton A. Mussert**, 1901 U.S. author **Mari Sandoz**, 1902 Brazilian soprano **Bidú Sayao**, 1906 Pioneer American aviatrix **Jacqueline Cochran**, 1912 U.S. comedian **Foster Brooks**, 1927 U.S. sci-fi writer **Zilpha Keatly Snyder**, 1928 Israeli sculptor **Yaacov Agam**, 1932 Italian fashion designer **Valentino**, 1947 U.S. futurist/trend forecaster **Faith Popcorn**, 1961 Filipino pianist **Cecile Licad**, 1963 English actress **Natasha Richardson**

May 12

1765 **Emma, Lady Hamilton:** One of the world's great beauties, which can be seen in the many portraits of her by contemporary artists, especially George Romney. Born Emma Lyon, she had a good nature, great charm and sexuality, and a remarkable life. At 16 she went to live in the house of a "procurer and abbess of a brothel." Had a number of affairs, entertaining her lovers' friends by dancing naked on a table. Became the mistress of Charles Greville, eventually marrying his elderly uncle Sir William Hamilton. Entered into a long-time affair with married Lord Nelson. On hearing of Nelson's death at the Battle of Trafalgar she wrote to a friend:

My heart broken and my head consequently weak ... I tell you truly—I am gone nor do I want to live. He that I loved more than life is gone. I feel and hope that I shall not be long after him ... in his grave all my happiness is buried.

1812 **Edward Lear:** English landscape painter and writer. Known for popularizing limericks and nonsense verse, including his best-known set of verses, "The Owl and the Pussycat." Also published volumes of bird and animal drawings, and seven illustrated travel books.

They dined on mince, and slices of quince,/ Which they ate with a runcible spoon;/ And hand in hand, on the edge of the sand,/ They danced by the light of the moon.

1820 **Florence Nightingale:** "Lady with the Lamp." English nurse and hospital reformer. Headed team of nurses who tended to the wounded in Crimean War. Founded the Nightingale School and Home for Nurses. Labored all her life for establishment of more nursing schools.

The very first requirement in a hospital is that it should do the sick no harm.

1828 **Dante Gabriel Rossetti:** English poet and painter. Driving force of Pre-Raphaelite Brotherhood. Wrote lyric poems, distinguished by mysticism and fantasy. Paintings: *The Girlhood of Mary Virgin* and *Ecce Ancilla Domini*. Poems: "The Blessed Damozel" and "My Sister's Sleep."

Love is the last relay and ultimate outposts of eternity.

1850 **Henry Cabot Lodge:** American politician and historian. Represented Massachusetts as a congressman from 1887 to 1893 and as a senator from 1893 to 1924. As chairman of the Senate Foreign Relations Committee he led the successful fight against American participation in the League of Nations, arguing that membership would threaten United States sovereignty.

I would rather see the United States respected than loved by other nations.

1888 **Theodor Reik:** Austrian-born U.S. psychoanalyst and author. Emphasized the role of intuition in treatment, diverging from orthodox Freudian views. Books: *Listening with the Third Ear* and *Curiosities of the Self.*

We are all in a race for dear life: that is to say, we are fugitives from death.

1889 **Otto Frank:** German-born Father of Ann Frank. He moved his family to The Netherlands from Germany to escape the Nazi anti–Jewish decrees. In July 1942, he took his family, consisting of his wife Edith and two daughters Margot and Anne, into hiding in the upper rear rooms of a building in Amsterdam. They were eventually joined by four other Jews. They were concealed for two years with the aid of Franks' colleagues, until they were betrayed by an anonymous informant. All were sent to concentration camps, with only Otto surviving. After the war he was given Anne's diaries and papers that had been found in their ransacked hiding place. The first Dutch edition of *The Diary of Anne Frank* was published in 1947.

How could I have known how much it meant for her to see a patch of blue sky, to observe the flying seagulls, or how important that chestnut tree was to her, when she had never shown an interest in nature before. But once she felt like a caged bird, how she longed for it. Even just the thought of the open air gave her comfort, but she kept all these feelings to herself.

1909 **Katharine Hepburn:** Four-time Oscar winning American actress with eight additional nominations. Nominated for five Emmys, winning for *Love Among the Ruins*. Also nominated for two Tony awards. Among her best films: *A Bill of Divorcement*, *Alice Adams*, *Bringing Up Baby*, *The Philadelphia Story*, *Woman of the Year*, *Adam's Rib*, *The African Queen*, *Long Day's Journey Into Night*, *The Lion in Winter* and *On Golden Pond*. Maintained a longtime romance and friendship with married Spencer Tracy. In 1999, the American Film Institute ranked her as the greatest actress of all time.

Plain women know more about men than beautiful ones do. But beautiful women don't need to know about men. It's the men who have to know about beautiful women.

1915 **Mary Kay Ash:** American cosmetics executive. Founder and Chairman Emeritus of Mary Kay Cosmetics. Stressed positive attitude of the representatives who sold her products in cosmetic parties.

If you think you can, you can. And if you think you can't, you're right.

1918 **Julius Rosenberg:** American communist, who along with his wife Ethel were tried, convicted, and executed for spying for the Soviet Union. Decades later, decrypted Soviet communications indicated that Julius was involved in espionage, although no evidenced of particular acts of espionage or any involvement by Ethel was provided. His last words:

We are innocent. That is the whole truth. To forsake this truth is to pay too high a price even for the priceless gift of life. For life thus purchased we could not live out in dignity.

1925 **Lawrence "Yogi" Berra:** Joined the New York Yankees as catcher-outfielder (1947). At the end of 17 years, he had hit 358 HRs. Appeared in the most World Series games (75). MVP (1951, 1954, 1955). Elected to Hall of Fame (1972). Managed Yankees and New York

Mets to pennants. Famous for his wacky observations, including:

This is like déjà vu all over again.— You can observe a lot just by watching.— Baseball is ninety percent mental. The other half is physical.— Nobody goes there anymore because it's too crowded.— I don't want to make the wrong mistake.

1925 **John Simon:** Serbian-American literary, theater and film critic. Was theater critic at *New York* magazine for 36 years. Also has made regular contributions to *The New Leader*, *The New Criterion*, and *National Review*. Some suggest that his acerbic and even cruel descriptions of actors are due to the horrific things he must have seen as a teenager in Yugoslavia during World War II. Time magazine referred to him as "Count Dracula of Schubert Alley."

Miss Garland's figure resembles the giant-economy-size tube of toothpaste in girls' bathrooms: Squeezed intemperately at all points, it acquires a shape that defies definition by the most resourceful solid geometrician.

1937 **George Carlin:** Grammy-winning American stand-up comedian, actor and author. His most famous skits when he appeared on TV variety shows included the stupid disk jockey from "Wonderful WINO" and the hippie-dippie weatherman, Al Sleet. Noted for his irreverent attitude and his observations on language, especially his best-known routine "Seven Words You Can Never Say on Television."

I think we're already circling the drain as a species, and I'd love to see the circles get a little faster and a little shorter

OTHERS: 1670 King of Poland **August II**, 1754 Composer **Franz Anton Hoffmeister**, 1842 French composer **Jules Massenet**, 1868 U.S. publisher **Halsey William Wilson**, 1880 U.S. artic explorer **Lincoln Ellsworth**, 1903 English actor **Wilfrid Hyde-White**, 1907 English/U.S. detective writer **Leslie Charteris**, 1910 U.S. orchestra leader **Gordon Jenkins**, 1914 U.S. TV newsman **Howard K. Smith**, 1923 English biscuit manufacturer **Lord Laing**, 1929 U.S. songwriter **Burt Bacharach**, 1930 U.S. platform springboard diver **Pat McCormick-Keller**, 1933 Soviet poet **Andrei Voznesensky**, 1936 U.S. newscaster **Tom Snyder**, 1939 Nixon's press secretary **Ron Ziegler**, 1943 English rock singer **Billy Swan**

May 13

1792 Pope **Pius IX:** Italian pope with the longest papacy (1846–78). Convened First Vatican Council. Defined dogma of Immaculate Conception. In his encyclical *Quanta Cura*, He distinguished between individual licentiousness and the rights and liberties proper to the Catholic Church.

... kingdoms rest upon the foundation of the Catholic faith, and that nothing is so deadly, nothing so certain to engender every ill, nothing so exposed to danger, as for men to believe that they stand in need of nothing else than the free will which we received at birth, if we ask nothing further from the Lord; that is to say, if forgetting our Author, we abjure His power to show that we are free.

1813 **John Sullivan Dwight:** U.S. music critic, editor, and author. Member of the Transcendental Club and Brook Farm. Founder and editor *Dwight's Journal of Music*.

The Bible is a window in this prison of hope, through which we look into eternity.

1840 **Alphonse Daudet:** French novelist and short-story writer. Wrote humorous stories of provincial and Parisian life, "Letters from My Mill" and "Tartarin de Tarascon." His novels included *The Nabob* and *Sappho*.

Hatred— The anger of the weak.

1842 Sir **Arthur Sullivan:** British composer best known for his operatic collaborations and turbulent partnership with librettist William S. Gilbert and producer Richard D'Oyly Carte, producing thirteen operettas over a period of twenty years. The most successful were *HMS Pinafore*, *The Pirates of Penzance* and *The Mikado*. Sullivan's other compositions included the overture *In Memoriam*, the oratorio *The Prodigal Son*, the hymn "Onward, Christian Soldiers" and the song "The Lost Chord."

I am terrified at the thought that so much hideous and bad music will be put on records forever.

1856 **Peter Henry Emerson:** Cuban-born English physician, scientist, and photographer. Preferred photographing rural subjects displayed in a simplistic manner. In his book *Naturalistic Photography*, he argued that pictures should imitate nature rather than alter it. This was a departure from the then current practice in which the objective of photographers was to get everything sharp.

Photograph people as they really are— do not dress them up... The photographic technique is perfect and needs no ... bungling.

1882 **Georges Braque:** French painter, sculptor, stage, book and glass designer. Principle founder of modern art. With Picasso, developed cubism. Known for collage techniques, still lifes featuring geometrical shapes and low-key color harmonies. The first living artist to have his paintings exhibited in the Louvre. Paintings: *The Port of La Ciotat* and *The Black Birds*.

Art is made to disturb. Science reassures.

1907 Dame **Daphne du Maurier:** English novelist. Granddaughter of British caricaturist and novelist George du Maurier. Works of melodrama, period romances, Cornish settings and history. Novels: *Rebecca*, *Jamaica Inn*, Frenchman's *Creek* and *My Cousin Rachel*.

Writers should be read, but neither seen nor heard.

1914 **Joe Louis:** African-American boxer. Nicknamed "The Brown Bomber." World heavyweight champion (1937–49), the longest reign in division history. Professional record, 63–3 with 49 KOs. Defeated six previous or subsequent champions: Max Baer, Jack Sharkey, James J. Braddock, Max Schmeling, and Jersey Joe Walcott.

Once that bell rings you're on your own. It's just you and the other guy.

1923 **Beatrice Arthur:** Emmy-winning American actress and comedienne. Best known for her roles in the sitcoms *Maude* and *The Golden Girls*. Stage roles in *Threepenny Opera*, *Fiddler on the Roof* and her Tony-winning performance in *Mame*. Noted for her distinctive deep voice, acid wit, and near 5 ft. 10 in. height.

All this time I've just wanted to be blond, beautiful — and five feet two inches tall.

1927 **Clive Barnes:** English writer, journalist, TV producer, commentator and lecturer. Dance and theater critic for the *New York Post* and senior consulting editor of *Dance Magazine*. Author of *Inside American Ballet Theater*, *Best American Plays* and *Nureyev*. Made a Commander of the British Empire in 1975.

Television is the first truly democratic culture — the first culture available to everybody and entirely governed by what the people want. The most terrifying thing is what people do want.

1931 **Jim Jones:** Controversial preacher and religious cult leader. Established the evangelical group The People's Temple. Set up an agricultural commune of Jonestown in Guyana in 1977. An investigating committee arrived to look into charges that Jones used threats and manipulation to control his followers. Its leader Congressman Leo Ryan and four members of his party were murdered. Jones ordered more than 900 followers, many of them children, to drink a cyanide-laced drink. Jones died of a self-inflicted gunshot wound.

To me death is not a fearful thing. It's living that's cursed.

1950 **Stevie Wonder:** Blind African-American singer, songwriter, multi-instrumental artist, and producer. Winner of 17 Grammy awards. Inducted into Rock 'n' Roll Hall of Fame (1989). Hits: "For Once in My Life," "You Are the Sunshine of My Life," and "I Just Called to Say I Love You." Has spoken out against nuclear war, worked to end apartheid in South Africa, and raised funs for his eye-disease facility, Wonderland.

Just because a man lacks the use of his eyes doesn't mean he lacks vision.

OTHERS: 1717 Empress of Austria **Maria Theresa**, 1729 American glassmaker **Henry Stiegel**, 1769 King of Portugal **Joâo VI**, 1828 English social reformer **Josephine Butler**, 1857 English pathologist **Ronald Ross**, 1891 German actor **Fritz Rasp**, 1907 Archaeologist **Laurence Kirwan**, 1913 President of Liberia **William R. Tolbert**, 1937 Sci-fi author **Roger Zelazny**, 1939 U.S. actor **Harvey Keitel**, 1941 U.S. newspaper publisher **Marshall Field V**, 1941 U.S. singer **Ritchie Valens**, 1942 Jazz guitarist **Jim Douglas**, 1943 U.S. singer **Mary Wells**, 1946 Rock bassist **Danny Klein**, 1950 English singer **Peter Gabriel**, 1956 Vocalist **Darius Rucker**, 1961 Basketball player **Dennis Rodman**

May 14

1686 **Daniel Gabriel Fahrenheit:** German physicist and instrument maker. Made important improvements in the construction of thermometers, first using alcohol and later mercury. Introduced the thermometric scale known by his name, by setting zero at the freezing point of an equal mixture of ice and salt.

Pure water while freezing in the presence of pure ice always gives the same reading.

1727 **Thomas Gainsborough:** English landscape painter and fashionable portraitist. Developed an elegant formal portrait style inspired by Anthony Van Dyck. Painted landscapes for his own pleasure. Most famous painting is *Blue Boy*. His great landscapes include *The Harvest Wagon* and *The Watering Place*. His attributed last words:

We are all going to heaven, and Van Dyck is of the company.

1771 **Robert Owen:** Welsh factory owner, philanthropist whose ideas presaged socialism. In partnership with Jeremy Bentham, established innovative social and welfare programs. Sponsored several experimental utopian communities of "Owenites" in Britain and the U.S. Strongly supported early labor unions. In *A New View of Society*, he maintained that character is wholly formed in one's environment.

All the world old is queer save thee and me, and even thou art a little queer.

1880 **B.C. [Robert Charles] "Bertie" Forbes:** Scottish-born American journalist, publisher and writer. Founder, publisher and editor of the business and finance magazine bearing his name. His motto: "Information means money." His son Malcolm S. Forbes took over the foundering publishing empire, and turned into a success. He was followed by his four sons, most notably Malcolm Jr., who unsuccessfully ran for a presidential nomination in 1996 and 2000.

Books are like a mirror. If an ass looks in, you can't expect an angel to look out.

1900 **Hal Borland:** American naturalist and historical writer. Wrote "outdoor editorials" for the Sunday *New York Times* from 1941 until shortly before his death in 1978. Author of thirty-one books and a contributing editor to *Audubon Magazine*. His outdoor books are essays following the seasons through the year. They include *An American Year*, *Hill Country Harvest*, *Sundial of the Seasons*, and *Seasons*.

No winter lasts forever; no spring skips its turn.

1925 **Patrice Munsel:** "Princess Pat" also known as "Baby Diva." American operatic singer. At 18 the youngest singer ever accepted at the New York Met. Also appeared in films and Broadway musicals.

It thrills me no end when my own age group bursts out in whistles and cheers. Yet there is nothing in the world to compare with the feeling I get when I hear the "bravos" of that wonderful Metropolitan audience.

1929 **Gump Worsley:** Canadian hall-of-fame hockey goalie with the New York Rangers, Montreal Canadians, and Minneapolis North Stars. Calder Memorial Trophy winner and twice awarded the Vezina Trophy. When some goalies began wearing masks in the NHL, he refused to do, explaining:

Anyone who wears one is chicken. My face is my mask.

1936 **Bobby Darin:** American singer, pianist, guitarist, and actor. Ubiquitous presence in pop entertainment in the late 1950s and 60s. Oscar nominated for film *Captain Newman M.D.* Song hits: "Splish Splash," "Mack the Knife," and "Beyond the Sea." Died of heart failure, which occurred during his second open-heart surgery.

Conceit is thinking you're great; egotism is knowing it.

1944 **George Lucas:** American director, writer, and producer. Heads Lucasfilms. Formed Industrial Light and Magic special effects company. Directed the epic *Star Wars* and *American Graffiti*. Produced *The Empire Strikes Back, The Return of the Jedi* and *Indiana Jones* films. Returned to directing with the first *Star Wars* prequel *The Phantom Menace.*

The secret to film is that it's an illusion.

1952 **David Byrne:** Scottish-born American rock musician, composer and producer. Lead singer and guitarist with new wave rock group "Talking Heads." Biggest hit: "Burning Down the House." The group's releases reflected his interest in experimental pop and African rhythms.

To shake your rump is to be environmentally aware.

1969 **Cate Blanchett:** Australian actress. First person to win the Critics Circle Theatre award for Best Newcomer and Lead Actress in the same year for her performance in David Mamet's *Oleanna*. Nominated for an Oscar for her performance in the title character in *Elizabeth*, appeared in the *Lord of the Rings* trilogy as the Elf Queen, and won an Academy Award for her impersonation of Kate Hepburn in *The Aviator.*

If you know you are going to fail, then fail gloriously.

1971 **Sofia Coppola:** American director, actress, producer, and screenwriter. First American woman nominated for an Academy Award for Directing for *Lost in Translation*, winning an Oscar for its screenplay. Acting career was essentially finished when her performance in *The Godfather Part III* was heavily criticized. Cast by her father, director Francis Ford Coppola, for the role at the last moment when Winona Ryder fell ill. Niece of Talia Shire and cousin of Nicolas Cage and Jason Schwartzman.

Everyone in my family is in the film business; I knew I wanted to be creative and it was very important in my family to be artistic.

OTHERS: 1679 Dutch astronomer **Peder Horrebow**, 1781 German historian **Friedrich von Raumer**, 1867 German premier of revolutionary Bavaria **Kurt Eisner**, 1870 U.S. designer of fine books **Bruce Rogers**, 1881 Vaudeville female impersonator **Julian Eltinge**, 1885 German conductor **Otto Klemperer**, 1905 French social philosopher **Raymond Aron**, 1907 General/premier/president of Pakistan **Mohammad Ayub Khan**, 1909 International Chess Master **Vladimir Alatortsev**, 1917 U.S. bandleader **Norman Luboff**, 1926 British comedian **Eric Morecambe**, 1937 Baseball manager **Dick Howser**, 1943 Congressman Wilbur Mills' mistress **Elizabeth Ray**, 1961 English actor **Tim Roth**

May 15

1773 Prince **Clemens Von Metternich:** Chancellor of Austria (1809–48). His reactionary policies dominated Europe from the Congress of Vienna (1814–15) to the revolutions of 1848. Helped promote the marriage of Napoleon and Marie-Louise, the daughter of Emperor Francis I. By diplomacy and deceit, kept Austria neutral in the war between France and Russia. Forced to resign he fled to England and retired to his castle on the Rhine in 1851.

It is useless to close the gates against ideas; they overleap them.

1803 **Edward George Bulwer-Lytton, Lord Lytton:** British politician, literary patron, novelist and dramatist. His enormous outputs of works, very popular in his day, are all but forgotten today. Works: *The Last Days of Pompeii* (3 volumes), *Harold, the Last of the Saxon Kings*, and *King Arthur*. The opening lines of his novel *Paul Clifford*, "It was a dark and stormy night..." has led to an annual fiction prize for the most overwritten first sentence in a hypothetical novel.

Nothing is so contagious as enthusiasm; it moves stones, it charms brutes. Enthusiasm is the genius of sincerity, and truth accomplishes no victories without it.

1856 **L. (Lyman) Frank Baum:** American writer of children's books. Gained commercial success with his first book. *Father Goose*. Best known for creating the marvelous characters of a series of 14 books, beginning with the *Wonderful Wizard of Oz*. Ruth Plumly Thompson continued the series after Baum's death.

I have a feeling we're not in Kansas anymore.

1862 **Arthur Schnitzler:** Austrian playwright and novelist. Practiced medicine throughout his life. Known for psychological dramas and the exotic lives of his characters. Plays: *Anatol, Merry-Go-Round*, and *Playing with Love*. Most successful novel *None But the Brave*.

Tolerance means excusing the mistake of others. Tact means not noticing them.

1894 **Katherine Anne Porter:** American short-story writer, novelist. Her best known work is her only novel *Ship of Fools*, which received both a Pulitzer Prize and a National Book Award. Also wrote collections of stories: *Flowering Judas, Pale Horse, Pale Rider*, a set of three novellas, and the Pulitzer Prize winning *Collected Short Stories*.

The real sin against life is to abuse and destroy

beauty, even one's own — even more, one's own, for that had been put in our care and we are responsible for its well-being.

1902 **Richard J. Daley:** American political boss, mayor of Chicago (1955–76). Noted for making the Windy City run using an effective political machine and his mishandling of the protests at the Democratic National Convention (1968). Sometimes the mayor stumbled over saying what he meant.

The police are not here to create disorder; they're here to preserve disorder.

1904 **Clifton Fadiman:** American literary critic and author. Editor at Simon and Schuster (1929–35). Book editor of *The New Yorker* (1933–43). MC for radio program "Information Please" (1938–48).

When you travel, remember that a foreign country is not designed to make you comfortable. It is designed to make its own people comfortable.

1911 **Max Frisch:** Swiss dramatist and novelist. Began as a journalist and worked as an architect until 1955. Noted for his expressionist depictions of the moral dilemmas of modern life. Plays: *Santa Cruz, The Chinese Wall,* and *Andorra*: Novels: *A Wilderness of Mirrors* and *Man in the Holocene.*

It's precisely the disappointing stories, which have no proper ending and therefore no proper meaning, which sound true to life.

1915 **Paul A. Samuelson:** U.S. economist. Taught at MIT from 1940 until 1986. Famed for his widely used textbook, *Economics, An Introductory Analysis.* Basic theme is that the universal nature of consumer behavior is the key to economic theory. Has made important contributions to mathematical structure of economic theory. Nobel Prize (1970).

What we know about the global financial crisis is that we don't know very much.

1923 **Richard Avedon:** American photographer. From 1945 was a regular contributor to *Harper's Bazaar* and later was closely related with *Vogue.* Noted for strong black-and-white celebrity portraits and fashion photographs. Books include *Observations, Nothing Personal,* and *The Sixties.*

All photographs are accurate. None of them is truth.

1926 **Peter Shaffer:** British playwright. Wrote *Five Finger Exercise, Equus* and *Amadeus.* Wrote several novels in collaboration with his twin brother Anthony Shaffer, using the pseudonym Peter Anthony. Later plays include *The Gift of the Gorgon.*

Rehearsing a play is making the word flesh. Publishing a play is reversing the process.

1943 **David Cronenberg:** Canadian film director, screenwriter and actor. Began making horror films in 1970, many which became cult favorites, including *Scanners, The Dead Zone,* and *the Fly.* Later films included *Naked Lunch* and *M. Butterfly.*

Everybody's a mad scientist, and life is their lab. We're all trying to experiment to find a way to live, to solve problems, to fend off madness and chaos.

OTHERS: 1565 Master builder of Amsterdam **Henrick de Keyser**, 1845 Russian zoologist **Ilja Metsjnikov**, 1859 French physicist **Pierre Curie**, 1870 U.S. financial consultant **Henry Doherty**, 1889 Founder of Amalgamated Clothing Workers of America **Bessie Hillman**, 1891 Russian playwright **Mikhail Bulgakov**, 1894 French director **Jean Renoir**, 1905 U.S. actor **Joseph Cotten**, 1909 English actor **James Mason**, 1910 New York mayor **Robert F. Wagner**, 1918 U.S. country singer **Eddy Arnold**, 1927 English playwright **Anthony Shaffer**, 1937 Trinidad singer/guitarist **Trini Lopez**, 1940 U.S. basketball coach **Don Nelson**, 1953 Baseball player **George Brett**

May 16

1801 **William H. Seward:** U.S. politician and statesman. Secretary of state (1861–69) under Abraham Lincoln and Andrew Johnson. During the Civil War, he established a secret police force, which arrested thousands of citizens for disloyalty, that is, for disagreeing with Lincoln's war policies. Purchased Alaska from Russia for $7,200,000 in 1867, which at the time was proclaimed "Seward's Folly." The town of Seward and the Seward Peninsula, both in Alaska, are named for him.

Revolutions never go backward.

1832 **Philip D. Armour:** U.S. meat-packing executive. Introduced on-premise slaughtering and utilization of animal waste. First to use refrigerator cars to transport meat cross-country and to make canned meat products.

I like to turn bristles, blood, and the inside and outside of pigs and bullocks into revenue.

1881 **Anne O'Hare McCormick:** U.S. foreign correspondent with *New York Times* (1922–54). Member of the editorial board from 1936. First woman to receive Pulitzer Prize for foreign correspondence (1937). Wrote *The Hammer and the Scythe* (1928).

Today the real test of power is not capacity to make war but the capacity to prevent it.

1910 **Charles Luckman:** American architect and industrialist, acclaimed the "Boy Wonder of American Business," when named president of the Pepsodent toothpaste company at age thirty. Later he became president of Lever Brothers. Resigned to form an architectural firm, which designed the Prudential Center in Boston, the new Madison Garden in New York City, and the NASA Manned Spacecraft Center in Houston.

The trouble with America is that there are far too many wide-open spaces surrounded by teeth.

1912 **Studs [Louis] Terkel:** American radio personality and author. Got his nickname because he reminded people of James T. Farrell's fictional character Studs Lonigan. Blacklisted from TV in the 1950s for his leftist leanings, he worked at the same Chicago radio station for 45 years. His books focused on the history of the U.S.A., heavily relying on oral history. Works include: *Division Street: America, Hard Times, Working, The Good War* (Pulitzer Prize), *Race: What Blacks and Whites Think and Feel About the American Obsession,* and *Hope Dies Last: Keeping the Faith in Difficult Times.*

I think it's realistic to have hope. One can be a perverse idealist and say the easiest thing: "I despair. The world's no good." That's a perverse idealist. It's practical to hope, because the hope is for us to survive as a human species. That's very realistic.

1919 **[Wladziu Valentino] Liberace:** American pianist famous for giving concerts wearing flamboyant costumes and playing on ornate pianos holding candelabras. Highly successful playing primarily popular music, he hosted his own TV show, *The Liberace Show.* Appeared in films such as *Sincerely Yours.*

When the reviews are bad I tell my staff that they can join me as I cry all the way to the bank... You know that bank I used to cry all the way to? I bought it.

1928 **Billy Martin:** American baseball second baseman with four NY Yankees world champions in fifties. Five-time manager of Yankees, winning two pennants and a World Series. Also managed Minnesota, Detroit, Texas and Oakland.

When you're a professional you come back no matter what happened the day before.

1929 **John Conyers, Jr.:** African-American Democratic congressman from Michigan from 1961, the second longest serving member of the House of Representatives, only our ranked by his Michigan colleague, John Dingell. Only Judiciary Committee Member to serve on both the Watergate impeachment and the Clinton impeachment. Considered to be one of the most liberal members of Congress. Author of *Anatomy of an Undeclared War* (1972).

Many of us find it unacceptable to put our brave men and women in harm's way, based on false information.

1929 **Adrienne Cecile Rich:** American poet, scholar and critic. Her first volume of poems was *A Change of World.* Her growing involvement in the women's movement and a lesbian/feminist perspective politicized much of her later work. Her collection *Diving into the Wreck* and her nonfiction *Of Woman Born* both won National Book Awards.

Lying is done with words and also with silence.

1955 **Olga Korbut:** Belarus-born gymnast. First appeared in the 1969 championship at the age of 13. The diminutive athlete captivated the world at the Munich Olympics in 1972 with her charming smile and lithe grace. Won a gold medal as a member of the Soviet team, and also individual gold medals for the balance beam, on which she was the first person ever to do a backward somersault, and floor exercises, as well as silver for the parallel bars. After her retirement, she became a gymnastic coach.

Don't be afraid if things seem difficult in the beginning. That's only the initial impression. The important thing is not to retreat; you have to master yourself.

1957 **Joan Benoit Samuelson:** U.S. track and field runner. Twice won the Boston marathon. Winner of first women's Olympic marathon. Sullivan Award winner in 1985. Books: *Running Tide* and *Running for Women.*

I look at victory as milestones on a very long highway.

1966 **Janet Jackson:** African-American singer and actress. Youngest child of the Jackson music family, sister of Michael Jackson. Appeared on TV series *Good Times* and *Diff'rent Strokes.* Song Hits: "When I Think of You," "Miss You Much," "Love Will Never Do (Without You)" and "Someone to Call My Lover." Will be remembered for his costume malfunction at the halftime show of the 2004 Super Bowl.

I can't believe people got so upset at the sight of a single breast! America is so parochial, I may just have to move to Europe where they are more mature about things like that!

OTHERS: 1718 Italian mathematician **Maria Gaetana Agnesi**, 1804 Founder of 1st U.S. kindergarten **Elizabeth Palmer Peabody**, 1824 U.S. educator **Edmund Kirby-Smith**, 1866 U.S. sociologist **Ernest Watson Burgess**, 1892 Austrian/British tenor/conductor **Richard Tauber**, 1905 U.S. actor **Henry Fonda**, 1911 U.S. actress **Margaret Sullavan**, 1913 U.S. bandleader **Woody Herman**, 1924 President of Gambia **Dawada Kairaba Jawara**, 1931 Connecticut Senator/Governor **Lowell Weicker**, 1952 Irish actor **Pierce Brosnan**, 1955 U.S. actress **Debra Winger**, 1961 Sedanese tennis player **Yannick Noah**, 1970 Argentine tennis player **Gabriela Sabatini**

May 17

1749 **Edward Jenner:** English surgeon. Discovery of the smallpox vaccine. Taught the need of experimentation, he noticed that people who had been sick from the relatively harmless cowpox disease did not contract smallpox. His inoculations of people with cowpox greatly reduced the death rate from smallpox.

The joy I felt as the prospect before me of being the instrument destined to take away from the world one of the greatest calamities was so excessive that I found myself in a kind of reverie.

1805 **Robert Smith Surtees:** English sporting novelist. Passionately addicted to riding to hounds, most of his writings dealt with horses and riding. Creator of "Mr. John Jorrocks," a Cockney fox hunting London grocer. Editor of the *New Sporting Magazine* (1831–36).

More people are flattered into virtue than bullied out of vice.

1866 **Erik Satie:** Eccentric French café pianist before turning to composing after age 40.Wrote ballets, lyric dramas, and odd, witty and charming short piano pieces. Acknowledged as a forerunner of modern music.

Influenced and alienated his admirers Debussy, Ravel, and Les Six.

Why attack God? He may be as miserable as we are.

1875 **Joel E. Spingarn:** American critic, author, and educator. Professor of Comparative Literature at Columbia University. Founder of the publishing firm of Harcourt, Brace and Co. Literary works include *A History of Literary Criticism in the Renaissance.* One of the first Jewish leaders of the National Association for the Advancement of Colored People (NAACP). Chairman of the board from 1913 until his death. In 1913 established the Spingarn medal, an annual award recognizing outstanding achievement by an African-American in service to his race. Encouraged African-American writers during the Harlem Renaissance in the 1920s.

The army officials want the camp to fail. The last thing they want is to help colored men to become commissioned officers. The camp is intended to fight segregation, not encourage it.

1900 **Ayatollah Ruhollah Khomeini:** Born **Ruhollah Musawi.** Iranian religious and political leader. A Shiite Muslim who bitterly opposed the pro–Western regime of Shah Reza Pahlavi. Exiled from 1964 to 1979, Khomeini returned after the collapse of the Shah's government to be virtual head of a strict Muslim state. Condoned the seizure of 52 U.S. Embassy hostages in Teheran. Waged war on Iraq and blessed the execution of tens of thousands of Iranians.

Americans are the great Satan, the wounded snake.

1904 **Jean Gabin:** French film star of the period between the two World Wars. Specialized in playing tragic heroes. One of his most popular roles was Inspector Maigret. Other films: *The Lower Depths*, *Pepe le Moko*, *Grand Illusion*, *Napoleon* and *Les Misérables.* The child of music hall artists, he followed their lead, becoming a music hall and operetta star, playing leading man to the legendary actress Mistinguett. Speaking of his stage debut:

I understood immediately that to get success I had to make for the front door, not the back one. And the front door was the door of Mistinguett's dressing room.

1911 **Clark Kerr:** American educator and economist. Chancellor of the University of California (1952–58), president (1958–67). As he liked to say he was "fired with enthusiasm" by Governor Ronald Reagan. Chaired the Carnegie Commission on Higher Education (1967–73).

I find that the three major administrative problems on a campus are sex for the students, athletics for the alumni and parking for the faculty.

1911 **Maureen O'Sullivan:** Beautiful, demure brunette Irish-born actress. Mother of Mia Farrow with whom she appeared in *Hannah and Her Sisters.* Films included *The Barretts of Wimpole Street* and *Pride and Prejudice.* Best remembered for playing Jane to Johnny Weissmuller's Tarzan in the thirties series.

Cheetah bit me whenever he could. The apes were all homosexuals, eager to wrap their paws around Johnny Weissmuller's thighs. They were jealous of me and I loathed them.

1912 **Archibald Cox:** U.S. lawyer and professor. Named Watergate special prosecutor, and then fired by President Nixon in the "Saturday Night Massacre" when he rejected an administration compromise on disputed tapes. Wrote *The Warren Court and Role of the Supreme Court in American Government.*

Through the ages, men of law have been persistently concerned with the resolution of disputes in ways that enable society to achieve its goals with a minimum of force and maximum of reason.

1914 **Stewart Alsop:** American journalist. With his brother Joseph, wrote the informative and opinionated syndicated column "Matter of Fact." Editor of the *Saturday Evening Post* from 1958 to 1968. He wrote of battling a rare blood disease in *Stay of Execution.*

A dying man needs to die, as a sleepy man needs to sleep, and there comes a time when it is wrong, as well as useless, to resist... Death is, after all, the only universal experience except birth.

1918 **Birgit Nilsson:** Swedish opera singer, acclaimed as the greatest Wagnerian soprano of her time. Had a steely voice of exceptional power and stamina. From 1959 until her retirement in 1984 she was a popular figure at the Metropolitan Opera. When asked if she would object to additional stage seats added for one of her sold out concerts, she replied:

Sell everything ... and please don't forget the space on the piano lid.

1920 **Harriet Van Horne:** American newspaper columnist. Television and radio personality and critic at the *New York World-Telegram* and its successors the *World-Telegram and Sun* and the *World Journal Tribune.* Later a columnist for the *New York Post.* Also wrote for the *New York Times* Syndicate and the *Los Angeles Times* Entertainment Syndicate.

There are days when any electrical appliance in the house, including the vacuum cleaner, seems to offer more entertainment possibilities than the TV set.

OTHERS: 1444 Italian painter **Sandro Botticelli**, 1768 Queen of England **Caroline of Brunswick**, 1823 Contralto/composer **Charlotte Helen Sainton-Dolby**, 1873 French novelist **Henri Barbusse**, 1873 English novelist **Dorothy Miller Richardson**, 1886 Borbón King of Spain **Alfonso XIII**, 1889 French flutist **Marcel Moyse**, 1905 U.S. screenwriter **John Patrick**, 1908 Yugoslavian soprano **Zinka Milanov**, 1904 British CEO of Rolls Royce **Lord Tombs**, 1931 Jazz musician **Dewey Redman**, 1936 U.S. actor/director **Dennis Hopper**, 1942 U.S. singer/songwriter **Taj Mahal**, 1944 Concert pianist **Paul Crossley**, 1953 U.S. newscaster **Kathleen Sullivan**, 1956 U.S. boxer **Sugar Ray Leonard**

May 18

1048 **Omar Khayyam:** Persian mathematician, astronomer and poet. Calculated how to correct the Persian calendar. Invented a method of solving cubic equations by intersecting a parabola with a circle. Measured the length of the year as 365.24219858156 days. His fame spread to the West, not as a scientist, but for his verses, which were loosely translated into English by Edward Fitzgerald, published as the *Rubaiyat of Omar Khayyam*, with only about 50 of the 250 quatrains authenticated to be the work of the man, whose name means "tentmaker."

A hair divides what is false and true.

1692 **Joseph Butler:** English bishop, theologian, apologist and philosopher. Dean of St. Paul's Cathedral and later bishop of Durham. Attempted to reconcile enlightened self-interest with morality. Most famous for his *Fifteen Sermons on Human Nature* and *Analogy of Religion, Natural and Revealed.*

Things and actions are what they are, and the consequences of them will be what they will be: why then should we desire to be deceived?

1862 **Josephus Daniels:** U.S. editor, publisher, and diplomat. Secretary of the Navy during World War I. Ambassador to Mexico, 1933–42. Wrote *The Life of Woodrow Wilson* and *Editor in Politics*. Remembered for banning alcohol from U.S. Navy ships, which led to the phrase "cup of Joe" to refer to a cup of coffee.

Army: A body of men assembled to rectify the mistakes of the diplomats.

1872 Sir **Bertrand Russell:** English philosopher, mathematician and social reformer. One of the greatest philosophers and most complex and controversial figures of the 20th century, exerted a profound influence on modern thought. Prolific writer on a wide range of topics, including education, social science, politics, ethics, sexual freedom, and religion but best known for his work in mathematical logic and analytic philosophy. Most famous scientific contribution is *Principia Mathematica*, with Alfred North Whitehead. Received the Nobel Prize for Literature in 1950. After World War II, he became a leader of the world-wide campaign for nuclear disarmament. Used logic in an attempt to clarify issues in the foundations of mathematics as well as to settle philosophical questions.

Do not fear to be eccentric in opinion, for every opinion now accepted was once eccentric.

1883 **Walter Gropius:** German-American architect. Founder and director of the Bauhaus until 1928. Designer of its second center in Dessau. Worked in U.S. (1937–69). Chief among his ideas was that all design requires a systematic study of the particular needs and problems involved, without reference to previous forms or styles.

Our guiding principle was that design is neither an intellectual nor a material affair, but simply an integral part of the stuff of life, necessary for everyone in a civilized society.

1891 **Rudolph Carnap:** German-American philosopher. Member of the Vienna Circle and a proponent of United Science. Argued for an empiricist reconstruction of scientific knowledge. Emigrated to the U.S. in 1935 and became an American citizen in 1941. Professor at the University of Chicago (1936–52) and UCLA for the remainder of his career. Published works included *Meaning and Necessity; A Study in Semantics and Modal Logic, Logical Foundations of Probability* and *The Continuum of Inductive Methods.*

In logic there are no morals. Everyone is at liberty to build up his own logic, i.e. his own form of language, as he wishes.

1892 **Frank Capra:** Populist-influenced Italian-born U.S. director. Oscar winner for *It Happened One Night, Mr. Deeds Goes to Town, You Can't Take It with You* and the army documentary *Prelude to War*. Post war films included *Arsenic and Old Lace* and *It's a Wonderful Life.*

Film is one of the three universal languages, the other two: mathematics and music.

1902 **Meredith Willson:** American composer, conductor. Flautist with John Philip Sousa's band and the New York Philharmonic. Appeared with Tallulah Bankhead on radio's "The Big Show." Wrote *The Music Man* and *The Unsinkable Molly Brown.*

Barbershop quartet singing is four guys tasting the holy essence of four individual mechanisms coming into complete agreement.

1904 **Jacob Javits:** American politician and lawyer. Liberal Republican Congressman and Senator from New York State. For a time he was the only Jew in the U.S. Senate. Ranking minority member on the Foreign Relations Committee. Received the Presidential Medal of Freedom in 1983. New York's Javits Center is named in his honor.

Love your country. Don't be afraid to stick your neck out. And take a chance on the young.

1909 **Johnny Mercer:** American vocalist, lyricist and composer. Cofounder of Capitol Records. Contributed to many Broadway musical productions such as *St. Louis Woman* and *Seven Brides for Seven Brothers* and Hollywood films. His songs "On the Atchison, Topeka and the Santa Fe," "In the Cool, Cool, Cool of the Evening," "Moon River" and "Days of Wine and Roses" each won Academy Awards. Credited with over 1000 lyrics.

Once upon a time the world was sweeter than we knew. Everything was ours; how happy we were then, but then once upon a time never comes again.

1919 **Margot Fonteyn:** English prima ballerina. Considered one of the greatest dancers of the 20th century. Made debut at Vic-Wells Ballet in *Nutcracker* (1934). With Britain's Royal Ballet (1934–75). Formed partnership with Rudolf Nureyev (1962–79) in ballets such as *Swan Lake* and *Raymonda*. President Royal Academy of Dancing from 1954 to 1991.

Great artists are people who find the way to be themselves in their art. Any sort of pretension induces mediocrity in art and life alike.

1920 Pope **John Paul II [Karol Jozef Wojtyla]:** Polish religious leader. First non–Italian pope in 455 years (1978–2005). Author of an internationally best-selling book *Crossing the Threshold* (1994). Traveled more than any other pope. Some of his trips attracted the largest crowds ever assembled. Known for his energy, charisma, intellect and doctrinal conservatism. Is on a fast tract to sainthood since his death in 2005.

Science can purify religion from error and superstition. Religion can purify science from idolatry and false absolutes.

OTHERS: 1474 Art patron **Isabella d'Este, Marchioness of Mantua**, 1711 Italian astronomer **Ruggiero G. Boscovich**, 1744 Bohemian clarinetist/composer **Joseph Beer**, 1850 English physicist **Oliver Heaviside**, 1885 President of Brazil **Eurico Gaspar Dutra**, 1900 U.S. Senator **Kenneth Keating**, 1911 U.S. Blues singer **Big Joe Turner**, 1912 U.S. film director **Richard Brooks**, 1912 U.S. vocalist **Perry Como**, 1921 U.S. writer **Patrick Dennis**, 1924 U.S. sportscaster **Jack Whittaker**, 1931 U.S. actor **Robert Morse**, 1937 U.S. baseball player **Brooks Robinson**, 1946 U.S. baseball player **Reggie Jackson**, 1947 Republic of Ireland Prime Minister **John Bruton**, 1952 U.S. country singer **George Strait**

May 19

1762 **Johann Gottlieb Fichte:** German philosopher. Developed ethical idealism out of Immanuel Kant's work. He demonstrated that practical reason is the root of all knowledge and humanity by starting with the ego, which is independent and sovereign, as the principle from which all other knowledge is deducted. Reputation rests mainly on *Addresses to the German Nation* in which he attempted to rally German nationalists against Napoleon.

It is a mistake to say that it is doubtful whether there is a God or not. It is not in the least doubtful, but the most certain thing in the world, nay, the foundation of all other certainty — the only solid absolute objectivity — that there is a moral government of the world.

1795 **Johns Hopkins:** American philanthropist. Named for his great-grandmother, Margaret Johns. He was an important investor in the nations' first railroad, the Baltimore and Ohio. Never married, he was guided by the strong social consciousness of his Quaker faith to use his fortune to benefit humanity. In 1867, he arranged for the incorporation of the Johns Hopkins University and the Johns Hopkins Hospital. His bequest to found Johns Hopkins University was the largest in U.S. history, equivalent now to more than $88 million. When the university opened in 1876, it did so with the stated goal, endorsed by Hopkins:

The encouragement of research ... and the advancement of individual scholars, who by their excellence will advance the sciences they pursue, and the society where they dwell.

1859 Dame **Nellie Melba:** Australian operatic soprano. Star of London's Covent Garden and New York Met, from 1890s. Best known for her roles in *Lakmé*, *Faust*, and *La Traviata*. Famous for pure tone. Dessert "Peach Melba" named in her honor.

The first rule in opera is the first rule in life: see to everything yourself.

1879 Lady **Nancy Astor (Nancy Witcher Langhorne):** American-born English politician. She succeeded her husband as Conservative MP for Plymouth. First woman to sit in the British House of Commons. Advocated women's rights, temperance. Opposed socialism. Wrote *My Two Countries*.

I married beneath me, all women do.

1890 **Ho Chi Minh:** Legendary Vietnamese leader and evolutionist. Founded Communist Party of Vietnam (1930). Organized Vietminh which fought Japanese in World War II. Played direct role in the Geneva Accord dividing Vietnam into North and South. Directed successful military operations against the French. President of Democratic Republic of Vietnam (North) (1954–69). Leading force in the war between North and South Vietnam.

You will kill 10 of our men, and we will kill 1 of yours, and in the end it will be you who tire of it.

1915 **Pol Pot:** Cambodian prime minister, dictator and mass murderer. In 1975 his Khmer Rouge forces captured Phnom Penh, and ordered the entire population to evacuate the city. His intention was to return to "year zero" of an ethnically pure, agrarian, communist state. It resulted in the deaths of more than 2 million people. Was overthrown by the Vietnamese in 1979 and jailed.

It is up to history to judge.

1925 **Malcolm X [Malcolm Little]:** African-American militant black activist. Spoke for racial pride and Black Nationalism. Joined Black Muslims while in prison. Rose to position of leadership. Suspended in 1964 by Elijah Muhammad. Malcolm X formed Organization for African American Unity. Assassinated (1965).

You can't separate peace from freedom because no one can be at peace unless he has his freedom.

1929 **Harvey Cox:** Prominent American theologian and professor of divinity at the Harvard Divinity School. Widely known for his immensely popular publication *The Secular City*. Its thesis is that the church is primarily a people of faith and action, rather than institution. Argued that the church should be at the forefront of change in society.

There has never been a better raconteur than Jesus of Nazareth.

1930 **Lorraine Hansberry:** Youngest U.S. playwright and first African-American to win Best Play Award from the New York Drama Critic's Circle for her first work, *A Raisin in the Sun*. *To Be Young, Gifted and Black* was completed by her husband Robert Nemiroff after her death at age 34 of cancer.

Sometimes I can see the future stretched out in front of me — just as plain as day. The future

hanging over there at the edge of my days. Just waiting for me.

1941 **Nora Ephron:** American author, screenwriter, director. Daughter of screenwriters Henry and Phoebe Ephron. Oscar nominated for screenplays for *Silkwood* and *When Harry Met Sally*. Directed 1993 hit *Sleepless in Seattle*.

The desire to get married, which — I regret to say, I believe is basic and primal in women — is followed almost immediately by an equally basic and primal urge — which is to be single again.

1952 **Joey Ramone:** Real name **Jeffry Hyman**. Vocalist for the legendary punk rock group, the Ramones. Originally the drummer of the group, he was distinctive because of his 6 ft. 6 in. height and long black hair that almost completely covered his face. The heyday of the Ramones was the mid–1970s. After that they remained mostly an underground act. Died of lymphoma in 2001.

The Ramones own the fountain of youth. Experiencing us is like having the fountain of youth.

1953 **Victoria Wood:** British comedienne, actress, singer, and writer. Regarded as among the top sitcom writers in Britain. Her clever dialogue-based TV comedies include *Dinnerladies* and *The Royle Family*. Starred in several of her series including *Wood and Walters* (with Julie Walters) and *Victoria Wood as Seen on Television*.

I sometimes think that being widowed is God's way of telling you to come off the Pill.

OTHERS: 1469 Italian sculptor **Giovanni della Robbia**, 1860 Italy's premier **Victor E. Orlando**, 1864 Us naturalist/inventor **Carl Akeley**, 1879 British publisher **Lord Waldorf Astor**, 1899 Russian novelist **Leonid M. Leonov**, 1913 President of India **Neelam Sanjiva Reddy**, 1934 News anchor on PBS **Jim Lehrer**, 1935 TV personality **David Hartman**, 1941 U.S. nutritionist **Jane Brody**, 1945 English guitarist/vocalist **Peter Townshend**, 1948 Jamaican actress **Grace Jones**, 1949 U.S. football player **Archie Manning**, 1957 Basketball player **Bill Laimbeer**, 1961 U.S. pro bowler **Lisa Wagner**, 1963 U.S. pro golfer **Rebecca Bradley**

May 20

1768 **Dolley Madison:** American First Lady. Her first husband having died she married James Madison in 1794. She was famous as Washington hostess while her husband was secretary of state (1801–9) and president (1809–17) and a great asset to his career. In 1814, she saved many state papers and the Gilbert Stuart portrait of George Washington just before the British arrive in the city. She was granted a lifelong seat on the floor of the U.S. House of Representatives.

I would rather fight with my hands than my tongue.

1799 **Honoré de Balzac:** French novelist. Wrote more than 90 novels and tales. Considered a founder of the realistic school, or naturalism in the novel and one of the greatest fiction writers of all times. Depicted ordinary and undistinguished lives in meticulous detail. Books: *The Last Choudans*, *The Human Comedy*, *Father Goriot* and *Lost Illusions*.

Marriage must incessantly contend with a monster that devours everything: familiarity.

1806 **John Stuart Mill:** British philosopher and economist. Leading proponent of Utilitarianism. Prominent as a publicist in the reforming age of the 19th century. Writings: *System of Logic*, *The Enfranchisement of Women*, *The Subjection of Women*, *On Liberty* and *Utilitarianism*. Son of Scottish philosopher, historian and economist James Mill.

Conservatives are not necessarily stupid, but most stupid people are conservatives.

1825 **Antoinette Brown Blackwell:** First ordained U.S. minister. One of the first U.S. women to receive a college education. Active feminist, abolitionist and temperance advocates. Books: *The Sexes Throughout Nature*. Sister-in-law of social worker Henry B. Blackwell and Elizabeth Blackwell, who became the first modern female physician.

Nature is just enough; but men and women must comprehend and accept her suggestions.

1833 **John Marshall Harlan:** American jurist and Supreme Court Justice. Commanded a Union regiment in the American Civil War. Appointed to the highest court in the land by President Rutherford B. Hayes. Became on of the most forceful dissenters in the court's history. Favored the rights of blacks, trust busting and the federal income tax. His grandson of the same name served on the Supreme Court (1955–71).

Our constitution is color-blind, and neither knows nor tolerates classes among citizens. In respect of civil rights, all citizens are equal before the law. The humblest is the peer of the most powerful.

1890 **Allan Nevins:** American historian. Worked for 20 years as a journalist before joining the faculty of Columbia University. Best know works were the Pulitzer Prize winning biographies *Grover Cleveland* and *Hamilton Fish*, and his eight-volume history of the American Civil War. In 1948, he inaugurated the first oral history program in the U.S.

History is never about the melee. It is not allowed to be neutral, but forced to enlist in every army.

1894 **Adela Rogers St. Johns:** American journalist. Star reporter of the William Randolph Hearst papers. Covered the Lindbergh baby kidnapping and Bruno Hauptman's trial. Books: *A Free Soul* and *Some Are Born Great*.

God made man, and then said I can do better than that and made woman.

1904 **Margery Allingham:** British detective story writer. Published first work at age 8 and her first novel when 19. Wrote very popular stories about the fictional detective Albert Campion, including *Tiger in the Smoke* and *The China Governess*.

It is always difficult to escape from youth; its hopefulness, its optimistic belief in the privileges of desire, its despair, and its sense of outrage and injustice at disappointment, all these spring on a man inflicting indelicate agony when he is no longer prepared.

1908 **James Stewart:** Perhaps the most popular actor to appear in films. The tall, gangling, long-faced star with a slow hesitant drawl projected sincerity, honesty and trustworthiness. Oscar winner for *The Philadelphia Story.* Nominated for *Mr. Smith Goes to Washington, It's a Wonderful Life* and *Anatomy of a Murder.* A bomber pilot during World War II, super-patriot and conservative Stewart stayed in reserves, rising to rank of brigadier general.

The great thing about the movies ... is you're giving people little tiny pieces of time that they will never forget.

1915 **Moyshe Dayan:** Israeli general and public official. Guerilla fighter against Arab raiders. Joined the illegal Jewish defense force Hagana. Lost an eye fighting the Vichy French in Syria during World War II. Army chief of staff during the Suez crisis. Led invasion of Sinai Peninsula (1956). As defense minister, led Israeli forces to victory in Six Day War (1967). As foreign minister (1977–79) helped broker the Camp David Accords.

Freedom is the oxygen of the soul.

1918 **William David Ormsby-Gore, Lord Harlech:** British politician. Served in Harold Macmillan government as Minister of State for Foreign Affairs. In 1960 he was appointed British Ambassador to the United States, where he had a close personal relationship with President John F. Kennedy and his brother Bobby Kennedy. In 1965 he took up his seat in the House of Lords. A fierce opponent of oil-barrel politics.

In the end it may well be that Britain will be honored by historians more for the way she disposed of an empire than for the way she acquired it.

1946 **Cher [Cherilyn Sarkisian Lapierre]:** U.S. singer and actress. Had a successful television show with husband Sonny Bono (1971–77). Oscar winner for *Moonstruck.* Song Hits: "Gypsies, Tramps and Thieves," "Dark Lady" and "After All."

Men should be like Kleenex, soft, strong and disposable.

OTHERS: 1743 Haitian revolutionary leader **Toussaint-Louverture**, 1818 Founder of Wells Fargo **William G. Fargo**, 1841 Social reformer **Sara Louisa Oberholtz**, 1851 German inventor of flat phonograph record **Emile Berliner**, 1851 U.S. nun/cared for terminally ill cancer patients **Rose Hawthorne Lathrop**, 1891 U.S. leader of American Communist Party **Earl Browder**, 1899 U.S. actress **Estelle Taylor**, 1913 Architect **Henry Cadbury Brown**, 1927 U.S. pro football coach **Bud Grant**, 1937 U.S. pro golfer **Dave Hill**, 1940 Japanese baseball player **Sadaharu Oh**, 1940 Canadian pro hockey player **Stan Mikita**, 1941 Premier of Singapore **Goh Chok Sole**, 1944 English blues/rock singer **Joe Cocker**

May 21

427 BCE **Plato:** Originally known as **Aristocles.** Greek philosopher, whose name refers to his broad forehead, was a student of Socrates. Plato founded his famous school, called the Academy, in Athens. Developed a profound and wide-ranging philosophical system, Platonism, which became an essential part of Western philosophy. His many dialogues, in which the central character was often Socrates, include *Apology, Protagoras, Symposium, Republic,* and *Laws.*

A hero is born among a hundred, a wise man is found among a thousand, but an accomplished one might not be found even among a hundred thousand men.

1471 **Albrecht Dürer:** German Renaissance painter and engraver. Traveled widely and was greatly influenced by Italian painters. Known for penetrating self-portraits. Produced many paintings, but is better known for great series of designs on wood, including the *Apocalypse* and the *Triumphal Arch*, the largest known woodcut (100 square feet). His greatest engravings include *St. Jerome in His Study, Melencolia I,* and *The Knight, Death and the Devil.*

And since geometry is the right foundation of all painting, I have decided to teach its rudiments and principles to all youngsters eager for art.

1688 **Alexander Pope:** "Wicked Wasp of Twickenham." English poet and satirist. Suffered from poor health due to tuberculosis, asthma, and curvature of the back, which resulted in his diminutive stature of 4 ft. 6 in. Frequently engaged in literary vendettas. Regarded as the epitome of English neoclassicism. Best Known Works: "The Dunciad," "Epistle to Doctor Arbuthnot," "Essay on Criticism," "Rape of the Lock," and translations of the *Iliad* and *The Odyssey.*

For fools rush in where angels feat to tread.

1753 **Pierre Victurnien Vergniaud:** French revolutionist, eloquent orator and spokesman for the Girondins. As a member of the General Assembly, he was unable to persuade the body to spare the king's life and thus voted for the monarch's death. When the Girondists clashed with the rival revolutionary faction, the Montagnards, Vergniaud and his party members were arrested and sent to the guillotine.

There was reason to fear that the Revolution, like Saturn, might devour everyone of her children.

1780 **Elizabeth Gurney Fry:** English Quaker philanthropist and social reformer. Dedicated her life to promoting wide-ranging prison reforms, particularly the treatment of the poor and female prisoners. Also reached out to help the homeless, establishing a "nightly shelter" in London. Instituted the Brighton District Visiting Society, which consisted of volunteers who visited the homes of the poor to provide help and comfort them. Opened a training school for nurses, which inspired Florence Nightingale to take a team of Fry's nurses to assist wounded soldiers in the Crimean War.

Oh Lord, may I be directed what to do and what to leave undone.

1793 **Charles Paul de Kock:** French novelist and dramatist. Established a reputation for an endless series of novels about contemporary Parisian life. Novels: *Georgette, ou la Nièce du tabellion*, *La Grand yule*, *André le Savoyard* and *Le Barbier de Paris*. His licentious works are no longer widely read.

The best way to keep your friends is to never owe them anything and never lend them anything.

1844 **Henri Rousseau:** Primitive French painter. Worked many years as a minor customs official, earning him the nickname "le Douanier" (customs officer) by his friends. Produced painstaking portraits, exotic imaginary landscapes and dreams, such as "Sleeping Gypsy." Died a pauper, his genius only then recognized.

When I go out into the countryside and see the sun and the green and everything flowering, I say to myself, "yes indeed, all that belongs to me."

1876 **Cyrus S. Ching:** American government official, industrial relations executive. Enlightened industrialist who translated his concepts of human relationships into beneficial labor-management relationships. President Truman appointed him the first director of Federal Mediation and Conciliation Service.

I learned long ago never to wrestle with a pig. You get dirty, and besides, the pig likes it.

1898 **Armand Hammer:** American millionaire industrialist and philanthropist. Made his first millions in pharmaceuticals, but increased his fortune with whisky making, cattle raising and his investments in wildcat oil wells. Became head of the Occidental Petroleum Corp. Went to Soviet Russia in 1921 to provide medical aid to famine victims. Longtime advocate of broadening U.S.–Soviet trade ties.

Regrets and recriminations only hurt your soul.

1904 **Thomas Wright "Fats" Waller:** American composer, pianist. Played and recorded with Fletcher Henderson and Ted Lewis. Wrote score for Broadway musical *Early to Bed* and films *Hooray for Love* and *Stormy Weather*. Songs: "Ain't Misbehavin'," "Honeysuckle Rose" and "The Joint Is Jumpin'."

"Ain't Misbehavin'" was written while I was lodged in the alimony jail, and I wasn't misbehaving, you dig?

1921 **Andrei D. Sakharov:** Nobel Peace Prize–winning physicist, mainly responsible for the development of the Soviet H-bomb. Became a symbol of Soviet dissidence, campaigning for a nuclear test-ban treaty, peaceful international coexistence and improved civil rights within the U.S.S.R. Forbidden to travel to Oslo to receive the Nobel Peace Prize in 1975. Forced into exile at Gorky. Released in 1986, his honors were restored in 1989, the year of his death.

I could not stop something I knew was wrong and terrible. I had an awful sense of powerlessness

1944 **Mary Robinson:** Seventh and first female President of Ireland. Irish name **Máire Bhean Mhic Róibin**. As the Labor Party candidate, she defeated *Fianna Fáil's* Brian Lenihan in the 1990 presidential election. Credited with revitalizing and liberalizing a previously conservative political office. Immensely popular, she resigned the presidency four months ahead of the end of her term in 1997 to assume a post as the United Nations High Commissioner for Human Rights. In 2002, awarded the Sydney Peace Price for her outstanding work in that capacity.

I was elected by the women of Ireland, who instead of rocking the cradle rocked the system.

OTHERS: 1527 King of Spain **Philip II**, 1808 French poet/writer **Gérard de Nerval**, 1856 U.S. philanthropist **Grace Hoadley Dodge**, 1865 Danish archaeologist **C.J. Thomsen**, 1868 U.S. historian/editor **Clarence Walworth Alvord**, 1878 U.S. inventor of hydroplane **Glenn Hammond Curtiss**, 1901 Orchestra leader **Horace Heidt**, 1903 Angolan-born sci-fi writer **Manly Wade Wellman**, 1904 U.S. actor/director **Robert Montgomery**, 1906 U.S. tennis player **Helen Willis Moody Roark**, 1909 French banker **Guy Rothschild**, 1916 U.S. novelist **Harold Robbins**, 1917 U.S. actor **Raymond Burr**, 1917 U.S. Irish singer **Dennis Day**, 1926 U.S. poet/novelist **Robert Creeley**

May 22

1813 **Richard Wagner:** German composer, conductor, librettist, and author. One of the most influential figures in the history of Western music. The subject matter of most of his operas is drawn from Norse and Teutonic mythology and history. Works: *The Flying Dutchman*, *Tannhaüser*, *Lohengrin*, *Der Ring des Niebelunen*, *Tristan und Isolde* and *Der Meistersinger*. Started the now famous theater at Bayreuth, which opened with his last opera *Parsifal* in 1882. Wrote controversial essays, arguing that Jewish musicians, such as Felix Mendelssohn, were only capable of producing shallow music. Called for the abandonment of Jewish culture and assimilation of the Jews into the German culture. There is scant evidence that Hitler was influenced by these views, although the Nazis appropriated Wagner's music as their own in the 1930s.

The Jewish race is the born enemy of pure humanity and everything that is noble in it.

1844 **Mary Cassatt:** American impressionist artist. A close friend of Edgar Degas who influenced her style and encouraged her to exhibit her works. Noted for paintings of mother and child. Also renown for her etching and drypoint studies of domestic scenes.

I think that if you shake the tree, you ought to be around when the fruit falls to pick it up

1859 **Sir Arthur Conan Doyle:** English physician and novelist. Known chiefly for his popular series of tales concerning Sherlock Holmes and his good-natured companion, Dr. Watson: *A Study in Scarlet, The Sign of the Four, The Memoirs of Sherlock Holmes* and *Hound of the Baskervilles.* When Conan Doyle tired of Holmes and had him fall to his death in 1893, the public demands forced him to resurrect the sleuth.

When you have eliminated the impossible, whatever remains, however improbable, must be the truth.

1907 Lord **Laurence Olivier:** Generally regarded as the finest British actor of his generation. His first love always was the stage, especially in Shakespearean roles. Oscar for *Hamlet* and special Oscars for *Henry V* and Life Achievement. Nominated for *Wuthering Heights, Rebecca, Richard III, The Entertainer, Othello, Sleuth, Marathon Man* and *The Boys from Brazil.* In 1970 he was created a life peer, the first actor ever so honored. Married to actresses Vivian Leigh and Joan Plowright.

I take a simple view of living. It is keep your eyes open and get on with it.

1914 **Vance Packard:** American nonfiction writer. Author of popular sociological books, including *The Hidden Persuaders, The Status Seekers* and *The Waste Makers.*

Leadership appears to be the art of getting others to want to do something you are convinced should be done.

1922 **Judith Crist:** Nationally known American film and drama critic for *TV Guide.* Journalism professor, Columbia University. Books: *The Private Eye* and *The Cowboy and the Very Naked Girl.*

Film criticism became the means whereby a stream of young intellectuals could go straight from the campus film society into the professionals' screening room without managing to get a glimpse of the real world in between.

1924 **Charles Aznavour:** French-born Armenian foggy-voiced singer and actor. Toured with Edith Piaf and Les Compagnons de la Chanson. Gained fame in fifties for the motion picture *Shoot the Piano Player.*

To be aged, but not old.

1928 **T. Boone Pickens:** American businessman. Head of Mesa Petroleum, one of the largest independent oil companies in the world. Well-known for taking over undervalued companies in the 1980s. A supporter of George W. Bush, Pickens made a $2.5 million contribution to the Swift Boat Veterans to pay for their ads attacking John Kerry. In 2006, donated $165 million to his alma mater Oklahoma State University to upgrade the football stadium.

Be willing to make decisions. That's the most important quality in a good leader. Don't fall victim to what I call the ready-aim-aim-aim-aim syndrome. You must be willing to fire.

1930 **Robert Byrne:** American writer, quote collector and preeminent teacher and commentator on billiards. Author of seven novels, five collections of humorous quotations, seven books on billiards, and an expose of frauds in the literary world. In 2001 he was inducted into the Billiard Congress of America's Hall of Fame.

Winter is nature's way of saying, "up yours."

1930 **Harvey Milk:** American politician and the first openly gay city supervisor of San Francisco. Only weeks after the enactment of a gay rights bill, former city supervisor Dan White assassinated both Milk and Mayor George Moscone. White was convicted of voluntary manslaughter and sentenced to seven years and eight months in prison, a sentence widely denounced as too lenient. The Gay community erupted into the White Nights Riots. Less than a year after getting out of prison, White committed suicide. Milk, regarded a martyr for the gay rights movement, foresaw the possibility of his assassination, saying:

If a bullet should enter my brain, let that bullet destroy every closet door in the country.

1934 **Garry Wills:** American author and historian. Frequent contributor to the *New York Review of Books.* Won a 1993 Pulitzer Prize for General Non-Fiction for *Lincoln at Gettysburg: The Words That Remade America* and the National Medal for the Humanities in 1998. Other books include: *The Second Civil War, Inventing America: Jefferson's Declaration of Independence, Reagan's America* and *Under God: Religion and American Politics.*

Politicians make good company for a while just as children do — their self-enjoyment is contagious. But they soon exhaust their favorite subjects — themselves.

1936 **Jill Tweedie:** British feminist, writer and broadcaster. Mainly remembered for her column in the Guardian's Women's Page, "Letters from a faint-hearted feminist. Also known for her autobiography *Eating Children.*

Men, I feel are like wine — before buying, a real connoisseur takes a small sip, and spits them out.

OTHERS: 1772 Hindu reformer **Ram Mohan Roy**, 1841 French poet **Catulle Mendès**, 1879 Ukrainian-born actress **Alla Nazimova**, 1907 Belgian comic book creator **Hergé**, 1911 Russian-born psychologist/pianist **Anatol Rapoport**, 1914 American musician **Sun Ra**, 1922 U.S. Television producer **Quinn Martin**, 1934 American musician **Peter Nero**, 1936 U.S. psychiatrist **M. Scott Peck**, 1938 U.S. actress **Susan Strasburg**, 1940 U.S. TV reporter **Bernard Shaw**, 1941 U.S. actor **Paul Winfield**, 1942 Unabomber **Theodore Kaczynski,** 1943 Irish politician **Betty Williams**, 1950 English songwriter **Bernie Taupin**, 1959 English singer **Morrissey**, 1970 English model **Naomi Campbell**

May 23

1707 **Carolus Von Linnaeus:** Swedish botanist. His classification or artificial system of plants, known as the "sexual system," superseded Jussieu's natural system. His *Species plantarum* is considered the foundation of modern botanical nomenclature with plants being groped hierarchically into genera, classes and orders.

Nature does not proceed by leaps and bounds.

1734 **Franz Anton Mesmer:** German physician. Discoverer of cure by suggestion, *mesmerism,* which he attributed to magnetic force. Although his work has been discredited, it prepared the way for the use of hypnotism in medicine and investigation of hysterical symptoms. A learned commission denounced him as an imposter, causing him to retire to Switzerland.

I have made a discovery that will lift pain and misery.

1799 **Thomas Hood:** British humorist and poet. Gained recognition when with John Hamilton Reynolds, he published *Odes and Addresses to Great People* in 1825. Invented "picture-puns" and started *Hood's Monthly Magazine.*

To attempt to advise conceited people is like whistling against the wind.

1810 **[Sarah] Margaret Fuller:** U.S. editor, essayist, poet and teacher. First female journalist for the *New York Tribune.* Author of the remarkable feminist tract "Women in the Nineteenth Century," envisioning America as the one place where women might rise above men's tyranny.

Male and female represent the two sides of the great radical dualism. But in fact they are perpetually passing into one another. Fluid hardens to solid, solid rushes to fluid. There is no wholly masculine man, no purely feminine woman.

1844 **Abdu'l Bahá:** Son and successor of the Persian Prophet-founder-leader of the Bahá'i Faith, Bahá'u'l-láh. Called "The Centre of the Covenant" by his father, Abdu'l Bahá journeys to the West spread the Bahá'i message far beyond its roots. Writings: *Tablets of the Divine Plan, Foundations of World Unity* and *The Secret of Divine Civilization.*

The reality of man is his thought, not his material body. The thought force and the animal force are partners. Although man is part of the animal creation, he possesses a power of thought superior to all other created beings.

1854 **Edgar F. Smith:** American educator, chemist, and author. Professor of Chemistry, University of Pennsylvania. Provost (1911–20). Wrote *The Life of Robin Hare, Chemistry in Old Philadelphia* and *Priestley in America.*

You may tempt the upper class with your villainous demitasses/ But Heaven will protect the working girl.

1873 Rabbi **Leo Baeck:** German-Jewish scholar and leader of Progressive Judaism. His book *The Essence of Judaism* made him a famous proponent for the Jewish people. A chaplain in the Imperial Army in World War I, he survived the Theresienstadt concentration camp during World War II, at which time he began his great work *This People Israel.* After the war, he taught at Hebrew Union College in the U.S. and became Chairman of the World Union for Progressive Judaism.

A minority is always compelled to think. That is the blessing of being in the minority.

1875 **Alfred P. Sloan, Jr.:** U.S. automobile executive. President of General Motors (1923–37). Chairman of the Board (1937–56). The Alfred P. Sloan Foundation started the cancer research center Sloan-Kettering Institute.

The greatest real thrill that life offers is to create, to construct, to develop something useful. Too often we fail to recognize and pay tribute to the creative spirit. It is that spirit that creates our jobs.

1910 **Artie Shaw:** Born **Arthur Jacob Arshawsky.** U.S. jazz clarinetist, composer, bandleader and writer. During the Swing Era, his band had many musical hits, including "Begin the Beguine," "Stardust" and "Frenesi." First white bandleader to hire a black vocalist when Billie Holiday joined his band. Shaw was almost as famous for having been married eight times, including wives Betty Kern (daughter of Jerome Kern), Ava Gardner, Lana Turner and Evelyn Keyes.

No matter how carefully and assiduously and how deeply you bury shit, the American public will find it and buy it in large quantity. It's true, absolutely true.

1914 **Barbara Mary Ward:** Baroness Jackson of Lodsworth: English economist. Advocated European economic unity and help for the underdeveloped countries. Books: *The Rich Nations and the Poor Nations* and *Spaceship Earth.*

I have the impression that when we talk so confidently of liberty, we are unaware of the awful servitude ... of poverty when means are so small that there is literally no choice.

1958 **Drew Carey:** American comedian and actor, distinguished by his black-rimmed glasses and crew cut. After a period as a stand-up comedian, he starred in the TV sitcom, *The Drew Carey Show.* He also hosted the U.S. version of the improvisational comedy show, *Whose Line Is It Anyway.* Autobiography: *Dirty Jokes and Beer: Stories of the Unrefined.*

You know that look women get when they want sex? Me neither.

1974 **Ken Jennings:** U.S. software engineer for a healthcare-placement firm, who holds the record for the longest winning streak on the syndicated TV game show *Jeopardy!* Won 74 games before being defeated by Nancy Zerg on his 75th appearance. During this period he won $2,522,700. Won an additional $500,000 in the *Jeopardy! Ultimate Tourney of Champions,* a 15-week, 75-show. Jennings finished second to Brad Rutter, who won $2 million and supplanted Jennings as the number one overall winner of money on a game show.

Being a nerd really pays off sometimes.

OTHERS: 1052 King of France **Philip I**, 1100 Emperor of China **Qinzong**, 1820 U.S. engineer/inventor **James Buchanan Eads**, 1824 American Civil War general **Ambrose Burnside**, 1848 German aviation pioneer **Otto Lilienthal**, 1883 American actor **Douglas Fair-**

banks, Sr., 1884 Italian socialist **Corrado Gini**, 1891 Swedish writer **Pär Lagerkvist**, 1900 German war criminal **Hans Frank**, 1908 U.S. physicist **John Bardeen**, 1910 U.S. actor **Scatman Crothers**, 1920 U.S. singer **Helen O'Connell**, 1928 U.S. singer/actress **Rosemary Clooney**, 1933 British actress **Joan Collins**, 1934 U.S. inventor **Robert Moog**, 1943 Australian tennis player **John Newcombe**, 1951 Russian chess player **Anatoly Karpov**

May 24

1544 **William Gilbert:** English physician and physicist. Coined terms "electricity," "electric force," "electric attraction" and "magnetic poles." First to suggest the earth acted like a giant magnet and heavenly bodies were kept in place by magnetism. His book *On the Magnet* (1600) is the first major English book on science.

Look for knowledge not in books but in things themselves.

1743 **Jean-Paul Marat:** French revolutionary. Established the radical paper *The Friend of the People*. Advocated extreme violence during the French Revolution. Leader of the Montagnard faction. Assassinated by Girondin supporter, Charlotte Corday, in his bath, and thereafter was hailed as a martyr.

Of what use is political liberty to those who have no bread? It is of value only to ambitious theorists and politicians.

1794 **William Whewell:** English philosopher and historian. Spent most of his career at Cambridge University. Primarily remembered for his work on the theory of induction. Stressed the need to see the scientific process as a historical process. Works: *History of the Inductive Sciences* and *Philosophy of the Inductive Sciences*.

It is a test of true theories not only to account for but to predict phenomena.

1855 **Arthur Wing Pinero:** British actor and most successful playwright of his time. Wrote a series of successful farces such as *The Magistrate* before turning to dramas of social significance, including *The Second Mrs. Tanqueray* and *The Notorious Mrs. Ebbsmith*.

I believe the future is only the past again, entered through another gate.

1819 Queen **Victoria I:** Longest-reigning British monarch. Queen of Great Britain and Ireland (1837–1901). Restored dignity to the crown. Devoted to her husband Prince Albert with whom she had nine children. She grieved for her husband who died in 1861 to the end of her life, having his clothes laid out on his bed each evening.

The Queen is most anxious to enlist everyone in checking this mad, wicked folly of "Women's Rights." It is a subject which makes the Queen so furious she cannot contain herself.

1870 **Benjamin Cardozo:** American jurist. A successful courtroom lawyer, followed by election to the state of New York's Supreme Court, appointment to the Court of Appeals and to the U.S. Supreme Court in 1932. Generally siding with the liberals on the court he handed down important opinions on congressional power, control of inter-state commerce and the relationship of the Bill of Rights to states' rights.

Justice is not to be taken by storm. She is wooed by slow advances.

1870 **Jan C. Smuts:** South African statesman, soldier. Boer guerrilla leader in the South African War (1899–1902). Prime Minister of Union of South Africa. Played a significant role in drafting the Versailles Treaty after World War I and instrumental in the founding of the League of Nations.

When in doubt, do the courageous thing.

1878 **Harry Emerson Fosdick:** American clergyman and professor at Union Theological Seminary. Pastor of the interdenominational Riverside Church in New York City. Leading modernist during the 1920s fundamentalism controversy.

Christians are supposed not merely to endure change, nor even profit by it, but to cause it.

1882 **James Oppenheim:** American poet, author and editor. Founder and editor of *The Seven Arts*, an important early 20th century U.S. literary magazine. His novel *The Nine-Tenths* and his famous poem "Bread and Roses" examined labor troubles with Fabian and suffragist themes. Blacklisted for his opposition of the U.S.'s involvement in World War I.

The foolish man seeks happiness in the distance; the wise man grows it under his feet.

1918 **Coleman Young:** U.S. politician. First African-American member of the Democratic National Committee (1968) and first black mayor of Detroit (1974–92). Served longer than any other mayor in city's history. Revitalized the crime-ridden city by attracting new businesses and reinforcing the police department. Won Spingarn Award (1980).

Courage is one step ahead of fear.

1940 **Joseph Brodsky:** Russian-born poet. His independent spirit led to a five-year sentence to hard labor. Exiled from the U.S.S.R. in 1972, he settled in New York. Poet laureate of the U.S., 1991–92. Poetry collections include: *A Part of Speech*, *History of the Twentieth Century* and *To Urania*. Pulitzer Prize winner in 1987.

It is well to read everything of something, and something of everything.

1941 **Bob Dylan:** American singer, songwriter, guitarist and harmonica player. Born Robert Allen Zimmerman, he took his stage name from poet Dylan Thomas. Innovator of folk-rock style. Songs: "A Hard Rain's Gonna Fall," "Blowin' in the Wind," "Mr. Tambourine Man" and "Like a Rollin' Stone." Has redefined himself several times over the years, insisting that he is not the revolutionary influence so many believe him to be.

A hero is someone who understands the responsibility that comes with his freedom.

OTHERS: 15 BCE Roman commander **Julius Caesar Germanicus**, 1552 English bishop **John Jewel**, 1605

Patriarch of Russian Orthodox church **Nikon**, 1810 German rabbi/scholar **Abraham Geiger**, 1850 U.S. journalist **Henry Woodfin Grady**, 1878 U.S. engineer **Lillian Moller Gilbreth**, 1887 Ukrainian sculptor **Alexander Archipenko**, 1887 U.S. poet/college president **Mother Mary Madeleva, CSC**, 1899 French tennis player **Suzanne Lenglen**, 1899 French poet **Henri Michaux**, 1909 U.S. politician **Wilbur Mills**, 1914 German actress **Lilli Palmer**, 1934 Chicago Mayor **Jane Byrne**, 1944 American singer **Patti LaBelle**, 1945 Elvis' ex-wife **Priscilla Presley**, 1963 U.S. basketball player **Joe Dumars**

May 25

1803 **Ralph Waldo Emerson:** "The Sage of Concord." U.S. poet, essayist, lecturer and philosopher. Leading exponent of New England Transcendentalism. Known for challenging traditional thought in his essays and lectures in which he decreed the proper role of the scholar. With Margaret Fuller, he launched *The Dial*, an outlet for transcendental ideas. Works: *Nature*, *The American Scholar* and *Poems*.

A foolish consistency is the hobgoblin of little mind, ordered by little statesmen and philosophers and divines. With consistency a great soul has simply nothing to do.

1878 **Bill Robinson:** "Bojangles." African-American dancer and actor. Developed extraordinary tap-dancing skills. First black performer in white vaudeville as well as the first black to appear in the Ziegfeld's Follies. Best known for appearances in four films with Shirley Temple.

What success I achieved in the theater is due to the fact that I worked just as hard when there were ten people in the house as when there were thousands. Just as hard in Springfield, Illinois as on Broadway.

1879 Lord **Beaverbrook:** Originally **William Maxwell Aitken**. Canadian-born British publisher, statesman and financier. Made a fortune in Montreal as a financier. Moved to England and became active in politics as a Conservative. Beginning in 1916 he took over or founded newspapers, including the *London Daily Express*. Became a "press lord" and played a major role in building Great Britain's popular press.

Buy old masters. They fetch better prices than old mistresses.

1887 **Pio of Pietrelcina:** Originally **Francesco Forgione**. Italian priest and canonized saint, noted for his piety and his mystic experiences. In 1918, Padre Pio had his first occurrence of stigmata — bodily marks, pain and bleeding in locations corresponding to the crucifixion wounds of Jesus Christ. The phenomenon continued for the remaining fifty years of his life. Numerous physicians studied his stigmata, but reportedly could not explain the wounds that were never infected. At his death, his body appeared unwounded. Pio is the patron saint of stress relief and January blues. His advice:

Pray, Hope and Don't Worry!

1889 **Igor Sikorsky:** Russian-American aviation engineer and pioneer in aircraft design. Built and flew first multimotored plane. Developed first successful helicopter. Directed his company, a division of United Aircraft Corp. for nearly 30 years.

The helicopter ... approaches closer than any other vehicle to the fulfillness of mankind's ancient ideas of the flying horse and the magic carpet.

1898 **Bennett Cerf:** American author, publisher, editor and founder of Random House Publishers. Opponent of censorship. An inveterate punster and raconteur. Wrote a syndicated column and was a regular panel member on TV's *What's My Line?*

Gross ignorance is 144 times worse than ordinary ignorance.

1908 **Theodore Roethke:** American poet. His verse is characterized by introspection and intense lyricism. Taught at several universities, notably at the University of Washington. Poetry Collections: *Open House*, *The Waking* (Pulitzer Prize), *Words for the Wind* (Bollingen Prize, National Book Award) and *The Far Field* (National Book Award).

What we need are more people who specialize in the impossible.

1917 **Theodore Hesburgh:** American priest, educator. President of the University of Notre Dame for 30 plus years. A crusader for civil rights. Chaired Commission on Civil Rights (1969–72). Awarded Presidential Medal of Freedom and more than 100 honorary degrees.

My basic principle is that you don't make decisions because they are easy; you don't make them because they are cheap; you don't make them because they are popular; you make them because they are right.

1923 **John Weitz:** German-born American clothing designer, intelligence officer (spy) for the Office of Strategic Services (OSS) in World War II and historian. Born to a prosperous German family, educated in England and moved to the U.S. in 1940. Ian Fleming named Weitz as the prototype of his character, James Bond. Was one of the first designers to license his name for products such as socks, ties and cologne. Advertising slogan: "John Weitz designs for the woman who wishes her husband could afford her." Author of *Hitler's Diplomat: The Life and Times of Joachim von Ribbentrop* and *Hitler's Banker: Hjalmar Horace Greely Schacht*. Father of film directors Paul and Christopher Weitz whose movies include *About a Boy*.

Even overweight cats instantly know the cardinal rule: when fat, arrange yourself in slim poses.

1926 **Miles Davis:** American jazz trumpeter and bandleader. One of the most influential and admired musicians in jazz. Prophet of the "cool" school. His dark, brooding tone, fusing jazz harmonies with rock instrumentations and the use of a metal mute were major influences on jazz trumpet soloists. Albums: *Kind of Blue*, *The Birth of the Cool*, *Miles Ahead*, *We Want Miles* and *Bitches Brew*.

A legend is on old man with a cane known for what he used to do. I'm still doing it.

1929 **Beverly Sills:** "Bubbles." American coloratura soprano with an effervescent personality. One of the most celebrated opera stars in the world. With New York City Opera (1955–79). Director (1979–88). Medal of Freedom (1980). Repertoire: *Manon, La Traviata* and *Lucia di Lammermoor.*

I'm cheerful. I'm not happy, but I'm cheerful. There's a big difference... A happy woman has no cares at all; a cheerful woman has cares and learns to ignore that.

1939 **Dixie Carter:** American actress noted for portraying Southern women. Appeared in the soap opera *The Edge of Night* from 1974 to 1976. Performed in TV series: *Out of the Blue, On Our Own, Diff'rent Strokes,* and *Filthy Rich,* before landing her best known role, that of interior director Julia Sugarbaker in *Designing Women.* Married to actor Hal Holbrook.

It takes a mighty good man to be better than no man at all.

OTHERS: 1334 Emperor of Japan **Suko**, 1494 Italian painter **Jacopo da Pontormo**, 1725 American politician **Samuel Ward**, 1865 American YMCA leader **John Raleigh Mott**, 1898 U.S. boxer **Gene Tunney**, 1907 Burmese politician **U Nu**, 1925 Mexican poet **Rosario Castellanos**, 1925 U.S. actress **Jeanne Crain**, 1927 American writer **Robert Ludlum**, 1936 U.S. singer/songwriter **Tom T. Hall**, 1939 English actor **Ian McKellen**, 1944 English-born puppeteer/director **Frank Oz**, 1958 British musician **Paul Weller**, 1963 Canadian actor/comedian **Mike Myers**, 1956 English singer **Simon Fowler**, 1976 Dominican baseball player **Miguel Tejada**, 1978 Pro football linebacker **Brian Urlacher**

May 26

1689 Lady **Mary Wortley Montagu:** English author, traveler, medical pioneer, poet, essayist and eccentric. Prolific letter writer. Her witty epistles of Middle Eastern life, which she shared with her husband wile he was the ambassador in Constantinople, were published posthumously.

Satire should like a polished razor keen,/ Wound with a touch that's scarcely felt or seen.

1764 **Edward Livingston:** American jurist and statesman. Republican congressman from New York (1795–1801). Became district attorney for the state of New York and then mayor of New York City. Moved to Louisiana where he was appointed by the legislature to prepare a provisional code of judicial procedure, which came to be known as "The Livingston Code." Served in U.S. congress and the senate, representing Louisiana. Became Andrew Jackson's Secretary of State and later minister plenipotentiary to France.

There is a definite cost to doing nothing.

1822 **Edmond de Goncourt:** French writer. With his younger brother Jules, devoted his life largely to writing. Produced a series of social histories and a body of art criticism. In his will, Edmond established the Académie Goncourt, which annually awards the Prix Goncourt, France's most eminent literary prize, to authors of outstanding French literature.

It there is a God, atheism must seem to Him as less of an insult than religion.

1886 **Al Jolson:** American singer, actor. Rose to stardom on Broadway stage, becoming America's most popular entertainer. Jolson ushered in the sound era with *The Jazz Singer* (1927). He was never as good in films as when facing the adoring crowds whom he loved.

Wait a minute, wait a minute. You ain't heard nothin' yet, folks.

1895 **Dorthea Lange:** Originally **Dorothea Nutzhorn.** American photographer who studied at Columbia University. Established a studio in San Francisco. Best known for her social records of migrant workers, share-croppers, and tenant farmers during the depression, for her photo essay *Migrant Mother* and her documentation of the World War II internment of Japanese-Americans. Worked as a free lance photographer throughout the world.

The camera is an instrument that teaches people how to see without a camera.

1902 **Adolfo López Mateos:** Mexican politician. President of the country from 1958 to 1964. Liked by the people for his oratory skills and dedication to the poor. Known for his efforts in land redistribution to peasants, nationalization of foreign utilities companies, devotion to public health and promotion of education and literacy. Maintained good relations with the U.S., but remained neutral during the Cuban Missile Crisis.

A woman is a citizen who works for Mexico. We must not treat her differently from a man, except to honor her more.

1907 **John Wayne:** "Duke" Legendary American film actor personified for some the American ideals of loyalty, integrity, honesty and self-reliance. Others objected to his super-patriot pose. Won an Oscar for *True Grit.* Other films: *Stagecoach, Fort Apache, Red River, She Wore a Yellow Ribbon, The Spoilers* and *The Quiet Man.* Directed *The Alamo,* which he saw as a metaphor for America.

Never say sorry — it's a sign of weakness.

1908 **Robert Morley:** Rotund British actor, playwright. The delightful character actor is at his best being jovial or pompous. Oscar nominated for his first film, *Marie Antoinette.* Others: *Major Barbara, The Story of Gilbert and Sullivan* and *Oscar Wilde.*

It is a great help for a man to be in love with himself. For an actor, however, it is absolutely essential.

1920 **Peggy Lee:** Originally **Norma Deloris Egstrom.** American singer, songwriter and actress. Oscar nominated for performance in *Pete Kelly's Blues.* Possessed a smooth, slightly husky voice that usually was backed by jazz-influenced arrangements. Collaborated with her husband Dave Barbour to write several of her song hits "Manana," "Lover," "Fever" and "Is That All There Is."

I learned courage from Buddha, Jesus, Lincoln, Einstein and Cary Grant.

1928 **Jack Kevorkian:** "Dr. Death." Retired American pathologist, writer and inventor. Devised a suicide machine with which a person could commit suicide by merely pushing a button. Has assisted in the deaths of more than 100 people with incurable diseases. In 1998 he was convicted of murder and sentenced to 10–25 years in prison.

I want to use death to benefit humanity. Now, it's just a total waste.

1948 **Stevie Nicks:** American singer and songwriter. Best known for her work as vocalist and songwriter with the musical group formed by Mick Fleetwood. Co-wrote the songs "Rhiannon" and "Landslide" for the successful album *Fleetwood Mac.* This was followed by *Rumors,* one of the all-time best-selling albums, featuring songs such as Nicks "Gold Dust Woman." Her first solo album *Bella Donna* (1981), featuring "Stop Dragging My Heart Around," Leather and Lace" and "Edge of Seventeen."

By the time I was five, I was a little diva.

1951 **Sally Ride:** American astronaut and astrophysicist. Joined NASA in 1977. First American woman in space on Space Shuttle *Challenger* (June 18–24, 1983), as flight engineer. Preceded in space by Russians Valentina Treshkova in 1963 and Svetlana Saviskaya in 1982. Ride later became director of the California Space Institute at the University of California, San Diego.

I came into this because I wanted to fly in space. My intention after the flight is to come back to the astronaut office and get back in line and try to fly again.

OTHERS: 1264 Japanese shogun **Prince Koreyasu,** 1566 Ottoman Emperor **Mehmed III,** 1650 1st Duke of Marlborough **John Churchill,** 1667 French mathematician **Abraham de Moivre,** 1700 German social reformer **Nicolaus Zinzendorf,** 1893 U.S. actress **Norma Talmadge,** 1912 U.S. actor **Jay Silverheels,** 1913 British actor **Peter Cushing,** 1923 TV actor **James Arness,** 1938 Canadian opera singer **Teresa Stratas,** 1939 U.S. sports broadcaster **Brent Musburger,** 1941 South-African tennis player **Cliff Drysdale,** 1949 U.S. singer **Hank Williams Jr.,** 1964 U.S. guitarist/singer **Lenny Kravitz,** 1966 English actress **Helena Bonham Carter,** 1974 Swedish swimmer **Lars Frőlander**

May 27

1265 **Dante Alighieri:** Italian poet. A towering figure of European literature. His life was given direction by his spiritual love for Beatrice Portinari to whom he dedicated most of his poetry. His most famous work is the masterpiece *The Divine Comedy,* a profoundly Christian vision of human temporal and eternal destiny. It is the story of his imaginary journey through hell, purgatory and heaven with guides Vergil and Beatrice. By writing it in Italian rather than Latin, he made Italian a literary language.

There is no greater sorrow than to recall a time of happiness in misery.

1818 **Amelia Jenks Bloomer:** American social reformer. Campaigned for temperance and women's rights. Wrote on education and unjust marriage laws. Advocated dress reform which led to her wearing full trousers, nicknamed "bloomers."

The costume of women should be suited to her wants and necessities. It should conduce at once to her health, comfort and usefulness; and, while it should not fail to conduce to her personal adornment, it should make that end of secondary importance.

1836 **Jay Gould:** American financier, ruthless speculator and unscrupulous robber baron. First worked as a surveyor and then engaged in lumbering. In 1857 he became the principal shareholder in a Pennsylvania bank. Began to buy railroad bonds. Manipulated the shares to become president of the Erie Railway Co. While trying to corner the gold market in September 1869, he caused the "Black Friday" stock market crash. Gained control of the Union Pacific, Western Union, the New York *World* and the Manhattan Elevated Railroad.

I can hire one-half the working class to kill the other half.

1837 **Wild Bill Hickok:** American frontiersman, originally named **James Butler.** A legendary marksman, he was a Union scout and spy during the Civil War. After the war he was a tough sheriff and U.S. marshal who cleaned up Hays City and Abilene. Toured with Buffalo Bill's Wild West Show. Shot dead while playing poker in Deadwood in the Dakota Territory by Jack McCall. Ever since his hand a pair of aces and a pair of eights, all cards black, has been known as a "dead man's hand."

Never run away from a gun. Bullets can travel faster than you can. Besides, if you're going to be hit, you had better get in the front than in the back. It looks better.

1867 **[Enoch] Arnold Bennett:** British novelist, dramatist, critic and journalist whose best work describes life in the "Five Towns"—the Potteries in his native Staffordshire. Also wrote the three novels that make up *The Clayhanger Family.*

The moment you're born you're done for.

1878 **Isadora Duncan:** American dancer. Rejected the conventions of classical ballet. One of the first to interpret dance as a free form of art. Inspired by ancient Greece, she danced barefoot in a tunic without tights. Found great success in Europe. Inspired a wide range of avant-garde artists. Free spirit who believed in free love. Strangled in a freakish accident when her long scarf caught in the spokes of a car's wheel.

Any intelligent woman who reads the marriage contract, and then goes into it deserves all the consequences.

1907 **Rachel Louise Carson:** American marine biologist and science writer. Her books *The Sea Around Us, The Edge of the Sea* and particularly her seminal and prophetic *The Silent Spring* are known for their literary merit as well as their scientific content. She warned of the hazards to wildlife and humans of the indiscriminate use of insecticides.

The "control of nature" is a phrase conceived in arrogance, born in the Neanderthal age of biology and the convenience of man.

1911 **Hubert H. Humphrey:** American politician. Worked as a pharmacist before entering politics. Outstanding liberal Democratic Party leader. U.S. senator from Minnesota. Helped forge bipartisan support for the Nuclear Test-Ban Treaty and the Civil Rights Act. As Lyndon Johnson's vice president, he defended U.S. participation in the Vietnam War. Democratic presidential candidate (1968), narrowly losing to Richard Nixon.

A fellow that doesn't have any tears doesn't have any heart.

1912 **Sam Snead:** American golfer. Nickname: 'Slamming Sammy." Won 81 tournaments on the U.S. Professional Golfers Association Tour between 1936 and 1965. Credited with 135 victories worldwide. Also had six Senior Championships.

The only things I fear on a golf course are lightning and Ben Hogan.

1915 **Herman Wouk:** American novelist. Served aboard a destroyer-minesweeper during World War II, an experience that led to his best-selling novel *The Caine Mutiny*, for which he won a Pulitzer Prize. Other novels: *Marjorie Morningstar, The Winds of War*, and *War and Remembrance.*

Income tax returns are the most imaginative fiction being written today.

1923 **Henry Kissinger:** U.S. government official. Secretary of state for presidents Nixon and Ford. Nobel Peace Prize winner (1973), shared with Le Duc Tho of North Vietnam. Developed the first official U.S. contact with Communist China. Attempted to negotiate an Arab-Israeli peace agreement (1973–75). Initiated SALT talks (1969). Later became an international consultant, lecturer and writer.

Power is the greatest aphrodisiac.

1930 **John Barth:** American writer. Most of his writing is set in Maryland's eastern shore where he grew up. Taught at Johns Hopkins University from 1973 to 1995. Best-known works are his novels: *The End of the Road, The Sot-Weed Factor,* and *Giles Goat-Boy.* Also wrote *Lost in the Funhouse*, a collection of short stores and *Chimera*, three linked novellas.

Everyone is necessarily the hero of his own life story.

OTHERS: 1332 Tunisian historian **Ibn Khaldun**, 1794 U.S. financier **Cornelius Vanderbilt**, 1819 American composer **Julia Ward Howe**, 1871 French painter/graphic artist **Georges Rouault**, 1894 French writer **Louis-Ferdinand Céline**, 1894 American author **Dashiell Hammett**, 1897 British physicist **John Cockcroft**, 1908 U.S. composer **Harold Rome**, 1911 Mayor of Jerusalem **Teddy Kollek**, 1911 U.S. actor **Vincent Price**, 1912 American author **John Cheever**, 1917 Japanese Prime Minister **Yasuhiro Nakasone**, 1922 British actor **Christopher Lee**, 1935 U.S. beauty queen/actress **Lee Meriwether**, 1936 U.S. actor **Lou Gossett Jr.**, 1946 Danish musician **Niels-Henning Ørsted Pedersen**

May 28

1759 **William Pitt the Younger:** English statesman. Prime minister of England (1783–1801). Son of William Pitt, who trice was virtually prime minister. The Younger Pitt has been cited as England's greatest prime minister. Clamped down on radical agitation during French Revolutionary wars. Secured the Act of Union with Ireland but resigned when his proposal for Catholic emancipation was denied.

Necessity is the plea of every infringement of human freedom. It is the argument of tyrants; it is the creed of slaves.

1807 **Jean Louis Rodolphe Agassiz:** Swiss-born U.S. naturalist, zoologist, oceanographer, mining engineer and author. Founder of the Marine Biological Laboratory at Woods Hole, Massachusetts. Major work: *Contributions to the Natural History of the United States of America.* His wife Elizabeth Cabot Agassiz, herself a naturalist, helped organize and manager several of her husbands field expeditions.

Every scientific truth goes through three states: first, people say it conflicts with the Bible; next, they say it has been discovered before; lastly, they say they always believed it.

1884 **Edvard Beneš:** A founder of modern Czechoslovakia. Served as first foreign minister (1918–1935) and president (1935–38). Led exile regime in London during World War II. Returned home in 1945, serving as president until communist takeover of 1948.

I never feel sure of myself except when I am speaking the truth.

1888 **Jim Thorpe:** Originally James Francis. Outstanding predominately Indian-American athlete. Declared a pro, he was stripped of 1912 gold medals in Olympic pentathlon and decathlon. They were returned posthumously in 1983. All-American running back at Carlisle Indian School. Played major league football and baseball. Named Outstanding Athlete of 20th Century (1950). Served as the first president of what would become the National Football League. Had difficulty adjusting to retirement and fell into near-poverty and bouts of alcoholism. After decking Knute Rockne who once tried to tackle him, Thorpe said:

Son, they came to see old Jim play.

1908 **Ian Fleming:** English writer. Created the character of James Bond, Agent 007, licensed to kill for the British government. Books include: *From Russia with Love* and *Goldfinger, Dr. No,* and *Thunderball*, all of which were made into successful movies.

Men want a woman whom they can turn on and off like a light switch.

1911 **Randolph Churchill:** British writer. Son of Winston and Clementine Churchill. Unsuccessful politician. Noted for his irascibility, bad temper and drinking problem. Carved out a career for himself as a successful writer. Began the official biography of his father but died after finishing the second volume. The project was completed by Sir Martin Gilbert.

No statesmen ever will find it worth his pains, to tax our labor and exercise our brain.

1912 **Patrick White:** Australian writer. Wrote misanthropic novels that explored the possibility of savagery. Works: *The Aunt's Story*, *The Tree of Man*, *Riders in the Chariot*, and *The Eye of the Storm*. Also wrote plays and short stories. Awarded the Nobel Prize in 1973.

I forget what I was taught. I only remember what I have learnt.

1916 **Walker Percy:** American novelist. While working as a pathologist he contracted tuberculosis. While he recovered he decided on a writing career and conversion to Roman Catholicism. First and best novel *The Moviegoer* introduced his concept of spiritual emptiness found in the rootless modern world. Other works dealt with the New South transformed by industry and technology, including *Love in the Ruins*.

We love those who know the worst of us and don't turn their faces away.

1917 **Barry Commoner:** American biologist, educator and environmentalist. Advocated environmental protection and use of solar energy. Warned of the environmental threats posed by modern technology. Books: *Science and Survival* and *The Politics of Energy*.

If you can see the light at the end of the tunnel you are looking the wrong way.

1919 **May Swenson:** American poet, editor, translator and professor of poetry. Taught at Bryn Mawr, the University of North Carolina, the University of Californian at Riverside, Purdue University and Utah State University. Editor of New Directions published from 1959 to 1966. Served as Chancellor of The Academy of American Poets from 1980 to her death in 1989. Collections: *Another Animal*, *A Cage of Spines*, and *To Mix with Time*.

We play in the den of the Gods and snort at death.

1944 **Rudolph W. Giuliani:** American politician. Mayor of New York City from 1994 to 2001. Distinguished himself by his calming leadership after the attack on the Twin Towers by terrorists on September 11, 2001. Currently Chairman and CEO of Giuliani Partners LLC.

We only see the oppressive side of authority. Maybe it comes out of our history and our background. What we don't see is that freedom is not a concept in which people can do anything they want, be anything they can be. Freedom is about authority. Freedom is about the willingness of every single human being to cede to lawful authority a great deal of discretion about what you do and how you do it.

1968 **Kylie Minogue:** Australian singer, songwriter and actress. Well-known for her provocative music videos and her sex symbol celebrity. Holds the record for the highest concert ticket sales for a female performer. Hits: "The Locomotion," "Better the Devil You Know," and "Can't Get You Out of My Head." In the spring of 2005, she developed breast cancer and has since undergone chemotherapy treatment.

I don't try to be a sex bomb. I am one.

OTHERS: 1140 Chinese poet **Xin Qiji**, 1779 Irish poet **Thomas Moore**, 1818 American Confederate general **Pierre Beauregard**, 1845 Hungarian violinist **Leopold Auer**, 1858 Swedish inventor **Carl Rickard Nyberg**, 1910 U.S. singer **T-Bone Walker**, 1915 American linguist **Joseph Greenberg**, 1922 American boxing trainer **Lou Duva**, 1931 U.S. actress **Carroll Baker**, 1936 U.S. civil rights leader **Betty Shabazz**, 1938 U.S. basketball player **Jerry West**, 1944 U.S. singer **Gladys Knight**, 1945 U.S. physician/professional clown **Patch Adams**, 1945 U.S. singer **John Fogerty**, 1946 Indian poet **Satchidanandan**, 1949 U.S. musician **Wendy O. Williams**

May 29

1630 **Charles II:** English king of Britain and Ireland. As Prince of Wales, he sided with his father Charles I in the English Civil War. When his father was executed, he assumed the title of king, but was forced into exile for nine years, before he was summoned back to the throne. For the last four years of his life, he ruled without parliament.

It is upon the navy under the Providence of God that the safety, honor, and welfare of the realm do chiefly attend.

1736 **Patrick Henry:** American patriot, lawyer, and merchant. Delegate to Continental Congress. Governor of Virginia and four times reelected. Great orator whose stirring call to arms brought many to the struggle against the British.

If life is so dear, or peace so sweet, as to be purchased at the price of chains of slavery. Forbid it, Almighty God! I know not what course others may take but as for me, give me liberty or give me death.

1874 **G.K. [Gilbert Keith] Chesterton:** English essayist, novelist, journalist and poet. Father Brown was his detective creation, appearing in a series of books. The character first appeared in *The Innocence of Father Brown* (1911). Became a Catholic in 1922 and thereafter wrote mainly on religious topics, including books on the lives of St. Francis of Assisi and Thomas Aquinas.

To love means loving the unlovable. To forgive means pardoning the unpardonable. Faith means believing the unbelievable. Hope means hoping when everything seems hopeless.

1880 **Oswald Spengler:** German philosopher of history. Maintained that every culture is a distinct organic form that grows, matures and decays. Author of the morbidly prophetic *The Decline of the West.*

I maintain that today many an inventor, many a diplomat, many a financier is a sounder philosopher than all those who practice the dull craft of experimental psychology.

1892 **Max Brand:** Pseudonym of **Frederick Faust.** "King of the pulp writers." American novelist and screenwriter. Wrote the Dr. Kildare series and *Destry Rides Again.*

There has to be a woman, but not much of a one. A good horse is much more important.

1894 **Beatrice Lillie:** Canadian-British comedienne. Developed her comic genius in André Charlot produced revues. Established an international reputation as a high-spirited star of sophisticated comedies. Toured worldwide in *An Evening with Beatrice Lillie* between 1952 and 1956. An example of her quick wit is her remark to a waiter who spilled soup on her.

Never darken my Dior again.

1897 **Erich Wolfgang Korngold:** Austrian-American composer. G. Mahler and A. Schnabel praised his childhood compositions. Established his reputation with *Die tote Stadt* (1920). Moved to Hollywood in 1934 where he became best known for his film scores, including those for *Captain Blood, Anthony Adverse,* and *The Adventures of Robin Hood,* winning Academy Awards for the latter two.

As for my working habits, I like the idea of perfection. If a thing is not right it is done over and over again.

1903 **Bob Hope:** "Old Ski Nose." U.S. actor, comedian. Got his start in vaudeville in the twenties, where he perfected the character of the none-too-bright, not-too-brave, know-it-all who at the first sign of danger is apt to hide behind some female's skirt. Movies: *The Cat and the Canary, Road to Singapore, My Favorite Blonde* and *The Paleface.* Hosted a popular radio show and appeared in numerous TV specials. For more than 40 years he took variety shows to U.S. troops overseas.

I have seen what a laugh can do. It can transform almost unbearable tears into something bearable, even hopeful.

1912 **Pamela Hansford Johnson:** Prolific English critic and author. Wrote both psychological novels and literary studies. Her output included 27 novels, 7 short plays, six in collaboration with her second husband C.P. Snow, a number of critical works, short stories, verse, sociological studies, and a collection of autobiographical essays.

There are few things more disturbing than to find, in somebody we detest, a moral quality which seems to us demonstrably superior to anything we ourselves possess. It augurs nor merely an unfairness on the part of creation, but a lack of artistic judgment. Sainthood is acceptable only in saints.

1917 **John F. Kennedy:** Thirty-fifth American president (1961–63). Assassinated by Lee Harvey Oswald in Dallas, Texas, November 22, 1963, ending a thousand days in office, often referred to as "Camelot." First and thus far only Roman Catholic president. World War II hero. Congressman from Massachusetts (1947–53), Senator (1953–60).Established the Peace Corps and the Alliance for Progress. Forced U.S.S.R. to pull missiles from Cuba (1962).

For those to whom much is given, much is required.

1939 **Al Unser:** American automobile racer, born into a family of racers. Three-time USAC/CART national champion. Four-time Indy winner. Brother of Bobby Unser and father of Al Jr.

You may drive the freeways daily at top speeds with confidence and skill. But that doesn't qualify you as a race driver. Put an ordinary driver in an Indy-type race car and he'd probably crash before he got out of the pit area.

1955 **John Hinckley Jr.:** Obsessed with actress Jodie Foster, he manically thought to impress her by assassinating Ronald Reagan in 1981. As a result of his firing a revolver six times, the president was wounded by a ricocheted bullet, Press Secretary James Brady was permanently disabled, and a police officer and a secret service agent were wounded. He was tried and found not guilty by reason of insanity and subsequently has been confined to Saint Elizabeth's Hospital in Washington D.C.

Guns are neat little things, aren't they? They can kill extraordinary people with very little effort.

OTHERS: 1716 French naturalist **Louis Daubenton,** 1841 U.S. poet **Eugene F. Ware,** 1860 Spanish composer **Isaac Albéniz,** 1892 Argentine writer **Alfonsina Storni,** 1894 Austrian-born director **Josef von Sternberg,** 1906 British author **T. H. White,** 1913 American boxer **Tony Zale,** 1914 Nepalese sherpa **Tenzing Norgay,** 1922 Greek composer **Iannis Xenakis,** 1938 Baseball commissioner **Fay Vincent,** 1941 English guitarist **Roy Crewsdon,** 1948 U.S. soap opera star **Anthony Geary,** 1953 American composer **Danny Elfman,** 1958 U.S. actress **Annette Bening,** 1959 English actor **Rupert Everett,** 1982 Brazilian model **Ana Beatriz Barros,** 1984 U.S. basketball player **Carmelo Anthony**

May 30

1757 **Henry Addington, 1st Viscount Sidmouth:** British statesman. Elected to the House of Commons in 1784. Became Speaker of the House in 1789. When William Pitt the Younger resigned as Prime Minister after failure to achieve Catholic emancipation in Ireland, Addington replaced him as PM in 1801. Addington's poor management led to Pitt's return to power in 1804. Addington remained an important political figure until 1832.

I hate liberality— nine times out of ten it is cowardice, and the tenth time lack of principle.

1814 **Mikhail Bakunin:** Russian revolutionary and anarchist leader. Took part in revolutionary agitation in Germany, Austria and France before being extradited to Russia and exiled to Siberia. Founder of Nihilism. His revolutionary manifesto: *An Appeal to Slavs*. Returned to the West and had a famous quarrel with Karl Marx, which split the European revolutionary movement.

The passion for destruction is also a creative passion.

1888 **James A. Farley:** U.S. political leader, businessman. Managed Franklin D. Roosevelt's 1932 and 36 presidential campaigns. Powerful chairman of Democratic National Committee (1932–40). U.S. Postmaster General (1933–40).

A rigged convention is one with the other man's delegates in control. An open convention is when your delegates are in control.

1891 **Ben Bernie:** American radio bandleader. Known for mellifluous and humorous introductions and his trademark radio sign-off:

And now the time has come to lend an ear to au revoir. Pleasant dreams. Think of us ... when requesting your themes. Until the next time when ... possibly you may all tune in again. Keep the Old Maestro always ... in your schemes. Yowsah, yowsah, yowsah.

1892 **Stepin Fetchit [Lincoln Theodore Perry]:** U.S. actor. First African-American to receive featured billing. Played lazy, easily frightened comic characters now labeled as insulting stereotypes in *Show Boat*, *David Harum* and *Dimples*. First black entertainer to earn a million.

All the things that Bill Cosby and Sidney Poitier have done wouldn't be possible if I hadn't broken that law. I set up thrones for them to come and sit on.

1898 **Howard Hawks:** Considered the first American "auteur," having control of films from start to finish as screenwriter, producer and director. Films: *Scarface*, *Bringing Up Baby*, *Only Angels Have Wings*, *Sergeant York*, *Red River* and *Gentlemen Prefer Blondes*.

For me the best drama is one that deals with a man in danger.

1899 **Irving Thalberg:** American film executive. Became head of production at MGM in 1925. Known as "the boy wonder of Hollywood." Controlled MGM's output by supervising script selection and final editing. Responsible for the high quality of the studios' films. Married to actress Norma Shearer. Never expected to live to 30 because of a rheumatic heart condition, he died at 37 of pneumonia.

Always remember, there's nothing too good for the audience.

1901 **Cornelia Otis Skinner:** American stage actress and writer. Daughter of tragedian Otis Skinner. Best known for her staged one-woman melodramas and her monologues. Co-wrote the play *The Pleasure of His Company* and the book *Our Hearts Were Young and Gay*.

Woman's virtue is man's greatest invention.

1903 **Countee Cullen:** African-American poet. Won a New York City wide poetry contest as a teen. His first collection of poems, *Color* (1925) received critical acclaim. A leader of the Harlem Renaissance. Author of *The Black Christ*, *The Ballad of the Brown Girl* and *Color*. Taught in the city's public schools from 1934 to his death in 1946.

Never love with all your heart/ It only ends in aching.

1909 **Benny Goodman:** "The King of Swing." U.S. clarinetist and bandleader. His sensational broadcast from Los Angeles' Palomar Ballroom is seen as the beginning of the Swing era. Song hits: "Stompin' at the Savoy," "Don't Be That Way," Let's Dance," "Sing, Sing, Sing" and "Taking a Chance on Love." One of the first white bandleaders to include blacks in he musical groups.

If a guy's got it, let him give it. I'm selling music not prejudice.

1926 **Christine Jorgenson:** An ex–GI, named George, she became one of the first to have sex reassignment surgery. Became a spokesperson for transsexual and transgendered people.

While I'm not a complete woman, no one is a complete anything — male or female — including myself. But I still consider myself a woman.

1964 **Wynonna Judd:** Award winning country music singer. She sang as a duo with her mother Naomi as The Judds before working as a single. She is the half sister of actress Ashley Judd. Wynonna has 20 number one singes and a Grammy award. Her #1 country albums are *Wynonna (*1992), *Tell Me Why* (1993) and *What the World Needs Now Is Love* (2003).

There's a place for all types of country music as long as there is honesty and realness and a real human experience for the fans.

OTHERS: 1010 Chinese Emperor **Renzong**, 1220 Russian ruler **Alexander Nevsky**, 1800 German mathematician **Karl Feuerbach**, 1835 English poet laureate **Alfred Austin**, 1846 Russian jeweled egg maker **Peter Carl Fabergé**, 1859 French psychologist/neurologist **Pierre Marie Felix Janet**, 1886 American critic **Randolph Bourne**, 1908 U.S. voice actor **Mel Blanc**, 1908 Swedish physicist **Hannes Alfvén**, 1912 U.S. biochemist **Julius Axelrod**, 1912 Welch actor **Hugh Griffith**, 1918 Mexican poet **"Pita" Amor**, 1920 U.S. film director **Franklin Schaffner**, 1943 U.S. football player **Gale Sayers**, 1964 U.S. musician **Tom Morello**, 1972 Dominican baseball player **Manny Ramirez**

May 31

1819 **Walt Whitman:** "The Good Gray Poet." "The Bard of Democracy." U.S. poet, journalist, essayist. His *Leaves of Grass* was initially condemned as a vulgar, immoral book. Other works: "Drum Taps," "Crossing Brooklyn Ferry," "Song of Myself," and "Out of the Cradle Endlessly Rocking."

I am for those who believe in loose thoughts. I

share the midnight orgies of young men. I dance with the dancers and drink with the drinkers.

1857 Pope **Pius XI [Ambrogio Damiano Ratti]:** Italian religious leader. Papacy (1922–39). Best known for negotiating Lateran Treaty (1929), establishing the Vatican's independence from Italy.

To suffer and to endure is the lot of humanity.

1860 **Walter Sickert:** German-born English impressionist painter. Favored urban scenes and ordinary people as his subjects. Pupil of Whistler. Influenced by Degas. Used the latter's style to illustrate London low life. Paintings: *The Old Bedford Music Hall, The Camden Town Murder* and *Ennui.* His comment to unwelcome guests:

Come again when you can't stay so long.

1893 **Elizabeth Coatsworth:** American poet and children's writer. Her poetry included the collection *Compass Rose.* Also wrote a novel *Here I Stay,* children's stories such as *The Cat Went to Heaven* and a New England chronicle, *Maine Ways.* Her best writing was about animals, farming, and seafaring. Wife of author Henry Beston.

Only of one thing I am sure:/ when I dream/ I am ageless.

1894 **Fred Allen:** American comedian and humorist who started in vaudeville. Unchallenged master ad-libber. Created routines which influenced several later comic generations. Became a national institution on several witty and popular radio series featuring the famous Allen's Alley of colorful and beloved characters. These included Socrates Mulligan (Charlie Cantor), Senator Beauregard Claghorn (Kenny Delmar), Titus Moody (Parker Fennelly), Pansy Nussbaum (Minerva Pious) and Ajax Cassidy (Peter Donald). He and his good friend Jack Benny milked a "feud" on their radio programs for many years, with hilarious put downs.

Hanging is too good for a man who makes puns; he should be drawn and quoted.

1898 **Norman Vincent Peale:** American clergyman. Prominent religious author and radio preacher on national program *The Art of Living* for 54 years. Wrote *The Power of Positive Thinking.* Awarded the Presidential Medal of Freedom in 1984.

Imagination is the true magic carpet.

1911 **Maurice Allais:** French economist and physicist. Awarded the 1988 Nobel Prize in Economics "for his pioneering contributions to the theory of markets and efficient use of resources." Made contributions to decision theory and monetary policy. The Allais paradox, a decision problem he first presented in 1953 which contradicts expected utility theory is named for him.

In essence, the present creation of money, out of nothing by the banking system, is similar — I do not hesitate to say it in order to make people clearly realize what is at stake here — to the creation of money by counterfeiters, so rightly condemned by law.

1920 **Edward Bennett Williams:** Top American trial attorney whose clients included Frank Costello, Robert Vesco, Frank Sinatra, Michael Milken, the Reverend Sun Myung Moon, John Connally. Adam Clayton Powell, Jimmy Hoffa and Senator Joseph McCarthy. Owner of the Baltimore Orioles baseball team and the Washington Redskins football team.

The lawyer is neither expected nor qualified to make a moral judgment of the person seeking his help.

1926 **John G. Kemeny:** Hungarian-born U.S. mathematician, philosopher and educator. Helped design the world's first atomic bomb while working on the Manhattan Project. Pioneered the computer revolution by co-creating the programming language BASIC (*Beginner's All-Purpose Symbolic Instruction Code*), first to use a very simple syntax. It served simultaneously as an "interpreter," in that it analyzed (compiled) each line as it was written. As president of Dartmouth College during the tumultuous period of student protest during the Vietnam War, Kemeny maintained a relative calm on his campus by his personal popularity with the students. Chaired the commission that investigated the Three Mile Island nuclear power plant accident.

The man ignorant of mathematics will be increasingly limited in his grasp of the main forces of civilization.

1930 **Clint Eastwood:** American actor, director and producer. First gained attention it the TV western *Rawhide.* Famous for his tough guy roles. Appeared in "spaghetti westerns," directed by Sergio Leone, becoming an international star. Returned to Hollywood to appear in the very successful *Dirty Harry* films. Combined acting and directing in films such as *Unforgiven,* for which he won an Oscar for both functions and *Million Dollar Baby* for which he became the oldest director (74) to win a Best Director Award.

They say marriages are made in Heaven. But so is thunder and lightning.

1939 **Terry Waite:** British humanitarian and author. Best known for his work as a hostage negotiator in Lebanon as an envoy of the Church of England. Was able to secure the release of several prisoners of the Islamic Jihad, before being taking hostage himself. Imprisoned in February 1987, he wasn't released until November 1991. Today, he is involved in a great many charities.

The terrible thing about terrorism is that ultimately it destroys those who practice it. Slowly but surely, as they try to extinguish life in others, the light within them dies.

1943 **Joe Namath:** "Broadway Joe." U.S. football New York Jets' quarterback, with a fondness for New York nightlife. Two-time All-AFL, and once All-NFL. Promised and delivered a Super Bowl victory for the Jets in 1969. Pro Hall of Fame (1985).

Football is an honest game. It's true to life. It's a game about sharing. Football is a team game. So is life.

OTHERS: 1640 King of Poland **Michael Wiśniowiecki**, 1837 English clown **Joseph Grimaldi**, 1838 English philosopher **Henry Sidgwick**, 1872 English cartoonist **Heath Robinson**, 1908 American actor **Don Ameche**, 1912 U.S. senator **Henry "Scoop" Jackson**, 1922 English actor **Denholm Elliott**, 1923 Prince of Monaco **Rainier III**, 1924 U.S. ambassador/cabinet member **Patricia R. Harris**, 1938 American singer **Johnny Paycheck**, 1938 U.S. folk singer **Peter Yarrow**, 1948 British musician **John Bonham**, 1965 U.S. actress **Brooke Shields**, 1972 Norwegian cross-country skier **Frode Estil**

June 1

1563 **Robert Cecil:** First Earl of Salisbury, Trained in statesmanship by his father William Cecil, principal advisor to Queen Elizabeth I. Robert succeeded his father as chief minister in 1598. Guided the peaceful succession of Elizabeth by James I. Negotiated the end of the war with Spain and allied England to France.

Virtue consists of avoiding scandal and venereal disease.

1780 **Carl Von Clausewitz:** Prussian general and military historian. After serving with distinction in the Napoleonic Wars, he was appointed director of the War College. Wrote *On War*, which expounded philosophy of war. Advocate of Total War. His work had a tremendous effect on military strategies during the World Wars.

War is nothing more than the continuation of politics by other means.

1801 **Brigham Young:** President of the Mormon Church and colonizer, who significantly influenced the development of the American West. Assumed leadership of the Mormons after the murder of founder Joseph Smith. Led followers to the Great Salt Lake Basin in Utah, arriving July 24, 1847, announcing "This is the place."

We should never permit ourselves to do anything that we are not willing to see our children do.

1804 **Mikhail Glinka:** Russian civil servant and composer. Wrote opera, *Life for the Tsar*. His *Ruslan and Lyudmila* pioneered the style of the Russian national school of composers. Greatly influenced Pyotr Tchaikovsky and Nicolai Rimsky-Korsakov.

A nation creates music — the composer only arranges it.

1878 **John Masefield:** English poet, dramatist, and novelist. From 1930 until his death in 1967, poet laureate of London. Best known for his sea poems, *Salt Water Ballads* and the narrative poem "Reynard the Fox." His novels are romantic adventure stories. Also wrote literary criticism.

Love, freedom, comrades, surely makes amends for all the thorns through which we walk to death.

1924 **William Sloane Coffin, Jr.:** American clergyman. Leader in Vietnam peace movement. Chaplain, Yale University (1958–75). Pastor, Riverside Church, New York City from 1977.

The world is too dangerous for anything but truth and too small for anything but love. The word of the Lord falls with the force of a snowflake.

1926 **Andy Griffith:** American actor, who made his Broadway debut in *No Time for Sergeants*, a role he reprised in a film. Other movies include the acclaimed *A Face in the Crowd*. Starred in many TV series, including the popular sitcom *The Andy Griffith Show* and the dramatic series *Matlock*. His appealing native Blue Ridge drawl allowed him to create homespun characters.

If ah was to lose my accent, ah'd have to compete with actors and ah wouldn't do that for a hundred dollar bill!

1926 **Marilyn Monroe:** Originally **Norma Jean Mortenson**. Hollywood's most glamorous blonde sex symbol since Jean Harlow. A sense of tragedy surrounded the vulnerable star, who came to hate the image she and the studios created for her. Married three times, her husband included Joe DiMaggio and Arthur Miller. Films: *The Asphalt Jungle*, *Gentlemen Prefer Blondes*, *The Seven Year Itch*, *Bus Stop*, *Some Like It Hot* and *The Misfits*. Died at age 36 of an apparently self-administrated drug overdose.

If you can make a girl laugh — you can make her do anything.

1934 **Pat Boone:** American pop singer and actor. Direct descendent of American pioneer Daniel Boone. Known as "The Kid in White Buck Shoes," one of the most popular entertainers of the 1950 and 1960s. Hits included: "Ain't' That a Shame," "Love Letters in the Sand," "April Love," and "Friendly Persuasion." Wrote the theme song from the film *Exodus*, "This Land Is Mine." Films: *April Love*, *State Fair* and *Journey to the Center of the Earth*.

It seems that my wife Shirley was always pregnant until we found out what was causing it.

1937 **Morgan Freeman:** African-American actor, known for his mellifluous voice. "Easy Reader" on television's "The Electric Company." Moved on to Broadway and films. Oscar nominated for *Street Smart*, *Driving Miss Daisy*, *The Shawshank Redemption* and finally won for *Million Dollar Baby*. Publicly opposes the celebration of Black History Month, arguing that Black history is American history, and racism won't end until people stop calling people white or black.

I don't get off on romantic parts. But I often think if I had had my dental work done early on, well, maybe.

1937 **Colleen McCullough:** Australian neuroscientist and internationally acclaimed novelist. Worked in several hospitals before spending ten years teaching and doing research at the Yale Medical School. Novels include: *The Thorn Birds*, *Indecent Obsession* and the *Masters of Rome* series.

You don't have to walk in a man's shoes to know

where he's been. All you have to do is, buy him a new pair, to get him to where he's going.

1953 **David "Son of Sam" Berkowitz:** American serial killer who murdered six people and wounded several others in the 1970s. His victims were teen girls with long, dark hair, and young couples. His murderous sprees came to and end on August 10, 1977 when he was arrested and confessed. Sentenced to 365 years in prison. His nickname came from a neighbor Sam Carr, who according to Berkowitz was a high demon, who sent his evil Labrador Retriever to command Berkowitz to kill.

It was a command. I had a sign and I followed it. Sam told me what to do and I did it.

OTHERS: 1633 Italian astronomer **Germiniano Montanari**, 1790 Austrian playwright **Ferdinand Raimund**, 1796 French mathematician **Sadi Carnot**, 1843 Scottish fingerprinting pioneer **Henry Faulds**, 1882 English poet/critic **John Drinkwater**, 1890 U.S. actor **Frank Morgan**, 1921 U.S. bandleader **Nelson Riddle**, 1936 British cartoonist **Gerald Scarfe**, 1939 British race car driver **Jackie Stewart**, 1940, 1945 U.S. mezzo-soprano **Frederica von Stade**, 1947 English guitarist **Ron Wood**, 1973 German model **Heidi Klum**, 1974 Canadian singer **Alanis Morissette**, 1981 Venezuelan pitcher **Carlos Zambrano**, 1982 Belgian tennis player **Justine Henin-Hardenne**

June 2

1730 **Martha Washington:** American widow **Martha Dandridge Custis**, who married George Washington, first president of the United States. She brought considerable wealth to the union as well as two stepchildren. The Washingtons had no children of their own.

I've learned from experience that the greater part of our happiness or misery depends on our dispositions and not on our circumstances. I have learned too much of the vanity of human affairs to expect felicity from the scenes of public life.

1740 **Donatien Alphonse François, Marquis de Sade:** French nobleman and writer. Condemned to death in 1722 for his cruelty and sexual perversions but escaped. Later was imprisoned for 12 years by royal decree for staging orgies during which he whipped and sodomized prostitutes. While in the Bastille, he wrote *The 120 Days of Sodom*. After his release, wrote *Justine*, *Philosophy in the Bedroom* and *Juliette*. Died insane. His life and erotic writings spawned the word "sadism," deriving pleasure from inflicting pain.

There is no more lively sensation than that of pain; its impressions are certain and dependable, they never deceive as may those of the pleasures women perpetually feign and almost never experience.

1773 **John Randolph:** American statesman. As congressman from Virginia, he was the Democratic leader of the House of Representatives. Quarreled with Thomas Jefferson, opposed the War of 1812 and also the Missouri Compromise. Helped draft a new Virginia constitution in 1829.

That most delicious of all privileges — spending other people's money.

1840 **Thomas Hardy:** English novelist, poet and dramatist. Set most of his work in the imaginary county of Wessex in southwester England. Novels: *Far from the Madding Crowd*, *The Return of the Native*, *Tess of the D'Urbervilles* and *Jude the Obscure*. Poetry: *Wessex Poems* and *Winter Words*.

The real, if unavowed, purpose of fiction is to give pleasure by gratifying the love of the uncommon in human experience, mental or corporal.

1840 **John Lancaster Spalding:** American Catholic bishop. First bishop of Peoria, Illinois and a founder of the Catholic University of America. Remembered for the many churches, schools and institutions he founded. Two of his uncles also were bishops. His aunt was a nun and his sister was a Mother Superior in St. Louis.

As memory may be a paradise from which we cannot be driven, it may also be a hell from which we cannot escape.

1857 Sir **Edward Elgar:** British composer, regarded as having inaugurated the "English musical renaissance." The *Enigma Variations* and the oratorio *The Dream of Gerontius* established him as the leading figure in English music. Other works: *Pomp and Circumstances Marches*, two symphonies, concertos for violin and cello, and tone poems *Cockaigne* and *Falstaff*.

Music is in the air — you simply take as much of it as you want.

1868 **John Hope:** African-American educator and political activist. First black president of Morehouse College. Later became the president of Atlanta University. Helped found the Niagara Movement and organized the Commission on Interracial Cooperation of which he was the first president.

We have sat on the river bank and caught catfish with pin hooks. The time has come to harpoon a whale.

1886 **Grover Whalen:** American politician, businessman and public relations expert. Official greeter of the city of New York. Welcomed everyone to the city from Charles Lindbergh to Admiral Richard Byrd to Douglas MacArthur. Was the master of the ticker tape parades. President of the New York World Fair Corporation. First major political assignment was as chief of police. Known as a ruthless enforcer of the prohibition laws.

There is plenty of law at the end of a nightstick.

1890 **Hedda Hopper:** Originally **Elda Furry**. American actress and gossip columnist. Wife of matinee idol DeWolf Hopper. She appeared in more than 50 films. During her 28-year career as a radio columnist, she rivaled Louella Parsons in fame and power. Noted for her hats.

Our town worships success, the bitch goddess whose smile hides a taste for blood.

1899 **Edwin Way Teale:** U.S. naturalist and author. "America's naturalist." His genius was the ability to see the interconnectedness of all things. Won Pulitzer Prize for *Wandering Through Winter* (1966). Other works: *The Lost Woods* and *Autumn Across America.*

Time and space — time to be alone, space to move about — these may well become the great scarcities of tomorrow.

1904 **Johnny Weissmuller:** Romanian-born American athlete and actor. Free style swimmer who in the 1920s won five Olympic gold medals and set 67 world records. Most famous and popular Tarzan of them all, appearing as "The Ape Man" in 12 films. Credited with inventing the King of the Jungle's familiar yodeling call.

The main thing is not to let go of the vine.

1913 **Barbara Mary Crampton Pym:** English novelist. Worked most of her life at the International African Institute in London. Wrote seven popular novels, including: *Quartet in Autumn, A Very Private Eye, Jane and Prudence* and *Crampton's Hodnet.*

Miss Doggett again looked puzzled; it was as if she had heard that men only wanted one thing, but had forgotten for the moment what it was.

OTHERS: 926 Emperor of Japan **Murakami**, 1535 Pope **Leo XI**, 1624 King of Poland **John III**, 1907 American writer **Dorothy West**, 1920 Football team president **Tex Schramm**, 1920 Governor of Tennessee **Frank G. Clement**, 1922 Pro golfer **Charlie Sifford**, 1930 U.S. astronaut **Charles "Pete" Conrad**, 1936 American actress **Sally Kellerman**, 1940 King of Greece **Constantine II**, 1941 English musician **Charlie Watts**, 1944 U.S. composer **Marvin Hamlisch**, 1944 Field goal kicker **Garo Yepremian**, 1948 "The Beaver" **Jerry Mathers**, 1955 U.S. comedian **Dana Carvey**, 1960 U.S. race car driver **Kyle Petty**, 1978 U.S. model **Nikki Cox**, 1989 Ghanaian soccer player **Freddy Adu**

June 3

1635 **Philippe Quinault:** French dramatist. Collaborated with Jean-Baptiste Lully in the creation of the form of the "tragédie-lyrique" which became the model for French opera. Among his popular librettos are *Amadis, Roland* and *Armida.*

It is not wise to be wiser than is necessary.

1726 **James Hutton:** Scottish geologist. Founded the science of geology. Anticipated Darwin's idea of organic evolution by natural selection. The Huttonian theory emphasized the igneous origin of many rocks and rejected the assumption of causes other than those that could be seen still at work. Expounded these views in *A Theory of the Earth*, which forms the basis for modern geology.

The result, therefore, of our present inquiry is that we find no vestige of a beginning — no prospect of an end.

1771 **Sydney Smith:** English clergyman, essayist and wit. Helped found the *Edinburgh Review.* Moved to London where he made his mark as a preacher. Lectured at the Royal Institution on moral philosophy. His writings include several collections of articles, letters, and pamphlets on a variety of subjects.

Marriage resembles a pair of shears, so joined that they cannot be separated, often moving in opposite directions, yet always punishing anyone who comes in between them.

1804 **Richard Cobden:** British businessman, economist and politician. Made a fortune in the calico wholesale business. Wrote pamphlets on international free trade. Helped found the Anti–Corn-Law League. Elected to Parliament, where his speeches concentrated on the Corn Laws that regulated the import and export of grain, which were repealed in 1846. Argued for friendly relations with Russia and helped negotiate a commercial treaty with France.

For every credibility gap there is a gullibility gap.

1808 **Jefferson Davis:** American political leader, soldier, and farmer. U.S. Senator from Mississippi (1847–51 and 1857–61). U.S. Secretary of War (1853–57). President of the Confederate States of America (1861–65). Imprisoned and indicted for treason, but case was dropped.

If the Confederacy fails, there should be written on its tombstone, Died of a Theory.

1816 **Alfred Mercier:** Louisiana-born U.S. author of poems, novels and plays written in French. Founded a French literary society in New Orleans, L'Athénée Louisianais which published *Compte Rendu*, a periodical which contained the best of the French literature published in Louisiana at the time.

What we learn with pleasure we never forget.

1865 **George V:** King of the United Kingdom from 1910 to 1936. Second son of King Edward VII. His reign witnessed the Union of South Africa, World War I, The Irish Free State settlement, and the General Strike of 1926. He was succeeded successively by his sons Edward VIII and George VI.

My father was frightened of his mother. I was frightened of my father and I am damned well going to see to it that my children are frightened of me.

1906 **Josephine Baker:** African-American singer and dancer. Made her Broadway debut in *Shuffle Along.* In 1925, she went to Paris with a show called La Revue Nègre, which flopped. Appeared in an all-black act at the Folies Bergère and became the toast of France for five decades, as the epitome of *le jazz hot.* Became a French citizen in 1937 and during World War II joined the French Resistance, earning several medals. Tireless campaigner for racial equality in the U.S. Addressed the crowds at the Lincoln Memorial at the end of the March on Washington in March 1963. Of her somewhat scandalous stage image:

I wasn't really naked. I simply didn't have any clothes on.

1926 **Colleen Dewhurst:** Canadian-born American actress. Noted for her performances in stage productions of Eugene O'Neill plays. Tony awards for *All the Way Home* and *A Moon for the Misbegotten*. Films: *Annie Hall*, *Nun's Story* and *Dying Young*, which also starred her son by ex-husband George C. Scott, Campbell Scott.

We should try to bring to any power what we have as women. We will destroy it all if we try to imitate that absolutely unfeeling, driving ambition that we have seen coming at us across the desk.

1926 **Allen Ginsberg:** U.S. beat movement poet. Verses are loosely structured and spontaneous, largely drawn from experiments with hallucinogenic drugs and vision, as well as the teachings of Zen Buddhism. Poems: "The Howl," "Kaddish" and "Reality Sandwiches."

I saw the best minds of my generation destroyed by madness, starving hysterical naked, dragging themselves through the negro streets at dawn looking for an angry fix; angel-headed hipsters burning for the ancient heavenly connection to the starry dyn.

1931 **Bert Lance:** U.S. government official. President Jimmy Carter's director of U.S. Office of Management and the Budget. Forced to resign because of questionable banking practices.

If it ain't broke, don't fix it.

1936 **Larry McMurtry:** American screenwriter, novelist and essayist. Pulitzer Prize–winning novel *Lonesome Dove* was adapted into a hit television miniseries, which was set in the "old west" or contemporary Texas. Other novels have been adapted into highly successful films, including his first *Horseman, Pass By*, filmed as *Hud*, *The Last Picture Show* and *Terms of Endearment*. Wrote the screenplay for the highly acclaimed and award winning *Brokeback Mountain*.

The lives of happy people are dense with their own doings — crowded, active, thick.... But the sorrowing are nomads, on a plain with few landmarks and no boundaries; sorrow's horizons are vague and its demands are few.

OTHERS: 1659 Scottish astronomer **David Gregory**, 1853 English Egyptologist **William Matthew Flinders Petrie**, 1864 UA automobile designer **Ransom Olds**, 1877 French painter **Raoul Dufy**, 1887 U.S. concert tenor **Roland Hayes**, 1903 American tenor **Jan Peerce**, 1904 U.S. physician **Charles Drew**, 1911 U.S. actress **Paulette Goddard**, 1918 U.S. ecdysiast **Lili St. Cyr**, 1922 French director **Alain Resnais**, 1925 U.S. actor **Tony Curtis**, 1926 U.S. musician **Boots Randolph**, 1930 American author **Marion Zimmer Bradley**, 1942 U.S. songwriter/ musician **Curtis Mayfield**, 1950 U.S. musician **Suzi Quatro**, 1951 U.S. singer **Deniece Williams**, 1986 Spanish tennis player **Rafael Nadal**

June 4

470 BCE **Socrates:** Ancient Greek philosopher. Together with Plato and Aristotle he laid the philosophical foundations of Western culture. Although he wrote nothing, his personality and doctrines are displayed in Plato's dialogues and Xenophon's *Memorabilia*. Socrates' teaching method consisted mainly of asking problem questions, which ultimately led to revealing the student's unsupported assumptions and misconceptions. Accused of impiety and of corrupting the Athenian youth, he was condemned to death by suicide. Socrates' assertion that all teachers should embrace:

I cannot teach anybody anything, I can only make then think.

1738 **George III:** King of Great Britain and Ireland from 1760 to 1820. Ascended the throne during the Seven Years' War. England was in financial distress caused by the war and George tried to raise funds through taxation of the American colonies. Instead he lost the colonies as a result of the British defeat in the American Revolution. In 1811, the return of the madness that had afflicted him for short periods of his life caused Parliament to enact the regency of his son, the future George IV. His point of view, unfortunately shared by many leaders of nations:

A traitor is everyone who does not agree with me.

1843 **Charles C. Abbott:** American archaeologist and naturalist. Interested in determining the earliest human occupants of the New World. Best known as investigator of the Trenton Gravels site in New Jersey. Author of *Days Out of Doors* and *Notes of the Night*. Abbott's laws:

(1) If you have to ask, you're not entitled to know. (2) If you didn't like the answer, you shouldn't have asked the question.

1863 **Robert Fitzsimmons:** English-born New Zealand/U.S. boxer. Made boxing history by being the sport's first-three division world champion, jumping back and forth from Middleweight to Heavyweight to Light-Heavyweight. At 160 pounds took the world heavyweight championship from James J. Corbett. Lost it to James J. Jeffries.

The bigger they come, the harder they fall.

1878 **Frank N.D. Buchman:** American clergyman called "a surgeon of souls." Protestant evangelist, he was influential in the founding of Alcohol Anonymous and Moral Re-Armament movement (called the Oxford Group prior to 1938), a non-sectarian international attempt to change the world by changing one person at a time.

There is enough in the world for everyone's need, but not enough for everyone's greed.

1894 **Gabriel Pascal:** Transylvanian-born producer and director. Stage actor in Vienna. Entrusted by George Bernard Shaw with the filming of Shavian plays. His most famous production was *Pygmalion*, which he later adapted into the musical *My Fair Lady*.

Vestal virgins half-nude in a steambath. That is Hollywood's idea of sex. They must think the American male is so tired and impotent that he has

to have a vast exposure of female flesh to excite him.

1908 **Rosalind Russell:** American actress. Graduate of American Academy of Dramatic Arts. Was a hit on Broadway in *Wonderful Town* (1953). Often played strong-willed career women, but also was excellent in comedies. Oscar nominated for *Mourning Becomes Electra, My Sister Eileen, Sister Kenny* and *Auntie Mame.*

Success is a public affair. Failure is a private funeral.

1919 **Robert Merrill:** American operatic baritone. First performer to sing 500 performances at the Met. Roles: Escamillo (*Carmen*), Germont (*La Traviata*), Marcello (*La Bohème*) and Iago (*Otello*). Wrote two books of memoirs, *Once More From the Beginning* and *Between Acts.*

If you think you've hit a false note, sing loud. When in doubt, sing loud.

1926 **Robert Earl Hughes:** Once the heaviest known human. Began life weighing 11½ pounds. Progressed to 203 lbs at 6 years, 378 lbs at 10, 546 lbs at 13 and peaked at 1069 pounds with a waist of 122 inches and a chest of 124 inches. At his death he required a specially built coffin, the size of a packing case for a grand piano. There have been confirmations of at least 7 others who were heavier. Carol Yager tops the list at more than 1600 pounds and John Brower Minnock some 200 pounds lighter. When Hughes attended the Brown County Fair in his home town of Mt. Sterling, Illinois in the back of a pickup truck, he was a reluctant exhibit, frequently admonishing visitors:

Don't stare. Go away.

1937 **Robert Fulghum:** American Unitarian minister and author, primarily of short essays. Expounds his simple philosophy by seeing the world through the eyes of children. First to simultaneously have the number one and two spots on hardcover best-seller list with *All I Really Need to Know I Learned in Kindergarten* and *It Was on Fire When I Lay Down on It.*

Remember the Dick-and-Jane books and the first word you learned — the biggest word of all — LOOK.

1966 **Cecilia Bartoli:** Italian mezzo-soprano, best known for her Mozart and Rossini roles. One of the most popular opera singers of recent times. Made her Metropolitan Opera debut in 1996 as Despina in *Così fan tutte.* Her repertoire includes baroque and early classical era music of such composers as Gluck, Vivaldi, Haydn and Salieri.

The voice is an instrument that you really must take time to develop. It's like a good red wine. Give it time.

1975 **Angelina Jolie:** American actress noted for her exotic looks, her strange off-screen behavior, and her humanitarian work with refugees. The daughter of actor Jon Voight, she won an Oscar for Best Supporting Actress for her work in *Girl, Interrupted.* Also has received three Golden Globes. Once married to actor Billy Bob Thornton, she also has had a baby with Brad Pitt. Other films include the *Laura Craft* movies and *Mr. and Mrs. Smith.*

When other little girls wanted to be ballet dancers I kind of wanted to be a vampire.

OTHERS: 1694 French economist **François Quesnay,** 1751 English Chancellor **John Eldon,** 1754 Austrian scientific editor **Franz Xaver,** 1787 French geologist **Constant Prévost,** 1877 German biochemist **Heinrich Wieland,** 1916 American chemist **Robert F. Furchgott,** 1917 U.S. news commentator **Charles Collingwood,** 1917 U.S. Senator **Howard Metzenbaum,** 1924 U.S. actor **Dennis Weaver,** 1928 German-American sex therapist **Ruth Westheimer,** 1937 U.S. musician **Freddie Fender,** 1944 U.S. singer/actress **Michelle Phillips,** 1946 U.S. newswoman **Bettina Gregory,** 1953 Japanese entrepreneur **Susumu Ojima,** 1965 U.S. tennis player **Andrea Jaeger**

June 5

1723 **Adam Smith:** Scottish moral philosopher and political economist. His major work, *An Inquiry into the Nature and Causes of the Wealth of Nations* was the first systematic formulation of classical English economics. Advocated a laissez-faire economy.

Man is an animal that makes bargains: no other animal does this — no dog exchanges bones with another.

1757 **Pierre Jean George Cabanis:** French physiologist. Principal work, *On the relations between the physical and moral aspects of man,* consists in part of memoirs, and is a sketch of physiological psychology. Held that the soul is not an entity, but a facility; thought is the function of the brain.

Impressions arriving at the brain make it enter into activity; just as food falling into the stomach excites it to more abundant secretion of gastric juice.

1878 **Francisco "Pancho" Villa:** Mexican revolutionary and advocate of radical land reform Joined Francisco Madero's successful uprising against Dictator Poftirio Diaz. After Madero's assassination, Villa formed the Division of the North and with Venustiano Carranza led a successful revolt against the regime of Victoriano Huerta. Villa broke with the moderate Carranza and fled north. He raided a town in New Mexico and was pursued by a U.S. force led by General John J. Pershing. Granted a pardon after Carranza's overthrow, he was assassinated three years later. His dying words:

Don't let it end like this. Tell them I said something.

1883 **John Maynard Keynes:** English economist, known for his revolutionary theories. Denounced the provisions of the Treaty of Versailles after World War I in his prophetic work *The Economic Consequences of the Peace* in which he predicted the international economic crisis of the 1920s and 1930s. Originator of so-called New Economics. Advised wide government expenditure as a counter measure to deflation and depression. Works: *The End of Laissez-faire*, *A Treatise on Money* and *How to Pay for the War*.

Capitalism is the astonishing belief that the most wickedest of men will do the most wickedest of things for the greatest good of everyone.

1887 **Ruth Fulton Benedict:** American anthropologist. Taught at Columbia University from 1930 until her death in 1948. Leading member of the culture-and-personality movement in U.S. anthropology of the 1930s. Emphasized how a small part of the range of possible human behavior is emphasized in any one society. Best known works: *Patterns of Culture* and *Race: Science and Politics*.

No man ever looks at the world with pristine eyes. He sees it edited by a definite set of customs and institutions and ways of thinking.

1892 **Dame Ivy Compton-Burnett:** English novelist. Her novels were set in upper-class Victorian society, the characters usually belonging to one large family, spanning several generations. Works include *Brothers and Sisters* and *Mother and Son*.

There is more difference within the sexes than between them.

1898 **Federico García Lorca:** Spanish gifted musician, poet and playwright. In a career spanning only 19 years, ended when he was assassinated in the Spanish Civil War at Granada. He resurrected and revitalized the most basic strains of Spanish poetry and theater. His tragic poems placed him among the greatest 20th century poets. Also wrote successful prose plays including the trilogy *Blood Wedding*, *Yerma*, and *The House of Bernarda Alba*.

As I have not worried to be born, I do not worry to die.

1900 **Dennis Gabor:** Hungarian-born physicist. Moved to England in 1933, joining the Imperial College London as professor of applied electron physics. Credited with the invention of the technique of holography, a method of photographically recording and reproducing three-dimensional images. Nobel Prize winner in 1971.

Till now man has been up against Nature; from now on he will be up against his own nature.

1934 **Bill Moyers:** U.S. broadcast journalist. Personal assistant and White house press secretary to Lyndon B. Johnson. Publisher of *Newsday*. Contributing editor to *Newsweek*. Editor-in-chief of television's "Bill Moyers' Journal." Winner of more than 30 Emmy Awards for producing TV series or specials such as *A World of Ideas*, *Healing and the Mind* and *Genesis*.

Creativity is piercing the mundane to find the marvelous.

1939 **Margaret Drabble:** English author whose novels include the espionage thriller *The Needle's Eye*, *A Summer Bird-Cage*, *The Middle Ground* and *The Gates of Ivory*. Also has written literary biographies and edited the *Oxford Companion of English Literature*.

The rare pleasure of being seen for what one is compensates for the misery of being it.

1939 **Joe Clark:** Canadian statesman and youngest ever Prime Minister (1979–1980). Elected to the Federal parliament in 1972. Became the leader of the Progressive Conservative party in 1976. His minority government lost the general election and he was deposed as party leader. Served as Canada's minister for external affairs until he left politics to take a post with the United Nations in 1993.

Success and failure are both imposters and I take them both lightly.

1947 **David Hare:** Award-winning English playwright and director. Founded the Portable Theatre and became resident playwright at the Royal Court (1969–71). Plays, *Slag*, *Teeth 'n' Smiles* and *Plenty*.

No one but a fool is always right.

OTHERS: 1718 English furniture maker **Thomas Chippendale**, 1819 English mathematician/astronomer **John Couch Adams**, 1823 U.S. crime prevention reformer **George Thorndike**, 1850 Western lawman **Pat Garrett**, 1862 Swedish ophthalmologist **Allvar Gullstrand**, 1894 English publisher **Lord Thomson of Fleet**, 1895 Western actor **William Boyd**, 1905 Hall of Fame football player **Art Donovan**, 1915 U.S. critic **Alfred Kazin**, 1919 U.S. children's author **Richard Scarry**, 1925 U.S. singer **Bill Hayes**, 1928 English director **Tony Richardson**, 1932 Irish author **Christy Brown**, 1941 U.S. actor/screenwriter **Spalding Gray**, 1946 U.S. entertainer **Fred Stone**

June 6

1606 **Pierre Corneille:** French poet and dramatist. Considered the creator of French classical tragedy Trained as a lawyer, he went to Paris where his comedy *Mélite* was hugely successful. Became a favorite of Cardinal Richelieu. Wrote more comedies but in 1636 he produced the classical tragedy *El Cid*, which was followed by other major tragedies: *Horace*, *Cinna*, and *Poleucte*. Joined Molière and Quinault in writing the opera *Psyché*. His brother Thomas was also a playwright of merit.

The manner of giving is worth more than the gift.

1755 **Nathan Hale:** American schoolteacher and patriot, Revolutionary hero. Hanged by British as a spy. Gained immortality with his familiar last words, "I only regret that I have but one life to lose for my country." His words, upon being warned by a friend against taking the assignment that led to his arrest:

Every kind of service necessary to the public good becomes honorable by being necessary.

1799 **Alexander Pushkin:** Russian poet, playwright, novelist and short-story writer. Russia's greatest poet. In his country he holds the same place that Shakespeare does in England and Goethe does in Germany. Works: *Ruslan and Lyudmilla*, *Eugene Onegin*, *Boris Godunov* and *The Queen of Spades*. He died early, defending his wife's honor in a duel with her brother-in-law.

The illusion which exalts us is dearer to us than ten-thousand truths.

1860 **William R. Inge:** "The Gloomy Dean." English theologian and dean of St. Paul's Cathedral, who earned his byname for his pessimistic sermons and newspaper articles. Explored mystical aspects of Christianity in sermons and newspaper articles. Wrote *Outspoken Essays* and *Lay Thoughts of a Dean.*

The church is only a secular institution in which the half-educated speak to the half-converted.

1862 Sir **Henry Newbolt:** English author and poet, best known for his patriotic and nautical verse. Works included *Admirals All, The Island Race* and *Songs of the Sea.* During World War I he was an official war historian, producing *The Naval History of the Great War.*

To set the cause above renown. To love the game beyond the prize. To honor, while you strike him down, the foe that comes with fearless eyes. To count the life of battle good. And dear the land that gave you birth. And dearer yet the brotherhood.

1868 **Robert Falcon Scott:** British Antarctic explorer. Joined the navy in 1881. Commanded the National Antarctic Expedition of 1901–04, which explored the Ross Sea area and discovered what he named King Edward VII Land. Led a second expedition to the South Pole in 1912, only to discover that the Norwegian expedition headed by Roald Amundsen had beaten them by a month. All members of Scott's party died, their frozen bodies and diaries were found eight months later.

Had we lived I should have had a tale to tell of the hardihood, endurance and courage of my companions which would have stirred the heart of every Englishman. These rough notes and our dead bodies must tell the tale.

1875 **Thomas Mann:** German novelist, essayist. Nobel Prize winner for literature (1929). Forced into exile by Nazis (1939). Became a U.S. citizen (1944). Works: *Buddenbrooks, Death in Venice, The Magic Mountain* and *Doctor Faustus.* Awarded a Nobel Prize for Literature in 1929. His brother Heinrich also was a novelist.

Beauty can pierce one like a pain.

1886 **Paul Dudley White:** American physician and cardiac specialist. His most famous patient was President Dwight D. Eisenhower. This successful treatment made the public aware that heart disease need not be crippling. His major textbook, *Heart Disease,* established his international reputation.

A vigorous five-mile walk will do more good for an unhappy but otherwise healthy adult than all the medicine and psychology in the world.

1909 **Sir Isaiah Berlin:** Latvian-born British philosopher, historian and writer. Director of the Royal Opera House, president of the British Academy, translator of Turgenev, activist in Jewish affairs and first president of Wolfson College, Oxford. Most important works: *Karl Marx, The Hedgehog and the Fox, Historical Inevitability, The Age of Enlightenment,* and *Four Essays on Liberty.*

Only barbarians are not curious about where they come from, how then came to be where they are, where they appear to be going, whether they wish to go there, and if so, why, and if not, why not

1925 **Maxine Kumin:** American poet, novelist and essayist. Has been compared to Robert Frost because she frequently writes of the rhythms of rural New England life. Pulitzer Prize for Poetry in 1973. Author of: *No One Writes a Letter to a Snail, The Nightmare Factory* and *A Way of Staying Sane.* Won Pulitzer Prize for *Up Country* (1973).

Cherish your wilderness.

1939 **Marion Wright Edelman:** American lawyer, educator, activist, social reformer and children's advocate. Founder and President of the Children's Defense Fund. The first African American woman admitted to the Mississippi state bar. Received a MacArthur "genius" award and more than 65 honorary degrees. Books include *The Measure of Our Success: A Letter to My Children and Yours.*

Don't feel entitled to anything you didn't sweat and struggle for.

1954 **Harvey Fierstein:** American actor, singer and playwright. Best known for his semi-autobiographical play and film *Torch Song Trilogy,* which he wrote and starred in. Won a Tony for his performance in the play, which won a Tony for Best Play in 1983. Known for his gravelly voice. Has appeared both as a stand-up comedian and a drag queen. Wrote the book for the Jerry Herman musical *La Cage aux Folles,* earning him another Tony.

The great thing about suicide is that it's not one of those things you have to do now or you lose your chance. I mean, you can always do it later.

OTHERS: 1436 German mathematician **Regiomontanus**, 1599 Spanish painter **Diego Velázquez**, 1756 U.S. painter **John Trumbull**, 1804 U.S. publisher **Louis Antoine Godey**, 1840 British organist **Sir John Stainer**, 1890 U.S. bandleader **Ted Lewis**, 1898 Irish-born dancer/choreographer **Ninette De Valois**, 1901 First president of Indonesia **Sukarno**, 1903 Armenian composer **Aram Khachaturian**, 1906 German-born mathematician **Max Born**, 1907 Baseball player **Bill Dickey**, 1917 Dominican actress **Maria Montez**, 1918 U.S. biochemist **Edwin G. Krebs**, 1936 U.S. singer **Levi Stubbs**, 1955 U.S. actress/ comic **Sandra Bernhard**, 1956 Swedish tennis player **Björn Borg**, 1967 U.S. actor **Paul Giamatti**

June 7

1778 **George Bryan "Beau" Brummell:** English dandy and wit. Became an arbiter of elegancies. Influenced men toward simplicity and moderation in dress. Credited with inventing trousers to replace breeches. Close friend and protégé of the future King George IV, but they quarreled. Because of gambling debts, Beau fled to France, where he died in a lunatic asylum.

Starch makes the gentleman, etiquette the lady.

1848 **Paul Gauguin:** French painter. Abandoned his family to devote himself completely to his art. Set out for Tahiti, where he spent the rest of his life. Gradually evolved his own style, reflecting his hatred of civilization. Found his inspiration in primitive people. A highly original painter who had a great influence on impressionists. Also excelled in wood carvings of pagan idols.

In art, all who have done something other than their predecessors have merited the epithet of revolutionary; and it is they alone who are the masters. Art is either a revolutionist or a plagiarist.

1857 **Samuel McChord Crothers:** American Unitarian clergyman and essayist. His essays often appeared in the *Atlantic Monthly*. He treated human foibles with a gentle, humorous touch. In his preaching, he looked at old dogmas to discover what value remained in them. Encouraged his congregation to support social welfare projects.

The trouble with facts is that there are so many of them.

1897 **George Szell:** Hungarian-born U.S. conductor with Berlin State Opera, German Opera, Metropolitan Opera and Cleveland Orchestra. Made his debut at age 18, and before his 20th birthday had appeared with the Berlin Philharmonic as pianist, conductor and composer. When war broke out he settled in the U.S.

Conductors must give unmistakable and suggestive signals to the orchestra, not choreography for the audience.

1899 **Elizabeth [Dorothea Cole] Bowen:** Irish-born British novelist and short-story writer. Explored psychological relationships in the upper class. Works: *Encounters*, *The Death of the Heart* and *The Heat of the Day*.

Nobody speaks the truth when there is something they must have.

1909 **Peter Rodino:** Democratic congressman from New Jersey who served in the House of Representatives for 40 years. Chairman of the House Judiciary Committee that looked into the possible impeachment of President Richard Nixon. Rodino conducted the investigation in a fair and dignified way, to the benefit of the nation. He expressed what has come to be known as the "Rodino rules."

I ... have been guided by a simple principle, the principle that the law must deal fairly with every man. For me, this is the oldest principle of democracy. It is this simple but great principle which enables men to live justly and in decency in a free society.

1909 **Jessica Tandy:** English-born actress. Teamed with husband Hume Cronyn in plays such as *The Fourposter* and *The Gin Game*, for which she won a Tony. Most celebrated stage performance was as the original Blanche DuBois in *A Streetcar Named Desire* (1947). Oscar winner at 81 for *Driving Miss Daisy*. Speaking of her husband:

When he's late for dinner, I know he's either having an affair or is lying dead in the street. I always hope it's in the street.

1917 **Gwendolyn Brooks:** One of foremost African American poets of the 20th century. Reared in the Chicago slums, her poems depict the wounds and inequities inflicted on blacks. Pulitzer Prize for poetry for her verse narrative, "Annie Allen" (1950), the first awarded to an African American woman. Succeeded Carl Sandburg as poet laureate of Illinois. Among her other books are *In the Mecca* and *Primer for Blacks*.

Art hurts. Art urges voyages — and it is easier to stay at home.

1922 **Rocky Graziano:** American boxer. World middleweight champion (1946–47). Fought Tony Zale for title three times in 21 months, losing twice. Pro record 67–10–6 with 52 knockouts.

Fighting is the only racket where you're almost guaranteed to end up as a bum.

1943 **Yolande Cornelia "Nikki" Giovanni:** African American poet and author. Professor of writing and Literature at Virginia Polytechnic Institute and State University since 1987. Has written more than two dozen books, including volumes of poetry, illustrated children's books, and three collections of essays. Works: *Black Feeling, Black Talk, Black Judgment, Those Who Rode the Night Winds*, and *Sacred Cows ... and Other Edibles*.

There are two people in the world that are not likeable" a master and a slave.

1951 **Deborah Tannen:** American sociologist and professor of sociolinguistics at Georgetown University. Has written several books about how people in social situations talk to each other. Her goal is a theoretical understanding of talk and social interaction. Books include: *Talking form 9 to 5: Women and Men at Work, That's Not What I Meant!, You Just Don't Understand: Men and Women in Conversation* and *I Only Say This Because I Love You*.

Life is a matter of dealing with other people, in little matters and cataclysmic ones, and that means a series of conversations.

1954 **Louise Erdrich:** Native American born novelist, short story writer, essayist, critic and poet. Her fiction and poetry draws on her Chippewa heritage as she examines the complex relations among full and mixed blood Native Americans in their struggle for identity in White European American culture. Received the Wordcraft Circle Writer of the Year award in 2000 for *The Birchbark House*.

Columbus only discovered that he was in some new place. He didn't discover America.

OTHERS: 1502 Pope **Gregory XIII**, 1529 French lawyer **Étienne Pasquier**, 1770 British prime minister **Earl of Liverpool**, 1811 Scottish obstetrician **Sir James Young Simpson**, 1825 British author **R.D. Blackmore**, 1862

Austrian physicist **Philipp Lenard**, 1896 Hungarian politician **Imre Nagy**, 1896 U.S. World War I flying ace **Douglas Campbell**, 1917 U.S. singer/actor **Dean Martin**, 1928 Film director **James Ivory**, 1940 Welsh singer **Tom Jones**, 1946 Talk show host **Jenny Jones**, 1952 Northern Irish actor **Liam Neeson**, 1958 U.S. musician **Prince**, 1972 New Zealand actor **Karl Urban**, 1975 U.S. basketball player **Allen Iverson**, 1981 Russian tennis player **Anna Kournikova**

June 8

1810 **Robert Schumann:** German composer. Husband of pianist, teacher and composer Clara Wieck. Parallel to his piano work, he produced some of the finest lieder. Compositions: *Carnaval, Myrthen, Liederkreise, Papillons* and four symphonies. His mental deterioration, due to syphilis and a family history of mental illness landed him in a sanitarium where he died.

People compose for many reasons: to become immortal; because the pianoforte happens to be open; to become a millionaire, because of the praise of friends; because they have looked into a pair of beautiful eyes; or for no reason whatever.

1814 **Charles Reade:** English novelist and dramatist. Noted for historical romances and novels that exposed social injustice that led to reforms. His masterpiece was the long historical novel of the 15th century, *The Cloister and the Hearth*. Other works: *It Is Never Too Late to Mend* and *Put Yourself in His Place*. His recipe for a successful novel:

Make 'em laugh; make 'em cry; make 'em wait.

1869 **Frank Lloyd Wright:** American architect and writer. Considered the most abundantly creative genius of American architecture. His "organic architecture," using natural materials, and a low, gently spreading profile, is known as the Prairie Style. Projects: Guggenheim Museum, New York City; Kaufmann House, Bear Run, Pennsylvania; and Robie House, Chicago, Illinois. His buildings were meant to harmonize both with their inhabitants and their environment.

No house should ever be on a hill or on anything. It should be of the hill. Belonging to it. Hill and house should live together each happier for the other.

1903 **Marguerite Yourcenar:** Belgium-French-U.S. novelist, poet, essayist, critic and classical scholar. First woman elected to the Académie Française. Noted for her rigorously classical style and her erudition. Novels: *Memoirs of Hadrian* and *The Abyss*.

All happiness is a form of innocence.

1916 **Francis Crick:** British physicist, microbiologist and neuroscientist. Co-discoverer with James D. Watson of the double-helix structure of DNA, the basic substance of the chromosome and thus of heredity. Shared the Nobel Prize in Physiology or Medicine in 1962 with Watson and Maurice Wilkins. Crick has made significant contributions in laying the foundations of the field of molecular biology and the biological implications of the structure of DNA.

We've discovered the secret of life.

1917 **Byron R. "Whizzer" White:** All-American running back with University of Colorado. Played pro football with Pittsburgh and Detroit. Football Hall of Fame (1954). Lawyer, jurist. Associate justice of U.S. Supreme Court (1962–1993). His opinions on the Court were generally moderate to conservative.

The Court is most vulnerable and comes nearest to illegitimacy when it deals with judge-made constitutional law having little or no cognizable roots in the language or design of the Constitution.

1923 **Malcolm Boyd:** U.S. Episcopal priest, spoken-word artist and author. Became known as "The Espresso Priest" for his religiously-themes poetry readings at the "Hungry I" nightclub in San Francisco. Activist in civil and gay rights movements. The author of more than 30 books, including: *Are You Running with Me Jesus?* and *Free to Live, Free to Die*.

Prayer represents commitment. To pray is to say "I'm willing to get with it — love, responsibility, action."

1925 **Barbara Bush:** American first lady. Wife of George H. W. Bush, the 41st U.S. president and mother of George W. Bush, the 43rd. Probably more popular at the time than her husband. Co-wrote *Millie's Book*, with the White House pet.

Clinton lied. A man might forget where he parks or where he lives, but he never forgets oral sex, no matter how bad it is.

1929 **Bliss Carmen:** Canada's best known poet. Descended from American Loyalists. Attended the University of New Brunswick, Edinburgh and Harvard. Moved to New York where he was an influential writer and editor with *Cosmopolitan*, the *Atlantic Monthly* and other literary journals. Known for his anthology and editing the ten-volume *The World's Best Poetry* and *The Oxford Book of American Verse*.

What are facts but compromises? A fact merely marks the point where we have agreed to let investigation cease.

1929 **Jerry Stiller:** American comedian and actor. Teamed with his wife Ann Meara as a comic duo, whose routines emphasized their real-life relationship foibles. He appeared in the recurring role of George's Costanza's father Frank on the *Seinfeld* sitcom and in a similar role in *The King of Queens*. Father of actor and comedian Ben Stiller and actress Amy Stiller.

Creative comedy is like growing geraniums in a mine field.

1935 **Joan Rivers:** American comedian and talk show host. Her routines are typically about her unattractiveness and her bored husband. Appeared regularly on The Tonight Show and The Ed Sullivan Show. Became a popular headliner and recorded a successful album of her standup act called "Can We Talk?" After her husband Edgar Rosenberg committed suicide, she wrote about his passing in her books *Enter Talking* and *Still*

Talking. The last few years she has co-hosted red carpet specials with her daughter Melissa.

A man can sleep around, no questions asked, but if a woman makes nineteen or twenty mistakes she's a tramp.

1977 **Kanye West:** African American rap singer, hip hop producer and poet. In 2005 he was nominated for ten Grammies, making him the most nominated artist of the year. Won for Best Rap Album, *The College Dropout*, Best Rap song for "Jesus Walks" and Best R&B song for producing Alicia Keys' "You Don't Know My Name." In 2006 he was nominated for eight Grammies, winning three for Best Rap Album, Late Registration, Best Rap Song "Diamonds from Sierra Leone" and Best Rap Solo Performance for "Gold Digger."

This dark diction has become America's addiction.

OTHERS: 1625 Italian astronomer **Giovanni Cassini**, 1683 Italian violinmaker **Giuseppe Guarnerius**, 1813 U.S. naval commander **David Dixon Porter**, 1851 French physicist **Jacques-Arsine d'Arsonval**, 1903 Texas senator **Ralph Yarborough**, 1911 Baseball pitcher **Van Lingle Mungo**, 1918 U.S. actor **Robert Preston**, 1921 Indonesian President **Suharto**, 1924 U.S. comedian **George Kirby**, 1927 American painter **LeRoy Neiman**, 1934 English singer **Millicent Martin**, 1940 U.S. singer **Nancy Sinatra**, 1943 U.S. hurdler **Willie Davenport**, 1950 Brazilian actress **Sonia Braga**, 1957 U.S. cartoonist **Scott Adams**, 1958 U.S. actor **Keenen Ivory Wayans**, 1972 U.S. tennis player **Lindsay Davenport**

June 9

1672 **Peter I:** "The Great." Russian Czar (1682–1725). Modernized Russia. Embarked on a series of sweeping military, fiscal, educational, administrative and ecclesiastical reforms, many based on Western models. Moved his capital to the new city he built, St. Petersburg, his "window to the West." Some of his reforms were brutally implemented. Suspecting that his son Alexis was plotting against him, he had his heir tortured to death.

I have conquered an empire but I have not been able to conquer myself.

1791 **John Howard Payne:** American actor, playwright, editor and poet. Plays: *Love in Humble Life*, *The Signet Ring* and *The Wife and the Widow*. Most famous poem is "Home, Sweet Home."

Mid pleasures and palaces though we may roam,/ Be it ever so humble, there's no place like home.

1836 **Elizabeth Garrett Anderson:** English physician. Refused admission to medical schools, she studied privately with London physicians and was licensed to practice in 1865. General medical attendant of the New Hospital for Women. Worked to create a medical school for women. In 1908 she was elected mayor of Aldeburgh, the first woman mayor in England.

I asked my father what there was to make doctoring more disgusting than nursing, which women were always doing, and which ladies had done publicly in the Crimea. He could not tell me.

1892 **Cole Porter:** U.S. composer and lyricist. His style was clever and sophisticated. Musical comedies: *Jubilee*, *Kiss Me Kate* and *Can-Can*. Songs: "Night and Day," "Begin the Beguine," "You're the Tops" and "I Get a Kick Out of You." He was severely hurt in a riding accident in 1937, but despite permanent pain, he continued to compose.

In olden days a glimpse of stocking was looked on as something shocking but now, God knows, anything goes.

1893 **S.N. (Samuel Nathaniel) Behrman:** American playwright, screenwriter and journalist. His first play, the sophisticated comedy *The Second Man*, made him famous and was tagged the "American Noel Coward." Wrote over 25 comedies. His more serious plays were noted for addressing complex social and moral issues.

A wonderful discovery, psychoanalysis. Makes quite simple people feel they're complex.

1900 **Fred Waring:** U.S. conductor. His chorus, the Pennsylvanians, made many tours and radio and television appearances beginning in 1923.

Poems can be read or spoken, melodies can be played or whistled, but words and music were blended into song, and a song was written to be sung.

1916 **Robert McNamara:** American Secretary of Defense during the John F. Kennedy and Lyndon B. Johnson presidencies. Initially supported U.S. involvement in the Vietnam War but by 1967 sought peace negotiations. Disagreed with the bombing of North Vietnam. Resigned in 1968 to become president of the World Bank. He was one of the "Whiz Kids" hired to revitalize the Ford Motor Company and in 1960 became the corporation's president.

A computer does not substitute for judgment any more than a pencil substitutes for literacy. But writing without a pencil is no particular advantage.

1916 **Les Paul:** U.S. guitarist and inventor. With wife Mary Ford had numerous hits, including "How High the Moon," "The World Is Waiting for the Sunrise" and "Vaya Con Dios." Pioneered over-dubbing, multi-tracking as a multi-recording guitarist with Ford singing harmony for herself. He invented the first solid-body electric guitar and was instrumental in developing modern day multitrack recording. Took his design to the Gibson Guitar Company in 1947. The "Gibson Les Paul" guitar became a favorite of rock band musicians.

Heavy metal music is five guys on the stage sounding like World War III.

1922 **George Axelrod:** U.S. dramatist, screenwriter, producer and director. Plays: *The Seven Year Itch* and *Will Success Spoil Rock Hunter?* Screenplays: *Breakfast at Tiffany's*. (Academy Award nomination), *Bus Stop* and the *Manchurian Candidate*.

A humorist ... can himself be horrified out of laughter, which is a terrible thing. We're not seeing things funny, partly because we're scared to death. In a grotesque horrible way, life itself has become pretty much of a joke. And you can't make a joke on a joke.

1931 **Jackie Mason:** American Rabbi and stand-up comedian. Delights in causing controversy by being "politically incorrect." Starred in successful Broadway one-man show, *The World According to Me.* In 2005 he started a daily talk show, "The Jackie Mason Show."

It's no longer a question of staying healthy. It's a question of finding a sickness you like.

1939 **Letty Cottin Pogrebin:** American writer and social activist. An early leader in the women's movement who combined her feminist ideas with Jewish values. Co-founded *Ms.* Magazine and the National Woman's Political Caucus. Has written 9 books, including the memoir *Getting Over Growing Older*, a book on time and aging. Expressed her fused Jewish-feminist identity in her book *Deborah, Goldie and Me: Being Female and Jewish in America.*

If knowledge is power, clandestine knowledge is power squared; it can be withheld, exchanged, and leveraged.

1981 **Natalie Portman:** Israeli-born American actress. Began her career at age 12 in *Léon*, in which she is protected from crooked cops who slaughtered her family by a professional hitman. Beginning at 14 she appeared in three *Star Wars* films as Padmé Amidala. Had a small but showy role in *Cold Mountain*. Won a Golden Globe and was nominated for an Academy Award for her awesome performance in *Closer*. A graduate from Harvard with a degree in psychology, she has co-authored two research papers which were published in professional scientific journals. Says she'd rather be smart than be a movie star.

Smart women love smart men more than smart men love smart women.

OTHERS: 1508 Slovenian protestant reformer **Primož Trubar**, 1595 King of Poland **Wladislaus IV**, 1640 Holy Roman Emperor **Leopold I**, 1781 British inventor **George Stephenson**, 1822 U.S. horticulturist **Peter Henderson**, 1843 Austrian novelist **Bertha von Suttner**, 1908 U.S. actor **Robert Cummings**, 1927 U.S. writer **R. Wright Campbell**, 1930 U.S. news correspondent **Marvin Kalb**, 1934 U.S. singer **Jackie Wilson**, 1939 U.S. sportscaster **Dick Vitale**, 1952 Israeli singer **Uzi Hitman**, 1961 Canadian-born actor **Michael J. Fox**, 1961 U.S. director/ producer/writer **Aaron Sorkin**, 1963 American actor **Johnny Depp**, 1973 U.S. football player **Tedy Bruschi**, 1978 British singer/guitarist **Matthew Bellamy**

June 10

1213 **Fakhruddin 'Iraqi:** Persian metaphysician, poet and Sufi mystic. Considered by many Sufis to be the greatest of all Masters and his writings are revered as great treasures. Especially regarded for its musical and poetic expressions. He spoke of Reality in terms of Love, the Beloved, and the lover. Love refers to the Absolute of Essence, while lover and Beloved refer to seeker and Sought. Major work *Lama'at Divine Flashes.*

Before this there was one heart but a thousand thoughts. Now all is reduced to there is no love but Love.

1895 **Hattie McDaniel:** U.S. character actress. A former radio singer, she sang a duet with Will Rogers in her first major role in *Judge Priest*. In 1939 she was an Oscar winner for her portrayal of wise Mammy in *Gone with the Wind*, the first African-American so honored. Her roles were mainly maids and she starred as one in the radio comedy *The Beulah Show*. Other notable film appearances: *China Seas*, *Alice Adams*, *Show Boat*, and *Song of the South*.

Why should I complain about making $7000 a week playing a maid? If I didn't, I'd be making seven dollars a week actually being one!

1904 **Frederick Loewe:** Austrian-American songwriter. A piano prodigy, the youngest soloist ever to appear with the Berlin Philharmonic Orchestra. Moved to the U.S. in 1924 and wrote music for Broadway revues. Met Alan Jay Lerner in 1942, with whom he collaborated on five successful Broadway musicals, including *Brigadoon* and *My Fair Lady*. Their film musicals included *Gigi* and *Camelot*. From his letter read at a memorial service for Lerner:

It won't be long before we'll be writing together again. I just hope they have a decent piano up there.

1910 **Howlin' Wolf:** American musician originally named **Chester Burnett**. An influential blues singer, songwriter and harmonic player. An imposing figure with one of the loudest and most memorable voices of all the class 1950s blues singers. Songs: "How Many More Years," "Evil," "Smokestack Lightnin,'" and "Little Red Rooster."

I don't play anything but the blues, but now I could never make no money or nothin' but the blues. That's why I wasn't interested in nothin' else.

1911 **Terence Rattigan:** English playwright. Wrote *French Without Tears*, *The Winslow Boy*, *The Browning Version* and *Separate Tables*. Wrote screenplays for the film adaptations of his plays and for *The Yellow Rolls-Royce* and the musical version of *Goodbye Mr. Chips*.

A novelist may lose his reader for a few pages; a playwright never dares lose his audience for a minute.

1915 **Saul Bellow:** Canadian-born American novelist of Jewish moral and modern urban dwellers, disaffected by society, but not destroyed in spirit. Received the National Book Award for *The Adventures of Augie March* and a Pulitzer Prize for *Humboldt's Gift*. Awarded a Nobel Prize in 1976.

A novel is balanced between a few true impressions and the multitude of false ones that make up most of what we call life.

1921 **Philip, Duke of Edinburgh:** Duke of Edinburgh. Greek-born consort of Queen Elizabeth II of England. Served in combat with the Royal Navy during World War II. Known for speaking his mind and controversial observations.

Dontopedology is the science of opening your mouth and putting your foot in it. I've been practicing it for years.

1922 **Judy Garland:** American actress and singer born **Frances Gumm.** Possessed a sweet but powerful voice with a remarkable emotional range. Fondly remembered by many singing "Over the Rainbow" in *The Wizard of Oz.* Among her most successful films in her troubled life: *Meet Me in St. Louis, Easter Parade* and *A Star Is Born.* Acclaimed for her serious role in *Judgment at Nuremburg.* Mother of entertainers Liza Minnelli and Lorna Luft. Her reliance on drugs led to her early death in 1969.

Behind every cloud is another cloud.

1926 **Nat Hentoff:** American newspaper columnist, editor, critic, biographer and civil libertarian. A free speech absolutist, pro-life advocate, and anti-death penalty advocate. Author of *Does Anybody Give a Damn? Nat Hentoff on Education, Our Children Are Dying, The First Freedom: The Tumultuous History of Free Speech in America* and *The War on the Bill of Rights and the Gathering Resistance.* A strong critic of the Bush administration policies such as the Patriot Act.

Since the reign of George III, resistance has been our legacy and to this day still is.

1928 **Maurice Sendak:** American children's book author and illustrator. Wrote and illustrated *Where the Wild Things Are,* which won the Carnegie Medal. It perturbed parents but delighted children and sold hugely all over the world. He later collaborated on opera productions.

There must be more to life than having everything.

1933 **F. Lee Bailey:** U.S. attorney and author. Founded a detective agency to conduct his case research. Represented Albert DeSalvo (the Boston Strangler), Patty Hearst, Dr. Sam Sheppard, Capt. Ernest Medina and was a member of the O.J. Simpson defense team.

Can any of you seriously say the Bill of Rights could get through Congress today? It wouldn't even get out of committee.

1965 **Elizabeth Hurley:** English model, actress, producer and designer. Probably better known for her beauty and her love life than her acting. Face of Estée Lauder's ReNutriv Skin Line. Donates the proceeds of a lipstick named for her, Elizabeth Pink, to the Breast Cancer Fund. Films: two *Austin Powers* movies and *Bedazzled.*

A bit of lusting after someone does wonders for the skin.

OTHERS: 1637 French Jesuit missionary and explorer **Jacques Marquette,** 1735 American physician **John Morgan,** 1810 German ornithologist **Hermann Schlegel,** 1861 French physicist **Pierre Duhem,** 1862 American actress **Mrs. Leslie Carter,** 1885 U.S. film critic **Jack Kroll,** 1901 British lyric writer and librettist **Eric Maschwitz,** 1923 Czech-born newspaperman **Robert Maxwell,** 1926 U.S. actress **June Haver,** 1929 U.S. astronaut **James McDivitt,** 1929 U.S. science writer **Edward O. Wilson,** 1931 Brazilian singer **João Gilberto,** 1943 U.S. journalist **Jeff Greenfield,** 1951 Football QB **Dan Fouts,** 1953 U.S. politician **John Edwards,** 1982 American figure skater **Tara Lipinski**

June 11

1572 **Ben Jonson:** English dramatist and poet. Worked as a bricklayer and performed military service in Flanders. Joined a company of players and killed one of their members in a duel. Shakespeare appeared in Jonson's play *Every Man in His Humor.* Best known for his dramatic satires *Volpone, Epicoene, The Alchemist* and *Bartholomew Fair.* His lyric genius is ranked second only to Shakespeare.

Drink to me only with thine eyes,/ And I will pledge with mine;/ Or leave a kiss upon the cup,/ And I'll not look for wine.

1588 **John Wither:** British poet and pamphleteer While imprisoned for his *Abuses Stript and Whipt,* he wrote a book of five pastorals, *The Shepherd's Hunting,* followed by a love elegy, *Fidelia.* Released, he soon found himself locked away again for the satirical self-confession, *Wither's Motto.* Served as a major-general under Oliver Cromwell, but after the Restoration lost his position and property, and was imprisoned again on suspicion of having written the satire on parliament, *Vox Vulgi.* Finest poem: *Fair Virtue, or the Mistress of Philarete.*

Shall I, wasting in despair,/ Die because a woman's fair?/ Or make pale my cheeks with care/ Cause another's rosy are?

1776 **John Constable:** English painter. A large inheritance allowed him to concentrate on painting. A master of watercolor as well as oil painting. Noted for painting his romantic views of the English countryside directly from nature. Paintings: *Haywain, The White Horse, Salisbury Cathedral* and *Waterloo Bridge.*

There is nothing ugly; I never saw an ugly thing in my life: for let the form of the object be what it can,— light, shade, and perspective will always make it beautiful.

1864 **Richard Strauss:** German composer. Best known for his symphonic poems, such as *Till Eulenspiegel's Merry Pranks* and *Thus Spoke Zarathustra.* His operas, including the scandal-causing *Salome, Der Rosenkavalier* and *Aridane auf Naxos,* were well-received. Remained in Austria during World War I, but later was cleared of any collaboration with the Nazi regime.

The human voice is the most beautiful instrument of all, but it is the most difficult to play.

1868 **Edward Verrall Lucas:** Prolific English journalist and writer of nearly 100 books. Remembered mostly now for his essays and books about London and travel, and his biography of Charles Lamb. Provided extensive material for *Punch* magazine and wrote a column for the *Sunday Times*.

I have noticed that the people who are late are often so much jollier than the people who have to wait for them.

1880 **Jeannette Rankin:** American social worker, feminist, pacifist and politician. Elected to the House of Representatives in 1916 as a Republican representing Montana, becoming the first woman to serve in Congress. Introduced the first bill to give women the right to vote and was instrumental in the adoption of a bill granting married women independent citizenship. Voted against declaring war on Germany. Failing in her bid to be elected to the U.S. Senate she returned to social work. Reelected to the House in 1940, she was the only legislator to vote against declaring war on Japan. At age 87, she led 5,000 women on a march to Capitol Hill in a protest of the Vietnam War.

I want to stand by my country, but I cannot vote for war. I vote no.

1888 **Anna Akhmatova:** Pseudonym of **Anna Andreeyevna Gorenko**. Ukrainian-born poet. Her early works *Evening* and *Beads* were collections of lyrical poems. *Requiem* is a poetic cycle on the Stalin purges. Soviet authorities condemned her work for its preoccupation with love and God. After the publication of *Anno Domini* in 1922, she was officially silenced until 1940 when she published *The Willow*. After World War II, she was again denounced and her verse banned. After Stalin's death she was "rehabilitated" and today is recognized as one of the greatest of all Russian poets.

My love for you's so strong/That no one could kill it — not even you.

1910 **Jacques-Yves Cousteau:** French ocean explorer, filmmaker, and author. Invented the aqualung, which has made possible the sport of scuba diving. Founded the French Office of Underseas Research (now the Center of Advanced Marine Studies). In later years he issued dire warnings about human destruction of the oceans. Wrote *The Silent World* and *The Living Sea*. His film *The Golden Fish* won an Academy Award in 1960.

The best way to observe a fish is to become a fish.

1913 **Vince Lombardi:** Legendary U.S. football coach of the Green Bay Packers. One of the most successful coaches in the history of football. He led the Packers to five NFL championships and victory in the first two Super Bowls during his ten-year tenure. Following a one-year retirement, he returned to coach the Washington Redskins during the 1969 season, but lasted only one season, being diagnosed with cancer that killed him in the fall of 1970. Famous for his coaching philosophy and motivational skills.

The greatest accomplishment is not in never failing, but in rising again after you fail.

1920 **Hazel Scott:** West Indian–born jazz pianist, singer, actor and feminist. Popular entertainer in Paris (1965–67). Played bebop, blues, and ballads. Most successful recording was "Tico Tico." First African American woman to have her own TV show. Publicly opposed McCarthyism and racial segregation. Show was canceled in 1950 when she was accused of being a Communist sympathizer. Married to politician Adam Clayton Powell (1945–60).

I have always respected everyone's religion. As I say, there is only one God and a lot of confused people.

1925 **William Styron:** American author concerned with oppression in its myriad forms. Noted for his treatment of tragic themes and his use of rich, classical prose style. Author of Pulitzer-winning *The Confessions of Nat Turner*, which deals with an 1831 Virginia slave uprising and *Sophie's Choice,* dealing with the Holocaust.

A good book should leave you with many experiences, and slightly exhausted. You should live several lives while reading it.

1949 **Ingrid Newkirk:** English-born American animal rights activist. Co-founder with Alex Pacheco and president of People for the Ethical Treatment of Animals (PETA). Books: *Free the Animals*, *You Can Save the Animals*, and *Making Kind Choices*.

Recognize meat for what it really is: the antibiotic and pesticide-laden corpse of a tortured animal.

OTHERS: 1540 English poet **Barnabe Googe**, 1704 Portuguese composer **Carlos Seixas**, 1723 German astronomer **Johann Palitzsch**, 1737 Polynesian king **Kamehameha**, 1741 American physician **Joseph Warren**, 1842 German industrialist **Carl von Linde**, 1847 Leader of English women's movement **Millicent Garrett Fawcett**, 1876 U.S. anthropologist **Alfred L. Kroeber**, 1900 News panelist **Lawrence Spivak**, 1907 U.S. philanthropist **Paul Mellon**, 1932 South African playwright **Athol Fugard**, 1933 U.S. comic actor **Gene Wilder**, 1937 U.S. pathologist **Robin Warren**, 1947 U.S. politician **Henry Cisneros**, 1956 Football QB **Joe Montana**, 1982 U.S. basketball player **Diana Taurasi**

June 12

1659 **Yamamoto Tsunetomo:** Japanese samurai who for thirty years devoted his life to the service of the Saga domain. When his master died, he did not commit tsuifuku (ritual suicide) because his lord had expressed a dislike for the practice. Renounced the world and retired to a hermitage in the mountains. Came to believe that becoming one with death in one's thoughts was the highest attainment of purity. Views are contained in the *Hagakure* (*Hidden behind the Leaves*). In the 1930s it was one of the most famous representatives of *bushido* (the samurai code), used to encourage World War II Japanese soldiers to battle to the death.

I have found the essence of Bushido: to die!

1802 **Harriet Martineau:** English social and historical writer. Works: *Illustrations of Political Economy, Poor Laws and Paupers Illustrated* and *Society in America.* Published two novels and translated and condensed Auguste Comte's *Philosophie positive.*

Anyone must see at a glance that if men and women marry those whom they do not love, they must love those whom they do not marry.

1819 **Charles Kingsley:** English clergyman, poet and novelist. A Christian socialist, he was deeply involved in social reform. His novels greatly influenced social developments in Great Britain during the Victorian era. Wrote: *Westward Ho!, Hereward the Wake* and the children's book *The Water Babies.*

There are two freedoms; the false, where man is free to do what he likes; the true, where man is free to do what he ought.

1827 **Johanna Spyri:** Swiss author, who wrote of her love of homeland and a feeling for nature. Best remembered for her classic novel *Heidi,* the story of a young orphan girl who is sent to live with her grandfather in the Swiss Alps.

Oh, I wish that God had not given me what I prayed for! It was not so good as I thought.

1892 **Djuna Barnes:** American novelist, poet and illustrator. Began her career as a reporter and illustrator for magazines. Her works, many of which she illustrated; include the outstanding novel *Nightwood,* which tells of the homosexual and heterosexual loves of five remarkable people. Also famed for her verse play *The Antiphon.*

The heart of the jealous knows the best and most satisfying love, that of the other's bed, where the rival perfects the lover's imperfections.

1897 Sir **Anthony Eden:** British politician and statesman. Elected to the House of Commons in 1923. Was foreign secretary (1935–38), but resigned to protest PM Neville Chamberlain's policy of appeasement. Held the same post twice more (1940–45) and (1951–55). Succeeded Winston Churchill as Prime Minister in 1955. Helped establish the Southeast Asia Treaty Organization. Fell from favor when the Egyptians seized the Suez Canal.

Corruption never has been compulsory.

1915 **David Rockefeller:** American banker, financier and philanthropist. Grandson of John D. Rockefeller and brother of Nelson Rockefeller. Earned a PhD and served in World War II. Joined the staff of the Chase National Bank and effected its merger with the Bank of Manhattan. Served as chairman of the board of the Chase Manhattan Bank (1969–81).

If necessity is the mother of invention, discontent is the father of progress.

1919 **Uta Hagen:** German-born American actress, acting teacher and writer. Primarily known for stage roles. Because of blacklisting she had only very limited film roles. Wrote *Respect for Acting* and *Challenge for the Actor.* Students at her New York acting school HB Studios included Matthew Broderick, Jason Robards, Sigourney Weaver, Whoopi Goldberg, Jack Lemmon, Al Pacino and Robert De Niro.

To maintain one's ideals ignorance is easy.

1924 **George Herbert Walker Bush:** Forty-first U.S. president and father of the 43rd president George Walker Bush. Senior Bush was the youngest World War II fighter pilot. Ambassador to the U.N. (1971–73). Republican National Chairman (1973–74). Headed the CIA (1976). Ronald Reagan's vice-president. As president he helped impose a U.N. approved embargo against Iraq in 1990 to force its withdrawal from Kuwait and when Iraq refused, he authorized a U.S.–led offensive that became the Persian Gulf War. Lost his bid for a second term to Bill Clinton in 1992.

People say I'm indecisive, but I don't know about that.

1929 **Brigid Brophy:** English novelist, essayist, critic, biographer and dramatist. Expressed controversial opinions on marriage, wars, sex and pornography. Because of her outspokenness, has been labeled "one of our leading literary shrews." Works: *The Crown Princess and Other Stories, The Burglar, Pussy Owl: Superbeast, Religious Education in State Schools* and *Beardsley and His World.*

Whenever people say "we mustn't be sentimental," you can take it they are about to do something cruel. And if they say, "We must be realistic," they mean they are going to make money out of it.

1929 **Anne Frank:** German-Jewish girl. Kept a diary given to her on her thirteenth birthday. In it she chronicles the events of her life and the lives of her families during two years of hiding from the Nazis. It later was published as *The Diary of a Young Girl.* It has been translated into many languages and is one of the most widely read books. Anne and her family were captured and sent to a concentration camp at Bergen-Belsen where she died of typhus.

I keep my ideals, because in spite of everything I still believe that people are really good at heart

1932 **Rona Jaffe:** American novelist. Wrote her first and best known novel, *The Best of Everything,* while an associated editor for a publishing firm. The subject of the book was women working in the publishing world who were victims of dastardly men. Wrote the controversial novel *Mazes and Monsters* about people going crazy after playing a game very similar to the popular Dungeons & Dragons.

A blond in a red dress can do without introductions — but not without a bodyguard.

OTHERS: 1107 Emperor of China **Gaozong**, 1519 Grand Duke of Tuscany **Cosimo I de' Medici**, 1577 Swiss astronomer/mathematician **Paul Guldin**, 1806 U.S. pioneer bridge builder **John Augustus Roebling**, 1897 Polish composer **Alexandre Tansman**, 1911 Yugoslavian communist politician **Miovan Djilas**, 1916 American film producer **Irwin Allen**, 1917 U.S. actress **Priscilla Lane**, 1920 American cartoonist **Dave Berg**, 1928 American singer **Vic Damone**, 1930 U.S. comic actor/singer **Jim Nabors**, 1941 American sportscaster **Marv Alpert**, 1941 U.S. musician **Chick Corea**, 1974 Japanese major league baseball player **Hideki Matsui**, 1981 Brazilian model **Adriana Lima**

June 13

1752 **Fanny Burney: Madame d'Arblay**. English novelist. Educated herself by reading English and French literature. Chiefly known for her *Diaries and Letters* and novels published anonymously: *Evelina, Cecilia* and *Camilla.*

How little has situation to do with happiness!

1795 **Thomas Arnold:** English educator. Set the pattern for English public-school system while headmaster at Rugby. Introduced the form and prefect systems to keep disciple and something he called "muscular Christianity," graphically described in *Tom Brown's School Days* by Thomas Hughes. Father of poet Matthew Arnold.

My object will be, if possible, to form Christian men, for Christian boys I can scarcely hope to make.

1831 **James Clerk Maxwell:** Scottish mathematician and physicist. Especially known for his application of mathematics to the study of electricity. Showed that magnetism, electricity, and light were simply different manifestations of the same fundamental laws. Developed the theory of electromagnetism and was the first to predict the existence of electromagnetic radiation, and to describe light as an electromagnetic wave. Recast the discoveries of British physicist Michael Faraday in mathematical form, describing all of these by a unique, elegant, and concise system of equations, the fundamental laws of electromagnetism, usually referred to as *Maxwell's equations.*

The only laws of matter are those that our minds must fabricate and the only laws of mind are fabricated for it by matter.

1865 **William Butler Yeats:** Irish poet and dramatist. Son of J.B. Yeats, a well-known Irish painter. Established his reputation in 1888 with "The Wanderings of Oisin." Best known plays were *The Countess Cathleen, The Land of Heart's Desire* and *Cathleen in Houlihan.* Cofounder of a theater society that would become the Abbey Theatre. Best known poems: "Bzyantium," "Easter 1916," and "Leda and the Swan."

Education is not the filling of a pail, but the lighting of a fire.

1893 **Dorothy L. Sayers:** English mystery novelist. Created sophisticated amateur detective Lord Peter Wimsey, who appeared in novels including *Murder Must Advertise* and *The Nine Tailors.* Earned a reputation as a leading Christian apologist with her plays *The Zeal of Thy House* and *The Devil to Pay.*

As I grow older and older. And totter toward the tomb, I find that I care less and less who goes to bed with whom.

1894 **Mark Van Doren:** American poet, critic and novelist. *Collected Poems 1922–38* earned him a Pulitzer Prize. Also wrote critical biographies of Thoreau, Dryden, Shakespeare and Hawthorne. Edited the *Oxford Book of American Prose* and wrote three novels. Brother of critic and biographer Carl Van Doren.

Memory holds together past and present, gives continuity and dignity to human life ... the companion ... the tutor, the poet, the library, with which you travel.

1897 **Paavo Nurmi:** Finnish athlete who won nine gold medals at three Olympic Games. Set 22 world records in races ranging in distance from 1500 meters to 10,000 meters. His stature stands outside the Olympic Stadium in Helsinki.

Mind is everything: muscles — pieces of rubber. All that I am, I am because of my mind.

1903 **Harold "Red" Grange:** Nicknamed "The Galloping Ghost." All-American football running back at the University of Illinois. Played pro ball with the Chicago Bears and New York Yankees. Against Michigan in 1924, he accumulated 402 total yards and 5 touchdowns. Became a sports commentator on radio and TV. On his trademark ability to evade tacklers:

No one ever taught me and I can't teach anyone. If you can't explain it, how can you take credit for it?

1911 **Luis Alvarez:** U.S. experimental nuclear physicist. During World War II developed radar navigation and landing systems for aircraft. Developed the bubble-chamber which allowed him to discover new subatomic particles. Won Nobel Prize (1968).

There is no democracy in physics. We can't say that some second-rate guy has a much right to opinion as Fermi.

1928 **John Forbes Nash:** Brilliant but troubled American mathematician. Established the mathematical principles of Game Theory, known as Nash equilibrium, an attempt to explain the dynamics of threat and action among competitors. Awarded the Nobel Prize in Economics in 1994. Throughout his life he suffered from mental illness, chronicled in the popular book *A Beautiful Mind* by Sylvia Nasar, the basis of a highly fictionalized account in the award-winning movie of the same name.

I would not dare to say that there is a direct relation between mathematics and madness, but there is no doubt that great mathematicians suffer from maniacal characteristics, delirium and symptoms of schizophrenia.

1937 **Eleanor Holmes Norton:** African-American lawyer who is the non-voting Delegate to the U.S. House of Representatives from the District of Columbia. Has served as an assistant legal director of the American Civil Liberties Union, chair of the New York City Commission on Human Rights and Chairwoman of the U.S. Equal Opportunity Commission.

Men without jobs do not form families.

1969 **Laura Kightlinger:** American comic actress. Worked as a writer and consulting produced to the TV sitcom *Will & Grace,* as well as appearing in a recurring role in the series. Host of *Stand-Up Stand-Up* for Comedy Central. Wrote a collection of short autobiographical stories *Quick Shots of False Hope*.

I want to be so famous that drag queens will dress like me in parades when I'm dead.

OTHERS: 37 CE Roman statesman/general **Gnaeus Julius Agricola**, 823 Holy Roman Emperor **Charles the Bald**, 1773 English scientist **Thomas Young**, 1786 U.S. general **Winfield Scott**, 1809 German author **Heinrich Hoffman**, 1875 Texas governor **Miriam "Ma" Ferguson**, 1881 1st woman film director **Lois Weber**, 1892 English actor **Basil Rathbone**, 1899 Mexican composer **Carlos Chávez**, 1915 U.S. tennis player **Don Budge**, 1917 Latin American novelist **Augusto Roa Bastos**, 1926 American comic actor **Paul Lynde**, 1935 Bulgarian artist **Christo**, 1953 American comedian **Tim Allen**, 1973 U.S. model **Leeann Tweeden**, 1986 U.S. twin actresses **Mary-Kate and Ashley Olsen**

June 14

1811 **Harriet Beecher Stowe:** U.S. novelist. Daughter of Presbyterian minister and revivalist Lyman Beecher. Sister of clergyman and orator Henry Ward Beecher. Best known as the author of *Uncle Tom's Cabin* which aroused considerable anti-slavery feelings prior to the Civil War. With her sister Catherine Esther Beecher, she produced *The American Woman's Home*, which was an influential guide for generations of American housewives.

The bitterest tears shed over graves are for words left unsaid and deeds left undone.

1855 **Robert M. Lafollette, Sr.:** U.S. politician, lawyer. Leader of the Progressive movement which championed the little guy against established interests. Wisconsin congressman (1885–91), reform governor (1900–6) and senator (1907–25). Progressive Party presidential candidate (1924), receiving nearly five million votes.

We are opposed to the excessive use of money in campaigns. It is the weapon of special interests. It is the instrument of evil. It debauches manhood and corrupts the electorate. It serves every bad cause and embarrasses every good one.

1873 **Georges Gurdjieff:** Armenian mystic and philosopher. In 1919 he founded the Institute for the Harmonious Development of Man in Georgia, reestablishing it three years later in France. He and his followers lived communally, engaged in discussions of philosophy, ritual exercises and dance. Taught that ordinary living was akin to sleep and through spiritual discipline it was possible to achieve heightened levels of vitality and awareness.

A man will renounce any pleasures you like but he will not give up his suffering.

1904 **Margaret Bourke-White:** U.S. photo-journalist. Began her career as an industrial and architectural photographer. An innovator in photo essays with *Life* magazine (1936–69). Covered World War II for *Life* magazine. First woman photographer to be attached to the U.S. armed forces. An official U.N. correspondent during the Korean War. Books: *Eyes on Russia* and *Halfway to Freedom*.

Saturate yourself with your subject and the camera will all but take you by the hand.

1907 **René Char:** French poet. Wrote philosophical poems charged with vivid imagination. His poems and aphorisms reflect both his Provençal origins and his years of active participation in the World War II French resistance as the leader of a Maquis group in Provence. Verses deal with the place of the poet and beauty among the chaos and struggle of human existence.

A poet must leave traces of his passage, not proof.

1909 **Burl Ives:** U.S. folk singer and actor. Left college to hitchhike around the country, collecting songs from hoboes and drifters. Recorded over 100 albums. Songs: "Blue Tail Fly," "The Foggy, Foggy Dew," "Frosty the Snowman" and "Big Rock Candy Mountain." Oscar winner for *The Big Country*. Memorable as "Big Daddy" in *Cat on a Hot Tin Roof*.

Ballad singing has been going on ever since people sang at all. It comes up like an underground stream and then goes back again. But it always exists.

1928 **Ernesto "Che" Guevara:** Argentine-born Latin American guerrilla and revolutionary. Theoretician and tactician of guerrilla warfare. Trusted aide of Fidel Castro in the Cuban revolution. Left Cuba in 1965 to become a guerrilla leader in the Congo and then in South America. Captured and executed in Bolivia.

The revolution is not an apple that falls when it is ripe. You have to make it fall.

1933 **Jerzy Kosinski:** Polish-born U.S. author. His novels espouse a belief in survival at any cost. Wrote *The Painted Bird*, *Being There* and *Passion Play*. Spoke of his horrific experiences as a Jew in World War II in Poland and Russia. After his death, it became known that much of his past had been fabricated. From his suicide note:

I am going to put myself to sleep now for a bit longer than usual. Call the time Eternity.

1946 **Donald Trump:** American real estate tycoon. Built New York's Trump Tower and Atlantic City casinos. His enthusiastic self-promotion made him a celebrity of the eighties. Faced near bankruptcy in 1990, but later embarked on a vast building project on New York's West Side.

Without passion you don't have energy, with out energy you have nothing.

1961 **Boy George** (Born **George Alan O'Dowd):** British singer and musician. Gained a large degree of fame for his androgynous style and his musical group Culture Club in the 1980s. The band's breakthrough hit was the very popular "Do You Really Want To Hurt Me?" Albums: *Kissing to Be Clever* and *Color by Numbers*. Currently he is a popular disk jockey.

There's the illusion that homosexuals have sex

and heterosexuals fall in love. That's completely untrue. Everybody wants to be loved.

1968 **Yasmine Bleeth:** American actress. Popular TV soap opera actress. Best known for her role on TV's *Baywatch*, and her form-fitting red lifeguard swimming suit. Began her career at age six months appearing in a baby shampoo commercial. Overcame a cocaine addiction. Outspoken advocate of breast cancer research and early detection, prompted by the misdiagnosis of the disease that killed her mother.

I love a man who can wear my underwear.

1969 **Steffi Graf:** German tennis star, considered one of the greatest players of all time. Equally successful on all different surfaces. Won 22 Grand Slam singles title. In 1988 she became the only player to achieve the "Golden Slam"—capturing all four Grand Slam titles and the Olympic Gold Medal in the same year. Married to Andre Agassi.

When you lose a couple of times, it makes you realize how difficult it is to win.

OTHERS: 1444 Indian mathematician **Nilakantha Somayaji**, 1736 French physicist **Charles Augustin de Coulomb**, 1801 American religious leader **Heber C. Kimball**, 1856 Russian mathematician **Andrey Markov**, 1864 German physician **Alois Alzheimer**, 1868 U.S. pathologist **Karl Landsteiner**, 1877 French mezzo-soprano **Jane Barthori**, 1903 American logician **Alonzo Church**, 1917 Norwegian mathematician **Atle Selberg**, 1919 U.S. actress **Dorothy McGuire**, 1925 White House Press Secretary **Pierre Salinger**, 1926 Baseball pitcher **Don Newcombe**, 1929 U.S. composer **Cy Coleman**, 1952 U.S. basketball coach **Pat Summitt**, 1958 U.S. speed skater **Eric Heiden**

June 15

1767 **Rachel Robards Jackson:** U.S. first lady. Caused a scandal by marrying Andrew Jackson before divorcing her first husband.

Believe me; this country [Florida] has been greatly overrated. One acre of our fine Tennessee land is worth a thousand here.

1843 **Edvard Grieg:** Norwegian composer of choral works, dances and sonatas for various instruments. Developed into a strongly national composer. Wrote a piano concerto, orchestral suites, violin sonatas, and numerous songs and piano pieces. Best known for his *Peer Gynt Suite*.

I am sure my music has a taste of codfish in it.

1881 **William McFee:** Writer of sea stories, born on the *Erin's Isle*, a three-master owned by his sea captain father. Became a marine engineer and moved to the U.S. in 1911. Most famous novels: *Casuals of the Sea*, *North of Suez*, *No Castle in Spain*, *The Beachcomber*, *The Derelicts* and *The Watch Below*.

People don't seem to realize that doing what's right is no guarantee against misfortune.

1884 **Harry Langdon:** American actor in minstrel shows, circuses, burlesque, vaudeville and silent films. His baby face innocence, handicapped by indecisiveness and bemused bewilderment about the wider world was featured in the likes of *Tramp, Tramp, Tramp*, *The Strong Man* and *Long Pants*.

Comedy is the satire of tragedy.

1902 **Erik Ericson:** German-born psychologist, writer and educator. Opened new relationship between psychoanalysis and social sciences. Introduced term "identity crisis." Books: *Childhood and Society*, *Gandhi's Truth* and *Young Man Luther*. Taught at the University of California at Berkeley, until the 1950s which he left when he refused to sign a loyalty oath.

If life is to be sustained, hope must remain, even where confidence is wounded, trust impaired.

1914 **Saul Steinberg:** Romanian-American artist and cartoonist. Settled in the U.S. in 1942. Known for his *New Yorker* magazine covers combining styles of cubism and pointillism. His works were often surrealistic or whimsically nightmarish visions of contemporary America.

People who see a drawing in the "New Yorker" will think automatically that it's funny because it's a cartoon. If they see it in a museum, they think it is artistic; and if they find it in a fortune cookie they think it is a prediction.

1916 **Herbert Simon:** American social scientist. In *Administrative Behavior* he argued that corporate decision-making shouldn't be limited means of achieving maximum profits; rather there are a multiplicity of factors that should be considered. Award Nobel Prize in Economics in 1976. Worked in the field of Artificial Intelligence.

Anything that gives us new knowledge gives us an opportunity to be more rational.

1921 **Errol Garner:** African-American jazz pianist and composer. Developed an international following as a concert performer. Entirely self-taught, he formed a three piece group that achieved fame with one of the best selling jazz albums *Concert by the Sea*. Best known composition: "Misty."

In playing the organ you have to wear narrow shoes or your feet get stuck.

1922 **Morris K. Udall:** "Mo." American politician, lawyer and former professional basketball player. Lost an eye following an infection as a child and wore a glass eye from then on. U.S. Representative from Arizona (1961–1991), succeeding his brother Stewart who was appointed Secretary of the Interior in Kennedy's cabinet. Noted for his liberal views, self-depreciating wit and easy manner. Chairman of House Interior and Insular Affairs Committee. Sought Democratic presidential nomination (1976).

I have learned the difference between a cactus and a caucus. On a cactus, the pricks are on the outside.

1932 **Mario Cuomo:** U.S. politician, noted for his liberal views, particularly for his steadfast opposition to the death penalty and his unwavering pro-choice views on abortion. Governor of New York (1982–94).

Defeated by George Pataki in the 1994 Republican landslide. Often mentioned as a Democratic presidential candidate, but declined to make a run.

The price of seeking to force our beliefs on others is that someday they may force their beliefs on us.

1937 **Waylon Jennings:** American country music singer and guitarist. Toured with Buddy Holly and gave up his seat to J.P. Richardson (The Big Bopper) on the plane that crashed killing all aboard including Holly, Richardson and Ritchie Valens. Jennings became addicted to amphetamines and later switched to cocaine. First of the performers of the so-called outlaw country movement. Albums: *Ladies Love Outlaws*, *Lonesome, On'ry and Mean*, *Honky Tonk Heroes*, and with Willie Nelson, *Waylon and Willie*.

Honesty is something you can't wear out.

1943 **Xaviera Hollander:** Indonesian-born former call girl and madam. Wrote the best-selling *The Happy Hooker: My Own Story* in 1971. Wrote a sex advice column for *Penthouse* magazine, called "Call Me Madam." Latest book *Child No More* is the story of losing her mother.

Actually, if my business was legitimate, I would deduct a substantial percentage for depreciation of my body.

OTHERS: 1594 French painter **Nicolas Poussin**, 1624 German orientalist **Hiob Ludolf**, 1805 Chicago's 1st mayor **William Butler Ogden**, 1882 English illustrator/caricaturist **Hablot Knight Browne**, 1882 Prime Minister of Romania **Ion Antonescu**, 1894 U.S. composer **Robert Russell Bennett**, 1914 U.S.S.R. Communist Party General Secretary **Yuri Andropov**, 1941 American singer/composer **Harry Nilsson**, 1947 U.S. photographer **John Hoagland**, 1948 Pro football coach **Mike Holmgren**, 1949 Baseball player/manager **Dusty Baker**, 1954 American comic actor **James Belushi**, 1958 Baseball player **Wade Boggs**, 1963 U.S. actress **Helen Hunt**, 1969 U.S. singer/actor **Ice Cube**

June 16

1583 Count **Axel Oxenstierna:** Swedish statesman. Chancellor of Sweden for 42 years. His country's greatest civil servant. Negotiated favorable peace treaties with Denmark, Sweden and Poland. Regent during Queen Christina's minority, effectively ruling the country.

Behold, my son, with what little wisdom the world is ruled.

1613 **John Cleland:** English Cavalier poet, known for his popular elegies and satires. A staunch Royalist, as a member of the Long Parliament for Cambridge he opposed to the election of Oliver Cromwell costing him his fellowship at St. John's College. Appointed judge advocate at Newark by Charles I. Was forced to surrender and spent the rest of his life wandering around the country.

Love melts the rigor which the rocks have bred; a flint will break upon a feather bed.

1829 **Geronimo:** Chiricahua Apache leader in the 1870s. Led a force of 4,000 from the barren Arizona reservation on which they had been forced to live. After years of bloodshed, he was captured, but escaped once again with some of his followers. Surrendered under a promise to return him to Arizona, but the promise was not kept, and he was put to hard labor. Late in life he converted to Christianity and dictated his autobiography, *Geronimo: His Own Story*.

I cannot think that we are useless or God would not have created us. There is one God looking down on all of us. We are all children of one God. The sun, the darkness, the winds are all listening to what we have to say.

1890 **Stan Laurel:** British-born U.S. comedian, teamed with Oliver Hardy to form a beloved comedy team in more than 100 films, 27 of which were features. The first great screen comedy team converted simple everyday situations into convoluted tangles of stupidity. Laurel was the featherbrained member of the team, characteristically scratching his head and at the first sign of trouble, sobbing uncontrollably.

If any of you cry at my funeral, I'll never speak to you again.

1902 **Barbara McClintock:** American geneticist. Experiments with variations in the coloration of kernels of corn led her to the discovery that genetic information is not stationary. Her pioneering work, not recognized for many years, finally earned her the Nobel Prize for Medicine in 1983.

When you know you're right, you don't care what others think. You know sooner or later it will come out in the wash.

1912 **Enoch Powell:** English conservative politician, scholar and racist. Enlisted in World War II as a private, rose to the rank of brigadier. Minister of housing and minister of health. His outspoken views opposing non-white immigration, racial discrimination and the common market led to his dismissal from the shadow cabinet. Books: *A Nation Not Afraid*, *Medicine and Politics* and *No Easy Answers*.

To write a diary every day is like returning to one's own vomit.

1915 **John Tukey:** American operations analyst and statistician. Working at Bell Laboratories and Princeton University, he made matchless contributions to statistics and seamlessly brought together the work of scientific, governmental, technological and industrial worlds. Coined the term "bit," an abbreviation of "binary digit." Noted that "software" as he called it, is "at least as important as the 'hardware' of tubes, transistors, wires, tapes, and the like."

Far better an approximate answer to the right question, than the exact answer to the wrong question, which can always be made more precise.

1917 **Katharine Graham:** U.S. publisher. Consistently voted one of the most influential women in the United States. After her husband's suicide she succeeded him as president of the *Washington Post* (1963–67);

publisher (1968–78); chairman and CEO from 1973. Her best-selling autobiography *Personal History*, earned a Pulitzer Prize in 1997.

A mistake is simply another way of doing things.

1937 **Erich Segal:** American novelist and professor of classics at Yale University. Wrote the phenomenally popular and soapy romantic *Love Story*, which was made into an equally popular and soapy movie. Had his characters mouth the ridiculous assertion, which became a catch-phrase, "Love means never having to say you're sorry." Followed this success with a less well-received sequel *Oliver's Story*.

True love comes quietly, without banners or flashing lights. If you hear bells, get your ears checked.

1938 **Joyce Carol Oates:** American writer, university professor. Winner of the National Book Award for 1970 novel *Them*. Also received four O. Henry awards. Often writes of people whose all-consuming lives end in violence and self-destruction due to circumstances they neither cause nor control.

The use of language is all we have to pit against death and silence.

1951 **Roberto Duran:** Panamanian boxer. Held world titles at four different weights, lightweight, welterweight, junior middleweight and middleweight. Only boxer to have fought in five different decades. Had 69 wins by knockouts. Remembered for quitting in the 8th round of a fight with Sugar Ray Leonard. Frustrated by his opponent's antics and style, he said "No más, no más" (no more, no more).

Getting hit motivates me. It makes me punish the guy more. A fighter takes a punch, hits back with three punches.

1971 **Tupac Shakur:** African-American hip hop artist, poet and actor. Highest selling rap artist ever, 67 million albums worldwide. Most of his songs were about growing up amidst the violence and hardships in the U.S. ghettos. Often in trouble with the law and feuding with fellow rappers, he served almost 8 months in prison for sexual assault. He was shot and killed in September, 1996, possibly by a street gang.

My mama always used to tell me: "If you can't find somethin' to live for, you best find somethin' to die for."

OTHERS: 1313 Italian writer **Giovanni Boccaccio**, 1801 German mathematician/physicist **Julius Plücker**, 1806 English physician **Edward Davy**, 1858 Swedish King **Gustaf V**, 1888 Russian physicist **Alexander Friedman**, 1903 American soprano **Helen Traubel**, 1910 U.S. actor **Jack Albertson**, 1916 Basketball player **Hank Luisetti**, 1920 U.S. author/photographer **John Howard Griffin**, 1920 President of Mexico **José López Portillo**, 1930 Hungarian cinematographer **Vilmos Zsigmond**, 1939 U.S. C&W singer **Billy "Crash" Craddock**, 1940 Oregon Governor **Neil Goldschmidt**, 1941 U.S. recording company executive **Lamont Dozier**, 1970 U.S. pro golfer **Phil Mickelson**

June 17

1703 **John Wesley:** English evangelist, theologian. Founder of Methodist movement. In 1738 during the reading of Luther's preface to the Epistle to the Romans, he experienced an assurance of salvation which he felt driven to bring to others.

Catch on fire with enthusiasm and people will come for miles to watch you burn.

1818 **Charles Gounod:** French composer and songwriter. Organist of the Eglise des Missions Etrangères in Paris. Reputation largely rests on his hugely popular masterpiece the opera *Faust*. Also published Masses, hymns, and anthems. Other Operas: *Roméo et Juliette* and *Mireille*.

Musical ideas sprang to my mind like a flight of butterflies, and all I had to do was to stretch out my hand to catch them.

1871 **James Welden Johnson:** African-American poet, novelist and diplomat. Practiced law and was U.S. Consul in Venezuela and Nicaragua. Secretary of the NAACP. Professor of creative literature at Fisk University. Wrote *The Autobiography of an Ex-Colored Man*, *Black Manhattan* and edited *American Negro Poetry*.

You are young, gifted and Black. We must begin to tell our young. There's a world waiting for you. Yours is the quest that's just begun.

1882 **Igor Stravinsky:** Russian-born American composer. Famous for his Diaghilev ballets, *The Firebird*, *Petrouchka* and *The Rite of Spring*. Essentially an experimenter, he also composed *Oedipus Rex*, an opera-oratorio, and the choral *Symphony of Psalms*. Also wrote the opera *The Rake's Progress* and *Requiem Canticles*.

My music is best understood by children and animals.

1898 **M.C. (Maurits Cornelius) Escher:** Dutch graphic artist. Designed fascinating images that showed his unique perspective of the world and the worlds of his imagination. Created a number of captivating landscapes, portraits, and geometric designs, but he is best known for his tessellations, that is, coverings of the plane with congruent figures. Famed for his popular bizarre optical illusions and Surrealistic depictions of unexpected metamorphoses of objects.

Order is repetition of units. Chaos is multiplicity without rhythm.

1900 **Martin Bormann:** German Nazi politician. One of Adolf Hitler's closest advisers. Participated in the abortive Munich putsch of 1923. Made Reichsminster in 1941 and remained with Hitler until the Fuhrer's suicide. His exact fate is uncertain, but a skeleton uncovered by an exactor in Berlin in 1972 has been confirmed to be Bormann's by forensic experts.

Every educated person is a future enemy.

1907 **Steuart Henderson Britt:** American advertising consultant. Cofounder with George R. Freichs of The Freichs Group, which specialized in qualitative and quantitative research in consumer and professional markets. Books: *Market Management and Administra-*

tive Action and *Psychological Experiments in Consumer Behavior.* Passionately believed in the power of advertising.

Doing business without advertising is like winking at a girl in the dark. You know what you are doing, but nobody else does.

1914 **John Hersey:** American novelist and journalist. Born to missionaries in China. Worked as a correspondent in the Far East, Italy and Russia (1937–46). Pulitzer Prize for *A Bell for Adano.* Others: *Hiroshima* (originally a story for *The New Yorker*), *The Wall* and *The Conspiracy.*

A Yankee, a real Yankee — that's a person who's an idealist even after he's come to see how hopeless life is.

1918 **Ajahn Chah:** Thai Buddhist monk. One of the greatest meditation masters of the 20th century. Established monasteries of Wat Nong Pah Pong and Wat Pah Nanachat in Northeast Thailand. His followers use meditation for calming and for insight. His talks were recorded, transcribed, translated and published as books.

Looking for peace is like looking for a turtle with a mustache. You won't be able to find it. But when your heart is ready, peace will come looking for you.

1919 **Kingman Brewster:** U.S. educator and diplomat. President of Yale University (1963–77). Known for the improvements he made in Yale's faculty, curriculum and admission policies. Skillfully handled Vietnam War Protests. During his tenure women were admitted as undergraduates. U.S. Ambassador to Great Britain and later Master of University College, Oxford.

Universities should be safe havens where ruthless examination of realities will not be distorted by the aim to please or inhibited by the risk of displeasure.

1943 **Newt Gingrich:** Republican congressman from Georgia. Best known as the Speaker of the House of Representatives (1995–1999). Named *Time* Magazine's Man of the Year in 1995 for his role in leading the Republican Revolution in Congress, ending 40 years of Democratic majority in the House. He defined a Contract with America, which listed the promises that the Republicans would present as acts of Congress. Investigated for ethics violations, but all charges were dropped. Pressed to resign as Speaker in 1998, he declined to remain in Congress even though he won his 11th election.

The idea that a congressman would be tainted by accepting money from private industry or private sources is essentially a socialist argument.

1945 **Tommy Franks:** Retired American general. Served as the Commander-in-Chief of United States Central Command, overseeing U.S. Armed Forces in a 25-country region, including the Middle East. Led the attack on the Taliban in Afghanistan after the 9–11 attacks and led the invasion of Iraq in 2003.

If terrorists succeeded in using a weapon of mass destruction against the U.S. or one of our allies, it would likely have catastrophic consequences for our cherished republican form of government.

1980 **Venus Williams:** African-American professional women's tennis player. Won 33 singles championships, including 5 Grand Slam tournaments. Has two Olympic gold medals for singles and doubles in 2000. Older sister of tennis champion Serena Williams.

I'd like to imagine that in order to beat me a person would have to play almost perfect tennis.

OTHERS: 1239 King of England **Edward I**, 1691 Italian painter/architect **Giovanni Paolo Pannini**, 1811 Icelandic independence fighter **Jón Sigurdsson**, 1832 English physicist/chemist **William Crookes**, 1860 U.S. theatrical manager/impresario **Charles Frohman**, 1867 Irish-U.S. inventor shorthand system **John Robert Gregg**, 1904 U.S. actor **Ralph Bellamy**, 1910 U.S. country musician **Red Foley**, 1923 Football player **Elroy "Crazylegs" Hirsch**, 1933 French violinist **Christian Ferras**, 1945 London Mayor **Ken Livingstone**, 1945 Belgian cyclist **Eddy Merckx**, 1946 U.S. singer **Barry Manilow**, 1958 U.S. musician/activist **Jello Biafra**, 1964 German swimmer **Michael Gross**

June 18

1581 Sir **Thomas Overbury:** English poet and courtier. Became involved in numerous court intrigues and scandals, one of which resulted in his death in the Tower of London. Posthumously published works: "The Wife" and "Crumm's Fal'n from King James's Table."

You cannot name any example in any heathen author but I will better it in Scripture.

1812 **Ivan Goncharov:** Russian novelist. Served for 30 years as a minor government official. Best known for the extremely successful novel *Oblomov*, one of the greatest and most typical examples of Russian realism. The title character has been likened to Shakespeare's *Hamlet.*

It is a trick among the dishonest to offer sacrifices that are not needed or not possible, to avoid making those that are required.

1850 **Cyrus Curtis:** American publisher. In Philadelphia he founded *The Tribune and Farmer*, from its women's section he formed the *Ladies Home Journal.* In 1890, organized the Curtis Publishing Co., whose other periodicals would include *The Saturday Evening Post, The Country Gentleman*, and *The Philadelphia Inquirer.*

There are two kinds of people who never amount to much: those who cannot do what they are told, and those who can do nothing else.

1869 **Carolyn Wells:** American writer, humorist, poet, playwright and anthologist. Wrote over 170 mysteries, nonsense tales and children's books, including *At the Sign of the Sphinx, A Satire Anthology* and *Book of Limericks.*

Advice is one of those things it is far more blessed to give than to receive.

1886 **George Leigh Mallory:** English mountaineer. Last seen climbing toward the summit of the highest mountain in the world. Mt. Everest, on the morning of June 8, 1924. In 1999, an American expedition found his frozen body at about 27,000 feet on the north face of the mountain. Answered "because it's there" when asked why he wanted to climb Mt. Everest, although some people incorrectly insist it was said by Sir Edmund Hillary. Mallory elaborated:

What is the use of climbing Mount Everest? And my answer must at once be, it is no use. There is not the slightest prospect of any gain whatsoever.

1903 **Jeanette MacDonald:** American soprano and actress. Performed on Broadway for nine years before lured to Hollywood. Best known for her appearances with Maurice Chevalier and Nelson Eddy in films including *The Love Parade, The Merry Widow, Naughty Marietta, Maytime* and *New Moon.* For many her best performance was in the film *San Francisco,* giving a rousing rendition of the title song.

If I ever published my memoirs they will be called The Iron Butterfly.

1913 **Sylvia Field Porter:** U.S. financial reporter and author of *Money Book,* which in 1975 sold over a million copies. Leading financial columnist with the *New York Post* (1935–77) and the *New York Daily News* commencing in 1978. *Sylvia Porter's Income Tax Guide* has been published annually since 1960.

One of the soundest rules to remember when making forecasts in the field of economics is that whatever is to happen is happening already.

1915 **Red Adair:** American oil field firefighter. World famous for his innovative approaches to the extremely hazardous profession of extinguishing and capping blazing, erupting oil wells. Served with a bomb disposal unit during World War II. Over his career, his company battled more than 2,000 land and offshore oil well, natural gas and other spectacular fires. When he was 75, he extinguished oil well fires in Kuwait during the Gulf War of 1991.

I've done made a deal with the devil. He said he's going to give me an air-conditioned place when I go down there, if I go there, so I won't put all the fires out.

1937 **Gail Godwin:** American novelist and short-story writer. Her fiction is about personal freedom in the relations between the sexes and the choices women make. Author of *Glass People, Dream Children, A Mother and Two Daughters,* and *The Odd Woman.* Along with her longtime companion Robert Starer, she wrote ten musical works, including a chamber opera.

None of us suddenly becomes something overnight. The preparations have been in the making for a lifetime.

1942 **Roger Ebert:** American film critic, lecturer and writer. Writes a column for the *Chicago Sun-Times,* which is syndicated to more than 200 newspapers in the U.S. and abroad. Long time co-host of a syndicated TV program, giving thumbs-up or thumbs-down on current films. Pulitzer Prize winner for film criticism in 2003. Wrote the screenplay for the 1970 cult film *Beyond the Valley of the Dolls,* directed by Russ Meyer.

Every great film should seem new every time you se it.

1942 **Thabo Mvuyelwa Mbeki:** President of South Africa. Son of an anti-apartheid activist, Following South Africa's first all-race elections in 1994, Mbeki became Nelson Mandela's deputy president. Respected for his competence in running the government's day-to-day workings and his contributions to South Africa's economic growth strategy.

Those who oppressed us described us as the Dark Continent!

1942 **Paul McCartney:** English musician, singer and songwriter. Met John Lennon in the mid–1950s, with whom he formed the Quarryman, which became the Beatles. With Lennon, he wrote scores of songs, many of which are the most popular on the 20th century, including: "Yesterday," "Michelle," "Hey Jude," "And I Love Her" and "Eleanor Rigby." After the breakup of the Beatles, McCartney formed the Band Wings with his first wife Linda Eastman. Their hit albums included *Band on the Run* and *Wings at the Speed of Sound.* Knighted in 1997.

In the end, the love you take is equal to the love you make.

OTHERS: 1854 U.S. journalist/publisher **E.W. Scripps**, 1857 U.S. industrialist **Henry Clay Folger**, 1868 Hungarian admiral **Miklós Horthy**, 1877 American artist **James Montgomery Flagg**, 1884 French politician **Édouard Daladier**, 1896 American dramatist **Phillip Barry**, 1906 U.S. band leader **Kay Kyser**, 1913 American composer **Sammy Cahn**, 1924 U.S. basketball player **George Mikan**, 1926 U.S. syndicated columnist **Tom Wicker**, 1931 President of Brazil **Fernando Henrique Cardoso**, 1937 U.S. Senator **Jay Rockefeller**, 1939 Baseball player **Lou Brock**, 1952 Italian-U.S. actress **Isabella Rossellini**, 1964 Saddam's son **Uday Hussein**

June 19

1566 **James I:** King of England (1603–25). Son of Mary, Queen of Scots. On her forced abdication became James VI, King of Scots (1567–1625). Succeeded Elizabeth I as English monarch.

[Smoking is] a custom loathsome to the eye, hateful to the nose, harmful to the brain, dangerous to the lungs, and in the black stinking fume thereof nearest resembles the horrible Stygian smoke of the pit that is bottomless.

1608 **Thomas Fuller:** English clergyman, scholar and writer. One of the wittiest and most prolific authors of the 17th century. Works: *The Holy State, the Profane State* and his most famous work, *History of the Worthies of Britain.*

If you have one true friend you have more than your share.

1623 **Blaise Pascal:** French philosopher, scientist, mathematician and writer. Considered one of the greatest minds in Western intellectual history. With Pierre de Fermat, developed the modern theory of probability. Formulated the first laws of atmospheric pressure and equilibrium of liquids. The *Provincial Letters*, written in defense of the Jansenists, a strict sect of Christianity founded by a Flemish theologian Cornelius Jansen, are considered "a monument in the evolution of French prose." Pascal's notes on apologetics were published after his death as *Pensées* ("Thoughts").

It is not certain that everything is uncertain.

1834 **Charles H. Spurgeon:** English Baptist preacher. Drew such enormous crowds to his humorous sermons that the 6000 seat Metropolitan Tabernacle was erected for him. Wrote 50 popular volumes of sermons and collections of pithy sayings.

A man who does nothing never has time to do anything.

1856 **Elbert Hubbard:** U.S. writer, essayist, lecturer ad editor. After years as a successful businessman, established in 1893 the Roycrofters, a craft community in East Aurora, N.Y. Best known as the author of *A Message to Garcia*, which embodied his ideas about a community of workers.

If you can't answer a man's arguments, all is not lost; you can still call him vile names.

1881 **James J. Walker:** "Jimmy." Dapper, debonair and flamboyant, fun-loving mayor of New York City (1925–32). Forced to resign as a result of an investigation into widespread corruption in his administration. Wrote the popular song "Will You Love Me in December."

I never knew a girl who was ruined by a book.

1896 **Wallis Simpson, Duchess of Windsor:** Twice divorced U.S. socialite who met and fell in love with the United Kingdom's Edward, Prince of Wales. When he became king, she was unacceptable as a prospective British queen. Edward renounced the throne to marry her. They became a well-publicized international couple, living mostly in France.

A woman can't be too rich or too thin.

1903 **Lou Gehrig:** U.S. baseball first baseman with the New York Yankees who set a record for consecutive games played (2,130), later broken by Cal Ripken, Jr. Gehrig died of a muscle wasting disease, now known by his name. He demonstrated his bravery at a Yankee stadium ceremony to honor him, saying:

Two weeks ago, I got a bad break. Yet today, I count myself the luckiest man on the face of the earth.

1919 **Pauline Kael:** American film critic, author. Columnist for *The New Yorker* magazine. Books: *I Lost It at the Movies, Kiss Kiss Bang Bang* and *5001 Nights at the Movies*.

Good movies make you care, make you believe in possibilities again.

1945: **Aung San Suu Kyi:** Burmese politician and devout Buddhist nonviolent, pro-democracy activist in Mynanmar (Burma). Helped found the National League for Democracy. The military junta placed her under house arrest and with the exception of a few releases; she has been confined since 1989. In 1990, her party won the general elections and she should have become Prime Minister but the military refused to give up power. She won the Sakharov Prize for Freedom of Thought and the Nobel Peace Prize.

The value systems of those with access to power and of those far removed from such access cannot be the same. The viewpoint of the privileged is unlike that of the underprivileged.

1947 **Salman Rushdie:** Indian-born British writer. His first novel, *Midnight's Children*, is an allegorical story of Modern India. This was followed by *Shame*, a condemnation of politics and sexual morality in Pakistan. He was denounced for blasphemy and condemned to death by Iran's Ruhollah Khomeini for his novel, *The Satanic Verses*, which included some episodes about the life of Muhammad, outraging Muslim leaders. He was forced into hiding for years.

It is very, very easy not to be offended by a book. You just have to shut it.

1953 **Adrienne Gusof:** American freelance writer, lecturer, humorist and motivational speaker. Writes extensively about relationships and sexuality. Wrote the advice column for an international magazine and currently is the advice columnist for an on-line e-zine. Noted for her short quips such as:

Living in a vacuum sucks, Opportunity knocked. My doorman threw him out and Not only is life a bitch, but it is always having puppies.

OTHERS: 1310 Japanese shogun **Prince Morikuni**, 1764 Founder of Royal Geographical Society **John Barrow**, 1856 U.S. literary agent **Elisabeth Marbury**, 1861 English military man **Douglas Haig**, 1865 English actress **Dame May Whitty**, 1877 U.S. actor **Charles Coburn**, 1897 U.S. comic actor **Moe Howard**, 1902 U.S. bandleader **Guy Lombardo**, 1908 U.S. actress **Mildred Natwick**, 1910 U.S. chemist **Paul Flory**, 1914 U.S. Senator **Alan Cranston**, 1914 Country musician **Lester Flatt**, 1945 Serbian-Bosnian politician **Radovan Karadžić**, 1970 Indian politician **Rahul Gandhi**, 1978 German basketball player **Dirk Nowitzki**

June 20

1604 **Friedrich Von Logau:** German epigrammatist. His epigrams appeared in two collections under the pseudonym Salomon von Golaw (an anagram of his name) in 1638 and 1655. Lived in the turbulent times of the Thirty Years' War. Satirized court life, the uselessness of war, the lack of German national pride and German imitation of French customs, dress and speech.

Though the mills of God grind slowly, yet they grind exceedingly small. Though with patience He stands waiting, with exactness grinds He all.

1674 **Nicholas Rowe:** 18th century English barrister and tragic dramatist. First person to produce a critical edition of Shakespeare's plays, dividing them into acts and scenes. Named English poet laureate in 1715. Tragedies produced at Lincoln Inn Fields include: *Tamberlane*, *The Fair Penitent*, *Ulysses*, *The Royal Convert* and *Lady Jane Grey*.

Guilt is the source of sorrow, 'tis the fiend, th' avenging fiend, that follows us behind, with whips and stings.

1723 **Adam Ferguson:** Scottish man of letters, philosopher, historian, and patriot. Member of the Scottish common sense school of philosophy. Works: *Essay on the History of Civil Society* and *Principles of Moral and Political Science*.

The history of mankind is confined within a limited period, and from every quarter brings an intimation that human affairs have had a beginning.

1743 **Anna Laetitia Barbauld:** née **Aikin**. English writer, who published several popular volumes of prose for children with her brother John Aikin. When her mentally unstable husband committed suicide, she threw herself into literary pursuits. Edited the 50 volume The British Novelists. Her poem in heroic couplets, "Eighteen hundred and eleven," foretold the decline of the British Empire and the rise of America's prosperity.

The most characteristic mark of a great mind is to choose some one important object, and pursue it for life.

1852 **George Iles:** Gibraltar-born American miscellaneous writer. Editor: *Little Masterpieces of Science* and *Little Masterpieces of Autobiography*.

Hope is faith holding out its hand in the dark.

1858 **Charles W. Chestnutt:** African-American writer, school principal, attorney and founder of a legal stenography firm. Son of emancipated blacks, he wrote works on social justice. His story "The Goophered Grapevine" was the first published work of a black fiction writer. He was an important influence on later writers.

Sins, like chickens, come home to roost.

1905 **Lillian Hellman:** American dramatist and left-winged activist. One of the most persuasive voices in American theater. Plays include: *The Children's Hour*, *Watch on the Rhine*, *Another Part of the Forest* and *The Little Foxes*. Lived for many years with detective writer Dashiell Hammett, who encouraged her writing. Her autobiographical works include *An Unfinished Woman* and *Pentimento*, of which writer Mary McCarthy said "Every word she writes is a lie, including 'and' and 'the.'"

Since when do we have to agree with people to defend them from injustice?

1909 **Errol Flynn:** Hard-living Tasmanian-born roguish actor who starred in many swashbuckling films, including *Captain Blood*, *The Charge of the Light Brigade* and *The Adventures of Robin Hood*. His off-screen reputation for drinking and womanizing became legendary, eventually affecting his career. His autobiography: *My Wicked, Wicked Ways*.

The public has always expected me to be a playboy, and a decent chap never lets his public down.

1924 **Chet Atkins:** American country guitarist and recording executive. His signature style of playing guitar is the bass rhythm played with his thumb and the melody picked with three fingers. Pioneered the use of the electric guitar in country music. Recorded more than 100 albums. As an RCA executive, produced hit recordings for Elvis Presley, Waylon Jennings and Jim Reeves.

Once you become predictable, no one's interested any more.

1936 **Dan Greenburg:** American humorist, novelist, journalist, screenwriter and playwright. His best selling books include *How to Be a Jewish Mother*, *How to Make Yourself Miserable*, and *How to Avoid Love*. Children books include *The Bed Who Ran Away from Home* and *Arnold the Elephant*.

Cats are dangerous companions for writers because cat watching is a near-perfect method of writing avoidance.

1942 **Brian Wilson:** American singer and songwriter. Best known as a founding member and main producer, composer and arranger for The Beach Boys. Formed in the early 1960s the group consisted of his brothers Carl and Dennis, cousin Mike Love and friend Al Jardine. Top hits include: "Surfin' USA," "Fun, Fun, Fun," "California Girls," and "Good Vibrations." Forced to overcome mental illness and drug abuse.

Beware the lollipop of mediocrity; lick it once and you'll suck forever.

1946 **Andre Watts:** German-born U.S. pianist. Son of an African-American soldier and a Hungarian mother. Appeared with the Philadelphia Orchestra at age nine. At age 16 he appeared on TV under Leonard Bernstein's conducting. An international favorite, known for his 19th century repertoire.

It's not enough to play the best you can — it takes a certain amount of luck. It's like blessings from on high. Or being kissed by the gods. If people hear you, and want to hear you again, you can sustain a career.

OTHERS: 1723 English theologian **Theophilus Lindsey**, 1785 French poet **Marceline Desbordes-Valmore**, 1819 German-born French composer **Jacques Offenbach**, 1868 U.S. philanthropist **Helen Miller Shepard**, 1876 U.S. civil engineer **Arthur E. Morgan**, 1894 U.S. philanthropist **George Delacorte**, 1899 French Resistance leader **Jean Moulin**, 1906 British novelist **Catherine Cookson**, 1924 World War II hero/actor **Audie Murphy**, 1931 U.S. actor **Martin Landau**, 1945 Canadian singer **Anne Murray**, 1949 U.S. musician **Lionel Ritchie**, 1952 American actor **John Goodman**, 1953 U.S. singer **Cyndi Lauper**, 1960 English guitarist **John Taylor**, 1967 Australian actress **Nicole Kidman**

June 21

1639 **Increase Mather:** American colonial clergyman. Father of Puritan leader Cotton Mather. Pastor of Second Church of Boston. President of Harvard (1685–1701). His *Case of Conscience Concerning Evil Spirits Personating Men* helped end the Salem witchcraft trials.

It were better that ten suspected witches should escape, than that one innocent person should be condemned.

1806 **Augustus De Morgan:** English mathematician, logician and bibliographer. Most important work: *Formal Logic; or the Calculus of Inference, Necessary and Probable* (1847). His *Budget of Paradoxes* is a delightful satire on some of the most eccentric people the world has ever known, including those who believed they had squared the circle, invented perpetual motion, demonstrated that the Earth is flat, proved that astronomers were wrong in claiming planetary orbits to be ellipses, and refuted Newton's laws of motion.

Great fleas have little fleas upon their back to bite 'em. / And little fleas have lesser fleas, and so on ad infinitum./And the great fleas themselves, in turn, have greater fleas to go on,/While these again have greater still, and greater still, and so on.

1880 **Arnold Gesell:** American psychologist and pediatrician. Director of the Clinic for Child Development at Yale University. Also taught at the Yale School of Medicine. Devised standard scales for measuring the progress of infant development. Books include: *An Atlas of Infant Behavior* and *Child Development.* Brother of jurist Gerhard Gesell.

Every generation rediscovers and re-evaluates the meaning of infancy and childhood.

1882 **Rockwell Kent:** American painter, book designer and illustrator, explorer, writer, sailor and political activist. Had a tremendous output of pen-and-ink drawings, wood engravings, lithographs, textiles, oils and watercolors, which was inspired by the great outdoors. Harassed for his radical leftist politics. Awarded the Lenin Peace Prize in Moscow in 1967.

If to the viewer's eyes, my world appears less beautiful than his, I'm to be pitied and the viewer praised.

1892 **Reinhold Niebuhr:** American theologian. Dealt with the failure of Christianity to confront social problems. Critic of capitalism and advocate of socialism. Emphasized the persistent evil in human nature and social institutions. Writings: *Moral Man and Immoral Society, Christian Realism and Political Problems* and *Essays in Applied Christianity.*

God grant me the serenity to accept the things I cannot change, the courage to change the things I can, and the wisdom to know the difference.

1903 **Al Hirschfeld:** American caricaturist. Especially known for his stylish drawings in the New York Times from 1929 till his death at age 99. His caricatures of casts of Broadway plays, which accompanied reviews in the *Times,* were very popular. Readers enjoyed finding the name of his daughter Nina that he hid in all of his drawings. Also produced watercolors, lithographs, etchings and sculptures.

Life isn't a science. We make it up as we go.

1905 **Jean-Paul Sartre:** French philosopher, dramatist, novelist and critic. His works dramatize the discovery of the meaningless of life, the precondition for his philosophy of Existentialism. Works: *Nausea, The Flies, No Exit,* and *The Roads to Freedom.* Declined the Nobel Prize for Literature in 1964.

Man is condemned to be free; because once thrown into the world, he is responsible for everything he does.

1912 **Mary McCarthy:** American writer, reviewer, critic, and satirist. Served on the staff of the *Partisan Review* (1947–48).Begin writing at the urging of her second husband critic and essayist Edmund Wilson. Works: *Memories of a Catholic Girlhood, The Company She Keeps, The Groves of Academe* and *The Group.*

You mustn't force sex to do the work of love or love to do the work of sex.

1921 **Gower Champion:** American dancer and choreographer. Teamed with his then wife Marge Champion, appearing in movie musicals *Show Boat* and *Lovely to Look At.* Noted for his successful Broadway musical comedies: *Lend an Ear, Bye Bye Birdie, I Do! I Do!* and *Hello Dolly!* Won seven Tony Awards, but did not live to received the last two, for choreography and direction of *42nd Street.* At the curtain call of its opening night, producer David Merrick stunned the cast and audience by announcing that Champion had died that afternoon of a rare form of blood cancer.

I use dancing to embellish, extend or enlarge upon an existing emotion.

1921 **Judy Holliday:** American comic actress. Academy Award winner for revising her Broadway role as "Billie Dawn" in *Born Yesterday.* Other films: *Adam's Rib, The Solid Gold Cadillac* and *Bells Are Ringing,* which she had also starred in on Broadway. Investigation of allegations that she was a communist did not result in her being blacklisted from movies, but she was not allowed to perform on radio and TV for about 3 years.

Acting is a very limited form of expression and those who take it seriously are very limited people. I take it seriously.

1921 **Jane Russell:** American actress. Discovered by Howard Hughes, who starred her in the movie *The Outlaw,* which did not have a general release until five years after it was made. Censors of the production code considered too much of her voluptuous bust was shown. Hughes designed a special bra to lift up her breasts even more, but she claims she didn't wear it, but told him she did. Her other films included *Paleface* and *Gentlemen Prefer Blondes.*

Sometimes the photographers would pose me in a low-necked nightgown and tell me to bend down and pick up the pails. They were not shooting the pails.

1935 **Françoise Sagan:** French novelist. Best known for her earliest work *Bonjour Tristesse*, written in four weeks when she was just 18. It was followed by *A Certain Smile*. Both novels are direct testaments of adolescent wisdom and precocity.

Every little girl knows about love. It is only her capacity to suffer because of it that increases.

OTHERS: 1732 German composer **Johann Christoph Friedrich Bach**, 1781 French mathematician/physicist **Siméon-Denis Poisson**, 1825 English historian **William Stubbs**, 1850 U.S. naturalist **Daniel Carter Beard**, 1884 British field marshal **Claude Auchinleck**, 1891 Italian architect **Pier Luigi Nervi**, 1891 German conductor **Hermann Scherchen**, 1898 American botanist **Donald C. Peattie**, 1914 Canadian economist **William Vickrey**, 1927 American politician **Carl B. Stokes**, 1928 U.S. opera singer **Judith Rankin**, 1931 U.S. government official **Margaret Heckler**, 1944 English musician **Ray Davies**, 1947 Iranian activist **Shirin Ebadi**, 1953 Prime Minister of Pakistan **Benazir Bhutto**

June 22

1767 Baron **Karl Wilhelm von Humboldt:** German philologist and statesman. Prussian Minster at Rome. First minister of public instruction and minister to Vienna. First to study the Basque language scientifically and also studied the languages of the East and the South Sea Islands.

True enjoyment comes from the activity of the mind and exercise of the body; the two are ever united.

1805 **Giuseppe Mazzini:** Italian propagandist and revolutionary founder of the secret society Young Italy Association. Traveled through Europe advocating republicanism and insurrection. Worked vainly to make the new Italy a republic. Was one of a triumvirate governing the Roman Republic, which was overthrown after only two months by the French.

Slumber not in the tents of your fathers. The world is advancing.

1844 **Margaret Sidney:** Pen name of **Harriet Mulford Stone Lothrup**. U.S. author. Married the founder of the Lothrop publishing company. Lived in the former home of Louisa May Alcott and Nathaniel Hawthorne. Remembered for *Five Little Peppers and How They Grew* and others in the children's series.

Corners are for little people; but when people who know better do wrong, there aren't any corners they can creep into, or they'd get into them pretty quick.

1887 Sir **Julian Huxley:** British biologist and writer. Grandson of T.H. Huxley. Secretary of the Zoological Society of London (1935–42). Applied his scientific knowledge to politics and social problems. Formulated a pragmatic ethical theory based on the principle of natural selection. First director-general of UNESCO.

The major ethical problem of our time is to achieve global unity for man.

1898 **Erich Maria Remarque:** German–U.S. novelist. Best known for his internationally successful antiwar novel *All Quiet on the Western Front*, inspired by his services in World War I. Also wrote *Three Comrades*, *A Time to Live and a Time to Die* and *The Night in Lisbon*. Nazis banned his novels in 1933. Emigrated to the U.S.A., where he became a naturalized citizen and married actress Paulette Goddard.

A hospital alone shows what war is.

1906 **Gilbert Highet:** Scottish-American classicist, critic and literary historian. Sought to raise the level of mass culture. Published essays and books, as well as hosting his own radio program. Believed it was the duty of the intellectual to support freedom and defend pluralism. Books: *The Classical Tradition: Greek and Roman Influences on Western Literature*, *The Art of Teaching*, and *Man's Unconquerable Mind*.

A teacher must believe in the value and interest of his subject and a doctor believes in health.

1906 **Anne Morrow Lindbergh:** American author and aviation pioneer. Daughter of lawyer and diplomat Dwight W. Morrow. Wife of famed aviator Charles Lindbergh. Later served as his copilot and navigator. First woman to earn a first class glider pilot's license. The pair chartered air routes between continents. Her first born, Charles A. Lindbergh was kidnapped and murdered, prompting the couple to leave America. Books: *The Gift from the Sea*, *Dearly Beloved*, and *War Within and Without*.

Don't wish me happiness — I don't expect to be happy — it's gotten beyond that, somehow, Wish me courage and strength and a sense of humor — I will need them all.

1906 **Billy Wilder:** Vienna-born U.S. director, screenwriter, and producer. Oscar winner as best director and screenwriter for *The Lost Weekend* and *The Apartment* (which also earned Best Picture Oscar). Oscar for directing *Stalag 17* and for screenwriter for *Sunset Boulevard*. Nominated either as director or screenwriter 13 other times.

If you're going to tell people the truth, be funny or they'll kill you.

1910 **Katherine Dunham:** American dancer, choreographer and anthropologist. Noted for her interpretation of primitive and ethnic dances. Organized first professional African American dance troupe, for which she choreographed revues based on her anthropological researches in the Caribbean. Also choreographed for Broadway shows, operas and movies.

Go within every day and find the inner strength so that the world will not blow your candle out.

1913 **Lawrence G. Lovasik:** American priest and writer. Missionary in America's coal and steel regions. Founded the Sisters of the Divine Spirit, a congregation of home and foreign missionaries. His many books include *The Hidden Power of Kindness: A Practical Handbook for Souls*, and *One Deed at a Time*, in which the author preaches that by being kind, man has the power to make the world a happier place in which to live.

It is just as cowardly to judge an absent person as it is wicked to strike a defenseless one. Only the ignorant and narrow-mined gossip, for they speak of persons instead of things.

1933 **Dianne Feinstein:** née **Goldman**. American Democrat politician. First, and so far, only female mayor of San Francisco. Won a special election in 1992 to the U.S. Senate. Member of the U.S. Senate Committees on: Appropriations, Rules and Administration, Intelligence, Judiciary, and Energy and Natural Resources. Her positions on major issues have earned her criticism from both the left and the right. Firm supporter of capital punishment and legal abortion. Has made several gun control proposals.

Ninety percent of leadership is the ability to communicate something people want.

1964 **Dan Brown:** American author of thriller novels. Recorded a children's album, *Angels and* Demons, which included the song "All I Believe." Fourth novel, *The Da Vinci Code*, became a world-wide best-seller and one of the most popular books of all time. Other novels: *Digital Fortress*, *Angels and Demons*, and *Deception Point*.

Two thousand years ago, we lived in a world of Gods and Goddesses. Today, we live in a world solely of Gods. Women in most cultures have been stripped of their spiritual power.

OTHERS: 1757 British explorer **George Vancouver**, 1856 English author **H. Rider Haggard**, 1903 U.S. bank robber **John Dillinger**, 1903 Baseball pitcher **Carl Hubbell**, 1909 U.S. producer **Michael Todd**, 1910 German computer pioneer **Konrad Zuse**, 1921 U.S. director/producer **Joseph Papp**, 1922 American fashion designer **Bill Blass**, 1930 Murder victim **Charles Lindbergh III**, 1936 U.S. singer/songwriter/actor **Kris Kristofferson**, 1941 U.S. journalist **Ed Bradley**, 1944 British singer **Peter Asher**, 1947 U.S. singer **Howard Kaylon**, 1948 U.S. basketball player **Pete Maravich**, 1949 U.S. actress **Meryl Streep**, 1954 U.S. actor/comedian **Freddie Prinze**, 1962 U.S. basketball player **Clyde "The Glide" Drexler**

June 23

1668 **Giambattista Vico:** Italian jurist, and philosopher of law and cultural history. Exponent of a new science of humanity. Influenced many later scholars including Goethe and Marx. His *New Science* (1725) is recognized as a landmark in European intellectual history. Attempted to systematize the humanities into a single human science.

Men first fell necessity, then look for utility, next attend to comfort, still later amuse themselves with pleasure, thence grow dissolute in luxury, and finally go mad and waste their substance.

1876 **Irvin S. Cobb:** American playwright, novelist, journalist, editor, and actor. Noted for his "Judge Priest" stories. First winner of the O. Henry Award for the best short story of the year in 1922.

Humor is merely tragedy standing on its head with its pants torn.

1894 **Edward VIII [Duke of Windsor]:** King of England who resigned in 1936, abdicating his throne for twice married American Wallis Simpson. Spent the rest of his life traveling through international society.

I have found it impossible to carry the heavy burden of responsibility and to discharge my duties as king as I would wish to do without the help of the woman I love.

1894 **Alfred Kinsey:** American zoologist who authored several studies of the sexual life of human beings. Books: *Sexual Behavior of the Human Male* and *Sexual Behavior of the Human Female*. Criticized for his research methods and misuse of sampling methods and statistical inferences.

The only unnatural sex act is that which you cannot perform.

1910 **Jean Anouilh:** French dramatist and screenwriter. One of the leading playwrights of the contemporary theater. Influenced by the neoclassicism inspired by Giraudoux. Wrote *Antigone*, *The Waltz of the Toreadors* and *Becket*.

Beauty is one of the rare things that do not lead to doubt of God.

1910 **Gordon B. Hinkley:** Fifteenth President of The Church of Jesus Christ of Latter-day Saints. Considered by members of the Church to be a living Prophet and Witness of Jesus Christ. Books: *Go Forward with Faith*, *Standing for Something* and *Way to Be!*

Your faith will perform miracles especially when you get your hands and feet involved.

1912 **Alan Turing:** British mathematician, logician and cryptographer. Brilliant original thinker and the theoretical founder of the computer revolution. As a code breaker he helped win World War II. His search for the relationship between mind and matter made him a pioneer in the field of computer science. Research into the relationships between machines and nature led to the creation of the field of artificial intelligence. Arrested, tired and convicted for performing a homosexual act. Given the alternatives of prison or submission to psychoanalysis and injections for a year in an effort to "cure" his disease, he chose the latter.

A computer would deserve to be called intelligent if it could deceive a human into believing that it was human.

1927 **Bob Fosse:** American dancer, choreographer, and director. Tony winner for *Pippin*, *Pajama Game*, *Dancin,' Damn Yankees*, *Sweet Charity* and *Redhead*, the last three starring his wife Gwen Verdon. Oscar winner for *Cabaret*. Directed the film *All That Jazz*, a thinly disguised autobiography, which detailed his drug use, womanizing and killing pace of living.

My friends know that to me happiness is when I am merely miserable and not suicidal.

1936 **Richard Bach:** American writer. Most of his books have been semi-autobiographical and contain

New Age philosophy. Believes that our true nature is not bound by space or time. Best known as the author of hugely successful *Jonathan Livingston Seagull*, a fable about a seagull who flew for the sake of flying. Other works: *Illusions*, *One*, *Out of My Mind* and *The Ferret Chronicles*.

Compelling reason will never convince blinding emotion.

1940 **Wilma Rudolph:** American sprinter. A sickly child who wore an orthopedic shoe until she was 11.Winner of three Olympic Gold medals for track in 1960: 100 meters, 200 meters and 4x400 meter relay. First American woman to win three track-and-field gold medals in a single Olympics.

Winning is great, sure, but if you are really going to do something in life, the secret is learning how to lose. Nobody goes undefeated all the time. If you can pick up after a crushing defeat, and go on to win again, you are going to be a champion someday.

1943 **James Levine:** American conductor. Debuted as a pianist at age 10 with the Cincinnati Symphony Orchestra. Great guest appearance as conductor of *Tosca* led to his appointment as principal conductor and later musical director and artistic director of the Metropolitan Opera. Director of Chicago's Ravinia Festival (1973–93).

Where my tastes in music are concerned, I'm a real maximalist. But where my attitude about the function of the conductor in a performance is concerned, I'm a real minimalist.

1948 **Clarence Thomas:** African-American jurist. Chairman of the Equal Employment Opportunity Commission (1982–90) Appointed to the U.S. Supreme Court to replace Thurgood Marshall as the Court's Second black justice. His confirmation hearing was complicated by the accusation of sexual harassment brought by a former subordinate, law professor Anita Hill. Narrowly confirmed by the Senate, he has served as a quiet conservative.

I don't fit in with whites, and I don't fit in with Blacks. We're in a mixed-up generation, those of us who were sent out to integrate society.

OTHERS: 47 BCE Egyptian Pharaoh **Ptolemy XV**, 1534 Japanese warlord **Oda Nobunaga**, 1763 Empress of France **Josephine**, 1875 Swedish sculptor **Carl Milles**, 1898 English novelist/journalist **Winifred Holtby**, 1907 English economist **James Meade**, 1911 U.S. advertising executive **David Ogilvy**, 1913 U.S. Secretary of State **William P. Rogers**, 1923 Football team owner **Art Modell**, 1929 American singer **June Carter Cash**, 1936 Greek Prime Minister **Costas Simitis**, 1937 President of Finland **Martti Ahtisaari**, 1943 U.S. internet pioneer **Vint Cerf**, 1957 American actress **Frances McDormand**, 1963 Scottish golfer **Colin Montgomerie**, 1949 U.S. football player **LaDainian Tomlinson**

June 24

1542 Saint **John of the Cross:** Spanish Carmelite friar, mystic and poet. With Saint Teresa of Avila, reformed the Carmelite order. The reformation process was resisted by a large number of Carmelite friars who imprisoned him, kept him in isolation and publicly lashed him before the community at least once a week. While imprisoned he composed his most famous poem "Spiritual Canticle." It and his "Dark Night of the Soul" are judged to be among the best poems ever written in Spanish.

In the evening of life, we will be judged by love alone.

1558 **Theodore Beza:** French theologian and religious reformer. Writer of witty but indecent verses but after surviving an illness that almost took his life; he went to Geneva to join John Calvin. The duo founded the academy of Geneva. Beza became professor of theology and rector there. On Calvin's death, became leader of the Genevese Church.

We divide this Word into two principal parts or kinds: the one is called the "law," the other the "Gospel." For all the rest can be gathered under the one or the other of these two headings... Ignorance of this distinction between Law and Gospel is one of the principal sources of the abuses which corrupted and still corrupts Christianity.

1813 **Henry Ward Beecher:** American clergyman and social reformer. Son of Minister Lyman Beecher. First pastor of the Plymouth Congregational Church in New York City. Spoke out in favorite of temperance and against slavery, the Civil War and Reconstruction. Advocate of reconciliation with the South. Wrote for *The Independent*, and after 1870 edited *The Christian Union*.

The dog was created specially for children. He is a god of frolic.

1831 **Rebecca Harding Davis:** American author and journalist. Her novella *Life in the Iron Mills* is believed to mark the transition from Romanticism to Realism in American literature. Sought to effect social changes for blacks, women, Native Americans, immigrants, and the working class.

Down these mean streets a man must go who is not himself mean, who is neither tarnished nor afraid. He is the hero, he is everything. He must be a complete man and a common man and yet an unusual man. He must be, to use a rather weathered phrase, a man of honor, by instinct, by inevitability, without a thought of it, and certainly without saying it. He must be the best man in his world and a good enough man for any world.

1839 **Augustus Franklin Swift:** American meat packer. Worked at the butcher trade from age 14. Developed his own business. Revolutionized the meatpacking industry by shipping dressed beef instead of live steers to purchasers in the east. Established Swift & Co., pioneering the use of waste products to make glue margarine, soap, and fertilizer.

Don't let the best you have done so far be the standard for the rest of your life.

1842 **Ambrose Bierce:** American journalist, author and editor. His often vitriolic wit, fascination with the supernatural and precise use of language won him the nickname "Bitter Bierce." Works: *The Fiend's Delight, Can Such Things Be?* and *The Devil's Dictionary*, in which he provided stinging definitions, such as "Absurdity, n.: A statement or belief manifestly inconsistent with one's own opinion."

All are lunatics, but he who can analyze his delusions is called a philosopher.

1848 **Brooks Adams:** American geopolitical historian. Critic of capitalism. Son of diplomat Charles Francis Adams. Grandson of John Quincy Adams. Traveled extensively in Europe, the Middle East and India. Major work, *The Law of Civilization and Decay*. A prophet of American doom, he saw the wave of new immigrants as a corruption of the nation.

Politics, as a practice, whatever its profession, has always been the systematic organization of hatreds.

1912 **Norman Cousins:** American political journalist, educator, author, peace advocate, essayist and editor of *Saturday Review* (1937–72). Believed that "there is a need for writers who can restore to writing its powerful tradition of leadership in crisis." Wrote a collection of non-fiction books, including *Who Speaks for Man?*, which advocated a World Federation and nuclear disarmament. Battled heart disease and a form of arthritis with massive doses of vitamin C and by training himself to laugh. He detailed his struggle in *Anatomy of an Illness as Perceived by the Patient*.

Laughter is a powerful way to tap positive emotions.

1915 Sir **Fred Hoyle:** British mathematician, astronomer, cosmologist and writer of popular science works and fiction. Formulated a mathematical basis for the steady-state theory of the universe, making the expansion of the universe and the creation of matter interdependent. This theory fell out of favor with the development of the Big-Bang model.

There is a coherent plan in the universe, though I don't know what it's a plan for.

1935 **Pete Hamill:** American journalist and author. Began his career with the *New York Post* in 1960. Written for numerous national magazines, worked as a syndicated columnist and served as editor-in-chief of the *New York Daily News*. Books include 8 novels, two collections of stories, including *Downtown: My Manhattan*, and his bestselling memoir *A Drinking Life*.

It's odd being an American now. Most of us are peaceful, but here we are again, in our fifth major war of this century.

1946 **Robert Reich:** American writer and politician. Secretary of Labor (1993–97) in the Clinton administration. Born with Fairbanks disease, which topped his height at 4 ft. 10½ in. Rhodes Scholar at Oxford. Author of *The Work of Nations*, in which he warned that America faced deep social divisions. Currently a professor at the University of California, Berkeley's Goldman School of Public Policy.

In Washington, it's dog eat dog. In academia, it's exactly the opposite.

1955 **Gurumayi Chidvilasananda:** Guru of Siddha Yoga, a new religious group teaching traditional Hindu or yogic practices both in India and the West. She received the authority of the Siddha Yoga from Swami Muktananda, before his death in 1982. Mission is to awaken seekers to their own potential for enlightenment. Followers believe that the Guru is a perfected human being, having achieved full realization of the Divine in one's lifetime.

Recognize that you have the courage within you to fulfill the purpose of your birth. Summon forth the power of your inner courage and live the life of your dreams.

OTHERS: 1386 Italian saint **Giovanni da Capistrano**, 1450 Venetian navigator **John Cabot**, 1532 English politician **Robert Dudley**, 1771 French chemist **E.I. Du Pont**, 1834 U.S. journalist **George Arnold,** 1850 British field Marshal **Horatio Kitchener**, 1883 Austrian-born physicist **Victor Franz Hess**, 1895 American boxer **Jack Dempsey**, 1899 Native Canadian Indian actor **Chief Dan George,** 1903 U.S. actor/singer **Phil Harris**, 1906 French cellist **Pierre Fournier**, 1916 American writer **John Ciardi**, 1930 French film director **Claude Chabrol**, 1931 U.S. golfer **Billy Casper**, 1942 U.S. musician **Mick Fleetwood**, 1945 New York Governor **George Pataki**

June 25

1852 **Antoni Gaudí i Cornet:** Spanish architect. Most famous exponent of Catalan "modernisme," a branch of the Art Nouveau movement. Best known for the extravagant and ornate still unfinished church of the Holy Family in Barcelona, on which he toiled from 1884 until his death in 1926. Wishing to mimic nature, he integrated the parabolic arch, organic shapes and water fluidity in his architecture. Eight of his structures have been designated UNESCO World Heritage Sites.

Those who look for the laws of Nature as a support for their new works collaborate with the Creator.

1858 **Georges Courteline:** French writer, born **Georges Victor Marcel Moinaux**. Blessed with a quick wit, he became a leading dramatist, producing many plays as well as a number of novels. Best known for his satirical comedies that often made fun of wealthy elitists and government bureaucracies.

It is better to waste one's youth that to do nothing with it at all.

1865 **Robert Henri:** American realist painter. Major influence in what has come to be called the Ashcan movement. Established his own influential art school in New York City (1908). Formed the group known as *The Eight*.

Good composition is like a suspension bridge—each line adds strength and takes none away

1873 **Arthur Chapman:** U.S. journalist, historical writer and poet. Contributed the sub-genre of American poetry known as Cowboy Poetry. Author of *The Story of Colorado* and *The Pony Express*. Most famous poem, "Out Where the West Begins," first appeared in his "Center Shots" column in the *Denver Republican*.

Out where the handclasp's a little stronger,/ Out where the smile dwells a little longer,/ That's where the West begins.

1875 **Ernest Benn:** Managing director of the family publishing company, Benn Brothers. Hired "publishing genius" Victor Gollancz, who convinced his employer to publish a series of art books, which were a great literary and financial success. Benn gave Gollancz credit for making Ernest Benn Ltd. the biggest thing in publishing history, but parted company with him over who controlled the business.

Politics is the art of looking for trouble, finding it whether it exists or not, diagnosing it incorrectly, and applying the wrong remedy.

1887 **George Abbott:** American playwright, director, producer, and screenwriter. Remained active at 100 years of age. Plays: *Three Men on a Horse* and *The Boys from Syracuse*. Stage musicals: *The Pajama Game* and *Damn Yankees*. Directed over 100 theatrical pieces, winning six Tony awards.

Don't think you're funny. It'll never work if you think you're funny.

1900 **Moses Hadas:** American educator, translator and author. Professor of Greek at Columbia University. Wrote: A History of Greek Literature and A History of Rome. His translations introduced German and Greek works to English readers.

Thank you for sending me a copy of your book. I'll waste no time in reading it.

1900 **Louis Mountbatten:** 1st Earl Mountbatten of Burma. British admiral of the Fleet. Chief of Combined Operations Command in World War II, playing a key role in planning D-Day. Appointed supreme commander in SE Asia in 1943. Received the Japanese surrender at Singapore. Appointed the last Viceroy of India in 1947, First Sea Lord in 1954. Assassinated by Irish terrorists in 1979.

Sailors, with their built-in sense of order and discipline, should really be running the world.

1903 **George Orwell:** Pen name of **Eric Arthur Blair**. English novelist, essayist and critic. War correspondent in World War II for the BBC and *The Observor*. Most remembered for his novels attacking totalitarianism, *Nineteen Eighty-Four* and *Animal Farm*.

Power is not a means, it is an end. One does not establish a dictatorship in order to safeguard a revolution; one makes the revolution in order to establish the dictatorship.

1908 **Willard Von Orman Quine:** Most famous, most widely cited, American philosopher of the second half 20th century. Made no separation between philosophy and logic. Revolutionized developments in epistemology, metaphysics, philosophy of language, and philosophy of mathematics. Proved that the real numbers exist—exist philosophically, not just mathematically. Seminal work: *Two Dogmas of Empiricism*.

Logic chases truth up the tree of grammar.

1923 **Dorothy Gilman:** American Novelist. Began her writing career producing fiction for children, under her married name, Dorothy Gilman Butters. Created Mrs. Pollifax, the kindly, gentle grandmother who becomes a CIA agent, and is the heroine of fourteen novels, starting with *The Unexpected Mrs. Pollifax*. Other works: *A Nun in the Closet* and *Thale's Folly*.

A man from hell is not afraid of ashes.

1933 **James Howard Meredith:** First African-American to enroll at the University of Mississippi. Attorney General Robert Kennedy sent 500 federal marshals to protect him, when Governor Ross Barnett blocked his path to the admissions office. When white militants laid siege to the campus, Kennedy sent 5000 troops to restore order. Meredith recounted his experience in *Three Years in Mississippi*. Organized the "Walk Against Fear," a march from Memphis to Jackson, Mississippi, during which he was shot and wounded by a white supremacist.

My answer to the racial problem in America is not deal with it at all. The founding fathers dealt with it when they made the Constitution.

Others: 1814 French geologist **Gabriel Auguste Daubrée**, 1834 U.S. Episcopal bishop/social reformer **Henry Codman Potter**, 1893 U.S. actress **Charlotte Greenwood,** 1900 U.S. novelist/ critic **V.F. Calverton**, 1903 U.S. street singer **Arthur Tracy**, 1907 German physicist **J. Hans D. Jensen**, 1913 Martinique writer **Aime Cesaire**, 1924 U.S. director **Sidney Lumet**, 1925 U.S. architect **Robert Venturi**, 1928 Russian physicist **Alexei Abrikosov**, 1940 English writer **A.J. Quinnell**, 1942 U.S. basketball player **Willis Reed**, 1945 U.S. vocalist/songwriter **Carly Simon**, 1949 Miss America /TV hostess **Phyllis George**, 1963 English singer **George Michael,** 1966 Congo basketball player **Dikembe Mutombo**

June 26

1753 Comte **Antoine de Rivarol:** French writer and epigrammist. Remembered for his pithy wit and maxims. Wrote the sarcastic *Petit Almanach de nos grands hommes*, in which he pitilessly ridiculed his many subjects. Also made a distinguished translation of Dante's *Inferno*.

Ideas are a capital that bears interest only in the hands of talent.

1824 **William Thompson, Lord Kelvin:** British physicist and mathematician. Carried out fundamental research in thermodynamics, helping to prove the law of conservation of energy. Also presented the dynamical theory of heat. Devised a temperature scale named for him based on absolute zero. Coined term "kinetic energy."

The true measure of a man is what he would do if he knew he would never be caught.

1842 **Alfred Marshall:** British economist. Examined and extended the ideas of classical economists, such as Adam Smith and David Ricardo. One of the founders of the neoclassical school of economics. Best known work *Principles of Economics* introduced the concepts of elasticity of demand, consumer's surplus, and the representative firm.

Capital is that part of wealth which is devoted to obtaining further wealth.

1865 **Bernard Berenson:** Vilnius-born American art critic and historian. Moved to Italy in 1900. Leading authority on Italian Renaissance art. Wrote *Aesthetics and History* and *The Italian Painters of the Renaissance*. Bequeathed his villa and art collection to Harvard University, which converted it into the Center for Italian Renaissance Culture.

I would like to stand on a busy street corner, hat in hand, and beg people to throw me all their wasted hours.

1869 **Martin Andersen-Nexö:** Danish writer and social reformer. Won fame throughout Europe with his novel *Pelle the Conqueror*, describing his life of poverty, and the growth of the Labor Movement. His other major work: *Ditte, Daughter of Man*. His works helped raise social consciousness in Denmark and throughout Europe.

Every mother hope that her daughter will marry a better man than she did, and is convinced that her son will never find a wife as good as his father did.

1892 **Pearl Buck:** née **Sydenstricker**. U.S. novelist born in China to missionary parents. Lived in China from infancy until 1935 when she returned to the U.S.A. Pulitzer Prize for *The Good Earth*. Nobel Prize in Literature (1938). Other novels: *A House Divided*, *Dragon Seed* and *The Time Is Noon*. Five of her novels were written under the pseudonym **John Sedges**.

The young do not know enough to be prudent, and therefore they attempt the impossible — and achieve it, generation after generation.

1893 **Dorothy Fuldheim:** American journalist. Became the first woman in the country with her own news show. Later co-hosted a long-running afternoon show "The One O'clock Club." Conducted more than 15,000 interviews, including Helen Keller, Anastas Mikoyan and the Duke of Windsor. Named one of America's Most Admired Women by a Gallup Pole. Autobiographical reminiscences: *I Laughed, I Cried, I Loved* and *A Thousand Friends*.

This is a youth-oriented society, and the joke is on them because youth is a disease from which we all recover.

1901 **Stuart Symington:** American businessman and politician. Served as Secretary of the Air Force (1947–1950). Elected Democratic senator from Missouri, serving from 1953 to 1976. Advocate of a strong national defense. Helped establish the U.S. Air Force Academy. Ran for the Democratic presidential nomination in 1960, with the backing of Harry Truman, but lost to John F. Kennedy.

If civilians are going to be killed, I would rather have them be their civilians than our civilians.

1914 **Babe (Mildred Ella) Didrikson Zaharias:** All-around American athlete. All-American basketball player, won two gold medals at the 1932 Olympics in the high hurdles and the high jump. Excelled in swimming, tennis, and rifle-shooting. Turning her attention to golf, won 17 Amateur Championships before turning pro, winning the U.S. Women's Open three times. Helped found the Ladies Professional Golf Association. Voted female "Athlete of the Half Century" in 1950.

It's not enough to swing at the ball. You've got to loosen your girdle and really let the ball have it.

1916 **Virginia Satir:** American psychologist and educator. Called "The Mother of Family System Therapy" and "everyone's family therapist." Written or co-written twelve books, including *Conjoint Family Therapy* and *The New Peoplemaking*. Helped people reshape their means of problem solving into more positive ways, preaching that "problems are not the problem; coping is the problem."

We must not allow other people's limited perceptions to define us.

1931 **Colin Wilson:** British novelist and writer on philosophy, sociology and the occult. One of the angriest of Britain's Angry Young Men. Author of *The Outsider*, a study of alienation, which experienced great success. Novels: *Ritual in the Dark* and *Adrift in Soho*. Many of his more than 70 books deal with the psychology of crime, the occult, human sexuality and his existential philosophy.

The average man is a conformist, accepting miseries and disasters with the stoicism of a cow standing in the rain.

1961 **Greg Lemond:** American cyclist. Before there was Lance Armstrong, there was Greg Lemond. Called "Huck Finn with steel thighs" by *Sports Illustrated*. Three-time winner of the Tour de France.

Training doesn't get easier; you just get faster.

OTHERS: 1689 President of Harvard University **Edward Holyoke**, 1702 English religious leader **Philip Doddridge**, 1819 Possible inventor of baseball **Abner Doubleday**, 1866 Financier of Egyptian excavations **Lord Carnarvon**, 1898 German aircraft designer **Willy Messerschmidt**, 1904 Hungarian-born actor **Peter Lorre**, 1909 Elvis Presley's manager **Col. Tom Parker**, 1914 Orchestra leader **Richard Maltby**, 1922 U.S. actress **Eleanor Parker**, 1926 Canadian astronomer **Frank Scott Hogg**, 1933 Italian conductor **Claudio Abbado**, 1933 Actor **Noriyuki "Pat" Morita**, 1937 U.S. physicist **Robert C. Richardson**, 1942 Minister of Brazilian Culture **Gilberto Gil**, 1974 U.S. baseball player **Derek Jeter**

June 27

1846 **Charles S. Parnell:** Ardent Irish nationalist and Member of Parliament. First president of the Home Rule Party. Allied with the Liberals in support of PM Gladstone's Home Rule Bill. His influence and cause were harmed when he was named as correspondent in a divorce case of his mistress Katherine O'Shea and was forced to retire as leader of the Irish nationalists.

Why should Ireland be treated as a geographical fragment of England — Ireland is not a geographical fragment, but a nation.

1869 **Emma Goldman:** Lithuanian-born U.S. anarchist, feminist and birth control advocate. Known as "Red Emma." Emigrated to the U.S.A. in 1885. Lectured on anarchism. Founded and edited the anarchist magazine *Mother Earth* (1906). Imprisoned in 1893 for inciting a riot in New York City and during World War I for opposing and obstructing the military draft. Deported to the U.S.S.R. (1919).

No real social change has ever been brought about without a revolution — Revolution is but thought carried into action.

1872 **Paul Laurence Dunbar:** African-American poet and novelist. Son of escaped slaves. First black writer to attempt to make a living by his writings and was the first to gain national prominence. His reputation rests upon his verse and short stories written in black dialect. Verse collections: *Oak and Ivy*, *Lyrics of Lowly Life* and *Majors and Minors.* Published four novels including *The Sport of the Gods.*

I know why the caged bird sings, ah me, when his wing is bruised and his bosom is sore; when he beats his bars and he would be free, it is not a carol of joy or glee, but a prayer that he sends from his heart's deep core.

1880 **Helen Keller:** American educator, lecturer and writer. Born deaf and blind. Learned to communicate with the help of teacher Anne Sullivan. Became an example of achievement despite supreme handicaps. Her autobiography is titled *The Story of My Life.* It was dramatized by William Gibson in the Pulitzer Prize winning play *The Miracle Worker*, filmed in 1962.

The best and most beautiful things in the world cannot be seen or even touched. They must be felt with the heart.

1884 **Gaston Bachelard:** French philosopher and poet. His range of interests and influence were found among the history of science, psychoanalysis, and literary criticism. Works: *La Psychoanalyse du feu* and *La Flamme d'une chandelle.*

So, like a forgotten fire, a childhood can always flare up again within us.

1888 **Antoinette Perry:** American actress and director. Long career on the stage as an actress from 1905 and a director from 1928, Founded the American Theatre Wing (1941). The annual "Tony" Awards of the New York Theater are named for her.

Why, when I was a child, I didn't say, as most children do, that I was going to become an actress. I felt that I was an actress and no one could have convinced me that I wasn't!

1894 **Jacques Deval:** Pseudonym of **Jacques Bouleran**. French–U.S. novelist and playwright. Came to the U.S. in the 1930s. Served in the U.S. Army during World War II and afterwards returned to France. Produced more than 40 works in French and English. Plays included *Lorelei*, *Her Cardboard Lover*, *Mademoiselle*, and *Tovarich.*

God loved the birds and invented trees. Man loved the birds and invented cages.

1927 **Bob Keeshan:** Beloved American television actor. Star and title character of the longest-running children's program, *Captain Kangaroo* (1955–81). Appeared as the silent clown Clarabelle who communicated by honking horns on television's *Howdy Doody Show.* Won Five Emmy Awards, Three Peabody Awards, Kennedy Center Honors and Introduction into the Clown Hall of Fame.

Play is the work of children. It's very serious stuff.

1930 **H. [Henry] Ross Perot:** American multimillionaire businessman and politician. Founder of Electronic Data Systems. Chairman and CEO until he was bought out by GM in 1986. Spent a large amount of his fortune on an unsuccessful presidential bid in 1992, capturing 19% of the popular vote, but received no electoral votes.

If someone is blessed as I am is not willing to clean out the barn, who will?

1938 **Alan Coren:** British writer and journalist. Joined *Punch* as an assistant editor in 1963, becoming editor in 1978. Also was the editor of *The Listener.* Published several humorous books: *Present Laughter* and *More Like Old Times.*

I wonder sometimes if manufacturers of foolproof items keep a fool or two on their payroll to test things.

1949 **Vera Wang:** Chinese-American fashion designer, famous for her wedding gown collection. Trained as a figure skater. Competed in the 1968 U.S. Figure Skating Championship. When she didn't make the Olympic team, she turned her attention to fashion. Worked for Ralph Lauren before opening her design salon. Designed wedding gowns for Mariah Carey, Jennifer Lopez, Jessica Simpson and Victoria Beckham.

I brought color to bridal. There was one whole season of blush. If you think about the bareness, the illusion (fabric), the corsets that I did in bridal, they were trends in ready-to-wear, too.

1951 **Mary McAleese:** Belfast-born Catholic lawyer. Succeeded Mary Robinson as Reid Professor of Criminal Law at Trinity College in 1975 and then in 1997 succeed Robinson as President of Ireland. This was the first time in history that a woman had succeeded another woman as an elected head of state anywhere in the world. Has since been reelected to a second seven year term.

We are a vibrant first-world country, but we have a humbling third-world memory.

OTHERS: 1717 French botanist **Louis Guillaume**, 1850 U.S. translator **Lafacadio Hearn**, 1869 German embryologist **Hans Spemann**, 1900 African-American actor **Lorenzo Tucker**, 1913 U.S. billiards player **Willie Mosconi**, 1918 U.S. backstroke swimmer **Adolph Kiefer**, 1920 U.S. screenwriter I.A.L. **Diamond**, 1924 U.S. editorial cartoonist **Paul Conrad**, 1931 Canadian industrialist **Charles Bronfman**, 1932 American soprano **Anna Moffo**, 1938 U.S. politician **Bruce Babbitt**, 1941 Polish film director **Krzysztof Kieślowski**, 1946 First ordained female rabbi **Sally Priesand**, 1955 French actress **Isabelle Adjani**, 1975 American actor **Tobey Maguire**, 1977 Spanish soccer player **Raúl**

June 28

1491 **Henry VIII:** King of England. His book on the Sacraments, in reply to Martin Luther, earned him the title "Defender of the Faith" from the Pope. The Catholic Church denied him an annulment of his marriage with his brother's widow Catherine of Aragon, who gave him no male heir. As a result, he founded the Church of England with himself as head and suppressed monasteries. Divorced Catherine and married five more times. Two of his wives were beheaded for infidelity, including Anne Boleyn, who gave birth to the future Queen Elizabeth I.

He who I favor wins.

1577 **Peter Paul Rubens:** German painter, educated in Antwerp, where he began to study art. Moved to Venice, where he became a diplomat to Spain for the Duke of Mantua. Executed many portraits and paintings on historical subjects. His various patrons included Archduke Albert of Antwerp and Marie de Médicis. Major works: the triptych "The Descent from the Cross," and "Peace and War."

My talent is such that no undertaking, however vast in size ... has every surpassed my courage.

1712 **Jean-Jacques Rousseau:** Swiss-born French philosopher, author, political theorist and composer. Largely self-taught. Father of French Romanticism. His most famous and influential work, *The Social Contract*, which was a great influence on French revolutionary thought, introducing the slogan "Liberty, Equality, Fraternity." Other works: *Discourse on the Origin and Foundations of Inequality Amongst Men*, in which he emphasized the natural goodness of human beings, and his major work on education, *Emile*, written in novel form.

Man was born free, an everywhere he is in chains.

1824 **Paul Broca:** French physician, anatomist and anthropologist. A child prodigy, simultaneously held baccalaureate degrees in literature, mathematics, and physics, before entering medical school at age 17, graduating 3 years later. Professor of surgical pathology at the University of Paris. First to locate the motor speech center in the brain. Pioneer in the study of physical anthropology and contributed significantly to the comparative anatomy of primates.

The least questioned assumptions are often the most questionable.

1844 **John Boyle O'Reilly:** Irish-born poet, novelist and editor. A member of the Irish Republican Brotherhood, which caused him to be transported to Western Australia. Escaped to the U.S. to become a prominent spokesman for Irish sentiment and culture. Editor of the Boston newspaper *The Pilot*. His collections of poems included: *Songs, Legends and Ballets, The Statues in the Block* and *In Bohemia*.

Doubt is brother-devil to Despair.

1867 **Luigi Pirandello:** Italian dramatist, short-story writer and novelist. Wrote powerful and realistic novels, such as The *Late Mattia Pascal*, before turning to the theater. Known for symbolic dramas and satires. Plays: *Six Characters in Search of an Author, As You Desire Me* and *Right You Are if You Think You Are*. Nobel Prize for Literature (1934).

Life is full of infinite absurdities, which strangely enough, do not even need to appear plausible, since they are true.

1873 **Alexis Carrel:** French biologist and surgeon. Received Nobel Prize for Physiology or Medicine (1912) for development of blood vessel suture technique. Did much research on the prolongation of the life of tissues. Helped Henry Dakin develop a solution for sterilizing deep wounds.

The quality of life is more important than life itself.

1892 **E.H. Carr:** British historian and international relations theorist. Author of *The History of Russia, The Moral Foundation for World Order* and *What Is History?* Also wrote biographies of Feodor Dostoyevsky, Karl Marx and Mikhail Bakunin.

The function of the historian is neither to love the past nor to emancipate himself from the past, but to master and understand it as the key to the understanding of the present.

1905 **Ashley Montagu:** British-American anthropologist and author. Worked on human biosocial evolution. Argued against the view that cultural phenomena are genetically determined. Wrote UNESCO's "Statement on Race." Author of more than 60 books. Publications: *The Natural Supremacy of Women, The Prevalence of Nonsense, Man's Most Dangerous Myth: The Fallacy of Race*, and *The Elephant*.

Science has proof without certainty. Creationists have certainty without any proof.

1909 **Eric Ambler:** English author and playwright, noted for suspense and thriller stories, usually with an espionage background: *Epitaph for a Spy, The Mask of Dimitrios*, and the *Intercom Conspiracy*. Received the Crime Writers' Association Award four times, as well as the Edgar Allan Poe award (1964).

For the skeptic there remains only one consolation: if there should be such a thing as

superhuman law it is administered with subhuman inefficiency.

1928 **Mel Brooks:** American actor, director, screenwriter and producer. Writer for Sid Caesar's television "Show of Shows." Best-known films: *The Producers*, *Blazing Saddles* and *Young Frankenstein*, each earning him an Oscar nomination for story or screenplay. Transformed *The Producers* into a long-running Broadway musical hit later filmed.

Humor is just another defense against the universe.

1946 **Gilda Radner:** American actress and comedian. Best known for her five-year stint as one of the original members of TV's *Saturday Night Live*. Famous for her hilarious characterizations Roseanne Roseannadanna, Baba Wawa, and Emily Litella. Diagnosed with ovarian cancer, she suffered extreme physical and emotional pain as a result of chemotherapy. Wrote a memoir about her struggle, called *It's Always Something*, a catch-phrase she made popular on SNL. Her cancer spread and she lapsed in a coma, dying three days later with her second husband Gene Wilder at her side.

I wanted a perfect ending. Now I've learned, the hard way, that some poems don't rhyme, and some stories don't have a clear beginning, middle and end. Life is about not knowing, having to change, taking the moment and making the best of it, without knowing what's going to happen next.

OTHERS: 1243 Emperor of Japan **Go-Fukakusa**, 1490 Bishop/elector **Albert of Mainz,** 1831 German violinist **Joseph Joachim**, 1887 Irish-born U.S. author **Ernest Boyd**, 1906 French guitarist/composer **Napoleon Coste**, 1902 U.S. composer **Richard Rodgers**, 1906 German physicist **Maria Goeppert-Mayer**, 1916 Scottish politician **William Whitelaw**, 1921 Prime Minister of India **P.V. Narasimha Rao**, 1930 President of Brazil **Itamar Franco**, 1939 Budget director **Leon Panetta**, 1947 U.S. writer **Mark Helprin**, 1948 U.S. actress **Kathy Bates**, 1960 U.S. football player **John Elway**, 1965 U.S. baseball player **Mark Grace**, 1966 U.S. actor **John Cusack**, 1966 U.S. actress **Mary Stuart Masterson**

June 29

1798 **Giacomo Leopardi:** Italian poet and scholar. A gifted congenitally handicapped (hunchbacked) child who by 16 had read all the Latin and Greek classics. Suffered throughout his life from chronic ailments and unrequited love, which became the basis of his lyric poetry. Among his most noted lyric poems are the collections *Canzoni, Versi,* and *I canti morali*.

People are ridiculous only when they try or seem to be that which they are not.

1801 **Frederic Bastiat:** French economist, legislator and writer. Championed private property, free markets, and limited government. Believed that the free market was inherently a source of " economic harmony" among individuals, as long as the government was restricted to protecting the lives, liberties and properties of citizens from theft or aggression.

The state is the great fictitious entity by which everyone seeks to live at the expense of everyone else.

1819 **Thomas Dunn English:** American physician editor, playwright, novelist and poet. Edited a humorous periodical *John Donkey*. Settled in New Jersey where he practiced medicine, served in the state legislature and wrote several novels. Also wrote more than 20 plays and collections of poems. The vigorous verse "Gallows Goers" had a vast circulation during the national debate regarding capital punishment (1845–1850).

Ambition is the germ from which all growth of nobleness proceeds.

1858 **George W. Goethals:** American engineer, trained at West Point. Administrator and chief engineer of the Panama Canal project (1907–14). The first civil governor of the Canal Zone.

Faith in the ability of a leader is of slight service unless it is united with faith in his justice.

1861 **William James Mayo:** American surgeon. A specialist in stomach surgery. Cofounder with his brother Charles of the Mayo Clinic at St. Mary's Hospital in Rochester, Minnesota. Set up the Mayo Foundation for Medical Education and Research at the University of Minnesota.

Lord, deliver me from the man who never makes a mistake, and also from the man who makes the same mistake twice.

1863 **James Harvey Robinson:** American historian. A founder of the New School for Social Research; he was the first director. Exerted an important influence on the study and teaching of history. Editor of the Annals of the American Academy of Political and Social Science. President of the American Historical Society.

We find it hard to believe that other people's thoughts are as silly as our own but they probably are.

1865 **William Borah:** U.S. politician and lawyer. Republican senator from Idaho. An isolationist, who advocated disarmament. Played a major role in preventing the U.S. from joining the League of Nations.

No more famous chimera ever infested the brain of man than that you can control opinions by law or direct beliefs by stature, and no more pernicious sentiment ever tormented the human heart than the barbarous desire to do so.

1868 **George Ellery Hale:** American astronomer. Director of the Yerkes Observatory, Wisconsin (1892–1904) and at Mt. Wilson, California (1904–23), where he initiated the construction of some of the world's largest telescopes. The Mt. Palomar and Mt. Wilson observatories were established under his guidance, which operated jointly (1948–80) as the Hale Observatories.

Like buried treasures, the outposts of the universe have beckoned to the adventurous from immemorial times.

1900 **Antoine-Marie-Roger de Saint-Exupéry:** French author and aviator. A commercial and wartime pilot. Opened transatlantic airmail routes to South America and Africa. Declared missing after a flight to North Africa during World War II. Wrote popular children's fable for adults, *The Little Prince.*

Man's "progress" is but a gradual discovery that his questions have no meaning.

1903 **Robert Traver:** Pseudonym of **John Donaldson Voelker**. American jurist and author. Born and spent most of his life in the Upper Peninsula of Michigan, the setting for his best known novel, *Anatomy of a Murder*. Other books: *Anatomy of a Fisherman*, *The Jealous Mistress*, and *Trout Magic*.

A writer judging his own work is like a deceived husband — he is frequently the last person to appreciate the true state of affairs.

1933 **John Bradshaw:** American educator, theologian and author. Best known for his PBS television programs: *The Eight Stages of Man*, *Creating Love*, *Eating Disorders*, *Adult Children of Dysfunctional Families* and *Surviving Divorce*. Author of five *New York Times* bestsellers, including *Homecoming*. Survived his dysfunctional family, alcoholic father, and his alcohol addiction.

Children are curious and are risk takers. They have lots of courage. They venture out into a world that is immense and dangerous. A child initially trusts life and the processes of life.

1941 **Stokely Carmichael:** Trinidad and Tobago-born African American civil rights activist. Developed the Black Power concept. Leader of the Student Nonviolent Coordinating Committee. Changed the group's focus from integration to black liberation. Moved to Guinea in West Africa with his wife, singer Miriam Makeba, where he wrote *Stokely Speaks: Black Power Back to Pan-Africanism*. Adopted the name **Kwame Ture** in honor of African leaders Kwame Nkrumah and Ahmed Sékou Touré.

Our grandfathers had to run, run, run. My generation's out of breath. We ain't running no more.

OTHERS: 1517 Flemish physician **Rembert Dodoens**, 1830 U.S. sculptor **John Quincy Adams Ward**, 1901 U.S. singer **Nelson Eddy**, 1905 Radio actor **Ed Gardner**, 1908 U.S. composer **Leroy Anderson**, 1911 Royal Consort of The Netherlands **Bernhard**, 1914 Czech conductor **Rafael Kubelik**, 1922 Yugoslavian poet **Vasko Popa**, 1926 Emir of Kuwait **Jaber Al-Ahmad Al-Jaber Al-Sabah**, 1930 Italian journalist **Oriana Falacci**, 1944 U.S. actor **Gary Busey**, 1944 Archbishop of Boston **Sean O'Malley**, 1945 Sri Lanka president **Chandrika Kumaratunga**, 1948 English drummer **Ian Paige**, 1963 German violinist **Anne-Sophia Mutter**, 1972 U.S. activist **Samantha Smith**

June 30

1685 **John Gay:** English playwright and poet. Best known for his satire, *The Beggar's Opera*, whose target was Sir Robert Walpole and the court of George II. It had an unprecedented run of 62 performances.

We must respect the other fellow's religion, but only in the sense and to the extent that we respect his theory that his wife is beautiful and his children smart.

1782 **Ann Taylor:** English author. Collaborated with her sister Jane to write *Original Poems for Infant Minds*. It included the famous nursery rhyme *Twinkle, Twinkle, Little Star*.

Who ran to help me when I fell, And would some pretty story tell, Or kiss the place to make it well? My mother!

1803 **Thomas Lovell Beddoes:** English poet. Eldest son of physician and writer Thomas Beddoes. Published a murder drama, *The Bride's Tragedy*. His Gothic-Romantic drama *Death's Jest-book* was published one year after his suicide.

If there were dreams to sell, what would you buy?/ Some cost as passing bell;/ Some a light sigh,/ That shakes from Life's fresh crown/ Only a roseleaf down.

1884 **Georges Duhamel:** French poet, man of letters and novelist. Studied medicine and became an army surgeon. The experience provided the background for his novel *Civilization*. Sought to uphold traditional values and safeguard individual liberties. Best known works are his novel cycles *Salavin* and *The Pasquier Chronicles*.

Do not trust your memory; it is a net full of holes; the most beautiful prizes slip through it.

1892 **Oswald Pohl:** Nazi official and general of the Waffen-SS. Put in charge of the concentration camps. Captured after the war he was sentenced to death by an American military tribunal and was hanged after a long series of delays. Pohl insisted he was only a "simple functionary."

In no way am I responsible or guilty for the murder of the 5 million Jews or the death of others in the concentration camps... The fact that I was in charge of all the concentration camps in Germany from 1942 until the end is beside the point.

1893 **Harold Laski:** English political scientist and Socialist. A Marxist although not a Communist. Believed the state responsible for social reform. Chairman of the Labor Party (1945–6). Books: *Authority in the Modern State*, *A Grammar of Politics* and *The American Presidency*.

As a scandal is the second breath of life my name is down for an early copy.

1897 **Allan K. Chalmers:** American educator and author. Headed the second defense committee for the Scottsboro Boys, nine young black men were accused of the rape of two white girls in Scottsboro, Alabama in 1931. They spent years of false imprisonment even after one of the accusers admitted the rapes never took place. As a result of the injustice of the Alabama legal system, there were protests all over the world. Chalmers wrote a book about the case, *They Shall Be Free*.

The Grand essentials of happiness are:

something to do, something to love, and something to hope for.

1911 **Czesław Miłosz:** Polish-born writer and poet. Founder of the catastrophist school of Polish poetry. Co-founder of the literary periodical *Zagary*. Worked for the Warsaw underground during the war. Opposed to the Communist regime, he exiled himself, eventually emigrating to the U.S. Books include *Hymn of the Pearl* and *Hymn of the Earth*. Nobel Prize for Literature in 1980.

The voice of passion is better than the voice of reason. The passionless cannot change history.

1917 **Lena Horne:** African-American singer and actress. Began her career as a dancer at Harlem's Cotton Club. Blessed with stunning good looks and an attractive husky voice. Became a popular singer with the Noble Sissle and the Teddy Wilson bands. First African-American signed to a long term film contract, although her scenes were often excised for distribution in the South. Films: *Cabin in the Sky*, *Stormy Weather* and *Death of a Gunfighter*. Blacklisted in the early 1950s for her friendship with Paul Robeson and her outspokenness about discrimination.

You have to be taught to be second class; you're not born that way.

1917 **Buddy (Bernard) Rich:** American bandleader and drummer. Known for the clarity and speed of his drumming. Played with several of the great swing bands, notably Artie Shaw and Tommy Dorsey before forming his big band. Also worked with some of the finest jazz musicians in small ensembles that appeared in concerts and on recordings. Objected to efforts to classify music.

There are only two kinds of music ... good and bad.

1936 **Dave Van Ronk:** American folk and blues singer, guitarist and song writer. Through an early interest in jazz he gravitated toward black music. Regular player in New York's Greenwich Village at the famous *Washington Square*. For a time his most dedicated follower was Bob Dylan. Albums included: *Dave Van Ronk Sings the Blues*, *Gambler's Blues*, and *Black Mountain Blues*.

Honesty is the cruelest game of all, because not only can you hurt someone — and hurt them to the bone — you can feel self-righteous about it at the same time.

1950 **H.H. Swami Tejomanyananda:** Hindu teacher, monastic head, story teller (Kathakaar), author and head of Chinmaya Mission Worldwide. Referred to as **Guruji**. Author of original Sanskrit compositions. Uses his melodious voice to continue the ancient Hindu tradition of a traveling story teller. His books include *Hindu Culture — An Introduction*, a clear description of the basics of Hinduism.

A principal in spiritual living is "Remember the rights others have over you, and forget the rights you have over others!" We have duties, not rights and demands.

OTHERS: 1470 King of France **Charles VIII**, 1717 Czech-born composer **Johann Stamitz**, 1789 French painter/graphic artist **Horace Vernet**, 1817 English botanist **Joseph Dalton Hooker**, 1891 U.S. pro wrestler **Man Mountain Dean**, 1891 English painter **Stanley Spencer**, 1893 German politician **Walter Ulbricht**, 1903 U.S. lawyer/politician **Robert E. Hannegan**, 1906 U.S. film director **Anthony Mann**, 1917 U.S. actress **Susan Hayward**, 1929 U.S. singer **June Valli**, 1934 U.S. magician **Harry Blackstone, Jr.**, 1936 U.S. actress **Nancy Dussault**, 1938 U.S. Runner **Billy Mills**, 1939 Mexican poet/writer **José Emilio Pacheco**, 1966 U.S. boxer **Mike Tyson**, 1985 U.S. swimmer **Michael Phelps**

July 1

1646 **Gottfried Wilhelm Leibniz:** German philosopher, mathematician and diplomat. Major contribution to mathematics was discovering the fundamental principles of infinitesimal calculus, independently of Newton. An individual of extraordinary breadth of knowledge, he made major contributions to optics, mechanics, statistics, and probability theory and was a pioneer in the use of binary systems and modern symbolic logic. Set forth the fundamental concepts of the computer, constructing a calculating machine.

In symbols one observes an advantage in discovery which is greatest when they express the exact nature of a thing briefly and, as it were, picture it; then indeed the labor of thought is wonderfully diminished.

1742 **Joseph Hall:** English clergyman and writer. Bishop of Exeter and of Norwich. Moral philosopher, who also wrote satires. Works: *Contemplations*, *Christian Meditations*, *Episcopacy* and *The World Different and the Same*.

A reputation once broken may possibly be repaired, but the world will always keep their eyes on the spot where the crack was.

1742 **Georg Christoph Lichtenberg:** German physicist and satirist. Among the first scientists to introduce experiments with apparatus in their lectures. Remember for his investigations in electricity. Kept notebooks from his student days until the end of his life, which only became known to the world after his death, published by his sons. His literary fame owes itself to his reflections found therein. Widely considered one of the best aphorists in Western intellectual history.

A book is a mirror: if an ass peers into it, you can't expect an apostle to look out.

1804 **George Sand:** (pseudonym of **Amandine Aurore Lucille Dupin**) French Romantic novelist of tales of love that transcend convention. Her lovers included Merimee, de Musset and Chopin. Wrote over 100 books. Works: *Valentine*, *La Mare au diable*, *La Petite Fadette* and autobiographical works of her notorious affairs.

We cannot tear out a single page of our life, but we can throw the whole book in the fire.

1882 **Susan Glaspell:** American novelist, playwright, theatrical producer and theater owner/operator. With her husband, novelist and playwright George Cram Cook founded the influential Provincetown Players theater group. Plays: *Woman's Honor, Inheritors* and the Pulitzer Prize winning *Alison's House.* Novels *The Glory of the Conquered* and *The Morning Is Near Us* and a biography of her husband *The Road to Temple.*

Seems nothing draws men together like killing other men.

1904 **Mary Steichen Calderone:** American physician. Principal founder and first director of the Sex Information ad Education Council of the United States. Brought the uncomfortable subject of sex education to the forefront of public debate and paved the way for discussions about sexually transmitted diseases, such as AIDs and unwanted pregnancy. Daughter of noted photographer Edward Steichen.

I don't want to control anybody's mind or anybody's heart — I just want to free people from the concept of sex as evil instead of a gift from God.

1908 **Estée Lauder:** American cosmetics executive. Worked her way up in the cosmetics industry by selling face cream made by her uncle. Founder Estée Lauder, Inc. in 1946. Had great success with *Youth Dew* bath oil in the fifties. Named one of the Ten Top outstanding women in business in 1970. Published her autobiography, *Estée: a Success Story* in 1985.

It seems obvious from the start that I should use my womanness as an asset rather than a liability.

1915 **Jean Stafford:** American short story writer and novelist. Novels: *Boston Adventure* and *The Mountain Lion.* Wrote *Children Are Bored on Sunday* and *A Mother in History*, an interview with the mother of Lee Harvey Oswald. Her *Collected Stories* won a Pulitzer Prize (1970).

She did observe with some dismay, that, far from conquering all, love lazily sidestepped practical problems.

1938 **Diane Ravitch:** American historian of education, educational policy analyst, author and former U.S. Assistant Secretary of Education. Critic of multiculturalism. Advocate of higher standards in public life. Books: *The Great School Wars, Against Mediocrity, Challenges to the Humanities, The Schools We Deserve,* and *The Language Police*, a criticism of both left-wing and right-wing attempts to stifle the study and expression of views with which these groups oppose.

The person who knows "how" will always have a job. The person who knows "why" will always be his boss.

1941 **Sally Quinn:** American Journalist. Hired by Ben Bradlee, executive editor of *The Washington Post,* to be a reporter for the paper's *Style* section. One of the paper's most celebrated writers, renowned for her irreverent and often controversial profiles of celebrities and publications. Novels: *Regrets Only* and *Happy Endings.* Also wrote *We're Going to Make You a Star*, about her short-lived experience as a co-anchor for "CBS Morning News." Married Bradlee in 1991.

The football season is like pain. You forget how terrible it is until it seizes you again.

1941 **Twyla Tharp:** American dancer, director and choreographer. Choreographed more than one hundred twenty-five dances for dance companies and five movies. Won two Emmy Awards and a Tony. Her dance programs include "Cutting Up," created for Mikhail Baryshnikov and Billy Joel's award-wining dance musical *Movin' Out.* Created dance numbers for films: *Hair, Ragtime,* and *Amadeus.*

Dancing is like bank robbery. It takes split-second timing.

1951 Lady **Diana Frances Spencer:** Princess of Wales. Married Charles, Prince of Wales in 1981. Had two sons, William and Henry. Most photographed woman in the world and most popular member of the royal family. Separated in 1992 they were divorced in 1996. Killed in a car accident in Paris along with her companion Dodi al-Fayed. A massive public outpouring of grief for "Princess Di" followed.

Being a princess isn't all it's cracked up to be.

OTHERS: 1633 Swiss theologian **Johann Wilhelm Heidegger**, 1869 U.S. grammarian **William Strunk Jr.**, 1892 American novelist **James M. Cain**, 1899 U.S. father of Gospel music **Thomas A. Dorsey**, 1899 English actor **Charles Laughton**, 1902 French-born U.S. film director **William Wyler**, 1903 English pilot **Amy Johnson**, 1909 U.S. sportscaster **Bill Stern**, 1912 U.S. environmentalist **David R. Brower**, 1916 U.S. actress **Olivia de Havilland**, 1921 1st president of Botswana **Seretse Khama**, 1931 French actress/dancer **Leslie Caron**, 1942 Canadian actress **Geneviéve Bujold**, 1952 Canadian comic actor **Dan Aykroyd**

July 2

1714 **Christoph Willibald Gluck:** German composer. Best known for operas based on simplicity: *Orfeo ed Eurydice, Alceste* and *Paride ed Elena.* Paris was divided in the famous Gluck and Niccolò Piccinni controversy, between supporters of French and Italian operatic styles.

The greatest beauties of melody and harmony become faults and imperfections when they are not in their proper places.

1877 **Herman Hesse:** German-Swiss novelist and poet. Nobel Prize winner for Literature in 1946. Author of lyrical, symbolic, ironic novels including: *Rosshalde, Siddhartha, Steppenwolf* and *Magister Ludi.* Became a cult figure after his death.

Eternity is a mere moment, just long enough for a joke.

1903 Sir **Alec Douglas-Home:** Later **Baron Home of the Hirsel**. British politician and statesman. Member of the House of Lords until he renounced his peerage. Held several cabinet posts as well as becoming leader of the House of Lords (1957–60). Foreign Secretary (1960–63) and Prime Minister (1963).

Why employ intelligent and highly paid

ambassadors and then go and do their work for them? You don't buy a canary and sing yourself.

1906 **Han A. Bethe:** German-born American physicist and Nobel laureate in 1967.During World War II, director of theoretical physics for the atomic bomb project at Los Alamos. Collaborated with Ralph Alpher and George Gamow on the "alpha, beta, gamma" theory of the origin of the chemical elements during the early development of the universe.

If we fight a war and win it with H-bombs, what history will remember is not the ideals we were fighting for but the methods we used to accomplish the. These methods will be compared to the warfare of Genghis Khan who ruthlessly killed every last inhabitant of Persia.

1908 **Thurgood Marshall:** American lawyer for the National Association for the Advancement of Colored People. Appointed the first African-American Supreme Court Justice by Lyndon Johnson in 1967. As chief of the legal staff of the NAACP, argued the case of *Brown v. Board of Education of Topeka* before the Supreme Court. Historical victory declared racial segregation in public schools unconstitutional.

In recognizing the humanity of our fellow beings, we pay ourselves the highest tribute.

1918 **Robert W. Sarnoff:** Russian-born American communications executive. Radio operator who picked up the distress calls from the *Titanic*. Proposed the production of Marconi radio music boxes. Became general manager and later president of NBC. Set up the NBC radio network, ordered the construction of the RCA building, and established the fist U.S. TV service. Converted NBC to first all-color television network (1956).

Whatever course you have chosen for yourself, it will not be a chore but an adventure if you bring to it a sense of the glory of striving.

1925 **Patrice Lumumba:** Congolese (now Zaire) leader. Founded and led the Congolese National Movement. As premier he was the leading negotiator with Belgium for independence. First Prime Minister of the newly independent Congo. Warring factions plunged the country into chaos. Deposed in September 1960 and soon after was assassinated, becoming a national hero.

When you civilize a man, you only civilized an individual, but when you civilize a woman, you civilize a whole people.

1926 **Medgar Evers:** African-American civil rights martyr. Field secretary of Mississippi's NAACP. Traveled throughout the state recruiting members and organizing economic boycotts. Shot to death in front of his home (1963). A white segregationist was charged but set free after two trials in 1964 resulted in hung juries. Finally convicted at a third trial 30 years later.

I'm looking to be shot any time I step out of my car... If I die, it will be for a good cause. I've been fighting for America just as much as the soldiers in Vietnam.

1929 **Imelda Marcos:** First Lady of the Philippines when Ferdinand Marcos was the president (1965–86). Regime marked by increasing repression, misuse of foreign financial aid and political murders. When the couple was forced into exile in 1986, they fought demands from U.S. courts investigating charges of financial mismanagement and corruption. He died in 1989 and she was sentenced to 18 years imprisonment.

People say I'm extravagant because I want to be surrounded by beauty. But tell me, who wants to be surrounded by garbage?

1932 **Dave Thomas:** American founder of Wendy's Old Fashioned Hamburgers restaurant chain. Appeared in over 800 commercials, more than anyone else in history. Worked with Kentucky Fried Chicken founder Col. Harlan Sanders, to make the business a successful franchise. Opened his first Wendy's in 1969. By the time of his death in 2002, there were more than 6,000 in North America.

I think the harder you work the more luck you have.

1942 **Vicente Fox:** President of Mexico, whose election in 2000, ended 71 years of uninterrupted rule by the Institutional Revolutionary Party. Served as Coca Cola's chief executive in Mexico (1975–79). Elected to the National Chamber of Deputies in 1987 and governor of Guanajuato in 1995. As president sought to improve relations with the U.S.

I am the guardian of power, not its owner.

OTHERS: 1489 Archbishop of Canterbury **Thomas Cranmer**, 1856 Indian nationalist leader **Bal Gangadhar Tilak**, 1862 English physicist **William Henry Bragg**, 1865 Prussian feminist/socialist writer **Lili Braun**, 1884 German neurologist **Alfons Maria Jakob**, 1879 U.S. football coach **Bob Zuppke**, 1914 U.S. conductor **Frederick Fennell**, 1923 Polish writer **Wisława Szymborska**, 1927 U.S. actor **Brock Peters**, 1937 U.S. race car driver **Richard Petty**, 1939 U.S. politician **John H. Sununu**, 1947 U.S. TV producer **Larry David**, 1956 U.S. actress/model **Jerry Hall**, 1964 Baseball player **Jose Canseco**, 1986 U.S. actress **Lindsay Lohan**

July 3

1683 **Edward Young:** English poet, dramatist, literary critic and country clergyman. Author of *Night Thoughts*, occasioned by, among other sorrows, the death of his wife. *Death and Immortality* was written in defense of Christian orthodoxy against freethinkers. Many of its lines have passed into proverbial use.

Procrastination is the thief of time/ Year after year it steals, till all are fled,/ And to the mercies of a moment leaves/ The vast concerns of an eternal scene.

1746 **Henry Grattan:** Irish patriot and statesman. Member of the Irish House of Commons. Brilliant orator and leader of the fight for Ireland's independence. Opposed the Act of Union (1800) that merged the Kingdoms of Ireland and Great Britain. His patriotism was untainted by self-seeking. When a more extreme Catholic Party under the leadership of Daniel O'Connell evolved his influence gradually declined.

At twenty years of age, the will reigns; at thirty, the wit; and at forty, the judgment.

1860 **Charlotte Perkins Gilman:** American lecturer, economist, author, and poet. An early theorist in the feminist movement. Lectured on women's issues as well as wider social concerns. Founded and edited the journal *Forerunner.* Wrote *In This Our World, Women and Economics* and *The Man-Made World.* Committed suicide when she was diagnosed with incurable cancer.

There is no female mind. The brain is not an organ of sex. Might as well speak of a female liver.

1878 **George M. Cohan:** "The Yankee Doodle-Boy." American actor, singer, dancer, songwriter, and producer. As a child acted in vaudeville in a family theatrical group, The Four Cohans. Starred in numerous Broadway musicals. His songs include: "I'm a Yankee Doodle Dandy," "Give My Regards to Broadway" and "You're a Grand Old Flag." A super, flag-waving patriot he claimed to have been born on July 4th.

Many a bum show has been saved by the flag.

1879 **Alfred Korzybski:** Polish-born American semanticist. Propounded what he called "General Semantics," an approach to the subject that rejects Aristotelian language structure, which he believed tended to confuse words with things for which they stand. Among his writings: *Science and Sanity: An Introduction to Non-Aristotelian Systems* and *General Semantics.*

The affairs of man are conducted by our own, man-made rules and according to man-made theories. Man's achievements rest upon the use of symbols.... We must consider ourselves as a symbolic, semantic class of life, and those who rule the symbols, rule us.

1883 **Franz Kafka:** Prague-born German novelist and short-story writer. His work centered on the problematic existence of modern man. Wrote of guilt-ridden, isolated men in an aimless world. At his death of tuberculosis, he asked Max Brod to burn all of his writing, including his three novels *The Metamorphosis, The Trial* and *Amerika.* Instead Brod edited and published the works, along with Kafka's diaries.

The meaning of life is that it stops.

1888 **Ramón Gómez de la Serna:** Spanish writer, usually known simply as Ramón. Wrote many well-known biographies, novels, plays, essays and short sketches. Center of Spanish avant-garde during the 1930s. Went into exile in 1936, spending the remainder of his life in Argentina. Invented the literary form of which he was almost the only one to use, *greguerta,* which combined humor with a metaphysical conceit.

A piano store looks like a funeral parlor for music.

1900 **John Mason Brown:** America's outstanding lecturer and critic-at-large. Drama critic and editor for *Saturday Review* (1944–55). Author of *Letters From Greenroom Ghosts, Two on the Aisle* and *Through These Men.*

The critic is a man who prefers the indolence of opinion to the trials of action.

1906 **George Sanders:** Russian-born American actor. Snobbish character actor advanced from B-movie detective series to a comfortable career in some excellent films, usually featuring his trademark sneer, world-weary boredom, unhidden contempt for inferiors (everyone) and his perfect diction. Academy Award as Best Supporting Actor for *All About Eve.* Committed suicide because he was bored.

Acting is like roller skating. Once you know how to do it, it is neither stimulating nor exciting.

1913 **Dorothy Kilgallen:** American journalist, columnist, radio and TV personality. Covered the trials of Bruno Hauptmann and Dr. Sam Sheppard. Wrote syndicated column "Voice of Broadway." Co-hosted a radio talk show with husband Richard Kollmer. Became a panelist on TV's *What's My Line?* in 1950. Died of a fatal combination of alcohol and seconal at age 52. Not clear if it is was suicide or an accidental death.

Doorman — a genius who can open the door of your car with one hand, help you in with the other, and still have one left for the tip.

1937 **Tom Stoppard:** Czech-born British author, dramatist and screenwriter. Worked as a freelance journalist and theater critic while writing radio plays. *Rosencrantz and Guildenstern Are Dead* made his reputation. Others: *Travesties* and *The Real Thing* (Won a Tony in 1982). Screenplays include *Brazil, Empire of the Sun, Shakespeare in Love* and *Enigma.*

My whole life is waiting for the questions to which I have prepared answers.

1947 **Dave Barry:** American writer and Pulitzer Prize winning humorist. Best known for his weekly syndicated newspaper column, written for *The Miami Herald* from 1983 to 2005. Fiction: *Big Trouble* (made into a movie) and *Tricky Business.* Non-fiction: *The Taming of the Screw, Dave Barry's Guide to Marriage and/or Sex,* and *Dave Barry's Money Secrets.*

You can only be young once. But you can always be immature.

OTHERS: 1567 French explorer **Samuel de Champlain,** 1728 Scottish architect **Robert Adam,** 1731 Continental Congress president **Samuel Huntington,** 1738 American painter **John Singleton Copley,** 1854 Czech composer **Leoš Janáček,** 1888 U.S. playwright **Dana Burnett,** 1893 U.S. composer **Howard Dietz,** 1893 U.S. musician **Mississippi John Hurt,** 1909 U.S. Secretary of Agriculture **Earl Butz,** 1927 British film director **Ken Russell,** 1928 English novelist **Evelyn Anthony,** 1939 U.S. President of NOW **Eleanor Smeal,** 1947 U.S. actress/singer **Betty Buckley,** 1959 British journalist **Julie Burchill,** 1962 U.S. actor **Tom Cruise**

July 4

1804 **Nathaniel Hawthorne:** American novelist and short-story writer. His family participated in the Salem witch trials and later in the Quaker persecutions, leaving him always with a sense of guilt. Made this a theme in his work. Best known for *Twice-Told Tales, Mosses* *from an Old Manse, The Scarlet Letter, The House of the Seven Gables* and *The Marble Faun.*

Happiness is a butterfly, which when pursued, is always just beyond our grasp, but which, if you will sit down quietly, may alight upon you.

1807 **Giuseppe Garibaldi:** Italian patriot and military leader in the movement for Italian unification and independence. An ardent Republican, after serving in the army of the short-lived Roman Republic, fled to the U.S. where he became a naturalized citizen. Returning to Italy he led his band of one thousand men known as the Red Shirts, conquering the Kingdom of the Two Sicilies and Naples. Defeated in an attempt to capture Rome. His famous cry:

Rome or death.

1826 **Stephen C. Foster:** American songwriter. Several of his compositions are still popular more than a century and a half after they were written, including "Beautiful Dreamer," "Swanee River," "My Old Kentucky Home" and "Jeannie with the Light Brown Hair," written for his wife, Jane McDowall. Not successful in an attempt to make a living as a professional songwriter, he died impoverished at age 37. In his pocket on a scrap of paper was written:

Dear friends and gentle hearts.

1872 **Calvin Coolidge:** "Silent Cal." American politician. First came to national attention when as governor of Massachusetts, he broke the Boston police strike. In 1920 became Republican vice-presidential nominee. Thirtieth president of the United States, succeeding Warren G. Harding who died in office (1923). Reelected by a large majority in 1924. Famous for his taciturn nature and frugality.

No man has ever listened himself out of a job.

1900 **Louis Armstrong:** Also known as "Satchmo" and "Pops." American musician, bandleader, composer, singer, and actor. Leading trumpeter in jazz history. Made more than 1,500 recordings. Originated the "scat" vocal, which is wordless vocalizing. Hit songs featuring his distinctive gravelly voice include: "Potato Head Blues," "A Kiss to Build a Dream On," "What a Wonderful World," "Do You Know What It Means to Miss New Orleans," and "Hello Dolly."

What is Jazz? When you got to ask what it is, you'll never get to know.

1902 **Meyer Lansky:** Originally **Maier Suchowljansky**. Russian-born American mobster. As a youth, joined Bugsy Siegel in a crime spree. Together with Lucky Luciano, formed a national crime syndicate. Developed gambling operations in Cuba and elsewhere in the Caribbean. Involved in narcotics-smuggling, prostitution, labor-racketing, and extortion rackets. Convicted on income-tax evasion, but did not go to jail.

All pro sports, as well as the NCAA, should thank God every day we have sports betting here... We have the only agency in the world that regulates the honesty of the games.

1905 **Lionel Trilling:** American critic and scholar. One of the dominant critical voices of his era. Theorized that the function of criticism is to search for the ideas by which every age can be evaluated. His essays combined social, psychological and political insights with literary criticism. Author of *The Liberal Imagination, The Opposing Self, Beyond Culture* and *Mind in the Modern World.*

Immature artists imitate. Mature artists steal.

1912 **Virginia Graham:** American writer, playwright and radio/television personality. Began her career on radio as the host of "Weekday." Best known as the hostess of the nationally syndicated TV talk shows "The Virginia Graham Show," "Girl Talk" and "Food for Thought. One of the co-founders of the Cerebral Palsy Foundation.

In society it is etiquette for ladies to have the best chairs and get handed things. In the home the reverse is the case. This is why ladies are more sociable than gentlemen.

1918 **Ann Landers** and **Abigail Van Buren:** Pseudonyms of twins **Pauline Esther** and **Esther Pauline Friedman**. Syndicated advice columnists whose columns appeared in 1,000 newspapers around the country, with a readership of more than 70 million each.

Ann's advice: ***The naked truth is always better than the best dressed lie.***

Abby's advice: ***The less you talk, the more you're listened to.***

1927 **Neil Simon:** American playwright. Worked as a comedy writer for Sid Caesar in the 1950s. Probably the most commercially successful playwright in Broadway history. Plays: *Barefoot in the Park, The Odd Couple, Biloxi Blues, Brighton Beach Memoirs* and *Lost in Yonkers*, which won a Tony award and a Pulitzer Prize. Wrote the books for several musicals, including *Sweet Charity*, and *Promises, Promises.*

If no one ever took risks, Michelangelo would have painted the Sistine floor.

1930 **George Steinbrenner:** "The Boss" Owner of the American Shipbuilding Company and principal owner of the New York Yankees since 1973. Hands-on owner, obsessed with winning, he's famous or perhaps infamous for his willingness to pay any price to lure free agents to his club, as well as his feuds and his hirings and firings. In his first 23 years as owner he changed managers 20 times, which included firing Billy Martin on five different occasions. Over the years he has had 11 general managers.

Owning the Yankees is like owning the Mona Lisa. That's something you never sell.

1938 **Bill Withers:** African-American singer-song writer. Served in the U.S. Navy for nine years. Turned his attention to singing his own songs, having his first success with the single "Ain't No Sunshine" from his album *Just As I Am.* His second album *Still Bill* features the very popular "Lean on Me." Recorded albums from 1971 to 1985. Other songs: "Use Me," "Lovely Day," and "Two of Us."

Ain't no sunshine when she's gone/ And she's always gone too long/ Anytime she goes away.

OTHERS: 1847 U.S. circus impresario **James A. Bailey**, 1882 MGM studio head **Louis B. Mayer**, 1883 U.S. cartoonist **Rube Goldberg**, 1902 U.S. actor/Senator **George Murphy**, 1909 Welsh pianist **Alec Templeton**, 1911 U.S. bandleader/TV personality **Mitch Miller**, 1917 Spanish bullfighter **Manolete**, 1920 U.S. hotel operator **Leona Helmsley**, 1927 Italian actress **Gina Lollobrigida**, 1942 U.S. football player **Floyd Little**, 1943 U.S. reporter/talk show host **Geraldo Rivera**, 1946 U.S. peace activist **Ron Kovic**, 1958 Australian guitarist **Kirk Pengilly**, 1962 U.S. tennis player **Pam Shriver**

July 5

1755 **Sarah Kemble Siddons:** "Queen of Tragedy." Welsh actress. Married actor William Siddons. Toured the country before joining Drury Lane, receiving public acclaim. Member of the permanent cast at Covent Garden from 1806. Famed for her dignity, deep rich voice and dramatic gestures. Best known performances as tragic-heroine's Isabella in *The Fatal Marriage* and Lady Macbeth in *Macbeth*.

Alas, how wretched is the being one who depends on the stability of public favor!

1803 **George Borrow:** English traveler and linguist. Studied the languages of the countries he visited. One of the most imaginative minor prose writers of the 19th century. Published picturesque accounts, based on his experiences: *The Zincali, or an account of the gypsies in Spain*, *The Bible in Spain*, *Lavengro*, *The Romany Rye* and *Wild Wales*.

If you must commit suicide ... always contrive to do it as decorously as possible; the decencies, whether of life or of death should never be lost sight of.

1810 **P.T. Barnum:** American showman. Extraordinary entrepreneur. Opened the New York City museum in 1842 where for the next 27 years he featured freaks and wonders, including midget Tom Thumb and the Swedish Nightingale, Jenny Lind. Famed for his observation "There's a sucker born every minute." In 1871 he formed the Barnum and Bailey Circus.

Money is a terrible master but an excellent servant.

1843 **Mandell Creighton:** English historian and bishop of London. Chief works are *Simon de Montfort*, *History of the Papacy During the Reformation Period* and *Queen Elizabeth*.

The real object of education is to leave a man in the condition of continually asking questions.

1853 **Cecil Rhodes:** British colonial statesman and prime minister of Cape Colony, South Africa. Made a fortune at the Kimberley diamond diggings and formed the DeBeers Consolidated Mines Co. The territory of British South Africa and Bechuanaland was later named Rhodesia after him. Organized the British defenses during the Boer War. His will founded scholarships at his old school Oxford for Americans, Germans and colonials (Rhodes Scholars). Said on the day he died:

So little done, so much to do.

1879 **Wanda Landowska:** Warsaw-born harpsichordist and music teacher. Became a prominent pianist in Europe and was appointed professor of the harpsichord at the Berlin Hochschule in 1912. In 1927, she established a school in Paris for the study of old music. Emigrated to the U.S. in 1940, where she composed and wrote prolifically. Best-known work: *La Musique ancienne*.

The power and magic of music lie in its intangibility and its limitlessness. It suggests images, but leaves us free to choose them and to accommodate them to our pleasure.

1889 **Jean Cocteau:** French poet, novelist, dramatist, actor, painter, essayist, filmmaker and director. In the vanguard of almost every experimental artistic movement in the 1st half of the 20th century and produced work in nearly every genre of artistic expression. Most famous modernistic ballets: *Parade* and *Le Boeuf sur le toit*. Plays include *Antigone* and *Orphée*. Novels: *La Belle et la bête* and *Les Enfants terribles*.

Art is a marriage of the conscious and the unconscious.

1899 **Marcel Achard:** French playwright, screenwriter, director. Presided over the Cannes Film Festival (1958–59) and the Venice Festival (1960). Films: *The Merry Widow*, *Mayerling* and *The Earrings of Madame De*.

The career of a writer is comparable to that of a woman of easy virtue. You write first for pleasure, later for the pleasure of others and finally for money.

1909 **Andrei A. Gromyko:** U.S.S.R. diplomat. Appointed to the staff of the Soviet embassy in Washington in 1939 and was named ambassador in 1943. After World War I, became a permanent delegate to the U.N. Security Council. Notorious for an austere and humorless demeanor when dealing with representatives of the Western nations during the Cold War. Became Soviet president in 1985, serving for three years before being replaced by Mikhail Gorbachev.

The world may end up under a Sword of Damocles on a tightrope over the abyss.

1911 **Georges Pompidou:** French politician and statesman. Helped draft the constitution for the Fifth Republic (1959). Negotiated a settlement in Algeria (1961). Prime minister in 1962. Played a key role in resolving the political crisis of 1968. Dismissed by his increasingly jealous patron Charles de Gaulle. Following de Gaulle's resignation in 1969 he was elected president.

There are three roads to ruin: women, gambling and technicians. The most pleasant is with women, the quickest is with gambling, but the surest is with technicians.

1915 **Barbara "Babe" Paley:** American model, editor of a high fashion magazine, socialite and charity worker. Wife of William S. Paley. Frequently chosen by the New York Dress Institute as one of the best dressed.

I have seldom known a person, who deserted the truth in trifles and then could be trusted in matters of importance.

1958 **Bill Watterson:** American creator of the comic strip *Calvin & Hobbes.* Awarded the National Cartoonist Society Humor Comic Strip Award for 1988 and their Reuben Award for 1986. Fought against anything he felt cheapened his work. Refused to merchandise *Calvin and Hobbes* images and turned down an offer to make it into an animated series.

Things are never quite as scary when you've got a friend.

OTHERS: 1675 Accuser at Salem witch trials **Mary Walcott**, 1781 Founder of Singapore **Stamford Raffles**, 1801 U.S. naval commander **David Farragut**, 1857 German women's rights activist **Clara Zetkin**, 1880 U.S. educator **Everett D. Martin**, 1888 U.S. physiologist **Herbert Spencer Gasser**, 1902 U.S. diplomat **Henry Cabot Lodge Jr.**, 1904 British writer **Harold Acton**, 1923 U.S. football coach **John McKay**, 1924 Hungarian cellist **János Starker**, 1950 U.S. musician **Huey Lewis**, 1951 Baseball pitcher **Goose Gossage**, 1963 U.S. actress **Edie Falco**, 1970 U.S. rapper **Mac Dre**, 1979 French tennis player **Amélie Mauresmo**

July 6

1747 **John Paul Jones:** Scottish-born naval hero of the American Revolution. Commanded the U.S. ship *Bonhomme Richard* in celebrated victory over the British Frigate *Serapis.* Later became an admiral with the Russian navy, winning victories over Turks.

I wish to have no connection with any ship that does not sail fast; for I intend to go in harm's way.

1875 **Roger W. Babson:** American educator, statistician, business forecaster, and writer. Founded the Babson Report Service and other stock market counseling services, which advised clients on when to buy and sell their stocks, bonds, and commodities. Established the Babson Institute (later Babson College) in 1919 and Webster College to train women in business in 1927.

The successful man is the one who had the chance and took it.

1899 **Mignon Good Eberhart:** American novelist. Author of fifty-one suspense novels including *The Patient in Room 18, Mystery of Hunting's End, The Case of Susan Dare* and *R.S.V.P. Murder.* Received the Grand Master Award from the Mystery Writers of America, an organization of which she served as president.

I seat myself at the typewriter and hope, and lurk.

1907 **Frida Kahlo:** Mexican artist. Began painting while convalescing from a serious accident. Sent her works to painter Diego Rivera, whom she later married. Many of her Surrealistic and often shocking paintings were striking self-portraits. Her recurring themes were pain, which she suffered throughout the remainder of her life, and the suffering of women.

My painting carries with it the message of pain.

1913 **Gwyn Thomas:** Welsh schoolteacher-turned writer, dramatist, and TV personality. Wrote *The Keep, The Love Man* and *Where Did I Put My Pity?* A regular on the BBC radio and later TV series *Brains Trust,* a discussion program. Plays include *The Ship* and *The Dig.*

There are still parts of Wales where the only concession to gaiety is a striped shroud.

1921 **Nancy Davis Reagan:** American actress and wife of Ronald Reagan, former actor and president of the United States. Had great influence on her husband with whom she appeared in the film *Hellcats of the Navy.* There remarkable love story continued to the end, as she cared for him as Alzheimer's slowly eroded his mind and body.

There is no moral middle ground. Indifference is not an option... For the sake of our children, I implore each of you to be unyielding and inflexible in your opposition to drugs.

1927 **Bill Haley:** U.S. musician and singer. Pioneer of rock and roll music. Formed various country and western groups with a touch of rhythm and blues. With the Comets his hits included: "Rock Around the Clock, "Shake Rattle and Roll" and "See You Later, Alligator."

I sat down one night and wrote the line rock, rock, rock everybody. I was going to use the "stomp"— like rock, rock, rock and then stomp, stomp, stomp. But that didn't fit. I went from one word to another and finally came up with "roll."

1927 **Pat Paulsen:** American comedian and presidential candidate. Regular on "The Smothers Brothers Comedy Hour," as a deadpan editorialist providing double-talk commentary on the issues of the day. In 1968 he launched his Presidential campaign, with an emphasis on brilliant satiric comedy. Campaign slogan: "I've upped my standards. Now, up yours." Received the International Platform Associations prestigious "Mark Twain Award" for outstanding work in the field of comedy.

All the problems we face in the United States today can be traced to an unenlightened immigration policy on the part of the American Indian.

1935 **Dalai Lama (Tenzin Gyatso):** Spiritual and temporal head of Tibet. Proclaimed the *tulku* (reincarnation) of the 13th Dalai Lama at the age of three. Worshipped by the adherents of Lamaism as a living God. The People's Republic of China seized control of Tibet. In 1959 he set up the government of Tibet in exile in Dharamsala, India. Nobel Peace Prize winner (1989), in recognition of his nonviolent campaign to end China's domination of Tibet. Writings: *Ethics for a New Millennium, A Simple Path, The Wisdom of Forgiveness* and *The Heart of Compassion.*

My religion is very simple. My religion is kindness.

1946 **George W. Bush:** American politician. Elected 43rd President of the United States under a cloud of controversy about ballots in Florida, which wasn't settled until a split U.S. Supreme Court ruled in his favor. After the 9–11 attack on the Twin Towers in New York, he ordered the invasion of Afghanistan, which resulted in the overthrow of the Taliban government, allies of the al-Qaeda terrorists leader, Osama bin Laden. Convinced Iraq had weapons of mass destruction, he directed the overthrow of the Saddam Hussein government, but has had a much more difficult time in establishing the peace and a stable Iraqi government. Despite a growing belief that the war was unnecessary and is turning into another Vietnam, he was reelected to a second term, but his popularity steadily declined.

I just want you to know that, when we talk about war, we're really talking about peace.

1946 **Jamie Wyeth:** Third-generation American artist. Son of Andrew Wyeth, one of the country's most popular painters, and the grandson of Newell Convers Wyeth, a famous illustrator of classic novels. Long a sensitive observer of his rural surroundings in Delaware and Pennsylvania, Jamie paints livestock and other animals as well as portraits of people. Works are found in many public collections, including National Gallery of Art, John F. Kennedy Library, Museum of Modern Art, and Brandywine River Museum.

I doubt things. Being satisfied by something is a real danger for me. I hope I never lose that. That would be death.

1950 **John Lindley Byrne:** English-born American author and comic book artist. Most famous works have been Marvel Comic's *X-Men* and *Fantastic Four* and the 1986 re-vamping of the DC Comic's *Superman* franchise. Also produced original works *Next Men* and *Danger Unlimited.*

I feel not unlike a small boy, waking from a bad dream to find reality not much of an improvement.

OTHERS: 1766 Scottish-born poet **Alexander Wilson**, 1785 English botanist **William Jackson Hooker**, 1796 Tsar of Russia **Nicholas I**, 1832 Mexican Emperor **Maximilian**, 1838 Croatian scholar **Vatroslav Jagic**, 1917 U.S. opera soprano **Dorothy Kirsten**, 1923 President of Poland **Wojciech Jaruzelski**, 1925 U.S. singer/game show producer **Merv Griffin**, 1927 U.S. actress **Janet Leigh**, 1931 U.S. singer/actress **Della Reese**, 1936 Irish comedian **Dave Allen**, 1937 U.S. singer "Duke of Earl" **Gene Chandler**, 1939 English pentathlete **Mary Peters**, 1946 U.S. actor/director **Sylvester Stallone**, 1975 U.S. rapper **50 Cent**

July 7

1860 **Gustav Mahler:** Czechoslovakian-born Austrian composer. Conductor and artistic director of Vienna State Opera House. Resigned after ten years to devote himself to composition. His musical credo was "the content must shape the form." An important bridge between the late romantic 19th century style and the revolutionary work of Schoenberg. Works include: *Resurrection Symphony, Symphony of a Thousand,* and *The Song of the Earth.*

If a composer could say what he had to say in words he would not bother trying to say it in music.

1884 **Lion Feuchtwanger:** German-Jewish novelist. Established his place in the literary world with novel *Jud Süss. Erfolg* ("Success") was a thinly veiled criticism of the Nazi Party and Hitler. Hitler was appointed Chancellor while Feuchtwanger was on a speaking tour in the U.S. His home was ransacked, manuscripts of projected works destroyed and his German citizenship revoked, declared "Enemy of the State number one." Settled in France, where he wrote exposures of Nazi racist policies. When Germany invaded France, he was imprisoned in an internment camp, but escaped and received asylum in the U.S.

There's only a step from the sublime to the ridiculous, but there's no road leading from the ridiculous to the sublime.

1887 **Marc Chagall:** Russian-born French painter. Developed a style of great poetry and brightness. Noted for his illustrations for Gogol's novel *Dead Souls.* Painted a ceiling at the Paris Opera and a massive mural for the Metropolitan Opera at Lincoln Center in New York.

All colors are the friends of their neighbors and the lovers of their opposites.

1893 **Vladimir Mayakovsky:** Russian poet Joined the Social Democratic Party in 1908 and spent much of the next two years in prison for his political activities. First published work was a small book of four poems, *Ya* (I), marking him as one of the more original new poets. Poems characterized by hyperbolic imagery, forceful rhythm and often coarse language. Greeted the Revolution by composing propaganda verses, which he read before crowds of workers throughout the country.

Art is not a mirror to reflect the world, but a hammer with which to shape it.

1899 **George Cukor:** American director. Famous as a woman's director for the sensitivity he showed in portraying strong intelligent female characters in films such as *Little Women, Dinner at Eight, Camille, The Women, The Philadelphia Story, Adam's Rib, Born Yesterday* and *My Fair Lady,* the latter his only Oscar after five nominations.

You can't have any successes unless you can accept failure.

1906 **Leroy "Satchel" Paige:** Legendary African-American baseball pitcher with the Negro Leagues. At age 42 he made it to the Major Leagues where he gave strong evidence of what he might have done had the color ban been lifted when he was a young man.

How old would you be if you didn't know how old you are?

1911 **Gian Carlo Menotti:** Italian-born American composer and librettist. His best known operas are *The Medium, Amahl and the Night Visitors* and *The Saint of Bleecker Street.* Staged his own works, replete with dramatic strokes.

Art is the unceasing effort to compete with the beauty of flowers — and never succeeding.

1915 **Margaret Walker:** African-American novelist, poet and educator. Wrote *For My People*, which celebrated the black identity. Other volumes of poems: *Prophets for a New Day* and *October Journey*. Most celebrated book is *Jubilee*, a fictionalized account of her great-grandmother's life during and after slavery.

When I was about eight, I decided that the most wonderful thing, next to a human being, was a book.

1922 **Pierre Cardin:** French fashion designer. Joined the Paquin fashion. Designed the costumes for Jean Cocteau's film *Beauty and the Beast*. Opened his emporium in the 1950s. Designed gowns for costume balls, and ready-to-wear collections for both men and women. Master of the bias cut.

The jean! The jean is the destructor! It is a dictator! It is destroying creativity. The jean must be stopped!

1933 **David McCullough:** American historian, editor, essayist, educator, lecturer and author. Called a "master of the art of narrative history." Narrator of numerous documentaries including Ken Burn's *The Civil War* and *Napoleon*. Past president of the Society of American Historians and elected to the American Academy of Arts and Sciences. Bestselling books: *The Johnstown Flood*, *Truman*, *John Adams* and *1776*.

You can't be a full participant in our democracy if you don't know our history.

1940 **Ringo Starr:** British drummer with the Beatles, replacing Pete Best. With their breakup his solo work included "It Don't Come Easy," "Photograph" and "You're Sixteen." Participated in *The Concert for Bangladesh* organized by George Harrison in 1971. Did his best solo work with his bestselling 1973 album *Ringo*.

I think the main point of the situation is that those pieces of plastic that we did are still some of the finest pieces of plastic around.

1972 **Lisa Leslie:** An original member of American Women's National Basketball Association, playing for the Los Angles Sparks. At 6' 5" she is one of the leagues' top-performing and popular players. First to perform a dunk in a league game. Helped lead the U.S.' national women's basketball team to gold medals in the Olympic Games of 1996 and 2000. Also a fashion model with aspirations of becoming an actress.

I'm strong, I'm tough, I still wear my eyeliner.

OTHERS: 1053 Emperor of Japan **Shirakawa**, 1586 English statesman **Thomas Howard**, 1746 Italian astronomer **Giuseppe Piazzi**, 1752 French inventor **Joseph-Marie Jacquard**, 1901 Italian director **Vittorio De Sica**, 1903 Scottish historian **Stephen Runciman**, 1906 Croatian-born mathematician **Willem Feller**, 1907 U.S. writer **Robert A. Heinlein**, 1915 Russian-born actor **Yul Brynner**, 1917 U.S. political leader **Lawrence O'Brien**, 1919 U.S. defense attorney **William Kunstler**, 1927 U.S. composer/bandleader **Doc Severinsen**, 1959 Playboy model **Jessica Hahn**, 1980 U.S. figure skater **Michelle Kwan**

July 8

1621 **Jean La Fontaine:** French author. Prolific writer of comedies, lyrics, elegies, ballads and licentious tales. A vagabond, dreamer, and lover of pleasure. Best remembered for his *Fables Choisies, Mises en Vers*, which are among the masterpieces of French literature.

Nothing is more dangerous than a friend without discretion; even a prudent enemy is preferable.

1790 **Fitz-Greene Halleck:** American poet. With young poet Rodman Drake, who died at 25, wrote *The Croaker Papers*, a series of satirical and humorous verses, and another satire, *Fanny*. His visit to Europe, traces of which are found in his later poetry. Served as private secretary to John Jacob Astor.

I cannot spare the luxury of believing that all things beautiful are what they seem.

1839 **John D. Rockefeller:** American financier and philanthropist. Founded an oil company that became Standard Oil Trust. Founded the University of Chicago and Rockefeller Foundation. Gave over $500 million in aid of medical research, universities and Baptist churches. His philanthropy was continued by his son and other descendants.

If you want to succeed you should strike out on new paths, rather than travel the worn paths of accepted success.

1867 **Käthe Kollwitz:** German sculptor and graphic artist. Deeply involved with and sympathetic to the struggles of the oppressed poor. Expressed her abhorrence of war, poverty, and exploitation in her works: *Weaver's Revolt* and *Peasant's War*, and a series of eight prints on the theme of *Death*.

Growing old is partly an inescapable process of accommodations and adjustments.

1885 **Ernst Bloch:** German Marxist philosopher and atheist theologian. When the Nazis came to power fled to Switzerland, and eventually to the U.S. Works were very influential during the student protest movements in 1968. Works: *Atheism in Christianity*, *The Spirit of Utopia*, and *The Principle of Hope*.

So the sick man has the feeling not that he lacks something but that he has too much of something. His discomfort, as something which is hanging around him and superfluous, has to go; pain is proud flesh. He dreams of the body which knows how to keep comfortably quiet.

1892 **Richard Aldington:** British poet, novelist, translator and scholar. Member of a group that introduced *imagism*. Poetry collections: *Images of War* and *Soft Answers*. Novels: *Death of a Hero* and *All Men Are Enemies*. Biographies of D.H. Lawrence and Lawrence of Arabia. Once married to American poet Hilda Doolittle.

Nationalism is a silly cock crowing on his own dunghill.

1893 **Fritz Perls:** German-born psychiatrist and psychotherapist. Coined the term "Gestalt Therapy," which he and his wife Laura Perls developed from the 1940s. Their approach was similar but not identical to Gestalt psychology and the Gestalt Theoretical Psychotherapy of Hans-Juergen Walter. Books: *Ego, Hunger and Aggression*, *Gestalt Therapy* and *In and Out the Garbage Pail.*

I am not in this world to live up to other people's expectations, nor do I feel that the world must live up to mine.

1913 **Walter Kerr:** American journalist, critic and playwright. Drama critic for the *New York Herald Tribune* and *New York Times*. Won a Pulitzer Prize for Criticism in 1978. Husband of playwright Jean Kerr with whom he coauthored the musical *Goldilocks*, which won two Tony awards. Books: *How Not to Write a Play*, *Criticism and Censorship*, *Tragedy and Comedy*, and *The Silent Clowns*.

Half the world is composed of idiots, the other half of people clever enough to take indecent advantage of them.

1926 **Elisabeth Kübler-Ross:** Swiss-born American psychiatrist, thanatologist and writer. Appalled by hospital treatment of dying patients, began a series of lectures featuring terminally ill patients. Proposed the Five Stages of Grief: denial, anger, bargaining, depression, and acceptance. Books: *On Death & Dying*, *Death: The Final Stage of Growth*, *On Children & Death*, *AIDS & Love*, and *The Tunnel and the Light*.

We are not powerless specks of dust drifting around in the wind, blown by random destiny. We are, each of us, like beautiful snowflakes—unique, and born for a specific reason and purpose.

1934 **Marty Feldman:** British writer, comedian, and actor. Famous for bulging eyes, a result of a thyroid condition. Began his show business career as a trumpet player but soon started writing comedy sketches for British TV. Movies: *The Adventures of Sherlock Holmes's Smarter Brother* and *Young Frankenstein*. Directed and starred in *The Last Remake of Beau Geste*.

Comedy, like sodomy, is an unnatural act.

1952 **A. Whitney Brown:** American writer and humorist. Best known for his recurring appearances on *Saturday Night Live* during the 1980s, where acting as a news correspondent he delivered funny opinion pieces in the segment called "The Big Picture." Appeared on *The Daily Show*, in a similar capacity.

That is the saving grace of humor, if you fail no one is laughing at you.

1953 **Anna Quindlen:** American bestselling author, columnist and journalist. Her liberal opinion column, *Public and Private*, which appears in the *New York Times*, won the Pulitzer Prize for Commentary in 1992. She currently writes a column for *Newsweek*. Books: *A Short Guide to a Happy Life*, *Thinking Out Loud*, and *Happily Ever After*.

The thing that is really hard, and really amazing, is giving up on being perfect and beginning the work of becoming yourself.

OTHERS: 1836 British politician **Joseph Chamberlain**, 1838 German inventor **Ferdinand Graf von Zeppelin**, 1851 English archaeologist **Arthur Evans**, 1882 Australian composer **Percy Grainger**, 1895 Russian physicist **Igor Tamm**, 1898 English novelist **Alec Waugh,** 1904 French mathematician **Henri Cartan**, 1906 U.S. architect **Philip Johnson**, 1907 U.S. politician **George W. Romney**, 1914 U.S. singer **Billy Eckstine**, 1923 U.S. hurdler **Harrison Dillard**, 1929 U.S. author **Shirley Ann Grau**, 1931 TV executive **Roone Arledge**, 1932 U.S. singer **Jerry Vale**, 1942 Senator **Philip Gramm**, 1946 Ballerina **Cynthia Gregory**, 1951 Actress **Anjelica Huston**, 1958 Actor **Kevin Bacon**, 1961 U.S. country singer **Toby Keith**

July 9

1764 **Ann Radcliffe:** English novelist known for her tales of terror in the convention of Gothic romances set in Italy: *The Romance of the Forest*, *The Mysteries of Udolpho* and *The Italian*.

One act of beneficence, one act of real usefulness, is worth all the abstract sentiment in the world.

1811 **Sara Payson Parton:** Pen Name "Fanny Fern." American author. Wrote weekly column for Bonner's *New York Ledger* (1856–72). Caused a scandal with the publication of her best-selling book *Ruth Hall*, a thinly-veiled autobiography, in which people recognized themselves and did not appreciate how they were portrayed. Vocal feminist, constantly writing in defense of women's rights.

There are no little things. "Little things" are the hinges of the universe.

1856 **Nikola Tesla:** Croatian-born American inventor and researcher. Worked for Thomas Edison and George Westinghouse, but preferred independent research. His inventions made production and distribution of alternating-current electric power possible. Established an electric-power station at Niagara Falls. Many of his theories, which would later prove to be correct, were ridiculed and he died alone.

The spread of civilization may be likened to a fire; First, a feeble spark, next a flickering flame, then a mighty blaze, ever increasing in speed and power.

1858 **Franz Boas:** German-born American anthropologist. His lifelong work was the study of the Indian tribes of the Pacific Northwest. Directed the Jesup North Pacific Expedition (1896–1905), which investigated the relationships between the aboriginal people of Siberia and North America. Argued that all human groups have actually evolved equally but in different ways. Established newer and simpler anthropological concepts outlined in *Race, Language and Culture*.

If we were to select the most intelligent, imaginative, energetic, and emotionally stable third of mankind, all races would be present.

1889 **Don Herold:** American cartoonist, illustrator and humorist. Wrote and illustrated many books and contributed to several national magazines. Publications: *So Human, There Ought to Be a Law, Strange Bedfellows, Love That Golf, Drunks Are Driving Me to Drink,* and *Adventures in Golf.*

Women give us solace, but if it were not for women we should never need solace.

1894 **Dorothy Thompson:** American journalist, writer, radio commentator and activist. Established her reputation as a foreign correspondent in Germany and Vienna during the 1920s. Wrote the widely syndicated column *On the Record.* Married to novelist Sinclair Lewis. Author of *The Courage to Be Happy, Political Guide* and *I Saw Hitler!*

Peace has to be created, in order to be maintained. It is the product of Faith, Strength, Energy, Will, Sympathy, Justice, Imagination, and the triumph of principle. It will never be achieved by passivity and quietism.

1901 **Barbara Cartland:** Prolific British author of approximately 600 books, mostly Gothic romances that have sold over 600 million copies. Step-grandmother of Princes Diane. Earned a place in *Guinness Book of Records* for writing 26 books in 1983. Non-fiction includes biographies, and books on health food, vitamins and beauty.

Among men, sex sometimes results in intimacy; among women, intimacy sometimes results in sex.

1908 **Paul Brown:** American football coach and executive. One of the most innovative coaches of all time. Considered the "father of the modern offense." Coached Ohio State (1941–43), Cleveland Browns (1946–62) and Cincinnati Bengals (1968–76). Elected to Hall of Fame (1967). The Cleveland team was named for its highly popular coach, following a poll taken by the *Cleveland Plain Dealer.*

Football is a game of errors. The team that makes the fewest errors in a game usually wins.

1911 **John Archibald Wheeler:** American theoretical physicist. Spent most of his career (1938–76) at Princeton University, before finally moving to the University of Texas. Helped develop the hydrogen bomb. Searched for a unified field theory and with physicist Richard Feynman worked on the concept of action at a distance.

We are not only observers. We are participators. In some strange sense this is a participatory universe.

1936 **June Jordan:** African-American poet, bisexual activist, writer, scholar and journalist. Founded the Poetry for People at the University of California, Berkeley, where she was a full professor in the departments of English, Women Studies, and African American Studies. Publications: *Who Look at Me, Fannie Lou Hamer, Some Changes, Dry Victories,* and the autobiographical *Soldier: A Poet's Childhood.*

But everybody needs a home so at least you can have some place to leave which is where most other folks will say you must be coming from.

1937 **David Hockney:** English graphic and pop artist. His portraits, self-portraits, still lifes, and quiet scenes of friends are characterized by a frank, mundane realism and brilliant colors. Work includes a set of satirical etchings, *The Rake's Progress.* Also achieved prominence at a set designer for the opera and ballet.

The moment you cheat for the sake of beauty, you know you're an artist.

1945 **Dean R. Koontz:** Prolific American author, best known for his popular suspense novels. Published mainstream suspense and horror fiction, under his name and several pseudonyms. Dogs often figure in his novels, as he is an avid dog lover. Novels: *Whispers, Watchers, Dark Rivers of the Heart,* and *One Door from Heaven.* Also has written children's books, essays, short stories, poetry and screenplays.

Human beings can always be relied upon to exert, with vigor, their God-given right to be stupid.

OTHERS: 1577 English colonist **Thomas West**, 1578 Holy Roman Emperor **Ferdinand II**, 1686 American politician **Philip Livingston**, 1819 U.S. inventor **Elias Howe**, 1878 U.S. newscaster **H.V. Kaltenborn**, 1879 Italian composer **Ottorino Respighi**, 1894 Russian physicist **Pyotr L. Kapitsa**, 1916 British Prime Minister **Edward Heath**, 1927 U.S. singer **Ed Ames**, 1929 King of Morocco **Hassan II**, 1932: U.S. Secretary of Defense **Donald Rumsfeld**, 1936 U.S. conductor **David Zinman**, 1943 Astronaut **John Casper**, 1947 U.S. football player/murder suspect **O.J. Simpson**, 1956 Actor **Tom Hanks**, 1963 Musician **Courtney Love**

July 10

1509 **John Calvin:** French theologian and Protestant reformer. Forced to flee France because of his radical views, he settled in Geneva. Founder of Calvinism, which recognized only the Bible as a source of knowledge and of authority of questions of belief. Its chief principles were the total depravity of man, the absolute power of the will of God, the superiority of faith to good works, and divine predestination of those to be saved, the Elect.

However many blessings we expect from God, His infinite liberality will always exceed all our wishes.

1723 Sir **William Blackstone:** English jurist and writer. Gave the first lectures on English common law at Oxford. Best known for *Commentaries on the Laws of England,* which for more than a century were fundamental to any study of English law. Served as judge of the Court of Common Pleas. Advocated prison reform.

The public good is in nothing more essentially interested, than in the protection of every individual's private nights

1813 **Arthur Helps:** English historian and novelist. While at Trinity College, Cambridge, he was a member of the elite group of intellectuals, the Conversazione

Society. Better known as "The Apostles" the society was established in 1820 for the purposes of discussion of social and literary questions. Publications: *Thoughts in the Cloister and the Crowd, Conversations on War and General Culture, Talk About Animals and Their Masters, The Life of Columbus,* and *Thoughts Upon Government.*

Routine is not organization, any more than paralysis is order.

1830 **Camille Pissarro:** French artist. Known as the "Father of Impressionism." Painted rural and urban French life, particularly landscapes around Pontoise and scenes from Montmartre. Had sympathy for peasants and laborers. Mentor to Paul Cezanne and Paul Gauguin.

Blessed are those who see beautiful things in humble places where other people see nothing.

1842 **Adolphus Busch:** German-born brewer. Emigrated to the U.S. at the age of eighteen. Joined the St. Louis brewery owned by his father-in-law Eberhard Anheuser. A good businessman, Busch was responsible for pioneering the pasteurization of beer. He established the Budweiser brand and served as president of the Anheuser-Busch Brewing Association from 1879 until his death in 1913. The company continues to be headed by his descendants.

You can only drink thirty or forty glasses of beer a day, no matter how rich you are.

1867 **Finlay Peter Dunne:** American humorist. Creator of "Mr. Dooley," an imaginary Irishman who presided over a small saloon on Chicago's West Side, spreading both his wit and his wisdom. The more than 700 essays featuring Mr. Dooley speaking in his Irish dialect were collected in books including *Mr. Dooley in Peace and War, Mr. Dooley's Philosophy* and *Mr. Dooley Says.*

A fanatic is a man that does what he thinks the Lord would do if He knew the facts of the case.

1871 **Marcel Proust:** French novelist. Memories of visits to relatives in Auteuil in Illiers provided the basis for the imaginary village of Combray, the setting for the early part of his most famous work, *Remembrance of Things Past.* His Jewish background, homosexuality and hypochondria were farmed out to characters in the work, and extensively analyzed by the narrator, that is, Proust.

The real voyage of discovery consists not in seeking new landscapes but in having new eyes.

1875 **Mary McLeod Bethune:** African-American educator. Daughter of former slaves. Devoted her life to ensuring the right to education and freedom from discrimination for African Americans. Encouraged people to: "Invest in the human soul. Who knows, it might be a diamond in the rough." Advisor to President Franklin D. Roosevelt on the problems of minority groups. Attempted to get his support for a proposed law against Lynching.

The drums of Africa still beat in my heart. They will not let me rest while there is a single Negro boy or girl without a chance to prove his worth.

1888 **Toyohiko Kagawa:** Japanese pacifist, social reformer and Christian evangelist. Leader in the Japanese labor movement and in the establishment of cooperatives. Repeatedly arrested for his part in labor activism. While in prison wrote two of his more than 150 books, novels *Crossing the Deathline* and *Shooting the Sun.* Organized the Japanese Federation of Labor and the National Anti-War League in 1928. Arrested in 1940 for apologizing to the Chinese for Japan's occupation. Member of the transitional government that offered surrender to the U.S.

Love is creation raised to a higher degree.

1920 **David Brinkley:** American television journalist. Joined NBC in 1943 and became Washington correspondent for NBC News (1951–81), Co-anchored NBC's nightly Huntley-Brinkley Report (1956–70) with Chet Huntley. Later Brinkley hosted a weekly TV news and interview program and provided analysis of the news.

Numerous politicians have seized absolute power and muzzled the press. Never in history has the press seized power and muzzled the politicians.

1923 **Jean Kerr:** American playwright, novelist and humorist. Best known for *Please Don't Eat the Daises, The Snake Has All the Good Lines,* and her *play Mary, Mary.* Wife of critic Walter Kerr.

Even though a number of people have tried, no one has yet found a way to drink for a living.

1943 **Arthur Ashe:** U.S. tennis player. First African American to win U.S. Championship and Wimbledon and first black member of the U.S. Davis Cup team, which he helped win five championships. Critic of racial injustice, including South Africa's apartheid policy. In 1992 announced that he had been infected with AIDs from a blood transfusion during surgery. Devoted his time to increasing public awareness of the disease. Died in 1993.

True heroism is remarkably sober, very undramatic. It is not the urge to surpass all others at whatever cost, but the urge to serve others at whatever cost.

OTHERS: 1452 Scottish King **James II**, 1592 French historian **Pierre d'Hozier**, 1682 English mathematician **Roger Cotes**, 1802 Scottish writer **Robert Chambers**, 1835 Polish composer **Henryk Wieniawski**, 1875 English writer **Edmund Clerihew Bentley**, 1899 U.S. actor **John Gilbert**, 1921 U.S. boxer **Jake LaMotta**, 1923 U.S. author **Earl Hammer Jr.**, 1927 New York mayor **David Dinkins**, 1931 Canadian writer **Alice Munro**, 1945 British tennis player **Virginia Wade**, 1947 U.S. musician **Arlo Guthrie**, 1968 Algerian athlete **Hassiba Boulmerka**, 1980 U.S. singer **Jessica Simpson**

July 11

1274 **Robert the Bruce:** King of Scots. Hero of the Scottish War of Independence. As Earl of Carrick, swore fealty to Edward I of England, but joined the

Scottish revolt under William Wallace. Killed his political rival John Comyn in 1306 and was crowned king at Scone. After Edward's death, the English were expelled from Scotland, but sporadic war continued until at the Treaty of Northampton (1328) where the independence of Scotland and Bruce's right to the throne were recognized.

History is written by those who hang heroes.

1558 **Robert Greene:** Elizabethan prose writer and dramatist, known as a university wit and a writer of rogue literature. In his brief life of some 34 years, he had thirty-eight publications. Plays: *Friar Bacon and Friar Bungay, The Scottish History of James IV and England.* Warned his fellow playwrights to beware of the upstart actor William Shakespeare who was encroaching on their territory by writing plays himself.

Stop shallow water from running, it will rage; tread on a worm and it will turn.

1754 **Thomas Bowdler:** English author who wrote expurgated editions of Shakespeare's works in ten volumes and Gibbon's *Decline and Fall.* The term "bowdlerize" has been with us since.

I acknowledge Shakespeare to be the world's greatest dramatic poet, but regret that no parent could place the uncorrected book in the hands of his daughter, and therefore I have prepared the Family Shakespeare.

1767 **John Quincy Adams:** Sixth American president (1825–29), elected to the office by the House of Representatives, as none of the four candidates (the others: Andrew Jackson, Henry Clay and William H. Crawford) received a majority. Eldest son of John Adams, the second U.S. president. Returned to the House of Representatives for nearly seventeen years after his presidency. Secretary of State under President James Monroe. Largely responsible for the promulgation of the Monroe Doctrine.

Always vote for principle, though you may vote alone, and you may cherish the sweetest reflection that your vote is never lost.

1838 **John Wanamaker:** American merchant. Father of the department store and of modern advertising. Founded a Philadelphia store bearing his name, with the principal "One price and goods returnable." In 1889 he began the First Penny Savings Bank in order to encourage thrift. That same year appointed Postmaster General by President Benjamin Harrison. His son and successor Rodman Wanamaker is credited with founding the Professional Golf Association of America and the Millrose Games.

Courtesy is the one coin you can never have too much of or be stingy with.

1857 **Alfred Binet:** French psychologist. Major figure in the development of experimental psychology in France. With Theodore Simon developed influential scales for the measurement of intelligence of children. Works: *Experimental Study of Intelligence* and *A Method of Measuring the Developing of the Intelligence of Young Children.*

The scale, properly speaking, does not permit the measure of the intelligence, because intellectual qualities are not superposable, and therefore cannot be measured as linear surfaces are measured.

1888 **Bartolomeo Vanzetti:** Italian anarchist with Nicola Sacco convicted and executed for murders during a robbery. Doubt of their guilt created an international storm of protest. Vindicated by a proclamation of Governor Dukakis on the fiftieth anniversary of their executions. Case inspired numerous literary works, including Edna St. Vincent Millay's poem "Justice Denied in Massachusetts," Upton Sinclair's novel *Boston* and Maxwell Anderson's play *Winterset.* Vanzetti's final statement:

Our words — our lives — our pains; nothing! The taking of our lives, lives of a good shoemaker and a poor fish peddler — all! That last moment belongs to us — that agony is our triumph.

1899 **E.B. (Elwyn Brooks) White:** American humorist, essayist, and novelist. Regularly contribute to *The New Yorker*'s "Talk of the Town." His essays were blessed with his sharp satirical style. Author of the classic children's books, *Stuart Little* and *Charlotte's Web.* Poetry collections: *The Lady Is Cold* and *The Fox of Peacock.*

Analyzing humor is like dissecting a frog. Few people are interested and the frog dies of it

1913 **Kofi Abrefa Busia:** Ghanaian politician. Became leader of Ghana Congress Party in opposition to Kwame Nkrumah. Forced to flee the country he became a Professor of Sociology and Culture at the University of Leiden in the Netherlands. Returned to Ghana with the overthrow of Nkrumah's government by the military. Formed the Progress Party, which won the parliamentary elections in 1969, with Busia as the new Prime Minister. His government was overthrown by the army in 1972.

Diplomacy means the art of nearly deceiving all your friends, but not quite deceiving all your enemies.

1915 **Ingrid Bengis:** Russian-American feminist writer and novelist. Born to Russian Jewish immigrants to the United States. Moved to St. Petersburg, Russia (1991), to seek her spiritual roots. Immediately immersed in "catastroika," a period of immense turmoil. In her novel *Metro Stop Dostoevsky: Travels in Russian Time,* she relates the realities and rhythms of Russian life in a search for its soul as one world collapses and another begins.

Imagination has always had powers of resurrection that no science can match.

1926 **Frederick Buechner:** American author. While still an undergraduate at Princeton, he began his first novel *A Long Day's Dying.* His most critically acclaimed novel, *Godric,* is the semi-fictionalized story of a medieval saint, Godric of Finchale. Told from Godric's point of view, the book won the Pulitzer Prize in 1981. Other works: *Speak What We Feel, The Son of Laughter* and *The Sacred Journey.*

Lust is the craving for salt of a man who is dying of thirst.

1934 **Giorgio Armani:** Italian fashion designer. Left medical school to become a buyer for a department store before becoming a fashion designer. Introduced ready-to-wear clothing for men and women in 1974. Leader in the pared-down, unstructured silhouette in menswear and the wide-shoulder look for women executives.

The difference between style and fashion is quality.

OTHERS: 1561 Spanish poet **Luis de Góngora**, 1628 Japanese warlord **Tokugawa Mitsukuni**, 1657 Prussian King **Frederick II**, 1826 Russian folklorist **Alexander Afanasyev**, 1846 French novelist/essayist **Léon Bloy**, 1876 French poet/artist **Max Jacob**, 1892 U.S. character actor **Thomas Mitchell**, 1897 Alabama sheriff **Eugene "Bull" Connor**, 1913 U.S. writer **Cordwainer Smith**, 1915 World War II air hero **Colin P. Kelly**, 1924 Brazilian physicist **César Lattes**, 1930 U.S. literary critic **Harold Bloom**, 1953 U.S. boxer **Leon Spinks**, 1957 Jamaican musician **Michael Rose**, 1959 U.S. guitarist **Richie Sambora**, 1975 U.S. rapper **Lil' Kim**

July 12

100 BCE **Gaius Julius Caesar:** Roman general, statesman, orator and writer. Formed the first triumvirate with Pompey and Crassus. When Crassus died, Caesar and Pompey had a falling out. The Senate demanded Caesar's resignation. Instead he crossed the Rubicon into Italy and entered into a civil war with Pompey. Victorious, he was named dictator. Went to Egypt where he engaged in the Alexandrine War and a very public affair with Queen Cleopatra. Returning to Rome, his person was declared sacred. His ambitious plans for Rome were unfulfilled when he was assassinated on the Ides of March, by conspirators led by Brutus and Cassius, who believed they were striking a blow for the restoration of the republic.

Cowards die many times before their actual deaths.

1813 **Claude Bernard:** French physiologist. His aim was to establish scientific method in medicine. His motto was "Art is I; science is we." Insisted that all living creatures were bound by the same laws as inanimate matter. In his major work, *An Introduction to the Study of Experimental Medicine* (1865), he described what makes a good scientific theory and what makes a scientist a true discoverer.

The true worth of an experimenter consists in his pursuing not only what he seeks in his experiment, but also what he did not seek.

1817 **Henry David Thoreau:** American essayist, naturalist and poet. Part of the Transcendentalist circle. A mystic, supported himself by a variety of occupations, including pencil-maker, teacher, tutor and surveyor. Built a wooden hut at Walden Pond, living there for two years and later wrote his famous work *Walden, or Life in the Woods*, recognized as a literary masterpiece and one of the seminal books of the century. Only other book published in his lifetime: *A Week on the Concord and Merrimack River.*

If a man does not keep pace with his companions, perhaps it is because he hears a different drummer. Let him step to the music he hears, however measured or far away.

1849 **William Osler:** Canadian physician. Considered by many as the Father of Modern Medicine. With William Henry Welch, William Stewart Halsted and Howard Kelly founded Johns Hopkins Hospital, where Osler was the first chief-of-staff. In 1905, he was appointed to the Regius Chair of Medicine at Oxford, which he held until his death in 1919. A prolific writer with his most famous work being *Principles and Practice of Medicine*, which appeared in many editions and translations for the next 50 years.

The good physician treats the disease; the great physician treats the patient who has the disease.

1854 **George Eastman:** American inventor and philanthropist. Abandoned a career in banking to take up producing photography equipment and film. Invented a successful roll-film and the "Kodak" box camera. Manufactured the transparent celluloid film used by Edison and others in experiments that led to the making of motion pictures. His suicide note: "My work is done. Why wait?"

Light makes photography. Embrace light. Admire it. Love it. But above all, know light. Know it for all you are worth, and you will know the key to photography.

1884 **Amadeo Modigliani:** Italian painter and sculptor. Painted his subjects, usually the poor of Montmartre in elongated, mannerist style. His first one-man show In Paris, featuring some very frank nudes, was closed on the first day on charges of indecency. His health was delicate and his life was marked by poverty, drink and drug addiction. Recognition of his genius came only after his death.

If a women poses for you, she gives herself to you.

1895 **R. [Richard] Buckminster Fuller:** American architect, engineer and theoretician. Sought solutions to global living by gaining the maximum benefits from a minimum expenditure of energy and materials. Most famous creation is the geodesic dome. Its basic unit is the tetrahedron, which when combined with octahedrons forms the most economic space-filling structures.

Faith is much better than belief. Belief is when someone else does the thinking.

1904 **Pablo Neruda:** Pen name of **Ricardo Neftali Reyes**. Chilean poet, diplomat and politician. The appearance of *Twenty Love Poems and a Song of Despair* in 1924 established him as one of Chile's most important poets. Appointed to various consular posts in Europe and Asia. Elected to the Chilean senate but was expelled when the Communist party, of which he was a militant member, was declared illegal. He became the people's poet. Awarded the Nobel Prize for Literature in 1971.

A child who does not play is not a child, but the man who doesn't play has lost forever the child who lived in him and who he will miss terribly.

1908 **Milton Berle:** "Uncle Miltie." "Mr. Television" and "The Thief of Bad Gags." American comedian. Began his career in vaudeville at age 5. Star of one of the most popular television shows of all time in the golden age of television. Opened his show by making an entrance in a different outrageous costume. Hosted the first charity telethon for the Damon Runyon Cancer Fund. First entertainer inducted into the International Comedy Hall of Fame.

If evolution really works, how come mothers only have two hands?

1917 **Andrew Wyeth:** American artist. His photographic realism and advocacy of traditional values made his works very popular. Best-known work is *Christina's World*. Each day, Christina, a crippled friend and neighbor of Wyeth dragged herself over the field from her house to visit her family's graves. In 1986, Wyeth revealed that he had made more than 240 drawings and paintings of his neighbor Helga Testorf, which as the "Helga Pictures" are greatly valued for dwelling on a single subject over a long period of time.

I prefer winter and fall, when you feel the bone structure of the landscape — the loneliness of it, the dead feeling of winter. Something waits beneath it, the whole story doesn't show.

1920 **Pierre Berton:** Canadian journalist and writer. Worked in Klondike mining camps during his university years. At 31 became managing editor of *MacLean's*. Permanent panelist on *Front Page Challenge*. Host of *The Pierre Berton Show*, *Heritage Theatre* and *The Secret of My Success*. Books: *The National Dream* and *The Last Spike*.

A Canadian is someone who knows how to make love in a canoe.

1937 **Bill Cosby:** African-American actor, comedian and TV producer. In the series *I Spy* (1965–68), became the first black actor to star in a dramatic role on network television. Appeared on children's programs *Sesame Street* and *The Electric Company*. Star of a succession of "Cosby" series as one of the most popular and respected stars in the history of TV. Outspoken advocate of African American youths making the most of educational opportunities.

Through humor, you can soften some of the worst blows that life delivers. And once you find laughter, no matter how painful your situation might be, you can survive it.

OTHERS: 1675 Italian composer **Evaristo Abaco**, 1730 English potter **Josiah Wedgwood,** 1824 French painter **Eugène Boudin**, 1828 Russian philosopher **Nikolai Chernyshevsky**, 1850 German anthropologist **Otto Schoetensack**, 1868 German poet **Stefan George**, 1886 Danish actor/humanitarian **Jean Hersholt**, 1895 Norwegian soprano **Kirstin Flagstad**, 1895 U.S. lyricist **Oscar Hammerstein II**, 1920 U.S. actress **Beah Richards**, 1925 U.S. auto executive **Roger B. Smith**, 1934 U.S. pianist **Van Cliburn**, 1937 French PM **Lionel Joslin**, 1948 U.S. fitness trainer **Richard Simmons**, 1971 U.S. figure skater **Kristi Yamaguchi**

July 13

1527 **John Dee:** Eminent Elizabethan mathematician, astronomer, geographer, astrologer, alchemist and more than a mere dabbler in magic. Unsuccessfully prosecuted for sorcery and heresy. Believed the model for Shakespeare's Prospero in *The Tempest*. Wrote on navigation, geography and calendar reform. Strong advocate of the establishment of English maritime supremacy in order to form a British Empire. Advisor to English voyages of discovery, preparing nautical information, including charts for navigation in the Polar Regions.

A marvelous neutrality have these things Mathematical, and also a strange participation between things supernatural, immortal, intellectual, simple, and indivisible, and things natural, mortal, sensible, compounded and divisible.

1793 **John Clare:** English poet. Born into a barely literate, impoverish family. Wrote *Poems Descriptive of Rural Life and Scenery* and *The Rural Muse*, for which he became famous as a peasant poet, but only briefly. Best poems were startlingly original, ranking high among English nature verses.

He could not die when trees were green,/ For he loved the time too well.

1844 **Robert Bridges:** English poet and physician. Appointed poet laureate in 1913. Advocated the return to the diction of the 18th century. Cofounder of the Society for Pure English. Works: *Milton's Prosody*, *Poetical Works*, and the *Treatment of Beauty*. Wrote plays on classical subjects and critical essays.

When death to either shall come — I pray it be first to me.

1859 **Sidney Webb:** British socialist reformer. Joined the Fabian Society and wrote the tract, *Facts for Socialists*. With his wife Beatrice Potter Webb wrote the influential *The History of Trade Unionism*. They cofounded the London School of Economics and helped reorganize the University of London. He served in Parliament (1922–29) and as colonial secretary (1929–31). Impressed by the Soviet Union, the Webbs wrote *Soviet Communism: A New Civilization?*

The inevitability of gradualness cannot fully be appreciated.

1886 Father **Edward J. Flanagan:** American Roman Catholic priest who founded Boys Town where vocational training was supplemented with religious and social education. Believed there was no such thing as a bad boy.

It costs so little to teach a child to love, and so much to teach him to hate.

1894 **Isaak Babel:** Ukrainian-born writer. First published stories appeared in a journal edited by Maksim Gorky. Recorded his experiences with a cavalry detachment fighting in Poland in a volume of stories entitled *Red Cavalry*. This was followed by *Odessa Tales*. Disappeared in 1938, a victim of the purges, and reputedly was executed or died in a concentration camp. His realization of the powerful effect of concision of literature is revealed in a line from one of his stories:

No steel can pierce the human heart so chillingly as a period at the right moment.

1903 Lord **Kenneth M. Clark:** English art historian. Leading scholar of the Italian Renaissance. Widely known for his popular BBC television series "Civilization" and a book of the same name. His massive *Catalogue of Drawings of Leonardo da Vinci* was the first chronological record of the artist's work. Wrote and lectured on a wide range of subjects: 19th century poetry, English landscape paintings, Chinese and modern art.

Opera, next to Gothic architecture, is one of the strangest inventions of Western man. It could not have been foreseen by any logical process.

1904 **James K. Feibelman:** American educator, author and philosopher. Wrote some 45 books on various subjects including *Understanding Oriental Philosophy*, *Death of the God in Mexico*, and *Inside the Great Mirror: A Critical Examination of the Philosophy of Russell, Wittgenstein, and Their Followers*.

That some good can be derived from every event is a better proposition than that everything happens for the best, which it assuredly does not.

1934 **Wole Soyinka:** Pen name of Akinwande Oluwole Soyinka. Nigerian poet, playwright and essayist. Became instrumental in developing an indigenous theatre in Nigeria. Plays are preoccupied with the themes of sacrifice and martyrdom, drawing heavily on Nigerian folk motifs. Works: *A Dance of the Forests, A Play of Giants, The Season of Anomy,* and *Poems from Prison*. Nobel Prize winner for Literature in 1986.

The greatest threat to freedom is the absence of criticism.

1935 **Jack Kemp:** American professional football quarterback, politician and government official. Played for the Buffalo Bills. U.S. Congressman from New York (1971–89). Supported conservative policies but also civil-rights measures. Secretary of Housing and Urban Development (1989–93). Robert Dole's VP nominee in 1996.

When people lack jobs, opportunity, and ownership of property they have little or no stake in their communities.

1940 **Paul Prudhomme:** New Orleans-born chef who served his apprenticeship throughout the U.S.A., before returning to the Crescent City to open a series of restaurants. His K-Paul's Louisiana Kitchen became widely known for traditional Cajun and Creole cooking and his own innovations. His reputation was aided by numerous TV appearances, cooking videos, and best-selling cookbooks.

We cooked for 300 people in tuxedos the Saturday before the hurricane (Katrina) hit. Then we cooked for 1,200 people in National Guard uniforms the Sunday after it hit.

1942 **Harrison Ford:** American film actor. Initial efforts as an actor were so unsatisfactory; he made his living as a master carpenter, a craft he still pursues as a hobby. Known for his wry charm and good looks. Films: *Star Wars* and sequels, *Raiders of the Lost Ark* and sequels, *Witness* (Oscar Nomination), *The Fugitive*, *Patriot Games* and *Firewall*.

The actor's popularity is evanescent; applauded today, forgotten tomorrow.

OTHERS: 1590 Pope **Clement X**, 1607 Czech-born actor **Václav Hollar**, 1608 Holy Roman Emperor **Ferdinand III**, 1821 Ku Klux Klan leader **Nathan Bedford Forrest**, 1858 Us ethnographer **Stewart Culin**, 1864 U.S. entrepreneur **John Jacob Astor IV**, 1905 U.S. critic **Bosley Crowther**, 1913 TV host **Dave Garroway**, 1913 Dutch high jumper **Carolina Gisolf**, 1918 Italian race car driver **Alberto Ascari**, 1921 Australian composer **Ernest Gold**, 1933 British novelist **David Storey**, 1944 Hungarian inventor/sculptor **Ernö Rubik**, 1957 U.S. film director **Cameron Crowe**, 1966 North Korean gymnast **Myong Hui Choe**

July 14

1634 **Pasquier Quesnel:** French Jansenist theologian and director of the Paris Oratory. Author of the Nouveau *Testament en français avec des réflexions morales* (1687–94, *New Testament in French with Thoughts on Morality*). Refusing to denounce Jansenism he was banished from Paris and fled to Brussels in 1641. He was imprisoned in 1703 but escaped to Amsterdam.

The truth only irritates those it enlightens, but does not convert.

1834 **James Abbott McNeil Whistler:** Expatriate American painter, etcher and lithographer. Preoccupied with aesthetic considerations over social or literary significance, that is, "art for art's sake." Best known for *Arrangement in Gray and Black No. 1*, popularly known as *Whistler's Mother*. His character is revealed in the collection of his early writings: *The Gentle Art of Making Enemies*.

I maintain that two and two continue to make four, in spite of the whine of the amateur for three, or the cry of the critic for five.

1858 **Emmeline Pankhurst:** English suffragist. Founded the Women's Franchise League (1889) and with her daughter Christabel the Women's Social and Political Union (1903). At the outbreak of World War I she turned her attention to the industrial mobilization of women. Conducted hunger strikes when arrested for arson and bombings. Her motto: "Trust in God. She will provide."

We have to free half of the human race, the women, so they can help free the other half.

1898 **Albert "Happy" Chandler:** U.S. politician and baseball executive. Governor of Kentucky, U.S. Senator and second commissioner of baseball, succeeding Kenesaw Mountain Landis. Backed Branch Rickey's move to make Jackie Robinson the first black in the major leagues, saying:

I don't believe in barring Negroes from baseball just because they are Negroes.

1903 **Irving Stone:** American writer known for his biographical novels of famous historical figures: *Lust for Life*, based on the life of Vincent Van Gogh, *Adversary in the House*, based on the life of Eugene Debs, *The Agony and the Ecstasy*, based on the life of Michelangelo, *The Passions of the Mind*, based on the life of Sigmund Freud, and *For the Defense*, based on the life of Clarence Darrow.

To try to understand another human being, to grapple for his ultimate depths, that is the most dangerous of human endeavors.

1904 **Isaac Bashevis Singer:** Polish-born Yiddish novelist, short-story writer, critic and journalist. Stories often are set in Poland of the past. Emigrated to New York, following his brother novelist Israel Joshua Singer. Worked as a journalist for the *Jewish Daily Forward*, which published most of his short stories. Works: *The Magician of Lublin*, *Lost in America* and *The Golem*. Nobel Prize for Literature (1978).

The very essence of literature is the war between emotion and intellect, between life and death. When literature becomes too intellectual— when it begins to ignore the passions, the emotions— it becomes sterile, still, and actually without substance.

1912 **Woodrow Wilson "Woody" Guthrie:** American folksinger. Sang in the hobo and migrant camps of the Great Depression; musical spokesman for labor and populist sentiment. Wrote over 1000 songs. Most famous for "Dust Bowl Ballads," describing the forced migration of Oklahoma families from their barren land. Hits: "So Long It's Been Good to Know You,)" "Hard Traveling," "Union Maid," and "This Land Is Your Land," which became an unofficial national anthem.

This land is your land, this land is my land. From California to the New York Island. From the redwood forest to the Gulf Stream waters. This land was made for you and me.

1913 **Gerald Ford:** U.S. politician. Republican Congressman from Michigan (1949–73). When Vice President Spiro Agnew resigned, Richard Nixon appointed Ford to replace him. When the Watergate scandal forced Nixon to resign, Ford became the first person to serve as president who had not been elected to either that post or vice president. Later Ford pardoned Nixon. Jimmy Carter defeated Ford in the 1976 presidential election.

If the government is big enough to give you everything you want, it is big enough to take away everything you have.

1916 **Natalia Ginzburg:** Italian author, essayist and playwright. Unsentimentally dealt with family relationships, employing a simple conversational style. Wrote about World War II life under fascism and of the Resistance movement. Works: *The Dry Heart*, *A Light for Fools*, and *Voices in the Evening*.

Everyday silence harvests its victims. Silence is a mortal illness.

1918 **Ingmar Bergman:** Swedish film director, scriptwriter and producer. Worked repeatedly with a devoted group of actors and crew. Director of Stockholm's Royal Dramatic Theatre (1963–66). Films: *The Seventh Seal*, *Wild Strawberries*, *The Virgin Spring*, *Through a Glass Darkly*, *Smiles of a Summer Night*, *Cries and Whispers*, *Fanny and Alexander* and his filmed for TV production *Scenes from a Marriage*.

The theater is like a faithful wife. The film is the great adventure, the costly, exciting mistress.

1937 **Jerry Rubin:** American political and social activist in the 1960s and 1970s and author. Co-founder with Abbie Hoffman of the Youth International Party ("Yippies"). Defendant in the "Chicago Seven" trial, brought on by the riots at the 1968 Chicago Democratic National Convention. Convicted under anti-riot provision in the Civil Rights Act. Later became a businessman and entrepreneur.

The power to define the situation is the ultimate power.

1951 **Esther Dyson:** American computer publisher. Daughter of noted physicist and mathematician Freeman Dyson and sister of scientific historian George Dyson. Formed EDventure Holdings, a company specializing in analyzing the impact of emerging technologies and markets on the economy and society. Publishes a monthly technology-industry newsletter and a syndicated column for the *New York Times*.

It may not always be profitable at first for businesses to be online, but it is a certainly going to be unprofitable not to be online.

OTHERS: 1454 Florentine humanist **Poliziano**, 1602 French statesman **Jules Cardinal Mazarin**, 1610 Grand Duke of Tuscany **Ferdinando II de' Medici**, 1801 German physiologist **Johannes Peter Müller**, 1860 U.S. Western novelist **Owen Wister**, 1868 English archaeologist/spy **Gertrude Bell**, 1906 Greek-born U.S. businessman **Tom Carvel**, 1910 U.S. animator **William Hanna**, 1912 Canadian literary critic **Northrop Frye**, 1918 U.S. playwright **Arthur Laurents**, 1924 Scottish pharmacologist **James W. Black**, 1932 U.S. football player **Roosevelt Grier**, 1937 Japanese politician **Yoshiro Mori**, 1952 U.S. singer **Chris Cross**

July 15

1606 **Rembrandt [Harmenszoon Van Rijn]:** Dutch painter and etcher. Established himself as the finest portrait painter in Amsterdam. Status declined as his style diverged from popular taste, causing him to sink into financial difficulties. He declared bankruptcy and his property, including his art collection, were sold. Well known for his dramatic use of light and shadows. Painted more than 100 self-portraits, establishing a record of the gradual alteration of his features. Works: *The Company of Captain Franz Banning Cock*, better known as *The Night Watch*, and *Supper at Emmaus*.

Painting is the grandchild of nature. It is related to God.

1796 **Thomas Bullfinch:** American mythologist and writer. Throughout his life held a business position, devoting leisure time to writing. *Age of Fable* is still used in schools as an introduction to the mythology of Greece, Rome, Scandinavia and Celtic lands. He also wrote the very popular *Age of Chivalry*.

In ages when there were no books, when noblemen and princess could not read, history or tradition was monopolized by the story-tellers.

1836 **William Winter:** American drama critic, historian, essayist and poet. Drama critic with the *New York Times* (1861–66) and *New York Tribune* (1866–1909). Works: *Henry Irving, Shakespeare's England, The Life and Art of Edwin Booth*, and *Life and Art of Richard Mansfield*.

Cities, unlike human creatures, may grow to be so old that at last they will become new.

1848 **Vilfredo Pareto:** French-born Italian economist and sociologist. Began his career as an engineer and directed an Italian railway company. Wrote several influential textbooks in which he demonstrated a mathematical approach to economics. *The Mind and Society* was a sociological tract presented a theory of the superiority of an elite class, anticipating certain Fascist principles.

Give me the fruitful error any time, full of seeds, bursting with its own corrections. You can keep your sterile truth for yourself.

1850 **Mother Francis Xavier (Maria Francesca) Cabrini:** Italian-born nun. Founder of the Missionary Sisters of the Sacred Heart (1886). Emigrated to the U.S., where she became renowned for her social and charitable work. Founded convents, orphanages and hospitals in Europe and the U.S. Canonized in 1946, becoming the first U.S. saint.

To become perfect, all you have to do is to obey perfectly. When you renounce your personal inclinations you accept mortification countersigned with the cross of Christ.

1892 **Walter Benjamin:** German literary critic and essayist. His thesis was rejected by the University of Frankfurt, forcing him to abandon plans for an academic career. A revision of his thesis, published as *The Origin of German Tragic Drama*, was his longest and most ambitious work. He applied his personal form of Marxist social criticism to film, art, European cities, and the works of Proust and Baudelaire.

Memory is not an instrument for exploring the past but its theater. It is the medium of past experience, as the ground is the medium in which dead cities lie interred.

1906 **Richard W. Armour:** American humorist noted for historical satires and literary scholarship. Wrote a number of humorous articles for *The Saturday Evening Post*, including: "To the Collector of the Internal Revenue" and "Warning for Empty-handed Husbands." Books: *It All Started with Columbus* and *Twisted Tales from Shakespeare*.

Politics, it seems to me, for years, or all too long, has been concerned with right or left instead of right or wrong.

1919 **Iris Murdoch:** Irish-born novelist and philosopher. Philosophy works *Sartre, Romantic Rationalist* and *The Sovereignty of Good*. Her Novels have been called psychological detective stories, portraying complicated and sophisticated sexual relationships: *Under the Net, The Bell, A Severed Head, The Red and the Green*, and *The Philosopher's Pupil*. Married literary critic John Bayley, who chronicled her decline due to Alzheimer's disease in *Elegy for Iris: A Memoir*, made into a very fine movie.

We live in a fantasy world, a world of illusion. The great task is to find reality.

1922 **Leon Lederman**: American physicist. Son of Russian-Jewish immigrants. Discovered a new particle, the long-lived K-meson, which had been predicted from theory. Shared the 1988 Nobel Prize with colleagues Melvin Schwartz and Jack Steinberger for their work with neutrinos.

Physics isn't a religion. If it were, we'd have a much easier time raising money.

1946 **Linda Ronstadt:** American singer. Began her career singing folk music with her band the *Stone Poneys*. Her repertoire as a solo artist covers a wide range of musical genres, including traditional country, rhythm & blues, new wave, opera, and mariachi. Nominated for 27 Grammy Awards, winning eleven. Hit songs: "You're No Good," "When Will I Be Loved," "Hurt So Bad," "Blue Bayou" and "I Can't Help It."

The thing you have to be prepared for is that other people don't always dream your dream.

1949 **Carl Bildt:** Swedish politician and diplomat. Member of the Riksdag (Swedish Parliament), leader of the Liberal Conservative Moderate Party and Prime Minister (1991–94). His government program was one of liberalizing and reforming the Swedish economy and gaining membership for Sweden in the European Union, with the latter achieved in 1994. Served as mediator in the Balkans conflict.

All the communities are in favor of peace, but sometimes different versions of peace.

1950 **Jesse Ventura:** "The Body." American professional wrestler and politician. Elected Governor of Minnesota (1999–2003) running as a candidate for the Reform Party of Minnesota. Regarded as one of the first politicians to effectively use the Internet as a medium for reaching out to voters. Did not seek a second term, believing that government should be a single term responsibility of every citizen. Vetoed a bill to promote recitation of the Pledge of Allegiance in public schools, saying:

I believe patriotism comes from the heart.

Patriotism is voluntary. It is a feeling of loyalty and allegiance that is the result of knowledge and belief. A patriot shows their patriotism through their action, by their choice [such as voting, attending community meetings and speaking out when needed]. No law will make a citizen a patriot.

OTHERS: 1573 English architect **Inigo Jones**, 1704 German religious leader **August Gottlieb Spangenberg**, 1779 U.S. educator/poet **Clement Moore**, 1808 English Catholic archbishop **Henry Cardinal Manning**, 1871 Japanese writer **Kunikida Doppo**, 1899 Irish leader **Sean F. Lemass**, 1926 Moroccan author **Driss Chraïbi**, 1930 French philosopher **Jacques Derrida**, 1931 U.S. author **Clive Cussler**, 1933 English guitarist **Julian Bream**, 1935 U.S. actress **Diahann Carroll**, 1946 Sultan of Brunei **Hassanal Bolkiah**, 1950 Newspaper columnist **Arianna Huffington**, 1953 Haitian political leader **Jean-Bertrand Aristide**

July 16

1194 Saint **Clare of Assisi:** Follower of St. Francis of Assisi. At the age of 18, she entered the Benedictine order. With her sister St. Agnes co-founded the Poor Ladies of San Damiano, later known as the Poor Clares. The order opened houses throughout Europe. Members lived on alms and focused on prayer and penitence. Worked many years to have an austere "Primitive Rule" for the order approved by the Pope. Notified of the approval two days before her death.

The Lord often reveals what is the best to the least.

1486 **Andrea del Sarto:** Italian painter, whose named derives from his father's occupation, "of the tailor." After an apprenticeship with Piero Di Cosimo he was commissioned by the Servites to paint a series of frescoes for the Church of the Annunciation. Established as one of the most outstanding painters of Florence, where his most celebrated works can be found.

Oh, but a man's reach must exceed his grasp, or what's a heaven for?

1723 Sir **Joshua Reynolds:** English painter, known for his portraits. Leading proponent of painting in the "Grand Manner" as exemplified by the Italian Renaissance works of Michelangelo, Raphael, and Titan. First president of Royal Academy (1768–1792). Paintings: *Dr. Samuel Johnson* and *Sarah Siddons as the Tragic Muse*.

Few have been taught to any purposes who have not been their own teachers.

1821 **Mary Baker Eddy:** American religious leader, editor and author. Founder of the Christian Science movement and the *Christian Science Monitor* newspaper. Published *Science and Health* and *Rudimental Divine Science,* expositions of her ideas and official statement of the organization she headed. Taught that pain, disease, old age, and death were "errors," that nothing but truth or mind can heal. The doctrines of Christian Science are summarized by Eddy as:

The prayer that reforms the sinner and heals the sick is an absolute faith that all things are possible to God.

1862 **Ida Bell Wells:** African-American journalist, reformer, and civil rights activist. Advocate for blacks' and women's rights. After three of her friends were lynched, she launched anti-lynching campaign. Wrote for the *Chicago Conservator*. Co-founded Chicago's Alpha Suffrage Club, possibly the first black women's suffrage organization. First president, American Negro League.

In slave times the Negro was kept subservient and submissive by the frequency and severity of the scourging, but, with freedom, a new system of intimidation came into vogue; the Negro was not only whipped and scourged; he was killed.

1872 **Roald Amundsen:** Norwegian explorer Member of the 1897 Belgian expedition, the first to winter in the Antarctic. Planned an expedition to the North Pole, but when Robert E. Peary achieved the feat, turned his attentions to the South Pole. Led the expedition that reached the pole in December 1911, one month before Robert Falcon Scott's disastrous attempt. Returned to Norway and founded a successful shipping business. Disappeared while flying a rescue mission to locate a downed dirigible.

Adventure is just bad planning.

1880 **Kathleen Norris:** American author of over 80 wholesome novels whose formula usually was "get a girl into trouble, and then get her out again." It allowed her to sell more than 10 million copies. They include: *Certain People of Importance* and *Over at the Crowleys*.

When you are unhappy, is there anything more maddening than to be told that you should be contented with your lot?

1889 **Shoeless Joe Jackson:** American baseball player. Outstanding hitter with the Chicago White Sox. Achieved the third highest career batting average in baseball history. A certain hall-of-famer had he not been implicated in the Black Sox Scandal in which some of his teammates were paid by gamblers to lose the 1919 World Series to the Cincinnati Reds. His production during the ill-fated series was outstanding and he was acquitted of any guilt in a trial. However, baseball commissioner Kenesaw Mountain Landis banned him and seven other players from baseball for life.

God knows I gave my best to baseball at all times and no man on earth can truthfully judge me otherwise.

1896 **Trygve Lie:** Norwegian government official. Foreign minister of Norway's government-in-exile during World War II. Helped draft provisions for the United Nations Security Council. First secretary general of the U.N. Dealt with Arab intervention in Israel, the India-Pakistan conflict over Kashmir and U.N. intervention in the Korean War.

A real diplomat is one who can cut his neighbor's throat without having the neighbor notice it.

1907 **Barbara Stanwyck:** Originally **Ruby Stevens.** Born into poverty, surviving with out parents as a chorus girl from age 15. Remarkably popular American actress in over 80 films, usually as strong-willed, independent women: Movies: *Meet John Doe, Ball of Fire, Stella Dallas, Double Indemnity* and *Sorry, Wrong Number,* Oscar nominated for the last four. Received an honorary Academy Award (1981).

Egotism — usually just a case of mistaken nonentity.

1928 **Anita Brookner:** English art historian and novelist. Authority on 18th century painting. First female Slade professor at Cambridge University and reader at the Courtauld Institute of Art. Came late to novel writing, but between 1981 and 1988, she published 8 novels, including *Family and Friends, A Friend from England* and *Hôtel du Lac,* for which she won the Booker Prize.

A man can go from being a lover to being a stranger in three moves flat but a woman under the guise of friendship engage in acts of duplicity which come to light very much later. There are different species of self-destruction.

1958 **Michael Flatley:** Irish-American step dancer. First non–European to win the All-Ireland World Championship for traditional dance in 1975. Created the initial choreography for *Riverdance.* With fellow lead dancer Jean Butler, led the show to great worldwide success. Left to form his own dance shows, first *Lord of the Dance,* followed by *Feet of Flames* and most recently *Celtic Tiger.*

I'm not an egomaniac like a lot of people say. But I am the world's best dancer, that's for sure.

Others: 1611 Queen of Poland **Cecylia Renata**, 1704 English inventor **John Kay**, 1722 English sculptor **Joseph Wilton**, 1902 Russian psychologist **Alexander Luria**, 1903 Canadian band singer **Carmen Lombardo**, 1907 U.S. popcorn farmer **Orville Redenbacher**, 1911 U.S. actress/dancer **Ginger Rogers**, 1924 U.S. beauty queen/TV personality **Bess Myerson**, 1926 U.S. biologist **Irwin Rose**, 1941 Jamaican reggae singer **Desmond Dekker**, 1948 Panamanian actor/musician **Rubén Blades**, 1948 Israeli violinist/conductor **Pinchas Zuckerman**, 1967 U.S. comic actor **Will Ferrell**, 1976 Israeli tennis player **Anna Smashnova**

July 17

1674 **Isaac Watts:** English Non-conformist minister. Published four collections of verse. Also wrote a number of theological and educational works. Regarded as the father of English hymnody. Hymns: "O God, Our Help Is Ages Past," "Behold the Glories of the Lamb" and "Jesus Shall Reign."

For Satan finds some mischief still for idle hands to do.

1744 **Elbridge Gerry:** American politician, signer of the Declaration of Independence and fifth U.S. vice president, serving under James Madison. Member of the Democratic-Republican Party. As governor of Massachusetts his name was given to the art of gerrymandering — a process by which electoral districts are drawn with an aim to aid the party in power.

The evils we experience flow from the excess of democracy. The people do not want virtue, but are dupes of pretended patriots.

1763 **John Jacob Astor:** German-born American businessman. Amassed a fortune trading furs all over North America and real estate. One of the most powerful financiers in the country. At his death he was the richest man in the country. Left a legacy to found a public library in New York City. His version of "money can't buy happiness":

I am the most miserable man on earth.

1810 **Martin Farquhar Tupper:** Prolific English writer of verse and prose. Author of *Proverbial Philosophy,* a series of moralizing commonplaces in free verse, which achieved huge, worldwide popularity. Remained a best-selling in Great Britain and the U.S. for more than a generation. Much of his other writings are now forgotten.

If thou are master to thyself, circumstances shall harm thee little.

1876 **Maxim Litvinov:** Soviet politician and diplomat. Joined the Russian Social Democratic Party in 1898 and exiled to Siberia in 1903. After the Bolshevik Revolution, he was appointed ambassador to England. As people's commissar for foreign affairs, gained U.S. recognition of Soviet Russia in 1934. Ambassador to the U.S. (1941–3) and vice-minister of foreign affairs (1943–6).

Peace is indivisible.

1889 **Erle Stanley Gardner:** American detective story writer. A trial lawyer by profession he created the character of lawyer Perry Mason and became one of the most successful writers of crime detection in the history of U.S. publishing. Wrote well over 100 books, beginning with *The Case of the Velvet Claws.* His confident wisecrack upon submitting a manuscript to a publisher:

It's a dammed good story. If you have any comments, write them on the back of a check.

1898 **Berenice Abbott:** American photographer. Worked in Paris as an assistant to Man Ray and Eugene Atget. Set up her studio (1925), making portraits of Parisian expatriate artists, writers, and collectors. Best known works are black and white architectural, documentary images of New York City in the 1930s. Many of her photographs were published in *Changing New York* (1939).

Photography can only represent the present. Once photographed, the subject becomes part of the past.

1899 **James Cagney:** American actor/dancer. Toured in vaudeville as a song-and-dance man. Went to Hollywood and played the first of a series of gangster films, *Public Enemy,* followed by *Angels with Dirty Faces* and considerably later *White Heat.* Academy Award for his portrayal of George M. Cohan in *Yankee Doodle Dandy.*

Other films: *Man with a Thousand Faces*, *Mister Roberts*, *One Two Three*, and *Ragtime*.

Though I soon became typecast in Hollywood as a gangster and hoodlum, I was originally a dancer, an Irish hoofer, trained in vaudeville tap dance. I always leapt at the opportunity to dance in films later on.

1902 **Christina E. Stead:** Australian-born novelist and Hollywood screenwriter. Common thread of novels is her treatment of subtly destructive obsessions. Best known work *The Man Who Loved Children* depicts marriage as savage warfare between love and independence. Others: *Seven Poor Men of Sydney* and *Dark Places in the Heart*.

If all the rich men in the world divided up their money among themselves, there wouldn't be enough to go around.

1912 **Art Linkletter:** Canadian-born American broadcaster, TV personality and author. Hosted popular radio and television shows, "House Party" and "People Are Funny." Author of more than 20 books including the best-selling *Kids Say the Darndest Things* and *Old Age Is Not for Sissies*.

Things turn out best for the people who make the best out of the way things turn out.

1917 **Phyllis Diller:** Fright-wigged, gravel-voices American stand-up comedienne and actress. Housewife discovered later in life at the Purple Onion nightclub. Guest star on numerous TV shows. Appeared in a few movies. Occasionally makes appearances as a concert pianist with symphony orchestras.

Women want men, careers, money, children, friends, luxury, comfort, independence, freedom, respect, love, and three-dollar pantyhose that won't run.

1935 **(Johann) Peter Schickele:** American composer and musical parodist. Composed more than 100 original works for symphony orchestra, choral groups, chamber ensemble, film and TV. Known for his portrayal of "the deservedly forgotten Baroque-ish composer and least loved of the twenty-odd sons of Johann Sebastian Bach," P.D.Q. Bach. These musical parodies have earned four Grammy Awards for Best Comedy Performance Album. Schickele has invented a wide range of unusual instruments, including the dill piccolo (for playing sour notes), the left-handed sewer flute and the tuba mirum.

There are a lot of singers in big cities who make their living singing in all sorts of different kinds of churches: synagogues, churches of different denominations, and it has been said of these singers that they're "Pantheists"; pantheists being people who believe in all gods whose churches hire singers.

OTHERS: 1698 French Mathematician **Pierre Maupertuis**, 1831 Emperor of China **Xianfeng**, 1839 U.S. inventor **Ephraim Shay**, 1859 Puerto Rico journalist **Luis Muñoz Rivera**, 1877 Hungarian conductor **Ernst von Dohnanyi**, 1888 Israeli writer **Shmuel Yosef Agnon**, 1901 Polish poet **Bruno Jasieński**, 1916 U.S. soprano **Eleanor Steber**, 1917 Baseball player **Lou Boudreau**, 1918 President of Guatemala **Carlos Arana Osorio**, 1935 Canadian actor **Donald Sutherland**, 1951 U.S. actress **Lucie Arnaz**, 1954 Chancellor of Germany **Angela Merkel**, 1954 U.S. author **J. Michael Straczynski**, 1963 King of Lesotho **Letsie III**

July 18

1635 **Robert Hooke:** Restoration England's physicist, chemist, and mathematician Called England's Leonardo Da Vinci. In *Attempt to Prove the Motion of the Earth* (1674), he offered a theory of planetary motion based on the correct principle that the Earth moves in an ellipse around the Sun. Known for the law of stress and strain named for him. In its simplest form, it states that, provided the elastic limit is not exceeded, the deformation of a material is proportional to the force applied to it.

The truth is, the Science of Nature has already too long made only a work of the brain and fancy. It is now high time that it should return to the plainness and soundness of observations on material and obvious things.

1811 **William Makepeace Thackeray:** India-born English novelist and satirist. First came to public attention with *The Yellowplush Papers*, *A Shabby Genteel Story* and *The Paris Sketch Book*. From 1842 to 1851 he was on the staff of *Punch*. Most of his major novels were published as monthly serials with illustrations by the author. Novels: *Vanity Fair*, *The Memories of Barry Lyndon* and *The Rose and the Ring*.

Women like not only to conquer, but to be conquered.

1887 **Vidkun Quisling:** Norwegian politician and fascist. Collaborated with Nazis when German invaded Norway in 1940. Appointed Führer of Norway. The Hird was a Norwegian military unit of "storm troopers" who handled security for Quisling's government. His name has come to be used to describe a traitor. Arrested in 1945, he was so despised; Norway broke with its centuries-old policy against capital punishment and executed him on October 23, 1945.

In the new order we are all servants of society, and the Hird is the guarantee that the thesis of common good before individual interests is put into practice.

1902 **Jessamyn West:** American writer. A Quaker, best known for *The Friendly Persuasion*, which was made into a movie starring Gary Cooper and Dorothy McGuire. It was nominated for an Academy Award for "best picture." Other Works included: *Except for Me and Thee*, the sequel to *Friendly Persuasion*, *A Mirror for the Sky* and *Double Discovery*.

A taste for irony has kept more hearts from breaking than a sense of humor for it takes irony to appreciate the joke whish is on oneself.

1906 **S.I. (Samuel Ichiye) Hayakawa:** American psychologist, semanticist and politician. Wrote the lauded *Language in Thought and Action.* President of San Francisco State College during the turbulent anti-war protest years (1968–73). Defeated incumbent Democratic U.S. Senator John V. Tunney in 1977. His term was undistinguished, due to worsening senility. Often fell asleep at his desk on the Senate floor, earned him the nickname "Sleeping Sam."

In a very real sense, people who have read good literature have lived more that people who cannot or will not read.

1906 **Clifford Odets:** American playwright. Outstanding proletarian dramatist, whose works are marked by a strong social conscience, and derive from the conditions of the Great Depression. One of the founders of the Group Theatre. Plays: *Waiting for Lefty, Golden Boy* and *The Country Girl.* Film scripts include *The General Died at Dawn, None but the Lonely Heart* (which he directed) and *The Big Knife.*

Life shouldn't be printed on dollar bills.

1913 **[Richard] "Red" Skelton:** American comedian and actor. As a child of 10 he toured with a medicine show. Later became very popular on radio, television and in movies. Noted for his broad humor and warm personality. Created characters "The Mean Widdle Kid," "Clem Kadiddlehopper," "Deadeye" and "Freddie the Freeloader."

I have a sixth sense, not the other five. If I wasn't making money they'd put me away.

1918 **Nelson Mandela:** South African political Leader of African National Congress. Sentenced to life imprisonment (1964), for conspiracy to overthrow South African government. An international cause célèbre. Released from prison by President F.W. De Klerk in 1990. Mandela and De Klerk shared the 1993 Nobel Peace Prize for their efforts to end apartheid and bring about the transition to nonracial democracy. First black president of South Africa.

I learned that courage was not the absence of fear, but the triumph over it. The brave man is not he who does not feel afraid, but he who conquers that fear.

1921 **John Glenn, Jr.:** U.S. astronaut and politician. Flew 59 missions as a Marine Corps pilot in World War II and 90 more in the Korean War. Selected as a member of the Mercury project's space flight training. In 1962 aboard Friendship 7, first man to orbit the Earth. U.S. Democratic senator from Ohio (1975–99). At 77 made his second spaceflight aboard space shuttle Discovery, the oldest person to go into space.

We have an infinite amount to learn both from nature and from each other.

1933 **Yevgeny Aleksandrovich Yevtushenko:** Russian poet. Descendant of Ukrainians exiled to Siberia. Much of his poetry expressed the impatience of the younger Soviet generation with the society of Stalin. He had some trouble with Soviet officials, especially with the publication of "Babi Yar," which charged the Soviet Union with anti-Semitism.

Why is it that right-wing bastards always stand shoulder to shoulder in solidarity, while liberals fall out among themselves?

1937 **Hunter S. Thompson:** American journalist and author. In 1965, infiltrated the Hell's Angels motorcycle gang and published his experiences. Created a writing genre known as "gonzo journalism." His extremely subjective and often wildly funny writings gained a large underground following. Other Works: *Fear and Loathing in Las Vegas* and *The Great Shark Hunt.* Died from a self-inflicted gunshot wound.

I wouldn't recommend sex, drugs or insanity for everyone, but they've always worked for me.

1950 Sir **Richard Branson:** English entrepreneur. Best known for Virgin group of business organizations: Virgin Records, Virgin Atlantic Airlines, Virgin Mobile, Virgin Express, Virgin Healthcare Foundation and Virgin Galactic, meant to take paying passengers into suborbital space. The name "Virgin" was chosen when a female friend who helped set it us commented "We're all virgins at business.

Business opportunities are like buses, there's always another one coming.

OTHERS: 1013 Crippled monk/scientist **Hermannus Contractus**, 1504 Swiss religious reformer **Heinrich Bullinger**, 1720 English ornithologist **Gilbert White**, 1850 U.S. poet **Rose Hartwick Thorpe**, 1853 Dutch physicist **Hendrik Lorentz**, 1865 English playwright **Laurence Housman**, 1890 U.S. corporate president **Charles E. Wilson**, 1908 Mexican actress **Lupe Velez**, 1909 President of Afghanistan **Mohammed Daoud Khan**, 1911 Canadian actor **Hume Cronyn**, 1929 U.S. figure skater **Dick Button**, 1940 Baseball player/manager **Joe Torre**, 1941 U.S. singer **Martha Reeves**, 1947 U.S. entrepreneur/politician **Steve Forbes**

July 19

1637 **Thomas Ken:** English clergyman Prebendary of Winchester cathedral and royal chaplain to Charles II. Appointed Bishop of Bath and Wells. When he refused to publish the Declaration of Indulgence issued by James II in his diocese, he was imprisoned, tried for sedition, and acquitted. After the Revolution of 1688, refused to swear allegiance to William of Orange and stripped of his bishopric.

Redeem thy misspent time that's past. And live this day as if thy last.

1799 **Sophie Rostopchine Segur:** Russian-born French writer of famous books for children based on stories she told her children and grandchildren. Her central character was "Sophie," a girl with many trials and tribulations.

God keeps the wicked to give them time to repent.

1834 **Edgar Degas:** French painter. Associated with the Impressionists. Known for his mastery of motion. His most famous medium was pastels. Portrayed ballet dancers at work, milliners, laundresses, and women at their toilette. Derived much of his intimacy of presentation from his familiarity with Japanese prints, introduced in France around 1860.

Art is not what you see, but what you make others see.

1860 **Lizzie Borden:** Accused American murderess. On August 4, 1892, she was charged with murdering her father and stepmother with an axe in their Fall River, Massachusetts home. Her trial was eagerly followed all over the country. Acquitted, the crime was never solved. Subject of numerous ditties that failed to accept the verdict. Most famous of these is the anonymous quatrain. "Lizzie Borden took an axe/ And gave her mother forty whacks/ When she saw what she had done/ She gave her father forty-one."

Oh, Mrs. Churchill, do come over, someone has killed father.

1865 **Charles Horace Mayo:** Gifted American surgeon. Originated modern procedures in goiter surgery, neurosurgery and orthopedic surgery. With brother William James Mayo co-founded the Mayo Clinic Foundation for Medical Education and Research (1915). Currently the clinic employs about 500 physicians who care for more than 200,000 patients each year.

The definition of a specialist as one who knows "more and more about less and less" is good and true.

1896 **A.J. [Archibald Joseph] Cronin:** Scottish-born physician and author of best-selling novels *Hatter's Castle*, *The Stars Look Down*, *The Citadel* and *The Keys of the Kingdom*. *Dr. Findlay's Casebook*, a popular and long-running British TV series, was based on several of his books.

The virtue of all achievement is victory over oneself.

1898 **Herbert Marcuse:** German-born American political philosopher and sociologist. Author of *Eros and Civilization* and *One-Dimensional Man*. Argued that mass materialism stifles all diversity and saw American society as one that systematically impeded freedom. Believed that students and minority groups would be the most successful agents of change. Student radicals espoused many of his views, although it appeared they did not completely understand them.

Obscenity is a moral concept in the verbal arsenal of the establishment, which abuses the term by applying it, not to expressions of its own morality but to those of another.

1917 **William Scranton:** American politician. Republican governor of Pennsylvania (1963–67) Served as U.S. Ambassador to the United Nations (1976–77). During 1964, there was a move to "Draft Scranton" by Republicans who were wary of ultraconservative Barry Goldwater. After leaving politics he served on the boards of several high-profile American corporations.

The value of government to the people it serves is in direct relationship to the interest citizens themselves display in the affairs of state.

1921 **Rosalyn S. Yalow:** American nuclear physicist, who turned to nuclear medicine. Developed the radioimmunoassay method to detect and measure peptide hormones, such as insulin, in the blood, which has led to better control of digoxin in heart disease and diagnosis of neural diseases such as spina bifida in the fetus. Recipient of the Nobel Prize in Physiology or Medicine in 1977.

The excitement of learning separates youth from old age. As long as you're learning you're not old.

1922 **George McGovern:** U.S. politician and historian from South Dakota. Elected to the U.S. House of Representatives (1957–61) and Senate (1963–81). As Democratic candidate for president in 1972 campaigned on an immediate end of the war in Vietnam and a broad program of social reform. Lost by a wide margin to Richard Nixon. Failed to win reelection to the Senate and returned to teaching.

The highest patriotism is not a blind acceptance of official policy, but a love of one's country deep enough to call her to a higher plain.

1927 **Jan Myrdal:** Swedish author, political writer and wine columnist. Known for "reports," travel notes from Asian countries, including *Report from a Chinese Village*. His autobiographical works detailing his childhood and his conflicts with his authoritarian parents, sociologists and economists Alva Myrdal and Gunnar Myrdal, both who were Nobel Prize recipients, he for economics, she for peace.

There is a third dimension in traveling, the longing for what is beyond.

1946 **Ilie Nastase:** Romanian tennis player. First player from an Iron Curtain country to win the U.S. Open (1972). Twice number one in the world (1972, 1973). Won French Open (1973). Noted for his temper, earning him the nickname "Nasty Nastase."

As long as I can get angry then I play well. If I play well I can beat anyone. I am happy because I am getting angry.

OTHERS: 1670 English composer **Richard Leveridge**, 1688 Italian missionary **Giuseppe Castiglione**, 1789 English painter **John Martin**, 1814 U.S. firearms inventor **Samuel Colt**, 1817 U.S. Army Nurse **Mary Ann Bickerdyke**, 1883 Austrian animator **Max Fleischer**, 1906 Norwegian composer **Klaus Egge**, 1920 U.S. violinist **Robert Mann**, 1929 U.S.S.R. gymnast **Sofia Muratova**, 1934 Portuguese Prime Minister **Francisco Sá Carneiro**, 1938 Indian astrophysicist **Jayant Narlikar**, 1941 Russian dancer **Natalya Bessmertnova**, 1941 U.S. singer **Vikki Carr**, 1947 English guitarist **Brian May**, 1963 Hungarian swimmer **Sandor Wladar**

July 20

1304 **Francesco Petrarch:** Italian clergyman, poet and scholar. Primary interest was Latin and Greek literature. Founder of Renaissance Humanism. His beloved was Laura, the subject of his collection of lyrics called "Rime" (verses) or "Canzoniere" (song book). Possibly she was Laure de Noves, married to Hugo de Sade. She inspired him with a passion famous for its constancy and purity. Had a major influence on many subsequent writers, notably Chaucer.

Five enemies of peace inhabit with us: avarice, ambition, envy, anger, and pride; if these were to be banished, we should infallibly enjoy perpetual peace.

1591 **Anne Hutchinson**, née **Marbury:** English-born American colonial religious liberal. Preached theological ideas for which she was tried for heresy and sedition. Banished from the Massachusetts Bay Colony she and some friends acquired territory for the Narragansett Indians of Rhode Island, where they set up a democracy. Resettled in what is now Pelham Bay in New York State. She and most of her family were killed in an Indian massacre. Her curse on her accusers in the Bay State.

Take heed how you proceed against me; for I know that for this you go about to do to me, God will ruin you and your posterity and this whole state.

1873 **Alberto Santos-Dumont:** Brazilian-born aviation pioneer. Billed himself as the first "sportsman of the air." Designed, built and flew a variety of air balloons before developing the first practical dirigible airship. Made the first fully public flight of an airplane in Paris in October of 1906, two years before the Wright brothers' first successful public flight. Brazilians acclaim Santos-Dumont as the "Father of Aviation."

The balloon seems to stand still in the air while the earth flies past underneath.

1880 Count **Hermann Keyserling:** "The wandering philosopher." Estonian-born German social philosopher and mystic. Ideas centered on the theme of spiritual regeneration, conditioned by his contact with many cultures, during his far-flung travels. Books: *The Travel Diary of a Philosopher* and *Creative Understanding*.

The greatest American superstition is a belief in facts.

1890 **George II, King of Greece:** (1922–24 and 1935–47). Followed his father King Constantine I into exile in 1917, and returned with him in 1920. Succeeded to the throne upon his father's abdication. In 1923, he compiled with a request by the government to leave the country while the National Assembly considered the question of the future form of government. Officially deposed when a republic was proclaimed in 1924, but a military coup in 1935 restored him to the throne. Fled to Great Britain after the Nazi invasion of Greece. Died in 1947 and was succeeded by his brother Paul.

The most important tool for a King of Greece is a suitcase.

1895 **Laszlo Moholy-Nagy:** Hungarian-born American painter, photographer and art teacher. Produced "photograms," that is, non-representative photographic images made directly without a camera. Leading avant-garde artist in the New Photographers movement in Europe. Work included film-making and typography integrated with photographic illustration. Headed the new Bauhaus School in Chicago.

The number of ways for a person to occupy time is probably more unlimited than the number of ways in which matter occupies space.

1900 **Oren Arnold:** American writer of heroic tales of the west. Wrote of Superstition Mountain and the legend of the Spanish gold discovered by a Dutch miner. Despite the efforts of many to locate it, it remains lost. Also wrote biographies of Mexican Revolutionary Pancho Villa and Native American activist Carlos Montezuma. Books: *Ghost Gold, Before the Alamo* and *Sourcebook of Family Humor*.

Don't expect too much of Christmas Day. You can't crowd into it any arrears of unselfishness and kindliness that may have accrued during the past twelve months.

1919 Sir **Edmund Hillary:** New Zealand mountain climber and Antarctic explorer. With Sherpa Tenzing Norgay, the first to reach the summit of the highest (29,028 feet) mountain in the world, Mt. Everest (May 29, 1953). In 1958 he participated in the first crossing of Antarctica by vehicle.

Nobody climbs mountains for scientific reasons. Science is used to raise money for the expeditions, but you really climb for the hell of it.

1920 **Elliot Richardson:** American lawyer and politician. Member of the cabinet of President Nixon, who managed to avoid being tainted by the Watergate Scandal. Served as Secretary of the Department of Health, Education and Welfare (1970–73) and after the resignation of John Mitchell appointed Secretary of Defense. Also served in the Gerald Ford administration.

There is an increasingly persuasive sense not only of failure, but of futility. The legislative process has become a cruel shell game and the service system has become a bureaucratic maze, inefficient, incomprehensible, and inaccessible.

1925 **Frantz Fanon:** French West Indian psychoanalyst and social philosopher. Edited the newspaper the *National Liberation Front*. In his widely read book *The Wretched of the Earth*, he urged colonized peoples to purge themselves of their degradation by violence. Died of leukemia at age 36.

Fervor is the weapon of choice of the impotent.

1939 **Judy Chicago:** Originally, **Cohen** changed for the place of her birth. American multimedia artist. Developed the concepts of "vaginal iconography" and "central core" imagery. Notable work is *The Dinner Party*, consisting of a triangular table with place settings for 39 important women represented by ceramic plates with feminine imagery. The table runners are embellished with embroidery styles typical of their eras.

Because we are denied knowledge of our history, we are deprived of standing upon other's shoulders and building upon each other's hard earned accomplishments. Instead we are condemned to repeat what others have done before us and thus we continually reinvent the wheel. The goal of The Dinner Party is to break that cycle.

1946 **Carlos Santana:** Mexican-born American Grammy-winning musician and Latin-rock guitarist. Original member of The Santana Blues Band, which featured a blend of salsa, rock, blues, and jazz. Hits: "Soul Sacrifice," "Black Magic Woman," and "No One to Depend On." Made a major comeback at the end of the millennium with album *Supernatural*, containing the hit singles "Smooth" and "Maria Maria."

First of all, the music that people call Latin or Spanish is really African. So Black people need to get credit for that.

OTHERS: 1659 French painter **Hyacinthe Rigaud**, 1661 French founder of New Orleans **Pierre Le Moyne d'Iberville**, 1804 English anatomist/zoologist **Richard Owen**, 1847 German artist **Max Liebermann**, 1850 U.S. merchant **John Graves Shedd**, 1890 Screen femme fatale **Theda Bara**, 1902 Irish composer **Jimmy Kennedy**, 1924 American writer **Thomas Berger**, 1929 U.S. businessman **Mike Ilitch**, 1933 U.S. publisher **Nelson Doubleday**, 1933 U.S. author **Cormac McCarthy**, 1936 U.S. Senator **Barbara Mikulski**, 1938 British actress **Diana Rigg**, 1938 U.S. actress **Natalie Wood**, 1945 U.S. singer/songwriter **Kim Carnes**

July 21

1515 Saint **Philip Neri:** Florence-born churchman. Spent his young manhood in works of charity and instruction. Became a priest in 1551. Gathered disciples to what became the Congregation of the Oratory. The community was finally established at Vallicella, where he built the church Chies Nuova on the site of Santa Marian.

He who wishes to be perfectly obeyed should give few orders.

1664 **Matthew Prior:** English poet and diplomat. Chiefly known for his epigrams, satires and society verse. Works: "A Better Answer (to Chloe Jealous)," "A Letter to the Lady Margaret Cavendish When a Child," and "The Secretary." Took part in European treaty negotiations, including the Treaty of Ryswick and the Peace of Utrecht, which became known as "Matt's Peace."

Who walks the fastest, but walks astray, is only furthest from his way.

1885 **Frances Parkinson Keyes:** American novelist. Best-known work is a murder mystery set in New Orleans a few weeks before Mardi Gras, called *Dinner at Antoine's*. Others: *Silver Seas and Golden Cities*, *Honor Bright*, *The Great Tradition*, *Fielding's Folly*, and *The Rose and the Lily*.

Women were cats, all of them, unless they were fools, and there was no way of getting even with them, ever, except by walking off with the men they wanted.

1899 **Hart Crane:** American poet. Among the first to attempt to express the spirit of a mechanized 20th century in poetry. Known for unique, creative and imaginative talent. First published poetry in a number of little magazines. First collection, *White Buildings* appeared in 1926, notable for several poems, especially "For the Marriage of Faustus and Helen." Despondency caused him to jump to his death from a ship.

There are no stars to-night/ But those of memory/ Yet how much room for memory there is/ In the loose girdle of soft rain.

1899 **Ernest Hemingway:** Macho American novelist and short-story writer. Went to Europe as an ambulance driver in World War I and was seriously wounded at age 18. Later a correspondent for the *Toronto Star* in Paris, where he met Ezra Pound and Gertrude Stein, whose writing greatly influenced his. Awarded a Nobel Prize for Literature (1954). Committed suicide (1961). Works: *The Sun Also Rises*, *A Farewell to Arms*, *For Whom the Bell Tolls* and *The Old Man and the Sea* for which he was awarded a Pulitzer Prize.

There is nothing to writing. All you have to do is sit down at a typewriter and bleed.

1911 **Marshall McLuhan:** Canadian cultural critic and communication theorist. Established the Center for Culture and Technology at the University of Toronto to research the cultural and psychological consequences of mass media and technology. Author of *The Mechanical Bride*, *The Gutenberg Galaxy*, *Understanding Media* and his most influential work *The Medium Is the Message*.

A point of view can be a dangerous luxury when substituted for insight and understanding.

1920 **Isaac Stern:** Outstanding Russian-born American violinist. Carnegie Hall debut was a triumph. Honors include: Officer of the Légion d'honneur of France, Kennedy Center Honors Award, and Wolf Prize of Israel. In 1960 he formed a famous trio with pianist Eugene Istomin and cellist Leonard Rose. Energetic worker for the cause of human rights. Instrumental in saving Carnegie Hall from demolition and helped establish the National Endowment for the Arts.

I have a responsibility to pass on to the next generation what I learned from my teachers, it keeps me young and reminds me where I came from. Teaching young artists is like giving water to a flower.

1923 **Rudolph A. Marcus:** Canadian chemist. Employed at the Polytechnic Institute of Brooklyn, the University of Illinois and Caltech. His work, which has clarified fundamental phenomena such as photosynthesis, cell metabolism, and simple corrosion, earned him a Nobel Prize for Chemistry in 1992.

Being exposed to theory, stimulated by a basic love of concepts and mathematics, was a marvelous experience.

1934 **Jonathan Miller:** British physician, writer, actor and director. Research fellow, history of medicine, University College. Appeared in the play *Beyond the Fringe*, which he co-authored. Directed films, television and plays. Directed celebrated opera productions and wrote the BBC medical series *The Body in Question* and *States of Mind*.

Humor is vague, runaway stuff that hisses around the fissures and crevices of the mind, like some sort of loose physic gas.

1944 **Buchi Emecheta:** Nigerian novelist. Orphaned in early childhood, she was educated at a missionary school. Married at 17, went to London with her husband. At age 22, she left him and earned a degree in sociology, while raising five children and writing. Novels: *In the Dutch*, *Second Class Citizen*, *The Slave Girl* and *The Rape of Shavi*. Her play *A Kind of Marriage* was produced on BBC television.

Black women all over the world should re-unite and re-examine the way history has portrayed us.

1944 **Paul Wellstone:** American politician and two-term Senator from Minnesota. Leading spokesman for the progressive wing of the Democratic Party. Known for his work for peace, the environment, labor, health care and support for victims of domestic violence. Called "the conscience of the Senate." Only senator to vote against authorization for the war in Iraq. Killed at age 58 with seven others including his wife and one of his three children in a plane crash into a dense northern Minnesota forest.

The people of this country, not special interest big money, should be the source of all political power.

1948 **Garry Trudeau:** American cartoonist. At Yale University created the daily comic strip *Doonesbury*. It is now syndicated in nearly 1400 newspapers worldwide. First comic strip artist to win a Pulitzer Prize for Editorial Cartooning (1975). Received an Oscar in the category for Animated Short Film, for *The Doonesbury Special*. Plays include the 1988 HBO miniseries "Tanner '88," directed by Robert Altman. Married journalist Jane Pauley in 1980.

Well, it's a humor strip. So my first responsibility has always been to entertain the reader... But if, in addition, I can help move readers to thought and judgment about issues that concern me, so much the better.

1952 **Robin Williams:** Multi-talented American comedian and actor. First gained attention for stand-up routines in San Francisco clubs. Starred in the TV series "Mork and Mindy." Has an uncanny improvisational skill. First film roles were not well-received, but his Academy-Award nominated performance in *Good Morning, Vietnam*, established him as an important film personality. Received a second nominator for the unorthodox teacher in *Dead Poets Society* and won an Oscar in 1997 for Best Supporting Actor in *Good Will Hunting*. Voice of the genie in the animated hit *Aladdin*.

You're only given a little spark of madness. You mustn't lose it.

OTHERS: 1620 French astronomer **Jean Picard**, 1710 German physician **Paul Möhring**, 1816 German news service founder **Paul Julius von Reuter**, 1903 U.S. financier **Roy Neuberger**, 1922 U.S. singer **Kay Starr**, 1924 U.S. comic actor **Don Knotts**, 1926 Canadian film director **Norman Jewison**, 1930 American golfer **Gene Littler**, 1933 U.S. author **John Gardner**, 1938 U.S. Attorney General **Janet Reno**, 1939 U.S. director of National Intelligence **John Negroponte**, 1945 English writer **Wendy Cope**, 1946 U.S. lawyer/judge **Kenneth Starr**, 1948 English singer **Cat Stevens**, 1949 U.S.S.R. pairs figure skater **Ludmila Smirnova**

July 22

1822 **Gregor Mendel:** Austrian botanist and Augustinian monk. Discovered the basic statistical laws of heredity. His famous work was done on the edible pea, in which he studied seven characteristics, such as stem height and flower color. The plants were self-pollinated and the seeds of their off-spring studied. His research was largely ignored until 16 years after his death.

My scientific studies have afforded me great gratification; and I am convinced that it will not be long before the whole world acknowledges the results of my work.

1844 **William Archibald Spooner:** English Anglican priest and scholar. Source of the word, "spoonerism," a linguistic flip-flop of words made by accidentally transposing letters or syllables, producing rhyming substitutes that still make some sense. For instance: "a half formed wish" becomes "a half-wormed fish." Spooner's toast to Queen Victoria came out as: Three cheers for our queer old dean." Perhaps his most famous spoonerism occurred when he scolded a student:

Sir, you have tasted two whole worms; you have hissed all my mystery lectures and been caught fighting a liar in the quad, you will leave Oxford by the next town drain.

1849 **Emma Lazarus:** American poet and essayist. Indignant because of Russian pogroms, she went about defending and glorifying the Jewish people Poetry: *Admetus and Other Poems* and *Songs of a Semite*, including her best poem "Dance to Death," Her sonnet, "The New Colossus" is inscribed on the pedestal of the Statue of Liberty.

Give me your tired, your poor,/ Your huddled masses yearning to breathe free,/ The wretched refuse of your teeming shore,/ Send these the homeless, tempest-tossed, to me:/ I lift my lamp beside the golden door.

1882 **Edward Hopper:** American painter of precise representations, not only of a scene, but also of the mood. Solitary detachment is suggested by sharp, sometimes harsh light. His urban scenes, such as *Nighthawks*, strongly influenced the Pop and New Realist painters of the 1960s and 70s.

My aim in painting has always been the most exact transcription possible of my most intimate impression of nature.

1890 **Rose Kennedy:** American public figure, philanthropist, mental health activist. Daughter of Boston political boss John F. Fitzgerald. Wife of multimillionaire businessman Joseph P. Kennedy. Mother of nine children, including President John F. Kennedy and Senators Bobby and Teddy Kennedy.

Life isn't a matter of milestones but of moments.

1891 **Ely Culbertson:** American bridge expert. Inventor and popularizer of contract bridge. Developed the first successful bidding system. Author of *Contract Bridge Complete*. Devoted his later years to working for world peace. Devised a peace plan in 1940 that included ideas later adopted by the U.N.

A deck of cards is built like the purest of hierarchies, with every card a master to those below it, a lackey to those above it.

1893 **Karl Menninger:** American physician and pioneer in psychiatric treatment. Cofounder, with his father Charles Frederick Menninger, of the Menninger Diagnostic Clinic in 1920. With his brother William, established the Menninger Sanitarium and Psychopathic Hospital, a major center for the study and treatment of mental health problems. Formed the Menninger Foundation followed by the Menninger School of Psychiatry, which Karl directed.

What's done to children, they will do to society.

1898 **Stephen Vincent Benét:** American poet, short-story writer and novelist. Works were marked by American themes. Collections of verse: *Heavens and Earth*, *The Ballad of William Sycamore* and *Tiger Joy*. Most famous poem, "John Brown's Body," won a Pulitzer Prize (1929). Unfinished American epic "Western Stars" earned a posthumous Pulitzer (1944). Brother of American poet and critic William Rose Benét.

Life is not lost by dying; life is lost minute by minute, day by dragging day, in all the thousand small uncaring ways.

1898 **Alexander Calder:** American painter and sculptor. Known for his airily exuberant *mobiles*, the name Marcel Duchamp gave to Calder's sculptures of wire and brightly painted metal cutouts. Later he went on to *stabiles*, large, abstract immobile sculptures for public buildings, parks and gardens. Also composed portraits done in wire and constructed a miniature circus.

To an engineer, good enough means perfect. With an artist, there is no such thing as perfect.

1900 **Edward Dahlberg:** American critic, novelist, essayist and poet. Traveled around the U.S. as a hobo, which provided material for his first two novels *Bottom Dogs* and *From Flushing to Calvary*, hailed as prime examples of proletarian literature. Books of criticism attacked contemporary culture and dissented from prevailing literary assessments of authors Ernest Hemingway, William Faulkner and F. Scott Fitzgerald.

Every decision you make is a mistake.

1908 **Amy Vanderbilt:** American journalist. Etiquette expert wrote a syndicated newspaper column and regular revisions of her 1952 *Amy Vanderbilt's Complete Book of Etiquette*. Published her famous book after five years of research. Hosted two TV programs, "It's in Good Taste" and "The Right Thing to Do." Served as a consultant for various agencies and organizations, including the U.S. Department of State.

Good manners have much to do with the emotions. To make them ring true, one must feel them, not merely exhibit them.

1923 **Robert Dole:** U.S. politician. Republican Senator from Kansas. Senate minority leader (1987–94). Majority leader (1985–87 and 1995–96). One of the few Republicans who could bridge the gap between the moderate and conservative wings of the party. Republican nominee for Vice-President in 1976 on a ticket headed by Gerald Ford and Presidential candidate in 1996, defeated by incumbent Bill Clinton. Served with the U.S. Army in Northern Italy. Hit by Nazi machine gun fire, resulting in a paralyzed right arm.

History buffs probably noted the reunion at a Washington party a few weeks ago of three ex-presidents: Carter, Ford and Nixon — See No Evil, Hear No Evil and Evil.

OTHERS: 1510 Duke of Florence **Alessandro de' Medici**, 1559 Italian monk **Lawrence of Brindisi**, 1711 Russian physicist **Georg Wilhelm Richmann**, 1784 German mathematician **Friedrich Bessel**, 1887 German physicist **Gustav Hertz**, 1893 English director **James Whale**, 1916 French boxer **Marcel Cerdan**, 1924 U.S. singer **Margaret Whiting**, 1932 Dominican fashion designer **Oscar De La Renta**, 1936 U.S. author **Tom Robbins**, 1939 English actor **Terence Stamp**, 1940 Canadian-born *Jeopardy* host **Alex Trebeck**, 1941 U.S. musician **George Clinton**, 1941 Canadian jockey **Ron Turcotte**, 1944 Baseball pitcher **Sparky Lyle**

July 23

1823 **Coventry [Kersey Dighton] Patmore:** English poet and assistant librarian at the British Museum. Associated with the Pre-Raphaelite brotherhood. Best known works: "The Angel in the House," a long poetic celebration of married life, and mystical and religious themes as in "The Unknown Eros."

To him that waits all things reveal themselves, provided that he has the courage not to deny, in the darkness, what he has seen in the light.

1834 **James Gibbons:** American religious leader. Archbishop of Baltimore. Largely responsible for the growth pt the Roman Catholic Church in the U.S. In 1886, appointed the country's second cardinal. Held that the Constitution was man's greatest governmental achievement. Founder and first chancellor of Catholic University. Author of many books including *The Faith of Our Fathers* and *Our Christian Heritage*.

There are no office hours for leaders.

1874 **"Sunny Jim" Fitzsimmons:** American thoroughbred racehorse trainer. Began as a stable-boy, then a none-too-successful stint as a jockey and when he became too heavy for that he turned to training. Over a period of some seventy years, his steeds won over 2,275 races, including two Triple Crown winners, Gallant Fox in 1930 and Omaha in 1935. Speaking of champion horses:

It's what you can't see that matters.

1886 **Salvador de Madariaga y Rojo:** Spanish writer, diplomat and historian. Served as ambassador to the U.S. and France, and was Spain's permanent delegate to the League of Nations (1931–36). Moved to England when the Spanish Civil War broke out and did not return to Spain until the death of Francisco Franco. Works: *Englishmen, Frenchmen, Spaniards, Spain*, and *The Rise and Fall of the Spanish American Empire.*

The Anglo-Saxon conscience does not prevent the Anglo-Saxon from sinning; it merely prevents him from enjoying his sin.

1888 **Raymond Chandler:** American detective story writer. Although holding the deepest respect for "civilized culture," he made his mark writing about the seamy low-life of California. Master of hard-boiled fiction. Created brash but honorable private eye Philip Marlowe. Books: *The Big Sleep, Farewell, My Lovely, The Lady in the Lake*, and *The Long Goodbye.*

Down these mean streets a man must go who is not himself mean; who is neither tarnished nor afraid.

1891 **Haile Selassie I:** Descendent of the Queen of Sheba. Led the 1916 revolution and became regent and heir to the throne. As Emperor of Ethiopia, westernized his country's institutions. First ruler to address both the League of Nations and the United Nations. Pleas for help to the League against the invasion of Mussolini's troops into Abyssinia were ignored. His rule was restored in 1941 when the English liberated his country. Deposed in 1974 in favor of the crown prince when a disastrous famine led to economic chaos, industrial strikes, and mutinies in the armed forces.

Throughout history, it has been the inaction of those who could have acted; the indifference of those who should have known better; the silence of the voice of justice when it mattered most; that has made it possible for evil to triumph.

1906 **Marston Bates:** American zoologist and author. Studies of mosquitoes in the 1930s and 40s greatly contributed to the understanding of the epidemiology of yellow fever in northern South America. Insisted that the biosphere must be respected in law and government, that people were entitled to clean, beautiful surroundings, and that the protection of the environment was non-negotiable. Wrote *The Prevalence of People, Man in Nature* and *The Nature of Natural History.*

Research is the process of going up alleys to see if they are blind.

1907 **Elspeth Josceline Grant Huxley:** Kenyan-born English writer, journalist, broadcaster, colonial officer and an environmental and government advisor. Written many novels and essays on her native land and its problems, including: *Lord Delamare and the Making of Kenya* and *The Flame Trees of Thika.* Early in her life she was an advocate of colonialism, but later called for the independence of African countries.

Only man is not content to leave things as they are but must always be changing them, and when he has done so, is seldom satisfied with the result.

1913 **Michael Foot:** British politician. With two other journalists, Frank Owen and Peter Howard, he published the best seller, *Guilty Men*, which attacked the appeasement policy of Neville Chamberlain. Won a seat in parliament in 1945 and when Labor lost the general election in 1979, Foot was elected Leader of the Labor Party (1980). Wrote highly regarded biographies and worked for nuclear disarmament.

Men of power have no time to read; yet the men who do not read are unfit for power.

1947 **Don Imus:** American radio personality and "shock jock." Best known for his sarcasm and harsh language directed towards his guests on his popular radio show, *Imus in the Morning.* Long career with New York's WNBC was interrupted for two years in 1977 so that he could deal with his cocaine and vodka habits and his unprofessionalism. Created some remarkable characters, none more so than radio evangelist Billy Sol Hargus of the "First Church of the Gooey Death and Discount House of Worship." Established The Imus Ranch in Santa Fe, New Mexico, a charitable organization that operates for children with cancer.

My goal is to goad people into saying something that ruins their life.

1967 **Philip Seymour Hoffman:** American film and stage actor. Dependable supporting actor who inhabits his roles playing diverse and idiosyncratic characters. First gained notice in *Scent of a Woman*, followed by impressive appearances in *Boogie Nights, The Big Lebowski, Magnolia, The Talented Mr. Ripley* and *Almost Famous.* Capped his career thus far with his Oscar winning 2005 appearance as writer Truman Capote in the acclaimed film *Capote.*

The only true currency in this bankrupt world is what you share with someone else when you're uncool.

1973 **Monica Lewinsky:** White House intern, thrust into the public limelight for her affair with President Clinton, which led to his impeachment for perjury and obstruction of justice. Her involvement in the sexual relationship became known when her confidante Linda Tripp turned over secret recordings of her phone conversations with Monica to Independent Counsel Kenneth Starr. Lewinsky became the center of intense media attention and the butt of many jokes. On Larry King Life, discussing weight loss through the Jenny Craig Program:

I've learned not to put things in my mouth that are bad for me.

OTHERS: 1626 Ottoman Jewish religious leader **Sabbatai Zevi**, 1705 English topographer **Francis Blomefield**, 1777 German painter **Philipp Otto Rugge**, 1816 U.S. tragic actress **Charlotte Coleman**, 1888 Serbian fascist **Milan Stoyadinovich**, 1898 American economist **Jacob Marschak**, 1899 President of Germany **Gustav Heinemann**, 1918 Baseball player **Pee Wee Reese**, 1936 Punjabi revolutionary **Shiv Kumar Batalvi**, 1936 baseball pitcher **Don Drysdale**, 1936 U.S. Supreme Court Justice **Anthony Kennedy**, 1965

U.S. guitarist **Slash**, 1971 U.S. singer/fiddler **Alison Krauss**, 1989 English actor **Daniel Radcliffe**

July 24

1660 **Charles Talbot, 1st Duke of Shrewsbury:** One of the seven signatories of the letter inviting William, the Prince of Orange to assume the English throne. Talbot contributed funds to defray the expenses of the projected invasion and landed with William in England from Holland in November 1688. Held various administrative positions, including Secretary of State. Accused of treason, he retired into private life, living abroad, mostly in Rome. Expressed his abhorrence of public life, declaring that if he had a son he

... would sooner bind him to a cobbler than a courtier and a hangman than a statesman.

1725 **John Newton:** English clergyman and composer. Pressed into service aboard the HMS Harwich, he became involved in the slave trade. Converted to Christianity during a storm at sea. After much soul-searching recognized the horrors of slavery and the hypocrisy of his participation as a Christian. Returned to England to become a priest. Made curate at Olney, Buckinghamshire. Produced the *Olney Hymns*, the most famous of which was "Amazing Grace." In 1982 he was inducted into the Gospel Music Hall of Fame.

Many have puzzled themselves about the origin of evil. I am content to observe that there is evil, and that there is a way to escape from it, and with this I begin and end.

1783 **Simón Bolívar:** "The Liberator." Venezuela-born South American statesman and soldier. Freed Latin American people from the oppressive Spanish rule, leading to the independence of Columbia, Venezuela, Peru and Bolivia. When he gave up presidency, class structure returned to Latin America society. Spanish and Portuguese born were at the top, followed by the creoles, with ancestors from Europe. At the bottom of the societal pyramid were the mulatto, African American and Native American people. The politically strong seized power, denying Latin Americans a place in the republic of which Bolivar dreamed.

The Liberator of Venezuela renounces forever and declines irrevocably any office except the post of danger at the head of our soldiers in defense of the salvation of our country.

1802 **Alexandre Dumas (Père):** French novelist and dramatist. Wrote nearly 300 volumes. Became famous at age 27 for his play *Henry III*. Other plays *Napoleon Bonaparte* and *Antony*. It became his intention to present the history of France in novels. Author of *The Count of Monte Cristo*, and *The Three Musketeers*. Lived a life of gusto with many mistresses, one of whom blessed him with an illegitimate son, known as Dumas fils (son), who also wrote novels.

Repentance is not so much remorse for what we have done as the fear of the consequences.

1819 **Josiah Gilbert Holland:** U.S. editor, poet and novelist. Works, popular in his day, include: *The Bay-Path, Single and Married, Garnered Sheaves* and *The Mistress of the Manse*. Sometimes wrote using the pen-name Timothy Titcomb. Cofounder with Roswell Smith of *Scribner's Monthly*, editor (1870–81).

The most precious possession that ever comes to a man in this world is a woman's heart.

1853 **William Gillette:** American actor, playwright and stage-manager. "Aristocrat of the stage." Considered to be one of the greatest actors in U.S. history. Replaced much dialogue with physical action. Although he appeared in many other plays, including *Secret Service* and *The Admirable Crichton*, he is most famous for giving a distinctive image to Conan Doyle's famous detective Sherlock Holmes, introducing the now-familiar deerstalker cap, the cloak, the curved pipe, the magnifying glass, the violin, and the syringe. In his lifetime Gillette performed his adaptation of the Holmes story some 1,300 times.

I want to make money on Holmes quick, so as to be through with it!

1878 Baron **Edward J.M. Dunsany:** Irish author, playwright and poet. After service in the Boer War he became active in the Abbey Theatre. He used the background of fairies and other supernatural creatures to satirize human behavior. Best known works: *The Glittering Gates, A Night at an Inn* and *The Laughter of the Gods*.

Logic, like whiskey, loses its beneficial effect when taken in too large quantities.

1895 **Robert Graves:** English poet, novelist and critic. Wrote lucid, dryly humorous verse as well as exquisite love poems. His collections of poems included *Fairies and Fusiliers*, much of which dealt with the psychological effects of World War I. Historical novels: *I, Claudius, Claudius the God, The Golden Fleece* and *Homer's Daughter*. Produced the translation with commentary, *The Greek Myths*.

If I were a girl, I'd despair. The supply of good women far exceeds that of the men who deserve them.

1898 **Amelia Earhart:** American aviatrix. Worked as a military nurse in Canada during World War I and later was a social worker. First woman to make a solo flight across the Atlantic Ocean in 1932. Three years later she became the first person to fly solo from Hawaii to California. Disappeared without a trace with her navigator Fred Noonan in 1937 in the South Pacific while attempting to fly around the world. Speculation about her fate continues to this day. Some believe she was captured and executed by the Japanese.

Never interrupt someone doing what you said couldn't be done.

1916 **John D. MacDonald:** American mystery writer. Created the character Travis McGee, a Florida-based private investigator. All his McGee novels have a color in the title. *A Flash of Green, Bright Orange for the Shroud* and *Pale Gray for Guilt*. Also produced a novel of ecological concern, *Condominium*.

Integrity is not a conditional word. It doesn't

blow in the wind of change with the weather. It is your inner image of yourself, and if you look in there and see a man who won't cheat, then you know you never will.

1920 **Bella Abzug:** American feminist, lawyer and politician. As a lawyer she took on numerous union, civil-rights, and civil-liberties cases. Represented several people charged by Senator Joe McCarthy. Prominent peace campaigner, she founded Women Strike for Peace in 1961 and later the National Woman's Political Caucus. First Jewish woman elected U.S. representative (1971–77), championed the Equal Right Amendment, abortion rights, and child-care legislation and opposed the Vietnam War.

Our struggle today is not to have a female Einstein get appointed as an assistant professor. It is for a woman schlemiel to get as quickly promoted as a male schlemiel.

1932 **William Ruckelshaus:** American attorney and civil servant. First head of the Environmental Protection Agency, later Deputy U.S. Attorney General. In 1973, in what is known as the "Saturday Night Massacre," Ruckelshaus and his boss Elliot Richardson resigned from the Justice Department rather than obey President Nixon's order that they fire Watergate special prosecutor Archibald Cox, investigating official misconduct on the part of the president and his aides.

The best way to win an argument is to begin by being right.

OTHERS: 1860 Czech artist **Alfons Mucha**, 1864 German writer **Frank Wedekind**, 1867 English writer **E.F. Benson**, 1874 Christian writer **Oswald Chambers**, 1900 U.S. writer **Zelda S. Fitzgerald**, 1916 U.S. band singer **Bob Eberly**, 1939 Australian political cartoonist **Pat Oliphant**, 1936 U.S. comedienne **Ruth Buzzi**, 1947 U.S. pianist **Peter Serkin**, 1949 U.S. comedian **Michael Richards**, 1952 U.S. film director **Gus Van Sant**, 1963 UB basketball player **Karl Malone**, 1964 Baseball player **Barry Bonds**, 1968 U.S. singer/actress **Kristin Chenoweth**, 1969 U.S. actress/singer **Jennifer Lopez**

July 25

1799 **David Douglas:** Scottish botanist, plant collector and explorer. Traveled through North America as a collector for the Horticultural Society of London. Discovered many trees, shrubs and herbaceous plants that he introduced to Britain. The *Douglas fir* and the *Douglas squirrel* are named after him.

A forest of these trees is a spectacle too much for one man to see.

1844 **Thomas Eakins:** American artist. Studied in Paris and became known for his portraits and scenes of sporting events. His best-known work is "The Gross Clinic," a realistic depiction of a surgical operation. Exercised considerable influence on art through his teaching.

The big artist keeps an eye on nature and steals her tools.

1848 **Arthur James Balfour:** English statesman and philosopher. Major force in the Conservative party for 50 years. First Lord of the Treasury and Leader of the House of Commons. Prime minister during a period (1902–5), which saw the end of the Boer War. As foreign secretary under Lloyd George, he is known for the *Balfour Declaration* which promised the Zionists a home in Palestine.

It is unfortunate, considering that enthusiasm moves the world, that so few enthusiasts can be trusted to speak the truth.

1853 **David Belasco:** U.S. producer and playwright. A theatrical giant who made major innovations in staging. Important influence on standards of theatrical production. Managed the Madison Square Garden theatre and the Lyceum, before building his own theater in 1906. Associated with 374 plays. His best known plays include *The Heart of Maryland*, *The Girl of the Golden West* and *The Return of Peter Grimm*.

If you can't write your idea on the back of my calling card, you don't have a clear idea.

1880 **Morris Raphael Cohen:** Russian-born U.S. philosopher and educator. Author of *Reason and Nature: Logic in the Scientific Method*, *Law and Social Order*, *Preface to Logic*, *Faith of a Liberal* and his autobiography *A Dreamer's Journey*.

Cruel persecutions and intolerance are not accidents, but grow out of the very essence of religion, namely, its absolute claims.

1884 **Davidson Black:** Canadian anthropologist and professor of anatomy. His contributions to anthropology in studying protohuman remains and in identifying "Peking Man" in 1927 brought him international fame. The fossil remains found in the Zhoukaudian cave of about 40 individuals and more than 100,000 artifacts have been uncovered. Its strata date to 460,000–230,000 years ago.

The Peking man was a thinking being, standing erect, dating to the beginning of the Ice Age.

1890 **Dorothy Bernard:** South African-born American actress. One of the first American film stars as a member of the original Biograph stock company, predating Mary Pickford and the Gish sisters. Played Eponine in a film version of *Les Misérables* and Jo March in *Little Women*, both in 1918. Starred in the TV situation comedy *Life with Father* (1953–55), in a role in which she appeared on tour from 1939 to 1949.

Courage is fear that has said its prayers.

1902 **Eric Hoffer:** American social philosopher who received no formal education because of a temporary blindness. Worked as a longshoreman and wrote articles, books and aphorisms in his spare time. During the 1920 and 30s, he worked as a migrant laborer in California, keeping a library card in each town he passed through. Author of *The True Believer*, *The Passionate State of Mind* and *In Our Time*. Set forth the belief that it was possible to have social change without revolution.

We lie loudest when we lie to ourselves.

1905 **Elias Canetti:** Bulgarian-born author. All his books are written in German. His novel *Auto-da-Fé* depicts in gruesome detail the madness of a reclusive sinologist when he is exposed to the horrors of the world. Canetti's life-long preoccupation with the relationship of the individual to society resulted in his nonfiction masterpiece *Crowds and Power*. He was awarded the Nobel Prize in Literature in 1981.

All the things one has forgotten scream for help in dreams.

1927 **Midge Decter:** American neoconservative journalist, editor and author. Founded and executive director for The Committee for Free World. Its members envisioned themselves committed to the defense of the non-communist world "against the rising menace of totalitarianism. " She is one of the original drivers of the neo-conservative movement. Neoconservatives advocate the use of military force, unilaterally if necessary, to replace autocratic regimes with democratic ones. Publications: *Losing the First Battle, Winning the War, The Liberated Woman and Other Americans, Liberal Parents, Radical Children*, and *The New Chastity and Other Arguments Against Women's Liberation.*

Women's Liberation calls it enslavement but the real truth about the sexual revolution is that it has made of sex an almost chaotically limitless and therefore unmanageable realm in the life of women.

1954 **Walter Payton:** "Sweetness" African-American football running back for all 13 years of his professional career with the Chicago Bears. Quiet and humble off the field; a relentless and hard-nosed competitor on it. Held the career rushing record for 18 years until it was surpassed by Emmitt Smith. At Jackson State University, fourth in the voting for the Heisman Trophy. Elected to the Pro Football Hall of Fame in 1993. Died in 1999 from a rare liver disease called primary sclerosing cholangitis.

I want to be remembered as the guy who gave his all whenever he was on the field.

1956 **Iman (Abdulmajid):** Beautiful and mysterious Somali-born supermodel and actress. Daughter of the Somali ambassador to Saudi Arabia. Attended high school in Egypt and studied political science at Nairobi University in Kenya. Recruited as a model by U.S. photographer Peter Beard. Once married to pro basketball player Spencer Haywood; now married to British rock star David Bowie.

A self-esteem issue doesn't change whether you're considered beautiful or not because it's about what's inside you.

OTHERS: 975 German bishop/chronicler **Thietmar**, 1421 English politician **Henry Percy**, 1562 Japanese warlord **Kato Kiyomasa**, 1870 U.S. illustrator **Maxfield Parrish**, 1883 Italian composer **Alfredo Casella**, 1886 Danish big-game hunter **Bror von Blixen-Finecke**, 1894 U.S. actor **Walter Brennan**, 1903 U.S. saxophonist **Johnny Hodges**, 1920 English scientist **Rosalind Franklin**, 1924 U.S. Senator **Frank Church**, 1928 U.S. Jazz bassist **Keter Betts**, 1929 Indian politician **Somnath Chatterjee**, 1935 U.S. actress **Barbara Harris**, 1937 English archeologist **Colin Renfrew**, 1978 First test tube baby **Louise Brown**

July 26

1796 **George Catlin:** U.S. author and self-taught portrait painter. Long interested in American Indian life, began a series of visits to various tribes on the Great Plains and became famous for some 500 paintings and sketches of American Indian scenes. Published several illustrated books on Native American life. Most of his paintings were acquired by the Smithsonian Institution where they are exhibited.

No tragedian ever trod the stage, no gladiator ever entered the Roman Forum, with more grace and manly dignity, than did Four Bears as he arrived for his sitting.

1856 **George Bernard Shaw:** Irish dramatist, critic and social reformer. Took up various causes and joined several literary and political societies, notably the Fabian Society. Freethinker, supporter of women's rights and advocate of equality of income, the abolition of private property and a radical change in voting system. His plays and essays were his way of promoting his theories: *Arms and the Man, Mrs. Warren's Profession, Man and Superman, Major Barbara, Pygmalion* and *Saint Joan*. Other writings: *Common Sense About the War* and *The Intelligent Woman's Guide to Socialism and Capitalism.*

Life does not cease to be funny when people die any more than it ceases to be serious when people laugh.

1875 **Carl Jung:** Swiss psychologist. Professional career began at the Burghőlzli mental hospital in Zurich. First one to apply psychoanalytic ideas to the study of schizophrenia. Collaborated with Sigmund Freud but broke away from him to go into a long period of self-analysis. Found the school of "Analytical Psychology," described in his autobiographical *Memories, Dreams, and Reflections*. Believed that the mind was a self-regulating system and anticipated Existentialism. Formulated the introvert and extrovert types.

Everything that irritates us about others can lead us to an understanding of ourselves.

1875 **Antonio Machado:** Spanish poet and playwright. Leading poet of the Generación Del 98, a group of Spanish writers profoundly affected by the outcome of the Spanish-American War. Greatest and most characteristic verse is in the volume *Campos De Castilla*, containing poems steeped in the landscape and history of Spain. Before becoming estranged by taking opposing sides in the Spanish Civil War, he collaborated with his brother Manuel Machado, also a poet, on a number of plays.

Travelers, there is no path, paths are made by walking.

1885 **André Maurois:** Pen name of **Émile Herzog**. French biographer, novelist, and essayist. Despite not publishing his first book until he was 33, created a vast literary output. Biographies: *Ariel* (about poet Shelley), *Disraeli, Proust, Lélia* (about George Sand) and *Prométhée* (about Balzac). Histories: *The Miracle of England* and *The Miracle of France*. Novels: *Atmosphere of Love* and *The Family Circle*.

A happy marriage is a long conversation which always seems too short.

1893 **George Grosz:** German-American artist. Associated with the Dada movement before World War I. Arrested on several occasions for irreverence or blasphemy. With the rise of Hitler, left Germany for the U.S. in 1932. Known for venomous satirical caricatures and lithographs attacking militarism, the vaporous bourgeois and narrow-minded capitalists. *Ecce Homo* is a collection of his drawings.

It is an old ploy of the bourgeoisie. They keep a standing "art" to defend their collapsing culture.

1894 **Aldous Huxley:** English novelist, essayist, satirist and critic. Grandson of biologist Thomas Huxley. Early novels are witty, despairing evocations of society in the 1920s. Increasingly interested in political and philosophical issues. Preoccupation with mysticism dominated much of his later work. Books: *Point Counter Point, Eyeless in Gaza, Heaven and Hell, Brave New World* and *The Perennial Philosophy*.

That men do not learn very much from the lessons of history is the most important of all the lessons that History has to teach.

1906 **Gracie Allen:** American malaprop-prone scatterbrained and delightfully zany comedienne. In films and on radio and television with her husband and partner straight-man George Burns, until her untimely death in 1964. Noted for her scatterbrain answers to his questions. Made 13 films together, including *The Big Broadcast* films of 1932, 36, and 37.

The President of today is just the postage stamp of tomorrow.

1921 **Jean Shepherd:** American radio show host, writer and first-class storyteller. Always told stories in the first person, feeling that made the tale more believable to the listener. Did a nightly radio show in New York City during the 50s, 60s, and 70s. Remembered for classic movie *A Christmas Story*, a holiday staple on TV. Books: *In God We Trust, All Others Pay Cash* and *A Fistful of Fig Newtons*. Wrote columns for the *Village Voice*. Also recorded 6 LPs.

Can you imagine 4,000 years passing and you're not even a memory? Think about it friends. It's not just a possibility, it's a certainty.

1926 **Don Carter:** American professional bowler. "Mr. Bowling." Won Five World Invitational Championships. Bowling Writers Association of America's Bowler of the Year a record six times. First president of the Professional Bowlers Association. First pro bowler to earn a six-figure annual income.

One of the advantages bowling has over golf is that you seldom lose a bowling ball.

1928 **Stanley Kubrick:** American director whose films have received extremely divided opinions of their value: *Paths of Glory, Spartacus, Lolita, Dr. Strangelove, 2001: A Space Odyssey, A Clockwork Orange, The Shining* and *Eyes Wide Shut*.

If it can be written, or thought, it can be filmed.

1943 **Mick Jagger:** English rock star. Lead singer with the Rolling Stones, whose name was adapted from a Muddy Waters song. Jagger and Keith Richards wrote most of the group's songs, characterized by a driving backbeat, expressive instrumental accompaniments and biting and satirical lyrics. Biggest hits: "I Can't Get No Satisfaction," "Ruby Tuesday," "Honky Tonk Woman," and "Angie."

It's all right letting yourself go, as long as you can get yourself back.

OTHERS: 1739 U.S. VP **George Clinton**, 1782 Irish composer **John Field**, 1802 Mexican president **Mariano Arista**, 1874 Russian-born conductor **Serge Koussevitzky**, 1897 U.S. author **Paul Gallico**, 1903 U.S. Senator **Estes Kefauver**, 1907 Hungarian gymnast **Istvan Pelle**, 1908 President of Chile **Salvador Allende**, 1922 U.S. film director **Blake Edwards**, 1929 Bulgarian pianist **Alexis Weissenberg**, 1940 Congressional aide **Mary Jo Kopechine**, 1945 English actress **Helen Mirren**, 1954 U.S. tennis player **Vitas Gerulaitis**, 1956 U.S. figure skater **Dorothy Hamill**, 1959 U.S. actor **Kevin Spacey**, 1964 U.S. actress **Sandra Bullock**

July 27

1768 **Charlotte Corday:** French noblewoman and patriot. Sympathized with the aims of the French Revolution, but was horrified by the actions of the Jacobins. Managed to obtain an audience with the revolutionary leader Jean Paul Marat while he was in his bath. She assassinated him with a hidden knife because she saw him as the persecutor of the Girondists. She was guillotined for the crime four days later.

I told my plan to no one. I was not killing a man, but a wild beast that was devouring the French people. In Paris, they cannot understand how a useless woman, whose longer life could have been of no good, could sacrifice herself to save her country.

1824 **Alexandre Dumas (Fils):** French dramatist. Bastard son of the novelist Alexandre Dumas. His works include: *La Dame aux camélias* (*The Lady of the Camellias*), later adapted into the play *Camille*, which inspired Giuseppe Verdi to write *La Traviata*. Dumas also wrote essays, letters, and speeches. Best known for his plays, such as *Le Demi-monde* (*The Half-World*) and *Le Fils naturel* (*The Natural Son*).

If God were suddenly condemned to live the life which He has inflicted upon men, He would kill Himself.

1852 **George Foster Peabody:** U.S. banker and philanthropist. Director of Federal Reserve Bank of New York (1914–21). Donated his estate, Yaddo, Saratoga

Springs, New York, for an arts center. Peabody Awards for excellence in broadcasting are named for him.

Education is a debt due from present to future generations.

1870 **Hilaire Belloc:** French-born English poet, historian and essayist. Prolific and versatile writer of poetry and verses; essays on religious, social and political topic; biography; travel; literary criticism; and novels. Author of *The Bad Child's Book of Beasts, Cautionary Tales* and *On Nothing*. Biographies include Danton, Marie Antoinette, Cromwell and Charles II.

When I am dead, I hope it may be said: "His sins were scarlet, but his books were read."

1906 **Leo Durocher:** "The Lip." Good-field, no-hit shortstop with the New York Yankees, the St. Louis Cardinals' Gashouse Gang and the Brooklyn Dodgers. Combative and fiery Manager of Dodgers and Giants, leading the former to one pennant in 1941 and the latter to two in 1951 and 1954, winning the World Series in 1954. Also managed the Chicago Cubs and Houston Astros. Married actress Larraine Day.

I never did say that you can't be a nice guy and win. I said that if I was playing third base and my mother rounded third with the winning run, I'd trip her up.

1909 **Alan Chadwick:** English-born proponent of organic gardening. Established the Student Garden Project at the University of California, Santa Cruz. Introduced the French Intensive and Biodynamic systems of food and flower production to America. Chadwick-inspired gardens and farms spread across the country. The Chadwick Gardens is a world renowned research center for helping world farmers use organic gardening to obtain higher yields of food in small spaces with a minimal use of chemicals.

We are the living links in a life force that moves and plays around and through us, binding the deepest soils with the farthest stars.

1912 **Igor Markevitch:** Ukrainian-born conductor. Studied with Nadia Boulanger and was "discovered" by Diaghilev, who commissioned a Piano Concerto, which premiered at Covent Garden. Recognized as one of the leading Russo-French modernist composers. Married Nijinsky's daughter. In World War II he joined resistance movement in Italy. After the war, became an Italian citizen and embarked on a second career as an internationally acclaimed conductor and teacher.

Baton technique is to a conductor what fingers are to a pianist.

1916 **Elizabeth Hardwick:** American literary critic, novelist, short story writer and educator. Early associated with the *Parisian Review*. One of the founders in 1962 of the New York Review of Books, to which she was a frequent contributor and editor. Essays are insightful, sophisticated, witty and often acerbic. Author of *The Simple Truth, A View of My Own, Seduction and Betrayal: Women and Literature* and her highly acclaimed novel *Sleepless Nights*. Married to poet Robert Lowell (1949–72).

Adversity is a great teacher, but this teacher makes us pay dearly for its instruction; and often the profit we derive, is not worth the price we paid.

1922 **Norman Lear:** American television producer. Wrote and produced films including *Come Blow Your Horn* and *Divorce American Style*. Turned his attention to creating and producing hit series such as: *All in the Family*, which earned him four Emmys, *Maude, Stanford and Son, The Jeffersons* and *Mary Hartman, Mary Hartman*. Founded People for the American Way, a progressive activist group to speak out for Bill of Rights guarantees and to monitor violations of constitutional freedoms.

Life is made up of small pleasures. Happiness is made up of those tiny successes. The big ones come too infrequently. And if you don't collect all these tiny successes, the big ones don't really mean anything.

1924 **Vincent Canby:** American journalist and senior film critic with the *New York Times* from 1969 to 1993. In writing his obituary fellow *Times* critic Janet Maslin said his writing was "conversational prose that conveyed a bracing disdain for sentiment. His scholarship and cultural perspective were never flaunted but were as solid as his journalism." Wrote several novels and plays, but refused to publish an anthology of his reviews.

Good fiction reveals feelings, refines events, locates importance and, though its methods are as mysterious as they are varied, intensifies the experience of living our lives. Hack fiction exploits curiosity without really satisfying it or making connections between it and anything else in the world.

1938 **Gary Gygax:** American computer game creator. Best known as the author of the tremendously popular fantasy role-playing game *Dungeons & Dragons*. It was co-created with Dave Arneson and co-published with Don Kaye. In 1966, He and others created the *International Federation of Wargamers*.

The secret we should never let the gamemasters know is that they don't need any rules.

1948 **Peggy Fleming:** American figure skater. Defined her own figure skating style which saw her win five U.S. titles, three World Tiles, and the gold medal in the 1968 Olympics in Grenoble, France. After the Olympics she starred in the first of five TV specials. Spokesperson for the National Osteoporosis Foundation. Due to an early detection and successful surgery she survived breast cancer, diagnosed in 1998.

The first thing is to love your sport. Never do it to please someone else. It has to be yours.

1975 **Alex Rodriguez:** American baseball player. "A-Rod." Regarded as one of the best players in Major League baseball, and perhaps is destined to be one of the all-time great players. As a free-agent, he signed a 10-year deal with the Texas Rangers worth $252 million. As good as he was with the Rangers; he couldn't make them a winner. Traded to the New York Yankees, where Derek Jeter was the shortstop; A-Rod moved to third base. Youngest player to reach 300 homeruns and youngest to reach 400.

Enjoy your sweat because hard work doesn't guarantee success, but without it you don't have a chance.

OTHERS: 1452 Duke of Milan **Ludovico Sforza**, 1667 Swiss mathematician **Johann Bernoulli**, 1781 Italian composer **Mauro Giuliani**, 1848 Hungarian physicist **Roland, Baron von Eőtvős**, 1857 Puerto Rican political leader **José Celso Barbosa**, 1881 German chemist **Hans Fischer**, 1886 German architect **Ernst May**, 1901 U.S. crooner **Rudy Vallee**, 1903 Russian actor **Nikolai Cherkasov**, 1917 French actor **Bourvil**, 1918 U.S. cellist **Leonard Rose**, 1939 Northern Ireland poet **Michael Longley**, 1942 U.S. tennis player **Dennis Ralston**, 1964 U.S. bassist **Karl Mueller**, 1972 U.S. sports reporter **Jill Arrington**, 1979 Mexican boxer **Jorge Arce**

July 28

1456 **Jacopo Sannazaro:** Neapolitan poet. Academic name **Acticus Syncerus**. Most remembered for the humanistic classic *Arcadia*, a pastoral romance masterpiece that illustrated the possibilities of poetical prose in Italian. His elegant style influenced much of the courtly literature of the 16th century. Acclaimed the "Christian Virgil" for his sacred poem in Latin, "De partu Virginis" (On the Virgin's Parturition).

Man is only miserable so far as he thinks himself so.

1804 **Ludwig Andreas Feuerbach:** German philosopher and Bible critic. Analyzed religion from a psychological and anthropological viewpoint in *The Essence of Christianity* and *The Essence of Religion*. Asserted that Christianity is a man-made myth, satisfying man's need to imagine perfection and that the nature of man, of the species is God.

In practice all men are atheists, they deny their faith by their actions.

1844 **Gerard Manley Hopkins:** English poet and Jesuit priest. Came under the influence of the Oxford movement and Cardinal Newman and was received into the Catholic Church. Known for his poems on religion and nature. Author of "The Windhover," "The Caged Skylark," and "The Leaden Echo and the Golden Echo."

The world is charged with the grandeur of God.

1866 **Beatrix Potter:** English writer and illustrator of stories for children. Her drawings and watercolors made her stories all the more enchanting. They include: *The Tale of Peter Rabbit*, which begins with the classic line, "Once upon a time there were four little rabbits, and their names were Flopsy, Mopsy, Cottontail and Peter," *The Roly-Poly Pudding* and *Jemima Puddleduck*.

Thanks goodness I was never sent to school; it would have rubbed off some of the originality.

1887 **Marcel Duchamp:** French painter of the Dada movement. Anticipated many elements of Pop Art by erasing the boundaries between works of art and everyday objects, as is the case with his *Fountain*, which depicts an ordinary urinal. His futuristic *Nude Descending a Staircase* was an experiment in depicting motion on a canvas. His brother Raymond Duchamp-Villon was a cubist sculptor.

I have forced myself to contradict myself in order to avoid conforming to my own taste.

1902 **Karl Popper:** Austrian-born philosopher of science. Formulated and answered a major question in the philosophy of science, namely, how to distinguish between science, such as astronomy, and pseudoscience, such as astrology. Professed that truth can be uncovered and established as truth only after it has been subjected to logical refutation. Works: *The Logic of Science* and *Conjectures and Refutations*.

Science must begin with myths and the criticism of myths.

1909 **Malcolm Lowry:** English novelist. His literary quality was recognized only after his death. Reputation is based on his autobiographical novel *Under the Volcano*, set in Mexico, where he lived (1936–37). Also wrote *Dark Is the Grave Wherein My Friend Is Laid*, a collection of short stories and *Ultramarine*, an impressionistic, experimental sea story.

Good God, if our civilization were to sober up for a couple of days it'd die of remorse on the third.

1915 **Charles Townes:** American Physicist. In the early 1950s, he and his students at Columbia University constructed the first *maser*, a device that produces and amplifies electromagnetic radiation in the microwave range of the spectrum and showed that a similar device producing visible light was possible. Shared the 1954 Nobel Prize for his role in the invention of the maser and later the laser.

This is a very unusual universe.

1927 **John Ashbery:** American poet and art critic. Poems noted for their elegance, exquisite rhythms, and obscurity. Collections include: *Turandot and Other Poems*, *Some Trees*, *Rivers and Mountains* and *Self-Portrait in a Convex Mirror*, which earned a 1975 Pulitzer Prize.

There is the view that poetry should improve your life. I think people confuse it with the Salvation Army.

1929 **Jacqueline Lee Bouvier Kennedy Onassis:** American first lady. Wife of assassinated President John F. Kennedy. Speaking of her late husband: "Now he is a legend when he would have preferred to be a man." Later married Aristotle Onassis. Editor with Doubleday at the time of her death.

If you bungle raising your children, I don't think whatever else you do matters very much.

1943 **Bill Bradley:** U.S. senator from New York. All-American basketball player at Princeton. Rhodes Scholar at Oxford. Helped the U.S. team win Olympic Gold Medal in 1964. All-Star small forward with New

York Knicks, helping them win two NBA championships. As U.S. Senator from New Jersey, sought to raise public awareness of race relations and poverty. Critic of campaign-financing practices. Unsuccessfully sought Democratic nomination for president in 2000.

Ambition is the path to success. Persistence is the vehicle you arrive in.

1954 **Hugo Chávez:** President of Venezuela (1983–). Known for his democratic socialist governance, promotion of Latin American integration and criticism of U.S. foreign policy. Launched a massive program to combat disease, illiteracy, poverty, and other social ills in his country. On the international stage, supports alternative models of economic development, and advocated cooperation among the poor nations, especially those in Latin America. After Hurricane Katrina battered the Gulf Coast, his government was the first to offer aid, including tons of food, water, mobile hospital units, medical specialists, power generators, and one million barrels of petroleum. Bush administration refused the aid, claiming Chávez was playing the "oil card" on the geopolitical stage, a charge Chávez readily admits and promises to do use it over and over again.

I have said it already. I am convinced that the way to build a new and better world is not capitalism. Capitalism leads us straight to hell.

OTHERS: 1165 Muslim mystic **Ibu al-'Arabi**, 1659 French Huguenot pastor **Charles Ancillon**, 1867 American-born astronomer **Charles Dillon Perrine**, 1901 U.S. labor leader **Harry Bridges**, 1904 Russian physicist **Pavel A. Cherenkov**, 1907 U.S. inventor **Earl Tupper**, 1915 U.S. musician **Frankie Yankovic**, 1922 Belgian-born undersea explorer **Jacques Piccard**, 1934 U.S. dancer/choreographer **Jacques d'Amboise**, 1937 U.S. pianist **Peter Duchin**, 1938 President of Peru **Alberto Fujimori**, 1945 U.S. cartoonist **Jim Davis**, 1951 Spanish architect **Santiago Calatrava**, 1958 Canadian cancer activist **Terry Fox**

July 29

1805 **Alexis de Tocqueville:** French sociologist and historian. Sought to advance the rule of the people while at the same time controlling undesirable tendencies. Books: *Democracy in America*, a subtle analysis of the strength and weaknesses of a democratic society in evolution, which won the Montyon Prize from the French Academy in 1836, and his profound social and political study or pre–Revolutionary France, *The Old Regime and the Revolution*.

There are two things which a democratic people will always find very difficult — to begin a war and to end it.

1869 **Booth Tarkington:** American novelist and playwright. Novels for children include *Penrod* and its sequels, which describe the adventures of a boy and his friends in a small Midwestern city and *Seventeen*. Other works *The Gentleman from Indiana*, *Monsieur Beaucaire*, and his two Pulitzer winners, *The Magnificent Ambersons* and *Alice Adams*. Also wrote twenty-five plays, most notably *The Man from Home*.

Cherish all your happy moments: they make a fine cushion for old age.

1877 **Charles William Beebe:** American zoologist, literary naturalist and explorer. Curator from 1899 of ornithology for the New York Zoological Society. Explored ocean depths down to almost 1000 meters in a bathysphere. Books: *Galapagos, The Arcturus Adventure, World's End* and *Beneath Tropic Seas*.

The marsh to him who enters in a receptive mood, holds, besides mosquitoes and stagnation, melody, the mystery of unknown waters, and the sweetness of Nature undisturbed by man.

1878 **Don [Donald R.P.] Marquis:** American newspaperman, poet, and humorist. Wrote columns "The Sun Dial" for the *New York Sun* and "The Lantern" for the *New York Tribune*. Created Archy, the cockroach, and Mehitabel, the cat, newspaper philosophers of the 1920s. Wrote about Clem Hawley, the Old Soak, an uninhibited enemy of prohibition, and Hermione and her Little Group of Serious Thinkers, noted for their platitudes.

Procrastination is the art of keeping up with yesterday.

1883 **Benito Mussolini:** "Il Duce." Italian founder of Fascism. Advanced a program of economic controls and national expansion that appealed to many Italians in the troubled years after World War I. Let his followers on a famous march on Rome, which resulted in his being appointed prime minister. Stifled all opposition and became dictator in 1922. Attacked Ethiopia (1935) and made an alliance with Hitler (1939). Entered World War II with the fall of France. After the Allies invaded Italy he was deposed but rescued by the Germans, who installed him as a ruler of a puppet state. Captured by Italian partisans and shot along with his mistress Clara Petacci. Their bodies were hung upside down for all to see.

It's good to trust others but, not to do so is much better.

1905 **Dag Hammarskjöld:** Swedish diplomat and political economist. President of the board of the Bank of Sweden. Chair of the Swedish delegation to the United Nations. Second Secretary General of the U.N. (1953–61). Dealt with the Suez Crisis, conflicts in Lebanon and Jordan, and civil strife in the newly formed Republic of the Congo. Died in a plane crash while on a mission in Africa. Posthumously awarded the Nobel Peace Prize in 1961.

Pray that your loneliness may spur you into finding something to live for, great enough to die for.

1905 **Stanley Kunitz:** Jewish-American poet. Dubbed a "poet's poet." His collection *Selected Poems, 1928–1958* won a Pulitzer Prize. Other collections: *The Testing-Tree, The Coat Without a Seam* and *Passing Through*. Served two years (1974–76) as the Poet Laureate Consultant in Poetry to the Library of Congress, later became the modern Poet Laureate program.

Old myths, old gods, old heroes have never died. They are only sleeping at the bottom of our mind, waiting for our call. We have need for them. They represent the wisdom of our race.

1906 **Diana Vreeland:** French-born fashion columnist and editor. Career began in 1937 as a columnist for *Harper's Bazaar*. Joined *Vogue* in 1962, where she was editor-in-chief until she was fired in 1971. Became a consultant to the Costume Institute of the Metropolitan Museum of Art in New York.

Elegance is innate. It has nothing to do with being well dressed. Elegance is refusal.

1907 **Melvin Belli:** American lawyer and writer. "The King of Torts." Silver-haired and silver-tongued headline-making trial lawyer. Famous for his personal injury cases and instrumental in setting up some of the foundations of modern consumer rights law. Clients included: Zsa Zsa Gabor, Errol Flynn, Chuck Berry, Muhammad Ali, Sirhan Sirhan, Lana Turner, Mae West, Lenny Bruce, Martha Mitchell and Jack Ruby. Books: *Modern Trials* (6 volumes), *Trial Tactics*, and *Criminal Law*.

There is never a deed so foul that something couldn't be said for the guy; that's why there are lawyers.

1929 **Jean Baudrillard:** French philosopher, and cultural theorist. Best known for formulating the notion of hyperreality. Claimed that the U.S. constructed a world more "real" than real, where its inhabitants are obsessed with timelessness, perfection, and objectification of the self. Works: *America* and *The Gulf War Did Not Take Place*.

It was as if the outcome had been devoured in advance by a parasitic virus, the retro-virus of history. This is why one could offer the hypothesis that this would not have taken place. And now that it is over, one can finally take account of its non-occurrence.

1938 **Peter Jennings:** Canadian-American television journalist. From 1968, he worked as a foreign correspondent, reporting from the Middle East during the Yom Kipper War and the Lebanese civil war. He was ABC's reporter-on-scene during the Munich Olympics Massacre of Israeli athletes by Palestinian terrorist. From 1983 through April 1, 2005, he was the sole anchor of ABC's *Evening News*. Long-time smoker, informed viewers that he had been diagnosed with lung cancer, and was beginning chemotherapy treatment. Succumbed to the disease on August 7, 2005.

Almost 10 million Americans are living with cancer. I am sure I will learn from them how to cope with the facts of life that none of us anticipated.

1953 **Ken Burns:** American producer and director of acclaimed historical and biographical documentaries for television and film, using original prints and photographs. Zooming in on a portion of a still picture or panning the subjects seems to add life to the photos. Among his best known presentations are the miniseries *The Civil War*, *Baseball* and *Jazz*. His documentaries have been nominated for two Academy Awards. *The Civil War*, *Baseball*, and *Unforgivable Blackness* each won Emmys.

Good history is a question of survival. Without any past, we will deprive ourselves of the defining impression of our being.

OTHERS: 1605 German poet **Simon Dach**, 1801 English publisher **George Bradshaw**, 1843 German linguist **Johannes Schmidt**, 1849 Austrian Zionist leader **Max Nordau**, 1865 Russian composer **Alexander Glazunov**, 1872 U.S. folklorist **Eric Alfred Knudsen**, 1876 Russian-born actress **Maria Ouspenskaya**, 1887 Hungarian-born composer **Sigmund Romberg**, 1892 U.S. actor **William Powell**, 1898 U.S. physicist **Isidor Isaac Rabi**, 1904 Indian pioneer aviator **J.R.D. Tata**, 1905 U.S. actress **Clara Bow**, 1925 Greek composer **Mikis Theodorakis**, 1936 U.S. politician **Elizabeth Dole**, 1957 Russian gymnast **Nellie Kim**

July 30

1511 **Giorgi Vasari:** Painter, architect and art historian. Painted mannerist portraits and religious themes. Architect of the Uffizi in Florence. Best known for *Lives of the Most Eminent Painters and Sculptors*, a valuable, if not totally accurate source of information of Italian artists, and more importantly, Renaissance thought and aesthetics. First to call the Renaissance the rebirth of fine art.

Men of genius sometimes accomplish most when they work the least, for they are thinking out inventions and forming in their minds the perfect idea that they subsequently express with their hands.

1763 **Samuel Rogers:** English poet, wit and patron of men of letters. Noted for his sarcasm and biting wit. Much of what he had to say is preserved in Alexander Dyce's *Recollections and G.H. Powell's Reminiscences*. Rogers' best known poetic work is *The Pleasures of Memory*.

It doesn't signify whom one marries, for one is sure to find the next morning that it is someone else.

1818 **Emily Brontë:** One of three English sister novelists. As a child, she kept a journal, the *Gondal Chronicle*, on the wars and intrigues of the Royalists and Republicans in a mysterious Northern England county. Based on her novel *Wuthering Heights* and her poetry she is generally agreed to be the greatest talent in the family. Poems: "The Prisoner," "Remembrance" and "The Visionary."

Any relic of the dead is precious, if they were valued living.

1857 **Thorstein B. Veblen:** American economist and social philosopher. Known for his criticism of 19th century capitalism. Author of *The Theory of the Leisure Class*, an American classic in economics and sociology. Other works by the innovative and influential social critic: *The Instinct of Workmanship, The Theory of Business Enterprise* and *The Vested Interests.*

The outcome of any serious research can only be to make two questions grow where only one grew before.

1863 **Henry Ford:** U.S. auto manufacturer. With the 1908 Model T, he produced a car that sold for $500 allowing working people to afford cars. Employees worked an eight-hour schedule and were paid above the average wage earner in the industry. Pioneered the assembly-line production method. In 1928 developed the Model A to replace the Model T. In 1932 introduced the V-8 engine. Signed first union-shop contract in the industry (1941). Wrote a book on folk and social dancing.

Don't find fault, find a remedy; anybody can complain.

1889 **Casey Stengel:** U.S. baseball player. As manager, led the New York Yankees to ten American League pennants, five in consecutive years, and seven World Series championships. Also managed the New York Mets, a hapless expansion team, loved for their futility, prompting "Old Case" to ask *Can't Anyone Here Play This Game?* Famed for garbled but colorful explanations, dubbed "Stengalese."

The key to being a good manager is keeping the people who hate me away from those who are still undecided.

1898 **Henry Moore:** English sculptor and graphic artist. Developed his style of bold, smooth usually human forms. Worked with bronze, stone, concrete and wood. Often grouped together two or more forms to create one sculptural entity. Particularly well-known for a series of reclining nudes. Completed commissions for UNESCO's Paris headquarters, Lincoln Center, and the National Gallery of Arts.

The secret of life is to have a task, something you devote your entire life to, something you bring everything to, every minute of the day for the rest of your life. And the most important thing is, it must be something you cannot possibly do.

1909 **C. Northcote Parkinson:** English political scientist. Wrote many books on historical, political and economic subjects. Won fame for serio-comic takes on bureaucrats and their malpractices in *Parkinson's Law, the Pursuit of Progress.* Part of the law is that subordinates multiply at a fixed rate, regardless of the amount of work produced. The main assertion of the law is:

Work expands to fill the time available for its completion. General recognition of this fact is shown in the proverbial phrase, "It is the busiest man who has time to spare."

1940 **Patricia Schroeder:** American lawyer and politician. Worked for the National Labor Relations Board (1964–66). Democratic congresswoman from Colorado (1973–1997). First woman to serve on the House Armed Services Committee. Prime mover behind the Family and Medical Leave Act. Now president and CEO of the Association of American Publishers.

I have a brain and a uterus, and I use both.

1947 **Arnold Schwarzenegger:** Austrian-born U.S. bodybuilder, action screen star and politician. Won many body building contests. Films: *Pumping Iron, Conan the Barbarian, The Terminator* and *True Lies.* Elected Republican Governor of California, in a recall election that removed sitting governor Democrat Gray Davis, despite sexual harassment charges by a number of women, who claimed he groped them. Found it harder to govern than to criticize from the outside. In a 2005 special election, voters soundly rejected all the ballot initiatives the governor had proposed to reform state government.

It's simple, if it jiggles, it's fat.

1956 **Anita Hill:** American lawyer, educator and author. At the confirmation hearing of Supreme Court Justice Nominee Clarence Thomas, she accused him of sexual harassment at the time she was his assistant at the U.S. Department of Education. When Thomas became chairman of the U.S. Equal Employment Opportunity Commission, Hill joined the Commission's legal staff. Thomas made a blanket denial of the accusations and after an extensive debate in the Senate was narrowly confirmed.

I did what my conscience told me to do, and you can't fail if you do that.

1974 **Hilary Swank:** American actress. Two time Academy Award Winner for Best Actress, as the troubled real-life transman Brandon Teena in for *Boys Don't Cry* and as a waitress-turned boxer in *Million Dollar Baby.* She was paid $75 a day for her role as the girl playing a boy, earning a total of $3000. First drew attention, appearing as the female protégé of a sensei played by Pat Morita.

One thing I've learned: You never know where life is taking you, but it's taking you.

OTHERS: 1855 U.S. sculptor **James Edward Kelly**, 1855 German industrialist **Georg Wilhelm Siemens**, 1880 U.S. newspaper publisher **Robert R. McCormick**, 1889 Russian-born Television inventor **Vladimir Zworykin**, 1904 Mexican poet **Salvador Novo**, 1914 Irish Int. Olympic Committee President **Lord Killanin**, 1921 U.S. pianist **Grant Johannesen**, 1930 U.S. economist **Thomas Sowell**, 1934 Baseball commissioner **Bud Selig**, 1938 French politician **Hervé de Charette**, 1939 U.S. film director **Peter Bogdanovich**, 1941 Canadian singer/composer **Paul Anka**

July 31

356 BCE **Alexander the Great:** Ancient King of Macedon. Greatest military leader of antiquity. Succeeded his assassinated father Philip II of Macedonia when he was 20 and immediately took Thessaly and Thrace, and when he brutally razed Thebes, other Greek states surrendered without a fight. In 334 BCE he defeated the Persian army and is said to have cut the

Gordian knot in Phrygia, which according to legend meant he was to rule all of Asia. Took Syria, Phoenicia, Tyre and Egypt, where he founded the city of Alexandria. Fell ill at Babylon after a long bout of feasting and drinking and died at age 33.

There is nothing impossible to him who will try.

1689 **Samuel Richardson:** English novelist, known for his interest in the psychological aspects of character. Apprenticed to a printer, he later set up his own printing business. Published his *The Apprentice's Vade Mecum,* a book of advice on morals and conduct. Novels: *Pamela, or Virtue Rewarded. Clarissa Harlow* and *Sir Charles Grandison.*

For the human mind is seldom at stay: if you do not grow better, you will most undoubtedly grow worse.

1880 **Munshi Premchand:** Born **Dhanpat Rai Srivastava.** One of the greatest literary figures of modern Hindu and Urdu literature. Wrote more than 300 stories, a dozen novels and two plays. Employed simple language, using the dialect of the common people. Unlike other writers of his day, who wrote mostly fantasy, he commented on the realistic issues of the day — corruption, debt, poverty, colonialism, etc. Many consider his last novel *Godan* (*The Gift of a Cow*) to be his best.

Like timidity, bravery is also contagious.

1901 **Jean Dubuffet:** French painter, sculptor and printmaker. Champion of "art brut," the naive and powerful artwork of prisoners, psychotics and other unusual amateurs. Executed crude images making use of sand, plaster, tar, gravel, and ashes bounded together with varnish and glue. Sculpted works from junk materials, which were met with public outrage. Later produced huge fiberglass sculptures for public spaces.

Art doesn't go to sleep in the bed made for it. It would sooner run away than say its name: what it likes to be is incognito. Its best moments are when it forgets what its own name is.

1912 **Milton Friedman:** U.S. economist. Leading conservative economist and advocate of monetarism. Oversaw the economic transition after the overthrow of Salvador Allende in Chile. Author of *Studies in the Quantity Theory of Money* and *a Monetary History of the United States, 1867–1960.* Awarded Nobel Prize for Economics in 1976.

If you put the federal government in charge of the Sahara Desert, in 5 years there'll be a shortage of sand.

1912 **Irv Kupcinet:** "Kup." American talk show host and columnist for the *Chicago Sun-Times.* Launched "Kup's Column" in 1943 which ran for the next six decades. In it he provided inside gossip of local and national celebrities and political figures. Pioneer in TV talk shows, which under various different names ran on Saturday nights for 27 years, earning him 15 local Emmy Awards and a Peabody.

An optimist is a person who starts a new diet on Thanksgiving Day.

1919 **Curt Gowdy:** American sports announcer. Longtime voice of the Boston Red Sox. Covered many nationally-televised sporting events. Broadcasted 13 World Series, 16 Baseball All-Star Games, nine Super Bowls, 14 Rose Bowls, eight Olympic Games and 24 NCAA Final Fours. Famous for his slightly graveled voice, easy style and occasional malapropism.

Folks, this is perfect weather for today's game. Not a breath of air.

1919 **Primo Levi:** Italian writer and chemist. Captured by the Nazis, sent to Auschwitz as a slave laborer. Wrote about his survival in concentration camps: *If This Is a Man, or Survival in Auschwitz, The Reawakening,* and *The Drowned and the Saved.* Best-known work is *The Periodic Table,* a collection of 21 meditations, each named for a chemical element.

I am constantly amazed by man's inhumanity to man.

1921 **Whitney Young, Jr.:** African-American civil rights leader. Executive director of the National Urban League. Called for a "Marshall Plan" for the nation's blacks to help them catch up after generations of discrimination. Author of *To Be Equal* and *Beyond Racism.* Received a Presidential Medal of Freedom in 1969. Drowned while on a visit to Africa.

It is better to be prepared for an opportunity and not have one than to have an opportunity and not be prepared.

1943 **William Bennett:** American politician and best-selling author. Appointed United States Secretary of Education (1985–88) by Ronald Reagan. Director of the Office of National Drug Control Policy during the George H.W. Bush administration. Publication of *The Book of Virtues: A Treasury of Great Moral Stories,* which he edited, made him a leading voice for conservative morality, an image that was damaged when it became known that he was addicted to high-stakes gambling.

Sometimes we need to remind ourselves that thankfulness is indeed a virtue.

1950 **Steve Miller:** American science fiction writer. Reviewer of music and books, reporter, editor, professional chess tournament director, librarian, manager of a computer store, and resource specialist for *The Maine Meeting Place,* an electronic bulletin board system for the disabled. His works appear in more than 100 newspapers, magazines and journals. Host of the weekday radio program *Morning in America.*

The question to everyone's answer is usually asked from within.

1965 **J.K. Rowling:** Pen Name of **Joanne "Jo" Rowling.** English novelist. First person to become a billionaire by writing books. Worked as a researcher and bilingual secretary for Amnesty International. At that time she had the idea for a story of a young boy who attends a school of wizardry. Produced six books in the series, beginning with *Harry Potter and the Philosopher's Stone,* and currently is writing the seventh. All have been or will be filmed, and have proved to be almost as successful as the books themselves.

There is no good or evil: only power and those too weak to seek it.

OTHERS: 1527 Holy Roman Emperor **Maximilian II**, 1598 Italian sculptor/architect **Alessandro Algardi**, 1724 French lexicographer **Noël François de Wailly**, 1803 U.S. inventor **John Ericsson**, 1843 Austrian poet **Peter Rosegger**, 1860 U.S. artist/naturalist **Mary Vaux Walcott**, 1867 U.S. businessman **S.S. Kresge**, 1887 German sociologist **Hans Freyer**, 1916 U.S. game show producer **Bill Todman**, 1930 Russian clown **Oleg Popov**, 1944 U.S. economist **Robert C. Merton**, 1944 U.S. producer/motion picture executive **Sherry Lee Lansing**, 1951 Australian aborigine tennis star **Evonne Goolagong**, 1958 U.S. businessman **Mark Cuban**

August 1

10 BCE **Emperor Claudius:** Roman emperor (41–54). Grandson of Empress Livia, brother of Germanicus, and nephew of Emperor Tiberius. Devoted himself to historical studies, and perhaps because of his physical difficulties and remaining in the background, he survived the vicious in-fighting of the imperial family. Became emperor almost by accident after his predecessor Caligula was assassinated. Nowhere near the bumbling, frightened and humane individual depicted in fictional accounts. Could be just as brutal to his enemies as his predecessors.

Conquering new lands is an excellent way of showing that I am a mighty Roman leader.

1744 **Jean-Baptiste Lamarck:** French naturalist and pre–Darwin evolutionist. Published the well-received *French Flora* in 1773 and the next year became keeper of the royal garden. Major works: *Philosophie zoologique*, in which he postulated that, acquired characteristics can be inherited by future generations, and *Natural History of Invertebrate Animals*.

Time and favorable conditions are the two principal means which Nature has employed in giving existence to all her productions. We know that her time has no limit and that consequently she always has it at her disposal.

1779 **Francis Scott Key:** American poet and attorney. After watching the bombardment of Ft. McHenry during the War of 1812 from a British man-of-war, he wrote the poem "The Star-spangled Banner." It was later set to music by John Stafford Smith and adopted as the U.S. National Anthem in 1931.

Then in that hour of deliverance, my heart spoke. Does not such a country, and such defenders of their country, deserve a song?

1779 **Lorenz Oken:** German naturalist. Real name was **Lorenz Ockenfuss.** Extended to the physical sciences the philosophical principles which Immanuel Kant applied to mental and moral science. Maintained that "the animal classes are virtually nothing else than a representation of the sense-organs, and that they must be arranged in accordance with them." His prolific speculations foreshadowed cell theory in the proposition that all organic beings originate from and consist of vesicles or cells. Main work: *Natural History for All Social Ranks* (13 vols.).

The law of causality is a law of polarity. Causality is valid only in time, is only a series of numbers. Time itself has no causality. Causality is an act of generation.

1815 **Richard Henry Dana, Jr.:** American lawyer and writer. Quit Harvard University to ship as a common seaman aboard the brig *Pilgrim*, which sailed from Cape Horn to California. He wrote vividly and realistically of his experiences in *Two Years Before the Mast*, which was published anonymously in 1840.

Everything was "shipshape" and Bristol fashion.

1818 **Maria Mitchell:** First acknowledged woman astronomer in the United States. Her father was a dedicated astronomer who encouraged his daughter to aspire to high goals; doing everything he could to further her knowledge of mathematics and astronomy. In 1847, standing on the roof of her parents home she discovered a new comet. First woman member of American Academy of Arts and Sciences. President of the American Association for the Advancement of Women.

Besides learning to see, there is another art to be learned — not to see what is not

1819 **Herman Melville:** American novelist and poet. Spent his youth aboard ships which formed the basis for his books *Typee*, *Omoo* and his masterpiece *Moby Dick*. A critical and popular failure at the time of its publication, it is recognized as one of the best, truly American novels. He died virtually forgotten, with his work *Billy Budd*, still in manuscript form.

If is better to fail in originality than to succeed in imitation.

1881 **Rose Macaulay:** English writer. Published thirty-five books, mostly novels, but also biographies and travel books. Novels: *Potterism*, *The World, My Weariness* and *The Towers of Trebizond*. Maintained an affair with writer and former Jesuit priest Gerald O'Donovan from 1918 until his death in 1942.

Adultery is a meanness and a stealing, a taking away from someone what should be theirs, a great selfishness, and surrounded and guarded by lies lest it should be found out. And out of meanness and selfishness and lying flow love and joy and peace beyond anything that can be imagined.

1895 **Benjamin E. Mays:** African-American educator. Son of former slaves. Inspired by Frederick Douglass, Paul Laurence Dunbar and Booker T. Washington, he became a Baptist minister. Earned a Ph.D. from the University of Chicago. President of Morehouse University for 27 years. First African-American president of the Atlanta Board of Education. Advisor to several U.S. presidents. Students included Julian Bond, Andrew Young and Dr. Martin Luther King Jr.

The tragedy of life doesn't lie in not reaching your goal. The tragedy lies in having no goal to reach.

1932 **Meir Kahane:** American orthodox rabbi, author, and political activist. Founder of the Jewish Defense League in the U.S., labeled a terrorist organization by the FBI and Kach, an Israeli political party, declared racist by the Israeli government and outlawed. Kahane was a member of the Israeli Knesset before being banned from political candidacy by Israel's Anti-Racist Law of 1988. Maintained that Israel should limit citizenship to Jews and create a Jewish religious state. Assassinated in New York City in 1990.

Never, ever deal with terrorists. Hunt them down and, more important, mercilessly punish those states and groups that fund, arm, support, or simply allow their territories to be used by the terrorists with impunity.

1936 **Yves St. Laurent:** Algerian-French fashion designer. Hired at age 17 to be Christian Dior's assistant. With Dior's death four years later, headed the House of Dior. Opened his fashion house in 1962. Quickly emerged as one of the world's most influential designers. Responsible for the "chic beatnik" and "little boy" looks in the 1960s. Produces perfumes *Opium* and *Paris.*

Isn't elegance forgetting what one is wearing?

1942 **Jerry Garcia:** American guitarist. Cofounder and vocalist of the psychedelic rock group *The Grateful Dead,* influential rock band that emerged from various San Francisco groups. For 30 years, the group toured almost constantly, developing a fanatically devoted fan base, known as deadheads. Garcia died in 1995 of a heart attack, exacerbated by sleep apnea. Albums: *Grateful Dead, Anthem of the Sun, American Beauty* and *Live Dead.*

Talk about your plenty, talk about your ills, one man gathers what another man spills.

OTHERS: 1313: Japanese Emperor **Kogon**, 1555 English spiritualist **Edward Kelley**, 1579 Spanish writer **Luis Vélez de Guevara**, 1770 American explorer **William Clark**, 1858 Austrian composer **Hans Rott**, 1885 Hungarian chemist **George de Hevesy**, 1920 U.S. platform Diver **Sammy Lee**, 1921 U.S. tennis player **Jack Kramer**, 1927 English conductor **Raymond Leppard**, 1930 French sociologist **Pierre Bourdieu**, 1930 English songwriter **Lionel Bart**, 1937 U.S. Senator **Al D'Amato**, 1942 Italian actor **Giancarlo Giannini**, 1946 Australian epidemiologist **Fiona Stanley**, 1978 U.S. football player **Edgerrin James**

August 2

1754 **Pierre Charles L'Amant:** French engineer, architect and urban planner. Moved to America to fight the British in the Revolutionary War. Designed ceremonial and monumental works, introducing symbolic and allegorical European decorative motifs to America. Hired by George Washington to design the basic plan for Washington, D.C. Constantly feuding with Secretary of State Thomas Jefferson, he was dismissed in 1792 for his imperious attitude and died in poverty. However, his plan was generally followed.

After much ... search for an eligible situation ... I could discover no one so advantageous to greet the congressional building as that on the west end of Jenkins Heights, which stands as a pedestal waiting for a monument.

1820 **John Tyndall:** Largely self-educated British physicist and natural philosopher. Best known for his research on radiant heat, the acoustics properties of the atmosphere and the blue color of the sky. His famous address to the British Association in Belfast in 1874, on the relation between science and theology led to acute controversy.

Science keeps down the weed of superstition not by logic, but by rendering the mental soil unfit for its cultivation.

1858 Sir **William Watson:** English poet, who wrote lyrical and political verse. Known for his brief, epigrammatic poems. Gained his reputation with *Wordsworth's Grave and other Poems* and *Lachrymae musarium,* verses on the death of Tennyson. Poems are now largely forgotten; except for his anthology piece "April, April, Laugh thy girlish laughter."

Hate and mistrust are the children of blindness.

1865 **Irving Babbitt:** U.S. educator, scholar and literary critic. With Paul Elmer Moore, founded modern humanistic movement, a philosophical and critical movement that fiercely criticized Romanticism. It stressed the value of reason and restraint. Author of *Rousseau and Romanticism* and *Democracy and Leadership.*

A democracy, the realistic observer is forced to conclude, is likely to be idealistic in its feeling about itself, but imperialistic about its practice.

1867 **Ernest Dowson:** English poet of the decadent school. Part of the London literary society that included Richard Le Gallienne, Aubrey Beardsley and Oscar Wilde. Contributed poems to the *Yellow Book,* the *Savoy* and anthropologies published by the Rhymers' Club group at Oxford. His most famous poem is "Non Sum Qualis Eram Bonae sub Regno Cynarae" (in verses), containing the familiar refrain: "I have been faithful to thee, Cynara! in my fashion."

They are not long, the days of wine and roses.

1871 **John French Sloan:** American artist. Member of the realistic urban "Ashcan School." Organizer of the Armory Show and other independent showings. Art editor of *The Masses* and contributor to *Harper's* and *Collier's.* Works: *Women Drying Their Hair* and *Backyards, Greenwich Village.* His remembrances and ideals are found in *The Gist of Art.*

Since we have to speak well of the dead, let's knock them while they're alive.

1894 **Westbrook Pegler:** American newspaper columnist. Wrote a nationally syndicated sports feature for the *Chicago Tribune.* In 1933, joined the *New York World-Telegram* to write the column "Fair Enough," venting the opinions of the "average man" on the world of international events.

My hates have always occupied my mind much

more actively and have given greater spiritual satisfaction than my friendships.

1905 **Myrna Loy:** Very popular American film actress. In early films often appeared in exotic foreign and vampish roles, such as Fu Manchu's daughter. Sophisticated and appealing performances in *The Thin Man* and its sequels, *The Best Years of Our Lives*, *Mr. Blandings Builds His Dream House* and *Cheaper by the Dozen* made her appear as the perfect wife. However she was married five times. Worked for the Red Cross during World War II and later for UNESCO.

Life, is not having and a getting, but of being and a becoming.

1912 **George H. T. Kimble:** British-born director of the American Geographical Society. One of the first (1950s) to alert the world that the climate of the North Atlantic region is growing unmistakably warmer. Through his writings and lectures attempted to acquaint the Western world with Africa. Books: several volumes under the general title of *Tropical Africa*, *Geography in the Middle Ages*, and *Our American Weather.*

The darkest thing about Africa has always been our ignorance of it.

1924 **James Baldwin:** African-American novelist and essayist. At fourteen preached in Harlem storefront churches. Novels: *Go Tell It on the Mountain*, based on his experiences of religious awakening, *Another Country*, *Tell Me How Long the Train's Been Gone* and *If Beale Street Could Talk*, which movingly dealt with a black man's emotional and sexual torments. Books of essays: *Notes of a Native Son*, *Nobody Knows My Name* and *The Fire the Next Time*. Plays: *The Amen Corner*, *Blues for Mister Charlie* and *One Day When I Was Lost.*

I imagine one of the reasons people cling to their hates so stubbornly is because they sense, once hate is gone ... they will be forced to deal with pain.

1933 **Peter O'Toole:** Talented and eccentric Irish actor. Studied at the Royal Academy of Dramatic Art before making his London stage debut in 1956. Starred as Hamlet in the National Theatre's inaugural production in 1905. Won international acclaim and an Academy Award nomination for his performance in *Lawrence of Arabia*. Also Oscar nominated for roles in *Beckett*, *The Lion in Winter*, *Goodbye, Mr. Chips*, *The Ruling Class*, *The Stunt Man*, *My Favorite Year* and *Venus*. Often played eccentrics and heavy drinkers.

When did I realize I was God? Well, I was praying and I suddenly realized I was talking to myself.

1942 **Isabel Allende:** Peruvian-born Chilean writer. Daughter of Chilean ambassador to Peru and niece of Chilean president Salvador Allende, killed in a violent coup in 1973, forcing her into exile in Venezuela. One of the most popular novelists in the world, having sold over 35 million copies, translated into 27 different languages. Works: *The House of Spirits*, *Paula*, *Of Love and Shadows* and her play *El Embajador.*

Erotica is using a feather; pornography is using the whole chicken.

OTHERS: 1533 Swiss scholar **Theodor Zwinger**, 1696 Ottoman Sultan **Mahmud I**, 1788 German chemist **Leopold Gmelin**, 1835 U.S. inventor **Elisha Gray**, 1868 King of Greece **Constantine I**, 1892 U.S. columnist **John Kieran**, 1892 U.S. film studio head **Jack Warner**, 1900 U.S. singer/actress **Helen Morgan**, 1912 Croatian statistician **Vladimir Zerjavic**, 1922 U.S. Senator **Paul Laxalt**, 1924 U.S. actor **Carroll O'Connor**, 1925 Argentinean dictator **Jorge Rafael Videla**, 1926 U.S. department store mogul **Betsy Bloomingdale**, 1950 U.S. judge **Lance Ito**, 1960 U.S. Actress **Apollonia**

August 3

1808 **Hamilton Fish:** U.S. politician from New York State. Although Great Britain was officially neutral during the Civil War, it allowed the construction in England of the Confederate cruiser *Alabama*, which destroyed 68 Union ships. U.S. Ambassador Charles Francis Adams demanded the British take responsibility for damages. As Secretary of State in the Grant administration, Fish acted as a member of the arbitration tribunal. Signed the Washington Treat of 1871, establishing certain wartime obligations of neutrals and awarded the U.S. damages of $15.5 million.

If our country is worth dying for in time of war let us resolve that it is truly worth living for in time of peace.

1867 **Stanley Baldwin:** British politician. Managed his family's diversified industries before becoming a member of the House of Commons (1908–37). Conservative prime minister during the general strike of 1926 (1923–29) and at the time of Edward VIII's abdication (1935–37). Strengthen the military, but showed little concern for the aggressive policies of Germany and was criticized for not protesting Italy's invasion of Ethiopia.

War would end if the dead could return.

1887 **Rupert Brooke:** English poet. Wrote two volumes of romantic and patriotic poetry in the early years of World War I. Died at 28 of blood poisoning on his way to the Dardanelles and was buried there. His best known poem "The Soldier" expresses idealism in the face of death and includes the famous line: "If I should die, think only this of me;/ That there's some corner of a foreign field/ That is forever England."

A book may be compared to your neighbor. If it be good, it cannot last too long; if bad, you cannot get rid of it too early.

1900 **Ernie Pyle:** American war correspondent during World War II who wrote about the everyday trials and tribulations of the ordinary soldier. Reported on the U.S. campaigns in North Africa, Sicily, Italy, and France. Pulitzer Prize winner (1944). Killed by Japanese machine gun fire (1945) during the Okinawa invasion. Compilations of his columns include *Ernie Pyle in England*, *Brave Men*, and *Last Chapter.*

War makes strange giant creatures out of us little routine men who inhabit the earth.

1901 **Stefan Wyszynski:** Polish Catholic cardinal. Founded the Christian Workers University and joined the Polish resistance in World War II. As Polish Catholic primate, refused to consent to communist demands. Placed under house arrest (1953–56). After his release, he struck a compromise on church and state matters with the Polish government to avoid a potential Soviet invasion. Thereafter he maintained the unity of the church in an uneasy coexistence with the communist government.

The Poles do not know how to hate, thank God.

1905 **Dolores Del Rio:** Exotically beautiful Mexican movie star. **Born Dolores Martinez Asúnsolo y López Negrete.** At the age of 16 she married screenwriter Jamie del Rio. Also married to art director Cedric Gibbons and had a torrid affair with Orson Welles, ten years her junior. Appeared in numerous U.S. films, beginning in the silent era: *What Price Glory, Bird of Paradise,* and *Journey into Fear*. Later an important actress in Spanish-language films.

Beauty does not come with cream and lotions. God gave us beauty, but whether that beauty remains or changes is determined by our thoughts and deeds.

1905 **Maggie Kuhn:** American lifelong social activist. In the 1930s and 40s, taught as the YWCA, educating women about unionizing, women's issues, and social issues. Caused controversy by establishing a human sexuality class. In 1971, founded the senior citizen's political activist group "The Gray Panthers," which worked to reverse the tendency to treat old people like children, finding retirement homes to be "glorified playpens." Professed that old age wasn't a disease, but "a struggle and survivorship triumph over all kinds of vicissitudes and disappointments, trials and illnesses."

The ultimate indignity is to be given a bedpan by a stranger who calls you by your first name.

1918 **James MacGregor Burns:** Political writer, presidential biographer and authority on leadership studies. Established the (James MacGregor Burns) Academy of Leadership at the University of Maryland. Best known for contributions to the Transformational, Aspirational and Visionary schools of leadership theory. Pulitzer Prize and National Book Award in 1971 for *Roosevelt: Soldier of Freedom 1940–1945*.

Transformational leadership occurs when one or more persons engage with others in such a way that leaders and followers raise one another to higher levels of motivation and morality.

1920 **P.D. James:** Pen name of **Phyllis Dorothy James White**. English mystery writer created intelligent, perceptive, poet, Inspector Adam Dalgleish. Books: *A Mind to Murder, The Black Tower,* and *An Unsuitable Job for a Woman*. Her husband's confinement to mental hospitals and her work with the police as a juvenile delinquency specialist is reflected in her writing, seen in her empathy for the suffering of chronic illness and slow death of her characters.

Human kindness is like a defective tap, the first gush may be impressive but the stream soon dries up.

1924 **Leon Uris:** American novelist. Joined the Marines at the beginning of World War II. Radioman at Guadalcanal, Tarawa, and New Zealand. Best-selling novel *Battle Cry* is the story of Marine training and combat. Forte is the semi-historical novel: *Exodus* about the Jewish resettlement in Palestine and creation of the Jewish state of Israel, *Trinity*, a fictional version of the troubles between the Catholics and Protestants in Northern Ireland, and *QB VII*, about the role of a Polish doctor in a German concentration camp.

Often we have no time for our friends but all the time in the world for our enemies.

1937 **Diane Wakoski:** American poet. Associated with the "deep image" movement and the Beats. Published over forty books of poetry, including: *Emerald Ice, Medea the Sorceress, Coins and Coffins, Greed, Parts I and II* and her best known, *Motorcycle Betrayal Poems.*

Poems reveal secrets when they are analyzed. The poet's pleasure is finding ingenious ways to enclose her secrets should be matched by the reader's pleasure in unlocking and revealing these secrets.

1941 **Martha Stewart:** American entrepreneur and general lifestyle guide. Born **Martha Helen Kostrya.** As a model, she appeared in several TV commercials and magazines. Began a catering business in 1976, the beginning of what would become a domestic arts business empire. Imprisoned in 2004 for lying to investigators of her alleged insider trading. Released in 2005 she is as popular and successful as ever.

All the things I love is what my business is about.

OTHERS: 1509 French scholar/painter **Étienne Dolet**, 1801 English gardener/architect **Joseph Paxton**, 1811 U.S. inventor **Elisha G. Otis**, 1832 Croatian composer **Ivan Zajc**, 1872 King of Norway **Haakon VII**, 1900 "Monkey trial" defendant **John T. Scopes**, 1902 U.S. orchestra leader **Ray Block**, 1903 Tunisian politician **Habib Bourguiba**, 1905 Austrian Catholic archbishop **Cardinal Franz König**, 1925 U.S. football coach **Marv Levy**, 1926 U.S. singer **Tony Bennett**, 1940 U.S. actor **Martin Sheen**, 1946 British politician **Jack Straw**, 1948 French Prime Minister **Jean-Pierre Raffarin**, 1951 Canadian hockey player **Marcel Dionne**

August 4

1792 **Percy Bysshe Shelley:** English Romantic poet. Privately published a series of Gothic-horror novelettes and verses while still in his teens. Shared a triangular relationship with May Godwin and her stepsister. Moved his household permanently to Italy to escape creditors, ill-health, and "social hatred." Championed liberty and rebelled against the strictures of English politics and religion. His passionate search for personal love and social justice was channeled into poems ranking with the greatest in the English language. Author of "Prometheus Unbound," "The Cloud," "Ozymandias" and "Epipsychidion."

Poetry is a mirror which makes beautiful that which is distorted.

1839 **Walter Pater:** English man of letters, critic and essayist. First became known with his *Studies in the History of the Renaissance* and for his philosophical romance, *Marius the Epicurean*. As a result of his *Appreciations with an Essay on Style* he was widely acknowledged as a master of English prose.

A museum ... often induces the feeling that nothing could ever have been young.

1840 Baron **Richard von Krafft-Ebing:** German neurologist and psychiatrist. Much of his work was on forensic psychiatry. Widely known for his studies of sexual aberrations and particularly for his collection of case histories *Psychopathia Sexualis* (1886). Coined the terms paranoia, sadism, and masochism.

Purely sensual love is never true or lasting, for which reason first love is, as a rule, but a passing infatuation, a fleeting passion.

1859 **Knut Hamsun:** Norwegian novelist, dramatist and poet. Born **Knut Pedersen**. Gained fame with his first novel, *Hunger*. Other works: *Mysterier*, *Pan* and *The Growth of the Soil*. Focused on the inner turmoil of the individual, but later widened his attention to include the effects of society on the individual, frequently featuring a wandering hero. Awarded the Nobel Prize for Literature in 1920.

In old age we are like a batch of letters that someone has sent. We are no longer in the past, we have arrived.

1870 Sir **Harry Lauder:** Scottish entertainer. Beloved star of the British music hall and American vaudeville singing Scottish songs, many of his own composition, and delivering recitations while dressed in traditional kilt. Most famous song: "Roamin' in the Gloamin'." Knighted in 1919 for his work in organizing entertainment for troops during World War I.

A bank account makes interesting reading, better than most novels.

1899 **Ezra Taft Benson:** American cabinet official and religious leader. Eisenhower's controversial Secretary of agriculture and head of the Mormon Church. Strong supporter of the John Birch Society, an organized in 1958 by Robert H. Welch, Jr., a retired candy maker to combat communism and promote ultraconservative causes.

Some of the greatest battles will be fought within the silent chambers of your own soul.

1900 **Elizabeth Bowes-Lyon, Queen Mother of the United Kingdom:** English monarch. Queen-consort of King George VI and mother of Queen Elizabeth II. Won the endearing love of the British subjects during the World War II bombings of England by adamantly refusing to take her daughters and herself out of the country to safety. The royal pair traveled extensively visiting heavily damaged towns.

The children will not leave unless I do. I shall not leave unless their father does, and the King will not leave the country in any circumstances whatever.

1904 **Witold Gombrowicz:** Polish novelist and dramatist. First successful novel was *Ferdydurke*, which dealt with the problems of immaturity and youth, and a critical examination of class roles in Polish society and culture, especially among the nobility. Work benefited from the virulent criticism of it by the nationalistic Warsaw establishment. Shortly before the outbreak of World War II, moved to Buenos Aires, Argentina and did not return because his works were banned by the communist Polish government.

I educated myself by reading books, especially those that were forbidden, and by doing nothing—for the freely wandering mind of the loafer is that which best develops the intelligence.

1912 **Raoul Wallenberg:** Swedish diplomat. Posted as First Secretary to the Swedish embassy in Budapest in 1941. Responsible for saving nearly 100,000 Budapest Jews from transportation to Auschwitz by designing a Swedish protection passport. Arrested by the Soviets in 1945. Evidence released from archives of Stalin's secret police reveals that he was executed by the Soviets as an alleged American spy in 1947. One week before being taken into "protective custody," he made the following statement:

For me there's no choice. I've taken on this assignment and I'd never be able to go back to Stockholm without knowing inside myself I'd done all a man could do to save as many Jews as possible.

1920 **Helen Thomas:** American journalist. Born to Lebanese immigrant parents. Joined the UPI news agency in Washington D.C. in 1943. Broke through a number of barriers to women reporters and won great respect in her field. Especially known for her coverage of American presidents and her bold and tireless pursuit of information. She became the reporter first recognized during press conferences.

This is the worst president ever. He (George W. Bush) is the worst president in all of American history.

1960 **José Luis Rodríguez Zapatero:** President of the Spanish Government when his party, the Spanish Socialist Workers' Party, won the 2004 general election. Withdrew Spanish troops from Iraq, reacting to polls that showed that more than 90% of Spaniards opposed the America-led invasion. Claimed he had made the decision before the March 2004 Madrid terrorist train bombings. On the domestic front, mostly concerned with social issues, including divorce and legalizing same-sex marriages, contributing to a growing tension between government and the Catholic Church.

Wars such as that which has occurred in Iraq only allow hatred, violence and terror to proliferate... You can't bomb a people just in case.

1961 **Barack Hussein Obama, Jr.:** American politician and U.S. Senator from Illinois. Received international media coverage for his keynote address at the 2004 Democratic National Convention while still an Illinois State Senator. Born in Honolulu, Hawaii to economist Barack Obama, Sr., a native of Kenya, and S. Ann Dunham, who divorced when their son was two years old. Initially practiced the Muslim religion, but later converted to Christianity. Known as a highly-principled supporter of liberal causes, is highly regarded for his ability to build coalitions and persuade opponents.

I'm so overexposed, I'm making Paris Hilton look like a recluse.

OTHERS: 1521 Pope **Urban VII**, 1701 Scottish classical scholar **Thomas Blackwell**, 1719 German mineralogist/geologist **Johann Gottlob Lehmann**, 1805 Irish mathematician **William Rowan Hamilton**, 1834 English mathematician **John Venn**, 1909 U.S. runner **Glenn Cunningham**, 1909 Brazilian landscape designer **Roberto Burle Marx**, 1912 Russian mathematician **Aleksandr D. Aleksandrov**, 1913 U.S. poet **Robert Hayden**, 1921 Canadian hockey player **Maurice Richard**, 1936 Algerian writer/filmmaker **Assia Djebar**, 1958 U.S. middle distance runner **Mary Decker Slaney**, 1942 New Zealand PM **David Lange**

August 5

1802 **Niels Henrik Abel:** Norwegian mathematician. At age 16, gave the first proof of the general binomial theorem. Proved that the general equation of the fifth degree ("the quintic") is not solvable by algebraic means. Instrumental in establishing mathematical analysis on a rigorous basis. Never in his brief lifetime, did he receive the recognition his genius deserved, but after his death of pneumonia, brought on by poverty and neglect, fellow mathematician Charles Hermite said of him: "Abel has left mathematicians enough to keep them busy for 500 years."

It appears to me that if one wants to make progress in mathematics, one should study the masters and not the pupils.

1850 **Guy de Maupassant:** French short-story writer and novelist. Pupil of Gustave Flaubert. Member of the naturalist school. Style was direct and simple, with attention paid to realistic detail. Stories are drawn mostly from humble Norman peasant life. Stories: "The Necklace" and "The Umbrella." Novels: *Bel-Ami* and *Pierre et Jean.*

It is better to be unhappy in love than unhappy in marriage, but some people manage to do both.

1876 **Mary Ritter Beard:** American historian and writer of feminism and the labor movement. Wrote *On Understanding Women* and *Women as a Force in History.* Married to historian Charles A. Beard with whom she collaborated on: *Rise of American Civilization* and *The American Spirit: A Study of the Idea of Civilization in the United States.*

In their (women) quest for rights they have naturally placed emphasis on their wrongs rather than their achievements and possessions, and have retold history as a story of their long martyrdom.

1886 **Bruce Barton:** American author, advertising executive and congressman. Co-founded BBDO advertising agency in 1919, heading it until 1961. Politically conservative; staunch opponent of Franklin D. Roosevelt. Served two terms in the House of Representatives (1937–41). Famous for bestselling guides to personal success. In his *The Man Nobody Knows*, Jesus Christ is depicted as a successful salesman and role model for the modern businessman. Also wrote *The Book Nobody Knows* and *What Can a Man Believe?*

When you are through changing, you are through.

1890 **Naum Gabo:** Russian-American Sculptor. Born **Naum Pevsner**. With his brother Antoine Pevsner issued the Realist Manifesto, in which they set out the principles of European Constructivism. One of the earliest artists to experiment with kinetic sculptor, produced abstract sculptors using materials such as glass, plastic and wire to achieve a sense of movement.

Art has no need of philosophical arguments, it does not follow the signposts of philosophical systems; Art like life, dictates systems to philosophy.

1899 **Conrad Potter Aiken:** American poet, novelist and critic. Work reflects his intense interest in psychoanalysis and the development of identity. Forms and sounds of music pervade his poetry. Pulitzer Prize in 1929 for *Selected Poems* and a National Book Award in 1953 for *Collected Poems.* Novels: *Blue Voyage* and *King Coffin.* Edited Emily Dickson's *Selected Poems*, which was largely responsible for establishing her posthumously literary reputation.

Separate we come, and separate we go. And this be it known, is all that we know.

1906 **John Huston:** U.S. film director, screenwriter and actor. Son of actor Walter Huston, father of Anjelica Huston. Dealt with the struggles of flawed men, whose best-laid plans are undone by their human weaknesses. Oscar winner as director and screenwriter for *The Treasure of the Sierra Madre.* Nominated as director for *The Asphalt Jungle, Moulin Rouge* and *Prizzi's Honor.* Eight other nominations for Best Screenwriting. Autobiography: *An Open Book.*

After all, crime is only a left-handed form of human endeavor.

1906 **Wassily Leontief:** Russian economist who did research on how changes in one economic sector effect other sectors. Arrested several times for his opposition to Communism. In 1931 he went to the U.S. to work for the National Bureau of Economic Research. In 1973 he won the Bank of Sweden Prize in Economic Sciences in Memory of Albert Nobel. Publications: *Studies in the Structure of the American Economy, The Future of the World Economics* and *Essays in Economics.*

If fewer people can produce the goods and services the country needs, what happens to the other people?

1930 **Neil Armstrong:** U.S. astronaut. Won three Air Medals in the Korean War after which he became a civilian research pilot for the forerunner of NASA. Member of the second group of astronauts. Command pilot of *Gemini* 8, which completed the first manual docking maneuver. On the *Apollo 11* mission, he became the first man to step on the moon, saying "That's one small step for a man, one giant leap for mankind."

It suddenly struck me that that tiny pea, pretty and blue, was the Earth. I put up my thumb and shut one eye, and my thumb blotted out the planet Earth. I didn't feel like a giant. I felt very, very small.

1937 **Herb Brooks:** American hockey coach, best known for leading the U.S. hockey team to a gold medal in the 1980 Winter Olympic Games, The American team, composed of college-aged players, defeated the heavily favored Soviet team, which had won the previous four Olympic gold medals, an event that has been called the *Miracle on Ice*. They then went on to defeat Finland to take the gold. Later coached the New York Rangers, Minnesota North Stars, New Jersey Devils and Pittsburgh Penguins in the NHL

Great moments are born from great opportunities.

1946 **Jimmy Webb:** American pop music composer. Had hit songs in the 1960s, 70s, 80s, and 90s. Only person to receive Grammy Awards in all three categories: music, lyrics and orchestration. His top ten hits have been sung by a disparate group of vocalists, including "By the Time I Get to Phoenix" and "Wichita Lineman" by Glen Campbell; "All I Know" by Art Garfunkel; "MacArthur Park" by Richard Harris, and "Up, Up and Away" by The Fifth Dimension.

We as songwriters are in the same position as a professional fisherman. Our fishing grounds are kind of fished out.

1962 **Patrick Ewing:** American basketball player. Born in Kingston, Jamaica, he grew to 7 feet tall. Had an All-American career at Georgetown University. Was the number one overall college draft pick in 1985. As a center for the New York Knicks, holds many team records, an All-Star 11 times in 13 seasons. Is only the 12th player in NBA history to score more than 20,000 points and have over 10,000 rebounds.

Whenever my body heals and the pain and all the swelling goes away is when I'll be ready.

OTHERS: 1604 "Apostle to the Indians" **John Eliot**, 1623 Italian composer **Antonio Cesti**, 1662 Scottish historian **James Anderson**, 1811 French composer **Ambroise Thomas**, 1813 Norwegian poet **Ivar Aasen**, 1815 English explorer **Edward John Eyre**, 1860 "Elephant Man" **Joseph Carey Merrick**, 1872 Brazilian physician **Oswaldo Cruz**, 1890 Austrian composer **Erick Kleiber**, 1897 Danish politician **Aksel Larsen**, 1911 U.S. actor **Robert Taylor**, 1923 U.S. Attorney General **Richard G. Kleindienst**, 1923 President of Singapore **Devan Nair**, 1944 U.S. actress **Loni Anderson**, 1975 Indian actress **Kajol Mukherjee**

August 6

1638 **Nicolas Malebranche:** French philosopher, scientist, and theologian. Although he admired Descartes' physics and method he found fault with the latter's metaphysics. In his principle work *The Search for Truth*, asserted that God arranges an exact correspondence between our notions of material objects and the objects themselves. His views embroiled him in conflict with the Jansenists, although his solution of Cartesian dualism won him many disciples.

Just as our eyes need light in order to see, our minds need ideas in order to conceive.

1715 **Luc de Clapiers, Marquis de Vauvenargues:** French moralist and essayist. In his small amounts of work, which are still of interest, he shares his detached thoughts on questions of moral philosophy and literary criticism. He thinks nobly of man and has been called a modern Stoic. Well-known for his aphorisms and maxims.

When a thought is too weak to be expressed simply, it is clear proof that it should be rejected.

1809 **Alfred, Lord Tennyson:** English poet. Often regarded as the chief representative of the Victorian era in poetry. Although very popular in his lifetime, his work has been criticized for shallowness and sentimentality. Works: "Locksley Hall," "The Charge of the Light Brigade," "In Memoriam" and "Enoch Arden."

Knowledge comes, but wisdom lingers.

1868 **Paul Claudel:** French playwright, diplomat and poet. Brother of French sculptor Camille Claudel. His brilliant diplomatic career began in 1892. French ambassador to Japan (1921–27) and the United States (1927–33). At the same time he pursued a literary career, using poetry and drama to express his conception of the grand design of creation. Poetic dramas: *Break of Noon, The Hostage, Tidings Brought to Mary* and his masterpiece *The Satin Slipper*.

It is fortunate that diplomats have long noses since they usually can't see beyond them.

1874 **Charles Fort:** American journalist, writer and researcher into the abnormal and unexplained. *Forteana* is sometimes used to describe various anomalous phenomena. Called "essentially a satirist highly skeptical of human beings — especially scientists' claims to ultimate knowledge." Investigated phenomena for which science could not account and as a result they were rejected or ignored. These appeared in seven books, most notably *The Book of the Damned, New Lands, Lo!* and *Wild Talents*.

The ideal state is meekness, or humility, or the semi-invalid state of the old. Year after year I am becoming nobler and nobler. If I can live to be decrepit enough, I shall be a saint.

1881 Sir **Alexander Fleming:** Scottish bacteriologist. First to use antityphoid vaccines on human beings and pioneered the use of Salvarsan against syphilis. Discovered penicillin in 1928. He shared the 1945 Nobel Prize for Physiology or Medicine with Howard Florey and Ernst Chain, who perfected a method of producing the volatile drug.

One sometimes finds what one is not looking for.

1883 **Scott Nearing:** American sociologist, conservationist, peace activist, educator, writer and radical. Fought against child labor and abuses of big business. Retired to become a homesteader in Maine. Books: *Poverty and Riches*, *Democracy Is Not* Enough, *Living the Good Life* and *The Conscience of a Radical.*

War drags human beings from their tasks of building and improving, and pushes them en masse into the category of destroyers and killers.

1893 **Wright Patman:** American lawyer and politician. Member of the U.S. House of Representatives from Texas (1928–76). Chairman of the House Banking Committee for 13 years. Sponsored the legislation that established the Small Business Administration.

The dollar represents a one dollar debt to the Federal Reserve System. The Federal Reserve Banks create money out of thin air to buy Government Bonds from the U.S. Treasury ... and have created out of nothing a ... debt which the American people are obliged to pay with interest.

1911 **Lucille Ball:** American actress, comedienne and astute businesswoman. Made her greatest mark with TV series "I Love Lucy," with then-husband Desi Arnaz and her solo shows that followed. Preeminent female star of the early decades of television. President of Desilu, one of the world's largest television production companies. Famous for her red hair, rasping voice and being alternately brassy and feminine.

Once in his life, every man is entitled to fall madly in love with a gorgeous redhead.

1916 **Richard Hofstadter:** American historian, who made important contributions to the study of American social, political, and cultural history. Received Pulitzer Prizes for *The Age of Reform* and *Anti-Intellectualism in American Life*. Long-time professor at Columbia University, prompting him to remark: "No one who lives among intellectuals is likely to idolize them unduly."

If there is anything more dangerous to the life of the mind than having no independent commitment to ideas, it is having an excess of commitment to some special and constricting idea.

1917 **Robert Mitchum:** American actor. Made his screen debut acting in Hopalong Cassidy westerns. Got noticed for his performance in *The Story of G.I. Joe*. Whether a hero or a villain he was known for his laconic, sleepy-eyed and deceptively casual manner. Films: *Out of the Past, Crossfire, The Night of the Hunter, Cape Fear, and Farewell, My Lovely*. Starred in the TV series based on Herman Wouk's *The Winds of War* and *War and Remembrance.*

Every two or three years I knock off for a while. That way I'm constantly the new girl in the whorehouse.

1927 **Andy Warhol:** Originally **Andrew Warhola**. American artist, filmmaker and leading exponent of the Pop Art Movement. Known for paintings of soup cans and celebrities. Adroit self-promoter, he conceived of the artist as a celebrity. Made several avant-garde films, noted for their pointlessness. Considered one of the most important and influential American cultural figures of the late 20th century.

I am a deeply superficial person.

OTHERS: 1180 Japanese emperor **Go-Toba,** 1504 Archbishop of Canterbury **Matthew Parker**, 1619 Italian singer **Barbara Strozzi**, 1697 Holy Roman Emperor **Charles VII**, 1766 English chemist **William Hyde Wollaston**, 1881 U.S. gossip columnist **Lucille Parsons**, 1889 English poet **John Middleton Murry**, 1892 U.S. actor **Hoot Gibson**, 1902 U.S. gangster **Dutch Schultz**, 1922 English entrepreneur **Sir Freddie Laker**, 1932 British painter **Howard Hodgkin**, 1943 U.S. computer scientist **Jon Postel**, 1962 Hong Kong actress **Michelle Yeoh**, 1970 Film director **M. Night Shyamalan**, 1990 U.S. beauty queen/murder victim **JonBenét Ramsey**

August 7

1560 Countess **Erzabet (Elizabeth) Bathory:** Hungarian terror of Transylvania. Perpetuated incredible sadistic cruelties of vampirism and mutilation upon pretty servant and peasant girls in an underground torture chamber, earning her the title, "Blood Countess." Allegedly believed bathing in the blood of female virgins would maintain her beauty. Number of her victims has been estimated as nearly 600. While her accomplices in blood orgies were ultimately brought to trial and either beheaded or burned alive, because of her noble birth, she was found to be criminally insane and was walled up with in a room of her castle, where she died of natural causes at the age of 54. Her incantation for protection by the deity Isten:

When I am in danger send ninety-nine cats to come with speed and ... keep Elizabeth safe from harm.

1742 **Nathaniel Greene:** Military officer during the American Revolutionary War. At the beginning of the conflict, merely a militia private, but acquired many volumes on military tactics and taught himself the art of war. Congress appointed him a brigadier of the Continental Congress and General George Washington assigned him the command of Boston. Emerged from the war with a reputation as the most military gifted officer, second only to Washington.

I am determined to defend my rights and maintain my freedom or sell my life in the attempt.

1867 **Emil Nolde:** German expressionist painter, printmaker and watercolorist. Solitary painter, fervently religious and racked by a sense of guilt. Created such works as *Dance Around the Golden Calf* and *Marsh Landscape*. As a graphic artist, primarily noted for star black-and-white crudely incised woodcuts. Although a member of the Nazi party, his work was considered "degenerate" and he was forbidden to paint.

Clever people master life; the wise illuminate it and create fresh difficulties.

1876 **Mata Hari:** Pseudonym of **Margaretha Geertruida Zelle Macleod**. Dutch dancer and courtesan.

Lived in Java and Sumatra. After returning to Europe she began dancing in Paris, virtually nude. Soon had many lovers. Joined the German Secret Service during World War I. Passed on military secrets that she wormed out of her Allied lovers. Convicted of spying, she was executed by a French firing squad.

I am a woman who enjoys herself very much; sometimes I lose, sometimes I win.

1885 **Billie Burke:** American actress. The toast of Broadway in the early part of the century. Married Florenz Ziegfeld. Starred in numerous silent films, but is best remembered as a fluttery matron in a number of films, including the *Topper* series, and as Glinda, the good witch in *The Wizard of Oz*.

Age is something that doesn't matter, unless you are a cheese.

1903 **Louis B. Leakey:** Kenya-born British anthropologist, archaeologist and paleontologist. Convinced that Africa was the cradle of mankind, in 1959, with his wife Mary, unearthed the skull of "Zinjanthropus." In 1964, found remains of *Homo habilis* and in 1967 discovered *Kenyapithecus africanus*. Fostered field research of primates in their natural habitat, choosing three female researchers, later dubbed "Leakey's Angels." Jane Goodall studied chimpanzees in Tanzania; Dian Fossey made an extensive study of the mountain gorillas in Rwanda; and Birutė Galdikas studied orangutans in Borneo.

We decided to leave a part of each and every excavated area exactly as we had found it, protecting the specimens from rain and excessive sun.

1904 **Ralph Bunche:** African-American diplomat and educator. Taught political science at Howard University (1928–50). Directed the U.N. Trusteeship department (1947–54). Principal Secretary of U.N. Palestine Commission. 1950 Nobel Prize for mediating Palestine conflict (1948–49).

There are no warlike people, just warlike leaders

1929 **Don Larsen:** American baseball player. In an otherwise unremarkable career he was the first and thus far only pitcher to hurl a perfect game in World Series play. It occurred in the 1954 series won by his team the New York Yankees in seven games over the Brooklyn Dodgers.

Sometimes a week might go by when I don't think about that game, but I don't remember when it happened last.

1942 **Garrison Keillor:** American author, humorist, musician, satirist, story teller and radio personality. In 1974 he created and hosted the public radio humor and musical show *Prairie Home Companion*, which still airs today with a wide and loyal following. Each episode features a story from fictional Lake Wobegon, Minnesota, "where the women are strong, the men are good looking, and all the children are above average." Books: best-selling *Lake Wobegon Days*, *Leaving Home*, *The Sandy Bottom Orchestra* and *Good Poems for Hard Times*.

I believe in looking reality straight in the eye and denying it.

1945 **Alan Page:** All-American football defensive end for the University of Notre Dame. Played professionally at tackle with the Minnesota Vikings as part of its legendary "Purple People Eaters" front line. First defensive player to win the NFL's Most Valuable Player award. Earned a law degree while continuing his career with the Chicago Bears. In a distinguished legal career, first African-American ever elected to state wide office, winning a seat as an Associate Justice of the Minnesota State Supreme Court Justice in 1992. Reelected in 1998, the largest vote-getter in Minnesota history. Speaking of his first election:

I felt like I played a very tough football game with no hitting above the waist.

1966 **Jimmy Donal "Jimbo" Wales:** American founder and President of the Wikimedia Foundation, which operates the free internet encyclopedia Wikipedia. A *wiki*, a shortened form of the Hawaiian *wiki wiki*, meaning "quick," is a website that allows anyone visiting it to add, remove, or otherwise alter the content, quickly and easily. As a futures and options trader, earning enough money to "support himself and his wife for the rest of their lives," enabling him to set up and fund his peer-reviewed, open–content encyclopedia.

The purpose is really contained in the word "freely licensed," which is to make available to anyone in the world, in any language, a curriculum they can copy, redistribute and modify for whatever purpose they may have, for free.

1975 **Charlize Theron:** Gorgeous South African-born model and actress. Attended the Joffrey Ballet School, but a knee injury ended her career as a ballet dance. Moved to Hollywood, and after a few small roles, her career skyrocketed in the late 1990s, culminating in her Academy Award winning performance as serial killer Aileen Wuornos in the 2003 film *Monster*. To do so, she had to hide her beauty. Other films: *North Country* (Oscar nomination), *The Legend of Bigger Vance*, and *The Cider House Rules*.

There's only so much you can do, but if somebody doesn't give you a chance there is nothing you can do.

OTHERS: 317 Roman emperor **Constantius II**, 1400 French composer **Guillaume Dufay**, 1598 Swedish poet **Georg Stiernhielm**, 1726 American revolutionary leader **James Bowdoin**, 1779 German geographer **Carl Ritter**, 1844 French geologist **Auguste Michel-Lévy**, 1911 U.S. director **Nicholas Ray**, 1925 Indian scientist **M.S. Swaninathan**, 1926 U.S. comedian **Stan Freberg**, 1927 U.S. politician **Edwin W. Edwards**, 1928 Canadian magician **James Randi**, 1929 U.S. evangelist **Ruth Carter Stapleton**, 1940 Prime Minister of Belgium **Jean-Luc Dehaene**, 1942 U.S. singer **B.J. Thomas**, 1955 Russian writer **Vladimir Sorokin**

August 8

1694 **Francis Hutchinson:** Irish philosopher and one of the founding fathers of the Scottish Enlightenment. Exponent of the moral-sense theory of ethics. Published anonymously the essays for which he is best known: the *Inquiry concerning Beauty, Order, Harmony and Design*, the *Inquiry concerning Moral Good and Evil, Thoughts on Laughter* and *Observations on the Fable of the Bees*. His main work, *A System of Moral Philosophy*, was published posthumously.

That action is best which produces the greatest happiness for the greatest numbers.

1839 **Nelson A. Miles:** American General. Fought in the Army of the Potomac during the Civil War, rising to the rank of brigadier general. Served as Confederate president Jefferson Davis' jailer and was criticized for keeping his prisoner shackled in his cell. Fought the American Indians on the Western frontier, capturing both Chief Joseph and Geronimo. Forever remembered with shame for allowing the massacre at Wound Knee.

If the graves of the thousands of victims who have fallen in the terrible wars of the two races had been placed in line the philanthropist might travel from the Atlantic to the Pacific and from the Lakes to the Gulf, and be constantly in sight of green mounds.

1866 **Matthew Henson:** African-American explorer. Accompanied Admiral Robert Peary on all his polar expeditions. Placed the American flag at the Geographic North Pole in 1909. Wrote about his artic explorations in *A Negro Explorer at the North Pole*. Because of racist views of the time, he never gained the fame lavished on Peary. In 2000, the National Geographic Society awarded the Hubbard Medal to Henson posthumously.

As I stood there at the top of the world and thought of the hundreds of men who had lost their lives in the effort to reach it, I felt profoundly grateful that I had the honor of representing my race.

1883 **Emilano Zapata:** Mexican revolutionary leader of a Mexican agrarian movement. National hero of Mexico. General of the Liberation Army of the South. Supported Francisco Madero's overthrow of dictator Porfirio Díaz. Some land reforms were accomplished but Zapata was dissatisfied and mobilized his army once again. Madero was overthrown by Victoriano Huerta, who suppressed land reforms. Lured to a meeting with a Mexican officer who claimed to wish to defect, Zapata was riddled by bullets by soldiers. In a letter to Pancho Villa, he wrote:

Ignorance and obscurantism have never produced anything other than flocks of slaves for tyranny.

1884 **Sara Teasdale:** American lyrical poet. Major themes were love, nature's beauty, and death. Received the Columbia University Poetry Society Prize (the forerunner of the Pulitzer Prize for Poetry) for her *Love Songs* (1917). Other poetry collections: *Helen of Troy and Other Poems, Dark of the Moon* and *Strange Victory*. In 1933, took an overdose of sleeping pills, lay down in a warm bath, and fell asleep, from which she never awoke.

When I can look life in the eyes, grown calm and very coldly wise, live will have given me the truth, and taken in exchange — my youth.

1896 **Marjorie Kinnan Rawlings:** American author, environmentalist, and supporter of civil rights at a time when few southerners were willing to take that stand. Lived in remote rural Florida and wrote novels with rural themes and settings. Best known work is *The Yearling*, the story of a boy and his pet deer, which won a Pulitzer Prize for fiction. Other Novels: *South Moon Under, Cross Creek*, and *The Sojourner*.

A woman has got to love a bad man once or twice in her life, to be thankful for a good one.

1902 **Paul Dirac:** English theoretical physicist. One of the most gifted mathematical thinkers of the 20th century. Driven by a search for beauty and elegance in the equations he developed. Best known for his work in quantum mechanics and his theory of the spinning electron. Formulated a quantum theory for the motion of electrons in electric and magnetic fields. Famous "Dirac equation" reconciled Austrian physicist Erwin Schrödinger's earlier quantum theory and Einstein's theory of relativity. Dirac's work earned him the Nobel Prize for Physics (1933), shared with Schrödinger.

God used beautiful mathematics in creating the world.

1908 **Arthur J. Goldberg:** U.S. government official, jurist and labor lawyer. Played an important role in the merger of the CIO and AFL. U.S. Secretary of Labor (1961–62). Associate Justice of the Supreme Court (1962–65). Argued that imposition of the death penalty was condemned by the international community and should be regarded as "cruel and unusual punishment." His stand encouraged attorneys to challenge the death penalty, with the effect that executions ceased for most of the 1960s and 70s. Resigned to replace the late Adlai Stevenson as U.S. ambassador to the U.N. (1965–68).

If Columbus had an advisory committee he would probably still be at the dock.

1922 **Rudi Gernreich:** Austrian-born American fashion designer and gay activist, who invented the "unisex fashion." Introduced plastic fabrics in futuristic modes. Most famous for designing topless bathing suits (monokini) and evening gowns, and the thong swimsuit. His clothes embodied the contradictions of his time, especially as regarding the emerging independent roles of women.

UNISEX clothing is an anonymous sort of uniform of an indefinite revolutionary cast.

1929 **Ronnie Biggs:** British criminal involved in the Great Train Robbery of 1963 when. £2.6 million was stolen from a mail train. Convicted and imprisoned, he escaped, and fled to Australia and then Brazil. When British police located him in Rio de Janeiro, he couldn't be extradited because he was the father of a Brazilian child. Reportedly returned to England in disguise while a documentary about the robbery was made. After suffering a stroke, returned to England for the free health care program and was imprisoned.

There's a difference between criminals and crooks. Crooks steal. Criminals blow some guy's brains out. I'm a crook.

1931 **Roger Penrose:** English mathematical physicist. Emeritus Rouse Ball Professor of Mathematics at the University of Oxford. In 1965, Penrose and physicist Steven Hawking proved that singularities, such as black holes, could be formed from the gravitational collapse of dying immense stars. As a result they were jointly awarded the Eddington Medal of the Royal Astronomical Society. Publications: *The Emperor's New Mind, Shadows of the Mind, The Large, the Small and the Human Mind,* and *The Road to Reality: A Complete Guide to the Laws of the Universe.*

Consciousness is the phenomenon whereby the universe's very existence is made known,

1937 **Dustin Hoffman:** U.S. actor on stage and screen. Studied with Lee Strasberg, becoming a dedicated method actor. Came to prominence for his Academy Award nominated role in *The Graduate,* playing a disaffected college graduate. His reputation as a perfectionist, often found him in conflict with directors. Won Oscars for *Kramer vs. Kramer* and *Rain Man.* Also nominated for *Midnight Cowboy, Lenny* and *Tootsie.* Starred on Broadway as Willy Loman in *Death of a Salesman.*

A good review from the critics is just another stay of execution.

OTHERS: 1602 French mathematician **Gilles de Roberval**, 1646 German-born painter **Godfrey Kneller**, 1673 Scottish spy **John Ker**, 1814 Suffragist/1st U.S. woman judge **Esther Morris**, 1891 German violinist **Adolf Busch**, 1901 U.S. physicist **Ernest O. Lawrence**, 1905 French composer **André Jolivet**, 1907 U.S. musician/arranger **Benny Carter**, 1915 U.S. track coach **James "Jumbo" Elliott**, 1921 U.S. country singer **Webb Pierce**, 1921 Indian medical scientist. **V. Ramalingaswami**, 1921 U.S. actress/swimmer **Esther Williams**, 1958 U.S. reporter/TV host **Deborah Norville**, 1981 Swiss tennis player **Roger Federer**

August 9

1593 **Izaak Walton:** English writer. Best known for *The Compleat Angler,* a discourse on the pleasures of fishing, combines practical information about angling with folklore, quotations from diverse writers, pastoral interludes of songs and ballads and glimpses of idyllic rural life. Also wrote admiring biographies of Sir Henry Wotton, Richard Hooker and George Herbert. Prose work is distinguished by great simplicity, grace of style, and humor.

Good company in a journey makes the way seem shorter.

1631 **John Dryden:** English poet, dramatist and critic. Most of his early writing was for the theatre and included several rhymed heroic plays: *The Indian Queen, The Indian Emperour* and *Conquest of Granada.* Noted for tragic-comedies, *Secret Love, Marriage à-la-Mode* and *The Assignation.* Famed for satiric and didactic verse: *The Hind and the Panther* and *Absalom and Achitophel. His Essay on Dramatic Posey* was one of the chief models for modern prose.

Love is not in our choice but in our fate.

1653 **John Oldham:** English poet. Published several Pindaric odes, but is most remembered for his ironical *Satire against Virtue* and *Satires upon the Jesuits.* Also translated and wrote imitations of Juvenal, Horace, Bion, Moschus and Boileau. Died of smallpox at age 30 and was commemorated by Dryden in well-known lines beginning: "Farewell, too little and too lately known."

While some no other cause for life can give, but a dull habitude to live.

1809 **William Barrett Travis:** South Carolina-born Texan lawyer and army officer. On February 3, 1836 became the commander of the regular soldiers at the Alamo with James Bowie commanding the volunteers. Troops of Mexico's Santa Anna began their assault on the Alamo on February 23, 1836. After fighting off the attack for thirteen days, the greatly outnumbered defenders, including Travis, Bowie and legendary Davy Crockett, were all killed. During the siege Travis wrote a letter addressed "To the People of Texas and All American in the World," calling for aid to be sent to his garrison, containing the promise:

[If this call is neglected] I am determined to sustain myself for as long as possible, and die like a soldier who never forgets what is due to his own honor and that of his country. Victory or Death.

1871 **Leonid Andreyev:** Russian writer. Studied law at the universities of St. Petersburg and Moscow and during this period, depression led him to several suicide attempts. Encouraged by Maxim Gorky, he turned to writing. His early realistic works were concerned with sensational themes of the awakening sexuality of a young man, insanity and murder. Searched for sensational effect and symbolic import in his novels and plays. Works: *In the Fog, Thought, The Red Laugh, He Who Gets Slapped* and *The Life of Man.*

The loss of reason in war seems to me honorable, like the death of a sentry at his post.

1896 **Jean Piaget:** Swiss psychologist and educator. Pioneer investigator of the origin and development of children's intellectual faculties. Theories center on his principle that children perceive the world differently than adults and that their development proceeds in genetically determined stages, always following the same sequence. Significant Works: *The Language and Thought of the Child, The Psychology of Intelligence* and *The Growth of Logical Thinking from Childhood to Adolescence.*

The current stage of knowledge is a moment in history, changing just as rapidly as the sate of knowledge in the past has ever changed and, in many instances, more rapidly.

1896 **Lev S. Vygotsky:** Russian psychologist. Pressured to modify his theories to match the prevailing political ideology, he refused and his work was expunged several years after his death. Unlike Piaget, he saw a child's development as the result of interaction with others and believed that the culture within which the child is raised influences the operations a child will develop. His view makes instruction central to a child's development of mental processes. Posthumous work *Thought and Language* was initially suppressed as a threat to Stalinism.

The only good kind of instruction is that which marches ahead of development and leads it.

1922 **Philip Larkin:** British librarian, novelist and poet. Led the post World War II antiromantic movement. Wrote subtle, cynical and witty poems critical of contemporary life. Novels: *Jill* and A *Girl in Winter.* Poetry collections: *The North Ship, The Less Deceived, The Whitsun Weddings* and *High Windows.* Edited *The Oxford Book of Twentieth Century English Verse.* Developed an interest in jazz music, resulting in his volume of essays, *All What Jazz.*

Why should I let the toad work/Squat on my life?/ Can't I use my wit as a pitchfork/ And drive the brute off?

1927 **Marvin Minsky:** American computer scientist, electrical engineer, mathematician and educator. Spent his entire career at MIT. Significant contributions to artificial intelligence, cognitive psychology, neural networks and the theory of Turing machines. Pioneer in robotics, he influenced many projects working to build into machines human capacity for commonsense reasoning. His ideas are reflected in his *The Society of Mind.*

No computer has ever been designed that is ever aware of what it is doing; but most of the time, we aren't either.

1928 **Bob Cousy:** U.S. basketball player and coach. All-American at Holy Cross. One of the best ball-handling guards and playmakers led the Boston Celtics to six NBA championships. Ten times all-star. After his playing days, coached at Boston College and the Cincinnati Royals. Elected to Hall of Fame (1970).

My game strength was court savvy.

1938 **Ron Laver:** Australian professional tennis player nicknamed the "Rocket." Member of Australia's Davis Cup team at 18, remaining on the squad until he turned pro in 1963. Second male player, after Don Budge, to win the Grand Slam of Tennis (1962), and first to repeat the feat seven years later. By the time of his retirement in 1971, he was tennis' them all-time leading money winner.

An otherwise happily married couple may turn a mixed doubles game into a scene from Who's Afraid of Virginia Woolf?

1939 **Romano Prodi:** Italian politician and former President of the European Commission (1999–2004). Served as Minister of Industry and held numerous posts on various commissions through the 1980s and 90s. Twice came under investigation, charged with conflict of interest over contracts awarded to his economic research company, but was acquitted. Prime Minister in 1996, but his government fell in 1998 when the Communist party withdrew its support.

Nobody can be rich and stupid for more than one generation.

OTHERS: 1201 English chronicler **Arnold Fitz Thedmar**, 1848 German composer **Johann Michael Bach**, 1674 Czech architect **František Maximilián Kaňka**, 1726 Italian Jesuit scientist **Francesco Cetti**, 1757 Scottish civil engineer **Thomas Telford**, 1776 Italian chemist **Amedeo Avogadro**, 1845 Canadian religious figure **Brother Andre**, 1899 Australian author **P.L. Travers**, 1902 French violinist **Zino Francescatti**, 1913 U.S. politician **Herman Talmadge**, 1914 Finnish author **Tove Jansson**, 1957 U.S. actress **Melanie Griffith**, 1963 U.S. pop singer/actress **Whitney Houston**, 1967 U.S. sports figure **Deion Sanders**

August 10

1753 **Edmund Jennings Randolph:** American public official and lawyer. Joined the Continental Army as aide-de-camp to George Washington. Delegate to the Continental Congress (1779–1782), where he introduced the Virginia Plan as an outline for a new national government. First U.S. Attorney General (1789–94). U.S. Secretary of State (1794–95). A scandal erupted when an intercepted French message implied he was prone to bribery, leading to his resignation. In 1807, served as defense counsel during Aaron Burr's trial for treason.

Our chief danger arises from the democratic parts of our constitution.

1810 **Camillo di Cavour:** Italian statesman. Influenced by revolutionary ideas from an earlier age, he founded the liberal newspaper *Il Risorgimento*, becoming a leading figure of the Risorgimento (Resurgence), the 19th century movement for Italian unification. Elected to the Parliament, he held several cabinet posts. By exploiting international rivalries succeeded in unifying Italy under the House of Saxony, with him as first prime minister of the new kingdom (1861).

I have discovered the art of deceiving diplomats. I tell them the truth and they never believe me.

1845 **Kunanbaev Ibragim Abai:** Kazakh poet, philosopher, composer and educator. Founder of modern Kazakh literature was afforded a European post education in Russia. Early promoter of the Russian language and culture among the Kazakhs. Helped legitimize Kazakh as a written language by employing the vernacular for his translations of European writings. Until his time, his country's poetry was mostly oral.

When summer in the mountains gains its peak,/ When gaily blooming flowers begin to fade,/ When nomads from the sunshine refuge seek/ Beside a rapid river, in a glade,/ Then the grassy meadows here and there/ The salutatory neighing can be heard/ Of varicolored stallion and mare.

1858 **Anna Julia Haywood Cooper:** African-American author, educator and scholar. Received a Ph.D. in history from the University of Paris-Sorbonne in 1925, only the fourth African-American to earn a doctorate. Taught at Saint Augustine's Normal School in Raleigh, North Carolina and at the M Street School in Washington D.C., where she also was principal. Books: *A Voice from the South: By a Woman from the South* and *The Attitude of France on the Question of Slavery between 1789 and 1848.*

Let woman's claim be as broad in the concrete as in the abstract.

1869 **Laurence Binyon:** British poet and art historian. Best known for his highly respected translation of Dante's *Divine Comedy* into *terza rima*, an Italian verse form in chain-rhymed *tercets* (stanza of three lines), the second line of each stanza rhyming with the first and third of the next. His collections of Poems: *The North Star* and *The Burning of the Leaves.* Wrote pioneering works on Oriental art and translated Japanese poems.

They shall grow not old, as we that are left grow old/Age shall not weary them, nor the years condemn/At the going down of the sun and in the morning/We will remember them.

1874 **Herbert C. Hoover:** American statesman and thirty-first president of the U.S.A. An engineer, he headed Allied relief operations during World War I. Secretary of Commerce in 1921 and seven years later the Republican candidate for president. As president, done in by the Great Depression and for opposing direct governmental assistance to the unemployed, losing to Franklin D. Roosevelt (1932). Participated in famine relief work after World War II. The Hoover Dam is named for him.

Older men declare war. But it is the youth that must fight and die.

1881 **Witter Bynner:** American poet and Chinese literature scholar. Composed "Canticle of Praise," a long dramatic ode for an armistice celebration at the end of World War I. Traveled to China, where he translated 18th century Chinese poetry. Settled in Santa Fe, drawn into a literary circle dominated by Mabel Dodge Luhan, who once accused Bynner of single-handedly introducing homosexuality into New Mexico. His works: *The New World, The Persistence of Poetry* and *A Book of Lyrics.*

I am a miser of my memories of you/ And will not spend them.

1884 **Panaït Istrati:** Romanian writer nicknamed *The Maxim Gorky of the Balkans.* Believing in the ideals of the Bolshevik revolution he traveled to Russia, planning to become a citizen, but later disillusioned by the extent of Stalin's dictatorship. Wrote several books expressing his disenchantment, including, *The Confession of a Loser.* Other works: *The Bandits, Adrien Zagraffi's Childhood,* and *The Sponge-Fisher.*

Because the kindness of a single human is more powerful than the meanness of a thousand; the evil extinguishes together with the one who provoked it; the good continues to beam after the disappearance of the just.

1897 **Reuben Nakian:** "Grand Old Man of American Sculpture." Maintained innovative spirit and creativity for more than 70 years. Constantly rethinking and revising his modes of sculptural expression. Explored and mastered the use of new media, everything from clay, plaster, metal, paper, to Styrofoam. Used Greek and Roman mythology in his works: *Voyage to Crete, Rape of Lucrece, Mars, Venus* and *Birds in Flight.*

Sculpture should have a powerful human content. Sculpture should be poetry.

1928 **Jimmy Dean:** American singer, actor and sausage entrepreneur. Host of the Washington D.C. program *Town and Country Time*, which gave Patsy Cline and Roy Clark their starts. Best known song "Big Bad John," number one on the Billboard charts and the 1962 Grammy winner for Best Country & Western Recording. His mid–1960s variety show gave network exposure to country music entertainers such as Roger Miller, George Jones, Charlie Rich and Buck Owens. After the show ended, he founded the Jimmy Dean Sausage Brand, which prospered, in part because of his good-natured commercials.

I can't change the direction of the wind, but I can adjust my sails to reach my destination.

1928 **Eddie Fisher:** American singer. Protégé of Eddie Cantor. Hit songs: "Any Time," "Wish You Were Here," "I'm Walking Behind You," and "Oh! My Pa-Pa." Wed actress Debbie Reynolds, dubbed "America's Couple." Three years later, consoling Elizabeth Taylor, widow of Mike Todd, led to break-up of his marriage. Wed Taylor shortly thereafter, but got his comeuppance when she and Richard Burton found each other while making *Cleopatra.* Speaking ungallantly of his ex:

Debbie Reynolds was indeed the girl next door. But only if you lived next door to a self-centered, totally driven, insecure, untruthful phony.

1942 **Betsey Johnson:** Rule-breaking American fashion designer of some of the most over-the-top fashions, including ripped fishnets, vinyl, wild leathers, biker chic, and the ditzy look. Dubbed "The Madwoman of Seventh Avenue," designed clothes that were sexy but whimsical and always emphasized the femininity of woman wearing them. Celebrities who favor her designs: Minnie Driver, Courtney Love, Salma Hayek and Helena Bonham Carter.

Like red lipstick on the mouth, my clothes wake up and brighten and bring the wearer to life ... drawing attention to her beauty and specialness ... her moods and movements ... her dreams and fantasies.

OTHERS: 1360 Italian jurist **Francesco Zabarella**, 1489 German statesman/reformer **Jacob Sturm von Sturmeck**, 1560 German composer **Hieronymus Praetorius**, 1645 Italian Catholic missionary **Eusebio Kino**, 1839 Russian physicist **Aleksandr G. Stoletov**, 1890 Canadian politician **Angus L. MacDonald**, 1898 "The Tin Man" **Jack Haley**, 1902 U.S. actress **Norma**

Shearer, 1902 Swedish chemist **Arne Tiselius**, 1905 U.S. journalist **Era Bell Thompson**, 1909 U.S. luthier **Leo Fender**, 1912 Brazilian novelist **Jorge Amado**, 1940 "Righteous Brother **Bobby Hatfield**, 1945 White House counsel **Harriet Miers**

August 11

1833 **Robert G. Ingersoll:** American lawyer, statesman, orator and writer. "The Great Agnostic." Noted for defense of free-thinking in religious matters. Influenced by Voltaire and Paine. Powerful advocate of scientific rationalism and a humanistic philosophy. Sought-after golden-tongue orator. Books: *The Gods, Some Mistakes of Moses* and *Why I Am an Agnostic.*

In nature there are neither rewards nor punishments — there are consequences.

1865 **Gifford Pinchot:** First American professional forester and conservationist. Appointed to the National Forest Commission in 1896 by President Grover Cleveland, charged with developing a plan for the nation's Western forest reserves. First chief of the U.S. Forest Service. Reformed the management and development of forests in the U.S. Advocated scientific conservation for the planned use and renewal of the nation's forest reserves. Coined the name "conservation" as applied to natural resources.

Conservation means the wise use of the earth and its resources or the lasting good of men.

1882 **Horace Meyer Kallen:** German-born U.S. educator and philosopher. Opposed over-simplification of vital philosophical problems. Maintained that denying complications only multiplies them as denying the reality of evil only exacerbates evil. Argued that cultural diversity and national pride were compatible, and that ethnic diversity and respect for ethnic and racial differences strengthens the nation. Books: *The Education of Free Men, Cultural Pluralism and the American Idea* and *Liberty, and Laughter and Tears.*

Education is the first resort as well as the last for worldwide solution of the problems of freedom.

1892 **Hugh MacDiarmid:** Pseudonym of **Christopher Murray Grieve**. Scottish poet and critic. Leading figure of Scottish Renaissance. Early works written in *Lallans*, language reconstructed from ancient Scottish dialects. Ardent Marxist and co-founder the Scottish Nationalist Party. Author of *Scots Unbound, First and Second Hymn to Lenin, A Drunk Man Looks at the Thistle* and *At the Sign of the Thistle.*

Killing is the ultimate simplification of life.

1897 **Louise Bogan:** American poet and Critic. Served as poetry critic for *The New Yorker* (1931–69). Influenced by the English Metaphysical poets. Books: *Body of This Death, The Sleeping Fury, Achievements in American Poetry, Selected Criticism,* and *The Blue Estuaries: Poems 1923–1968.*

The art of one period cannot be approached through the attitudes (emotional or intellectual) of another.

1905 **Erwin Chargaff:** American biochemist who discovered the base-pairing rules in DNA. Showed that a single organism contains many different kinds of RNA but that its DNA is essentially one kind, characteristic of the species and even of the organism. His rules were of great value as a clue to the double helix structure put forth by Francis Crick and James Watson (1953).

Science is wonderfully equipped to answer the question "How?" but it gets terribly confused when you ask the question "Why?"

1913 **Angus Wilson:** British novelist, short-story writer, and biographer. Established his reputation with his short stories in the collection *The Wrong Set.* Other works include best-selling novels *Hemlock and After, Anglo-Saxon Attitudes,* the political satire *The Old Men at the Zoo* and the chronicle of three generations of a family, *No Laughing Matter.* The subjects of his biographies were Emile Zola, Charles Dickens and Rudyard Kipling.

I have no concern for the common man except that he should not be so common.

1921 **Alex Haley:** African-American writer. Early adventures stories led to regular assignments with *Playboy* magazine, including an interview with American-Nazi leader George Lincoln Rockwell. Best known for *Roots,* which traced his ancestry back to its origins in Africa. Calls the work, a mixture of fact and fiction, "faction." His twelve year labor of research earned him a special Pulitzer Prize in 1977.

Either you deal with what is the reality, or you can be sure that the reality is going to deal with you.

1925 **Carl T. Rowan, Jr.:** African-American newspaper columnist and diplomat. Besides writing a nationally syndicated column, he was a radio commentator and a panelist on television public affairs programs. Ambassador to Finland (1963–64) and director of the U.S. Information Agency (1964–65).

A minority group has "arrived" only when it has the right to produce some fools and scoundrels without the entire group paying for it.

1933 **Jerry Falwell:** American fundamentalist Baptist clergyman and lobbyist. Leading exponent of the "electronic church." Founded the conservative political lobbying organization, Moral Majority. Professes that those who are not born-again Christians are failures as human beings. Critical of other evangelists, asserted that "Billy Graham is the chief servant of Satan in America." Some believe he holds American Taliban-like aspirations for ultraconservative Christianity.

The idea that religion and politics don't mix was invented by the Devil to keep Christians from running their own country.

1943 **Pervez Musharraf:** Pakistani general and current president. Took power on October 12, 1999 after a bloodless *coup d'état* succeeding Muhammad Rafiq Tarar. Following the September 11, 2001 terrorist attacks, he sided with the U.S. against the Taliban government in Afghanistan. Unequivocally condemned all acts of terrorism and pledged to combat Islamic extremism and lawlessness within Pakistan. Survived several assassination attempts and made peace overtures to India.

Islam teaches tolerance, not hatred; universal brotherhood, not enmity; peace, not violence.

1950 **Steve Wozniak:** American computer engineer, who greatly contributed to the personal computer revolution of the 1970s. With Steven Jobs founded Apple Computer and created Apple I and Apple II. Wrote most of the software that ran on Apple. Badly injured in 1981 when he crashed his private plane, took a leave of absence before returning in 1983 to work on the revolutionary Macintosh computer. Severed all ties with Apple in 1985, the same year he was awarded the National Medical of Technology.

Never trust a computer you can't throw out a window.

OTHERS: 1673 English physician **Richard Mead**, 1807 U.S. politician **David Rice Atchison,** 1837 French politician **Marie François Carnot**, 1858 Dutch physician/pathologist **Christiaan Eijkman**, 1863 French President **Gaston Doumergue**, 1892 Japanese novelist **Eiji Yoshikawa**, 1897 English author **Enid Blyton**, 1900 U.S. sprinter **Charles Paddock**, 1912 German astronomer **Eva Ahnert-Rohlfs**, 1912 Thai Prime Minister **Thanom Kittikachorn**, 1919 French violinist **Ginette Neveu**, 1938 Slovenian chemist **Branko Stanovnik**, 1941 U.S. Congress-woman **Elizabeth Holtzman,** 1946 U.S. journalist **Marilyn Vos Savant**,

August 12

1696 **John Balguy:** English divine and philosopher. Under the non de plume of **Silvius**, published *A letter to a Deist concerning the Beauty and Excellency of Moral Virtue, and the Support and Improvement which it receives from the Christian Religion*. Purported to show, that while a love of virtue for its own sake is the highest principle of morality, religious rewards and punishments are most valuable, and in some cases absolutely indispensable, as sanctions of conduct. Other works: *The Foundation of Moral Goodness, Divine Rectitude*, and *Essay on Redemption*.

Contentment is a pearl of great price, and whoever procures it at the expense of ten thousand desires makes a wise and a happy purchase.

1696 **Maurice Greene:** English composer and organist. Appointed Master of the King's Musick in 1735. His *Cathedral Music* was completed after his death by his student and successor. Wrote much vocal music, both sacred and secular, including the oratorio "The Song of Deborah" and "Barak." The *Chaplet Songs* included "Ye Purple Blooming Roses," "The Flea, a Passionate Love Song" and "Chloe."

In vain the Force of Female Arms,/ In vain their offer'd Love:/ Their Smile, their Air,/ nor all their Charms,/ My passion can remove,/ For all that's Fair and Good./ I find in Chloe's Form,/ in Chloe's Mind.

1774 **Robert Southey:** English poet and author. One of the Lake Poets. Best remembered for the ballad "The Battle of Blenheim." Poet laureate (1813–43). Later became better known for his prose than his poetry, including a biography of Lord Nelson, a naval history and his collection of letters.

Never let a man imagine that he can pursue a good end by evil means, without sinning against his own soul. The evil effect on himself is certain.

1831 **Helena Petrovna Blavatsky:** Known as **Madame Blavatsky**. Ukrainian-born theosophist and occultist. Settled in New York City in 1875, where with Henry Steel Olcott, founded the Theosophical Society. Later carried on her work in India. Although her psychic powers were widely acclaimed, they didn't withstand an investigation by the Society for Psychical Research.

The Path that leadeth on is lighted by one fire — the light of daring burning in the heart. The more one dares, the more one will obtain.

1859 **Katherine Lee Bates:** American poet, educator, editor and writer. For many years, professor of English literature at her alma mater Wellesley College. Lived with partner Katharine Corman, founder of the Wellesley College Economics department. Best known as the author of "America the Beautiful." "America! America!/ God shed His grace on thee/ And crown thy good with brotherhood/ From sea to shining sea!" It first appeared in print in *The Congregationalist*, a weekly journal, for Independence Day in 1895. The words are usually sung to the music written by Samuel A. Ward for his hymn *Materna* (1882).

Love planted a rose, and the world turned sweet.

1866 **Jacinto Benavente y Martínez:** Spanish dramatist. Intended to enter the legal profession, but turned to writing. After publishing some poems and short stories won acclaim as a dramatist, writing more than 150 plays, several satirical society comedies. Masterpiece is the allegorical *The Bonds of Interest* (1907). Nobel Prize for Literature in 1922.

The worst thing that bad people can do is make us doubt good people.

1867 **Edith Hamilton:** German-born American educator and author. Credited with popularizing classical Greek and Roman literature. Historical works: *The Greek Way* and *The Roman Way*. Her *Mythology* was a standard textbook for many years. At age 90, she was made an honorary citizen of Athens.

A people's literature is the great textbook for real knowledge of them. The writings of the day show the quality of the people as no historical reconstruction can.

1876 **Mary Roberts Rinehart:** American novelist, mystery story writer, journalist, playwright and suffragist. Her novels combined humor and ingenuity. Invented the "Had I But Known" school of detective fiction. Author of *The Circular Staircase*, later dramatized as *The Bat*. Wrote numerous stories about a dauntless spinster called Tish, and her middle-aged cronies, Aggie and Lizzie.

I hate those men who would send into war youth to fight and die for them; the pride and cowardice of these old men, making their wars that boys must die.

1880 **Christy Mathewson:** "Big Six." Righthanded pitcher with the New York Giants for 17 years. Won 30 or more games three consecutive years (1903–5). Had 373 career victories. One of the first five players elected to the National Baseball Hall of Fame in 1936.

Many baseball fans look upon an umpire as a sort of necessary evil to the luxury of baseball, like the odor that follows an automobile.

1881 **Cecil B. DeMille:** American film director, producer and screenwriter. His first feature film, The Squaw Man (1913), was so successful, he remade it two more times. Most closely identified with epic spectacles such as: *The Ten Commandments* (1923 and 1956), *The King of Kings, The Sign of the Cross, Cleopatra* (1934), *The Plainsman*, and *The Greatest Show on Earth*. Host on radio's *Lux Playhouse* for many years.

Give me two pages of the Bible and I'll give you a picture.

1887 **Erwin Schrödinger:** Austrian physicist. Published four papers (1926) that laid the foundation of the wave behavior of matter within quantum mechanics. Tied the so-called Schrödinger's equation to almost every aspect of physics, making it the fundamental equation of quantum mechanics. An extremely powerful mathematical tool, it determines the behavior of the wave function that describes the wavelike properties of a subatomic system. Nobel Prize for Physics in 1933.

Thus, the task is not so much to see what no one has seen, but to think what nobody has yet thought, about that which everybody sees.

1911 **Cantinflas:** Born **Mario Moreno Reyes**. Mexican circus clown, acrobat and actor. Such an icon of the Spanish-speaking world that today in Mexico there's even a verb based on his name —*cantinflear*— meaning to use a lot of words, but end up saying very little, one of his trademark routines. Famous playing the wise fool, finding dignity in poverty, and revealing the ingenuity of the working class. Won International fame with *Around the World in 80 Days*. Charlie Chaplin called him the greatest comic ever born.

Always I project optimism.... Chaplin makes sometimes to cry. Cantinflas makes only to laugh — never to cry.

OTHERS: 1503 King of Denmark and Norway **Christian III**, 1644 Bohemian composer **Heinrich Ignaz Biber**, 1647 German writer **Johann Acker**, 1753 English artist **Thomas Bewick**, 1865 Finnish composer **George Norman Douglas**, 1880 British author **Radclyffe Hall**, 1885 French physicist **Jean Cabannes**, 1886 Australian journalist/newspaper owner **Keith Murdoch**, 1892 U.S. actor **Alfred Lunt**, 1906 U.S. animator **Tedd Pierce**, 1927 U.S. country singer **Porter Wagoner**, 1930 Hungarian — U.S. businessman **George Soros**, 1971 U.S. tennis player **Pete Sampras**

August 13

1422 **William Caxton:** First English printer, translator and publisher. Exerted an important influence on English literature. Translated a French Romance about the Trojan War and in order to satisfy the demand for copies of the work, he learned the printing trade. *Recuyell of the Historyes of Troye* became the first book ever printed in English. Set up a printing business, and produced nearly 80 books, many his translations of works by Boethius, Chaucer and John Gower.

Love lasteth long as the money endureth.

1699 **John Dyer:** Welch poet. His first poem, "Grongar Hill" was an immediate success. While visiting Italy, he composed "The Ruins of Rome," about 600 lines of Miltonic blank verse. Ordained in 1741, made his living serving several Lincolnshire parishes. Longest work, *The Fleece*, in four books (1757), dealt with the tending of sheep, the preparation of the wool, weaving, and woolen manufacturing.

And he that will this health deny,/ Down among the dead men let him lie.

1818 **Lucy Stone:** American suffragist, abolitionist, woman's rights activist, social reformer and editor. First opponent in battle for women's rights was her father, who refused her money for higher education. Taught for several years to earn enough to attend the progressive Oberlin College. After graduation, she lectured against slavery and for woman suffrage. Founded and edited *Woman's Journal* (1870).

A wife should no more take her husband's name than he should hers. My name is my identity and must not be lost.

1851 **Felix Adler:** German-born American educator and founder of the New York Society for Ethical Culture, which emphasized the need for stronger morality in all personal, professional, and political relationships. Established the first kindergarten for New York City's poor. This later grew into the first vocational school, combining manual training and ethical instruction. Author of *The Moral Instruction of Children, Life and Destiny* and *An Ethical Philosophy of Life*.

Ethical religion can be real only to those who are engaged in ceaseless efforts at moral improvement. By moving upward we acquire faith in an upward movement, without limit.

1895 **Bert Lahr:** U.S. comedian in burlesque, vaudeville, radio and the stage. Best known for his unforgettable performance as the "Cowardly Lion" in *The Wizard of Oz*. Won a 1964 Tony Award as Best Actor in a Musical for *Foxy*. Nominated the previous year for a Tony as Best Actor in a Drama for *The Beauty Part*. Died before the completion of his last film *The Night They Raided Minsky's*.

After The Wizard of Oz I was typecast as a lion, and there aren't all that many parts for lions.

1899 **Alfred Hitchcock:** "Master of Suspense." British film director of stylish thrillers with intricate plots and novel camera techniques. Moved to Hollywood in 1939, where most of his subsequent movies were suspenseful psychological spine-tingling drams, filled with black humor. British Films: *The Lodger, Blackmail, The 39 Steps* and *The Lady Vanishes.* American films: *Rebecca, Notorious, Strangers on a Train, Rear Window, Psycho* and *North by Northwest.* Made a cameo appearance in each of his movies, something fans always looked for. Also hosted a successful TV series, *Alfred Hitchcock Presents.*

I never said actors are cattle; what I said was all actors should be treated like cattle.

1912 **Ben Hogan:** One of the most prominent U.S. golfers. Four-time PGA Player of the Year. Of the major tournaments, he won four U.S. Opens, two Masters, two PGA and one British Open. Sixty-three career wins. In 1948, became the first person in 26 years to win all three U.S. major titles. Despite a life-threatening car accident he recovered and returned to with a further three titles in 1953.

As you walk down the fairway of life you must smell the roses, for you only get to play one round.

1916 **Daniel Schorr:** American radio and television correspondent. Last active journalist of Edward R. Murrow's legendary CBS team. After serving with the U.S. Army Intelligence during World War II, began a 20-year career as a foreign correspondent. CBS's chief Watergate correspondent. Suspended for leaking a secret House Intelligence Commission report on the CIA to the *Village Voice.* Helped create Ted Turner's Cable News Network. Since 1985, primarily works for National Public Radio and writes articles for *The Christian Science Monitor.*

The Ship of State, it has been said, is the only kind of ship that leaks mainly from the top.

1919 **George Shearing:** English-born American jazz pianist. Blind from the age of three. His jazz quarter had a succession of highly popular recordings including "September in the Rain" and his own composition "Lullaby of Birdland." Appeared regularly in concerts with singer Mel Torme duding the 1880s and 90s. His interest in classical music resulted in appearances with concert orchestras during the 50s and 60s.

If you establish an identity, you build a monster — and that's right, you've got to live with it. Of course, you can enjoy it too.

1926 **Fidel Castro:** Cuban revolutionary leader. Organized a failed rebellion in 1953. Captured, served time in prison and then went to Mexico where he met Che Guevara, with whom he continued to plot Batista's removal. Gradually managed to organize guerrilla bands throughout the island. On January 1, 1959, he and his followers seized control. Transformed Cuba into the first communist state in the Western hemisphere. Private commerce and industry were nationalized and U.S.–owned land and businesses were expropriated. The U.S.'s unsuccessful attempt to overthrow him with the disastrous Bay of Pigs expedition led to the Cuban Missile Crisis.

They talk about the failure of socialism but where is the success of capitalism in Africa, Asia and Latin America?

1948 **Kathleen Battle:** African-American lyric contralto. Almost totally inexperienced singer was hired to perform at the 1972 "Festival of Two Worlds" in Spoleto, Italy. Famed for portrayals of ingénues and heroines in Mozart operas *Die Zauberflöte* and *Don Giovanni.* Reputation for being difficult to work with and diva temperament, which resulted in the Metropolitan Opera canceling her contract for unspecified "unprofessional actions." Five time Grammy winner's repertoire includes sacred music, jazz, and spirituals.

The question is not ... if art is enough to fulfill my life, but if I am true to the path I have set for myself, if I am the best I can be in the things I do. Am I living up to the reasons I became a singer in the first place?

1987 **Helen Araomi:** Nigerian researcher, poet, human rights activist and musician. In her poetry she weaves fantasy and reality, castigating inequality and corruption that inundates her country, in particular the unjust treatment of African women and children. Most recurring themes are: humor, war, peace, children's rhymes and faith. Poems: "Aids is real," "Black is beauty," "Injustice," "Nigeria" and "Smiles and frowns."

Knowledge is like an endless sea. We can't know everything.

OTHERS: 1584 English politician **Theophilus Howard**, 1625 Danish physician **Rasmus Bartholin**, 1666 English scholar **William Wotton**, 1721 French bibliographer **Jacques Lelong**, 1803 Russian philosopher **Vladimir Odoevsky**, 1814 Swedish physicist **Anders Jonas Angström**, 1823 English-born historian **Goldwin Smith**, 1860 U.S. sharpshooter **Annie Oakley**, 1866 Italian industrialist **Giovanni Angelli**, 1872 German chemist **Richard Willstätter**, 1907 Scottish architect **Basil Spence**, 1912 Italian-born biologist **Salvador Luria**, 1913 1st President of Cyprus **Makarios III**, 1982 U.S. speed skater **Shanni Davis**

August 14

1863 **Ernest L. Thayer:** American journalist, writer and poet. Hired by Harvard classmate William Randolph Hearst as humor columnist for the *San Francisco Examiner* (1886–88), using the nickname "Phin." His last piece for the paper on June 3, 1888 was a ballad called "Casey" ("Casey at the Bat"). Although Thayer wrote it, it was actor De Wolf Hopper who made it popular, by reciting it on stage. Much evidence points to Boston star and Hall-of-Famer Mike "King" Kelly being the model for legendary "Casey."

Oh! somewhere in this favored land the sun is shining bright;/ The band is playing somewhere, and somewhere hearts are light;/ And somewhere men are laughing and some-where children shout,/

But there is no joy in Mudville — mighty Casey has struck out.

1867 **John Galsworthy:** English novelist and playwright. Master of the didactic drama, Wrote social satires and portrayals of the British upper middle class. Best known for his novel series, *The Forsythe Saga*. Received the Order of Merit in 1929 and the Nobel Prize for Literature in 1932.Other novels: *From the West Winds*, *The Island Pharisee*, and *The Dark Flower*. Plays: *Strife*, *The Skin Game* and *Old English*.

Idealism increases in direct proportion to one's distance from the problem.

1925 **Russell Baker:** American journalist, humorist, essayist, and biographer. Author of the nationally syndicated *New York Times* column "Observer" (1962–98). Astute political commentator with biting cerebral wit. Pulitzer Prize in 1979 in recognition of his distinguished commentary and as second Pulitzer for his autobiography *Growing Up*. Edited the anthologies *The Norton Book of Light Verse* and *Russell Baker's Book of American Humor*. Host of the PBS series "Masterpiece Theatre" from 1993.

Inanimate objects are classified scientifically into three major categories — those that don't work, those that break down and those that are lost. The goal of all inanimate objects is to resist man and ultimately defeat him.

1928 **Lina Wertmüller:** Italian actress, director and playwright for the theater before turning to movies. Traveled through Europe, producing avant-garde plays, working as a puppeteer, stage manager, set designer, publicist and radio/TV scriptwriter. Directed a string of pictures, all starring Giancarlo Giannini: *The Seduction of Mimi*, *Swept Away* and *Seven Beauties*. The last earned her Academy Award nominations for Best Screenplay and Best Director, becoming the first woman nominated for a directing Oscar.

I don't think suicide is so terrible. Some rainy winter Sunday where there's a little boredom, you should always carry a gun. Not to shoot yourself, but to know exactly that you're always making a choice.

1930 **Earl Weaver:** American baseball manager with the Baltimore Orioles (1968–82, 1985–86). "Earl of Baltimore" won 1,480 games, six American League East titles, four pennants and the 1970 World Series. Named Manager of the Year by *The Sporting News* in 1977 and 1979. Pioneered the use of radar guns to track the speed of pitchers. Elected to the Hall of Fame by the Veterans Committee in 1996.

The key to winning baseball is pitching, fundamentals, and three run homers.

1943 **Jimmy Johnson:** American football coaster and broadcaster. First coach to win both a NCAA Division 1 National Championship (in 1987, during his five years at the University of Miami) and a Super Bowl (in 1992 and 1993 with the Dallas Cowboys). Johnson left the Cowboys to become a TV analyst after the 1993 season due to a falling out with owner Jerry Jones. In 1996, replaced legendary Don Shula as coach of the Miami Dolphins but retired after 2000 season.

The difference between ordinary and extraordinary is that little extra.

1947 **Danielle Steel:** Born **Danielle Fernandes Schuelein-Steel.** American author of romance novels, one of the best-selling writers in the history of the U.S., more than 530 million copies of her books sold. In addition to adult novels, written series of books for children. Twenty-one of her novels have been adapted for TV. French government named her a "Chevalier" of the distinguished Order of Arts and letters. Novels include: *Miracle*, *Dating Game*, *The Kiss*, *A Perfect Stranger*, *Full Circle*, *Daddy*, *Vanished* and *Wings*.

Sometimes, if you aren't sure about something, you have to just jump off the bridge and grow wings on your way down.

1950 **Gary Larson:** American cartoonist. Creator of *The Far Side*, a comic panel, first appeared in the *Seattle Times* in 1978, and syndicated in 1980 by Chronicle Features. Using surreal themes, his panels frequently showed parallels between the behavior of humans and animals. Successfully used "mixed metaphors." His creation is considered by many to be the greatest single-panel strip of all time. After fourteen years of drawing the panel, he retired in 1995.

By the time they had diminished from 50 to 8, the other dwarves began to suspect "Hungry."

1954 **Mark Fidrych:** Baseball pitcher with the Detroit Tigers. Nicknamed "The Bird" for his resemblance to *Sesame Street's* Big Bird. In his rookie season (1976) won 19 games, led the leaguer in ERA (2.34) and complete games (24), starting pitcher in the All-Star Game, won the American League Rookie-of-the-year Award, and finished second in the voting for the Cy Young Award. His antics made him a national celebrity. Strutted around the mound after each out, talk to himself, talk to the ball and insisted balls be removed from the game that "had hits in them." Regrettably his celebrity was brief. The very next year tore the cartilage in his knee and developed arm problems. Despite attempts to make a comeback he was forced to retire at age 29.

When you're a winner you're always happy, but it you're happy as a loser you'll always be a loser.

1959 **Earvin "Magic" Johnson:** All-American basketball player at Michigan State University, 12-time All-Star and winner of three Most Valuable Player Awards with the NBA Los Angeles Lakers for 13 seasons. Regarded as one of the purest passers and best point guards in the game's history. Led the Lakers to five NBA championships. Voted to the NBA's 50th Anniversary All-Time. Announced that he was HIV–positive and had to retire from the game (1991). Since then worked to educate and raise awareness of the disease. Frequently speaks to inner-city kids, encouraging them to stay in school, telling them:

You don't have to be Magic to be special. You're already special, you're you.

1960 **Sarah Brightman:** English soprano and actress. Met her future husband Andrew Lloyd Webber when she auditioned for and won a role in his new musical *Cats*. Starred in a number of his musicals, including *The Phantom of the Opera*, in which the role of Christine was written specifically for her. The couple divorced in 1990, and the next year she met producer Frank Peterson, who helped her become an international star. Her albums are a creative blend of pop, classical and electronics. Albums: *Timeless*, *La Luna*, *Encore*, and *Harem*.

I can't be a wife. I'm not that sort of person. Wives have to compromise all the time. You do have to be fairly selfish when you have a gift. You cannot afford to let too many outside things get in the way.

1966 **Halle Berry:** Academy-Award–winning U.S. actress and model. First African-American woman to win an Oscar for Best Actress (in 2002 for *Monster's Ball*). Won an Emmy and a Golden Globe in 1999 for Outstanding Lead Actress for her portrayal of Dorothy Dandridge in the HBO movie *Introducing Dorothy Dandridge*. Acquired unilateral hearing loss after being beaten severely by a former boyfriend. Other Films: Jungle Fever, *Losing Isaiah*, *Swordfish*, and *Die Another Day*.

While being called beautiful is extremely flattering, I would much rather be noticed for my work as an actress.

Others: 1575 English-born poet **Robert Hayman**, 1586 Rhode Island colonist **William Hutchinson**, 1599 English classical scholar **Méric Casaubon**, 1714 French painter **Claude Joseph Vernet**, 1777 Danish physicist **Hans Christian Ørsted**, 1851 U.S. gambler/gunfighter **Doc Holliday**, 1861 Librarian of Congress **Herbert Putnam**, 1866 Belgian mathematician **Charles Jean de la Vallée-Poussin**, 1882 English art historian **Gisela Richter**, 1910 French composer **Pierre Schaeffer**, 1916 Co-owner New York Football Giants **Wellington Mara**, 1941 U.S. guitarist/songwriter **David Crosby**, 1952 U.S. swimmer **Debbie Meyer**

August 15

1195 Saint **Anthony of Padua:** Lisbon-born Franciscan friar. "Evangelical Doctor," "Wonder-Worker" and "Hammer of Heretics." Renown for his personal holiness. One of the most famous disciples of St. Francis of Assisi, devoted to Mary, the Virgin Mother. Patron saint of seekers of lost articles. Maintained that as Jesus was designated the "Son of God," Mary is designated as "Mother of God."

Actions speak louder than words; let your words teach and your actions speak... It is useless for a person to flaunt the law if their actions undermine it.

1769 **Napoléon Bonaparte:** Emperor of France (1804–15). In 1799 launched a successful coup d'état and installed himself as First Consul. Declared France as a hereditary empire and crowned himself emperor. Enacted many internal reforms in the economy and legal system, introducing the Napoleonic Code and reconstructed France's educational system. Conquests were put to an end by Wellington and the English fleet at Trafalgar. Forced to abdicate in 1814. Escaped his exile at Elba the next year and enjoyed a brief triumph, reestablishing himself as emperor for the Hundred Days, but his army was crushed at the Battle of Waterloo. Went into exile on the remote island of Ste. Helena where he died six years later.

Men are more easily governed through their vices than through their virtues.

1771 Sir **Walter Scott:** Prolific Scottish novelist, poet and lawyer. Derived most of his material from Scottish history and legend. One of the first authors to develop an international reputation. Co-founder of the Quarterly Review, a journal in which made several anonymous contributions revealing Tory sympathies. Ballads include "The Lay of the Last Minstrel," "Marmion" and "The Lady of the Lake." Classic novels: *Rob Roy*, *Ivanhoe* and *Quentin Durward*.

Breathes there a man, with soul so dead,/ Who never to himself hath said,/ This is my own, my native land!

1785 **Thomas De Quincey:** English essayist and critic. While studying at Oxford, he experimented with opium to relieve the pain of facial neuralgia. Became a lifelong addict, whose experiences inspired him to write his best known work *Confessions of an English Opium Eater* (1822). Because of its poetic and imaginative prose, it became a masterpiece of English literature. Best known essay is "On the Knocking at the Gate in Macbeth."

If once a man indulges himself in murder, very soon he comes to think little of robbing; and from robbing he next comes to drinking and Sabbath-breaking, and from that to incivility and procrastination.

1803 Sir **James Douglas:** Canadian statesman. "Father of British Columbia." Joined the Hudson's Bay Company in 1821 rising to the position of a senior member in charge of operations west of the Rocky Mountains. Governor of Vancouver (1851–64). When gold was discovered on Fraser River in 1858, he extended his authority to the mainland to preserve Britain's Pacific foothold. When Britain created the colony of British Columbia, he was its first governor (1858–64).

I like to think of thought as living blossoms borne by the human tree.

1872 **Sri Aurobindo:** Originally **Aravinda Akroyd Ghose**. Indian writer, nationalist, Hindu mystic, evolutionary philosopher, poet, yogi and guru. Renounced nationalism and politics for yoga and Hindu philosophy. Followers believe him to have been an avatar, that is, an incarnation of the Supreme Being. Writings include *The Life Divine*, *The Synthesis of Yoga*, *The Secret of the Veda* and *Aurobindo on Himself*.

Life is life — whether in a cat, or dog or man. There is no difference there between a cat or a man. The idea of difference is a human conception for man's own advantage.

1879 **Ethel Barrymore:** Originally **Ethel Blythe**. American actress. Sister of actors Lionel and John Barrymore. One of her greatest stage successes was W. Somerset Maugham's comedy, *The Constant Wife* (1926). Also graced the screen in films such as *None But the Lonely Heart* for which she won an Academy Award for Best Supporting Actress (1944), *Farmer's Daughter*, *Pinky*, and *The Spiral Staircase*. Winston Churchill had considered proposing to her, but as she was both an American and a Roman Catholic, who could not remarry after divorcing Russell Griswold Colt, it didn't happen.

For an actress to be a success she must have the face of Venus, the brains of Minerva, the grace of Terpsichore, the memory of Macaulay, the figure of Juno, and the hide of a rhinoceros.

1887 **Edna Ferber:** American novelist and short-story writer. In the 1920s and 30s considered the greatest American female novelist. Member of the famed and fabled Algonquin Round Table, a group of wits who met each day for lunch at New York's Algonquin hotel. Novels include the Pulitzer Prize–winning *So Big*, *Show Boat* and *Giant*. Wrote several plays in collaboration with George S. Kaufman: *The Royal Family*, *Dinner at Eight* and *Stage Door*.

Big doesn't necessarily mean better. Sunflowers aren't better than violets.

1888 **T.E. Lawrence:** "Lawrence of Arabia." British archaeologist, military strategist and author. Fluent in Arabic, drafted into Military Intelligence with the rank of Captain. Planned, organized and led a national rebellion of the Arab people, giving them their first opportunity in 400 years to become a Middle East power. Wrote *The Seven Pillars of Wisdom* in which he described his bitterness when his success was undone and the Arab efforts betrayed by the European powers. Offered the position of Viceroy of India, he, resigned his commission and enlisted in the ranks of the Royal Air Force. Died in a motorcycle accident.

Many men would take the death sentence without a whimper to escape the life sentence which fate carries in her other hand.

1912 **Julia Child:** Originally **Julia McWilliams**. American chef, cooking consultant, writer and television personality. It was her husband, U.S. Foreign Service officer Paul Cushing Child, who introduced her to fine cuisine. She learned to cook to please him and to entertain their large social circle. Author of *Mastering the Art of French Cooking*, *The French Chef Cookbook* and *The Way to Cook*. Created the popular PBS series *The French Chef* (1962–73) and other cooking shows. Helped audiences of her shows and reader of her books appreciate fine food and wine.

I was 32 when I started cooking; up until then, I just ate.

1924 **Phyllis Schlafly:** American conservative political activist. Foe of feminism in general and the Equal Rights Amendment in particular. Champion of conservative causes, reflected in the title of her books: *Feminist Fantasies, Pornography's Victims, Equal Pay for Unequal Work, The Power of the Christian Woman* and *A Choice Not an Echo*. Opposed abortion and gay marriage. Embarrassed by the public outing of her eldest son as a gay man. Started the *Phyllis Schlafly Report*, a political newsletter that is still published.

It's very healthy for a young girl to be deterred from promiscuity by fear of contracting a painful, incurable disease, or cervical cancer, or sterility, or the likelihood of giving birth to a dead, blind, or brain-damaged baby even ten years later.

1925 **Oscar Peterson:** Canadian jazz pianist and composer. Considered the greatest virtuoso of modern jazz piano. Influenced by Art Tatum and Nat King Cole, his playing is characterized by cascades of notes and an effervescent swing. Showed his roots in both swing and bebop, with new improvised technique standards of harmonic complexity, convoluted melodic lines and frequent shifting of rhythmic accent.

The music field was the first to break down racial barriers, because in order to play together, you have to love the people you are playing with, and if you have any racial inhibitions, you wouldn't be able to do that.

1944 **Linda Ellerbee:** Born **Linda Jane Smith**. Outspoken American broadcast journalist and writer. Reporter for *The Today Show* and *Good Morning America*. Host of *Nick News*, a kid's TV issues program on Nickelodeon. Cohost of television's "Our World." Autobiography, *And So It Goes*, was published in 1986. Became overweight in the 1980s and used a highly-published healthy-eating program to lose 50 pounds. At the same time, she survived breast cancer.

I think laughter may be a form of courage. As humans we sometimes stand tall and look into the sun and laugh, and I think we are never more brave than when we do that.

OTHERS: 1001 Scottish king **Duncan I**, 1432 Italian poet **Luigi Pulci**, 1613 French scholar **Gilles Ménage**, 1845 English painter/illustrator **Walter Crane**, 1856 Ukrainian writer **Ivan Franko**, 1883 Croatian sculptor **Ivan Meštrović**, 1890 French composer **Jacques Ibert**, 1892 French physicist **Louis duc de Broglie**, 1893 New Zealand astronomer/computing pioneer **Leslie Comrie**, 1896 Austrian-born biochemist **Gerty Cori**, 1896 Russian inventor **Leon Theremin**, 1900 Polish poet **Jan Brzechwa**, 1912 English actress **Dame Wendy Hiller**, 1916 Albanian writer **Aleks Çaçi**, 1935 U.S. presidential advisor **Vernon Jordan Jr.**

August 16

1645 **Jean de la Bruyère:** French writer and satiric moralist. Sympathies lay with the ancients in their literary battle with the moderns. His most famous work: *Characters, or the Manners of the Century* earned him an immense reputation, but it gained him almost as many enemies as admirers. The first part, which was a translation of Theophrastus, raised no alarm, but the second consisted of maxims, reflections and characterizations of men and women of the time.

It is a sad thing when men have neither the wit to speak well nor the judgment to hold their tongues.

1766 **Carolina Nairne:** née **Lady Oliphant**. Scottish song writer. Lived in Edinburgh but traveled widely in Ireland and Europe after her husband's death. Collected traditional airs and wrote songs to them using the pseudonym "Mrs. Bogan of Bogan." These were published in *The Scottish Minstrel* and posthumously as *Lays from Strathearn*. Included was the lament for Prince Charles Edward Stewart:

Will ye no come back again?/ Better lo'ed ye canna be,/ will ye no come back again?

1860 **Jules Laforgue:** French poet associated with the Symbolists. With Gustave Kahn, is considered to have invented free verse. Volumes of Poetry include: *Les Complaintes*, *L'Imitation de Notre-Dame la lune*, and *Moralités légendaires*. Exerted considerable influence on T.S. Eliot, Ezra Pound, James Joyce, Hart Crane, and Wallace Stevens.

What a day-to-day affair life is.

1862 **Amos Alonzo Stagg:** U.S. football innovator. "The Grand Old Man of Football." All-American football player at Yale University (1889). Lived an amazing 102 years. Coached the University of Chicago for 41 years and 14 more years at College of the Pacific, named "Coach of the Year" in 1943, at age 81.Teams won 314 games. Charter member of the College Football Hall of Fame. Played in the first public basketball game at Springfield College in 1892. Created five-man basketball and organized the University of Chicago National Interscholastic Basketball Tournament, held annually (1917–1931).

Winning isn't worth while unless one has something finer and nobler behind it.

1868 **Bernarr McFadden:** American publisher. In boyhood he was not expected to survive when stricken with tuberculosis. Refusing to accept the prognosis, he began a regimen to restore his health. This included breathing fresh air 24 hours a day and nourishing his body with wholesome foods. Not only did he recover but he developed himself into the embodiment of strength and radiant vitality. A health fanatic, considered an eccentric parachuting from planes on his 81st, 83rd and 84th birthdays. Originator of the saying, "feed a cold, starve a fever." Published *McFadden's Encyclopedia of Physical Culture*.

Sickness is a crime. Don't be a criminal.

1894 **George Meany:** American labor leader. First active in the plumber's union, then with the New York State Federation of Labor. Elected secretary-treasurer of the American Federation of Labor (AFL) in 1939 and President in 1952. Helped reunify labor by bringing together the AFL and CIO. President of the merged AFL–CIO (1955–79). Awarded Presidential Medal of Freedom (1964).

It was almost on a par with religion... I grew us with faith in the trade union movement.

1911 **E.F. Schumacher:** German-born British economist. Interned in Britain while studying at Oxford at the outbreak of World War II. After the war he was an economic advisor to the British Control Commission in Germany, followed by service with the National Coal Board. His concern for the Third World was expressed in *Small Is Beautiful*. Founded the Intermediate Technology Development Group to develop tools and ideas appropriate to the culture and traditions of the people to use them.

Our ordinary mind always tries to persuade us that we are nothing but acorns and that our greatest happiness will be to become bigger, fatter, shinier acorns; but that is of interest only to pigs. Our faith gives us knowledge of something better: that we can become oak trees.

1913 **Menachem Begin:** Russian-born Israeli political leader. During World War II joined the Polish army and escaped to Palestine, becoming leader of the Irgun Zvai Leumi in 1943. Led the opposition in the Knesset. Prime minister, (1977–1983). Shared 1978 Nobel Peace Prize with Anwar Sadat for signing historic Camp David accord, which led to an Israel-Egypt peace treaty. Invading Lebanon in 1983 turned world opinion against him and he was forced to resign.

Israel is still the only country in the world against which there is a written document to the effect that it must disappear.

1920 **Charles Bukowski:** "The Laureate of the Low Life." German-born American author and poet. Began publishing short stories in the mid 1940s and his first poetry collection, *Flower, Fist, and Bestial Wail*, was published in 1959. A literary savage who wrote of the seamy side of life where he lived, led to his cult status. Works: *Ham on Rye* and *Confessions of a Man Insane Enough to Live with Beasts*.

Some people never go crazy. What truly horrible lives they must live.

1923 **Shimon Peres:** Polish-born Israeli statesman. Emigrated to Palestine in 1934 and joined the Zionist military organization, the Hagana, in 1947. After Israel received independence, held various defense positions. Helped establish the Israel Labor Party in 1967. Prime Minister (1984–86). As foreign minister in the Yitzhak Rabin government, he, Rabin and Yasser Arafat shared the 1994 Nobel Peace Prize. Became prime minister again in 1995 when Rabin was assassinated.

Television has made dictatorships impossible, but democracy unbearable.

1946 **Massoud Barzani:** Iran-born Iraqi Kurdish politician. Head of the Autonomous Kurdish Government in Iraq and the leader of the Kurdistan Democratic Party. Established a government in Southern Kurdistan (Northern Iraq) with the Patriotic Union of Kurdistan. Member of the U.S.–led occupation "Iraq Interim Governing Council."

Let me tell you, politics is much more difficult than war, ... In politics, there are so many more fronts.

1958 **Madonna [Ciccone]:** American entertainer and singer. "Queen of Pop." Great self-promoter who constantly reinvents herself to maintain an audience who wonders what shocking thing she will do next. Claimed she lost her virginity as a "career move." Hits: "Holiday," "Like a Virgin," "Like a Prayer," "Vogue," "Take a Bow," "Music," "Die Another Day" and "Hung Up." Films: *Dick Tracy, A League of Their Own* and *Evita.*

I'm tough, ambitious, and I know exactly what I want. If that makes me a bitch, okay.

OTHERS: 1355 Countess of Ulster **Philippa Plantagenet**, 1378 Chinese Emperor **Hongxi**, 1650 Italian cartographer/encylopediest **Vincenzo Coronelli**, 1832 German psychologist **Wilhelm Wundt**, 1884 Luxembourg-born editor/publisher **Hugo Gernsback**, 1892 U.S. cartoonist **Otto Messmer**, 1895 Swiss novelist **Albert Cohen**, 1897 U.S. circus owner **Robert Ringling**, 1928 U.S. actress **Ann Blyth**, 1930 U.S. football player/ announcer **Frank Gifford**, 1931 U.S. singer **Eydie Gorme**, 1954 Canadian film director **James Cameron**, 1968 Slovenian alpine skier **Mateja Svet**, 1974 Hungarian swimmer **Krisztina Egerszegi**

August 17

1601 **Pierre de Fermat:** French mathematician. "Prince of Amateurs." Developed the modern theory of numbers; discovered the basic principles of analytic geometry, independently of René Descartes; shared with Blaise Pascal the founding of the theory of probability; and advanced the principle that light when reflected, always takes the path for which the travel time is the least. Most famous for making the likely mistaken claim of having found a proof of his "Last Theorem," asserting the impossibility of expressing any number that is a power greater than two as the sum of two like powers. His results were contained in voluminous correspondences with friends, notes in the margins of his books, and challenges to others to find proofs of theorems he devised.

I have so little aptitude in writing out my [mathematical] demonstrations that I have been content to have discovered the truth, and to know the means of proving it when I shall have reason to do so.

1786 **Davy Crockett:** Legendary American. frontiersman and politician. His motto: "Be sure you're right — then go ahead." Distinguished himself with Andrew Jackson during the Creek War of 1814. Elected to Tennessee legislature and to Congress. Killed in the defense of the Alamo in San Antonio, Texas. After losing his reelection bid to congress, he bluntly expressed his feelings:

Since you have chosen to elect a man with a timber toe to succeed me, you may all go to hell and I will go to Texas.

1862 **Maurice Barrès:** French novelist and politician. As a member of the Chamber of Deputies (1889–93), championed nationalism, individualism, provincial patriotism and national energy. His series of novels titled *Les Basions de l'Est* served as successful French propaganda during World War I. Other works: *Le Culte du Moi* and *Colette Baudoche.*

The politician is an acrobat; he keeps his balance by doing the opposite of what he says.

1882 **Samuel Goldwyn:** Originally **Samuel Gelbfiss**, and then **Samuel Goldfish**. Polish-born American movie producer and founder of Metro-Goldwyn-Mayer (MGM) in 1924. Famed for his relentless ambition, bad temper, and genius for publicity. A colorful personality, legendary for his malapropisms, known as Goldwynisms: "Don't improve it into a flop," "Let's have some new clichés," "A verbal contract isn't worth the paper it's written on" and "Anyone who would go to a psychiatrist should have his head examined." As an independent producer, he hired top screenwriters, directors and actors for classic films including: *Wuthering Heights, The Little Foxes, and The Best Years of Our Lives,* of which he said:

I don't care if it doesn't make a nickel. I just want every man, woman and child in America to see it.

1887 **Marcus M. Garvey:** Jamaican-born American black nationalist leader. "Black Moses." Founded the Universal Negro Improvement Association. Editor of *Negro World,* in which he preached the message of a "new Negro," proud of being black. Advocated an independent black economy within the framework of black capitalism. Established black-run businesses, including the Black Star shipping line. Promoted a "Back to Africa" movement. Once boasting 2 million followers, his influence rapidly declined after he spent two years in prison for mail fraud and upon his release was deported.

I know no national boundary where the Negro is concerned. The whole world is my province until Africa is free.

1890 **Harry L. Hopkins:** U.S. public official. Director of the Federal Emergency Relief Administration. Organized the Works Projects Administration during President Roosevelt's first term. U.S. Commerce Secretary (1938–40). Resigned to make several trips representing Roosevelt in London and Moscow to discuss assistance and military strategy. Directed Lend-Lease program. His assessment of those who opposed the government projects of the New Deal:

You know some people make fun of people who speak a foreign language, and dumb people criticize something they do not understand, and that is what is going on up here — God damn it!

1892 **Mae West:** American actress in stock, burlesque, vaudeville, Broadway and the movies. Wrote suggestive plays, condemned as being obscene. Busty blonde embraced for her frank expression of her sexuality. The show business legend's movies include: *She Done Him Wrong, I'm No Angel, My Little Chickadee* and *Myra Breckinridge.* Famed for her double-entendre wisecracks: "I used to be Snow White, but I drifted," "Too much of a good thing ... can be wonderful," "A hard man ... is good to find," "I'm the lady who works at Paramount all day ... and Fox all night" and "She's the kind of girl who climbed the ladder of success ... wrong by wrong."

Just a little more loving and a lot less fighting and the world would be all right.

1904 **John Hay Whitney:** "Jock." American multimillionaire sportsman, publisher and diplomat. Multifaceted career as financier, horse breeder, and philanthropist. Owned New York *Herald Tribune*. Ambassador to Great Britain. Funded "Opportunity Fellowships" for people with exceptional promise who had not had the fullest opportunity to develop their abilities.

The role we can play every day, if we try, is to take the whole experience of every day and shape it to involve American man. It is our job to interest him in his community and to give his ideas the excitement they should have.

1911 **Elinor Smith:** American professional pilot. Flew her first solo flight at age 15, and the next year became the world's youngest licensed pilot. In 1928 she flew under all four East River suspension bridges and the same year set a light plane altitude record, one of four world records she would set during her career. Toured the American air show circuit and became the first female test pilot. Worked to preserve the history of Long Island aviation and promoted the creation of an air museum.

Becoming a professional pilot was for me the most desirable goal in the world, and I was not going to allow age or sex to bar me from it.

1926 **Jiang Zemin:** "Core of the third generation" of Communist Party Chinese leaders. Minster of Electronic Industries in 1983 and then Mayor of Shanghai. General Secretary of the party (1989–2002), President of the People's Republic of China (1993–2003). During his leadership, China experienced substantial economic growth, reforms and improved relationship with other countries, while the Communist Party maintaining its tight control over the nation.

It takes two hands to clap.

1932 **V.S. Naipaul:** Trinidadian novelist and journalist of Indian descent. Writes satirical stories of the vanishing culture of the East Indian in Trinidad. Author of *In a Free State* and *A Bend in the River*. Won the Nobel Prize for Literature in 2001.

Most people are not really free. They are confined by the niche in the world that they carve out for themselves. They limit themselves to fewer possibilities by the narrowness of their vision.

1959 **David Koresh:** Born **Vernon Wayne Howell**. Self-proclaimed head of the Branch Davidians. Believed he was the reincarnation of both King David and King Cyrus of Persia. When the cult began trading in guns, Bureau of Alcohol, Tobacco and Firearms (ATF) agents raided their Waco, Texas compound. Following a 51-day standoff, Attorney General Janet Reno ordered the Davidians removed by force. During the assault a fire broke out, killing Koresh and 85 of his followers. A spectator at the siege was Timothy McVeigh, who two years later to the day blew up the Murrah Federal Building in Oklahoma City.

These people remain here because I have thoroughly opened to them the seven seals.

OTHERS: 1578 Italian painter **Francesco Albani**, 1828 French neurologist **Jules Bernard Luys**, 1844 King of Ethiopia **Menelik II**, 1878 Irish writer **Oliver St. John Gogarty**, 1904 Austrian musicologist **Leopold Nowak**, 1913 "Deep Throat" Watergate informant **W. Mark Felt**, 1920 U.S. singer **Georgia Gibbs**, 1920 Irish-born actress **Maureen O'Hara**, 1929 U.S. U-2 spy pilot **Francis Gary Powers**, 1930 English poet **Ted Hughes**, 1941 U.S. baseball player **Boog Powell**, 1943 U.S. actor **Robert De Niro**, 1943 Japanese ski-jumper **Yukio Kasaya**, 1952 Argentine tennis player **Guillermo Vilas**, 1966 U.S. skateboarder **Rodney Mullen**

August 18

1792 Lord **John Russell:** British statesman. One of four members of the government entrusted with framing the first Reform Bill (1832). Prime Minister (1846–52). Mismanagement of the Crimean campaign and bungling of the Vienna conference destroyed his popularity, forcing him out of office for four years, but returned as foreign secretary and again became prime minister (1865–66).

It is impossible that the whisper of a fraction should prevail against the voice of a nation.

1807 **Charles F. Adams:** U.S. diplomat and public official. Grandson of John Adams and son of John Quincy Adams. Father of Henry Brooks Adams. Member of the House of Representatives (1858–61). Minister to Great Britain (1861–68). Published the life and works of his father and grandfather and edited the letters of his grandmother, Abigail Adams.

The American experiment is the most tremendous and far reaching engine of social change which has ever either blessed or cursed mankind.

1834 **Marshall Field:** American merchant and philanthropist. Founder of Chicago's premier department store, Marshall Field and Co. recently taken over by Macy's. Pioneering activities in retail merchandising were continued and extended into publishing by successive generations of his family. Left a large part of his fortune to the University of Chicago and the Field Museum of Natural History.

Right or wrong, the customer is always right.

1900 **Vijaya Lakshmi Pandit:** Indian diplomat and politician. Sister of Indian Prime Minister Jawaharlal Nehru. Following India's independence in 1947, nation's first envoy to the Soviet Union. (1947–49) and to the U.S. and Mexico (1949–51) Headed the Indian delegation to the United Nations (1946–68) and became the first woman President of the United Nations General Assembly (1953). Harsh critic of her niece Indria Gandhi, after the latter became Prime Minister in 1966.

The more we sweat in peace the less we bleed in war.

1917 **Caspar Weinberger:** American politician and Secretary of Defense under Ronald Reagan (1981–87). Known for his related roles in the Strategic Defense Imitative program (dubbed *Star Wars*). Oversaw a massive rebuilding of U.S. military strength, which created economic and military pressures that were associated with Perestroika and the beginning of the end of the Cold War with the Soviet Union. Resigned after reluctantly participating in the transfer of missiles to Iran during the Iran-Contra Affair.

The United Nations is totally incapable of doing any kind of job as pacifying or removing terrorism from a country like Iraq.

1919 **Walter Hickel:** American Republican politician. Governor of Alaska (1966–69) and U.S. Secretary of the Interior (1969–70). President Nixon dismissed him from the position after Hickel wrote a letter after the shooting of college students at Kent State University critical of Nixon's Vietnam War policy and failure to address the concerns of young people. Reelected governor of Alaska (1990–1994).

To turn your mind off from your heart when you make a decision affecting human lives is to isolate yourself from reality and morality.

1922 **Shelley Winters:** American actress began her career as a sexpot, but as her looks were more common than sultry, allowed to prove her worth as an actress. Won Academy Awards as Best Supporting Actress for *The Diary of Anne Frank* and *A Patch of Blue*. Nominated for *A Place in the Sun* and *The Poseidon Adventure*. Married four times. Had many affairs which she detailed in her autobiographies. Her lovers included William Holden, Burt Lancaster and Marlon Brando.

All marriages are happy. It's trying to live together afterwards that causes all the problems.

1922 **Alain Robbe-Grillet:** French novelist. Worked some time as an agronomist and then in a publishing house. First novel, *The Erasers* (1953) proved to be very controversial. Used an unorthodox narrative structure and concentrated on external reality. Originator of the "antinovel" which described images without commentary. Author of *The Voyeur, Jealousy* and *Last Year at Marienbad*.

A new form will always seem more or less an absence of any form at all, since it is unconsciously judged by reference to the consecrated forms.

1925 **Brian Wilson Aldiss:** English science fiction writer and novelist. Literary editor of the *Oxford Mail* (1958–69). Best known for *The Hand-Reared Boy, Non-stop, The Moment of Eclipse* and *The Helliconia Spring*. Produced histories of science fiction: *Billion Year Spree* and *Trillion Year Spree*.

Science fiction is no more written for scientists than ghost stories are written for ghosts.

1927 **Rosalyn Carter:** First Lady of the United States (1977–81). Wife of President Jimmy Carter. Her husband's trusted political partner and confidante. Dubbed "The Steel Magnolia," by the White House press corps, for her combination of Southern sweetness and tenacious drive. Active in human right causes and a member of the board of advisors of Habitat for Humanity.

A leader takes people where they want to go. A great leader takes people where they don't necessarily want to go, but ought to be.

1933 **Roman Polanski:** Originally **Rajmund Roman Liebling**. French-born Polish film director. Had a terrifying World War II childhood in Poland. Made films in Poland and England before settling in Hollywood in 1968. The next year his eight-month pregnant wife Sharon Tate and three others were slaughtered by the Manson family. He fled the United States for Europe to escape conviction of raping a 13-year-old. Films: *Knife in the Water, Rosemary's Baby, Chinatown, Frantic* and the Academy Award–winning *The Pianist*.

Normal love isn't interesting. I assure you that it's incredibly boring.

1934 **Roberto Clemente:** Puerto Rican Major League baseball player. Right-handed right-fielder with the Pittsburgh Pirates, known for his remarkable throwing arm. 4-time NL batting champion and NL MVP in 1996. Had exactly 3000 hits. Died on New Years Eve, 1972, in the crash of an air plane loaded with relief supplies that he had collected for Nicaraguan earthquake victims. Elected to the Hall of Fame posthumously in 1973, the first Hispanic American to be so honored.

Any time you have an opportunity to make a difference in this world and you don't, then you are wasting your time on Earth.

OTHERS: 1414 Persian poet **Jami**, 1450 Croatian poet **Marko Maurulić**, 1587 1st English child born in North America **Virginia Dare**, 1596 Flemish Jesuit writer **Jean Bolland**, 1685 English mathematician **Brook Taylor**, 1750 Italian composer **Antonio Salieri**, 1774 U.S. explorer **Meriwether Lewis**, 1830 Emperor of Austria **Franz Josef I**, 1873 U.S. songwriter **Otto Harbach**, 1904 Polish-born cosmetics entrepreneur **Max Factor**, 1928 Owner of Cincinnati Reds **Marge Schott**, 1934 U.S. attorney **Vincent Bugliosi**, 1935 U.S. decathlete **Rafer Johnson**, 1936 U.S. actor **Robert Redford**, 1955 Egyptian scientist **Taher Elgamal**

August 19

1686 **Eustace Budgell:** English writer. A principal contributor of miscellaneous essays to *The Spectator*. Signed some 37 papers with an X. Founded the weekly *Bee* (1733–35). Lost a fortune in the South Sea Company collapse. Drowned himself in the Thames.

Friendship is a strong and habitual inclination in two persons to promote the good and happiness of one another.

1793 **Samuel Griswold Goodrich:** American publisher who wrote under the pseudonym **Peter Parley**. Published some 200 volumes, mostly for the young, beginning *with The Tales of Peter Parley About Amer-*

ica. Edited the Boston-located periodical *The Token* (1828–42) to which he contributed moralistic poems, tales and essays for children.

Abuse is the weapon of the vulgar.

1858 **Edith Nesbit:** English poet and novelist. Married the Fabian journalist Hubert Bland. Best known for her children's books, which she turned to in order to help with the family finances. Her stories of the Bastaple family included: *The Story of the Treasures Seekers*, *Five Children and It*, and *The Railway Children*.

It is a curious thing that people only ask if you are enjoying yourself when you aren't.

1865 **John Cotton Dana:** Highly influential American librarian and museum director and student of printing and its arts. Founded the Newark, New Jersey Museum (1909), directing it until his death (1929). It included contemporary American commercial products as folk art. President of the American Library Association, which annually gives the John Cotton Dana Public Relations Award to libraries.

Who dares to teach must never cease to learn.

1870 **Bernard Baruch:** American businessman and statesman. Held several key government posts including, serving on the Council of National Defense and chairman of the War Industries Board during World War I. U.S. representative to the U.N. Atomic Energy Commission (1946), which proposed a World Atomic Authority. Author of *American Industry in the War* and *A Philosophy of Our Time*.

Two things are bad for the heart — running up stairs and running down people.

1871 **Orville Wright:** Self-taught American engineer and aviation pioneer. With his older brother Wilbur invented the first heavier-than-air machine to make a sustained flight (December 17, 1903 at Kitty Hawk, North Carolina). Encouraged by their success, patented their flying machine and formed an aircraft production company. In 1915 Orville sold his interests in the business to turn his attention to aviation research.

If we worked on the assumption that what is accepted as true really is true, then there would be little hope for advance.

1882 **George Wesley Bellows:** American painter, draftsman, and lithographer. American Ashcan painter. Painted boxing scenes and landscapes. After 1913, his work took on social messages and often depicted urban poverty. Paintings: *Forty-two Kids*, *Up the River*, *Stag at Sharkeys* and *The Cliff Dwellers*. In 1926 he revived lithography in the U.S., and his prints are as important as his painting. These include the classics: *Billy Sunday*, *Dance in a Mad House* and *Dempsey and Firpo*.

Art strives for form, and hopes for beauty.

1883 **Gabrielle "Coco" Chanel:** French fashion designer. After serving as a nurse in World War I, she opened a couture house in Paris. Revolutionized women's fashions after World War I with straight, simple lines. Freed women from the restriction of corsets designed her first "chemise" dress in 1925. Noted also for her "little black dress" and costume jewelry. Her world famous perfume Chanel No. 5 brought her great wealth and a dazzling social life.

A woman is closest to being naked when she is well dressed.

1902 **Ogden Nash:** American poet who wrote humorous and satirical verse. Noted for sophisticated whimsy and satire. Made use of puns, distorted rhymes, and clever free verse. Much of his work was originally published in *The New Yorker* magazine, where he held an editorial position. Wrote lyrics for *One Touch of Venus*, and *Two's Company*. Many collections include: *Free Wheeling* and *Bed Riddance*.

People who work sitting down get paid more than people who work standing up.

1903 **James Gould Cozzens:** American writer. Literary maverick, whose novels generally dealt with the moral dilemmas and compromises of upper-middle-class people, which were both praised and savaged by critics. Wrote the Pulitzer Prize winning *Guard of Honor*. Other works: *Confusion*, *Ask Me Tomorrow*, *The Just and Unjust*, and *By Love Possessed*.

A cynic is just a man who found out when he was about ten that there wasn't any Santa Claus, and he's still upset.

1919 **Malcolm S. Forbes:** American publisher and editor of *Forbes* magazine (1957–90). Took over the floundering publishing business founded by his father, Scottish immigrant Bertie Charles Forbes, and turned it into a success. Notorious for his extravagance and elaborate parties. Had a passionate interest in ballooning and Fabergé eggs.

Education's purpose is to replace an empty mind with an open one.

1946 **Bill Clinton:** Originally **William Jefferson Blythe III**. Adopted by his widowed mother's second husband Roger Clinton. Governor of Arkansas (1979–81, 1983–92) and 42nd president of the United States (1992–2000). During his two terms, there was sustained economic growth and successive budget surpluses, the first in three decades. At all stages of his political career he was beset by charges of womanizing and became only the second U.S. president to be impeached. He was charged with perjury and obstruction of justice in his denial to a grand jury that he had an affair with White House intern Monica Lewinsky but was acquitted in his Senate trial.

For too long we've been told about "us" and "them." Each and every election we see a new slate of arguments and ads telling us that "they" are the problem, not "us." But there can be no "them" in America. There's only us.

OTHERS: 1398 Spanish poet **Marqués de Santillana**, 1646 English Astronomer Royal **John Flamsteed**, 1686 Italian composer **Nicola Porpora**, 1743 French courtesan **Madame Du Barry**, 1785 U.S. clockmaker **Seth Thomas**, 1875 Croatian explorer **Stjepan Seljan**, 1878 Philippines President **Manuel Quezon**, 1881 Romanian composer **Georges Enescu**, 1906 U.S. inventor TV pioneer **Philo T. Farnsworth**, 1915 U.S. screenwriter

Ring Lardner Jr., 1921 *Star Trek* creator **Gene Roddenberry**, 1930 Irish-born author **Frank McCourt**, 1931 U.S. jockey **Willie Shoemaker**, 1934 U.S. transsexual tennis player **Dr. Renee Richards**

August 20

1785 **Oliver Hazard Perry:** U.S. naval hero and older brother of naval officer Matthew C. Perry. With the outbreak of the War of 1812 he was ordered to Erie, Pennsylvania to direct the construction of his command of ten small ships, for service on the Great Lakes. Defeated the English fleet despite having his flagship virtually destroyed. Transferred his command to the Niagara, and soon forced the English to surrender. Sent to General William Henry Harrison his famous message:

We have met the enemy and they are ours.

1829 **H.P. (Henry Parry) Liddon:** Anglican canon and theologian. Powerful advocate of the Oxford movement of the late 19th century, which sought to emphasize the Church of England's Catholic inheritance as a source of legitimacy and deeper spiritually. In 1866 he delivered his Bampton Lectures on *The Divinity of Our Lord.*

What we do upon some great occasion will probably depend on what we already are; and what we are will be the result of previous years of self-discipline.

1833 **Benjamin Harrison:** American politician. Grandson of the 9th U.S. president William Henry Harrison. Became the 23rd U.S. president (1889–93) despite having a smaller popular vote than President Grover Cleveland, winning in the Electoral College. Signed the Sherman Antitrust Act (1890), the first legislation to prohibit business combinations in restraint of trade. Failed in his reelection bid, losing to Cleveland, who once more became president.

I pity the man who wants a coat so cheap that the man or woman who produces the cloth will starve in the process.

1847 **Boleslaw Prus:** Born **Aleksander Glowacki**. Polish journalist, short-story writer and novelist. One of the most important literary figures of the Polish Positivist period. Began his distinguished 40 year career as a journalist, writing regular weekly columns, at age 25 and wrote short stories as a sideline. Novels: *The Outpost, The Doll, The New Woman* and *Pharaoh.*

Don't count on luck. If it doesn't come — it won't disappoint you. If it comes — it may surprise you.

1881 **Edgar A. Guest:** English-born American journalist and poet. Syndicated author of sentimental verse for the *Detroit Free Press.* Thoroughly realistic about his work; knew it was folksy doggerel, but he liked it and millions of ordinary folks did as well. Wrote "A Heap o' Livin'," "Just Folks," "When Day Is Done," and "Life's Highway." Prose work *Making a House a Home* and *Between You and Me.*

I'd rather see a sermon than hear one any day; I'd rather one should walk with me than merely tell the way: The eye's a better pupil and more willing than the ear, fine counseling is confusing, but example's always clear.

1886 **Paul Tillich:** German-born American Protestant theologian and philosopher. Applied aspects of depth psychology and existentialism to his interpretation of Christian doctrine. Sought to mediate between traditional Christian culture and the secular orientation of modern society. Major works: the three volumes *Systematic Theology* and *Dynamics of Faith.*

Neurosis is the way of avoiding non-being by avoiding being.

1890 **H.P. (Howard Philips) Lovecraft:** American author of nightmarish horror tales of demonism in the Poe tradition. From 1923 he was a regular contributor to *Weird Tales.* All but one of his books was published after his death. Since became a cult figure, Works: *The Shadow Over Innsmouth, The Case of Charles Dexter Ward,* and *At the Mountains of Madness.*

We live on a placid island of ignorance in the midst of black sea of infinity, and it was not meant that we should voyage far.

1892 **George Aiken:** American politician. Republican Governor of Vermont (1937–41) and U.S. Senator (1941–75). Proponent of many progressive programs such as Food Stamps and public works projects for rural America. Ideas didn't set well with many Old Guard Republicans. Frequently called a communist. People of his state admired him so much he only spent $17.09 on his final election. Critic of Vietnam War policy. Advised President Johnson to "Declare the U.S. the winner and begin de-escalation.

If we were to wake up one morning and find everyone was the same race, creed and color, we would find some other cause for prejudice by noon.

1901 **Salvatore Quasimodo:** Italian poet, critic and translator. After publication of poetry collection, *Waters and Land* gradually became leader of Hermeticism, modernist poetic movement characterized by unorthodox structure, illogical sequences, and highly subjective language. Also published a wide range of translations and wrote essays. Nobel Prize for Literature in 1959.

Poetry is the revelation of a feeling that the poet believes to be interior and personal, but which the reader recognizes as his own.

1910 **Eero Saarinen:** Finnish-born American architect and furniture designer. Son of architect Eliel Saarinen, the foremost Finnish architect of his time. Eero's designs for expressionist modern buildings include: General Motors Technical Center, U.S. Embassy in London, Trans World Airline terminal at New York's Kennedy Airport. Also responsible for the parabolic "Gateway to the West" in St. Louis.

Always design a thing by considering its next larger context — a chair in a room, a room in a house, a house in an environment, an environment in a city plan.

1921 **Jacqueline Susann:** American model, actress and writer. Best-selling author of novels *Valley of the Dolls* and *The Love Machine*, which broke sales records. She made no literary claims for her works, admitting they were to provide her readers with access to the sensational world of show business. Plagued by health problems, the recurrence of her breast cancer in 1973 took her life at age 56, after staying in a coma for seven weeks.

When I write I do five drafts. The first is on inexpensive white paper. I don't try for style, I just spill it out.

1928 **Luciano De Crescenzo:** Italian engineer and author. At age 50 he decided to write a book about his birthplace, Naples. The result was *Therefore Spoke Panorama*, whose introduction contains a one-sentence summary of his philosophy: "Naples isn't simply a city; it is a part of the human spirit that I know I can find in everyone, whether or no they are Neapolitan." Other Books: *Seems Yesterday*, *History of the Greek Philosophy*, *Order and Disorder*, and *Great Greek Myths*.

We are each of us angels with only one wing, and we can only fly by embracing one another.

OTHERS: 1561 Italian composer **Jacopo Peri**, 1625 French dramatist **Thomas Corneille**, 1719 Czech astronomer **Christian Mayer**, 1779 Swedish chemist **Jöns Jakob Berzelius**, 1860 French statesman **Raymond Poincaré**, 1897 Norwegian writer **Tarjei Vesaas**, 1905 U.S. musician **Jack Teagarden**, 1908 Baseball manager **Al Lopez**, 1913 U.S. neurobiologist **Roger Wolcott Sperry**, 1931 U.S. boxing promoter **Don King**, 1937 Russian film director **Andrei Konchalovsky**, 1942 U.S. singer **Isaac Hayes**, 1944 Indian Prime Minister **Rajiv Gandhi**, 1944 All-Star baseball player **Craig Nettles**, 1956 U.S. actress **Joan Allen**

August 21

1567 Saint **Francis de Sales:** French Roman Catholic bishop of Geneva. Distinguished preacher and devotional writer. *Introduction to a Devout Life* was an instant classic, first manual of piety addressed to those living in a society. Founded a congregation of nuns of the Visitation. Active in the struggle against Calvinism, successfully converting the Calvinistic population of Chablais. Canonized in 1665.

Do not wish to be anything but what you are, and try to be that perfectly.

1789 **Augustin-Louis Cauchy:** One of the greatest mathematicians of the 19th century and a leading representative of the French school of analysis. Introduced new standards of rigor in calculus from which grew the modern field of analysis. In *Cours d'analyse de l'École Polytechnique* (1821), by developing the concepts of limits and continuity, he provided the foundation for calculus essentially as it is today. Whether due to a pompous personality or zealous piety, he annoyed many who still acknowledged his tremendous mathematical talent.

It is therefore ridiculous to suppose that religion can turn anybody's head, and if all the insane were sent to insane asylums, more philosophers than Christians would be found there.

1798 **Jules Michelet:** French historian. Lectured on history at the École Normale. Professor of history at the Collège de France (1838–51). Noted for his vivid accounts of French history. Greatest works, the 24-volume *Histoire de France* and the 7-volume *Histoire de la Révolution*. Collaborated with his second wife on several nature books.

Woman is a miracle of divine contradictions.

1872 **Aubrey Beardsley:** English illustrator. Best known for his fantastic and erotic black-and-white drawings. His drawings appeared in the *Yellow Book* magazine and in his collection *Book of Fifty Drawings*. The most important illustrator of his day, his work is found in editions of Oscar Wilde's *Salomé*, Alexander Pope's *Rape of the Lock*, and Ben Jonson's *Volpone*. His fictional pieces were collected and published posthumously as *Under the Hill*. Career lasted only eight years. He died of tuberculosis at age 26.

No language is rude that can boast polite writers.

1887 **Carmel White Snow:** American fashion editor-in-chief with *Harper's Bazaar* (1934–58). Broadened the scope of fashion journalism to encompass art, fiction, and photography. Promoted Parisian designers. Launched the careers of some of the era's greatest figures in fashion and art. Championed the concept of "a well dressed woman for the well dressed mind."

Elegance is good taste, plus a dash of daring.

1890 **William M. Henry:** American journalist and pioneer in broadcast journalism. Covered sports, politics, and a rich variety of human behavior. Award-winning columnist ("By the Way") with Los Angeles *Times* (1911–70). Awarded the Presidential Medal of Freedom in 1970 by President Nixon.

Keep a secret, it's your slave. Tell it, and it's your master.

1904 **[William] "Count" Basie:** African-American pianist, bandleader and composer. Formed his own band in 1935 and by the following year it was established as one of the most popular in the country. Led big bands until his death in 1984. Basie music was characterized by the trademark "jumping" beat and the contrapuntal accents of his piano. Hits: "One O'Clock Jump," "Basie Boogie" and "I Left My Baby."

Of course, there are a lot of ways you can treat the blues, but it will still be the blues.

1930 Princess **Margaret Rose, Countess of Snowdon:** The second daughter of King George VI and sister of Queen Elizabeth II. Romance with Group-Captain Peter Townsend couldn't lead to marriage because he was divorced. Married Anthony Armstrong-Jones who was created Earl of Snowden. They had two children, but the marriage was dissolved in 1978. When Elizabeth gave birth to the new Prince of Wales, she joked, "I suppose, I'll now be known as Charley's Aunt."

Do you realize you are looking into the most beautiful eyes in the world?

1932 **Melvin Van Peebles:** African-American actor, director, screenwriter and composer. Helped break some of the color barriers in the film trade unions. Appeared as an actor in such films as *Jaws: The Revenge*, *Posse*, and *The Hebrew Hammer*. Directed: *Watermelon Man*, *Sweet Sweetback's Baadasssss Song*, and *Identity Crisis*. Subject of a documentary, *How to eat you're Watermelon in White Company (and enjoy It)*.

I make a film like I cook for my friends. I hope they like it, but if they don't, I'm prepared to enjoy it all by myself.

1936 **Wilt Chamberlain:** African-American basketball center, 7'4". Played two years for the University of Kansas. Led NBA in scoring seven times and rebounding eleven times. Four-time MVP; 31,419 career points. Led Philadelphia 76ers and LA Lakers to NBA titles. In 1962 he scored a record 100 points in a single game.

The world is made up of Davids. I am a Goliath, and nobody roots for Goliath.

1950 **Arthur Bremer:** Shot George C. Wallace on May 15, 1972, leaving him paralyzed for life. Six months earlier, Bremer was arrested for carrying a concealed weapon and fined for disorderly conduct. Despite his arrest he was able to purchase the pistol with which he would do "something bold and dramatic, forceful and dynamic." Wrote in his diary that he planned to assassinate either Richard Nixon or Wallace. Preferred to gun down Nixon; he couldn't get close enough, so he settled on Wallace. Only sorry that his victim hadn't died, he was convicted and sentenced to 63 years in prison.

Today I am a trillionth part of history.

1956 **Kim Cattrall:** English-born actress, who grew up in British Columbia, Canada. Appeared in a number of TV programs before beginning her movie career. Films: *Tribute*, *Police Academy*, *Mannequin*, *Star Trek VI: The Undiscovered Country* and *The Heidi Chronicles*. Best known for her role as sexually adventuresome Samantha Jones in the HBO series *Sex in the City*, which gave her international recognition.

Practically all the relationships I know are based on a foundation of lies and mutually accepted delusion.

OTHERS: 1165 Capetian king of France **Philip II Augustus**, 1597 English antiquarian **Roger Twysden**, 1660 French scientist/engineer **Hubert Gautier**, 1725 French painter **Jean-Baptiste Greuze**, 1754 Scottish inventor **William Murdoch**, 1813 Belgian chemist **Jean Stas**, 1826 German anatomist **Karl Gegenbaur**, 1906 U.S. movie animator **Friz Freleng**, 1915 Danish singer **Rasquel Rastenni**, 1924 U.S. sports announcer **Jack Buck**, 1933 English opera singer **Janet Baker**, 1936 U.S. playwright **Mart Crowley**, 1938 U.S. singer **Kenny Rogers**, 1944 Australian film director **Peter Weir**, 1969 Canadian figure skater **Josée Chouinard**

August 22

1862 **Claude Debussy:** French composer. Influenced by the Symbolist poets and Impressionist painters, which led him to a highly original compositional style. Experimented with novel techniques and effects. Produced pictures in sound and extended this new idiom to orchestral music. Regarded as the founder of musical impressionism. Best known pieces include *Claire de lune*, *Prélude a l'Après-midi d'un Faun*, *La Mer* and his only opera *Péleas et Mélisande*.

There is nothing more musical than a sunset.

1891 **Jacques Lipchitz:** Lithuanian-French-American sculptor. Trained as an engineer and turned to sculpture after moving to Paris in 1909. One of the founders of the Cubist school of sculptor. Produced what he called "transparent sculptures," open-spaced, curvilinear bronzes, which greatly influence the course of sculpture for the next quarter century. Developed a dynamic style noted for heavy stone abstractions and monumental figures. Works include: *Harpist*, *The Prayer* and *Bellerophon Taming Pegasus*.

All my life as an artist I have asked myself: What pushes me continually to make sculpture? I have found the answer. Art is an action against death. It is a denial of death.

1893 **Dorothy Parker**, née **Rothschild:** U.S. poet, satirist, short-story writer and book reviewer for *The New Yorker* and screenwriter. Drama critic for *Vanity Fair* (1917–20). Member of the Algonquin Round Table group. Contributed to several film scripts, including *The Little Foxes* and *A Star Is Born*. Famed for her spontaneous and acerbic bon mots: "Brevity is the soul of lingerie, as the Petticoat said to her Chemise," "This is not a novel to be tossed aside lightly, it should be thrown with great force" and "One more drink and I'd have been under the host."

There's a hell of distance between wisecracking and wit. Wit has truth in it; wisecracking is simply calisthenics with words.

1902 **Leni Riefenstahl:** German film director and actress. Former ballet and modern dancer. Became Adolf Hitler's favorite director. *Triumph of Will* vividly illustrated Hitler's charismatic appeal and *Olympia* was an epic documentary of the 1936 Olympics held in Berlin. After the war she was blacklisted by the Allies. Claimed political ignorance not sympathy for the Nazis was behind her wartime activities.

In 1934 people were crazy and there was great enthusiasm for Hitler. We had to try and find that with our camera.

1904 **Deng Xiaoping** or **Teng Hsiao-p'ing:** Powerful leader of the Chinese Communist party leader. Vice premier of the People's Republic and general secretary of the Chinese Communist Party. Fell from favor during the Cultural Revolution but was rehabilitated under the sponsorship of Zhou Enlai. His protégés premier Zhao Ziyang and secretary general Hu Yaobang embraced Deng's reform program. His massacre of student protestors in Tiananmen Square in 1989 permanently tarnished the reputation of the man credited with the transformation of China into a major player on the world stage.

Do not debate! is one of my inventions.

1908 **Henri Cartier-Bresson:** French photographer. Studied painting, but after a trip to West Africa he adopted photography as his means of artistic expression. Known for spontaneous, sequential images in still photography, developed from his fascination with film. With Robert Capa and David Seymour, founded the cooperative Magnum Photos. Best known collections: *The Decisive Moment* and *The Europeans*.

The photograph itself doesn't interest me. I want only to capture a minute of reality.

1920 **Ray Bradbury:** American science fiction writer. Primarily a short-story writer who has created some of the finest examples of the genre. His tales combine social criticism with fanciful science fiction. Best known for the short-story collections: *The Martian Chronicles* and *I Sing the Body Electric!* and novels *Fahrenheit 451* and *Something Wicked This Way Comes*. Volumes of verse: *Where Robot Mice & Robot Men Run Around in Robot Towns*, and *The Ghosts of Forever*.

There are worst crimes than burning books. One of them is not reading them.

1926 **Honor Blackman:** British actress. Some sources give her birthday as December 12, 1927. Played string of "English Rose" type film roles for the Rank Organization. Mostly remembered for the sexy Judo expert "Dr. Cathy Gale" in the TV series *The Avengers* and as the delicious "Pussy Galore" in James Bond movie *Goldfinger*. Other films: *A Night to Remember*, *Life at the Top* and *Age of Innocence*.

Men who are insecure about their masculinity often challenge me to fight.

1934 **H. Norman Schwarzkopf:** American general. "Stormin' Norman." Commanded troops of Desert Storm in the Persian Gulf War with Iraq of 1991. In 1988 he was appointed Commander-in-Chief of the U.S. Central Command. His plans for Operation Desert Shield and Operation Desert Storm are credited with shortening the war with Iraq. After retirement in 1991, wrote *It Doesn't Take a Hero*.

Leadership is a potent combination of strategy and character. But if you must be without one, be without strategy.

1935 **E. Annie Proulx:** American journalist and author who did not begin writing fiction until her fifties. Pulitzer Prize for Fiction and the National Book Award for fiction for her second novel *The Shipping News*. O. Henry Prize for the year's best short story in consecutive years, for "Brokeback Mountain" and "The Mud Below." When neither Ang Lee's film adaptation of *Brokeback Mountain* nor its star Heath Ledger won Oscars, she wrote a vitriolic commentary in which she blasted the awards show and the voters.

Roughly 6000 film industry voters, mostly in the Los Angeles area, many living cloistered lives beyond wrought-iron gates or in deluxe rest homes, out of touch not only with the shifting larger culture and the yeasty ferment that is America these days, but also out of touch with their own segregated city, decide which films are good.

1939 **Carl Yastrzemski:** "Yaz." Major league baseball player. Hall-of-Fame left-fielder with the Boston Red Sox. Won the Triple Crown and MVP award in 1967 with a .326 batting average, 44 home runs (tied with Harmon Killebrew) and 121 runs-batted-in. That was the year of "The Impossible Dream," as the Red Sox rebounded from a 9th place finish the previous year to winning the pennant, losing the World Series to the St. Louis Cardinals. Eighteen-time All-Star and outstanding defensive player, retired in 1983 at age 44, after 23 years, the longest career with one team in history.

I think about baseball when I wake up in the morning. I think about it all day and I dream about it at night. The only time I don't think about it is when I'm playing.

1941 **[Duane Charles] "Bill" Parcells:** "The Big Tuna." Highly regarded NFL football coach. Head coach of the New York Giants (1983–90). Led them to two Super Bowl victories (1986, 1990). Coached the New England Patriots (1993–96) and the New York Jets (1997–99). Retired, but was lured back to coaching by Dallas Cowboys' owner Jerry Jones (2003). His colorful comment on leaving the Patriots over player personnel decisions dispute with owner Robert Kraft:

They want you to cook the dinner; at least they ought to let you shop for some of the groceries.

OTHERS: 1601 French writer **Georges de Scudéry**, 1647 French physicist **Denis Papin**, 1764 French architect **Charles Percier**, 1771 English inventor **William S. Maudslay**, 1834 U.S. astronomer **Samuel Pierpont Langley**, 1836 U.S. artist **Archibald M. Willard**, 1860 German TV pioneer **Paul Nipkow**, 1867 Swiss nutritionist **Maximilian Bircher-Benner**, 1874 German philosopher **Max Scheler**, 1880 U.S. cartoonist **George Herriman**, 1900 Russian lexicographer **Sergei Ozhegov**, 1915 Polish economist **Edward Szczepanik**, 1917 U.S. guitarist/singer **John Lee Hooker**, 1956 U.S. baseball player **Paul Molitor**

August 23

1754 **Louis XVI:** King of France (1774–93). Reforms of his ministers failed to prevent the revolution. Convicted of treason by the National Convention which abolished the monarchy. Only hours after saying farewell to Queen Maria Antoinette and their children he was conveyed to the scaffold at the Place de la Revolution with a large escort of cavalrymen. Took two hours to make the trip through a massive crowd that had gathered to witness the execution. His last words before being guillotined:

I die innocent of all the crimes laid to my charge; I pardon those who have occasioned my death; and I pray to God that the blood you are going to shed may never be visited on France. May my blood cement your happiness!

1769 **Georges Curvier:** French zoologist and anatomist. Developed comparative anatomy and the technique of showing, from a few bones, a probable reconstruction of the entire animal of an extinct species. Did much to establish the modern classification of animals, expanding on the work of Carl Linnaeus by adding another broader level, the phylum. First to classify fossil mammals and reptiles, founding vertebrate paleontology. Rejected theories of evolution. Last words to the nurse who was applying leeches to his body:

Nurse, it was I who discovered that leeches have red blood.

1849 **William E. Henley:** English poet, playwright, critic and editor. Suffered from tubercular arthritis. Recovering from having a foot amputated to save the other, wrote *Hospital Sketches,* a sequence of poems first published in 1875. Friend of Robert Louis Stevenson who used him as a model for Long John Silver in *Treasure Island.* Henley's best known poem "Invictus" concludes with the familiar lines:

It matters not how strait the gate,/ How charged with punishment the scroll,/ I am the master of my fate;/ I am the captain of my soul.

1852 **Arnold Toynbee:** English economic historian and social reformer, committed to the improvement of the living conditions of the working class. First to identify and name the British "Industrial Revolution." A collection of his lectures, published posthumously in 1884, became a classic of British economic history. Criticized "party Historians" who sought to read into the past the controversies of the present.

You must pursue facts for their own sake, but penetrated with a vivid sense of the problems of your own time. This is not a principle of perversion, but a principle of selection. You must have some principle of selection, and you could not have a better one than to pay special attention to the history of the social problems which are agitating the world now, for you may be sure that they are problems not of temporary but of lasting importance.

1855 **Barrett Wendell:** American educator and author. First teacher at Harvard University to offer American literature as an object of systematic historical and critical study. Wrote *A Literary History of America, Liberty, Union and Democracy, The Mystery of Education* and *The Traditions of European Literature.* Biographies of Cotton Mather, William Shakespeare and Sir Walter Raleigh.

I wonder if anyone ever reached the age of thirty-five in New England without wanting to kill himself.

1869 **Edgar Lee Masters:** American lawyer, poet and novelist. Member of the literary renaissance, the Chicago Group. Wrote biographies of Vachel Lindsay, Walt Whitman, Mark Twain and Abraham Lincoln. Best known work is his satirical *Spoon River Anthology,* a book of dramatic monologues, written in free verse, spoken from beyond the grave by people buried in an Illinois cemetery.

I am Anne Rutledge who sleep beneath these weeds,/ Beloved in life of Abraham Lincoln,/ Wedded to him, not through union,/ But through separation.

1883 **Jonathan Wainwright:** "Skinny." U.S. army general in command of the forces in the Philippines after General Douglas MacArthur's departure. Forced to surrender, he survived the infamous "Bataan Death March." During the forced march of 63 miles by 70,000 U.S. and Filipino prisoners of war to a concentration camp, some 10,000 died along the way. After the war, the Japanese commander of the march was convicted by a U.S. military tribunal and hanged. Released in 1945, Wainwright was awarded the Congressional Medal of Honor.

Peace is a militant state, which is not secured by wishful thinking.... If we are to be sure of our liberty, we must be ready to fight for it.

1884 **Will Cuppy:** American humorist and journalist. Best known for his mock-scientific observations of nature. Satirized with dry and subtle humor everything from arrogant experts to modern society and popular culture. Wrote weekly column," Mystery and Adventure," for the *New York Herald Tribune* on current detective stories. Edited three collections of crime and mystery stories. Author of *How to be a Hermit, How to Tell Your Friends from the Apes, Murder Without Tears,* and *The Decline and Fall of Everybody.*

The Dodo never had a chance. He seems to have been invented for the sole purpose of becoming extinct and that was all he was good for.

1888 **Morris L. Ernst:** American lawyer, author and editor. Author of *Hold Your Tongue!, Adventures on Libel and Slander, How High Is Up, Lawyers and What They Do* and *A Love Affair with the Law.* Editor with Judith A. Posner of *The Comparative International Almanac.* Most famous for his defense in the censorship case against James Joyce. Other clients included Rafael Trujillo, dictator of the Dominican Republic and Frank Costello, New York organized crime boss arrested for tax evasion.

Man's fear of ideas is probably the greatest dike holding back human knowledge and happiness.

1911 **J.V. [James Vincent] Cunningham:** American educator, literary critic and poet. Theory was that verse is metrical speech. Volumes of verse: *The Helmsman, The Exclusions of a Rhyme, and Collected Poems and Epigrams.* Literary criticism: *Woe or Wonder* and *Tradition and Poetic Structure.*

I like the trivial, vulgar and exalted.

1912 **Gene Kelly:** Athletic American dancer, actor, director and choreographer. In 1941 he choreographed *Billy Rose's Diamond Horseshoe* and had the title role in *Pal Joey.* Free-flowing, imaginative routines revolutionized the Hollywood musical. Academy Award nominated for *Anchors Aweigh.* Received a special Oscar for his versatility and achievements in the art of choreography. Other film musicals: *On the Town, An American in Paris* and *Singing in the Rain.* Director: *Invita-*

tion to the Dance, A Guide for the Married Man and *Hello Dolly!*

The male dancer's place in the arts has been terribly misrepresented.... I want to show that there's a definite analogy between sport and dancing.

1932 **Mark Russell:** American political satirist, pianist and singer. Has appeared for more than 25 years of public broadcasting network PBS at least twice a year. Plays piano and sings between periods of talking. Known for making up new words for popular tunes, which express the political situation he is addressing. First rose to popularity at the time of the Watergate scandal. Continues to spoof politicians, particularly presidents, be they Democrats, Republicans, third party or independent.

The scientific theory I like best is that the rings of Saturn are composed entirely of lost airline luggage.

OTHERS: 686 Frankish Ruler **Charles Martel**, 1623 Polish astronomer **Stanislaw Lubieniecki**, 1783 English civil engineer **William Tierney Clark**, 1847 U.S. physicist **Sarah Frances Whiting**, 1875 English radio pioneer **William Eccles**, 1903 Scottish violist **William Primrose**, 1921 U.S. economist **Kenneth Arrow**, 1924 Israeli writer **Ephraim Kishon**, 1924 U.S. economist **Robert Solow**, 1931 U.S. microbiologist **Hamilton O. Smith**, 1933 California governor **Pete Wilson**, 1934 U.S. actress **Barbara Eden**, 1946 English drummer **Keith Moon**, 1951 Queen of Jordan **Noor**, 1963 Race car driver **Kenny Wallace**

August 24

1578 **John Taylor:** English poet and Thames waterman. Pressed for the navy and was present at the battle of Cadiz. Wrote rollicking verse and prose. Each of his many journeys resulted in a booklet with an odd title. In 1630 published *All the Workes of John Taylor, the Water Poet*. Gave the world the familiar line "*To call a spade a spade.*"

God sends meat, and the devil sends cooks.

1591 **Robert Herrick:** English clergyman and Cavalier poet. Known for pastoral and love lyrics. A Royalist he lost his parish in rural Devonshire during the English Civil War, and lived happily in London in the society of poets until the Restoration. Author of short poems that made ideal song lyrics and became among the most popular songs of the period: "To the Virgins," and "To Make Much of Time." Some of his excellent religious verses are found in his collection of poems, *Hesperides*.

It takes great wit and interest and energy to be happy. The pursuit of happiness is a great activity. One must be open and alive. It is the greatest feat man has to accomplish.

1759 **William Wilberforce:** English statesman, philanthropist and reformer. During a tour of the continent he converted to evangelical Christianity. Campaigner for 19 years against oppression and slavery in the British Empire. Also set about to put an end of the slave trade abroad and the total abolition of slavery. Helped found the *Christian Observor*, and wrote *A Practical View of Christianity*. His name was given to Wilberforce College in Ohio.

If to be feelingly alive to the suffering of my fellow-creatures is to be a fanatic, I am one of the most incurable fanatics ever to be permitted to be at large.

1810 **Theodore Parker:** American Unitarian clergyman, abolitionist, reformer and author. Leader of antislavery movement. Social reform ideas, opposed by the conservatives of his time, were later widely adopted. Founded *Massachusetts Quarterly Review*. Wrote *A Discourse of Matters Pertaining to Religion* and *Sermons for the Times*.

Let others laugh when you sacrifice desire to duty; if they will. You have time and eternity to rejoice in.

1872 Sir **Max Beerbohm:** English essayist and caricaturist. Dubbed "the incomparable Max" by George Bernard Shaw. Legendary for his wit and powers of satire. Applied irony to society's foibles and to the idiosyncrasies of writers, artists and politicians. Best known for caricatures of literary and political figures published in *The Poet's Corner*. Dramatic criticism is collected in *Around Theatres* and *More Theatres*.

We must stop talking about the American dream and start listening to the dreams of Americans.

1894 **Jean Rhys:** Pseudonym of **Gwen Williams**. West Indian–born English novelist. After World War I, she married a Dutch poet, Max Hamer, and moved to the continent, living mostly in Paris. Published *The Left Bank and Other Stories* set in Paris or the West Indies. Best-known novel: *Wide Sargasso Sea*, a prequel to Charlotte Bronte's *Jane Eyre*. Others: *Quartet, After Leaving Mr. Mackenzie* and *Good Morning Midnight*.

Age seldom arrives smoothly or quickly. It's more often a succession of jerks.

1895 **Richard J. Cushing:** American Roman Catholic Cardinal. Archbishop of Boston (1944–70). Master fundraiser and prime mover in the development of new parishes and charitable institutions in the Boston archdiocese. Director of the Boston office of the Society for the Propagation of the Faith. Known for his close ties to the Kennedy family and his anti-communism.

Saints are all right in Heaven, but they're hell on Earth.

1898 **Malcolm Cowley:** American novelist, journalist, editor, poet and translator. Member of the American colony in France in the 1920s, leading him to write *Exile's Return*, about expatriate members of the "Lost Generation." Wrote an important study of William Faulkner's works in *The Portable Faulkner*, followed by *The Faulkner-Cowley File: Letters and Memoirs 1944–1962*. Other books: *The Literary Situation, Fitzgerald and the Jazz Age*, and *The Dream of the Golden Mountains*.

Be kind and considerate with your criticism.... It's just as hard to write a bad book as it is to write a good book.

1899 **Jorge Luis Borges:** Argentinean poet, critic, essayist and short-story writer. Afflicted by a growing hereditary blindness, which was total by the mid 1950s. Member of the Spanish avant-garde Ultraist literary group. Noted for highly original fictional narratives, metaphorical allegory and fantasy-woven tales: *Ficciones*, *The Aleph*, *Dreamtigers*, and *Extraordinary Tales*. Collection of poems: *Fevor de Buenos Aires.*

Reality is not always probable, or likely.

1922 **René Lévesque:** Canadian reporter, minister of the government of the province of Quebec, founder of the Parti Québécois, and 23rd Premier of Quebec. An important figure of the Quebec nationalist movement. Sought to negotiate the political independence for Quebec. On May 20, 1980, a referendum on his party's sovereignty-association plan. In an 86% turnout of eligible voters, the plan was opposed by 60% and 40% in favor.

... I have confidence that one day ... there's a normal rendezvous with history that Quebec will hold, and I have confidence that we shall be there, together, to witness it.

1929 **Yasser Arafat:** Palestinian leader and President of the Palestinian Authority. Co-founded the guerrilla organization Fatah (1956), which became the leading military component of the Palestinian Liberation Organization (PLO), which he led (1969–2004). PLO was formally recognized in 1974. First leader of a non-governmental organization to address the U.N. In 1993 formally recognized Israel. The next year he shared the Nobel Peace Prize with Israeli leaders Yitzhak Rabin and Shimon Peres.

Whoever stands by a just cause cannot possibly be called a terrorist.

1947 **Paulo Coelho:** Brazilian novelist. When he resisted his parents intention that he become an engineer in order to pursue his lifelong dream of becoming an author, his father had him committed to a mental institution on three different occasions, where he underwent electroconvulsive therapy. At age 38 finally published his first novel, *Pilgrimage: A Contemporary Quest for Ancient Wisdom.* A most original author, his works deals with obsessive soul-searching. His best-known work is the modern classic *The Alchemist.* Other Works: *The Valkyries*, *The Fifth Mountain*, *Eleven Minutes*, and *The Zahir.*

I think writing is a way to allow yourself to go into the mystery of your soul.

OTHERS: 1113 French conqueror of Normandy **Geoffrey Plantagenet**, 1552 Italian painter **Lavinia Fontana**, 1669 Italian composer **Alessandro Marcello**, 1787 Antarctica explorer **James Weddell**, 1880 U.S. inventor **Joshua Lionel Cowen**, 1884 Creator of Charlie Chan **Earl Derr Biggers**, 1890 Hawaiian swimmer **Duke Kahanamoku**, 1927 U.S. economist **Harry Markowitz**, 1938 Icelandic politician **Halldór Blöndal**, 1951 U.S. novelist **Orson Scott Card**, 1960 U.S. baseball player **Cal Ripken, Jr.**, 1965 U.S. basketball player **Reggie Miller**, 1973 U.S. actor/comedian **David Chappelle**

August 25

1530 **Ivan IV Vasilyevitch: Ivan Grozny (Terrible).** Grand Duke of Muscovy. First ruler of Russia to assume the title tsar. Nickname *Grozny* means "inspiring fear or terror, dangerous, or awesome." Revised the law code, created a standing army and subordinated the church to the state. Introduced laws restricting the mobility of the peasants, which led to serfdom. Formed a secret police loyal only to him, as a tool to keep the hereditary nobles, the boyars, in line. Unbalanced and violent. Beat his daughter-in-law for wearing indecent clothing, which caused her to miscarriage and a heated argument with his son and heir resulted in the latter's death. Ivan IV died as had been prophesized on March 18, 1854. At his 1547 coronation, he spoke of the doctrine of the Third Rome:

Two Romes fell, but the third — Moscow — shall stand, and a fourth shall never be! And in that Third Rome — as ruler of Muscovy — as sole Master from this day forth shall I reign.

1744 **Johann Gottfried von Herder:** German poet, critic, theologian and philosopher. Maintained that the truest poetry is that of the people. Great influence on Johan Goethe during the latter's *Strum and Drang* period and on the growing German Romanticism. Love for the songs of the people found expression in *Stimmen der Völker in Liedern*, a collection of folksongs. His masterpiece *Ideas for the Education of Mankind* recognized the importance of the historical method and anticipated evolutionary theories.

Say oh wise man how you have come to such knowledge? Because I was never ashamed to confess my ignorance and ask others.

1836 **Bret Harte:** American short-story writer, novelist, poet and humorist. Often showed thieves and vagabonds as more admirable that conventional law-abiding people. Helped found and edit *The Overland Monthly*. Stories: "The Luck of the Roaring Camp," "The Outcasts of Poker Flat" and "Plain Language from Truthful James." U.S. consul in Germany and Scotland, and a favorite in European literary circles.

The creator who could put a cancer in a believer's stomach is above being interfered with by prayers.

1850 **Edgar Wilson "Bill" Nye:** American journalist, humorist and lecturer. Nye, Mark Twain and Artemus Ward are considered to be responsible for making American humor a distinct and truly national branch of literature. Founder and editor of the *Laramie Boomerang*. Works: *Bill Nye's History of the United States*, *Bill Nye and Boomerang*, *Forty Liars and Other Lies* and *Bailed Hay*. Late wrote two books with the "Hoosier poet" James Whitcomb Riley and appeared with him on the lecture circuit.

Winter lingered so long in the lap of spring, that it occasioned a great deal of talk.

1889 **William Feather:** American publisher and author. Founder of the William Feather Co., printers and publishers in Cleveland, Ohio in 1916. Editor and publisher *The William Feather Magazine*. Works: *As We Were Saying, Haystacks and Smokestacks, Business of Life* and *Talk About Women.*

Plenty of people miss their share of happiness, not because they never found it, but because they didn't stop to enjoy it.

1909 **Ruby Keeler:** Originally **Ethel Hilda Keeler**. Canadian-born actress and dancer. Dancer on Broadway, but when she married Al Jolson, she moved to Hollywood and became a star in Warner Bros. musicals. After divorcing Jolson, she retired, but returned to Broadway in 1971 to star in *No, No, Nanette*, which ran for 861 performances. Best remembered for the chorus girl who replaces the Broadway star on opening night in *42nd Street*. Other films: *Gold Diggers of 1993, Footlight Parade, Dames, Go Into Your Dance*, with Jolson, and her favorite *Colleen.*

It's amazing. I couldn't act. I had that terrible singing voice, and now I can see I wasn't the greatest tap dancer in the world either.

1913 **Walt Kelly:** American cartoonist Creator of the comic strip "Pogo," whose message was a satirical and penetrating look at American society and its problems. It features the title character, an opossum, and his friends of the Okefenokee Swamp. Kelly used his characters to satirize prominent political figures. During the Vietnam War, Pogo's observation "We have met the enemy and he is us" became a familiar sign at anti-war protests.

We are confronted with insurmountable opportunities.

1918 **Leonard Bernstein:** Gifted American conductor and composer. Fame came when he was unexpectedly asked to fill in as conductor for ill Bruno Walter on short notice at a 1943 broadcast. Equally at home with symphonic music and Broadway shows. Initiated a television series, "Young People's Concerts" with the New York Philharmonic. Musical compositions: symphonies *Jeremiah, The Age of Anxiety*, and *Kaddish*; an opera written for TV, *Trouble in Tahiti*; the ballet *Fancy Free*:; the operetta, *Candide*; musicals *On the Town, Wonderful Town*, and *West Side Story*; and *Mass*, commissioned for the opening of the John F. Kennedy Center of the Performing Arts.

To achieve great things, two things are needed; a plan, and not quite enough time.

1919 **George C. Wallace:** American politician. As governor kept his pledge "to stand in the schoolhouse door" to prevent black students enrolling at the University of Alabama. Yielded in the face of the federalized National Guard. American Independent Party presidential candidate in 1968. Served as governor again (1971–79). Shot while campaigning for the Democratic Presidential nomination in 1972. Paralyzed from his waist down. In the 1980s he renounced his segregationist views and was reelected governor with the help of black voters.

I draw the line in the dust and toss the gauntlet before the feet of tyranny, and I say segregation now, segregation tomorrow and segregation forever!

1927 **Althea Gibson:** American tennis player. First African-American to win a major tournament, the French (1956). U.S. singles champ (1957 and 1958). Wimbledon champion the same years. In all won 11 Grand Slam events. Became the first African-American to be voted Female Athlete of the Year by the Associated Press (both years 1957 and 1958). Later appeared in some films and played professional golf.

Shaking hands with the Queen of England was a long way from being forced to sit in the colored section of the bus station going into downtown Wilmington, North Carolina.

1930 **Sean Connery:** Scottish actor. Made his London stage debut in the chorus of *South Pacific*. Best known in the role of Ian Fleming's character James Bond in seven popular 007 films, beginning in 1962 with *Dr. No*. Other movies: *The Man Who Would Be King, The Name of the Rose* and *The Hunt for Red October*. Won an Academy Award for Best Supporting Actor for *The Untouchables*. Knighted by Queen Elizabeth II, but insisted that the ceremony take place in his beloved Scotland.

I like women. I don't understand them, but I like them.

1944 **Conrad Black: Baron Black of Crissharbour**: Canadian-born British financier and newspaper magnate. At one point, the Chicago-based Hollinger International, of which he was CEO, ranked as one of the world's largest media empires. His board ousted him in 2003 after an investigation turned up evidence that he and several partners paid themselves millions of dollars without company approval. The company filed suit against Black, asking $200 million in damages. In 2005, arrest warrants for Black and several other Hollinger executives on a series of fraud charges involving more than $2 billion were issued.

Keep a little perspective guys. This isn't Enron. This isn't WorldCom.

OTHERS: 1635 Welsh privateer **Sir Henry Morgan**, 1724 British painter **George Stubbs**, 1802 Austrian poet **Nikolaus Lenau**, 1819 U.S. private detective **Allan Pinkerton**, 1850 French scientist **Charles Richet**, 1900 German physician **Hans Adolf Krebs**, 1903 Hungarian physicist **Árpád Élő**, 1912 East Germany President **Erich Honecker**, 1916 U.S. actor **Van Johnson**, 1921 Canadian-born game show host **Monty Hall**, 1931 TV host **Regis Philbin**, 1938 English author **Frederick Forsyth**, 1946 Baseball pitcher **Rollie Fingers**, 1954 English musician **Elvis Costello**, 1960 U.S. film director **Tim Burton**, 1970 German model **Claudia Schiffer**

August 26

1676 Sir **Robert Walpole:** English statesman. Entered politics largely by accident when his two elder brothers died, leaving him the family estate and wealth. Formidable speaker quickly rose through the ranks of his party, becoming first lord of the Treasury and Chancellor of the Exchequer. King George I could not speak English and soon ceased to attend parliamentary proceedings, leaving Walpole a free hand as the leader of the government. Regarded as the first British prime minister (1721–42). Presented with No. 10 Downing Street, which became the permanent London home of English prime ministers.

Our supreme governor, the mob.

1743 **Antoine Laurent Lavoisier:** French chemist, regarded as father of modern chemistry. Defined the role of oxygen, which he named. Concluded that human energy was derived from oxidation of hydrogen and carbon. Worked on a scheme for improving the water supply to Paris and on the methods of purifying water. He offended Marat, who had him brought up on charges of counter-revolutionary activity. Convicted and guillotined the next day. Speaking of his friend, mathematician Joseph-Louis Lagrange said: "It took them only an instant to cut off that head, but a century will not be sufficient to produce another like it."

I consider nature a vast chemical laboratory in which all kinds of composition and decompositions are formed. Vegetation is the basic instrument the creator uses to set all nature in motion.

1745 **Henry Mackenzie:** Scottish writer. "Man of Feeling." Crown attorney in the Scottish Court of Exchequer and comptroller of taxes. Identified as "one of the most illustrious names connected with polite literature in Edinburgh." Contributor to *The Scots Magazine* and *General Intelligencer*. Novels: *The Man of Feeling, The Man of the World*, and *Julia de Roubigné*. A founder of the Royal Society of Edinburgh.

Mankind, in the gross, is a gaping monster that loves to be deceived, and has seldom been disappointed.

1873 **May Lamberton Becker:** American editor and writer. Editor: Reader's Guide of the *New York Herald Tribune* "Books." Wrote: *Books as Windows, Adventures in Reading, Choosing Books for Children, Introducing Charles Dickens*, and *Presenting Miss Jane Austen*. Compiler of the seven volume *Golden Tales* series: *Our America, Old South, New England, Prairie States, Far West, Canada* and *Southwest*.

We grow neither better nor worse as we get old, but more like ourselves.

1875 **John Buchan, Lord Tweedsmuir:** Scottish writer and governor general of Canada. Known for his swift-paced romantic adventure stories. Author of *Prester John*, a romance of South Africa, and his spy novels, featuring his hero Richard Hannay: *The Thirty-Nine Steps, Greenmantle*, and *The Three Hostages*. Biographies include lives of Oliver Cromwell and his Scottish contemporary James Graham Montrose.

Without humility there can be no humanity.

1880 **Guillaume Apollinaire:** French poet and critic. Born in Rome of Polish descent. Helped launch poetry into unexplored channels. His work was bizarre, symbolist and fantastic. Collections: *L'Enchanteur pourissant, Le Bestaire, Les Alcools*, and *Calligrammes*. While recuperating from a wound received during World War I, wrote the play *Les Marmelles de Tirésias*, for which he coined the term "surrealist."

Memories are hunting horns whose sound dies on the wind.

1885 **Jules Romains:** Pseudonym of **Louis-Henri-Jean Darigoule**. French novelist, dramatist and poet. Founded the literary movement known as Unanimism, based on the psychological concept of group consciousness and collective emotion and the need for the poet to merge with transcendent consciousness. Later he defined it as "representation of the world without judgment." Principal work *Cycle Men of Good Will*, a 27 volume set, gives an intricate view of French life from 1908 to 1933. Novels: *The Death of Nobody* and *The Boys in the Back Room*. His plays were considered masterpieces of French theater.

Healthy people are invalids who don't know it.

1904 **Christopher Isherwood:** English-born American novelist, short-story writer and memoirist. Described the social corruption and disintegration of Germany during Hitler's rise to power in *Berlin Stories*. Sketch about "Sally Bowles," a cabaret entertainer with more beauty, eccentricity and wit than talent was dramatized by John Van Druten as *I Am a Camera*, and was the basis of the Broadway and film musical *Cabaret*. *Christopher and His Kind* is a frank account of the homosexual affairs of his youth.

I am a camera with its shutter open, quite passive, recording, not thinking.

1914 **Julio Cortázar:** Argentine author, born in Brussels. Lived in exile in Paris after the election of Juan Perón. Novels: *The Winners, Hopscotch, Sixty-two: A Model Kit, Rayuela* and *A Change of Light*. His short stories include "Blow-up," which was adapted for a film by Italian director Michelangelo Antonioni.

The evolution from happiness to habit is one of death's best weapons.

1921 **Benjamin Bradlee:** American journalist and editor. Joined the Washington *Post* and worked for *Newsweek*. Became managing editor of the *Post* in 1965. Encouraged investigating journalism. Supported the Watergate investigation of reporters Bob Woodward and Carl Bernstein, resulting in a constitutional crisis and the resignation of President Richard Nixon. Wrote *Conversations with Kennedy* (1975).

News is the first rough draft of history.

1935 **Geraldine Ferraro:** American Democratic politician. U.S. congresswoman from New York (1978–84). Picked by Walter Mondale to be his running mate as Vice-Presidential candidate (1984), first woman of a major party to run for the office. Investigations of her husband's finances hurt the campaign. Twice ran unsuccessfully for the U.S. Senate. Speaking of the Reagan administration economic policies:

I'd call it a new version of voodoo economics, but I'm afraid that would give witch doctors a bad name.

1960 **Branford Marsalis:** American tenor and soprano saxophonist and bandleader. Oldest of four brothers, all of whom are jazz musicians, as was their father Ellis Marsalis. Began his professional career playing with the Art Blakely big band. Started his own band in 1986. Albums: *Do the Right Thing, Mo' Better Blues, I Heard You Twice the First Time* and *Footsteps of our Fathers.* With Harry Connick, Jr., came up with an initiative to help restore the New Orleans' musical heritage after hurricane Katrina.

The record industry is changing, and sooner or later we had to face the reality that there's not a lot of room at major labels for my kind of creative music — not just jazz — that doesn't generate large sales.

OTHERS: 1740 French balloonist **Joseph Montgolfier**, 1775 German writer **William Joseph Behr**, 1873 U.S. inventor **Lee DeForest**, 1874 U.S. novelist **Zona Gale**, 1882 German-born physicist **James Franck**, 1896 Bulgarian revolutionary **Ivan Mihailov**, 1898 U.S. art collector **Peggy Guggenheim**, 1900 German engineer **Hellmuth Walter**, 1901 U.S. general **Maxwell Taylor**, 1906 U.S. polio researcher **Albert Sabin**, 1911 U.S. orchestra leader **Lester Lanin**, 1922 U.S. journalist **Irving R. Levene**, 1941 Swiss film director **Barbet Schroeder**, 1946 U.S. Secretary of Homeland Security **Tom Ridge**, 1952 U.S. swimmer **John Kinsella**

August 27

1770 **Georg Wilhelm Hegel:** German idealist philosopher. Conceived of consciousness and the external object as forming a unity in which neither factor can exist independently. Mind and nature are two abstractions of one indivisible whole. Had great influence on modern movements of existentialism, Marxism, positivism and analytical philosophy. For Hegel the task of philosophy was to comprehend the rationality of what already exists. Karl Marx and others used this dialectic to show the inevitability of radical change.

What experience and history teaches us that people and governments have never learned anything from history, or acted upon principles deducted from it.

1777 **Thomas Campbell:** Scottish poet, balladwriter and journalist. In 1799 published instantaneously successful *The Pleasures of Hope*, a rhetorical and didactic poem dealing with popular topics of the day, the French Revolution, the partition of Poland and slavery. Works: "Glenara," "Lord Ullin's Daughter," "Ye Mariners of England," *Specimens of the British Poets, Life of Mrs. Siddons*, and "The Pilgrim of Glencoe."

To live in hearts we leave behind/ Is not to die.

1865 **Charles G. Dawes:** American Republican politician. 30th Vice President of the United States (1925–29) under Calvin Coolidge. Appointed by the Allied Reparations Commission president of the committee that produced the Dawes Plan, a $200 million loan that enabled Germany to pay enormous war debts after World War I. Recipient of the Nobel Peace Prize in 1925. Ambassador to Great Britain (1929–32).

Mediocrity requires aloofness to preserve its dignity.

1871 **Theodore Dreiser:** American journalist, editor and novelist. Pioneered naturalism in American literature. Leading light of Chicago Group. Novels: *Sister Carrie, Jennie Gerhardt* and *An American Tragedy*, which brought him great popularity after years of publishing works largely ignored. Praised for his powerful realism and sincerity. In the 1930s devoted his energy to the radical reform movement.

Words are but the vague shadows of the volumes we mean. Little audible links, they are, chaining together great inaudible feelings and purposes.

1876 **Eugene G. Grace:** American industrialist. Chairman of Bethlehem Steel. Touched off an Anti-Trust investigation when he planned a merger with Youngstown Sheet and Tube. Stockholders bitterly complained and labor protested after the great crash when he received a bonus of $1,623,000. During World War II he was acknowledged as the leader of the steel industry in America.

Do one thing at a time and do that one thing as if your life depended upon it.

1877 **Lloyd C. Douglas:** American Lutheran minister and author. Served in pastorates in Indiana, Ohio, Washington, D.C., Michigan, Ohio, California and finally in Montreal, Quebec. Wrote his first novel, *The Magnificent Obsession*, at age 50. It was an immediate success. His works were of a moral, didactic and distinctly religious tone. Other novels: *Green Light, White Banners, The Robe* and *The Big Fisherman.*

If a man harbors any sort of fear, it percolates through all his thinking, damages his personality, makes him landlord to a ghost.

1890 **Man Ray:** Originally **Emmanuel Radnitsky**. American painter, sculptor, photographer and filmmaker. Only American to play a major role in both the Dada and Surrealist movements. Developed the rayograph (cameraless pictures) technique in photography, by placing objects on light-sensitive paper, and the technique of solarization, which makes part of the image negative and part positive. Important avant-garde film maker in the 20s.

I photograph the things that I do not wish to paint, the things which already have an existence.... I paint what cannot be photographed, that which comes from the imagination or from dreams, or from an unconscious drive.

1896 **Kenji Miyazawa:** Japanese poet and author of children's literature. The only works published before his death was a collection of free-verse poems *Spring and Asura* and a collection of children's stories, *The Restaurant of Many Orders.* After he died many more of his works were discovered and published, including:

Gingatetsudō no Yoru, Kazeno Matasaburo and his poem "Ame ni mo Makezu," which defines the Japanese ideal.

We must embrace pain and burn it as fuel for our journey.

1908 **Lyndon B. Johnson:** Democratic Texan politician. Thirty-sixth U.S. president succeeding assassinated President John F. Kennedy. Exercised his political skill learned as a Senator from Texas and majority leader to pass civil rights and antipoverty legislation. Anti–Vietnam War sentiment caused him not to seek re-nomination in 1968. His special skills were summarized by Georgia Senator Richard Russell: "He doesn't have the best mind in the Senate; he isn't the best orator, he isn't the best parliamentarian. But he's the best combination of all of these qualities.

Doing what is right isn't the problem. It is knowing what's right.

1908 **Frank Leahy:** American Football coach. Played tackle for Knute Rockne at the University Notre Dame. Head coach at Boston College, guiding them to a 20–2 record, including an undefeated 1940 season, a Sugar Bowl victory, and a share of the national championship. Returned to his alma mater 1941, his tenure as head coach interrupted by service with U.S. Navy. Returned to Notre Dame in 1946. During his 13-year tenure, Notre Dame had six undefeated seasons, five national championships, record of 107 wins, 13 losses, 9 ties, and an unbeaten streak that reached 39 games.

Egotism is the anesthetic that dulls the pain of stupidity.

1910 **Mother Teresa of Calcutta:** Born **Agnes Gonxha Bojaxhiu** in Yugoslavia. Nun and nurse. Went to the slums of India as young woman. Founded the Missionaries of Charity in Calcutta, which served the blind, the aged, lepers, the disabled and the dying. Indian government awarded her the Padmashri ("Lord of the Lotus") for her service to the people. Her order has hundred of centers in more than 90 countries, with some 4,000 nuns and hundreds of thousands of lay workers. Nobel Peace Prize (1979). Pope John Paul II issued a special dispensation to expedite the process of declaring her a saint.

If you cannot feed a hundred people, then just feed one.

1932 Lady **Antonia Fraser:** English biographer and author of contemporary mysteries featuring Jemima Shore. Painstakingly researched biographies: *Mary Queen of Scots, Oliver Cromwell, King James I of England* and *Charles II*. Other works: *The Weaker Vessel: Women's Lot in Seventeenth Century England* and *Quiet as a Nun*. Married playwright Harold Pinter.

I decided as usual justice lay in the middle— that is to say nowhere.

OTHERS: 1655 English politician **John Hervey**, 1730 German philosopher **Johann Georg Hamann**, 1858 Italian mathematician **Giuseppe Peano**, 1865 U.S. Egyptologist **James Henry Breasted**, 1870 Mexican poet **Amado Nervo**, 1874 German chemist **Carl Bosch**, 1875 Women's rights activist **Katharine McCormick**, 1886 English violist **Rebecca Clarke**, 1899 British author **C.S. Forester**, 1906 U.S. serial killer **Ed Gein**, 1909 U.S. musician **Lester Young**, 1915 U.S. physicist **Norman F. Ramsey**, 1916 U.S. comic actress **Martha Raye**, 1929 U.S. author **Ira Levin**, 1957 German golfer **Bernard Langer**, 1979 Chinese diver **Tian Liang**

August 28

1592 **George Villiers, 1st Duke of Buckingham:** Charming English courier and statesman. Favorite of James I and the future Charles I. Appointed lord high admiral in 1619. His arrogance and abuse of power made him extremely unpopular. His erratic foreign policy led to a series of disasters, including failed military expeditions in Spain and France. When a bill to impeach him was introduced by the House of Commons in 1626, Charles dissolved Parliament. While planning a second attack on France, Buckingham was assassinated at Portsmouth by a discontented subaltern and the people of London rejoiced.

The world's a forest, in which all lose their way; though by a different path each goes astray.

1749 **Johann Wolfgang von Goethe:** German poet, playwright and novelist. Directed the city of Weimar's theater and did research in science. Inspired by William Shakespeare. Generally considered the founder of modern German literature. Leading romantic "Strum und Drang" ("Storm and Stress") dramatist. Best known for his masterpiece the poetic play *Faust* and his autobiographical *The Sorrows of Young Werther.* Visit to Italy inspired the classical dramas *Iphigenie in Tauris* and *Tasso.*

There is no crime of which I do not deem myself capable.

1774 **Elizabeth Ann Seton:** American educator and religious leader. Founded the Sisters of St. Joseph, the first American religious community, a teaching order instrumental in establishing American parochial schools. Born **Elizabeth Ann Bayley**, she was reared as an Episcopalian. At age 19 she was the belle of New York and married wealthy businessman William Magee Seton. They had five children before his business failed and he died of tuberculosis. At age 30, she was widowed, penniless, with five small children to raise. Drawn to Catholicism, she converted in 1805. She opened a school in Baltimore, which from the beginning followed the lines of a religious community. Canonized in 1975, the first U.S.–born saint.

Live simply, so that all may simply live.

1857 **Liam O'Flaherty:** Irish author whose novels are set in County Mayo, which include *The Neighbor's Wife, The Informer, The Puritan* and *Famine*. Best known for his short stories that deal unsentimentally with life or more often death, from an animal's point of view: "The Cow's Death," The Wounded Cormorant," and "The Seal." Described by writer Sean O'Faolain as "an inverted romantic."

It is impossible for a creative artist to be either a Puritan or a Fascist, because both are a negation

of the creative urge. The only thing the creative artist can be opposed to are ugliness and injustice.

1882 **Belle Benchley:** Born **Belle Jennings**. Director of Zoological Gardens of San Diego (1922–53). The "Zoo Lady," the only female zoo director in the world. Considered an innovator in working with and understanding animals. In the book *My Life in a Man-Made Jungle* (1940) she wrote about her experiences as "housekeeper, chief dietician and consulting physician as well as homemaker. First and thus far the only woman president of the American Zoological Association (1949–50).

Animals have their moods just as we do and do not always desire attention.

1896 **Arthur Calwell:** Australian politician. Lifetime member of the Australian Labor Party (ALP). During the years 1945–49, he oversaw the program for a massive influx of one million Europeans into Australia. In 1960 he became the leader of the ALP opposition.

It is better to be defeated on principle than to win on lies.

1899 **Charles Boyer:** Suave French actor with come-hither eyes and a rich accented voice. The "great lover" of the screen began his career as a leading man in French theater and films including *Mayerling* and *Liliom*. Romantic roles in American movies: *Private Worlds, Algiers, All This and Heaven Too* and *Gaslight*. Settled into fine character roles, often playing charming roués. Denied that he was a ladies-man. Devoted and faithful husband of English actress Pat Paterson for 44 years. Four days after her death, he committed suicide.

That love at first sight should happen to me was Life's most delicious revenge on a self opinionated fool.

1899 **Rufino Tamayo:** Mexican painter and graphic artist. Engrossed in tribal sculpture as curator at the National Museum of Anthropology. His distinctive style blended pre–Columbian Mexican folk art with Cubism and Surrealism. A 1950 exhibition at the Venice Biennale brought him international fame. Designed murals *Mexico Today* and *Birth of Nationality* for Mexico City's Palace of Fine Arts and murals in the UNESCO's Paris headquarters.

We are tragic people; we have always lived under pressure, and when you live like that, there is no reason to be happy.

1903 **Bruno Bettelheim:** Austrian-born American psychologist and educator. With the Nazi occupation of Austria, arrested and sent to the concentration camps Dachau and Buchenwald, which led to his long-term study of the psychological effects of totalitarianism, *Individual and Mass Behavior in Extreme Situations* (1943). Fled Europe for the U.S. in 1939 Became especially involved with emotionally disturbed children. Among his most influential books are *Love Is Not Enough, Truants from Life, and Children of the Dream*. In *The Uses of Enchantment*, he discusses the psycho-social importance of fairy tales.

Play teaches the habits most needed for intellectual growth.

1906 **John Betjeman:** English poet and architectural authority. Poet laureate (1972–84). His poems celebrate the English countryside, nostalgically evoking the Victorian era. Poetry collections: *Continual Dew, New Bats in Old Belfries* and *A Few Late Chrysanthemums*. Wrote a verse autobiography, *Summoned by Bells*. His collections of architectural essays include: *Ghostly Good Taste* and *A Pictorial History of English Architecture*.

Childhood is measured out by sounds and smells and sights, before the dark hour of reason grows.

1913 **(William) Robertson Davies:** One of Canada's most read and popular authors. Novelist, playwright, essayist and critic. Known as a novelist for his *Deptford Trilogy: Fifth Business, The Manticore* and *World of Wonders*, first person narratives that blend philosophy, humor, the occult and ordinary life. Other Works: *Cornish Trilogy: The Rebel Angels, What's Bred in the Bone* and *The Lyre of Orpheus*. His blend of fantasy, sardonic wit, and grotesque elements earned his style the designation "Ontario Gothic."

One of the most difficult tasks for the educated and sophisticated mind is to recognize that some clichés are also important truths.

1965 **Shania Twain:** Gorgeous raven-haired Canadian singer and songwriter, born **Eilleen Regina Edwards**. Set several records for record sales for female artists and for country artists. Her album *Come On Over* was the all-time biggest-selling album by a female artist. Only female artist to have three certified Diamond albums. Recipient of five Grammy Awards. Number One Country Hits: "Any Man of Mine," "No One Needs to Know," and "You're Still the One." "Shania" is an Ojibwa word meaning "I'm on my way."

I don't want my body to be a distraction from my talent or my brain.

OTHERS: 1853 Russian engineer **Vladimir Shukhov**, 1867 Italian composer **Umberto Giordano**, 1894 Austrian conductor **Karl Böhm**, 1899 U.S. cinematographer **James Wong Howe**, 1908 U.S. ornithologist **Roger Tory Peterson**, 1910 Dutch economist **Tjalling Koopsman**, 1913 U.S. cantor/tenor **Richard Tucker**, 1916 U.S. sociologist **C. Wright Mills**, 1917 U.S. comic book artist **Jack Kirby**, 1924 New Zealand author **Janet Frame**, 1925 U.S. actor/dancer **Donald O'Connor**, 1928 Canadian Prime Minister **Paul Martin**, 1943 Baseball manager **Lou Pinella**, 1952 U.S. writer **Rita Dove**, 1982 U.S. singer **LeAnn Rimes**

August 29

1619 **Jean Baptiste Colbert:** French economist, government official and businessman. Finance minister to Louis XIV (1665–85). Vigorous reformer put order back in the nation's finances. Boosted industry and commerce. Built French navy to one of the most formidable in Europe and initiated state manufactures. Reform movements couldn't keep step with the demands of King's war policies and extensive royal building program. At the end of Louis' reign, the French economy was once again in bad shape.

The art of taxation consists in so plucking the goose as to get the most feathers with the least hissing.

1632 **John Locke:** English philosopher. Leading proponent of liberalism. In his most famous treatise, *An Essay Concerning Human Understanding*, an inquiry into the nature of knowledge, he rejected the rationalist view that a thinker could only work out by reason alone the truth of the universe. Locke argued that knowledge of the world could only be gained through experience. Laid the foundations for British empiricism and pragmatism. Also wrote *Two Treatises on Civil Government*, which refutes absolutism and the divine right of kings. Greatly influenced the framers of the U.S. Constitution.

There is frequently more to be learned from the unexpected questions of a child than the discourses of men.

1809 **Oliver Wendell Holmes, Sr.:** American physician, professor, poet and essayist. Father of jurist Oliver Wendell Holmes, Jr. First dean of the Harvard Medical School. Author of "Old Ironsides" and "The Deacon's Masterpiece." Contributed "The Autocrat of the Breakfast Table" to the *Atlantic Monthly*. Famed for his wit and originality, Holmes was in great demand as a guest and speaker.

Stupidity often saves a man from going mad.

1862 Count **Maurice Maeterlinck:** Belgian poet, playwright and essayist. Disciple of the Symbolist movement. In 1889 he produced his first volume of poetry, *Les Serres chaudes* and his prose play, *La Princesse Maleine*. Three years later he completed his play Pelléas et Mélisandre, upon which Claude Debussy based his opera of the same name. Also wrote several popular expansions of scientific subjects, including *La Vie des abeilles* and a number of philosophical works. Nobel Prize for Literature in 1911.

How strangely do we diminish a thing as soon as we try to express it in words.

1876 **Charles Franklin Kettering:** U.S. engineer, inventor and manufacturer in the automobile industry. Designed the motor for the first electric starter for gasoline motors. Prior to his venture into the automobile industry, he developed the first electric cash register and co-founded the Dayton Engineering Laboratories (DELCO). Made advances in aircraft design, fuels, and diesel engines. Interest in science, led to the building of the Sloan-Kettering Institute for Cancer Research and the C.F. Kettering Foundation.

Problems are the price of progress. Don't bring me anything but trouble. Good news weakens me.

1898 **Preston Sturges:** Originally **Edmund Preston Biden**. American film director and scriptwriter. Cosmetics inventor of a kissproof lipstick before beginning a career of writing and directing freewheeling comedies. Films blended wit, slapstick and social consciousness. Parodied politics, advertising, sex and hero worship. Hits: *The Lady Eve*, *Sullivan's Travels*, *The Palm Beach Story*, *The Miracle of Morgan's Creek*, and *Hail the Conquering Hero*. Script for *The Great McGinty* won an Academy Award.

A pretty girl is better than a plain one. A leg is better than an arm. A bedroom is better than a living room. An arrival is better than a departure. A birth is better than a death. A chase is better than a chat. A dog is better than a landscape. A kitten is better than a dog. A baby is better than a kitten. A kiss is better than a baby. A pratfall is better than anything.

1915 **Ingrid Bergman:** Swedish-born actress of incredible beauty and remarkable radiance and vitality. Winner of Oscars for *Gaslight*, *Anastasia* and *Murder on the Orient Express*. Superb in *Casablanca*, *The Bells of St. Mary's* and *Notorious*. Among the most popular actresses in the world until she deserted her husband to have an affair with director Roberto Rossellini, whom she married shortly after delivering twin girls. All was forgiven after *Anastasia*, and she returned to Hollywood in triumph.

A kiss is a lovely trick designed by nature to stop speech when words become superfluous.

1920 **Charlie "Bird" Parker:** Self-taught American jazz saxophonist. Worked out the rhythmic and harmonic ideas that would form the basis of the bebop style. Formed an important musical association with trumpeter Dizzy Gillespie and joined Billy Eckstine's orchestra. Leading spirit of modern jazz, pioneering new "cool" movement. Alcohol and heroin took his life at age 35. Compositions such as "Now's the Time" and "Ornithology" are standard jazz pieces.

I kept thinking there's bound to be something else. I could hear it sometimes, but I couldn't play it.

1922 Mr. **Blackwell (Richard Blackwell):** Born **Richard Selzer**. American fashion designer and critic. Best known for his annual "ten-worst-dressed women of the year" awards, given since 1960. Accompanying comments are very catty: Britney Spears—"An over-the-hill Lolita"; Paris Hilton—"Vapid Venus of Beverly Hills"; Martha Stewart—"Dresses like the centerfold for the *Farmer's Almanac*"; Camilla Parker-Bowles—"A dilapidated Yorkshire pudding"; Cher—"A million beads and one overexposed derriere"; Princess Anne—Lumpy, dumpy and frumpy" and finally:

Elizabeth Taylor looks like two small boys fighting under a mink blanket.

1936 **John McCain:** American Republican politician and Senator from Arizona. On October 26, 1967 shot down over Vietnam and held as a prisoner of war for five-and-a-half years, mostly in the infamous Hanoi Hilton. Released in 1973, he returned to active duty. Won a seat in the U.S. House of Representatives (1981) and in 1986 was elected to succeed retiring Senator Barry Goldwater. Despite criticism for his behavior on the Senate Select POW/MIA Committee and his involvement in the Keating Scandal, ran for the presidential nomination in the 2000 elections and is likely to do so again in 2008.

War is wretched beyond description, and only a fool or a fraud could sentimentalize its cruel reality.

1940 **James "Jim" Brady:** Assistant to the President and White House Press Secretary under Ronald Reagan. Shot when John Hinckley, Jr. attempted to assassinate Reagan on March 30, 1981. Almost died and is permanently disabled. Ever since he and his wife Sarah have been ardent supporters of gun control. They found the Center to Prevent Gun Violence. The Brady Handgun Violence Prevention Act is named for him.

The Senate passed a pretty good bill and we don't want to see it put into the dumpster.

1958 **Michael Jackson:** Unusually successful entertainer. Known admiringly as the "King of Rap" and disparagingly as "Wacko Jacko." Made over $70 million with his *Thriller* album. Numerous single hits include: "Ben," "Beat It," "Bad" and "The Way You Make Me Feel." Built an amusement park and private zoo on his Neverland Ranch, where economically disadvantaged and terminally ill children and their parents are entertained. Widely criticized for his frequent sleepover parties in which he has shared his bed with young boys. Has trice been accused of sexual abuse. Tried and acquitted of the latter allegations in 2005.

Lies run sprints, but the truth runs marathons. The truth will win this marathon in court.

OTHERS: 1628 English statesman **John Granville**, 1756 Polish mathematician **Jan Śniadecki**, 1777 Russian Sinologist **Nikita Y. Bichurin**, 1780 French painter **Jean Ingres**, 1805 English theologian **Frederick Maurice**, 1810 Founding father of Argentine Republic **Juan Bautista Alberdi**, 1844 English Socialist poet **Edward Carpenter**, 1917 U.S. actress **Isabel Sanford**, 1923 British actor/director **Richard Attenborough**, 1924 U.S. singer **Dinah Washington**, 1935 U.S. film director **William Friedkin**, 1938 U.S. Secretary of the Treasury **Robert Rubin**, 1946 U.S. high jumper **Bob Beamon**, 1985 Serbian warlord **Dušan Jocić**

August 30

1748 **Jacques-Louis David:** French Neoclassical painter. Elected a member of the Committee for Public Safety and voted for the execution of Louis XVI. Artistic director of great national fétes founded on classical customs. Works: *Belisarius*, *Oath of the Horatti*, *Death of Socrates*, and *Brutus Condemning His Son*, and his masterpiece *The Rape of the Sabines*. Twice imprisoned after the death of Robespierre and narrowly escaped with his life. Appointed court painter by Napoleon, but after the Bourbon Restoration, banished as a regicide and died in Brussels.

To give a body and a perfect form to one's thoughts, this — and only this — is to be an artist.

1797 **Mary Wollstonecraft Shelley:** English novelist, daughter of William Godwin and Mary Wollstonecraft. Second wife of poet Percy Bysshe Shelley. They lived abroad throughout their married life. Best known for her first and most impressive Gothic novel *Frankenstein, or the Modern Prometheus*.

No man chooses evil because it is evil; he only mistakes it for happiness, the good he seeks.

1871 **Ernest Rutherford:** New Zealand-born British experimental physicist. While still in New Zealand he invented a sensitive radio-wave detector just six years after Heinrich Hertz first discovered radio waves. Laid the groundwork for the development of nuclear physics by investigating radioactivity. Discovered and named alpha, beta and gamma radiation and "half-life" phenomenon of radioactivity. First to achieve a man-made nuclear reaction. Nobel Prize in chemistry (1908).

We haven't got the money, so we've got to think.

1893 **Huey P. Long:** "The Kingfish." Demagogic political boss of Louisiana in the 1930s. Earned the wrath of the wealthy and the support of the poor as an exponent of a "share-the-wealth" social services and public works programs. Notorious for his corruption and demagoguery. Governor (1928–32); U.S. Senator (1932–35). Squandered public funds on extravagant personal projects, including the construction of a marble and bronze state house in Baton Rouge. Assassinated by the son of a man he had vilified in 1935.

The time has come for all good men to rise above principle.

1901 **John Gunther:** American foreign correspondent and author. Traveled wherever the news was being made in the world. Books: *Inside Europe*, *Inside Asia*, *Latin America*, *U.S.A.*, *Inside Africa* and *Russia Today*. Did more than any other reporter to make America cognizant of other countries' attitudes and accomplishments. *Death Be Not Proud* is a memoir off his son's death at age 17 of cancer.

There are no generalizations in American politics that vested selfishness cannot cut through.

1901 **Roy Wilkins:** African-American journalist and civil rights leader. In 1931 he was the executive assistant secretary of the. Editor of the National Association for the Advancement of Colored People (NAACP)'s newspaper, *Crisis* (1934–49) Executive director of the NAACP (1955–77). Articulate spokesman for the moderate wing of the civil rights movement. Sought equal rights through changes in laws. Helped organize the 1963 March on Washington.

The players in this drama of frustration and indignity are not commas or semicolons in a legislative thesis; they are people, human beings, citizens of the United States.

1907 **Shirley Booth:** American stage, screen and television actress. Mellow-faced, plumpish with a childlike air of simplicity. Broadway hits: *Three Men on a Horse*, *The Philadelphia Story*, *My Sister Eileen*, and *Goodbye My Fancy*. Academy Award for recreating her Tony Award winning Broadway role of frowzy Lola Delaney in *Come Back Little Sheba*. Widely popular for her television series, "Hazel," as a wisecracking maid.

Actors should be overheard, not listened to, and the audience is 50 percent of the performance.

1918 **Ted Williams:** "The Splendid Splinter." American outfielder with the Boston Red Sox. Powerfully built, attractive, publicity-shy and feared by the opposition, a seeker of personal athletic perfection, but also a brooding victim of complex hostilities. One of the greatest hitters of all time, the Hall of Famer is the last man to hit .400 in a season (.406 in 1941).Had a lifetime batting average of .344 and hit 521 career home runs. His baseball career was interrupted twice by his service with the Marines, first during World War II and then in the Korean conflict.

Why do they cheer me for hitting a homer and then boo me for grounding out the next time up? I'm still the same guy, ain't I...? They can go to hell.

1927 **Geoffrey Beene:** American fashion designer. Studied fashion in New York City and Paris. Noteworthy for unconventional designs, Started his New York Company in 1962, featuring high-quality, read-to-wear clothing for women and me. His subtly colored and distinctively simple designs brought him eight Coty Awards.

Before I ever think of a design I have to select the fabrics, so fabrics are the inspiration for any collection.

1930 **Warren Buffett:** American entrepreneur. Learned to invest in companies selling stock below their intrinsic value. Turned an initial investment of $105,000 into his Buffett Partnership (1956–69), which was worth $105 million by the time of its dissolution. Said to be the first person to make $1 billion in the stock market. His financial reports are read eagerly by stock-market novices and experts alike.

It takes 20 years to build a reputation and five minutes to ruin it. If you think about that, you'll do things differently.

1943 **R. [Robert] Crumb:** American cartoonist, with no formal art training, but obsessed with drawing from childhood. Moved to San Francisco in 1967, becoming a prominent member of the hippie counterculture. Founder of underground "commix" satirical magazines, which poked fun at American culture. Featured characters included Fritz the Cat, the Furry Freak Brothers and Mr. Natural, considered classics of the genre.

Killing yourself is a major commitment; it takes a kind of courage. Most people just lead lives of cowardly desperation. It's kinda half suicide hen you just dull yourself with substances.

1943 **Jean-Claude Killy:** French skier. European champion in 1965, and the following year won the world-combined championship, consisting of downhill, shalom, and giant shalom. In 1967 won the first World Cup for men and repeated the fete in the following year. At the Winter Olympics that year, he second skier in history to sweep the alpine events.

To win you have to risk loss.

OTHERS: 1377 Ruler of Persia **Shah Rukh**, 1705 English philosopher **David Hartley**, 1720 English brewer/politician **Samuel Whitbread**, 1884 Swedish chemist **Theodor Svedberg**, 1896 Canadian actor **Raymond Massey**, 1906 U.S. actress **Joan Blondell**, 1908 U.S. actor **Fred MacMurray**, 1912 U.S. physicist **Edward Mills Purcell**, 1913 British economist **Richard Stone**, 1922 U.S. mezzo-soprano **Regina Resnik**, 1930 U.S. basketball coach **Jerry Tarkanian**, 1935 U.S. singer **John Phillips**, 1954 President of Belarus **Alexander Lukashenko**, 1972 U.S. actress **Cameron Diaz**, 1982 U.S. tennis player **Andy Roddick**

August 31

12 CE **Caligula:** Born **Gaius Julius Caesar** son of Germanicus. Roman emperor (0037–0041), notorious as a cruel tyrant, believed to be mentally unstable. Remembered for naming his horse Incitatius to a consulship. Gained the nickname *Caligula*, Latin for "little boots," as an infant because of the military boots he wore. His brief reign as emperor began when he succeeded Tiberius and ended with his assassination. His final words as he was being stabbed to death by his own Praetorian guards: "I am still alive!" Expressed his desire to cut off the heads of the citizens of Rome:

Would that the Roman people had a single neck.

1811 **Théophile Gautier:** French poet, novelist and critic. Extreme romanticist. Stressed perfection of form. Forerunner of the Parnassian school. Poetry: "La Comédie de la mort," "Émaux et camées" and "Albertus." Celebrated Novel: *Mademoiselle de Maupin*. Theatrical criticisms were contained in *L'Historie de l'art dramatique en France*.

Chance is a pseudonym of God when he did not want to sign.

1821 **Hermann von Helmholtz:** German scientist. Perhaps the most versatile scientist of his century. Did first class work in physics and physiology, both theoretical and experimental. Probably the last scholar whose work ranged over the sciences, mathematics, philosophy, and the arts. Discoverer of the law of conservation of energy, he achieved major results in theories of electricity and magnetism, and on the physiology of vision and hearing.

Whoever, in the pursuit of science, seeks after immediate practical utility may rest assured that he seeks in vain.

1870 **Maria Montessori:** Italian educator. Her success with mentally retarded children led her in 1907 to apply similar methods to younger children of normal intelligence. Originated *The Montessori Method* (1909) that advocates an informal child-centered approach, allowing the children to set their own pace. Stresses development of initiative, and sense and muscle training as well as free but guided instructive play of the child, using a variety of sensory materials. Ideas became an integral part of modern nursery and infant-child education.

The greatest sign of success for a teacher ... is to be able to say, "The children are now working as if I did not exist."

1874 **Edward Lee Thorndike:** American psychologist. Formulated theories of educational psychology and in the psychology of animal behavior, which led to the theory of connectionism. Remembered for his research with cats escaping from puzzle boxes. Intended to discover whether or not cats escaping from the puzzle boxes used insight. Concluded that cats did consistently show gradual learning. Works: *The Principles of Teaching*, *Psychology of Learning* and *The Measurement of Intelligence*.

Never will you get a better psychological subject than a hungry cat.

1879 **Alma Schindler Mahler Gropius Werfel:** Austrian composer, author and companion of geniuses. Married Gustav Mahler. He told her: "The role of composer falls to me, yours is that of loving companion!" Although he had five of her *Lieder* printed, she realized that spending 10 years as a loving companion wasted her musical development. After Mahler's death, she had a passionate affair with painter Oskar Kokoschka, who depicted her as *The Tempest*. She left him in 1915 to marry architect Walter Gropius. Later she wed young poet Franz Werfel, whom she inspired and organized his life and his fame.

God granted me the privilege of knowing the brilliant works of our times before they left the hands of their creators. And if I was allowed to assist these knights for a while, then my existence is justified and blessed.

1884 **George Sarton:** Belgian-born American historian of science. Dominant authority on the subject, founding its principal journals *Isis* (1912) and *Osiris* (1936). Wrote the monumental 13 volume *Introduction to the History of Science* (1927–48), which reached to the 14th century. More volumes were completed by others after his death Defined science as "systematized positive knowledge, or what has been taken as such at different ages and in different places.

There are but few saints among scientists, as among other men, but truth itself is a goal comparable with sanctity.

1885 **(Erwin) Dubose Heyward:** American novelist, poet and dramatist. Drew on the life of South Carolina African-Americans for much of his writing. Charleston, South Carolina's Catfish Road is the setting for his best known and first novel *Porgy*. He and his wife dramatized it, which became the basis for George Gershwin's opera *Porgy and Bess*. Other novels include *Mambas' Daughter*, set in Charleston's black community, which was also successfully dramatized.

Compassionate the mountains rise/ Dim with the wistful dimness of old eyes/ That, having looked on life out of mind,/ Know that the simple gift of being kind/Is greater than all the wisdom of the wise.

1908 **William Saroyan:** American author, short story writer and playwright. His first book, *The Daring Young Man on the Flying Trapeze* (1934), is a collection of brash, original and irreverent short stories, celebrating the joy of living despite of poverty, hunger and insecurity due to the Great Depression. His play, *The Time of Your Life* (1939) won the New York Drama Critics Circle Award and a Pulitzer Prize, which he rejected. With his cousin Ross Bagasarian he wrote the song "Come On-a My House," with which Rosemary Clooney had a smash hit.

The role of art is to make a world which can be inhabited.

1935 **Eldridge Cleaver:** African-American political activist and author. Convicted and imprisoned for an assault with intent to kill. While in prison he wrote *Soul on Ice*, influential in the black power movement. Later wrote *Soul on Fire*. After release from prison became a prominent member of the Black Panther Party, serving as Minister of Information. In 1968, charged with attempted murder, he jumped bail, and fled to Algeria. Returned to the U.S. (1975) and denounced the Black Panthers, becoming a conservative Republican.

Respect commands itself and it can neither be given nor withheld when it is due.

1936 **Marva Collins:** American teacher and educational reformer. Started Chicago's one-room school, Westside Preparatory (1975) in an impoverished neighborhood. Noted for successfully applying a modified Socratic teaching method with children, many of whom have been labeled learning-disabled by public schools. Material is selected with abstract content meant to challenge students. Students are taught to test their reasoning. Among her many awards is a National Humanities Medal in 2004.

Trust yourself, Think for yourself. Act for yourself, Speak for yourself. Imitation is suicide.

1945 **Itzhak Perlman:** Israeli violinist and teacher. One of the greatest violinists of the late 20th century. Contracted polio at age four. Learned to walk with the aid of crutches and generally is seated when playing. Tours extensively and made a large number of records. He has been a soloist for a number of film scores, including *Schindler's List* and *Memoirs of a Geisha*. Received a Kennedy Center Honor in 2003.

Child prodigy is a curse because you've got all those terrible possibilities.

OTHERS: 161 CE Roman Emperor **Commodus**, 1569 Mughal Emperor of India **Jahangir**, 1834 Italian composer **Amilcare Ponchielli**, 1880 Queen of the Netherlands **Wilhelmina I**, 1897 U.S. actor **Frederic March**, 1903 U.S. entertainer **Arthur Godfrey**, 1905 Film producer/writer **Dore Schary**, 1907 President of the Philippines **Ramon Magsaysay**, 1913 British radio astronomer **Bernard Lovell**, 1918 U.S. composer **Alan Jay Lerner**, 1924 U.S. comedian **Buddy Hackett**, 1935 U.S. baseball player/manager **Frank Robinson**, 1945 Irish musician **Van Morrison**, 1949 U.S. actor **Richard Gere**, 1958 U.S. track star **Edwin Moses**

September 1

1789 Lady **Marguerite Blessington:** Irish-born English socialite and writer. Known for her great beauty.

Headed an intellectual salon at her Kensington mansion, Gore House, where she wrote many sketches of London life. Formed a relationship with Comte d'Orsay. Best known work was a memoir *Conversations with Lord Byron*. Lived extravagantly and hopelessly in debt she fled to Paris with d'Orsay in 1849, where she died two months later.

Mountains appear more lofty the nearer they are approached, but great men resemble then not in this particular.

1868 **Frank McKinney "Kin" Hubbard:** U.S. humorist and caricaturist. Made sketches of several Hoosier characters and printed them in the *Indianapolis News* with succinct captions, such as "Ther's some folks standin' behind the President that ought to git around where he kin watch them." Proved so popular, he was encouraged to continue the series, and thus his "home-cured philosopher," Abe Martin, a farmer from Brown County, Indiana, was born and featured in 26 books.

The only time some fellows are seen with their wives is after they're indicted.

1875 **Edgar Rice Burroughs:** American novelist. Best known as the creator of Tarzan, the Ape Man, whom he featured in 23 books. *Tarzan of the Apes* was published in 1912, and immediately became a cultural sensation. Burroughs also wrote popular science fiction/fantasy stories featuring earthly adventurers transported to various planets.

If people were paid for writing rot such as I read in some of those [pulp fiction] magazines... I could write stories just as rotten.

1907 **Walter Reuther:** American labor leader. As a sixteen-year-old tool-and-die maker In Wheeling, Vest Virginia, discharged for organizing a worker's protest against Sunday and holiday work. Founded and served as director of the U.S Auto Workers (1935–70). President of the CIO (1952–55). Architect of merger of the AFL with the CIO (1955). Ardent anticommunist.

If it walks like a duck, and quacks like a duck, then it just may be a duck.

1923 **Rocky Marciano:** American heavyweight boxer. By mid–1951 he had won all 38 of his professional fights, all but five by knockout. Only fighter ever to knockout Joe Louis. Eliminated three other contenders for the title before taking the championship belt with a 13th round knockout of Jersey Joe Walcott in 1952. He successfully defended his title six times before retiring undefeated in 1956. Died in a plane crash ten years later.

Why waltz with a guy for 10 rounds if you can knock him out in one?

1933 **Ann W. Richards:** Born **Dorothy Ann Willis**. American teacher and Democratic politician. In 1982 became the first woman elected to statewide office in Texas in fifty years. As state treasurer she was credited with greatly modernizing the treasury's operations. Delivered the keynote address at the 1988 Democratic National Convention. Elected governor of Texas in 1991. Noted for many appointments of women and minorities to important positions. Lost her reelection bid to George W. Bush in 1995.

I have always had the feeling I could do anything and my Dad told me I could. I was in college before I found out he might be wrong.

1933 **Conway Twitty:** Born **Harold Jenkins**. American country music singer. Changed his name in 1957 and scored his first hit with the ballad "It's Only Make Believe." During the next eight years he had three gold records. Hits: "Hello Darlin,'" and with Loretta Lynn "After the Fire Is Gone," "Lead Me On," "Louisiana Woman, Mississippi Man" and "As Soon As I Hang Up the Phone."

A good country song takes a page out of somebody's life and puts it to music.

1935 **Seiji Ozawa:** Japanese-born conductor. Studied to be a pianist, but after breaking two fingers playing rugby, changed to composition and conducting. Conducted the Nippon Hosso Kyokai Symphony Orchestra in 1954 and shortly thereafter he conducted the Japan Philharmonic Orchestra. Music director of the Boston Symphony Orchestra from 1973 to 2002, when he took residency as the Music Director of the Vienna State Opera.

To make music, all the members of the orchestra must have the same idea about the music. Only the conductor can decide that one idea and I think that is his most important job.

1938 **Alan Dershowitz:** American lawyer and jurist. Worked on a number of high-profile legal cases. Represented defendants including Claus von Bulow, whose conviction for trying to kill his wife, Dershowitz got overturned. Other clients: Patricia Hearst, Leona Helmsley, Jim Bakker, Mike Tyson, O.J. Simpson and Harry Reems. Books: *Reversal of Fortune*, *The Case for Peace: Why Terrorism Works* and *Supreme Injustice: How the High Court Hijacked Election 2000.*

All sides in a trial want to hide at least some of the truth. The defendant wants to hide the truth because he's generally guilty. The defense attorney's job is to make sure the jury does not arrive at that truth. The prosecution wants to make sure the process by which the evidence was obtained is not truthfully presented, because as often as not, that process will raise questions.

1939 **Lily Tomlin:** American comedian and actress. Got her break with television's "Laugh-In," creating characters such as Edith Ann, the devilish little girl in the big rocking chair and Ernestine, the sarcastic nasal telephone operator. Films: *9 to 5* and *Nashville*, for which she was Oscar nominated. Grammy Award for the comedy album "This Is a Recording." Tony Award for her one-woman show "The Search for Signs of Intelligent Life in the Universe."

Man invented language to satisfy his deep need to complain.

1944 **Leonard Slatkin:** Internationally recognized American conductor. Music Director of the National

Symphony Orchestra and Principal Guest Conductor of the Los Angeles Philharmonic at the Hollywood Bowl. Five Grammy awards and fifty other nominations. Son of noted conductor-violinist Felix Slatkin and cellist Eleanor, founding members of the famed Hollywood String Quartet. Married to soprano Linda Hohenfeld.

I use my hand like a sculptor, to mold and shape the sound I want to clarify.

1950 **Phil McGraw: Dr. Phil**, American TV talk show host and clinical psychologist. The format of his syndicated daily show, *Dr. Phil*, is offering advice to guests on a different topic for each telecast. Author of self-help behavioral books on topics such as weight loss and relationships. Despite criticism of exploiting his guests with "pop psychology" and simplistic advice, has a considerable cult following.

Anger is nothing more than an outward expression of hurt, fear and frustration.

OTHERS: 1453 Spanish general **Gonzalo Fernández Córdoba**, 1653 German composer **Johann Pachelbel**, 1711 English composer **William Boyce**, 1726 French chess player **François-André Danican Philidor**, 1791 U.S. religious writer **Lydia Sigourney**, 1795 U.S. journalist **James Gordon Bennett**, 1848 Swiss entomologist **Auguste-Henri Forel**, 1849 U.S. educator **Elizabeth Harrison**, 1854 German composer of opera *Hansel and Gretel* **Engelbert Humperdinck**, 1905 Puerto Rican dancer **Elvera Sanchez**, 1920 U.S. writer **Liz Carpenter**, 1922 Canadian actress **Yvonne De Carlo**, 1937 U.S. golfer **Al Geiberger**, 1946 English singer **Barry Gibb**, 1957 Cuban singer **Gloria Estefan**, 1968 9/11 terrorist leader **Mohammed Atta**

September 2

1838 **Lydia Kamekaeha Liliuokalani:** Last sovereign to rule Hawaii before annexation of the islands by the U.S. Tried to restore traditional monarchy. Opposed the reciprocity treaty giving commercial concessions to the U.S. In 1893, declared deposed by Sanford B. Dole and the Missionary Party. An uprising in her name was suppressed and the rebels arrested. To win pardons for her supporters she abdicated. A talented musician, she composed the song, "Aloha Oe."

Farewell to thee, farewell to thee,/ Thou charming one who dwells among the bowers,/ One fond embrace before I now depart/ Until we meet again.

1839 **Henry George:** American economist, land reformer and writer. While visiting New York City he saw the paradox of progress and poverty developing hand-in-hand. Seeking an explanation of the anomalies of capitalistic economics, he published *Progress and Poverty* (1879), which analyzed wealth in terms of land and its value; asserting that to work the land is a natural right and the rent demanded by landlords is a violation of economic law and an obstacle to general prosperity. Other works: *Social Problems* and *The Science of Political Economy.*

What has destroyed every previous civilization has been the tendency to the unequal distribution of wealth and power.

1850 **Eugene Field:** American poet and journalist. Wrote column "Sharps and Flats," for the *Chicago Daily News.* Pioneer in writing the featured personal column, filled with a variety of bits and pieces, ranging from satirical attacks on pretensions of Chicago's nouveaux rich to free translations of the classics. Known as "the poet of childhood" for his poems "Little Boy Blue" and "Wynken, Blynken and Nod."

All human joys are swift of wing,/ For heaven doth so allot it:/ That when you get an easy thing,/ You find you haven't got it.

1852 **Paul Bourget:** French conservative writer of novels, short-stories, plays, poetry, criticism and travel books. Occupies an important place in the development of the psychological novel. Works: *Cruelle enigme, Le Disciple, Cosmopolis* and *L'E'tape.* Critical works include *Nouveaux Essais de psychologie contemporaine.* His later novels were increasingly moralistic and didactic.

Flirting is the sin of the virtuous and the virtue of the sinful.

1866 **Hiram Johnson:** American lawyer and political leader. Opposed the political machine in Sacramento over which his attorney father presided. Elected Governor of California in 1910 on a reform platform and reelected in 1914. His administration was the most progressive in the nation. Ended the domination of the government by the Southern Pacific Railroad. Elected to the U.S. Senate (1917) and served five terms. Implacable isolationist opposed U.S. entry in World War I, The League of Nations and the World Court.

The first casualty of war is truth.

1901 **Adolph Rupp:** Legendary U.S. basketball coach with the University of Kentucky. Held the record for career victories (879). Led his teams to four National championships. Coach of the Year three times. When someone once told him, "Winning isn't everything!" He replied, "Then why do we keep score?" Has been accused of being a racist for not having African Americans on his teams.

I wouldn't give an iota to make a trip from the cradle to the grave unless I could live in a competitive world.

1904 **Elizabeth Borton de Trevino:** American children's author and journalist. Newberry Medal winner for *I, Juan de Pareja* (1966). Living in Boston as a journalist, she was given an assignment in Monterrey, Mexico, where she met and married Luis Trevino. Described their courtship and marriage in *My Heart Lies South: The Story of My Mexican Marriage.* Other books: *El Guero* and *Leona: A Love Story.*

Art should be Truth, and Truth unadorned, unsentimentalized, is Beauty.

1917 **Cleveland Amory:** American author. A society "Boswell" and stern social historian. After the publication of his first book, *The Proper Bostonians*, some described him as "Boston's Benedict Arnold." Described his time as the President of the *Harvard Crimson* as "meaning so much that, while life afterward might go on, nothing else really mattered." Source for insights of yesterday's "Old Guard" and today's society, which he called "Publiciety." Other books: *The Last Resorts* and *Who Killed Society?*

The New England conscience does not stop you from doing what you shouldn't — it just stops you from enjoying it.

1931 **Alan K. Simpson:** American lawyer and politician. U.S. Republican Senator from Wyoming (1979–97). Republican whip (1985–95). Chairman of Committee on Veteran's Affairs. Although his father, a former governor of Wyoming, was one of only six U.S. senators to vote against the Civil Rights Act of 1964, Simpson has been an outspoken advocate for abortion rights, gay and lesbian rights, and equality for all persons regardless of race, color, creed, gender or sexual preference.

If you have integrity, nothing else matters. If you don't have integrity, nothing else matters.

1948 **Christa McAuliffe:** American astronaut. A New Hampshire high school Social Studies teacher. President Reagan made the decision that the first ordinary American to travel on board a space shuttle would be "one of America's finest, a teacher." Chosen from 11,500 applicants, she called her impending trip into space to be the Ultimate Field Trip. Just 73 seconds after lift-off on January 28, 1986, the space shuttle *Challenger* exploded, killing Christa and the other six crew members.

I touch the future, I teach. I really appreciate that sentiment. That's going with me.

1952 **Jimmy Connors:** American tennis player. Won eight Grand Slam singles titles and two Grand Slam doubles titles. Brash and extremely competitive, he was not averse to doing anything that might give him an edge in his matches. Played to the crowd, and verbally abused opponents and officials. The "Brash Basher from Belleville" (his home town) had a high-profile romance with teen tennis prodigy Chris Evert. Considered one of the top male tennis players of all time.

People don't seem to understand that it's a damn war out there.

1966 **Salma Hayek:** Mexican actress born in Coatzacoalcos, Veracruz. Her first big break was landing the title role in the hugely successful soap opera "Teresa." Arriving in Hollywood at age 24, she found that Latin actresses were usually typecast as the mistress's maid or a local prostitute. After a number of bit parts, she teamed with Antonio Banderas in the now cult classic, *Desperado*. Exhibited her exceptional talent and established as a serious actress when she co-produced *Frida* (2002), the story of legendary Mexican painter Frida Kahlo. The film was nominated for six Oscars, including best actress for Hayek.

I've stolen a couple of hearts and they are in my private collection. My heart has been stolen too — but I've gone and got it back every single time!

OTHERS: 1243 English politician **Gilbert de Clare**, 1548 Italian architect **Vincenzo Scamozzi**, 1661 German organist **Georg Böhm**, 1726 English prison reformer **John Howard**, 1804 Argentine writer **Esteban Echeverria**, 1841 Japanese reformer **Ito Hirobumi**, 1850 U.S. baseball manufacturer **Albert Spalding**, 1853 German physicist **Wilhelm Ostwald**, 1884 U.S. missionary **Frank C. Laubach**, 1918 U.S. author **Allen Drury**, 1918 Watergate figure **Martha Mitchell**, 1923 French mathematician **René Thom**, 1936 U.S. computer chip manufacturer **Andrew Grove**, 1937 U.S. Baseball commissioner **Peter Ueberroth**, 1948 U.S. football player **Terry Bradshaw**, 1965 U.S. boxer **Lennox Lewis**

September 3

1499 **Diane de Poitiers:** French Duchess of Valentinois. Mistress of Henri, dauphin of France. She inspired him with a profound passion. When he became King Henri II, she was for all purposes his queen, while his lawful wife, Catherine de Medici, lived in comparative obscurity. Diane was a patron of the arts. When Henri died, Catherine forced her to restore the crown jewels and leave the court.

The years that a woman subtracts from her age are not lost. They are added to other women's.

1811 **John Humphrey Noyes:** American social reformer Believed the millennium occurred in 70 CE based on Christ's expectation that the event would occur within one generation of His death. Founded a communistic community in Putney, Vermont, devoted to perfection. Christ's teaching that in heaven there would be no marriage convinced him that on earth all men are married to all women, as members of a "complex marriage." The group's radical sexual practices forced them to flee to New York where he established the Oneida Community. Oneidans turned to the production of silverware as their main source of income.

There is no more reason why sexual intercourse should be restrained by law, than why eating and drinking should be — and there is little occasion for shame in the one case as in the other.

1849 **Sarah Orne Jewett:** U.S. writer and hostess. Her sketches of a New England town, "Deephaven" were published in the *Atlantic Monthly* in 1877. Other Works: *A Country Doctor*, *A Marsh Land*, *Country Byways*, *The King of Folly Island and Other People* and *Tales of New England*. Her writing resembled nineteenth century fiction, especially that of Gustave Flaubert, whom she greatly admired.

God would not give us the same talent if what were right for men were wrong for women.

1856 **Louis H. Sullivan:** U.S. architect. Founder of "Chicago School" of architecture, diametrically opposed to useless tradition and devoted to modernism. Noted for his architectural maxim: "Form ever follows function," the basis for all modern design. Gained international fame with the Chicago Auditorium Theater building. Others: St. Louis' Wainwright Building, the first skyscraper, and the Carson, Pirie, Scott department store in Chicago. Among his apprentices was Frank Lloyd Wright.

Our architecture reflects truly as a mirror.

1914 **Dixie Lee Ray:** American politician, teacher, supporter of the environment and marine biologist. Director of the Pacific Science Center in Seattle, Washington. Chairperson of Atomic Energy Commission, where she created the Department of Safety in order to make the use of nuclear energy safer. U.S. assistant Secretary of State for oceans and international environment and science affairs. Governor of Washington (1977–80).

The general public has long been divided into two parts: those who think science can do anything, and those who are afraid it will.

1923 **Mort Walker:** American cartoonist, best known for creating the newspaper comic strip *Beetle Bailey* in 1950 and *Hi and Lois* in 1954. After more than 50 years in the business, he still supervises the daily work at his studio. In 1974 he founded the Museum of Cartoon Art and in 1989 was inducted into the Museum of Cartoon Art Hall of Fame.

Seven days without laughter makes one weak.

1926 **Alison Lurie:** American novelist and editor of children's literature. Pulitzer Prize for her 1984 novel *Foreign Affairs*, about American academics in England. Other novels: *Love and Friendship*, *The Nowhere City*, *Imaginary Friends*, *The Truth About Lorin Jones*, and *Truth or Consequences*. Co-editor of the Garland Library of Children Classics (73 volumes).

We can lie in the language of dress or try to tell the truth; but unless we are naked and bald, it is impossible to be silent.

1927 **Hugh Sidey:** U.S. correspondent and author. Former Washington Bureau Chief. Covered the White House for decades. Wrote the column "The Presidency," for *Time* magazine. Covered the nation's chief executives from Dwight D. Eisenhower through Bill Clinton, traveled with them, saw them in times of triumph and moments of disappointment. Wrote *John F. Kennedy, President* and *Lyndon Johnson in the White House*.

Bureaucrats are the only people in the world who can say absolutely nothing and mean it.

1931 **Dick Motta:** U.S. basketball coach with several pro teams. Infamous for his quick temper and eccentricities. Effective strategist who knew how to bring out the best of his players. His 1978 Washington Bullets won the NBA championship. Ranks third in career victories (856) behind Lenny Wilkins and Red Auerbach. Originated the phrase: "It (the opera) ain't over till the fat lady sings."

War is the only game where it doesn't pay to have the home-court advantage.

1938 **Caryl Churchill:** English dramatist. Most of her plays, predominately radical and feminist in tone, performed at the Royal Court Theatre. Her greatest commercial success is *Serious Money*, a satire of the world of financial brokers. Also wrote: *Cloud Nine*, *Top Girls* and *Mad Forest*.

England, that little gray island in the clouds where governments don't fall overnight and children don't sell themselves in the street and my money is safe.

1940 **Eduardo Galeano:** Uruguayan essayist, journalist and historian. Best-known works include *Memory of Fire* and *The Open Veins of Latin America*, translated into some 20 languages. Work combines documentary, fiction, journalism, political analysis and history. As a result of a military coup in 1973, forced to leave Uruguay and settle in Argentina, where he founded and edited a cultural magazine, *Crisis*. Most widely read Latin American writers. Twice received the prestigious Casa de las Américas prize.

We are all moral until the first kiss and the second glass of wine.

1947 **Kjell Magne Bondevik:** Norwegian Lutheran minister and politician. Prime Minister of Norway (1997–2000 and from 2001–2005). During his first term as Prime Minister he admitted that he was suffering from depression, becoming the highest ranking world leader to admit to suffering from a mental problem while in office. He took three weeks off while he treated the problem and then returned to office.

Unfortunately, religion, like patriotism, is easy to misuse for political purposes.

OTHERS: 1568 Italian composer **Adriano Banchieri**, 1596 Italian violinmaker **Nicolo Amati**, 1693 British politician **Charles Radclyffe**, 1695 Italian composer **Pietro Locatelli**, 1710 Swiss naturalist **Abraham Trembley**, 1860 U.S. merchant **Edward Filene**, 1869 Austrian chemist **Fritz Pregl**, 1875 Austrian auto engineer **Ferdinand Porsche**, 1899 Australian biologist **Frank Burnet**, 1905 U.S. physicist **Carl Anderson**, 1907 U.S. anthropologist **Loren Eiseley**, 1908 Russian mathematician **Lev Pontryagin**, 1910 U.S. singer **Kitty Carlisle**, 1913 U.S. actor **Alan Ladd**, 1942 U.S. musician **Al Jardine**, 1965 U.S. actor **Charlie Sheen**, 1986 U.S. snowboarder **Shaun White**

September 4

1768 Viscount **François-Auguste-René de Chateaubriand:** French writer. Interested in exotic locations and primitive tribes. Visited the U.S. in 1791 and on his return to France, fought for the royalist side that was defeated at Thionville in 1792. Lived in exile in England until 1800. Author of novels of North and South American Indians: *Atala* and the autobiographical *René*. Also set his work in Greece, the Holy Land and the Near East. Later wrote *Memoirs from Beyond the Tomb*.

Justice is the bread of the nation, it is always hungry for it.

1896 **Antonin Artaud:** French playwright, actor, director and dramatic theorists. In a series of manifestos, collected in The Theatre and Its Double, he called for a return to the primitive and the ritualistic in drama, in opposition to the realistic theater of a dominant rationalistic culture. Conceived the Theater of Cruelty, intended to release feelings usually repressed in the unconsciousness. Major influence on modern dramatists such as Albert Camus and Jean Genet. Declared insane in 1936, he was confined to an asylum.

There is in every madman a misunderstood genius whose idea, shining in his head, frightened people, and for whom delirium was the only solution to the strangulation that life had prepared for him.

1905 **Mary Renault:** Pen name of English novelist **Mary Challans**, who recreated ancient worlds. Early works based on her experiences as a wartime nurse. Moved on to historical novels, most of which are lively first-person narratives set in ancient Greece or Asia Minor. They include *The Last of the Wine, The Bull From the Sea, The King Must Die, Fire from Heaven* and *The Persian Boy.*

In hatred as in love, we grow like the thing we brood upon. What we loathe, we graft into our very soul.

1906 **Max Delbrück:** German-born U.S. biologist and biophysicist. Pioneered techniques in molecular biology by studying genetic changes which occur when viruses invade bacteria. His firm belief in an "informational basis" in molecular biology bore fruit in the hands of other scientists whom he inspired. Shared the Nobel Prize in Physiology or Medicine in 1969.

Any living cell carries with it the experience of a billion years of experimentation by its ancestors.

1908 **Richard Wright:** African-American expatriate novelist. Wrote "I like to live in France because it is a free country... The Negro problem in America has not changed in 300 years." First book was a collection of short stories called *Uncle Tom's Children.* Proceeded to write powerful books exploring the way blacks were mistreated and shaped by white society. His most famous work is *Native Son* and his autobiographies: *Black Boy* and *American Hunger.*

Blues, spirituals, and folk tales recounted from mouth to mouth ... all these formed the channels through which the racial wisdom flowed.

1917 **Henry Ford, II:** U.S. automobile executive. Grandson of Henry Ford and son of Edsel B. Ford. From the day his father died on cancer in 1943 (he blamed the way his grandfather treated his son for the early death), young Ford was groomed to take over. First as a VP, then president in 1945, and when Henry I died in 1947, chairman of the Board. Improved relations with labor and emphasized "human engineering," which consisted of improvement of dealer relations, community relations and employee relations. Nurtured the giant educational and cultural Ford Foundation. His motto: "Don't complain. Don't explain."

You will find men who want to be carried on the shoulders of others, who think that the world owes them a living. They don't seem to see that we must all lift together and pull together.

1918 **Paul Harvey [Aurandt]:** "Voice of U.S. Heartland." American radio commentator with ABC news since 1957. Syndicated columnist for *Los Angeles Times* since 1954. Began his daily *Paul Harvey News and Comment* for ABC radio in 1951. His folksy commentary, smooth baritone voice and dramatic use of the pause made him very popular. He even read the commercials as enthusiastically as his conservative commentary on the news.

If "pro" is the opposite of "con" what is the opposite of "progress?"

1924 **Joan Delano Aiken:** English writer of adult fantasy, crime/mystery, romance/gothic, and children's fantasy. First success occurred in 1941 when the British Broadcast Corporation featured some of her short stories on their Children's Hour program. Works: *All You Ever Wanted and Other Stories, The Wolves of Willoughby Chase,* which won the Lewis Carroll Shelf Award and *Night Fall,* which won America's Edgar Allen Poe Award for juvenile mystery.

Stories ought not to be just little bits of fantasy that are used to wile away an idle hour; from the beginning of the human race stories have been used — by priests, by bards, by medicine men — as magic instruments of healing, of teaching, as a means of helping people come to terms with the fact that they continually have to face insoluble problems and unbearable realities.

1925 **Forrest Carter:** American writer. *The Education of Little Tree,* a heartwarming memoir of Carter as a young Cherokee boy being raised a simple old Cherokee couple after his parents die, not only is fiction, it is virtually a hoax. Also wrote *The Outlaw Josey Wales,* as Asa Carter. Rabid segregationist, leader of his own Ku Klux Klan terrorist organization and a hate mongering racist all his life. He published a racist broadsheet, *The Southerner.* Claimed that he wrote Wallace's infamous "Segregation Forever!" speech. Reportedly, Carter died from choking on his own vomit while in a fist fight with his son.

The Indian never fishes or hunts for sport, only for food. Grandpa said it was the silliest damn thing in the world to go around killing something for sport.

1926 **Ivan Illich:** Austrian-born American social critic and theorist. Ordained a Roman Catholic priest in 1951. Resigned priestly duties. Cofounder and director, *Center for Intercultural Culture.* Most celebrated works are *De-Schooling Society,* a critical discourse on education as practiced in modern economics and *Toward a History of Needs.*

Man must choose whether to be rich in things or in the freedom to use them.

1927 **John McCarthy:** American computer scientist. Coined the term "artificial intelligence." Originated research on general purpose time-sharing systems. Frequent lecturer whose talks are sprinkled with his words of wisdom: "As the Chinese say, 1001 words is worth more than a picture," "Compassion is contempt with a human face," "When there's a will to fail, obstacles can be found," "Language is froth on the surface of thought," and "He who refuses to do arithmetic is doomed to talk nonsense."

Here's a way to tell scientific intelligence from legal intelligence. Both may start from the idea that something cannot be done and think up arguments to explain why. However, it is possible that the scientist may discover a flaw in the argument that leads him to change his mind and discover a way to do it. He will be pleased. The legal thinker will merely try to patch the flaw in the argument, because once he has chosen a side, all his intelligence is devoted to finding arguments for that side.

1949 **Tom Watson:** U.S. PGA golfer. Has eight victories in the Major tournaments, including five British Open titles. Early in his career, had a reputation as an "also ran." Could not seem to win tournaments. Byron Nelson offered his assistance and before long Watson was rewarded with his first victory in the 1974 Western Open. Six times U.S. PGA Player of the Year. Earned Vardon trophy 3 times and the Bobby Jones Award.

Confidence in golf means being able to concentrate on the problem at hand with no outside interference.

OTHERS: 1241 King of Scotland **Alexander III**, 1717 English dissenting minister **Job Orton**, 1802 U.S. missionary physician **Marcus Whitman**, 1824 Austrian composer **Anton Bruckner**, 1824 U.S. poet **Phoebe Cary**, 1846 U.S. architect **Daniel Burnham**, 1846 Irish nationalist **John Dillon**, 1892 French composer **Darius Milhaud**, 1913 U.S. chemist **Stanford Moore**, 1920 U.S. Food columnist **Craig Claiborne**, 1934 Welsh economist **Clive Granger**, 1937 Australian swimmer **Dawn Fraser**, 1941 Brazilian philosopher **Marilena Chaui**, 1959 Austrian skier **Armin Kogler**, 1960 U.S. actor **Damon Wayans**, 1968 U.S. baseball catcher **Mike Piazza**, 1981 African-American singer **Beyoncé Knowles**

September 5

1568 **Tommasso Campanella:** Italian philosopher and poet. Entered the Dominican order in 1583. Tried to reconcile the naturalistic themes of the Renaissance with Counter-Reformation orthodoxy. His empirical, anti–Scholastic philosophy caused him to be imprisoned by the Spanish Inquisition for heresy. He was imprisoned again for conspiracy against Spanish rule and heresy (1599–1726). In prison wrote his famous utopian work *City of the Sun*.

The world is a living image of God.

1638 **Louis XIV:** "The Sun King." King of France (1643–1715). Obsessed with France's greatness he adopted aggressive foreign and commercial policies. Made the state an absolute monarchy. Expanded French territory, persecuted Huguenots, built the palace at Versailles and sowed the seeds of the Revolution during his great grandson's reign.

Has God forgotten all I have done for Him?

1791 **Giacomo Meyerbeer:** Originally **Jakob Liebmann Meyer Beer**. German operatic composer. A prodigy who played Mozart's D-minor piano concerto in public at age seven. Attracted attention as a pianist in Venice, and after studying in Italy, he produced opera in the new style, originated by Gioacchino Rossini, which were well received. Lived mostly in Berlin where he was appointed *Kapellmeister* in 1842. Works: *Robert le Diable* and *Huguenots*.

Please accept a promise from me in his name that I will always live in the religion in which he died.

1857 **Konstantin Tsiolkovsky:** Russian rocket scientist and inventor. Self-educated and handicapped by deafness from childhood, his visionary ideas on the use of rockets for space exploration were published in 1903. Worked out the basic theory of rocketry and multistage rocket technology. Independent of James Clerk Maxwell, he developed the kinetic theory of gases.

The Earth is the cradle of humanity, but mankind cannot stay in the cradle forever.

1888 Sir **Sarvepalli Radhakrishnan:** Indian statesman and philosopher. Best known for introducing the thinking of western idealist philosophers into Indian thought. An Oxford don who was knighted in 1931. Ambassador to UNESCO (1946–48) and later to the U.S.S.R. (1949–52). First vice-president of India (1952–61) and second president (1962–67). Author of *The Religion We Need* and *Religion in a Changing World*.

It is not God that is worshipped but the group or authority that claims to speak in His name. Sin becomes disobedience to authority not violation of integrity.

1902 **Daryl F. Zanuck:** American film producer. Began as a scriptwriter for Warner Brothers, and soon became executive producer. Led the change to sound films with *The Jazz Singer* in 1929 and introduced the gangster film with *Little Caesar*. Co-founded 20th Century Fox where he served as controlling executive, later president, then chairman and CEO (1971–79). Films made during his tenure *The Grapes of Wrath*, *How Green Was My Valley*, *Gentleman's Agreement*, *The Sound of Music* and *Patton*.

For God's sake don't say yes until I've finished talking.

1905 **Arthur Koestler:** Hungarian-born English novelist and essayist. An idealist, disillusioned by communism, science, Yoga and Zen, to name a few. Author of *Darkness at Noon*, which exposed the Stalinist purges of the 1930s, *The Sleepwalkers*, a study of the Copernican revolution in astronomy, *Scum of the Earth* and *The Ghost in the Machine*. Increasingly interested in parapsychology, he endowed a university chair in the subject at Edinburgh.

Creative activity could be described as a type of learning process where teacher and pupil are located in the same individual.

1912 **John Cage:** Highly inventive U.S. composer, pianist, writer, philosopher and artist. Studied with

Arnold Schoenberg and is noted for his experimental approach to music, including the use of silence and the role of chance. Pioneer of aleatory music, in which the composition is randomly determined by the use of a computer or dice. All his work since the 1950s is influenced solely by his idea that Zen and other Eastern philosophies are more relevant in art than Western traditions. Compositions: *Music for Wind Instruments*, *Music of Changes* and *Fontana Mix*.

I can't understand why people are frightened of new ideas. I'm frightened of the old ones.

1929 **Bob Newhart:** American standup comedian and actor. His 1960 comedy album, *The Button Down Mind of Bob Newhart* went straight to number one on the charts and received the Grammy Award for Album of the Year. Had his own TV show, the popular *Bob Newhart Show* (1972 to 78). He returned to primetime TV with a new sitcom, *Newhart* (1982–90). Also appeared in movies: *Hot Millions*, *Catch-22*, and *In & Out*.

Laughter gives us distance. It allows us to step back from an event, deal with it and then move on.

1936 **John Danforth:** American Republican politician, statesman and Episcopal priest. Succeeded retiring Senator Stuart Symington in the U.S. Senate (1976–95). Political moderate, in 2005 he wrote two op-ed pieces in the *New York Times* criticizing the increasingly blurry line between church and state brought about by some Christian conservatives in the Republican Party. He believes that right-wing preachers have "hijacked" the Republican Party. Author of *Faith and Politics: How the "Moral Values" Debate Divides America and How to Move Forward Together* (2006).

There is something about a political party adopting a particular religious agenda, a sectarian religious agenda, as its own, that is divisive.

1936 **Jonathan Kozol:** American educator and author. Harvard graduate with honors taught fourth grade at a public school in a poor black neighborhood of Boston. Fired for reading Langston Hughes poetry to his class. Became a prominent figure in the Boston civil rights scene. Wrote *Death at an Early Age*, a probing criticism of American education, which won the National Book Award (1968). Other works: *Rachel and Her Children: Homeless Families in America* and *Amazing Grace: The Lives of Children and the Conscience of a Nation*.

I believe the questions that we should be asking about justice and injustice in America are not chiefly programmatic, technical or scientific. They are theological. But I disagree with those who think we should be asking questions of theology primarily to those who live in poverty. I think we need to ask these questions of ourselves.

1950 **Cathy Lee Guisewite:** American cartoonist. Creator of the "Cathy" cartoon strip, which amusingly shows how difficult it is to be an independent career woman today. When Guisewite married, she allowed her creation to marry her longtime boyfriend. In 1993, received the Reuben Award for Outstanding Cartoonist of the Year from the National Cartoonists Society. Earned an Emmy in 1987 for her animated TV special *Cathy*.

Food, love, career, and mothers, the four major guilt groups.

OTHERS: 1187 King of France **Louis VIII**, 1480 French scholar **Geofroy Tory**, 1494 German *Meistersinger* **Hans Sachs**, 1667 Italian mathematician **Giovanni Saccheri**, 1735 German composer **Johann Christian Bach**, 1750 Scottish poet **Robert Fergusson**, 1787 French mineralogist **François Beudant**, 1807 Irish philologist **Richard C. Trench**, 1847 American outlaw **Jesse James**, 1867 U.S. composer **Amy Beach**, 1897 U.S. market researcher **Arthur Neilsen**, 1916 African-American novelist **Frank Yerby**, 1921 U.S. film executive **Jack Valenti**, 1924 Federal Reserve Chairman **Paul Volcker**, 1934 U.S. TV actress **Carol Lawrence**, 1940 U.S. film actress **Raquel Welch**, 1942 German director **Werner Herzog**

September 6

1656 **Guillaume Dubois:** French cardinal and statesman. Tutor and then the secretary to the Duc de Chartres, who as Philippe, duc d'Orléans was appointed regent, with Dubois as his leading minister. Virtually all powerful, he was appointed foreign minister and Archbishop of Cambral in 1720, cardinal in 1721 and prime minister in 1722.

To become a great man it is necessary to be a great rascal.

1757 **Marie Joseph du Motier, Marquis de Lafayette:** French soldier and statesman. Hero of the American Revolution, friend of George Washington and beloved by the American people. Given the rank of major general by Congress. Negotiated French military support for American cause. Aided victory at Yorktown, remarking on British surrender: "The play is over. The fifth act has come to an end." He also asserted "Humanity has won its battle. Liberty now has a home."

When the government violates the people's rights, insurrection is, for the people and for each portion of the people, the most sacred of the rights and the most indispensable of duties.

1766 **John Dalton:** English meteorologist and chemical theorist. Made his scientific reputation in 1801 with his Law of Partial Pressures, which states that the pressure of a gas mixture is the sum of the pressures that the pressure of each gas would exert if it were present alone and occupied the same volume as the whole mixture. Proposed an atomic theory linked to quantitative chemistry. His theory made it possible to interpret the laws of chemical combination and the conservation of mass.

These observations have tacitly led to the conclusion, which seems universally adopted, that all bodies of sensible magnitude, whether liquid or solid, are constituted of a vast number of extremely small particles, or atoms of matter...

1795 **Frances "Fanny" Wright:** Scottish-American social reformer, writer, and lecturer. After touring widely she published *Views of Society and Manners in America* (1821). In 1824, she bought and freed slaves and settled them at a socialist, interracial community she established at Nashoba, Tennessee. With Robert Dale Owen, published a socialist journal, *Free Enquirer*. Defied convention by lecturing widely, attacking slavery, religion, traditional marriage and unequal treatment of women.

I am neither Jew nor Gentile, Mohammedan nor Theist; I am but a member of the human race.

1800 **Catherine Esther Beecher:** American educator. Daughter of Lyman Beecher and sister of Harriet Beecher Stowe. Promoted higher education for women. In 1824 she opened the Hartford Female Seminary, a private school for girls (including Harriet). Published *A Treatise on Domestic Economy for the Use of Young Women at Home and at School*, which emphasized the importance of women's work in society. Founded the American Woman's Educational Association (1852).

The tea-kettle is as much an English institution as aristocracy or the Prayer-Book.

1860 **Jane Addams:** American social worker, humanitarian and advocate of international peace. Founded Chicago's Hull House, one of first American social settlements (1889). It was modeled on Toynbee Hall, London. Acclaimed first citizen of Chicago. Active in pacifist and suffrage movements. First woman to win Nobel Peace Prize (1931), shared with Nicholas Murray Butler.

The good we secure for ourselves is precarious and uncertain until it is secured for all of us and incorporated into our common life.

1888 **Joseph P. Kennedy:** American executive, businessman, financier, ambassador and diplomat. Dreamed of becoming a millionaire by age 35 he made it by 25, when he became the youngest bank president in the country. Married Rose Fitzgerald, daughter of Boston's first native-born Irish Catholic mayor "Honey Fitz." They had nine children, including President John F. Kennedy, and Senators Robert Kennedy and Ted Kennedy. He branched out into shipbuilding and the motion picture industry, taking actress Gloria Swanson as his mistress. Franklin D. Roosevelt appointed him Ambassador to the Court of St. James in London. Began preparing his son Joe Jr. to become president of the U.S., but when he was killed in World War II, he turned his attention to John, who he instructed during the 1960 presidential campaign:

Don't buy a single vote more than necessary. I'll be damned if I'm going to pay for a landslide.

1899 **Billy Rose:** Professional name of **William Samuel Rosenberg.** American entertainment entrepreneur and prolific songwriter. Owner of several New York theaters and night clubs. Produced shows: *Jumbo*, *Aquacade* and *Carmen Jones*. Songs: "It's Only a Paper Moon," "Me and My Shadow" and "Without a Song." Second husband of musical comedy star Fanny Brice.

It's hard for a fellow to keep a chip on his shoulder if you allow him to take a bow.

1917 **Barbara "Bobo" Rockefeller:** American model, actress and socialite, born **Jievute.** At age 16 she won a Miss Lithuania contest. Began a modeling and acting in New York City. While appearing in *Tobacco Road*, she met proper Bostonian Richard Sears, Jr., who gave her the nickname "Bobo." They married and after seven years they divorced amicably. Married Winthrop Rockefeller in 1948. After six years of marriage to "Winnie" and nearly five years of litigation, the then world-record divorce settlement was $2 million in trust funds and $750,000 cash for Bobo, plus a $2 million trust fund for their son.

There is one big advantage in having the name Rockefeller — you can go any place without making reservations ahead. But the rest, it just makes everything harder, and more expensive. You're a big dollar sign.

1928 **Robert M. Pirsig:** American author. Best known for his first book *Zen and the Art of Motorcycle Maintenance: An Inquiry into Values* (1974). In this mostly autobiographical story of a man's motorcycle trip across North America with some friends and his son, outlines his ideas about the Good. In 1974, awarded a Guggenheim Fellowship, which allowed him to complete his follow-up book, *Lila: An Inquiry into Morals* (1991), in which he elaborates a Metaphysics of Quality.

It is a puzzling thing. The Truth knocks on the door and you say, "Go away, I'm looking for the truth," and so it goes away. Puzzling.

1954 **Carly Fiorina:** Controversial American executive. President of Hewlett-Packard Corporation in 1999, Chairman in 2000, and forced to resign in 2005. Recognized as the most powerful woman in business for six years in a row. Accelerated lay-offs to increase profits and antagonized American workers by her comment to Congressional Members defending moving U.S. jobs overseas: "There is no job that is America's God-given right anymore. We all have to compete for jobs."

Do not be afraid to make decisions; do not be afraid to make mistakes.

1958 **Jeff Foxworthy:** American stand-up comedian. Best known for one of the highest-selling comedy of all times, *You Might Be a Redneck If...* (1993). Its success led to his starring in a TV sitcom, *The Jeff Foxworthy Show*, but it lasted only one season. Toured for three other comedians in the "Blue Collar Comedy Tour" for three years, in which they specialized in common-man comedy. Books: *No Shirt, No Shoes, No Problem* and a cookbook, *The Redneck Grill*.

You many be a redneck if... You have spent more on your pickup truck than on your education. If you own a home with wheels on it and several cars without.

OTHERS: 1535 Flemish historian **Emanuel van Meteren**, 1711 Founder U.S. Lutheran Church **Henry Muhlenberg**, 1802 French naturalist **Alicide d'Orbigny**, 1829 Polish physician **Marie Zakrzewska**, 1875 American lawyer/writer **Arthur Train**, 1879 German actor **Max Schreck**, 1890 U.S. Flying Tigers leader

Claire Chennault, 1925 U.S. blues singer **Jimmy Reed**, 1937 Spanish illustrator **Sergio Aragones**, 1939 Japanese molecular biologist **Susumu Tonegawa**, 1939 U.S. country singer **David Allan Coe**, 1944 U.S. actress **Swoosie Kurtz**, 1944 English bass player **Roger Waters**, 1947 U.S. actress **Jane Curtin**, 1971 Irish musician **Dolores O'Riordan**, 1975 U.S. baseball first baseman **Derrek Lee**

September 7

1533 **Elizabeth I:** English Queen (1558–1603). Daughter of Henry VII and Anne Boleyn. After the death of Edward VI, she backed her half-sister Mary for the throne, but her Protestantism aroused the suspicions of the Catholic queen, who imprisoned Elizabeth in the Tower of London. After Mary's death, Elizabeth ascended to the throne and led her nation in one of its greatest periods. Repealed all of Mary's Catholic legislation and firmly established the Church of England. Her fleet defeated the Spanish Armada (1588). With her death in 1603, the Tudor dynasty game to an end and the throne passed peacefully to the Stuart James VI of Scotland as James I of England.

I know I have the body of a weak and feeble woman, but I have the heart and stomach of a king and of a king of England too.

1707 **Georges-Louis Leclerc de Buffon:** French naturalist and polymath. Surveyed much of biology and had early ideas on evolution of species. Translated Stephen Hales and Isaac Newton into French, introduced calculus into probability theory, and worked on microscopy, tensile strength, cosmology and geology, and the origin of life. Curator of the Jardin du Roi. Best known for his 36-volume beautifully-illustrated *Histoire naturalle* (1749–88).

The human mind cannot create anything. It produces nothing until after having been fertilized by experience and meditation; its acquisitions are the gems of its production.

1860 **Anna Mary "Grandma" Moses:** American folk painter. Best known for paintings of rural life. Started painting in her late 70s. Her paintings on Masonite, which she explains "will last many years longer than canvas," were discovered in 1939 by a New York art collector hanging in a Hoosick, New York drugstore. Since then her work whose fanciful childlike touches evoked nostalgia by their simplicity and warmth, have been widely admired. Paintings: *The Old Checkered House*, *Black Horses* and *From My Window*.

Life is what we make it, always has been, always will be.

1870 **Aleksandr I. Kuprin:** Russian novelist. Gave up an army career for literature. Ranks next to Antonin Chekhov as a teller of short stories. Those that have been translated include: *The Duel*, *The River of Life*, *A Slav Soul*, *The Bracelet of Garnets* and *Sasha*.

I am a wanderer passionately in love with life. I wanted to live the inner life of every man I saw, look at the world through his eyes.

1887 Dame **Edith Sitwell:** English poet and prose writer. An eccentric who habitually dressed in medieval costume. Dresses in a tiara, floor-length cape, and Tibetan bracelets as she gives readings of her poetry. Known for her experimental patterns of sound and imagery. Her later poems evoked the symbolism of death, faith and rebirth, which she says are the "hymns of praise to the glory of life." Typical of her preoccupation with experimentation is the popular *Facade*, poems read to a background of music, composed by Sir William Walton. Poems: "Daphne," "The Strawberry" and "The Little Ghost Who Died for Love."

I am patience with stupidity but not with those who are proud of it.

1900 **Taylor Caldwell:** English-born American novelist. Began writing novels as a child, the first a tale of seduction at the time of Nero. Her second husband, Marcus Reback was her collaborator, business manager, researcher, editor and partner. Best-selling novels include: *Dynasty of Death*, *This Side of Innocence*, *Dear and Glorious Physician* and *Captains and the Kings*.

Contrary to general opinion, women are not so sentimental as men, but are much more hardheaded.

1909 **Elia Kazan:** "Gadge." Istanbul-born American actor, screenwriter, producer and director. Directed five Pulitzer Prize dramas: *The Skin of Our Teeth*, *A Streetcar Named Desire*, *Death of a Salesman*, *Cat on a Hot Tin Roof*, and *JB*. Oscar winner as director for *Gentleman's Agreement* and *On the Waterfront*. Nominated for *A Streetcar Named Desire*, *East of Eden* and *America, America*. His career was clouded when Kazan testified before the Un-American Activities Committee in 1952 that he had been a Communist in the 30s and named other members among his colleagues. Lillian Hellman and Arthur Miller publicly and bitterly denounced his action, which he claimed was motivated by his disillusionment with communism because of the atrocities of Stalin.

The writer, when he is also an artist, is someone who admits what others don't dare reveal.

1914 **James Van Allen:** Discovered the magnetosphere, the radiation belts that are named for him. Used left over German V-2 rockets to carry instruments to measure cosmic radiation into the upper atmosphere, and in 1958 put a Geiger radiation counter on the first American satellite, Explorer I. Explorer satellites revealed a region of high levels of radiation at a height of several hundred kilometers above the Earth. Further investigation revealed that there are two toroidal (donut-shaped) belts, created by charged particles from the Sun being trapped by the Earth's magnetic field.

I'm one of the most durable and fervent advocates of space exploration, but my take is that we could do it robotically at far less cost and far greater quality of results.

1924 **Daniel Inouye:** American politician. Recipient of the Medal of Honor during World War II when he lost his right arm during the campaign in Europe. Currently the senior Senator from Hawaii, have served in the Senate for 43 years, third in longevity behind fellow Democrats Robert Byrd and Ted Kennedy. First American of Japanese descent to serve in the U.S. House of Representatives and when he succeeded Oren E. Long, the first in the Senate. Served on the Senate Watergate Committee and chaired the Iran Contra special investigating committee.

The ability to criticize and question our leaders is at the essence of democracy.

1931 **Al McGuire:** U.S. basketball coach and television color commentator. Played 4 years of basketball at St. John's University. After college he played a few years in the NBA. Began his illustrious coaching career first as an assistant at Dartmouth College, and completed it with Marquette University (1964–77), where his record was 295–80,capping it when Marquette won the 1977 NCAA championship and then quit coaching.

I think the world is run by C students.

1936 **Buddy Holly:** Originally **Charles Hardin Holley**. American singer and songwriter, born in Lubbock, Texas. Played in country music bands while still in high school. Later switched to rock-n-roll and with his band, the Crickets, produced some of the most distinctive and influential work in rock music. Songs included: "That'll Be the Day," "Peggy Sue" and "Oh, Boy." Died in a plane crash at age 22 along with singers Richie Valens and The Big Bopper (Jape Richardson). Among the first inducted into the newly-formed Rock and Roll Hall of Fame.

Death is often referred to as a good career move.

1950 **Peggy Noonan:** American journalist, author and political analyst. Speechwriter for Presidents Ronald Reagan and George W.H. Bush. Coined the catch phrases used by Bush, "a kinder, gentler nation, and popularized H.G. Wells' "a thousand points of light." Pushed Bush to pledge "Read my lips: no new taxes" in his 1988 nomination acceptance speech. When he was unable to keep his promise, it contributed to his defeat in 1992. Noonan is now a columnist for The Wall Street Journal. Books: *The Case Against Hilary Clinton, When Character Was King: A Story of Ronald Reagan* and *John Paul the Great: Remembering a Spiritual Father.*

A speech is poetry: cadence, rhythm, imagery, and sweep! A speech reminds us that words, like children, have the power to make dance the dullest beanbag of a heart.

OTHERS: 1524 Swiss theologian **Thomas Erastus**, 1717 Austrian Jesuit missionary **Martin Dobrizhoffer**, 1829 U.S. geologist **Ferdinand Vandiver Hayden**, 1866 French writer **Tristan Bernard**, 1867 U.S. financier/art collector **J.P. Morgan**, 1885 U.S. writer **Elinor Wylie**, 1889 Dutch aviation pioneer **Albert Plesman**, 1905 U.S. Treasurer **Ivy Baker Priest** 1908 U.S. heart surgeon **Michael DeBakey**, 1912 U.S. electrical engineer **David Packard**, 1930 King of Belgium **Baudouin I**, 1930 jazz saxophonist **Sonny Rollins**, 1942 African-American actor **Richard Roundtree**, 1945 Canadian hockey player **Jacques Lemaire**, 1946 Chilean biologist **Francisco Varela**, 1949 U.S. singer **Gloria Gaynor**

September 8

1474 **Ludovico Ariosto:** Italian epic and lyric poet. Author of *Orlando Furioso*, an epic of Roland and other knights of Charlemagne recognized as a classic example of Renaissance literature. Edmund Spenser used its narrative form as a model for his *Faerie Queene*. Besides this great work, Ariosto also wrote comedies, satires, sonnets and a number of Latin poems.

When the devil grows old he turns hermit.

1830 **Frédéric Mistral:** French poet and Provençal patriot. His passionate odes to his native Provençe and its people had much in common with mediaeval troubadour poetry. Selected works: *Mirèio*, which Charles Gounod used as the basis of his opera *Mireille, The Song of the Rhone* and *Les Olivadou*. Shared the Nobel Prize for Literature in 1904 with Spanish dramatist José Echegaray. Mistral used the funds he received with the prize to develop his museum of ethnography, which he had founded in Arles.

Aioli epitomizes the heat, the power, and the joy of the Provençal sun, but it has another virtue — it drives away flies.

1841 **Antonín Dvořák:** Czech composer whose musical style was eclectic. Combined ethnic folk elements with Viennese musical tradition of Joseph Haydn and Johannes Brahms. In the U.S. from 1892 to 95 as director of the New York Conservatory, he suggested the way to develop a truly national American style of music was to base it on the melodies of Negroes and Indians. Famous for his symphony *From the New World*. Other works: *Stabat mater, Carnival Overture, Symphony, Te Deum* and *Rusalka*.

All the great musicians have borrowed from the songs of the common people.

1873 **Alfred Jarry:** French writer, best known for his five-act satirical farce *Ubu the King*, which is often cited as a forerunner of surrealism and the Theater of the Absurd. After army service, he returned to Paris where he devoted himself to writing, the company of friends, who appreciated his witty, unpredictable conversation and to alcohol, which he called "my sacred herb" and referred to absinthe as "the green goddess." Novels: *The Supermale* and *Exploits and Opinions of Dr. Faustroll, pataphysician* According to Jarry who invented it, pataphysics deals with the laws that govern exceptions and explains the universe supplementary to the real one.

God is the tangential point between zero and infinity.

1886 **Siegfried Sassoon:** English poet and prose writer. Known for his anti-war poetry and fictionalized autobiographies. Seriously Wounded in France in World War I. Published *The Old Huntsman* and *Counter Attack* while still in the army. Met Wilfrid Owen at a sanatorium and published the latter's poetry when he was killed at the front. In Sassoon's postwar poetry, a strong attachment to the countryside is notable in his semi-autobiographical trilogy beginning with *Memoirs of a Fox-Hunting Man*.

Soldiers are citizens of death's gray land,/ Drawing no dividend from time's to-morrows.

1897 **Jimmie Rodgers:** First country music superstar. Known as "The Father of Country Music," "The Singing Brakeman" and "The Blue Yodeler." Before his meteoric journey from poverty to fame to early death, he worked at the highly dangerous job of railroad brakeman. His recordings of old mountain ballads and the sentimental songs about home, family, sweethearts, and railroads made him an icon. Hit songs: "Waiting for a Train," "In the Jailhouse Now," "Train Whistle Blues" and "Blue Yodel No. 9." The epitaph on his statue at the Jimmie Rodgers Memorial Museum in Meridian, Mississippi reads:

His is the music of America. He sang the songs of the people he loved, of a young nation growing strong. His was an America of glistering rails, thundering boxcars, and rain-swept nights, of lonesome prairies, great mountains and a high blue sky. He sang of the bayous and the cornfields, the wheated plains, of the little towns, the cities, and the winding rivers of America.

1900 **Claude Pepper:** American politician. Elected Democratic U.S. Senator from Florida (1936–50), where he supported legislation that created Social Security, minimum wages and medical assistance for the elderly. Elected a U.S. congressman (1963–89). Champion for senior citizens. Instrumental in passage of law against mandatory retirement based solely on age. Asserted, "Ageism is as odious as racism and sexism."

If more politicians in this country were thinking about the next generation instead of the next election, it might be better for the United States and the people.

1911 **Euell Gibbons:** American outdoorsman and naturalist. Led a colorful life as a cowboy, farmer, hobo, alcoholic, carpenter, Depression-days communist and beachcomber. Author of books promoting eating wild foods, including *Stalking Wild Asparagus*, *Stalking the Blue-Eyed Scallop*, *Stalking the Healthful Herb*, and *Stalking the Good Life*. Died of a heart attack, the result of his smoking and adding saturated fats to his wild food diet.

Nature is typified by cooperation and mutualism. It's everywhere. The production of fruit and the scattering of seed by animals is one example. Flowers and bees are another... There are thousands and thousands examples of mutual aid ... of one life form absolutely dependent upon another.

1915 **Hugh "Duffy" Daugherty:** American football coach with Michigan State. NCAA coach of the year (1965). He was known for his wit, good humor, and wisdom. Began his football career playing for Syracuse University. Assistant coach under Clarence "Biggie" Munn first at Syracuse and then at Michigan State. When Munn became the university's athletic director, he appointed Daugherty head coach, a position he held for 19 years.

Football isn't a contact sport, it's a collision sport. Dancing is a contact sport.

1922 **Sid Caesar:** American comedian, best at parody, pantomime and mimicking foreign languages at high speeds. Did ground-breaking comedy work on television with "The Admiral Broadway Review," "Caesar's Hour" and "The Sid Caesar Show." Emmy winner (1952, 1957). Started his professional career as a musician, playing sax and clarinet with the bands of Charlie Spivak, Shep Fields and Claude Thornhill. In 1950 he joined *Your Show of Shows*, making TV magic on live telecasts with Imogene Coca, Carl Reiner, and Howard Morris, written by talented writers including Neil Simon, Mel Brooks, and Woody Allen.

Comedy has to be based on truth. You take the truth and you put a little curlicue at the end.

1924 **Grace Metalious:** American author. Best known for her steamy novel of small-town life, *Peyton Place*, which sold 6 million copies in the first 17 months. It was rejected by several publishers, who couldn't foresee the fascination readers would have with the scandals and passions of a hypothetical New England town. The sex-ridden novel was made into a movie of the same name as was her sequel *Return to Peyton Place*.

Even Tom Sawyer had a girl friend and to talk about adults without talking about their sex drives is like talking about a window without glass.

1932 **Patsy Cline:** American singer. First country singer to cross over to pop music. Won first place on Arthur Godfrey's TV show with "Walking After Midnight," her first crossover hit. Joined the Grand Ole Opry in 1960. Seriously injured in a car crash, she returned to the Opry in 1962 and recorded hits such as "I Go to Pieces" and "Crazy." Killed in airplane crash at age 30. Subject of the film *Sweet Dreams* (1985).

You want me to act like we've never kissed, you want to forget; pretend we've never met, and I've tried and I've tried, but I haven't yet... You walk by, and I fall to pieces.

OTHERS: 1157 King of England **Richard the Lionhearted**, 1588 French priest/mathematician **Marin Mersenne**, 1592 Dutch Governor of New Amsterdam **Peter Stuyvesant**, 1672 French organist **Nicolas de Grigny**, 1778 German poet **Clemens Brentano**, 1837 U.S. geologist **Raphael Pumpelly**, 1873 German film director **Max Reinhardt**, 1889 U.S. politician **Robert A. Taft**, 1901 South African PM **Hendrik F. Verwoerd**, 1921 Welch entertainer **Harry Secombe**, 1922 U.S. politician **Lyndon LaRouche**, 1925 British comedian **Peter Sellers**, 1930 South Vietnam Premier **Nguyen Cao Ky**, 1938 U.S. Senator **Sam Nunn**, 1947 U.S. writer **Ann Beattie**, 1960 English bassist **David Steele**, 1971 U.S. singer **Pink**

September 9

1585 Duc **Armand Jean du Plessis de Richelieu:** French cardinal and statesman. Chief Minister to Louis XIII (1624–42). Virtual ruler, he built France into a world power. Centralized the government. Made alliances with the Netherlands and German Protestant powers. Described as " the frail gentleman in the red robe who united a quarrelsome France that Louis XIV was to inherit." Founder of the French Academy and the Jardin des Plantes.

If you give me six lines written by the hand of the most honest of men, I will find something in them which will hang him.

1828 Count **Leo Tolstoy:** Russian novelist, social reformer and moral philosopher. Also wrote short-stories, plays and essays. With Dostoyevsky made the realistic novel an important literary genre. Subsequently espoused a moral code based on the love of humankind, renouncing property, and repudiating organized religion. Wrote commentaries on the gospels and made translations of them. In *Confession*, he describes the metaphysical torments that beset him. Novels: *The Cossacks, War and Peace, Anna Karenina* and *Resurrection*, and his story *The Death of Ivan Ilyich*.

In the name of God, stop a moment, look around you.

1868 **Mary Hunter Austin:** American writer and feminist. Had a deep commitment to socialism and mysticism. Became associated with John Reed, Walter Lippmann and others of the group of writers whose center was Mabel Dodge. Austin's best writing was concerned with nature or Indian life. Books: *The Land of Little Rain, The Basket Woman, A Woman of Genius* and *The Land of Journey's End*.

What women have to stand on squarely is not the ability to see the world in the way men see it, but the importance and validity of their seeing it in some other way.

1887 **Alfred M. Landon:** U.S. Republican politician and oilman. Millionaire at 40 as a wildcat oil prospector. Governor of Kansas (1933–37). Carried only two states in his overwhelming defeat for the presidency by Franklin D. Roosevelt in 1936. Leavened the disappointment of his loss with humor, saying "As Maine goes, so goes Vermont." As Governor he endorsed many of the most controversial aspects of the New Deal. Despite opposing him in the election, he admired and respected Roosevelt. When asked in 1962 to describe his political philosophy:

I would say practical progressive, which means that the Republican Party or any political party has got to recognize the problems of a growing and complex industrial civilization. And I don't think the Republican Party is really wide awake to that.

1890 Colonel **Harland Sanders:** U.S. restaurateur. Originator of Kentucky Fried Chicken. First restaurant in Corbin, Kentucky. Governor Ruby Laffoon made him a Kentucky Colonel in 1935 in recognition of his contribution to the state's cuisine. In 1939, his restaurant was first listed in Duncan Hines' *Adventures in Good Eating*. Began franchising his chicken business at age 60. Today more that a billion KFC dinners are served annually in more than 80 countries and territories around the world.

Feed the poor and get rich or feed the rich and get poor.

1898 **Beverley Nichols:** Prolific English writer on subjects ranging from religion to politics to travel. Author of six novels, five detective mysteries, four children's stories, six autobiographies, and six plays. Best remembered today for his gardening books, *Down the Garden Path, A Thatched Roof, A Village in a Valley, Merry Hall, Laughter on the Stairs* and *Sunlight on the Lawn*.

Marriage — a book of which the first chapter is written in poetry and the remaining chapters in prose.

1900 **James Hilton:** English novelist, book reviewer and journalist. Produced best-selling novels *Lost Horizon*, about the mystical "Shangri-La," *Goodbye Mr. Chips*, in celebration of his father's life as a Latin and Greek teacher and *Random Harvest*, about a man suffering from amnesia. Moved to Hollywood in 1935, where he wrote several screenplays.

Surely there comes a time when counting the cost and paying the price aren't things to think about anymore. All that matters is value — the ultimate value of what one does.

1907 **Leon Edel:** Canadian-born American educator and biographer. Most famous work is his five-volume biography of Henry James (*Henry James, The Imagination of Genius*, 1953–72). It epitomizes biography as a literary form. The second and third volume earned Edel a Pulitzer Prize and a National Book Award in 1963. Other biographies on James Joyce and the Bloomsbury Group.

The secret of biography resides in finding the link between talent and achievement. A biography seems irrelevant if it doesn't discover the overlap between what the individual did and the life that made this possible. Without discovering that, you have shapeless happenings and gossip.

1908 **Cesare Pavese:** Italian novelist, poet, editor and translator. Translated the work of many major American writers. The dominant themes of his own work contrast city and country life, man's solitude and his need to establish a rapport with other human beings. Books: *The Political Prisoner, The Harvesters* and *The Moon and the Bonfires. The Burning Brand: Diaries 1935–1950* is his tormented diary, which tells much of his long-contemplated suicide.

We do not remember days, we remember moments. The richness of life lies in memories we have forgotten.

1911 **Paul Goodman:** American poet, literary critic and fictionist. Described himself as an "Enlightenment Man of Letters" a "utopian sociologist" and a "conservative anarchist." Played a provocative role as a bohemian-artist dissenter in New York intellectual circles. Achieved a dissident role of considerable notoriety and influence in the last years of his. Most persuasive and influential radical stance was as libertarian critic of American education. Social Criticism: *Growing Up Absurd* and *Compulsory Mis-Education*. Novels: *The Empire City* and *Making Do*.

When the Devil quotes Scriptures, it's not,

really, to deceive, but simply that the masses are so ignorant of theology that somebody has to teach them the elementary texts before he can seduce them.

1918 **Jimmy the Greek Snyder:** Born **Demetrios George Synodinos**. American bookmaker and sports commentator. Before he quit gambling, he would bet up to $250,000 on a single football game. Fired from CBS after an off-hand remark during a national broadcast that African Americans were naturally superior athletes because they had been bred to produce stronger offspring during slavery.

Roulette is a pleasant, relaxed and highly comfortable way to lose your money.

1932 **Alice Thomas Ellis:** Penname of **Anna Lindholm Haycraft**. English novelist and columnist. Novels: *The Sin Eater*, *Unexplained Laughter*, and *The Birds of the Air*. A conservative, traditionalist Catholic, she was unhappy with the changes in the Church triggered by the Second Vatican Council. In her column for the *Catholic Herald*, she provoked an outcry when she attacked Derek Worlock, the Archbishop of Liverpool, shortly after his death. She blamed him for what she believed to be an invasion of the Church by heresy.

Men were made for war. Without it they wandered greyly about, getting under the feet of the women, who were trying to organize the really important things of life.

1960 **Mario Batali:** American chef. His flagship restaurant is Babbo Ristorante e Enoteca, located in Greenwich Village. Hosts two Food Network programs, "Molto Mario" and "Ciao America." Named "Man of the Year" in the chef category by *GQ* magazine in 1999, the James Beard Foundation's "Best Chef: New York City" Award in 2002 and the James Beard Foundation Award "Outstanding Chef of the Year" in 2005. Books: *Simple Italian Food*, *The Batali Cookbook*, and *Molto Italiano*.

There are all kinds of myths going on in the Italian culture, and the way they celebrate is through their food. It's the tradition of the table where the Italians celebrate most of their triumphs and successes.

OTHERS: 1629 Dutch admiral **Cornelis Tromp**, 1737 Italian physician/physicist **Luigi Galvani**, 1754 British ship's captain **William Bligh**, 1823 U.S. paleontologist/anatomist **Joseph Leidy**, 1834 English novelist **Joseph Henry Shorthouse**, 1877 U.S. baseball player/manager **Frank Chance**, 1878 U.S. poet **Adelaide Crapsey**, 1924 U.S. actress **Jane Greer**, 1928 African-American musician **Julian "Cannonball" Adderley**, 1929 French singer **Claude Nougaro**, 1932 U.S. actress **Sylvia Miles**, 1935 Israeli actor **Chaim Topol**, 1941 African-American singer **Otis Redding**, 1941 U.S. computer scientist **Dennis Ritchie**, 1949 Football quarterback **Joe Thiesmann**, 1960 British actor **Hugh Grant**

September 10

1487 **Julius III:** Born **Giammaria Ciocchi del Monte in Rome**. Last of the High Renaissance Popes (1550–55). First president of the Council of Trent. In the ten week conclave to elect a successor to Pope Paul III, he was the compromise candidate. Promoted Jesuits and initiated church reforms. Founded Collegium Germanicum. Caused a scandal when he created his first Cardinal, an illegitimate, teenaged, virtually illiterate street urchin he had picked up on the streets of Parma some years earlier and who had been adopted by the Pope's brother.

Do you not know, my son, with what little understanding the world is ruled?

1758 **Hannah Webster Foster:** American author. Novels: *The Coquette, or, The History of Eliza Wharton* and *The Boarding School*. Her daughters were also novelists. Harriet Vaughan Foster Cheney wrote: *A Peep at the Pilgrims in Sixteen Hundred Thirty-Six* and *The Rivals of Acadia*. Her sister Eliza Lanesford Foster Cushing wrote: *Saratoga: A Tale of the Revolution* and *Esther: A Sacred Drama*.

True courage consists not in fleeing from the storms of life, but in bravely steering through them with patience.

1839 **Charles Sanders Peirce:** American mathematician, astronomer, chemist, geodesist, surveyor, cartographer, metrologist, spectroscopist, engineer, inventor, psychologist, lexicographer, historian of science, mathematical economist, lifelong student of medicine, book reviewer, dramatist, actor, short story writer, phenomenologist, semiotician, logician, rhetorician and metaphysician. Joined the U.S. Coast Guard and Geodetic Survey in 1861, where he remained for thirty years circles. Regarded as one of the world's great logicians. Best known as the founder of the philosophical movement *pragmatism*. Proposed that belief or an idea is to be understood by the actions, uses, and habits to which it gives rise.

The pragmatist knows that doubt is an art which has to be acquired with difficulty.

1885 **Carl Van Doren:** American editor, critic and biographer. Lectured in English Literature at Columbia University (1911–30). Literary editor of the *Nation* (1919–22), the *Century Magazine* (1922–25) and managing editor of the *Cambridge History of American Literature* (1917–21). His biography *Benjamin Franklin* won a Pulitzer Prize (1938). Also edited Franklin's *Letters and Papers* (1947). Brother of poet Mark Van Doren.

The race of men, while sheep in credulity, are wolves for conformity.

1890 **Franz Werfel:** Expressionist poet, playwright and novelist, born in Prague, lived in Vienna and in 1938 moved to France. Best known for novels, the epic *The Forty Days of Musa Dagh* (1933) and the story of the Lourdes visionary, *The Song of Bernadette* (1941).

Religion is the everlasting dialogue between humanity and God. Art is its soliloquy.

1892 **Arthur Holly Compton:** U.S. physicist and professor. Famous for his work in radioactivity and cosmic rays. Made key contribution to the development of the quantum theory of energy. Nobel Prize winner (1927). Reported in code by telephone to James Bryant Conant that the first chain reaction had been initiated thusly, "The Italian Navigator has reached the New World." Courant: "And How did he find the natives?" Compton: "Very friendly."

If cooperation is thus the lifeblood of science and technology, it is similarly vital to society as a whole.

1896 **Elsa Schiaparelli:** Italian-born French fashion designer. Daring innovations, use of accessories and colors, such as shocking pink, enlivened the fashion scene for 40 years. Originated the padded shoulder line in 1932. The "Schiaparelli look" consists of a trim silhouette, dramatic colors, and imaginative touches in ornamentation and accessories. During World War I she was active in French War Relief in the U.S. and lectured on "Clothes Make the Woman."

Women insisted on looking like little girls, even if they were old, with a silhouette that with some wishful thinking could be called slim, and built-up faces that looks as if they had cried "Stop!" to death.

1903 **Cyril Connolly:** English essayist, critic, iconoclast and sometimes novelist. Called himself one of the "Mandarins" of modern English letters, a term he used to differentiate the aristocrats of literature from the realists and revolutionists. Founded and edited the magazine *Horizon* (1939–50). Author of *Enemies of Promise, The Unquiet Grave* and *The Evening Colonnade.*

Whom the gods wish to destroy they first call promising.

1929 **Arnold Palmer:** Arguably the most popular American golfer. His charisma played a major role in popularizing television golf tournaments. On the course his fans affectionately known as "Arnie's Army" followed him around the course, constantly growing till it reached its largest number at the 18th hole. Won four Masters, two British Opens and one U.S. Open. Two-time PGA Player of the Year. First player to win over $1 million in career. He participated in his last master's in 2005, his 50th consecutive appearance in the premiere golf event.

Golf is deceptively simple and endlessly complicated.

1934 **Charles Kuralt:** Likeable CBS newsman. Hosted TV's human-interest segment of *CBS Evening News,* "On the Road with Charles Kuralt" and *CBS Sunday Morning.* Told stories of remarkably interesting ordinary Americans he encountered in his travels. Wrote *North Carolina Is My Home* and when he died he was buried on the campus of the University of North Carolina at Chapel Hill. Two years after his death, his reputation was sullied when it became known that for decades he had a second "wife" and family in Montana, while his official family lived in New York City.

The everyday kindness of the back roads more than makes up for the acts of greed in the headlines.

1948 **Margaret Trudeau:** Former Canadian First Lady. At age 18, the carefree "flower child" met Pierre Trudeau, then Canadian Minister of Justice, while on a vacation in Tahiti. Although thirty years older, he pursued her, but kept their romance a secret until elected Prime Minister in 1968. Astonished the country by marring the vivacious 22-year-old Margaret. During the marriage, she was frequently criticized for her behavior in her public appearances. They separated in 1977 and she became a jet-setter, delighted to tell of her affairs in interviews and her book *Beyond Reason.*

I want to be more than a rose in my husband's lapel.

1949 **Bill O'Reilly:** American commentator, syndicated columnist, journalist, editor and author. Best known as the host of the FOX News Network TV editorial program *The O'Reilly Factor,* on which he offers his fiercely opinionated point-of-view on national and international events. His guests are of all political stripes and from all social spectrums. Sometimes his passion gets the better of him and he rudely berates his guests, but generally they are allowed to present their side of arguments. Darling of the conservative right, maintains he is not a conservative, preferring to call himself a traditionalist and a populist.

Conservative people tend to see the world in black and white, good and evil. Liberals see grays. In any talk format, you have to pound home a strong point of view. If you're not providing controversy, people won't listen, or watch.

OTHERS: 1550 Spanish Amada Commander **Alonso de Guzmán El Bueno**, 1588 English composer **Nicholas Lanier**, 1753 English architect **Sir John Soane**, 1839 U.S. publisher **Isaac Kauffman Funk**, 1852 Seminole chief **Alice Brown Davis**, 1861 Danish sculptor **Niels Hansen Jacobsen**, 1886 U.S. poet/novelist **Hilda Doolittle** 1896 Chinese military leader **Ye Ting**, 1917 Chilean author **Miguel Serrano**, 1922 Peruvian singer **Yma Sumac**, 1934 U.S. baseball player **Roger Maris**, 1938 German fashion designer **Karl Lagerfeld**, 1941 U.S. paleontologist /evolutionary biologist **Stephen Jay Gould**, 1941 English conductor **Christopher Hogwood**, 1945 Blind Puerto Rican singer **José Feliciano**

September 11

1700 **James Thomson:** Scottish-born poet. Known for his savage melancholy, atheism, and political radicalism. Author of "A Poem to the Memory of Sir Isaac Newton." His "The Seasons," which was immensely influential, one of the most popular and frequently reprinted of English poems. Wrote the ode "Rule, Britannia!" that appeared originally in the last scene of the dramatic piece *Alfred, a Masque.*

But who can paint/ Like nature? Can

imagination boast/ Amid its gay creation, hues like hers?

1723 **Johann Bernhard Basedow:** German educational reformer. Greatly influenced by Jean Jacques Rousseau's *Emile.* Founded the Philanthropinum, an institute for qualifying teachers, where he applied his educational principles in training disciples, who were to spread them throughout Germany. He attracted few scholars, but his ideas were well received and similar institutions sprang up all over the country. He was the first to conduct gymnastics as part of education. However, he was unsuited for managing his institute and his intractality constantly put him at odds with colleagues. He resigned as director in 1778. At his death he stated:

I want an autopsy made for the benefit of men.

1798 **Franz Ernst Neumann:** German mineralogist, physicist and mathematician. Early papers were mostly concerned with crystallography. Next he devoted himself to optics and became one of the early searchers for a true dynamical theory of light. Later, he attacked the problem of giving mathematical expression to the conditions holding for a surface separating two crystalline media. His last publication was on spherical harmonics.

The greatest luck is the discovery of a new truth; to that, recognition can add little or nothing.

1862 **O. Henry:** Pen name of **William Sydney Porter**. Master American short-story writer. Distinguished for his popular sentimental and deftly-plotted tales of ordinary people and his perception of the romantic aspects of everyday life. Spent three years in prison for embezzlement, when he "borrowed" money to help his consumptive wife. Founded a literary magazine, *Rolling Stone.* It was while imprisoned that he adopted his pseudonym and began to write stories: "The Gift of the Magi," "The Last Leaf" and the collection *Cabbages and Kings.*

Life is made up of sobs, sniffles and smiles, with sniffles predominating.

1877 Sir **James Hopwood Jeans:** British mathematician, astrophysicist, and science popularizer. His claim that matter is continuously created throughout the Universe was a forerunner of steady-state theory. Books: *The Universe Around Us* (1929), *The Mysterious Universe* (1930) and *Physics and Philosophy* (1942). To show the relative size of things, which range "from electrons of a fraction of a millionth of a millionth of an inch in diameter, to nebulae whose diameters are measured in hundreds of thousands of millions of miles," asserted that a model of the universe in which the sun was represented by a "speck of dust 1/300 of an inch in diameter" would have to extend 4 million miles in every direction to encompass even a few neighboring galaxies."

The universe begins to look more like a great thought than a great machine.

1885 **D.H. Lawrence:** English novelist, short-story writer, poet and essayist. Known for his idealistic theories about sexual relations. His work expresses his belief in emotion and the sexual impulse as creative and true to human nature. Many of his books were banned as obscene. He was persecuted during World War I for supposed pro–German sympathies. Novels: *Women in Love, Lady Chatterley's Lover* and the semiautobiographical *Sons and Lovers.*

I never saw a wild thing/ Sorry for itself.

1903 **Theodor W. Adorno:** German social philosopher and musicologist. Member of the "Frankfurt School" at the Institute for Social Research, whose other members included Max Horkheimer and Herbert Marcuse. Emigrated to the U.S. in 1934 to teach at the exiled New School of Social Research, returning with the institute to Frankfurt in 1960. Argues that all past philosophy is systematically vitiated, because it is vulnerable to exploitation. Works: *Negative Dialectics* and sociological writings on music, art, and mass culture.

But he who dies in despair has lived his whole life in vain.

1913 **Hedy Lamarr:** Austrian-born actress, with a face of almost flawless beauty, who long held the title of the most glamorous actress in films. Gained worldwide notoriety in 1933 as 17-year-old **Hedwig Keisler** by appearing completely nude in the film *Ecstasy.* Her first of five husbands unsuccessfully attempted to buy up all the existing prints of the film. In Hollywood the exquisite brunette beauty appeared in *Algiers, White Cargo* and *Samson and Delilah.*

If you use your imagination, you can look at any actress and see her nude ... I hope to make you use your imagination.

1917 **Jessica Mitford:** English-born American writer. Sister of Nancy Mitford. Lifelong champion of civil rights. Moved to the U.S.A. and became a communist. Author of the autobiographical *Hons and Rebels,* Best-known book: *The American Way of Death.* Others: *The Trial of Dr. Spock* and *The Making of a Muckraker.*

You may not be able to change the world, but at least you can embarrass the guilty.

1924 **Tom Landry:** Former Dallas Cowboys football coach. The only coach the team had from its formation in 1960 until he was fired in 1989 by the new owner. Won two Super Bowls. Had 271 career victories and NFL-record 20 consecutive winning seasons (1966–85). Credited with introducing flex defense and reviving the shotgun offense.

Leadership is getting someone to do what they don't want to do, to achieve what they want to achieve.

1935 **Arvo Pärt:** Estonian composer. Emigrated in 1980 settling in East Berlin. Many compositions include orchestral choral, piano and chamber works; evince an eclectic range of musical techniques including neo–Baroque, aleatory methods, minimalism and impressionism. In his religious work he evoked old polyphonic forms and medieval harmonies.

I could compare my music to white light which contains all colors. Only a prism can divide the

colors and make them appear; this prism could be the spirit of the listener.

1939 **Charles Geschke:** American inventor and businessman. Co-founder with John Warnock of Adobe System, the graphics and publishing software company (1982). Focus on family and church were always priorities for him and his wife Nan. While speaking about the impact of the digital revolution on print media, to the U.S. Catholic bishops at their 1998 annual meeting he interrupted his remarks by saying as a Catholic he had a message to deliver:

We as a religion have cut ourselves off from 50 percent of the population. I would never do that in running my business. I want to say this to the hierarchy — make women much more essential in what you do. It will be essential as we enter the 21st century.

OTHERS: 1522 Italian naturalist **Ulisse Aldrovandi**, 1821 U.S. publisher of "dime" novels **Erastus Flaval Beadle**, 1825 German critic **Eduard Hanslick**, 1865 Latvian poet **Rainis**, 1902 U.S. politician/composer **Jimmie Davis**, 1913 U.S. football coach **Paul "Bear" Bryant**, 1917 Philippines President **Ferdinand Marcos**, 1922 Civil rights leader **Charles Evers**, 1923 Hindu guru **Swami Madhavananda**, 1935 2nd man in space **Gherman Titov**, 1940 U.S. film director **Brian de Palma**, 1945 German soccer player **Franz Beckenbauer**, 1946 U.S. entertainer **Lola Falana**, 1949 U.S. miler and long distance runner **Marty Liquori**, 1967 U.S. singer **Harry Connick, Jr.**

September 12

1575 **Henry Hudson:** English navigator in the service of Holland. Discovered the North American bay, river and strait which bear his name. In 1607 and 1608 he conducted two voyages in search of a Northeast Passage to Asia. In 1609 he explored the Northeast coast of America, sailing up the Hudson River to the site of Albany. His final voyage was in 1610, when he attempted to winter in Hudson Bay. His crew mutinied and set him and a few others adrift, never to be seen again.

You cannot fly like an eagle with the wings of a wren.

1725 **Guillaume Le Gentil:** French astronomer. First to catalogue the dark nebula sometimes known as Le Gentil 3 in the constellation Cygnus. Remembered for his unfortunate experience when trying to observe the transit of Venus in 1761 at Pondicherry, a French colony in India. After much difficulty due to a war between France and Britain, he arrived at Pondicherry, built a small observatory and waited. Although the entire month had been beautifully sunny, on the fateful day it was cloudy and he saw nothing, almost driving him crazy.

That is the fate which often attends astronomers ... exiling myself from my motherland, only to be the spectator of a fatal cloud, which arrived in front of the Sun at the precise moment of my observation, snatching from me the fruit of my efforts and exertions.

1829 **Charles Dudley Warner:** American essayist, editor and novelist. Editor of the *Hartford Evening Press* (1861–67) and co-editor of the *Hartford Courant* (1867–1900). Collaborated with Mark Twain on the novel *The Gilded Age*. Editor of the multi-volume *Library of the World's Best Literature*. Also the author of essays including "My Summer in a Garden," "My Winter on the Nile," and "A Little Journey in the World."

It is fortunate that each generation does not comprehend its own ignorance. We are thus enabled to call our ancestors barbarous.

1880 **H.L. Mencken:** American newspaperman, editor and critic with the *Baltimore Sun* (1908–56). Literary editor of the *Smart Set*. Editor (1914–23). With George Jean Nathan founded the iconoclastic *The American Mercury* magazine (1924). Author of *The American Language* (1919, with supplements, 1945 and 48), *A Book of Prefaces, Treatise on Right and Wrong* and *A Mencken Chrestomathy*. A bad-tempered, crude and intolerant writer, famous for his biting wit: "A cynic is a man who, when he smells flowers, looks around for a coffin," "Love is the delusion that one woman differs from another," "Faith may be defined briefly as an illogical belief in the occurrences of the improbable" and:

Injustice is relatively easy to bear; what stings is justice.

1888 **Maurice Chevalier:** French singer and musical comedy star. Trademarks consisted of a jutting lower lip, a straw hat and a bow tie. Identified with him is the song, "Louise," introduced in his first American film, *Innocents of Paris*. Discovered by and had an affair with the legendary Mistinguette in 1909. Films in the U.S. include *The Love Parade*, *Love in the Afternoon* and *Gigi*. Even in old age he usually played a charming rogue who couldn't resist women who couldn't resist him. Spent World War II in France and was suspected of Nazi collaboration, but was vindicated.

Many a man has fallen in love with a girl in a light so dim he would not have chosen a suit by it.

1891 Don **Pedro Albizu Campos:** Advocate for Puerto Rican independence. Called "El Maestro" by his followers. Under his direction, the Nationalist Party of Puerto Rico became a major force in the fight for independence. Urged the Puerto Rican people to reclaim their cultural history and national symbols such as the flag and the national anthem. In and out of U.S. prisons, spending some 25 years locked away from the mid 1930s until the early sixties. Never accepting the U.S. rights to govern Puerto Rico, and citing the legal precedent of the Boston Tea Party, he said:

If they won't listen to legal reason, then we must take up arms against the invaders.

1891 **Arthur Hays Sulzberger:** American journalist. Publisher of the *New York Times*, the long–called "good gray" newspaper, whose motto is "all the news that's fit to print." Married Iphigene Ochs, daughter of publisher of the *Times*, Adolph Ochs in 1917 while he was a World War I Army officer. Returning to civilian life, he went to work for the *Times*. Within two years he was vice-president and assistant to the publisher.

Freedom of the press, or, to be more precise, the benefit of freedom of the press, belongs to everyone — to the citizens as well as the publisher... The crux is not the publisher's "freedom to print"; it is, rather, the citizen's right to know.

1892 **Alfred A. Knopf:** American publisher. With his wife Blanche Wolf Knopf founded Alfred A. Knopf, Inc., Publishers (1915). Published the best-selling *Green Mansions* by W.H. Hudson. Knopf introduced the American reading public to Thomas Mann, Theodore Dreiser, Willa Cather, H.L. Mencken, T.S. Eliot, Clarence Day and D.H. Lawrence.

The writer who can't do his job looks to his editor to do it for him, though he won't dream of sharing his royalties with that editor.

1913 **Jesse Owens:** Born **James Cleveland Owens**. African-American athlete. One of the world's top track performers of all times. Won four gold medals for the 100 meter, 200 meter, 4 by 100 relay and the long jump at the Berlin Olympics in 1936. His victories were a source of embarrassment to exponents of "Aryan supremacy" and Hitler snubbed him because of his race.

I wasn't invited to shake hands with Hitler, but I wasn't invited to the White House to shake hands with the President either.

1917 **Han Suyin:** Pen name of **Elizabeth Comber**, born **Rosalie Elizabeth Kuanghu Chow**. Chinese-born Eurasian physician and novelist. Wrote several books on modern China, novels set in East Asia and autobiographical works. Cultural and political conflicts between East and West in modern history play a central role in her works. Her most famous novel, *A Many-Splendoured Thing*, about a Eurasian physician in Hong Kong who falls in love with a married Caucasian news correspondent.

There is nothing stronger in the world than gentleness.

1921 **Stanisław Lem:** Polish writer of science fiction and theoretical criticism. Trained as a physician, at one time he was Poland's best-selling and most widely translated author. Much of his work is touched by black humor and a sense of the grotesque. Works: *The Star Diaries, The Invincible*, and A *Perfect Vacuum*.

A man who for an entire week does nothing but hit himself over the head has little reason to be proud.

1940 **Mickey Lolich:** American major league left-handed pitcher who played almost his entire career with the Detroit Tigers. Nicknamed "Lo Lo," the master of the now lost art of completing games, finishing 29 games which he started in 1968. Most remembered for his work in the 1968 World Series, when he won three complete games as the Tigers defeated the St. Louis Cardinals.

All the fat guys watch me and say to their wives, "See, there's a fat guy doing okay. Bring me another beer."

OTHERS: 1494 French king **Francis I**, 1605 English antiquarian **William Dugdale**, 1688 Czech sculptor **Ferdinand Brokoff**, 1690 Belgian theologian **Peter Dens**, 1788 U.S. religious leader **Alexander Campbell**, 1812 U.S. industrialist **Richard Hoe**, 1818 U.S. weapons inventor of first machine gun **Richard Gatling**, 1852 English Liberal politician/Prime Minister **Herbert Asquith**, 1897 French physicist **Irene Joliot-Curie**, 1902 U.S. actress, "Wicked Witch of the West" **Margaret Hamilton**, 1907 Irish poet **Louis MacNeice**, 1914 British actor 007's *Q* **Desmond Llewelyn**, 1916 U.S. race car driver **Tony Bettenhausen**, 1931 U.S. country singer **George Jones**, 1944 Native American activist **Leonard Peltier**, 1980 Chinese basketball player **Yao Ming**, 1986 U.S. singer **Emmy Rossum**

September 13

1506 **John Leland:** English antiquarian, authorized by King Henry VIII to have access to the libraries of Cathedrals, Abbeys, Priories and any other places where records and ancient writings were stored. He collected and transcribed many documents that almost certainly would have been lost. In order to complete his task, he traveled widely through England and Wales. He described his work:

I trust so to open this window, that the light shall be seen, so long, that is to say, by the space of a whole thousand years stopped up, and the old glory of your renowned Britain.

1819 **Clara Wieck Schumann:** Brilliant German pianist. married composer Robert Schumann. After his death she toured widely as a pianist, often playing her husband's compositions. As a teacher of piano at the Hoch Conservatorium at Frankfurt am Main (1878–92), she contributed greatly to the improvement of modern piano playing technique. As a composer, she wrote a piano concerto and "Drei Romanzen" for violin and piano.

Composing gives me great pleasure ... there is nothing that surpasses the joy of creation, if only because through it one wins hours of self-forgetfulness, when one lives in the world of sound.

1830 **Marie Ebner-Eschenbach:** Born **Countess Dubsky** in Moravia. Austrian novelist. Known for sensitive portrayals of life in Austrian villages and castles. The plots of her stories were often based on her memories of her youth and the legends and folklore that she learned from a nursemaid. Her masterpiece is *The Child of the Parent.* In 1900 she was awarded an honorary doctorate from the University of Vienna, the first received by a woman.

Those who understand only what can be explained understand very little.

1857 **Milton S. Hershey:** American businessman. After visiting the Columbian Exposition of 1895, bought chocolate manufacturing equipment and 40,000 acres of undeveloped land north of Lancaster. Founded his chocolate empire, the Hershey Chocolate

Company and the "company town" of Hershey, Pennsylvania. Largest milk chocolate maker in the world. Unable to have children, Hershey and his wife opened the Hershey Industrial School in 1909. Nine years later he transferred the majority of his assets, including his control of the chocolate company, to the formation of the Hershey Trust Fund for philanthropic ventures, which is now worth billions.

Caramels are only a fad. Chocolate is a permanent thing.

1860 **John J. Pershing:** "Black Jack." American general. Led campaign against Pancho Villa in Mexico. Head of the United States Expeditionary Force in Europe during World War I. Congress created a new rank for him — General of the Armies of the United States. He had to form and train an army that grew in a year and a half to nearly 3 million men. Pulitzer Prize winner (1932) for *My Experiences in the World War*. Allegedly pronounced at the grave of the Marquis de Lafayette, "Lafayette, we are here," although it may have been uttered by Charles E. Stanton.

A competent leader can get efficient service from poor troops, while on the contrary an incapable leader can demoralize the best of troops.

1874 **Arnold Schoenberg:** Austrian-born American composer and music theorist. Had a revolutionary influence on modern music through his use of the twelve-tone scale and development of the concepts of atonality and serialism. Abolished the distinction between consonance and dissonance in his *Three Piano Pieces* (1900). As a Jewish professor of music at the Universities of Vienna and Berlin, he and his music were denounced. Emigrated to the U.S.A. in 1933 and became a citizen in 1941.

In music there is no form without logic, there is no logic without unity.

1876 **Sherwood Anderson:** American short-story writer, novelist, poet and journalist. First Major work: *Winesburg, Ohio*, a collection of short stories about small-town life. Other works: *Dark Laughter*, *Beyond Desire* and *Death in the Woods*.

Everyone in the world is Christ and they are all crucified.

1894 **J.B. Priestley:** English novelist, dramatist and essayist. Noted for distorting the past, present and future in works such as the picturesque novel *The Good Companions*, *Dangerous Corner* and *When We Are Married*. Plays include *Time and the Conways* and *An Inspector Calls*. During and after World War II he was a popular radio broadcaster on current affairs.

I know only two word of American slang, "swell" and "lousy." I think "swell" is lousy, but "lousy" is swell.

1905 **Claudette Colbert:** Originally **Claudette Chauchoin**. Urbane French-born U.S. actress. Her first films accented sex, as in *Sign of the Cross* and *Cleopatra*. Was at her best in sophisticated comedies such as *Midnight* and *The Palm Beach Story*. Oscar winner for *It Happened One Night*. Nominated for *Private Worlds* and *Since You Went Away*. Never allowed the right side of her face to be photographed.

It matters more what's in a woman's face than what's on it.

1911 **Bill Monroe:** Born **William Smith Monroe**. American country and western musician. "Father of Modern Bluegrass Music." By the age of 18 he was an accomplished musician and to make ends meet during the Great Depression he and two of his brothers played at local dances and parties. In 1945 he formed his classic bluegrass group, whose performers included Lester Flatt and Earl Scruggs. His song "Blue Moon of Kentucky" became a country classic.

Country music belongs to America.

1916 **Roald Dahl:** Welsh writer. Wrote *Charlie and the Chocolate Factory* that has twice been adapted for film, the first starring Gene Wilder as Willy Wonka and the second, Johnny Depp. Also wrote *James and the Giant Peach* and the screenplay for the film *Chitty-Chitty-Bang-Bang*. Married to actress Patricia Neal until their divorce in 1983.

A little nonsense now and then is relished by the wisest men.

1925 **Mel Tormé:** American singer and author. Dubbed "The Velvet Fog" by his publicist to describe his smooth style, a name he hated. Formed the Mel-Tones, which had several hits, the biggest being "What Is This Thing Called Love?" Became a solo artist in 1947 and had one #1 hit, "Careless Love." Composed the very popular standard "The Christmas Song," which was a big hit for Nat King Cole. In the early 1980s, he collaborated with pianist George Shearing on several excellent albums.

To me, nostalgia is nothing more than a mindless plundering of the past for the commonplace.

1938 **Judith Martin:** Etiquette expert, columnist and author. Her amusing advice appears under the name *Miss Manners*. Column appears in more than 300 newspapers. Prior to her big success, she was a copy girl in the women's section of the *Washington Post*. Most of her time there was spent in answering etiquette questions, which gave her an idea for a new career, started in 1978.

Chaperons don't enforce morality; they force immorality to be discreet.

OTHERS: 1087 Byzantine Emperor **John II Comnenus**, 1520 English statesman **William Cecil**, 1739 Russian statesman **Grigori Potemkin**, 1802 German philosopher **Arnold Ruge**, 1851 U.S. bacteriologist tracked the carrier of yellow fever **Walter Reed**, 1857 Polish rebel **Michal Drzymala**, 1855 U.S. psychiatrist/neurologist **Adolf Meyer**, 1873 Greek mathematician **Constantin Carathéodory**, 1894 Polish poet **Julian Tuwin**, 1918 Argentine singer **Dick Haymes**, 1923 French photographer **Édouard Boubat**, 1924 French composer **Maurice Jarre**, 1937 U.S. animator **Don Bluth**, 1940 Puerto Rican politician **Óscar Arias**, 1950 U.S. actress **Nell Carter**, 1961 U.S. guitarist **Dave Mustaine**, 1977 U.S. singer **Fiona Apple**

September 14

1486 **Heinrich Cornelius Agrippa von Nettesheim:** German astrologer and alchemist. Extensively read Kabbalistic and Hermetic literature. Most influential writer of Renaissance esoterica. Besides his fascination with alchemy and magic, he was knowledgeable in law, theology, medicine and philosophy. His most famous work is *Of Occult Philosophy or Magic*, which appeared in three books: *Natural Magic*, *Celestial Magic* and *Ceremonial Magic*.

Magic is a faculty of wonderful virtue, full of most high mysteries, containing the most profound contemplation of most secret things, together with the nature, power, quality, substance and virtues thereof, as also the knowledge of whole Nature, and it doth instruct us concerning the differing agreement of things amongst themselves, whence it produceth its wonderful effects, by uniting the virtues of things through the application of them one to another.

1769 Baron **Friedrich Heinrich Alexander von Humboldt:** German naturalist and explorer. Traveled throughout Europe, the Americas and Russian Asia collecting plants, studying rivers and ocean currents. Made the first isothermic and isobaric maps. The crowning task of his life, accomplished in his seventy-sixth year was his five-volume work *Kosmos*; in which he attempted to unify the various branches involved in the knowledge of the world.

People often say that I'm curious about too many things at once... But can you really forbid a man from harboring a desire to know and embrace everything that surrounds him?

1849 **Ivan Pavlov:** Russian physiologist. Researched blood circulation and conditioned reflects. His study with dogs is known to every student in a general psychology course. Showed by experiment with dogs how the secretion of saliva can be stimulated not only by food but also by the sound of a bell associated with the presentation of food, and that this sound can elicit salivation even when food is not present. Nobel Prize (1904) for his work on digestion.

While you are experimenting, do not remain content with the surface of things. Don't become a mere recorder of facts, but try to penetrate the mystery of their origin.

1857 **Alice Stone Blackwell:** American suffragist. Blackwell led the movement to reconcile the two competing factions of the women's suffrage movement, merging them into the National American Woman Suffrage Movement. Editor-in-chief of the *Woman's Journal*. Launched America's first international human rights movement by founding a society known as "Friends of Armenia."

Justice is better than chivalry if we cannot have both.

1864 Lord **Robert Cecil:** Viscount of Chelwood. English conservative statesman and author. One of the leading architects of the League of Nations. President of the League of Nations Union (1923–45). Awarded Nobel Peace Prize (1937). Wrote books on commercial law, the church and peace.

Example is more forcible that precept. People look at my six days in the week to see what I mean on the seventh.

1883 **Margaret Higgins Sanger:** American founder of the birth control movement in the U.S. Her experiences as a nurse led her to distribute the pamphlet *Family Limitations* in defense of birth control. Legal proceedings were initiated against her for disseminating "obscene" literature, but were dropped. Founded the National Birth Control League (1914), serving as its first president and later became president of the International Planned Parenthood Foundation.

A free race cannot be born to slave mothers. A woman cannot choose but give a measure of that bondage to her sons and daughters.

1886 **Jan Masaryk:** Czech foreign minister and diplomat. Son of Tomáš Masaryk, a founder of modern Czechoslovakia during World War I. Jan helped establish the Czech Republic. Ambassador to Great Britain (1925–38). Resigned in protest at the betrayal of his country by the Munich pact, in which without any Czech representations, Britain and France agreed to Hitler's demand to annex the part of Czechoslovakia known as the Bohemian Sudetenland. As part of the agreement Poland and Hungry occupied Moravia, Slovakia, and Ruthenia. After the war, became foreign minister, but shortly after the communist coup in Czechoslovakia in February 1948, he either committed suicide or was murdered.

If you have sacrificed my nation to preserve the peace of the world, I will be the first to applaud you. But if not, gentlemen, God help your souls.

1916 **Eric Bentley:** English-born American critic, editor and translator. Written many plays and books, including *A Century of Hero Worship*, *The Playwright As a Thinker*, *What Is Theatre?*, *The Life of the Drama* and *Are You Now or Have You Ever Been*. Has a preference for what he calls the "heroic failure," drama that is more personal than marketable. Argued that William Shakespeare and George Bernard Shaw were popular despite their greatness not because of it. Drama critic for the *New Republic* (1952–56).

Ours is the age of substitutes: instead of language, we have jargon; instead of principles, slogans; and, instead of genuine ideas, bright ideas.

1917 **Sydney J. Harris:** English-born American author and journalist. With the *Chicago Daily News*, from 1941 to 1986. Wrote syndicated column, "Strictly Personal" (1944–86). Author of *A Majority of One*, *Last Things First* and *Pieces of Eight*. Many years a member of the Usage Panel of the *American Heritage Dictionary*.

The whole purpose of education is to turn mirrors into windows.

1920 **Lawrence R. Klein:** American economist. For creating computer models to forecast economic trends in the field of econometrics, awarded the Bank of Sweden Prize in Economic Sciences in Memory of Alfred Nobel (1980). Member of the American Communist Party while working at the Cowles Commission for Research in Economics, where he built his model of the U.S. economy. He ran afoul of Senator Joseph McCarthy's "witch-hunt." Denied tenure at the University of Michigan, where he developed with Arthur Goldberger, the so-called Klein-Goldberger macroeconomic model. Moved to Great Britain until the communism hysteria died down.

An early fascination with higher mathematics at the university level blossomed into speculative thinking that could provide a basis for dealing with economic issues.

1934 **Kate Millet:** American writer, critic, sculptor, philosopher and feminist. Involved in the civil-rights movement of the 1960s. Champions women's issues groups. Member of CORE since 1965. Published the influential *Sexual Politics* in 1870, which advocates radical feminism. Also wrote *Going to Iran*, about her experiences in and her expulsion from Iran in 1979 during her campaign for women's rights in that country.

Aren't women prudes if they don't and prostitutes if they do?

1946 **Oliver Stone:** American film director, screenwriter and producer. His adaptation of Billy Hayes' novel *Midnight Express* earned him his first Oscar. Known for political films about recent American history such as *JFK* and *Nixon*. Drawing on his personal experiences during the Vietnam War, *Platoon* and *Born on the Fourth of July* earned him two additional director Academy Awards. Other movies: *Wall Street* and *Natural Born Killers*.

I've been to war, and it's not easy to kill. It's bloody and messy and totally horrifying, and the consequences are serious.

OTHERS: 1388 Danish geographer **Claudius Swart**, 1656 British antiquarian **Thomas Baker**, 1735 English social reformer **Robert Raikes**, 1737 Austrian composer **Michael Haydn**, 1804 British ornithologist **John Gould**, 1867 U.S. artist/illustrator **Charles Dana Gibson**, 1887 U.S. boxing champ **Stanley Ketchel**, 1899 U.S. movie producer **Hal Wallis,** 1908 U.S. actor "The Lone Ranger" **Clayton Moore**, 1913 Guatemalan President **Jacobo Arbenz**, 1920 Uruguayan writer **Mario Benedetti**, 1928 U.S. labor leader **Albert Shanker**, 1936 U.S. physician **Ferid Murad**, 1938 "Star Trek "actor **Walter Koenig**, 1940 U.S. basketball coach **Larry Brown**, 1942 U.S. Secretary of Navy **John Lehman**, 1944 U.S. actress **Joey Heatherton**, 1973 U.S. rapper **Nas**

September 15

1254 **Marco Polo:** Venetian merchant and traveler, who joined his father and uncle on a journey from Europe to Asia beginning in 1271, traveling along the "silk road" arriving at the court of Kublai Khan around 1274. The Polos remained in China for 17 years. The Mongol emperor sent Marco to several fact-finding missions to distant lands. The Polos returned to Vienna in 1295 by sailing from China to Persia and then overland to Turkey. Marco's tale of his travels, *Il Milione*, was an immediate success, although it has been suspected to be more fiction than fact.

I have not told half of what I saw.

1613 **François de la Rochefoucauld:** French moralist and classical writer. Devoted to the Queen, Marie de' Medici, his adventures in political intrigues and a series of love affairs led to him being forced into exile. Author of five editions of *Réflexions ou sentences et maximes morales*, pessimistic epigrams which owed their origin to his belief that human behavior is based on self-love. When his *Mémoirs* gave wide offence, he denied he had written it.

No persons are more frequently wrong, than those who will not admit they are wrong.

1789 **James Fenimore Cooper:** First American novelist to achieve worldwide fame. Best known for "The Leatherstocking Tales, "the adventure stories featuring frontiersman Natty Bumpo, a natural man uncorrupted by civilization. Novels: *The Last of the Mohicans*, *The Pathfinder* and *The Deerslayer*. Cooperstown, New York, besides being the location of Baseball's Hall of Fame, boasts a Cooper shrine, preserving scenes, names and traditions associated with him and his characters.

Everybody says it, and what everybody says must be true.

1857 **William Howard Taft:** American politician, 27th U.S. President (1909–13) and Chief Justice of the Supreme Court (1921–30). Appointed head of the commission to set up a civilian government in the Philippines and was the island nation's first civilian governor. Served as U.S. Secretary of War under President Theodore Roosevelt, who supported Taft's presidential victory in 1908. However by 1912, a rift in the Republican Party pitted Taft against Roosevelt running on the Bull Moose Party ticket, giving the election to Democrat Woodrow Wilson.

Don't write so you can be understood; write so that you can't be misunderstood.

1876 **Bruno Walter:** Originally **Bruno Walter Schlesinger**. German-born American conductor. Achieved the reputation as the perfect classicist among contemporary conductors. Foremost conductor of Mahler's symphonies. After moving to the U.S.A. in 1939, he often conducted the New York Philharmonic, the Metropolitan Opera and the Los Angeles Philharmonic.

Music springs from and is replenished by a hidden source which lies outside the world of reality. Music ever spoke to me of a mysterious world beyond, which moved my heart deeply and eloquently intimated its transcendental nature.

1889 **Robert Benchley:** American humorist, actor and drama critic. Noted for his sharp, but not cruel satirical remarks. His classic comedy monologue *The Treasurer's Report* launched his comedy career. Made more than 40 movie shorts including *How to Sleep*, which won an Academy Award. Wrote drama criticism for the *New Yorker*, for which he also wrote the column, "The Wayward Press," using the pseudonym Guy Fawkes.

A dog teaches a boy fidelity, perseverance, and to turn around three times before sitting down.

1890 Dame **Agatha Christie:** English novelist and playwright. Mystery writer of some 75 novels, who has sold more than 100 million copies featuring Belgian detective Hercule Poirot, introduced in her first novel, *The Mysterious Affair at Styles*, and eccentric amateur detective, the spinster Miss Marple, who began her snooping in *Murder at the Vicarage*. Author of novels *Death on the Nile* and *And Then There Were None*. Plays: *The Mousetrap*, which set a record for the longest continuous run, and *Witness for the Prosecution*.

One doesn't recognize the really important moments in one' life until it's too late.

1894 **Jean Renoir:** French motion picture director. Son of painter Pierre Auguste Renoir. Discovered a passion for the cinema while recovering from wounds he suffered during World War I. His films showed a deep appreciation of the unpredictability of human character. Among his most famous films are the moving antiwar *Grand Illusion*, *The Rules of the Game*, *The Diary of a Chambermaid* and *The River*.

A director makes only one movie in his life. Then he breaks it into pieces and makes it again.

1903 **Roy Acuff:** American country-western musician. Singer, songwriter and fiddler, dubbed the "King of Country Music." Gained immediate popularity with "The Great Speckled Bird" and "The Wabash Cannonball." National radio star on the Grand Ole Opry. With Fred Rose, he founded Acuff-Rose Publishing Co. in 1942, the first publishing house exclusively for country music. Elected the first living member of the Country Music Hall of Fame in 1962.

Don't be a blueprint. Be an original.

1904 **Sheilah Graham:** Originally **Lily Sheil**. London-born American columnist. Reported on Hollywood film town happenings in a syndicated column that appeared in 125 newspapers. Best remembered as the mistress of F. Scott Fitzgerald, who she helped regain his health and stature as a writer. With writer Gerald Frank, she wrote *Beloved Infidel*, the story of their four-year romance.

No one has a closet friend in Hollywood.

1914 **Creighton Abrams:** American general. Trained at West Point. Commanded a tank battalion during World War II. Broke through German lines to relieve U.S. troops at Bastogne in 1944. Served in the Korean War (1950–53). Commanded U.S. forces in Vietnam (1968–72) and supervised the gradual withdrawal of American troops. Chief of Staff, U.S. Army, 1972–74.

When eating an elephant take one bite at a time.

1945 **Jessye Norman:** Exceptionally gifted African-American soprano. Has imposing stage presence. Won the Munich International Music Competition in 1968. Made her operatic debut as Elizabeth in *Tannhaüser*, in 1969. Met debut as Cassandra in 1983. Repertory includes classical German pieces and French moderns. Considered by many as the greatest soprano of her generation.

I am grateful that my horizons were not narrowed at the outset.

OTHERS: 53 CE Roman emperor **Trajan**, 973 Central Asian mathematician/astronomer **al-Biruni**, 1830 Mexican President **Porfirio Diaz**, 1881 Italian automobile designer **Ettore Bugatti**, 1890 Swiss composer **Frank Martin**, 1894 Swedish physicist **Oskar Klein**, 1904 Italian king **Umberto II**, 1907 U.S. scream queen actress **Fay Wray**, 1913 U.S. Attorney General **John N. Mitchell**, 1914 Argentine writer **Adolfo Bioy Casares**, 1924 U.S. musician/pianist **Bobby Short**, 1926 French mathematician **Jean-Pierre Serre**, 1928 U.S. comedian **Norm Crosby**, 1929 U.S. physicist **Murray Gell-Mann**, 1938 U.S. baseball pitcher **Gaylord Perry**, 1961 U.S. football quarterback **Dan Marino**

September 16

1098 **Hildegard of Bingen:** German abbess, mystic writer and composer. When she told her confessor of visionary experiences, she was encouraged by the abbot of the monastery of St. Disibod and the local archbishop to begin the ten-year task of writing what would become *Scivias*, a report of 25 visions that summed up Christian doctrine on the history of salvation. Wrote many hymns and began her second visionary work, *Book of Life's Merits*, on moral instruction. Last major work was *Book of the Divine Work*, on the relationship of humans to God and to each other.

Man contains the entire creation within himself, and the breath of life that never dies is within him.

1678 **Henry St. John, 1st Viscount Bolingbroke:** English statesman, orator and man of letters. Leader of Tory party during reign of Queen Anne. Responsible for negotiating the Peace of Utrecht in 1713. Discharged by King George I and impeached by the Whig Parliament of 1715, he fled to France to briefly support the pretender to the British throne James Edward Stuart. Major works: *Dissertation Upon Parties* and *Letters on the Study of History*.

Wise men spend their time in mirth; it is only fools who are serious.

1875 **James Cash Penney:** American businessman and entrepreneur. Founder and board chairman of the J.C. Penney Company, which once operated more than 1700 department stores nationally. He lost a fortune in 1929, but bounced back. Relinquished daily management operation in 1917 to Earl Corder Sams, but remained chairman of the board until 1946, and then honorary chairman until his death in 1971.

Give me a stock clerk with a goal and I'll give you a man who will make history. Give me a man with no goals and I'll give you a stock clerk.

1883 **Thomas Ernest Hulme:** English critic and philosopher. Noted for *Speculations* (1924) and *Language and Style* (1929). Killed in World War I, but T.S. Eliot and Ezra Pound popularize his ideas. Distinguished classicism and "realistic" from humanism and romanticism. Claimed that humanism erroneously described man as "naturally" good and capable of perfection, whereas classicism truthfully depicted man as intrinsically bad or limited. Asserted that this could be overcome by order and tradition to "something fairly decent."

Language is by its very nature a communal thing; that is, it expresses never the exact thing but a compromise — that which is common to you, me and everybody.

1885 **Karen Horney:** German-born American psychoanalyst and psychiatrist. Outgrew Freud's concepts, adopting principles similar to those of Adler. In the 1920s she began publishing papers that took issue with orthodox Freudianism. Best know for exposing the male chauvinist bias in Freudian analysis of women. Author of *Our Inner Conflicts* and *Neuroses and Human Growth*.

Like all sciences and all valuations, the psychology of women has hitherto been considered only from the point of view of men.

1887 **Nadia Juliette Boulanger:** French composer, conductor and outstanding teacher of musical composition. Studied at the Conservatorie (1897–1904), where she won several prizes. Went on to write many vocal and instrumental works. Later devoted herself to teaching at the Conservatorie and the École Normale de Musique, where she had international influence.

Do not take up music unless you would rather die than not do so.

1887 **Louise Arner Boyd:** American explorer of the Arctic and socialite, who financed an expedition to find the explorer Roald Amundsen, who had disappeared in 1928. She traveled almost 10,000 miles across the Arctic Ocean, but found no trace of the Norwegian. Best known for leading a series of scientific expeditions to the coasts of Greenland during the 1930s. At age of sixty-eight, she became the first woman to fly over the North Pole, photographing the area.

It is perhaps worth warning prospective photographers of the menace of lone musk ox bulls in certain localities ... charging in a series of full-speed rushes.

1893 **Albert Szent-Györgyi:** Hungarian-born American biochemist. Discovered actin, which is responsible for muscle contraction. Emigrated to the U.S. where he became director of the Institute of Muscle Research at Woods Hole, Massachusetts (1947–75). First to isolate vitamin C. Awarded Nobel prize in physiology (1937).

A discovery is said to be an accident meeting a prepared mind.

1893 Sir **Alexander Korda:** Originally **Sándor Lázló Kellner**. Hungarian-born English film director and producer. Began his career as a journalist before producing films, first in Budapest, then Vienna, Berlin and Hollywood, before moving the U.K. in 1932. Major figure in British filmmaking. Founded London Film Productions. Films include: *The Private Life of Henry VIII, Rembrandt, The Four Feathers, The Scarlet Pimpernel, The Thief of Bagdad, The Third Man* and *Richard III.*

It's not enough to be Hungarian; you must have talent too.

1924 **Lauren Bacall:** Born **Betty Perske**. Sultry-eyed, husky-voiced American model and actress. Dubbed "The Look" after the former model costarred with Humphrey Bogart in the film *To Have and Have Not.* Married Bogart and later Jason Robards, Jr. Other films include: *The Big Sleep, Key Largo* and *How to Marry a Millionaire*. Also appeared in a number of Broadway plays and musicals, winning a Tony Award for *Applause*.

Imagination is the highest kite one can fly.

1925 **B.B. King:** Born **Riley B. King**. American singer and guitarist. Influenced early by gospel music. Known as the "Beale Street Blues Boy," later shortened to B.B. His first hit, "Three O'Clock Blues" was followed by a long succession of other rhythm and blues classics. By the late 1960s gained a white audience for his singing and the music he played on his guitar he calls "Lucille." Other hits: "Everyday I Have the Blues," "The Thrill and Gone," and probably his finest album, *Live at the Regal*, as well as Grammy Award–winning album *There Must Be a Better World Somewhere*.

Jazz is the big brother of the blues. If a guy's playing blues like we play, he's in high school. When he starts playing jazz it's like going on to college, to a school of higher learning.

1926 **Robert H. Schuller:** American clergyman and televangelist who invented the drive-in church. Bases his sermons on the positive aspects of Christianity, rather than preaching death and damnation for sinners. Preaches each Sunday to nearly 10,000 people, some sitting in pews, some in cars. His television program "The Hour of Power" has an audience of more than 3 million. Books: *To the Good Life, Self-Love* and *Don't Throw Away Tomorrow*.

What would you do if you knew you could not fail?

OTHERS: 1387 King of England **Henry V**, 1507 Emperor of China **Jiajing**, 1518 Venetian painter **Tintoretto**, 1797 Italian scholar **Antonio Panizzi**, 1823 U.S. historian **Francis Parkman**, 1827 French geologist **Jean Albert Gaudry**, 1853 German physician **Albrecht Kossel**, 1881 English art critic **Clive Bell**, 1858 British PM **A. Bonar Law**, 1886 Alsatian sculptor/painter **Jean Arp**, 1905 Czech poet **Vladimir Holan**, 1914 U.S. radio-TV personality **Allen Funt**, 1923 Singapore leader **Lee Kuan Yew**, 1925 U.S. musician **Charlie Byrd**, 1927 U.S. actor **Peter Falk**, 1934 U.S. basketball player **Elgin Baylor**, 1939 South African writer **Breyten Breytenbach**, 1956 U.S. illusionist **David Copperfield**

September 17

1580 **Francisco Gómez de Quevedo y Villegas:** Spanish satirist, moralist and poet. Remembered mostly for his vitriolic satires exposing the follies and vices of humankind. One of his satiric poems got him imprisoned in the monastery of San Marcos in Leon. When he was released four years later, his health was ruined. Best works: the picturesque novel *El Buscón* and the *Sueños*, a series of burlesque descriptions of hell.

In short, not only are things not what they seem, they are not even what they are called!

1643 **Gilbert Burnet:** Scottish theologian and historian. Took an active role in the political and religious controversies of the time. Lost favor at Court because of his criticisms of the policies of James II. Adviser to the Prince of Orange. After the Glorious Revolution he returned to England and appointed Bishop of Salisbury. Publications: *History of the Reformation of the Church of England*, *History of My Own Times* and *History of the Dukes of Hamilton*.

That is not the best sermon which makes the hearers go away talking to one another, and praising the speaker, but which makes them go away thoughtful and serious, and hastening to be alone.

1743 Marquis **Antoine Marie Jean de Condorcet:** French mathematician, statesman, revolutionary and philosopher. Leading thinker of the Enlightenment. Made contributions to the theory of probability. Devised a state education system. Elected to the National Convention as a Girondin, but was condemned by the Revolutionary Tribunal. While in hiding he wrote the famous *Sketch for a Historical Picture of the Progress of the Human Mind*. He was captured and took poison to avoid the guillotine.

All errors in government and in society are based on philosophical errors which, in turn, are derived from errors in natural science.

1883 **William Carlos Williams:** American poet, playwright, essayist and fiction writer. Trained as a pediatrician, he maintained a lifelong medical practice. Noted for making the ordinary appear extraordinary. Considered patron saint of American poets. Pulitzer Prize for *Pictures from Brueghel and Other Poems*. Most important prose works include: *In the American Grain* and *Make Light of It: Collected Stories*.

Poets are damned but they are not blind, they see with the eyes of the angels.

1907 **Warren E. Burger:** American jurist and lawyer. Active in the Republican Party. President Nixon appointed him Chief Justice of the Supreme Court (1969). Strict constructionist in criminal matters, contrary to expectations of some, did not try to reverse the tide of activist decisions on civil rights issues and criminal law made during the tenure of he predecessor, Earl Warren. Burger voted with the majority in Roe vs. Wade, which established a woman's right to have an abortion without restrictive interference from the government.

Judges rule on the basis of law, not public opinion, and they should be totally indifferent to pressures of the times.

1916 Lady **Mary Florence Stewart:** English author of romances of the natural and supernatural. Interest in myth led her to produce her main work, a trilogy about King Arthur and Merlin: *The Crystal Cage*, *The Hollow Hills* and *The Last Enchantment*. Also wrote *Madam, Will You Talk*, *Nine Coaches Waiting* and *This Rough Magic*.

It is harder to kill a whisper than even a shouted calumny.

1918 **Chaim Herzog:** Born in Belfast, Northern Ireland. Emigrated to Palestine in 1935. Joined the British army and by the end of World War II was the head of British intelligence in northern Germany. Returned to Palestine and headed the Israel Defense Forces Military Intelligence Branch for a number of years. Israel's Ambassador to the U.N. and sixth President of Israel, serving two five-year terms. Publications: *War of Atonement: The Inside Story of the Yom Kippur War* and *The Arab-Israeli Wars*.

I do not bring forgiveness with me, nor forgetfulness. The only ones who can forgive are dead; the living have no right to forget.

1923 **Hank Williams:** American singer, guitarist and songwriter. Most famous songs: "Lonesome Blues," "My Bucket's Got a Hole in It," "Cold, Cold Heart," "Jambalaya," "Hey, Good Lookin'" and "Your Cheatin' Heart." Gained international fame as a performer of both country and western, and popular music. Died of a drug and alcohol abuse.

Hear that lonesome whippoorwill? He sounds too blue to fly. The midnight train is whining low, I'm so lonesome I could cry.

1935 **Ken Kesey:** American author. Associated with the "Beat" movement. Ward attendant in a mental hospital and used the experience to write his most famous work, *One Flew Over the Cuckoo Nest*, which is a grim satire set in a mental hospital and draws distinctions between sanity and insanity, as well as questions of freedom and responsibility. *Sometimes a Great Notion* is a complex narrative saga of conflicts and loyalties in an Oregon logging family.

To hell with facts! We need stories!

1939 **David Souter:** American jurist. In 1990, President George W.H. Bush appointed him to the First U.S. Circuit Court and later that year to the U.S. Supreme Court. Conservative in his early decisions, he has since moved toward the center on most issues.

It is impossible, maybe undesirable, to take partisanship out of the political process.

1945 **Phil Jackson:** "The Zen Master." American basketball player and coach. Played basketball at the University of Dakota, Valuable reserve and fan favorite for the New York Knicks, winning his first NBA title ring in 1973. As head coach of the Chicago Bulls (1989–98), acquired six additional championship rings. Won three more with the Los Angeles Lakers. Known for his triangle offense ball playing scheme developed by Tex Winter. Takes a holistic approach to coaching his players, influenced by Eastern philosophy.

Always keep an open mind and a compassionate heart.

1955 **Rita Rudner:** American writer and comedian. Delivers comical monologues with a soft-spoken voice. Noted for her "niceness" and her lethal but non-aggressive wit. With her husband Martin Bergman, wrote the screenplay for the film *Peter's Friends*, in which she also appeared. Books: *Naked Beneath My Clothes* and *Tickled Pink: A Comic Novel.*

Men reach their sexual peak at eighteen. Women reach theirs at thirty-five. Do you get the feeling that God is playing a practical joke?

OTHERS: 1639 Mennonite bishop **Hans Herr**, 1677 English physiologist **Stephen Hales**, 1730 Prussian army officer **Friedrich von Steuben**, 1820 French dramatist **Émile Augier**, 1826 German mathematician **Bernhard Riemann**, 1884 U.S. composer **Charles T. Griffes**, 1890 U.S. radio journalist **Gabriel Heatter**, 1900 U.S. hotelier **John W. Marriott**, 1904 U.S. comic actor **Jerry Colonna**, 1927 U.S. football quarterback/kicker **George Blanda**, 1927 Puerto Rican baseball player **Orlando Cepeda**, 1928 English actor **Roddy McDowall**, 1929 English race car driver **Stirling Moss**, 1931 U.S. actress **Anne Bancroft**, 1934 U.S. tennis player **Maureen Connolly**, 1948 U.S. actor **John Ritter**

September 18

1475 **Cesare Borgia:** Duke of Valentinois, illegitimate son of Pope Alexander VI and brother of Lucrezia Borgia. His father initially groomed Cesare for a Church career. Elevated to the rank of Cardinal at the age of 22. Appointed commander of the papal armies, briefly employing Leonardo da Vinci as military architect and engineer. When his father died, Cesare's political enemies, led by the new pope Julius II, had him imprisoned and exiled to Spain. Died at the siege of Viana in 1507, age thirty-one. Machiavelli's *The Prince* was at least partially based on Borgia's life and exploits.

When I lived, I provided for everything but death, now I must die, and am unprepared.

1709 **Samuel Johnson:** Celebrated English lexicographer, essayist, poet and moralist. "Hercules of Literature." Literary drudge "greater than anything he wrote" and "literary dictator" of his time. A circle of celebrities gathered around him known as the Literary Club, including James Boswell, his biographer. Works: *Dictionary of the English Language*, an edition of Shakespeare's works, 10-volume *Lives of the Poets, The Rambler* and *The Idler.*

Patriotism is the last refuge of the scoundrel.

1718 **Nikita Ivanovich Panin:** Russian statesman born in Gdańsk, Poland. Political mentor to Catherine the Great, whom he supported when she overthrew her husband, Tsar Peter III, and declared herself empress in 1762. Called Panin her encyclopedia, because of his great learning and accomplishments. He advocated the Northern Alliance, a combination of Russia, Prussia, Poland, and Sweden against the Bourbon-Habsburg League. Sought closer ties with Frederick the Great of Prussia. His opposition to the partition of Poland led Catherine to replace him with a more compliant minister.

Two men please God — who serves Him with all his heart because he knows Him; who seeks Him with all his heart because he knows Him not.

1750 **Tomas de Iriarte:** Spanish poet. Began his literary career at age 18 translating French plays for the royal theater of the king of Spain. In 1770 under the anagram of **Tirso Imarete**, published an original comedy, *Hacer que hacemos*. Most noted for the *Fábulas literarias* (1781), humorous attacks on literary men and their methods.

The foolish and vulgar are always accustomed to value equally the good and the bad.

1779 **Joseph Story:** U.S. jurist. Pioneer in founding and directing Harvard Law School. Associate justice of the Supreme Court (1811–45). Celebrated for his legal writings — among them the first patent act — which helped to form American legal thought.

Human wisdom is the aggregate of all human experience, constantly accumulating, selecting, and reorganizing its own materials.

1827 **John Townsend Trowbridge:** American poet, editor and author of books for boys. Pen name: Paul Creyton. Contributing and managing editor of *Our Young Folks* (1865–73). Wrote *Jack Hazard* and *Toby Trafford* series. Best known poem: "Darius Green and His Flying Machine."

The tears of the you who go their way, last a day;/ But the grief is long of the old who stay.

1895 **John G. Diefenbaker:** Canadian politician. Leader of Progressive Conservative Party. Prime minister (1957–63). Called his program "Canada First," pointing to what he believed had been Canada's unfavorable trade balance wit the U.S.A. Suffered political downfall over controversy of producing nuclear weapons.

Freedom is the right to be wrong, not the right to do wrong.

1905 **Agnes de Mille:** American dancer and choreographer. Niece of film director Cecil B. DeMille. Incorporated the first popularly-successful use of indigenous dance motifs into American theater. Choreographed ballet *Rodeo*, the first to include tap dancing. Choreographed films: *Carousel, Gentlemen Prefer Blondes* and *Oklahoma!* Tony Award winner (1947 and 1962). Autobiographies: *Dance to the Piper* and *And Promenade Home.*

The truest expression of a people is in its dances and its music. Bodies never lie.

1905 **Greta Garbo:** Born **Greta Lovisa Gustafsson**. Swedish-born actress. Discovered by film director Mauritz Stiller, who remained her trusted friend. Louis B. Mayer saw her first important film *The Saga of Gösta Berling* and in 1925 she arrived in Hollywood, unable to speak a word of English, with a contract with MGM. Her much publicized romance with screen matinee idol John Gilbert did not end in marriage as he would have liked. Twice nominated for Academy awards for *Anna Christie* and *Ninotchka*. The remarkable beauty retired from films at the age of 36 in 1939 to escape her blazing celebrity. Withdrew resolutely into the shadows of a personal privacy, leaving the world only Garbo the legend. Other films: *Flesh and the Devil, Mata Hari, Grand Hotel, Queen Christina, Anna Karenina* and *Camille*.

Life would be so wonderful if we only knew what to do with it.

1952 **Rick Pitino:** American basketball coach. Standout guard for the University of Massachusetts. The only coach in NCAA history to take three different teams to the Final Four: Providence (1987), Kentucky (1993, the national championship in 1996 and 1997), Louisville (2005). As successful as he has been at the collegiate level, his experiences as a coach with the NBA New York Knicks (1987–89) and Boston Celtics (1997–2001) proved to be extremely frustrating. Wrote a motivational self-help book *Success Is a Choice*.

Excellence is the unlimited ability to improve the quality of what you have to offer.

1961 **James Gandolfini:** American actor. Best known for his acclaimed performances in the role of Mafia boss Tony Soprano in HBO's series *The Sopranos*. Tony is a troubled family man, but also a vicious killer when his business calls for eliminating someone. Gandolfini won three Emmys for Best Actor in a Drama. Film appearances: *All the King's Men, The Mexican* and *Get Shorty*.

I'm an actor ... I do a job and I go home. Why are you interested in me? You don't ask a truck driver about his job.

1971 **Lance Armstrong:** American road racing cyclist. Famous for winning the Tour de France a record seven consecutive years (1999–2005). Few years earlier he had overcome surgery and extensive chemotherapy to treat testicular cancer that had metastasized to his brain and lungs. Named *Sports Illustrated* magazine's Sportsman of the Year in 2002. In many parts of Europe, he is suspected of taking performance-enhancing drugs, but no hard evidence to substantiate these claims has been produced.

Pain is temporary. It may last a minute, or an hour, or a day, or a year, but eventually it will subside and something else will take its place. If I quit, however, it lasts forever.

OTHERS: 1684 German composer **Johann Walther**, 1752 French mathematician **Adrien-Marie Legendre**, 1812 U.S. politician **Herschel V. Johnson**, 1819 French physicist **Leon Foucault**, 1838 Dutch artist **Anton Mauve**, 1863 Swiss theologian **Hermann Kutter**, 1870 U.S. anthropologist **Clark Wissler**, 1889 Australian politician **Doris Blackburn**, 1905 African-American actor **Eddie "Rochester" Anderson**, 1916 Italian actor **Rossano Brazzi**, 1923 British architect **Peter Smithson**, 1925 U.S. baseball pitcher **Harvey Haddix**, 1933 U.S. actor **Robert Blake**, 1934 U.S. singer **Jimmie Rodgers**, 1939 U.S. singer/actor **Frankie Avalon**, 1959 Baseball 2nd baseman **Ryne Sandberg**, 1971 U.S. actress **Jada Pinkett Smith**

September 19

1737 **Charles Carroll:** American revolutionary leader. In 1776 accompanied Benjamin Franklin on a diplomatic mission to Canada. As a member of the Continental Congress, he was the Only Roman Catholic signer of the Declaration of Independence. One of Maryland's first two U.S. Senators (1789–92).

Without morals a republic cannot subsist any length of time; they therefore who are decrying the Christian religion, whose morality is so sublime and pure (and) which insures to the good eternal happiness, are undermining the solid foundation of morals, the best security of free governments.

1778 Lord **Henry Peter Brougham:** English statesmen and noted legal reformer. As Attorney General he successfully defended Queen Caroline at her trial. As Lord Chancellor of England (1830–34), responsible for setting up the Central Criminal Court and the Judicial Committee of the Privy Council. Played an important role in the improvement of education, law reform and the abolition of slavery in the British Empire. Helped found London University.

War is a crime which involves all other crimes.

1811 **Orson Pratt:** American leader in the Latter Day Saints movement and an original member of the Quorum of Twelve Apostles. Ordained an elder by the Prophet Joseph Smith, Jr. and after serving in a number of missions was elevated to a High Priest. Preached in Scotland, introducing his missionary tract, *An Interesting Account of Severable Remarkable Visions*, which contained the earliest known printed account of Joseph Smith's First Vision.

All the modern Christian churches have no more authority to preach, baptize, or administer any other ordinance of the gospel than the idolatrous Hindoos have.

1894 **Rachel Field:** American novelist, playwright and poet. Editor of several collections of fairy tales. Author of popular children's fiction: *Hitty, Her First Hundred Years*, her Newberry medal winning novel for young adults and *Calico Bush*. Adult fiction: *Time Out of Mind*, a story of Maine characters and *All This and Heaven Too*, a story of a French woman who is the pivot about which a famous crime revolves.

The public is more easily swayed by persons than by principles.

1904 **Bergen Evans:** American educator, lexicographer and author. English professor who became the master of ceremonies for TV's the *$64,000 Question*. Wrote "The Skeptic's Corner" for *American Mercury* (1946–50). Author of "The Last Word," a syndicated daily newspaper feature. Host of several language-oriented television shows.

Freedom of speech and freedom of action are

meaningless without freedom to think. And there is no freedom of thought without doubt.

1908 **Mika Waltari:** Finnish novelist. Best known for the historical novel *The Egyptian*, whose theme is the corruption of humanistic values in a materialistic world. Frequently suffered from insomnia and depression. One of the most prolific Finnish writers, he is the author of 29 novels, 15 novellas, 6 collections of stories or fairy tales, 6 collections of poetry and 26 plays.

A decision once taken brings peace to a man's mind and eases his soul.

1911 **William Golding:** English novelist. Master of strange situations and ironic twists. First book was the contemporary classic *Lord of the Flies*, about savagery taking over among a group of English schoolboys marooned on a Pacific Island. Other works: *Pincher Martin*, *The Spire*, *Rites of Passage* and *The Paper Men*. Nobel Prize for Literature (1983).

Sleep is when all the unsorted stuff comes flying out as from a dustbin upset in a high wind.

1919 **Mary Midgley:** British moral philosopher. Best known for her popular works on religion, science, and ethics. Concerned with what she considered attempts to substitute science for the humanities. Her first book, *Beast and Man*, was an examination of human nature. Other works: *Evolution as A Religion*, *Science as Salvation: a Modern Myth and Its Meaning*, and *Myths We Live By*.

Mourning and desolation are not our inventions. But because we can anticipate them, can think about them, and experience them widely in imagination, we have a graver problem — one, of course, which forms part of the price we pay for the joys and uses of imagination.

1921 **Paulo Freire:** Brazilian educator and writer. His educational ideas were developed from his experience teaching literacy to Brazilian peasants. Employs interactive methods, where students are encouraged to question the teacher. Appointed director of the Brazilian National Literacy Program. Jailed following a military coup. Forced into exile, he returned in 1979 to help form the Worker's Party. His most important work is *Pedagogy of the Oppressed*.

Washing one's hands of the conflict between the powerful and the powerless means to side with the powerful, not to be neutral.

1922 **Damon Knight:** American science fiction writer, editor and critic. Recipient of the Hugo Award. Founded the Science Fiction and Fantasy Writers of America. Co-founder of the National Fantasy Fan Federation, the Milford's Writers' Conference and the Clarion Writers Workshop. The Damian Knight Memorial Master Award for lifetime achievement was named in his honor. Novels: *Hell's Pavement*, *Mind Switch*, *The Observers* and *Double Meaning*.

The popularity of conspiracy theories is explained by people's desire to believe that there is some group of folks who know what they're doing.

1922 **Emil Zátopek:** Czech athlete. Long distance runner. In his career he set world records for nine different distances. Won gold medals in the 5000, 10,000, and marathon in the 1952 Olympic Games. His wife Dana Ingrova Zatopkova also won a gold medal that year for the javelin.

It's at the borders of pain and suffering that the men are separated from the boys.

1932 **Mike Royko:** U.S. newspaper syndicated columnist. Pulitzer Prize winner for commentary (1972). His irreverent, acerbic, insightful political and social essays reflect his working-class origins, exposing injustices visited on ordinary people. His one-rule diet: "if you enjoy it, you can't eat it. If you don't like it, you can eat all you want." Published collections of his columns and the best-selling *Boss*, on former Chicago mayor Richard Daley.

The subject of criminal rehabilitation was debated recently in City Hall. It's an appropriate place for this kind of discussion because the city has always employed so many ex-cons and future cons.

OTHERS: 866 Byzantine Emperor **Leo VI**, 1551 King of France **Henry II**, 1749 French mathematician **Jean-Baptiste Delambre**, 1759 English entomologist **William Kirby**, 1905 Watergate special prosecutor **Leon Jaworski**, 1907 U.S. Supreme Court Justice **Lewis F. Powell, Jr.**, 1909 Austrian automobile pioneer **Ferry Porsche**, 1912 U.S. editor **Clifton Daniel**, 1912 German conductor **Kurt Sanderling**, 1920 U.S. sports writer **Roger Angell**, 1921 U.S. pro football player **Charlie Conerly**, 1931 U.S. singer **Brook Benton**, 1934 Beatles manager **Brian Epstein**, 1940 U.S. singer "Righteous Brothers" **Bill Medley** 1941 Italian politician **Umberto Bossi**, 1949 English fashion model **Twiggy Lawson**

September 20

1807 **Giovanni Ruffini:** Italian wrier and patriot. Supporter of Giuseppe Mazzini. Ruffini was condemned to death for his participation in the mazziniani movements. He escaped to exile. Returned to Italy and was elected Deputy to the Piermont Parliament. Later Ambassador to Paris. His most celebrated novels are *Lorenzo Benoni* and *Dottor Antonio*, which provoked English and French sympathies for the fate of Italy.

The teacher is like the candle which lights others in consuming itself.

1842 Lord **James Dewar:** British-Scottish physicist. Studied at Edinburgh and became a professor at Cambridge, where he pursued a wide range of experimental research. First to liquefy and then solidify hydrogen. Research in low-temperature preservation led to the Thermos bottle. With Frederick Abel he invented cordite, the first smokeless powder, long used as the standard British military propellant.

Minds are like parachutes, they only function when they're open.

1851 **Henry Arthur Jones:** English playwright. Strongly influenced by Norwegian playwright Henrik

Ibsen. Achieved prominence in the field of melodrama. Contributed greatly to Victorian society drama. Author of over 60 plays including *The Silver King, The Middleman, Mrs. Dane's Defense, The Dancing Girl* and *The Liars*. Critical works: *The Renaissance of the English Drama* and *The Theatre of Ideas.*

O God! Put back Thy universe and give me yesterday.

1878 **Upton Sinclair:** American crusading socialist, vegetarian, telepathist, teetotaler, and veteran of many political and literary battles. Known as "the last of the muckrakers." Espoused socialism and concern for social and political problems. His 1906 best-seller, *The Jungle*, a thundering call for reform in the meat packing industry. Other battling books: *The Metropolis, The Profits of Religion, King Coal,* and *Oil!* His novel *Dragon's Teeth*, earned a Pulitzer Prize.

Is it altogether a Utopian dream, that once in history, a ruling class might be willing to make the great surrender, and permit social change to come about without hatred, turmoil, and waste of human life.

1880 **Elizabeth Kenny:** Australian nurse and health administrator. Established a backyard clinic to treat long-term poliomyelitis victims and cerebral palsy patients. Developed a new treatment for polio during the 1930s. Established clinics in Brisbane, backed by the State government but oppose by the medical profession. Moved to the U.S.A. in 1940 with an introduction to the Mayo Clinic in Rochester, Minnesota, where her methods were widely acclaimed. The Sister Kenny Institute was established in Minneapolis in 1942. Autobiography: *And They Shall Walk.*

Some minds remain open long enough for the truth not only to enter but to pass through by way of a ready exit without pausing anywhere along the route.

1885 **Ferdinand "Jelly Roll" Morton:** American jazz pianist, singer, bandleader, arranger and composer. Style was tinged with Creole elements and ragtime. Unaccompanied piano solos made best sellers of his compositions: "New Orleans Blues," "Wolverine Blues," "Jelly Roll Blues" and "King Porter Stomp." Led his band, the Red Hot Peppers, blending lyricism and stomping rhythms. Disputed W.C. Handy's claim as the originator of jazz and the blues.

New Orleans is the cradle of jazz and I myself happened to be the creator in the year 1902. In 1908 Handy didn't know anything about the blues and he doesn't know anything about jazz and stomp to this day. I myself figured out the peculiar form of mathematics and harmonies that was strange to all the world but me.

1901 **Charles Abrams:** American lawyer and author. Helped create the New York Housing Authority and lobbied President Kennedy to issue an executive order banning discrimination in federally subsidized housing projects. Wrote: *The Future of Housing, Forbidden Neighbors, Man's Struggle for Shelter in an Urbanizing World* and *The City Is the Frontier.*

A city is the pulsating product of the human hand and mind, reflecting man's history, his struggle for freedom, creativity, genius — and his selfishness and errors.

1902 **Stevie [Florence Margaret] Smith:** English poet and novelist, who drew on suburban life and religion in much of her work. Poems: "A Good Time Was Had By All," "Me Again," "Not Waving but Drowning." Novels: *Novel on Yellow Paper, Over the Frontier,* and *The Holiday.*

Nobody heard him, the dead man,/But still he lay moaning./I was much further out than you thought, and not waving but drowning./I was much too far out all my life,/And not waving but drowning.

1917 **Arnold "Red" Auerbach:** Second winningest basketball coach in history, 1,037 victories, including playoff games in 20 years. Led Boston Celtics as general manager-coach to nine NBA titles, eight in a row. Retired in 1966 to become the team's general manager and club president. Famous for lightning a cigar when he knew his team was victorious.

An acre of performance is worth a whole world of promise.

1927 **Rachel Roberts:** Welsh actress. Direct and intense, she made her film mark with her breakthrough and BAFTA–winning performance in *Saturday Night and Sunday Morning*, Equally brilliant in *This Sporting Life*, which earned her another BAFTA and an Oscar nomination. Once married to actor Rex Harrison. Died from an overdose of barbiturates.

A new actress is pretty commonly seen in the press, but you don't often see such mystery behind who the character is.

1928 **Joyce Brothers:** Originally **Joyce Diane Bauer**. American psychologist, columnist and author. Publishes a daily syndicated newspaper column since 1960. First brought to wide public attention when she won the top prize on the TV game show *The $64,000 Question*, on which she appeared as an expert on the subject of boxing. Had a monthly column in Good Housekeeping magazine for almost 40 years, hosted her TV show, published several best-selling books.

The best proof of love is trust.

1934 **Sophia Loren:** Italian actress. Dubbed "the stick" when at 12 she haunted breadlines near Naples. Tall, statuesque, sensuous, sultry, green-and-gold eyed star of 23 Italian films before becoming an international sensation Films: *The Key, Desire Under the Elms, Two Women* (Oscar winner), *Yesterday, Today and Tomorrow, Marriage Italian Style, Arabesque* and *Grumpier Old Men.* Married producer Carlo Ponti, who launched her movie career.

I think the quality of sexiness comes from within. It is something that is in you or it isn't and it really doesn't have much to do with breasts or thighs or the pout of your lips.

OTHERS: 1833 Italian pacifist **Ernesto Teodoro Moneta**, 1861 Librarian of Congress **Herman Putnam**, 1873

Canadian film director **Sidney Olcott**, 1889 U.S. athlete **Charles Reidpath**, 1910 French yachtsman **Jacques-Baptise LeBrun**, 1922 U.S. pianist **William Kapell**, 1923 Irish poet **Geraldine Clinton Little**, 1924 U.S. fashion designer **James Galanos**, 1925 U.S. singer **Gogi Grant**, 1929 U.S. comic actress **Anne Meara**, 1935 U.S. football running back/actor **Jim Taylor**, 1941 U.S. glass artist **Dale Chihuly**, 1948 U.S. writer **George R.R. Martin**, 1951 Canadian hockey player **Guy Lafleur**, 1975 Colombian race car driver **Juan Pablo Montoya**, 1967 U.S. rock singers **Gunnar and Matthew Nelson**

September 21

1452 **Girolamo Savonarola:** Italian monk and reformer. Roman Catholic prophet and eloquent preacher of the Dominican order. Crusaded against political and religious corruption won him popular support. In 1494 he led a revolt in Florence that expelled the ruling Medici family and established a democratic republic. His denunciations of Pope Alexander VI led to his excommunication in 1497. Arrested in 1498 he was tortured, hanged and burned for heresy.

Lord! Teach me the way my soul should walk.

1849 Sir **Edmund William Gosse:** English man of letters. Son of English naturalist Philip Henry Gosse. Assistant librarian at the British Museum, translator at the Board of Trade and in 1904 appointed librarian to the House of Lords. Through his studies and translations of Northern European Literature and other critical works he introduced Henrik Ibsen's works to English-speaking readers. Published two volumes of poetry, *On Viol and Flute* and *Collected Poems*.

Never mind whom you praise, but be very careful who you blame.

1866 **Charles Jean Henri Nicolle:** French physician and bacteriologist. Pupil of Louis Pasteur and director of the Pasteur Institute at Tunis (1903–32). Nobel Prize winner in physiology or medicine (1928) for discovering that typhus fever is transmitted by the body louse. As a result the armies of World War I introduced delousing as a compulsory part of military routine.

Chance favors only those who know how to court her.

1866 **H.G. Wells:** English science-fiction novelist, sociological writer and historian. Threw himself into contemporary issues — free love, Fabianism, progressive education, scientific theory, world government and human rights. Wrote over 100 books and countless articles, achieving unparalleled fame in his lifetime. Pioneered English science fiction with his allegory set in the year 802701, *The Time Machine*. Other Science Fiction: *The Island of Dr. Moreau*, *The Invisible Man* and *The War of the Worlds*. Most important work of nonfiction, *Outline of History*.

A time will come when a politician who has willfully made war and promoted international dissension will be as sure of the dock and much surer of the noose than a private homicide. It is not reasonable that those who gamble with men's lives should not stake their own.

1874 **Gustav Holst:** English composer. Wrote operas, including *Savitri* (1916) and *At the Boar's Head* (1925); ballets, songs, and choral works, including *Hymns from the Rig Vesla* (1911) and *The Hymn of Jesus* (1920). Probably best known for his orchestral suites, in particular *The Planets* (1918). Lifelong friend of Ralph Vaughn Williams with whom he shared an enthusiasm for English folk music.

There is no room in music for the second-rate — it might as well be the nineteenth-rate.

1902 **Luis Cernuda:** Spanish poet and literary critic. After the proclamation of the Second Spanish Republic, he worked to support a more liberal and tolerant Spain. During the Spanish Civil War, an anti-fascist he fled to England before settling in Mexico. Major opus is *Reality and Desire*. Broke new ground with *Forbidden Pleasures*, an avant-garde work, using surrealism to explore his sexuality. Crucial ground-breaking figure for homosexual writing in Spain.

Everything beautiful has its moment and then passes away.

1907 **Helen Foster Snow:** American writer. Journalistic pen name **Nym Wales**. One of the first Americans to encounter the fledgling Chinese Communist Party and Mao Zedong. Traveled to China where she married British novelist and scientist C.P. Snow. They spent nearly ten years in Asia during the time of the Japanese conquest of Manchuria, Sino-Japanese War and the conflict between Chiang Kai-Chek's Nationalists and the Communists for ultimate power in China. She considered Chiang Kai-check a fascist. Most famous works are *My China Years* and *Inside Red China*.

One can judge a civilization by the way it treats its women.

1909 **Kwame Nkrumah:** African founder of the nation of Ghana. "Gandhi of Africa." Leader against white domination and favored Pan-Africanism. Formed Convention People's Party, whose slogan was "Self-government now," to fight for independence of Gold Coast. First prime minister of Ghana (1957–66). Suppressed dissent. Overthrown by a military coup in 1966 while visiting China. Returned to Ghana where he was appointed the new head of state.

Freedom is not something that one people can bestow on another as a gift. They claim it as their own and none can keep it from them.

1916 **Françoise Giroud:** Originally **Françoise Gourdji**. Swiss-born French feminist, politician, journalist, broadcaster and editor. Cofounder of magazines *Elle* and *L'Express*, which she also edited. Prime Minister Giscard d'Estaing appointed her to the post of Minister for the Status of Women. Writings: *Ce que je crois*, *La Comédie du pouvoir* and the bestseller *Les hommes et les femmes*.

Desire can be as fragile as it is sudden.

1947 **Stephen King:** Maine-born American author of enormously popular novels, most of whom have been adapted to film. One of the world's best-selling authors. His novels blend horror, the macabre, fantasy and science fiction: *Carrie, The Shining, The Dead Zone, Firestarter, Cujo, Stand By Me, Misery* and the series *The Green Mile.*

If I cannot horrify, I'll go for gross-out. I'm not proud.

1947 **Marsha Norman:** American dramatist and novelist. Themes include the nature of responsibility. Her first produced play, *Getting Out* (1977), features a murderer represented by a double character. Won a 1983 Pulitzer Prize for her play *'night Mother* (1982), dealing with the relationship between a woman who is about to commit suicide and her mother. Her novel *Fortune Teller* (1987) examines the ethics of abortion.

Dreams are illustrations ... from the book your soul is writing about you.

1951 **Aslan Maskhadov:** Leader of the separatist movement in the southern Soviet republic of Chechnya. Senior military figure on the Chechen side during the war with Russia (1994–96). Credited with the Chechen victory. President of the Chechen Republic of Ichkeria in 1997. Returned to leading the guerrilla movement against the Russian army during the Second Chechen War. Denied responsibility for increasingly brutal terrorist acts carried out by followers of his political opponent. Reportedly killed in March 2005 during an engagement against Russian Special Forces.

Independence is not a whim or an ambition. It is the necessary condition of our survival as an ethnic group.

OTHERS: 1645 French explorer **Louis Joliet**, 1756 Scottish engineer/road-builder **John MacAdam**, 1863 U.S. actor **John Bunny**, 1895 Russian poet **Sergei Yesenin**, 1912 U.S. animator **Chuck Jones**, 1912 Hungarian pianist **György Sándor**, 1919 Argentine philosopher/physicist **Mario Bunge**, 1919 Pakistani scholar **Fazlur Rahman**, 1929 English philosopher **Bernard Williams**, 1931 U.S. actor **Larry Hagman**, 1934 Canadian singer/songwriter **Leonard Cohen**, 1935 U.S. actor **Henry Gibson**, 1944 U.S. actress/novelist **Fannie Flagg**, 1950 U.S. actor **Bill Murray**, 1953 Dutch race car driver **Arie Luyendyk**, 1957 U.S. film director **Ethan Coen**, 1967 U.S. singer **Faith Hill**, 1981 U.S. celebrity/actress **Nicole Richie**

September 22

1694 **Philip Dormer Stanhope, 4th Earl of Chesterfield:** English statesman, orator and man of letters. Best known for wit and wisdom of his letters to his son, written between 1737 and 1768, which provide a classic portrayal of an ideal 18th century gentleman. His name is used as a synonym for courtly manners.

Religion is by no means a proper subject of conversation in a mixed company.

1788 **Theodore Edward Hook:** English novelist and wit. Achieved early fame as the author of 13 successful comic operas and melodramas. Well known punster and practical joker. Started the Tory journal *John Bull.* Author of *Impromptu at Fulham, Gilbert Gurney* and *William Weare.* In an 1825 article in *John Bull,* he prophesied the Chunnel:

A tunnel underneath the sea from Calais straight to Dover, Sir. The squeamish folks may cross by land from shore to shore, with sluices made to drown the French, if they would ever come over, Sit, has been long talk'd of, till at length 'tis though a monstrous bore.

1791 **Michael Faraday:** English physicist and chemist who contributed greatly to the understanding of electromagnetism. Made the greatest electrical discovery, the generation of electricity by means of magnetism. Creator of classical field theory. Although many scientists have their major ideas before they are 30, Faraday's talents only became obvious in his 40s. Also an effective popularizer of science, he gave annual Christmas lectures for young people beginning in 1826, continued to this day, only now they are televised.

The five essential entrepreneurial skills for success are concentration, discrimination, organization, innovation and communication.

1847 **Alice Meynell:** née **Thompson.** English mystical poet, literary critic and essayist. Author of "A Thrush Before Dawn," "The Laws of Verse," "The Poet to the Birds" and "In Early Spring." Volumes of essays: *The Rhythm of Life, The Color of Life* and *Hearts of Controversy.* Married author and journalist Wilfrid Meynell with whom she edited several periodicals.

There is nothing in the world more peaceful than apple-leaves with an early moon.

1885 **Erich Von Stroheim:** Austrian-born director, actor and screenwriter. Dubbed "the man you love to hate," he played mainly villains, such as the sadistic Prussian officer in Jean Renoir's *Le Grande Illusion.* As director made costly, lengthy films including his masterwork *Greed.* Others: *The Merry Widow, The Wedding March* and *Queen Kelly.* Nominated for a Best Supporting Academy Award for his role *in Sunset Boulevard.*

When you ask me why I do such pictures I am not ashamed to tell you the true reason: only because I do not want my family to starve.

1895 **Paul Muni:** Originally **Muni Weisenfreund.** Austrian-born American actor. Appeared on the English-speaking stage from 1926. Broadway hits: *Counselor-at-Law, Key Largo, A Flag Is Born* and *Inherit the Wind,* for which he won a Tony Award. Movies: *I Am a Fugitive from a Chain Gang, Black Fury, The Story of Louis Pasteur* (Academy Award as Best Actor), *The Good Earth, The Life of Emile Zola, Juarez,* and *A Song to Remember.* A distinguished "star" character actor, although he dismissed the star designation.

I don't want to be a star. If you had to label me anything, I'm an actor — I guess. A journeyman actor. I think "star" is what you call actors who can't act.

1901 **Charles B. Huggins:** Canadian-born surgeon and cancer researcher. At the University of Chicago from 1927, where he was professor of surgery and head of the Ben May Laboratory for Cancer Research. Recipient of the Nobel Prize in Physiology or Medicine, notably for his discovery of hormonal treatment for cancer of the prostate gland.

Nature can refuse to answer but she cannot give a wrong answer.

1902 **Howard Jarvis:** U.S. political activist and politician. Anti-tax crusader. Founded a Taxpayer's Association, which succeeded in getting California voters to approve Proposition 21, which slashed property taxes by fifty-seven percent, but also resulted in a loss of many services that citizens had grown accustomed to having. He can be seen in the 1980 movie *Airplane!* as the remarkably patient taxi passenger.

The only way to cut government spending is not to give them the money to spend in the first place.

1910 **Marjorie Holmes:** Prolific American writer of inspirational books: *I've Got to Talk to Somebody, God* and *Who Am I God?* Holmes ruminations about the meaning of life are monologues directed to God, but are not talks with God and the nature of the God to whom she directs her remarks is not clear, but He isn't a God of a church or a community. Other titles in her series: *How Can I Find You, God?* and *Lord, Let Me Love.*

Thank you, God, for the dignity and beauty of self. The precious innate self. The only thing that can't be taken from us. The only thing we really own.

1920 **Bob Lemon:** American right-handed baseball pitcher with the Cleveland Indians. Hall-of-Famer began his career as a light-hitting third baseman. When he switched to pitching, the sinker-ball pitcher won 20 or more games seven times. Teamed with Bob Feller, Early Wynn and Mike Garcia to form one of the greatest starting pitcher staffs in baseball history. Managed the Kansas City Royals, the Chicago White Sox and had two stints as skipper of the New York Yankees, leading them to a pennant, but not a World Series. Fired twice by owner George Steinbrenner in a period of slightly more than one full season.

Baseball was made for kids, and grown-ups only screw it up.

1927 **Tommy Lasorda:** Colorful American baseball manager with the L.A. Dodgers since 1975. Led his team to two World Series victories (1981, 1988). Had a cup-of-coffee in the major leagues as a left-handed pitcher, first with the Brooklyn Dodgers and then the Kansas City Athletes. Lasorda, who bleeds Dodgers blue, succeeded Walter Alston as manager in 1976, remaining in the position until 1996. After retiring he became an executive with the Dodgers.

There are three types of baseball players: those who make it happen, those who watch it happen, and those who wonder what happened.

1931 **Fay Weldon:** British feminist, novelist and author of TV screenplays. Wrote the award-winning first episode of *Upstairs, Downstairs.* Novels have the recurring themes of the nature of women's sexuality and experience in a man's world. Works: *The Fat Woman's Joke, The Life and Loves of a She-Devil, Puffball,* and *The Cloning of Joanna May.*

Men are irrelevant.

OTHERS: 1515 Queen of Henry VII **Anne of Cleves**, 1601 Queen of Louis XIII **Anne of Austria**, 1715 French physician **Jean-Étienne Guettard**, 1717 Swedish astronomer **Pehr Wargentin**, 1722 Scottish writer **John Home**, 1741 German zoologist **Peter Simon Pallas**, 1892 U.S. humorist **Frank Sullivan**, 1902 Romanian-born producer/actor **John Houseman**, 1918 Polish-born violinist **Henryk Szeryng**, 1922 Chinese physicist **Chen Ning Yang**, 1924 English novelist **Rosamunde Pilcher**, 1932 Swedish boxing champ **Ingemar Johansson**, 1948 Ex-husband of Britain's Princess Anne **Mark Phillips**, 1958 Italian tenor **Andrea Bocelli**, 1958 U.S. musician **Joan Jett**, 1976 Brazilian soccer player **Ronaldo**

September 23

480 BCE **Euripides:** Athenian tragic poet. Abandon painting for literature writing more than 80 dramas, of which 19 survive, including *Medea*, *Orestes* and *Electra.* One of three Greek playwrights of tragic drama whose work has survived to the modern age with frequent productions. The other two are Aeschylus, called the founder of Greek drama, and Sophocles. The trio were contemporaries of the comic dramatist and poet Aristophanes.

Friends show their love — in times of trouble, not in happiness.

63 BCE **Augustus Caesar:** First Roman Emperor. Great nephew and adopted son of Julius Caesar. As emperor centralized power. Patron of agriculture and the arts. Friend of Horace, Virgil and other celebrated individuals who made the Augustin age of literature famous. Introduced Pax Romana, an era of peace. His excellent advice: "Make haste slowly." Accomplished much construction and civic improvement.

I found Rome a city of bricks and left it a city of marble.

1215 **Kublai Khan:** "The last of the great Khans." Grandson of Genghis Khan. Founder and the first Emperor (1279–1294) of the Chinese Yuan Dynasty. Worked to minimize the influence of regional lords who had held immense power before and during the Song Dynasty. Introduced paper currency and encouraged Chinese arts. His court was visited by many Europeans, most notably Marco Polo. The Khan's summer palace was in Shangdu, which literally translates as upper capital or Xanadu, inspiring Samuel Taylor Coleridge to write his spectacular poem "Kublai Khan," allegedly came to him in an opium-induced dream.

In Xanadu did Kubla Khan/ A stately pleasure-dome decree:/ Where Alph, the sacred river, ran/ Through caverns measureless to man/ Down to a sunless sea.

1800 **William Holmes McGuffey:** American educator. Wrote and published *Eclectic Readers*, better known as the *McGuffey Peerless Pioneer Readers*, which made him famous and are still yearned for by some backward-looking educational reformers. It wasn't until he became Professor of Philosophy at the University of Virginia in 1845 that he created his books that sold over 122 million copies, helping millions of kids learn to read.

The Christian religion is the religion of our country. From it are derived our notions on character of God, on the great moral Governor of the universe. On its doctrines are founded the peculiarities of our free institutions. From no source has the author drawn more conspicuously than from the sacred Scriptures. From all these extracts from the Bible I make no apology.

1838 **Victoria Claflin Woodhull:** American writer, editor and reformer. Supported by Cornelius Vanderbilt, she and her sister Tennessee Claflin opened a very successful stock brokerage office in 1868. Founded *Woodhull and Claflin's Weekly* and was involved with a socialist group called *Pantarchy*, which advocated the principles of equal rights for women, free love and a single moral standard. First woman candidate for U.S. presidency, even though she and all other women did not have the right to vote. Works: *Scientific Propagation of the Human Race* and with her sister, *The Human Body the Temple of God.*

I am a free lover. I have an inalienable constitutional and natural right to love whom I may, to love as long or as short a period as I can, to change that love every day if I please.

1852 **William Stewart Halsted:** American surgeon. Pioneer of scientific surgery. Professor at Johns Hopkins from 1886, where he established the first surgery school in the United States. Developed a cocaine injection for local anesthesia, becoming an addict in the process, but was cured. Devised successful operative techniques, including those for cancer of the breast. Championed the use of rubber gloves and sterile conditions in surgery.

The only weapon with which the unconscious patient can immediately retaliate upon the incompetent surgeon is hemorrhage.

1863 **Mary Eliza Church Terrell:** African-American educator, writer and social reformer. Her father, a former slave, made a fortune in real estate, making her possible to become educated with a Master's degree from Oberlin College and travel throughout Europe to study languages. Devoted her life to speaking out against racial discrimination and women's inequality. First president of the National Association of Colored Women and co-founder of the National Association for the Advancement of Colored People.

Not only are colored women with ambition and aspiration handicapped on account of their sex, but they are everywhere baffled and mocked on account of their race.

1865 Baroness **Emmuska Orczy:** Originally **Magdalena Rosalia Marie Josepha Barbaro**. Hungarian-born British novelist. Became famous for the swashbuckling *The Scarlet Pimpernel*, her first success in her long career of writing popular adventure romances. It was set in the era of the French Revolution, when an English dandy rescues French aristocrats sentenced to the guillotine. In his disguise as an ineffective dandy, he spouts the famous doggerel.

We seek him here, we seek him there,/ Those Frenchies seek him everywhere./ Is he in heaven?—Is he in hell?/ That demned, elusive Pimpernel.

1889 **Walter Lippmann:** Influential U.S. journalist. In 1913, he, Herbert Croly and Walter Weyl were the founding editors of *The New Republic* magazine. During World War I, he was an advisor to Woodrow Wilson and assisted in drafting Wilson's Fourteen Points. Syndicated political columnist for the *New York Herald-Tribune* (1931–62) and *The Washington Post* (1962–67). Pulitzer Prize for International Reporting in 1962. Author of *A Preface to Politics*, *The Good Society*, and *Unity and the Common Market.* First to bring the phrase "cold war" to common currency in his 1947 book of that name.

Most men, after a little freedom, have preferred authority with the consoling assurances and the economy of effort it brings.

1920 **Mickey Rooney:** Originally **Joe Yule, Jr.** Multi-talented American actor. Began his career with his family in their vaudeville act when he was two. Made his film debut in 1926 playing a midget. Appeared in the Andy Hardy series of films, as a cocky, energetic teen, who usually found that his father knew best. Often appeared in films with Judy Garland: *Babes in Arms* and *Strike Up the Band.* Other films: *A Midsummer Nights' Dream*, *Boys Town*, and *The Human Comedy.* The diminutive star was married eight times, including Ava Gardner, his first (1942–43). Nominated for an Oscar for Best Actor in a Supporting Role for *The Black Stallion.* Received an honorary Academy Award in 1983.

You always pass failure on your way to success.

1930 **Ray Charles:** Originally **Ray Charles Robinson.** African-American pianist and singer, blind since the age of six. Learned to write songs in Braille, initially in the rhythm 'n' blues style, but later delved into jazz, soul and country. A musical genius. Songs: "What'd I Say," "Georgia on My Mind," "Hit the Road Jack," "I Can't Stop Loving You," "Busted" and "Crying Time." His album *Modern Sounds in Country and Western Music* sold more than a million copies. The film *Ray*, based on his life, earned its star Jamie Foxx an Academy Award.

What is a soul? It's like electricity— we don't really know what it is, but it's a force that can light a room.

1949 **Bruce Springsteen:** "The Boss." American singer and songwriter. Taught himself to play guitar and worked in several groups before forming his own 10-piece band in the early 1970s. Leader in the rock and roll field and voice of dissident youth. Hits: "Hungry Heart," "Dancing in the Dark," "Born in the

U.S.A.," "My Hometown," "War" and "Philadelphia." Sensitive lyrics voice his working-class sympathies, giving him vast appeal, especially for his concerts.

The best music is essentially there to provide you something to face the world with.

OTHERS: 1650 English bishop **Jeremy Collier**, 1713 King of Spain **Ferdinand VI**, 1745 American pioneer **John Sevier**, 1819 French physicist **Hippolyte Fizeau**, 1870 U.S. folk song collector **John Lomax**, 1880 Scottish physician/biologist **John Boyd Orr**, 1890 German general **Friedrich Paulus**, 1897 U.S. actor **Walter Pidgeon**, 1900 Russian-born U.S. sculptor **Louise Nevelson**, 1901 Czech writer **Jaroslav Seifert**, 1916 Assassinated Italian politician **Aldo Moro**, 1926 U.S. saxophonist/composer **John Coltrane**, 1938 Austrian actress **Romy Schneider**, 1943 Spanish singer **Julio Iglesias**, 1959 U.S. comic actor **Jason Alexander**, 1961 U.S. astronaut **Willie McCool**

September 24

1501 **Girolamo Cardano:** Also known by the Latin version of his name **Jerome Cardan**. Gained fame, or perhaps notoriety, for being the most outstanding mathematician of his time, a physician, an astrologer, a scientist, a philosopher, a gambler, and a rascal. Described as a turbulent man of genius, lunatic, hypochondriac, perverted, dishonest, unscrupulous, pirate, indiscreet, quarrelsome, conceited, heretic, humorless, but capable of generosity, kindness and merciless self revelation. In 1545 produced his masterpiece *The Great Art, or the Rules of Algebra*. Passion for gambling and games. As a physician he often prescribed gambling as therapy for those suffering from anxiety and grief. Late in his life, he wrote *Book on the Games of Chance*.

Even if gambling were altogether an evil, still on account of the very large number of people who play, it would seem to be a natural evil. Thus it is not absurd for me to discuss gambling, not in order to practice it, but in order to point out the advantages in it, and, of course, the disadvantages, so they may be reduced to a minimum.

1717 **Horace Walpole:** Son of English statesman Sir Robert Walpole, twice prime minister. Fourth Earl of Oxford. English author, man of letters, connoisseur, collector and memorialist. His *Memoirs* covering the years from 1746 to 1791 are considered the most important and accurate source for the history of England of that period. *The Castle of Otranto*, reputedly the earliest English gothic novel. His *Correspondence* marked him as the most outstanding letter writer in the entire history of the literature of England.

History is a romance that is believed; romance, a history that is not believed.

1755 **John Marshall:** American lawyer, jurist and fourth chief justice of the Supreme Court (1801–35). Founder of the American system of constitutional law. His opinions did more than any other to determine the way which the U.S. constitution has been construed or understood ever since his tenure U.S. Secretary of State (1800–1).

The law does not expect a man to be prepared to defend every act of his life which may be suddenly and without notice alleged against him.

1825 **Frances Ellen Watkins Harper:** American writer, poet and abolitionist. First known African-American novelist. The themes of her writings reflected the causes she supported — antislavery, black women, and education. Author of *Poems on Miscellaneous Subjects*, *Idylls of the Bible* and *The Sparrow's Fall and Other Poems*. Wrote two novels: *Iola Leroy; of Shadows Lifted* and *Sketches of Southern Life*.

What matters if they do forget the singer, so they don't forget the song.

1843 **Samuel Augustus Willoughby Duffield:** American Presbyterian clergyman, hymnologist and poet. Author of *The Heavenly Land*, *Warf and Woof*, *English Hymns: Their Authors and History* and *The Latin Hymn-Writers and Their Hymns*.

A mind without occupation is like a cat without a ball of yarn.

1878 **C.F. (Charles Ferdinand) Ramuz:** Swiss poet, author and essayist, who wrote in French, mainly about peasant life in his native canton of Vaud. Produced 20 novels, including: *The Reign of the Evil One*, *The End of All Men*, *The Triumph of Death* and what is widely held to be his best work, *When the Mountain Fell*.

Man never has what he wants, because what he wants is everything.

1890 Sir **Alan P. Herbert:** British humorist and novelist. Called to the bar, but never practiced law. Established a reputation in his twenties as a witty author of verses. Joined the periodical *Punch* in 1924. Wrote the successful review *Riverside Nights* with Nigel Playfair and contributed a series of brilliant libretti for comic operas. Novels: *The Secret Battle*, *The Water Gipsies* and *Holy Deadlock*. Campaigned against jargon and officialese in many humorous articles.

If nobody said anything unless he knew what he was talking about, a ghastly hush would descend upon the earth.

1895 **Tommy Armour:** American golf professional and teaching pro. Won his first tournament before World War I. Won Both the U.S. Open and the Canadian Open in 1927; PGA Championship in 1930 and British Open in 1931. As a teacher his four fundamentals of golf are grip, stance, coordination and power, but he also stresses thinking, noting: "People who wouldn't think of doing a dumb thing anywhere else, are dumb all over a gold course."

Golf is an awkward set of bodily contortions designed to produce a graceful result.

1896 **F. Scott Fitzgerald:** American novelist, short-story writer and screenwriter. With the success of his collections of short stories, *Flappers and Philosophers* (1920) and *Tales of the Jazz Age* (1922) he came to be recognized as spokesman for the youthful rebellion of the era. Author of *This Side of Paradise, The Great Gatsby* and *The Last Tycoon.* His wife Zelda became mentally ill and he progressively became dependent on alcohol and to have money problems.

You don't write because you want to say something, you write because you have something to say.

1931 **Anthony Newley:** British actor, singer, and composer. At age 14 appeared as the Artful Dodger in David Lean's film *Oliver Twist* (1948). In 1961 he collaborated with Leslie Bricusse on the hit stage show *Stop the World I Want To Get Off* and later the partnership produced *The Roar of the Greasepaint, The Smell of the Crowd.* His biggest song hit was "What Kind of Fool Am I?" Married four times, once to actress Joan Collins, of whom he said: "she's a commodity who would sell her own bowel movement."

My only regret is that in a show business career you can have no private life.

1936 **Jim Henson:** Originally **James Maury**. American puppeteer and producer. Created the Muppets (melding "marionettes "and "puppets") in 1954, which appeared as regulars on television's "Sesame Street" and in a series of movies. Henson was the voice of Kermit the Frog and created Miss Piggy. Also produced and directed *The Muppet Movie* and its sequels. His career was cut short when he died of pneumonia in 1990.

The most sophisticated people I know — inside they are all children.

1951 **Pedro Almodóvar:** Internationally acclaimed Spanish film director and screenwriter. Saved his money earned working for a phone company to buy a camera. Made short films with the help of his friends and became a star of the pop culture of the late 70s Madrid scene. Written, directed, acted and produced nearly 30 films, centered on relationships that occur in improbable situations. Films: *Dark Habits, Women on the Verge of a Nervous Breakdown* (Oscar for Best Foreign Language Film), *Tie Me Up! Tie Me Down!, All About My Mother* and *Talk to Her.*

I was born at a bad time for Spain, but a really good one for cinema.

OTHERS: 15 CE Roman Emperor **Vitellius**, 1564 British navigator/samurai **William Adams**, 1625 Dutch politician **Johan de Witt**, 1724 Irish brewer **Sir Arthur Guinness**, 1795 French sculptor **Antoine Barye**, 1801 Ukrainian scientist **Mikhail V. Ostrogradsky**, 1802 French paleontologist **Adolphe d'Archiac**, 1871 English athlete **Lottie Dod**, 1884 German weapons designer **Hugo Schmeisser**, 1898 Australian-born pharmacologist **Howard Walter Florey**, 1899 Australian portrait artist **Sir William Dobell**, 1905 Spanish biochemist **Severo Ochoa**, 1909 Polish architect **Gerard Ciolek**, 1921 U.S. sportscaster **Jim McKay**, 1946 U.S. football player **"Mean" Joe Greene**

September 25

1764 **Fletcher Christian:** British mutineer. Described by Captain Bligh as being 5 feet 9 inches tall, with a very dark complexion (consistent with the believe that he was born on the Island of Man), dark-brown hair, strong-made, bowlegged, of a nervous disposition and subject to violent sweating. When he led the mutiny on the H.M.S. Bounty, he was a 23-year-old first-mate, who had served on various ships with Bligh, with whom he had a close friendship. After the mutineers set Bligh at sea in an open boat, they took refuge on Pitcairn Island with some Tahitian men and women, including his lover Maimiti, where they found a settlement.

From now on, they'll spell mutiny with my name. I regret that.

1782 **Charles Robert Maturin:** Irish poet and novelist. Took holy orders and for a time ran a school. One of the leading writers of the Gothic novel. His most memorable work is *Melmouth the Wanderer*, the story of a man who sold his soul to the devil in exchange for a long life. Other books: *The Fatal Revenge, The Wild Irish Boy* and *The Albigenses.*

'Tis well to be merry and wise,/ 'Tis well to be honest and true;/ It is best to be off with the old love,/ Before you are on with the new.

1793 **Felicia Dorthea Browne Hemans:** English poet. Author of 24 volumes of verse which expressed romantic themes of childhood, innocence, liberty, inspiration and nature. She responded to the concerns of women of her time by idealizing and romanticizing woman's role and relationships. Captured much of the ethos of her day. Best known for *The Homes of England, The Landing of the Pilgrim Fathers*, and *Casabianca.*

The boy stood on the burning deck,/ Whence all but he had fled;/ The flame that lit the battle's wreck,/ Shone round him o'er the dead.

1881 **Lu Xun:** Pen name of Chinese writer Zhou Shuren, considered one of the most influential Chinese writers of the 20th century. Made significant contributions to every modern literary genre except for the novel. Founder of the modern vernacular literature. Called the "chief commander of China's modern cultural revolution" and "champion of common humanity." Stories: "A Madman's Diary," "Storm in a Teacup," "The Flight of the Moon" and "Opposing Aggression." Essay Collections: *Call to Arms, Old Tales Retold* and *Wild Grass.*

To be suspicious is not a fault. To be suspicious all the time without coming to a conclusion is the defect.

1897 **William Faulkner:** Among the greatest American writers. Most of his novels are set in fictional Yoknapatawpha County, Mississippi in which he explored the decay of the ante-bellum aristocracy and the rise of the crass and unscrupulous Snopes clan. Novels: *The Sound and the Fury, Sanctuary, Intruder in the Dust, Requiem for a Nun, A Fable, for which he belatedly received a Pulitzer Prize* and a second posthumously for *The Reivers.* In his 1949 Nobel Prize for literature speech he declared:

I believe man will not merely endure, he will prevail. He is immortal, not because he, alone

among creatures, has an inexhaustible voice but because he has a soul, a spirit capable of compassion and sacrifice and endurance.

1906 **Dmitri Shostakovich:** Preeminent Russian composer of the Soviet generation. Composed chamber and symphonic works. Alternated between political and satirical composition, later attempting to work closer to the government's official prescription. His style and compositions largely defined the nature of new Russian music. Wrote 11 symphonies, among them *May the First* and the outstanding *Ninth Symphony*; operas; the ballet *The Golden Age*; piano works; sonatas; and string quartets.

There can be no music without ideology.

1930 **Shel Silverstein:** American poet, cartoonist and composer, often compared to Dr. Seuss. Best known for his children's stories and his poetry. Credited for helping young readers develop an appreciation of poetry. Books, which he also illustrates: *Uncle Shelby's ABZ Book, Uncle Shelby's Story of Lafacadio, the Lion Who Shot Back, The Giving Tree Where the Sidewalk Ends, The Missing Piece* and *Falling Up*. Wrote the music and lyrics for "A Boy Named Sue," which earned Johnny Cash a Grammy Award in 1970.

I will not play tug o' war. I'd rather play hug o' war. Where everyone hugs instead of tugs. Where everyone giggles and rolls on the rug. Where everyone kisses, and everyone grins, and everyone cuddles, and everyone wins.

1931 or perhaps 1929 **Barbara Walters:** American television personality. Appeared regularly on "20/20" (1979–2004). One of the highest paid journalists in America. Opened doors for women in the big-paying, high — profile TV jobs. Television's first anchorwoman. Best known for her interviews with personalities in the world of entertainment and politics, among who have been: Boris Yeltsin, Margaret Thatcher, Fidel Castro, Indira Gandhi, Moammar Qaddafi, Katharine Hepburn, and Monica Lewinsky.

The sports page records people's accomplishments; the front page usually records nothing but man's failures.

1932 **Glenn Gould:** Canadian concert pianist. Debuted at age 15 with Toronto Symphony. Planned to concentrate on composing but the acclaim for his first recording, J.S. Bach's *Goldberg Variations*, launched him on an international career as a pianist. His Bach interpretations set new standards for their technical brilliance and subtle intelligence. Disliking playing in public, he left the concert stage for recording studios.

A record is a concert without halls and a museum whose curator is the owner.

1952 **Christopher Reeve:** American actor, director and spokesman for disabled people and a strong supporter of stem cell research. Best known for his film portrayal of Superman. In 1995 thrown from a horse and was paralyzed from the neck down. Later admitted that he contemplated suicide after realizing the extent of his disability, but credited his wife Dana with pulling him out of his depression, by telling him "I'll be with you for the long haul, no matter what. You're still you and I love you." The Reeves opened the Christopher and Dana Reeve Paralysis Resource Center in 2001. He died of heart failure at age 52 in 2004. A non-smoker, she died of lung cancer a year-and-a-half later.

A hero is an ordinary individual who finds the strength to persevere and endure in spite of overwhelming obstacles.

1968 **Will Smith:** Charismatic and energetic African-American actor, singer, producer and author. Starred on TV's comedy series *The Fresh Prince of Bel Air* (1900–96). He released a string of hit singles: "Men in Black" and "Getting Jiggy Wit It," and "Just the Two of Us" for his young son, Trey. Married to Jada Pinkett, with whom he has two children. Nominated for an Academy Award for his portrayal of Muhammad Ali in the film *Ali*.

Too many people spend money they haven't earned for things they don't want, to impress people they don't like.

1969 **Catherine Zeta-Jones:** Beautiful, exotic Welsh actress, singer and dancer. Gained international fame for *The Mask of Zorro* with Antonio Banderas and *Entrapment* with Sean Connery. Won an Academy Award for Best Supporting Actress for her role in *Chicago*. Married actor Michael Douglas, 25 years her senior, in 2000, with whom she has two children and shares a birthday. Other films: *Traffic, Intolerable Cruelty*, and *Ocean's Twelve*.

For a marriage to be a success, every woman and every man should have her and his own bathroom.

OTHERS: 1358 Japanese shogun **Ashikaga Yoshimitsu**, 1525 English explorer **Steven Borough**, 1599 Swiss sculptor **Francesco Borromini**, 1644 Danish astronomer **Ole Rømer**, 1683 French composer **Jean-Philippe Rameau**, 1773 Italian entomologist **Agostino Bassi**, 1839 German paleontologist **Karl von Zittel**, 1866 U.S. geneticist **Thomas Hunt Morgan**, 1903 Latvian painter **Mark Rothko**, 1905 U.S. sportswriter **Red Smith**, 1918 Baseball player/announcer **Phil Rizzuto**, 1927 English conductor **Sir Colin Davis**, 1936 U.S. actress/dancer **Juliet Prowse**, 1944 U.S. actor/producer **Michael Douglas**, 1947 U.S. supermodel **Cheryl Tiegs**, 1961 U.S. actress **Heather Locklear**, 1965 Basketball player **Scottie Pippin**

September 26

1774 **Johnny Appleseed:** Originally **John Chapman**. American frontier nurseryman and environmentalist. Little is known of his life until he appeared in Pennsylvania around 1800, gathering apple seeds from orchards. According to legend, he planted and tended to a trail of seedling orchards along the line of the coming migration of settlers into the western territory. Even during this period the source of information about him and his activities has been passed along by oral tradition. Dressed eccentrically, wearing a tin plate for a hat.

Appears to have been also a religious mystic and a Swedenborgian missionary. Noted for his kindness and generosity both to man and beast.

I could not enjoy myself better anywhere — I can lay on my back, look up at the stars and it seems almost as though I can see the angels praising God, for he made all things good.

1783 **Jane Taylor:** English children's writer. With her sister Ann, she published *Original Poems for Infant Minds* (1894), which was translated into several languages. It was followed by *Rhymes for the Nursery*, which contains one of the best-known verses of the English language, "Twinkle, twinkle, little star." In 1816 Jane Taylor produced *Essays in Rhyme.* Regularly contributed to *Youth's Magazine.*

Who ran to help me when I fell,/ And would some pretty story tell,/ Or kiss the place to make it well?/ My mother.

1874 **Lewis Hine:** American photographer and social activist. Interested in the potential of the camera for recording social conditions. Made an extensive photographic study of the immigrants arriving at Ellis Island and followed their lives in the tenants and sweatshops of the city. Worked for the National Child Labor Committee, traveling to factories, mills and mines where children worked long hours in deplorable health and safety conditions. His eloquent photo collections shocked the nation and became a powerful propaganda force for reform. After World War I, he recorded the European relief work of the Red Cross and made a remarkable study of the construction of the Empire State Building.

If I could tell the story in words, I wouldn't need to lug around a camera.

1888 **J. Frank Dobie:** American educator, storyteller, folklorist, historian and author. Going back-and-forth between teaching at the University of Texas in Austin and running his uncle's ranch, he found that, "in the university I am a wild man; in the wilds I am a scholar and a poet." Blended both environments by collecting the legendary tales of Texas and the frontier. Editor of the Texas Folklore Society, which broke with the practices of the American Folklore Society. Dobie and his followers collected and presented folklore and a living, participatory endeavor. Defended his refusal to seek a doctoral degree:

The average Ph.D. thesis is nothing but transference of bones from one graveyard to another.

1888 **T.S. [Thomas Stearns] Eliot:** American-born English poet, critic and dramatist. Recognized as one of the major poets of the 20th century. Poetry revolutionized the literary conventions of the Romantics and Victorians. Described himself as "classical in literature, royalist in politics and Anglo-Catholic in religion." Developed the concept of "dissociation of sensibility," described in his literary and social criticism. Awarded the Nobel Prize for Literature and the Order of Merit in 1948. Works: "The Love Song of J. Alfred Prufrock," "The Waste Land," "The Hollow Men," "Ash Wednesday," *Old Possum's Book of Practical Cats* and plays *Murder in the Cathedral* and *The Cocktail Party.*

I grow old ... I grow old.../ I shall wear the bottoms of my trousers rolled./ Shall I part my hair behind? Do I dare to eat a peach?/ I shall wear white flannel trousers, and walk upon the beach,/ I have heard the mermaids singing, each to each./ I do not think they will sing to me.

1889 **Martin Heidegger:** German philosopher. Main exponent of 20th century Existentialism. Published his magnum opus *Being and Time* (1927), which strongly influenced Jean-Paul Sartre and other existentialists. Employed the method of phenomenology, which emphasizes the immediacy of experience, the attempt to isolate it and set off from all assumptions of existence or casual influence and lay bare its essential structure. In 1933 he joined the Nazi Party and supported Hitler's policies, asserting: "The Fuhrer alone is the present and future German reality and its law."

Every man is born as many men and dies as a single one.

1897 **Paul VI [Giovanni Batista Montini]:** Catholic Church diplomat for most of his career, until named Bishop of Milan in 1954. Became a cardinal in 1958. Pope from 1963 to 1978. Carried through the Vatican II reforms, including revisions to the mass. Relaxed rules on fasting and removed a number of questionable saints from the church's calendar. Issued the encyclical *Humanae Vitae*, condemning birth control. Promoted Ecumenism as the first pope to travel widely.

No more war! Never again war! If you wish to be brothers, drop your weapons.

1898 **George Gershwin:** Foremost American composer. His melodic talents and genius for rhythmic invention made him a genuinely important American composer. Wrote many popular songs and musicals with his lyricist brother Ira. Produced musical comedies using fashionable jazz formulas in original and ingenious ways. His most ambitious undertaking was the composition of *Porgy and Bess*, an American opera in a folk manner, based on a book by Dubose Heyward. More serious music: *Rhapsody in Blue* and *An American in Paris.* Songs: "I Got Rhythm," "Summertime," "Someone to Watch Over Me," "But Not for Me," and "They Can't Take That from Me."

Life is a lot like jazz ... it's best when you improvise.

1914 **Jack LaLanne:** American fitness, exercise and nutritional advocate. Known as "the father of fitness." Opened his own health spa where he encouraged clients to better themselves through weight-training. Designed much of the equipment that is now standard in the fitness industry. First to encourage women to weight-lift. Presented fitness and exercise advice on TV (1951–84). At 91, he continues to work out every morning for two hours. His advice: "If man made it, don't eat it; if it tastes good, spit it out" and,

I can't die. It would ruin my image.

1946 **Andrea Dworkin:** American feminist. Critic of contemporary misogynistic society. Portrays society as promoting the hatred of women by debasing images of them, creating an atmosphere conducive to rape and woman-battering. Worked to have pornography legally condemned as an infringement of equal rights. Publications: *Woman Hating, Take Back the Night: Women on Pornography* and *Pornography: Men Possessing Women.*

Men know everything — all of them — all the time — no matter how stupid or inexperienced or arrogant or ignorant they are.

1946 **Christine Todd Whitman:** American Republican politician. Governor of New Jersey (1994–2001) and administrator of the Environmental Protection Agency (EPA, 2001–2003). Her tenure in the latter capacity has been criticized for her disavowal of the validity of a government-commissioned report suggesting human contribution to global warning. Contrary to the EPA's conclusions, assured New Yorkers that no threat was posed to their health by toxins released in the 9–11 attacks on the World Trade Center. Wrote *It's My Party, Too: Taking Back the Republican Party ... And Bringing the Country Again* (2005) critical of the policies of the Bush administration.

When you're dealing with people who think that Sponge Bob Square Pants is more important that social security, you have a problem.

1948 **Olivia Newton-John:** British-born Australian actress and singer. Granddaughter of German Nobel-prize winning physicist Max Born. Father Brin Newton-John was attached to the Enigma project at Bletchley Park, and was the officer who took Rudolf Hess into custody when he parachuted into Scotland in 1941. Her mother, Irene, translated and published *The Born-Einstein Letters* (1971). Her first album, *Olivia Newton-John*, made her one of the most popular British singers. "I Honestly Love you" was her first single to chart #1 in the U.S., followed by other hits: "Have You Never Been Mellow," "Hopelessly Devoted to You" and "Physical." Of her film career, only *Grease* stands out.

I love that quiet time when nobody's up and the animals are all happy to see me.

OTHERS: 1711 English politician **Richard Grenville-Temple**, 1791 French painter **Théodore Géricault**, 1869 Armenian composer **Komitas**, 1876 U.S. social worker **Edith Abbott**, 1877 Italian neurologist **Ugo Cerletti**, 1877 Swiss pianist **Alfred Cortot**, 1891 French conductor **Charles Munch**, 1892 U.S. sociologist **Robert S. Lynd**, 1895 U.S. actor **George Raft**, 1907 English art historian **Anthony Blunt**, 1925 U.S. country singer **Marty Robbins**, 1926 U.S. singer **Julie London**, 1930 German tenor **Franz Wunderlich**, 1936 South African activist **Winnie Mandela**, 1945 Brazilian singer **Gal Costa**, 1947 U.S. singer **Lynn Anderson**, 1954 U.S. guitar player **Craig Chaquico**, 1981 African-American Tennis player **Serena Williams**

September 27

1389 **Cosimo de' Medici:** Italian statesman and patron of the arts. Also known as "Cosimo the Elder." First of the Medici political dynasty, rulers of Florence during the Italian Renaissance. Worked to create peace in Northern Italy through the creation of a balance of power between Venice and Milan, during the Lombardy wars, and discouraging foreign powers from interfering. Patron of Fra Angelico, Fra Lippo Lippi, and Donatello, whose famed *David* was commissioned by Cosimo.

We read that we ought to forgive our enemies, but we do not read that we should forgive our friends.

1627 **Jacques Benigne Boussuet:** French bishop and theologian and court preacher. First to advocate the theory of political absolutism. Made the argument that government was divine and that kings perceived their power from God.

The greatest weakness of all is the great fear of appearing weak.

1722 **Samuel Adams:** American revolutionary patriot and statesman. Helped organize the Boston Tea Party and the Sons of Liberty. Wrote pamphlets against the British. Member of the Continental Congress (1774–81). Signer of the Declaration of Independence. Governor of Massachusetts (1794–97).

It does not require a majority to prevail, but rather an irate, tireless minority keen to set brush fires in people's minds.

1821 **Henri Frédéric Amiel:** Swiss writer whose fame rests upon his 16,900 page *Journal intime*, begun in 1847, which is a masterpiece of self-analysis. His remarkable diary was published in part first in 1883 in 2 volumes and translated by Mrs. H. Ward two years later. Since then it has been reedited and augmented.

Truth is not only violated by falsehood; it may be equally outraged by silence.

1840 **Alfred Thayer Mahan:** U.S. admiral and naval theorist. Wrote 20 books on naval history and global strategy, which greatly influenced the policies of the super powers during the late 19th and early 20th centuries. Major work: *The Influence of Sea Power upon History*.

We are to have a navy adequate to the sense of our needs; and that sense is bound to expand as our people appreciate more and more ... that a country's power and influence must depend upon her hold upon regions without her own borders, and to which the sea leads.

1840 **Thomas Nast:** German-born American caricaturist and editorial cartoonist. Best known for his Christmas drawings over a 24-year period. His sketches of Santa Claus are those now most identified with the secular saint. Chose the North Pole to be Santa's home, where he had a toy factory there with workers who were elves. Conceived the notion that bad children didn't get presents and started the custom of writing to Santa. Other notable images: Republican elephant, Democratic donkey, image of Columbia as a woman, and Uncle Sam. Biting wit focused on political corruption, and was instrumental in the downfall New York's Boss Tweed, who complained:

Let's stop those damned pictures. I don't care so much what the papers write about me — my constituents can't read, but damn it, they can see pictures.

1871 **Grazia Deledda:** Italian novelist, who wrote mainly stories of the lives and sensual passions of the peasants of her native Sardinia. Won a reputation for her superb lyricism and the intensity of her writing in novels such as, *Ashes*, *Ivy*, and *The Mother*. Nobel Prize for Literature in 1926.

According to an ancient Sardinian legend, the bodies of those who are born on Christmas Eve will never dissolve into dust but are preserved until the end of time.

1874 **Myrtle Reed: Mrs. James Sidney McCullough.** American novelist, essayist and poet. Pen name **Olive Green**. Works: *Lavender and Old Lace*, *Love Affairs of Literary Men*, *A Weaver of Dreams* and *A Spinner in the Sun*.

It saves trouble to be conventional, for you're not always explaining things.

1896 **Sam Ervin:** American politician and lawyer. U.S. senator from North Carolina (1954–75). Served on the Senate committee that censored Senator Joseph McCarthy and helped investigate labor racketeering. Became a folk hero as the chairman of the Senate Select Committee on Presidential Campaign Activities investigating the Watergate scandal. An eloquent expert on the constitution, he unceasingly pursued evidence against White House claims of executive privilege, which he labeled executive poppycock.

There is nothing in the Constitution that authorizes or makes it the official duty of a president to have anything to do with criminal activities.

1906 **William Empson:** British poet and critic. Tremendous influence on 20th century literary criticism and his rational metaphysical poetry. In particular, in his *Seven Types of Ambiguity* (1930), suggested that uncertainty or overlapping of meanings in the use of word can be an enrichment of poetry. Close examination of poetic texts helped lay the foundation for New Criticism. Other works: *Some Versions of Pastoral* and *The Structure of Complex Words*.

It is this deep blankness is the real thing strange./ The more things happen to you the more you can't/ Tell or remember even what they are.

1917 **Louis S. Auchincloss:** American novelist, short-story writer, essayist and biographer. Wrote his first novel *The Indifferent Children* (1947) using the name "Andrew Lee." Works deal with well-placed establishment figures: *The Rector of Justin*, *Powers of Attorney*, and *The Cat and the King*. Biographies of Edith Wharton, Cardinal Richelieu and an illustrated historical study of Queen Victoria.

Keep doing good deeds long enough and you'll probably turn out a good man in spite of yourself.

1949 **Mike Schmidt:** Hall of Fame third baseman with the Philadelphia Phillies. Perhaps the best at his position to have ever played the game. Led national league in home runs eight times; 548 career home runs; 3-time MVP and 10-time golden glove winner.

Philadelphia is the only city in the world where you can experience the thrill of victory and the agony of reading about it the next day.

OTHERS: 1643 American Puritan clergyman **Solomon Stoddard**, 1729 Austrian poet **Michael Denis**, 1805 Prussian orphanage builder **George Müller**, 1842 Belgian geologist **Alphonse Renard**, 1879 Austrian mathematician **Hans Hahn**, 1879 English composer **Cyril Scott**, 1907 French philosopher **Maurice Blanchot**, 1913 U.S. psychologist **Albert Ellis**, 1918 English radio astronomer **Martin Ryle**, 1920 U.S. actress **Jayne Meadows**, 1932 U.S. economist **Oliver E. Williamson**, 1934 U.S. sportscaster **Dick Schaap**, 1936 African-American TV dance show host **Don Cornelius**, 1943 Canadian singer/guitarist **Randy Bachman**, 1947 U.S. singer **Meat Loaf**, 1984 Canadian singer **Avril Lavigne**

September 28

551 BCE **Confucius:** China's most famous teacher, philosopher and political theorist. His teachings that have deeply influenced East Asian life and thought are known primarily through the *Analects*, a short collection of his discussions with his disciples, compiled posthumously. At 50 he began a 12-year journey around China, seeking the "Way." Spent the remainder of his life teaching an increasing number of disciples, sharing his experiences and an transmitting the old wisdom in a series of books, known as the *Five Classics* There are arguments over whether Confucianism should be considered a religion, as it makes little reference to theological or spiritual matters.

I hear and I forget. I see and I remember. I do and I understand.

1705 **Henry Fox:** English statesman. Squandered his inheritance and went to the Continent to escape from his creditors. Made the acquaintance of a wealthy woman, who as his patroness enabled him to return to England and enter parliament. His oratorical skills helped him progress in the House of Congress, holding various positions in several administrations, including Secretary of War (1741–46) and Leader of the House of Commons (1755–56, 62–63). As Paymaster of the Forces, he amassed a fortune from the interest on the outstanding balances in the accounts of his office.

Touch but a cobweb in Westminster Hall, and the old spider of the law is out upon you with all his vermin at his heels.

1841 **Georges Clemenceau:** French politician and statesman. Premier (1906–9 and 1917–20). Nicknamed "the Tiger," for his ferocious attacks on those he disliked. After World War I, presided over the Peace Conference in Paris that drew up the Treaty of Versailles. His successful desire for revenge against Germany and demand for incredible reparations is seen as a significant contributing factor to the horrendous economic conditions in the defeated nation, leaving it ripe for embracing the promises of Hitler and the Nazis.

America is the only nation in history which miraculously has gone directly from barbarianism to degeneration without the usual interval of civilization.

1887 **Avery Brundage:** Controversial American sports administrator. President of U.S. Olympic Committee (1929–53). President of the International Olympic Committee (1952–73). Guardian of what he considered the superiority of amateur sports against the menace of creeping professionalism. After visiting the Soviet Union in 1955, impressed with their athletic skills he said that he feared that the U.S. would be at a disadvantage in future competition because "we have become a race of grandstand and bleacher sitters." Saw no contradiction in the following two observations:

The Olympic Movement is a 20th century religion, where there is no injustice of caste, of race, of family, of wealth.... The ancient Greeks kept women athletes out of their games. They wouldn't even let them on the sidelines. I'm nor sure but that they were right.

1901 **William S. Paley:** American radio and television executive. Founder of the Columbia Broadcasting System (CBS), serving as president (1928–46) and chairman of the board (1946–90). Launched CBS News in 1933. Gave Edward R. Murrow "carte blanche" to assemble a crew of working newsmen rather than merely a group of mellifluous-sounding news readers. When asked at a stockholder's meeting why Murrow was paid more than Paley, he replied modestly, "Because he's worth more."

Who can refute a sneer?

1909 **Al Capp:** U.S. cartoonist. Creator of "Li'l Abner," a comic strip noted for broad satire of the mores and politics of the country. As time went by and protests against the war intensified, he became increasingly strident in his strips against those who did not share his political, social and moral beliefs. An example of his contemporary on aspects of the modern world with which he abhorred is the statement: "Abstract art is a product of the untalented, sold by the unprincipled to the utterly bewildered."

Young people should be helped, sheltered, ignored, and clubbed if necessary.

1915 **Ethel Rosenberg:** With her husband Julius, the first U.S. civilians executed for espionage. There is doubt that she actually was a spy. When Soviet communications were decrypted and made public, they indicated that Julius was actively involved in espionage, but they provided no specific acts of espionage for which he was convicted, nor that Ethel was involved. The primary witness against the couple was her brother David Greenglass, who confessed to having passed on secret information to the U.S.S.R. obtained at the top-secret Los Alamos laboratory. Sparred execution for his testimony, he asserted that Ethel and Julius had also passed secrets. Her last words:

We are the first victims of American fascism.

1924 **Marcello Mastroianni:** Darkly handsome Italian actor. Appeared in over 100 movies, Won international fame in films such as Luchino Visconti's *White Nights* and Federico Fellini's *La Dolce Vita*. Other films: *La Notte, Divorce—Italian Style, Yesterday, Today and Tomorrow, Ginger and Fred* and *Everybody's Fine.*

Woman is the sun, an extraordinary creature, one that makes the imagination gallop. Woman is also the element of conflict. With whom do you argue? With a woman, of course. Not with a friend, because he accepted all your defects the moment he found you. Besides, woman is mother—have we forgotten.

1925 **Arnold Stang:** American comedian and character actor, best known for playing nebbish types. One of the busiest second bananas. Traded quips on radio, TV and in films with Eddie Cantor, Jack Benny, Henry Morgan, Fred Allen, Fanny Brice, Milton Berle, Gertrude Berg, and Frank Sinatra. His trademark consisted of thick, horn-rimmed glasses, bow tie and a high-pitched New York accent. Radio work: "Let's Pretend," "The Henry Moran Show" and "The Goldbergs." Film work: *My Sister Eileen* and *The Man with the Golden Arm.* TV: "The Milton Berle Show" and the title role inn the animated "Top Cat."

Radio allows you to use your imagination. TV dinners describe what TV really is.

1934 **Brigitte Bardot:** Originally **Camille Javal**. French actress. Trained as a ballet dancer and worked as a model before becoming a blonde sex-kitten. A pouting child-woman in films directed by her husband Roger Vadim: *And God Created Woman* and *The Bride Is Much Too Beautiful.* Film image of petulant sexuality reinforced by her much publicized love life. Uncomfortable as an international symbol of sexual permissiveness, retired from films (1971).

It is better to be unfaithful than to be faithful without wanting to be.

1938 **Ben E. King:** Originally **Benjamin Earl Nelson**. African-American singer and songwriter. Plaintive baritone voice had all the passion of gospel. His honey smooth phrasing and crisp enunciation displayed on hits: "Spanish Harlem," "Here Comes the Night," and "A Man without a Dream." Best known for "Stand by Me," co-written with Jerry Leiber and Mike Stoller. Voted one of the Songs of the Century by the Recording Industry Association of America.

When the night has come/ And the land is dark? And the moon is the only light we'll see/ No, I won't be afraid/ Oh, I won't be afraid/ Just as long as you stand, stand by me.

1972 **Gwyneth Paltrow:** Tall, thin, delicate beautiful American actress. Daughter of actress Blythe Danner and film director Bruce Paltrow. Academy Award Winner for *Shakespeare in Love*. Began her acting career in the Williamstown Theatre production of *Picnic.* Married Chris Martin, lead singer of the band Coldplay, in 2003, with whom she has two children, Apple and Moses Other films: *The Talented Mr. Ripley, Emma, Sylvia* and *Proof.*

Beauty, to me, is about being comfortable in your own skin. That, or a kick-ass red lipstick.

OTHERS: 1573 Italian artist **Michelangelo Merisi da Caravaggio**, 1605 French astronomer **Ismael Bullialdus**, 1746 English philologist **Sir William Jones**, 1803 French author **Propser Mérimçe**, 1824 British poet **Francis Turner Palgrave**, 1856 U.S. children's author/educator **Kate Douglas Wiggin**, 1870 French composer **Florent Schmitt**, 1892 U.S. writer **Elmer Rice**, 1901 U.S. TV host **Ed Sullivan**, 1905 German boxer **Max Schmeling**, 1913 Tennis player **Alice Marble**, 1916 English actor **Peter Finch**, 1939 U.S. biologist **Stuart Kauffman**, 1947 PM of Bangladesh **Sheikh Hasina**, 1968 English actress **Naomi Watts**, 1987 U.S. actress **Hilary Duff**

September 29

1511 **Michael Servetus:** Spanish physician and theologian. While studying medicine in Paris he discovered the pulmonary circulation of blood. In his theological writings he denied the Trinity and divinity of Christ. His unorthodox teachings led to his condemnation by both Protestants and Roman Catholics. Escaped the Inquisition but was burned in Geneva by John Calvin for heresy.

To kill a man is not to defend a doctrine, but to kill a man.

1547 **Miguel de Cervantes [Saavedra]:** Great Spanish novelist, dramatist and poet. Wounded and lost the use of his left hand at the battle of Lepanto. Taken prisoner by pirates in 1575 and spent five years in captivity in Algiers. Spent the remainder of his life trying to scratch out a living as a writer and minor government official. His reputation as one of history's greatest novelists rests almost entirely on his masterpiece *Don Quixote* and twelve short stories known as the *Exemplary Tales.*

In order to attain the impossible, one must attempt the absurd.

1758 Lord **Horatio Nelson:** British naval commander. Called the most famous naval commander of the greatest maritime power in history. Defeated French in the Battle of the Nile (1798). Killed during the Battle of Trafalgar, in which the French fleet was destroyed. His long romance with Lady Emma Hamilton caused a scandal. While dying, he remarked, "Thank God I have done my duty."

I could not tread these perilous paths in safety, if I did not keep a saving sense of humor.

1810 **Elizabeth Gaskell:** English novelist Born **Elizabeth Stevenson**. Married Manchester Unitarian Minister William Gaskell. Shocked by the poverty of the city's textile workers, became involved in various charities and wrote a novel to illustrate the problems faced by the people living in industrial towns and cities. *Mary Barton: A Tale of Manchester Life* (1884) addressed key social issues such as urban poverty, Chartism, and the developing trade-union movement.

Like all energetic people, the more he had to do the more time he seemed to find.

1864 **Miguel de Unamuno y Jugo:** Spanish author and philosopher. Fierce critic of Spanish social and political life. Best known in English-speaking countries for his philosophical essays. In *La Vida de Don Quijote y Sancho* he perceives Don Quixote as the embodiment of Spanish genius. *The Tragic Sense of Life* is an unorthodox medication on man's religious aspirations, with God, not the first cause but the consequence of man's longing for immortality.

A lot of good arguments are spoiled by some fool who knows what he is talking about.

1901 **Enrico Fermi:** Italian-born U.S. physicist. Pioneered the study of neutrons and neutron bombardment. Awarded the Nobel Prize in Physics (1938) for his research in radioactive substances. With Albert Einstein and Leo Szilard, he urged President Roosevelt to develop a nuclear weapon before Germany did, leading to the establishment of the Manhattan Project. Fermi was a member of the group which made the first man-made nuclear chain reaction at the University of Chicago's Stagg Field in 1942. While he approved the military use of the fission bomb (A-bomb) against Japan, he opposed the development of the fusion bomb (H-bomb).

There are two possible outcomes: if the result confirms the hypothesis, then you've made a measurement. If the result is contrary to the hypothesis, then you've made a discovery.

1913 **Trevor Howard:** Prolific British actor. Created many memorable screen appearances: the married doctor whose not-to-be love for married Celia Johnson in *Brief Encounter* (1945) is one of the finest love stories every to appear on the screen; remarkable as the police major in *The Third Man* (1949), exceptionally worthy in Graham Greene's *The Heart of the Matter* (1953), a Christ-like figure fighting a losing battle to ban the hunting of elephants in flawed *The Roots of Heaven*, and Oscar nominated for the drunker father in *Sons and Lovers.*

I've been number two in films for donkey's years.

1923 **Oail Andrew "Bum" Phillips:** American football coach. In 1975, Phillips was named head coach and general manager of the Houston Oilers, serving in that capacity through 1980; the team's winningest coach. Head coach of New Orleans Saints (1981–85). Known for wearing his trademark cowboy hat on the sidelines but not in enclosed stadiums because he was taught not to wear a hat indoors.

You don't know a ladder has splinters until you slide down it.

1935 **Jerry Lee Lewis:** American rock 'n' roll singer and piano player. Influenced by blues and gospel musicians. Known for His energetic and uninhibited live performances, standing and jumping around as he plays his piano. Biggest hits: "Whole Lotta Shakin' Goin' On" and "Great Balls of Fire." Cousin of evangelist Jimmy Swaggart and country and western singer Mickey Gilley.

If I'm going to Hell, I'm going playing the piano.

1939 **Molly Haskell:** American author and film critic. Movie reviewer first with *The Village Voice*, then the *New York Magazine* and *Vogue*. Books include *From Reverence to Rape: the Treatment of Women in Movies* (1973, revised and reissued in 1989) and a collection of essays and interviews, *Holding My Own in No Man's Land: Women and Men in Films and Feminists* (1997).

For a woman there is nothing more erotic than being understood.

1942 **Madeline Kahn:** Delightfully funny American actress and comedienne in quirky roles. Sang on and off Broadway and in nightclubs before her screen debut. Oscar nominations for *Paper Moon* and *Blazing Saddles*. Others: *Young Frankenstein* and *High Anxiety*. In 1989 she starred in a Broadway revival of *Born Yesterday* and earned a Tony Award for her performance as sister Gorgeous in Wendy Wasserstein's *The Sisters Rosensweig*.

Husbands should be like Kleenex: soft, strong and disposable.

1943 **Lech Wałęsa:** Polish political leader and labor union official. An electrician, he worked at the Lenin Shipyard at Gdańsk but was fired for his antigovernment activities. Joined workers on strike in 1980 and soon became the leader of Solidarity, the only independent trade union in the Communist world (1980). Won Nobel Peace Prize (1983). Elected president in a landslide in 1990, and helped guide Poland into a free-market economy.

He who puts out his hand to stop the wheel of history will have his fingers crushed.

OTHERS: 1388 1st Duke of Clarence **Thomas of Lancaster**, 1561 Flemish mathematician **Adriaan van Roomen**, 1636 Archbishop of Canterbury **Thomas Tenison**, 1639 English politician **William Russell**, 1640 French sculptor **Antoine Coysevox**, 1725 British statesman **Robert Clive**, 1838 U.S. architect **Henry Hobson Richardson**, 1893 Russian conductor **Fabien Sevitzky**, 1895 U.S. parapsychologist **J.B. Rhine**, 1901 Italian philosopher/poet **Lanza del Vasto**, 1907 U.S. cowboy actor/singer **Gene Autry**, 1927 U.S. Senator **John Tower**, 1931 U.S. nuclear physicist **James Watson Cronin**, 1931 Swedish actress **Anita Ekberg**, 1936 Italian PM **Silvio Berlusconi**, 1956 British miler **Sebastian Coe**

September 30

1207 **Jalal ad-Din ar-Rumi:** Persian poet and mystic. Met Shams ad-Din, a holy man who revealed the mysteries of divine majesty and beauty. Their intimate relationship scandalized Rumi's followers, who had Shams murdered. The Collected Poetry of Shams contains Rumi's verses of love for Shams. Main work, *Spiritual Couplets* widely influenced Muslim thought and literature.

Sell your cleverness and buy bewilderment.

1861 **William Wrigley, Jr.:** American manufacturer. Founded Wrigley chewing gum empire. President of the company from 1891 to 1932. Owner of the Chicago Cubs baseball team. Played an instrumental role in the history of Catalina Island, off the shore of Los Angeles, arranging so it would always remain protected for all generations to enjoy.

When two men in business always agree, one of them is unnecessary.

1895 **Lewis Milestone:** Originally **Lev Milstein**. Russian-born U.S. director and screenwriter. Academy Award for Best Director for the masterful anti-war *All Quiet on the Western Front* (1929–30). Told by a studio executive that the ending of *All Quiet on the Western Front* was too depressing, he responded, "I've got your happy ending. We'll let the Germans win the war." Other Films: *The Front Page, Rain, The General Died at Dawn, Of Mice and Men, The Purple Heart,* and *A Walk in the Sun*.

Hollywood has no future. All we have out here is the past. And God knows, it hasn't much present.

1905 **Michael Powell:** British film director. Teamed with screenwriter Emeric Pressburger to form a production company, turning out colorful and experimental movies: *The Thief of Bagdad, The Life and Death of Colonel Blimp, Stairway to Heaven, Black Narcissus, The Red Shoes,* and *The Tales of Hoffman*.

Everyone has heard of Canterbury if only because they murder archbishops there.

1921 **Deborah Kerr:** Originally **Deborah Jane Kerr-Trimmer**. English actress. Often cast in prim roles. Oscar nomination for *Edward, My Son, From Here to Eternity, The King and I, Heaven Knows, Mr. Allison, Separate Tables* and *The Sundowners*. Received a special Academy Award in 1994.

Personally, I think if a woman hasn't met the right man by the time she's 24, she may be lucky.

1922 **Jesse Unruh:** American political leader. Known as "Big Daddy." Powerful and influential California assemblyman and California State Treasurer. National figure in Democratic Party politics, often feuding with fellow Democrat Pat Brown, Governor of California. Unruh aided the presidential campaigns of John F. Kennedy and Robert Kennedy.

Money is the mother's milk of politics.

1924 **Truman Capote:** Born **Truman Streckfus Persons.** American author and playwright. Early works were in the Southern gothic tradition. Wrote of alienated individuals in slightly surreal stories. Later works noted as "non-fiction novels." Works include: *Other Voices, Other Rooms, Breakfast at Tiffany's* and *In Cold Blood*. In 2005 Philip Seymour Hoffman won a Best Actor Oscar for portraying Capote in a film of that name. Another film about Capote was released in 2006.

Finishing a book is just like you took a child out in the yard and shot it.

1928 **Elie Wiesel:** Hungarian-born journalist and author. A survivor of Auschwitz concentration camp, his books deal with the experiences of survivors of the

Holocaust. Attempted to resolve the ethical torment of why it happened and what it revealed about human nature. Books: *Night*, *A Beggar in Jerusalem*, *The Testament* and *The Forgotten*. In 1986 he won the Nobel Peace Prize.

The opposite of love is not hate, it's indifference. The opposite of art is not ugliness, it's indifference. The opposite of faith is not heresy, it's indifference. And the opposite of life is not death, it's indifference. Because of indifference, one dies before one actually dies.

1931 **Angie Dickinson:** Born **Angeline Brown**. Long-legged American actress. Best known for her television series "Police Woman" (1974–78) and films *Rio Bravo*, *The Sins of Rachel Cade* and *Dressed to Kill*. Formerly married to composer Burt Bacharach.

I dress for women and I undress for men.

1935 **Johnny Mathis:** African-American singer. High school track star; invited to try out for the 1956 Olympics but chose a musical career instead. Mellow voiced pop star with hits: "A Certain Smile," "Twelfth of Never," "Misty," "Chances Are" and "The Shadow of Your Smile."

They're disappointed if you don't do the old songs.

1964 **Trey Anastasio:** American musician, guitarist, songwriter and singer. Frontman for the psychedelic cult band Phish. Throughout his career, he has participated in various projects not associated with the group. Albums: *One Man's Trash*, *Trampled by Lambs and Pecked by Doves*, *Trey Anastasio*, *Shine* and *Plasma*.

Set the gearshift for the high gear of your soul, you've got to run like an antelope out of control.

1980 **Martina Hingis:** Swiss tennis player. Born in what is now Slovakia. Known as the "Swiss Miss." Won five Grand Slam single titles and nine Grand Slam double titles. Set a series of "youngest ever" records, before ligament injuries to her ankles forced her to retire at 21, but she made a comeback in 2005.

One day you can be a kid, but another day you have to be like this is your job, you play tennis. You have to work for that.

OTHERS: 1530 Italian philologist/physician **Geronimo Mercuriali**, 1550 German mathematician **Michael Maestlin**, 1631 Judge at Salem witch trials **William Stoughton**, 1700 Polish writer **Stanisław Konarski**, 1715 French philosopher **Étienne Bonnot de Condillac**, 1800 British architect **Decimus Burton**, 1870 French physicist **Jean Baptiste Perrin**, 1870 U.S. banker **Thomas W. Lamont**, 1882 German physicist **Hans Geiger**, 1898 French actress **Renée Adorée**, 1904 Welsh poet **Waldo Williams**, 1908 Ukrainian violinist **David Oistrakh**, 1915 U.S. Governor **Lester Maddox**, 1939 French chemist **Jean-Marie Lehn**

October 1

1799 **Rufus Choate:** One of the most able American lawyers and most scholarly of American public men. His numerous orations and addresses were remarkable for their pure style, grace and elegance of form, and their wealth of classical allusion. Elected to the U.S. Congress as a Whig, resigning after serving two terms. But after pursuing a successful Boston law practice, he succeeded Daniel Webster in the U.S. Senate.

A book is the only immortality.

1847 **Annie Besant:** Born **Annie Wood**. English social reformer, Fabian socialist theosophist, and Indian independence advocate. Ardent proponent of birth control and socialism, influenced by George Bernard Shaw. Longtime residence of India, where she was involved in politics. Instrumental in acquainting Europeans with Hindu thought. President of the Indian National Congress (1917–23). Publications: *The Gospel of Atheism* and *Theosophy and the New Psychology*.

Better remain silent, better not even think, if you are not prepared to act.

1885 **Louis Untermeyer:** American poet and critic. Turned to poetry only after he realized that he lacked the talent to become a concert pianist. One of the first to recognize the importance of anthology as a device for critical survey. Made translations of Heine, Horace, etc. and wrote biological works: *Heritage American Poets Series—Longfellow to Emily Dickinson*. Publications: *Modern American and British Poetry*, *A Treasury of Great Poems* and *A Treasury of Ribaldry*. A famous punster, he said, "Punning, like poetry is something everyone belittles and everyone attempts."

Every poet knows the pun is Pierian, that it springs from the same soil as the Muse, a matching and shifting of vowels and consonants, an adroit assonance sometimes derided as jackassonance.

1893 **Faith Baldwin:** Prolific American writer of many popular romantic novels. Spokeswoman for the misunderstood and struggling wife, mother, or working woman. Works: *Alimony*, *The Office Wife*, *Weekend Marriage*, *He Married a Doctor*, *Skyscraper*, *They Who Love* and *Evening Star*. Also wrote poetry, serials and short stories.

Character builds slowly, but it can be torn down with incredible swiftness.

1904 **Vladimir Horowitz:** Russian-born American virtuoso pianist. One of the 20th century's greatest musicians. Considered by many to have been the most flawless technician of the piano. Following a successful debut at age 18, by age 22, he had performed as soloist with the great orchestras of nearly all the European capitals. Best know for his interpretations of Rachmaninoff, Chopin, Liszt, Prokofiev, Scriabin and Schumann. Married from 1933 to Wanda Toscanini, daughter of Maestro Arturo Toscanini.

I am a general. My soldiers are the keys and I have to command them.

1907 **Helen Brown Norden Lawrenson:** American social critic, editor and author. Editor of *Vanity Fair*. First woman to write for *Esquire* magazine with her article "Latins Are Lousy Lovers" (October 1939). However, the author was given as "Anonymous." It was revealed to be her work when reprinted in *The Bedside Esquire* (1940). Apparently she did a great deal of international field work on the subject, which became clear with her memoir, *Whistling Girl: Candid Confessions of a Chameleon*. It details her adventures in brothels, love affairs in Havana, membership in the Communist Party and interviews with Hollywood stars.

Girls without chemises/ Should stay away from breezes/ Or they many catch sneezes/ In addition to being the cynosure of all eyes/ When their skirts fly above their kneeses.

1911 **Fletcher Knebel:** American author of several novels. Spent 20 years as a journalist and the political columnist for Cowles Publications. Wrote 15 books, most of them fiction, and all with political themes. Best known, co-written with Charles Bailey II, was *Seven Days in May*, about an attempted military coup in the United States. Other novels: *Convention, Night of Camp David* and *Vanished*.

Our forefathers made one mistake. What they should have fought for was representation without taxation.

1924 **James Earl "Jimmy" Carter:** Democratic politician and Governor of Georgia (1971–75). 39th president of the U.S. (1971–81), first to be elected from the Deep South. Features of his presidency were the return of the Panama Canal Zone to Panama and the Camp David Agreements for Peace in the Middle East. High inflation and the Iran hostage crisis contributed to his defeat in 1980 by Ronald Reagan. Emerged as a leading mediator and peace negotiator throughout the world. Helped oversee elections in countries with insecure democratic traditions. Third U.S. president, after Theodore Roosevelt and Woodrow Wilson, to receive the Nobel Peace Prize (2002).

America did not invent human rights. In a very real sense, it is the other way around. Human rights invented America.

1924 **William H. Rehnquist:** American jurist. Active in the conservative wing of the Republican Party. At the U.S. Justice Department, he opposed civil-rights legislation and advocated greatly enlarged police power. Nominated to the Supreme Court by President Nixon in 1972 and Ronald Reagan appointed him Chief Justice in 1986. Led the court along a conservative path. Presided over the U.S. Senate during the impeachment trail of President Clinton.

Somewhere out there, beyond the walls of the courthouse, run currents and tides of public opinion which lap at the courtroom door.

1935 **Julie Andrews:** Originally **Julia Elizabeth Wells**. British actress and singer. Selected for the New York production of *The Boyfriend* (1954) and several long running Broadway musicals, most notably *My Fair Lady* and *Camelot*. Especially known for her starring roles in the musical films *Mary Poppins*, for which she won an Academy Award, and *The Sound of Music*, for which she was nominated. Films in which she tried to jettison her sweet and prim image: *S.O.B.*, *10*, and *Victor/Victoria*.

All love shifts and changes. I don't know if you can be wholeheartedly in love all the time.

1949 **Merle Kessler:** San Francisco–based writer, playwright and performer. Founding member of Duck's Breath Mystery Theater, which celebrated its 30th anniversary in 2005. Also writes under the pen name **Ian Shoales**, ranting about stupidities with cranky commentary since 1979. Featured on NPR's "Morning Edition," ABC's "Nightline," and online in *Salon Magazine*. His comments also air weekly on ABC's news program, "World News Now."

Football players, like prostitutes, are in the business of ruining their bodies for the pleasure of strangers.

1949 **Annie Leibovitz:** American photographer. Became known during her 13 years as staff photographer for *Rolling Stone Magazine*. In the 80s, photographed celebrities for a national advertising campaign for American Express charge cards. Since 1983, she worked as a portrait photographer for *Vanity Fair*. Published five books of her photographs, including: *American Olympians*, *Women*, and *American Music*. Her longtime companion was Susan Sontag until the latter's death.

A thing that you see in my pictures is that I was not afraid to fall in love with these people.

OTHERS: 1207 King of England **Henry III**, 1507 Italian architect **Giacomo da Vignola**, 1620 Dutch painter **Nicolaes Pieterszoon Berchem**, 1760 English writer/politician **William Beckford**, 1771 French violinist/composer **Pierre Baillot**, 1791 Russian writer **Sergei Aksakov**, 1837 Civil War Commander of Black soldiers **Robert Gould Shaw**, 1881 U.S. engineer **William Boeing**, 1896 1st Pakistani PM **Liaquat Ali Khan**, 1904 Austrian-born physicist **Otto Frisch**, 1910 U.S. outlaw **Bonnie Parker**, 1914 U.S. historian **Daniel J. Boorstin**, 1920 U.S. actor **Walter Matthau**, 1930 Irish actor **Richard Harris**, 1936 U.S. ballet dancer **Edward Villella**, 1945 Panamanian baseball player **Rod Carew**

October 2

1800 **Nat Turner:** African-American slave uprising leader. Let 60 slaves in the "Southampton Insurrection" (1831), capturing an armory in Virginia. Believed he was divinely appointed to lead the slaves to freedom. Eluded capture for 6 weeks. Slave owners were so alarmed that regressive measures forbidding the educating any blacks were swiftly enacted. Widespread torture and execution followed. Turner and 16 others were hanged.

Having soon discovered to be great, I must appear so, and therefore studiously avoided mixing in society, and wrapped myself in mystery, devoting my time to fasting and prayer.

1851 **Ferdinand Foch:** Marshal of France appointed Commander-in-Chief of the Allied Armies in World War I in 1918. Largely responsible for the Allied victory at the first battle of the Marne (1914). Launched the Allied counter-offensive in July 1918 that brought about the negotiation of an armistice to end the war.

My center is giving away, my right is in retreat; situation excellent. I shall attack.

1869 Mahatma **Mohandas Gandhi:** Indian philosopher, political leader and social thinker. Practiced law in Bombay before moving to South Africa, where he opposed discriminatory legislation against Indians. Leader of the Indian nationalist movement against the British. Espoused nonviolent civil disobedience to achieve political and social changes. Civil disobedience campaign in 1920 caused violent disorder and led to his imprisonment. Led 200-mile march to the sea to collect salt as a symbolic defiance of Government monopoly (1922–24). Threatened "fasts to the death" were effective because of his international reputation as a holy man. Negotiated with the British Cabinet Mission, which recommended new constitutional structure, resulting in India's independence. Assassinated by a Hindu fanatic in 1948.

Be the change you want to see in the world.

1871 **Cordell Hull:** Democratic American politician, statesman and diplomat from Tennessee. Member of Congress (1907–33). U.S. Secretary of State (1933–44). Developed the Good Neighbor policy with Latin America. Promoted cooperation with the Soviet Union against Hitler. Planner of a postwar world organization. Known as the "Father of the United Nations." Nobel Peace Prize (1945).

Never insult an alligator until after you have crossed the river.

1879 **Wallace Stevens:** American poet. From 1916 worked for the Hartford Accident and Indemnity Company, where he remained until his death, promoted to vice-president in 1934. At the same time he published poems and his first volume of poetry *Harmonium*. Pulitzer Prize winner for his *Collected Poems* (1954). Poems: "Thirteen Ways to Look at a Blackbird," "Anecdote of the Jar," "Peter Quince at the Clavier," "and "The Man with the Blue Guitar."

A poet looks at the world as a man looks at a woman.

1890 **Groucho Marx:** Originally **Julius Henry Marx**. Fast-thinking, master of the ad-lib and the cynical pun American comedian, who with his brothers Chico and Harpo (sometimes Zeppo) were delightfully zany in Broadway shows and films: *Animal Crackers, Duck Soup, A Night at the Opera* and *A Day at the Races*. Groucho became identified with his crouched walk, incredible mustache (initially painted on), roving, leering eyes, framed by steel-rimmed glasses and an ever present cigar. Hosted the popular television quiz show, "You Bet Your Life."

A man's only as old as the woman he feels.

1904 **Graham Greene:** English novelist, short-story writer and playwright. Novels are psychological studies, adventure thrillers and stories of moral dilemmas. A converted Roman Catholic his works sometimes had specifically Catholic themes. A number of his stories were of the "chase" genre. The agony of the attempted escape of Greene's hunted and haunted characters is the agony of modern man. Works: *This Gun for Hire, The Third Man, The Power and the Glory, The Heart of the Matter, The End of the Affair, The Quiet American,* and *Our Man in Havana.*

Heresy is another word for freedom of thought.

1930 **Antonio Gala:** Difficult to classify Spanish writer. A poet, playwright, journalist and novelist; also has written short stories, essays and TV scripts. Poetry Collections: *La Zubia Sonnets, Love Poems,* and *Intimate Enemy.* Novels: *The Crimson Manuscript, Two-Headed Eagle,* and *Turkish Passion.* Awarded several prizes, not only for his poetry, but also for his contributions to theater and opera.

Happiness is realizing that nothing is too important.

1937 **Johnnie L. Cochran:** Renowned American attorney who made a name for himself successfully defending celebrities like O.J. Simpson, Puff Daddy, and Snoop Dogg in high profile cases. Most proud of his work with ordinary citizens who claimed to be abused by police. During the Simpson case, in a trial that divided the country, he is remembered for the phrase, "If the glove doesn't fit, you must acquit." It was said in a dramatic moment during which O.J. tried on a pair of bloodstained "murder gloves" to show jurors they did not fit. Many legal experts fell this was the turning point in the trial.

People in New York and Los Angeles, especially mothers in the African-American community are more afraid of police injuring or killing their children than they are of muggers on the corner.

1940 **Rex Reed:** American movie critic and actor. Co-host of the syndicated TV show *At the Movies.* Currently writes the column "On the Town with Rex Reed" for the *New York Observor.* Also a regular on TV's *The Gong Show.* Briefly flirted with an acting career. He was incredibly lame as a would-be transsexual in the incredibly lame film made from Gore Vidal's book *Myra Breckinridge.*

Hollywood is where if you don't have happiness you send out for it.

1945 **Don McLean:** American songwriter and singer. In his biggest hit "American Pie" (1971), he sings of "the day the music died," referring to the death of Buddy Holly. Also had a major hit with "Vincent" (also known as "Starry, Starry Night," about Vincent van Gogh, containing the line, "The world was never meant for one as beautiful as you." Other songs: "And I Love You So," "Castles in the Air," "Wonderful Baby," (a tribute to Fred Astaire) and "Superman's Ghost" (a tribute to George Reeves who portrayed Superman on TV in the 1950s).

I met a girl who sang the blues,/ And I asked her for some happy news;/ But she just smiled and turned away.

1951 **Sting [Gordon Sumner]:** English singer, songwriter and actor. Before going solo, he was the lead singer, principal composer and bass guitarist for the rock group The Police. Took his nickname from the yellow and black jersey he liked to wear, which was said to make him look like a bumblebee. Solo songs: "Fortress Around Your Heart," We'll Be Together," "All for Love," "You Still Touch Me," Brand New Day," and "After the Rain Has Fallen." Featured in the film *Dune* (1984) and appeared as Baron Frankenstein in *The Bride* (1985).

It takes a man to suffer ignorance and smile.

OTHERS: 1452 King of England **Richard III**, 1539 Italian cardinal **St. Charles Borromeo**, 1832 English anthropologist **Edmund B. Tylor**, 1847 German statesman/soldier **Paul von Hindenburg**, 1852 Scottish chemist **William Ramsay**, 1895 U.S. comedian **Bud Abbott**, 1901 French singer **Alice Prin**, 1914 U.S. rocket scientist **Jack Parsons**, 1921 U.S. test pilot **Albert S. Crossfield**, 1921 Archbishop of Canterbury **Robert Runcie**, 1926 English writer **Jan Morris**, 1928 U.S. "Little Rascals" actor **Spanky McFarland**, 1932 U.S. baseball player **Maury Wills**, 1948 U.S. fashion designer **Donna Karan**, 1949 U.S. musician **Richard Hell**, 1950 Indian actress **Persis Khambatta**, 1970 U.S. actress/TV personality **Kelly Ripa**, 1971 U.S. singer **Tiffany**

October 3

1690 **Robert Barclay:** Scottish writer. One of the most eminent writers belonging to the Religious Society of Friends. He wrote defenses of the sect, publishing *Truth Cleared of Calumnies* (1670) and a *Catechism and Confession of Faith* (1673). His greatest work, *An Apology for the True Christian Divinity* (1676) was an elaborate statement of the grounds for holding certain fundamental positions laid down in his fifteen *Theses Theologiae* (1676). His works, though eagerly read, failed to arrest the persecution of the Quakers, and Barclay was several times thrown into prison.

Since we have placed justification in the revelation of Jesus Christ and brought forth in the heart, there working his works of righteousness and bringing forth the fruits of the Spirit.

1800 **George Bancroft:** American historian and Democratic statesman. Called the "Father of American History." Author of the 10-volume *A History of the United States* and *The History of the Formation of the Constitution of the United States.* As U.S. Secretary of the Navy he established the Naval Academy at Annapolis in 1845, gave the orders that led to the occupation of California and dispatched Zachary Taylor into the debatable land between Texas and Mexico. In 1866, Congress chose Bancroft to deliver the special eulogy on Abraham Lincoln.

Conscience is the mirror of our souls, which represents the errors of our lives in their full shape.

1804 **Townsend Harris:** American diplomat. President of New York City's board of education and helped found the Free Academy, which later would become City College of New York. In 1847 he embarked on trading voyages in the Pacific and Indian Oceans. Appointed first U.S. Consul to Japan. At first unwelcomed, changing Japanese attitudes and Harris' perseverance resulted in a commercial treaty in 1858, opening Japanese ports to U.S. trade.

If a man use opium once he cannot stop it, and it becomes a life-long habit to use opium; hence the English wish to introduce it into Japan.

1858 **Eleanora Duse:** Internationally acclaimed Italian stage actress, known as "The Duse." A rival of Sarah Bernhardt. She had a thousand faces and provided psychological motivation for her roles. Her great powers were best shown in the works of her lover Gabriele D'Annunzio, who wrote *La Gioconda* and *Francesca da Rimini* for her, and as Henrik Ibsen's dramatic heroines Hedda Gabbler and Elida in *The Lady from the Sea.*

The weaker partner in a marriage is the one who loves the most.

1867 **Pierre Bonnard:** French painter and printmaker. Studied law and briefly was a successful barrister. Decided to become an artist in 1891. First show was at the *Galerie Durand-Ruel* (1896). In the 1920s, was a member of Les Nabis, a group of young artists committed to creating work of symbolic and spiritual nature. Known for intense use of colors, in nude paintings of his wife, flowers, interior views and landscapes.

You reason color more than you reason drawing... Color has a logic as severe as form.

1872 **Emily Post:** Born **Emily Price** to a wealthy Baltimore family. Began her career writing novels and society journalism. Moved to shape the nation's manners with *Etiquette: The Blue Book of Social Usage* (1922). American dictator of decorum and authority on social behavior. Always a stickler for fundamentals, she nevertheless crafted her advice by applying good sense and thoughtfulness to basic human interactions. Wrote a newspaper column and gave advice on radio broadcasts. In 1946, founded the Emily Post Institute for the Study of Gracious Living.

Ideal conversation must be an exchange of thought, and not, as many of those who worry most about their shortcomings believe, an eloquent exhibition of wit or oratory.

1889 **Carl von Ossietzky:** German pacifist. Reluctant conscript in the German army in World War I; cofounder of *No More War* (1922). Edited a weekly publication that exposed German military leaders' secret rearmament activities. Convicted of treason in 1931, his sentence was commuted, but when Hitler came to power he was again arrested and sent to a concentration camp (1933). While in the prison hospital he was awarded the Nobel Peace Prize (1935). Outraged, Hitler decreed that no German could accept a Nobel Prize. Ossietzky died of tuberculosis while still imprisoned.

We cannot appeal to the conscience of the world when our own conscience is asleep.

1897 **Louis Aragon:** French poet, novelist and critic. Early on associated with Cubism and Dada. His post–World War I poems were among the most obscure of the surrealism movement, writing *Nightwalker.* After becoming a Communist, he devoted his art to social revolution, heading Communistic cultural committees, writing for *L'Humanite* and eventually editing the newspaper *Ce Soir*, and later the weekly *Les Lettres Françaises*. During World War II, evacuated from Dunkirk to England, he was an intellectual spirit of the French Resistance. Poem: "The Red Front." Novel: *The Century Was Young*.

Of all possible sexual perversions, religion is the only one to have been scientifically systematized.

1900 **Thomas C. Wolfe:** American author. His autobiographical novel *Look Homeward Angel* was rejected by publishers until Scribner's recognized its virtues. He angered many people in his home town of Ashville, North Carolina, because it was thinly veiled and often a cruel portrait of townspeople and family. Died of tubercular meningitis when he was 38, leaving two books unfinished and countless others that never took shape. His editor at Harper & Brothers assembled the two novels, *Of Time and the River* and *You Can't Go Home Again*.

If a man has talent and cannot use it, he has failed. If he has talent and uses only half of it, he has partly failed. If he has talent and learns to use the whole of it, he has gloriously succeeded, and won a satisfaction and a triumph few men can ever know.

1916 **James Herriot:** Pseudonym of **James Alfred Wight**. Scottish veterinarian and writer. His experiences as a Yorkshire country vet are the basis of his engaging and very popular books, all with titles taken from an Anglican hymn book: *All Creatures Great and Small* (1972), *All Things Bright and Beautiful*, *All Things Wise and Wonderful* and *The Lord God Made Them All*. He also published *Dog Stories*, a collection of fifty tales about dogs.

If having a soul means being able to love and loyalty and gratitude, then animals are better off than a lot of humans.

1925 **Gore Vidal:** U.S. novelist, playwright and critic. Known for his outspoken, irreverent, sophisticated and often bitter satires of public and private corruption. Novels: *Myra Breckinridge* and *Burr*. Screenplay: *Suddenly Last Summer*. Television play: *Visit to a Small Planet*. Play: *The Best Man*. Essays: *Rocking the Boat*, *Reflections upon a Sinking Ship* and *Matters of Fact and Fiction*.

There is no such things as a homosexual or a heterosexual person. There are only homo- or heterosexual acts. Most people are a mixture of impulses if not practices.

1954 **Al Sharpton:** African-American Pentecostal minister, political activist and civil rights activist. Ordained and licensed as a minister at age 10. Founded the National Youth Movement (1971) to fight drugs and raise money for impoverished youths and the National Action Network to increase voter education and confronting racism and violations of civil and human rights. Never held public office, but ran for the U.S. Senate from New York, three times, for Mayor of New York once, and in 2004, he sought the Democratic Party nomination of President of the United States.

I do believe the Democratic Party has moved far to the right. I do believe that the party has a bunch of elephants running around in donkey clothes.

OTHERS: 1605 Chinese revolutionary **Li Tzu-ch'eng**, 1720 German poet **Johann Peter Uz**, 1790 Chief Cherokee Nation **John Ross**, 1863 Russian explorer **Pyotr Kozlov**, 1885 U.S. playwright **Sophie Treadwell**, 1896 Spanish poet **Geraldo Diego**, 1898 U.S. film director **Leo McCarey**, 1899 U.S. comedic actress of "The Goldbergs" **Gertrude Berg**, 1919 U.S. economist **James M. Buchanan**, 1928 Danish dancer **Erik Bruhn**, 1933 Australian tennis player **Neale Fraser**, 1938 U.S. singer **Eddie Cochran**, 1941 U.S. musician **Chubby Checker**, 1951 U.S. baseball player **Dave Winfield**, 1954 U.S. musician **Stevie Ray Vaughan**, 1959 U.S. golfer **Fred Couples**, 1969 U.S. singer **Gwen Stefani**, 1973 Canadian actress **Neve Campbell**

October 4

1542 Saint **Robert Bellarmine:** Italian cardinal and theologian. Entered the Jesuits and was ordained at Louvain. Quickly obtained a reputation both as a professor and a preacher, drawing both Catholics and Protestants from distant parts to hear his sermons. Considered to be one of the most influential Catholic theologian of his time and a powerful defender of the teachings of the Church. He wrote, "Freedom of belief is pernicious, it is nothing but the freedom to be wrong.

To assert that the earth revolves around the sun is as erroneous as to claim that Jesus was not born of a virgin.

1814 **Jean François Millet:** French painter. Leading member of the Barbizon school. Pre-eminent in his portrayal of French peasant life, painting landscapes and rural scenes. Among his best known works are *Angelus* and *The Man with the Hoe*.

Art will never come except from some small disregarded corner where an isolated and inspired man is studying the mysteries of nature.

1858 **Michael Pupin:** Eminent Serbian-born American physicist, chemist electrical scientist, inventor and teacher. His invention, known as "Pupin coil" (1894) greatly extended the range of long-distance telephones. When the American rights were acquired by American Telephone and Telegraph, Pupin became very wealthy. His autobiography, *From Immigrant to Inventor* won a Pulitzer Prize in 1924. He held that modern science supported and enhanced belief in God.

Truth is beautiful and divine no matter how humble its origin.

1884 **Damon Runyon**: U.S. journalist and author. Wrote syndicated sports column, "Both Barrels," and more general column, "The Brighter Side." One of his most famous lines is "The race is not always to the swift, nor the battle to the strong, but that's the way to bet." Wrote short stories *Guys and Dolls* (1932), wryly dealing with the seamier side of New York City, using a jargon of his own invention. Died of cancer in 1946 and one of the earliest cancer fundraising campaigns is named for him.

I long ago came to the conclusion that life is 6 to 5 against.

1895 **[Joseph F.] Buster Keaton:** American actor and film director. Among the greatest screen comedians. Rivaled Charlie Chaplin in popularity. Typically portrayed a dignified, restrained young man with bags under his eyes and a deadpan expression, which let to his being called "The Great Stone Face." After starring in vaudeville, he began making films in 1917 in Fatty Arbuckle comedies. Silent movies: *One Week, The Navigator, Sherlock, Jr., The General, Steamboat Bill, Jr.*, and *The Cameraman.*

I don't act anyway. The stuff is injected as we go along. My pictures are made without script or written direction of any kind.

1928 **Alvin Toffler:** American author and futurist. Formerly an associate editor with *Fortune* magazine, his early work focused on the impact of technology. Turned to examining the reaction to changes in society. Wrote: *The Culture Consumers, Future Shock* and *The Third Wave.* Describes future shock as "the shattering stress and disorientation that we induce in individuals by subjecting them to too much change in too short a time.

The illiterate of the 21st century will not be those who cannot read and write, but those who cannot learn, unlearn, and relearn.

1934 **Sam Huff:** American football player. Linebacker with the New York Giants and Washington Redskins after earning All-American honors at West Virginia University. Considered one of the most physical defensive players in the history of the National Football League. Five-time Pro Bowler was elected to the Pro Football Hall of Fame in 1982.

You can run on a football field but you can't hide.

1941 **Jackie Collins:** English-born romance novelist. Sister of actress Joan Collins. Books are quite popular with readers but not with critics, who dismissed them for what they were — pure escapism. Her first *novel The World Is Full of Married Men*, delighted readers who enjoyed being shocked by its raunchy sexual content. Others: *Hollywood Wives, Hollywood Husbands, Rockstar, Lady Boss* and *American Star.* To date her 24 novels have sold over 400 million copies.

The biggest critics of my books are people who never read them.

1941 **Anne Rice:** American author of horror and fantasy stories. Born **Howard Allen O'Brien** in New Orleans, the city where most of her stories take place. Most famous for *The Vampire Chronicles*, a series of novels whose protagonist has been transformed into a vampire. Also published erotica under the pen names Anne Rampling and A.N. Roquelaure. Her fans consider her works among the best in modern popular fiction. Critics find her tales redundant and even boring, after all how many times can one be shocked by a vampire's gruesome blood gathering.

People who cease to believe in God or goodness altogether still believe in the devil.... Evil is always possible. And goodness is eternally difficult.

1942 **Bernice Johnson Reagon:** African-American historian and musician. Founded the *a cappella* ensemble *Sweet Honey in the Rock* in 1973. Active member of the civil rights movement in the 1960s as a member of the *Freedom Singers.* Specialist in African-American oral history, performance and protest traditions. Featured on the Emmy-nominated PBS documentary *The Songs Are Free: Bernice Johnson Reagon with Bill Moyers.* Conceptual producer of the Peabody Award–winning radio series, *Wade in the Water, African American Sacred Music Traditions.*

There is nowhere you can go and only be with people who are like you. Give it up.

1943 **H. Rap Brown:** African-American civil rights leader, black activist, and Justice Minister of the Black Panther Party. Most known for his proclamation, "violence is as American as cherry pie." Chairman Student Nonviolent Coordinating Committee before joining the Black Panthers. Converted to Islam while in prison five years for a robbery conviction, and now goes by the name **Jamil Abdullah al-Amin**. Opened a grocery store in Atlanta and preached against drugs and gambling. In 2002, he was convicted of killing a sheriff's deputy and was sentenced to life imprisonment.

The power structure serves the system and the system is the thing which demands exploitation of the people.

1946 **Susan Sarandon:** Born **Susan Abigail Tomalin** Talented and intelligent U.S. actress with great large expressive eyes. Memorable in the cult classic *The Rocky Horror Show, Pretty Baby, Atlantic City* (Oscar nominated), *Bull Durham, Thelma and Louise* (Oscar nominated) and *Dead Man Walking* (Oscar). Married Chris Sarandon, divorced in 1979, but retained her married name as her professional name. Since 1988, she has been in a relationship with actor Tim Robbins. They have two children and are both active in liberal causes.

I was told that I have an overabundance of original sin.

OTHERS: 1160 Countess of the Vexin **Alys**, 1515 German painter **Lucas Cranach**, 1562 Danish astronomer **Christian Sørensen Longonontanus**, 1625 French child prodigy **Jacqueline Pascal**, 1723 German entomologist **Nikolaus Poda von Neuhaus**, 1822 U.S. President **Rutherford B. Hayes**, 1861 U.S. painter of western scenes **Frederic Remington**, 1892 Austrian politician **Engelbert Dollfuss**, 1903 Computer pioneer **John Vincent Atanasoff**, 1914 Australian politician **Jim Cairns**, 1916 Russian physicist **Vitaly Ginzburg**, 1918 Japanese chemist **Kenichi Fukui**, 1924 U.S. actor **Charlton Heston**, 1944 U.S. baseball manager **Tony La Russa**, 1947 British politician **Ann Widdecombe**

October 5

1703 **Jonathan Edwards:** American Presbyterian clergyman, educator, philosopher and theologian.

Third president of Princeton. His theology was highly influenced by Newtonian science and Lockean psychology. Stimulated the religious revival known as "Great Awakening." Called "the greatest American mind of the Colonial period and the last medieval American, at least among intellectuals. Best known sermon: "Sinners in the Hands of an Angry God." Author of *Freedom of the Will* (1754).

Resolution One: I will live for God. Revolution Two: If no one else does, I still will.

1713 **Denis Diderot:** French encyclopedist, materialistic philosopher, novelist, satirist, dramatist and art critic. Noted letter writer of the eighteenth century. Always controversial, his *Philosophical Thoughts* (1746) was burned by the Parliament of Paris for its anti-Christian sentiments. Imprisoned for his *Essay on Blindness* (1749). Mainly known for his 20-year effort, compiling and editing with a few others, the 28-volume *Encyclopédie ou Dictionnaire Raisonné des Sciences, des Arts et des Métiers*, a major work of the age of Enlightenment.

We swallow greedily any lie that flatters us, but we sip only little by little at a truth we find bitter.

1879 **John Erskine:** American educator, author and musician. Students included Mark Van Doren, Mortimer J. Adler, Clifton Fadiman and Rexford G. Tugwell. His emphasis on studying the classics was a forerunner of the "great books" program adopted by several universities. Works: the satirical novel in modern setting, *The Private Life of Helen of Troy, The Delight of Great Books, What Is Music?* and *My Life as a Teacher*. Gave occasional public concerts as a pianist and was the first president of the new Julliard School in New York City.

Opinion is that exercise of the human will which helps us to make a decision without information.

1882 **Robert H. Goddard:** U.S. physicist and rocketry pioneer. In *A Method of Reaching Extreme Altitudes* he predicted the breaking free of earth's gravity and traveling to the moon and beyond. Had more than 200 rocketry patents and it is probable that one cannot design a rocket, build one, or launch it without borrowing from among his patents. Developed the first successful liquid-fuelled rocket, launched in 1926. Three years later, launched the first instrumental rocket. NASA's Goddard Flight Center is named in his honor.

Just remember — when you think all is lost, the future remains.

1902 **Ray Kroc:** American fast food entrepreneur. Founder of the McDonald's chain of fast-food restaurants. Manufacturer of milk-shake machines in the 1950s, he bought the rights to operate stands similar to those of Mac and Dick McDonald, who sold hamburgers, French fries and milkshakes. Kroc established strict standards of quality, hygiene, service and value. Made franchise arrangements with individual restaurant owners. Offered training that emphasized automation and standardization. Today, there are McDonalds almost everywhere in the world and the number of hamburgers sold keeps growing and growing, making it the world's largest food-service retailer.

Are you green and growing or ripe and rotting?

1908 **Joshua Logan:** U.S. producer and director of many Broadway shows, including *Annie Get Your Gun, Mr. Roberts, South Pacific* and *Fanny*. Directed films *Bus Stop, Picnic* and *Paint Your Wagon*. Organized the summer theatre group called The University Players (1931–35) on Cape Cod, where the careers of Henry Fonda and Margaret Sullivan were launched. Broadway star Mary Martin said of him: "Director Logan inspires both newcomers and mature stars to rise above their usual capacity."

Fear is the great destroyer of the theatre. Because I have experience my own emotional setback I instinctively recognize fear when I see it in others and I rush to try and eradicate it.

1911 **Flann O'Brien:** Originally **Brian Ó Nuallain**. Irish humorist, novelist, dramatist and newspaper columnist. Wrote a column for the *Irish Times* for 26 years under the penname **Myles na Gopaleen**. A selection of his columns appears in *The Best of Myles* (1968). Most famous for his literary experiment, *At Swim-Two-Birds* (1939), a novel that combines folklore, legend, humor, poetry and linguistic games. Other novels: *The Hard Life* and *The Dalkey Archive*.

The majority of the members of the Irish parliament are professional politicians, in the sense that otherwise they would not be given jobs minding mice at crossroads.

1936 **Václav Havel:** Czech dissident dramatist and political leader. First publicly performed play was *The Garden Party* (1963). Other plays: *The Increased Difficulty of Concentration* and *Largo desolato*. In 1968 he became politically active, publishing the *Charter 77* manifesto. His activities cost him five years in prison. Became famous for his articulation of "Post-Totalitarianism," which enables people to "live within a lie," in his 1985 work *The Power of the Powerless*. Became a leading figure in the non-violent resistance movement, the Velvet Revolution of 1989. First freely elected president of Czechoslovakia in 55 years (1990).

Anyone who takes himself too seriously always runs the risk of looking ridiculous; anyone who can consistently laugh at himself does not.

1937 **Barry Switzer:** American football. Winning percentage is fourth-best in college history with a record of 157–29–4 at the University of Oklahoma, which he led to three national championships. The program was racked with several scandals. He resigned when several of his players had brushes with the law after the 1988 season. Resurfaced in 1994 with the Dallas Cowboys, owned by his former player and longtime friend Jerry Jones. Dallas won the Super Bowl in his second season. After 3 seasons, he resigned with a 45–26 NFL career record. Autobiography: *Bootlegger's Boy*.

Some people are born on third base and go through life thinking they hit a triple.

1938 **Teresa Heinz Kerry:** American philanthropist and wife of Senator John Kerry. Born **Maria Teresa Thierstein Simões-Ferreria** in the Portuguese colony of Mozambique. Married billionaire and future U.S. Senator from Pennsylvania Henry John Heinz III in 1966. He died in an airplane crash in 1991, and she inherited his vast fortune. Met John Kerry at the 1992 Earth Summit conference held in Rio de Janeiro. They were married in 1995. During her husband's 2004 campaign for the presidency, she fell prey to some of the trick questions of the media, and made comments that made her look bad. Chairs the Howard Heinz Endowment and the Heinz Family Philanthropies, disbursing funds to many social and environmental causes.

I hope it comes as no surprise that I have something to say.

1951 **Robert Frederick Xenon "Bob" Geldof:** Irish singer, songwriter, actor and political activist. Lead singer with the Irish rock group The Boomtown Rats. Hits: "Rat Trap" and "I Don't Like Mondays." In 1984 a news report on the famine in Ethiopia inspired him to co-write the song "Do They Know It's Christmas?" with Midge Ure. Put together a group called Band Aid, consisting of leading British and Irish pop musicians to record the song, raising millions of pounds for the relief of the famine He organized the massive charity concert Live Aid, which raised unprecedented sums for the cause (1985). He was awarded an honorary knighthood by Queen Elizabeth II.

It's really very simple, Governor. When people are hungry they die. So spare me your politics and tell me what you need and how you are going to get it to these people.

1959 **Maya Lin:** Chinese-American artist and architect. While still an undergraduate at Yale University, won a public design competition for the Vietnam Memorial in Washington, D.C. The stone-cut masonry "Wall" officially opened in 1982. It is granite and V-shaped. One side points towards the Lincoln Memorial and the other towards the Washington Monument. In 2003, she served on the selection jury of the World Trade Center Site Memorial Committee.

To fly we have to have resistance.

OTHERS: 1641 French mistress of Louis XIV **Marquise de Montespan**, 1721 Italian painter **Francesco Guardi**, 1781 Czech mathematician/philosopher **Bernard Bolzano**, 1824 Baseball statistician **Henry Chadwick**, 1829 U.S. President **Chester A. Arthur**, 1889 Venezuelan writer **Teresa de la Parra**, 1903 U.S. geophysicist **M. King Hubbert**, 1922 U.S. cartoonist **Bill Keane**, 1923 U.S. militant anti–Vietnam war priest **Philip Berrigan**, 1923 British actress **Glynis Johns**, 1930 German economist **Reinhard Selten**, 1941 Argentine President **Eduardo Duhalde**, 1952 English writer **Clive Barker**, 1958 U.S. comedian **Bernie Mac**, 1965 Canadian hockey player **Mario Lemieux**, 1975 English actress **Kate Winslet**

October 6

1510 **Rowland Taylor:** English Anglican clergyman and martyr of the Tudor period. Did not support the Roman Catholic position of clerical celibacy, nor did he hold to view of transubstantiation, the belief that the bread and wine taken during Holy Communion becomes the body and blood of Jesus Christ. Queen Mary I set to reverse the Protestant reforms of her predecessors and strictly enforce Roman Catholicism. In doing so she executed hundreds of "heretics," Among them Taylor, who was excommunicated, refused to recant and was burned at the stake.

And although I know, that there is neither justice nor truth to be looked for at my adversaries hands, but rather imprisonment and cruel death; yet I know my cause to be so good and righteous, and the truth so strong upon my side, that I will be God's grace go and appear before them and to their bears resist their false doings.

1801 **Hippolyte Lazare Carnot:** French statesman. Elected deputy for Paris in 1839, he sat with the radical group opposed to Louis Philippe and in favor of the republic. Chosen minister of education, he founded *École d'administration*, intended to prepare governmental administrators, sponsored adult education, proposed a law for obligatory and free primary education, and another for the secondary education of girls. Opposed the *coup d'état* of Louis-Napoleon Bonaparte, refusing to take the oath of loyalty to the emperor. Died three moths after his eldest son was elected president of the republic.

In a free country there is much clamor, with little suffering; in a despotic state there is little complaint, with much grievance.

1803 **Heinrich William Dove:** German physicist and meteorologist. Published more than 300 papers, among them more than 100 articles on topics of experimental physics. Described as "the Father of Meteorology." Gave descriptions of the temperature regime of the earth (including soils, springs, oceans, and air) and explanations about storms, rain, air pressure and other phenomena.

When we professors are uncertain about some principle, we begin by saying "as is well known."

1820 **Jenny [Johanna Maria] Lind:** "The Swedish Nightingale." Swedish soprano operatic and concert star. Had a remarkably pure and controlled voice, becoming a master of coloratura, singing parts written for her by Giacomo Meyerbeer and Giuseppe Verdi. Her earnings were largely devoted to the founding and endowment of musical scholarships. In retirement she taught voice at the Royal College of Music in London.

I have brightness in my soul, which strains toward Heaven. I am like a bird.

1868 **George H. Lorimer:** American literary editor-in-chief for *Saturday Evening Post* (1899–1937). Commissioned Frank Norris, Willa Cather, Jack London, Rudyard Kipling, Theodore Dreiser, Sinclair Lewis, G.K. Chesterton, H.G. Wells, and Stephen Crane to write articles and stories for the publication The editor's conservative views were evident in the articles published in the magazine, which Upton Sinclair described as "standardized as soda crackers; originality is taboo, new ideas are treason, social symphony a crime, and the one virtue is to produce larger and larger quantities of material things."

You got to get up each morning with determination if you're going to go to bed with satisfaction.

1887 **Le Corbusier [Charles Edouard Jeanneret]:** Swiss architect and city planner, who adopted his pseudonym, which means "the builder," in 1920. A founder of modern fundamentalist architecture, his early work is characterized by the same desire to define simple volumes and to achieve geometric order that can be seen in his paintings and in Cubism. Never sacrificed beauty to utility. Redefined the family dwelling as "a machine for living. Buildings: *Palace of the League of Nations*, Geneva; *National Museum of Western Art*, Tokyo; and *Carpenter Visual Art Center*, Harvard University.

Space and light and order. Those are the things that men need just as much as they need bread or a place to sleep.

1895 **Caroline Gordon:** American writer. Played gracious hostess to some of the world's greatest writers, Ford Madox Ford, T.S. Eliot, Flannery O'Connor, William Faulkner, F. Scott Fitzgerald and Ernest Hemingway. Published ten novels, including *Penhally, Aleck Maury, Sportsman, None Shall Look Back* and *The Women on the Porch*. Also published *How to Read a Novel.*

A well-composed book is a magic carpet on which we are wafted away to a world that we cannot enter in any other way.

1905 **Helen Wills Moody:** American tennis player who dominated women's tennis for over a decade. Won eight Wimbledon, seven U.S. and four French single titles (1923–38). Female Athlete of the Year (1935). Great rivalry with Helen Jacobs drove her to continue to play during the 1938 Wimbledon final, despite being severely handicapped by injury.

Concerning the limits and limitations of the women's game — why should we believe there are any?

1908 **Carole Lombard:** Born **Jane Alice Peters**. American actress. Beautiful blonde comedienne in films *Twentieth Century*, *My Man Godfrey* (Oscar nomination), *Nothing Sacred* and *To Be or Not to Be*. Glamorous and sophisticated; shone playing for laughs in witty and wacky screwball comedies. At the time of her death in a plane crash, while on a war bond campaign, she was married to Clark Gable.

I live by a man's code, designed to fit a man's world, yet at the same time I never forget that a woman's first job is to choose the right shade of lipstick.

1914 **Thor Heyerdahl:** Norwegian ethnologist, adventurer and popularizer of science. His 4300 mile Kon-Tiki expedition (1947) established the possibility that Polynesians may have originated in South America. The story of his adventure was published as *Kon-Tiki* and became a best-seller in 52 languages. In 1955 he set sail for Easter Island, which resulted in another bestseller *Aku-Aku,* whose title refers to the guardian spirit of Easter Islanders. His Ra expedition confirmed the possibility that pre–Columbia cultures may have been influenced by Egyptian civilization.

One learns more from listening than speaking. And both the wind and the people who continue to live close to nature still have much to tell us which we cannot hear within university walls.

1917 **Fannie Lou Hamer,** née **Townsend:** African-American civil rights activist. Propelled to fight social injustice by her experiences of forced sterilization and being fired for attempting to vote. Plantation worker until 1962 when she went to work for The Student Non-Violent Co-Coordinating Committee. Campaigned for civil rights, promoting voter registration and school desegregation. Founded the Mississippi Freedom Democratic Party. Founding member of the National Women's Political Caucus (1971).

I'm sick and tired of being sick and tired.

1929 **Shana Alexander:** U.S. author, columnist and journalist. Her father Milton Ager wrote the songs "Ain't She Sweet" and "Happy Days Are Here Again." Mother Cecilia Ager: star reporter and film critic for *Variety*. Alexander appeared in the "Count Counterpoint" of television's "60 Minutes" (1975–79), opposite the conservative viewpoints of James J. Kilpatrick. Columnist of "The Feminine Eye" for *Life* magazine and a columnist and contributing editor to *Newsweek*. Nonfiction: *Anyone's Daughter* about Patty Hearst and *Very Much a Lady* about murderer Jean Harris.

The sad truth is that excellence makes people nervous.

OTHERS: 1459 German navigator **Martin Behaim**, 1552 Italian missionary to China **Matteo Ricci**, 1773 French king **Louis-Philippe**, 1831 German mathematician **Richard Dedekind**, 1838 Italian patriot **Giuseppe Cesare Abba**, 1846 U.S. engineer **George Westinghouse**, 1887 Mexican novelist **Martin Luis Guzman**, 1888 French pilot **Roland Garros**, 1906 U.S. actress **Janet Gaynor**, 1910 British politician **Barbara Castle**, 1927 Austrian pianist **Paul Badura-Skoda**, 1930 Syrian President **Hafez al-Assad**, 1942 Swiss actress **Britt Ekland**, 1948 Northern Ireland politician **Gerry Adams**, 1950 U.S. author **David Brin**, 1963 U.S. actress **Elizabeth Shue**, 1973 U.S. basketball player **Rebecca Lobo**

October 7

1576 **John Marston:** English dramatist, satirist and divine. Wrote satirical verses and plays for the new professional children's companies, playing in private indoor theaters. Published *The Metamorphosis of Pigmalion's Image and certaine satyres* and *The Scourge of Villanie* using the penname **Kinsadyer**. Some satires were directed against literary rivals. Dramatic works: *The History of Antonio and Mellida, The Malcontent*, and *The Parasitaster.*

Speak, speak, let terror strike slaves mute,/ Much danger makes great hearts more resolute.

1849 **James Whitcomb Riley:** "The Hoosier Poet." Considered by some critics as the Robert Burns of America. Wrote poems rich in the habits, speech and outlook of rural and small-town Indiana folk. Poems: "When the Frost Is on the Punkin," "The Old Swimming Hole," "Little Orphan Annie" and "The Raggedy Man."

It's no use to grumble and complain/ It's just as cheap and easy to rejoice. When God sorts out the weather and sends rain — Why, rain's my choice.

1879 **Joe Hill:** Swedish-born U.S. labor organizer and songwriter. Joined the Industrial Workers of the World (IWW) in 1910. Organized strike activities for the radial labor organization. Songs: "The Preacher and the Slave" and "There Is Power in Union." Executed in Utah for a murder he probably didn't commit, making him a martyr and folk hero in the radical labor movement. Last words, "I die like a true rebel. Don't waste any time mourning — organize!"

Work and pray, live on hay. You'll get pie in the sky when you die.

1885 **Niels Bohr:** Danish physicist. Revolutionized physics by combining elements of quantum theory with classic mechanics. Worked on U.S. atom bomb project. Organized first Atoms for Peace conference (1955). Because his wife was Jewish, Bohr was not safe in German occupied Denmark, so he escaped to Sweden and from there to England. Awarded the Nobel Prize in physics (1922); when he left his homeland, he dissolved the heavy gold of the metal in acid. The inconspicuous solution escaped detection and after the war his medal was recast from it.

How wonderful that we have met with a paradox. Now we have some hope of making progress.

1897 **Elijah Muhammad:** Originally **Elijah Poole**. American Black Muslim leader. Son of former slaves and sharecroppers. Had a spiritual revelation in 1930 and fell in with the Nation of Islam. By 1934, Poole changed his name, took over the movement and proclaimed himself the "Messenger of Allah." Argued for the separation of the races, scorned integration attempts and stressed the need for African-Americans to establish their own economic power-base. When died he was succeeded by his son Wallace, who led the movement closer to traditional Islam.

I am doing all I can to make the so-called Negroes see that the white race and their religion (Christianity) are their open enemies, and to prove to them that they will never be anything but the devil's slaves and finally go to hell with them for believing and following them and their kind.

1900 **Heinrich Himmler:** German Nazi leader. Joined the Nazi party in 1925 and in 1929 was placed in charge of the SS (Schutstaffel, projective force). Developed the unit into Hitler's personal bodyguard. Himmler also directed the secret police (Gestapo) and initiated the systematic elimination of Jews. Minister of the interior and finally commander-in-chief of the home forces. Fled Hitler's Chancellery bunker during the destruction of Berlin. When the Allies realize who they had captured, he committed suicide.

The best political weapon is the weapon of terror. Cruelty commands respect. Men may hate us, but we don't ask for their love, only for their fear.

1907 **Helen Clark MacInnes:** Scottish-born American writer. Author of over 20 books, most of which were suspense-thrillers with European settings, authentically depicted and best-selling adventure stories drawn from World War II events. Books: *Above Suspicion, Assignment in Brittany, Home Is the Hunter* and *The Salzburg Connection.*

Expect the worst and you won't be disappointed.

1927 **R.D. Laing:** Scottish existentialist psychiatrist and author. Counterculture guru in the 1960s. Held controversial views of schizophrenia, outlined in his book *The Divided Self.* Claims a schizophrenic suffers from "ontological insecurity." By this he means, "the schizophrenic does not take for granted his own person as being an adequately embodied, alive, real, substantial and continuous being. Taught that psychiatrists should not attempt to cure mental illness, a term he despised, but encourage patients to view themselves as going through an enrichment period.

Life is a sexually transmitted disease and the mortality rate is one hundred percent.

1931 **Desmond Tutu:** First native African Anglican bishop of Johannesburg, South Africa. Eloquent and outspoken advocate of the rights of black South Africans. Emphasized non-violent protests and encouraged other countries to apply economic pressure on the South African government. Award the Nobel Peace Prize (1984). In 1996, appointed chairman of the Truth and Reconciliation Commission, charged with hearing evidence of human-rights violations during white rule.

We may be surprised at the people we find in heaven. God has a soft spot for sinners. His standards are quite low.

1934 **Imamu Baraka:** African-American poet and playwright, born **LeRoi Jones**. Published his first book of poems, *Preface to a Twenty-Volume Suicide Note* (1961). Others: *The Dead Lecturer, Black Magic* and *Hard Facts.* Won an Obie Award for the play *The Dutchman* (1964). Active in organizing blacks for social and political action, calls for black separatism and the elimination of the white race.

There is no violent revolution except as a result of the Black mind expanding, trying to take control of its own space.

1943 **Oliver North:** American marine officer and politician. Involved in the Iran-Contra Affair, in which the National Security Council illegally authorized the sales of weapons to Iran in an attempt to secure release of U.S. hostages held in Lebanon by pro-Iranian terrorist groups. President Reagan reluctantly sacked North, who was indicted for conspiracy to defraud the government. Found guilty of obstructing Congress, destroying documents and accepting illegal gifts. He was sentenced to two years' probation. Later all charges against him were dropped.

I was provided with additional input that was radically different from the truth. I assisted in furthering that version.

1952 **Vladimir Putin:** Russian president. KGB official responsible for determining the fate of assets in countries where Russian missions had closed. Boris Yeltsin promoted him to deputy head of his administration. And one year later he was named prime minister. Yeltsin then stepped down as president in Putin's favor. In 2000, won a resounding electoral victory, partly due to his efforts to prevent Chechnya from seceding. Relationship with the United States and in particular with President Bush has been at times quite supportive and at others quite critical.

Whoever does not miss the Soviet Union has no heart. Whoever wants it back has no brain.

OTHERS: 1573 Archbishop of Canterbury **William Laud**, 1697 Italian artist **Canaletto**, 1728 Signed Declaration of Independence **Cesar Rodney**, 1746 U.S. hymn composer **William Billings**, 1888 U.S. Vice-President **Henry A. Wallace**, 1911 U.S. bandleader/singer **Vaughn Monroe**, 1917 U.S. actress **June Allyson**, 1929 British author **Robert Westall**, 1931 U.S. basketball coach **Cotton Fitzsimmons**, 1937 Polish politician **Maria Szyszkowska**, 1939 English chemist **Harold Kroto**, 1950 Tanzanian politician **Jakaya Kikwete**, 1952 U.S.S.R. gymnast **Ludmilla Tourischeva**, 1955 French-born cellist **Yo-Yo Ma**, 1957 British figure skater **Jayne Torvill**, 1968 U.S. singer **Toni Braxton**

October 8

1713 **Alison Cockburn,** née **Rutherford:** Scottish poet and songwriter. Famous wit and brilliant hostess of lively soirées that brought together most of the literary elite of 18th century Edinburgh. Queen of society for 60 years. Best known for the first version of the ballad "The Flowers of the Forest."

The almighty maker of souls has various methods of restoring them to the divine image; it is impossible his power can fail; it is impossible for his image to be entirely obliterated; it is impossible that misery, sin, and discord can be eternal!

1720 **Jonathan Mayhew:** Noted American clergyman and patriot. Minister of Old West Church, Boston, Massachusetts. Espoused liberal theological views, he made his church practically the first Unitarian Congregational church in New England. Politically, he urged the necessity of colonial union to secure colonial liberties. He bitterly opposed the Stamp Act and is credited with coining the phrase "no taxation without representation."

Let us not profess ourselves vassals to the lawless pleasures of any man on earth.

1833 **E.C. [Edmund Clarence] Stedman:** American author, poet, journalist, editor, anthologist and businessman. His poetry, once very popular, have not worn well. Chief literary importance rests on his criticism and anthologies: *Victorian Poets, Poets of America. A Victorian Anthology, An American Anthology,* and *Nature of Poetry.*

My lips till then has only known,/ The kiss of mother and of sister,/ But somehow, full upon her own/ Sweet, rosy, darling mouth,/ — I kissed her.

1890 **Eddie Rickenbacker:** American aviator. Champion race-card driver, establishing a world's speed record. Commanding officer of the 94th Aero Squadron, leading his men to a record 69 victories — 26 of which he scored himself. Awarded the Congressional Medal of Honor, the Croix de Guerre, the Legion of Honor and the Distinguished Service Cross. Reported his wartime experiences in *Fighting the Flying Circus* (1919). In 1942, while on a War Department inspection tour of Pacific air bases, his B-17 went down. Adrift for 22 parching days, he bullied and babied his companions through the agonizing ordeal. Wrote about the adventure in *Seven Came Through* (1943).

Courage is doing what you're afraid to do. There can be no courage unless you're scared.

1895 **Juan Perón:** Argentine Army officer who seized power in 1944 with a group of other officers. Elected president in 1946, his government (1946–55) was something of a populist dictatorship, which made genuine efforts to raise the living standards of the poor, but also was filled with petty corruption and repressed opposition. Severe economic problems led to his overthrow by a coup in 1955, forced into exile. Returned in 1971, winning the presidential election in 1973. Followed in office in 1974 by his third wife, Isabel Martínez de Perón, displaced by a military coup in 1976.

Perónism is humanism in action; Perónism is a new political doctrine, which rejects all the ills of the politics of previous times; in the social sphere it is a theory which establishes a little equality among men, which grants them similar opportunities and assures them of a future so that in this land there may be no one who lacks what he needs for a living, even though it may be necessary that those who are wildly squandering what they possess may be deprived of the right to do so, for the benefit of those who have nothing at all...

1912 **John W. Gardner:** U.S. educator, public official and reformer. President of the Carnegie Foundation for the Advancement of Teaching. U.S. secretary of Health, Education and Welfare (1965), directing Lyndon B. Johnson's various "war on poverty" programs. Organized and Chaired "Common Cause," a citizens" lobbying group.

Life is the art of drawing without an eraser.

1915 **William E. "Bill" Vaughan:** American journalist and author. Wrote a nationally syndicated column,

"Starbeams" for more than 30 years. With wit and without maliciousness he deflated the self-important and celebrated the many interesting facets of American life. Some of his memorable and timeless comments: "Muscles come and go, flab stays"; "The tax collector must love poor people — he's creating so many of them"; "The Vice Presidency is sort of like the last cookie on the plate. Everybody insists he won't take it, but somebody always does." And,

A citizen of America will cross the ocean to fight for democracy, but won't cross the street to vote in a national election.

1920 **Frank Herbert:** American science fiction writer. First novel was *The Dragon of the Sea* (1956), about a search for a saboteur in an undersea war. Developed an interest in the evolution of intelligence. Best known as author of the *Dune* series, large scale heroic adventure stories containing serious ideas about ecology and religion.

The beginning of knowledge is the discovery of something we do not understand.

1927 **Jim Elliot:** American Christian missionary to Ecuador. Arrived in Ecuador in 1952, planning to evangelize the Quechua Indians. Elliot, four other missionaries and their pilot made contact from their airplane with the famously violent Huaorani Indians, using a loudspeaker and letting down a basket filled with gifts. A few months later, the missionaries built a base camp nearby to the tribe, along the Curaray River. They were joined from time to time by curious Indians. Encouraged by these visits, they were not alarmed when a larger party arrived. However, the Indians killed the five missionaries, whose mutilated bodies were later found downstream.

He is no fool who gives what he cannot keep to gain that which he cannot lose.

1941 **Jesse Jackson:** American Baptist preacher and civil rights leader. Joined Martin Luther King in civil rights marches and protests. Worked on building the political machine that gave Chicago its first African-American mayor. Charismatic orator sought Democratic presidential nomination several times, in an effort to increase voter registration and place black issues on the national agenda. Tried to build what he called a rainbow coalition of ethnic-minority and socially-deprived groups.

If my mind can conceive it, and my heart can believe it, I know I can achieve it.

1946 **Dennis Kucinich:** American Democratic Congressman. Elected to Cleveland's City Council at age 23. At age 31, became mayor of the city, the youngest mayor of a major city in the U.S. His tenure was characterized by bombastic confrontations, rejection of needed federal funds to rebuild downtown, and charges that his young staff didn't possess the experience and know-how to do their jobs. Not reelected in 1979. In 1996 elected to the U.S. House of Representatives. In the 2004 presidential primary season, he offered himself as the progressive candidate, but won no primaries.

We have weapons of mass destruction we have to address here at home. Poverty is a weapon of mass destruction. Homelessness is a weapon of mass destruction. Unemployment is a weapon of mass destruction.

1964 **Ian Hart:** English actor. First gained wide recognition for portraying John Lennon in the film *Backbeat* (1995). Other films: *The End of the Affair*, as detective Parkis, hired by Ralph Fiennes to spy on Julianne Moore, *Harry Potter and the Sorcerer's Stone*, as Professor Quirinus Quirrell, and *Finding Neverland*, as Sir Arthur Conan Doyle.

There's a statistical theory that if you give a million monkeys typewriters and set them to work, they'd eventually come up with the complete works of Shakespeare. Thanks to the internet, we now know this isn't true.

OTHERS: 1676 Spanish scholar **Benito Jerónimo Feijóo y Montenegro**, 1713 Polish rabbi/Talmudist **Yechezkel Landau**, 1715 French missionary **Michael Benoist**, 1765 Irish lawyer **Harman Blennerhassett**, 1870 French organist **Louis Vierne**, 1888 German psychiatrist **Ernst Kretschmer**, 1889 U.S. airline founder **C.E. Woolman**, 1895 Albanian king **Zog I**, 1901 U.S. psychologist **Doris Allen**, 1901 Norwegian composer **Eivind Groven**, 1917 U.S. author **Walter Lord**, 1918 Danish chemist **Jens Christian Skou**, 1936 U.S. gossip columnist **Rona Barrett**, 1939 Australian actor **Paul Hogan**, 1943 U.S. comic actor **Chevy Chase**, 1949 U.S. actress **Sigourney Weaver**, 1970 U.S. actor **Matt Damon**

October 9

1261 **Diniz:** Known as **Denis** or **Dionysius** in English. King of Portugal (1279–1325). Poet and patron of literature. Founded the university at Lisbon later moved to Coimbra. Stimulated commerce and industry. Encouraged agriculture, giving special favors to nobles who pursued farming, leading to him being sometimes called *o Lavrador* (the farmer). Laid down laws to restrict further acquisitions of land by the church and confiscated the lands of the Templars.

History is philosophy learned by examples.

1835 **Camille Saint-Saëns:** Celebrated French composer. Acquired a reputation as a virtuoso on the organ and a master of improvisation. Abilities as a performer were extraordinary. His compositions included: choral work *Hail California*, a ballet *Javotte*, the opera *Samson et Dalila*, and his ingenious suite *Carnival of the Animals*, which he wrote in 1880, but would not allow to be published in his lifetime.

There is nothing more difficult than talking about music.

1884 **Helene Deutsch:** née **Rosenbach**. Austrian-born American psychoanalyst and colleague of Sigmund Freud. Last of the original Freudians. First psychoanalyst to specialize in women. Author of *The Psychology of Women*. Fled Germany in 1935, immigrating to the United States, settling in Cambridge,

Massachusetts, where she continued her career until her death in 1982.

The embattled gates to equal rights indeed opened up for modern women, but I sometimes think to myself: "That is not what I mean by freedom — it is only social 'progress.'"

1890 **Aimee Semple McPherson:** née **Kennedy**, aka **Sister Aimee**. Canadian-born American religious leader. Best known female evangelist of her day. Renown for her healing ministry and the controversy surrounding her activities, embroiling her in many civil suits and her unexplained five-week disappearance in 1926. Founded the International Church of the Foursquare Gospel. Built the Angelus Temple in Los Angeles. Had her own radio station, Bible school, magazine, and social service agency. Books: *This Is That*, *In the Service of the King* and *Give Me My Own God*.

Right here let us make it plain, that each individual is either a sinner or a saint. It is impossible to be both; it is impossible to be neutral, there is no half-way business in God. Either you are the child of the Lord or you are serving the devil — there is no middle territory.

1892 **Ivo Andrić:** Serbo-Croatian diplomat and writer. Nicknamed, "the Yugoslav Tolstoy." Member of the diplomatic service, he was minister in Berlin at the outbreak of World War II in 1939. Main works: *The Bridge on the Drina* and *Bosnian Story*, both published in 1945, earned him the 1961 Nobel Prize for Literature.

One shouldn't be afraid of the humans. Well, I am not afraid of the humans, but of what is inhuman in them.

1892 **Marina Tsvetaeva:** Major Russian poet, dramatist and memoirist. Published her first collection of poetry, *Evening Album*, in 1910. Much of her early poetry of her middle period, in particular *The Swans Encampment*, was anti–Bolshevik in spirit. Emigrated to Paris in 1922, a symbol of Russia-in-exile, where she wrote memoirs of Russian poets. Returned to Russia in 1939, but was evacuated to a remote town in 1941 and hanged herself.

A deception that elevates us is dearer than a host of low truths.

1899 **Bruce Catton:** U.S. historian and journalist. Information director for several governmental agencies. From his experiences came his book *War Lords of Washington* (1948). Deeply interested in the American Civil War, and from 1952 devoted full time to writing Civil War histories: *Mr. Lincoln's Army*, the Pulitzer Prize winning *A Stillness at Appomattox*, *Grant Moves South* and *Gettysburg: The Final Fury*.

Our American heritage is greater than any one of us. It can express itself in very homely truths; in the end it can lift up our eyes beyond the glow in the sunset skies.

1900 **Alistair Sim:** Highly gifted British character actor with marvelously doleful eyes. Former elocution professor had a penchant for playing eccentric types, delighting audiences with his droll wit and sly comic characterizations. For many he was the definitive Ebenezer Scrooge, in a classic 1951 film. Other charming films: *Laughter in Paradise*, *An Inspector Calls*, *The Belles of St. Trinan's* and *The Green Man*.

It was revealed to me many years ago with conclusive certainly that I was a fool and that I had always been a fool. Since then I have been as happy as any man has a right to be.

1934 **Jill Ker Conway:** Australian-born American historian, educator and writer. Taught at the University of Toronto (1964–75), serving as Vice President (1973–75). Became the first woman president of Smith College (1975–85). Author of *True North*, *The Female Experience in 18th and 19th Century America: A Guide to the History of American Women*. Speaking of her autobiography *The Royal Road from Coorain*, she stated that her purpose was to

... communicate to people very directly about the authenticity of women's motivation for work, about how a person strives to find some creative expression. The moral of my mother's life was while she had challenging work, she was indomitable and when she didn't she fell apart. It's very much the vogue to talk about women as developing their moral consciousness through a connectedness to mother, but I think that's misleading. My book is deliberately a story of separation — of independence and breaking away.

1940 **John Lennon:** English musician, singer and songwriter. Founding member of the Beatles, as rhythm guitarist, keyboard player and vocalist. He and Paul McCartney wrote most of the hit songs of the group. Songs after the group's breakup: "Imagine" and "Starting Over." With his second wife Japanese artist Yoko Ono, made peace protests by staying in bed while being filmed and interviewed. At the birth of his son Sean, Lennon retired from music and became a house husband for five years. Murdered by a deranged fan December 8, 1980.

A dream you dream alone is only a dream. A dream you dream together is reality.

1941 **Trent Lott:** Republican U.S. Senator from Mississippi since 1989. Senate Majority Leader when Bob Dole resigned from the Senate. To satisfy right-wing supporters, Lott pushed the impeachment trial of President Clinton even when it was clear he would not be convicted. Lott was forced to resign his leadership role when at the 100th birthday party of staunch segregationist Senator Strom Thurmond of South Carolina, he made the mistake of saying publicly what he apparently believed privately, namely that had Thurmond been elected president in 1948 on the Dixiecrat ticket, "we wouldn't have had all these problems over these years."

Racial discrimination does not always violate public policy.

1970 **Annika Sörenstam:** Swedish golfer. Arguably the best golfer on the Ladies Professional Golf Association tour. World Amateur champion in 1992. Won seven collegiate titles during her career at the University of Arizona. College Player of the Year and NCAA Pac-10 champion in 1901. Since joining the LPGA Tour in 1994, she has won 67 official tournaments, including nine majors. Tops the LPGA's career money list by several million dollars. Holder of various all-time scoring records, including the lowest score, 59.

If you think about it, the golf ball doesn't know which country you're in.

OTHERS: 1201 French founder of Sorbonne **Robert de Sorbon**, 1221 Italian chronicler **Salimbene di Adam**, 1518 French mathematician **Claude Bachet de Méziriac**, 1796 English Egyptologist **Joseph Bonomi the Younger**, 1840 British artist **Simeon Solomon**, 1859 French officer **Alfred Dreyfus**, 1873 Hungarian violinist **Carl Flesch**, 1873 German physicist **Karl Schwarzschild**, 1873 U.S. entrepreneur **Charles Walgreen**, 1888 Russian politician **Nikolai I. Bukharin**, 1908 French filmmaker **Jacques Tati**, 1911 U.S. photographer **Joe Rosenthal**, 1928 Finnish composer **Einojuhani Rautavaara**, 1946 Turkish PM **Tansu Çiller**, 1953 U.S. actor **Tony Shalhoub**, 1975 English musician **Sean Lennon**

October 10

1813 **Giuseppe Verdi:** Italian musician and opera composer. Genius for dramatic, lyric, and tragic stage music. Operas: *Rigoletto*, *Il Trovatore*, *La Traviata*, *Aïda* and *Otello*. At the death of Gioacchino Rossini, Verdi conceived the idea of honoring his memory by a collective composition of a *Requiem*, to which several Italian composers would contribute a movement each, Verdi reserving the last section, *Libera me*, for himself. Completed in 1869, it was never performed in its original form.

I would be willing to set even a newspaper of a letter, etc. to music, but in the theatre the public will stand for everything except boredom.

1834 **Aleksis Kivi:** Originally **Stenvall**. Finnish author. By writing in Finnish and not in Swedish he established the western dialect of the modern literary language of Finland. Considered the father of the Finnish theatre and novel. Works: the novel, *Seven Brothers*, the rural comedy *The Cobbler on the Hearth* and the tragedy *Kullervo*.

God is forbearing and merciful, and He will always forgive us, if we pray with a sincere heart.

1861 **Fridtjof Nansen:** Norwegian explorer, scientist, humanitarian and statesman. In 1882 made a voyage into the artic regions and on his return was made keeper of the natural history department of the museum of Bergen. In summer 1888, made a journey across Greenland from east to west. Greatest achievement was the partial accomplishment of his scheme for reaching the North Pole by letting his ship *Fram* get frozen into the ice north of Siberia and drift with a current setting towards Greenland.

It is better to go skiing and think of God, than go to church and think of sport.

1885 **Walter Anderson:** Belarus-born German ethnologist. Professor of folklore at the University of Tartu in Estonia (1920–39). A driving force behind the comparative geographic-historical method of folkloristics. Seminal figure in the development of folklore studies in Estonia and the Baltic region and as a result had an indirect role in the development of Estonian nationalism in the period just prior to the annexation of Estonia by the Soviet Union. Best known for his monograph *Kaiser und Abt*.

Good listeners, like precious gems, are to be treasured.

1895 **Lin Yutang:** Chinese-born government official, writer, speaker, and philosopher. Professing to be "happily a pagan," he believed the only religion for modern man was a kind of mysticism, consisting of a reverence and respect for the moral order of the universe and the effort to live in harmony with it. Books: *My Country and My People*, *Wisdom of Confucius*, *Between Tears and Laughter*, *On the Wisdom of America* and *The Secret Name*.

Stated in the simplest terms, science is but a sense of curiosity about life, religion is a sense of wonder at life, art is a taste for life, and philosophy is an attitude toward life.

1898 **Lilly Daché:** French-born American milliner. First innovations were hats molded to the head. Created a sensation was a black cloche trimmed with black and white checkered ribbon, red cherries and pink cherry blossoms. In 1949 she made her first dress collection. She also extended her business with a line of cosmetics, accessories and a beauty salon. Books: *Talking Through My Hat* and *Lilly Daché's Glamour Book*.

Glamour is what makes a man ask for your telephone number. But it is also what makes a woman ask for the name of your dressmaker.

1900 **Helen Hayes:** American stage and screen actress. Her legitimate stage triumphs include: *Caesar and Cleopatra*, *What Every Woman Knows*, *Victoria Regina* and *Mrs. McThing*. On the occasion in 1959 when a Broadway Theater was reamed The Helen Hayes in her honor, she declared, "An actress's life is so transitory! Suddenly you're a building." Oscar winner for *The Sin of Madelon Claudet* and *Airport*.

Age is not important unless you're a cheese.

1901 **Alberto Giacometti:** Swiss sculptor and painter. Developed a style related to the Cubist sculpture of Alexander Archipenko and Jacques Lipchitz, partly inspired by African and Oceanic art. His signature style was in creating thin, attenuated sculptors of solitary, skeletal figures and heads. Work evokes a sense of existential tragedy comparable to that produced by the existential writers.

All I can do will only ever be a faint image of what I see and my success will always be less than my failure or perhaps equal to the failure.

1913 **Claude Simon:** Major French novelist in the genre of the *Nouveau roman*. The absence of story, time and punctuation is his hallmark. His novels give extremely detailed and precise descriptions of sensual impressions, while leaving their essence or significance unclear. Novels, *The Wind, The Grass, The Palace* and *The Road to Flanders*. Relatively unknown when he was awarded the Nobel Prize for Literature (1985).

For me, the big chore is always the same: how to begin a sentence, how to continue it, how to complete it.

1917 **Thelonious Monk:** American jazz pianist and composer. One of the most influential and original modern jazz musicians. Contributed to the development of bebop. Performed with Coleman Hawkins, Cootie Williams and Dizzy Gillespie before recording under his own name. Best-known composition "Round Midnight" has become a jazz standard.

All musicians are subconsciously mathematicians. All musicians stimulate each other. The vibrations get scattered around.

1930 **Harold Pinter:** English playwright, screenwriter, novelist, poet, director and actor. Established himself as one of the most original voices in the English-speaking theater. Offers existential glimpses of bizarre or terrible moments in people's lives. Plays: *The Caretaker, The Collection, The Birthday Party, The Homecoming* and *The Dumb Waiter*. Oscar nominated for screenplays *The French Lieutenant's Woman* and *Betrayal*.

The past is what you remember, imagine you remember, convince yourself you remember, or pretend you remember.

1948 **Cyril Neville:** African-American singer and percussionist. Youngest of the New Orleans funk band The Neville Brothers, known as "The First Family of New Orleans" and "Professors of the Uptown Funk." Angry after the events of hurricane Katrina, Neville, who now resides in Austin, Texas, pledges he will not return to the Crescent City, saying "The gumbo has spilled into the chili." Caught flak for walking onstage at Madison Square Garden wearing T-shirt, emblazoned with: "Ethnic cleaning in New Orleans."

Somebody said on TV the other night that New Orleans had died. New Orleans was murdered. Neglect and greed murdered New Orleans.

OTHERS: 1684 French painter **Antoine Watteau**, 1731 British chemist/physicist **Henry Cavendish**, 1780 Scottish physician **John Abercrombie**, 1791 U.S. agriculturist **Henry L. Ellsworth**, 1870 Russian writer **Ivan A, Bunin**, 1906 Indian novelist **R.K. Narayan**, 1924 Australian author **James Clavell**, 1924 U.S. filmmaker **Ed Wood**, 1930 U.S. Senator **Adlai Stevenson III**, 1933 U.S. murdered hairstylist **Jay Sebring**, 1946 U.S. dancer/actor **Ben Vereen**, 1948 French singer **Séverine**, 1951 Fiji statesman **Ratu Epeli Ganilau**, 1958 U.S. country singer **Tanya Tucker**, 1963 U.S. journalist/murdered hostage **Daniel Pearl**, 1969 Pro football QB **Bret Favre**, 1974 Race car driver **Dale Earnhardt, Jr.**

October 11

1675 **Samuel Clarke:** English philosopher, metaphysician, moralist and a defender of rational theology. Chaplain to the Bishop of Norwich to Queen Anne. His Boyle lectures of 1704–5 contained his "Demonstration of the Being and Attributes of God" and expounded a "mathematical" proof of God's existence.

There was plainly wanted a divine revelation to recover mankind out of their universal corruption and degeneracy.

1756 **Mason Locke Weems**, generally known as **Parson Weems**. American printer and author best known as the source of all the half-truths about George Washington, found in his *The Life of Washington*. Among these is the pious story of how age six George could not tell a lie, so he confessed to his father that he had cut down a cherry tree with his little hatchet. Other works: *Life of General Francis Marion, Life of Benjamin Franklin* and *Life of William Penn*.

... to be a truly great, a man must have not only great talents, but those talents must be constantly exerted on great, i.e., good actions — and perseveringly too — for if he should turn aside to vice — farewell to heroism.

1844 **Henry John Heinz:** American food manufacturer. Began his career at age 8 peddling produce from his family's garden. By age 16, he employed others to tend and sell his wares. In 1876, with his brother and cousin, he confounded F & J Heinz Company, reorganized later as H.J. Heinz Company, of which he was president (1905–19). He invented the advertising slogan "57 Varieties" in 1896. Promoted the pure food movement in the U.S.A.

To do a common thing, uncommonly well, brings success.

1872 **Harlan Fiske Stone:** American lawyer and jurist. Associate justice of the Supreme Court (1925–41) and Chief Justice (1941–46). A liberal who believed in judicial restraint, and except where questions of individual liberty were involved, courts should defer to legislatures. Only Supreme Court Justice who occupied each of the nine seats on the court as he moved up in seniority.

Democracy cannot survive without the guidance of a creative minority.

1884 **Eleanor Roosevelt:** American diplomat and humanitarian. Wife of President Franklin D. Roosevelt. Affectionately called "The First Lady of the World." she often served as her husband's legs and ears. As an invaluable advisor, brought to his attention the problems of the nation that she saw in her far flung-travels. Wrote the column, "My Day." U.S. representative to the U.N. (1945, 1947–52, 1961). Chair of the U.N. Human Rights Commission. Named "World's Most Influential Woman."

Great minds discuss ideas; Average minds discuss events; Small minds discuss people.

1897 **Nathan Twining:** U.S. Air Force General. Directed air assaults against Solomon Islands and New Guinea during World War II. In 1944 went to the Mediterranean as commander of the 15th Air Force, which under his direction carried out the famous Ploesti oilfield raids. Chairman, Joint Chiefs of Staff (1957–60).

This "flying saucer" situation is not at all imaginary or seeing too much in some natural phenomenon. Something is flying around. The phenomenon is something real and not visionary or fictitious.

1906 **Charles Revson:** American cosmetics manufacturer. President, chairman and CEO of Revlon, Inc., which he founded with two partners in 1932, the largest cosmetics and fragrance manufacturer. Introduced opaque nail polish and matching colors for lips and nails.

In the factory we make cosmetics; in the drug store we sell hope.

1910 **Joseph Alsop, Jr.:** U.S. political columnist. With his brother, Stewart Alsop, wrote the syndicated column "Matter of Fact." Passionate anti-communist and strong supporter of U.S. policies in Vietnam. Even their friends called them "prophets of doom." Joe said "The readers of our political columns may perhaps suspect that it has not always been fun for us. But it has. The truth is, thank God, we like a fight." Books: *We Accuse*, written with his brother, *Men Around the President* and *American White Paper*, written with Robert E. Kintner.

The plain truth is that the reporter's trade is for young men. Your feet, which do the legwork, are nine times more important than your head, which fits the facts into the story.

1914 **J. Edward Day:** American businessman, U.S. Postmaster General in the administration of John F. Kennedy, and lawyer. Responsible for reducing the postal deficit through rate increases and for introducing zip codes. Replying to a request from an individual to be honored with a stamp (but never mailed the letter).

We cannot put the face of a person on a stamp unless said person is deceased. My suggestion, therefore, is that you drop dead.

1918 **Jerome Robbins:** Born **Jerome Rabinowitz.** American choreographer, dancer, ballet master and director. First directorial credit was in 1954 when he co-staged with George Abbott the musical *Pajama Game*. Choreographed film *The King and I.* and codirected *West Side Story* (Oscar), which he codirected. Broadway shows: *Gypsy* and *Fiddler on the Roof.* Producer Leland Hayward said of him, "In dance he has completely revolutionized the theater.

Dance is like life, it exists as you're flitting through it, and when it's done, it's over.

1919 **Art Blakey:** Later **Abdullah Ibn Buhaina**. American Jazz drummer. Worked with Fletcher Henderson's big band before joining Billy Eckstine's ensemble (1944–47). Prodigious technique and thunderous attack assured his role as one of the principal drum stylists in modern jazz. Formed the Jazz Messengers, one of the most enduring ensembles in modern jazz, with Horace Silver in 1954. Its aggressive blues-inflected approach made it the archetypal hard-bop unit.

Jazz is known all over the world as an American musical art form and that's it. No America, no jazz. I've seen people try to connect it to other countries, for instance to Africa, but it doesn't have a damn thing to do with Africa.

1989 **Michelle Wie:** Hawaiian born Korean-American golfer, known for her long drives. Turned pro in 2005, although too young to become a member of the LPGA. By the time she was 10 she was the youngest player to qualify for a USGA amateur championship. In 2002 youngest player to qualify for an LPGA event, the Takefuji Classic Finished fourth in the 2004 Kraft Nabisco Championship, only four shots behind the winner.

I don't like boys. They're kind of annoying.

OTHERS: 1616 German writer **Andreas Gryphius**, 1661 French diplomat **Melchior de Polignac**, 1758 German astronomer **Heinrich Olbers**, 1782 Danish poet **Steen Steensen Bilcher**, 1821 English founder YMCA **George Williams**, 1885 French writer **François Mauriac**, 1895 Croatian composer **Jakov Gotovac**, 1896 Slavic linguist **Roman Jakobson**, 1900 U.S. football player/baseball umpire **Cal Hubbard**, 1925 U.S. novelist **Elmore Leonard**, 1932 U.S. country singer **Dottie West**, 1946 Japanese gymnast **Sawao Kato**, 1957 Welsh comedienne **Dawn French**, 1961 Egyptian pop star **Amr Diab**, 1962 U.S. actress **Joan Cusack**, 1985 U.S. actress **Michelle Trachtenberg**

October 12

1537 Lady **Jane Grey:** Queen of England for ten days. Great granddaughter of King Henry VII married in 1553 to Lord Guildford Dudley, son of the Duke of Northumberland, who persuaded King Edward VI to set aside the claims to the throne of his sisters Mary and Elizabeth. When Edward died Jane reluctantly accepted the crown. Although Mary was a Roman Catholic, she had the support of the people. The Lord Mayor of London announced that Mary was queen on July 19. Jane and her young husband were both executed in 1554.

Although it hath pleased God to hasten my death by you, by whom my life should rather have been lengthened, yet can I patiently take it, that I yield God more hearty thanks for shortening my woeful days. And now, good people, while I am alive, I pray you assist me with my prayers.

1602 **William Chillingworth:** Controversial English scholar and theologian. In *The Religion of Protestants a Safe Way to Salvation*, he argued that the Bible is the sole authority in spiritual matters, and that individuals had the right to interpret it. Also wrote a number of anti–Jesuit papers, published in the posthumous *Additional Discourses.*

Passionate expression and vehement assertion are no arguments, unless it be of the weakness of the cause that is defended of them, or of the man that defends it.

1710 **Jonathan Trumbull:** Originally spelled **Trumble.** Colonial statesman and patriot. Governor of Connecticut. Friend and counselor of George Washington. Dedicated the resources of his state to the fight for independence during the Revolutionary War. Trumbull College at Yale and Trumbull, Connecticut, are named for him. Of his six children, Jonathan Jr. became governor of Connecticut and John Trumbull is known as the "Painter of the American Revolution."

If you ask an American who is his master? He will tell you he has none, nor any governor but Jesus Christ.

1775 **Lyman Beecher:** American preacher and author. One of the most influential pulpit orators of his time. Preached against Unitarianism and Catholicism. Supported traditional Calvinism. Father of Henry Ward Beecher and Harriet Beecher Stowe. Wrote *A Plea for the West* and *Works.*

No great advance has been made in science, politics, or religion without controversy.

1866 **James Ramsey MacDonald:** British journalist, politician and statesman. One of the founders of the British Labor Party. In Parliament, opposition to World War I made him unpopular. Asked to form a government by King George V, becoming the first Labor Prime Minister in 1924, albeit of a minority government. Also served as PM in a minority government 1929–34, at which time he set a historic precedent by naming Margaret Bondfield, the first female minister.

We have all taken risks in making war. Isn't it time that we should take risks to secure peace?

1872 **Ralph Vaughan Williams:** English composer. Wrote nine symphonies. Considered the most important English composer of his generation. Style was tonal and his music was often derived from English folk and classical tradition. Operas: *Sir John in Love, Hugh the Drover* and *The Pilgrim's Progress.* Other works: the orchestral *Fantasia on a Theme by Thomas Tallis,* A *London Symphony* and *Fantasia on Greensleeves.*

If I many venture to give my own definition of a folk song, I should call it "an individual flowering on a common stem."

1875 **Aleister Crowley:** Real name **Edward Alexander.** Prolific English poet, author and philosopher. Wrote books on magic and occult lore. A legendary figure, notorious for his celebration of Black Magic rites. A diabolist who claimed to be the Beast from the Book of Revelation. Joined the Order of the Golden Dawn, a group of theosophists involved in Cabbalistic magic. Books: *Songs of the Spirit* and *The Diary of a Drug Fiend.*

I was asked to memorize what I did not understand; and, my memory being so good, it refused to be insulted in that manner.

1896 **Eugenio Montale:** Italian poet, prose writer, editor and translator. Awarded a Nobel Prize in 1975 for his pessimistic poetry *Cuttlefish bones* and *Occasions.* In 1989, it was revealed that much of his literary journalism, such as his regular column in the *Corriere della Sera* newspaper, was actually written by American Henry Frost.

Man cannot produce a single work without the assistance of the slow, assiduous, corrosive worm of thought.

1932 **Dick Gregory:** American stand-up comedian and political activist. Got a big break when he was hired by Hugh Hefner to work at the Chicago Playboy Club. Soon began appearing nationally on TV. Became an activist for civil rights and against the Vietnam War. Noted for his fasts in behalf of causes he supported. Books: *Nigger, From the Back of the Bus* and *Up from Nigger.* Ran for the president in 1968 as a write-in candidate. Nutrition guru in the 1980s, advocating a diet of raw fruits and vegetables.

I never learned hate at home. I had to go to school for that.

1935 **Luciano Pavarotti:** Italian opera tenor. One of the most famous living singers and today's best-selling classical vocalist. Became an internationally known celebrity in 1990 singing Giacomo Puccini's aria, "Nessun Dorma" from *Turandot,* which achieved pop status, and remains his trademark song. Noted for his two concerts with tenors Jose Carreras and Placido Domingo and conductor Zubin Mehta. The first recorded live from the ancient Baths of Caracalla in Rome became the biggest selling classical record of all time. Operatic roles include Rodolfo in *La Bohème,* Cavaradossi in *Tosca,* the Duke of Mantua in *Rigoletto,* and Nemorino in *L'Elisir d'amore.*

Learning about music by reading about it is like making love by mail.

1935 **William Raspberry:** Pulitzer Prize–winning African-American journalist. Syndicated urban affairs columnist for the *Washington Post.* Knight Professor of Communications and Journalism at the Stanford Institute of Public Policy at Duke University. Writes on minority issues. Author of *Looking Backward at Us,* a collection of his columns from the 1980s.

We must teach our young girls to honor and respect the temple of their bodies. We must make our boys understand the difference between making a baby and being a father.

1950 **Susan Anton:** American actress. Won the Miss California title in 1969 and was second runner-up in the Miss America pageant in 1970. Appeared in TV commercials as the Muriel Cigar Girl, leading to regular appearances on the Merv Griffin Show. Starred on Broadway in David Rabe's play *Hurleyburly.* Co-starred with Keith Carradine in the Tony Award–winning musical *The Will Rogers Follies.* For three years she was part of the cast of TV's *Baywatch.*

Sometimes because a woman is beautiful, she's not encouraged to do more, although she may have so much more to offer.

OTHERS: 1490 Italian composer **Bernardo Pisano**, 1537 King of England **Edward VI**, 1725 French entomologist **Étienne Louis Geoffroy**, 1798 Emperor of Brazil **Pedro I**, 1840 Polish Shakespearian actress **Helena Modjeska**, 1860 U.S. inventor **Elmer Sperry**, 1894 U.S. biblical scholar **Charles Hodge**, 1904 Chinese writer **Ding Ling**, 1905 U.S. radio actress **Jane Sherwood Ace**, 1906 U.S. baseball player/manager **Joe Cronin**, 1923 Founder of Weight Watchers **Jean Nidetch**, 1934 U.S. architect **Richard Meier**, 1947 U.S. journalist **Chris Wallace**, 1953 French politician **Serge Lepeltier**, 1968 Australian actor/singer **Hugh Jackman**, 1975 U.S. runner **Marion Jones**, 1982 Irish singer **Molly Bennett**

October 13

1821 **Rudolf Virchow:** Distinguished German physician, sanitarian, biologist and politician. Founder of modern cellular pathology. First to describe leukemia. In his book *Cellular Pathology*, he proposed that disease is not due to sudden invasions or changes, but to slow processes in which normal cells give rise to abnormal ones, probably indicating that the cause of one's death has been present in a benign form for a long time before attacking the body.

The task of science is to stake out the limits of the knowable, and to center consciousness within them.

1853 **Lillie Langtry:** née **Le Breton**. British actress. Nickname "The Jersey Lily" originated in the title of the portrait of her by John Millais. Famed for her beauty. Best roles included Rosalind in *As You Like It*. Allegedly the mistress of the Prince of Wales, who became King Edward VII. Toured the United States. Langtry, Texas, is named for her. Autobiography, *The Days I Knew* (1909).

Sympathy is charming, but it does not make up for pain.

1885 **Harry Hershfield:** American cartoonist, humorist and raconteur. Devoted almost all of his nearly 90 years to telling funny stories, both in words and pictures. Created his most successful comic strip "Abie the Agent" in 1914, which entertained millions until 1940. Wrote joke books. Served as toastmaster at about 200 banquets a year, known as "New York's Best After Dinner Speaker." Panelist on the radio program "Can You Top This?"(1940–54).

It isn't the size of the dog in the fight, but the size of the fight in the dog, that counts.

1902 **Arna Bontemps:** African-American writer of the Harlem Renaissance. Author of *God Sends Sunday*, *Pogo and Fifina* (with Langston Hughes), *Story of the Negro* and *Hold Fast to Dreams*. With Countee Cullen he adapted his novel *God Sends Sundays* into the play *St. Louis Woman*. Wrote prolifically for children, most notably nonfiction works on black Americans and black history.

God suffer little men/ The taste of soul's desire.

1909 **Herblock:** Pen name of **Herbert L. Block**. American cartoonist and author. First published his cartoons in the *Chicago Daily News*. Later worked for the Newspaper Enterprise Association (1933–43). Leading spokesman for liberalism. Attacked injustices in politics, bib business, labor and economics. Best known for his 1950s cartoon attacking Senator Joseph McCarthy [coining the word "McCarthyism"] and his shots at President Richard Nixon. Won three Pulitzers. Books: *Herblock's Here and Now*, *Herblock's Special for Today* and *Straight Herblock*.

I've often summed up the role of the cartoonist as that of the boy in the Hans Christian Anderson story who says the emperor has no clothes on.

1925 **Lenny Bruce:** American entertainer and comedian. Constantly arrested for saying things in clubs and concerts that are considered tame today. For better or for worst, comics like Richard Pryor, Chris Rock and Eddie Murphy owe him a debt for leading the way into controversial subjects. Unfortunately, too many so-called comedians of today benefit from his freedom but unlike Bruce have no ideas to explore through the vehicle of humor.

If something about the human body disgusts you, the fault lies with [God] the manufacturer.

1925 **Margaret Thatcher:** née **Roberts.** British politician. Elected leader of the Conservative Party in 1975, the first woman party leader in British politics. Served as Britain's only woman prime minister in 800 years of parliamentary history (1979–90). Under her leadership the Conservative Party moved towards a more right-wing position. Established a personal political philosophy, spoken of as "Thatcherism," based on her resolution to persevere despite objections form her critics and doubt among her supporters.

If my critics saw me walking over the Thames they would say it was because I couldn't swim.

1941 **Paul Simon:** American singer and songwriter. Formed a folk-singing duo with Art Garfunkel, with Simon writing most of the songs. Their first LP, *Wednesday Morning, 3 A.M.* was not initially successful but one of its songs, "The Sound of Silence" was. Other albums: *Parsley, Sage, Rosemary, and Thyme*; *Bookends*; and *Bridge Over Troubled Water.* Contributed the soundtrack of the 1967 film *The Graduate*, including the hit "Mrs. Robinson. " Simon pursued a solo career with albums: *There Goes Rhymin' Simon*, *Still Crazy After All These Years* and *Graceland*.

The words of the prophets are written on the subway walls and tenements halls and whispered in the sounds of silence.

1946 **Edwina Currie [Jones]:** née **Cohen**. Former British Conservative Party Member of Parliament. Junior Health Minister, but forced to resign when she issued a warning about salmonella in British eggs that was criticized for being hysterical. Novels: *A Parliamentary Affair* and *A Woman's Place*. Published her *Diaries* (2002), which created a sensation, revealing that she had a four-year affair with John Major before he became Prime Minister.

One wants to mutter deeply that apart from having two good legs I also have two good degrees and it is just possible that I do know what I'm talking about.

1952 **Beverly Johnson:** African-American supermodel and businesswoman. Broke the color barrier by becoming the first African-American to appear on the cover of *Vogue*. Created the Beverly Johnson Signature Collection of Wigs. Spokesperson for the *Healthy U* uterine health information awareness campaign.

Everyone should have enough money to get plastic surgery.

1962 **Jerry Rice:** American football player. Generally regarded as the greatest pass catcher in Pro history. Selected to the Pro Bowl 13 times, Member of three Super Bowl winning teams with the San Francisco 49ers. Holds records for most career TD receptions (197), career receptions (1549) TDs (208) and consecutive games with a reception (274). In 2005–6, paired with dancer Anna Tebunskaya to finish second in the competition on TV's *Dancing with the Stars.*

To me it was never about what I accomplished on the football field... It was about the way I played the game.

1970 **Nancy Kerrigan:** U.S. figure skating star. Attacked with a tire iron, by those who didn't wish her to be competition for skater Tonya Harding. Kerrigan captured the silver medal in 1992 Winter Olympics.

Part of being a champ is acting like a champ. You have to learn how to win and not run away when you lose. Everyone has had bad stretches and real successes. Either way, you have to be careful not to lose your confidence or get too confident.

OTHERS: 1474 Italian painter **Mariotto Albertinelli**, 1566 Irish politician **Richard Boyle**, 1696 English statesman **John Hervey**, 1714 Dutch philologist **Pieter Burmann the Younger**, 1880 Russian poet **Sasha Cherny**, 1909 U.S. jazz musician **Art Tatum**, 1917 U.S. actress **Larraine Day**, 1917 U.S. puppeteer of "Kukla, Fran and Ollie" **Burr Tillstrom**, 1921 Italian-born actor/singer **Yves Montand**, 1931 U.S. baseball player **Eddie Matthews**, 1934 Greek singer **Nana Mouskouri**, 1942 Dallas Cowboys owner **Jerry Jones**, 1954 French historian **Claude Ribbe**, 1960 White House Press Secretary **Ari Fleischer**, 1972 U.S. Olympic swimmer **Summer Sanders**, 1980 U.S. musician **Ashanti**, 1982 Australian swimmer **Ian Thorpe**

October 14

1644 **William Penn:** English Quaker founder of the colony of Pennsylvania as a refuge for persecuted Quakers. Champion of religious toleration, liberty, freedom and justice that he helped establish in the new world, idea that are the basis of democracy. Maintained good relationships with surrounding colonies and the Native Americans. In 1697 presented plan for forming a union of the colonies, but it was never acted upon. Laid out the city street plan of Philadelphia. Wrote: *The Great Case of Liberty of Conscience.*

Right is right, even if everyone is against it; and wrong is wrong, even if everyone is for it.

1814 **Thomas Osborne Davis:** Irish writer and politician. Chief organizer of the Young Ireland movement. Established *The Nation* newspaper with two others. Dedicated his life to Irish nationalism. A Protestant, he preached peace between the Catholics and Protestants. Wrote stirring ballads, published as *Spirit of the Nation*. At the fore of Irish nationalist thinking. Built the idea that Ireland must be free by promoting Irish identity.

A people without a language of its own, is only half a nation.

1888 **Katherine Mansfield:** Pseudonym of **Kathleen Mansfield Beauchamp**. New Zealand's most famous writer. Had a lasting influence on the literary genre of short-story writing. Her first major work was *Prelude* (1917), a recreation of the New Zealand of her childhood, which confirmed her standing as an original and innovative writer. Other Collections: *The Garden Party* and those published after her death, including *The Dove's Nest and Other Stories*, *Something Childish and Other Stories*, and *The Little Girl and Other Stories*.

This is not a letter but my arms around you for a brief moment.

1890 **Dwight D. Eisenhower:** "Ike." Thirty-fourth American president. Five-star general in the U.S. Army; supreme allied commander in Europe. Led the invasion that defeated Germany. President of Columbia University (1948–50). He likely could have had either the Republican or Democratic nomination for president, before declaring he was a Republican. As U.S. president ended Korean War. Held office in a period of international tension, with the Cold War dominating international politics, and the growing civil rights movement at home. Sent troops to Little Rock, Arkansas, to force compliance with desegregation order.

When people speak to you about a preventive war, you tell them to go and fight it. After my experience, I have come to hate war. War settles nothing.

1894 **e.e. cummings:** Literary signature of **Edward Estlin Cummings**, American poet and painter. Most all the words in his poetry were written in lower case, using an unorthodox typography, and idiosyncratic punctuation. For example: from his poem "My Sweet Old Etcetera," (dreaming,/ et/ cetera, of/ Your smile/ eyes knees and of your Etcetera). Used a highly experimental approach to style and diction. The lyrical power of his poetry gradually became recognized. Other verses: "Buffalo Bill's," "Spring is like a perhaps hand," and "One Times One."

The world is mud-luscious and puddle-wonderful.

1894 **Lillian Gish:** Adopted name of **Lillian de Guiche**. American actress whose film career spanned 75 years. "The First Lady of the Silent Screen." Deceptively frail, she possessed a vibrant spirit that the camera always caught. Most celebrated work was with legendary director D. W. Griffith, playing virtuous heroines. Silent films: *Broken Blossoms, Way Down East, and Orphans of the Storm.* Appeared in several Broadway plays in the thirties. Talkies: *Duel in the Sun* and *The Night of the Hunter.* Received a special Academy Award in 1971.

A happy life is one spent in learning, earning, and yearning. What you get is a living; what you give is a life.

1906 **Hannah Arendt:** German-born American philosopher and political scientist. Went to the U.S.A. in 1940 as a refugee from the Nazis in Germany. Took an active role in various Jewish organizations and wrote about Jewish affairs. Author of *The Origins of Totalitarianism, The Human Condition* and *Men in Dark Times.*

Storytelling reveals meaning without committing the error of defining it.

1910 **John Wooden:** American basketball coach. His UCLA teams won ten national titles (1964–65, 1967–73, 1975). Named Coach of the Year six times. College Player of the Year (1932). Only member of Basketball Hall of Fame inducted as both player and coach.

Talent is God-given. Be humble. Fame is man-given. Be grateful. Conceit is self-given.

1914 **Brendan Gill:** American critic, author and journalist. Chiefly known for his pieces in the *New Yorker,* where he spent some 60 years, many of them as a film critic, theatre critic and architecture critic. Leading preservationist led the fight to save New York City's Grand Central Station. Books include: *Here at the New Yorker.*

Parody is homage gone sour.

1916 **C. Everett Koop**. United States Surgeon General. Took a relatively hard line on abortion, published the 1988 report stating that nicotine has an addictiveness similar to that of heroin or cocaine, and warned the nation of the dangers of the AIDs disease. Somewhat eccentric and flamboyant, well-known for his mustacheless beard and colorful bow ties, he generally wore the Surgeon General's ceremonial military uniform during much of his day-to-day work.

You can't talk of the dangers of snake poisoning and not mention snakes.

1932 **Bernie S. Siegel:** American surgeon and self-help therapist. Preached patient empowerment and the choices to live life fully and die in peace. In 1978 started Exceptional Cancer Patients, a specific form of individual and group therapy utilizing patient's dreams, drawings, and images. His goal: "I want to heal people, not tell then what day they are going to die." Author of *How to Live Between Office Visits* and *Love, Medicine and Miracles.*

If you watch how nature deals with adversity, continually renewing itself, you can't help but learn.

1939 **Ralph Lauren:** Born **Ralph Lifschitz**. American fashion designer. Although he never had any formal fashion education, his fashion empire has grown into a billion-dollar business. Since the inception of Polo, in 1967, he has created many other brands. Among these : Big & Tall, Polo Golf, Polo Jeans, Ralph Lauren Black Label, clothing for women and recently Rugby, intended to appeal to the college set.

I don't design clothes. I design dreams.

OTHERS: 1257 King of Poland **Przemysl II**, 1643 Mughal Emperor of India **Bahadur Shah I**, 1712 British PM **George Grenville**, 1801 Belgian physicist **Joseph Plateau**, 1857 U.S. automobile pioneer **Elwood Haynes**, 1861 Croatian geographer **Artur Gavazzi**, 1872 U.S. athlete **Ray Ewry**, 1882 Irish politician/patriot **Eamon de Valera**, 1892 U.S. diplomat **Summer Welles**, 1904 French World War II resistance fighter **Christian Pineau**, 1906 Egyptian founder Muslim Brotherhood **Imam Hassan al Banna**, 1911 Vietnamese politician **Le Duc Tho**, 1927 English actor **Roger Moore**, 1930 President of Zaire **Joseph Mobutu**, 1970 Czech supermodel **Daniela Peštová**, 1978 U.S. singer/actor **Usher**

October 15

70 BCE **Virgil:** In full **Publius Vergilius Maro**. Greatest Latin poet. Studied rhetoric and philosophy in Rome. Beame one of the court poets gatherer around the minister, Maecenas. Most famous work is the almost completed epic poem, *The Aeneid,* about the founding of Rome, requested by the Emperor. By the 3rd century his poems, considered classics even in his own time, ranked as sacred books. Other works: *Eclogues* and *Georgics or Art of Husbandry.*

Woman is always a fickle and changeable thing.

1814 **Mikhail Lermontov:** Russian author. His poem, written on the death of poet Alexander Pushkin, caused his exile to the Caucasus. Reinstated, he was banished a second time following a duel with the son of the French ambassador. Fortunately, the Caucasus inspired his best poetry: "The Novice" and "The Demon" as well as his novel *A Hero of Our Time,* a masterpiece of prose writing. His death was the result of another duel, when he was only 27.

O vanity! You are the lever by means of which Archimedes wished to lift the earth.

1844 **Friedrich Nietzsche:** German philosopher, classical scholar, critic and poet. Determined to give his age new values. Most famous for his theory of the "superman" which he developed in *Thus Spake Zarathustra,* asserting that "Man is a rope stretched between the animal and the Superman — a rope over an abyss." Other works: *Beyond Good and Evil, The Birth of Tragedy* and *Ecce Homo.* Much of his esoteric doctrine appealed to the Nazis. Was a major influence on existentialism.

The true man wants two things: danger and play. For that reason he wants woman, as the most dangerous plaything.

1869 **Francisco Largo Caballero:** Spanish politician, who joined the Socialist Party in 1894 and rose to become head of the party's trade union federation in 1925. Cooperated with the dictatorship of Miguel Primo de Rivera, then served in the Second Republic as labor minister. After the electoral victory of the Popular Front, he became prime minister and attempted to unify the leftist parties. An extreme-left uprising in Barcelona during the Spanish Civil War caused a cabinet crisis, forcing him to resign. Went into exile and was interned by the Germans during World War II.

If common sense has not the brilliancy of the sun, it has the fixity of the stars.

1881 **P. G. [Pelham Grenville] Wodehouse:** English-American novelist, short-story writer, librettist and humorist. Noted for his literary skill. His whimsical novels featured the Honorable Bertie Wooster and Jeeves his valet. Much of the humor in the series is derived from the contrast between the bumbling. dimwitted, but charming Wooster and the efficient servant Jeeves. Books: *My Man Jeeves*, *The Inimitable Jeeves*, *Carry On, Jeeves!*, and *Pigs Have Wings*.

It is a good rule of life never to apologize. The right sort of people does not want apologies, and the wrong sort takes a mean advantage of them.

1908 **John Kenneth Galbraith:** Canadian-born American economist, educator, government official and author. Maintained that more national wealth should be used for public welfare. Harvard professor, ambassador to India, Chairman of the Americans for Democratic Action. Author of *American Capitalism: The Concept of Countervailing Power*, *the Nature of Mass Poverty*, *the Affluent Society* and *the New Industrial State*.

Meetings are indispensable when you don't want to do anything.

1917 **Arthur Schlesinger, Jr.:** American political commentator and author. His book *The Age of Jackson* stimulated a reexamination of the Jacksonian era of American history, winning a Pulitzer Prize. Other publications: the three volume analytic and sympathetic history of the New Deal, *The Age of Roosevelt*; his account of the Kennedy presidency, *A Thousand Days*; and *The Imperial Presidency*, about the Nixon administration.

When lies must be told, they should be told by subordinate officials. At no point should the president be asked to lend himself to a cover operation. There seems to be merit in Secretary Rusk's suggestion that someone other than the president make the final decision and do so in his absence — someone whose head can later be placed on the block if things go terribly wrong.

1920 **Mario Puzo:** American novelist. Author of *The Godfather*, the saga of a Mafia family that was a bestseller for five years. Claimed he had never met a gangster prior to writing his masterpiece. Won Oscars for the screenplays of *The Godfather I* and *The Godfather II*, produced and directed by Francis Ford Coppola, with whom he wrote the screenplay for *The Godfather, Part III*. Puzo also wrote screenplays for *Earthquake* and *Superman*. Working on the outline of a fourth Godfather novel at the time of his death in 1999.

Like many businessmen of genius he learned that free competition was wasteful, monopoly efficient. And so he simply set about achieving that efficient monopoly. A lawyer with his briefcase can steal more than a hundred men with guns.

1923 **Italo Calvino:** Italian journalist, writer and essayist. First novel, *The Path to the Nest of Spiders*, inspired by his involvement in the Italian Resistance during World War II. Later he turned to fantasy and allegory. *Cosmicomics* is a collection of whimsical narratives about the creation and evolution of the universe. Other fantasies are fully realized in his trilogy of fables, *Our Forefathers*, *Baron in the Trees*, and *The Nonexistent Knight and the Cloven Viscount*.

A classic is a book that has never finished saying what it has to say.

1924 **Lee A. Iacocca:** American business executive. Advanced from engineer to president of Ford Motor Co. His brash manner let to his dismissal by Henry Ford II in 1978. The next year he took over the nearly bankrupted Chrysler Corporation and persuaded Congress to lend Chrysler $1.5 billion in 1980. Carried out layoffs, wage cuts, and plant closings to make the company more efficient. Placed the emphasis on manufacturing more fuel-efficient cars. Within a few years Chrysler showed a profit. Wrote the best-selling autobiography *Iacocca*.

In the end, all business operations can be reduced to three words: people, product and profits. Unless you've got a good team, you can't do much with the other two.

1931 **Avul Pakir Jainulabdeen Abdul Kalam:** Indian scientist and engineer often referred to as the Missile Man of India. Member of India's Defence Research and Development Organization and the Indian Space Research Organization. Made significant contribution as Project Director to the development of India's first indigenous Satellite Launch Vehicle. Elected India's 11th president in 2002. Books: *India 2020: A Vision for a New Millennium* and *Guiding Souls: Dialogues on the Purpose of Life*.

You have to dream before your dreams can come true.

1959 **Sarah Ferguson:** Duchess of York. Known as "Fergie." Married Prince Andrew, Duke of York in 1986 with whom she had two daughters before divorcing amicably in 1996. Has been the center of a number of tabloid scandals. Struggling with her weight, tabloids unkindly dubbed her "The Duchess of Pork." After slimming down, she developed more self-confidence and became a spokesperson for Weight Watchers. Raised funds for children's charities and has spent time in Sierra Leone, raising money for wounded and orphaned children of the civil war. Wrote a best-selling autobiography, *My Story*.

Lord grant me the serenity to accept the things I cannot change, the courage to change the things I can, and the wisdom to hide the bodies of those people I had to kill because they pissed me off.

OTHERS: 1542 Indian Mughal emperor **Akbar**, 1608 Italian mathematician **Evangelista Torricelli**, 1674 British poet **Robert Herrick**, 1829 U.S. astronomer **Asaph Hall**, 1830 U.S. author **Helen Hunt Jackson**, 1858 U.S. heavyweight boxing champion **John L. Sullivan**, 1905 British writer **C.P. Snow**, 1909 U.S. reporter **Robert Trout**, 1926 French philosopher **Michel Foucault**, 1926 U.S. author **Evan Hunter**, 1926 U.S. actress/wife of Howard Hughes **Jean Peters**, 1926 German conductor **Karl Richter**, 1940 Australian immunologist **Peter Doherty**, 1942 U.S. actress/director **Penny Marshall**, 1944 President of Albania **Sali Berisha**, 1945 U.S. baseball pitcher **Jim Palmer**, 1959 U.S. chef **Emeril Lagasse**, 1981 Russian tennis player **Elena Dementieva**

October 16

1758 **Noah Webster:** American teacher, lexicographer and publisher. Wrote best-selling grammar and spelling books. Worked for the establishment of a distinctive American version of the English language. His *American Dictionary of the English Language*, published in 1828, took 25 years to write. Periodically revised to keep abreast of the times it is now called *Webster's New International Dictionary*.

Language is not an abstract construction of the learned, or of dictionary makers, but is something arising out of the work, needs, ties, joys, affections, tastes, of long generations of humanity, and has its bases broad and low, close to the ground.

1854 **Oscar Wilde:** Irish-born poet, novelist and playwright. Eccentric dresser with many idiosyncrasies. His flamboyant aestheticism, scorn for sports, and collections of blue china won him hostile attention. He was spoofed in Gilbert & Sullivan's *Patience*. At Magdalen College, Oxford he won the Newdigate Prize for his poem "Ravenna." Accused of homosexual practices, tried, convicted and imprisoned. *The Ballad of Reading Gaol* is based on his experiences there. Major works: the novel *The Picture of Dorian Gray*, and the plays Lady *Windermere's Fan*, and *The Importance of Being Earnest*.

The only difference between a caprice and a lifelong passion is that the caprice lasts a little longer.

1861 **J.B. (John Bagwell) Bury:** Eminent Irish historian, classical scholar, byzantinist and philologist. Writings ranged from ancient Greece to the 19th century papacy. Led a revival of Byzantine history, which had been neglected for many years by English-speaking historians. Books: *History of the Roman Empire From Its Foundation to the Death of Marcus Aurelius*, *History of Greece to the Death of Alexander the Great*, and *History of the Eastern Empire from the Fall of Irene to the Accession of Basil I.*

History is a science, no more and no less.

1886 **David Ben-Gurion:** Polish-born Israeli statesman. Leading statesman in the struggle to make Palestine a refuge for the Jewish people and an independent nation. Following the Balfour Declaration, he joined the British Army's Jewish Legion during World War I. In the 1920's led several political organizations, including the Jewish Agency, world Zionism's highest directing body. First prime minister of Israel (1948–52 and 1954–63). Called the "Father of the Nation."

If an expert says it can't be done, get another expert.

1888 **Eugene G. O'Neill:** American playwright. Joined the experimental theater group The Provincetown Players, who staged his early one-act plays. Winner of four Pulitzer prizes in drama for *Beyond the Horizon*, *Agatha Christie*, *Strangle Interlude* and semi-autobiographical family tragedy *Long Day's Journey Into Night*. First U.S. playwright awarded a Nobel Prize for literature. Other Plays: *The Emperor Jones*, *Mourning Becomes Electra*, *Ah, Wilderness* (his only comedy) and *The Iceman Cometh*.

Life is a solitary cell whose walls are mirrors.

1890 **Michael "Mick" Collins:** Irish nationalist and patriot. Created a special assassination squad known as *The Twelve Apostles* to kill British agents. By the time he was 30 years old, the British offered a bounty of £10,000 for information leading to his capture or death Participated in the negotiations leading to the Anglo-Irish Treaty, which provided for a new Irish State, a dominion of the British Empire. Commander of the Free State's military forces in the civil war between two factions of the Sinn Féin, the anti-treaty IRA and the Free State troops. For ten days head of state until he was assassinated in an ambush by anti-treaty IRA men.

To go for a drink is one thing. To be driven to it is another.

1890 **Paul Strand:** American photographer. Rejected soft-focus pictorialism in favor of the minute detail and rich tonal affect using large-format cameras for his strong, clear, close up photographs of natural objects. Emphasized abstract form and patter in his photographs, such as *Wall Street*. Much of his later work was devoted to North American and European scenes and landscapes.

It is one thing to photograph people. It is another to make others care about them by revealing the core of their humanness.

1898 **William O. Douglas:** U.S. jurist. As chairman of the Securities and Exchange Commission he engineered the reorganization of the nation's stock exchange, instituting measures for the protection of small investors, and began government regulation of the sale of securities. Appointed Associate Justice of the Supreme Court by President Roosevelt in 1939. His 36-year tenure was the longest of anyone who served on the court. Committed liberal, urged the Court take bold steps in application of the Constitution. Author of *A Living Bill of Rights* and *Of Men and Mountains*.

The Constitution is not neutral. It was designed to take the government off the backs of people.

1918 **Louis Althusser**: Algerian-born French philosopher. Argued that the idea that economic systems determine family and political systems is simplistic. Attempted to show how the ruling class ideology of a particular period is a crucial form of class control. Structuralist analysis of capitalism views individuals and groups as agents of the structure of social relations, rather than as independent influences on history. Works: *For Marx, Lenin and Philosophy* and *Essays in Self-Criticism.*

Ideology ... is indispensable in any society if men are to be formed, transformed and equipped to respond to the demands of their conditions of existence.

1925 **Angela Lansbury:** English-born actress. At 18 she held her own among the likes of Charles Boyer, Ingrid Bergman and Joseph Cotton, nominated for Best Supporting actress for her portrayal of the sassy maid in *Gaslight.* Nominated twice again for *The Picture of Dorian Gray* and *The Manchurian Candidate.* Other respected film appearances: *State of the Union, The Long, Hot Summer, The Dark at the Top of the Stairs,* and *Bedknobs and Broomsticks.* Won Tony Awards for her Broadway performances in *Mame, Dear World, Gypsy,* and *Sweeny Todd.* Starred in the long-running TV mystery series, *Murder, She Wrote.*

I just stopped playing bitches on wheels and people's mothers. I have only a few more years to kick up my heels!

1927 **Günter Grass:** German novelist and playwright. Member of the Hitler Youth movement, drafted at age 16, wounded and became a prisoner of war. Worked as a writer and sculptor first in Paris and then in Berlin. Literary spokesman for Germans who grew up during the Nazi dictatorship. Author of *The Tin Drum, Cat and Mouse* and *Dog Years,* written with grotesque humor and socialist feelings. Received a Nobel Prize for Literature in 1999.

The job of a citizen is to keep his mouth open.

1931 **Charles W. Colson:** Chief Counsel for President Richard Nixon. Authored the 1971 memo listing Nixon's major political opponents, which came to be known as the "Enemies List." As a member of the Committee to Re-Elect the President, he and John Ehrlichmann appointed E. Howard Hunt to the White House Special Operations Unit (the so-called "Plumbers"), formed to stop leaks in t he Nixon administration. Served 18 months in prison for obstructing justice. Became a born-again Christian and founded Prison Friendship. Worked to promote prisoner rehabilitation and reform of the U.S. prison system. Books: *Born Again, Loving God* and *The Good Life.*

I'd walk over my own grandmother to re-elect Richard Nixon.

OTHERS: 1430 King of Scotland **James II**, 1708 Swiss experimental physiologist **Albrecht von Haller**, 1714 Italian geologist **Giovanni Arduino**, 1726 Polish painter **Daniel Chodowiecki**, 1888 U.S. activist **Paul Popenoe**, 1900 Italian painter **Primo Conti**, 1903 French storyteller **Cecile de Brunhoff**, 1908 Albanian dictator **Enver Hoxha**, 1914 King of Afghanistan **Zahir Shah**, 1919 U.S. writer **Kathleen Winsor**, 1921 U.S. actress **Linda Darnell**, 1936 Russian serial killer **Andrei Chikatilo**, 1940 U.S. basketball player **Dave DeBusschere**, 1941 U.S. baseball player/commentator **Tim McCarver**, 1958 U.S. actor/director **Tim Robbins**, 1962 Australian musician **Flea**, 1980 U.S. basketball player **Sue Bird**

October 17

1725 **John Wilkes:** English politician and journalist. Prominent member of the Hell-fire Club, which staged orgies at the home of Sr. Francis Dashworth. Established a newspaper *The New Briton* in which he criticized the government to such an extent that on one occasion he was charged with libel but was acquitted. Opponents acquired a copy of Wilkes' privately distributed *Essay on Women,* which they considered obscene and read passages from it the House of Lords, forcing Wilkes to flee to France. When he returned he was imprisoned for 22 months and had his seat in parliament vacated. Later became Lord Mayor of London and returned to parliament. When the Earl of Sandwich predicted, "You shall either die of the pox or on the gallows," Wilkes replied:

That sir depends on whether I embrace your mistress or your politics.

1813 **Georg Büchner:** German playwright. Pioneer of Expressionist Theater. Studied medicine and became involved in revolutionary politics. Fled to Zürich where he died of typhoid at the age of 24. Best-known works are the poetical dramas *Dantons Tod* and *Woyzeck,* which was the basis for the opera of the same name by Alban Berg.

The Revolution is like Saturn — it eats its own children.

1864 **Elinor Glyn:** née **Sutherland**. English novelist. Best-selling romantic novels, considered daring and naughty at the time, were turned into film vehicles for vivacious flapper silent film star Clara Bow. Author of *Man and Maid, Did She?, The Third Eye, Three Weeks* and *It.* A sort of Jackie Collins of her era, her works were nonsense, ungrammatical and extremely popular.

A madness of tender caressing seized her. She purred as a tiger might have done, while she undulated like a snake.

1898 **Shinichi Suzuki:** Japanese violinist and teacher. Studied music in Tokyo and Berlin. With three of his brothers, formed the Suzuki Quartet. Famed for his mass instruction methods of teaching young children to play the violin. His methods have found popularity throughout the world and have been adapted to other instruments.

Music exists for the purpose of growing an admirable heart.

1898 **Simon Vestdjik:** Regarded as one of the greatest Dutch writers of the 20th century. Produced 52 novels, as well as poetry, essays on music and literature, and several works on philosophy. Remembered mainly for his psychological, autobiographical and historical novels: *Back to Ina Damman*, *The Garden Where the Brass Band Played* and *Ivory Watchman*.

The poetical intention, if concentrated enough, is already poetry, or rather is the essence of poetry, and the only thing that lends meaning to the poetry. Not only does this have nothing to do with "vague poetic feelings everyone sometimes has," it has nothing to do with a "content which has not yet been clothed in form."

1915 **Arthur Miller:** American playwright and author. Pulitzer Prize for his perfect play *Death of a Salesman*. Miller had brushes with the authorities over his early Communist sympathies. Commented on the political persecution led by Senator Joe McCarthy and the House Un-American Activities Committee in *The Crucible*, which dealt with the Salem witch trials. Others: *All My Sons, A View from the Bridge, After the Fall, Incident at Vichy* and *Playing for Time*. Wrote the screenplay for *The Misfits*, starring Marilyn Monroe to whom he had been married.

The theater is so endlessly fascinating because it is so accidental. It's so much like life.

1917 **Alfred Kahn:** U.S. governmental administrator. Appointed chairman of the New York Public Service Commission, which was responsible for the regulation of electric, gas, telephone and water companies. President Jimmy Carter appointed him to head the Civil Aeronautics Board. He deregulated passenger air travel, which increased traffic volume, reduced fares and decreased the number of empty seats on airline flights. In 1978, Carter appointed him "inflation czar," that is Chairman of the Council on Wage and Price Stability.

You may have heard that a dean is to faculty as a hydrant is to a dog.

1918 **Rita Hayworth:** Originally **Margarita Carmen Cansino**. Beautiful redheaded actress and dancer. For most of her male admirers, her top performance was the title character in *Gilda*. First seen in the film when she seductively tosses her luxurious hair. Hayworth often complained, "Men fall in love with Gilda and wake up with me." Other Films: *Blood and Sand, Cover Girl, Pal Joey* and *Separate Tables*. Among her five husbands were Orson Welles and Aly Khan. Died of Alzheimer's disease.

After all, a girl is — well, a girl. It's nice to be told you're successful at it.

1920 **Montgomery Clift**: American actor. Among the founding members of the Actors Studio in 1947. Acclaimed for his intelligent and sensitive portrayals of introspective, troubled men. Made his film debut in 1948 in *The Search*, for which he received an Academy Award nomination. Also nominated for Oscars for *A Place in the Sun, From Here to Eternity* and *Judgment at Nuremberg*. Other films: *The Heiress, I Confess, Raintree County* and *Freud*. An automobile accident scarred his face, ruining his good looks. Died of a heart attack at age 45.

Failure and its accompanying misery is for the artist his most vital source of creative energy.

1930 **James Earl "Jimmy" Breslin:** U.S. author and Pulitzer-winning syndicated columnist. Known as the tough-talking voice of his native Queens. First established himself as a sportswriter. Whether it is sports, social issues or politics he writes with passion and personal involvement. Often focuses on injustice and corruption Author of *Can't Anybody Around Here Play This Game, Table Money* and *The Gang That Couldn't Shoot Straight*.

The office of president is a bastardized thing, half royalty and half democracy, that nobody knows whether to genuflect or spit.

1946 **Adam Michnik:** Polish activist and editor-in-chief of *Gazeta Wyborcza* (*Election Gazette*), the largest Polish newspaper. A dissident during the Communist rule of Poland he was imprisoned for six years. *Solidarity* activist in the struggle against marital law during the 1980s. Became a strong opponent of Lech Walesa and the new Solidarity leadership. Criticized by some former dissidents for his opposition to punishing non-criminal members of the former Communist Party.

I think it's always dangerous to make political arguments in a religiously ideological way. And it's very dangerous to treat as traitors to the nation those who think differently.

1972 **Eminem:** Born **Marshall Bruce Mathers III**. The name "Eminem" comes from his initials M.M. Nicknamed "Slim Shady." American rap and hip hop artist. One of today's most popular and controversial rappers. Became a crossover sensation with his debut single "My Name Is." The song also generated a law suit brought by his mother, which earned her almost nothing. His 2000 album, *The Marshall Mathers LP*, sold a reported 7 million copies. His 2003 song "Lose yourself" from the film *8 Mile*, in which he starred, became the first rap song to win an Academy Award.

Don't do drugs, don't have unprotected sex, don't be violent. Leave that to me.

OTHERS: 1253 French saint **Ivo of Kermartin**, 1563 Flemish cartographer **Jodocus Hondius**, 1623 Swiss theologian **Francis Turretin**, 1889 Russian philosopher **Nikolai Chernyshevsky**, 1900 U.S. actress **Jean Arthur**, 1909 U.S. jazz drummer **Cozy Cole**, 1912 Pope **John Paul I**, 1921 Soviet gymnast **Maria Gorokhsoskaya**, 1930 U.S. nutritionist **Robert Atkins**, 1936 Japanese seismologist **Hiroo Kanamori**, 1938 American daredevil **Evel Knievel**, 1946 U.S. pole vaulter **Bob Seagren**, 1948 Canadian actress **Margot Kidder**, 1948 U.S. actor, "Norm" of *Cheers* **George Wendt**, 1962 Ecuadorian-born cartoonist **Mike Judge**, 1962 Canadian comedian **Norm MacDonald**, 1969 South African golfer **Ernie Els**

October 18

1547 **Justus Lipsius:** Flemish humanist, classical scholar and political theorist. His view that a government should recognize only one religion, and that dissent should be extirpated by fire and sword almost ended in being applied to him. Leading editor of Latin prose texts. Produced editions of Tacitus and Seneca. Wrote a series of works designed to revive ancient Stoicism in a form that would be compatible with Christianity. The most famous was *On Constancy.*

Man is but a dream of a shadow.

1662 **Matthew Henry:** English non-conformist minister. *Exposition of the Old and New Testament is* less a critical view of the Bible passages than a devotional and practical commentary. Finished after his death by other clergymen. Its simple piety, good-sense and high moral tone, written with discriminating thought made it one of the finest examples of a devotional text. Other works: *The Communicant's Companion, A Method of Prayer* and *A Scriptural Catechism.*

He whose head is in heaven need not fear to put his feet in the grave.

1741 **Pierre Choderlos de Laclos:** French artillery officer and author. Wrote one of the earliest psychological novel *Les Liaisons Dangereuses,* which depicts the immorality of the times, in particular the corrupt aristocrats who enjoy the sport of seducing innocents. The book created an immediate sensation and was banned for years. He rose to the rank of general under Napoleon.

There is no woman in the world who does not abuse the power she has been able to acquire.

1785 **Thomas Love Peacock:** English writer, poet and satirical novelist. Novels include: *Headlong Hall, Nightmare Abbey* and *Crotchet Castle.* Caricatured contemporary figures as thinly disguised eccentrics involved in often ridiculous conversation. His satirical essay "The Four Ages of Poetry," prompted poet Percy Bysshe Shelley to pen a serious rebuttal in his *Defense of Poetry.*

The waste of plenty is the resource of scarcity.

1859 **Henri Louis Bergson:** French-born philosopher. *Creative Evolution* became one of the classics of the 20th century. The basic premise of his intellectual system is a faith in direct intuition as a means of obtaining knowledge. Considered a living exponent of his maxim, "The inertia of mankind has never given way except to the push of genius." Nobel Prize for literature (1927). Also wrote *Time and Free Will, Laughter* and *The Creative Mind.*

Homo sapiens, the only creature endowed with reason, is also the only creature to pin its existence on things unreasonable.

1889 **Fannie Hurst:** American novelist, playwright, Zionist, and women's rights worker. One of the most popular novelists in America during the period from the 1910s to the 1940s. Her works captured elements of lower and middle-class urban life, especially ethnic and racial minorities Several of her novels were brought to the screen, occasionally with her as screenwriter, and were well-received "weepers" or as they were often referred to, "women's movies": *Back Street, Imitation of Life, Young at Heart, Humoresque,* and *Four Daughters.* Active in reform organizations, including the Urban League. Among the first to join the Lucy Stone League, an organization that fought for the right of women to preserve their maiden name after marriage.

Art transcends war. Art is the language of God and war is the barking of men. Beethoven is bigger than war.

1904 **A.J. [Abbott Joseph] Liebling:** American journalist and author. On the staff of *The New Yorker* (1935–69). Contributed incisive commentaries on what he called "the wayward press." Books: *Back Where I Came From,* a kindly view of New York City, *The Wayward Pressman* and *Chicago: The Second City,* a not so kindly view of The City of Big Shoulders, Chicago.

If you just try long enough, you can always manage to boot yourself in the posterior.

1911 **Maharishi Mahesh Yogi:** Originally **Mahad Prasad Varma.** Indian religious leader. Founder of Transcendental Meditation (TM). Visited the U.S.A. in 1959, preaching the virtues of TM. Among his famous followers were the Beatles. Returned to India in the late 1970s and then settled in the Netherlands in 1990. His organization, which includes real estate, schools, and clinics, was estimated at worth more than $3 billion in the late 1990s.

The important thing is this: to be able, at any moment, to sacrifice what we are for what we could become.

1925 **Melina Mercouri:** Greek actress and a notable interpreter of contemporary Greek music. Wife of Blacklisted American director Jules Dassin who directed her in her best known film *Never on Sunday.* Other films: *Stella, Topkapi* and *Gaily, Gaily.* Elected to parliament and became Greece's Minister of Culture. One of her fervent campaigns was to have the Elgin marbles returned to Greece. These are a collection of ancient Greek sculptures and architectural fragments, removed from the Parthenon in Athens by Lord Elgin, ambassador to the Ottoman Empire, shipped to England and currently located in the British Museum.

This past must emerge from the museums in order to become a source of inspiration and creativity, to become the instruments and the joy of the people.

1950 **Wendy Wasserstein:** American playwright. Noted for her comic portrayals of single women. Won a Tony Award and the 1989 Pulitzer Prize for Drama for *The Heidi Chronicles,* a play about an unfulfilled feminist lecturer reflecting on the gains and failures of the women's movement. Others: *Any Woman Can't, When Dinah Shore Ruled the Earth* (written with Christopher Durang), *Uncommon Women, The Sisters Rosensweig* and *An American Daughter.*

Don't live down to expectations. Go out there and do something remarkable.

1951 **Terry McMillan:** African-American writer and educator. Her novels explore the lives of African-American women. Both *Waiting to Exhale* and *How Stella Got Her Groove Back* were made into films. The latter is the story of a 43-year-old single mother on vacation in Jamaica where she allows herself to have an affair with a man 20 years her junior, a fictional retelling of her own experience with a much younger man she met at a Jamaican resort and married three years later. Filed for divorce in 2005, reporting that the marriage was a "fraud" because her husband had lied about his sexual Orientation — and married only to gain U.S. citizenship.

It takes me forever to say my prayers these days, but I don't care, because this time around, I want to make sure God doesn't have to do any guesswork.

1956 **Martina Navratilova:** Czechoslovakian-born American tennis star. Holds the record for career singles championships in professional tennis, 167 tournament titles, when she retired in 1994. Number one player in the world 7 times. Has 9 Wimbledon singles titles, 18 Grand Slam singles titles and 37 Grand Slam doubles titles. Her intense rivalry with Chris Evert was one of the selling points of the women's game during the 1970s and 80s. Books include *Martina* and *Feet of Clay.*

Labels are for filing. Labels are for clothing. Labels are not for people.

OTHERS: 1569 Italian poet **Giambattista Marini**, 1701 French historian **Charles Le Beau**, 1777 German writer **Heinrich von Kleist**, 1868 Swedish author **Ernst Didring**, 1893 Japanese Macrobiotics founder **Georges Ohsawa**, 1898 Austrian singer/actress **Lotte Lenya**, 1919 Canadian PM **Pierre Trudeau**, 1921 U.S. Senator **Jesse Helms** 1927 U.S. actor **George C. Scott**, 1928 U.S. sports commentator **Keith Jackson**, 1932 Lithuanian politician **Vytautas Landsbergis**, 1934 U.S. evangelist **Chuck Swindoll**, 1939 U.S. football player/coach **Mike Ditka**, 1939 U.S. assassin **Lee Harvey Oswald**, 1948 U.S. author **Ntozake Shange**, 1961 U.S. musician **Wynton Marsalis**

October 19

1433 **Marsilio Ficino:** Italian philosopher and scholar. The Renaissance's first and most influential Platonist. Early in life he studied the philosophy of Plato and that of the Neo-Platonists in the Florentine household of Cosimo de' Medici. Translated Greek works into Latin and wrote commentaries on the ancient works. Desired to reconcile Platonism and Neo-Platonism with Christian thought. Major work *The Platonic Theory of the Immortality of Souls.*

Artists in each of the arts seek after and care for nothing but love.

1605 **Thomas Browne:** English writer and scholar. Steadfast Royalist noted for his antiquarian scholarship. A trained scientist and philosophical skeptic, he was nevertheless melancholy, mystical and credulous. His best-known work is *Religio Medici*, a journal of his reflections on the mysteries of God, nature and man. Other works: *Hydriotaphia, or Urn Burial, Vulgar Errors, The Garden of Cyrus* and *Christian Morals.*

A rich man's joke is always funny.

1680 **John Abernethy:** Irish Presbyterian minister. Grandfather of the renowned surgeon John Abernethy. Noted debater in the synods and assemblies of his church and a leading evangelist. When assigned to Usher's Quay, Dublin, he declined to accede. His refusual was regarded as ecclesiastical high-treason. In the Church a bitter quarrel and struggle broke out between the "Subscribers" and the "Non-Subscribers." Non-subscriber Abernethy stood firm for religious freedom and repudiated the ecclesiastical courts. He opposed the entire questions of tests for membership in the Irish Presbyterian Church. He fought for freedom of conscience and opinion of all, including Roman Catholics and Dissenters.

[I stand] against all laws that, upon account of mere differences of religious opinions and forms of worship, excluded men of integrity and ability from serving their country.

1784 **Leigh Hunt:** English journalist, essayist, poet and political radical. Had a wining way with words, as for example: "Colors are the smiles of nature," "If you are ever at a lost to support a flagging conversation, introduce the subject of eating" and "Your second-hand bookseller is second to none in the worth of the treasures he dispenses." Author of the poems "Abou Ben Adhem" and "Jenny Kissed Me."

Say I'm weary, say I'm sad,/ Say that health and wealth have missed me./ Say I'm growing old, but add/ Jenny kissed me.

1895 **Lewis Mumford:** American social critic. Described himself as a "generalist," whose forte is "not in finding or fabricating the pieces, but in putting them together into a significant picture." Wrote on architecture and the city. Among his major achievements was the four-volume *Renewal of Life* series, which established him as one of the foremost humanist philosophers of the industrial age. In *Values for Survival* (1946) he took the then unpopular view that the atom bombing of Hiroshima and Nagasaki was a descent into barbarianism.

Every generation revolts against its fathers and makes friends with its grandfathers.

1901 **Arleigh Burke:** Colorful battling American admiral of the U.S. Navy during World War II and the Korean War. Nicknamed "31-knot Burke" because of the way he habitually entered combat in his World War II Pacific actions. Negotiator at the Korean Truce Talks in 1951. As Chief of Naval Operations, he was the principal naval adviser to President Eisenhower and a member of the Joint Chiefs of Staff.

Any commander who fails to exceed his authority is not of much use to his subordinates.

1910 **Subrahmanyan Chandrasekhar**: Indian-born American astrophysicist. Developed the theory of white dwarf stars. Showed that when a star has exhausted its nuclear fuel, an inward gravitational collapse occurs, which normally will be eventually halted by the outward pressure of the star's highly compressed an ionized gas. At this point the star will have diminished to an extremely dense state, known as a white star, which has the unusual property that the greatest its mass, the smaller its radius. Like his uncle, Indian physicist C.V. Raman, Chandrasekhar won a Nobel Prize (1983).

Science is a perception of the world around us. Science is a place where what you find in nature pleases you.

1922 **Jack Anderson:** American investigative newspaper columnist. One of the fathers of modern investigative journalism. Won the 1972 Pulitzer Prize for National Reporting for his investigation on secret American policy decision-making between the U.S. and Pakistan during the 1970 Indo-Pakistan War. Took over Drew Pearson's syndicated column "Washington Merry-Go-Round" when Pearson died in 1969. A few months after Anderson's death the FBI attempted to gain access to his files on the grounds that certain information they contained could hurt U.S. government interests.

The incestuous relationship between government and big business thrives in the dark.

1937 **Peter Max:** Originally **Peter Finkelstein**. German-born American Pop artist. Multi-dimensional artist who focuses on contemporary events. Opened a design studio and gained success as a designer for books, posters, and products. Produces "cosmic imagery," including mass media as a "canvas" for his artistic expression. Work was influential and much imitated in advertising design. His decorative designs are on a Boeing 777 Continental, Dale Earnhardt's #3 Millennium race car, and U.S. postage stamps.

I never know what I'm going to put on the canvas. The canvas paints itself. I'm just the middleman.

1938 **Renata Adler:** Milan-born German-American writer, film critic and philosopher. Joined the *New Yorker* magazine in 1962. *A Year in the Dark* is her record of her brief experience as a film critic for the *New York Times* (1968–9). Books: *Speedboat* and *Pitch Dark Reckless Disregard* is an account of General William Westmoreland's libel suit against CBS.

Idle people are often bored and bored people, unless they sleep a lot, are cruel. It is not an accident that boredom and cruelty are great preoccupations of our time.

1942 **Andrew Vachss:** American author. Leading advocate for child safety and protection. Contributing editor of *Parade Magazine*. On the "Enemies List" of the International Pedophile Liberation Front, an organization of predatory pedophiles that promotes child molestation and child pornography. Vachss' recommendations for safe-guarding children are increase penalties, abolish statue of limitations, enact federal laws and recognize that Child Pornography is an international crime. In a 2006 *Parade* article, he wrote:

No child is capable, emotionally or legally, of consenting to being photographed for sexual purposes. This, every image of a sexually displayed child — be a photograph, a tape, or a DVD — records both the rape of the child and an act against humanity.

1946 **Philip Pullman:** English writer. Best-selling author of the trilogy of fantasy novels, *His Dark Materials*, consisting of *Northern Lights*, *The Subtle Knife* and *The Amber Spyglass*. The first volume won the Carnegie Medal for children's fiction in the U.K. in 1995. Certain Christian groups claim that he actively pursues an anti–Christian agenda. Some see the series as a direct rebuttal of C.S. Lewis's Christianity-inspired series, *The Chronicles of Narnia*, which Pullman denounced as propaganda.

Adam and Eve are like the imaginary number, like the square root of minus one... If you include it in your equation, you can calculate all manner of things, which cannot be imagined without it.

OTHERS: 1688 English anatomist **William Cheselden**, 1720 American Quaker preacher **John Woolman**, 1721 French Orientalist **Joseph de Guignes**, 1784 Canadian fur trader **John McLoughlin**, 1833 Australian poet **Adam Linsday Gordon**, 1862 French movie pioneer **Auguste Lumière**, 1908 Norwegian composer **Geirr Tveitt**, 1916 French immunologist **Jean Dausset**, 1916 Ukrainian pianist **Emil Gilels**, 1931 English author **John Le Carré**, 1939 U.S. soprano **Benita Valente**, 1945 U.S. actor **Divine**, 1951 NOW President **Patricia Ireland**, 1956 Italian physician **Carlo Urbani**, 1962 U.S. boxer **Evander Holyfield**, 1966 U.S. writer/director **Jon Favreau**, 1969 U.S. cartoonist **Trey Parker**

October 20

1469 Guru **Nanak Dev:** Founder of Sikhism. Spent long hours in meditation and religious discussions with Muslim and Hindu holy men. One day at age 30, he plunged into a river for his bath and did not reappear. Believed to have drowned, but 3 days later he reappeared on the same spot, a changed man. There was a divine light in his eyes. He gave up his belongings and made extensive travels to spread the message of God that had been revealed to him. At the time of his death he lay down and covered himself with a sheet, while his followers prayed. When they lifted the sheet, they found nothing except fresh flowers. His doctrine was set out later in the *Adi-Granth*.

There are worlds and more worlds below them and there are a hundred thousand skies over them. No one has been able to find the limits and boundaries of God. If there be any account of God, than alone the mortal can write the same; but Gods account does not finish and the mortal himself dies while still writing.

1632 Sir **Christopher Wren:** English architect, renowned mathematician and professor of astronomy. Buried under the choir of his most famous construction, St. Paul's Cathedral. The devastating London fire of 1666 gave him the opportunity to distinguish himself as an architect. Besides St. Paul's his legacy includes the towers of Westminster, many churches and public buildings as well as numerous private houses. A tablet on the spot bears the inscription "Si monumentum requiris, circumspice" (If thou seekest a monument, look around).

Architecture aims at Eternity.

1785 **Pauline Bonaparte:** Napoleon's favorite and youngest sister. A classical beauty, noted for her charm, fetish for bathing, moral laxity and innumerable scandalous affairs. When her many love affairs became an embarrassment, Napoleon arranged for her to marry one of his generals, Charles Leclerc. This hardly slowed down her affairs, often with junior officers and ordinary soldiers. After Leclerc died of yellow fever, Napoleon arranged a marriage to Italian Prince Camillo Borghese, with whom she was already quite intimate. When Napoleon was exiled to Elba, she liquidated her assets into cash and moved to care for him, the only member of his family to visit him. As she lay dying, she had a servant bring her a mirror, into which she gazed and announced:

I am not afraid to die. I am still beautiful.

1854 **Arthur Rimbaud:** French Symbolist poet and adventurer. His verse chiefly written before the age of 20, were violent, blasphemous poems. Probably his finest poem was "The Drunken Boat." Notable works: *Les Illuminations* and *A Season in Hell.* Lived with lyric poet Paul Verlaine in a homosexual relationship for two years, engaging in a wild and dissipated life. After a violent quarrel, Verlaine was imprisoned for attempting to shoot Rimbaud. After that Rimbaud led a vagabond life.

Life is a farce which everyone has to perform.

1859 **John Dewey:** American philosopher, psychologist, and author. Believed that the exigencies of a democratic and industrial society demanded new educational techniques. Adherent of pragmatism, maintaining that there is only the reality of experience. His watchword was "learning by doing." Helped inaugurate the theories and practice of progressive education. Author of: *Democracy and Education*, *The Theory of Inquiry* and *Problems of Man.*

Education is a social process; education is growth; education is not a preparation for life but is life itself.

1874 **Charles Ives:** One of the most remarkable American composers. Created music so original, so universal, and yet so deeply national in its source of inspiration that it profoundly changed the direction of American music. He anticipated many technological innovations, such as polytonality, atonality, and even 12-tone formations. Unique quality of his music was the combination of simple motifs, often derived from American church hymns and popular ballads. Works: *Concord Sonata*, *3 Places in New England*, *The Housatonic at Stockbridge*, *Lincoln, the Great Commoner*, and *A Symphony: Holidays.*

But maybe music was not intended to satisfy the curious definiteness of man. Maybe it is better to hope that music may always be transcendental language in the most extravagant sense.

1884 **Béla Lugosi:** Originally **Béla Blasko**. Hungarian-born actor. Played lead roles on the Hungarian stage from 1901 and in films from 1915. Went to the U.S.A. in 1921. Notable success in the Broadway play *Dracula.* Repeated the role in Tod Browning's 1931 film version, introducing himself to audiences speaking "I — am — Drac — ula," in his heavy accented, deliberated enunciation. It would prove to be his greatest role but it also typecast him in horror films.

In Hungary acting is a profession. In America it is a decision.

1892 **Jomo Kenyatta:** Born **Kamau wa Ngengi**. African politician affectionately called the "Grand Old Man." Founded the Pan-American Federation with Kwame Nkrumah. His relationship with the British government was ruined by his supposed involvement with the Mau Mau. In 1953 he was sentenced to seven years in prison at hard labor. As president (1964–78) of an independent Kenya he instituted a relatively peaceful land reform, but corruptly gave many choice parcels of land to his relatives and supporters, and he himself became the new nation's largest landowner. Books: *Facing Mount Kenya*, *Kenya: The Land of Conflict* and *The Challenge of Uhuru.*

When the missionaries arrived, the Africans had the land and the Missionaries had the Bible. They taught how to pray with our eyes closed. When we opened them, they had the land and we had the Bible.

1900 **Wayne Morse:** American politician and lawyer. One of the country's leading labor arbitrators. Elected to the Senate as a Republican from Oregon with New Deal inclinations, he refused to support Eisenhower for the presidency and declared himself an independent. Later a Democrat. A fighter and individualist, he rejected so-called "party responsibility, claiming "It's an alibi for doing what a close-knit group of machine politicians think ought to be substituted for representative government." Opposed the Vietnam War from the onset. One of only two members of Congress, to vote against The Gulf of Tonkin Resolution, which authorized escalated U.S. involvement in Indochina.

The liberal, emphasizing the civil and property rights of the individual, insists that the individual must remain so supreme as to make the state his servant.

1907 **Arlene Francis:** American actress, born **Arline Francis Kazanjian.** Appeared in 25 Broadway plays and in several films, including *One, Two, Three* with James Cagney. Well-known New York radio personality, hosting several radio shows. First woman to host a non musical or dramatic program with "Home," a morning TV show on topics of interest to women. Best known as a panelist (1950–1975) on the long-running TV game show, "What's My Line?"

Trouble is a sieve through which we sift our acquaintances. Those too big to pass through are our friends.

1917 **Bobby Locke:** South African professional golfer. Played in the British Open when he was eighteen, finishing as low amateur. Turned pro and was a prolific tournament winner in his native country. After serving in the South Africa Air Force during World War II he went to the U.S.A. to join the PGA tour. Played 59 events, winning eleven and finishing in the top three in thirty. Success was due to his outstanding putting ability. Offered expert and duffer alike the excellent advice.

Putting is in fact a game in itself. Drive for show. But putt for dough. You can tell a good putt by the sound it makes.

1925 **Art Buchwald:** American humorist and syndicated columnist. One of the nation's best known satirists. Moved to Paris in 1948 and wrote a popular column, reviewing the city's nightlife for the *International Herald Tribune*. After moving to Washington D.C., he poked fun at issues in the news. His sharp satirical work won a Pulitzer Prize in 1982. Books: *I'll Always Have Paris, How Much Is That in Dollars?* and *I Think I Don't Remember.*

Tax reform is taking the taxes off things that have been taxed in the past and putting taxes on things that haven't been taxed before.

OTHERS: 1463 Italian philosopher **Alessandro Achillini**, 1616 Danish physician **Thomas Bartholin**, 1660 English statesman **Robert Bertie**, 1677 King of Poland **Stanislaus I**, 1719 German statistician **Gottfried Achenwall**, 1819 Persian founder Bábi Faith **The Báb**, 1822 English novelist **Thomas Hughes**, 1889 U.S. actress, foil of Marx Bros. **Margaret Dumont**, 1904 English actress **Anna Neagle**, 1913 U.S. banjo player **Grandpa Jones**, 1918 German journalist **Robert Lochner**, 1931 U.S. baseball star **Mickey Mantle**, 1935 U.S. actor/singer **Jerry Orbach**, 1937 Baseball pitcher **Juan Marichal**, 1958 U.S. actor **Viggo Mortensen**, 1971 U.S. rap artist **Snoop Dogg**

October 21

1762 **George Colman the Younger:** English dramatist and miscellaneous writer. Son of lawyer and playwright George Colman the Elder. The Younger's witty conversation made him very popular in society. Made his fame with the musical romantic comedy *Inkle and Yarico*. Other dramatic works: *The Iron Chest, The Heir-in-*Law, which became famous for the character Dr. Pangloss, a greedy, pompous pedant, and *John Bull.* Wrote coarse humorous poetry which was very popular, including: *My Night Gown and Slippers* and *Poetical Vagaries.*

His heart runs away with his head.

1772 **Samuel Taylor Coleridge:** English lake poet, philosopher, essayist and critic. Master of the art of conversation. An important spokesman for English Romanticism. Major works: "Christabel, a tale of spiritual seduction set in a medieval castle," "Kubla Khan," the opium-vision, which begins with the line, "In Xanadu did Kubla Khan/ A stately pleasure dome decree," and "The Rime of the Ancient Mariner," a powerful metaphysical account of a nightmare sea-voyage.

Poetry: the best words in the best order.

1790 **Alphonse Marie de Lamartine:** First truly romantic poet in French literature. Produced many volumes of biography, memoirs, political and historical works, novels and travel writings. Served as Minister of Foreign Affairs at the time of the short-lived provisional government after the 1848 Revolution. Overthrown by Napoleon III. Author of *Méditations poétiques, Jocelyn, Histoire de la Révolution* and *Histoire des Girondins.*

There is a woman at the beginning of all great things.

1833 **Alfred Nobel:** Swedish industrialist, inventor and philanthropist. Invented and perfected a safe and manageable form of nitroglycerin, he called *dynamite*, and later, smokeless gunpowder and gelignite. Created an industrial empire and amassed a huge fortune. Left the bulk of his estate to establish Nobel prizes for peace, literature, physics, chemistry and medicine. In 1969, a sixth prize, for economics, was initiated in his honor.

I intend to leave after my death a large fund for the promotion of the peace idea, but I am skeptical as to its results.

1846 **Edmondo De Amicis:** Notable Italian novelist and short-story writer. Author of popular travel books and children's stories. His best-known book is the children's novel *Heart*. Published the first day of school in Italy in 1886, its success was immense. Over a few months it was printed in 40 Italian editions and translated into ten languages. Part of this overwhelming reception was its praise of the creation of Italy in the previous decade.

A woman is always a mystery: one must not be fooled by her face and her heart's inspiration.

1891 **Ted Shawn:** "Papa." First American male to achieve a world reputation in dance. Temporarily paralyzed by diphtheria, his physician advised him to take up dancing as a form of physical therapy. Dancing not only cured his paralysis, it set him his career path. In 1914 he met Ruth St. Denis, whom he married and formed the Denishawn Company and School. During the next 15 years the team changed the course of dance history. He purchased a run-down farm in the Berkshires and established the renowned Jacob's Pillow Dance Festival. His orchestrated premieres helped establish the emerging talents of Agnes de Mille, Anna Sokolow, Alvin Ailey and Robert Joffrey.

Dance is the only art of which we ourselves are the stuff of which it is made.

1901 **Joseph Sill Clark:** American politician. A silk-stocking Republican-turned–Democrat. Elected U.S. senator from Pennsylvania (1956). Offered some excellent advice: "A leader should not get too far in front of the troops or he will be shot in the ass." Fellow of the American Academy of Arts and Sciences and a member of the American Philosophical Society.

Defeat is not bitter unless you swallow it.

1912 **Georg (György) Solti:** Hungarian-born conductor. Brilliant conducting debut at the Budapest Opera with Mozart's *The Marriage of Figaro*. The rising wave of anti–Semitism in Hungary forced him to move to Switzerland. After World War II, appointed musical director of the Bavarian State Opera and later the same position in Frankfurt. Among his numerous other positions, was music director of the Chicago Symphony, where he became famous for the "Chicago sound," a synonym for excellence.

My life is the clearest proof that if you have talent, determination and luck, you will make it in the end. My motto is "Never give up."

1914 **Martin Gardner**: American recreational mathematician, magician and author of the long-running "Mathematical Games" column in *Scientific American*. Author or editor of more than 100 books on mathematics and science, including: *Magic Numbers of Dr. Matrix, The No-Sided Professor and other tales of fantasy, humor, mystery, and philosophy*, and *Did Adam and Eve Have Navels.*

If God creates a world of particles and waves, dancing in obedience to mathematical and physical laws, who are we to say that he cannot make use of those laws to cover the surface of a small planet with living creatures?

1917 **[John Burks] Dizzy Gillespie:** African-American jazz trumpeter, bandleader, composer and arranger. Received his nickname because of his wild manner of playing, making grimaces and gesticulating during his performances. One of the true jazz innovators of his era. Known for bullfrog-cheek playing style. Accidentally bent his horn in 1953, and continued to play it that way, claiming he could hear it better. A leader of the Bebop movement. Compositions: "Night in Tunisia," "Groovin' High" and "Blue 'n' Boogie."

I think the idea is now for blacks to write about the history of our music. It's time for that, because whites have been doing it all the time. It's time for us to do it ourselves and tell it like it is.

1929 **Ursula Le Guin:** née **Kroeber**. Prolific American science fiction writer and literary critic. Much of her work focuses on subjective views of a universe incorporating numerous habitable worlds, each spawned by beings from the "Hain." Her creation of new cultures shows up the deficiencies modern day society. Books: *Plant of Exile*, *Left Hand of Darkness*, and *The Lathe of Heaven*.

The creative adult is the child that has survived.

1956 **Carrie Fisher:** U.S. actress, author and script doctor. Daughter of Eddie Fisher and Debbie Reynolds. First movie appearance was in the romantic comedy *Shampoo*. Best known for as Princess Leia in the *Star Wars* trilogy. Wrote the autobiographical *Postcards from the Edge*, which was made into a movie. Publicly addressed her problems with drugs, bipolar disorder and addiction to prescription anti-depressants.

I think of my body as a side effect of my mind.

OTHERS: 1581 Italian painter **Domenico Zampieri**, 1650 French admiral **Jean Bart**, 1712 British economist **James Denham Steuart**, 1762 Dutch statesman **Herman Willem Daendels**, 1891 U.S. advertising executive **Leo Burnett**, 1904 Irish poet **Patrick Kavanaugh**, 1908 Lithuanian violinist **Alexander Schneider**, 1921 English composer **Malcolm Arnold**, 1924 Cuban singer **Celia Cruz**, 1928 Baseball pitcher **Whitey Ford**, 1940 British musician **Manfred Mann**, 1943 U.S. football player **Brian Piccolo**, 1949 PM of Israel **Benjamin Netanyahu**, 1957 German physicist **Wolfgang Ketterle**, 1959 Japanese actor **Ken Watanabe**

October 22

1811 **Franz Liszt:** Hungarian pianist and composer. True romantic and creator of the modern form of the symphonic poem. Innovating genius of modern piano technique. Liked to attach descriptive titles to his works such as "Fantasy, Reminiscence and Illustrations." Other Compositions: "Les Préludes" and 20 "Hungarian Rhapsodies" and many piano compositions. Legend has it that Liszt was a man of fantastic sexual powers. He was a great lover of mostly married women, but never married.

The musician above all who is inspired by nature without copying it, exhales in sound his life's most intimate secrets.

1821 **Collis P. Huntington:** Connecticut-born American railroad magnate. Promoted the Central Pacific Railroad's expansion across the West, linked with the Union Pacific Railroad in 1869 by the golden spike, creating the first transcontinental railroad. In 1871, oversaw construction of the Chesapeake and Ohio Railway across Virginia and West Virginia reaching to the Ohio River. At an age when most men retired, he built Newport News Shipbuilding, the largest privately owned shipyard in the world.

We shall build good ships; at a profit if we can, at a loss if we must, but always good ships.

1887 **John Reed:** American journalist, poet and revolutionary. Wrote for the radical socialist journal *The Masses*. Covered the revolutionary fighting in Mexico. War correspondent during World War I becoming a close associate of Lenin. Witnessed firsthand the Russian Revolution of 1917, described in his book *Ten Days That Shook the World*. Headed the U.S. Communist Labor Party. Indicted for sedition he fled to Russia where he died of typhus in 1920. Buried in Red Square within the Kremlin wall.

War means an ugly mob-madness, crucifying the truth tellers, choking the artists, sidetracking reforms, revolutions, and the working of social forces.

1890 **Joseph Nye Welch:** Lead attorney for the U.S. Army while it was under investigation by Joseph McCarthy's Senate Permanent Subcommittee on Investigation for Communist activities. Most dramatic moment was his emotion-packed exchange with the Wisconsin Senator on June 10, 1954. Angered by Welch's persistent cross-examination of Roy Cohn, McCarthy charged that a young attorney with Welch's law firm was a member of an organization that had been exposed as giving legal aid to the Communist Party. Nearly in tears by this unexpected attack, Welch's reply was greeted by applause from the assemblage.

Until this moment, Senator, I think I had never

gauged your cruelty or your recklessness. Have you no sense of decency, sir, at long last? Have you left no sense of decency? If there is a God in heaven, it [the attack] will do neither you nor your cause any good.

1913 **Robert Capa:** Originally **Endré Ernö Friedmann**. Hungarian-born war photographer. Adopted his new name, because it sounded American. Covered five wars: The Spanish Civil War, the Second Sino-Japanese War, World War II across Europe, the 1948 Arab-Israeli War and the First Indochina War. Among his famous photos is that of the instance a Spanish loyalist soldier is hit by a bullet and is falling dead. On D-Day, June 6, 1944, he swam ashore with the first assault wave on Omaha beach and photographed the first couple of hours of the invasion.

If your pictures aren't good enough, you aren't close enough.

1917 **Joan Fontaine.** Originally **Joan de Beauvoir de Havilland**. Japanese-born British actress. Younger sister of actress Olivia de Havilland. Became a star with her performance in *Rebecca* (1940) for which she was nominated for an Academy Award as Best Actress. Won the Oscar in 1941 for *Suspicion*, beating out her sister, nominated for *Hold Back the Dawn*. In the 1940s Fontaine excelled in romantic melodramas: *The Constant Nymph*, *Jane Eyre* and *A Letter from an Unknown Woman*.

The main problem in marriage is that for a man sex is a hunger like eating. If the man is hungry and can't get to a fancy French restaurant, he goes to a hot dog stand. For a woman, what is important is love and romance.

1919 **Doris Lessing:** née **Taylor**. English novelist and short-story writer. Born in Persia (now Iran) to a British army captain. Family moved to Southern Rhodesia (now Zimbabwe) where she became involved in politics, helping start a non-racialist left-wing party. First published novel was *The Grass Is Singing* (1950), a study of the sterility of white civilization in Africa. *The Golden Notebook* (1962), an experimental novel about a woman writer's struggle to discover the meaning of "self," a classic of feminist literature.

There is only one real sin, and that is to persuade oneself that the second-best is anything but the second-best.

1920 **Timothy Leary:** American psychologist who experimented with psychedelic drugs in the sixties. Forced to leave his position at Harvard, he became a guru to the counterculture generation, advising them to "Turn on. Tune in. Drop out." Co-authored *The Psychedelic Experience* (1964) with Ralph Metzner ostensibly based upon the Tibetan Book of the Dead. Two years later Leary formed the League of Spiritual Discovery, a religion with LSD as it sacrament.

Women who seek to be equal with men lack ambition.

1925 **Robert Rauschenberg:** American avant-garde artist, with roots in Dada and the ready-mades of Marcel Duchamp. Best known for his collages and "combines," which incorporate a variety of junk splashed with paint. Sometimes categorized as a pop artist, works include *Gloria* and *Summer Rental*. Later used silkscreen to transformer images from the commercial print media and his photographs to canvas.

I always have searched for a point of view that a participant could change.

1930 **Dory Previn:** née **Langdon**. American poet, composer and singer. She and her first husband André Previn received several Academy Award nominations for their motion picture songwriting. Much of her writing deals with her troubled relation with her paranoid father and several of her songs were inspired by the breakup of her marriage when her husband left her for actress Mia Farrow. Songs: "Reflections in a Mud-Puddle," "One Last Dance with My Father," "Mister Whisper" and "Beware of Young Girls."

Men wander/ women weep/ women worry/ while men sleep.

1936 **Bobby Seale:** American civil rights activist. Along with Huey P. Newton co-founded the Black Panther Party in 1966. One of the original Chicago Eight defendants charged with conspiracy and inciting a riot at the 1968 Democratic National Convention in Chicago. Sentenced to four years in prison for contempt of court due to his frequent outbursts. Today, he is a businessman marketing a line of Barbeque products.

We don't hate anybody because of their color. We hate oppression!

1943 **Cathérine Deneuve:** Originally **Cathérine Dorléac.** Beautiful French actress, whose remoteness and image of exterior calm concealing passion or intrigue has made her a leading screen personality since the 1960s. Nominated for an Academy Award as Best Actress for *Indochine*. Other films: *The Umbrellas of Cherbourg*, *Repulsion*, *Belle de Jour* and *The Last Metro*.

Opportunities are often things you haven't noticed the first time around.

OTHERS: 1511 German astronomer **Erasmus Reinhold**, 1729 German botanist **Johann Reinhold Forster**, 1844 Canadian Métis political leader **Louis Riel**, 1865 Estonian painter **Kristjan Raud**, 1881 U.S. physicist **Clinton Davisson**, 1903 U.S. geneticist **George Wells Beadle**, 1903 U.S. actor of "The Three Stooges" **Curly Howard**, 1904 U.S. blonde actress **Constance Bennett**, 1913 Vietnamese Emperor **Bao Dai**, 1927 South African politician **Allan Hendrickse**, 1938 British actor **Derek Jacobi**, 1942 U.S. singer/actress **Annette Funicello**, 1945 British long jumper **Shelia Sherwood**, 1963 U.S. figure skater **Brian Boitano**, 1973 Japanese baseball player **Ichiro Suzuki**

October 23

1733 **Francis Jeffrey:** Literary critic and Scottish judge. Co-founder with Sydney Smith and editor of *The Edinburgh Review* (1802–29). Prolific and biased writer of strictures on Wordsworth, Keats and Byron.

Wrote appreciatively of Sir Walter Scott, Lord Byron and especially John Keats.

Beware prejudices. They are like rats, and men's minds are like traps; prejudices get in easily, but it is doubtful if they ever get out. Opinions founded on prejudice are always sustained with the greatest violence.

1844 **Sarah Bernhardt:** Originally **Henriette Rosme Bernard.** Greatest French actress of the 19th century and one of the best known figures in the history of the stage. Revered Parisian stage tragedienne. Excelled as Cordelia in Shakespeare's *King Lear*, the title role in Jean Racine's *Phédre* and the male roles of Hamlet. Illegitimate daughter of a Dutch prostitute. Told by her mother that she would die at an early age, she kept a coffin with her at all times, in which she slept and made love.

The truth, the absolute truth, is that the chief beauty for the theatre consists in fine bodily proportions.

1869 **John W. Heisman:** American football coach and one of the game's greatest innovators. Coached at nine colleges from 1892 to 1927, winning 185 games. Responsible for legalizing the forward pass in 1906. Originated the center snap and the "hike" count signals of the quarterback in starting play. As director of athletics, Downtown Athletic Club, New York City (1928–36), he instituted in 1935 the trophy for Best College Player of Year, which is named for him.

Gentlemen, it is better to have died a small boy than to fumble this football.

1906 **Gertrude Ederle:** American swimmer. First woman to swim the English Channel. It took her 14 hours 11 minutes to swim from Cap Griz Nez to Kinsdown, nearly two hours faster than the existing men's record. Won a gold medal at the 1924 as a member of the U.S. 400-meter relay team, and two bronze medals. Later turned professional and became a swimming instructor and fashion designer.

To me, the sea is like a person — like a child that I've known a long time. It sounds crazy, I know, but when I swim in the sea I talk to it. I never feel alone when I'm out there.

1920 **Frank Rizzo:** Philadelphia law-enforcement official and politician. Heavy-handed tough-talking police commissioner expanded the police force, won the loyalty of his officers and kept the crime rate lower than any other major U.S. city. However, he was accused of racism and encouraging police brutality. Campaigned as a law-and-order Democrat for mayor and served two terms (1971–79). In 1979 the U.S. District Court accused Rizzo and 18 high-ranking city and police officials with violating the rights of the citizens of the city, but all charges were eventually dismissed.

A conservative is a liberal who got mugged the night before.

1923 **Ned Rorem:** American composer and diarist. At age 75, premiered his magnum opus, *Evidence of Things Not Seen*, a song-cycle for four singers and piano. Composed three symphonies, four piano concertos and an array of other orchestral works, six operas, and hundreds of songs and cycles. His *Paris Diary* (1969) brought him a degree of notoriety, being candid about his and others' sexuality, describing his relationship with Leonard Bernstein and Noel Coward.

Inspiration could be called inhaling the memory of an act never experienced.

1925 **Johnny Carson:** American television personality. "King of Late-Night." Longtime host of the "Tonight Show," succeeding Jack Paar in 1962. Six-time Emmy winner. For 30 years he amused his audience skewing politicians and celebrities, bantering with his guests, presenting broadly played comedy skits by his "Mighty Carson Players" and appearing as the spoof clairvoyant "Carnac the Magnificent."

The only thing money gives you is the freedom of not worrying about money.

1931 **Jim Bunning:** Baseball pitcher and Republican U.S. Senator from Kentucky. Compiled 224 wins. One of only five players to pitch a no-hitter in both leagues, the second a perfect game. Elected to Baseball's Hall of Fame in 1996. One of the Senate's most conservative members. Congressional experts and colleagues have accused him of a lackluster performance that has caused strains between him and the G.O.P.

The war against terror is every bit as important as out fight against fascism in World War II. Or our struggle against the spread of Communism during the Cold War.

1935 **Juan "Chi Chi" Rodriguez:** Puerto Rican golfer: Famed for his signature "toreador dance," where he makes believe that a birdie putt is a "bull" and that his putter is a "sword" with which he kills the bull. Represented Puerto Rico on 12 World Cup Teams. In 1989, voted the Bob Jones Award, highest honor given by the U.S. Golf Association.

I don't exaggerate — I just remember big.

1940 **Pelé:** Nickname of **Edson Arantes do Nascimento**. Also known as "The King" and "The Black Pearl." Legendary Brazilian soccer player. Considered the complete midfield and attacking player, exceptional at dribbling and passing. Led Brazil to three World Cup titles (1958, 1962 and 1970). Scored 1,281 goals in 22 years. Brazilian government declared him an Official national treasure to prevent him from joining a team in another country.

Enthusiasm is everything. It must be taut and vibrating like a guitar string.

1942 **Michael Crichton:** American author, film and television producer. Best-known for techno-thrillers. Only person to have had the number one movie, the number one book, and the number one TV show in the U.S. at the same time (respectively *Disclosure*, *Disclosure*, and *ER*). Best-selling novels: *The Great Train Robbery*, *The Terminal Man*, and *Jurassic Park*.

Historically, the claim of consensus has been the first refuge of scoundrels; it is a way to avoid debate by claiming that the matter is already settled.

1954 **Ang Lee:** Taiwanese-born director and producer. *Pushing Hands* (1992) received 8 nominations in Taiwan's premier film festival. *The Wedding Banquet* (1993) won the Golden Bear at the Berlin Film Festival and was nominated as the Best Foreign Language Film at both the Golden Globe and Academy Awards. Lee gained international success with *Crouching Tiger, Hidden Dragon* (2000), earning an Oscar nomination as Best Director. Won the Director's Academy Award for *Brokeback Mountain* (2005).

I did a woman's movie, and I'm not a woman. I did a gay movie, and I'm not gay. I learned as I went along.

OTHERS: 1698 French architect **Ange-Jacques Gabriel**, 1715 Tsar of Russia **Peter II**, 1762 American inventor **Samuel Morey**, 1801 German composer **Albert Lortzing**, 1817 French lexicographer **Pierre Athanase Larousse**, 1865 U.S. nature writer **Neltje Blanchan**, 1885 Canadian artist **Lauren Harris**, 1896 French engineer **André Lévêque**, 1904 U.S. golf teacher **Harvey Penick**, 1908 Russian physicist **Ilya Frank**, 1927 Polish philosopher **Leszek Kolakowski**, 1956 U.S. country singer **Dwight Yoakum**, 1959 U.S. musician **"Weird Al" Yankovic**, 1962 U.S. football player **Doug Flutie**

October 24

1632 **Antonie van Leeuwenhoek:** Dutch naturalist and microbiologist. Known as the "Father of Microscopy" and the first biological scientist. Had endless curiosity and an open mind, free of the scientific dogma of his day. Made some of the most important discoveries in the history of biology. First to see protozoa and bacteria under the microscope. His researches, which were widely circulated through letters describing what he had seen with his microscopes, opened up the entire work of microscopic life to the awareness of scientists.

Whenever I found out anything remarkable, I have thought it my duty to put down my discovery on paper, so that all ingenious people might be informed thereof.

1788 **Sarah Josepha Hale:** née **Buell**. Pioneer American poet, journalist and magazine editor, first woman to hold such a position. Editor of *Juvenile Miscellany* (1826–28); *Ladies Magazine* (1828–37), and spent the next 40 years as editor of what would be called *Godey's Magazine and Lady's Book*. Partly due to her efforts the national Thanksgiving celebration was established. *Poems for Children* (1830) contain her best-known poem, "Mary Had a Little Lamb."

I've learned to judge men by their own deeds;/ I do not make the accident of birth/ The standard of their merit.

1830 **Belva Ann Bennett Lockwood:** American lawyer, women's rights activist, suffragist, pacifist and politician. Skilled and vigorous supporter of women's rights. First woman to practice law before the U.S. Supreme Court. Helped promote various reforms, including the Equal Pay Act for female civil servants (1872). Twice ran for the U.S. presidency as the candidate of the National Equal Rights Party. Member of the nominating committee for the Nobel Peace Prize.

We shall never have equal rights until we take them, nor respect until we command it.

1868 **Alexandra David-Néel:** French oriental scholar, explorer and writer. Toured internationally as an opera singer. In 1911 she visited the Dalai Lama in exile in Darjeeling and studied Tibetan Buddhism. Expelled from India in 1916 for illegally traveled to Tibet, she when to Burma, Japan and Korea, arriving in Beijing. Made a 2,000 mile trek through Northern Tibet, Mongolia and across the Gobi Desert disguised as a Tibetan pilgrim. Described her adventure in *My Journey to Lhasa* (1927).

Who knows the flower best? The one who reads about it in a book or the one who finds it wild on the mountainside?

1882 Dame **Sybil Thorndike:** English actress who enjoyed success from 1904 on British and U.S. stages and in films from 1921. Best know for her lead role in George Bernard Shaw's *Saint Joan*. Helped make the Old Vic a famous center of Shakespearian productions, collaborating with her husband, actor-manager Sir Lewis Casson. On their golden wedding anniversary, they appeared together in *Eighty in the Shade*, a play written for them by Clarence Dane.

It's only people who are hysterical who can play hysterical parts.

1890 **Mainbocher:** American fashion designer born **Main Rousseau Bocher**. Noted for his elegant and expensive evening gowns. One of his creations was the wedding dress designed for Wallis Simpson, the Duchess of Windsor. Editor of French *Vogue* (1923–29). Also designed uniforms for WAVES, the Girl Scouts, Red Cross and SPARS.

I have never known a really chic woman whose appearance was not, in large part, an outward reflection of her inner self.

1891 **Brenda Ueland:** American feminist and freelance writer for many publications. Best-known for her book *If You Want to Write: A Book about Art, Independence and Spirit*. Carl Sandburg called it "the best book ever written on how to write." Concerned with animal welfare, regularly spoke out against vivisection. By her own account she had many lovers as well as three marriages, all of which ended in divorce. Physically active well into her old age. Regularly walked up to 9 miles a day, and worked on improving her handstands.

So you see, imagination needs mooding — long, inefficient, happy idling, dawdling and puttering.

1904 **Moss Hart:** American playwright, director and screenwriter. Wrote the Pulitzer Prize winning *You Can't Take It with You* and *The Man Who Came to Dinner* with George S. Kaufman. *Lady in the Dark*, written in collaboration with Kurt Weill and Ira Gershwin was one of the many successful musicals he directed. Earned a Tony Award for directing My *Fair Lady* (1959). Autobiography *Act One* (1959) became a bestseller.

All the mistakes I ever made were when I wanted to say "No" and said "Yes."

1914 **Jackie Coogan:** U.S. actor who made his screen debut at 18 months with his vaudevillian parents. Regular attraction at age four with the Annette Kellerman revue. Charlie Chaplin's costar at six in *The Kid*, winning the hearts of audiences as a bright-eyed ragamuffin in a tattered cap and oversized trousers. Had a prolific television career, appearing in some 1400 shows. Best remembered as Uncle Fester in *The Addams Family*.

All actors are really crazy.

1923 **Denise Levertov:** English-born American poet and essayist. Works question political and cultural issues. Emigrated to the U.S.A. in 1948. Appointed poetry editor of *The Nation* in 1961. Outspoken on many issues including Vietnam and feminism. Author of *With Eyes in the Back of Our Heads*, *The Double Image*, *The Jacob's Ladder*, *Footprints*, and collection of essays *Poet in the World*.

Images/ split the truth/ in fractions.

1925 **Luciano Berio:** Italian composer. Noted for pioneering electronic music. Co-founded, with Bruno Maderna, Studio di Fonologia (1955), an electronic music studio in Milan. Composer in Residence at Tanglewood in Lennox, Massachusetts. Reputation as a composer was made with his *Sinfornia*, a composition for voice and orchestra that premiered in 1968. Other compositions: *Circles*, *Sequenza III* and *Recital I (for Cathy)*.

The relation between practical and spiritual spheres in music is obvious, if only because it demands ears, finger, consciousness and intellect.

1929 **George Crumb:** American composer of hauntingly beautiful scores. Often juxtaposes contrasting musical styles. These range from music of the western art-music tradition, to hymns and folk music, to non–Western music. Compositions include: *Ancient Voices of Children*, *Night of the Four Moons*, *Black Angels*, *Music for a Summer Evening*, and his largest score, *Star-Child* won a 2001 Grammy for Best Contemporary Composition.

In a broader sense, the rhythms of nature, large and small— the sounds of wind and water, the sounds of birds and insects— must inevitably find their analogues in music.

OTHERS: 1804 German physicist **Wilhelm Weber**, 1891 Dominican Republic President **Rafael Trujillo**, 1901 Polish-born actress/dancer **Gilda Gray**, 1903 U.S. FBI agent **Melvin Purvis**, 1915 Italian baritone **Tito Gobbi**, 1915 U.S. cartoonist **Bob Kane**, 1915 Textile heir **Roger Milliken**, 1926 U.S. football QB **Y.A. Tittle**, 1929 Bulgarian writer **Yordan Radichkov**, 1930 U.S. singer "The Big Bopper" **J.P. Richardson**, 1930 Norwegian scientist **Johan Galtung**, 1932 French physicist **Pierre-Gilles de Gennes**, 1936 English musician with "Rolling Stones" **Bill Wyman**, 1939 U.S. actor **F. Murray Abraham**, 1948 U.S. civil rights activist **Kweisi Mfume**, 1961 U.S. Congresswoman **Mary Bono**, 1972 Convicted wife killer **Scott Peterson**

October 25

1800 **Thomas Babington Macaulay, 1st Baron Macaulay:** British poet, historian and politician. As a Member of Parliament he used his powers as an orator in the Reform Bill debates. Secretary of War (1939–41). Famous for "Horatius at the Bridge" and his five-volume *History of England from the Accession of James II*. Sydney Smith described him as "like a book in breeches" and William Lamb said: "I wish that I was as cocksure of anything as Tom Macaulay is of everything."

The measure of a man's real character is what he would do if he knew he would never be found out.

1811 **Évariste Galois:** French mathematician whose genius was cruelly disregarded during his lifetime. His work was not understood until eleven years after his death and his mathematical reputation rests on less than 100 pages of mostly posthumously published memoirs. Died in a duel, spending the last night of his life writing letters acquainting others with his work, which since has kept generations of mathematicians busy. The next morning he was fatally wounded and abandoned. When his younger brother arrived, Évariste told him, "Don't cry, I need all my courage to die at twenty."

Genius is condemned by a malicious social organization to an eternal denial of justice in favor of fawning mediocrity.

1838 **Georges Bizet:** Originally **Alexandre Césare Léopold Bizet**. French composer. Most famous work, is his masterpiece the four-act opera *Carmen*. It was completed just before his untimely death from heart disease. Won the Prix de Rome for *Le Docteur miracle* (1857). His incidental music to Léon Daudet's play *L'Arlésienne* (1872) was enormously popular.

As a musician I tell you that if you were to suppress adultery, fanaticism, crime, evil, the supernatural, there would be no longer be the means for writing one note.

1881 **Pablo Picasso:** Spanish-born artist. Founder of Cubism and leader of the surrealistic movement in France. Most influential painter of the 20th century. Contributed to art in the areas of painting, drawing, graphics, sculpture and theatrical design. During his Blue Period (1901–4), he produced a series of striking studies of the poor in haunting attitudes often of despair and gloom. Created more than 50,000 works. Had a succession of mistresses who inspired him and were his models. Best known paintings: *Seated Nude*, *Three Musicians*, *Mandolin and Guitar* and *Guernica*.

People want to find "meaning" in everything and everyone. That's the disease of our age, an age that is anything but practical but believes itself to be more practical than any other age.

1888 **Richard E. Byrd:** American admiral, aviator and explorer. Made first flight over the North Pole (1926) and the South Pole (1928). Conducted five Antarctic exploration expeditions. Used aircraft, radio, and modern technology to support, rather than replace, traditional methods of exploring on foot with dogs and sleds. Brother of Harry Byrd, U.S. Senator from Virginia.

Give wind and tide a chance to change.

1902 **Henry Steele Commager:** American historian. Advocate of the "long view." Favorite subject is the growth of America. Author of *The American Mind, The Great Constitution, Crusaders for Freedom, Majority Rule and Minority Rights* and editor of the fifty-volume *Rise of the American Nation* series.

A free society cherishes nonconformity, it knows that from the non-conformist, from the eccentric, have come many of the great ideas of freedom. Free society must fertilize the soil in which non-conformity and dissent and individualism can grow. If our democracy is to flourish, it must have criticism; if our government is to function, it must have dissent.

1912 **Minnie Pearl:** Stage name of **Sarah Ophelia Colley Cannon**. American country comedian. Frequently appeared on the *Grand Ole Opry* and a regular on TV's *Hew Haw* (1970–91). Wore a large hat with a price tag ($1.98) hanging off the side. Greeted audiences with her catch phrase delivered at the top of her voice, "Howdeeee! I'm just as proud to be here!" Her character was that of a man-hungry spinster from "Grinder's Switch." Monologues talked lovingly of her comical relatives, especially "Brother," who was somehow both slow-witted and wise, simultaneously.

God has a plan for all of us, but He expects us to do our share of the work.

1914 **John Berryman:** American poet. Poems are distinguished by precise technical control and continued experiments with style. One of the "confessional poets." Wrote *The Dispossessed* and *77 Dream Songs*. Contemporary critics hailed his *Homage to Mistress Bradstreet*, in which he used the 17th century American poet Anne Bradstreet as his mistress and alter ego, as the most important book of poetry since T.S. Eliot's *Four Quartets*. Also wrote a biography of Stephen Crane.

Life friends, is boring. We must not say so.
After all, the sky flashes, the great sea yearns,
we ourselves flash and yearn, and moreover my
mother told me as a boy (repeatedly) "Ever to
confess you're bored means you have no inner
resources." I conclude now that I have no inner
resources, because I am heavily bored.

1924 **Billy Barty:** American actor. Hollywood's most endearing dwarf. At 3-feet 9-inches, a bundle of energy and talent. Began performing at age three. In feature films from 1933 and had a busy TV career. Active in the cause of advancing the rights of persons of small stature. Founded Little People of America (1957) and the Billy Barty Foundation (1975). Films: *Gold Diggers of 1933, A Midsummer Night's Dream*, and *Under the Rainbow*.

We are your brothers, your daughters, your friends. We just happen to be wrapped in a smaller package.

1941 **Anne Tyler:** American novelist who writes against a background of Southern life. Chronicler of modern American family. Author of *Morgan's Passing, Dinner at the Homesick Restaurant* and *The Accidental Tourist*. Won the Pulitzer Prize for *Breathing Lessons* (1959).

People always call it luck when you've acted more sensibly than they have.

1942 **Helen Reddy:** Australian-born singer and songwriter. Had a television series in the early sixties. Her three U.S. #1 singles sold more than 15 million albums and 10 million singles. The first Australian to win a Grammy. Biggest hits: "I Don't Know How to Love Him," "I Am Woman," the feminist anthem she co-wrote with Ray Burton, "Delta Dawn" and "Angie Baby."

I am woman, hear me roar, in numbers too big to ignore, and I know too much to go back and pretend.

1944 **James Carville:** American Democratic political consultant, commentator and author. "Ragin' Cajun" gained national attention as a strategist of the 1992 presidential campaign of Bill Clinton. Co-host of CNN's *Crossfire*. Books: *All's Fair: Love, War and Running for President*, written with his wife, Mary Matalin, a Republican political consultant. Also wrote: *We're Right, They're Wrong: A Handbook for Spirited Progressives, The Horse He Rode In On: The People vs. Kenneth Starr*, and *Suck Up, Buck Up*.

As with mosquitoes, horseflies, and most bloodsucking parasites, Kenneth Starr was spawned in stagnant water.

OTHERS: 1683 British politician **Charles FitzRoy**, 1767 Swiss writer **Benjamin Constant**, 1806 German philosopher **Max Stirner**, 1825 Austrian composer **Johann Strauss II**, 1856 Croatian paleontologist **Dragutin Gorjanovic-Kramberger**, 1865 Polish general **Józef Dowbór-Mušnicki**, 1889 French film writer **Abel Gance**, 1895 Israeli PM **Levi Eshkol**, 1908 Swiss writer **Edmond Pidoux**, 1913 Nazi war criminal **Klaus Barbie**, 1927 U.S. singer **Barbara Cook**, 1935 U.S. astronaut **Russell Schweickart**, 1940 U.S. basketball coach **Bobby Knight**, 1954 U.S. hockey player with the Olympic "Miracle" team **Mike Eruzione**, 1971 Japanese violinist **Midori**

October 26

1759 **Georges Jacques Danton:** French revolutionary leader. During the early days of the Revolution, one of the most influential people in Paris. Dominated the Commission of Public Safety after the overthrow of the monarchy. Became critical of the revolutionary for its excesses, lost power to the Jacobins and was guillotined for treason.

Show my head to the people, it is worth seeing.

1800 **Helmuth Karl, Count Von Moltke:** Prussian field marshal. Headed general staff (1858–88). Reorganized Prussian Army which was victorious in the Austro-Prussian and Franco-Prussian wars, leading to German unification. Ranked with Otto von Bismark as a builder of the German Empire.

In the long run luck is awarded to the efficient.

1846 **Tennessee Celeste Claflin:** American writer, editor and women's rights worker. Cofounder with her older sister Victoria Woodhull of *Woodhull and Claflin's Weekly*, the first to print the Communist Manifesto in English Through her interest in spiritualism, met millionaire Cornelius Vanderbilt, who shared her enthusiasm. He financed the sisters, becoming the first very successful women stockbrokers in the United States. Claflin became a society hostess in London, while continuing to espouse women's rights.

The world enslaves our sex by the mere fear of an epithet; and as long as it can throw any vile term at us, before which we cower, it can maintain our enslavement.

1883 **Napoleon Hill:** American author. Interviewed some 500 successful men (Thomas Edison, Henry Ford, John D. Rockefeller, Theodore Roosevelt, Woodrow Wilson, George Eastman, and Alexander Graham Bell). The result of his 20-year project was *The Law of Success* (1928). Gave the formula for rags-to-riches success. Elaborated his success formula in his most famous work *Think and Grow Rich*, still in circulation, having sold more than thirty million copies.

If you can't do great things, do small things in a great way.

1886 **Vincent Starrett:** Canadian-born critic, editor, bibliophile and novelist. His classic work, *The Private Life of Sherlock Holmes* (1934), made him internationally famous. Co-founder of the Baker Street Irregulars, whose members are devoted to the great detective. His mystery novels include: *The Unique Hamlet, The Great Hotel Murder* and *The Quick and The Dead.*

The day before yesterday always has been a glamour day. The present is sordid and prosaic. Time colors history as it does a meerschaum pipe.

1911 **Mahalia Jackson:** Outstanding emotional contralto African-American gospel and blues singer. Sang in the choir of the Great Salem Baptist Church in Chicago and from 1932 appeared with the Johnson Gospel Singers. Songs: "Move On Up a Little Higher," "Prayer Changes Things" and "We Shall Overcome." Refused all secular engagements, however, she did sing at John F. Kennedy's inauguration.

Anybody that sings the blues is in a deep pit, yelling for help. Blues are the songs of despair, but gospel songs are the songs of hope.

1916 **François Mitterrand:** French socialist politician. Held ministerial posts in 11 governments from 1947 to 1958. Founded the French Socialist Party in 1971. President of the Republic (1981–85). His program of reform was hampered by deteriorating economic conditions. Forced to work with right-wing prime minister Jacques Chirac during his first term and conservative Edouard Balladur during his second.

France could have all the socialism its capitalistic economy could support.

1919 **Mohammed Reza Pahlavi:** Shah of Iran (1941–79). His family's dynasty was founded by his father, Reza Kahn, an army officer who seized power in 1921 and was proclaimed shah in 1925. He was forced by foreign powers to abdicate in 1941 in favor of his son, who took over in 1956, with U.S. support. He pursued a course of rapid industrialization that led to unrest and his eventual overthrow. Tolerated no political opposition. Deposed during the Islamic Revolution of 1979.

My main mistake was to have made an ancient people advance by forced marches toward independence, health, culture, affluence, comfort.

1942 **Bob Hoskins:** Squat, barrel-chested dynamic British character actor. Natural and spontaneous he easily slipped into films, rapidly working himself up from supporting parts to character leads. Nominated for an Academy Award for *Mona Lisa* (1986). Other films: *The Cotton Club, The Lonely Passion of Judith Hearne, Who Framed Roger Rabbit, Mermaids*, and *Mrs. Henderson Presents.*

Most dictators were short, fat, middle-aged and hairless. Besides Danny DeVito, there's only me to play them.

1945 **Pat Conroy:** American novelist. His novels alienated him from members of his family, made him *persona non grata* at his alma mater, almost drove him to suicide, and entertained millions with stories heavily influenced by the tragedies of his family. His father was a violent and abusive man. Growing up in such an environment is the subject of *The Great Santini* and *The Prince of Tides.* His experiences at The Citadel in Charleston, South Carolina, are found in *The Lords of Discipline. The Water Is Wide* is based on his experiences of teaching the children of remote Daufuskie.

That's one great thing about the novel. You can right wrongs. You're building the world you want.

1948 **Hillary Rodham Clinton:** American politician and lawyer. One of the most influential women in America as first lady and chief adviser of the 42nd president of the U.S. Bill Clinton. Enormously popular and greatly admired at the same time she is greatly vilified. Headed her husband's Health Care Task Force, which ran into problems with its plans for health-care reforms. Elected to the U.S. Senate from New York in 2000 and is expected to seek the Democratic nomination for the presidency in 2008.

We are Americans. We have the right to participate and debate any administration.

1959 **Juan Evo Morales Ayma:** Popularly known as **Evo**. President of Bolivia. Claims to be the first indigenous head of state since the Spanish conquest 450 years ago. Leader of the *cocalero* movement, a federation of coca leaf-growing farmers, resisting the U.S.'s efforts to eradicate coca in the Bolivian province of Chapare. Also leader of the Movement for Socialism political party, which was involved in the recent Gas Wars.

I don't mind being a permanent nightmare for the United States.

OTHERS: 1685 Italian composer/harpsichordist **Domenico Scarlatti**, 1694 Swedish composer **Johan**

Helmich Roman, 1757 Austrian philosopher **Karl Reinhold**, 1794 Russian architect **Konstantin Thon**, 1854 U.S. food-products manufacturer **C.W. Post**, 1865 U.S. businessman **Benjamin Guggenheim**, 1873 Danish Prime Minister **Thorvald Stauning**, 1874 British chemist **Martin Lowry**, 1911 Scottish poet **Sorley MacLean**, 1946 Game show host **Pat Sajak**, 1947 U.S. actress of "Charlie's Angels" **Jaclyn Smith**, 1952 English poet **Andrew Motion**, 1967 New Zealand singer **Keith Urban**, 1984 Figure skater **Sasha Cohen**

October 27

1466 **Desiderius Erasmus:** Dutch humanist. Great Renaissance scholar. First editor of the Greek version of the New Testament and exposed that the Vulgate edition of the Bible was a second-hand document. Defended reason, tolerance and faith. Opposed the notion of predestination. Although opposed to dogmatism and church abuses, remained impartial during Martin Luther's conflicts with the Pope. Author of *Praise of Folly* and *The Education of a Christian Prince.*

When I get a little money, I buy books; and if any is left, I buy food and clothes.

1728 **James Cook:** English naval explorer and cartographer. After surveying the St. Lawrence River in 1759, he made three voyages to Tahiti, New Zealand and Australia, and to the South and North Pacific attempting to find the Northwest Passage and charting the Siberian coast. Made several visits to the Hawaiian or Sandwich Islands, he last time in 1779, when he was stabbed to death in a scuffle with some islanders over stolen items.

Do just once what others say you can't do and you will never pay attention to their limitations again.

1782 **Niccolò Paganini:** Italian violinist, violist, guitarist and composer. A virtuoso soloist from the age of nine. Invented all the virtuoso techniques that have since been included in violin compositions. His violin compositions ingeniously exploited the full potential of the instrument. His signature violin is known as "Cannone Guarnerius," the name he gave it to reflect the "cannon" sound it produced.

I am not handsome, but when women hear me play, they come crawling to my feet.

1858 **Theodore Roosevelt:** Twenty-sixth president of the United States (1901–9), the youngest (at 42) to become president as vice-president when William McKinley was assassinated. Colonel with the Rough Riders in Cuba during the Spanish-American War. Aggressively broke up trusts and regulated business. Carried on a jingoistic foreign policy ("Speak softly and carry a big stick. Acquired the Panama Canal Zone. Introduced the Pure Food and Drug Act. Leading conservationist of natural resources but was a big game hunter in Africa. Nobel Peace Prize in 1906 for his part in ending the Russo-Japanese War. Lost presidential election as head of his Progressive or "Bull Moose" Party in 1912.

The only man who makes no mistakes is the man who never does anything.

1889 **Enid Bagnold:** English playwright, novelist and children's writer. Best-known for *National Velvet,* the story of a girl who wins the Grand National race on a piebald horse won in a raffle. It was made into a successful movie, starring a young Elizabeth Taylor. Other novels: *Serena Blandish* and *The Loved and the Envied.* Plays: *The Chalk Garden* and *A Matter of Gravity.*

It must be pleasant to reach that age when one can go to the lavatory without explanation.

1906 **Alfred Whitney Griswold:** American historian and President of Yale University (1951–63). Sharp-witted diagnostician of the country's ills and idiosyncrasies; embodied a charismatic authority. Attacked "opportunistic politicians" who fanned hatred of Communism into a "neurotic obsession." Lamented that conversation "has fallen on evil days ... drowned in singing commercials." Denounced athletic scholarships as "the greatest educational swindles ever perpetrated on American youth," its aim is not the education of the youth but the entertainment of its elders."

Books won't stay banned. They won't burn, ideas won't go to jail. In the long run of history, the censor and the inquisitor have always lost. The only sure weapon against bad ideas is better ideas.

1914 **Dylan Thomas:** Welsh poet, short-story writer and playwright. Individualistic poetic style, noted for lyrical power, puns, intricate meanings and vivid metaphors. His rich metaphoric language and emotional intensity in his early work, *The Map of Love,* made him famous. Verse has been compared to surrealist painting. Works: *Portrait of the Artist as a Young Dog, A Child's Christmas in Wales* and *Under Milk Wood.* His recitations of his work greatly contributed to his fame. Died of an alcohol overdose in New York while on tour.

Do not go gentle into that good night,/ Old age should burn and rave at close of day;/ Rage, rage against the dying of the light.

1923 **Roy Lichtenstein:** American painter. Founder and foremost practioners of Pop art. Work borrows heavily from popular advertising and comic book styles, which ha admitted to being "as artificial as possible." Most of his best-known artworks are relatively close, but not exact, copies of comic book panels. In the late 70s his style was more surrealistic. In addition to paintings he also made sculptures in metal and plastic.

I want my images to be as critical, as threatening and as insistent as possible.

1932 **Sylvia Plath:** American author and poet. Won a Fulbright Fellowship to Newnham College, Cambridge, where she studied English and married poet Ted Hughes. Suffered from deep depression. Best known for her volume of poetry, *Ariel,* written shortly before her suicide and The *Bell Jar,* a novel about her mental collapse during her student years. Won the Pulitzer Prize for poetry posthumously for *Collected Poems,* edited by her husband.

Perhaps when we find ourselves wanting everything, it is because we are dangerously close to wanting nothing.

1940 **John Joseph Gotti, Jr.**: American organized crime boss. Known as "The Dapper Don" for wearing $2000 hand-tailored suits and reveling in media attention, and "The Teflon Don," because he was avoided conviction on racketeering and assault charges. Head of the Gambino crime family, one of the five major New York Mafia families (1986–92). Convicted of 13 counts of murder, conspiracy to commit murder, loansharking, racketeering, obstruction of justice, and tax evasion. Sentenced to life-imprisonment without possibility of parole (1992). Incarcerated in a federal prison where he was kept in a solitary confinement cell 23 hours a day. Died of throat cancer (2002).

Don't carry a gun. It's nice to have them close by, but don't carry them. You might get arrested.

1940 **Maxine Hong Kingston:** Chinese-American writer. Works reflect her cultural heritage, blending fiction with nonfiction. *The Woman Warrior* and *China Men* were awarded the National Book Critics Award for nonfiction. Her only novel, *Tripmaster Monkey*, is based on the mythical Chinese character Sun Wu Kong. Awarded the 1977 National Humanities Medal by President Bill Clinton.

I learned to make my mind large, as the universe is large, so that there is room for contradictions.

1950 **Fran Lebowitz:** American humorist, essayist and writer. Best known for her sardonic social commentary on American life. Columnist for Andy Warhol's *Interview*, followed by a stint at *Mademoiselle*. Author of: *Social Studies*, *Metropolitan Life* and *Observer*. Has appeared as a judge on TV's *Law & Order*.

Romantic love is mental illness. But it's a pleasurable one. It distorts reality, and that's the point of it. It would be impossible to fall in love with someone that you really saw.

OTHERS: 1744 English painter **Mary Moser**, 1811 U.S. inventor **Isaac Singer**, 1842 Italian statesman **Giovanni Giolitti**, 1844 Swedish pacifist **Klas Arnoldson**, 1917 African freedom fighter **Oliver Tambo**, 1918 U.S. actress **Teresa Wright**, 1924 African-American actress **Ruby Dee**, 1926 U.S. government official/Nixon's Chief of Staff **H.R. Haldeman**, 1922 U.S. baseball player/broadcaster **Ralph Kiner**, 1931 Egyptian writer **Nawal El Saadawi**, 1933 U.S. pianist **Floyd Cramer**, 1939 British actor with "Monty Python's Flying Circus" **John Cleese**, 1945 Brazilian president **Luis Inácio Lula da Silva**, 1947 U.S. hostage **Terry Anderson**, 1978 Singapore musician **Vanessa-Mae**, 1980 Estonian singer **Tanel Padar**

October 28

1902 **Elsa Lanchester:** Originally **Elizabeth Sullivan**. British-born actress. Studied dancing with Isadora Duncan and later taught dancing. Married Charles Laughton in 1929. Lacking conventional beauty she never appeared as the lead in any films, but gave memorable performances in supporting roles. At her best in eccentric or comic parts. Films with Laughton: *The Private Life of Henry VIII*, *Rembrandt* and *Witness for the Prosecution*. Nominated for An Academy Award for the latter and for *Come to the Stable*. Best known as the title character in *Bride of Frankenstein*.

One thinks of a film star as a kind of gaily colored bird, forever giving itself a final preening under bright lights. Whereas it's all hard work, aspirins, and usually purgatives.

1903 **Evelyn Waugh:** English writer. Wrote satirical and darkly humorous novels, which depict the British aristocracy and high society. In his more serious work, he is greatly influenced by his conservative Catholic outlook. Novels: *Decline and Fall*, *Vile Bodies*, *A Handful of Dust*, *The Loved One*, *Brideshead Revisited* and the *Sword of Honor* trilogy. Wrote short stories, three biographies, travel accounts and his extensive diaries.

What a man enjoys about a woman's clothes are his fantasies of how she would look without them.

1907 **Edith Head:** American motion picture costume designer. Won eight Academy Awards including for the stylish suits worn by Paul Newman and Robert Redford in *The Sting*. Designed opulent dresses for many of the major stars of the era, including Elizabeth Taylor, Audrey Hepburn, Bette Davis and Barbara Stanwyck. Some of her most notable designs are found in: *The Heiress*, *All about Eve*, *Roman Holiday* and *Sabrina*.

Your dresses should be tight enough to show you're a woman and loose enough to show you're a lady.

1910 **Francis Bacon:** Anglo-Irish artist. Collateral descendent of the Elizabethan philosopher of the same name. With no formal training, he started painting, drawing and participating in gallery exhibitions. Known for bold, abstract and frequently grotesque or nightmarish imagery. Painted expressionist portraits, distorted by terror. Gained instant notoriety in 1944 for a series of controversial paintings, *Three Studies for Figures at the Base of a Crucifixion*. Other works: *Studies After Velaquez* and *Portrait of Pope Innocent X*.

The job of the artist is always to deepen the mystery.

1914 **Jonas Salk:** American physician and researcher. Working with other scientists to classify polo virus, he confirmed earlier studies that identified three strains. Showed that dead virus of each strain could induce antibody formation without producing disease, thus developing the first poliomyelitis vaccine. Founding director of the Salk Institute (1975). Awarded the Presidential Medal of Freedom (1977).

Intuition will tell the thinking mind where to look next.

1926 **Bowie Kuhn:** American sports executive. Elected Commissioner of Major League Baseball (1969–84). Tenure marked by labor strikes, owner disenchantment, drug abuse and the end of baseball's reserve clause, which tied players to the team they signed with, unable to seek a better deal with other clubs. Curt Flood challenged the clause, demanding that he be declared a free agent. Kuhn denied the request, resulting in Flood's suit alleging that Major League Baseball violated federal antitrust laws. Although Flood did not prevail, the end of the reserve clause was near.

I believe in the Rip Van Winkle theory: that a man from 1910 must be able to wake up after being asleep for seventy years, walk into a ballpark and understand baseball perfectly.

1929 **Joan Plowright:** English stage and film actress. Member of the English Stage Company at the Royal Court Theater, London in 1956, playing opposite Laurence Olivier whom she married in 1961. Joined the National Theatre in its first season, the company's lead actress until 1974. Films: *The Entertainer, Equus, Avalon* and *Enchanted April*, for which she won a Golden Globe for Best Supporting Actress. Won a Tony for her role in *A Taste of Honey* on Broadway.

Nothing is so sexy in a man as talent.

1938 **Anne Perry:** Originally **Juliet Hulme**. English-born novelist and convicted murderer. Moved with her family to New Zealand. Together with school friend Pauline Parker, murdered Parker's mother, beating the woman to death, hitting her 45 times with a brick. Too young for the death penalty, they spent only five years in prison. Events formed the basis of the film *Heavenly Creatures*. After her release she returned to England, changed her name and published her first novel *The Cater Street Hangman* (1979). Most of her 47 novels are historical mysteries or fantasies.

My major interest is in conflict of ethics, especially involving honesty with one's self, which is why the Victorian scene, with its layers of hypocrisy, appeals to me.

1939 **Jane Alexander:** Originally **Jane Quigley**. American stage and screen actress. Among her most famous roles as Eleanor Roosevelt in the television film *Eleanor and Franklin* and its sequel. Nominated four timed for Academy Awards: *The Great White Hope, All the President's Men, Kramer vs. Kramer* and *Testament.* Appointed chairwoman of the National Endowment for the Arts in 1993.

No one's conception of art is going to be acceptable to everybody.

1949 **Bruce Jenner:** American decathlete. Became an American champion in the decathlon and won a gold medal at the 1976 Summer Olympics. That year he received the James E. Sullivan Award as the top amateur athlete in the U.S. Struggled with dyslexia. After retiring from competition, he built a successful career as a motivational speaker.

I spent twelve years training for a career that was over in a week. Joe Namath spent one week training for a career that lasted twelve years.

1955 **William H. "Bill" Gates:** American corporation executive and philanthropist. Chairman and CEO of Microsoft Corporation, the world's largest software film, which he cofounded at age 19 with Paul G. Allen. Part inventor, part entrepreneur, part-time salesman and full-time genius. Criticized for having built Microsoft's business through unfair, illegal, or anticompetitive business practices. Forbes International has ranked him the world's wealthiest individual for 12 straight years. In 1999, Gates and his wife Melinda created the largest charitable foundation in the U.S.A. They have donated about 52% of their total wealth to charitable organizations and scientific research programs.

As we look ahead into the next century, leaders will be those who empower others.

1967 **Julia Roberts:** Lovely movie star and former model. Able to attract audiences to movies on her presence alone. First came to prominence in *Mystic Pizza.* Oscar nominated for Best Supporting Actress for *Steel Magnolias.* Really clicked with *Pretty Woman*, which made her a top box-office draw. Oscar winner for *Erin Brockovich.* Other films *Sleeping with the Enemy, My Best Friend's Wedding, Notting Hill, Runaway Bride, Ocean's Eleven and Ocean's Twelve.* Named one of *People* Magazine's "50 Most Beautiful People in the World" a record-setting nine times.

I'm too tall to be a girl. I'm between a chick and a broad.

OTHERS: 1510 Spanish duke/priest **Saint Francis Borgia**, 1585 Dutch religious reformer **Cornelius Jansen**, 1718 Croatian missionary **Ignacije Szentmartony**, 1793 U.S. firearms manufacturer **Eliphalet Remington**, 1846 French chef **Georges Escoffier**, 1907 Northern Ireland poet **John Hewitt**, 1912 English epidemiologist **Richard Doll**, 1914 English chemist **Richard Millington Synge**, 1915 U.S. screenwriter **Paul Jarrico**, 1922 German composer **Gershon Kingsley**, 1922 Zimbabwe politician **Simon Muzenda**, 1936 U.S. country musician **Charlie Daniels**, 1942 Dutch speed skater **Kees Verberk**, 1944 U.S. actor **Dennis Franz**, 1967 U.S. video game designer **John Romero**, 1974 U.S. actor **River Phoenix**

October 29

1656 **Edmond Halley:** (In the new style, his birthday is given as November 8) English astronomer. Pioneered understanding of trade winds, tides, cartography, naval navigation, mortality tables, and stellar proper motions. In his most important scientific work, *A Synopsis of the Astronomy of Comets*, he applied Newton's Laws of Motion to all available data on comets. His calculations led him to deduce that the comet he observed in 1682 was periodic and was the same comet that had appeared in 1607, 1531, 1456, 1380, and 1305. Predicted that it would reappear in 76 years. Halley achieved lasting fame, even though he had been dead for fifteen years, when the comet was observed on December 25, 1758, only a few days later than Halley expected. Demonstrated conclusively that comets were celestial bodies, not meteorological phenomena, as previously believed.

Now we know/ The sharply veering ways of

comets, once/ A source of dread, no longer do we quail/ Beneath appearances of bearded stars.

1740 **James Boswell:** Scottish lawyer, biographer and diarist. His fame survives because of his masterpiece, *The Life of Samuel Johnson, LL.D.* considered the greatest of English biographies. Also revealed to be one of the world's greatest diarists when his journal was published in the 20th century.

He who praises everyone, praises nobody.

1815 **Daniel Decatur Emmett:** American musician and composer. Remembered today chiefly for writing *Dixie*. Wrote it as a walkaround while he was with Bryant's Minstrels in New York City. Became immediately popular and with the outbreak of the Civil War, troops of both the North and the South marched off to war to its tune. But by the end of 1861, identified as a Southern tune. This did not set well with Ohio born Emmett, who was not a Southern sympathizer.

Look away! Look away! Look away! Dixie Land.

1837 **Abraham Kuyper:** Dutch theologian, statesman, journalist and Prime Minister of the Netherlands (1901–05). After serving as a pastor he founded a Calvinist-oriented newspaper and was elected to the national assembly. Formed the Anti-Revolutionary Party, first organized Dutch political party. Combined orthodox religious convictions and a progressive social agenda. Founded the Free University of Amsterdam and the Reform Churches in the Netherlands.

Do not bury our glorious orthodoxy in the treacherous pit of spurious conservatism.

1875 **Marie of Romania:** British-born Queen of Romania. Her mother, Marie, was the only surveying daughter of Tsar Alexander of Russia and her father, Alfred, was the second son of Queen Victoria. Married Ferdinand, the heir to the Romanian throne in 1893. When his father King Carol died, it wasn't seemly to have the pomp and circumstances of a huge crowning ceremony, which finally occurred in 1922. Marie was a rare combination of royal snobbery, common, sense, intelligence, and kindness. Not afraid to move into the 20th century, was often referred to as a "modern queen."

Fashion exists for women with no taste, etiquette for people with no breeding.

1882 **Jean Giraudoux:** French dramatist, novelist, essayist and diplomat. Spent 30 years in the French diplomatic corps. Became known for his avant garde poetic novels such as *Suzanne et le Pacifique*. Created an impressionistic form of drama emphasizing dialogue and style rather than realism. Author of: *Tiger at the Gates*, *Ondine* and *The Madwoman of Chaillot*.

There are truths which can kill a nation.

1891 **Fanny Brice:** American actress, singer and comedienne played with vaudeville and burlesque shows, the Ziegfeld Follies, Broadway, films and radio. Her biggest hit was "My Man." Portrayed by Barbra Streisand on Broadway and two films. Very popular as radio's "Baby Snooks."

Personal beauty is a greater recommendation than any letter of reference.

1897 **Joseph Paul Goebbels:** German Nazi propaganda minister. Gifted speaker, he edited the party's journal and created the Führer myth around Adolf Hitler. Instituted party demonstrations that helped convert the masses to Nazism. Ran the national propaganda machinery of the Third Reich. He and his wife poisoned their six children and then committed suicide at Hitler's Berlin bunker towards the end of World War II.

If you tell a big lie enough and keep repeating it, people will eventually come to believe it. The lie can be maintained only for such time as the State can shield the people from the political, economic, and/or military consequences of the lie. It thus becomes vitally important for the State to use all of its powers to repress dissent, for the truth is the mortal enemy of the lie, and thus by extension, the truth is the greatest enemy of the State.

1910 **A.J. [Alfred Jules] Ayer:** British philosopher, professor of logic and author. Closely associated with the British humanist movement. First president of the Agnostics' Adoption Society. Noted for promoting logical positivism. Known for his verification principle, according to which a sentence is meaningful only if it has verifiable empirical import. Books: *Language, Truth and Logic*, *The Problem of Knowledge* and *The Central Question of Philosophy*.

The principles of logic and metaphysics are true simply because we never allow them to be anything else.

1921 **William Henry "Bill "Mauldin:** American cartoonist and author. During World War II, his sardonic cartoons for *Stars and Stripes* featured GIs "Willie" and "Joe," enlisted men who managed to retain their humanity amidst the onslaughts of battles and army hierarchy. Later worked for the *St. Louis Post-Dispatch* and the *Chicago Sun-Times* as a political cartoonist. Pulitzer Prizes in 1945 and 1959. Books: *Up Front*, *Bill Mauldin's Army* and *I've Decided I Want My Seat Back*.

When we realize that we aren't God's given children, we'll understand satire. Humor is really laughing off a hurt, grinning at misery.

1925 **Dominick Dunne:** American writer and investigative journalist. Describes the way high society interacts with the judiciary system. Covered the famous trials of O.J. Simpson, Claus von Bulow, Michael Skakel, the Menendez brothers, and the murderer of his daughter actress, Dominique Dunne. Latter led him to write *Justice: A Father's Account of the Trial of His Daughter's Killer*. Novels: *The Two Mrs. Grenvilles*, *An Inconvenient Woman* and *A Season in Purgatory*. Father of actor writer Griffin Dunne and brother-in-law of Joan Didion.

When you're down and out, there's no meaner place to live than in Hollywood. You can get away with your embezzlements and your lies and your murders, but you can never get away with failing.

1971 **Winona Ryder:** American actress who gave some remarkably mature performances as a teenager and has developed into a beautiful talented young woman. Films: *Beetlejuice, Heathers, Bram Stoker's Dracula* and Oscar nominated performances in *The Age of Innocence* and *Little Women.*

I've learned that it's OK to be flawed.

OTHERS: 1017 Holy Roman Emperor **Henry III**, 1690 English antiquarian **Martin Folkes**, 1704 British admiral **John Byng**, 1827 French chemist/ politician **Marcellin Berthelot**, 1873 Columbian poet **Guillermo Valencia**, 1879 German Chancellor **Franz von Papen**, 1880 Soviet physicist **Abraham Ioffe**, 1920 Venezuelan-born immunologist **Baruj Benacerraf**, 1926 Canadian tenor **Jon Vickers**, 1938 Israeli cartoonist **Ralph Bakshi**, 1938 President of Liberia **Ellen Johnson-Sirleaf**, 1945 U.S. singer/actress **Melba Moore**, 1947 U.S. actor **Richard Dreyfuss**, 1953 Canadian hockey player **Denis Potvin**, 1968 Norwegian speed skater **Johann Olva Koss**, 1981 U.S. swimmer **Amanda Beard**

October 30

1735 **John Adams:** Second U.S. president (1797–1801). Lawyer, statesman, diarist, letter writer and diplomat. One of the Founding Fathers of the United States of America. Signer of the Declaration of Independence. Helped draft the Declaration of Independence. Helped draft the Treaty of Paris, ending the Revolutionary War. Washington's vice president. Washington and Adams were the only Federalist Presidents. The Alien and Sedition Acts were passed during his term of office, meant to restrict the public activities of political radicals who sympathized with the French Revolution and criticized Adams' policies. Father of John Quincy Adams, 6th U.S. president.

The government of the United States is not in any sense founded upon the Christian religion.

1751 **Richard Brinsley Sheridan:** Irish-born English dramatist, parliamentary orator and statesman. Wrote satirical comedies of manners. Best known for his masterpieces *The Rivals* and *The School for Scandal.* Other plays included *The Duenna, A Trip to Scarborough* and *The Critic*, furnishing brilliant roles for outstanding actors, including Minnie Maddern Fiske (billed as Mrs. Fiske) and Joseph Jefferson. Oddly, Sheridan had grown up with a dislike of the theater and declared that he never saw a play if he could avoid it. Chose playwriting, only when he could find nothing else to do to support himself. He lived beyond his means and was constantly in financial difficulties.

There's no possibility of being witty without a little ill-nature; the malice of a good thing is the barb that makes it stick.

1762 **André Marie de Chénier:** French poet, born in Istanbul, where his father was the French consul. Wrote idylls and elegies and experimented in didactic and philosophic verse. Active in the early part of the French Revolution, he was horrified by Jacobin excesses. Contributed denunciatory pamphlets to the *Journal de P*aris, an organ of moderate royalist positions. Arrested by order of Robespierre, imprisoned for 140 days and guillotined only three days before the end of the Terror. While imprisoned he wrote his last and most famous ode, *La Jeune Captive.* His philosophical poetry, for *instance L'Invention*, was his poetic expression of the scientific ideas of his age.

What is virtue? Reason put into practice:— talent? Reason expressed with brilliance;— soul? Reason delicately put forth, and genius is sublime reason.

1840 **William Graham Sumner:** American educator, sociologist and economist. One of the leading proponents of laissez-faire economics and Social Darwinism. Opposed socialism. Criticized welfare programs for disrupting the rightful stratification and unjustly burdening "the forgotten man," the citizen who worked hard and pulled his own weight. Books: *Andrew Jackson as a Public Man, Protectionism: the–ism which Teaches That Waste Makes Wealth* and The *Forgotten Man and Other Essays.*

If you want a war, nourish a doctrine. Doctrines are the most frightful tyrants to which men are ever subject, because doctrines get inside a man's reason and betray him against himself. Civilized men have done their fiercest fighting for doctrines.

1871 **Paul Valéry:** French poet, essayist and critic. Deeply influenced by the Symbolist Movement, wrote many poems published in magazines. Widely known for *La jeune parquet*, followed by *Album de vers ancines, 1890–1900* and *Charmes ou poémes*, which contained "Le cinetière mari" ("The Graveyard of the Sea"), establishing him as the outstanding French poet of his time. His notebooks were published posthumously as the famous *Cahiers.*

An artist never really finishes his work, he merely abandons it.

1877 **Irma S. Rombauer:** American author of cookbooks. Wrote the all-time best-selling *The Joy of Cooking* (1931). An American institution, the only cookbook chosen by the New York Public Library during its centennial celebration as one of the 150 most influential books of the century. While she was alive, in editions of her book she engaged her readers with a constant dialogue, telling stories about herself and her family, sprinkling the test with witticism and corny puns. Made in clear that cooking was neither a magical science nor an esoteric art, but part of everyday work of most women and some men and could be fun with her help.

Nothing stimulates the practiced cook's imagination like an egg.

1882 **William F. Halsey, Jr.:** "Bull." U.S. admiral. Commander of the U.S. Navy's Third Fleet during World War II, which played a major role in the defeat of the Japanese. Japanese surrender was signed aboard his flagship, the U.S.S *Missouri.* In *Narrative Account of the South Pacific Campaign* (1944), he asserted that success was due to a fighting team effort, maintaining that no one service won the battle. His motto: "Hit hard, hit fast, hit often." Retired as a five-star admiral.

There are no great people in this world, only

great challenges which ordinary people rise to meet.

1885 **Ezra Pound:** American poet, editor, translator and critic. Chief promoter of Imagism, a movement stressing free phrase rather than forced metric: *Mauberley*, *Cantos*, *The Spirit of Romance*, *How to Read*, and *ABC of Reading*. One of the most influential and controversial figures in modern literature. T.S. Eliot asserted "If it had not been for the work that Pound did ... the isolation of American poets might have continued for a long time." Arrested for making some 300 pro–Fascist radio broadcasts from Italy during World War II. Declared mentally unstable, but never tried for treason.

If a man isn't willing to take some risk for his opinions, either his opinions are no good or he's no good.

1886 **Zoë Akins:** U.S. playwright, poet, novelist and screenwriter. Author of *Déclassée*, a social melodrama; *Daddy's Gone a-Hunting*, a sentimental portrayal of a failing marriage, *The Greeks Had a Word for It*, a comedy about Ziegfeld showgirls. Her dramatization of Edith Wharton's *The Old Maid* won a Pulitzer Prize (1935). Wrote two novels, *Forever Young* and *Cake Upon the Water*. Also contributed to the screen adaptation of the musical *Showboat*.

Nothing seems so tragic to one who is old as the death of one who is young and this alone proves that life is a good thing.

1896 **Ruth Gordon:** née **Jones**. American actress, screenwriter and playwright. Her first Broadway starring appearance in Booth Tarkington's *Seventeen* received a scathing review from *New York Herald Tribune* critic Heywood Broun. Had personal triumphs in *Ethan Frome* and *A Doll's House*. In the 1940s, she concentrated on writing plays and screenplays, often in collaboration with her second husband Garson Kanin. They received Oscar nominations for *A Double Life*, *Adam's Rib* and *Pat and Mike*. In her mid–60s she delighted audiences of all ages with a series of feisty, eccentric film roles. Nominated for An Academy Award for *Inside Daisy Clover* and won for *Rosemary's Baby*. Other films: *Where's Poppa?* and *Harold and Maude*.

Never give up. And never, under any circumstances, face the facts.

1915 **Fred Friendly:** Originally **Ferdinand Friendly Wachenheimer**. American broadcast producer and journalist. In the 1950s collaborated with Edward R. Murrow to produce the radio series *Hear It Now* and the television series *See It Now*. Also produced *CBS Reports*. President of CBS News (1964–66). Advisor for the Ford Foundation. Instrumental in establishing the Public Broadcasting System Network.

[Murrow] taught us many valuable lessons about responsibility, and to always question authority, because without it authority often goes unchecked.

1928 **Daniel Nathans:** American microbiologist. Used the restriction enzyme isolated from a bacterium by Hamilton O. Smith to investigate the structure of the DNA of a monkey virus, the simplest virus known to produce cancer. His construction of a genetic map of the virus was the first application of restriction enzymes to the problem of identifying the molecular basis of cancer. Nobel Prize in Physiology or Medicine in 1978.

You have to make your bets, and they don't all pay off, but this is where fundamental discoveries are going to come from.

OTHERS: 1839 French artist **Alfred Sisley**, 1844 U.S. chemist **Harvey Wiley**, 1847 Italian physicist **Galileo Ferraris**, 1857 French neurologist **Georges Gilles de la Tourette**, 1861 French sculptor **Antoine Bourdelle**, 1893 U.S. body-builder **Charles Atlas**, 1895 U.S. physician **Dickinson Richards**, 1909 Indian physicist **Homi J. Bhabha**, 1917 Soviet Field Marshal **Nikolai Ogarkov**, 1930 Spanish cinematographer **Nestor Almendros**, 1930 U.S. jazz trumpeter **Clifford Brown**, 1932 French film director **Louis Malle**, 1934 Dutch flutist **Frans Brüggen**, 1936 Ukrainian gymnast **Polina Astkhova**, 1937 French film director **Claude Lelouch**, 1939 U.S. singer **Grace Slick**, 1945 U.S. actor, "The Fonz" **Henry Winkler**

October 31

1620 **John Evelyn:** English writer, whose diary, covering the years from 1631 to 1706, is considered an invaluable source of information on the social, cultural, religious and political life of 17th century England. His interests ranged from gardening to numismatics. Held several offices during the reign of King Charles II.

Friendship is the golden thread that ties the hearts of all hearts of all the world.

1795 **John Keats:** English poet. Called the poet's poet. Probably the most talented of the English romantic poets. "The Eve of St. Agnes," containing some of his most striking sensuous imagery, established him a permanent place in world literature. Keats embraced art for art's sake. Author of: "Endymion," "Hyperion," Ode on a Grecian Urn" and "Ode to a Nightingale." Not all his contemporaries appreciated his work. Lord Byron described it as "a sort of mental masturbation." Died of consumption at age 25 after recovering from a suicide attempt.

Beauty is truth, truth beauty,— that is all Ye know on earth, and all you need to know. A thing of beauty is a joy forever. Its loveliness increases. It will never pass into nothingness.

1815 **Karl Weierstrass:** German mathematician. "Father of modern analysis." What is most remarkable is that he spent much of his early life and career isolated from other outstanding mathematicians while he taught various subjects in secondary schools. It wasn't until he was about forty that his genius was recognized and he secured a university position. He broadened the understanding of the notion of "function," gave the modern δ, ε definition of limit, discovered and applied uniform convergence and gave a theory of irrational numbers as series of rational numbers.

A mathematician who is not also a poet will never be a complete mathematician.

1860 **Juliette Gordon Low:** American youth leader and social reformer. After meeting General Sir Robert Baden-Powell, who had founded the Boy Scouts in Britain in 1908, she founded the Girl Scouts of America at Savannah, Georgia, in 1912. Girl Scout Week, observed annually, begins with the last Sunday in October, honoring the founder.

To put yourself in another's place requires real imagination, but by so doing each Girl Scout will be able to live among others happily.

1863 **William G. McAdoo:** U.S. government official and lawyer. Organized the Hudson and Manhattan Railway companies. U.S. Secretary of the Treasury (1913–18). Floated $18 billion in loans to finance America's World War I efforts. Founder and chairman of the Federal Reserve Board. Son-in-law of President Woodrow Wilson. Director General of U.S. Railroads (1917–19) and Later U.S. Senator from California (1933–38).

It is impossible to defeat an ignorant man in argument.

1887 **Chiang Kai-Shek:** "Generalissimo." Chinese statesman and soldier. Considered "the symbol of Chinese unity and resistance against Japan." Staged a coup to establish himself as head of the Nationalist Government (1928–49), succeeding Dr. Sun Yat-Sen, the first president of the Chinese Republic. Fought Communists as well as the Japanese during World War II. Defeated by the Communists, resumed presidency exile on Taiwan (1949–75). His wife and chief advisor, Mayling Soong, was the member of the famous Soong family and sister of Sun Yat-sen's wife Chingling Soong.

Don't be disquieted in time of adversity. Be firm with dignity and self-reliant with vigor.

1895 **B.H. Liddell Hart:** British military historian and strategist. Developed a set of principles that he considered to be the basis of all good strategy; principles ignored by the majority of World War I commanders. Reduced his set of principles to a single phrase, the *indirect approach*, and two fundamentals: 1. Direct attacks against an enemy firmly in position almost never work and should not be attempted. 2. To defeat the enemy one must first upset his equilibrium, which is not accomplished by the main attack, but must be done before the main attack can succeed. The Germans adopted similar strategies against the British and its allies in World War II with the practice of *Blitzkrieg*.

Helplessness induces hopelessness, and history attests that loss of hope and not loss of lives is what decides the issue of war.

1900 **Ethel Waters:** African-American actress and singer. In her youth, acted as alarm girl for the prostitutes of her dreary neighborhood, and was a scrubwoman at Swarthmore College. At 17 sang in clubs and vaudeville, billed as "Sweet Mama Stringbean." First to sing W.C. Handy's "St. Louis Blues." One-time torso shaker other hits: *Dinah*, *Stormy Weather* and *Heat Wave*. Nominated for an Academy Award for *Pinky*. Other films: *Cabin in the Sky*, *The Member of the Wedding* and *The Sound and the Fury*. Her biography, *His Eye Is on the Sparrow*, created a nation-wide stir.

I can come when I please/ I can go when I please/ I can flit, fly and flutter, like the birds in the trees.

1930 **Michael Collins:** American astronaut and test pilot. Selected as a member of the third group of fourteen astronauts in 1963. Made two space flights. During Gemini 10, he and command pilot John W. Young performed two rendezvoused with different spacecraft. Manned the command module of *Apollo II* while Neil Armstrong and Buzz Aldrin walked on the moon.

I knew I was alone in a way that no earthling has ever been before.

1937 **Dan Rather:** American broadcast journalist. Anchorman of "The CBS Evening News" (1981–2005), succeeding the legendary Walter Cronkite. First TV journalist to report President John F. Kennedy had died of wounds received from an assassin. Reporting during the period of national mourning following the assassination brought him to the attention of CBS News management. Legendary for hardnosed coverage of the Watergate Investigation and Impeachment proceedings. Frequently accused of liberal bias in employing a double standard on how and which news stories to report, but was highly regarded within his profession.

A tough lesson in life that one has to learn is that not everybody wishes you well.

1944 **Richard F. "Kinky" Friedman:** American singer, songwriter, novelist and politician. His nickname is a reference to his hair. In the early 1970s he formed a band, *The Texas Jewboys*. Found cult fame as a country and western singer with songs such as "We Reserve the Right to Refuse Service to You," "Get Your Biscuits in the Oven and Your Buns in Bed," "Ride 'em Jewboy" and "They Ain't Makin' Jews Like Jesus Anymore." When his music career stalled he turned to writing detective novels, starring himself and a regular column for the magazine *Texas Monthly*.

I'd felt that a man without a woman was like a neck without a pain.

1950 **Jane Pauley:** American television news anchor and journalist. Co-host of *The Today Show* (1976–89). Shared anchor duties with Tom Brokaw and later Bryant Gumbel. Replaced by Deborah Norville in 1989, her supporters accused NBC of ageism. Hosted the short-lived *Real Life with Jane Pauley* and as deputy anchor for *NBC Nightly News*. Her autobiography, *Skywriting: A Life Out of the Blue*.

New Yorkers, by reputation, are fast-talking, assertive and easily annoyed; I fit right in.

OTHERS: 1291 French composer **Philippe de Vitry**, 1538 Italian historian **Caesar Baronius**, 1622 French artist **Pierre Paul Puget**, 1632 Flemish painter **Johannes Vermeer**, 1711 Italian scholar **Laura Bassi**, 1724 English writer **Christopher Anstey**, 1831 Italian neurologist **Paolo Mantegazza**, 1875 Indian freedom fighter **Vallabhbhai Patel**, 1912 U.S. actress/singer **Dale**

Evans, 1920 Welsh novelist **Dick Francis**, 1920 German photographer **Helmut Newton**, 1922 U.S. saxophonist **Illinois Jacquet**, 1922 Cambodian King **Norodom Sihanouk**, 1925 English chemist **John Poole**, 1927 U.S. actress **Lee Grant**, 1947 U.S. runner **Frank Shorter**, 1961 New Zealand film director **Peter Jackson**

November 1

1500 **Benvenuto Cellini:** Italian writer, engraver, unrivaled goldsmith and sculptor. Work characterized by elaborate virtuosity. Late Florentine sculptures include the bronze *Perseus with the Head of Medusa* in the Loggia dei Lanza in Florence and the bust of Cosimo I de' Medici. One of his most famous works was a gold saltcellar encrusted with enamel for Francis I of Fontainebleau. Fame owes much to his autobiography which achieved immediate popularity for its lively account of his tumultuous life, racy style and its vivid picture of Renaissance Italy.

One can pass on responsibility, but not the discretion that goes with it.

1636 **Nicholas Boileau-Despréaux:** French poet and literary critic. Gained wide recognition as the legislator and model for French neoclassicism with his didactic poem *Art poétiques*, based on Horace's *Ars Poetica*. Most influential exponent of classical standards for poetry. Official royal historian. Books include the semicomic *Lutrin*.

A fool always finds a greater fool to admire him.

1871 **Stephen Crane:** American novelist, short-story writer and poet. Often called the first American author. Best known work is *The Red Badge of Courage*, an epic of the American Civil War. Also wrote short stories, poetry and worked as a war correspondent in Greece. Other works: *Maggie: A Girl of the Streets*, *The Black Rider*, *The Open Boat*, and *War Is Kind*.

A man said to the universe/ "Sir, I exist!"/ "However," replied the universe,/ "The fact has not created in me/ A sense of obligation."

1880 **Sholem Asch:** Polish-born American novelist and dramatist. One of the best known Yiddish writers. Most of his writing details the experience of Jews in Eastern European villages or as immigrants in the U.S. Works include the *play The God of Vengeance*, the novels, *Mottke the Thief*, *Judge Not* and *Chaim Lederer's Return*. Biblical novels: *The Nazarene*, *The Apostle*, and *Mary*, in which he explored the common heritage of Judaism and Christianity.

The lash may force men to physical labor; it cannot force them to spiritual creativity.

1880 **Grantland Rice:** "Dean of American Sports Writers." Some would say he established the Golden Age of Sports with inspirational writing, transforming talented athletes into mythical-like figures, establishing them as demigods. Among those he consciously set out to rise to heroic status were Jack Dempsey, Babe Ruth, Bobby Jones, Bill Tilden, Red Grange and Knute Rockne. Comparison of the 1924 Notre Dame Football backfield, dubbed the "Four Horsemen of Notre Dame," with the Four Horsemen of the Apocalypse immortalized quarterback Harry Stuhldreher, left halfback Jim Crowley, right halfback Don Miller and fullback Elmer Layden.

Does the road wind up-hill all they way? Yes, to the very end. Will the day's journey take the whole long day?/ From morn to night, my friend.

1886 **Hermann Broch:** Austrian author and essayist. His trilogy, *The Sleepwalkers* (1930–33), records the disintegration of values in the late 19th and early 20th century Germany. Best known works are *The Death of Virgil* (1945), which represents the last 18 hours of the poet's life and *The Spell*, a portrayal of a stranger's domination of a village. Other works: *The Guiltless* and *The Tempter*.

No one's death comes to pass without making some impression, and those close to the deceased inherit part of the liberated soul and become richer in their humanness.

1887 **Isaac Goldberg:** American critic, editor and author. Lectured on music and belles-lettres. Addicted to radio, talkies, musicals, comedies, puns, toys of every description and volumes of esthetics. Literary editor of *American Freeman* (1923–32). Wrote: *The Story of Gilbert and Sullivan*, *Tin Pan Alley: A Chronicle of the American Popular Music Racket* and *George Gershwin: A Study in American Music*.

There is that smaller world which is the stage and that larger stage which is the world.

1892 **Alexander Alekhine:** Russian-born chess master and former World Chess Champion. Famous for his fierce and imaginative attacking style. In 1927, he won the title of World Chess Champion from José Raúl Capablanca, surprising the chess world. From 1927 to 1935, dominated world chess, finally being defeated by Max Euwe, the loss being attributed to his alcoholism. During World War II, Alekhine played in several tournaments held in Germany or German-occupied territory and allegedly wrote a number of anti–Semitic articles.

Chess first of all teaches you to be objective.

1923 **Gordon R. Dickson:** Canadian-born science fiction writer. Spent most of his life in Minneapolis, Minnesota. Won three Hugo awards. Best known for his *Childe Cycle* books. Novels include: *Necromancer*, *Time Storm*, *The Spirit of Dorsai* and *The Dragon Knight*. Short stories: "Soldier, Ask Not," "Mutants," and "The Man Who Worlds Rejected."

Some people like my advice so much that they frame it upon a wall instead of using it.

1924 **Victoria de los Angeles:** Originally **Victoria López Cima.** Spanish lyric soprano. Born in Barcelona where she gave her first public concert in 1944 and made her operatic debut at the Liceo theatre the next year. Subsequently she performed at all the great houses throughout the world. Noted for her 19th century Italian roles and interpretations of Spanish songs. Her repertoire included Carmen, Dido, Puccini's heroines, Mozart roles and Elizabeth in *Tannhaüser*.

Even the common gypsy women have a pride and reserve. They stay faithful to one man at a time, no matter what. That is my Carmen.

1935 **Gary Player:** South African professional golfer. Dubbed the *Black Knight* for his habit of dressing mostly in black on the course. Won each of the Masters, U.S. Open, PGA and British Open twice. Along with Arnold Palmer and Jack Nicklaus, often referred to as one of the "Big Three" golfers of his era. In addition to his wins on the PGA tour (24), Player won more than 100 other tournaments. Also won 12 senior tournaments.

A good golfer has the determination to win and the patience to wait for the breaks.

1973 **Aishwarya Rai:** Indian model and actress. Miss World of 1994. Often called "The Most Beautiful Woman in the World." Appeared in her first film in 1997. Breakthrough performance came in 1999 in the film *Hum Dil De Chuke Sanam.* Her song "Kajra Re," from the movie *Bunty Aur Babli,* was voted the best song of 2005 in a poll in the *Hindustan Times.* Made her first foreign film appearance as the heroine in *Bride and Prejudice,* a Hollywood-funded Bollywood version of Jane Austen's *Pride and Prejudice.* Devout Hindu, Rai has been described as being "a paragon of age-old, dutiful Indian femininity."

Right now, I'm following the Buddhist principle: Smile as abuse is hurled your way and this too shall pass.

OTHERS: 1539 French lawyer/scholar **Pierre Pithou**, 1607 German poet **Georg Philipp Harsdorffer**, 1643 English historian **John Strype**, 1661 French dramatist **Florent Carton Dancourt**, 1704 German encyclopedist **Paul Daniel Longolius**, 1727 Founder of Moscow University **Ivan I. Shuvalov**, 1778 King of Sweden **Gustav IV**, 1877 British composer **Roger Quilter**, 1880 German meteorologist **Alfred Wegener**, 1902 German conductor **Eugen Jochum**, 1914 Hassidic rabbi **Moshe Teitelbaum**, 1927 German-born film director **Marcel Ophuls**, 1934 Swiss-born automobile executive **Umberto Agnelli**, 1935 Palestine-born literary critic **Edward Said**, 1942 U.S. magazine publisher **Larry Flynt**

November 2

1734 **Daniel Boone:** American frontiersman and explorer. Captured by Shawnee Indians and was adopted by their chief. Escaped to warn Boonesborough of an impending attack. Legendary hero who helped blaze a trail through the Cumberland Gap, a notch in the Appalachian Mountains near the juncture of Virginia, Tennessee and Kentucky. Greatly influenced the extension of the new nation westward.

I have never been lost, but I will admit to being confused for several weeks.

1755 **Marie Antoinette:** Austrian-born queen-consort of France's Louis XVI. Famed for her beauty. As bride of the dauphin of France, her youth and inexperience led to criticism of her extravagance and disregard for conventions. As queen she further earned the dislike of her subjects by her devotion to the interests of Austria and her opposition to measures devised to relieve the financial distress of the nation. Revolutionary forces seized her family and treated them as common criminals. Found guilty of treason, she was guillotined. Bore herself with dignity and resignation at her trial, telling the tribunal:

I was a queen, and you took away my crown; a wife and you killed my husband; a mother, and you deprived me of my children. My blood alone remains: take it, but do not make me suffer long.

1795 **James Knox Polk:** Tennessee lawyer, Democratic statesman and 11th President of the United States. Under his leadership, the U.S. fought the Mexican War and acquired vast territories along the Pacific coast, including the annexation of California, and Texas admitted to the Union.

Although ... the Chief Magistrate must almost of necessity be chosen by a party and stand pledged to its principles and measures, yet in his official action he should not be the President of a party only, but of the whole people of the United States.

1815 **George Boole:** English mathematician. Set the path for a great deal of current computing and information technological innovation, such as digital recordings, computer programming, electrical engineering, satellite pictures, telephone circuits, television, and the Internet. Wrote the first work on symbolic logic, *The Laws of Thought,* in which he explored the analogy between the symbols of algebra and those of logic as used to represent logical forms and syllogisms. His formalism became the basis of what is now known as Boolean algebra.

No matter how correct a mathematical theorem may appear to be, one ought never to be satisfied that there was not something imperfect about it until it also gives the impression of being beautiful.

1865 **Warren G. Harding:** Twenty-ninth U.S. president. Republican Senator from Ohio. Promised a "return to normalcy." However, seemed befuddled by the demands of his office and frequently admitted he didn't know what to do about certain national problems. His administration was plagued by scandal. Died suddenly while on a speaking tour in California, before the worst revelations of his administration's incompetence and corruption was made public. Prime candidate for the title of worst U.S. president ever.

I have no trouble with my enemies. I can take care of my enemies in a fight. But my friends, my goddamned friends, they're the ones who keep me walking the floors at nights!

1897 **Richard Russell:** American politician and lawyer. U.S. senator from Georgia. Leader of the powerful and solid Democratic Southern Bloc. Chairman of Senate Armed Forces Committee (1951–69). President pro tem of the Senate (1969–71).Denounced the civil rights bill in 1957 as "cunningly contrived, based on bayonet rule and designed to destroy the separate system for the races on which the social order of the Southern states is built."

If we have to start over with another Adam and Eve, I want them to be Americans.

1911 **Odysseus Elytis:** Greek poet born into a prosperous Cretan family. Published verse influenced by French Surrealism in the 1930s. Early poems reveal his love of the Greek landscape and the Aegean Sea. During World War II joined the antifascist resistance. One of his best-known poems is *The Axion Esti*. Later works include *The Sovereign Sun* and *The Little Mariner*. Nobel Prize for Literature in 1979.

You'll come to learn a great deal if you study the insignificant in depth.

1913 **Burt Lancaster:** American gymnast, acrobat and actor. A touring acrobat with various circuses for six years. Made his New York stage debut in *A Sound of Hunting*, which earned him his memorable film debut as "The Swede" in Ernest Hemingway's *The Killers*. Successful both in action roles and more sensitive parts. Oscar winner for *Elmer Gantry*. Nominated for *From Here to Eternity*, *Birdman of Alcatraz* and *Atlantic City*. Formed a production company with agent Harold Hecht and producer James Hill.

This idea that to do any worthwhile work you've got to lead a turbulent emotional life is all nonsense. I have a very balanced life. To portray an unbalanced character on the screen, you don't have to be unbalanced. I only have to observe some of my friends.

1938 **Patrick Buchanan:** Conservative American syndicated political columnist, writer, television commentator and politician. Twice unsuccessfully sought the Republican nomination for president and in 2000 ran for the presidency as the Reform Party candidate. His platform included protectionist trade policies, immigration reduction, and opposition to multiculturalism, abortion and gay rights. White House advisor and speechwriter when Nixon took office. Returned to the White House in 1985 as White House Communications Director for the Ronald Reagan administration.

Our culture is superior because our religion is Christianity and that is the truth that makes men free.

1942 **Shere D. Hite:** Originally **Shirley Diana Gregory**. American researcher and writer on cultural research in human sexuality. In 1976, she published *The Hite Report*. A Nationwide Study of Female Sexuality, based upon five years of research. Followed in 1981 by *The Hite Report on Male Sexuality*, *The Hite Report of Women* and *The Hite Report on the Family*. Research methods criticized for allegedly not using random samples for her questionnaires.

Every family is a "normal" family — no matter whether it has one parent, two or no children at all. A family can be made up of any combination of people, heterosexual or homosexual, who share their lives in an intimate (not necessarily sexual) way.... Whenever there is lasting love, there is a family.

1946 **Giuseppe Sinopoli:** Distinguished Italian conductor and composer. Earned a degree in psychiatry while concurrently studied composition privately with Franco Donatoni in Paris. His medical training led him to probe deeply into the scores he conducted, often resulting in startlingly revealing but controversial interpretations. As a composer he pursues contemporary modes of expression. Appeared as guest conductor and principal conductor throughout the world.

The conductor must make it possible to eliminate himself in the music. If the orchestra feels him doing that, then everything will go well.

1961 **k.d. lang (kathy dawn):** Canadian singer and songwriter. Does not use capital letters in her name as a tribute to poet e.e. cummings. Won her first of four Grammy Awards for Best Female Country Vocal Performance for her 1989 album, *Absolute Torch and Twang*. Other albums: *Angel with a Lariat*, *Shadowland*, *Even Cowgirls Get the Blues*, and *Ingénue*, which contained her most popular song, "Constant Craving." Champions lesbian causes and animal rights.

Look. Art knows no prejudices, art knows no boundaries, art doesn't really have judgment in its purest form. So just go, just go.

OTHERS: 1699 French painter **Jean-Baptiste-Siméon Chardin**, 1739 Austrian composer **Carl Ditters von Dittersdorf**, 1808 French writer **Jules Barbey d'Aurevilly**, 1844 Ottoman Sultan **Mehmed V**, 1877 Shia Imam **Aga Khan III**, 1885 U.S. astronomer **Harlow Shapley**, 1894 German scientist **Alexander Lippisch**, 1897 U.S. mobster **Vito Genovese**, 1906 Russian poet **Daniil Andreev**, 1927 U.S. artist **Steve Ditko**, 1929 President of Pakistan **Muhammad Rafiq Tarar**, 1929 U.S. physicist **Richard E. Taylor**, 1934 Australian tennis star **Ken Rosewall**, 1936 California Judge **Rose Bird**, 1960 Croatian war criminal **Tihomir Blaskic**, 1974 U.S. rap artist **Nelly**, 1982 Japanese actress/singer **Kyoko Fukada**

November 3

39 CE **Lucan: Marcus Annaeus Lucanus.** Latin poet and prose writer, born in Cordova, Spain. Nephew of the philosopher Seneca the Younger. His only extant work *Pharsalia*, an epic in ten books, concentrates on the civil war between Julius Caesar and Pompey. An aristocrat and a rebel, he regretted the loss of the Republic and despised the reigns of the Caesars. Joined a conspiracy against Nero, betrayed, and ordered to commit suicide at age twenty-five.

We all praise fidelity; but the true friend pays the penalty when he supports those whom Fortune crushes.

1793 **Stephen F. Austin:** Anglo-American colonizer of Texas. Brought the first 300 families, known in Texas history as the "Old Three Hundred" to the region of the city and county now named for him. After the defeat of Santa Anna in 1836, The Republic of Texas was created. Austin ran for president of Texas, but was defeated by Sam Houston. Hearing of Austin's death that same year, Houston remarked: "The Father of Texas is no more." Austin's last words:

The independence of Texas is recognized! Don't you see it in the papers?

1794 **William Cullen Bryant:** American poet, editor and lawyer. Influential newspaper editors of the mid-nineteenth century, first distinctively American poet and leading abolitionist. Saw John Brown as a martyr to the cause. Although a leading Democrat he supported Abraham Lincoln, encouraged liberal causes and espoused a less severe religion. Poems: "Thanatopsis," "To a Waterfowl" and "The Yellow Violet." Translated the *Iliad* and the *Odyssey.*

Poetry is that art which selects and arranges the symbols of thought in such a manner as to excite the imagination the most powerfully and delightfully.

1831 **Ignatius Donnelly:** American writer, lawyer and politician. Enthusiasms focused on the theme that hidden meanings exist beyond the obvious level of everyday phenomena. Known by his political opponents as "The Prince of Cranks" and by his admirers as the "Sage of Nininger," for his establishment of the mini-utopia in Nininger City, Minnesota. Served in the U.S. Congress (1863–69). Supported women's suffrage and anti-slavery movements. In *Atlantis: The Antediluvian World* he sought to prove the existence of the lost continent in the Atlantic, however, his theories were short on facts.

The only politics worth studying is the amelioration of the condition of the great mass of mankind.

1879 **Vilhjalmur Stefansson:** Canadian explorer and ethnologist of Icelandic descent. Lived among the Eskimos (1906–12). Led the Canadian expedition that explored vast areas of Canadian Arctic and mapped the Beauport Sea (1913–18). Discovered new lands in the Arctic Archipelago. Books: *My Life with the Eskimo* and *The Friendly Artic.*

The philosophers of the Middle Ages demonstrated both that the Earth did not exist and that it was flat. Today they are still arguing whether the world exists, but they no longer dispute about whether it is flat.

1895 Grand Duchess **Olga of Russia (Olga Nikolaevna Romanova):** Oldest daughter of Nicholas II of Russia and Alexandra of Hesse. Although known for her compassionate heart and desire to help others, she also had a temper and could be bluntly honest. During World War I, served as a nurse, but her duty ended when she had a nervous breakdown. Only 22 when she and her family were executed by the Bolshevik secret police after a year of imprisonment following the February/March Revolutions of 1917.

Remember that the evil which is now in the world will only get more powerful, and that it is not evil which conquers evil, but only love.

1901 **André Malraux:** French archaeologist, art critic, soldier, historian, novelist, statesman and revolutionary. Participated in two rightist-oriented de Gaulle governments. *Man's Fate*, based on the Chinese Revolution, has been called "one of the profound revolutionary documents of our times." Other works: *The Conquerors, The Royal Way, Days of Wrath* and *Man's Hope* (based on the Spanish Civil War). *The Voices of Silence* is his huge spiritual history of art.

The great mystery is not that we should have been thrown down here at random between the profusion of matter and that of the stars; it is that from our very prison we should draw, from our own selves, images powerful enough to deny our nothingness.

1909 **James "Scotty" Reston:** Scottish-born American journalist, editor and author. Called a "reporters' reporter." Wrote syndicated column "Washington" for the *New York Times.* Among his major scoops were the Yalta Papers, the Oppenheimer case, the Eisenhower doctrine and the last public words of Stalin. Helped formulate the Robert A. Taft Senate speech, which turned the Republican policy away from isolationism. Books: *Sketches in Sand* and *Prelude to Victory.*

In any war, the first casualty is common sense, and the second is free and open discussion.

1918 **Russell Long:** American politician and lawyer. Son of Huey P. Long. U.S. Democratic senator from Louisiana (1951–86). Longtime Senate finance committee chairman. In 1959 he figured in the effort to have his uncle, Earl Long, committed to a mental institution after the Governor's uncontrollable outbursts in the Louisiana Senate.

A tax loophole is something that benefits the other guy. If it benefits you, it is tax reform. Tax reform means, "Don't tax you, don't tax me. Tax that fellow behind the tree."

1949 **Larry Holmes:** American boxer. Nicknamed "The Easton Assassin" for the Pennsylvania town where he lived. Considered one of the best fighters in the history of heavyweight boxing. Won his first 48 professional challenge fights. Won 69 fights, 44 by knockouts. WBC heavyweight boxing champion (1978–83) and IBF heavyweight boxing champion (1983–85). Successfully defended his WBC title 17 times and the IBF title 3 times.

All fighters are prostitutes and all promoters are pimps.

1952 **Roseanne:** Born **Roseanne Cherrie Barr.** American comedian, actress, writer and talk-show host. Began her career as a stand-up comedian, in which she represented herself as the typical American middle-class housewife, or "domestic goddess" as she called homemakers. Her ABC TV series, *Roseanne*, ran from 1988 to 1997, after which she hosted her talk show, *The Roseanne Show*, which ran for two years. Returned to stand-up comedy.

The thing women have yet to learn is nobody gives you power. You just take it.

1953 **Dennis Miller:** American comedian, political and social commentator, TV personality and actor. His monologues and standup routines often feature similes and metaphors involving obscure allusions to little-known people, places and things. Launched a late night syndicated talk show, *The Dennis Miller Show*. Later hosted *Dennis Miller Live* on which he interviewed just one guest with whom he discussed the day's topic. Books: *The Rants, Ranting Again, I Rant, Therefore I Am*, and *The Rant Zone*.

You know there is a problem with the education system when you realize that out of the 3 R's only one begins with an R.

OTHERS: 1618 Mughal Emperor of India **Aurangzeb**, 1718 English statesman **John Montagu, 4th Earl of Sandwich**, 1801 German publisher **Karl Baedeker**, 1801 Italian composer **Vincenzo Bellini**, 1845 U.S. Chief Justice **Edward Douglass White**, 1893 U.S. biochemist **Edward A. Doisy**, 1901 King of Belgium **Leopold III**, 1903 U.S. photographer **Walker Evans**, 1908 U.S. football player **Bronko Nagurski**, 1918 U.S. baseball pitcher **Bob Feller**, 1920 Australian writer **Oodgeroo Noonuccal**, 1921 U.S. actor **Charles Bronson**, 1933 British actor **Jeremy Brett**, 1933 U.S. presidential candidate **Michael Dukakis**, 1933 Indian economist **Amartya Sen**, 1948 British singer **Lulu**, 1950 U.S. writer **Joe Queenan**

November 4

1740 **Augustus Montague Toplady:** Anglican divine. Originally a follower of John Wesley, he later adopted extreme Calvinist views. Chiefly known as the writer of hymns and poems, including "Rock of Ages" and the collections *Poems on Sacred Subjects* and *Psalms and Hymns for Public and Private Worship*. Best-known prose work: *Historic Proof of the Doctrinal Calvinism of the Church of England*.

Rock of ages, cleft for me,/ Let me hide myself in Thee!/ Let the Water and the Blood/ From thy riven Side which flow'd, /Be of sin the double cure; /Cleanse me from its guilt and pow'r.

1771 **James Montgomery:** British hymnologist, poet and journalist. Wrote 23 books of verse and 400 hymns, with approximately 100 still in use: "Hail to the Lord's Anointed," Angels from the Realm of Glory," and "For Ever with the Lord." Also wrote secular poetry, notably, his collection *The Wanderer of Switzerland*, and lectured at the Royal Institution. Edited the *Sheffield Iris* for 32 years, and then founded *The Electric Review*.

Friend after friend departs; who hath not lost a friend?/ There is no union here at hearts that hath not here its end.

1873 **George E. Moore:** English philosopher. One of the fathers of analytic philosophy. *Principia Ethica* (1903) had a marked influence on contemporary intellectuals and writers. With colleagues Bertrand Russell, Alfred North Whitehead and young Ludwig Wittgenstein, he worked on problems of linguistic analysis and epistemology. Works: *Ethics, Philosophical Studies*, and *Some Main Problems of Philosophy*.

A man travels the world in search of what he needs and returns home to find it.

1879 **Will Rogers:** American actor, wit and folk hero. Popular entertainer and homespun philosopher. His shrewd comment upon men and affairs made his name a household word throughout America. Starred with the Ziegfeld Follies and in films: *A Connecticut Yankee, State Fair, David Harum* and *Judge Priest*. Died in a plane crash with Wiley Post near Point Barrow, Alaska.

Democrats never agree on anything, that's why they're Democrats. If they agreed with each other, they would be Republicans.

1906 **Bob Considine:** American journalist and author. Wrote syndicated column "On the Line" for 40 years, starting in 1937. Started as a sportswriter, replacing Damon Runyon in the Hearst organization. Once turned out 20,000 words at one sitting on *General Wainwright's Story*. Other books: *Innocents at Home, Man Against Fire* and *The Babe Ruth Story*.

Call it vanity, call it arrogant presumption, call it what you wish, but I would grope for the nearest open grave if I had no newspaper to work for, no need to search for and sometime find the winged word that just fits, no keen wonder over what each unfolding day many bring.

1912 **Pauline Trigere:** French-born American high fashion designer. Had a feeling for classic American look. Designer, model and symbol of the American fashion industry for more than half a century. Wore only her designs, generally punctuated with her trademark turtle pins. In 1961, she was the first name designer to use an African-American model. Won three Coty American Fashion Critics' Awards.

Fashion is what people tell you to wear. Style is what comes from your own inner thing.

1916 **Walter Cronkite:** American newspaperman, wire correspondent and broadcast journalist. Landed beside the first troops in Normandy on D-Day. United Press correspondent in Moscow (1946–48). Joined CBS in 1950. Narrator for *Air Power* and the long-running Peabody award winner *You Are There*. Also narrated *Twentieth Century*, a dramatization of events in recent history. CBS news anchor from 1962 to 1981. Described as "the most trusted man in America." His sign-off phrase: "And that's the way it is..."

In seeking truth you have to get both sides of a story.

1918 **Art Carney:** American actor. Best known as New York City sewer worker Ed Norton on television's "The Honeymooners." Because of his imitating ability, he frequently substituted for Franklin D. Roosevelt in his famous "Fireside Chats" when the president was too ill to speak. Originated the role of Felix Ungar opposite Walter Matthau as Oscar Madison in Neil Simon's *The Odd Couple* (1965). Won an Oscar at age 55 for portraying a 72-year-old man in *Harry and Tonto*.

I don't tell jokes, and if I tried, I couldn't hold an audience's attention for five minutes. I never

think of myself as a comedian. I do acting jobs in comedy situations.

1923 **Alfred "Freddie" Heineken:** Dutch brewer, who after World War II built the family business, founded by his grandfather in 1864, and the company's Heineken beer into an international success. Designed the familiar green bottle and the logo bearing the brand name. Richest man in the Netherlands with an estimated fortune of more than $3.6 billion. In 1983, kidnapped for three weeks before being released unharmed. Financed a film on the condition his mistress would star, but when she dumped him, he put the movie on the shelf for more than thirty years.

I consider a bad bottle of Heineken a personal insult.

1946 **Laura Bush:** Originally **Laura Lane Welch**. American First Lady. Wife of George W. Bush. After college, she taught in elementary schools and worked as a librarian in both the Houston and Austin school systems. Married George W. Bush on November 5, 1977. Much more of a traditional president's wife than her predecessor, she confines herself to championing education causes, women's health issues and patriotism in American schools.

I said "George, if you want to end world tyranny, you have to stay up later." Nine o'clock and Mr. Excitement here is in bed, leaving me to watch "Desperate Housewives" with Lynne Cheney. Ladies and gentlemen, I am a desperate housewife.

1946 **Robert Mapplethorpe:** Controversial American photographer whose pictures meant to show gay sexuality as beautiful shocked and offended many in and out of the art world. His most common themes were flowers, portraits of famous people, nude works that included homoerotic imagery and explicit content spanning classic nude forms to acts of S & M. Work regularly displayed at publicly-funded exhibitions and their content outraged many conservative and religious groups who opposed supporting his kind of art, especially funds from the National Endowment for the Arts. Died of complications of AIDS at 42.

I'm looking for the unexpected. I'm looking for things I've never seen before.

1969 **Sean Combs:** aka **P. Diddy**, **Puff Daddy**, **Puffy** and **Diddy**. American record producer, entertainment mogul and rap artist. Founder and CEO of *Bad Boy*, one of the driving forces in moving hip hop music into the mainstream. Developed acts: Father MC, Mary J. Bilge, Notorious B.I.G., Boyz N Da Hood, and Carl Thomas. His songs: "Shake Ya Tailfeather," "Bad Boy for Life," and "I'll Be Missing You."

It's okay to be crazy, but don't be insane.

OTHERS: 1575 Italian painter **Guido Reni**, 1845 Indian revolutionary **Vasudeo Balwant Phadke**, 1862 English novelist **Eden Phillpotts**, 1865 U.S. scientist/surgeon **Chevalier Jackson**, 1876 U.S. sculptor **James Fraser**, 1908 Polish physicist **Józef Rotblat**, 1909 Peruvian novelist **Ciro Alegria**, 1912 Russian composer **Vadim Salmanov**, 1913 U.S. actor **Gig Young**, 1929 U.S. actress **Doris Roberts**, 1932 Austrian President **Thomas Klestil**, 1937 U.S. M*A*S*H actress **Loretta Swit**, 1937 Canadian politician **Michael Wilson**, 1944 U.S. knuckleball pitcher **Joe Niekro**, 1951 Romanian President **Traian Bāescu**, 1955 Finnish Prime Minister **Matti Vanhanen**

November 5

1549 **Philippe de Mornay:** French Huguenot apologist with the work *Dissertation sur l'église visible* and as a diplomat the next year when he undertook a confidential mission for Admiral de Coligny to William the Silent, prince of Orange. After escaping the St. Bartholomew's Day Massacre with the aid of a Catholic friend, de Mornay took refuge in England. He returned to France and became a close advisor of Henry, King of Navarre, until the latter abjured his Protestantism to become King of France. His last words:

Die to live, live to die.

1613 **Isaac de Benserade:** French poet. Began his literary career with the tragedy *Cléopâtre* (1635). Received a pension from Richelieu, which ceased when the cardinal died. Became a favorite at court, writing ballets. He is most remembered for his sonnet *Job*. Placed in competition with *Urania* of Voiture, leading to a dispute on their relative merits that divided the whole count into two parties, the Jobelins and the Uranists.

In bed we laugh, in bed we cry;/ and born in bed, in bed we die;/ the near approach a bed may show, of human bliss to human woe.

1850 **Ella Wheeler Wilcox:** American poet. Completed a novel before she was ten and later wrote at least two poems a day. Wrote nearly 40 volumes of sentimental poetry. Books of Verse: *Drops of Water*, *Shells*, *Maurine* and *Poems of Passion*. Her best known poem, "Solitude" contains the line:

Laugh, and the world laughs with you;/ Weep, and you weep alone;/ For the sad old earth must borrow its mirth,/ But has trouble enough of its own.

1855 **Eugene V. Debs:** American socialist leader and labor organizer. First president of the American Railway Union. In 1884 he led a successful national strike for better wages. Helped establish the Socialist Party of America. Socialist Party presidential candidate five times between 1900 and 1920. His pacifism caused him to be imprisoned from 1918 to 1921. Author of *Walls and Bars*.

Intelligent discontent is the mainspring of civilization. Progress is born of agitation. It is agitation or stagnation.

1857 **Ida Minerva Tarbell:** Pioneer American muckraker journalist, writer and editor. Books: the two-volume *The History of the Standard Oil Company*, *The Business of Being a Woman*, *The Ways of Women* and *In the Footsteps of Lincoln*. Her exposé of John D. Rockefeller and his interests resulted in federal action and eventually in the breakup of the Standard Oil Company of New Jersey under the 1911 Sherman Anti-Trust Act.

Imagination is the only key to the future. Without it none exists — with it all things are possible.

1885 **Will Durant:** American lecturer and writer. Author of *The Story of Philosophy*, the ten-volume *The Story of Civilization*, the last four written in conjunction with his wife Ariel, and *The Lessons of History*. Found fault with the usual practice of writing history in separate longitudinal sections, which "does injustice to the unity of human life." Goal for his massive history was "to portray in each period the total complex of a nation's institutions, adventures and ways."

Education is a progressive discovery of our own ignorance.

1892 **J.B.S. [John Burdon Sanderson] Haldane:** English-Indian physiologist and geneticist. Conducted basic studies of sex-linkage in chromosomes and of mutation rate. Showed that enzyme reactions obey laws of thermodynamics. Intent upon bringing talents of one field of work in solving problems in quite a different area. Together with his students at Oxford, his work on deep sea diving and mountain ascents laid the basis for modern respiration physiology. Author of *Science and Ethics* and *Biochemistry of Genetics*.

It is my supposition that the Universe is not only queerer than we imagine, is queerer than we can imagine.

1911 **Roy Rogers:** Born **Leonard Slye** in Cincinnati, Ohio. American actor and singer. Appeared with his second wife, actress, singer and writer Dale Evans in motion pictures, radio, TV, rodeos, and stage appearances. His numerous recordings of old Western tunes resulted in his being known as the "King of the Cowboys." His tag-line: "Until we meet again, may the good Lord take a liking to you."

When my time comes, just skin me and put me up there on Trigger, just as nothing had ever changed.

1913 **Vivien Leigh:** Originally **Vivian Mary Harley**. Indian-born English actress. Once married to Laurence Olivier. Academy Awards for *Gone with the Wind* and *A Streetcar Named Desire*. Other films: *Waterloo Bridge*, *The Roman Spring of Mrs. Stone* and *Ship of Fools*. Allegedly David O. Selznick was burning his Atlanta set when her first met Leigh and knew at once as her delicate features were outlined by the flames that he had found his Scarlett O'Hara. Plagued with TB and physical exhaustion throughout her arduous career the disease took her life in 1967.

It is much easier to make people cry than to make them laugh.

1934 **Jeb Stuart Magruder:** American government official. As Deputy Director of the Committee to Re-elect the President was involved in the Watergate scandal. Cooperated with federal prosecutors. Allowed to plead guilty to a one-count indictment of conspiracy to obstruct justice, defraud the U.S., and eavesdrop on the Democratic national headquarters. Served seven months in prison. Wrote *An American Life: One Man's Life to Watergate*.

I know what I have done, and Your Honor knows what I have done. Somewhere between my ambition and my ideals, I lost my ethical compass.

1943 **Sam Shepard:** Born **Samuel Shepard Rogers IV**. American playwright, writer and actor. His play *Buried Child* received a 1979 Pulitzer Prize. Other plays: *Curse of the Starving Class*, *True West*, *A Lie of the Mind* and *The Gate of Hell*. As an actor: *Renaldo and Clara*, *Days of Heaven*, *Frances*, *The Right Stuff* and *The Pelican Brief*.

We've been sold a brand-new idea of patriotism. It never occurred to me that patriotism had to be advertised. Patriotism is something you deeply felt. You didn't have to wear it on your lapel or show it in your window or on a bumper sticker. That kind of patriotism doesn't appeal to me at all.

1952 **Bill Walton:** American basketball player and sports commentator. Center for John Wooden's UCLA team for three seasons. Member of two NCAA championship teams, which compiled an NCAA record 88 consecutive game winning streak. Three-time NCAA Player of the Year and winner of the Sullivan Award for the Best Amateur Athlete (1973). Drafted by the NBA's Portland Trailblazers. Member of their 1977 championship team. Nine years later earned a second championship ring with Boston Celtics.

No matter how good you get, there's always something further out there.

OTHERS: 1271 Persian ruler **Mahmud Ghazan**, 1667 German painter **Ludwig Agricola**, 1701 Venetian painter **Pietro Longhi**, 1854 French chemist **Paul Sabatier**, 1884 English poet **James E. Flecker**, 1890 Czech painter **Jan Zrzavý**, 1891 U.S. football coach **Greasy Neale**, 1900 U.S. politician **Martin Dies, Jr.**, 1905 U.S. actor **Joel McCrea**, 1906 U.S. astronomer **Fred Lawrence Whipple**, 1919 U.S. accordionist **Myron Floren**, 1920 U.S. economist **Douglass North**, 1921 Hungarian pianist **Georges Cziffra**, 1941 U.S. singer/actor **Art Garfunkel**, 1947 English singer **Peter Noone**, 1963 U.S. actress **Tatum O'Neal**, 1973 U.S. baseball player **Johnny Damon**

November 6

1494 **Suleiman the Magnificent:** Longest serving Sultan of the Ottoman Empire (1520–66). Known in the Islamic World as the Lawgiver, stemming from his complete reconstruction of the Ottoman legal system. Under his leadership, the Ottoman Empire reached its zenith. Personally led his armies to conquer Belgrade, Rhodes and most of Hungry, besieged Vienna, and annexed vast territories in North Africa and the Middle East. Fair ruler, although he had two of his sons strangled in order to avoid a succession battle. Opposed corruption and was a patron of artists and philosophers.

Noted as one of the greatest Islamic poets and an accomplished goldsmith. Described himself as:

Slave of God, master of the world, I am Suleiman and my name is read in all the prayers in all the cities of Islam. I am the Shah of Bagdad and Iraq, Caesar of all the lands of Rome, and the Sultan of Egypt. I seized the Hungarian crown and gave it to the least of my slaves.

1558 **Thomas Kyd:** English dramatist and scrivener. Author of the most popular drama of his day, *The Spanish Tragedy*, published anonymously in 1592. Early example of revenge tragedy, very popular on the Elizabethan stage. Only work published under his name was a translation of Robert Garnier's *Cornelia.* Credited with a share in several plays, including *The Tragedy of Solyman and Perseda* and a lost pre–Shakespearean version of *Hamlet.*

Evil news fly faster still than good.

1671 **Colley Cibber:** English actor, theater manager and playwright. Excelled at comic roles and won recognition as a dramatist with his comedy, *Love's Last Shift* (1696). Joint manager of Drury Lane, where he spent most of his career. Appointment as English Poet Laureate was ridiculed leading him to write *Apology for the Life of Mr. Colley Cibber, Comedian* (1740).

Oh! How many torments lie in the small circle of a wedding ring.

1854 **John Philip Sousa:** "The March King." American bandmaster and composer. Among his 140 marches are: "Stars and Stripes Forever," "El Capitan," "Semper Fidelis" and "The Washington Post." Led U.S. Marine Band (1880–92). Afterward directed his own band, which gained international fame. The sousaphone, a sort of tuba, which projects the sound forward rather than sideways, was named in his honor.

Composers are the only people who can hear good music above bad sounds.

1860 **Ignacy Jan Paderewski:** Polish pianist, composer and statesman. One of the most famous international pianists of his time and also received acclaim for his compositions Repeatedly on tour in the United States, he was known and loved not only for his musical genius but also for championing Polish freedom. First Prime Minister of an independent Poland, but resigned after only ten months in office and resumed his musical career. In 1939 briefly served as President of the Polish government in Paris. Emigrated to the U.S. when France surrendered to Germany in 1940.

Piano playing is more difficult than statesmanship. It is harder to wake emotions in ivory keys than it is in human beings.

1861 **James Naismith:** Canadian-American educator and physical education instructor. At the YMCA Training School (now Springfield College) in Massachusetts, was asked to devise a new indoor winter sport. Completed the assignment by inventing the game of basketball, which at the time consisted of two teams of nine players each who attempted to throw a ball into one of two peach baskets. Later coached basketball at the University of Kansas (1898–1937) and is also credited with inventing the protective helmet used by football players.

The appeal of basketball is that it is an easy game to play, but difficult to master.

1870 Lord **Herbert Samuel:** English statesman, philosopher, social legislator, administrator and Liberal Party leader (1931–35). Social worker in the London slums before entering the House of Commons. Effected legislation that established juvenile courts and the Borstal system for youthful offenders. As Postmaster General he nationalized the telephone system. First British high commissioner for Palestine (1920–25). Philosophical works: *Practical Ethics* and *Belief in Action.*

The virtue of some people consists wholly in condemning the vices in others.

1880 **Robert Musil:** Austrian-German novelist. The long novel *The Man Without Qualities* is considered one of the most important modernist novels. Set in Vienna on the eve of World War I, it deals with the moral and intellectual decline of the Austro-Hungarian Empire as seen through the eyes of the books protagonist an ex-mathematician who has failed to engage with the world around him. Other works: *The Confusions of Young Torless* and *Five Women.*

Progress would be wonderful — if only it would stop.

1887 **Walter Johnson:** American baseball pitcher. Nicknamed "Big Train" for his overpowering and effective fastball. Holds the record for most career shutouts (110) and ranks second to Cy Young in wins (416). Held the record for strikeouts (3508) until his record was broken in 1983 by Nolan Ryan. Played for the Washington Senators (1907–27), and subsequently became a baseball manager.

I throw as hard as I can when I think I have to throw as hard as I can.

1892 **Harold Ross:** American editor. Coeditor of *Stars and Stripes* (1917–19); editor of *The American Legion Weekly* (1919–24); and *Judge* (1925). Founded *The New Yorker* magazine, editor from 1925 to his death in 1951. Envisioned his creation as a smart and sophisticated periodical, promising, "*The New Yorker* will be the magazine which is not edited for the old lady in Dubuque." It soon attracted established writers and artists as well as new young talent drawn by its innovative style and Ross' encouragement.

Editing is the same as quarrelling with writers — same thing exactly.

1921 **James Jones:** American novelist, who wrote realistically of American Army life. Best-selling *From Here to Eternity* (National Book Award) astonished reviewers and readers with its ungrammatical prose, length of 861 pages, sexual content and unhappy ending. Many critics called it the most illiterate book of the year and Clifton Fadiman dubbed Jones "President of the Unedited Generation." However it sold four million copies. Followed by *Some Came Running*, which ran some 400 pages longer, but was just as steamy. To prove he could play the literary game he wrote *The Pistol*, consisting of 158 pages, impeccable grammar and without emphatic sex. Had another success with *The Thin Red Line.*

In spite of all the training you get and the precautions you take to keep yourself alive, it's largely a matter of luck that decides whether or not you get killed.

1931 **Mike Nichols:** Originally **Michael Igor Peschkowsky**. German-born American actor and stage and film producer and director. Teamed with Elaine May in a sophisticated Broadway revue of brilliant social-satire routines. Oscar winner for directing *The Graduate*. Others: *Who's Afraid of Virginia Woolf? Carnal Knowledge*, *Silkwood*, *Working Girl*, *The Birdcage*, and *Closer*. Directed the TV mini series "Angels in America." One of the few people to have an Emmy, Grammy, Oscar and a Tony Award. Recipient of Kennedy Center Honors in 2003.

Being with an insanely jealous person is like being in the room with a dead mammoth.

OTHERS: 1391 English politician **Edmund de Mortimer**, 1510 English physician **John Carius**, 1661 King of Spain **Charles II**, 1692 French poet **Louis Racine**, 1753 Russian sculptor **Mikhail Kozolvsky**, 1814 Belgian inventor of the saxophone **Adolphe Sax**, 1833 Norwegian author **Jonas Lie**, 1851 U.S. journalist/economist **Charles Dow**, 1893 President of Ford Motor Co. **Edsel Ford**, 1896 Radio comedian Fibber McGee **Jim Jordan**, 1916 U.S. composer/ conductor **Ray Conniff**, 1939 U.S. civil rights activist **Michael Schwerner**, 1946 U.S. Oscar-winning actress **Sally Field**, 1949 Cuban-born trumpeter **Arturo Sandoval**, 1955 U.S. journalist **Maria Shriver**, 1971 Zambian actress **Thandie Newton**, 1976 U.S. football player/ Army hero **Pat Tillman**

November 7

994 **Muhammad ibn Hazam:** Spanish-born Islamic scholar and theologian. Imprisoned for supporting the Umayyad caliphate in the Spanish civil war. Taught that legal theory must rely on a literal interpretation of the Qur'an and tradition. His beliefs were often attacked and his books publicly burned. Famed for his mastery of Arabic, he wrote about 400 books not only on law and theology, but logic, literature and history as well. Only about 40 of the books survive.

No one is moved to act or resolves to speak a single word, who does not hope by means of action or word to release anxiety from his spirit.

1832 **Andrew Dickinson White:** American diplomat, historian, and educator. Co-founder and first president of Cornell University. With Daniel Coit Gilman, first president of Johns Hopkins University, and Charles W. Eliot, president of Harvard (1869–1909), one of the "chief builders of the modern American university. Co-founder and first president of the American Historical Association.

The greatest and most ennobling, perhaps, of scientific truths ... was forced, in coming before the world, to sneak and crawl.

1867 Madame **Marie Sklodowska Curie:** Celebrated Polish-French chemist and physicist. Co-discovered with her husband Pierre of a new element, which they named polonium in honor of her native country. The same year they announced the discovery of radium. Coined word radioactive. In 1903 she presented her doctoral thesis, the first advanced scientific degree to be awarded to a woman in France. The same year she and Pierre shared the Nobel prize. He was killed in an accident in 1906. Madame Curie continued her work with radioactivity and in 1911 received the Nobel Prize for Chemistry, becoming the only individual to appear twice on the list of Nobel laureates. First woman member of French Academy of Medicine.

Nothing in life is to be feared, it is only to be understood. Now is the time to understand more, so that we may fear less.

1879 **Leon Trotsky:** Born **Lev Davidovich Bronstein.** Russian Communist theorist and agitator. Joined the Bolsheviks in 1917. Helped organize Russia's 1917 October Revolution with Lenin. Built up the Red Army that ultimately defeated the White Russian forces in the Civil War. After Lenin's death, Trotsky alienated Josef Stalin and others with his views that socialism within the Soviet Union could not come about until revolution had occurred in Western Europe and worldwide. Trotsky lost in a power struggle with Stalin, was expelled from the party and exiled in 1929. He settled in Mexico in 1937, where three years later he was murdered with an axe by a Stalinist assassin.

The end may justify the means as long as there is something that justifies the end.

1897 **Herman J. Mankiewicz:** American screenwriter, director and producer. Many of his contributions as a writer and producer of early sound films went uncredited. His supreme achievement was the screenplay for Citizen Kane for which he shared an Academy Award with Orson Welles. Shared another Oscar for *Pride of the Yankees*. Had many problems with gambling and drinking as well as feuds with studio executives. Contributed to the screenplays for *Dinner at Eight*, *Christmas Holiday* and *The Enchanted Cottage*.

I know a lot of $75-a-week writers [in Hollywood], but they're all making $1500 a week.

1903 **Konrad Z. Lorenz:** Austro-German zoologist and founder of the science of ethology — the study of animal behavior in a natural environment. Believed that it was important to learn about animals in nature rather than in laboratories. Proposed that all animal behavior is explicable in terms of adaptive evolution. Caused considerable controversy when he applied the same theories to human beings. Shared the 1973 Nobel Prize.

I believe I've found the missing link between animal and civilized man. It is us.

1913 **Albert Camus:** Algerian-born French philosopher, novelist, dramatist and journalist. A close associate of Jean-Paul Sartre and his circle. An intellectual leader of the French Resistance in World War II. Called the "conscience of the younger European generation." Author of: *The Stranger*, in which a man commits a casual and meaningless murder, *The Plague*, in which a modern city is laid waste by pestilence, and *The Fall*, in which a girl drowns herself while the man who loves her watches and does nothing. Nobel Prize for Literature (1957).

Every revolutionary ends up as an oppressor or a heretic.... Revolt and revolution both wind up at the same crossroads: with police or folly.

1918 **Billy Graham:** Originally **William Franklin Graham, Jr.** American evangelist. Attended Bob Jones College and the Florida Bible Institute. Ordained a Southern Baptist clergyman in 1939. Won many converts with tent revivals and radio broadcasts. One of the first evangelists to utilize television in his crusades. Established the series "Hour of Decision" in 1951. By this time he was established as fundamentalism's leading spokesman. Became a spiritual advisor to a series of U.S. presidents.

The framers of our Constitution meant we were to have freedom of religion, not freedom from religion.

1922 **Al Hirt:** New Orleans virtuoso trumpeter and bandleader. Nicknamed "He's the King!" and "The Round Mound of Sound." Studied classical trumpet at the Cincinnati Conservatory before entering the U.S. Army, where he was a bugler and played with the 82nd Army Air Force Band. After the war he performed with various swing bands. Returned to New Orleans to work with various Dixieland groups and his own bands. Recorded more than 50 albums. Chosen the World's Top Trumpeter twelve times by *Playboy* magazine. Hit singles include "Cotton Candy" and "Java."

A little bit of this, a little bit of that. I never had any specific style.

1926 Dame **Joan Sutherland:** Australian opera singer. One of the world's leading coloratura sopranos in the 1960s and 1970s. Made her début as Dido in Henry Purcell's *Dido and Aeneas* in Sydney. Joined the Royal Opera in London in 1952, remaining as resident soprano for seven years. Married her accompanist and coach Richard Bonygne, who became her principal conductor. Gained international fame with her roles in Donizetti's *Lucia de Lammermoor* and Handel's *Samson*. Retired in 1990.

You don't only just use your voice, you use support from the lungs and diaphragm and everything gets old, whether you like it or not.

1943 **Joni Mitchell:** Born **Roberta Joan Anderson**. Canadian-born singer, songwriter, guitarist and pianist. Wrote highly original and personal songs, featuring beautiful lyrical imagery. First gained attention among folk song audiences. Albums: *Song to a Seagull, Colors, Ladies of the Canyon, The Hissing of Summer Lawns* and *Turbulent Indigo*. Hit songs: "Both Sides Now," "Woodstock" and her biggest hit: "Help Me."

Moons and Junes and Ferris wheels/ The dizzy dancing way you feel/ As every fairy tale comes real/ I've looked at love that way.

1956 **Judy Tenuta:** American stand-up comedian and actress. Describes herself as a "multi-media Bondage Goddess" and "the Aphrodite of the Accordion." Verbally abuses countless herds of mortal swine (that is her audiences) and converts them to her religion "Judyism." Preaches that all women should be worshipped as "Love Goddesses." Has two smash comedy CDs. Twice nominated for Grammy Awards for her "Attention Butt-Pirates and Lesbetarians" and "In Goddess We Trust."

How many of you have ever started dating because you were too lazy to commit suicide?

OTHERS: 1598 Spanish painter **Francisco Zurbarán**, 1619 French writer **Gédéon Tallemant des Réaux**, 1687 English archaeologist **William Stukeley**, 1818 German physician **Emil du Bois-Reymond**, 1838 French writer **Auguste Villiers de l'Isle-Adam**, 1846 Austrian pianist **Ignaz Brüll**, 1878 Austrian-American chemist/physicist **Lise Meitner**, 1888 Indian physicist **Sir C.V. Raman**, 1901 Northern Ireland painter **Norah McGuinness**, 1903 U.S. actor **Dean Jagger**, 1905 English composer **William Alwyn**, 1915 U.S. scientist **William Morrison**, 1927 Japanese computer game executive **Hiroshi Yamauchi**, 1937 U.S. singer of "Peter, Paul & Mary" **Mary Travers**, 1942 British supermodel **Jean Shrimpton**

November 8

1847 **Bram Stoker:** Originally **Abraham.** Irish novelist. Worked in the civil service for 10 years and the manager of Henry Irving for 27 years. His masterpiece, the successful gothic novel, *Dracula*, was based on vampire legends, and became almost a literary genre of its own. His other works, including *The Lure of the White Worm*, were not nearly so popular.

There are mysteries which men can only guess at, which age by age they may solve only in part.

1848 **(Friedrich Ludwig) Gottlob Frege:** German mathematician and logician. Founder of modern mathematical logic. Offered a derivation of arithmetical concepts from logic. Developed new theories regarding the nature of language, functions and concepts, and philosophical logic. In 1893, he published *Grundgesetze der Arithmetik* ("Basic Laws of Arithmetic"). In it he presented his new logical language that he used to define the natural numbers and their properties.

Having visual impressions is, of course, necessary for seeing things, but it is not sufficient. What must be added is not anything sensible. And it is precisely this that unlocks the outer world for us; for without this non-sensible something, each of us would remain locked in his inner world.

1858 **Tomoyuki Yamashita:** General of the Japanese Imperial Army during World War II. He was most famous for conquering the British colonies of Malaya and Singapore, earning the nickname "The Tiger of

Malaya." In 1944, he assumed the command of the 14th Area Army to defend the Philippines, abandoning Manila and retreating to the mountains of northern Luzon. With the surrender of Japan, he surrendered the remainder of his forces. From October 29 to December 7, 1945, he was tried for war crimes relating to the massacre of more than 100,000 Filipino citizens of Manila during fierce street fighting for the capital, which was against Yamashita's specific order. He was found guilty and hanged on February 23, 1946. Among his last words:

As I said in the Manila Supreme Court that I have done with all my capacity, so I don't stand ashamed in front of the Gods for what I have done when I have died.

1883 **Arnold Bax:** English composer and author. Master of music for George VI and Elizabeth II. Composed the march played at her coronation. His early work influenced the poetry of William Butler Yeats. Bax's compositions include seven symphonies, the orchestral works *Spring Fire*, *November Woods* and *Tintagel*, four piano sonatas, three string quartets and numerous vocal works.

You should make a point of trying every experience once, excepting incest and folk dancing.

1897 **Dorothy Day:** American journalist and radical social reformer. Devoted her life to the practical applications of her political and religious beliefs. Started the Catholic Worker's Movement. Developed program of social reconstruction, which she called the green revolution, establishing settlement houses and farm communities for those ruined by the Great Depression. This experience is described in her *House of Hospitality* (1939). Founded *The Catholic World*, a pacifist radical monthly that agitated against nuclear weapons. Autobiography: *The Long Loneliness.*

Don't call me a saint. I don't want to be dismissed so easily.

1900 **Margaret Mitchell:** American author who wrote but one novel, *Gone with the Wind*, which was turned into one of the most successful movies ever made. The book won the 1937 Pulitzer Prize in fiction. It took her ten years to complete her masterpiece, which sold over 25 million copies and was translated into 30 languages. Died in a car accident (1949).

Until you lose your reputation, you never realize what a burden it was or what freedom really is.

1916 **June Havoc:** Born Ellen Evangeline Hovick. Canadian-born actress, dancer, writer and theater director. She was a child vaudeville star under the tutelage of her smothering stage mother Rose. Billed as "Baby Jane," her sister Louise would become Gypsy Rose Lee, Queen of burlesque, famous for her "intellectual" striptease act. June left the act at 13 to elope with a boy in the troupe. She appeared in a number of movies, most notably: *Two Jacks and a Jill*, *My Sister Eileen* and *Gentleman's Agreement*. Not liking how she was depicted, June became estranged from her sister with the publication of the latter's memoirs, *Gypsy*, which was the basis for a smash Broadway musical and film. She reconciled with her sister just before Gypsy died of cancer.

You are all you will ever have for certain.

1916 **Frank McGuire:** American basketball coach. Played at St. John's University and coached at his alma mater. Led his team to the Final Four in 1952 and the next year began a ten your tenure as coach at North Carolina, winning the NCAA title in 1957 with a perfect team record of 32–0. Recruiting violations forced him to resign in 1961 and become the coach of the NBA Philadelphia Warriors. He next moved to South Carolina, becoming the winningest coach in the university's history (1964–1980).

In this country, when you finish second, no one knows your name.

1922 **Christiaan Barnard:** South African heart surgeon. Showed that intestinal atresia is caused by deficient fetal blood supply, which led him to development of a surgical procedure to correct the formerly fatal defect. Introduced open-heart surgery to South Africa, designed a new artificial heart value and performed animal heart transplants. In 1967 his team performed the first human heart transplant. Although the transplant was successful, patient Louis Washkansky died of pneumonia 18 days later. Barnard's motto: "Suffering isn't ennobling, recovery is."

It is infinitely better to transplant a heart than to bury it so it can be devoured by worms.

1927 **Patti Page:** Born **Clara Ann Fowler**. American singer, dubbed "The Singing Rage." The sweet, chic, and glossy blonde's first record "Confess," singing in close harmony with herself establish her as a pop artist. Rose to the top of the charts with "Tennessee Waltz," which sold over four million copies and the novelty tune "How Much Is That Doggy in the Window?" Hosted her TV show, the *Patti Page Show* and made a successful film debut in *Elmer Gantry*.

I was a kid from Oklahoma who never wanted to be a singer, but was told I could sing. And things snowballed.

1929 **Bobby Bowden:** American football player and coach. Head coach at Florida State University since 1976. In his 30 years there he had only one losing season — his first. Compiled a 268–5–4 record. His Seminoles won the College Football National Championship in 1993 and 1999. Son Tommy is the head coach at Clemson University; another son Terry was the head coach at Auburn University where he was the 1993 Coach of the Year. Bobby is a colorful figure who can turn lively phrases. Speaking of one of his players:

He doesn't know the meaning of the word fear, but then again he doesn't know the meaning of most words.

1931 **Morley Safer:** Canadian-born American broadcast journalist. Member of CBS' television newsmagazine "60 Minutes" reporting team. Joined CBS in 1964 as a London-based correspondent. Opened the CBS news bureau in Saigon. Reported on excesses of American troops against harmless civilians. London bureau chief for three years before joining "60 Minutes." Wrote the best-selling *Flashbacks: On Returning to Vietnam.*

Arrogance and snobbishness live in adjoining rooms and use a common currency.

1949 **Bonnie Raitt:** American artist, singer and songwriter. Daughter of Broadway musical star John Raitt. Famous for her bottleneck-style guitar playing. At age 20 she toured with the Rolling Stones. Her albums include: *Silver Lining, Longing in Their Hearts, Nick of Time.* Hit singles: "You Got It," "You," "I Can't Make you Love Me," "Something to Talk About" and "Runaway." Active in preserving the environment.

I would rather feel things in extreme than not at all.

OTHERS: 1491 Italian poet **Teofilo Folengo**, 1710 English writer **Sarah Fielding**, 1732 American patriot/lawyer **John Dickinson**, 1836 U.S. lithographer/game manufacturer **Milton Bradley**, 1854 Swedish physicist **Johannes Rydberg**, 1866 English automobile pioneer **Herbert Austin**, 1868 German mathematician **Felix Hausdorff**, 1869 Russian-born poet **Zinaida Gippius**, 1884 Swiss psychiatrist **Hermann Rorschach**, 1908 U.S. writer/journalist **Martha Gellhorn**, 1920 U.S. actress **Esther Rolle**, 1942 Puerto Rican jockey **Angel Cordero Jr.**, 1954 FEMA director **Michael D. Brown**, 1975 U.S. actress **Tara Reid**

November 9

1721 **Mark Akenside:** English poet and physician. In 1744 he published his best known work, the didactic poem, *The Pleasures of Imagination.* Caricatured by Tobias Smollett for his haughty and pedantic manner in *Adventures of Peregrine Pickle* (1761). Akenside served as one of the physicians to the Queen.

The man forgets not, though in rags he lies, and knows the mortal through a crown's disguise.

1832 **Émile Gaboriau:** French novelist, journalist and pioneer of modern detective fiction. Described as the Edgar Allan Poe of France. Introduced a young policeman based on the real-life thief turned policeman, Eugène François Vidocq. Detective novels: *L'Affaire Lerouge* (*The Widow Lerouge*), *Monsieur Lecoq* and *Les Esclaves de Paris* (*The Slaves of Paris*). Gaboriau had a huge following until the time Arthur Conan Doyle came along with Sherlock Holmes.

Woman submits to her fate; man makes his.

1869 **Marie Dressler:** Originally **Leila Marie Koerber**. Canadian-born actress in stock, light opera, legitimate stage and films. Described herself as "too homely for a prima donna and too ugly for a soubrette." Made her film début in *Tillie's Punctured Romance.* Oscar for *Min and Bill.* Hollywood's number-one box-office attraction for four years. Other films: *Anna Christie, Tugboat Annie* and *Dinner at Eight.*

Fate cast me to play the role of an ugly duckling with no promise of swanning. I have played my life as a comedy rather than the tragedy many would have made of it.

1877 **Muhammad Iqbāl:** Islamic poet and philosopher. His literary works, written in Urdu and Persian, were mostly verse in the Classical style, suitable for public recitation. Sought through his writings to arouse Muslims to take their place in the world. His most celebrated work was *Secrets of the Self* (1915) Known for efforts to direct his fellow Muslims toward the establishment of a separate Muslim state, Pakistan.

Everything that possesses life dies if it has to live in uncongenial surroundings.

1879 **John Haynes Holmes:** American Unitarian clergyman and author. Editor *Unity* (1921–46). Books: *Marriage and Divorce, Religion for Today, The Sensible Man's View of Religion, The Second Christmas* and *My Gandhi.* Editor of *The Life and Letters of Robert Collyer* and compiler: *Readings from Great Authors.*

I await the hour when a journalist can be driven from the press room for venal practices, as a minister can be unfrocked, or a lawyer disbarred.

1886 **Ed Wynn:** Originally **Isaiah Edwin Leopold**. American actor and comedian. Billed as "The Perfect Fool." Vaudeville headliner. Appeared in Ziegfeld Follies. Had a highly publicized feud with W.C. Fields. Was radio and television's Texaco Fire Chief. Won the first Emmy as best actor in a series. Oscar nominated for *The Diary of Anne Frank.* Other films: *The Great Man, The Absent-Minded Professor* and *Marjorie Morningstar.*

I look wonderful for a woman my age, but not for a man. I was downtown last week and saw a building as old as I am. It looked terrible.

1891 **Clifton Webb:** American stage and film actor. Professional ballroom dance in New York by age 19. By his mid–20s he was performing in musicals and dramas on Broadway and in London. Created the role of Charles Condomine in Noel Coward's *Blithe Spirit* and introduced Irving Berlin's "Easter Parade" on the Broadway Stage. Film success occurred in his middle age in *Laura* and *The Razor's Edge,* both of which earned him Oscar nominations. Webb and Sophia Loren were seated next to one another when notorious publicity hound Jayne Mansfield provocatively leaned over the table, prominently displaying her obvious physical assets. Webb quipped:

Please Miss Mansfield; we're wine drinkers at this table.

1915 **Sargent Shriver:** American international lawyer and administrator. Compiled an unparalleled record of public service. With wife Eunice Kennedy Shriver, conducted the National Conference on Prevention and Control of Juvenile Delinquency. President of the Chicago Board of Education. Organizer and first director of the Peace Corps. Director of the Office of Economic Opportunity in the Lyndon B. Johnson administration. Created VISTA, Head Start, Community Action, Foster Grandparents, Job Corps, Legal Services and Neighborhood Health Services. U.S. Ambassador to France (1968–70). Vice-President Candidate in 1972. President of Special Olympics.

Freedom is a crusade, to be carried on enthusiastically around the earth. There are

Americans who have not lost the enthusiasm and audacity of the American Revolution.

1918 **Spiro T. Agnew:** American Vice President under Richard Nixon. Republican governor of Maryland. Took the lead in a campaign against the media and opponents of the Vietnam War. Although not involved in the Watergate Scandal, he was investigated for extortion, bribery and income-tax violations during his governorship. He resigned his office in 1973 shortly before pleading "no contest" to a charge of income tax evasion. Fined $10,000 and sentenced to three years probation.

A spirit of national masochism prevails, encouraged by an effete corps of impudent snobs who characterize themselves as intellectuals.

1928 **Anne Sexton:** née **Harvey**. American poet. Her frankness about her personal experiences sparked controversy. Wrote "confessional verse." Began writing to assist her recovery after a suicide attempt. Pulitzer Prize for *Live or Die* (1967). Also wrote: *All My Pretty Ones*, *The Awful Rowing Toward God* and *The Poet's Story*. Her *Complete Poems* were published in 1981, seven years after she committed suicide.

Put your ear down close to your soul and listen hard.

1934 **Carl Sagan:** American astronomer and writer. Gained prominence as a popular science fiction writer and enthusiastic scientific commentary. *The Dragons of Eden* earned him a Pulitzer Prize for nonfiction (1978). Co-produced and narrated the TV series *Cosmos*. Its companion book was the best-selling English-language science book of all time. In the 1980s, studied the environmental effects of nuclear war, popularizing the term "nuclear winter."

A central issue of science is that to understand complex issues (or even simple ones), we must try to free our minds of dogma and to guarantee the freedom to publish, to contradict, and to experiment. Arguments from authority are unacceptable.

1935 **Bob Gibson:** U.S. baseball right-handed pitcher with St. Louis Cardinals. Won 20 games or more per season five times. Received two National League Cy Young Awards (1968 and 1970). MVP (1968). His ERA in 1968 of 1.12 is the fourth best of all time. Led Cards to two World Series victories (1964 and 67). Had 251 career wins. Hall of Famer. Had more than 3,000 career strike-outs, the first pitcher to do so since Walter Johnson.

In a world filled with hate, prejudice, and protest, I find that I too am filled with hate, prejudice, and protest.

OTHERS: 1664: English writer **Henry Wharton**, 1717 German archaeologist **Johann Joachim Winckelmann**, 1731 African-American farmer/surveyor/scientist **Benjamin Banneker**, 1810 German surgeon **Bernhard von Langenbeck**, 1841 King of the United Kingdom **Edward VII**, 1853 U.S. architect **Stanford White**, 1873 German neurologist **Otfrid Foerster**, 1877 Italian politician **Enrico De Nicola**, 1885 German mathematician **Hermann Weyl**, 1889 French internationalist **Jean Monnet**, 1905 German writer **Erika Mann**, 1921 Soviet gymnast **Viktor Chukarin**, 1922 Hungarian philosopher **Imre Lakatos**, 1929 Hungarian writer **Imre Kertész**, 1936 Latvian chess player **Mikhail Tal**, 1941 U.S. guitarist **Tom Fogerty**

November 10

1483 **Martin Luther:** German Augustinian friar. On a mission to Rome, he was appalled by the corruption he found there, particularly the sale of papal indulgences, sort of get out of hell tickets. Luther preached the doctrine of salvation by faith rather than works. On October 31, 1517, he posted 95 theses on indulgences on the church door at Wittenberg. Called for reformation of the Catholic Church, denying the supremacy of the Pope. His questioning of church practices led to the Protestant Reformation. Tried for heresy and excommunicated. Translated the Bible into fresh, idiomatic and readable German, resulting in an immeasurable effect on the popular religious life of its readers. Also wrote hymns of which "A Mighty Fortress Is My God" is the most familiar.

You are not only responsible for what you say, but also for what you do not say.

1620 **Ninon de Lenclos:** Originally **Anne.** French courtesan. One of the most flamboyant women of the 17th century. Popular figure in the salons, her beauty, wit and sexual frankness attracted famous men of her day. She undertook the amorous education of numerous young men, stressing the importance of refinement and good sense in sexual comportment. Wrote *La Coquette Vengee* (*The Flirt Avenged*, 1659). Her drawing room became a center for the discussion and consumption of the literary arts.

A man is given the choice between loving women and understanding them.

1697 **William Hogarth:** English painter and engraver. Tiring of conventional art forms, he satirized the institutions of his time through caricature with his "modern moral subjects." Best known for series of paintings: *The Harlot's Progress*, *The Rake's Progress* and his masterpiece *Marriage à la Mode*. He followed these with several prints of low life, such as the "industry and idleness" series.

I have generally found that persons who had studied painting least were the best judges of it.

1728 **Oliver Goldsmith:** Irish-born English poet, playwright and novelist. Noted for his comic verbal faux pas, although this may have been intentional. Author of: *The Citizen of the World*, the novel *The Vicar of Wakefield*, the play *She Stoops to Conquer* and the poem "The Deserted Village." Actor David Garrick wrote an epitaph: "Here lies Nolly Goldsmith, for shortness called Noll,/ Who wrote like an angel, and talk'd like poor Poll."

Success consists of getting up just one more time than you fall.

1759 **Friedrich von Schiller:** German poet, dramatist, philosopher and historian. As an army surgeon he began writing *Sturm and Drang* (Storm and Stress) verse and plays. First play *The Robbers* with its revolutionary appeal was an immediate success. Wrote the poem "Ode to Joy," set to music by Ludwig von Beethoven in his Choral Symphony. In the last decade of his life, wrote the dramatic trilogy, *Wallenstein, Maria Stuart* and *Wilhelm Tell.*

No greater grief than to remember days of gladness when sorrow is at hand.

1879 **Vachel Lindsay:** American vagabond poet. From 1906 traveled America like a troubadour. Reciting his popular ragtime rhymes in return for food and shelter. Attempted to convert America to a love of poetry. His works include: "General William Booth Enters Heaven," "The Congo" and "The Santa Fe Trail." First American poet invited to appear at Oxford University. While suffering from extreme depression he committed suicide.

You can't crush ideas by suppressing them. You can only crush them by ignoring them.

1880 Sir **Jacob Epstein:** Anglo-American sculptor. Studied with Auguste Rodin. Gained fame with his controversial bronze figures and unidealized portraits. Revolted against the ornate. Works: Busts of Joseph Conrad, George Bernard Shaw and Paul Robeson; symbolic Figures: Night" and "Day" and a bronze bust, "The American Soldier" in the Metropolitan Museum.

A wife, a lover, can perhaps never see what the artist sees. They rarely ever do. Perhaps a really mediocre artist has more chance of success.

1893 **John P. Marquand:** American novelist. Wrote popular stories for magazines, including a series about the keen-witted Japanese detective Mr. Moto. Best known for a series of novels: *The Late George Apley, Wickford Point* and *Point of No Return.*

His father watched him across the gulf of years and pathos which always must divide a father from his son.

1894 **Mabel Normand:** American silent screen actress. At 16 she went to work for Biograph, becoming an important star of the company, working mostly under the direction of Mack Sennett. Brilliant comedienne, very likely, the most talented female comic star of the silent screen. Starred in numerous shorts, some of which she also directed. Feature films: *Mickey, Peck's Bad Girl, Jinx, The Slim Princess* and *Suzanna.* Career was dealt a heavy blow, when the public became aware of her involvement with director William Desmond Taylor who was mysteriously murdered.

Say anything you like, but don't say that I like to work. That sounds like Mary Pickford, that prissy bitch. Just say I like babies and twist their legs. And get drunk.

1925 **Richard Burton:** Originally **Richard Walter Jenkins, Jr.** Welsh actor. Made his first film appearance in *The Last Days of Dolwyn,* where he met his first wife actress Sybil Williams. His reputation as a fine actor was established with his London performance in Christopher Fry's *The Lady's Not for Burning.* Nominated eight times for an Oscar, coming up empty handed each time. Nearly as well-known for his affair with and marriages to Elizabeth Taylor as his fine performances in *My Cousin Rachel, Becket, The Night of the Iguana* and *Who's Afraid of Virginia Woolf?*

I rather like my reputation, actually, that of a spoiled genius from the Welsh gutter, a drunk, a womanizer; it's rather an attractive image.

1940 **Russell Means:** American Indian political activist. An Oglala Sioux born on the Pine Ride Reservation. As a young man, he was a petty thief and an alcoholic. Turned his life around in 1968, joining the American Indian Movement (AIM) and shortly became one of its most prominent leaders. Led AIM's occupation of Wounded Knee. Tried and acquitted of murder and served a four-year sentence on charges stemming from a riot in Sioux Falls, South Dakota.

I don't want to talk about the environment and the American Indian viewpoint; I hate the word Native American. It's a government term, which was created in the year 1970 in the Department of Interior, a generic term that describes all the prisoners of the United States of America.

1946 **David Stockman:** American government official and businessman. U.S. Republican congressman from Michigan (1977–81). Outspoken and controversial director of the Office of Management and Budget (1981–85). Committed to President Reagan's plan to reduce governmental spending, but developed grown doubts and became disillusioned with the doctrine of supply-side economics, which he described as a "Trojan horse." Resigned in 1985 and wrote The *Triumph in Politics,* criticizing the Reagan administration.

Do you realize the greed that came to the forefront? The hogs were really feeding.

OTHERS: 745 Shia Imam **Musa al-Kazim**, 1341 English statesman **Henry Percy**, 1565 Swedish theologian **Laurentius Gothus**, 1668 French composer **François Couperin**, 1577 Dutch poet/jurist **Jacob Cats**, 1695 English physician/ astronomer **John Bevis**, 1710 Danish statesman **Adam Moltke**, 1801 U.S. social reformer **Samuel Gridley Howe**, 1845 Prime Minister of Canada **John Sparrow David Thompson**, 1886 German author **Arnold Zweig**, 1888 Russian aircraft designer **Andrei Tupolev**, 1896 U.S. baseball player/manager **Jimmy Dykes**, 1918 German chemist **Ernst Fischer**, 1928 Italian composer **Ennio Morricone**, 1942 U.S. economist **Robert Engle**, 1949 U.S. dancer/choreographer **Ann Reinking**

November 11

1633 **George Saville, 1st Marquess of Halifax:** English statesman, politician and author. As a privy councilor chosen to negotiate terms of peace with Louis XIV of France and the Dutch at Utrecht. Supported restricting the marriages in the royal family to Protestants but opposed the bill that passed to exclude Roman Catholics from the House of Lords. Assisted in passing into law the Habeas Corpus Act. Writings: *The Character of King Charles II, Letter to a Dissenter* and *The Lady's New Year's Gift, or Advice to a Daughter.*

If the laws could speak for themselves, they would complain of the lawyers in the first place.

1741 **Johann Kaspar Lavater:** Swiss writer, patriot, and theologian. Founder of physiognomics which he attempted to elevate into a science. It is the practice of trying to judge character and mental qualities by observation of bodily, especially facial, features. Wrote volume of verses, Schweizerlieder (1767) and *Essays on Physiognomics.*

He who seldom speaks, and with one calm well-times word can strike dumb the loquacious, is a genius or a hero.

1744 **Abigail Smith Adams:** American first lady. Wife of 2nd U.S. president John Adams. Mother of John Quincy Adams, 6th U.S. president. Keen mind and extensive reading marked her one of the most intelligent women of her day. Author of letters published by her grandson: *New Letters of Abigail Adams* and *The Adams-Jefferson Letters.* Contained lively and astute observations of her views on women's rights. Valuable pictures of the social and political life of the era.

If we mean to have heroes, statesmen and philosophers, we should have learned women.

1821 **Fyodor Dostoyevsky:** Russian novelist. Supreme master of the realistic novel. Arrested as a member of a socialist circle. After a macabre mock execution, sent to a Siberian penal colony for four years. During his confinement he underwent a religious crisis that led him to reject socialist and progressive views and replace them with a belief in the Russian Orthodox Church and Russian people. *Notes from the House of the Dead* was based on his imprisonment. Wrote *The Possessed, Crime and Punishment, The Idiot* and *The Brothers Karamazov*, demonstrating remarkable talent for character analysis and narrative tension.

The secret of man's being is not only to live but to have something to live for.

1833 **Aleksandr Borodin:** Russian composer and expert in medical chemistry. Made use of Russian folk themes in his music. Wrote operas, symphonies, chamber music and numerous songs. Considered composing an avocation not an occupation, saying, "Respectable people do not write music or make love as a career." Said to have influenced Debussy, Ravel, Stravinsky and Sibelius. Best known works are *In the Steppes of Central Asia, Symphony No. 2* and the unfinished opera, *Prince Igor*, which contains the "Polovtsian Dances," completed by Rimsky-Korsakov and Aleksandr Glazunov.

In opera, as in decorative art, details and minutiae are out of place. Bold outlines only are necessary; all should be clear and straight forward... The voices should occupy the first place, the orchestra the second.

1836 **Thomas Bailey Aldrich:** American short-story writer, poet and editor of the *Atlantic Monthly.* Born in Portsmouth, New Hampshire, the setting of his semi-autobiographical novel, *The Story of a Bad Boy.* Received wide acclaim for his poem "The Ballad of Babie Bell" in his collection *The Bells.* Other works: *Marjorie Daw, The Luck of the Irish* and *The Stillwater Tragedy.*

The man who suspects his own tediousness is yet to be born.

1885 **George S. Patton, Jr.:** American general in World War II "Old Blood and Guts." Member of the 1912 Olympic team, competing in the modern pentathlon. Commanded U.S. Army II Corps in North Africa (1942–43). Led 7th Army assault on Sicily (1943) and 3rd Army invasion of occupied Europe (1944). Outspoken advocate of military mobility and armor. Played a central role in stopping the German counteroffensive at the Battle of the Bulge. Criticized for slapping a hospitalized soldier he suspected of malingering, and was required to apologize publicly.

The object of war is not to die for your country but to make the other bastard die for his.

1897 **Charles "Lucky" Luciano:** Originally **Salvatore Lucania.** Italian born American mobster. Earned his nickname for his ability to evade arrest and win at craps. Joined crime boss Joe Masseria's gang and soon was directing the mobster's bootlegging, narcotics and prostitution rackets. Planned the assassination of both his boss and a rival gang leader Salvatore Maranzano. Developed a national crime syndicate. Jailed for extortion in 1936, directed his crime empire from his cell. Sentence was commuted for some services rendered to the government during World War II. Deported to Italy, where he continued to run drug traffic and smuggle aliens into the U.S.

Behind every great fortune, there is a crime!

1915 **William Proxmire:** American politician. U.S. Democrat Senator from Wisconsin. Elected to fill the remainder of the term vacated by the death of Senator Joseph McCarthy in 1957. As Chairman of the Committee on Banking, Housing and Urban Affairs, instrumental in devising the financial plan that saved New York City from bankruptcy. Early advocate of campaign finance reform, in his last two campaigns, refused to take any contributions. Known for his *Golden Fleece* awards, which identified wasteful government spending. From 1967 to 1986, he gave daily speeches on the need to ratify the Convention on the Prevention and Punishment of the Crime of Genocide. After 3,211 speeches, the convention was finally ratified.

I have spent my career trying to get Congressmen to spend the people's money as if it were their own. But I have failed.

1922 **Kurt Vonnegut, Jr.:** American author and journalist. Writes satirical stories of American culture and mores. Works mingle realism with science fiction, and fantasy. His novel *Slaughterhouse-Five; or The Children's Crusade* was inspired by the author's personal experiences of the bombing of Dresden in the Second World War. Other Works: *Cat's Cradle, Player Piano, Slapstick, Deadeye Dick* and Breakfast *of Champions.*

Another flaw in the human character is that everybody wants to build and nobody wants to do maintenance.

1925 **Jonathan Winters:** American comedic actor. His stand-up routines were famous for their madcap improvisation and strange voices. Recorded numerous comedy albums and appeared frequently on the Jack Parr Show, often as his character Maude Frickert, a sweet old lady with a barbed tongue. Starred in the TV show *The Wacky World of Jonathan Winters* (1972–74). Robin Williams calls Winters his idol and greatest influence.

Nothing is impossible. Some things are just less likely than others.

1928 **Carlos Fuentes:** Mexican, lawyer, diplomat, writer and short-story writer. Despite being born to a wealthy family, he represents the frustrated ideals of the Mexican revolution. Mines the nation's past, both the Indian and Christian cultures for insights into the Mexican mind and the society it creates. Gained international attention with *The Death of Artemio Cruz,* a metaphysical exposé of modern Mexico. Other Works: *Where the Air Is Clear, The Good Conscience,* and *The Old Gringo,* a fictionalized account of the last days of Ambrose Bierce in Mexico.

I don't think any good book is based on factual experience. Bad books are about things the writer also knew before he wrote them.

OTHERS: 1050 Holy Roman Emperor **Henry IV**, 1493 Italian poet **Bernardo Tasso**, 1743 Swiss naturalist **Carl Peter Thunberg**, 1764 Russian writer **Barbara Juliana von Krüdener**, 1828 Hindu saint **Sri Narayan Mahaprabhuji**, 1863 French painter **Paul Signac**, 1869 Italian king **Victor Emmanuel III**, 1891 U.S. baseball player **Rabbit Maranville**, 1898 French film director **René Clair**, 1903 U.S. film producer **Sam Spiegel**, 1904 U.S. government official/accused Soviet spy **Alger Hiss**, 1918 U.S. comic actor **Stubby Kaye**, 1919 Finish novelist **Kalle Päätalo**, 1929 German writer **Hans Magnus Enzensberger**, 1940 U.S. Senator **Barbara Boxer**, 1945 Nicaraguan president **Daniel Ortega**

November 12

1815 **Elizabeth Cady Stanton:** American women's rights activist. Leader of the woman-suffrage movement in the United States. Determined to readdress the inequality that she found in women's legal, political and industrial rights and in divorce law. With Lucretia Mott, organized the first women's rights convention (1848), which launched the women's suffrage movement and adopted a set of resolutions for improving the status of women that Stanton had composed. President of National Woman Suffrage Association (1868–70). Author of *Eight y Years and More.*

Thus far, women have been the mere echoes of men. Our laws and constitutions, our creeds and codes, and the customs of social life are all of masculine origin. The true woman is as yet a dream of the future.

1817 **Bahaullah:** Persian-born theologian and philosopher. Leader of the Bahá'i faith. Name means "The Glory of God" in Arabic. Religion emerged from Babism in 1863 when he announced that he was the messenger of God predicted by the Báb. Worship consists of reading from scriptures of all religions. The Bahá'i faith proclaims the essential unity of all religions and the unity of all humanity. It is concerned with social ethics and has no priesthood.

It is not for him to pride himself who loveth his own country, but rather for him who loveth the whole world. The earth is but one country and mankind its citizens.

1840 **Auguste Rodin:** French sculptor. Bequeathed most of his work to the French government. His first great work, The Age of Bronze was considered so lifelike that it was alleged that he had taken a cast from a live model. Commissioned by the Musées arts décoratifs to create *The Gates of Hell.* It was unfinished at the time of his death, but contains some of his best known pieces, including *The Kiss* and *The Thinker.*

I choose a block of marble and chop off whatever I don't need.

1866 **Sun Yat-Sen:** Chinese Kuomintang revolutionary leader and statesman. Worked to overthrow the Ch'ing Dynasty. While in exile organized the Revolutionary Alliance. Formed Nationalist Party (1912). Elected head of state (1921). Attempted to unite China. Established a secessionist government at Guangzhou in 1912 and reorganized his party along the lines of the Soviet Communist Party. As President of the Southern Chinese Republic (1923–25), maintained a period of uneasy cooperation with the Chinese Communists.

Revolution is not a dinner party.

1874 **Bert Williams:** Born **Egbert Austin Williams**. Pre-eminent African-American entertainer of his era. Bahamas-born Actor, mime, dancer, singer and songwriter. Key figure in the development of African American music. Great comic artist who was a Broadway headline star in the Ziegfeld Follies and an early star of silent films. Tragically, he was restricted to playing the role of the shuffling darky, a role he perfected. Wrote his signature song, the plaintive masterpiece "Nobody," in which he mournfully chants lyrics suffered by a down-and-outer: "When life seems full of clouds and rain/ And I am full of nothin' but pain/ Who soothes my thumpin,' bumpin' brain?/ Nobody."

I have never been able to discover anything disgraceful in being a colored man. But I have often found it inconvenient — in America.

1889 **Dewitt Wallace:** American publisher. Developed the idea of a pocket-sized digest of popular articles while recuperating from wounds suffered in World War I. Founded the *Reader's Digest* in 1922 with his wife Lila Bell Wallace. Editor until 1965. The couple established the Lila Wallace–Reader's Digest Fund to benefit the arts and culture.

We are living in a fast-moving world. People are anxious to get at the nub of matters.

1895 **Dolores Ibarruri (Gómez):** Spanish Basque politician, journalist and orator. Joined the Socialist party in 1917 Used the pseudonym "La Pasionaria," that is "the passionate flower" as a journalist for the worker's press. Helped found the Spanish Communist Party in 1920 and formed the Anti-Fascist parliament in 1936. During the Spanish Civil War famous for her orations exhorting the people to fight the Fascist forces of General Franco. When her cause was lost, she moved to the Soviet Union, returned at age 81 and was elected to the National Assembly.

Better to die on one's feet than to live on one's knees.

1908 **Harry A. Blackmun:** American jurist and Supreme Court justice (1970–94).Taught law (1935–41) while becoming a general partner in his Minnesota law firm. Resident counsel at the Mayo Clinic (1950–59). President Nixon appointed him to the high court. Perceived as a conservative, he became progressively more liberal. Wrote the majority decision in *Roe vs. Wade.*

Who is to say that 5 men 10 years ago were right whereas 5 men looking the other direction today are wrong.

1918 **Jo Stafford:** American singer. Trained to be a classical opera singer, she discovered that in the Depression there was little call for opera singers. Began her career singing with her sisters on their own radio show. In Los Angeles. Joined the vocal group the Pied Pipers, a quartet that sang with Tommy Dorsey's band. Went solo in 1944. Regular on radio, often with her husband Paul Weston's band. Had 93 hits from 1944 to 1957: "Shrimp Boats," "My Darling, My Darling," "You Belong to Me," "Jambalaya" and "Make Love to Me."

I just tried to remember the lyrics and not bump into the trumpet player.

1929 **Grace Kelly:** Exquisitely beautiful blonde actress and Monaco princess. First starring role was the new bride of Gary Cooper in the western classic *High Noon.* Nominated for a Best Supporting Actress for *Mogambo.* Earned the Best Actress Oscar for *The Country Girl.* Icy aloofness and haughty reserve masked an underlying dormant passion. Others: *Dial M for Murder, Rear Window* and *To Catch a Thief.* Rumored to have had affairs with most of her leading men, but settled down when she married Prince Ranier III, the ruler of the tiny principality of Monaco in a lavish wedding. Died in mysterious and fiery automobile crash at 52.

Hollywood amuses me. Holier-than-thou for the public and unholier-than-the-devil in reality.

1934 **Charles Manson:** American cult leader. Founded a commune in 1967 based on free love and complete subordination to him. Two years later he allegedly ordered his followers to carry out a series of grisly murders, including that of the actress Sharon Tate, who was far along in her pregnancy. Manson and a number of his followers received death penalties, but were saved by a Supreme Court ruling against capital punishment.

Look down at me and you see a fool; look up at me and you see a god; look straight at me and you see yourself.

1961 **Nadia Comaneci:** Romanian gymnast. In the 1976 Olympics, at the age of 14, earned seven perfect scores and three individual gold medals. Won two more gold medals in 1980. Retired in 1980 to become a coach of the Romanian national team. Defected to the U.S.A. in 1989, became a model, and married gymnast Bart Connor in 1996.

I don't run away from a challenge because I am afraid. Instead, I run toward it because the only way to escape fear is to trample it beneath your feet.

OTHERS: 1493 Italian sculptor **Bartolommeo Bandinelli**, 1528 Chinese general **Qi Jiguang**, 1651 Mexican poet/nun **Sor Juana Inés de la Cruz**, 1729 French explorer **Louis Antoine de Bougainville**, 1842 English physicist **Lord Rayleigh**, 1896 Indian ornithologist **Salim Ali**, 1915 French critic and writer **Roland Barthes**, 1922 U.S. actress **Kim Hunter**, 1929 German writer **Michael Ende**, 1936 U.S. boxing referee **Mills Lane**, 1943 U.S. actor **Wallace Shawn**, 1944 U.S. musician **Booker T. Jones**, 1944 U.S. TV sportscaster **Al Michaels**, 1945 Canadian musician **Neil Young**, 1968 Dominican baseball player **Sammy Sosa**, 1970 U.S. figure skater **Tonya Harding**, 1982 U.S. actress **Anne Hathaway**

November 13

354 Saint **Augustine:** Latin name **Aurelius Augustinus**. Church Father and philosopher. Born in what is now Algeria. After a period of skepticism, he converted to Christianity in 387. Established a monastic community in 395. For the rest of his life he preached and in his writings defined points of Christian doctrine. Developed a theory of sin, grace, and predestination, which not only became basic to Catholic doctrines, but would be used as justification for the tenets of Calvin, Luther and the Jansenists. Wrote: *On the Trinity, The City of God, On Nature and Grace* and *Confessions.*

Faith is to believe what we do not see; and the reward of this faith is to see what we believe.

1714 **William Shenstone:** Scottish writer and landscape gardener. Known for pastoral verse, including songs, odes, ballads, and elegies. Established his reputation with "The Judgment of Hercules." and "A Schoolmistress," written in Spenserian stanzas. Transformed the Leasowes, a grazing farm, into a *fe'rmme ornée*, an early example of a natural landscape garden, beautified with cascades, pools, vistas, urns and a grove to Virgil, encircled by a winding walk.

A liar begins with making falsehood appear like truth and ends with making truth itself appear like falsehood.

1761 **John Moore:** British soldier and general. First saw action in the American Revolutionary War. As a Major-General, served in the suppression of the republican rebellion in Ireland in 1798. Established the innovative training regime that produced Britain's first light infantry regiments. Put in charge of the defense of the coast from Dover to Dungeness against a possible invasion by Napoleon. Later took command of the British forces in the Iberian Peninsula and was fatally wounded in the Battle of Corunna, fighting the French. Celebrated in a poem by Charles Wolfe, *The Burial of Sir John Moore after Corunna.* When the French took Corunna, their commander ordered a monument be built over the grave of his respected adversary.

Your opinion is your opinion, your perception is your perception — do not confuse them with "facts" or "truth." Wars have been fought and millions have been killed because of the inability of men to understand the idea that everybody has a different viewpoint.

1785 Lady **Caroline Lamb:** "Caro." English novelist. Well educated, a natural wit, the vivacious young woman not only wrote prose and poetry, but also took to sketch portraiture. Most infamous for her open affair with Lord Byron, shocking London, which tolerated bed-hopping as long as it was done discreetly. Before she met Byron, she described him as "Mad, bad, and dangerous to know." He loved to pursue women, but once captured, he longed to leave them. She caricatured Byron in one of her three novels, *Glenarvon.* At the height of her passion she sent him a letter enclosed with a very personal gift — her pubic hair.

I asked you not to send blood but yet do — because it means love I like to have it. I cut the hair too close & bled much more than you need — do not you the same & pray put not scissors points near where quei capelli grow — sooner take it from the arm or wrist — pray be careful....

1833 **Edwin Booth:** American actor. Born into a notable theater family. Found the famous Players Club in New York (1889). World famous for his Hamlet, Iago and King Lear. When his brother John Wilkes Booth assassinated Lincoln, Edwin withdrew from the stage until 1866. Once remarked: "An actor is a sculptor who carves in snow."

But Nature cast me for the part she found me best fitted for, and I have had to play it, and must play if till the curtain falls.

1850 **Robert Louis Stevenson:** Scottish novelist, poet and essayist. Wrote fiction and travel books. Author of the very popular classical novels *Treasure Island, The Strange Case of Dr. Jekyll and Mr. Hyde* and *Kidnapped.* Also known for *A Child's Garden of Verses* and his letters. Known as "Tusitala," or "teller of tales," in Samoa, where he died at "Vailema," which has become the destination of literary travelers in the area.

Most of our pocket wisdom is conceived for the use of mediocre people, to discourage them from ambitious attempts, and generally console them in their mediocrity.

1856 **Louis D. Brandeis:** American jurist and Zionist leader. As a lawyer, known as the people's attorney, for his defense of the constitutionally of state hours-and-wages laws, devising a savings bank life insurance plan for working people and his efforts to strengthening the government's anti–Trust power. Appointed to the Supreme Court by Woodrow Wilson in 1912. As the fist Jewish justice, his appointment was vigorously opposed by some anti–Semitic groups. Noted for his devotion to freedom of speech. Brandeis University is named for him. Books: *Other People's Money, Business, a Profession* and *The Curse of Bigness.*

If we desire respect for the law, we must first make the law respectable.

1866 **Abraham Flexner:** American educator, educational pioneer, administrator of philanthropies and author. The Carnegie Foundation for Advancement of Teaching hired him to evaluate 155 U.S. and Canadian medical colleges. Many of the schools that he severely criticized were forced to close their doors and others revised their policies and curricula. Channeled over half a billion dollars provided by the Rockefeller Foundation to improve medical education. Founder and first director of the Institute of Advanced Study, Princeton, N.J. to which he brought some of the world's leading scientists. Observed: "Probably no nation is rich enough to pay for both war and education." Books: *The American College, A Modern College* and *Funds and Foundations.*

Without ideals, without effort, without scholarship, without philosophical continuity, there is no such thing as education.

1911 **John Jordan "Buck" O'Neil:** African-American baseball player and manager in Negro league baseball. Spent most of his stellar career as first baseman and manager of the legendary Kansas City Monarchs. His players who became Major League standouts include Ernie Banks, Elston Howard, Lou Johnson, Satchel Paige and Hank Thompson. First African-American coach in the Major Leagues with the Cubs in 1962. Chairs the Negro Leagues Baseball Museum Board of Directors. Candidate for Hall of Fame in a special vote for Negro League players, managers and executives in 2006, but did not receive the necessary votes, which many in baseball consider a great injustice.

It's just a few of us left, especially the old-times. The guys after Jackie Robinson, we got quite a few of those left. But the guys before Jackie Robinson, there are very few of us left.

1922 **Oskar Werner:** Born **Oskar Josef Bechliessmayer.** Intelligent sensitive Austrian actor. Drew international attention for his appearance in Marcel Ophüls' *Lola Montès.* Brilliant in François Truffaut's *Jules and Jim.* Oscar nominated for his performance in *Ship of Fools,* in which his scenes with Signore Signoret are among the most memorable in film history. Other films: *Decision Before Dawn* and *Fahrenheit 451.*

I am married to the theater, and the films are only my mistress.

1938 **Jean Seberg:** American actress. Petite and pert, the elfin blonde Iowa-born actress was emotionally fragile and unstable. Landed the title role in director Otto Preminger's *Saint Joan,* a box-office failure and her second film *Bonjour Tristesse* was only marginally more successful. Attained international attention staring with Jean-Paul Belmondo in Jean-Luc Godard's classic New Wave film, *Breathless*. Other films: *Lilith*, *Paint Your Wagon*, and *La Récréation*. Involvement in anti-war politics and association with members of the Black Panther party made her the target of an undercover campaign by the FBI to discredit her. Found dead in her car in a Paris suburb in 1979.

I never knew until I came here [Hollywood] that somebody could be really nice to you for years and really hate your guts. Happens all the time here.

1949 **Whoopi Goldberg:** Born **Caryn Johnson**. African-American actress, comedian and singer. Scored a personal hit with her touring one-woman *Spook Show*. Broadway triumph with *Whoopi Goldberg* (1984–5). Made a sensational film début in *The Color Purple*, earning an Academy Award nomination. Won an Oscar for Best Supporting Actress for *Ghost*. With Robin Williams and Billy Crystal organized a TV show, "Comic Relief," to raise money for the homeless.

I am where I am because I believe in all possibilities.

OTHERS: 1312 King of England **Edward III**, 1486 German theologian **Johann Eck**, 1710 French dramatist **Charles Simon Favart**, 1760 Chinese Emperor **Jiaging**, 1848 Prince of Monaco **Albert I**, 1853 U.S. actor **John Drew**, 1854 U.S. composer **George Whitefield Chadwick**, 1869 Russian feminist **Ariadna Trykova**, 1886 German dancer **Mary Wigman**, 1898 U.S. jockey **Earl Sande**, 1913 U.S. actor **Alexander Scourby**, 1918 U.S. actor **Jack Elam**, 1924 Japanese geneticist **Motoo Kimura**, 1935 Archbishop of Canterbury **George Carey**, 1936 Italian writer **Dacia Maraini**, 1941 U.S. baseball pitcher **Mel Stottlemyre**, 1942 U.S. musician **John Hammond**, 1979 U.S. basketball player **Ron Artest**

November 14

1840 **Claude Monet:** French landscape and still-life painter. Student of color. Applied scientific principles of light to the art of painting. His painting of Le Havre, entitled *Impression, Sunrise* (1872), gave the name to the Impressionist movement. Juxtaposed brushstrokes of color to create an effect of dappled, glowing light. Considered one of the all-time great landscape painters. Painted the same subject at different times of the day to explore the effect of light on color and form: *The Haystacks*, *Rouen Cathedral* and *Water Lilies*.

People discuss my art and pretend to understand as if it were necessary to understand, when it's simply necessary to love.

1889 **Jawaharal Nehru:** Indian patriot and statesman. Leader of the Indian National Congress, becoming its president in 1929. Prominent in India's effort toward unity and independence. Imprisoned nine times by the British for political activities. Second only to Mohandas Gandhi in influence. First prime minister of independent India (1947–64). Tried to pursue a policy of neutrality toward major powers. His daughter was Prime Minister Indira Gandhi.

Without peace, all other dreams vanish and are reduced to ashes.

1900 **Aaron Copland:** Exceptionally gifted American composer and conductor. Studied in France with Nadia Boulanger. Early works, such as his 1926 piano concerto, were in the jazz idiom but gradually developed a gentler symphonic style. Among his most popular works were those based on folk motifs such as the American ballets *Billy the Kid*, *Rodeo* and *Appalachian Spring*. Other works: *Lincoln's Portrait* and *Fanfare for the Common Man*.

So long as the human spirit thrives on this planet, music in some living form will accompany and sustain it and give it expressive meaning.

1904 **Marya Mannes:** American writer, journalist and critic. Studied sculpture in London. In the 1930s she did bronze portraits of Walter Damrosch, Sergei Rachmaninoff and Raoul de Roussy de Sales. Joined the staff of *The Reporter*, remaining with the magazine for 12 years, writing TV, theater and social criticism. Novels: *Message from a Stranger* and *They*.

All great lovers are articulate, and verbal seduction is the surest road to actual seduction.

1906 **Louise Brooks:** American actress and writer. Appearances in George White Scandals and The Ziegfeld Follies led to a Hollywood contract in 1925. A pretty, shapely brunette with a boyish-bob hair style, she was first cast in routine flapper comedies but gradually emerged as a talented actress in *A Girl in Every Port* and *Beggars of Life*. Made her mark on film history in Germany, giving remarkable performances in *Pandora's Box* and *Diary of a Lost Girl*. In the 1950 film cultists rediscovered her old films. Acclaimed for her collection of essays, *Lulu in Hollywood*, about her life and other screen personalities.

The great art of films does not consist of descriptive movement of face and body but in the movements of thought and soul transmitted in a kind of intense isolation.

1908 **Joseph McCarthy:** American right-wing politician. Republican Senator from Wisconsin (1947–57). Infamous for highly publicized investigations and unsubstantiated claims of communists in the government. Due to his witch hunt, many people were blacklisted and unable to find work. Led his crusade against the Truman administration, but when he turned his attack on the army in 1954, it was shown that he and his aides had falsified evidence. President Eisenhower renounced him and his tactics. Discredited and censured by the Senate for contempt and abuse.

I have here in my hand a list of two hundred and five people that were known to the Secretary of State as being members of the Communist Party and who nevertheless are still working and shaping the policy of the State Department.

1912 **Barbara Hutton:** Wealthy American socialite and heiress to the Woolworth department store chain fortune. Dubbed the "Poor Little Rich Girl" because of her troubled life. Born into a highly dysfunctional family, she inherited close to 50 million dollars from her mother's estate. Married and divorced seven times, including husbands Cary Grant, Porfirio Rubirosa, to whom she was married only 53 days and Count Curt Haugwitz Reventlow. The Count dominated her through verbal and physical abuse. Abused drugs and alcohol. Spent her fortune recklessly, giving money and jewelry to strangers willing to pay attention to her. Reportedly when she died, only $3000 of her fortune remained.

I've never seen a Brink's truck follow a hearse to the cemetery.

1922 **Veronica Lake:** Born **Constance Frances Marie Ockelman**. Glamorous American actress. Famous for her "peek-a-boo" hair style, with her long blonde locks falling over one eye. Style was copied by so many young women, that government officials asked her to change it because female war plant workers were catching their long hair in machines. Often appeared in films with actor Alan Ladd. In the 1950s disappeared from view, except for an occasional news story of her arrest for public drunkenness. Cleaned up her act and made a modest comeback in a few low-budget films. Movies: *Sullivan's Travels*, *This Gun for Hire*, *I Married a Witch* and *The Blue Dahlia*.

Hollywood gives a young girl the aura of one giant, self-contained orgy farm. Its inhabitants dedicated to crawling into every pair of pants they can find.

1935 **Hussein ibn Talal:** King of Jordan from 1953 until his death from cancer in 1999. Became king due to the mental incapacity of his father, who abdicated in favor of his eldest son. By 1967, he had lost his entire kingdom west of the river Jordan in the Arab-Israeli Wars. Suppressed the Palestine Liberation Organized, a guerrilla force against his rule on the remaining East Bank territories. Later a moderating force in Middle Eastern politics. Attempted to mediate when Iraq invaded Kuwait in 1990.

We should face reality and our past mistakes in an honest, adult way. Boasting of glory does not make glory, and singing in the dark does not dispel fear.

1947 **P.J. O'Rourke:** American gonzo journalist, political satirist and writer. Claimed that in college he was a left-leaning hippie, but emerged as a political observer and humorist with definite libertarian and sometimes conservative views. Joined National Lampoon in 1973. Went freelance in 1981, writing articles for *Playboy*, *Vanity Fair* and *Rolling Stone*. Publications: *Republican Party Reptile*, *Parliament of Whores*, *Give War a Chance*, and *Eat the Rich*.

You know your children are growing up when they stop asking you where they came from and refuse to tell you where they're going.

1948 **Charles, Prince of Wales:** First in line to succeed his mother, Elizabeth II, as monarch of Great Britain. Failure of his marriage to Princess Diana was played out in the world's newspapers and magazines. They had two sons William and Harry, but the marriage became estranged amid rumors of the infidelity of both parties. With Diana's death, he publicly appeared with his mistress Camilla Parker Bowles, whom he married in 2005. Charles is known for his advocacy of excellence in architecture and other causes.

Do you seriously expect me to be the first Prince of Wales in history not to have a mistress?

1954 **Condoleezza Rice:** Currently United States Secretary of State, replacing Colin Powell. Formerly President George W. Bush's National Security Advisor. Professor of political science at Stanford University and Provost (1993–9). Given name is derived from the Italian music-related expression, "Con dolcezza," meaning "with sweetness." Maintains that racial segregation taught her determination against adversity and the need for her to be "twice as good" as non-minorities. Has plenty of support for making a run for the presidency in 2008. Media would be delighted at the prospect of Rice fighting Hilary Clinton for the prize. However she has declared:

I will not run for president of the United States. How is that? I don't know how many ways to say "no" in this town.

OTHERS: 1650 King of England **William III**, 1719 Austrian composer **Leopold Mozart**, 1765 American steamship inventor **Robert Fulton**, 1771 French anatomist **Marie François Bichat**, 1779 Danish poet **Adam Oehlenschläger**, 1797 British geologist **Charles Lyell**, 1805 German composer/pianist **Fanny Mendelssohn**, 1859 Romanian politician **Alexandru Averescu**, 1878 Polish poet **Leopold Statt**, 1891 Canadian physician **Frederick Banting**, 1904 U.S. actor/director **Dick Powell**, 1907 Swedish writer **Astrid Lindgren**, 1907 U.S. cartoonist **William Steig**, 1912 Chinese-born civil engineer **T.Y. Lin**, 1919 German soprano **Lisa Otto**, 1924 Russian violinist **Leonid Kogan**, 1966 U.S. baseball pitcher **Curt Schilling**

November 15

1607 **Madeline de Scudéry:** French author of heroic romances, including the ten-volume *Artamène, ou le Grand Cyrus* (1649–53) and the ten-volume *Clélie, historie romaine* (1654–60). Interweaved improbable tales of love and war in antique settings with ingenious systems and codes of contemporary allusions. Her work influenced heroic plays at the court of King Charles II.

Love is a capricious creature which desires everything and can be contented with almost nothing.

1708 **William Pitt** the Elder: Earl of Chatham. "The Great Commoner." English statesman and orator. Secretary of State (1756–61 and 1766–68). As a great prime minister he built up the British Empire and made it respected at home and abroad. Led England during the Seven Years' War (1756–63). Sent General Wolfe to Canada, who won it for Great Britain. Encouraged Robert Clive in India. Advocated a conciliatory policy toward the American colonies.

If I were an American, as I am an Englishman, while a foreign troop was landed in my country, I

never would lay down my arms — never! Never! Never!

1731 **William Cowper:** English poet. Suffered from severe depression, had a complete breakdown and attempted suicide. Suffered from periods of acute melancholia, which took a religious form. Turned increasingly to evangelical Christianity for consolation. During a calm period he wrote his satires "Table Talk," "The Progress of Error," "Truth," "Expostulation," "Hope," "Charity," "Conversation" and "Retirement," which were published in 1782. Best known for his long poem "The Task." Made contributions to Olney Hymns, which include the following:

God moves in a mysterious way,/ His wonders to perform./ He plants his footsteps in the sea,/ and rides upon the storm.

1738 **William Herschel:** German-born English organist, composer and astronomer. Built better and better telescopes to see deeper and deeper into space. Astronomy ceased being only a hobby for him when he achieved distinction by discovering a new planet, now named Uranus. King George III became William's patron, allowing him to become a full-time astronomer. William's work was carried on with distinction by his son Sir John Herschel.

The phenomena of nature, especially those that fall under the inspection of the astronomer, are to be viewed, not only with the usual attention to facts as they occur, but with the eye of reason and experience.

1881 **Franklin P. Adams:** "F.P.A." American sportswriter, columnist and humorist. Column "The Conning Tower," appeared in New York newspapers (1913–41). Fondly remembered for his civilized wit and wide-ranging knowledge, exhibited on radio's *Information, Please* (1938–50). Wrote the well-known baseball verse: "Tinker and Evers and Chance." Wrote a score of books, including *Tobogganing on Parnassus* and *F.P.A. Book of Pretorians.*

Nothing is more responsible for the good old days than a bad memory.

1882 **Felix Frankfurter:** Austrian-born American jurist. Convinced the Sacco-Vanzetti case was "one of the most glaring cases of prejudiced trails in American history," an opinion unpopular in Massachusetts, where the trial took place. Books: *The Case of Sacco and Vanzetti, The Business of the Supreme Court, Mr. Justice Brandeis,* and *Mr. Justice Holmes and the Supreme Court.* Helped found American Civil Liberties Union (1920). Appointed to the Supreme Court in 1930 by FDR. A liberal who advocated judicial restraint. Insisted that a decision of the Supreme Court must be apolitical — neither liberal nor conservative, and impersonal.

As a member of this court I am not justified in writing my private notions of policy into the Constitution, no matter how deeply I may cherish them or how mischievous I may deem their disregard.

1887 **Marianne Craig Moore:** Brooklyn-born American poet. Verse is marked by wit and irony, deep moral concern and deep feelings. Pulitzer Prize winner (1951), the National Book Award (1952) and the gold medal of the National Institute for Arts and Letters (1953). Highly disciplined poems distilled moral and intellectual insights from close observation of objective detail. Works: *Observations, The Pangolin and Other Verse, What Are Years, Nevertheless* and *Collected Poems.*

There never was a war that was not inward. I must fight till I have conquered in myself what causes war.

1887 **Georgia O'Keefe:** American painter. One of the most original and important American artists. Married photographer Alfred Stieglitz. Pioneered abstract art in the U.S.A., but later moved towards a more figurative approach. Found her unique style in New Mexico where she painted flowers and desert scenes with a Surrealist flavor, sometimes with the blanched skull of a longhorn in the foreground.

To create one's world in any of the arts takes courage.

1891 **W. Averell Harriman:** American statesman, art collector, diplomat and banker. Had one of the longest and most varied administrative careers of anyone in public life: Ambassador to U.S.S.R. (1943–46). Ambassador to England (1946), Secretary of Commerce (1946–48) Economics Cooperation Administration Ambassador (1948–50), Special Assistant to the President (1950–51), Director of Mutual Security (1951–53), and Governor of New York (1955–58). Twice unsuccessfully tried to win the Democratic nomination of President (1952, 1956).

The dictatorship of the proletariat is a historically regressive idea for it makes the individual the servant of the state, robs him of his power of decision, and is thus at odds with the aspirations of mankind.

1891 **Erwin Rommel:** German field marshal. Early Nazi sympathizer. Commanded Hitler's headquarters guard during the attack of Poland. Led a Panzer tank division during the 1940 invasion of France. Commanded the Afrika Korps, achieving initial major successes, but was eventually driven into retreat by a strongly reinforced 8th Army. Withdrawn for North Africa and appointed to an Army Corps command in France. Returning to Germany wounded, he condoned the plot against Hitler's life. After its discovery, he was forced to commit suicide.

Don't fight a battle if you don't gain anything by winning.

1897 **Aneurin Bevan:** British Labor Party leader and former coal miner. Often spoken of as the "bad boy of English politics." Fiery, energetic and forceful, a chronic dissenter, charged with bringing disunity into Labor's ranks. During World War II, one of Winston Churchill's bitterest critics, maintaining that the Conservative Prime Minister was not pressing the fight vigorously enough. When the Labor Party was swept into power in 1945, as Minister of Health (1945–51), Bevan developed Britain's socialized medicine system.

Reactionary: A man walking backwards with his face to the future.

1942 **Daniel Barenboim:** Argentine-born Israeli pianist and conductor. Noted exponent of Mozart and Beethoven. Gained his reputation as pianist/conductor with the English Chamber Orchestra. Musical director of the Orchestre de Paris (1975–89). Married to cellist Jacqueline Du Pré from 1945 until her death in 1987. Became principal conductor of the Chicago Symphony Orchestra in 1991. Prominent advocate for peace in the Middle East.

Every great work of art has two faces, one towards its own time and one toward the future, toward infinity.

OTHERS: 1660 German historian **Hermann von der Hardt**, 1784 French king of Westphalia **Jerome Bonaparte**, 1852 Khedive of Egypt **Tewtik Pasha**, 1862 German dramatist **Gerhard Hauptmann**, 1874 Danish zoophysiologist **August Krough**, 1889 King of Portugal **Manuel II**, 1895 Polish writer **Antoni Slonimski**, 1899 President of Pakistan **Iskander Mirza**, 1906 U.S. Air Force General **Curtis LeMay**, 1907 German Colonel/attempted assassination of Hitler **Claus von Stauffenberg**, 1919 U.S. TV judge **Joseph Wapner**, 1925 U.S. senator **Howard Baker**, 1930 British author **J.G. Ballard**, 1932 English singer **Petula Clark**, 1940 U.S. actor **Sam Waterston**, 1945 Norwegian singer **Anni-Frid Lyngstad**

November 16

42 BCE **Tiberius Caesar:** Roman emperor (14 BCE–37 CE). Raised by his mother Livia and his stepfather Augustus. Forced to divorce his wife to marry Augustus' profligate daughter Julia. With the death of his sons, Augustus adopted Tiberius and made him his heir. Upon assuming the role of emperor it was apparent he was not suited for it. His rule was eroded by suspicion and insecurity, which resulted in a growing number of treason trials and executions. He left Rome in 26 CE for Capri, while effective control of the empire was left in the hands of the praetorian prefect Sejanus. Tiberius spent his last years in gloom and debauchery.

It is the duty of a good shepherd to shear his sheep not to skin them.

1811 **John Bright:** British radical statesman and orator. Populist reformer, who fought for parliamentary reform. Founded the Anti–Corn Law League (1839), engaging in free trade agitation through the country. Member of the Peace Society and energetically denounced the Crimean War (1854). Regarded as one of the most eloquent speakers of his time.

The angel of death has been abroad throughout the land; you may almost hear the beating of his wings.

1827 **Charles Eliot Norton:** American educator, editor, critic and translator. Cofounder of *The Nation* (1865). Coeditor with James Russel Lowell of the *North American Review* (1864–68). Author of *History of Ancient Art*. Wrote on Medieval church-building and edited the poems of John Donne, and Anne Bradstreet, and the letters of Thomas Carlyle. Translator of Dante's *The Divine Comedy*.

The voice of protest, of warning, of appeal is never more needed than when the clamor of fife and drum echoed by the press and too often by the pulpit, is bidding all men fall in and keep step and obey in silence the tyrannous word of command. Then, more than ever, it is the duty of the good citizen not to be silent.

1873 **W.C. (William Christopher) Handy:** African-American composer and bandleader. Joined a minstrel show as a cornet player and formed his own band in 1903. Moved to New York where he founded a publishing company. First to introduce the Negro "blues" style to printed music. Known as the "Father of the Blues," which was the title of a book he wrote. His most famous work is the classical standard "St. Louis Blues."

St. Louis woman, wid her diamon' rings,/ Pulls dat man 'round by her apron strings.

1889 **George S. Kaufman:** American playwright and screenwriter. Plays: *The Butter and Egg Man*, *The Royal Family*, *Dinner at Eight* (with Edna Ferber), *Of Thee I Sing* (with Morris Ryskind and Ira Gershwin), the 1939 Pulitzer Prize–winning *You Can't Take It with You* (with Moss Hart), *The Solid Gold Cadillac* (with Howard Teichmann), and *The Man Who Came to Dinner*. Involved in the most publicized Hollywood scandal of the 1930's. During a custody battle over her daughter, Mary Astor's diary was introduced in court. It listed her indiscretions and her secret affair with Kaufman. While her praise of his sexual prowess briefly hurt her career, it only made him more popular.

One man's Mede is another man's Persian.

1896 Sir **Oswald Mosley**: British fascist and physician. Successively a Conservative, Independent and Labor Member of Parliament, and a member of the 1929 Labor government. Resigned and founded the New Party (1931). Following a visit to Italy he joined the British Union of Fascists, becoming its leader. The Union is remembered for its anti–Semitic violence in the East End of London and its support for Hitler. Mosley was detained under the Defense Regulations during World War II.

A prophet or an achiever must never mind an occasional absurdity, it is an occupational risk.

1899 **Mary Margaret McBride:** Affable American radio commentator and syndicated columnist. Hosted a series of daytime talk shows (1934–54) on which she introduced a celebrity guest, described her newest hat, plugged sponsors' products with breathless conviction and dispensed homespun and advice. Managed to maintain her personification of the small-town girl—folksy, warmhearted, unpretentious, but sharp as a tack. Wrote a number of best-selling travel books. Never married, explaining:

If I'd married the first man that came along and settled down on a farm with children, I'd have made him miserable. I wanted to be famous. I even wanted to be wicked when I got to New York. I'd heard and knew all about wicked people. I wanted

to marry a man in Naples and have a daughter by him and then leave him, but it didn't work out.

1905 **Eddie Condon:** American guitarist, banjoist, jazz promoter and bandleader. Played guitar with Artie Shaw's big band in the late 1930s.Organized and promoted concerts at New York's town hall. Opened a jazz club in Greenwich Village (1958–67), a Mecca for Dixieland fans. Condon called Dixieland "virile jazz." Moved his club uptown to Manhattan's Sutton Hotel. Said, "There isn't a sheet of music in the place.... We improvise with discipline."

As it enters the ear, does it come in like broken glass or does it come in like honey?

1922 **José Saramago:** Portuguese novelist and man of letters. Too poor to finish his university education, he continued his studies while working as a welder's assistant. Moved into journalism and translation work. Published his first novel *Country of Sin* in 1947. His breakthrough novel was *Baltasar and Blimunda*. His novels *The Stone Raft* and *Blindness* mix magic realism with outspoken political commentary. Received the Nobel Prize for Literature in 1998.

What kind of world is this that can send machines to Mars and does nothing to stop the killing of a human being?

1930 **Chinua Achebe:** Originally **Albert Chinualumogo**. Nigerian novelist. Described how, imposed Western values lead to social and psychological disorientation of traditional African society. First novel, *Things Fall Apart*, heralded as a fresh voice in African literature, presented an unsentimentalized picture of the Ibo tribe. Others: *Arrow of God* and *Anthills of the Savanna*. Essays: *Beware, Soul Brother*, on his experiences during the Nigerian Civil War.

When old people speak it is not because of the sweetness of words in our mouths; it is because we see something which you do not see.

1935 **Elizabeth Drew:** American journalist and author. Deeply insightful analysis of the national political scene. Her account of the Watergate affair was published as *Washington Journal*. Regular on PBS televisions "Thirty Minutes with..." Books: *Politics and Money, On the Edge: The Clinton Presidency, The Corruption of American Politics, Citizen McCain* and *Fear and Loathing in George W. Bush's Washington*.

One problem with the President's claims of extraordinary powers as commander in chief is that the "war on terror" is by definition an open-ended one, with no time limit on the president's powers, as Bush interprets them, to do virtually whatever he wants in order to conduct that war.

1952 **Shigeru Miyamoto:** Japanese video game designer. Called one of the fathers of modern videogaming. Created *Donkey Kong, Mario, Pikmin* and *Legend of Zelda* video games for Nintendo. Games are characterized by refined control-mechanics and imaginative worlds in which players are encouraged to discover things for themselves, as well as basic storylines.

Video games are bad for you? That's what they said about rock-n-roll.

OTHERS: 1717 French mathematician **Jean le Rond d'Alembert**, 1720 Italian composer **Carlo Campioni**, 1766 French violinist **Rodolphe Kreutzer**, 1836 King of Hawaii **David Kalakaua**, 1880 Russian poet **Alexander Blok**, 1892 Chinese writer **Guo Moruo**, 1895 German conductor **Paul Hindemith**, 1896 U.S. opera singer **Lawrence Tibbett**, 1907 U.S. actor **Burgess Meredith**, 1924 U.S. runner **Mel Patton**, 1938 U.S. philosopher **Robert Nozick**, 1941 U.S. Secretary of Labor **Ann Dore McLaughlin**, 1953 British humorist **Griff Rhys Jones**, 1964 U.S. baseball pitcher **Dwight Gooden**, 1964 Canadian singer **Diana Krall**, 1970 U.S. actress **Martha Plimpton**, 1977 Ukrainian figure skater **Oksana Baiul**

November 17

9 CE **Vespasian:** Originally **Titus Flavius Vespasianus.** Roman Emperor (70–79). Founder of the Flavian dynasty. Served as tribune in Thrace, and as quaestor in Crete and Cyrene. During Claudius' reign, commanded a legion in Germany and in Britain. In 67 Nero sent him to subjugate the Jews. Proclaimed imperator by the legions in the East. When he reached Rome as Emperor, restored the government and finances to order, and set a personal example by the simplicity of his life style. Embarked on an ambitious building program, beginning the Colosseum. Extended and consolidated Roman conquests in Germany and Britain.

Woe is me; I think I am becoming a god.

1755 **Louis XVIII:** King of France. Younger brother of King Louis XVI. Fled to Belgium in 1791 to escape the fate of his executed brother. When his brother's heir Louis XVII died, Louis XVIII named himself king, living in exile. With Napoleon's defeat in 1814, Louis returned to France, where surviving nobles and clergy moved him to treat Republicans and Protestants severely. This opened the way for Napoleon's hundred day return in 1815. After the Battle of Waterloo Louis XVIII promised moderation and amnesty to all but traitors, but was helpless to prevent a backlash, called "White Terror," where Royalists slew hundreds of adherents of the Revolution and Protestants.

Punctuality is the politeness of kings.

1815 **Eliza Woodson Burhans Farnham:** American philanthropist, reformer and author. An early advocate of the importance of rehabilitation as a focus of prison internment. She took an interest in reform movements, but opposed political rights for women, fearing it would actually reduce the influence of women. Appointed a matron of the women's division of Sing Sing Prison, she initiated a highly advanced regime, allowing inmates to speak to one another and set up a system of privileges and useful training.

The human face is the organic seat of beauty.... It is the register of value in development, a record of Experience.

1887 **Bernard Law Montgomery:** British Army field marshal. Distinguished almost as much for his egotism as for his victories. His defeat of Germany's Erwin Rommel at El Alamein (1942) gave Britain a much needed lift. By 1944, he commanded all British and American ground forces at the Allied landings in Normandy. Led Allied forces through Europe into Germany (1944–45). In his memoirs criticized General Eisenhower's philosophy and military strategies, claiming the war would had ended earlier with less lost of life if his plan had been used.

Discipline strengthens the mind so that it becomes impervious to the corroding influence of fear.

1902 **Eugene Paul Wigner:** Originally **Jenó Pál Wigner**. Hungarian-born American mathematical physicist. To satisfy his father's wishes, he worked for a degree in chemical engineering, while studying his real loves mathematics and physics in his spare time. He completed a doctorate in engineering, but thereafter began the work for which he is famous, namely applying group theory to quantum mechanics. Worked on the Manhattan Project at the University of Chicago during World War II. Received the Nobel Prize for Physics in 1963.

The promise of future science is to furnish a unifying goal to mankind rather than merely the means to an easier life, to provide some of what the human soul needs in addition to bread alone.

1916 **Shelby Foote:** American writer, historian and novelist. Foremost living authority on the Civil War, served as the principal guide through the highly successful Civil War series produced for public television by documentary filmmaker Ken Burns. Author of the three volume *The Civil War: A Narrative*. Wrote six novels, including *Follow Me Down*, *Shiloh* and *Love in a Dry Season*. Cousin of Horton Foote, American author and playwright.

History is a pretty wretched subject to study in school, As I remember it, it was terrible. They required us to memorize so many things. There was a Treaty of Utrecht, and it has thirteen steps. I don't know one of those steps. But it had thirteen.

1930 **Bob Mathias:** American athlete. Suffered from anemia as a child and turned to athletics to gain strength. At age 17, he won a gold medal in the Olympic Decathlon, becoming the youngest athlete to every win an Olympic track and field gold medal. Decathletes are regarded as the finest all-around athletes in the world. He won a second decathlon gold medal four years later in 1952, the same year he played fullback on Stanford's Rose Bowl football team. Also served in the U.S. House of Representatives.

Throw your heart over the bar and your body will follow.

1937 **Peter Cook:** British comedian, satirist and writer. First achieved prominence as one of the writers and performers of *Beyond the Fringe*. Collaborated with Dudley Moore in the irreverent TX series, *Not Only ... But Also*. With it they created a new style of dry, absurdist television which was instantly successful with audiences. Cook and Moore appeared together in the classic film, *Bedazzled*, with Cook as the devil who promises nerdish Moore the love of an unattainable beauty in exchange for his soul. Cook repeatedly tricks Moore in a variety of ways.

You know, I go to the theater to be entertained. I don't want to see plays about rape, sodomy and drug addiction ... I can get that at home.

1942 **Martin Scorsese:** American director, screenwriter, producer and actor. He gave up his initial vocation to be a priest for the cinema. Most consistently innovative director working during the past 30 years. His body of work addresses themes of Italian-American identity, Catholic concepts of guilt and redemption, machismo and the violence endemic in America. Films: *Mean Streets*, *Taxi Driver*, *Raging Bull*, *Goodfellas*, *Cape Fear*, *The Age of Innocence*, *Casino*, *Gangs of New York* and *The Aviator*. Nominated six times for a Best Director Oscar, winning in 2007 for *The Departed*.

It seems to me that any sensible person can see that violence does not change the world and if it does, then only temporarily.

1944 **Danny De Vito:** American actor and director. Memorable for his role of Louie DePalma on television's "Taxi." The little man (5 feet tall) is a big entertainment phenomenon. Films: *Romancing the Stone*, *Twins*, *Ruthless People*, *Batman Returns* and *Hoffa*. Appeared in and directed *Throw Momma from the Train* and *The War of the Roses*. Major film producer including *Pulp Fiction*, *Get Shorty*, and *Erin Brockovich*.

There are two dilemmas that rattle the human skull: How do you hang on to someone who won't stay? And how do you get rid of someone who won't go?

1944 **Tom Seaver:** Nicknamed "Tom Terrific" and "The Franchise." American Hall of Fame baseball right-handed pitcher with the Mets, Reds and White Sox. National League Rookie of the Year in 1967 and won three Cy Young Awards (1969, 1973 and 1975).In 1969 Seaver won a league-high 25 games and he led the Mets to their first World Series championship. Had 311 wins and 3,640 strikeouts in 20 seasons.

My job isn't to strike guys out; it's to get them out, sometimes by striking them out.

1948 **Howard Dean:** American Democrat politician and physician. During his tenure as Governor Vermont paid off much of its debt, had a balanced budget 11 times, and taxes were twice lowered. Early frontrunner in the 2004 Democrat presidential nomination. Showed strong fundraising ability, pioneering the use of the Internet in campaigning. Elected Democratic National Chairman. Has come up with the 50-State Strategy. Rather than focusing just on "swing states," the goal is for the Democrats to be committed to winning elections at every level in every region of the country.

I think most people ... would be glad to pay the same taxes they paid when Bill Clinton was president, if only they could have the same economy as when Bill Clinton was president.

OTHERS: 1503 Italian painter **Agnolo Bronzino**, 1587 Dutch poet **Joost ven den Vondel**, 1681 French theologian **Pierre François le Courayer**, 1790 German mathematician **August Möbius**, 1793 British painter **Charles Eastlake**, 1799 U.S. artist **Titian Peale**, 1857 Polish neurologist **Joseph Babinski**, 1878 U.S. social worker **Grace Abbott**, 1895 Mexican author **Gregorio López y Fuentes**, 1901 U.S. director/teacher **Lee Strasberg**, 1906 Japanese auto pioneer **Soichiro Honda**, 1922 U.S. biochemist **Stanley Cohen**, 1925 U.S. actor **Rock Hudson**, 1925 English conductor **Charles Mackerras**, 1938 Canadian singer **Gordon Lightfoot**, 1966 French actress **Sophie Marceau**, 1938 Canadian producer **Lorne Michaels**.

November 18

1647 **Pierre Bayle:** French philosopher. Held that many long-standing beliefs, including much Christian tradition, were as questionable as the notion that comets presaged catastrophes. His *Historical and Critical Dictionary* (1696–1706) treats its biographical, theological and philosophical subjects in orthodox ways, but his dissent is found in voluminous footnotes. The work influenced Denis Diderot to complete his *Encyclopédie*.

It is pure illusion to think that an opinion that passes down from century to century, from generation to generation, may not be entirely false.

1797 **Sojourner Truth:** Originally **Isabella Van Wagener**. African-American evangelist, abolitionist and social reformer. Leading orator who fought for women's suffrage and the abolition of slavery. Born a slave in New York State and worked for a various owners before gaining her freedom. Having had visions since childhood, she felt called to change her name to Sojourner Truth in 1841. Preached to large crowds across America. In 1664 President Lincoln appointed her counselor to the freedmen of Washington. She continued to promote Negro rights, including educational opportunities. Autobiography: *The Narrative of Sojourner Truth* (1950).

Those are the same stars, and that is the same moon, that look down upon your brothers and sisters, and which they see as they look up to them, though they are ever so far away from us, and each other.

1836 **W.S. [William Schwenck] Gilbert:** English dramatist and writer of humorous verse. Best known for collaborating with composer Arthur Sullivan in writing a series of comic operas, originally produced in London by Richard D'Oyly Carte at the Savoy Theatre: *H.M.S. Pinafore*, *The Pirates of Penzance*, and *The Mikado*. As a librettist, Gilbert had a penchant for whimsy, nonsense and topical satire. The operas poked fun at contemporary Victoria life. Followers of Gilbert and Sullivan productions are called Savoyards after the theatre and their number is still considerable.

If you wish in this world to advance, your merits you're bound to enhance;/ You must stir it and stump it, and blow your own trumpet, or trust me, you haven't a chance.

1836 **Cesare L. Lombroso:** Italian alienist, criminologist and professor of psychiatry. Founder of the science of criminology. Interests centered on the relation between mental and physical disorder. Wrote: *Crime, Its Causes and Remedies*. His theory that there is a criminal type discernible from a normal person has been discredited.

The ignorant man always adores what he cannot understand.

1870 **Dorothy Dix:** Pseudonym of **Elizabeth M. Gilman**. American journalist and writer. Wrote syndicated advice column beginning in 1896. Letters addressed "Dear Dorothy" presented the personal and emotional problems of the writer. Dix proffered guidance in how to deal with their dilemmas. Allegedly, she formulated many of the most interesting questions put to her, giving her an opportunity to express her opinion on this or that topic. This gave rise to a political term in Australia and the United Kingdom. The term "Dorothy Dixer" applied to a question written by a minister and asked by a backbencher, allowing the minister to promote himself or criticize the opposition.

You never saw a very busy person who was unhappy.

1882 **[Percy] Wyndham Lewis:** English novelist, essayist and painter. Wrote notable satirical works, many essays expressing his vehement political and literary opinions and as a painter was a leading proponent of the cubist related school called vorticism. Together with Ezra Pound, T.S. Eliot, James Joyce and Ford Madox Ford promoted a return to classicism, blasting the trends towards romanticism. Works: novels *Blasting and Bombardiering*, *The Apes of God*, *The Revenge for Love* and essays *The Art of Being Ruled*, *Time and Western Man* and *The Hitler Cult and How I Will End*.

As a result of the feminist revolution, "feminine" becomes an abusive epithet.

1882 **Jacques Maritain:** Eminent French Catholic philosopher, theologian and man of letters. One of the forces behind the major religious revival at mid-century. Largely responsible for revising interest in scholasticism, philosophical realism, and Thomist philosophy. Renowned for his study of Saint Thomas Aquinas, *The Angelic Doctor*, and such books as *True Humanism* and *Art and Scholasticism*.

I don't see America as a mainland, but as a sea, a big ocean. Sometimes a storm arises, a formidable current develops, and it seems it will engulf everything. Wait a moment, another current will appear and bring the first one to naught.

1888 **Frances Marion:** Born **Marion Benson Owens**. One of the most renowned American female screenwriters of the 20th century. During World War I was one of the first female war correspondents to cover actual battles in Europe. After the war, became one of the busiest and highest paid screenwriters, credited with nearly 150 scenarios in the silent and early talkie eras. First female to receive an Oscar for a screenplay, winning for both *The Big House* and *The Champ*. Others: *Rebecca of Sunnybrook Farm*, *Anne of Green Gables*, *Anna Christie*, *Dinner at Eight*, and *Camille*.

De we really know anybody? Who does not wear one face to hide another?

1900 **Howard Thurman:** African-American theologian, clergyman and civil rights leader. Helped the Fellowship of Reconciliation establish the first integrated, intercultural Church in the U.S., the Church for the Fellowship of All Peoples in San Francisco. Author of 20 books, the most famous of which, *Jesus and the Disinherited*, deeply influenced Martin Luther King Jr., whose father had been a classmate of Thurman.

A dream is the bearer of a new possibility, the enlarged horizon, the great hope.

1925 **Gene Mauch:** U.S. baseball player and manager. Managed the Phillies (1960–68), Montreal Expos (1969–75), Minnesota Twins (1976–80), and California Angels (1981–8, 1985–87). Advocated "little ball," an emphasis on basic fundamentals such as bunting, sacrifice plays, and other means of advancing runners, rather than trying to score runs by home runs. Holds the dubious distinction of managing the most seasons without winning a pennant.

I'm not the manager because I'm always right, but I'm always right because I'm the manager.

1939 **Margaret E. Atwood:** Canadian novelist, short story writer, critic and poet. Most widely read writer in Canada and tireless campaigner for social justice. *The Circle Game*, a collection of poems, earned the Governor-General's award. Best known as a novelist: *The Handmaid's Tale* and *The Edible Woman*, *Alias Grace*, *Cat's Eye*, *Bluebeard's Egg* and *Oryx and Crake*.

If the national mental illness of the United States is megalomania, that of Canada is paranoid schizophrenia.

1946 **Alan Dean Foster:** American author of science-fiction and fantasy novels and movie novelizations. Best known for novels set in the Humanx Commonwealth, an interstellar union of races, including humankind and the insectoid Thranx. Novels: *Midworld*, *Cachalot*, *Sentenced to Prison*, *Flinx in Flux* and *Flinx's Folly*. Media novelizations: *Alien* (and its two sequels), *The Black Hole*, *Outland*, *Krull*, and *Starman*.

Freedom is just Chaos, with better lighting.

OTHERS: 1786 German composer **Carl Maria von Weber**, 1787 French photography inventor **Louis-Jacques Daguerre**, 1810 U.S. botanist **Asa Gray**, 1832 Swedish artic explorer **Nils Nordenskjöld**, 1866 U.S. painter **Jules Guérin**, 1874 U.S. author **Clarence Day**, 1897 British physicist **Patrick Blackett**, 1899 Hungarian-born conductor **Eugene Ormandy**, 1901 U.S. pollster **George Gallup**, 1906 U.S. scientist **George Wald**, 1908 U.S. actress **Imogene Coca**, 1916 Italian soprano **Amelita Galli-Curci**, 1927 U.S. musician **Hank Ballard**, 1942 U.S. actress **Linda Evans**, 1944 German fashion designer **Wolfgang Joop**, 1948 Football player **Jack Tatum**, 1966 Spanish poet **Jorge Camacho**

November 19

1600 **Charles I:** King of England and Ireland (1625–49). A firm believer in the Divine Right of Kings, his need for money to fight foreign wars put him into conflict with parliament and led to the English Civil Wars. Charged with high treason, he was beheaded. It was bitterly cold on January 30, 1649. Concerned that he might shiver and people would think he was trembling from fear, so he donned an extra shirt before stepping on the scaffold and as he did every day he knelt in prayer, tucked his hair under a white cap so it would not impede the blade of the executioner's axe. He lay down flat with his neck on the block. Among his final words were:

I am going from a corruptible to an incorruptible crown, where no disturbance can be.

1831 **James A. Garfield:** American educator and U.S. Republican congressman from Ohio. General in the Civil War with the Union forces. Compromise candidate for president, who narrowly won the election. Tenure of only 150 days in office was marked by struggles in the Republican Party over influence and cabinet posts. Shot in a Washington DC railroad station by Charles J. Guiteau, a disappointed office-seeker after only six and a half months in office. He lingered for 11 weeks before succumbing to his wounds and was succeeded by Vice President Chester Arthur.

All free governments are managed by the combined wisdom and folly of the people.

1862 **Billy Sunday:** American baseball player and fundamentalist evangelist. Blessed with great speed, he played in the major leagues with Chicago, Pittsburgh and Philadelphia. At the Pacific Garden Mission in Chicago, he accepted Jesus Christ as his savoir and was "born again." Ordained a preacher in the Presbyterian Church in 1903. Noted for "fire-and-brimstone" approach to evangelism, preaching against political liberalism, evolution, and alcohol. Told that conversions at revival meetings didn't last, he replied, "Neither do baths, but they do a world of good."

Hell is the highest reward the devil can offer you for being a servant of his.

1899 **Allen Tate:** American poet and critic. Founder of the seminal literary magazine, *The Fugitive*. Edited *Hound and Horn* and *The Sewanee Review*. Poems: "Ode to the Confederate Dead," "The Mediterranean" and "The Oath." Biographies: *Stonewall Jackson: The Good Soldier*, *Jefferson Davis: His Rise and Fall*, and *Robert E. Lee*.

Men expect too much, do too little.

1909 **Peter F. Drucker:** Austrian-born American management consultant, educator and writer. The rise of Nazism forced him to leave for England in 1933, before moving to the U.S. in 1937. Editorial columnist for *The Wall Street Journal* and frequent contributor to the *Harvard Business Review*. Author of thirty-one books: *The New Society, The Frontiers of Management,* and *The Post-Capitalist Society.*

Efficiency is doing things right, effectiveness is doing the right things.

1917 **Indira Gandhi:** Indian political leader. Prime minister (1967–77, 1978–84). Daughter of Jawaharlal Nehru. Had two sons, Rajiv who was assassinated and Sanjay who died in an air crash. In 1975 convicted of election malpractices she responded by declaring a "state of emergency" in India. Civil liberties were curtailed and censorship imposed. Briefly lost her position but returned to power after the 1980 general election. Assassinated by two of her Sikh bodyguards, resentful of her employment of troops to storm the Golden Temple at Amritsar and dislodge malcontents. The murder provoked a Hindu backlash in Delhi, involving the massacre of 3,000 Sikhs.

There are two kinds of people, those who do the work and those who take the credit. Try to be in the first group; there is much less competition.

1921 **Roy Campanella:** African-American Hall of Fame baseball catcher, Played nine years in the Negro leagues. First catcher to break organized baseball's color line. A mainstay of the Dodgers' domination of the National League in the late forties and fifties. Three-time MVP. Paralyzed from the neck down in a car accident following the 1957 season. Spokesman for the disable, setting a shining example of cheerfulness despite a brutal physical therapy program.

I never want to quit playing ball. They'll have to cut the uniform off me to get me out of it.

1926 **Jeane Jordan Kirkpatrick:** American political scientist, educator, diplomat, and member of the neoconservative movement. Served as Ronald Reagan's foreign policy advisor in the 1980 campaign. U.S. permanent representative to the United Nations (1981–95). Ardent anticommunist, noted for her "Kirkpatrick Doctrine," which advocated U.S. support for anticommunist governments throughout the world even it they were authoritarian dictatorships.

Democracy not only requires equality but also an unshakable conviction in the value of each person, who is then equal. Cross cultural experience teaches us not simply that people have different beliefs, but that people seek meaning and understand themselves in some sense as members of a cosmos ruled by God.

1936 **Dick Cavett:** American TV talk show host, known for in-dept, often serious issues discussions. Appeared many times on *The Tonight Show with Johnny Carson* as a stand-up comedian. Host of his talk show in various formats and on various TV and radio networks. Tackled taboo subjects that other talk show hosts avoided. Nominated for eleven Emmy Awards, he won three.

I eat at this German-Chinese restaurant and the food is delicious. The only problem is that an hour later you're hungry for power.

1938 **Ted Turner:** American broadcast entrepreneur, yachtsman, and sports teams' owner. Bought Atlanta TV station WJRJ (later WTBS), which became the flagship of the Turner Broadcasting System. Piloted the yacht, *Courageous,* to victory in the 1977 America's Cup. Launched CNN in 1980. *Time*'s "Man of the Year" (1991). Merged his broadcasting system with Time Warner. Once married to actress Jane Fonda.

If only I had a little humility, I'd be perfect.

1942 **Calvin Klein:** American fashion designer. Designer of elegant, modern classics. First designer to win three consecutive Coty awards for womenswear (1973–75). Besides his clothing, known for cosmetics, linens and other designer collections. Produces the perfumes "Eternity" and "Obsession." Some of his erotic advertising photographs have drawn public protest.

The best thing is to look natural, but it takes makeup to look natural.

1959 **Allison Janney:** Award-winning American actress on the stage, in films and most recently playing one of the major characters of the long-running TV series "West Wing." Had comedic roles in the soap opera "As the World Turns" and "The Guiding Light." Earned Tony award nomination for *A View from the Bridge*. Films: *Drop Dead Gorgeous, 10 Things I Hate About You, American Beauty, Nurse Betty, The Hours* and *How to Deal.*

One out of every forty American men wears women's clothing. We've had more than forty presidents. One of these guys has been dancing around the Oval Office in a prom dress.

OTHERS: 1617 French painter **Eustache Le Seur**, 1711 Russian writer **Mikhail Lomonosov**, 1722 Austrian physician **Leopold von Auenbrugger**, 1752 American military leader **George Rogers Clark**, 1770 Icelandic sculptor **Bertel Thorvaldsen**, 1805 French engineer/builder of Suez Canal **Ferdinand de Lesseps**, 1843 German philosopher **Richard Avenarius**, 1893 French trumpet player **René Voisin**, 1900 German writer **Anna Seghers**, 1912 Romanian cell biologist **George Emil Palade**, 1915 U.S. physiologist **Earl W. Sutherland Jr.**, 1929 Slovenian musician **Slavko Avsenik**, 1939 U.S. newscaster **Garrick Utley**, 1961 U.S. actress **Meg Ryan**, 1962 U.S. actress/director **Jodie Foster**

November 20

1858 **Selma Ottiliana Louisa Lagerlöf:** Swedish novelist, internationally famous. Work is characterized by a social and moral seriousness as in *The Miracle of Anti-Christ* and *The Outcast*. Wrote *Gösta Berling* saga, based on the traditions and legends of her native Varmland, and the children's classic *Wonderful Adventures of Nils*. First woman member of the Swedish Academy and first woman to win Nobel Prize for literature (1909).

There isn't much that tastes better than praise from those who are wise and capable.

1871 **Arthur Guiterman:** Austrian-born American writer and poet. Wrote historical and legendary ballads and humorous verse, such as "Of all cold words of tongue or pen/ The worst are these: 'I knew him when.'" Editor of *The Literary Digest*, Co-founded the Poetry Society of America and later served as its president. Author of: *Ballads of Old New York*, *I Sing the Pioneer*, *Prophets in Their Own Country* and *Lyric Laughter*.

Don't tell your friends about your indigestion. "How are you" is a greeting, not a question.

1884 **Norman Thomas:** American socialist leader, reformer, editor and ordained minister of the Presbyterian Church. Helped found ACLU. Six-time Socialist candidate for U.S. presidency. Self-styled "Old-Fashioned Socialist, who opposes the use of force and the confiscation of private property. Early anti-Communist, labeled Josef Stalin, "a pioneer, ahead of Hitler, in purges, concentration camps, and the techniques of modern regimentation. Books: *America's Way Out—A Program for Democracy*, *War—No Profit, No Glory, No Need*, and *The Test of Freedom*.

If you want a symbolic gesture, don't burn the flag; wash it.

1889 **Edwin P. Hubble:** U.S. astronomer. Staff astronomer at Carnegie Institution's Mount Wilson Observatory, California (1910–53). Observing redshifts in the light wavelengths emitted by the galaxies, he discovered that galaxies were moving away from each other at a rate constant to the distance between them, known as Hubble's Law. Able to calculate when the expansion began and confirmed the Big Bang theory. Calculated that the latter occurred about 2 billion years ago, but more recent estimates make it to be more like 20 billion years ago.

Equipped with his five senses, man explores the universe around him and calls the adventure Science.

1908 **Alistair Cooke:** Cultured and witty English–U.S. journalist. Film critic for BBC and London's correspondent for NBC, later American correspondent for BBC. In 1947 began a series of radio commentaries beamed to England, known as *Letters from America*. Description of the U.S. won the Peabody Award. Best known as the urbane host of "Omnibus" (1952–60) and PBS's "Masterpiece Theater" (1971–1992).

Golf is an open exhibition of overweening ambition, courage deflated by stupidity, skill soured by a whiff of arrogance.

1917 **Robert C. Byrd:** American politician and lawyer. Born **Cornelius Calvin Sale, Jr**. Given to the custody of an aunt and uncle who renamed him. Democrat U.S. Congressman (1953–59) and Senator from West Virginia (1959–). Longest-serving current member of Congress. Filibustered the Civil Rights Act of 1964, saying it abrogated principles of federalism. Opposed the Voting Rights Act, but voted for the Civil Rights Act of 1968. Remarkably effective in steering federal funds to West Virginia. Wrote *Losing America: Confronting a Reckless and Arrogant President* (2004).

It is money, money, money! Not ideas, not principles, but money that reigns supreme in American politics.

1921 **Jim Garrison:** Originally **Earling Carothers Garrison**. American author and politician. Democratic District Attorney of Orleans Parish, Louisiana (1962–73). Depending upon one's viewpoint, Garrison's attempts to uncover the actual conspiracy of the assassination of President John F. Kennedy was blocked by a federal government cover-up, or he bungled his chance to discover the truth, or it was just a wild goose chase. Books: *A Heritage of Stone*, *The Star Spangled Contract* and best-selling *On the Trail of Assassins*.

I'm afraid, based on my experience that fascism will come to American in the name of national security.

1923 **Nadine Gordimer:** South African novelist and short story writer. First book was *Face to Face*, a collection of short stories. Published her first novel *The Lying Days* (1953), in which a white girl triumphs over the provincial narrowness and racial bigotry of her parents' mining village existence. Apartheid and her characters' relation to it, is ever present in her fiction, most powerfully in *Conservationist*. Awarded the 1991 Nobel Prize for Literature.

Art is so wonderfully irrational, exuberantly pointless, but necessary all the same. Pointless and yet necessary, that's hard for a puritan to understand.

1924 **Benoit Mandelbrot:** French-born mathematician. Expert in an area where mathematics, science and art merge. Study of processes with unusual statistical properties, and of everyday forms of nature, such as mountains, clouds and the path traveled by lightning, made him a pioneer of Chaos Theory or Dynamical Systems. Went beyond Einstein's theories of the fourth dimension by establishing that besides including the first three dimensions, there also are gaps or intervals between them that are fractional dimensions.

Clouds are not spheres, mountains are not cones, coastlines are not circles, and bark is not smooth, nor does lightning travel in a straight line.

1925 **Robert F. Kennedy:** American Democrat politician. His brother John F. Kennedy's attorney general (1961–64). When Lyndon Johnson preferred Hubert H. Humphrey for the 1964 vice-presidential nomination, Kennedy resigned and was elected U.S. Senator from New York. In 1968 he campaigned for the Democratic Party's presidential nomination, but after a primary victory in California He was assassinated by Jordanian Sirhan Bissara Sirhan.

There are those who look at things the way they are and ask why ... I dream of things that never were, and ask why not?

1942 **Joseph R. Biden, Jr.:** U.S. Senator from Delaware (1973 —). Respected Senate voices on drug policy, crime prevention, and civil liberties. Wrote laws that created the nation's "Drug Czar," who oversees and coordinates national drug policy. Supported the war in Iraq, but argued that more soldiers are needed, the war should be internationalized, and the Bush administration should "level with the American people" about the cost and length of the conflict.

Relations with many of our oldest friends are, quite frankly, scraping the bottom right now.

1948 **John R. Bolton:** American diplomat. Under Secretary for Arms Control and International l Security. In this role, a key area of responsibility was the prevention of proliferation of Weapons of Mass Destruction. Very successful in pushing his personal ultraconservative agenda. Critics allege he tried to spin intelligence to support his views and political objectives. Nomination as U.N. Ambassador was the subject of a prolonged filibuster by Democrats. President Bush appointed him to the position via a recess appointment, to last until a new congress convenes in January 2007.

There is no such thing as the United Nations. If the UN's secretary building in New York lost 10 stories, it wouldn't make a bit of difference.

OTHERS: 270 Roman Emperor **Maximinus**, 1602 German physicist **Otto von Guericke**, 1752 English poet **Thomas Chatterton**, 1762 French entomologist **Pierre Latreille**, 1841 Prime Minister of Canada **Wilfrid Laurier**, 1864 Swedish writer **Erik Axel Karlfeldt**, 1866 First Baseball Commissioner **Kenesaw Mountain Landis**, 1886 Austrian zoologist **Karl von Frisch**, 1900 U.S. "Dick Tracy" cartoonist **Chester Gould**, 1909 U.S. Senator **Alan Bible**, 1914 Italian fashion designer **Emilio Pucci**, 1920 U.S. actress **Gene Tierney**, 1925 Jazz singer **June Christy**, 1937 German tenor **René Kollo**, 1938 U.S. comedian/singer **Dick Smothers**, 1946 U.S. guitarist **Duane Allman**, 1956 U.S. actress **Bo Derek**, 1957 U.S. Secretary of Education **Margaret Spellings**

November 21

1694 **Voltaire:** Pen name of **François Marie Arouet**. French satirist, philosopher, historian, dramatist and poet. One of the greatest minds of the 18th century. Crusader for enlightenment, tolerance and justice. Undisputed ruler of European letters for more than fifty years. Known for his enmity to organized religion, fanaticism, intolerance and superstition. Famed for his declaration of personal principles: "I disapprove of what you say, but I will defend to the death your right to say it." Writings: *Œdipe*, *Le Siècle de Louis XIV*, *Zadig*, *Candide*, *Irene* and *La Henriade*.

It is dangerous to be right in matters on which the established authorities are wrong.

1729 **Josiah Bartlett:** American Revolutionary patriot. Elected to the Colonial Legislature in New Hampshire. Known as a principled legislator, not susceptible to pressure from the Royal Governor, and as an active advocate against British aggression. First signer of the Declaration of Independence after John Hancock. In 1777 he participated in the ratification of the Articles of Confederation. First governor of the state of New Hampshire (1792–94).

Custom governs the world; it is the tyrant of our feelings and our manners and rules the world with the hand of a despot.

1851 **Désiré-Joseph Mercier:** Belgian Roman Catholic cardinal and educator. Under the auspices of Pope Leo XIII, he organized an institute for the study of the teachings of St. Thomas Aquinas. Foremost leader in the 19th century revival of interest in Thomastic scholasticism and its integration with modern developments. During World War I, he was the spokesman of Belgian opposition to the German occupation, causing him to be placed under house arrest.

We must not only give what we have; we must also give what we are.

1898 **René Magritte:** Belgian artist and surrealist painter. Wallpaper designer and commercial artist. After his first poorly received one-man show went to Paris until 1930. Produced works of dreamlike incongruity, such as *Rape*, in which he substitutes a torso for a face. Major paintings: *The Wind and the Song* and *the Human Condition*. Considered an early innovator of the "Pop Art" of the 1960s.

Art evokes the mystery without which the world would not exist.

1904 **Coleman Hawkins:** American jazz tenor saxophonist. Joined the Fletcher Henderson Orchestra, where he laid the foundations of the tenor saxophone's future pre-eminence as a jazz solo instrument. His recording of "Body and Soul" became a benchmark for all jazz saxophonists. Known for his full tone and improvisations. Always inventive and seeking new challenges, he later greatly influenced the bebop movement.

I made the tenor sax — there's nobody plays like me and I don't play like anyone else.

1907 **Jim Bishop:** American author and editor. Wrote books dealing with the events of a fateful day in history: *The Day Lincoln Was Shot*, *The Day Christ Died* and *The Day Kennedy Was Shot*. Once remarked, "I'm a reporter, a pretty good one, a pro. If my work is memorable it's because I've revived the ancient art of storytelling." Learning that Jackie Gleason claimed to be hurt by Bishop's biography of the comedian, Bishop remarked: "I went from Lincoln to Gleason to Christ and neither of the other two subjects has complained yet."

It is difficult to live in the present, ridiculous to live in the future, and impossible to live in the past. Nothing is as far away as one minute ago.

1920 **Stan Musial:** "Stan the Man." Hall of Fame baseball outfielder and first baseman with St. Louis Cardinals. Seven-time national league batting leader, three-time MVP. At the height of his career he held more than fifty National League and Major League records. Had 3,630 career hits in 3,026 games played. First to play in more than one thousand games at two different positions. Oddly enough he had the same number of hits on the road as at home, namely 1,815.

The key to hitting for high average is to relax, concentrate, and don't hit the fly ball to center field.

1921 **Vivian Blaine:** American actress, singer and dancer. Most famous for originating the role of Miss Adelaide, the long-suffering, perpetually engaged chorus girl in the long running Broadway show *Guys and Dolls*, and later in the film version. Every night she stopped the show with her rendition of "Adelaide's Lament." As a starlet at 20th Century Fox, known as the cherry blonde because of her extraordinary hair as shown in Technicolor in films such as *State Fair*.

I put all my intelligence, such as it is, into playing dumb blondes.

1922 **Abe Lemons:** American college basketball coach, who established himself as a "teacher of men," not only in sports, but in the values of life. Excelled as a player and coach for more than 40 years at Oklahoma City University (OCU). Spent 25 years coaching at OCU, posting a 432–264 record, 3 years at Pan American University, and the University of Texas, before returning for a second stint with OCU.

Finish last in your league and they call you idiot. Finish last in medical school and they call you doctor.

1929 **Marilyn French:** American writer and *feminist* scholar. Examined the limited role of women in a male-dominated world culture. In the massive bestseller and biting social commentary *The Women's Room* she traced the heroine's development from 1950s housewife to 1970s emancipated woman. Other novels: *The Bleeding Heart and Her Mother's Daughter.* Non-fiction scholarly treatments: *On Women, Men and Morals, The War Against Women* and *Women's History of the World.*

Men seem unable to feel equal to women; they must be superior or they are inferior.

1945 **Goldie Hawn:** American actress. Became a TV sensation as the bikini-clad, perennially giggling, blonde scatterbrain on *Rowan and Martin's Laugh-In* (1968–70). Showed there was much more to her that a giddy bimbo by winning a Best Supporting Actress Academy Award for *Cactus Flower*. Particularly adept in film comedy roles, including: *Butterflies Are Free, Shampoo, Private Benjamin, Foul Play* and *The First Wives Club*.

I have witnessed the softening of the hardest heart by a simple smile.

1965 **Björk:** Icelandic musician, singer, songwriter and actress, with a very quirky fashion sense. Released her first solo album *Debut* in 1993. Composed the music and starred in the movie *Dancer in the Dark*, winning the Best Actress Prize at the Cannes Film Festival. Criticized at the 73rd Annual Academy Awards when she arrived in her now famous "swan dress." Composed and sang "Oceania" for the Opening Ceremony of the Olympic Games in Athens (2004).

I'm a fountain of blood in the shape of a girl.

OTHERS: 1567 French saint **Anne de Xainctonge**, 1761 British actress/royal mistress **Dorothy Jordan**, 1787 Canadian-born shipping magnate **Samuel Cunard**, 1863 English editor **Arthur Quiller-Couch**, 1886 English diplomat **Harold Nicolson**, 1888 U.S. "silent" comedian **Harpo Marx**, 1908 U.S. children's author **Elizabeth George Speare**, 1912 U.S. actress/tap dancer **Eleanor Powell**, 1913 British director/ producer **Roy Boulting**, 1916 U.S. football quarterback **Sid Luckman**, 1921 Finnish composer **Joonas Kokkonen**, 1931 Australian composer **Malcolm Williamson**, 1937 U.S. actress "That Girl" **Marlo Thomas**, 1944 U.S. politician **Dick Durbin**, 1956 U.S. journalist **Ed Kaz**, 1963 U.S. actress "The Sure Thing" **Nicollette Sheridan**

November 22

1819 **George Eliot:** Pen name of **Mary Ann Evans**. Considered one of the most distinguished English novelists of her time. Her realist fiction provides insights into the internal reasons for the choices her characters made in their struggle to understand life. Novels: *Adam Bede, The Mill on the Floss, Silas Marner* and *Middlemarch*. Wrote a volume of essays, *Impressions of Theophrastus Such*; the poems "The Spanish Gypsy," "Agatha," and "The Legend of Jubal."

I'm not denying the women are foolish; God almighty made 'em to match the men.

1857 **George R. Gissing:** British novelist, critic and essayist. Brilliant academic career was ruined when trying to reform and support a young prostitute, caught stealing money from his classmates, expelled and imprisoned. Spent a year wandering in the U.S. before returning to England, where he married the girl and entered a life of misery and poverty. His novels *The Nether World* and *New Grub Street* are characterized by realism and psychological acuteness.

That is one of the bitterest curses of poverty; it leaves no right to be generous.

1868 **John Nance Garner:** American politician and lawyer. "Cactus Jack." One of Washington's most colorful and influential figures. Always could be counted upon to speak his mind about what was right and wrong about the government. Congressman from Texas (1903–33). Speaker of the House (1931–33) and Franklin D. Roosevelt's vice president (1933–41). Union leader John L. Lewis referred to Nance as "a poker-playing, whiskey-drinking evil old man." At age 90, he reported that he had given up cigars and whiskey, recommending for a long life:

Don't overeat... It will kill you faster than anything.

1869 **André Gide:** French novelist, humanist, editor and essayist. Published more than 80 works in what was essentially a religious search. As well known for his influence as a moralist and a thinker as for his literary contributions. *Les Cahiers d'André Walter* reflected his spiritual love for his cousin Madeleine and conviction that physical desire must be suppressed. Later rejected mortification of the flesh and discovered his homosexual leanings. Fiction autobiographical in the sense that each major figure represents an exaggerated personification of some aspect of his character. Other works; *The Fruits of the Earth, The Immoralist,* and *The Counterfeiters.* 1947 Nobel Prize for Literature.

Nothing prevents happiness like the memory of happiness.

1890 **Charles de Gaulle:** French general and statesman. Leader of the French government-in-exile during World War II. Stood as a symbol of France's greatness during its darkest times under the German occupation, who returned to restore it to freedom as the first President of the Fourth Republic, but found it wanting and waited for a second call to bring France the "Grandeur," he insisted belonged to it. After a revolt against the government by French Army officers, De Gaulle became the first President of the Fifth Republic (1958–69). Author of *The Edge of the Sword* and *The Call to Honor.*

I am a man alone ... I am a man who belongs to no one and who belongs to everyone ... I am ready to take the leadership of the Government of the French Republic. What France needs is a great soul in this hour of peril. I am that soul. I am the Jeanne d'Arc of this era.

1912 **Doris Duke:** American heiress and philanthropist. So-called "richest girl in the world," her father died left his only child a trust fund in excess of $30,000,000 and a trusteeship of the Duke Endowment — a gift of $40,000,000 with provisions for more through accumulated income from the operation of her father's businesses. Did a great deal of philanthropic work and was a major benefactor of medical research and child welfare. Left virtually all of her estimated $1.3 billion fortune to a charitable foundation.

People wouldn't have money long if they didn't ask how much things cost and then refuse to buy half of them.

1913 **Benjamin Britten:** English composer, conductor and pianist. Turned out scores for films and theater music for writers W.H. Auden, Christopher Isherwood and J.B. Priestley. Britten's operas: *Peter Grimes, Billy Budd, The Turn of the Screw, A Midsummer Night's Dream* and *Death in Venice.* Other compositions: *The Young Person's Guide to the Orchestra*, the choral work *Hymn to Saint Cecilia*, the ballet *The Prince of Pagodas* and his greatest success, *War Requiem*, written for the opening of the rebuilt Coventry Cathedral in 1962.

[Music has] the beauty of disappointment and never satisfied love. The cruel beauty of nature and everlasting beauty of monotony.

1918 **Claiborne Pell:** American politician and business executive. Democratic U.S. Senator from Rhode Island (1961–97). Largely responsible for creating the "Pell Grants" in 1973, which provide financial aid and funds to U.S. college students. Also the main sponsor of the bill which created the National Endowment for the Arts and the National Endowment for the Humanities. Author of: *Megalopolis Unbound* and *Power and Policy.*

In politics, the secret is always let the other man have your way.

1921 **Rodney Dangerfield:** Born **Jacob Cohen**. American comedian and actor, best known for his "I get no respect" comedy monologues. His very first of that theme was "I don't get no respect. I played hide-and-seek, and they wouldn't even look for me." Opened a Manhattan nightclub, "Dangerfield's," as a venue for many up-and-coming comedians: Jerry Seinfeld, Tim Allen, Roseanne Barr and Rita Rudner. Films: *Caddyshack, Easy Money* and *Back to School.* His comedy album *No Respect* earned him a Grammy. Reportedly, he smoked marijuana daily for sixty years.

My psychiatrist told me I was crazy and I said I want a second opinion. He said, okay, you're ugly too.

1924 **Geraldine Page:** American actress nicknamed "First Lady of the American Theater." Her performance in an Off-Broadway revival of Tennessee William's *Summer and Smoke* caused a sensation. She was the first individual from a non–Broadway production to receive the Drama Critics Award. Received her first of four Tony Award nominations for her portrayal of a pathetic fading movie star in Tennessee Williams' *Sweet Bird of Youth.* Won an Academy Award with her eighth nomination, for her unparalleled performance in *The Trip to Bountiful.*

I didn't want to be a Hollywood actress who ever so often does a Broadway play. I wanted to be a Broadway actress who ever so often does a movie.

1943 **Billie Jean King:** née **Moffitt**. American tennis player and women's rights pioneer. One of the dominant players in women's tennis, winning 20 titles at Wimbledon consisting of six singles, 10 women's doubles, and four mixed doubles. One of the founders of the Women's Tennis Association. As its first president she played a prominent role in enhancing the prizes and playing conditions for professional women tennis players. Books: *Tennis to Win, Secrets of Wining Tennis* and *Billie Jean King.* Defeated aging Bobby Riggs in a "Battle of the Sexes" match (1973).

No one changes the world who isn't obsessed.

1984 **Scarlett Johansson:** Glamorous and incredibly stunning American actress, who reminds one of the classy and elegant beautiful actresses of Hollywood's Golden Age. Her films, began with *The Horse Whisperer*, followed by her major roles in *Ghost World, Lost in Translation, Girl with a Pearl Earring, The Perfect Score* and *Match Point* have brought her acclaim, positive critical notice and four Golden Globe nominations.

If you're comfortable with yourself, then it's sexy. Maybe people think I look sexy because I feel sexy. I am a very liberated person that way. I'm very comfortable with my sexuality, my body, my face — well sometimes I'm not comfortable with my face, but it's stuck there and there's nothing I can do about it.

OTHERS: 1428 English politician **Richard Neville**, 1564 English conspirator **Henry Brooke**, 1643 French explorer **Robert Cavlier de La Salle**, 1719 German composer **Wilhelm Friedemann Bach**, 1722 Ukrainian poet/philosopher **Hryhori Skovoroda**, 1767 Tyrolean patriot **Andreas Hofer**, 1787 Danish linguist **Rasmus Rask**, 1849 German artist **Christian Rohlfs**, 1877

Hungarian poet **Endre Ady**, 1893 U.S. auto designer **Harley Earl**, 1899 U.S. pilot **Wiley Post**, 1902 Governor of Rhodesia **Humphrey Gibbs**, 1921 Irish author **Brian Cleve**, 1923 Canadian film director **Arthur Hiller**, 1940 U.S. director **Terry Gilliam**, 1950 U.S. musician/actor **Steve Van Zandt**, 1958 U.S. actress **Jamie Lee Curtis**

November 23

1221 **Alfonso X:** His nickname "El Sabio" is translated "The Learned." King of Galicia, Castile and Leon (1252–84). Patron of learning and literature. Founder of a Castilian national literature, causing the first general history of Spain be composed in Castilian, as well as a translation of the Old Testament made by Toledo Jews. Reign was inept because of his pursuit of the title of German king and Holy Roman emperor.

Had I been present at the creation, I would have given some useful hints for the better ordering of the universe.

1760 **François-Noël Babeuf:** "Gracchus." French journalist and political agitator. The execution of Robespierre ended the Reign of Terror, but Babeuf, who called himself Gracchus Babeuf— in tribute to the Roman reformers, the Gracchi — defended the deposed terror leaders. Together with a small circle of followers, he openly preached "insurrection, revolt and the constitution of 1793. He and a number of his associates were executed for their role in the "Conspiracy of the Equals" an armed insurrection set for May 11, 1796. At his trial, Babeuf said:

The natural right of men and their destiny is to be happy and free. Society is instituted to guarantee the more certainty to each member the natural right of his destiny. When these natural rights are not the lot of all, the social pact is broken.

1804 **Franklin Pierce:** American politician and 14th U.S. President (1853–57). Elected to the U.S. Congress as a Jacksonian Democrat from New Hampshire. Advocated the annexation of Texas with or without slavery. As president he defended slavery and the fugitive slave law. During his administration, the Missouri Compromise was repealed and the Kansas-Nebraska Act was passed, kindling a flame in the county that eventually led to the Civil War.

Frequently the more trifling the subject, the more animated and protracted the discussion.

1859 **Billy the Kid [William H. Bonney]:** Originally **Henry McCarthy**. American western bandit and gunfighter. Killer from age 12. Achieved legendary notoriety for his hold-ups and robberies in the Southwest. Captured by Sheriff Pat Garrett in 1880 and sentenced to hang, but escaped. Garrett tracked him down and shot him several months later. The Kid's last words appear on his gravestone:

Truth and History. 21 Men. The Boy Bandit King. He Died as He Lived.

1878 **Ernest J. King:** American admiral. During World War I, served on the staff of the U.S. Atlantic Fleet. Commanded the submarine base at Groton, Connecticut (1923–5).Commander-in-chief of U.S. fleet (1941–45) and chief of Naval Operations (1942–45). First to hold both positions at the same time. Principal architect of America's victory at sea during World War II, masterminding the carrier based campaign against Japan.

If a ship has been sunk, I can't bring it up. If it is going to be sunk, I can't stop it. I can use my time much better working on tomorrow's problem than by fretting about yesterday's. Besides, if I let these things get me, I wouldn't last long.

1887 **Boris Karloff:** Mild-mannered English-born stage and screen actor. Most famous as the monster in Frankenstein. Typecast in horror movies: *The Old Dark House*, *The Mummy*, *The Black Cat* and *The Body Snatcher*. Pointed out that the impulse to shudder is a universal one, that includes all ages, and that the success of the Mother Goose tales and the stories of the Brothers Grimm is due to the fact that they deal with "the quintessence of cruelty and savagery. Starred in Broadway productions of *Arsenic and Old Lace*, *Peter Pan* (as Captain Hook) and *The Lark*.

Suddenly, out of the eerie darkness and gloom, there swept on the screen, about eight times larger than life itself, the chilling horrendous figure of me as the Monster!

1897 **Willie "The Lion" Smith:** Born **William Bertholoff**. U.S. musician and ragtime pianist. Originator of piano style known as "Harlem Stride," developed as he gained a reputation as a hot piano player by playing for rent parties in Harlem private homes and small clubs. Mentor and teacher to young musicians such as Artie Shaw, Thelonious Monk and Duke Ellington. Won his title "the Lion" for bravery in World War I. Composed over a hundred songs, including some of the most memorable tunes in the jazz repertoire: "Echo of Spring," "Ripplin" Waters" and "Keep Your Temper."

Loud people are like a bad drink of whiskey — either you fight them or join them. Either way it's a bad idea.

1920 **Paul Celan:** Originally **Paul Antschel**. Romanian poet and essayist. When Romania came under Nazi rule, as a Jew, he was sent to a forced-labor camp. Moved to Vienna in 1947, where he published his first volume of poetry, *The Sand from the Urns*, followed by *Poppy and Memory*. Poem "Todesfuge" is one of the most famous expressions of the Holocaust. He published seven additional volumes of poetry before taking his own life by drowning in the Seine.

Reality is not simply there; it must be searched and won.

1922 **Manuel Fraga Iribarne:** Spanish statesman and politician. Key political figure both during the dictatorship of General Franco and in the subsequent democracy. As minister for Propaganda and Tourism (1962–69), played a major role in revitalizing the Spanish tourist industry. Term as Spain's ambassador to the United Kingdom ended with Franco's death. During the transition to a new government with Juan Carlos I as chief of state, Fraga's drastic measures as chief of state security damaged his popularity. He was one of the writers of the democratic constitution.

There are two kinds of men, those who love and create, and those who hate and destroy.

1926 **Sri Sathya Sai Baba:** Born **Satyanarayan Raju**. Controversial Indian spiritual leader. At 14 he had a series of strange experiences, asserting that the spirit of a guru known as Sai Baba, who had died 20 years earlier, had come into him. The youngster took the name Sathya Sai Baba and began to work "miracles," including materializing presents for his followers, healing the sick, and divining the thoughts of his disciples. Scandals, including the violent deaths of some of Baba's closest associates in his bedroom and the accusation of his sexual misconduct with teenage boys, have caused many disillusioned disciples to turn away from Sathya Sai Baba.

Life is a challenge, meet it! Life is a dream, realize it! Life is a game, play it! Life is Love, enjoy it!

1943 **Andrew Goodman:** American civil rights activist, who along with Mickey Schwerner and James Chaney worked as part of the "Freedom Summer" project to register black voters in Mississippi. On June 21, 1964, the three were arrested by Deputy Sheriff Cecil Price for allegedly driving 35 miles per hour in a 30 speed zone. Fined they were told to leave the county and on they way back to Meridian, Mississippi were ambushed and killed. It would be 41 years to the day that Edgar Ray Killen was found guilty not of the murder of the three civil rights workers, but of manslaughter.

It is true that the white man (and by this I mean Christian civilization in general) has proved himself to be the most depraved devil imaginable in his attitudes towards the Negro race.

1956 **Shane Gould:** Australian swimmer who won three gold medals, a silver and bronze in the 1972 Summer Olympics and retired from the sport at age 16. Only individual, male or female, to hold every world freestyle record from 100m to 1500m simultaneously, and the first female swimmer ever to win three Olympic gold metals in world record times. Commenting on drugging problems in Olympic sports:

It's up to athletes and coaches to apply pressure on behalf of the sports. On reflection, I find it quite frightening, gray areas have replaced black and white, and in modern society, concepts of right and wrong should be quite clear at the Olympics, and they are not. I am concerned with ethics involved.

OTHERS: 912 Holy Roman Emperor **Otto I the Great**, 1553 Italian botanist **Prospero Alpini**, 1705 English historian **Thomas Birch**, 1719 Irish actor **Spranger Barry**, 1837 Dutch physicist **Johannes Diderik van der Waals**, 1860 Swedish Prime Minister **Hjalmar Branting**, 1869 Danish engineer **Valdemar Poulsen**, 1876 Spanish composer **Manuel de Falla**, 1890 Russian artist **El Lissitzky**, 1897 Indian writer **Nirad C. Chaudhuri**, 1904 U.S. political power broker **John Bailey**, 1925 President of El Salvador **José Napoléon Duarte**, 1928 U.S. composer **Jerry Bock**, 1930 U.S. Secretary of Labor **William E. Brock**, 1944 U.S. screenwriter **Joe Eszterhaus**, 1953 French singer **Francis Cabrel**

November 24

1583 **Philip Massinger:** English dramatist. Wrote many of his works in collaboration with other dramatists, most notably John Fletcher. Best-known play is the satiric comedy *A New Way to Pay Old Debts*. Other plays: *The Duke of Milan*, *The Maid of Honor* and *The Two Noble Kinsmen*.

To doubt is worse than to have lost; and to despair is but to antedate those miseries that must fall on us.

1632 **Baruch [Benedict] de Spinoza:** Dutch-born philosopher of Portuguese Jewish descent. Unorthodox views led to expulsion from the Amsterdam synagogue. Rejected the Cartesian dualism of spirit and matter. Most eminent expounder of the doctrine of pantheism. Sought to formulate a metaphysical system that was mathematically deduced. Espoused a deterministic political doctrine, arguing that the individual surrenders his or her natural rights to the state in order to obtain security. Works: *A Treatise on Religious and Political Philosophy* and *Ethics*.

The world would be happier if men had the same capacity to be silent that they have to speak.

1713 **Laurence Sterne:** English novelist and clergyman. Best known for nine volumes of *The Life and Opinions of Tristram Shandy*, which parodied the developing conventions of the novel form and adopted devices, including a distinctive fluid narrative that greatly influenced the stylistic approaches of later writers. Considered both an accomplished scoundrel and a sentimental humorist. Work praised for its humor and condemned for its indecency.

You can always tell a real friend; when you've made a fool of yourself, he doesn't feel you have done a permanent job.

1853 **William Barclay "Bat" Masterson:** American gunfighter and lawman. In 1880 he was associated with Wyatt Earp in and around the infamous Tombstone, Arizona. A gambler and something of a dandy, he went to New York City in 1902, becoming a sports writer for the *New York Morning Telegraph*. In time, he became the paper's sports editor. Has become a permanent part of the legend that surrounds the westward expansion of America.

There are many in this old world of ours who hold that things break about even for all of us. I have observed, for example, that we all get the same amount of ice. The rich get it in the summertime and the poor get it in the winter.

1864 **Henri de Toulouse-Lautrec:** French artist. Reputation is based on color lithographs from the 1890s. Work is noted for its calligraphic line and flatness, influenced by Japanese prints. Known for his post–Impressionist depictions of Parisian night life. Physically misshapen by an accident that resulted in his legs not growing, he probed the emotions of dancers, actresses, singers and prostitutes of Montmartre. Particularly well-known for his *Moulin Rouge* series.

Marriage is a dinner than begins with dessert.

1877 **Alben W. Barkley:** American Kentucky politician and Vice President (1949–53). In 1912 he won a seat in the House of Representatives, serving seven terms, before being elected to the U.S. Senate in 1926. During his second tem he began a ten year reign as majority leader. Early convert to the New Deal. Chosen to be Harry Truman's running mate in 1948. After his term he returned to the Senate remaining there until his death in 1956.

The best audience is intelligent, well-educated, and a little drunk.

1885 **Anna Louise Strong:** Controversial American journalist and author. Known for her coverage of and alleged support for, communist movements in the U.S.S.R. and the People's Republic of China. Spoke out against the draft when the U.S. entered World War I. Became associated with the labor-owned daily newspaper, *The Union Record*, writing forceful pro-labor articles and promoting the new Soviet government. Traveled to Russia in 1921 as a correspondent for the American Friends Service Committee. In the late 1920s she traveled in China and other parts of Asia. Returned to the U.S.S.R. where she founded *Moscow News*, the first English-language newspaper in the city. Published Works: *The First Time in History, Children of the Revolution, My Native Land, The Soviets Expected It*, and *When Serfs Stood Up in Tibet*.

I am one of those who never knows the direction of my journey until I have almost arrived.

1888 **Dale Carnegie:** American writer and public speaking teacher. Author of the best-selling *How to Win Friends and Influence People*, a book of common sense advice, case histories and optimistic homilies. *How to Stop Worrying and Start Living* includes the wise advice: "First ask yourself: What is the worst that can happen? Then prepare to accept it. Then proceed to improve on the worst." Wrote a syndicated column and organized classes at the Dale Carnegie Institute for Effective Speaking and Human Relations.

You can conquer almost any fear if you will only make up your mind to do so. For remember, fear doesn't exist anywhere except in the mind.

1912 **Geraldine Fitzgerald:** Irish-born actress. Began her acting career at Dublin's Gate Theatre. Moved to New York where Orson Welles gave her American start in a Mercury Theater production. Oscar nominated for Best Supporting Actress in *Wuthering Heights*. Constantly fought with studio bosses over suitable roles. Lost the fight and her screen career faded. Made a triumphant appearance in the 1971 Broadway revival of Eugene O'Neill's *Long Day's Journey Into Night*. Other film roles: *Dark Victory, Wilson, OSS, Ten North Frederick, Arthur* and *Easy Money*.

I am proud of my rebellious moments, but I wish I'd handled them with more wit.

1912 **Garson Kanin:** American director, screenwriter and playwright. Became a Broadway actor in 1933, and directed his first play in 1937, leaving for Hollywood the next year. Wrote and directed Broadway hit *Born Yesterday*. Wrote hilarious screenplays with his wife Ruth Gordon: *Adam's Rib, Pat and Mike*, and *It Should Happen to You*. Directed: *Bachelor Mother* and *My Favorite Wife*. Books: *Tracy and Hepburn* and *Moviola*.

Books are men of higher stature; the only men that speak aloud for future times to hear.

1925 **William F. Buckley, Jr.:** Erudite and some say pretentious conservative American editor, columnist, writer and television commentator. Refers to himself as a libertarian. Founder and editor of the conservative *National Review* (1966–). His syndicated column appeared in over 200 newspapers. Host of PBS's television's "Firing Line," where he displayed a scholarly, non-confrontational and humorous approach to his conservatism. Author of *God and Man at Yale, Up From Liberalism* and *Let Us Talk of Many Things*.

I won't insult your intelligence by suggesting that you really believe what you just said.

1946 **Ted Bundy:** American serial killer, a term coined to describe him. Believed to have killed at least 26 females by bludgeoning them and sometimes by strangulation between 1974 and 1978. He is also believed to have raped many of his victims and of mutilating and molesting their bodies after they were dead. Convicted in 1979, sentenced to death and executed in Florida ten years later after a series of unsuccessful appeals.

We serial killers are your sons, we are your husbands, we are everywhere. And there will be more of your children dead tomorrow.

OTHERS: 1583 Spanish poet **Juan Martínez de Jáuregui y Aguilar**, 1655 King of Sweden **Charles XI**, 1713 Spanish missionary **Junipero Serra**, 1784 U.S. General/President **Zachary Taylor**, 1787 Austrian organist **Franz Gruber**, 1806 Inventor of Rugby **William Webb Ellis**, 1826 Italian author **Carlo Collodi**, 1895 U.S. architect **Cass Gilbert**, 1884 President of Israel **Itzhak Ben-Zvi**, 1895 President of Czechoslovakia **Ludvik Svoboda**, 1912 U.S. jazz pianist **Teddy Wilson**, 1925 Dutch physicist **Simon van der Meer**, 1938 U.S. basketball player **Oscar Robertson**, 1940 NFL Commissioner **Paul Tagliabue**, 1944 Nigerian scholar/diplomat **Ibrahim Gambari**, 1978 U.S. actress **Katherine Heigl**

November 25

1562 **Lope de Vega:** Outstanding Spanish playwright and poet of the Spanish Golden Age. Creator of the Spanish version of commedia dell'arte. Considered second only to Cervantes among Spanish writers. Virtually alone, created the Spanish national drama. Reputation was such that the phrase "Es de Lope" became a synonym for "perfection." Plays: *Peribáñez, El Mejor Alcalde, El acero de Madrid, Los melindres de Belisa El divino africano* and his best nondramatic work, *La Dorotea*, a long prose romance.

No viper has worse venom or keener fangs than a woman enraged because she has been scorned by a man.

1835 **Andrew Carnegie:** Scottish-born American business tycoon, financier and philanthropist. Founder of the Carnegie Steel Company, which eventually became U.S. Steel. Gifted with remarkable organizational ability, built his steel company into a giant that weathered the depression following the Panic of 1893 better than the rest, so he came to dominate the industry. Published an article entitled "Wealth" in which he gave the view that it was the duty of the rich to oversee the distribution of their surplus wealth for the betterment of civilization, observing, "The man who dies rich, dies disgraced." Benefactor of more than 2500 libraries. Creator of endowments for international peace.

People who are unable to motivate themselves must be content with mediocrity, no matter how impressive their other talents.

1846 **Carry Amelia Moore Nation:** American prohibitionist and social reformer. In 1890s she pursued a hatchet-swinging mission of destroying rum joints. Jailed and fined for disturbing the peace, she was not intimidated: Paid her bail and fines by selling souvenir hatchets. Despite her spectacular campaign, the enactment prohibition was largely due to the efforts of more sedate reformers, who did not associate themselves with Nation.

Men are nicotine-soaked, beer-besmirched, whiskey-greased, red-eyed devils.

1881 **John XXIII: Angelo Giuseppe Roncalli**, Roman Catholic pope (1958–63). Made a Cardinal and Patriarch of Venice in 1953. Elected pope in 1958 on the 12th ballot. Considered to be an interim Pope, he began a new era in the Roman Catholic Church by convening Vatican II Council (1962), to effect reforms in the Church and modernize its teachings, disciplines and organization. Invited Eastern Orthodox and Protestant observers to join the delegates. Sought to repair relations with the Jews. Died before the Council had concluded, but it made major changes in Catholic liturgy.

If God created shadows it was to better emphasize the light.

1893 **Joseph Wood Krutch:** American author, critic, editor and naturalist. Drama critic and associate editor, *The Nation* (1924–32). Critical works include *Edgar Allan Poe: A Study of Genius*, one of his first psychoanalytical interpretations of literature, *Five Masters: A Study in the Mutations of the Novel* and *The American Drama Since 1918*. Essay collections: *The Modern Temper, The Measure of Man* and *Human Nature and the Human Condition.*

Ever time a value is born, existence takes on a new meaning; every time one dies, some part of that meaning passes away. Logic is the art of going wrong with confidence.

1896 **Virgil Thomson:** American composer and music critic. Settled in Paris, where he wrote the dissonant but traditionally formed *Sonata da Chiesa*, the ultramodern *Symphony on a Hymn Tune*, and *Symphony Number 2*, both of the latter works drawing upon American folk themes. His opera-collage of American historical, folk and contemporary musical themes, *The Mother of Us All*, depicting the life of Susan B. Anthony, was first performed in 1947. Wrote scores for films: *The River* and *Louisiana Story,* for which he won a Pulitzer Prize.

Try a thing you haven't tried before three times — once to get over the fear of it, once to find out how to do it, and a third time to find out whether you like it or not.

1900 **Helen Gahagan Douglas:** American actress, opera singer and politician. Well known star on Broadway in the 1920s. Her only Hollywood movie was *She* (1935), playing: "The Ice Goddess"—"She who must be obeyed." Elected to the U.S. Congress representing California for three terms. Allegedly had an affair with Lyndon Johnson. Ran for the U.S. Senate in 1950, but was defeated by Richard Nixon in a race her supporters described as a prototypical smear campaign. Nixon called her "the Pink Lady," a reference to her supposed fellow traveler sympathies. She crowned her opponent with the nickname that stuck, "Tricky Dick."

Character isn't inherited. One builds it daily by the way one thinks and acts, thought by thought, action by action.

1900 **Rudolf Hoess:** German commandant of the Auschwitz concentration camp (1940–43), responsible for the murder of hundreds of thousands of people. After service in the German army in World War I he was sentenced to ten years in prison for his involvement in a political murder, but served only five years due to a general amnesty. Early member of the Nazi Party, rose through the ranks of the SS. Captured in 1946 by the British, Hoess was handed over to Poland and was sentenced to death by hanging, which took place on April 2, 1947.

We were all so trained to obey orders without even thinking that the thought of disobeying an order would never have occurred to anyone.

1904 **Ba Jin:** Also **Pa Chin**, penname of **Li Yaotang** or **Li Feigan**. One of the most important and widely read Chinese writers of the 20th century. Editor at several publishing firms and periodicals, as well as composing the works for which he is best known — *The Family, The Love Trilogy: Fog, Rain* and *Lightning* and the novellas *Autumn in Spring* and *A Dream of the Sea*. During the Cultural Revolution, persecuted as a counterrevolutionary. Defiantly shouted at the end of a televised public humiliation in the People's Stadium: "You have your thoughts and I have mine. This is the fact and you can't change it even if you kill me." Rehabilitated in 1977 and elected to many important national literary posts.

Only by not forgetting the past can we be the master of the future.

1914 **Joe DiMaggio:** "Jolting Joe" and "The Yankee Clipper." U.S. Hall of Fame outfielder with the New York Yankees, leading them to 10 World Series titles in 13 years. Most remarkable accomplishment is hitting safely in 56 straight games (1941). Fielding was equally remarkable — it wasn't that he made spectacular catches; he just seemed to glide to the right spot to glove the ball. Married actress Marilyn Monroe in 1954, but the union was dissolved a year later.

There is always some kid who may be seeing me for the first or last time. I owe him my best.

1915 **Augusto Pinochet:** Chilean President. Came to power in a violent coup, supported by the U.S., which deposed Salvador Allende, a Marist surgeon who was the first Socialist elected President. Pinochet suspended the constitution, dissolved Congress, imposed strict censorship, proscribed the leftist parties that constituted Allende's Popular Unity coalition, and halted all political activity. His reign was one of extensive human rights violations. Approximately 3000 Chileans are known to have been executed, and some 27,000 others were incarcerated and tortured. While traveling abroad to have back surgery, he was arrested in England, under an international arrest warrant, and placed under house arrest, charged with crimes against humanity. Because of his age and health he was eventually allowed to return to Chile.

Sometimes democracy must be bathed in blood.

1960 **John F. Kennedy, Jr.:** American scion to the Kennedy legacy. Spent his entire life under public scrutiny. His place in history was established when on his third birthday, the world was moved as he saluted his assassinated father's passing cabinet. In 1995, he launched the glossy magazine *George*, which took a slightly askew look at government and those governing. After being linked with many lovely women, he married Carolyn Bessette. On July 16, 1999, Kennedy, his wife and her sister perished in a plane crash off the coast of Massachusetts. Their ashes were scattered near where they died.

The worst thing, I think that can happen (to famous people) is that ... you retreat into your own private world. For what I do and just for how I want to live my life, I think it's really important to connect to normal life.

OTHERS: 1501 Confucian scholar **Li Hwang**, 1703 French astronomer/botanist **Jean-François Séguier**, 1714 Japanese mathematician **Yoriyuki Arima**, 1817 U.S. statesman **John Bigelow**, 1844 German automobile engineer **Karl Benz**, 1845 Portuguese novelist **José Maria de Eça de Queirós**, 1862 U.S. pianist **Ethelbert Nevin**, 1874 U.S. boxer **Joe Gans**, 1883 U.S. mystic **Harvey Spencer Lewis**, 1895 German pianist **Wilhelm Kempff**, 1915 U.S. physician **Lewis Thomas**, 1924 Japanese poet **Takaaki Yoshimoto**, 1939 U.S. economist **Martin Feldstein**, 1945 U.S. musician **Percy Sledge**, 1954 Former CEO of Enron **Jeffery Skilling**, 1960 U.S. singer **Amy Grant**, 1971 U.S. actress **Christine Applegate**

November 26

1792 **Sarah Moore Grimké:** American abolitionist. Revolted against the practice of slavery and with her sister Angelina move to Philadelphia to become a Quaker. Freed the slaves they had inherited from their father. She appealed to the women of the U.S. to support the fight against slavery. The sisters moved to New York in 1836 and broadened their campaign to include women's emancipation. Sarah's publications: *Epistle to the Clergy of the Southern States*, *The Condition of Women* and *American Slavery as it is: Testimony of a Thousand Witnesses.*

I ask no favor for my sex... All I ask of our brethren is that they take their feet from off our necks.

1832 **Mary Edwards Walker:** American feminist and first woman surgeon in the U.S. Campaigned for rational dress for women — believing such binding clothes as corsets were not healthy, revised marriage and divorce laws, and women's rights. During the Civil War she served as an unpaid field surgeon near the front lines. Frequently crossed battle lines, treating civilians. Served as supervisor of a female prison and head of an orphanage. After the war Generals Sherman and Thomas nominated her for The Congressional Medal of Honor, awarded by President Andrew Johnson.

You men are not our protectors... If you were, who would there be to protect us from?

1847 **Maria Fyodorovna:** Princess **Marie Sophie Frederikke Dagmar** of Denmark and Empress of Russia. Wife of Tsar Alexander III and was the mother of the last Tsar of the Romanov Dynasty, Nicholas II. Her elder sister Alexandra was the Queen Consort of King Edward VII and mother of George V of the United Kingdom. When the monarch was overthrown during the October Revolution of 1917, Maria lost two sons, Emperor Nicholas II and Grand Duke Mikhail, four granddaughters and a grandson, but refused to leave Russia. It was only in 1919 that she grudgingly consented to return to Denmark. She wrote to her son Grand Duke Georgy Alexandrovich:

Fortunately, God conceals the future from us and we know nothing about the future troubles and ordeals. Otherwise, we could not have enjoyed the present and life would have been a long torture.

1894 **Norbert Weiner:** "Father of Automation." Founded a new discipline —*cybernetics*— the study of control and communication in animals and machines. Coined the term from the Greek *kybernetes*, meaning "steersman." When a steersman moves a rudder, the course of his boat changes. When the steersman notes that the previous course change is too much, he once again moves the rudder, in the opposite direction. The feedback of the steersman's senses is the controlling agent that keeps the craft on its intended course. One of the most colorful and eccentric mathematical geniuses of the 20th century, Wiener is famed for his legendary other-mindedness that significantly contributed to the stereotypical image of mathematics professors. Books: *Cybernetics, The Human Use of Human Beings* and *I Am a Mathematician.*

The nervous system and the automatic machine are fundamentally alike in that they are devices, which make decisions on the basis of decisions that they made in the past.

1895 **William "Bill W." Griffith Wilson:** Co-founder of the mutual-help group, Alcoholics Anonymous with Dr. Robert H. Smith. Wilson became an alcoholic at age 22. While recovering from alcoholism he had a religious vision, after which he never drank another drop. It wasn't always easy to maintain his sobriety, until he discovered the key to AA, having problem drinkers help each other. Dr. Smith, an Akron, Ohio surgeon became his partner in establishing both the organization and its twelve steps. The phrase "Friends of Bill W" is sometimes used as a code for Alcoholics Anonymous.

Suddenly the room lit up with a great white light.... It seemed to me; in the mind's eye that I was on a mountain and that a wind not of air but of spirit was blowing. And then it burst upon me that I was a free man.

1905 **Emlyn Williams:** Welsh actor and playwright. Because of the kindness of an English school teacher, spared the hard life of a coal miner. Years later he retold the story in a play in which he starred, *The Corn Is Green.* First attracted notice as a playwright with *A Murder Has Been Arranged* and his first success as an actor in Edgar Wallace's *The Case of the Frightened Lady.* Other plays, which he wrote and appeared in: *Night Must Fall, The Light of Heart* and *The Wind of Heaven.* The tour of his one-man show, impersonating Charles Dickens and reading selections from his works was a smash hit, as was his similar appearance as Dylan Thomas.

The possibilities for mobilizing the experience, imaginations, and intelligence of workers, both employed and unemployed, are limitless.

1908 **Lefty Gomez:** American baseball pitcher. Nicknamed "El Goofy," a bit of a screwball who delighted in playing practical jokes on everyone from teammates to umpires. Most of his career was spent with the New York Yankees. Became a sought-after dinner speaker known for his humorous anecdotes about his playing days and the personalities he knew. 20-game winner four times and an All-Star every year from 1933 to 1939.

The secret of my success was clean living and a fast outfield.

1912 **Eugène Ionesco:** Romanian-French dramatist of the Theatre of the Absurd. Associated with Samuel Beckett, Arthur Adamov, Jean Ghelderode and Jean Genet. From 1933 to 1937, Ionesco produced a number of critical reviews — most devoted to lambasting Romanian literary figures. Grim grotesque farces are basically comic. His favorite play, *The Victims of Duty* was hooted off the stage in Darmstadt. Other Works: *The Bald Soprano, The Killer* and *Rhinoceros.*

It is not the answer that enlightens, but the question.

1912 **Eric Sevareid:** American broadcaster with a solid background as a newspaper journalist. CBS correspondent (1939–77). Covered the fall of France to the Germans and the early blitz war in London. Flew to China, where his report on the Chiang-Communism crisis was censored *in toto* by the State Department. During this tour of Asia, he was one of 19 Americans forced to parachute from a disable plane, landing in the Burmese jungle, rescued by headhunters. Returned to Europe, went with the troops on the first landings in Italy, following them through France and Germany. Commentator on CBS News (1964–77). Author of *Not So Wild a Dream* and *This Is Eric Sevareid.*

Brotherhood is not so wild of a dream as those, who profit from postponing it, pretend.

1922 **Charles M. Schulz:** American cartoonist. Took a correspondent course in cartooning and worked as a freelance cartoonist for a religious magazine and *The Saturday Evening Post* before creating "Peanuts," starring Charlie Brown, Lucy and Snoopy. The strip was originally called *Li'l Folks* (1950). Most widely circulated strip of all times. It deals with the frustrations of everyday life and the cruelty that exists among children, often with philosophical and psychological overtones. It has been adapted for television and stage. Schulz based Charlie Brown on himself.

Life is like a ten speed bicycle. Most of us have gears we never use. I have a new philosophy.

1938 **Porter Goss:** American politician and Central Intelligence Agency director. U.S. Congressman from Florida (1988–2004). Eight years chairman of the House Intelligence Committee and served on the House Rules Committee and House Select Committee for Homeland Security. President Bush chose him to replace George Tenet at the head of the U.S. Intelligence agency. Given the job of reforming the CIA after a series of intelligence failures, particularly in relation to the 9–11 attacks. Less than two years after his appointment Goss resigned without giving any reason for the move.

The Iraq conflict, while not a cause of extremism, has become a cause for extremists.

1938 **Tina Turner:** Born **Anna Mae Bullock.** Rhythm and blues–rock vocalist and actress. Part of a successful team with guitarist husband Ike Turner whose biggest hit is "Proud Mary." Others include: "Poor Fool" and "River Deep, Mountain High." Developed a sexy stage routine, which included frenzied dancing in micro-mini skirts, sweat from her shapely body flying in all directions. Hits as a solo star: "What's Love Got to Do with It?" "We Don't Need Another Hero" and "Typical Male." Films: *Tommy* and *Mad Max Beyond Thunderdome.*

There comes a point where it is just undignified to be a rock 'n' roll star.

OTHERS: 1607 American colonial clergyman **John Harvard**, 1678 French geophysicist **Jean Jacques d'Ortous de Mairan**, 1857 Swiss linguist **Ferdinand de Saussure**, 1876 Air-conditioning pioneer **Willis H. Carrier**, 1898 German chemist **Karl Ziegler**, 1899 German kidnapper of Lindbergh baby **Bruno Hauptmann**, 1915 U.S. pianist **Earl Wild**, 1924 U.S. pop sculptor **George Segal**, 1925 U.S. actress **Linda Hunt**, 1931 Argentine activist **Adolfo Pérez Esquivel**, 1933 U.S. singer **Robert Goulet**, 1934 U.S.S.R. runner **Ludmila Shevtsova**, 1938 U.S. impressionist **Rich Little**, 1946 U.S. football coach **Art Shell**, 1964 Swiss skier **Vreni Schneider**, 1972 Indian actor **Arjun Rampal**

November 27

1635 **Françoise Bertaut de Motteville:** French memoir writer. An observant and independent woman, her chief work is her *Mémoirs*, which in effect is a history and defense of her mistress Anne of Austria and gives a faithful picture of the life at court. Historians have always used *Mémoirs* as one of their chief sources of information on the mid-century conflict known as the *Fronde*.

The true way to render ourselves happy is to love our work and find in it our pleasure.

1874 **Charles A. Beard:** Among America's most distinguished historians. Collaborated with his equally distinguished historian wife, Mary Ritter Beard, on the four part series *The Rise of American Civilization*. He helped found the New School for Social Research in 1919. During the 1930s and 40s he was deeply concerned with U.S. foreign policy. His outlook tended toward isolationism and he severely criticized President Roosevelt's policies in the period leading to World War II. Books: *The Supreme Court and the Constitution*, *A Basic History of the United States*, and *President Roosevelt and the Coming of the War*.

You need only reflect that one of the best ways to get yourself a reputation as a dangerous citizen these days s to go about repeating the very phrases which our founding fathers used in the struggle for independence.

1874 **Chaim Weizmann:** Russian-born Israeli statesman and biochemist. His 1912 discovery of a bacterium that could convert carbohydrate to acetone proved was of considerable value to the British armaments industry during World War I. In return, the British government aided his negotiations leading to the Balfour Declaration (1917). In 1919 he obtained an agreement from Emir Faysal ibn Hussain on Jewish-Arab coexistence in Palestine. World Zionist Organization president (1920–29, 1935–46). First president of Israel (1949–52).

Miracles sometimes occur, but one has to work terribly hard for them.

1877 **Katharine Anthony:** American biographer of Catherine the Great, Elizabeth I, Louise May Alcott, Dolley Madison and Susan B. Anthony. Best-known for *The Lambs*, a controversial study of the British writers Charles and Mary Lamb. Other works: *Mothers Who Must Earn* and *Feminism in Germany and Scandinavia*. From 1920 on, she lived in Manhattan with her life-partner Elisabeth Irwin, the founder of the Little Red School House.

Principles are a dangerous form of social dynamite.

1909 **James Agee:** American novelist, film critic and screenwriter. Wrote film criticism for *Time* magazine and contributed articles to the *Nation*, *Partisan Review*, *Harper's* and the *Forum*. His masterwork and only novel, *A Death in the Family*, presents a young boy's view of his family after the death of his father. It was published posthumously and awarded a Pulitzer Prize in 1958. Wrote scripts for *The African Queen* and *Night of the Hunter*.

God doesn't believe in the easy way.

1912 **David Merrick:** Originally **David Marulois.** Colorful, dynamic and egotistical American theatrical producer. Had a 40 plus years of more than 80 Broadway hits and a number of legendary flops. From 1957 on he produced several Broadway attractions at the same time. Established as the most successful producer on Broadway. Famed for his unorthodox publicity stunts and feuding with critics. Productions: *Fanny*, *The Matchmaker*, *Gypsy*, *Becket*, *Oliver!*, *Hello, Dolly!* and *42nd Street*. Famous for his remark: "It's not enough that I should succeed — others should fail." Won six regular Tony awards and two honorary ones.

There's a horse's ass for every light on Broadway.

1917 **Buffalo Bob Smith:** American host and creator of television children's classic *The Howdy Doody Show*. The show starring the freckled, redheaded puppet, Howdy Doody, took place in Doodyville, a circus town that had both puppet and human inhabitants. Among these was the costumed clown Clarabelle, who never spoke, but spayed seltzer everywhere. The first person to portray Clarabelle was Bob Keeshan, who went on the become Captain Kangaroo. The show ran from 1947 to 1960 on NBC, and had 2,543 episodes, first show ever to hit the 2000 mark. The live audience of kids was called the Peanut Gallery and there was a huge waiting list for tickets.

Say kids, what time is it?

1921 **Alexander Dubček:** Czech politician. During World War II, took part in the underground resistance to Nazi occupation. After the war rose through the ranks of the Communist Party, becoming its head in 1968. Introduced liberal reforms in the brief period known as the *Prague Spring*, which came to an end with the Soviet Union's invasion in August 1968. Expelled from the party, he returned to prominence as speaker of the Czech parliament in 1989 after the Communist Party gave up its monopoly on power.

Let whatever is going to happen to me happen. I'm expecting the worst for myself and I'm resigned to it.

1927 **William E. Simon:** American government official and financier. U.S. Secretary of the Treasury

(1974–77) during the Nixon administration, and continued in the role under President Gerald Ford. Simon was an active member of the U.S. Olympic Committee for over 30 years, serving a four-year term as president during which the 1984 games were held in Sarajevo and Los Angeles. A well-known philanthropist, made a personal commitment to serve the sick and poor.

Bad politicians are sent to Washington by good people who don't vote.

1937 **Gail H. Sheehy:** American writer, lecturer and social critic. A therapeutic journalist to whom everything looks like a passage. Notable for books on life and the life cycle, passages through life's stages. Author of the landmark work, *Passages* and its best-selling sequel, *New Passages*. Her huge international bestseller, *The Silent P*assage, broke the taboo around menopause, which she calls "Second Adulthood."

Growth demands a temporary surrender of security.

1942 **Jimi Hendrix:** Originally **James Marshall**. American blues and rock guitarist and songwriter. Left-handed, he taught himself to play the guitar, which he held upside down. Fused African traditions of blues, jazz, rock and soul with techniques of British avant-garde rock to redefine the role of the electric guitar. Made a sensational appearance at the Monterey Pop Festival in 1967 and rose to stardom with his first album *Are You Experienced?* Subsequent albums were among the most influential of the 1960s. Died at age 27 of an apparent accidental overdose of barbiturates.

When the power of love overcomes the love of power, the world will know peace.

1957 **Caroline Bouvier Kennedy Schlossberg:** Daughter and only surviving child of President John F. Kennedy and his wife and Jacqueline. With Ellen Alderman, she wrote two books on civil liberties*: In Our Defense—The Bill of Rights in Action* and *The Right to Privacy*. A founder of the Profiles in Courage Award, given annually to someone who exemplifies the type of courage examined in her father's book of the same name. Speaking of John Murtha who called for the withdrawal of U.S. forces in Iraq and Alberto Mora who spoke out against the Bush administration's policy that condones torture and abuse of prisoners and suspected terrorists.

Congressman John Murtha and Alberto Mora exemplify the kind of courage my father admired most. When others were unwilling to do so, each man recognized a moral obligation to speak out against the policies he believed were misguided and contrary to our national interest.

OTHERS: 1582 French scholar **Pierre Dupuy**, 1701 Swedish inventor/astronomer **Anders Celsius**, 1804 German opera composer **Julius Benedict**, 1809 British actress **Fanny Kemble**, 1857 British physiologist **Charles Scott Sherrington**, 1865 Columbian poet **Jose Silva**, 1867 French composer **Charles Koechlin**, 1901 U.S. sportscaster **Ted Husing**, 1903 Norwegian chemist **Lars Onsager**, 1916 U.S. sports announcer **Chick Hearn**, 1925 British science writer **John Maddox**, 1925 British comedian **Ernie Wise**, 1932 Philippine politician **Benigno Aquino**, 1940 Martial artist/actor **Bruce Lee**, 1955 U.S. engineer/broadcaster **Bill Nye**, 1958 U.S. baseball catcher/ manager **Mike Sciosica**, 1968 French actor **Michael Vartan**

November 28

1628 **John Bunyan:** English lay preacher and writer. Nonconformist minister. Arrested and spent ten years in prison for refusing to obey royal edicts banning nonconformist preaching. During his incarceration, wrote prolifically. A narrative genius, his writing style has been praised for its simplicity, vigor and concreteness. His most celebrated work is *Pilgrim's Progress*, a vision of life told allegorically as if it were a journey. Also wrote *The Holy City, or the New Jerusalem, A Confession of My Faith, and a Reason of My Practice,* and *The Holy War.*

Sin is the dare of God's justice, the rape of His mercy, the jeer of His patience, the slight of His power, and the contempt of His love.

1757 **William Blake:** English poet, engraver, printer and mystic. Known for his mysticism and complex symbolism. First book of poems was *Poetic Sketches* (1783). Had visions which helped him create his own mythology. Works: *Songs of Innocence, Songs of Experience, The Book of Thel* and *The Marriage of Heaven and Hell.* Finest artistic work is found in the *21 Illustrations to the Book of Job.*

To see a world in a grain of sand and heaven in a wild flower. Hold infinity in the palms of your hand and eternity in an hour.

1820 **Friedrich Engels:** German social and political philosopher, historian and founder of "scientific socialism." Shocked by the widespread poverty, he found in England, he wrote *The Condition of the Working Class in England.* Met Karl Marx in Brussels in 1844 and collaborated with him on the *Communist Manifesto*. Engels edited the second and third volumes of *Das Kapital* after Marx's death and was largely responsible for the wider distribution of his friend's ideas. His interpretations of Marxism and his philosophical and historical studies: *Origins of the Family, Private Property, and the State* developed the philosophy of dialectical materialism. Maintained: "the state is not abolished, it withers away." Contributed to feminist theory, saw the concept of monogamous marriage as having arisen because of the domination of man over woman. Argued that men dominated women just as the capitalist class dominated workers.

The Communists disdain to conceal their views and aims. They openly declare that their ends can be attained only by the forcible overthrow of all existing conditions. Let the ruling classes tremble at a communistic revolution. The proletarians have nothing to lose but their chains. They have a world to win. Workers of all countries ... unite!

1829 **Anton Rubinstein:** Russian composer, pianist and conductor. Settled in St. Petersburg, where he enjoyed the patronage of the Grand Duchess Helen. Court pianist and conductor of the court concerts. Wrote three operas: *Dimitri Donskoy*, *The Siberian Hunters*, and *Thomas the Fool*. Founder of the St. Petersburg Conservatory of Music. During the season 1872–73 he made a triumphant American tour. In 1890 he established the Rubenstein Prize. Introduced European methods into education and established high standards of artistic performance.

A concert is like a bullfight— the moment of truth.

1881 **Stefan Zweig:** Austrian biographer, poet, essayist and dramatist. Work distinguished by his psychological insight into character. Best known work, *The Tide of Fortune*, a set of historical portraits. Emigrated to London in 1934 and acquired British nationality. Later moved to the U.S. and Brazil. Wrote numerous essays and biographies of major literary and historical characters. Books: *Balzac*, *Dickens* and *Dostoyevsky*. Only novel: *Beware of Pity*.

Every wave, regardless of how high and forceful it crests, must eventually collapse within itself.

1894 **Brooks Atkinson:** American journalist and critic. Book reviewer, editor and theater critic for the *New York Times*. One of the famed "seven on the aisle" of Broadway critics. Called "the autocrat of the aisle seat." Could kill a new show single-handedly with a bad review. Foreign correspondent for the *Times* in Chunking, China (1942–44) and in Moscow (1945–46). His coverage of the political scene in the Russian capital earned him a Pulitzer Prize in 1947.Published several historical novels and an account of his stay in Russia, *Over at Uncle Joe's*.

In every age "the good old days" were a myth. No one ever thought they were good at the time. For every age has consisted of crises that seemed intolerable to the people who lived through them.

1904 **Nancy Mitford:** English novelist, biographer and editor. One of six beautiful sisters who moved in London society. Members of her family are easily recognized in Mitford's satiric and witty novels about upper-class British life and biographies of Voltaire and Madame de Pompadour. The London *Times Literary Supplement* observed that she had "a talent for personal and social mockery, a wit and gift for detecting the absurdities of character." Her *Noblesse Oblige* was a diverting treatise on everyday speech that tipped-off whether one is "U" (upper class) or "non–U."

I love children, especially when they cry, for then someone takes them away.

1907 **Alberto Moravia:** Pen name of **Alberto Pincherle.** Italian journalist, essayist, short story writer, playwright and novelist. Master of unflinching realism in powerful studies of Italian lower and middle-class life. Achieved notice in U.S. with *Woman of Rome* (1949), a relentless, unsentimental study of the life of a prostitute. Often recorded the way his characters responses to the compelling drive for sex and money. His *Two Women*, a bitter but compassionate account of the effect of World War II on an Italian peasant and her daughter, was made into a movie that won Sophia Loren an Oscar.

Good writers are monotonous, like good composers. They keep trying to perfect the one problem they were born to understand.

1908 **Claude Lévi-Strauss:** Belgian-French social anthropologist. Came to view culture as a system of communication, analogous to a language. Founder of structural anthropology. Primarily concerned with such fundamental social and mental structures as kinship, myths, language, religion and art. Author of: *The Elementary Structures of Kinship*, *Tristes Tropiques*, *Structural Anthropology* and the four-volume *Mythologiques*.

Language is a form of human reason, which has its internal logic of which man knows nothing.

1918 **Madeleine L'Engle:** Originally **Madeline L'Engle Camp**. American author of children's books and editor. Pursued a career in the theater before publishing her first book, the autobiographical *The Small Rain*. In the Newbery Medal-winning *A Wrinkle in Time*, she introduced a group of children engaged in a cosmic battle against a great evil. The same kids surface in *A Swiftly Tilting Planet* and other books. Works also reflect her strong interest in modern science.

If it can be verified, we don't need faith... Faith is for that which lies on the other side of reason. Faith is what makes life bearable, with all its tragedies and ambiguities and sudden, startling joys.

1944 **Rita Mae Brown:** Prolific American poet, novelist, essayist and social activist. Early member of the National Organization for Women (NOW), but reigned because of the discrimination she experienced as a lesbian. Founding member of *The Furies*, a lesbian feminist newspaper collective, which held that heterosexuality was the root of all oppression. Wrote the classic essay, "The Woman-Identified Woman." Novels: *Rubyfruit Jungle*, *Sudden Death*, *Venus Envy* and *Southern Discomfort*.

Lead me not into temptation; I can find the way myself.

1962 **Jon Stewart:** Originally **Jonathan Stuart Leibowitz**. American comedian, actor, author and producer. Host of the comedy fake news show *The Daily Show* (1999–). In 2005, he and the show received Emmy Awards and he earned a Best Comedy Album Grammy Award for the audio book *America (The Book)*. In an exchange with Tucker Carlson on CNN's *Crossfire*, asserted that the show had failed in its responsibility to inform and educate viewers about politics and that Carlson and co-host Paul Begala were "partisan hacks."

I celebrated Thanksgiving in an old-fashioned way. I invited everyone in my neighborhood to my house, we had an enormous feast, and then I killed them and took their land.

OTHERS: 1632 Italian composer **Jean-Baptiste Lully**, 1681 French Protestant rebel leader **Jean Cavalier**, 1700

English Astronomer Royal **Nathaniel Bliss**, 1792 French philosopher **Victor Cousin**, 1793 Swedish poet **Carl Love Almqvist**, 1805 U.S. archeologist **John Stephens**, 1866 U.S. architect **Henry Bacon**, 1887 German head of the SA storm troopers, the "Brownshirts" **Ernst Röhm**, 1895 Spanish pianist **José Iturbi**, 1904 U.S. Senator **James Eastland**, 1925 U.S. actress **Gloria Grahame**, 1929 U.S. founder of Motown Records **Berry Gordy Jr.**, 1936 U.S. politician **Garry Hart**, 1942 U.S. football player **Paul Warfield**, 1943 U.S. composer **Randy Newman**, 1949 Russian ballet dancer/actor **Alexander Godunov**, 1950 U.S. actor **Ed Harris**

November 29

1627 **John Ray:** English naturalist. Famed for his systems of natural selection. His plant classification greatly influenced the development of systematic botany and is the basis of all modern zoology. It was the first system to divide flowering plants into monocotyledons (having an embryo with a single seed leaf) and dicotyledons (which have two seed leafs), with additional divisions made on the basis of leaf and flower characters and fruit types. Also noted for proverbs: "If wishes were horses beggars might ride," "Misery loves company," and "Hell is paved with good intentions."

Beauty is power; a smile is its sword.

1799 **Amos Bronson Alcott:** American philosopher, teacher and reformer. An unassailable optimist, he taught himself to read and write by forming letters with charcoal on the kitchen floorboards. Attracted to Johann Pestalozzi's innovative child-centered educational ideas, he became a long and varied career as a teacher. In his schools, he introduced art, music, nature study, field trips, and physical education into the curriculum, while banishing corporal punishment. Encouraged children to asked questions and taught through dialogue and example. His second daughter was novelist Louisa May Alcott.

To be ignorant of one's ignorance is the malady of the ignorant.

1811 **Wendell Phillips:** American abolitionist and orator. After attending the World Anti-Slavery Convention in London (1840), he became an outspoken abolitionist. His eloquence helped fire the antislavery cause during the period leading up the American Civil War. Critical of the Mexican War and Lincoln's handling of the Civil War. Lectured on social issues that he espoused including penal reform, woman suffrage, prohibition, labor unionization and improved treatment of American Indians.

Governments exist to protect the rights of minorities. The loved and the rich need no protection; they have many friends and few enemies.

1832 **Louisa May Alcott:** American novelist. Educated at home by her father transcendentalist Amos Bronson Alcott, and occasionally by family friends Ralph Waldo Emerson and Henry David Thoreau. During the Civil War she was a nurse in a Union hospital, and her letters from this period were published as *Hospital Sketches* (1864). Her most famous novel, *Little Women*, drew on her own home experience, with Jo being a self-portrait, sold millions of copies.

I am not afraid of storms, for I am learning how to sail my ship.

1895 **Busby Berkley:** Originally **William Berkley Enos.** American Hollywood choreographer and director. Acquired a reputation as one of Broadway's top dance directors with 21 musicals to his credit, including *A Connecticut Yankee* and *Sweet and Low*. Went to Hollywood in 1930 and with his inventive mind and the Warner Bros. studio's technical facilities, he gave Depression audiences larger-than-life escapist dance numbers in *42nd Street*, *Gold Diggers of 1933*, *Footlight Parade* and *Dames*. They were lavishly staged with extravagant mass choreography employing dozens of pretty girl dancers in gaudy, vulgar, suggestive, erotic and stupendous routines.

I wanted to make people happy, if only for an hour.

1898 **C.S. [Clive Staples] Lewis:** English novelist, literary scholar and essayist on Christian theology and moral problems. Also wrote science fiction. Works: the medieval study, *The Allegory of Love*; the science fiction, *Out of the Silent Planet*; essays in popular theology, *The Screwtape Letters;* the autobiographical *Surprised by Joy; and* a series of books of Christian allegory for children, set in the magic land of Narnia: *The Lion, the Witch, and the Wardrobe*.

You don't have a soul. You are a Soul. You have a body.

1902 **Inez Robb:** Nationally known American syndicated columnist, whose newspaper career spanned 50 years. Noted for her interviews with the world's famous and for covering all newsworthy events. *Assignment America* appeared in 140 newspapers. In addition to her five-day-a week column, she contributed to magazines. Covered national political conventions and noteworthy trials. Admitted to a gift for infuriating people, "I have all the instincts of a tramp — but a nice one." Speaking out against the House Un-American Activities Committee to link peace groups with Communism:

It is monstrous to permit peace and its advocacy to become criminal matters merely because the Russians have cynically used peace for propaganda.

1908 **Adam Clayton Powell, Jr.:** Democratic U.S. politician and clergyman. Prominent African-American leader. Pastor of the Abyssinian Baptist Church of New York City (1937–71). Founder and editor of *The People's Voice*. U.S. representative (1945–67 and 1969–70). Chairman of the House Education and Labor Committee. Expelled from the House for alleged improper acts, but was reelected and given back his congressional seniority by the U.S. Supreme Court.

A man's respect for law and order exists in precise relationship to the size of his paycheck.

1912 Sir **John Templeton:** American-born British philanthropist and founder of Templeton Mutual Funds. A Rhodes Scholar, known as the Marco Polo of his Oxford class, for his round-the-world post graduation journey... In his late 20s he opened his own money-management firm and began to put international investment on the map. In 1992 Franklin Resources bought his funds for $440 million. Since then he devoted much of his time to philanthropy. The John Templeton Foundation gives $40 million a year to projects that explore the intersection of science and religion.

The four most dangerous words in investing are, "This time it's different."

1914 **Taisen Deshimaru:** Japanese Zen Buddhist master. Following the Japanese attack on Pearl Harbor he was sent off to war. While on Bangka Island, taught zazen to the inhabitants. The Occupational Army was executing large numbers indiscriminately. Taisen took up their cause and was labeled a rebel. Shortly before he was to be executed, high Japanese officials released him. Sent to an American POW camp in Singapore from which he was released moths later. Ordained a monk in 1965, settled in Paris to transmit the teaching of Zen. He became kaikyosokan — head of Japanese Soto Zen for a particular country or continent. Died in 1982 after having solidly established Zen practice in Europe.

To receive everything, one must open one's hand and give.

1926 **Hugh Leonard:** Pseudonym of **John Keyes Byrne**. Irish dramatist. Output is vast and complex, encompassing theater, television, film, memoir, criticism and journalism. Plays: *The Big Birthday Suit, The Poker Session*, and *Time Was*. Awarded a 1978 Tony for his play, *Da*. Essays: *A Peculiar People and Other Foibles*. Autobiography: *Home Before Night*. Novel: *Parnell and the Englishwoman*.

The problem with Ireland is that it's a country full of genius, but with absolutely no talent.

1949 **Petra Kelly:** Originally **Petra Karin Lehmann**. German politician, campaigner on ecological issues and peace activist. Co-founder of the German Green Party in 1979, which by 1983 entered the Bundestag with 28 seats. Seven years later, dogged by internal struggles, they lost all their parliamentary seats. She died in an apparent suicide pact with her life-partner Gert Bastian, but there is suspicion that her involvement with the secret police of the former East Germany played a role in the deaths.

We, the generation that faces the next century, can add the solemn injunction, "If we don't do the impossible, we shall be faced with the unthinkable."

OTHERS: 1426 Venetian painter **Giovanni Bellini**, 1484 Swiss humanist **Joachim Vadian**, 1762 French zoologist **Pierre André Latreille**, 1781 Chilean poet **Andrés Bello**, 1797 Italian composer **Gaetano Donizetti**, 1803 Austrian physicist **Christian Doppler**, 1813 Slovenian linguist **Franz von Miklosich**, 1857 German pediatrician **Theodor Escherich**, 1874 Portuguese neurologist **Egas Moniz**, 1895 President of Liberia **William Tubman**, 1896 U.S. stuntman **Yakima Canutt**, 1910 Lithuanian writer **Antanas Skėma**, 1915 U.S. musician **Billy Strayhorn**, 1927 U.S. baseball announcer **Vin Scully**, 1932 President of France **Jacques Chirac**, 1954 U.S. film director **Joel Coen**, 1964 U.S. actor **Don Cheadle**

November 30

1554 Sir **Philip Sidney:** English courtier, soldier and poet. Displeased Queen Elizabeth I when he advised her against a projected marriage. Left the court, sent to Holland to assist in the struggle against Spain. Fatally wounded at Zutphen. Literary works, written in 1578–82, were published posthumously: a pastoral romance, *Arcadia, the Defence of Poesie*, and a sonnet cycle, *Astrophel and Stella*. Spenser dedicated his *The Shepheardes Calendar* to Sidney.

If you neglect your work, you will dislike it; if you do it well, you will enjoy it.

1667 **Jonathan Swift:** Irish-born English satirist, political writer and clergyman. Dean of St. Patrick's Cathedral in Dublin. Master of the art of irony. All his works appeared anonymously: *The Tale of a Tub*, in which he exposed religious and intellectual complacency, *The Battle of the Books, Journal to Stella* and his masterpiece *Gulliver's Travels*. Progressively identified with Irish causes, in such works as *The Draper's Letter* and the savagely ironic *A Modest Proposal*.

We have just enough religion to make us hate, but not enough to make us love one another.

1835 **Mark Twain:** Pen name of **Samuel Langhorne Clemens**. American humorist, novelist, short-story writer and lecturer. Took his pen name from the riverboat pilot slang for "two fathoms deep." Fame as a humorist and storyteller was established in a Nevada mining camp with the publication of *The Celebrated Jumping Frog of Calaveras County*. Introduced colloquial speech into American fiction: *The Adventures of Tom Sawyer, Life on the Mississippi, The Adventures of Huckleberry Finn*, all drawn from his personal experiences. Besides these world classics, wrote: *The Prince and the Pauper* and *A Connecticut Yankee in King Arthur's Court*. A number of ill-considered investments drove him into bankruptcy, forcing him to spend the latter portion of his life lecturing to raise money.

The most interesting information comes from children, for they tell all they know and then stop.

1874 **Winston Churchill:** English statesman and author. Descendent of John Churchill, Duke of Marlborough. Regarded as one of the greatest statesmen of the 20th century. Political conservative, though often considered a maverick. Prime minister, (1939–45 and 1951–55). Symbol of the British spirit, providing sterling leadership of the British people during World War II. A powerful orator and incomparable master of English prose. Noted for his ability to create memorable phrases that aroused both courage and hope. In a speech in Fulton, Missouri (1946), he coined the term *Iron Curtain*, warning of the Soviet Union's expansionist tendencies. Awarded Nobel Prize in Literature for *The Second World War*, a six volume history. Only man to be named an honorary citizen of the United States.

Courage is what it takes to stand up and speak; courage is also what it takes to sit down and listen.

1874 **Lucy Maud Montgomery:** Canadian novelist, best known as the author of the novel *Anne of Green Gables*, the story of an orphan Prince Edward Island girl adopted by an elderly brother and sister, who believed they were getting a boy. This was followed by six sequels, each with perennial appeal. Delightfully captured the mysteries and fears of early childhood as in *Magic for Marigold*.

There is one good thing about this world ... there are always sure to be more springs.

1907 **Jacques Barzun:** French-born American writer and educator. Brought his scholarly approach to the study of a diverse range of contemporary problems: *Race, a Study in Modern Superstition*, *The Teacher in America* and *The American University*. Analyzed contemporary art in *The Use and Abuse of Art*. In *Clio and the Doctors*, he traced the influence of psychoanalysis on the interpretation of history. Also wrote the highly acclaimed *Simple and Direct: A Rhetoric for Writers* (with Georgia Dunbar).

Political correctedness does not legislate tolerance; it only organizes hatred.

1924 **Shirley Chisholm:** née **St. Hill**. American politician and nursery school teacher. Expert in the education of young children and consultant to the New York Bureau of Child Welfare (1959–64), Elected to the New York State Assembly (1964–8). First African-American woman elected to the House of Representatives. Democratic congresswoman from New York for seven terms (1969–83). Opposed the Vietnam War and criticized the House seniority system. Author of: *Unbought and Unbossed* and *Good Fight*.

The emotional, sexual and psychological stereotyping of females begins when the doctor says: "It's a girl."

1924 **Allan Sherman:** American songwriter and parody singer. Discovered that the song parodies he performed to amuse his friends and family had commercial possibilities. His album of parodies, *My Son, the Folk Singer* (1962) was quickly followed by *My Son, the Celebrity*. These were Jewish-folk-culture rewritings of old folk songs. A takeoff on *Frère Jacques*, *Sarah Jackman*, in which he and Christine Nelson exchange family gossip, became a minor hit. In *My Son, The Nut*, he parodied classical and popular music. Probably the best cut is "Hello Muddah, Hello Fadduh" sung to the music *Dance of the Hours*, in which he portrays a boy writing a letter to his parents from summer camp.

Adultery — which is the only grounds for divorce in New York — is not grounds for divorce in California. As a matter of fact, adultery in Southern California is grounds for marriage.

1929 **Joan Ganz Cooney:** Highly honored American producer and educator. One of the visionaries and the chief moving force behind the creation of Children's Television Workshop (CTW). Recognized that TV could do more than entertain children, it could provide supplementary education at a fraction of the cost of classroom instruction. Demonstrated that quality educational programming could attract and maintain a mass audience with shows including the influential and long-running "Sesame Street" and "Electric Company."

Cherishing children is the mark of a civilized society.

1930 **G. Gordon Liddy:** American Republican politician. Former FBI agent who helped plan the Watergate break-in of the offices of the Democratic National Committee headquarters. As one of the White House "plumbers," he spent about $300,000 engineering political dirty tricks and the Watergate break-in. Convicted for conspiracy in the Daniel Ellsberg Case and for contempt of court; he spent four and a half years in prison. Has taken his arch-conservative political views to the airwaves on "The G. Gordon Liddy Show." Wrote his best-selling autobiography *Will*.

Obviously crime pays, or there'd be no crime.

1931 **Bill Walsh:** American football coach. Widely recognized for a keen ability to evaluate talent. As an assistant coach with Oakland Raiders, Cincinnati Bengals and Sand Diego Chargers gained a reputation as being a superb offensive coach who specialized in the passing game. As head coach and general manager of the San Francisco 49ers, with quarterbacked by Joe Montana led the team to three Super Bowl wins in ten years. NFL Coach of the Year (1981).

We have a lot of players in their first year. Some of them are also in their last year.

1936 **Abbie Hoffman:** Originally **Abbott.** Yippie political activist. Arrested for disrupting the Democratic Party Convention in Chicago (1968). Rose to prominence for his antics at the trial of the Chicago Seven. After his arrest for selling drugs in 1973 he went underground, underwent plastic surgery and used the alias "Barry Freed." Worked as a New York environmentalist until resurfacing in 1980. After serving a year in prison, he returned to his environmental work. Suffering from depression, committed suicide in 1989. Books: *Revolution for the Hell of It* and *Steal This Book*.

I believe in compulsory cannibalism. If people were forced to eat what they killed, there would be no more wars.

OTHERS: 539 French bishop **St. Gregory of Tours**, 1508 Italian architect **Andrea Palladio**, 1625 French jurist **Jean Domat**, 1670 Irish philosopher **John Toland**, 1722 Swiss painter **Theodore Gardelle**, 1756 German physicist **Ernst Chladni**, 1810 U.S. gunsmith **Oliver Winchester**, 1819 U.S. projector of Atlantic cable **Cyrus Field**, 1858 Indian physicist **Jagdish C. Bose**, 1817 German classical scholar **Theodor Mommsen**, 1863 Philippines Revolutionary leader **Andreas Bonifacio**, 1915 U.S. blues musician **Brownie McGhee**, 1915 Canadian chemist **Henry Taube**, 1929 U.S. TV host **Dick Clark**, 1937 British director **Ridley Scott**, 1955 British musician **Billy Idol**. 1962 U.S. athlete **Bo Jackson**

December 1

1792 **Nicolai Lobachevsky:** Russian mathematician. Called the "Copernicus of Geometry," revolutionized the subject by helping to create a whole new branch, non–Euclidean geometry. In 1829 he published "On the Principles of Geometry" in the *Kazan Messenger*, marking the official birth of non–Euclidean geometry. With his paper, he became the first mathematician to take the revolutionary step of publishing a geometry built on an assumption in direct conflict with the Parallel Postulate. János Bolyai and Carl Friedrich Gauss, independently discovered non–Euclidean geometry, share the honor for its introduction.

There is no branch of mathematics, however abstract, which may not some day be applied to phenomena of the real world.

1863 **Oliver Herford:** American humorist, poet, artist and illustrator. "The American Oscar Wilde." Wrote *The Rubaiyat of a Persian Kitty*, a clever parody of Omar Khayyam's *Rubaiyat*. Author and illustrator of *Little Book of Bores*, *Cynic's Calendar* and *The Deb's Dictionary*. Among his amusing and thoughtful observations: "There is no time like the pleasant," "The Irish gave the bagpipes to the Scots as a joke, but the Scots haven't seen the joke yet," Tact: to lie about others as you would have them lie about you," and:

If some people got their rights they would complain of being deprived of their wrongs.

1886 **Rex Todhunter Stout:** U.S. detective story writer. Before turning to writing, he invented a banking system adopted widely in the United States. Most famous creation is the fat private eye Nero Wolfe, an inimitable beer and orchid fancier, who appeared in mystery novels such as: *Too Many Crooks*, *Black Orchids*, and *Malice in Wonderland*.

To say that man is a reasoning animal is very different thing than to say that most of man's decisions are based on his rational process. That I don't believe at all.

1896 **Georgy Konstantnovich Zhukov:** Soviet marshal. During World War I, he received an order of St. George Cross twice. After the Russian Revolution in 1917, he joined the Bolshevik Party. Fought in the Russian Civil War. Later served as a military commander in the Belarusian Soviet Socialist Republic (1922–39). During World War II, Marshal Zhukov saved Moscow, turned back the Germans at Stalingrad and captured Berlin. After the war Stalin felt that the military hero was too popular and demoted him to a relatively insignificant post. Instrumental in bringing Nikita Khrushchev to power. Once told General Eisenhower:

If we come to a minefield, our infantry attacks as if it were not there.

1910 Dame **Alicia Markova:** Originally **Lilian Alicia Marks**. English-born prima ballerina often called "the Pavlova of her generation." Praised as an ethereal wisp of pure form, one critic described her as "the miracle that never fails." Ballet impresario, Sergei Diaghilev signed her for his company *Ballets Russes* and changed her name to avoid the then prejudice that only Russians could be good ballerinas. Remembered most fondly for her *Giselle*, as well as *The Dying Swan* and *Les Sylphides*.

My life is a series of pirouettes from one city to another.

1911 **Walter Alston:** American Major League baseball manager. His career as a major league player consisted on one plate appearance with the St. Louis Cardinals in 1936. Alston was hired to manage the Dodgers, a tenure that lasted from 1954 to 1976, with only a one year contract every year. His teams won seven National League pennants and four World Series (1955, 59, 63, 65). National League Manager of the Year six times and led NL All-star Teams to seven victories. Retired with 2,040 victories.

Look at misfortune the same way you look at success. Don't panic! Do your best and forget the consequences.

1913 **Mary Martin:** A major talents of the Broadway stage. Speaking of her first professional appearance, "I had my first love affair at five. I fell in love with my audience." The public reciprocated from the moment she sang "My Heart Belongs to Daddy" in the Broadway hit *Leave It to Me* (1938). Greatest triumph came as Navy nurse Nellie Forbush in Rogers and Hammerstein's *South Pacific* (1949). Washed her hair on stage for two years, singing "I'm Going to Wash That Man Right Out of My Hair." A reckless and ingratiating *Peter Pan*, flying above the stage, both on Broadway and television. Brilliantly created the role of Maria in *The Sound of Music*.

Stop the habit of wishful thinking and start the habit of thoughtful wishes.

1935 **Woody Allen:** Originally **Allen Stewart Konigsberg**. American actor, director, screenwriter, playwright, and jazz clarinetist. Frequently plays a neurotic New Yorker, often a semi-famous, semi-successful film/TV writer, director or producer, or a novelist. Allen has more Academy Award nominations (14) for Best Original Screenplay than anyone else, and if the nominations for acting and directing are included he has 21 nominations. Oscar winner as director and co-writer of *Annie Hall*. Other films: *Manhattan*, *Hannah and Her Sisters*, *Radio Days*, *Crimes and Misdemeanors*, *Manhattan Murder Mystery*, *Bullets Over Broadway*, *Mighty Aphrodite*, and *Match Point*. Made 13 movies with ex-lover Mia Farrow.

If you want to make God laugh, tell him about your plans.

1939 **Lee Trevino:** Charismatic Mexican-American golfer. In his second year on the PGA tour, he won the first of his two U.S. Opens. He won two straight British Opens (1971–72). Also won two PGA Championships, but never did very well at the Masters, whose course he did not like, not did he care for its stodgy atmosphere. Hit by lightning in 1975, causing him severe back pain for which he underwent surgery the next year. Trevino switched to the Senior Tour in 1989, winning seven titles his first year.

If you are caught on a golf course during a storm and are afraid of lightning, hold up a 1-iron. Not even God can hit a 1-iron.

1940 **Richard Pryor:** African-American comedian and actor. Gifted storyteller known for his unflinching examinations of race and custom in modern life, and frequent use of colorful language, vulgarities, and racial epithets in live comedy shows. Raised in his grandmother's house of prostitution, where his mother worked. In Hollywood, he gained recognition for his performance as a drug addicted piano player in *Lady Sings the Blues*. Best film work was in partnership with Gene Wilder in *Silver Streak* and *Stir Crazy*.

There's a thin line between to laugh with and to laugh at.

1944 **John Densmore:** American drummer and founding member of the rock group The Doors (1965–73). To the chagrin of his former bandmates Ray Manzarek and Robbie Krieger, he vetoed licensing the band's songs to be used in commercials, of the group's dark hits "Light My Fire," "People Are Strange" and "Breaking on Through," costing them millions of dollars. His reason:

People lost their virginity to this music, got high for the first time to this music. I've had people say kids died in Vietnam listening to this music, other people say they know someone who didn't commit suicide because of this music. On stage, when we played these songs, they felt mysterious and magic. That's not for rent.

1945 **Bette Midler:** American actress, comedian and singer. Sang at the Commercial Baths, a gay bathhouse in the city, where her piano accompanist was Barry Manilow, who produced her first major album *The Divine Miss M* (1973), followed by *Bette Midler*, both hit the tops of the music charts. Won four Grammy awards including one for the title number of the film *The Rose* (also nominated for an Academy Award for her performance) and "Wind Beneath My Wings" from *Beaches*. Other films: *Ruthless People*, *Outrageous Fortune*, and *The First Wives Club*.

The worst part of success is trying to find someone who is happy for you.

OTHERS: 1081 King of France **Louis VI**, 1083 Byzantine historian **Anna Comnena**, 1521 Japanese warlord **Takeda Shingen**, 1525 Czech physician **Tadeáš Hájek**, 1716 French sculptor **Etienne-Martin Falconet**, 1873 Russian poet **Valery Bryusov**, 1895 English author **Henry Williamson**, 1901 Hungarian violinist **Ilona Feher**, 1911 U.S. baseball executive **Calvin Griffith**, 1912 U.S. architect **Minoru Yamasaki**, 1923 U.S. CIA director **Stansfield Turner**, 1930 German historian **Joachim Hoffmann**, 1935 U.S. singer **Lou Rawls**, 1942 U.S. author **John Crowley**, 1951 U.S. bassist **Jaco Pastorius**, 1960 U.S. supermodel **Carol Ault**, 1962 U.S. comic book writer **Joe Quesada**, 2001 Toshi of Japan **Aiko**

December 2

1859 **Georges Seurat:** French painter. With Paul Signac originated the neo-Impressionist technique of Pointillism, which consists of paining using tiny dots of color, rather than long brushstrokes. Examples of his work are: *The Bathers*, *Asinères* and *Sunday on the Island of La Grande Jatte*. Departed from Impressionism by evolving a formal type of composition based on classical proportions of the golden section, rather than capturing fleeting moments of light and movement.

Some say they see poetry in my painting; I see only science.

1883 **Nikos Kazantzakis:** Crete-born Greek writer and lawyer, whose work represents a major contribution to Modern Greek literature. Best known as the author of *Zorba the Greek* and his epic autobiographical narrative poem, "The Odyssey, a Modern Sequel." Also wrote *The Greek Passion* and *The Last Temptation of Christ*.

A person needs a little madness, or else they never dare cut the rope and be free.

1884 **Ruth Draper:** American dramatist and monologist. Following successful solo appearances entertaining American troops in France in 1918, toured extensively. Her repertoire consisted of 36 monologues of her own devising, involving 57 distinct characters. Created her characters and settings by subtle modulation of feature, gesture and voice.

Try to look at everything through the eyes of a child.

1899 Sir **John Barbirolli:** Originally **Giovanni Battista Barbirolli.** English-born conductor and cellist of Franco-Italian origin. In 1925, founded the Barbirolli Chamber Orchestra and two years later was guest conductor for the London Symphony. Succeeded Toscanini as conductor of the New York Philharmonic, (1937–43). Permanent conductor of the Halle Orchestra in Manchester (1943–58). First foreign conductor invited to the Salzburg Festival after World War II.

Do you know why conductors live so long? Because we perspire so much.

1910 **J. Russell Lynes:** American critic, editor and chronicler of American manners, morals and foibles. In his essay, "Highbrow, Lowbrow, and Middlebrow" he declared "the highbrows are the elite, the middlebrows are the *bourgeoisie*, and the lowbrows are the *hoi polloi*." Books: *Snobs*, *Guests: Or, How to Survive Hospitality*, *The Tastemakers*, and *Confessions of a Dilettante*.

The true snob never rests; there is always a higher goal to attain, and there are, by the same token, always more and more people to look down upon.

1925 **Alexander M. Haig, Jr.:** U.S. Army general and Republican politician. Served in Korea and Vietnam. Became White House chief of staff during last days of the Nixon presidency. Returned to active military duty as Supreme NATO commander before becoming president of United Technologies Corporation.

U.S. Secretary of State (1981–82) under President Ronald Reagan. When Reagan was shot, and in the absence of Vice-President George Bush, Haig mistakenly believed he was in charge of the White House.

That's not a lie, it's a terminological inexactitude. Also a tactical misrepresentation.

1923 **Maria Callas:** Originally **Cecilia Sophia Anna Mary Kalogeropoulou**. Tempestuous, predictably unpredictable American–born prima donna. Studied at Athens Conservatory, making her debut there in the title role of *Tosca*. Her coloratura range and dramatic versatility allowed her to sing 43 roles in over 500 performances in every major international opera house. Made very public departures from ranking opera houses in Rome, Vienna, San Francisco, Milan and was banished from the New York Metropolitan roster, when she exhausted the patience of Rudolph Bing. Her open affair with shipping magnate Aristotle Onassis ended when he married Jacqueline Kennedy.

The proper concern of an artist is art, and I have devoted myself to music in an effort to elevate it from the routine and restore opera to what I believe it must have been during the Golden Age of the last century.

1925 **Julie Harris:** American stage and film actress noted for her sensitive approach to complex emotional roles. Became a Broadway star playing a 12-year-old tomboy in *A Member of the Wedding*, repeating the role in her Oscar-nominated screen debut. Earned the reputation of one of America's most distinguished stage actress: *I Am a Camera*, *The Lark*, and *Little Moon of Alban*. Renowned for her solo performance as Emily Dickinson in *The Belle of Amherst*. Memorable in films *East of Eden* and *Requiem for a Heavyweight*. Won several Tonys and Emmys.

Anyone who performs for the public must have a complete dedication, a complete concentration on what he's doing.

1931 **Edwin Meese, III:** American government official. Headed Ronald Reagan's transition team following the 1980 presidential election. Member of the National Security Council and 75th Attorney General of the United States. Tenure was highly controversial for his involvement in the Iran-Contra affair and for criticizing the Supreme Court for straying from the original intent of the U.S. Constitution. Investigated concerning allegations of influence-peddling and shady financial deals, but no charges were brought to a grand jury.

You don't have many suspects who are innocent of a crime. That's contradictory. If a person is innocent of a crime, then he is not a suspect.

1946 **Gianni Versace:** Italian fashion designer. Designed clothing for young aggressive and sexy women that melded classic and pop culture influences, often featuring wild prints, skin-tight with low cuts and high slits on the skirts. Produced seasonal fashion shows staged like rock concerts and media events at his lavish design headquarters in Milan. Shot and killed on the steps of his Miami Beach, Florida mansion, on July 15, 1997, allegedly by spree killer Andrew Cunanan, who was found dead by his own hand in a boathouse.

You dress elegant women. You dress sophisticated women. I dress sluts.

1973 **Monica Seles:** Yugoslav-born tennis player. Ranked number one in the world in 1991 and 1992 after winning the Australian, French and U.S. Opens each year. Stabbed in the back by a male assailant (1993) during a match in Hamburg, Germany. After her comeback 27 months later, she won every match she played until she was narrowly defeated in September 1995 by Steffi Graf in the U.S. Open final. Every contact of her racket with the ball was accompanied by a loud grunt, caused by the effort she put into her swing.

I don't want to be remembered just as someone who grunted and giggled. I also don't want to be "the one with the knife in the back."

1981 **Britney Spears:** American pop singer and cultural phenomenon. "Mouseketeer" at age 11 on *The New Mickey Mouse Club* show. International success with her debut album *Baby One More Time* (1999). Often derided as untalented, the former "good" girl of U.S. pop music has become an influential sex symbol with erotic dance routines, sexual innuendo and barely-there clothing.

I've turned from a little nice school girl, into this sexy, slutty seductress. And I like it ... I like it a lot.

OTHERS: 1578 Italian composer **Agostino Agazzari**, 1678 Dutch engineer **Nicolaas Cruquius**, 1728 Italian economist **Ferdinando Galiani**, 1760 U.S. politician **John Breckinridge**, 1817 German historian **Heinrich von Sybel**, 1863 U.S. circus owner **John Ringling**, 1885 U.S. physician **George R. Minot**, 1891 German painter **Otto Dix**, 1892 Russian pianist **Leo Ornstein**, 1914 U.S. composer **Adolph Green**, 1914 U.S. actor **Ray Walston**, 1930 U.S. economist **Gary Becker**, 1939 Israeli writer **Yael Dayan**, 1945 U.S. film director **Penelope Spheeris**, 1957 Norwegian politician **Dagfinn Høybråten**, 1968 U.S. actress **Lucy Liu**, 1970 U.S. comedian **Sarah Silverman**, 1978 Canadian singer **Nelly Furtado**

December 3

1755 **Gilbert Stuart:** American artist. First among American painters to develop true individuality in his portraits. "Father of American Portraiture" was given the opportunity of depicting almost every notable person of the Federal Period, including George Washington, Thomas Jefferson, Abigail Smith Adams, and James Madison. His portrait of Washington is featured on the U.S. dollar bill.

What a business is this of a portrait painter! You bring him a potato and expect he will paint you a peach.

1795 Sir **Rowland Hill:** British administrator and educator. Developed the modern postal service adopted. In his *Post-Office Reform* (1837), advocated a low and uniform rate of postage, to be prepaid by stamps. In 1840 a uniform penny rate was established. As secretary to the Post Office he introduced the world's first adhesive postage stamp. Helped found the Society for the Diffusion of Useful Knowledge (1826).

We can do more good by being good, than in any other way.

1807 **Gamaliel Bailey:** American editor and social reformer. Under his leadership the journal, *The National Era* became one of the foremost abolitionist periodicals in the country, combining both moral fervor and high literary quality. It contained the first appearance of Harriet Beecher Stowe's *Uncle Tom's Cabin.* Other contributors included Nathaniel Hawthorne, John Greenleaf Whittier and Theodore Parker.

Never respect men merely for their riches, but rather for their philanthropy; we do not value the sun for its height, but for its use.

1826 **George B. McClellan:** U.S. Union general in the American Civil War. Distinguished himself in several actions in the Mexican War. Appointed by Lincoln to reorganize the Union army, he was overly cautious when it came to confronting the enemy. His failure to follow up on his advantage when he forced General Lee to retreat at Antietam caused him to be recalled. Opposed Lincoln for the presidency in 1864, running as a Democrat on a peace platform.

When this sad war is over we will all return to our homes, and feel that we can ask no higher honor than the proud consciousness that we belonged to the Army of the Potomac.

1838 **Cleveland Abbe:** American astronomer and meteorologist. Known as "the Father of the Weather Bureau." Introduced an ambitious program of serious research by recruiting a corps of weather observers who reported to him by telegraph. Beginning in 1869 he made regular forecasts. His efforts were partially responsible for the establishment of a national weather service within the U.S. Signal Service. Helped establish the use of standard time throughout the U.S.

True science is never speculative; it employs hypotheses as suggesting points of inquiry, but it never adopts the hypotheses as though they were demonstrated propositions.

1842 **Ellen Henrietta Swallow Richards:** American chemist, sanitation engineer and ecologist. Leader in the movement to educate women in the sciences, setting up programs at MIT, where she taught sanitary chemistry (1884–1911). Established the first program in sanitary engineering at MIT. Organizer and first president of the American Home Economics Association. Co-founded what later became the American Association of University Women.

The faculty [of Vassar] do not consider it a mere experiment any longer that girls can be educated as well as boys.

1857 **Joseph Conrad:** Originally **Jozef Konrad Korzeniowski**. Ukraine-born novelist and short-story writer of Polish parentage. Preeminent writer of tales that vividly evoke the mysteries of sea life and exotic foreign settings. Explored the psychological isolation of the "outsider." Held a deeply pessimistic vision of the human struggle. Novels: *The Nigger of the Narcissus, Lord Jim, Nostromo, The Secret Agent,* and *Under Western Eyes.*

The belief in a supernatural source of evil is not necessary; men alone are quite capable of every wickedness.

1895 **Anna Freud:** Austrian-born British psychoanalyst. Daughter of Sigmund Freud. Moved with her terminally ill father to London in 1938, to escape Nazi domination of Austria. Organized a residential war nursery for homeless children. Founded the Hampstead Child Therapy Clinic, which she directed (1952–1982). Made important contributions to child psychoanalysis. Called repression the principal human defense mechanism. Works: *The Ego and Mechanisms of Defence, Normality and Pathology in Childhood* and *Beyond the Best Interests of the Child.*

If some longing goes unmet, don't be astonished. We call that Life.

1922 **Henry Anatole Grunwald:** Austrian-born American editor and author. Joined *Time* magazine while still in college, became a writer in the foreign news department in 1945 and six years later was named a senior editor. Managing editor of *Time* magazine (1968–77). Editor-in-chief of all Time Inc.'s publications (1979–87). U.S. Ambassador to Austria from (1988–1990).

Where is the line between making the most of one's potential and reaching for the unattainable? When is the line between education as a tool and education as a king of magic? The line is blurred and that is why when education fails, disillusionment is so bitter.

1930 **Jean-Luc Godard:** French director and screenwriter. Wrote film criticism for *Cathiers du cinéma* before astounding audiences with his first feature film, the improvised and very original *Breathless* (1960), establishing him as an apostle of the "New Wave" movement. Emphasized film as an essay, and cinema as a political and social instrument. Other Films: *My Life to Live, Pierrot le fou, Alphaville, A Woman Is a Woman, Passion* and *Hail Mary!*

A story should have a beginning, a middle, and an end ... but not necessarily in that order.

1948 **Ozzy Osbourne:** British singer and heavy metal rock musician. Nicknamed "The Godfather of Heavy Metal" "The Prince of Darkness," and "The Madman." Lead singer of the band Black Sabbath, until 1979 when he left or was fired. Since then he has been a popular solo artist. With his second wife and two of his children he appeared in the reality feature "The Osbournes," the highest rated show in the history of the MTV channel.

I can honestly say all the bad things that ever happened to me were directly attributed to drugs and alcohol. I mean, I would never urinate at the

Alamo at nine o'clock in the morning dressed in a woman's evening gown sober.

1965 **Katarina Witt:** German figure skater. Won the first of six European championships in 1983. Went on to win two Olympic gold medals (1984, 1988) and four World Championships (1984, 85, 87, 88). Popular with audiences who prized her grace, beauty and eloquence as much as her technical abilities. With Brian Boitano, their *Carmen on Ice* show received a 1990 TV Emmy.

Every man prefers to look at a well-shaped woman instead of a rubber ball.

OTHERS: 1560 Dutch critic **Jan Gruter**, 1684 Norwegian historian **Ludvig Holberg**, 1776 German neuroscientist **Johann Spurzheim**, 1800 Slovenian poet **France Prešeren**, 1838 British open-space activist **Octavia Hill**, 1884 1st President of India **Rajendra Prasad**, 1887 Japanese prime minister **Prince Naruhiko**, 1900 Swiss mountain guide **Ulrich Inderbinen**, 1911 Italian composer **Nino Rota**, 1921 U.S. soprano **Phyllis Curtin**, 1922 Swedish cinematographer **Sven Nykvist**, 1927 U.S. C&W singer **Ferlin Husky**, 1930 U.S. singer **Andy Williams**, 1931 U.S. singer **Jaye P. Morgan**, 1937 U.S. race car driver **Bobby Allison**, 1960 U.S. actress **Julianne Moore**, 1972 U.S. skateboarder **Bucky Lasek**, 1977 Polish ski-jumper **Adam Malysz**

December 4

1584 **John Cotton:** English-born Puritan clergyman, who had great influence in the Massachusetts Bay colony. Religious and intellectual leader of New England. Son-in-law was Increase Mather and his grandson was Cotton Mather. Became head of Congregationalism in the United States. Author of: *The Way of the Church of Christ in New England*.

If you pinch the sea of its liberty, though it be walls of stone or brass, it will beat them down.

1612 **Samuel Butler:** British poet remembered now mostly for his long satirical burlesque poem on Puritanism called *Hudibras*, which became immediately popular and was a special favorite of King Charles II. Wrote many short biographies, epigrams and verses. To distinguish him from the 19th century Samuel Butler, the 17th century subject is designated as Samuel "Hudibras" Butler.

Though analogy is often misleading, it is the least misleading thing we have.

1795 **Thomas Carlyle:** Scottish-born Englishman of letters. Historian, biographer, essayist and the leading social critic of his day. Called "the Sage of Chelsea." Made explosive attack on sham, hypocrisy and excessive materialism. Distrusted democracy and the mob. His reputation was established by the three volumes on the French Revolution. Best-known works are *Sartor Resartus* and a biography of Frederick the Great.

Show me the man you honor, and I will know what kind of man you are.

1835 **Samuel Butler:** English writer, painter and musician. Emigrated to New Zealand, becoming a successful sheep farmer, which he wrote about in *A First Year in Canterbury Settlement*. Returned to England where he wrote his satiric anti-utopian masterpiece, *Erewhon* and its sequel *Erewhon Revisited*, both of which challenged aspects of Darwinism. "Erewhon" is an inversion of "nowhere." Wrote the semi-autobiographical *The Way of All Flesh*, which parodies child-parent relations and the effects of inherited family traits.

An apology for the Devil: It must be remembered that we have only heard one side of the case. God has written all the books.

1861 **Lillian Russell:** Originally **Helen Louise Leonard**. American singer and actress. In the early 1880s, impresario Tony Pastor featured her as "The American Beauty" at his New York City Theater. For 35 years, maintained a position as one of the first ladies of the American stage. Noted for her flamboyant personality, love of jewelry, and her legendary affair with "Diamond Jim" Brady. Campaigned for Warren Harding in the 1920 election. Died in 1922 after completing a fact-finding mission to Europe on behalf of President Harding. Buried with full military honors.

We all have a fear of the unknown; what one does with that fear will make all the difference in the world.

1865 **Edith Cavell:** English nurse and heroine of World War I. Matron of the Berkendael Medical Institute, Brussels. Tended friend and foe alike during World War I. Brought before a German military tribunal on charges of helping Belgian and Allied fugitives escape capture. She openly admitted her actions and was executed by a firing squad. Her last words:

Standing as I do in view of God and eternity, I realize that patriotism is not enough. I must have no hatred or bitterness toward anyone.

1866 **Wassily Kandinsky:** Russian-born painter and theorist. Founded the Russian Academy and became head of the Museum of Modern Art. Pioneer of abstract art, producing non-representative works as early as 1910. His treatise *On the Spiritual in Art* (1912) urged the expression of inner and essential feelings in art rather than the representation of the natural world. Co-founded the Munich-based *Blaue Reiter* group of artists.

There is no must in art because art is free.

1875 **Rainier Maria Rilke:** Pseudonym of **René Karl Wilhelm Josef Maria Rilke**. Austrian poet. Most significant figure in 20th century German poetry. Three-part poem cycle *The Book of Hours* is an almost mystical conception of the relationship among God, men and nature, written from the perspective of a Russian monk. Rilke's conception of art as a quasi-religious vocation culminated in the hymnic lyrics he is best known for: "The Duino Elegies" and "The Sonnets to Orpheus."

I hold this to be the highest task for a bond between two people: that each protects the solitude of the other.

1892 **Francisco Franco:** Spanish general of the Nationalist forces in the Spanish Civil War (1936–39). In

1937 he became leader of the Falange (Fascist) Party and proclaimed himself "Caudillo" (leader) of Spain. Established a fascist dictatorship. Despite close relations with Italian and German Fascists, he resisted pressure from Germany and Italy, staying neutral during World War II. Arranged for the monarchy to return upon his death, naming Prince Juan Carlos as his successor and heir.

I am responsible only to God and history.

1912 **Pappy Boyington:** Originally **Gregory Boyington**. Organized the legendary Black Sheep Squadron in 1943. In 84 days of combat his unit shot down 98 Japanese planes, 28 of them being his kills, for which he was awarded the U.S. Medal of Honor. On the day of his last kill he was shot down by a Japanese Zero fighter. Fished out of the water by an enemy submarine, he spent 20 months in POW camps, where he endured beatings and near starvation. Believed to have died in the crash, after the war he seemed to have come back from the dead.

Flying is hours and hours of boredom sprinkled with a few seconds of sheer terror.

1921 **Deanna Durbin:** Originally **Edna Mae Durbin**. Canadian-born actress and singer who saved Universal Studios from bankruptcy with films such as: *Three Smart Girls*, *100 Men and a Girl* and *Mad About Music*. When she was 14, MGM featured her in a musical short, *Every Sunday*, with Judy Garland. The studio signed Garland to a contract and dropped Durbin, immediately signed by Universal. Matured from a peppy adolescent to a starry-eyed romantic beauty and Hollywood's highest paid woman star, before her sudden retirement in 1948.

Just as Hollywood pin-up represents sex to dissatisfied erotics, so I represented the ideal daughter millions of fathers and mothers wished they had.

1973 **Tyra Banks:** African-American supermodel. Tall, skinny and awkward adolescent, constantly teased by her classmates, worked out and filled out. Turned down by four modeling agencies because she wasn't "photogenic," she signed with Elite agency when she was 17. Moved to Paris for a year, modeling for many of the top names in fashion. First African American model to appear on the cover of *Sports Illustrated* swimsuit edition. Host and producer of TV's *America's Next Top Model*.

Black women have always been these vixens, these animalistic erotic women. Why can't we just be the sexy American girl next door?

OTHERS: 1443 Italian Pope **Julius II**, 1555 German historian **Heinrich Meibom**, 1580 English adventurer **Samuel Argall**, 1595 French writer **Jean Chapelain**, 1660 French composer **André Campra**, 1713 Italian dramatist **Gasparo Gozzi**, 1777 French writer **Madame Récamier**, 1800 Dutch physician **Emil Aarestrup**, 1822 English feminist **Frances Crabbe**, 1849 Oglala Sioux chief **Crazy Horse**, 1852 Russian physicist **Orest Khvolson**, 1895 Chinese philosopher **Fung Yu-lan**, 1903 U.S. writer **Cornell Woolrich**, 1931 Canadian hockey player **Alex Delvecchio**, 1938 Australian soprano **Yvonne Minton**, 1940 Welsh musician **John Cale**, 1949 actor **Jeff Bridges**, 1964 U.S. actress **Marisa Tomei**

December 5

1782 **Martin Van Buren:** American lawyer and politician. Eighth president of the United States (1837–41). First president born an American citizen. President Andrew Jackson appointed Van Buren Secretary of State. "The Little Magician," as Van Buren came to be known was elected Vice President on the Jacksonian ticket in 1832. Last sitting vice president before George Bush to be elected president. More and more opposed to the expansion of slavery, he blocked the annexation of Texas because it would add to slave territory.

It is easier to do a job right that to explain why you didn't.

1830 **Christina Georgina Rossetti:** One of the finest female Victorian English poets. Daughter of poet and painter Gabriel Rossetti and sister of Dante Gabriel Rossetti, also a poet and painter. Wrote mainly religious poetry. Master of the sonnet and known for her ballads. Her first lyrics, including "An End" and "Dream Lane" were published in *The Germ* (1850) under the pseudonym Ellen Alleyne. Best-known poems: "A Birthday," "When I Am Dead" and "Up-Hill."

Can anything be sadder than work left unfinished? Yes, work never begun.

1839 **George Armstrong Custer:** American cavalry officer. Prior to the Battle of Gettysburg, General Meade promoted him from first lieutenant to brevet brigadier general (temporary rank) of volunteers, making him one of the youngest generals in the Union Army. Served with distinction in several decisive battles. After the war, reduced to the rank of lieutenant colonel. Participated in the campaigns against the Indian tribes of the Great Plains. He and his entire command were wiped out by combined Sioux-Cheyenne forces at the Little Bighorn.

If I were an Indian ... I would greatly prefer to cast my lot among those of my people who adhered to the free open plains, rather than submit to the confined limits of a reservation....

1890 **Fritz Lang:** Austrian-born film director. Brought to the screen a vision of a world largely populated by criminals, psychopaths, prostitutes and maladjusted personalities — a deterministic world ruled by the inevitability of fate. German films: *The Spiders*, *Dr. Mabuse*, *Die Nibelungen*, *Metropolis* and the classic psychological thriller about a child murder, *M*. Invited by Joseph Goebbels to direct and supervise Nazi productions, Lang feared that it was only a matter of time before the Jewish background of his mother was discoverer. Fled to Paris, leaving behind most of his possessions and his wife Thea von Harbou, who divorced him and wrote and directed films for the Nazi propaganda machine. In 1934 Lang sailed for America. His first film was the powerful anti-lynching story, *Fury*.

I should say that I was a visual person. I experience with my eyes and never, or rarely, with my ears ... to my constant regret.

1897 **Nunnally Johnson:** U.S. screenwriter, producer and director. Went to Hollywood in 1932, where he became one of the screen's most prolific and respected writers. In 1943 he formed International Pictures, eventually absorbed by Universal. Scripts: *The Grapes of Wrath, Roxie Hart, The Keys of the Kingdom, The Gunfighter, My Cousin Rachel* and *How to Marry a Millionaire.*

This is the only place I ever heard of where the citizens practice stabbing themselves in the back in their spare time just by way of gymnasium workouts.

1901 **Walt Disney:** American animator who created an empire with cartoon character Mickey Mouse. Pioneer in the creation of animated motion-picture cartoons. Over the years, his films won 29 Oscars. The best of the Disney movies during his lifetime: *Snow White and the Seven Dwarfs, Pinocchio, Bambi* and *Peter Pan.* His company began producing features combining live action with animation, and later pure action films. TV producer of the very popular *Mickey Mouse Club* and a weekly anthology series *Disneyland.* Opened amusement parts, Disneyland and Disney World.

If you can dream it, you can do it.

1901 **Werner Karl Heisenberg:** German physicist. Formulated a non-relativistic form of quantum mechanics for which he was awarded the 1932 Nobel Prize for Physics. Best known for formulating the Uncertainty Principle, the impossibility of determining exactly both the position and momentum of a particle simultaneously. During the Third Reich, he chose to remain in Germany to maintain its scientific tradition, though he was not a member of the Nazi party. Put in charge of the atomic energy and weapons program, but no atomic bomb was produced.

What we observe is not nature itself, but nature exposed to our method of questioning.

1932 **Little Richard Penniman:** African-American rhythm-and-blues singer, pianist and rock musician. An energetic performer, with a penchant for the outrageous. First big hit was "Tutti Frutti" (1956). Other hits followed: "Long Tall Sally," "Lucille" and "Good Golly, Miss Molly." Underwent a religious conversion and became an ordained minister. Returned to music as a regular attraction in Las Vegas, while continuing to tour and make film appearances.

Elvis may have been the king of rock 'n' roll, but I am the queen.

1934 **Joan Didion:** American writer, whose work examines contemporary society with a sense of cultural despair. Worked and wrote for *Vogue, Saturday Evening Post, Esquire* and *National Review.* Her columns have been published as *Slouching Towards Bethlehem* and *The White Album.* Other Books: *Run River, A Book of Common Prayer,* and *Democracy.*

I write entirely to find out what I'm thinking, what I'm looking at, what I see and what it means. What I want and what I fear.

1935 **Calvin Trillin:** American journalist, humorist and novelist. Long time staff writer for The New Yorker. Also contributed a column "Uncivil Liberties" written for *The Nation* magazine, called by *U.S.A Today,* "simply the funniest regular column in journalism." Best known for writing about food and eating — especially Chinese food for which he has a legendary zest. Books: *With All Disrespect, If You Can't Say Something Nice, Enough's Enough* and *A Heckuva Job: More of the Bush Administration in Rhyme.*

I never did very well in math — I could never seem to persuade the teacher that I hadn't meant my answers literally.

1946 **José Carreras:** Spanish lyric tenor. Born in the Catalonia region of Spain, where his name is **Josep Carreras i Coll.** At the height of his success, he was diagnosed with acute lymphoblastic leukemia and given only a 10% chance of survival. After a year of treatment, including radiation, chemotherapy and a bone marrow transplant, he not only survived but was able to resume his career. Founded the José Carreras International Leukemia Foundation, a charity which does leukemia research and registers bone marrow donors. Hundreds of millions of people watched *The Three Tenors* (Carreras, Plácido Domingo and Luciano Pavarotti) concert at the opening of the World Cup in Rome.

When you arrive at a certain level it's very easy to say yes" that is the moment to learn to say no.

1968 **Margaret Cho:** Korean-American comedian. First female Asian-American to have a TV series, "All-American Girl," based on her life and comedy act. Her comedy is quite sexually explicit, sharp political commentary, descriptions of her problems with prejudice, substance abuse, eating disorders and her relationship with her mother. Has always been very popular in the gay and lesbian community, and she has always been a supportive advocate of them.

I love the word "faggot," because it describes my kind of guy! You see, I am a fag hag. Fag hags are the backbone of the gay community. Without us, you're nothing! We have been there all through history guiding your sorry ass through the underground railroad! ... We went to the prom with you!

OTHERS: 1377 Emperor of China **Jianwen**, 1495 Flemish grammarian **Nicolas Cleynaerts**, 1539 Italian theologian **Fausto Paolo Sozzini**, 1547 Dutch historian/geographer **Ubbo Emmius**, 1687 Italian violinist **Francesco Geminiani**, 1820 Russian poet **Afansy Fet**, 1822 U.S. college president **Elizabeth Cary Agassiz**, 1841 U.S. mining tycoon **Marcus Daly**, 1859 British admiral **John Jellicoe**, 1868 German physicist **Arnold Sommerfield**, 1870 Czech composer **Vitězslav Novák**, 1879 U.S. airplane manufacturer **Clyde Cessna**, 1898 U.S. soprano **Grace Moore**, 1901 U.S. psychiatrist **Milton H. Erickson**, 1902 U.S. politician **Strom Thurmond**, 1949 New Zealand evangelist **Ray Comfort**

December 6

1478 **Baldassare Castiglione, Count of Novilara:** Italian diplomat, courier and among the most important and influential European authors during the Renaissance. Chief work was *The Book of the Courtier*, which sets forth in a series of dialogues his conception of the ideal courtier and the norms of culture in a cultured society. Also wrote Italian and Latin poems and many letters illustrating political and literary history. His portrait by Raphael's is one of the masterpieces of the Louvre.

Employ in everything a certain casualness which conceals art and creates the impression that what is done and said is accomplished without effort and without its being thought about. It is from this, in my opinion that grace largely derives.

1823 **[Friedrich] Max Muller:** Anglo-German orientalist and comparative philologist. Studied Sanskrit and its kindred sciences of philology and religion. Began his edition of the *Rigveda*, sacred hymns of the Hindus, while in Paris. Over a period of 21 years he prepared and published 51 volumes of the *Sacred Books of the East*. His works stimulated widespread interest in the study of linguistics, mythology and religion.

Language is the Rubicon that divides man from beast.

1833 **John Singleton Mosby:** American Confederate guerrilla leader. Organized Mosby's Partisan Rangers, leading hit-and-run raids against scattered outposts of the Federals, who considered him nothing more than an outlaw. Noted for his gray cape, lined with scarlet and a long ostrich plume in his hat. Credited with originating the phrase "the solid south."

War loses a great deal of its romance after a soldier has seen his first battle.

1849 Lord **Charles John Darling:** English judge with unusual insight into human nature. A staunch Conservative Unionist. His appointment as a judge of the High Court of Justice was widely criticized as it was believed that he had given no indication of any "legal eminence." Appointed member of the Privy Council in 1917. Wrote: *Crime and Insanity*, *Murder and Its Punishment* and *Musings on Murder*.

Men would be great criminals did they need as many laws as they break.

1875 **Evelyn Underhill:** English Anglican theologian and mystic, whose writing helped established mystical theology. Disciple of theologian Baron Friedrich von Hügel, she traveled intellectually from agnosticism to Christianity. Wrote numerous books on mysticism, including *The Life of the Spirit* and *Mysticism*, which became a standard work.

Delicate humor is the crowning virtue of the saints.

1886 **Joyce Kilmer:** American poet killed in France during World War I. Best known poem is "Trees," winning its author national fame. Also wrote "Summer of Love," "The Circus" and "Main Street." Editor: *Dreams and Images: An Anthology of Catholic Poets*.

I think I shall never see/ A poem lovely as a tree/ Poems are made by fools like me/ But only God can make a tree.

1887 **Lynn Fontanne:** Originally **Lillie Louise Fontanne**. English-born stage actress, who settled in America in 1916, where she met her husband and long-time stage partner, Alfred Lunt. They specialized in high comedy and were particularly brilliant in Noel Coward plays. Broadway's Lunt-Fontanne Theatre, opened in 1958, was named for them.

I lied to everyone. I lie very well, being an actress.

1896 **Ira Gershwin:** Originally **Israel Gershwin**. American lyricist and author. In 1921 he wrote a hit show *Two Little Girls in Blue* with Vincent Youmans. By 1924, he was successful enough that he began collaborating with his precocious younger brother George Gershwin. Their hits included, "I Got Rhythm," "'S Wonderful" and "They Can't Take That Away from Me." After his brother's death he worked with many other composers, including Kurt Weill and Jerome Kern.

One can be very happy without demanding that others agree with them.

1898 **Alfred Eisenstaedt:** German-born American photographer. Moved to the U.S.A. in 1935 and became one of the first photographers working for *Life* magazine. Contributed more than 2500 picture stories and 90 cover photos. His images from his worldwide assignments and telling photographic essays established him the first and most important photojournalist. Publications include *Witness to Our Time*, *The Eye of Eisenstaedt* and *Photojournalism*.

When I have a camera in my hand, I know no fear.

1898 **Karl Gunnar Myrdal:** Swedish economist, politician and public servant. Noted for comprehensive economic and sociological analyses of issues such as population control, developing nations, and political and economic problems in southern Asia. Wrote *An American Dilemma*, *Rich Lands, Poor Lands: The Road to World Prosperity*, and *The Challenge of World Poverty: A World Anti-Poverty Program in Outline*. Shared the Nobel Prize for Economics in 1974. His wife, Alva Myrdal, sociologist, diplomat, U.N. administrator and antiwar activist shared the 1982 Nobel Peace Prize.

The big majority of Americans, who are comparatively well off, have developed an ability to have enclaves of people living in the greatest misery without almost noticing them.

1920 **Dave Brubeck:** American pianist, composer and bandleader. Style combines the disciplines of contemporary serious music with the expressive freedom of jazz improvisation. Music has been labeled "modern" or "progressive" jazz. Made his reputation as an experimental musician in 1946 with his Jazz Workshop Ensemble. More widely known for the Dave Brubeck Quartet, formed in 1951. Continues to tour and record into his 80s.

Jazz is about the only form of art existing today in which there is freedom of the individual without the loss of group contact.

1953 **Will Shriner:** American comedian, director, actor, writer, producer, and host. Over the years, he's hosted hundreds of hours of TV shows. Has appeared in twelve films, including the Academy Award nominated *Peggy Sue Got Married.* His twin brother Kin Shriner has appeared as Scotty Baldwin on *General Hospital* and its 1997 spin-off, *Port Charles,* since 1977. Their father, Herb Shriner was a popular humorist and TV host, often compared to Will Rogers.

I want to die in my sleep like my grandfather... Not screaming and yelling like the passengers in his car.

OTHERS: 1285 King of Castile **Ferdinand IV**, 1421 King of England **Henry VI**, 1586 Italian astronomer **Niccolo Zucchi**, 1640 French historian **Claude Fleury**, 1721 British philologist **James Elphinston**, 1805 German organ builder **Adolf Reubke**, 1841 French painter **Frédéric Bazille**, 1872 U.S. silent screen cowboy star **William S. Hart**, 1890 Japanese physicist **Yoshio Nishina**, 1892 British poet/novelist/critic **Sir Osbert Sitwell**, 1900 U.S. actress **Agnes Moorehead**, 1904 French pianist **Eve Curie**, 1905 U.S. boxer **James J. Braddock**, 1915 U.S. swimmer **Eleanor Holm**, 1919 Belgian-born literary critic **Paul de Man**, 1921 U.S. football quarterback/coach **Otto Graham**, 1933 Polish composer **Henryk Górecki**, 1971 U.S. AIDs victim/activist **Ryan White**

December 7

1823 **Leopold Kronecker:** German mathematician and logician. Obsessed with the notion that all of mathematics, save geometry and mechanics, should be treated as a branch of arithmetic. Achieved notoriety for his intransigent advocacy of a constructivist and finitism mathematical philosophy, according to which a mathematical object does not exist unless it can be constructed from natural numbers in a finite number of steps. Most vocal and harsh critic of the transfinite set theory of Georg Cantor.

God made the integers; all else is the work of man.

1847 **Solomon Schechter:** Romanian-born American Jewish rabbi, Hebraic scholar and educator. Founder and President of the United Synagogue of America, President of the Jewish Theological Seminary of America, and architect of the American Conservative Jewish movement. Brought back 100,000 manuscript fragments from the famous *Cairo geniza.* Among these, he identified the previously missing Hebrew version of Ecclesiastics. Books: *Studies in Judaism* and *Some Aspects of Rabbinic Theology.*

You cannot be anything if you want to be everything.

1873 **Willa Sibert Cather:** American novelist, poet and journalist. Wrote about independent women. Considered one of the outstanding 20th-century U.S. writers. Had a high regard for the industry and courage of pioneering immigrants to the U.S.A. and a deep hatred for the modern world. Pulitzer Prize winner for *One of Ours* (1922). Other Works: *A Lost Lady, Death Comes for the Archbishop, My Ántonia* (generally considered her best work), and *O Pioneers!*

There are some things you learn best in calm, and some in storm.

1885 **Zechariah Chafee, Jr.:** American lawyer and legal scholar. Leading thinker on the subject of civil liberties. Did more than anyone else in the early 20th century to shape the debate surrounding freedom of speech and the Constitution's First Amendment. Believed that a good law should be clear, rational and predicable. Advocate for international human rights through his work as a representative on the United Nations Subcommission on Freedom of Information and the Press (1947). Books: *Freedom of Speech, The Inquiring Mind* and *The Blessings of Liberty.*

The real value of freedom is not to the minority that wants to talk, but to the majority that does not wish to listen.

1888 **Heywood C. Broun:** American journalist, novelist and fighter of social injustice. Wrote a liberal-oriented column for several New York newspapers. Helped found the American Newspaper Guild, which annually presents reporting awards in his name for reporting done "in the spirit of Heywood Broun." Because of his huge bulk and untidy appearance, the well known and loved writer became known as a "one-man slum."

The great threat to the young and pure in heart is not what they read but what they don't read.

1888 **Joyce Cary:** Anglo-Irish novelist, trained as an artist. Used his experiences gained in Nigeria as a backdrop to some of his early novels: *Aissa Saved, The African Witch* and *Mister Johnson.* Author of humorous English social history featuring eccentric characters such as the likable scoundrel and painter Gully Jimson in *The Horse's Mouth.* Also wrote: *A House of Children, Charlie Is My Darling,* and *Prisoner of Grace.*

Reality becomes a prison to those who can't get out of it.

1915 **Eli Wallach:** American actor. Trained for the stage at New York's Neighborhood Playhouse. In the 1950s he was regarded as one of the American theater's most respected performer. Leading exponent of "the Method" approach to acting. First screen appearance as the unscrupulous seducer in Eliza Kazan's *Baby Doll.* Appeared in films and on the stage with his wife Anne Jackson. Other films: *The Magnificent Seven, The Misfits, Lord Jim, The Good, the Bad and the Ugly* and *The Godfather Part 3.*

Having the critics praise you is like having the hangman say you have a pretty neck.

1922 **Howard Zinn:** American historian, political scientist, author and political activist. At the center of the most important historical moments of the last thirty or so years. Supporter of the anti-war movement during the U.S.'s involvement in Vietnam. As a faculty member of Spelman College participated in the Civil Rights movement and served as adviser to the Student Nonviolent Coordinating Committee. Author of *A People's History of the United States, You Can't Be Neutral on a Moving Train: A Personal History of Our Time* and *Vietnam: The Logic of Withdrawal.*

Dissent is the highest form of patriotism.

1928 **(Avram) Noam Chomsky:** American linguistic scholar, political philosopher and activist. Introduced a radically new linguistic theory in his *Syntactic Structures,* strongly behaviorist and descriptive. Proposed that language stemmed from and was governed by certain innate and discoverable proclivities or logical structures in the mind. The theory, which he labeled "Cartesian," is strongly rationalistic and contains profound psychological and philosophical implications. Other books: *Aspects of the Theory of Syntax, Language and Mind* and *Problems of Freedom and Knowledge.* Opposition to the Vietnam War involved him in the sixties protest movement as a theorist in radical politics.

For the totalitarian mind, adherence to state propaganda does not suffice: one must display proper enthusiasm while marching in the parade.

1947 **Johnny Bench:** Hall-of-Fame American baseball catcher with the Cincinnati Reds (1967–83). National League Rookie of the Year in 1968 and Most Valuable Player in 1970 and 1972. Key member of the talented "Big Red Machine" team that won four National League pennants and captured two World Series titles. Regarded as one of the greatest defensive catchers to play the game, earning 10 Gold Gloves. Annually the best college catcher receives the Johnny Bench Award.

A catcher and his body are like the outlaw and his horse. He's got to ride the nag till it drops.

1949 **Tom Waits:** American cult singer, song writer and actor. Distinctive voice described by the MusicHound Rock Album Guide as sounding "like it was soaked in a vat of bourbon, left hanging in a smokehouse for a few months and then taken outside and run over by a car." *Bone Machine* (1992) won a Grammy for Best Alternate Music Album and *Mule Variations* (1999) won one for Best Contemporary Folk Album. Films: *The Cotton Club, Ironweed,* and *Bram Stoker's Dracula.* Refuses to allow his songs to be used in commercials and criticizes artists that do:

Apparently the highest compliment our culture grants artists nowadays is to be in an ad — ideally naked on the hood of a new car. I have adamantly and repeatedly refused this dubious honor.

1956 **Larry Bird:** One of the best all-around basketball players in the sport's history. All-American at Indiana State. Fierce competitor, outstanding team leader and all-pro with Boston Celtics. Outstanding defender, one of three players to win the NBA MVP award three years in a row. Led Celtics to three championships. Member of the "Dream Team" that won the gold medal at the 1992 Olympics.

First master the fundamentals.

OTHERS: 967 Persian mystic **Abu Sa'id ibn Aboa al-Chair,** 1598 Italian artist **Giann Lorenzo Bernini,** 1761 Wax museum director **Marie Tussaud,** 1784 British poet **Allan Cunningham,** 1810 German physiologist **Theodor Schwann,** 1863 Italian composer **Pietro Mascagni,** 1863 U.S. department store founder **Richard Sears,** 1872 Dutch historian **Johan Huizinga,** 1879 Czech composer **Rudolf Friml,** 1888 U.S. politician **Hamilton Fish, III,** 1894 U.S. painter **Stuart Davis,** 1910 U.S. bandleader **Louis Prima,** 1924 President of Portugal **Mário Soares,** 1932 U.S. actress **Ellen Burstyn,** 1942 U.S. singer **Harry Chapin,** 1945 Finnish singer **Marion Rung,** 1973 U.S. football player **Terrell Owens**

December 8

65 BCE **Quintus "Horace" Horatius Flaccus:** Latin poet and satirist. Became the unrivaled lyric poet of his times. Early works included books of *Satires* and *Epodes.* Greatest works: the three books of lyrical *Odes* and verse *Epistics,* including the treatise *Ars Poetica,* which set down rules for the composition of poetry. Themes of love, friendship and philosophy had a significant influence on Western poetry from the Renaissance through the 19th century.

Carpe diem! (Seize the day), Rejoice while you are alive; enjoy the day, live life to the fullest; make the most of what you have. It is later than you think.

1542 **Mary, Queen of Scots:** Became queen upon the death of her father James. Because she was Catholic, Protestant nobles forced her to abdicate in favor of her son, later to become King James I of England. Fled to England seeking help from her cousin Queen Elizabeth I. Instead was imprisoned and after 19 years of trying to obtain her freedom, found guilty of supporting a Catholic plot to assassinate Elizabeth. Beheaded at Fotheringhay Castle in 1587, at the age of 44. The event did not go well as the executioner was unable to sever her neck with one blow, and was forced to use a grinding motion on her to complete the task.

No more tears now: I will think upon revenge.

1626 **Christina:** Queen of Sweden (1644–54). Educated as a prince. Negotiated the Peace of Westphalia, ending the Thirty Years' War. One of the wittiest and most learned woman of her age, she was a great patron of the arts and an influence on European culture. Abdicated in 1654 and lived in Rome for the rest of her life. Although her avowed reason for he action was that the burden of ruling was too much for a woman, her real reason was an aversion to marriage. She announced:

I will die a bachelor.

1765 **Eli Whitney:** American inventor and manufacturer. Best known for inventing the cotton gin, a machine that automated the separation of cottonseed from the short-staple cotton fiber. The cotton gin revolutionized the cotton industry in the U.S., but it didn't make Whitney wealthy. Others copied and sold his design. In 1798, he invented a way to manufacture muskets by machine so that the parts were interchangeable, which finally made him rich. Originating the modern system of producing machines with interchangeable parts was his greatest achievement.

One of my primary objects is to form the tools so the tools themselves shall fashion the work and give to every part its just proportion.

1848 **Joel Chandler Harris:** American writer and humorist. Wrote for various newspapers, including the *Atlanta Constitution* (1876–1900). Created a vogue for a distinct style of Southern black dialect literature with stories drawing on folklore, featuring Uncle Remus. A wise, genial old black man weaved his philosophy of life through tales about Br'er Rabbit, Br'er Fox and other animals. Harris' work and the Disney film made from the Uncle Remus tales have been criticized for racial stereotyping.

I am in the prime of my senility.

1868 **[George] Norman Douglas:** Austrian-born British novelist, essayist, antiquary, autobiographer, editor, geologist, historian, humorist, literary critic, scientist, story writer, zoologist and travel writer. Best known for his explorations of the pleasures of the hedonistic life. Travel books demonstrate his love of landscapes and an ear for anecdotes about the legends of the people of the land. Best known book is the novel *South Wind.* Others: *Old Calabria, Birds and Beasts of the Greek Anthology,* and *Looking Back.*

Justice is too good for some people and not good enough for the rest.

1886 **Diego Rivera:** Mexican muralist. Sought to create a new national art based on revolutionary themes. Painted many public murals, the most ambitious is in the National Palace. His New York's Rockefeller Center mural aroused a storm of controversy for including the figure of Lenin. Rockefeller family ordered it destroyed. In Mexico, he created a revival of fresco painting that became the nation's most significant contribution to 20th century art. Took many lovers, but was married to artist Frida Kahlo from 1929 until her death in 1954.

If I ever loved a woman, the more I loved her, the more I wanted to hurt her. Frida was only the most obvious victim of this disgusting trait.

1889 **Hervey Allen:** American author and editor. Major American novelist of the 1930s and 40s, especially for his picturesque novel, *Anthony Adverse,* one of the biggest selling fictional works of the decade, made into a hugely successful motion picture. Before that he was one of the most popular poets of the "lost generation," and a bestselling author of historical fiction. Collaborated with DuBose Heyward, writing a volume of verse, *Carolina Chansons.*

The only time you really live fully is from thirty to sixty. The young are slaves to dreams; the old servants of regrets. Only the middle-aged have all their five senses in the keeping of their wits.

1894 **James Thurber:** American writer and cartoonist. Wrote memoirs, fables, reports, satires, fantasies, complaints, fairy tales and sketches, which led him to be called the "foremost humorist in America." His popular drawings and cartoons were featured in the *New Yorker* magazine. Described humor as "emotional chaos remembered in tranquility." Best known literary efforts are the play, *The Male Animal,* written in collaboration with Elliott Nugent, and *The Secret Life of Walter Mitty.* As a result of a childhood action he became totally blind late in his life.

If I have any beliefs about immortality, it is that certain dogs I have known will go to heaven, and very, very few persons.

1943 **Jim Morrison:** American poet and singer. After his death of a drug overdose achieved a cult position. One of the first rock sex symbols. Lead singer of the super group The Doors. Songs: "Light My Fire," "People Are Strange." "Hello I Love You," and "Love Her Madly." Wished to be accepted as a serious artist, publishing collections of poetry such as *An American Prayer* and *The Lords and The New Creatures.* Drinking and drug use had a bad effect on his singing. Went to Paris, hoping to follow a literary career, but was found dead in his bathtub.

I believe in long, prolonged, derangement of the senses in order to obtain the unknown.

1961 **Ann Hart Coulter:** Conservative American author. Raging pundit, a proud liberal basher to the delight of those sharing her views, but rather easy to dismiss because of the outrageousness of some of her comments: "My only regret with Timothy McVeigh is he did not go to the New York Times Building." Fired from the *National Review,* when she turned in a column with a final solution to the Muslim Problem, "we should invade their countries, kill their leaders and convert them to Christianity." Books: *High Crimes and Misdemeanors: The Case Against Bill Clinton* and *How to Talk to a Liberal (If You Must).*

Whether they are defending the Soviet Union or bleating for Saddam Hussein, liberals are always against America. They are either traitors or idiots, and on the matter of America's self-preservation, the difference is irrelevant.

1966 **Sinead O'Connor:** Irish singer and songwriter. First album *The Lion and the Cobra* scored with hit "Mandinka." Second album, *I Do Not Want What I Haven't Got,* went straight to number one. Combines pop, jazz and Celtic sounds in her songs. Known for a clean-shaven head, controversy-courting and uninhibited observations. Ordained a priest in the Latin Tridentine Church.

We have a tradition of passing our history orally and singing a lot of it and writing songs about it and there's king of a calling in Irish voices when they're singing in their Irish accent.

OTHERS: 1508 Frisian geographer **Gemma Frisius,** 1708 Holy Roman Emperor **Francis I,** 1730 Dutch physiologist **Jan Ingenhousz**, 1810 U.S. reformer **Elihu Burritt**, 1815 German painter **Adolph Menzel**, 1831 U.S. architect **James Hoban**, 1832 Norwegian novelist **Björnstjerne Björnson**, 1861 French sculptor **Aristide Maillol**, 1865 French mathematician **Jacques Hadamard**, 1865 Finnish composer **Jean Sibelius**, 1890 Czech composer **Bohuslav Martinů**, 1911 U.S. actor **Lee J. Cobb**, 1913 U.S. poet **Delmore Schwartz**, 1925 U.S. singer/actor **Sammy Davis Jr.**, 1933 U.S. comedian **Flip Wilson**, 1939 Irish flautist **James Galway**, 1953 U.S. actress **Kim Basinger**

December 9

1579 **Martin de Porres:** South American who spent his entire life in the Dominican Order in Lima, Peru, ministering to the sick and the poor. Known as "Martin of Charity" and "The Saint of the Broom "(for his devotion to his work, no matter how menial). At age 11 became a servant in the Dominican priory. Promoted to almoner, begging money from the rich to support the poor and sick. At 15, took vows as a Dominican brother. Placed in charge of the Dominican infirmary, provided tender cure for the sick and made some spectacular cures. Canonized in 1962, the first African-American to be made a saint.

Compassion is preferable to cleanliness: with a little bit of soap I can clean my bed, but think of the flood of tears I would require to clean from my soul the stain that harshness against this unfortunate would leave.

1608 **John Milton:** English poet and prose writer. One of the most respected of all English literary figures. Early works include: "L'Allegro," "Il Penseroso," "Comus" and "Lycidas." During the Civil War, emerged as the official apologist for the Commonwealth. Blind from 1652, he wrote his masterpiece, the epic *Paradise Lost*. First three books reflect the triumph of the godly, but the last books are tinged with despair. *Paradise Regained*'s theme is the triumph of reason over passion. Other works: "On His Blindness," *De Doctrina Christiana,* and *Samson Agonistes*.

The mind can make a heaven out of hell or a hell out of heaven.

1886 **Clarence Birdseye:** American businessman and inventor. Considered the founder of the modern frozen food industry. His two major contributions to the concept of freezing food were the importance of freezing food so rapidly that there would be no damage to the cellular structure — affecting, taste, texture and appearance — and freezing food in a package that could be sold directly to the consumer. Credited with over 300 patents.

Go around asking a lot of damn fool questions and taking chances. Only through curiosity can we discover opportunities, and only by gambling can we take advantage of them.

1898 **Emmett Kelly:** American clown with Ringling Brothers and Barnum and Bailey circus. With his tattered clothes, battered hat and woeful face, his alter ego, "Weary Willie" became the most famous clown in the 20th century. Kelly said he didn't "feel funny when I'm in this hobo character. I'm a misfit, a reject. Maybe it's Willy's attempt at a little dignity in spite of everything that tickles folks."

Incongruity, they say, is one of the main ingredients of humor. Maybe it's because everyone can feel superior to me. I honestly don't know.

1901 **Ödön (Edmond Josef) von Horváth:** Important 20th century German-language writer. When the Nazis came to power in Germany in 1933, he resettled to Vienna and when Germany annexed Austria, went to Paris. Always fearful of being struck by lightning, he was killed in June 1938 during a thunderstorm on the Champs Élysées, when he was hit by a falling tree branch. Works: *Don Juan Comes Back from War, Judgment Day*, and *Tales from the Vienna Woods*.

Nothing conveys the feeling of infinity as much as stupidity does.

1902 **Lucius Beebe:** American journalist and social arbiter. Wrote a syndicated noted society column, "This New York" (1934–44). Lover of good food, wine, society and gossip; a chronicler in a glorious style of New York's social and gastronomic doings. Also owed one of the most highly publicized wardrobes, noted for mink-lined morning coats, astrakhan-collared evening coats, derbies, fancy vests and diamond boutonnières. Books: *People on Parade* and *The 20th Century Limited*.

All I want is the best of everything and there's very little of that left.

1904 **Louis Kronenberger:** American writer. Drama critic for *Time* magazine from 1938. Delighted readers with clever one-liners, including his description of Gertrude Lawrence's performance in *Susan and God*: "There are moments when Miss Lawrence seems to be playing Susan and God at the same moment." and on *The Twentieth Century*: "The trouble with our age is all signposts and no destination." Compiled anthologies: *The Pleasure of Their Company* and *The Thread of Laughter*.

In the history of mankind, fanaticism has caused more harm than vice.

1906 **Grace Brewster Murray Hopper:** American mathematician, naval officer and computer pioneer. Called "Grandmother of the Computer Age." Remained an active-duty officer or a reservist for 43 years and in 1983 received a special Presidential appointment to the rank of Rear Admiral. At the time of her retirement in 1986, she was the oldest officer ever to serve on active duty. A true visionary, she conceptualized that a much wider audience could use the computer if there were tools that were both programmer-friendly and application-friendly. Co-inventor of computer language COBOL. Her maxim: "A ship in port is safe, but that's not what ships are built for."

Humans are allergic to change. They love to say, "We've always done it this way." I try to fight that. That's why I have a clock on my wall that runs counterclockwise.

1912 **Thomas "Tip" O'Neill:** Outspoken liberal politician and champion of working people. As Democratic representative from Massachusetts (1953–87), he openly criticized President Lyndon B. Johnson and the Vietnam War. Supported Eugene McCarthy's antiwar candidacy and in 1973 as majority leader voted to cut off funding for the air war in Vietnam. Savvy Speaker of the House (1977–87). Leading opponent of President Reagan's administrative domestic and defense policies. Called Reagan the most ignorant man who had ever occupied the White House.

All politics is local.

1916 **Kirk Douglas:** Born **Issur Danielovitch**. American film actor and producer. Father of actor-producer Michael Douglas. Began his screen career in *The Strange Love of Martha Ivers*. Became a star and a respected actor, nominated for Oscars for his performances in *Champion*, *The Bad and the Beautiful* and *Lust for Life*. Autobiography: *The Ragman's Son*. Other films: *Young Man with a Horn*, *The Big Carnival*, *Detective Story*, and *Paths of Glory*.

When you become a star, you don't change—everyone else does.

1922 **Redd Foxx:** Born **John Elroy Sanford**. African-American comedian. Began his career doing stand-up comedy on the infamous "chitlin" circuit in the 1940s and 50s. One of the premier "blue humor" comedians. Material was dirty, too dirty it was believed for white audiences. Able to tell some of his least offensive jokes on *The Ed Sullivan Show* and other variety shows. Had considerable success with TV's *Sanford and Son* (1972). Pioneer in breaking racial ground in the entertainment industry.

We were poor. If I wasn't a boy, I wouldn't have anything to play with.

1933 **Ashleigh Brilliant:** English-born author and syndicated cartoonist. Best known for *Pot-Shots*, a single-panel comic of illustrated one-liners, limited to 17 words apiece. The *Wall Street Journal* described him as "history's only full time, professional published epigrammatist. They include: "My life so far has been a long series of things I wasn't ready for," "Sometimes I get very impatient waiting for somebody to do the things only I can do," "Wait! Come back! There's part of my face you haven't stepped on yet" and

Life is the only game in which the object of the game is to learn the rules.

OTHERS: 1571 Dutch astronomer **Metius**, 1594 Swedish king **Gustavus Adolphus**, 1610 Italian castrato **Baldassare Ferri**, 1652 German physician **Augustus Rivinus**, 1748 French chemist **Claude Louis Berthollet**, 1847 English actor **George Grossmith**, 1850 U.S. soprano **Emma Abbott**, 1891 Belarusian poet **Maksim Bahdanovič**, 1858 Spanish soprano **Conchita Supervia**, 1897 British actress **Hermione Gingold**, 1899 French author **Jean de Brunhoff**, 1905 U.S. screenwriter **Dalton Trumbo**, 1926 U.S. physicist **Henry Kendall**, 1929 U.S. actor/director **John Cassavetes**, 1934 British actress **Judi Dench**, 1942 Football player **Dick Butkus**, 1947 U.S. politician **Tom Daschle**, 1962 U.S. actress **Felicity Huffman**

December 10

1815 **Ada Byron, Lady Lovelace:** British pioneer computer programmer, the mathematically gifted and talented only legitimate child of renowned English poet George Gordon, Lord Byron. Engaged in a life-long correspondence with Charles Babbage about his Analytical Engine. She wrote an article (1843), giving descriptive, analytical, contextual, and metaphysical information about the engine. Explained a process that developed into computer programming, and did so with great clarity and insight, demonstrating that she had inherited some of her father's gift for words.

In considering any new subject, there is frequently a tendency, first, to overrate what we find to be already interesting or remarkable; and secondly, by a sort of natural reaction, to undervalue the true state of the case, when we do discover that our notions have surpassed those that were really tenable.

1824 **George MacDonald:** Scottish novelist, poet and Christian minister. Best known as a writer of juvenile fantasies, Christian allegories and fairy tales. He was deeply admired and an inspiration to the likes of W.H. Auden, J.R.R. Tolkien and Madeleine L'Engle. Works: *At the Back of the North Wind*, *Phantastes*, *Lilith* and *The Princess and the Goblin*. Served as a mentor to Charles Dodgson (Lewis Carroll), encouraging him to publish his story of *Alice*.

It is not in the nature of politics that the best men are elected. The best men do not want to govern their fellowman.

1830 **Emily Dickinson:** "The Belle of Amherst." One of the outstanding American poets. At age 23 withdrew from all social contact, living a secluded life, dressed only in white, seldom leaving her room, even to greet guests who came to see her. Secretly wrote over 1,000 poems, only two of which were published in her lifetime. Most were published after her death by her sister Lavina. Works are intensely personal and spiritual, show great originality in thought and form.

Because I could not stop for Death—/ He kindly stopped for me—/ The Carriage held but just Ourselves—/ And Immortality...

1851 **Melvil Dewey:** American librarian, educator and pioneer in library science. Founder of the first library school (1887). One of the founders of the American Library Association. Created the Dewey decimal system of classifying books for libraries in 1876, which divides books into ten main groups that classify the general fields of knowledge. Each main group is further broken down into smaller groups, and so. Categories are represented by numbers from 000 to 999. Many university libraries have abandoned the Dewey decimal system for that used by the Library of Congress.

The time was when a library was very much like

a museum, and a librarian was a mouser in musty books... The time is when a library is a school, and the librarian is the highest sense a teacher.

1882 **Otto Neurath:** Austrian philosopher and social theorist. Associated with "physicalism," which aimed to establish an entirely materialist foundation of knowledge. Wrote about a moneyless "economy in kind" (or barter system). Austrian government assigned him to the planning ministry before he was forced to flee for Great Britain in the wake of the Nazi occupation. After World War II, the Marxist governments of Bavaria and Saxony employed him to help socialize their economies. Works: *International Picture Language* and *Modern Man in the Making.*

We are like sailors who must rebuild the ship on the open sea, never able to dismantle it in dry-dock and to reconstruct it there out of the best materials.

1883 **Alfred Kreymborg:** American author, poet, anthologist and editor. Founded *The Glebe* (1913), one of the first periodicals to sponsor experimental writing. Later founded *Others,* a magazine dedicated to experimental poetry. Poetry: *Blood of Things, Manhattan Men* and *No More War and Other Poems.* Also wrote popular puppet plays which he performed on tour with his wife. Autobiography: *Troubadour* (1925).

Satan the envious said with a sigh:/ Christians know more about their hell than I.

1891 **Nelly Leonie Sachs:** German-born Swedish-Jewish poet and playwright. Writings expressed the anguish of the persecuted Jewish people. Lived under Hitler's terror until 1940, when she escaped to Sweden. After World War II wrote plays and poetry about the plight of the Jewish people. Shared the Nobel Prize for Literature in 1966. Works: *In the Dwellings of Death, Flight and Metamorphosis* and *Journey into a Dustless Room.*

Someone/ will take the ball/ from the hands that play/ the game of terror.

1907 **[Margaret] Rumer Godden:** British novelist, poet and author of children's books. Spent half her life in India, which provided a backdrop for much of her fiction. Her greatest success was *Black Narcissus,* made into a stunningly photographed movie, starring Deborah Kerr as the leader of a team of English Anglican nuns attempting to establish a mission in the Himalaya region. In children's books, frequently writes from a child's point of view as in *The Greengage Summer.*

Memory is the only friend of grief.

1908 **Olivier Messiaen:** French composer and ornithologist. One of the most original modern composers, he makes use of a wide range of resources from Gregorian chants to oriental rhythms. Among his innovations is his the phonetic emulation of bird song in several of his works. To attain ornithological fidelity, he made a detailed study of the rhythms and pitches of singing birds in many regions of several countries.

I give bird songs to those who dwell in cities and have never heard them, make rhythms for those who know only military marches or jazz, and paint colors for those who see none.

1911 **Chester "Chet" Huntley:** American broadcast journalist. In 1956, NBC brought him and David Brinkley to New York as broadcasters at the Democratic and Republican conventions. They were teamed to anchor *NBC Nightly News* (1956–70). Accused both of being too liberal and not liberal enough, Huntley explained his hope for remembrance was that "by some accident of voice tome [he would provoke audiences to] think with their heads, not their viscera."

[I used to believe] the government was the answer to all our problems. But the ... government, I've concluded, is now an insufferable jungle of self-serving bureaucrats.

1913 **Morton Gould:** Extraordinarily talented and versatile American composer, conductor and pianist. A child prodigy he composed at age 6 and presented a concert of his works at age 16. Compositions range in style and texture from the ballet *Fall River Legend* to American spirituals and from American symphonettes to the Broadway hit *Billion Dollar Baby.* Works: *Spirituals for String Choir and Orchestra, Lincoln Legend, Cowboy Rhapsody,* and *Dialogues.*

I've always felt that music should be a normal part of the experience that surrounds people.

1914 **Dorothy Lamour:** American actress. Former Miss New Orleans. Band vocalist and radio performer before entering films in the mid–1930s. One of Hollywood's most popular stars during World War II. Beautiful brunette, of limited acting range, famed for making the sarong (about a yard or so of silk wrapped seductively around her body) popular in films *The Jungle Princess, The Hurricane* and *Aloma of the South Seas.* Biggest successes came in the "Road" movies as a sultry foil for Bing Crosby and Bob Hope. Speaking of that teaming:

I felt like a wonderful sandwich, a slice of white bread between two slices of ham.

OTHERS: 1588 Dutch scientist/philosopher **Isaac Beeckman**, 1602 English jurist **John Bradshaw**, 1692 Dutch portrait painter **Cornelis Pronk**, 1787 U.S. educator of the blind **Thomas Hopkins Gallaudet**, 1821 Russian poet **Nikolai Nekrasov**, 1822 Belgian composer/organist **César Franck**, 1870 Austrian architect **Adolf Loos**, 1872 German philosopher **Ludwig Klages**, 1909 U.S. choreographer **Hermes Pan**, 1917 Malaysian king **Yahya Petra**, 1920 U.S. writer **Reginald Rose**, 1947 Azerbaijani politician **Resul Quliyev**, 1948 Founded Palestine Liberation Front **Abu Abbas**, 1960 Irish actor **Kenneth Branagh**, 1972 Belgian-born singer **Brian Molko**, 1980 U.S. violinist **Sarah Chang**

December 11

1803 **[Louis-] Hector Berlioz:** French composer and conductor. Master of orchestration, who exercised a profound influence on the course of modern music. Musical works are conceived as musical embodiments of literary ideas. Passionately infatuated with the Irish actress Harriet Smithson, he wrote *Symphonie fantastique* to be an offering of adoration and devotion for her. They wed, however their marriage did not prove to be as lasting as the symphony. Other Compositions: *Grande messe des morts*, *Roméo et Juliette* and *La Damnation de Faust*.

Love cannot express the idea of music, while music may give an idea of love.

1810 **Alfred de Musset:** French romantic poet and playwright. His poetry probes introspectively into the ecstasies and despairs of love. In 1833, began a stormy love affair with George Sand, which colored much of his work thereafter. Traced the emotionally upheaval of his celebrated but disastrous love for her as it evolved from despair to final resignation. Works include: *Contes d'Espagne et d'Italie*, *Premières poesies*, and *Poèsies nouvelles*, which include the lyrics for which he is best known, *Les Nuits*.

How glorious it is — and also how painful — to be an exception.

1849 **Ellen Key:** Swedish feminist, reformer, essayist and educator. Developed a pioneering method of teaching that was anti-authoritarian. Called "Pallas of Sweden," writings, including *The Century of the Child*, advanced her liberal ideas on the feminist movement, child welfare, love, sex and marriage. Philosophy focused on the role of women in society, placing mothers in the home and women without children in the political arena.

Education can give you a skill, but a liberal education can give you dignity.

1863 **Annie Jump Cannon:** American astronomer. Became deaf from contracting scarlet fever. Graduated from Wellesley College in 1884, and studied astronomy at Radcliffe. In 1896 joined the famous group of women astronomers at Harvard College Observatory. Specialist in the classification of stellar spectra. "The Census Taker of the Sky," discovered 300 variable and five new stars and one double star. Classified the spectra of more than 350,000 stars.

A life spent in the routine of science need not destroy the attractive human element of a woman's nature.

1882 **Max Born:** German-born British theoretical physicist. Developed matrix mechanics, a mathematical basis for quantum mechanics, which accounted for the positions and momentum of the electron in the atom with. Shared 1954 Nobel Prize for Physics with Walter Rothe. Eldest child, Irene, mother of singer and actress Olivia Newton-John, translated and published *The Born-Einstein Letters*.

The belief that there is only one truth, and that oneself is in possession of it, is the root of all evil in the world.

1882 **Fiorella H. La Guardia:** "The Little Flower." American Republican politician. U.S. congressman from New York (1917–21, 1923–33). Resigned from congress to command U.S. bombing squadrons on the Italian-Austrian front in World War I. Returned to Congress. Called a "chronic dissenter," fought for child-labor laws and woman suffrage. Opposed Prohibition and pork-barrel legislation. Mayor of New York (1933–45). Began a slum-clearing program and low-cost-housing projects, improved the operations of the police and fire departments, battled gangsters and official corruption. Fondly remembered for reading the comics to the kiddies on radio during a newspaper strike.

Politics is very much like taxes — everybody is against them or everybody is for them as long as they don't apply to him.

1911 **Naguib Mahfouz:** Egyptian novelist and screenwriter. Major work, the *Cairo Trilogy* (1956–7) includes the novels *Palace Walk*, *Palace of Desire* and *Sukkariyah*, offering a penetrating overview of 20th century Egyptian society. In 1988 he became the first Arabic writer to receive the Nobel Prize for Literature. Other works: *Midaq Alley*, *Children of Gebelawi* and *Miramar*. Also wrote short story collections and more than 30 screenplays.

You can tell whether a man is clever by his answers. You can tell whether a man is wise by his questions.

1918 **Aleksandr Solzhenitsyn:** Russian novelist. His first work was *One Day in the Life of Ivan Denisovich*. Subsequent books were published only in the West. His open letter to the Fourth Congress of Soviet Writers denouncing censorship, led to his expulsion from the Writers' Union. In 1970, awarded the Nobel Prize in Literature. Exiled from the Soviet Union, moved to the U.S.A. in 1976. Returned to Russia after the fall of the U.S.S.R. Other Books: *Cancer Ward*, *The First Circle*, *The Gulag Archipelago* and *Lenin in Zurich*.

Own only what you can always carry with you: know languages, know countries, know people. Let your memory be your travel bag.

1922 **Grace Paley:** née **Goodside.** American short-story writer, poet, active feminist and pacifist. Fiction, noted for its convincingly realistic dialogue, is usually set in New York City, often with Jewish settings and themes. In 1961 she helped found the Greenwich Village Peace Center. Works: *Little Disturbances of Man*, *Enormous Changes at the Last Moment*, *365 Reasons Not to Have Another War*, and an essay collection, *Long Walks and Intimate Talks*.

Rosiness is not a worse windowpane than gloomy gray when viewing the world.

1931 **Bhagwan Shree Rajneesh:** Indian spiritual leader. Established an Ashram in Pune, Preached a doctrine mixing Eastern mysticism, individual devotion and a notorious sexual freedom. Amassed vast personal wealth. By 1970, had attracted some 200,000 devotees. Lived with followers in Oregon (1981–85) until deported for immigration fraud.

Logic ridicules love, and love smiles knowingly at the whole foolishness of logic.

1940 **David Gates:** American singer and songwriter. Embarked on a career as a songwriter and producer, working with Elvis Presley, Bobby Darin, Merle Haggard and Glenn Yarborough. Formed the group *Bread,* one of the most popular pop groups of the early 1970s, with a string of hits of well-crafted melodic soft rock songs, written by Gates: "Make It with You," "Baby I'm a Want You," "Diary," "Lost Without Your Love," "Guitar Man," and "Aubrey."

I found her diary underneath the tree/ And started reading about me/ The words begun to stick to tears to flow/ Her meaning now is clear to see/ The love she've waited for, was someone else not me.

1943 **John Kerry:** American Democratic politician. U.S. Senator from Massachusetts (1984–). Served in U.S. Navy (1966–69), in Vietnam as the commander of a Fast Patrol Craft, also known as a "Swift boat." Awarded three Purple Hearts, a Silver Star and a Bronze Star. During an unsuccessful presidential bid as the Democratic candidate in 2004, his military service became a distracting issue. His record was questioned by a group of Swift Boat Veterans, disgruntled by his opposition to the Vietnam War after returning home and his criticism of President Bush's handling of the War in Iraq.

While we must remain determined to defeat terrorism, it isn't only terrorism we are fighting. It's the beliefs that motivate terrorists. A new ideology of hatred and intolerance has arisen to challenge America and liberal democracy.

OTHERS: 1566 Portuguese composer **Manuel Cardosa**, 1712 Italian philosopher **Francesco Algarotti**, 1725 American statesman **George Mason**, 1843 German bacteriologist **Robert Koch**, 1882 Indian poet **Subramanya Bharathy**, 1883 British actor **Victor McLaglen**, 1890 U.S. painter **Mark Tobey**, 1908 U.S. composer **Elliott Carter**, 1913 French actor **Jean Marais**, 1916 Cuban bandleader **Prez Prado**, 1920 U.S. blues singer **Big Mama Thornton**, 1931 Puerto Rican dancer/singer/actress **Rita Moreno**, 1938 U.S. jazz pianist **McCoy Tyner**, 1939 U.S. political activist **Tom Hayden**, 1944 U.S. singer **Brenda Lee**, 1950 Greek shipping heiress **Christina Onassis**, 1954 U.S. bassist **Nikki Sixx**, 1973 U.S. MC **Mos Def**

December 12

1779 Saint **Madeleine Sophie Barat:** French nun. Founded the Society of the Sacred Heart of Jesus, which aimed to promote educational opportunities among all classes. The first Convent opened in 1801 at Amiens. Under her direction as superior the convent grew in academic excellence and established 100 further foundations throughout Europe. So well thought of, instead of allowing her to retire at 85, her order gave her an assistant to help run the order for the rest of her life. Canonized in 1925.

Your example, even more than your words, will be an eloquent lesson to the world.

1805 **William Lloyd Garrison:** American social activist, journalist and abolitionist. Foremost anti-slavery voice in the United States. Founded and published the paper *The Liberator* (1831–66), in which argued the case for abolition. Denounced slavery so vehemently that he was imprisoned. Founded the American Anti-Slavery Society. After slavery was abolished he turned his attention to woman's suffrage and the plight of the American Indian.

Enslave the liberty of but one human being and the liberties of the world are put in peril.

1821 **Gustave Flaubert:** French novelist of the school of naturalism. One of the great literary artists of the 19th century. Believed in perfection of form and the absolute value of art. Best known for *Madame Bovary,* which served as a model for later realists. It created a scandal and was condemned as immoral, leading to Flaubert being unsuccessfully prosecuted. It has held its place among the world classics. Other works: *Salammbô, La Temptation de St. Antoine* and *A Simple Heart.*

To be stupid, selfish, and have good health are three requirements for happiness, though if stupidity is lacking, all is lost.

1863 **Edvard Munch:** Norwegian painter and printmaker. His use of primary colors and torturously curved designs were a great influence of the German Expressionists. Obsessed with subjects such as death and love, his mature paintings are really non-representative. His most characteristic work is the famous pictures entitled, *The Scream,* in which an anonymous figure on a bridge clasps his hands to his ears and screams out, swirling lines of color contributing to the mood of desperation.

From my rotting body, flowers shall grow and I am in them and that is eternity.

1864 **Arthur Brisbane:** American journalist and editor. Managing editor, Joseph Pulitzer's *New York World* (1890–97); and editor of its rival William Randolph Hearst's New *York Evening Journal* (1897–1921). These two sensational and gossip-filled tabloids marked the beginning of "yellow journalism" in the United States. Brisbane was known as the master of the big, blaring headline and of atrocity stories. Wrote columns "Today" and "This Week."

A good friend can tell you what is the matter with you in a minute. He may not seem such a good friend after telling.

1893 **Edward G. Robinson:** Originally **Emmanuel Goldenberg.** Rumanian-born American actor and art collector. First major stage success was *The Racket* (1928), where he gave his first rendition of Al Capone. In 1930 he played the role that all-too often defined him, the title character in *Little Caesar,* which led to many additional gangsters and tough guy roles. Soft-spoken, cultured actor preferred to play warm, human roles. Other films: *Dr. Erlich's Magic Bullet, House of Strangers, Double In*demnity and *Key Largo.* Known for his collection of French Impressionists.

Some people have youth, some have beauty. I have menace.

1897 **Lillian Smith:** American author and lecturer on racial issues. Her popular but controversial novel *Strange Fruit* was about white-black tensions in a small, stupefied Southern town. Seven publishers refused it, claiming it was unsalable. Atlanta booksellers refused to stock it. It sold several million copies, translated into 15 languages and adapted to the stage. Also wrote: *Killers of the Dream, Now Is the Time* and *One Hour.*

Education is a private matter between the person and the world of knowledge and experience, and has little to do with school or college.

1915 **Frank Sinatra:** American baritone singer, with an impeccable musical phrasing and choice of material, and actor. Became the idol of bobby-soxers. Billed as "The Voice" and later "Ole Blue Eyes." Virtually a has-been whose singing style had changed, before his Oscar for *From Here to Eternity.* Loved, hated, lionized, held in contempt, his volatile nature was a godsend for the media, who gleefully reported his violent outbursts and his close ties to mob bosses. Other films: *Anchors Aweigh, Ocean's Eleven, The Manchurian Candidate,* and Oscar nominated for *The Man with the Golden Arm.* Hit Songs: "You'll Never Know," "Oh! What It Seemed to Be," "Chicago," and "All the Way."

Basically, I'm for anything that gets you through the night— be it prayer, tranquilizers or a bottle of Jack Daniels.

1918 **Joe Williams:** Born **Joseph Goreed.** African-American jazz singer. One of the most popular interpreters of ballads and blues in jazz. Joined the Lionel Hampton Orchestra with which he toured for several years. Came to national prominence as a singer with the Count Basie band. Later formed a jazz combo. His biggest hit was "Every Day I Have the Blues." Other songs: "Ev'ryday (I'll Fall in Love)," "A Man Ain't Supposed to Cry," and "All Right, Okay, You Win.

You can't rehearse a blues, darlin'.

1923 **Og Mandino:** American essayist and philosopher of salesmanship. Published *The Greatest Salesman in the World,* a parable of Hafid, an impoverished camel boy who achieves a life of material abundance with the aid of 10 mystical scrolls that contain simple but profound spiritual advice on how to succeed in life. Based on fundamental Christian beliefs, it was a huge success and he became one of the most popular motivational speakers in the U.S.

I will love the light for it shows me the way, yet I will endure the darkness because it shows me the stars.

1929 **John Osborne:** English playwright, producer and screenwriter. First of England's "angry young men, who wrote vigorously realistic plays about contemporary British working class life." Oscar winner for *Tom Jones* screenplay. When his play *Look Back in Anger* opened in London in 1956, the critics found it a social outrage and reviewers attacked him as a ruffian and intellectual upstart. He saw it rather as unmasking "the Establishment." Other plays: *The Entertainer, Luther* and *Inadmissible Evidence.*

Laughter's the nearest we ever get, or should get, to sainthood. It's the state of grace that saves most of us from contempt.

1972 **Wilson Kipketer:** Kenyan-born middle distance runner, a permanent resident of Denmark from 1990. Dominated the 800 meter event for a decade, remaining undefeated for a three-year period with 8 of the 11 currently all-time fastest times. The International Olympic Committee disallowed him from competing for Denmark in the 1996 Games because he was not a full citizen, although he had competed for Denmark in the 1995 World Championships. Finished a disappointing second in the 2006 games in Sydney and could only manage a Bronze in Athens in 2004.

I was pushed by myself because I have my own rule, and that is that every day I run faster, and try harder.

OTHERS: 1560 PM of France **Maximilien de Béthune** 1724 British admiral **Samuel Hood**, 1745 U.S. Supreme Court Chief Justice **John Jay**, 1862 French historian **Daniel Halévy**, 1864 U.S. critic/essayist **Paul Elmer More**, 1870 U.S. oil baron **Walter B. Sharp**, 1892 Austro-Hungarian rocket engineer **Herman Potočnik Noordung**, 1903 Japanese film director **Yasujiro Ozu**, 1919 British astrologist **Olivia Barclay**, 1923 TV game show host **Bob Barker**, 1924 New York Mayor **Ed Koch**, 1927 U.S. inventor **Robert Noyce**, 1938 U.S. singer **Connie Francis**, 1940 U.S. singer **Dionne Warwick**, 1943 U.S. saxophonist **Grover Washington Jr.**, 1952 U.S. gymnast **Cathy Rigby**, 1977 U.S. supermodel **Bridget Hall**

December 13

1585 **William Drummond:** Scottish poet and laird of Hawthornden. Works included pamphlets and verses in the Royalist cause. Many of his poems were laments written for Mary Cunningham, who died on the eve of their wedding. Best known prose work was *A Cypress Grove,* a meditation on death, and *Flowers of Zion.*

He who will not reason is a bigot; he who cannot is a fool; and he who does not is a slave.

1797 **Heinrich Heine:** Born **Chaim Henry Heine.** German lyric poet, satirist and journalist. Writings demonstrated his love for the German land and people while expressing biting irony about German institutions, customs and literary trends. Combining romanticism with irony, his poetry has been employed in more than 3,000 musical pieces, including those of Schubert, Schumann, Mendelssohn and Liszt. Works: *Trip to the Harz Mountains, The Romantic School,* and *Germany, a Winter Tale.*

True eloquence consists in saying all that is necessary, and nothing but what is necessary.

1871 **Emily Carr:** Canadian artist and writer. Best known for producing a large body of work on Native American themes. Her first book of short stories, *Klee Wyck* (1941) won the Governor-General's Award. Other writings: *The Book of Small, The House of All Sorts* and Growing Pains. Selections from her diary were published posthumously as *Hundreds and Thousands.*

Life's an awful lonesome affair. You come into the world alone and you go out of the world alone yet it seems to me you are more alone while living than even going and coming.

1887 **George Pólya:** Hungarian-born mathematician. Undisputed father of mathematical problem solving and one of the giants of classical analysis. Considered solving problems a practical art, which can be taught and learned. His *How To Solve It*, the two-volume set *Mathematics and Plausible Reasoning*, and *Mathematical Discovery* are classics. Student understanding rather than student memorization is the goal. Basic principles: *Understanding the problem*, *Devising a plan*, *Carrying out the plan*, and *Looking back* need not be limited to mathematics. General heuristics provides strategies for solving all kinds of problems.

If you can't solve a problem, then there is an easier problem you can solve: find it.

1887 **Alvin York:** Reluctant American World War I hero. Fundamentalist religious beliefs made him oppose war, but after being drafted, he reconciled his duty to his country with his religious convictions. While in France, he led a small army detachment against a German machine gun nest, killing 25 of the enemy and inducing 132 others to surrender. Acclaimed as the greatest American hero of the war, he was awarded the Congressional Medal of Honor and given a ticker-tape parade. A Founder of the American Legion, Gary Cooper portrayed him in the very popular 1941 film, *Sergeant York*.

The fear of God makes heroes. The fear of man makes cowards.

1903 **Carlos Montoya:** Popular Spanish-born flamenco guitarist and composer. Took great pains to learn the history of the music that was born out of the Moorish invasion of Spain. Created his personal style, inventing new ways of playing far removed from classical flamenco. Transformed flamenco guitar music from its traditional roots as accompaniment to Andalusian Roma (gypsy) folk dancers and singers to an internationally recognized musical art form.

I play the way I do because to me, that is exactly the way the flamenco guitar should sound ... strange that the unknowing public should agree, while the real flamenco aficionados clearly do not.

1906 Sir **Laurens van der Post:** Afrikaner-born South African author, farmer, soldier and explorer. Helped found an outspoken antiapartheid magazine *Voorslag*. Forced into exile for his progressive racial views, he went to Japan, became fluent in Japanese, and wrote his first novel *In a Province*. During World War II, he was a POW, later relating his experiences in *The Seed and the Sower* and *The Prisoner and the Bomb*. Farmed his land in South Africa and produced his major works: *Venture to the Interior, The Dark Eye in Africa*, and *A Far-Off Place*.

Human beings are perhaps never more frightening than when they are convinced beyond doubt that they are right.

1911 **Kenneth Patchen:** American poet and author, noted for surrealistic poems. Works range from humor, fantasy, and love lyrics to poems of social protest. Style distinguished by striking imagery, original language and free forms. Illustrated his verse with his abstract paintings and read his poems to jazz accompaniment. Among his more than thirty volumes of poetry are: *Panels for the Walls of Heaven, Memoirs of a Shy Pornographer* and *Hurrah for Anything*.

Now is then's only tomorrow.

1915 **Ross MacDonald:** Pseudonym of **Kenneth Millar**. American-Canadian writer of hard-boiled mysteries. Published his first private-eye novel in 1949, introducing private detective Lew Archer, a tough but humane low-key guy, who observes the action form the sidelines. Protagonist of eighteen novels and several short-stories. *The Moving Target* and *The Drowning Pool* were filmed with Paul Newman. The detective's name was changed to Harper, because of Newman's success with films beginning with the letter "H." Other books: *Find a Victim, The Underground Man,* and *The Blue Hammer*.

There's nothing wrong with Southern California that a rise in the ocean level wouldn't cure.

1920 **George P. Shultz:** American government official and statesman. Served on President Eisenhower's Council of Economic Advisers and in the Nixon administration as U.S. Secretary of Labor (1969–1970) and U.S. Secretary of the Treasury (1972–1974) and during the Reagan presidency as U.S. Secretary of State (1982–1989). A dove on foreign policy, he often clashed with the more hawkish members of the president's administration.

He who walks in the middle of the roads gets hit from both sides.

1957 **Steve Buscemi:** Prolific and talented American character actor, who the New York Post described as, "Pale and thin, with a face that resembles a strange mix of Don Knotts, Peter Lorre and David Carradine." Brooklyn-born, he was a New York fireman (1980–84). Showed up at his old firehouse the day after the World Trade Center tragedy, and worked twelve hour shifts for a week, digging through the rubble looking for missing firemen. Films: *Reservoir Dogs, Fargo, The Big Lebowski*, and *Romance and Cigarettes*. Recurring role on TV's "The Sopranos," directing four episodes.

My favorite review described me as the cinematic equivalent of junk mail.

1967 **Jamie Foxx:** Born **Eric Morlon Bishop**. African-American comedian, singer and actor. Made his mark as a stand-up comedian, before joining the TV show *In Living Color*. Grammy-Award nominated, multi-platinum selling R&B singer and Academy Award winner for portraying legendary blind singer Ray Charles in *Ray* (2005. Also nominated for Best Supporting Actor for *Collateral* (2005). On accepting his Oscar, paid tribute to his grandmother Estelle who raised him and had the greatest influence on his life.

She still talks to me now, only now she talks to me in my dreams. And I can't wait to go to sleep

tonight because we have a lot to talk about. I love you.

OTHERS: 1662 Italian philosopher **Francesco Bianchini**, 1724 German scientist **Franz Aepinus**, 1818 U.S. First Lady **Mary Todd Lincoln**, 1835 Episcopal bishop **Phillips Brooks**, 1856 U.S. educator **Abbott L. Lowell**, 1867 Norwegian explorer **Kristian Birkeland**, 1871 Dutch historian **Herman Colenbrander**, 1883 U.S. librarian/ archivist **Belle da Costa Greene**, 1890 U.S. playwright **Marc Connelly**, 1897 U.S. journalist **Drew Pearson**, 1911 Norwegian economist **Trygve Haavelmo**, 1913 U.S. boxer **Archie Moore**, 1923 African-American baseball player **Larry Doby**, 1925 U.S. comic actor **Dick Van Dyke**, 1934 U.S. film producer **Richard D. Zanuck**, 1943 African-Canadian baseball player **Ferguson Jenkins**

December 14

1503 **Nostradamus:** Latin name of **Michel de Notredame**. French physician and astrologer. His *Centuries* of predictions in rhymed quatrains appeared in two collections during the period 1555 to 1558. Generally expressed in obscure and enigmatical terms his prophecies brought him an exalted reputation. True-believers have worked diligently to show that major events of history were foreseen by their master. Most declarations that he had described the rise of Adolf Hitler and the assassination of John F. Kennedy are not credible, but the desire to believe in magical powers is strong.

After there is great trouble among mankind, a greater one is prepared. The great mover of the universe will renew time, rain, blood, thirst, famine, steel weapons and disease. In the heavens, a fire is seen.

1533 **Henry IV:** Called **Henry of Navarre**. First Bourbon King of France (1589–1610). Promulgated the Edict of Nantes, granting religious and civil liberties to French Protestants. A Calvinist, he led the Huguenot army at the battle of Jarnac. Survived the massacre of St. Bartholomew's Day by proclaiming himself a Catholic. Escaped and renounced his conversion. Became king after the murder of Henry III when once again he embraced Catholicism, explaining: "Paris is well worth a Mass."

I want there to be no peasant in my realm so poor that he will not have a chicken in his pot every Sunday.

1546 **Tycho Brahe:** Danish astronomer. Greatest astronomical observer of the pre-telescopic era. Made a remarkable star catalogue of over 1000 stars. Profoundly changed observational practices. Compiled extensive data on the planet Mars, which allowed his assistant Johannes Kepler to deduce his three laws of planetary motion and to demonstrate that the orbit of Mars was not a circle but an ellipse. Tycho first became famous for his discovery of a nova (a term he coined) in Cassiopeia in 1572, the first to record the appearance of a supernova.

Now it is quite clear to me that there are no solid spheres in the heavens, and those that have been devised by authors to save the appearances, exist only in the imagination.

1640 **Aphra Behn:** née **Johnson**. English dramatist, novelist and poet. Considered the first professional female author in England. Spent her early life in Surinam, where she met the enslaved Negro prince Oroonoko, subject of her novel, *Oroonoko, or the History of the Royals Slave*. A professional spy in Antwerp during the Dutch Wars, forwarded political and naval information for which she received no pay. Wrote poetry and novels, as well as several coarse Restoration plays, including *The Forced Marriage*, *The Rover* and *The Feigned Courtesans*.

Love ceases to be a pleasure, when it ceases to be a secret.

1883 **Morihei Ueshiba:** Japanese founder of *Aikidio* ("The Art of Peace"). History's greatest master of the martial arts. Studies transcended technical matters to include a moral and philosophical view of the world based on harmony in the face of aggression. Had three visions, the first the revelation that the Way of the Warrior is to manifest Divine Love. The second revealed that martial arts techniques were vehicles for the civilization of life. The third vision was of the Great Spirit of Peace, a path that could lead to the elimination of all strife and the reconciliation of mankind.

Loyalty and devotion lead to bravery. Bravery leads to the spirit of self-sacrifice. The spirit of self-sacrifice creates trust in the power of love.

1896 **James H. Doolittle:** American air force officer, daredevil, scientist, engineer and administrator. During World War II, called "the little man who is everywhere." Commanded 16 B-25 bombers which raided Tokyo in 1942, as a message that the United States had not been bombed into submission and helplessness by the Japanese attack at Pearl Harbor. By 1944, held the rank of Lt. General and acquired almost every high military honor available. In 1956 chosen chairman of the National Advisory Committee for Aeronautics.

If we should have to fight, we should be prepared to do so from the neck up rather than from the neck down.

1897 **Margaret Chase Smith:** American politician and columnist. Republican U.S. representative from Maine (1940–49) and U.S. Senator (1948–72), serving longer than any other woman. Sought Republican presidential nomination (1964). Waged some of the toughest battles in the U.S. Senate, emerging without a blemish on her reputation of being scrupulous honest and knowing what she was fighting about.

Moral cowardice that keeps us from speaking our minds is as dangerous to this country as irresponsible talk. The right way is not always the popular and easy way. Standing for what is right when it is unpopular is a true test of moral character.

1913 **Dan Dailey:** American dancer and actor. Began in show business as a child with a minstrel show.

Often in musicals about show business people. Nominated for an Oscar for *When My Baby Smiles At Me.* Other films: *Mother Wore Tights, Give My Regards to Broadway, Call Me Mister,* and *There's No Business Like Show Business.*

In Hollywood, after you get a little success, the next thing you usually get is a divorce.

1919 **Shirley Jackson:** American short-story writer, playwright, novelist and screenwriter. Noted for her tales dealing with the supernatural, in which the tone is odd, and macabre, with an impending sense of doom. Most famous story "The Lottery," is set in a small town where the residents gather for an annual ritual, a lottery, the winner of which is methodically murdered by the community. Novels: *The Road Through the Wall, The Haunting of Hill House,* and *Life among the Savages,* a fictional and disrespectful memoir of her children.

It has long been my belief that in times of great stress, such as a 4-day vacation, the thin veneer of family wears off almost at once, and we are revealed in our true personalities.

1932 **Charlie Rich:** American country singer and pianist. Nicknamed "The Silver Fox," because of his full head of gray hair. Fashioned himself as a smooth, middle-of-the-road balladeer. Best known hit songs "Behind Close Doors" and "The Most Beautiful Girl in the World." topped the charts, earning him Country Music Association's Best Male Vocalist of the Year and a Grammy for Best Album (1973). Other hits: "A Very Special Love Song," "I Don't See you in My Eyes Anymore," and "Are We Dreamin' the Same Dream."

I think a guy who's had just the right amount of booze can sing the blues a hell of a lot better than a guy who is stone sober.

1935 **Lee Remick:** Talented, attractive American actress who combined respectability with sensuality. Big break came when director Elia Kazan saw her in a TV show and offered the role of a sexy drum majorette in *Face in the Crowd,* starring Andy Griffith as a megalomaniac entertainer. Oscar nominated for *Days of Wine and Roses.* Other films *Anatomy of a Murder, The Long, Hot Summer, Sanctuary and The Omen.*

Breasts and bottoms look boringly alike.

1946 **Patty Duke:** U.S. actress who zoomed to stardom before 13 as young Helen Keller in Broadway's *The Miracle Worker.* Repeated the role in the film, winning an Oscar, the youngest person ever to do so at the time. Star of television's "The Patty Duke Show" (1963–66). Appeared in numerous TV movies and segments of series, winning three Grammys. Her adult film career was hurt by her turbulent personal life and her bouts of depression.

I joke around a lot about the manic times because they're funny. We manics do outrageous things and it is a part of our colorful nature.

OTHERS: 1625 French orientalist **Barthélemy d'Herbelot de Molainville**, 1631 English philosopher **Anne Conway**, 1678 English historian **Daniel Neal**, 1775 U.S. founder Kenyon College **Philander Chase**, 1866 British artist **Roger Fry**, 1884 U.S. playwright **Jane Cowl**, 1895 French poet **Paul Eluard**, 1908 U.S. comedian **Morey Amsterdam**, 1911 U.S. novelty bandleader **Spike Jones**, 1918 U.S. TV executive **James T. Aubrey**, 1938 Brazilian theologian **Leonardo Boff**, 1946 U.S. film executive **Michael Ovitz**, 1951 Dutch chess grandmaster **Jan Timman**, 1956 Liechtenstein skier **Hanni Wenzel**, 1960 U.S. gay rights activist **Bob Paris**, 1965 U.S. baseball player **Craig Biggio**, 1970 Polish singer **Anna Maria Jopek**

December 15

37 CE **Nero Claudius Caesar:** Fifth Emperor of Rome (54–68). Although his reign began with much promise, he was more interested in sex, singing and chariot races than governing. Suspected of planning the great fire of Rome which he blamed on Christians, many of whom were cruelly put to death. Rebuilt the city with great magnificence. To pay for his building projects, all of Italy and the provinces were plundered. Roman legions and his guards rose against him. He committed suicide, lamenting, "What an artist dies with me!"

Hidden talent counts for nothing.

1802 **János Bolyai:** Romanian mathematician who wrote a 24-page article, developing the propositions that could be derived from this denial of the Parallel Postulate and the other postulates and axioms of Euclid. Regarded such propositions common to all geometries as the basis of an *absolute geometry.* Wrote, "Out of nothing I Have created a strange new universe." Today, Carl Friedrich Gauss and Nikolai Lobachevsky share credit with Bolyai for the invention of non-Euclidean geometry.

Mathematical discoveries, like springtime violets in the woods, have their season which no man can hasten or retard.

1852 **Antoine Henri Becquerel:** French physicist who discovered radioactivity. Partly by chance, he found that uranium salt placed on a wrapped photographic plate caused this to blacken. Found the phenomenon was totally due to the uranium. His work was soon confirmed and became the starting point for all studies on radioactivity. Shared the Nobel Prize for Physics with the Curies in 1903.

Decisiveness is often the art of timely cruelty.

1888 **Maxwell Anderson:** American playwright, poet and lyricist. Many of his plays dealt with concepts of liberty and justice. Major success with historical dramas: *Elizabeth the Queen* and *Mary of Scotland.* Other plays: *What Price Glory, Winterset, Key Largo,* and *The Bad Seed.* Wrote the screenplay for *All Quiet on the Western Front.* Wrote the lyrics for "Lost in the Stars," "Cry, the Beloved Country" and "September Song" from *Knickerbocker Holiday.*

And the days dwindle down/ To a precious few,/ September, November—/ And these few precious days I'd spend with you,/ These golden days I'd spend with you.

1892 **J. Paul Getty:** American oilman, real estate tycoon and art collector. Used $15 million left to him by his father to gain control of some 100 companies. Gained control of the Pacific Western Oil Co., which was renamed Getty Oil. Lived a relatively quiet life, until *Fortune* magazine "outed" him by estimating his worth, making him an overnight celebrity. Despite worth more than a billion dollars, noted for his miserliness. Had a multi-million art collection.

Formula for success: Rise early, work hard, strike oil.

1897 **David McCord:** American poet and writer. Premier American writer of light verse, noted for creative, rhythmic and often whimsical poems. Best remembered for his poetry written for children. *Every Time I Climb a Tree*, a collection of poems, demonstrating the gift of "making serious ideas unforgettable and ordinary events extraordinary."

A handful of sand is an anthology of the universe.

1904 **Betty Smith:** Born **Betty Wehmer**. American novelist and playwright. Best known novel, *A Tree Grows in Brooklyn*, the heart-warming story of the life of a sensitive young girl growing up in a city slum. An instantaneous hit soon turned into a very successful film and later a musical. Others: *Tomorrow Will Be Better*, *Maggie-Now* and *Joy in the Morning*.

Look at everything as though you were seeing it either for the first or last time. Then your time on earth will be filled with glory.

1913 **Muriel Rukeyser:** American poet, biographer, translator and activist. Wrote on social and political issues. Technical and scientific ideas played an important role in her early poetry, as seen in her first collection, *Theory of Flight*. In the title poem, she used the airplane as a symbol of man's longing for freedom. Poetry collections: *Beast in View*, *Body of Waking*, and *Waterlily Fire*.

The universe is made of stories, not atoms.

1922 **Philip Rieff:** American sociologist and author. Speculated that a new character had arrived on the scene in Western culture. "Psychological man" was no longer inspired by religious faith or a strong sense of civic responsibility; rather, his energies turned inward, toward the care and maintenance of himself. Books: *Freud: The Mind of the Moralist*, *The Triumph of the Therapeutic: Uses of Faith After Freud*, *My Life Among the Deathworks* and *The Feeling Intellect*.

Reason cannot save us. Nothing can; but reason can mitigate the cruelty of living.

1923 **Freeman Dyson:** English theoretical physicist. Unified the independent versions of quantum electrodynamics (QED). Showed how the independent theories of Willis Lamb, Julian Swinger, Sin-Itiro Tomonaga and Richard Feynman related to each other and produced a single general theory of QED. Subsequently Dyson was involved in many areas of physics, as well as cosmology and making speculations of space travel.

You ask: what is the meaning or purpose of life? I can only answer with another question: do you think we are wise enough to read God's mind?

1931 **Edna O'Brien:** Irish novelist, short-story writer and playwright. Writes of the position of women in society, their seeking a sense of belonging, and finding no understanding from men. Portrays the Irish as violent, puritanical and hypocritical. Books banned in Ireland, partially because her frank expression of female sexuality. Works: *The Country Girls*, *Johnny I Hardly Knew You*, *A Fanatic Heart*, and *August Is a Wicked Month*.

I'm an Irish Catholic and I have a long iceberg of guilt.

1933 **Tim Conway:** Originally **Tom Conway**. American comic actor, best known as a regular on TV's *The Carol Burnet Show*. Notorious for making the cast members — especially Harvey Korman — break out of character and begin to laugh at his adlibs as he played memorable characters such as "The Old Man" and "Mr. Tudball." Called "the best second-banana in the business." Earlier starred in *McHale's Navy* as the inept second-in-command.

I've never really taken anything very seriously. I enjoy life because I enjoy making other people enjoy it.

OTHERS: 1610 Flemish painter **David Teniers**, 1832 French engineer **Alexandre Eiffel**, 1852 Viceroy of Egypt **Tewfik Pasja**, 1859 Russian initiator of Esperanto **L.L. Zamenhof**, 1860 Danish physician **Niels Ryberg Finsen**, 1861 U.S. automobile pioneer **Charles Duryea**, 1879 Czech chorographer **Rudolf von Laban**, 1899 British sprinter **Harold Abrahams**, 1896 Dutch sculptor **Paul Citroen**, 1907 Brazilian architect **Oscar Niemeyer** 1916 New Zealand physician **Maurice Wilkins**, 1922 U.S. disk jockey, popularized "rock 'n' roll" **Alan Freed**, 1928 Austrian artist **Friedensreich Hundertwasser**, 1940 U.S. football player **Nick Buoniconti**, 1952 U.S. director **Julie Traynor**

December 16

1485 **Catherine of Aragon:** Spanish daughter of King Ferdinand and Queen Isabella. Arthur, son of England's King Edward VII, died 6 months after their marriage. As the marriage was never consummated, the Pope allowed her to be betrothed to her brother-in-law Henry. The only surviving child of the union was a daughter; later Queen Mary I. Henry sought a means of having a legitimate male heir. When his wife wouldn't consent to a divorce and the Pope refused it, the king broke with the Catholic Church and had his marriage annulled.

In this world I will confess myself to be the king's true wife, and in the next they will know how unreasonably I am afflicted.

1584 **John Selden:** Erudite English lawyer, historian and antiquary. Supported the rights of Parliament in the struggle with the crown. Helped draft the Petition of Rights. His *England's Epinomis* and *Jani Anglorum* established him as the father of legal antiquarianism. Best known book, *Table Talk*, the record of his conversations kept by his secretary, was published after his death.

Pleasure is nothing else but the intermission of pain.

1714 **George Whitefield:** British-born minister, evangelist, and the greatest pulpit orator of the 18th century. Took holy orders in 1738, but was suspended for his unorthodox doctrines. Associated with John and Charles Wesley in the founding of Methodism. Often preached In America and was a charter trustee of the University of Pennsylvania.

It is a poor sermon that gives no offense; that neither makes the hearer displeased with himself or with the preacher.

1770 **Ludwig van Beethoven:** German composer and pianist of unsurpassed genius. Called the "unsurpassed master of instrumental music." Wrote symphonies, chamber music, concertos and piano sonatas. Usually played his own piano pieces and orchestral works until in his early thirties he began going deaf. Became seriously depressed because of his illness and contemplation of his resulting isolation, and the failure of his marital hopes. Works: *Pathétique*, *Pastoral Symphony*, *The Moonlight Sonata*, *Eroica*, *Fidelio*, and *9th Symphony (Ode to Joy)*.

What you are, you are by accident of birth; what I am, I am by myself. There are and will be a thousand princes; there is only one Beethoven.

1775 **Jane Austen:** English novelist, one of the great writers of social comedy. Had a talent for evaluating ordinary human behavior and the nuances of social interaction among the landed gentry. Of her six novels, set within the confines of middle-class provincial society, four were published anonymously during her lifetime; the others posthumously. Works: *Persuasion*, *Sense and Sensibility*, *Pride and Prejudice*, *Mansfield Park*, *Emma*, and *Northanger Abbey*.

One half of the world cannot understand the pleasures of the other.

1863 **George Santayana:** Spanish-born American skeptical philosopher, poet and novelist. Taught that everything has a natural basis. Author of: *Idea of Christ in the Gospels*, *Egotism in German Philosophy*, *The Sense of Beauty*, *The Life of Reason*, *Realms of Being*, the best-selling *The Last Puritan, volumes of poetry* and his autobiography, *Persons and Places*.

That life is worth living is the most necessary of assumptions, and, were it not assumed, the most impossible of conclusions.

1899 **Noël Coward:** English playwright, actor, composer and director. Wrote and appeared in plays on both sides of the Atlantic. A master of English prose, noted for versatility, wit and sophistication. Wrote much about the spoiled, snobbish British rich. Plays: *Private Lives*, *Cavalcade*, *Design for Living*, and *Blithe Spirit*. Authored films such as *In Which We Serve* and the magnificent love story *Brief Encounter*. Songs: "Room with a View," "Mad Dogs and Englishmen" and "Someday I'll Find You."

It's discouraging to think how many people are shocked by honesty and how few by deceit.

1901 **Margaret Mead:** American anthropologist. Carried out a number of field studies in the Pacific. Wrote both academic and popular books, including, *Coming of Age in Samoa* and *Culture and Commitment*. In *Sex and Temperament in Three Primitive Societies* and *Male and Female*, she challenged the conventions of Western society and urged a new look at traditional sex roles. Popular speaker on civil liberties, ecological sanity, feminism, and population control.

Never doubt that a small group of thoughtful committed citizens can change the world; indeed, it's the only thing that ever has.

1905 **Piet Hein:** Danish mathematician, scientist, inventor and poet. In addition to discovering the Soma cube, created many intricate mathematical games, including "Hex." Produced beautiful pieces of furniture, helping make Scandinavian design an international conception. Named his short pithy poems, *gruks*. "Example: "Double doors are justified/ because they're comfortably wide;/ therefore, you only half undo 'em."

Problems worthy of attack prove their worth by hitting back.

1917 **Arthur C. Clarke:** English science-fiction writer. Themes are exploration and the place humans have in the universe. Warned that given the Malthusian fact that population will outpace the earth's resources, the alternatives to which are chilling, and include infanticide, sterilization and rationing of children. Books: *The Other Side of the Sky* and *2001: A Space Odyssey*.

Sometimes I think we're alone in the universe, and sometimes I think we're not. In either case the idea is quite staggering.

1928 **Philip K. Dick:** American science fiction writer. Recurrent motif of alternate universes and the collapse of an artificial reality, when the main characters discover that the entire world has been mechanically imposed on their psyches and that "reality" are vastly different. Novels: *We Can Remember It for You Wholesale* (filmed as *Total Recall*) and *Do Androids Dream of Electric Sheep?* (Filmed as *Blade Runner*).

Reality is that which, when you stop believing in it, doesn't go away.

1980 **Sarah Pezdek-Smith:** American self-taught artist, jewelry designer, photographer, poet and writer. Created Rustic Relics Designs, offering one-of-a-kind jewelry, wearable art, fiber, glass, paper and metal art. Claims her work is "a spontaneous culmination of raw emotion, paint, vulnerability, ink, written words, and a true passion for what I do."

The strength of a woman can carry the weight of the world.

OTHERS: 1622 Dutch admiral **Kurt Adeler**, 1717 British writer **Elizabeth Carter**, 1775 French composer **François-Adrien Boieldieu**, 1776 German physicist **Johann Ritter**, 1834 French economist **Léon Walras**,

1865 Brazilian poet **Olavo Bilac**, 1869 Bulgarian revolutionary **Hristo Tatarchev**, 1882 Hungarian composer **Zoltán Kodály**, 1888 King of Yugoslavia **Alexander I**, 1895 Ethiopian emperor **Lidj Jasu**, 1920 U.S. TV Producer **George Schaffer**, 1927 U.S. football coach **Bill Arnsparger**, 1938 Norwegian actress **Liv Ullman**, 1941 U.S. journalist **Lesley Stahl**, 1946 Swedish Keyboardist with "Abba" **Benny Anderson**, 1946 British conductor **Trevor Pinnock**, 1962 U.S. football player **William "Refrigerator" Perry**

December 17

1493 **Philipus Auerolus Paracelsus:** Adopted name of **Theophrastus Bomnastus von Hohenheim**. Swiss physician and alchemist. Believed minerals and chemicals have medicinal uses. Although something of a charlatan and his books filled with mystical nonsense, his rejection of the ancients and insistence on the value of experimentation made him a leading figure in early science.

Poison is in everything, and no thing is without poison. The dosage makes if either a poison or a remedy.

1616 Sir **Roger L'Estrange:** English journalist, pamphleteer and translator. Place in the history of journalism established with his papers *The Public Intelligencer* (1636–66) and *The Observer* (1681–87). Translated Aesop's *Fables*, Seneca's *Morals*, and Cicero's *Offices*.

It is not the place, nor the condition, but the mind alone that can make anyone happy or miserable.

1706 **Gabriele Émilie Le Tonnelier de Breteuil, the Marquise du Châtelet:** French mathematician Translated Dutch satirist Bernard Mandeville's *Fable of the Bees*, a controversial collection of essays, which for her was a Feminist Manifesto. Made an impassioned plea for the rights of women, arguing that women should be encouraged to develop their natural talents and improve their minds. Major work was a translation of Newton's *Principia Mathematica*. Voltaire, one of her lovers, wrote of her after her death:

She was a great man whose only fault was in being a woman. A woman who translated and explained Newton ... in one word, a very great man.

1778 Sir **Humphrey Davy:** English chemist. Fame rests chiefly on the discovery that chemical compounds can be decomposed into their elements using electricity. Using electrolytic decomposition discovered the elements potassium, sodium, barium, strontium, calcium and magnesium. Identified and named the element chlorine after he demonstrated that oxygen was not a necessary constituent of acids.

Life is made up, not of great sacrifices or duties, but of little things, in which smiles, and kindnesses, and small obligations, given habitually, are what win and preserve the heart and secure comfort.

1807 **John Greenleaf Whittier:** Quaker American poet and social reformer. Crusading abolitionist as shown in his verse "Voices of Freedom" (1846). After the Civil War, turned from politics and dedicated himself completely to poetry. Poems: "Snow-Bound," "The Barefoot Boy" and his epic of the Civil War, "Barbara Fretchie."

Tradition wears a snowy beard, romance is always young.

1853 **Herbert Beerbohm Tree:** English writer and great character actor. Roles included Marc Antony, Macbeth, Hamlet, Falstaff, Fagin, Shylock and Micawber. Helped the career of George Bernard Shaw, by producing *Pygmalion* in 1914. Married Helen Maud Holt, an actress who appeared as Lady Tree and often played opposite him. Fathered several illegitimate children, including film director Carol Reed.

Every man is a potential genius until he does something.

1873 **Ford Madox Ford:** Born **Ford Herman Hueffer**. English literary critic, editor and novelist. Chiefly remembered for *The Good Soldier*. Set prior to World War I, it chronicles the tragedies of adultery and deceit in the lives of two "perfect couples." Founded the *English Review* (1908) and the *Transatlantic Review* (1924). Published works by Thomas Hardy, D.H. Lawrence, Joseph Conrad, Ernest Hemingway, James Joyce and Ezra Pound.

Only two classes of books are of universal appeal. The very best and the very worst.

1874 **William Lyon Mackenzie King:** Canadian statesman. Leader of the Liberal Party (1919–21). Prime Minister (1921–26, 1926–30 and 1935–48). Represented Canada at imperial conferences in London, where he played an important role of establishing the status of self-governing nations of the Commonwealth. Maintained the unity of the English and French-speaking populations.

If some countries have too much history, we have too much geography.

1894 **Arthur Fiedler:** American conductor who originated the free Esplanade concerts in Boston (1929–79). Conducted the Boston Symphony Pops concerts (1930–79). With a combination of musicianship and showmanship he made the Pops the best-known orchestra in the land. Fascinated by the work of firefighters, he traveled in his own vehicle to large fires. Made an "Honorary Captain" in Boston Fire Department. Died at age 85, succeeded by John Williams.

It's nice to eat a good hunk of beef but you want a light dessert, too.

1903 **Erskine Caldwell:** American novelist, short story writer and documentary pieces. One of the most widely read authors of the 20th century. Eighty million books sold in 43 languages. Themes centered around social injustice in terms of class, race and gender. Portrayed of rural poverty was criticized by some Southerners, including author Margaret Mitchell. Successfully fought attempts to ban his most well-known novel

God's Little Acre as being obscene in the courts. Other Works include *Tobacco Road*, which made American theater history when it ran for seven-and-a-half years on Broadway.

I think you must remember that a writer is a simple-minded person to begin with and go on that basis. He's not a great mind, he's not a great thinker, he's not a great philosopher, he's a story-teller.

1908 **Willard Frank Libby:** American chemist. Nobel Prize winner (1960) for his part in the invention of the carbon-14 method of dating ancient findings. In conjunction with his students James R. Arnold and Ernest C. Anderson, found that all organic materials contain carbon-14 atoms that decay at a measurable rate, thus beginning development of an "atomic clock" that determines geological age and clears up many mysteries of archaeology and anthropology.

Nuclear war would mean abolition of most comforts, and disruption of normal routines, for children and adults alike.

1929 **William L. Safire:** Originally **Safir**. American journalist, author and language maven. Pulitzer Prize for distinguished commentary. Wrote the Op-ed Column and the column *On Language* in the *New York Times Magazine*. Earlier, a senior White House speechwriter for President Nixon. Books: *Before the Fall: an Inside View of the Pre-Watergate White House*, *William Safire on Language*, and *What's the Good Word?*

The right to do something does not mean that doing it is right.

OTHERS: 1619 Royalist Commander in English Civil War **Prince Rupert of the Rhine**, 1632 English antiquarian **Anthony Wood**, 1749 Italian composer **Domenico Cimarosa**, 1796 Canadian novelist **Thomas Chandler Haliburton**, 1830 French publisher **Jules de Goncourt**, 1853 French physician **Émile Roux**, 1883 French actor **Raimu**, 1887 Czech painter **Josef Lada**, 1899 English Mathematician **Mary Cartwright**, 1903 British bandleader **Ray Noble**, 1916 British writer **Penelope Fitzgerald**, 1922 U.S. engineer/urban planner **Alan Voorhees**, 1930 U.S. magazine publisher **Bob Guccione**, 1936 British singer/actor **Tommy Steele**, 1938 New Zealand runner **Peter Snell**, 1946 Canadian actor **Eugene Levy**

December 18

1835 **Lyman Abbott:** American author, religious leader and Congregational minister. Editor of the *Outlook* (1881–1922). Powerful exponent of progressive practical Christianity. Corresponding secretary of the American Union Commission, a group of ministers and laypersons formed to help Southern reconstruction. Books: *Christianity and Social Problems* and *America in the Making*.

Every life is a march from innocence, through temptation, to virtue or vice.

1859 **Francis J. Thompson:** English poet and essayist. Best known for "The Hound of Heaven," a poem that describes the divine pursuit of the human soul. Other Works are noted for their rich imagery: *Sister Songs* and *New Poems*. His exceptional "Essay on Shelley" and *Life of St. Ignatius Loyola* were published after his death of tuberculosis in 1907.

An atheist is a man who believes himself to be an accident.

1870 **H.H. [Hector Hugh Munro]:** Pseudonym **Saki**. Burma-born English novelist and short-story writer. Wrote humorous and satiric stories of the supernatural and macabre. His story collections, full of eccentric wit and unconventional situations, include: *The Chronicles of Clovis*, and *Beasts and Superbeasts*. Novels: *The Unbearable Bassington* and *When William Came*. Killed on the Western Front during World War I.

We all know that Prime Ministers are wedded to the truth, but like other married couples they sometimes live apart.

1879 **Paul Klee:** Swiss artist. Became a member of the "Blaue Reiter" (Blue Rider) Munich group. Surrealist painter influenced by primitive African sculptures. Produced a very personal world of fancy, expressed with wit and subtle coloring. Nazis confiscated many of his works as degenerate, calling them "the work of a sick mind." Paintings: *Angelus Novus*, *Twittering Machine* and *The Mocker Mocked*.

A line is a dot that went for a walk.

1886 **Ty [Tyrus Raymond] Cobb:** American baseball outfielder, mostly with the Detroit Tigers, which he also managed (1921–26). "The Georgia Peach." First person elected to Baseball's Hall of Fame. Fierce competitor, hated by other players, even his own teammates. Claimed that baseball is like a war, a struggle for supremacy, a survival of the fittest. Hit .400 three times. Lifetime BA, .367, the highest ever. Had 4,191 career hits, the most until Pete Rose broke his record.

Speed is a great asset; but it's greater when it's combined with quickness — and there's a big difference.

1913 **Willy Brandt:** Originally **Karl Herbert Frahm**. West German politician. Mayor of Berlin (1957–66). Pro-western, anti-communist, gained international renown during the Berlin Wall crisis in 1961. As Chancellor of West Germany (1969–74) sought reconciliation between eastern and western Europe, culminating in the signing of the Basic Treaty with East German in 1972. Nobel Peace Prize winner (1971).

It often takes more courage to change one's opinion than to keep it.

1916 **Betty Grable:** American film actress and singer. Popularity at a peak during World War II, when GIs chose her their number one "Pinup girl." As a publicity stunt the studio insured her glamorous gams for a million dollars. Husbands were former child star Jackie Coogan and bandleader Harry James. Films: *Moon Over Miami*, *Pin-up Girl*, *The Dolly Sisters*, *Mother Wore Tights* and *How to Marry a Millionaire*.

There are two reasons why I'm in show business, and I'm standing on both of them.

1917 **Ozzie Davis:** African-American actor, producer, director and playwright. Had a stage triumph starring in *Purlie Victorious* (1961), which he authored. Repeated the role in a film version, called *Gone Are the Days*. With wife, actress Ruby Dee, active in civil rights and humanitarian causes. They helped organize and served as MCs for the 1963 civil rights March on Washington for Jobs and Freedom. He headed Third World Cinema, a film production company formed to encourage black and Puerto Rican talent. Recipient of Kennedy Center Honors (2004).

I find, in being black, a thing of beauty; a joy; a strength; a secret cup of gladness.

1946 **Steve Biko:** South African anti-apartheid activist. Leader of the Black Consciousness Movement. Popular figure for urging black self-reliance and supporting black institutions. South African government slapped him with orders severely restricting his movements, freedom of speech and associations. Detained four times, he died in police custody, allegedly as the result of beatings.

We regard witchcraft as part of the mystery of our cultural heritage.

1947 **Steven Spielberg:** U.S. film producer, director and screenwriter. Films have been among the most popular and successful in box-office history. Wasn't until *Schindler's List* that he received the recognition of his peers with an Oscar for Best Director and Best Picture. Earned another Academy Award for Best Director with *Saving Private Ryan*. Other films: *Close Encounters of the Third Kind, Raiders of the Lost Ark, E.T., the Extra Terrestrial, The Color Purple, Empire of the Sun,* and *Munich*.

I dream for a living.

1952 **Elayne Boosler:** American comedian and activist. Takes a slice of life approach to comedy. First female to get her own comedy special on cable when Showtime aired "Party of One." Active in progressive politics. Moderated a Democratic presidential candidate forum hosted by the National Organization of Women, which centered on the issue of women's rights.

The Vatican is against surrogate mothers. Good thing they didn't have that rule when Jesus was born.

1980 **Christina Aguilera:** American pop singer and songwriter. Known for powerful voice and ability to sing *a capella*. Won Grammys for Best New Artist and Best Female Pop Vocal Performance with her song "Beautiful." Debut album went 10 times platinum, producing four hit singles. Second album *Stripped* was also a best-seller. Its cover was a controversial sexually charged image of the singer, posing topless.

I'm an ocean, because I'm really deep. If your search deep enough you can find rare exotic treasures.

OTHERS: 1661 Swedish inventor **Christopher Polhem**, 1779 English pantomimist **Joseph Grimaldi**, 1802 U.S. humorist **George Dennison Prentice**, 1847 French composer **Augusta Holmès**, 1856 British physicist **Sir J.J. Thomson**, 1863 Archduke of Austria **Franz Ferdinand**, 1888 U.S. public works official **Robert Moses**, 1897 U.S. bandleader **Fletcher Henderson**, 1904 U.S. film director **George Stevens**, 1912 African-American General **Benjamin O. Davis Jr.**, 1913 U.S. basketball coach **Ray Meyer**, 1927 U.S. Attorney General **Ramsey Clark**, 1963 U.S. actor **Brad Pitt**, 1970 U.S. rapper **DMX**, 1978 U.S. actress **Katie Holmes**

December 19

1714 **John Winthrop:** American physicist and astronomer. Considered the first professional scientist in America. In May 1761, Winthrop and two of his students embarked for St. John's, Newfoundland to observe the Transit of Venus, the goal to determine the distance from the Earth to the Sun. Winthrop described the morning of the transit, when he and his two assistants watched from a hill where they had a good view of the part of the horizon where the Sun would rise:

Thus prepared, we waited for the critical hour, which proved favorable to our wishes. The morning of the 6th of June was serene and calm. The Sun rose behind a cloud that lay along the horizon, but soon got above it; and at 4 hours 18 minutes we had the high satisfaction of seeing that most agreeable sight, Venus on the Sun.

1820 **Mary Ashton Rice Livermore:** American health reformer, hospital administrator, suffragist, ardent abolitionist, temperance advocate, supporter of higher education for women, and writer. Married Rev. Daniel P. Livermore, with whom she edited the *New Covenant*, a Chicago church periodical (1857–69). Founded *The Agitator* (1869), which was later, merged into the *Woman's Journal*.

Above all the titles of wife and mother, although dear, are transitory and accidental, there is the title human being, which precedes and out-ranks every other.

1861 **Italo Svevo:** Pseudonym of **Ettmore Schmitz.** Successful Italian businessman and novelist, master of psychological portrayal. Had considerable success with *The Confessions of Zeno*, a study of inner conflicts, which received considerable critical attention in Europe. Two short-story collections, essays, dramatic works, correspondence and his unfinished *Further Confessions of Zeno* were published after his death in an automobile accident in 1928.

God gave us memory so that we might have roses in December.

1865 **Minnie Maddern Fiske:** née **Maria Augusta Davey**. Celebrated American stage actress, director and theater manager, instrumental in the development of the American theater. Made her New York debut at 17. Championed realistic theater and natural acting. Acclaimed for her Ibsen heroines, and as Becky Sharp and Mrs. Malaprop. Married to theatrical manager Harrison Grey Fiske. Also campaigned for humanitarian causes.

You must make your own blunders, must cheerfully accept your own mistakes as part of the scheme of things.

1888 **Fritz Reiner:** Budapest-born conductor. Found his greatest acclaim as conductor of the Chicago Symphony Orchestra (1953–62). One of the most notoriously tough task makers among the great conductors, a perfectionist who demanded no less of his musicians than he did of himself. Because of a heart attack, he was forced to conduct from a sitting position. Preparing to conduct a series of performances of Wagner's music at the Metropolitan Opera, he suffered a fatal second heart attack.

People say I hate musicians. They are wrong. I only hate the bad ones.

1902 Sir **Ralph Richardson:** Eminent English character actor of the British stage and screen. One of a trio of great English actors with Laurence Olivier and John Gielgud. Stage appearances include: *West of Suez* and *The Cherry Orchard.* Three times nominated for Broadway's Tony Award as Best Dramatic Actor: *The Waltz of the Toreadors, Home,* and *No Man's Land.* Nominated for an Academy Award for his performance as Dr. Sloper in *The Heiress.*

Acting is the ability to dream on cue.

1906 **Leonid I. Brezhnev:** Ukraine-born Soviet statesman. General Secretary of the Communist Party (1964–82). President of the Supreme Soviet (1977–82). First to hold both positions simultaneously. Developed the Brezhnev Doctrine, asserting the right of Soviet intervention in Warsaw Pact countries such as Czechoslovakia. Attempted to normalize relations with the West and to promote détente with the U.S. Signed the SALT I treaty with President Nixon.

We should not pour muck on ourselves.

1910 **Jean Genet:** French novelist and dramatist. Began writing while serving a life sentence in prison. Novel *Our Lady of the Flowers* caused a sensation for its portrayal of the criminal world. Other novels: *Querelle of Brest, The Thief's Journal* and *Miracle of the Rose*, all thinly veiled autobiographical accounts of the underworld. Major figure in the Theatre of the Absurd, an avant-garde convention emphasizing the illogical and purposeless nature of existence. Plays, *The Maids, The Balcony,* and *The Blacks* were designed to shock, revealed hypocrisy and complicity in an exploitative social order.

Repudiating the virtues of your world, criminals hopelessly agree to organize a forbidden universe. They agree to live in it. The air there is nauseating: they can breathe it.

1915 **Edith Piaf:** Popular name of **Edith Giovanna Gassion**. Internationally famous French singer. Began as a street singer in Paris, graduating to singing her chansons in cabarets and large music halls, becoming known as "Piaf," Parisian slang for "sparrow." Renown for songs of sadness and nostalgia and her emotional and powerful voice and delivery: "Milord," "Le Voyage du pauvre negre," "Mon Legionnaire, "La Vie en rose" and "Non, je ne regrette rein." Beset by illness, accidents and unhappiness, died at age 47.

I want to make people cry even when they don't understand my words.

1944 **Richard Leakey:** Nairobi-born palaeoanthropologist. Son of archaeologists Mary and Louis Leakey. Worked at Koobi Fora, part of a vast fossil site covering 500 square miles on the eastern shores of Lake Turkana, discovering well-preserved hominid remains that drew worldwide attention. Discovered crania of *Australopithecus boisei, Homo habilis* and *Homo erectus.*

Let us devote our minds — the one thing we have more of than other apes — and let's secure their future.

1961 **Reggie White:** African-American football player. Fearsome defensive end for the Philadelphia Eagles, Green Bay Packers and the Carolina Panthers. One of the greatest players in NFL history. Nicknamed the "Minister of Defense," a reference both to his football prowess and his Evangelical Christian ordination. Twice Defensive Player of the Year and named to the All Time NFL team. Died suddenly at age 43.

God places the heaviest burden on those who can carry the weight.

1972 **Alyssa Milano:** American actress. At age 10, she landed the role of Tony Danza's daughter in the TV sitcom *Who's The Boss?* By the time she had grown up, she had really grown up, and shed her sweet little girl image for a sexy, well-endowed adult. But her film career didn't click. Back on the small screen, has success on *Melrose Place* and *Charmed.*

I feel a lot healthier when I'm having sex. Physically, I feel all these jitters when I wake up in the morning. Just energy jitters. I take vitamins. I work out everyday. When I'm having sex, I don't have that.

OTHERS: 1036 Chinese poet/essayist **Su Tung-p'o**, 1498 German Reformation theologist **Andreas Oslander**, 1699 English printer **William Bowyer**, 1790 English Artic explorer **William Parry**, 1875 U.S. historian **Carter Woodson**, 1885 U.S. jazz bandleader, first African-American group to record **King Oliver**, 1894 U.S. baseball commissioner **Ford Frick**, 1901 German inventor **Rudolf Hell**, 1903 U.S. geneticist **George Snell**, 1920 U.S. TV host **David Susskind**, 1933 African-American actress **Cicely Tyson**, 1944 Canadian guitarist **Zal Yanovsky**, 1957 U.S. basketball player, general manager **Kevin McHale**, 1972 U.S. football player **Warren Sapp**, 1980 U.S. actor **Jake Gyllenhaal**

December 20

1579 **John Fletcher:** English comedy playwright. One of eight dramatists regularly under contract to London theaters. Plays achieved a popularity rivaling Shakespeare. Best known for working with Francis Beaumont on *Philaster, A King and No King* and *The Maid's Tragedy*. May have collaborated with Shakespeare on *Henry VIII*. Singularly authored: *The Chances*, *The Tamer Tamed*, and A *Wife for a Month*.

And he that will go to bed sober,/ Falls with the leaf still in October.

1780 **John Wilson Croker:** English lawyer, politician and essayist. One of the leading contributors on literary and historical subjects to the *Quarterly Review*. Had no sympathy for the younger school of poets, especially critical of John Keats. Croker's opinion of Mary Shelley's *Frankenstein*, which he assumed written by a man, possibly Percy Shelley:

Our taste and out judgment alike revolt at this kind of writing, and the greater the ability with which it may be executed the worse it is — it inculcates no lesson of conduct, manners or morality; it cannot mend, and will not even amuse its readers.

1838 **Edwin Abbott Abbott:** English schoolmaster, theologian and writer. Best known as the author of the mathematical satire *Flatland: A Romance of Many Dimensions*, published under the pseudonym A. Square. Still popular masterpiece explores what it would mean if inhabitants of a two-dimensional world were visited by phenomena from a dimension higher than their own. Besides popularizing the notion of multidimensional geometry, it is also a clever satire on the social, moral, and religious values of the period.

Alas, how strong a family likeness runs through blind and persecuting humanity in all Dimensions! Points, Lines, Squares, Cubes, Extra Cubes — we are all liable to the same errors, all alike the Slavers of our respective Dimensional prejudices.

1865 **Elsie de Wolfe:** Married name **Lady Mendl**. American socialite and interior decorator. Champion of "good taste." Introduced new anti–Victorian fashion of interior design, focusing on visual unity and the use of pale colors and mirrors to emphasize space. Published *The House of Good Taste* in 1913.

It is the personality of the mistress that the home expresses. Men are forever guests in our homes, no matter how much happiness they may find there.

1865 **Maud Gonne:** Married name of **Maud MacBride**. Irish actress, feminist and agitator for Irish independence. Founded the Daughters of Ireland. Called the Irish Joan of Arc. Played the heroine in W.B. Yeats play *Cathleen ni Houlihan,* joining his theater movement. Active in efforts to win release of Irish political prisoners, took part in the Easter Rising (1916). Her husband was executed as a rebel and she was imprisoned. Founder-member of Sinn Fein.

The English may batter us to pieces, but they will never succeed in breaking our spirit.

1868 **Harvey S. Firestone:** American industrialist and founder of the Firestone Tire & Rubber Company. Established a tire making firm in Akron, Ohio. Pioneered the principle of the detachable rim. From 1906 on, was the major supplier of tires to the Ford Motor Company. Strong opponent of organized labor, long resisted the unionization of his work force.

Never be bullied into silence. Never allow yourself to be made a victim. Accept no one's definition of your life, but define yourself.

1881 **Branch Rickey:** American baseball executive. Instituted the farm system in 1919. As president of the Brooklyn Dodgers made Jackie Robinson the first black to play in the modern major leagues (1947). Always lecturing, tutoring, motivating, cautioning and inspiring. Among his maxims about the game: "Baseball is a game of inches," and "The man with the ball is responsible for what happens to the ball."

Ethnic prejudice has no place in sports, and baseball must recognize that truth it if is to maintain stature as a national game.

1895 **Susanne K. Langer:** American philosopher and educator. Influential in the field of linguistics and aesthetics. Speaking of the arts: "Art is the objectification of feeling and the subjectification of nature. Works: *Philosophy in a New Key*, *Problems of Art, Feeling and Form* and *An Essay on Human Feeling*. In "Life-Symbols: The Roots of Myth," wrote:

... the fairytale is a form of "wishful thinking," and the Freudian analysis of it fully explains why it is perennially attractive, yet never believed by adults even in the telling. Myth, on the other hand, whether literally believed or not, is taken with religious seriousness, either as a historic fact, or as a "mystic" truth.

1902 **Sidney Hook:** Controversial American philosopher and author. Attempted to synthesize the ideas of Karl Marx and John Dewey. His political disposition began shifting to the Right at the time of the Great Purge in the Soviet Union and by 1940 he adopted a vehement anti–Communist stance, opposing all "totalitarianism." Books: *The Metaphysics of Pragmatism*, *Toward the Understanding Of Karl Marx*, and *John Dewey: An Intellectual Portrait*.

Idealism, alas, does not protect one from ignorance, dogmatism, and foolishness.

1902 **Max Lerner:** Russian-born American journalist, educator, editor and writer. Moralist who wrote columns for the *New York Post*, famous for their ability to relate to anything from an election or a murder to the American ethic. Produced the massive book *America as a Civilization*. Others: *Ideas for the Ice Age*, *Actions and Passions*, *Ideas Are Weapons*, and *Beyond the Power Principle*.

The so-called lessons of history are for the most part the rationalizations of the victors. History is written by the survivors.

1911 **Hortense Calisher:** American novelist and writer of short-stories of upper-middle class New Yorkers with deft character analysis and complex story lines. Many of her stories feature Hester Elkin and her large Jewish family living in New York City. Among her best known stories is "In Greenwich There Are Many Graveled Walks." Novels: *Queenie,* and *Standard Dreaming*.

A happy childhood can't be cured. Mine'll hang

around my neck like a rainbow, that's all, instead of a noose.

1946 **Uri Geller:** Famous but controversial alleged Israeli psychic and TV personality. Well-known for performances featuring claimed paranormal abilities such as telekinesis, dowsing and telepathy. Makes it appear that using only his mind metal objects are bent and watches slowed down or sped up without any apparent physical force being applied to them. Critics claim he is a charlatan and a con-man. He insists his powers are the result of being hit by a light from the sky when he was four.

I've stopped caring about skeptics, but if they libel or defame me they will end up in court.

OTHERS: 1539 German poet **Paul Melissus**, 1626 German statesman **Veit Ludwig von Seckendorff**, 1629 Dutch painter **Pieter de Hoogh**, 1717 French Statesman **Charles Gravier**, 1833 U.S. physician **Samuel Mudd**, 1841 French pacifist **Ferdinand Buisson**, 1861 Slovenian painter **Ivana Kobilca**, 1890 Czech chemist **Jaroslav Heyrovsky**, 1894 Canadian Prime Minister **Robert Menzies**, 1898 U.S. actress **Irene Dunne**, 1917 U.S. physicist **David Bohm**, 1927 South Korean President **Kim Young-sam**, 1946 U.S. TV producer **Dick Wolf**, 1947 Italian singer **Giglliola Cinquetti**, 1949 Malian politician **Soumaïla Cissé**

December 21

1118 Saint **Thomas à Becket:** English Archbishop of Canterbury. Chancellor of England (1155–62) under King Henry II. Brilliant administrator, diplomat and military strategist. Hoping to solidify royal control of the church, Henry appointed Becket, archbishop of Canterbury. Thomas embraced his new duties and opposed royal power over the church. Murdered in his cathedral by four of Henry's knights. Canonized three years after his death.

Many are needed to plant and water what the faith has spread so far and there so many people... No matter who plants or waters, God gives no harvest unless what is planted is the faith of Peter and unless he agrees to his teachings.

1804 **Benjamin Disraeli:** British Tory statesman and novelist. As Prime minister (1868 and 1874–80), instituted reforms in housing, public health and factory regulations. Ensured that Britain bought a controlling interest in the Suez Canal and made Queen Victoria Empress of India. Negotiated "peace with honor" at the Congress of Berlin. His novels *Connigsby, Vivien Grey, The Young Duke* and *Sybil* demonstrated an acute wit, sharp realism and a totally individual and often fantastic style.

The magic of first love is our ignorance that it can ever end.

1879 **Joseph Stalin:** Born **Iosif Vissarionovich Dzhugashvili**. Name "Stalin," is Russian for "man of steel." Followed Lenin into power, securing enough party support to eliminate Leon Trotsky. Launched a succession of five-year plans for the industrialization and collectivization of agriculture. Soviet dictator with appointment as general secretary of the Communist Party. Solidified his power by killing more than 10 million peasants. Purged the intelligentsia, removing all opposition. Signed a nonaggression pact with Hitler (1939). When Germany invaded, the U.S.S.R. joined the Allies. After the war seized control of much of Eastern and Central Europe.

Ideas are more powerful than guns. We would not let our enemies have guns, why should we let them have ideas.

1892 **Walter Hagan:** American pro golfer. Won two U.S. Opens, the first at age 21, four British Opens, the initial time made him the first American to win "the second oldest cup in sports," and five PGA championships. Acknowledged the best golfer of his day — at least until Bobby Jones appeared on the scene. Real forte was match play, and probably no one could beat him man-to-man over 18 holes.

You don't have the game you played last year or last week. You only have today's game. It may be far from your best, but that's all you've got. Harden your heart and make the best of it.

1905 **Anthony Powell:** English novelist and journalist. Wrote Comedies of manners and mild social satires aimed at the worlds of fashion, art, and the upper classes. Best-known for a 12-volume sequence of novels, *A Dance to the Music of Time,* a satirical and panorama portrayal of the fortunes of British upper-middle class life covering 50 years between the world wars.

Growing old is like being increasingly penalized for a crime you haven't committed.

1918 **Kurt Waldheim:** Austrian diplomat. Elected U.N. Secretary-General and was reelected. His bid for a third term was vetoed by China. Elected President of Austria (1986). It came out that he had lied about his service as an officer in a paramilitary Nazi unit and while serving in Greece and Yugoslavia he was "excellently informed" of atrocities by German troops and made no efforts to stop them. Waldheim attempted to excuse himself:

Yes, I admit I wanted to survive [by following orders] ... I have the deepest respect for all those who resisted. But I ask understanding for all the hundreds of thousands who didn't do that, but nonetheless did not become personally guilty.

1926 **Joe Paterno:** Legendary American football coach, affectionately known as "JoePa." Led Penn State to two national titles (1982 and 1986). Posted a 354–117–3 record in 40 seasons as head coach. As he approached 80, his teams did not do well, and there were many calls for him to retire, but in 2005, he showed he still had the stuff to produce a winning team, finishing 11–1, earning him AP Coach of the Year.

The will to win is important, but the will to prepare is vital.

1937 **Jane Fonda:** Beautiful, talented American actress. Daughter of screen star Henry Fonda. Won Academy Awards for her performances in *Klute* (1971) and *Coming Home* (1978) Nominated five other times for *They Shoot Horses, Don't They?*, *Julia*, *The China Syndrome*, *The Morning After*, and *On Golden Pond*, the only film she ever made with her father. In contrast to her reel life her real life has been filled with scandal and controversy. Her anti-war activities during the Vietnam War and radio broadcasts on behalf of the Communist regime, earned her the name of "Hanoi Jane" and the hatred of many veterans.

To be a revolutionary, you have to be a human being. You have to care about people who have no power.

1940 **Frank Zappa:** American composer, guitarist, satirist and song writer. His rock group Mothers of Invention recorded their groundbreaking double album debut *Freak Out!* in 1966, establishing Zappa as a major new voice in rock music. Other albums: *Absolutely Free*, *We're Only in It for the Money*, and *Weasels Ripped My Flesh*. Hit singles: "Don't Eat the Yellow Snow," "Dancin' Fool" and "Valley Girl."

Stupidity has a certain charm — ignorance does not.

1954 **Chris Evert: Christine Marie Evert Mill.** American professional tennis player famed for her powerful two-handed backhand. Won 18 Grand Slam singles titles, including a record 7 at the French Open. Her career win-loss record in single matches 1309–146 is the best of any pro player in history. Ranked number one in the world in five years. Romance with men's player Jimmy Connors captured the public's imagination in the 1970s, but a planned wedding was called off.

If you're a champion, you have to have it in your heart.

1957 **Ray Romano:** Emmy Award–winning American comic actor. Best known as the star of the long-running TV comedy series *Everybody Loves Raymond*, one of the most-watched sitcoms in CBS history. In 2004 he became the highest paid TV actor in history for his role as Raymond, reportedly $50,000,000.

If my father had hugged me even once, I'd be an accountant right now.

1959 **Florence Griffith Joyner:** American Olympic runner. Lovingly known as "Flo-Jo," famed for her glamorous trackwear (consisting of eye-catching one-legged leotards), vivid make-up and elaborately-decorated fingernails. Won three gold medals in 1988 Olympics for 100m, 200m and 4 x 400m relay, setting two world records in the process. Her performance led to charges of using steroids. Named co-chair of the President's Council on Physical Fitness and Sports.

When anyone tells me I can't do anything ... I'm just not listening anymore.

OTHERS: 1795 Scottish missionary **Robert Moffat**, 1805 British chemist **Thomas Graham**, 1818 U.S. ethnologist **Lewis H. Morgan**, 1823 French entomologist **Jean Henri Fabre**, 1840 Turkish poet **Kemal Bey**, 1843 New Zealand poet **Thomas Bracken**, 1850 Bohemian composer **Zdeněk Fibich**, 1860 U.S. Zionist leader **Henrietta Szold**, 1878 Polish philosopher **Jan Lukasiewicz**, 1886 German Egyptologist **Hermann Kees**, 1918, White House Chief of Staff **Donald Regan**, 1921 Cuban ballerina **Alicia Alonso**, 1922, U.S. ventriloquist/co-inventor artificial heart **Paul Winchell**, 1935 U.S. TV host **Phil Donahue**, 1944 U.S. orchestra conductor **Michael Tilson Thomas**, 1947 Spanish guitarist **Paco de Lucia**, 1974 U.S. golfer **Karrie Webb**

December 22

1639 **Jean Racine:** French dramatic poet greatly influenced by a combination of the Jansenist concept of original sin and the Greek concept of Fate. His main thematic preoccupations were passion and women. Made careful exposition of character and depiction of powerful spiritual conflicts. Regarded as the master of tragic pathos. Verse tragedies: *Andromaque*, *Britannicus*, *Iphigénie*, *Phèdre* and *Bérénice*.

The feeling of mistrust is always the last which a great mind acquires.

1823 **Thomas W. Higginson:** American clergyman and author. Passionate in his opposition to slavery, participated in numerous missions to help fugitive slaves. During the Civil War commanded the first troop of African-American soldiers in the Union Army. His experience resulted in the publication *Army Life in a Black Regiment*. Discovered Emily Dickinson and co-edited the first publication of her poetry.

Originality is simply a pair of fresh eyes.

1858 **Giacomo Puccini:** Italian operatic composer. Acknowledged ruler of the Italian operatic stage, whose sense of the dramatic, gift for melody and skillful use of the orchestra ensured that his works would remain among the most popular operas. Operas: *Manon Lescaut*, *La Bohème*, *Tosca*, *Madama Butterfly*, *The Girl of the Golden West* and *Turandot*, unfinished at his death, completed by a pupil, Franco Alfano.

Inspiration is an awakening, a quickening of all man's faculties, and it is manifested in all high artistic achievements.

1862 **Connie Mack:** Born **Cornelius McGillicuddy**. Owner and manager of the Philadelphia Athletics (1901–1950). "The Tall Tactician" is best remembered as a dignified leader in a business suit, waving his scorecard to place his fielders. Built two dynasties — with four pennants in five years (1910–14) and three in a row (1929–31). Had 3,776 wins, more than any other manager. When New York Giants manager John McGraw called the Athletes a "white elephant," that no one else wanted, Mack adopted the pachyderm as the teams mascot, and its image appeared on the players' uniforms.

You're born with two strikes against you, so don't take a third one on your own.

1869 **Edwin Arlington Robinson:** American poet, known for his long narrative verse and objective psychological portraits. Most of his poetry was set in a fictional

New England village, Tilbury Town. Poems: "Luke Havergal," "Richard Corey" and "Two Men." Three-time Pulitzer Prize winner in 1921 for *Collected Poems,* in 1925 for *The Man Who Died Twice* and in 1927 for *Tristram,* which following *Merlin* and *Lancelot,* was the final volume of his Arthurian trilogy.

Youth sees too far to see how near it is/ To seeing farther.

1883 **Edgard Varèse:** French-born composer. Pioneered the development of electronic music. Work is almost exclusively orchestral, often using unconventional percussion instruments: *Metal, Ionisation, Hyperprism, Deserts* and *Poème électronique.* Organized the first International Composers' Guild (1921), leading organ of progressive musicians.

Contrary to general belief, an artist is never ahead of his time but most people are far behind theirs.

1887 **Srinivasa Ramanujan:** Tamilian Indian mathematician, having little access to mathematicians or mathematical libraries, was forced to find his own way in rediscovering mathematical formulas and creating new ones, relying only on his remarkable intuition. In his brief life, earned the reputation as one of India's greatest geniuses. Made substantial mathematical contributions to analytical number theory, elliptic functions, and infinite series. Had it not been for the great English mathematician G.H. Hardy, his light might never have been shed upon the world of mathematics.

An equation for me has no meaning, unless it represents a thought of God.

1905 **Kenneth Rexroth:** American poet, critic and translator at the center of San Francisco's "Beat Movement" In prose and poetry he denounced the dehumanizing forces in modern society and called for a visionary union with nature: *The Phoenix and the Tortoise, The Signature of All Things, The Heart's Garden, the Garden's Heart* and *The Morning Star.*

Man thrives where angles would die of ecstasy and where pigs would die of disgust.

1912 **Claudia "Lady Bird" Johnson:** Born **Claudia Alta Taylor**, her nickname originating as an infant. American first lady. Widow of Lyndon Baines Johnson, 36th U.S. president. At age 93, currently the oldest surviving First Lady. With an inheritance, she built a great communication center in Austin, Texas. Known for her love of the environment and as First Lady she championed a capital beautification project to improve physical conditions in Washington, DC.

The clash of ideas is the sound of freedom.

1945 **Diane Sawyer:** American broadcast journalist. Press aide on the staff of Ron Ziegler, President Nixon's Press Secretary. Rumored to be Watergate's "Deep Throat," which she repeatedly denied. First woman to co-host "60 Minutes" (1984–89). Co-anchor of ABC's "Prime Time Live." Since January 1999 has been co-anchor on ABC's "Good Morning America." Married to director Mike Nichols since 1988.

I think the one lesson I have learned is that there is no substitute for paying attention.

1951 **Charles de Lint:** Netherlands-born Canadian fantasy author and story teller. Many of his tales are set in the mythical North American city of Newford. Maintains that his primary interest is "to explore the complexities of human relationships through mythic/folkloric material against a mostly contemporary urban setting." Novels: *Mulengro: A Romany Tale, From a Whisper to a Scream,* and *Moonlight and Vines.*

I want to touch the heart of the world and make it smile.

1951 **Jan Stephenson:** Australian golfer. LPGA Rookie of the Year (1974). Won three of the four modern major championships. Posed, apparently naked, in a tub of golf balls for a calendar of beautiful female golfers. Claimed she agreed to be a sex symbol to help attract fans, sponsors and money for the LPGA Tour. Recently criticized for calling for racial quotas on people of Asian descent in the LPGA.

If I were commissioner, I would have a quota on international players and that would include a quota on Asian players. As it is, they're taking American money. American sponsors are picking up the bill. There should be a qualifying school for Americans and a qualifying school for international players.

OTHERS: 1400 Italian sculptor **Luca della Robbia**, 1694 German writer **Hermann Reimarus**, 1696 Founder of Georgia **James Oglethorpe**, 1807 Norwegian poet **Johann Welhaven**, 1809 British tour director **Thomas Cook**, 1846 Dutch circus director **Oscar Carré**, 1847 Created modern Japanese navy **Togo Heihachiro**, 1853 Venezuelan pianist **Teresa Carreño**, 1856 U.S. Secretary of State **Frank B. Kellogg**, 1860 U.S. penmanship expert **Austin Palmer**, 1872 French veterinarian **Camille Guérin**, 1907 British actress **Peggy Ashcroft**, 1944 U.S. baseball pitcher **Steve Carlton**, 1962 English actor **Ralph Fiennes**

December 23

1790 **Jean François Champollion:** French founder of Egyptology. Entered the race to translate the hieroglyphics, or "sacred script" of ancient Egypt. Mainly through the use of the 2nd century BCE Rosetta Stone — discovered by Napoleon's Army nine years earlier — he developed a system of translation, placing the study of early Egyptian culture and history on a firm foundation. Described the damage done to him by the strain of the work that would take his life at age 41:

My poor head hurts, my tinnitus, the humming and buzzing noises, has worsened and leaves me neither day nor night. I have frequent spasms and am incapable of occupying myself seriously for more than a quarter hour...

1804 **Charles Augustin Sainte-Beuve:** Great French literary historian and critic. Major works include several books of "portraits" of literary contemporaries. Concentrated on the influence of social and other factors in the development of authors' characters. An early champion of French romanticism, he also was popular for his speeches in favor of liberty of thought.

Tell me who admires you and loves you, and I will tell you who you are.

1805 **Joseph Smith:** American founder of the Church of Jesus Christ of Latter-day Saints (Mormon Church). In 1827 claimed he had a revelation of the *Book of Mormon*, inscribed on gold plates and concealed for a thousand years in a hill near Palmyra, New York. Despite ridicule for its practice of polygamy, the Church gained converts. Imprisoned in Carthage, Illinois, he was killed by a mob that broke into the jail. Brigham Young led most of Smith's followers to the Great Salt Lake.

I am like a sheep going to the slaughter; but I am as calm as a summer's day.

1812 **Samuel Smiles:** Scottish author and social reformer. Devoted to the advocacy of political and social reform. Best known for his didactic work *Self Help*, a guide to self-improvement, containing short accounts of the lives of great men of industry with the admonition to "do thou likewise." Wrote many moral works: *Character*, *Thrift*, and *Duty*.

Hope is like the sun, which, as we journey toward it, casts the shadow of our burden behind us.

1860 **Harriet Monroe:** American poet and critic. Founded the highly respected magazine, *Poetry*. Secured the backing of wealthy patrons and invited contributions from a wide range of poets, including Vachel Lindsay, T.S. Eliot, Ezra Pound and Robert Frost. Wrote the "Columbian Ode," for the Chicago World's Columbian Exposition (1892), celebrating the 400th anniversary of the "discovery" of America.

The people must grant a hearing to the best poets they have; else they will never have better.

1881 **Juan Ramón Jiménez:** Spanish lyric poet. Born in Andalusia, made his birthplace famous by his delightful story of the young poet and his donkey, *Platero and I*, one of the classics of modern Spanish literature. Left Spain in 1936 because he had aligned himself with the Republican in the Spanish Civil War, settling in Puerto Rico. In the last period of his life, his output of poetry was immense and he emerged as a major poet. Nobel Prize for literature (1956).

If they give you ruled paper, write the other way.

1896 **Giuseppe Tomasi di Lampedusa**: Italian aristocrat and writer, born in Palermo, Sicily. Most famous for *The Leopard*, which chronicles the reactions of an aristocratic family to social and political upheavals by the conquests of Giuseppe Garibaldi. It was rejected by publishers throughout his life but published posthumously. Vilified by the Italian literary establishment, it has since been regarded as a masterpiece.

If we want everything to remain as it is, it will be necessary for everything to change.

1902 **Norman MacLean:** American scholar of Shakespeare and the Romantic poets. Wrote *Critics and Criticism: Ancient and Modern*. Best known for the Pulitzer Prize winning *A River Runs Through It*. In the memoir of his family growing up in Montana, fly fishing became the emblem of the dawning conservationist feelings among Montanans.

Eventually, all things merge into one, and a river runs through it. The river was cut by the world's greatest flood and runs over rocks from the basement of time. On some of the rocks are timeless raindrops.

1908 **Yousuf Karsh:** Turkish-born Canadian photographer and journalist. Long recognized as outstanding in the field of photographic portraiture. Best known for portraits of the great, the near-great and the merely wealthy of his time in *Life* magazine. With his portrait of Winston Churchill during World War II, he became one of the top-priced photographers of the day, sought by magazines, private individuals and advertising concerns that could pay his price. His book *Faces of Destiny* contains remarkable examples of his work.

Within every man and woman a secret is hidden, and as a photographer it is my task to reveal it if I can.

1923 **James Bond Stockdale:** American Navy Admiral, whose heroism earned him the Medal of Honor. Embodying the virtues of both warrior and philosopher, credited the tenets of Epictetus, one of the ancient Stoics, with helping him survive 7 1/2 years of abuse as the highest-ranking U.S. Navy officer held captive in Vietnam. Deliberately inflicted a near-mortal wound to his person in order to convince his captors of his willingness to give up his life rather than capitulate. In 1992 Ross Perot chose Stockdale as his Vice-Presidential running mate.

The worse thing that can happen is death, and that's not the worst thing in the world either.

1933 **Akihito:** Emperor of Japan since 1989, succeeding his father Hirohito (Shōwa). Renouncing the quasi-divine status previously enjoyed by Japanese Emperors. His reign is called the "achievement of universal peace. In 1959, he married Michiko Shoda, daughter of a flour company president, the first non-aristocrat to join the royal family. The world's only emperor continues his efforts to humanize and modernize the royal family.

I believe it is extremely important for the Japanese people to strive to accurately understand this past history along with the ensuing era.

1935 **Paul Hornung:** American football halfback and kicker. "The Golden Boy." Only player to win Heisman Trophy while playing on a losing team, Notre Dame (2–8) in 1956. His 176 points in 1960 is the all-time NFL record. Voted MVP 1961, while only playing on weekends because of military service. On Christmas leave he stunned the New York Giants with a record-smashing 19-point outburst as Green Bay won the NFL Championship Game. Suspended 1963 for betting on his team, but reinstated the next year.

I would still rather score a touchdown than make love to the prettiest girl in the U.S.

Others: 1582 Italian composer **Severo Bonini**, 1597 German poet **Martin Opitz**, 1732 English inventor **Richard Arkwright**, 1777 Tsar of Russia **Alexander I**, 1867 U.S. Cosmetics mogul **Madame C.J. Walker**, 1885 French artist **Pierre Brissaud**, 1918 German Chancellor **Helmut Schmidt**, 1918 Italian-born flamenco dancer **José Greco**, 1923 Italian conductor **Claudio Scimone**, 1926 U.S. poet **Robert Bly**, 1938 U.S. Internet pioneer **Bob Kahn**, 1943 U.S. comedian **Harry Shearer**, 1944 U.S. General **Wesley Clark**, 1946 U.S. soap actress **Susan Lucci**, 1964 U.S. musician **Eddie Vedder**, 1971 British socialite **Tara Palmer-Tomkinson**, 1978 Canadian model/actress **Estella Warren**

December 24

1166 King **John of England:** Known as **John Lackland**. While King Richard the Lionheart was imprisoned in Germany on his way back from the Third Crusade, his brother John tried to seize control of England, When Richard returned John was banished but the two later reconciled. Crowned king in 1199, John lost Normandy and most of his other French land. Heavy taxes and aggressive assertion of feudal privileges led to the outbreak of civil war. English barons forced him to sign the Magna Carta, a kind of civil rights document for nobles, at Runnymead on June 12, 1215. In the play *King John*, William Shakespeare has the monarch say:

Life is tedious as a twice-told tale vexing the dull ear of a drowsy man.

1745 **Benjamin Rush:** American humanitarian, medical pioneer and author. As a physician he was a dogmatic theorist who proposed that all diseases are fevers caused by over stimulation of the blood vessels. The remedy was bloodletting and purges. He advocated humane treatment of the insane and forwarded the idea that insanity often had physical causes was a significant advance in the treatment of the mentally ill. Wrote the first chemistry textbook and the first psychiatry treatise in America.

Controversy is only dreaded by the advocates of error.

1754 **George Crabbe:** English poet and writer of verse tales. His very popular poem "The Village," was written in heroic couplets, a protest against Oliver Goldsmith's *Deserted Village*. It was his attempt to show the misery of rural poverty. "The Parish Register," depicted life in a rural community and "The Borough," is the story of the isolated and violent Peter Grimes, which became the basis of Benjamin Britten's famous opera.

A great lie is like a great fish on dry land; it may fret and fling and make a frightful bother, but it cannot hurt you. You have only to keep still, and it will die of itself.

1818 **James Prescott Joule:** British physicist who established the mechanical theory of heat. At 18, began his study of heat developed by an electric current and by 1840 had deduced the law connecting the current and resistance of a wire to the heat generated, now known as Joule's Law. Established the principle of conservation of energy and the equivalence of heat and other forms of energy. In his honor the SI unit of energy is named the *joule*.

Believing that the power to destroy belongs to the Creator alone I affirm ... that any theory which, when carried out, demands the annihilation of force, is necessarily erroneous.

1822 **Matthew Arnold:** English essayist, educator, poet and critic. Eldest son of Thomas Arnold, famous headmaster of Rugby and pioneer in the reform of English public schools. First made his mark with *Poems: A New Edition* (1853–4), which contained "The Scholar Gipsy" and "Sohrab and Rustum." Confirmed his standing with *New Poems* (1967), which contained "Dover Beach" and "Thyrsis." Crusader for classicism, critical traditionalism and the notion that literature should ennoble man.

Journalism is literature in a hurry.

1838 **John Morley: 1st Viscount of Blackburn**. English Liberal statesman, journalist, and biographer. Edited the *Fortnightly Review* (1867–82) and *Pall Mall Gazette* (1880–3). Member of Parliament until his elevation to a peerage. Served as Irish secretary and secretary for India, then Lord President of the Council. Wrote biographies of Voltaire, Rousseau, Diderot, but most notable contribution to literature was as the official biography of Gladstone.

The great business of life is to be, to do, to do without and to depart.

1905 **Howard Hughes, Jr.:** American businessman, producer, and aviator. Inherited his father's prosperous manufacturing firm of oil-drilling equipment. Invested in films and romancing beautiful starlets, many of which were put on long term personal contracts without ever appearing in a film. Made his cinematic reputation as producer and director of Jean Harlow in *Hell's Angels*. *The Outlaw*, starring Jane Russell and her remarkable cleavage, was made in 1943 but not widely released until 1946. Founded an aircraft company and set several world air speed records. From 1966 on lived as a recluse, entirely cut off from the world. Continued to run his empire with an electronic communications network.

I'm not a paranoid deranged millionaire. Goddamit, I'm a billionaire.

1907 **I.F. [Isidor Feinstein] Stone:** American radical journalist. Hostile to the Cold War. Opposed U.S. involvement in Vietnam. Founded *I.F. Stone's Weekly* (1951), which had an influence far greater than the size of its readership. As sole author, he created a unique blend of wit, erudition and pointed political commentary. Known for his espousal of unpopular causes long before they were taken up by the liberal establishment.

Rich people march on Washington every day.

1922 **Ava Gardner:** American film actress. Even before making her first movie appearance she gained a great amount of publicity for her one year marriage to

Mickey Rooney. Before long the sloe-eyed, sensuous beauty with a magnetic quality of sexuality replaced Rita Hayworth as Hollywood's love goddess. Married and divorced bandleader Artie Shaw and Frank Sinatra, with whom she had a stormy relationship. Nominated for an Academy Award for *Mogambo*. Other films: *The Barefoot Contessa. The Sun Also Rises*, and *The Night of the Iguana*.

Deep down, I'm pretty superficial.

1924 **Carol Haney:** American actress and dancer. Her appearance as Bob Fosse's dance partner in *Kiss Me Kate*, earned her a starring role on Broadway in *The Pajama Game*, produced by George Abbott and choreographed by Fosse. Stole the show with her rendition of "Steam Heat." Won a Tony for her performance but later in the show's run suffered torn ankle ligaments, giving an opportunity for her understudy Shirley MacLaine. Haney received three Tony nominations as Best Chorographer for *Flower Drum Song, Bravo Giovanni* and posthumously for *Funny Girl*.

The only thing that happens over night is recognition — not talent.

1930 **Robert Joffrey:** Originally **Abdullah Jaffa Bey Kahn**. American dancer, choreographer and teacher of Afghan descent. Built the Joffrey Ballet (which he founded in 1956 with Gerald Arpino) into one of the nation's top companies, and achieved international fame. His ballets in the sixties combined rock music and multimedia techniques: *Persephone, Astarte, Remembrance* and *Postcards*.

Painters can explore one theme for four or five years and they go on. Catch a dance company with a similar work two seasons in a row and right away it's doomed.

1971 **Ricky Martin:** Born **Enrique Martin Morales**. Puerto Rican born American singer. Member of the Latin boy band Menudo and a solo artist since 1990. His album, *Me Amaras*, skyrocketed to the top of the Latin Charts. Named the Best New Latin Artist in the 1993 Billboard Video Awards. Hit songs include: "Vuelve," "Livin la Vida Loca," "Shake Your Bon-Bon," and "Y Todo Queda En Nada." Created the "Ricky Martin Foundation," which provides musical instruments for Puerto Rican public schools and helps victims of child prostitution and pornography.

The homosexual community wants me to be gay. The heterosexual community wants me to be straight. Every [writer] thinks, "I'm the journalist who's going to make him talk." I pray for them. I pray that they get a life and stop living mine.

OTHERS: 1475 German writer **Thomas Murner**, 1440 Portuguese navigator **Vasco da Gama**, 1491 Spanish founder of Jesuits **St. Ignatius of Loyola**, 1508 Italian humanist **Pietro Carnesecchi**, 1689 Dutch painter **French van Mieris**, 1798 Polish poet **Adam Mickiewicz**, 1809 U.S. frontiersman **Kit Carson**, 1880 U.S. cartoonist **Johnny Gruelle**, 1886 Hungarian director **Michael Curtiz**, 1910 U.S. writer **Fritz Leiber**, 1920 Russian World War II heroine **Evgeniya Rudneva**, 1929 U.S. author **Mary Higgins Clark**, 1931 Argentine composer **Mauricio Kagel**, 1946 U.S. bisexual activist **Brenda Howard**, 1950 U.S. poet **Dana Gioia**, 1957 President of Afghanistan **Hamid Karzai**, 1974 TV host **Ryan Seacrest**

December 25

1642 Sir **Isaac Newton:** English mathematician and scientist. One of the greatest minds in history. During the Great Plague (1665–66), Cambridge University closed for nearly two years. He made good use of the time, inventing the method of fluxions and discovering the law of universal gravitation. By 1666 he had developed his laws of motion. A controversy developed over who should be credited with the invention of the infinitesimal calculus. The debate showed Newton at his worst, as he and those he encouraged to do so, belittled and dismissed the contributions of Gottfried von Leibniz. Priority became a matter of national pride. English mathematicians so stubbornly adhered to the work of their master that their mathematical accomplishments suffered in comparison with those of the continent for a long period thereafter.

I was like a boy playing on the sea-shore, and diverting myself now and then finding a smoother pebble or a prettier shell that ordinary, whilst the great ocean of truth lay all undiscovered before me.

1821 **Clara (Clarrisa Harlowe) Barton:** American schoolteacher, humanitarian and founder of the American Red Cross. During the Civil War she helped obtain supplies and comforts for the wounded. Known as the "angel of the battlefield." Worked for the International Red Cross in the Franco-Prussian War. Due to her campaigning, the U.S.A. signed the Geneva Convention in 1882.

I may be compelled to face danger, but never fear, and while our soldiers can stand and fight, I can stand and feed and nurse them.

1870 **Rosa Luxemburg:** Revolutionary born in Russian Poland, known as "Red Rosa." Became a leader of the left-wing movement in Berlin, writing tracts such as "Reform or Revolution," which defended Marxism and advocated revolution. At the outbreak of World War I, she and Karl Liebknecht formed the Spartacus League, later to become the German Communist Party. Spent most of the war in prison. After her release in 1919, took part in an abortive uprising in Berlin, known as the Spartacus Revolt, in which she and Liebknecht were murdered.

Freedom is always and exclusively freedom for the one who thinks differently.

1886 **Franz Rosenzweig:** German–born Jewish theologian. Reacted against Idealism of G.W.F. Hegel, expounding an existential approach, emphasizing experiences and interests of the individual. His existentialist understanding of faith and belief eventuated in his major work *The Star of Redemption* (1921). Collaborated on a translation of the Old Testament with Martin Buber, attempting to restore what he believed was the existentialist tone of the original.

Happiness and life are two different things; and it's no wonder that men came to ascribe bliss to the dead alone.

1887 **Conrad Hilton:** America's best known hotelier. Learned the business by carrying luggage from the train station in San Antonio to a small hotel operated by his father. After returning from military service in World War I, his intention was to buy a bank, but couldn't make a deal, so bought a hotel instead. In 1920, with borrowed money, he formed a hotel syndicate. He bought and sold hotels, making tremendous profits. Autobiography, *Be My Guest*, listed ten ingredients for success, the first: "Find your own particular talent" and the second: "Be big. Think big. Act big. Dream big."

Success seems to be connected with action. Successful people keep moving. They make mistakes, but they don't quit.

1892 Dame **Rebecca West:** Pseudonym of **Cicily Isabel Fairfield Andrews**. Irish critic and novelist. Took her pen name from character she played on stage in a production of Ibsen's *Rosmersholm*. Best known for, *The Meaning of Treason* and *A Train of Power*, based on her coverage of the Nuremberg War Crimes as a reporter after World War II. Novels tend to be psychoanalytic studies: *The Return of the Soldier, The Judge, The Thinking Reed,* and *The Birds Fall Down*.

I only know that people call me a feminist whenever I express sentiments that differentiate me from a doormat or a prostitute.

1908 **Quentin Crisp:** Born **Denis Charles Pratt**. Flamboyant English writer, artist's model, actor and raconteur. Self-described as the "stately homo of England." Renowned for his sharp wit and flamboyant clothes. A Homosexual rights campaigner became a gay icon in the 1970s with the publication of his memoir *The Naked Civil Servant*, the story of a young homosexual in the less tolerant Britain of the 1930s. Book made into an award-winning film starring John Hurt. Crisp has often been hailed as the 20th-century Oscar Wilde. Asked if he was a practicing homosexual, he replied, "I didn't practice. I was already perfect."

An autobiography is an obituary in serial form with the last chapter missing.

1918 **Anwar al-Sadat:** Egyptian statesman and president (1970–81. Member of the coup led by Gamal Nasser's that deposed King Farouk. Served as vice-president and became president when Nasser died in 1970. In 1973 Sadat joined with Syria in a surprise attack on Israel, losing militarily, but gaining politically. In 1977 he went to Jerusalem to offer peace to Israel and signed the Camp David Peace Accord with Menachem Begin (1978). Shared the Nobel Peace Prize with Begin. His assassination by Muslim extremists in 1981 elicited shock and grief worldwide.

You are not a realist unless you believe in miracles.

1924 **Rod Serling:** U.S. television script-writer. Author of over 200 television plays. Won Emmy award for "Patterns" (1955). Continued to turn out naturalistic hard-hitting studies of the contemporary scene. His plays *The Rack, Requiem for a Heavyweight* and *Rank and File* were praised as fine examples of new adult drama. Created, wrote and hosted "The Twilight Zone" (1959–64) and "Night Gallery" (1970–73). Speaking of television he said:

The baby is still growing ... still matures and shifts around ... sometimes proves something with a ringing clarity and sometimes falls on its pratt in the middle of the unknown.

1927 **Nellie Fox:** Born **Jacob Nelson Fox**. Hall-of-fame baseball player. A second-baseman, he was a catalyst for the "Go-Go" White Sox of the 1950s. 12-time American League All-Star. Never struck out more than 18 times in a season. Once went a record 98 games without a strikeout. Led league in hits four times, putouts 10 times, fielding percentage six times and holds the record for most consecutive seasons leading the league in singles (1954–60).

I don't think anyone ever liked to play more than I did.

1946 **Jimmy Buffett:** American singer and songwriter. Best known for his "island escapism" lifestyle and music including hits such as "Margaritaville" and "Come Monday." Has written three No. 1 bestsellers, *Tales from Margaritaville, Where is Joe Merchant?* and *A Pirate Looks at Fifty*. Raised $3.4 million at his "Surviving the Storm" Hurricane Relief Concert to help victims in Florida, Alabama, and the Caribbean caused by four major hurricanes of 2004. Donated $500,000 to Hurricane Katrina relief.

We are the people our parents warned us about.

1950 **Karl Rove:** American Senior Advisor and chief political strategist for George W. Bush. Sometimes referred to by critics as "Bush's Brain." Serves as Deputy Chief of Staff, heading the Office of Political Affairs, the Office of Public Liaison and the Office of Strategic Initiatives. Chaired meetings of the secretive internal White House Iraq Group charged with developing a strategy to publicize the White House's claim that Saddam Hussein posed a threat to the U.S.

As people do better, they start voting like Republicans — unless they have too much education and vote Democratic, which proves there can be too much of a good thing.

OTHERS: 1583 English composer **Orlando Gibbons**, 1652 Scottish physician **Archibald Pitcairne**, 1861 Indian founder of Banaras Hindu University **Pandit Madan Mohan Malaviya**, 1876 Founder of Pakistan **Muhammad Al Jinnah**, 1878 Swiss-born auto pioneer **Louis Chevrolet**, 1883 French artist **Maurice Utrillo**, 1886 U.S. musician **Kid Ory**, 1890 U.S. Collector of odd facts **Robert Ripley**, 1906 Ukrainian-born film producer **Lew Grade**, 1907 African-American bandleader/singer **Cab Calloway**, 1925 Peruvian-born author **Carlos Castaneda**, 1936 Indian-born film producer **Ismail Merchant**, 1946 U.S. football player **Larry Czonka**, 1949 U.S. actress **Sissy Spacek**, 1958 African-American baseball player **Ricky Henderson**

December 26

1716 **Thomas Gray:** English poet. Wrote poems of wistful melancholy. Though his output was relatively small, he became the dominant poetic figure of his day. His two Pindaric odes "The Bard" and "The Progress of Posey" are regarded precursors of romanticism. "Elegy Written in a Country Churchyard" is his masterpiece.

Poetry is thoughts that breathe, and words that burn.

1780 **Mary Somerville:** née **Fairfax**. English mathematician, scientist, astronomer and geographer. Called the "Queen of nineteenth-century Science." Her translation and expansion of Pierre de Laplace's Celestial *Mechanics* won her acclaim and success. Another major work, *Physical Geography* is the first book in England on Earth's physical Surface. Her *On Molecular and Microscopic Science* was awarded a gold medal from the Royal Geographical Society. One of the first two women admitted to the Royal Astronomical Society, the other being Caroline Herschel.

Sometimes I find mathematical problems difficult, but my obstinacy remains, for if I do not succeed today, I attack them again on the morrow.

1792 **Charles Babbage:** English mathematician and inventor. One of the most original and innovative thinkers of his time. Attempted to perfect two calculating machines: a "difference engine" to calculate tables of logarithms and an "analytical engine" to perform computations using punched cards. No direct line of descent from Babbage's work to the electronic computers invented in the 1930s and 1940s exist as his work had been forgotten. His *On the Economy of Machinery and Manufactures* (1832) pioneered the field now known as *operations research*, the scientific analysis of business problems aimed at giving managers information that will allow them more effectively to run their businesses.

Errors using inadequate data are much less than those using no data at all.

1820 **Dion Boucicault:** Originally **Dionysius Lardner Boursiquot**. Irish-born American actor and playwright. Wrote the successful comedy *London Assurance* and *The Corsican Brothers*. Moved to the U.S.A. in 1853 where he played a prominent role in obtaining the copyright law for drama in America. Wrote the lyrics of song, "The Wearin' of the Green."

I wish Adam had died with all his ribs in his body.

1872 Sir **Norman Angell:** Originally **Ralph Norman Angell-Lane.** British pacifist and writer on political and economic issues. Set out to prove the economic futility of war even for the victors. Achieved an international reputation for writing *The Great Illusion*, which had a tremendous impact on the intellectual community. Study centers based on the book were established at universities and in industrial centers. Also wrote *The Grand Illusion*. Recipient of the Nobel Peace Prize in 1933.

The greatest service we can do the common man is to abolish him and make all men uncommon.

1891 **Henry Miller:** "Bohemian Desperado." American writer who while living in France for nine years wrote his classics, the essentially autobiographical *Tropic of Cancer* and *Tropic of Capricorn*, both banned in the U.S.A. until the 1960s because of their explicit sexual nature. *Big Sur and the Oranges of Hieronymus Bosch* tells about the quasi-utopian art colony at the Big Sur in California where he settled after returning to the U.S.

Life has to be given a meaning because of the obvious fact that it has no meaning.

1893 **Mao Zedong (Mao Tse-tung):** Founding father of the People's Republic of China. Became leader of the Chinese Communist Party after the Long March — the withdrawal of the Communists from Southeast to Northwest China (1934–5). Defeated both the invading Japanese and the rival Kuomintang nationalist forces led by Chiang Kai-shek. Served as Chairman of the Communist Party and President of the Republic (1949–76). Launched disastrous Great Leap Forward, an unsuccessful attempt to quickly make agrarian China an industrial power. In 1965, introduced the Cultural Revolution, intended to affect a return to the revolutionary Maoist beliefs. Ideas popularized by his *The Little Red Book*.

Classes struggle, some classes triumph, others are eliminated. Such is history; such is the history of civilization for thousands of years.

1894 **Jean Toomer:** Originally **Nathan Eugene**. African-American poet, lecturer and" Harlem Renaissance" writer. *Cane*, considered his best work, is an experimental novel depicting the experience of being black in the U.S.A. It had a strong influence on younger African-American writers. Ambivalent about his mixed racial heritage and preoccupied with spiritual matters, he avoided race issues in subsequent works, which include *Essentials* and *Portage Potential*.

We learn the rope of life by untying its knots.

1921 **Steve Allen:** Literate American emcee, comedian, actor, pianist, singer, poet, composer, critic, columnist, novelist and short story writer. One of the greatest single all-around talents in the entertainment industry. Created and hosted late-night TV programs The Tonight Show (1953–57) and The Steve Allen Show" (1957–60). Starred in the title role pf the movie biopic *The Benny Goodman Story*. Composed over 3000 songs, including "Picnic," "This Could Be the Start of Something Big" and "Impossible."

If there is a God, the phrase that must disgust him is — holy war.

1927 **Alan King:** Born **Irwin Alan Kinberg.** American comic and actor. Stand-up comedian in the Catskills, attaining stardom on the supper-club circuit. Appeared frequently on *The Ed Sullivan Show* and other TV variety shows. American suburbia was the target of much of his barbed humor as he took on entire industries, e.g. the airlines, to vent his frustration and anger over whet he saw as mistreatment and poor service. Books: *Anyone Who Owns a House Deserves It* and *Help! I'm a Prisoner in a Chinese Bakery.*

If you want to read about love and marriage, you've got to buy two separate books.

1939 **Lynn Morley Martin:** American Republican politician. Served in the U.S. House of Representatives (1980–91). First woman elected to a congressional leadership post in the role of vice chair of the House Republican Conference. Failed to win a U.S. Senate seat, possibly because of her ads making fun of her opponent, incumbent Paul Simon's trademark bow ties, which was seen as petty and mean-spirited. Chosen Secretary of Labor to replace Elizabeth Dole.

No matter what your religion, you should try to become a government program, for then you will have everlasting life.

1954 **Susan Butcher:** One of only two people to win the world-famous Iditarod sled-dog race at least four times. Holds the record for the fastest completion of the grueling 1,157 mile race from Anchorage to Nome. Finished in the top 10 in 11 out of 14 races. "My goal was never to be the first woman or the best woman. It was to be the best sled-dog racer." Speaking of her battle with the disease that took her life in 2006:

There was a lot of pain. I've broken a lot of bones out there, but it was what I loved doing. I didn't really choose to have leukemia. This is just a battle that was given to me.

OTHERS: 1194 Holy Roman Emperor **Frederick II**, 1536 Korean Confucian scholar **Yi I**, 1716 French poet **Jean Francois de Saint-Lambert**, 1736 Italian composer **Antonio Caldara**, 1751 Austrian missionary **St. Clement Hofbauer**, 1819 U.S. novelist **E.D.E.N. Southworth**, 1837 U.S. admiral **George Dewey**, 1902 Russian painter **Anatoli L. Kaplan**, 1904 Cuban writer **Alejo Carpentier**, 1914 U.S. actor **Richard Widmark**, 1938 Indian playwright **Bahram Beyzayi**, 1940 U.S. economist **Edward C. Prescott**, 1940 U.S. music producer **Phil Spector**, 1947 U.S. baseball player **Carlton Fisk**, 1949 East Timor Foreign Minister **José Ramos Horta**, 1954 African-American baseball player **Ozzie Smith**

December 27

1571 **Johannes Kepler:** German astronomer and mathematician. Called the "father of modern astronomy." Announced his first and second laws of planetary motion in 1609, which formed the groundwork for the discoveries of Newton. Promulgated his third law in *Harmonies of the World* (1619). First to describe accurately the elliptic orbits of the Earth and the planets around the Sun. First to explain accurately how the eyes see, how eyeglasses improve vision, and what happens to light in a telescope.

The diversity of the phenomena of nature is so great, and the treasures hidden in the heavens so rich, precisely in order that the human mind shalt never be lacking for fresh nourishment.

1654 **Jacob Bernoulli:** Also known as **Jakob, Jacques or James Bernoulli**. Swiss mathematician and scientist. Member of a distinguished family of mathematicians and scientists. As professor of mathematics at Basel, he was one of the chief developers of both the ordinary calculus and of the calculus of variations. First to use the term *integral* in solving Leibniz's problem of the isochronous curve. Wrote an important treatise on probability, *Ars Conjectandi* (*The Art of Conjecture*).

Even as the finite encloses and infinite series/ And in the unlimited limits appear,/ So the soul of immensity dwells in minutia/ And in the narrowness limits no limits inhere/ What joy to discern the minute in infinity!/ The vast to perceive in the small, what divinity!

1797 **Ghalib:** *Nom de plume* adopted by **Mirza Asadullah Beg Khan**. Renowned classical Urdu and Persian poet of India. Most famous for his *ghazals* (a lyric poem, generally short and graceful in form and typically dealing with love) written in Urdu. Before his time, letter writing in Urdu was highly ornamental. His informal letters were written as if he was actually talking to the recipient. His interest began to shift decisively away from Urdu poetry to Persian in the 1820s.

The beauty of the verse and the fragrance of the flower both from the same eternity commence/ This blooming red rose is sired by the spring and gives tongue to my lucid eloquence.

1822 **Louis Pasteur:** French chemist and founder of microbiological sciences and preventive medicine. Considered one of the greatest scientists of all time. Contributed important discoveries to nearly every branch of science, but above all he proved the germ theory of disease. Established that putrefaction and fermentation are caused by microorganisms. Demonstrated that sheep and cows "vaccinated" with the attenuated bacilli of anthrax received protection against the disease. Medicine was never the same after his work; infectious disease could now be combated by established techniques and research guided by a general theory. Founded the Institut Pasteur at Paris for the treatment of rabies.

Chance favors the prepared mind.

1896 **Arch Ward:** American promoter and sports editor of the Chicago Tribune (1930–55). Nicknamed the "Cecil B. de Mille of sports." Asked to come up with a sports event in connection with the 1933 World's Fair to be held in Chicago, he suggested a Major League All-Star Game. Meant to be a one-time event, it has become an annual institution. The following year Ward created the College All-Star Game, in which graduated college stars from the previous season opposed the reigning National Football League champions. Started the All-American Conference that inaugurated pro football in Los Angeles, San Francisco, Baltimore, Miami, and the league's most successful team, the Cleveland Browns.

The book is closed, the year is done./ The pages full of tasks begun./ A little joy, a little care,/ Along with dreams are written there./ This new day brings another year./ Renewing hope,

dispelling fear./ And we may find before the end,/ A deep content, another friend.

1896 **Carl Zuckmayer:** German/Swiss/U.S. playwright. Depicted real and vital individuals in *The Merry Vineyard* and *Schinderhannes*, both dramas dealing with folk characters of his own Rhenish homeland. In his great comedy *The Captain of Köpenick*, he voiced his opposition to militarism and bureaucratic regimentation which soon multiplied in Hitler's Germany. Rise of the Nazis forced him into exile and spent seven years in the U.S.A., where he wrote passionate protests against Hitler's government.

One-half of life is luck, the other half is discipline — and that's the important half, for without discipline you wouldn't know what to do with luck.

1901 **Marlene Dietrich:** German-born actress. Best early films were directed by her discoverer Josef von Sternberg, who changed her from a plump fraulein into a seductively androgynous woman of tawdry glamour. While filming in England (1937), she was visited by Ambassador Joachim von Ribbentrop with a personal offer from Hitler to return to German films. Turned down the offer causing her films to be banned in Germany. Made anti–Nazi propaganda broadcasts in German, helped sell war bonds, entertained U.S. troops and became an American citizen. Awarded Medal of Freedom. Films: *The Blue Angel*, *Shanghai Express*, *The Scarlet Empress*, and *Witness for the Prosecution*.

A man would prefer to come home to an unmade bed and a happy woman than to a neatly made bed and an angry woman.

1906 **Oscar Levant:** America pianist, composer and actor. As a concert pianist he became one of his foremost interpreters of the work of his close friend George Gershwin Neurotic, hypochondriacal, insomniac, self-declared genius and caustic wit. Frequently appeared on TV talk shows, bombarding viewers with social gripes and psychological hang-ups. Autobiographies: *A Smattering of Ignorance*, *The Importance of Being Oscar* and *The Memoirs of an Amnesiac*. Films: *Rhapsody in Blue* (as himself in the biopic of Gershwin), *An American in Paris* and *The Band Wagon*.

I'm a study of a man in chaos in search of frenzy.

1907 **Sebastian Haffner:** Pseudonym for **Raimund Pretzel.** German journalist and writer. Fled from Germany to England with his Jewish wife. Wrote for the London Sunday newspaper, *The Observor*. Books: *Germany: Jekyll & Hyde*, *The Meaning of Hitler* and *From Bismark to Hitler*. In 1939, he began work on a personal story of an ordinary citizen's reaction to the events leading up to Hitler's rise to power. Discovered by his son after his death, *Defying Hitler* is an insightful memoir, describing the response to the Reichstag fire, the interaction of opposing leaders, the Jewish Boycott, and the steady erosion pf personal freedom.

One was permanently occupied and distracted by an unending sequence of celebrations, ceremonies, and national festivities... The colossal emptiness and lack of meaning of these never-ending events was by no means unintentional. The population should become used to cheering and jubilation, even when there was no visible reason for it... Was it not wonderful to celebrate in the spring sunshine, in squares decked with flags.

1915 **William H. Masters:** U.S. human sexuality expert. With his wife, psychologist Virginia Johnson established the Reproductive Biological Research Foundation, where studies of the psychology and physiology of sexual intercourse were carried out. Couples were observed having sex under laboratory conditions, using biochemical equipment to record sexual stimulations and reactions. Published *Human Sexual Response* and *On Sex and Human Loving*.

When things don't work well in the bedroom, they don't work well in the living room either.

1930 **Wilfred Sheed:** English-born American novelist and journalist. His parents founded the Roman Catholic publishing house Sheed and Ward. He settled in New York City, working as a book and theater reviewer. Selected essays and reviews were published as *The Morning After*. His fiction, such as *Transatlantic Blues*, was based on his own experiences. Lightly satirical in tone, it describes a man who can neither accept nor abandon his Catholic faith.

The American male doesn't mature until he has exhausted all other possibilities.

1943 **Cokie Roberts: Mary Martha Corinne Morrison Claiborne Boggs Roberts** American broadcast journalist, political commentator and author. Daughter of Louisiana Congressman Hale Boggs. Her brother coined the name "Cokie" because he couldn't say "Corrine." With her husband Steven V. Roberts, contributing editor at *U.S. News & World Report*, writes a weekly column syndicated in major newspapers around the nation. Author of the national bestseller *We Are Our Mother's Daughters* and *Founding Mothers: The Women Who Raised Our Nation*.

There's a view in this country that everybody's going through what they are going through for the first time.

OTHERS: 1555 German theologist **Johann Arndt**, 1709 Dutch architect **Pieter de Swart**, 1721 Dutch philosopher **François Hemsterhuis**, 1773 English scientist/inventor **George Cayley**, 1802 Norwegian landscape painter **Thomas Fearnley**, 1855 German ethnologist/mythologist **Paul Ehrenreich**, 1879 English actor **Sidney Greenstreet**, 1896 U.S. writer **Louis Bromfield**, 1907 Belgian philosopher **Emile de Strijker**, 1910 U.S. poet **Charles Olson**, 1917 Finnish writer **Onni Palaste**, 1934 Russian gymnast **Larissa Latynina**, 1943 Spanish musician **Joan Manuel Serrat**, 1948 French actor **Gérard Depardieu**, 1951 Mexican president **Ernesto Zedillo**, 1969 U.S. author/journalist **Sarah Vowell**

December 28

1822 **William Rounseville Alger:** American clergyman and author. Active abolitionist. His Boston Fourth of July oration in 1857 created a sensation for its bold treatment of the slavery question. Contributor to the publications *Old and New* and the *Christian Examiner*, editing the latter during the 1960s. Major literary efforts included: *Symbolic History of the Cross of Christ*, *The Friendships of Women* and *Life of Edwin Forrest, the American Tragedian*.

Man often makes up in wrath what they want in reason.

1856 **[Thomas] Woodrow Wilson:** American politician and educator. Twenty-eighth president of the United States (1912–20). President of Princeton University (1902–10). Elected Governor of New Jersey and was the Democratic presidential candidate. Defeated Theodore Roosevelt, an independent, and Republican incumbent William Howard Taft. Maintained U.S. neutrality in World War I, campaigning for re-election on the theme that he had "kept us out of war." When German renewed submarine attacks on unarmed passenger ships, he asked Congress for a declaration of war. At the end of hostilities, personally headed the U.S. delegation to the peace treaty, proposing the establishment of the League of Nations, which he could not get Congress to approve. Suffered a partially paralyzing stroke while on a cross-country speaking tour to gain support for his program. Nobel Peace Prize winner (1919).

We are citizens of the world. The tragedy of our times is that we do not know this.

1882 Sir **Arthur Stanley Eddington:** English astronomer, physicist and mathematician. Gave the first direct confirmation of Einstein's theory of relativity with observations of stars during a total solar eclipse. Founded the science of astrophysics. First to propose that the tremendous heat production at a star's core is what keeps it from collapsing under its own gravity. His ideas led him to the conclusion that unifying quantum theory and general relativity theory would allow for the calculation of certain universal constants. He asked:

What do we really observe? Relativity theory has returned the answer — we only observe relations. Quantum theory returns another answer — we only observe probabilities.

1902 **Mortimer J. Adler:** American philosopher, educator and writer. Taught at the University of Chicago (1930–52) when his friend Robert Maynard Hutchins was its president. The two educational rebels revamped the curriculum, emphasizing direct study of the classics rather than diluted commentaries. Instituted the "Great Books" program reprinting a set of classics in 54 volumes, with an index of great ideas, the *Syntopicon* (a synthesis of topics), as Adler's mammoth contribution to the project. He defined a "classic" as a book that everyone talks about but nobody reads.

In the case of good books, the point is not how many of them you can get through, but rather how many can get through to you.

1903 **Earl "Fatha" Hines:** African-American pianist and bandleader. Had a profound effect on the development of jazz piano. Had amazing technical command and tireless energy. Breaking with the stride tradition, he emulated the single-note instruments, in creating melodic variations with the right hand. His solo improvisation became known as "trumpet style Piano" and had considerable influence on later jazz pianists. Recorded many songs now considered jazz classics most notably "Weather Bird."

I always challenge myself. I get out in deep water and I always try to get back. But I get hung up. The audience never knows, but that's when I smile the most, when I show the most ivory.

1903 **John von Neumann:** One of the 20th century's preeminent scientists and greatest polymaths of all time. In his all too brief life, everywhere the Hungarian-born genius cast his eyes, a major intellectual revolution sprung up. Consultant on the Manhattan Project at Los Alamos, New Mexico during World War II that developed the atomic bomb. Spearheaded a mathematical treatment of shock waves and the development of the "high explosive lens," essential to its success. Suggested the concept of the stored program computer that sparked the computer revolution. One of the founders of game theory, focusing on model strategies leading to optimum success in situations involving chance or free choice.

There's no sense in being precise when you don't even know what you're talking about.

1911 **Sam Levenson:** American comedian and author. Former schoolteacher known for gentle satire on everyday life. The improbable comic sensation made numerous TV guest appearances leading to a network show of his own, "Sam Levenson Show." Also a regular panel member on shows such as *This Is Show Business* and *Masquerade Party*. On TV, on lecture platforms, and in night clubs he continued his serio-comic "kitchen talks" about urban children.

I like life. It's something to do. Somewhere on this globe every 10 seconds there is a woman giving birth to a child. She must be found and stopped.

1931 **Guy deBord:** French social reformer, writer and filmmaker. Like the Dadaists and the Surrealists before him, wished to supersede the categorization of art and culture as separate activities and to transform them into part of everyday life. In his major work *The Society of the Spectacle*, takes the position that spectacle, or the domination of life by images, subsumes all other forms of domination. Ideas had an enormous influence on the student rebellion in 1968.

Ideas improve. The meaning of words participates in the improvement. Plagiarism is necessary. Progress implies it. It embraces and author's phrase, makes use of his expressions, erases a false idea, and replaces it with the right idea.

1934 Dame **Maggie Smith:** British actress. Nominated for Academy Awards six times, winning Best Actress for *The Prime of Miss Jean Brodie* and Best Supporting Actress for *California Suite*. Other nominations for: *Othello*, *Travels with My Aunt*, *A Room with a View* and *Gosford Park*. Member of the Old Vic Company

(1959–63). Memorable playing Desdemona to Olivier's Othello for the National Theatre. Other films: *The Lonely Passion of Judith Hearne*, *My House in Umbria*, and as Professor Minerva McGonagall in the Harry Potter movies.

It's true I don't tolerate fools, but they don't tolerate me, so I am spiky. Maybe that's why I'm quite good at playing spiky elderly ladies.

1946 **Bill Lee:** Intelligent, articulate, and outspoken American left-handed pitcher mostly with the Boston Red Sox (1969–79). "The Spaceman," was one of the game's few counterculture symbols. Talked to animals, championed environmental causes, sprinkled marijuana on his pancakes, pondered Einstein and Vonnegut, and studied Eastern philosophers and mystics. Best year was 1973 when he won 17 games and made the All-Star team in 1973. Pitched in two games in the 1975 World Series against the Cincinnati Reds. His autobiography: *The Wrong Stuff*.

You take a team with twenty-five assholes and I'll show you a pennant. I'll show you the New York Yankees.

1954 **Denzel Washington:** African-American leading man of films and TV. First success with television's "St. Elsewhere." Won an Oscar for Best Supporting Actor for the film *Glory*. Nominated for his performance in the title role of *Malcolm X*. Won another Oscar for Best Actor for *Training Day* a far less outstanding performance and film, becoming one of several actors who were selected by voters for the Award to make up for not giving it for a superior effort. Others: *Mississippi Masala*, *Philadelphia*, *The Hurricane*, and *The Manchurian Candidate*.

Luck is where opportunity meets preparation.

1969 **Linus Torvalds:** Finnish computer engineer and programmer, best know for initiating the development of the operating system Linux at the University of Helsinki, when he was 21. Linux has made its author into a cult figure. He did not claim his right to receive payment from people who used his work. Instead, he published in on the Internet and invited other programmers to improve it and send their results to him. Linux remains a free program — anybody can use it without charge, on condition that any improvements they make on it must also be freely available to other users.

Software is like sex: it's better when it's free.

OTHERS: 1619 French writer **Antoine Furetière**, 1631 Dutch painter **Ludolf Backhuysen**, 1763 Canadian brewery founder **John Molson**, 1866 Polish historian **Szymon Askenazy**, 1879 U.S. aviation pioneer **Billy Mitchell**, 1888 German director **F.W. Murnau**, 1902 Chinese writer **Shen Congwen**, 1908 U.S. actor **Lew Ayres**, 1924 Uganda president **Milton Obote**, 1929 Canadian hockey goalie **Terry Sawchuk**, 1937 Indian industrialist **Ratan Tata**, 1944 U.S. chemist **Kary Mullis**, 1946 U.S. musician **Edgar Winter**, 1953 French pianist **Richard Clayderman**, 1956 British violinist **Nigel Kennedy**, 1972 U.S. tennis player **Patrick Rafter**, 1972 U.S. football kicker **Adam Vinatieri**

December 29

1721 Madame **de Pompadour:** Also **Jeanne-Antoinette Poisson**. French mistress of Louis XV, king of France. At nine a fortune teller predicted she would become the mistress of a king. From that time on she was called *Reinette*, meaning "little queen." When Louis XV's mistress Duchess de Chateauroux died in 1744, she was established as his official mistress. For 20 years, this woman of remarkable grace, beauty and wit, swayed state policy and became a patroness of the arts. Influenced the king on the treaty that allied France with former enemy Austria, leading to the French defeat in the Seven Years' War.

Champagne is the only wine that leaves a woman beautiful after drinking it.

1798 **L.P. [Laurens Perseus] Hickok:** American Presbyterian clergyman, educator, and author. Appointed Professor of Moral Philosophy, Vice President, and later President of his alma mater Union College. Wrote *A System of Moral Science: The Logic of Reason* and *Creation: Or, the Knowledge in the Reason of God and His Work*.

Genius is the highest type of reason; talent is the highest type of understanding.

1808 **Andrew Johnson:** American Democratic politician from Tennessee. With little formal education became U.S. congressman, governor and U.S. Senator, During the Civil War he was military governor of his state before becoming vice-president in Abraham Lincoln's second term. After Lincoln's assassination he became the 17th U.S. President (1865–69). His conciliatory polices toward the South were opposed by Congress. He vetoed congressional measures leading to his impeachment, brought to trial, and acquitted.

It's a damn poor mind that can only think of one way to spell a word.

1809 **William E. Gladstone:** British liberal statesman, author and orator. Prime minister (1868–74, 1880–85, 1886, 1892–94). Entered parliament as a Conservative but in 1867 became leader of the Liberal Party. Established a system of national education. His reforms of Parliament went a long way towards universal male suffrage. One of the first members of Parliament to give serious study to the colonial problems. Worked unsuccessfully for Irish Home Rule.

No man ever becomes great or good except through many and great mistakes.

1809 **Albert Pike:** American lawyer, soldier and Freemason. In the Civil War, commissioned a brigadier general in command of a brigade of American Indians, who performed badly, taking scalps and fleeing Union artillery. Best known for his work as a 33rd degree Mason. Rewrote the rituals of the society in the unpublished *Morals and Dogma of the Ancient and Accepted Scottish Rite of Freemasonry*."

Faith begins where Reason sinks exhausted.

1814 **Edwin Hubbel Chapin:** American clergyman, author, speaker, writer and pastor. Editor of *The Mag-*

azine and Advocate, a periodical devoted to the interests of Universalism. Espoused causes of temperance, abolition of slavery, and anti-capital punishment. Preached on the obligation to care for all people, stressing their innate worth. Books: *The Crown of Thorns: A Token for Sorrowing*, written following the death of his first born child, *The Positions and Duties of Liberal Christians*, and *Three Discourses on Capital Punishment*.

Never does the human soul appear so strong as when it forgoes revenge and dares to forgive an injury.

1876 **Pablo Casals:** Spanish cellist, conductor and composer. Called by Fritz Kreisler, "the best who draws a bow" and "king of all string players." Founded the Barcelona Orchestra (1919). Left Spain at the outbreak of the Spanish Civil War. Principal cellist of the Paris Opera. Compositions consist of choral and chamber music. Received the United Nations Peace Prize for his composition *Hymn to the United Nations*.

Music is the divine way to tell beautiful, poetic things to the heart.

1907 **Robert Weaver:** American government official and economist. First African-American to serve in the U.S. cabinet as first Secretary of the newly formed Department of Housing and Urban Development (HUD, 1966–69). During World War II he held several posts concerned with mobilizing black labor. Wrote *Negro Labor: A National Problem* and *The Negro Ghetto*.

We're caught in the middle. We're holding this bag and we're waiting for someone to tell us who to give it to.

1917 **Tom [Thomas J.] Bradley:** American politician. First African-American mayor of a predominantly white city, Los Angeles (1973–93). Spent 22 years in the city's police department, while earning a law degree. During five terms as mayor helped transform Los Angeles into a bustling business and trading center, overseeing a massive growth and hosting the 1984 Olympic Games. Spingarn Award (1983).

A child is a quicksilver fountain/ spilling over with tomorrows and tomorrows/ and that is why/ she is richer than you and I.

1919 **Jim Murray:** One of America's most widely read sports columnists. Fourteen time Sportswriter of the Year. Following tours of duty with *Sports Illustrated*, *Time* magazine, the *Los Angles Examiner*, and others, wrote a sports column for Los Angeles Times (1961–98). Named "America's Best Sportswriter" by the National Association of Sportscasters and Sportswriters. Pulitzer Prize for Commentary (1990).

Don Quixote would understand golf. It is the impossible dream.

1936 **Mary Tyler Moore:** American actress. Famous on TV even before her face was seen. As secretary in the series *Richard Diamond, Private Eye* (1957–9), only her sexy legs were shown and her sultry voice heard. Most successful in the series "The Dick Van Dyke Show" and "The Mary Tyler Moore Show." Showed her versatility as a serious actress, winning an Emmy for *First, You Cry*, a Tony for *Whose Life Is It Anyway* and an Oscar nomination for *Ordinary People*.

Having a dream is what keeps you alive... Overcoming the challenges makes life worth living.

1952 **Gelsey Kirkland:** American ballet dancer who formed a celebrated partnership with Russian-born dancer Mikhail Baryshnikov. Youngest member of the New York City Ballet, where she became principal dancer in 1972. Choreographers created ballets for her, including George Balanchine's *The Firebird*, Jerome Robbins' *An Evening Waltz* and Antony Tudor's *The Leaves Are Falling*. Moved to the American Ballet Theater in 1975 to join with Baryshnikov to form the decade's most celebrated ballet team.

I danced with passion to spite the music.

OTHERS: 1776 Scottish developer of waterproof fabric **Charles Macintosh**, 1796 German physicist **Johann Christian Poggendorff**, 1808 U.S. inventor/businessman **Charles Goodyear**, 1843 Queen of Romania **Elizabeth**, 1881 American boxer **Jess Willard**, 1908 German theologian **Helmut Gollwitzer**, 1910 British economist **Ronald Coase**, 1936 U.S. football player **Ray Nitschke**, 1937 Owner of Miami Dolphins **Wayne Huizenga**, 1938 U.S. actor **Jon Voight**, 1947 U.S. comic actor **Ted Danson**, 1953 Israeli singer **Gali Atari**, 1954 Prince of Japan **Norihito**, 1967 Canadian journalist **Ashleigh Banfield**, 1972 British actor **Jude Law**

December 30

1847 **John Peter Altgeld:** German-born American politician and social reformer. Democratic Governor of the state of Illinois (1893–1897). Considered one of the few incorruptible politicians. Spearheaded the nation's most stringent child labor and workplace safety laws, appointed women to important positions in the state government and vastly increased state funding for education. Recalled for pardoning three anarchists convicted of complicity in the 1886 Haymarket Riots. Memorialized in the Vachel Lindsay poem "The Eagle Forgotten."

Freedom of thought and freedom of speech in our great institutions are absolutely necessary for the preservation of our country. The moment either is restricted, liberty begins to wither and die.

1865 **(Joseph) Rudyard Kipling:** British writer, born in Bombay, India. Set many of his works in the India of the Raj. Poems: "The White Man's Burden," Mandalay," and "Gunga Din." Children's stories: *The Jungle Book* and the *Just So Stories*. First British writer awarded the Nobel Prize for Literature (1907). Putting aside question of glorification of empire and vision that the white man must civilize the heathen of the world, his extraordinary ear for language and precise use of vivid imagery earns deserved recognition.

I kept six honest serving men/ they taught me all I know:/ Their names are What and Why and When/ And How and Where and Who.

1869 **Stephen Leacock:** English-born Canadian humorist and economist. Author of over 60 books. Distinguished professor of economics with McGill University, Montreal. Researches added measurably to world wisdom in his specialty. Favorite teacher for his knowledge and insight which he shared with humor that illustrated his subject and drove the lessons home. Best known for humorous *Literary Lapses*, *My Discovery of England* and *Nonsense Novels*.

In ancient time they had no statistics so they had to fall back on lies.

1873 **Alfred Emanuel "Al" Smith:** Democratic New York politician. Governor of the state (1918–20, 1922–28). In his nominating speech at the National Convention in 1924, Franklin D. Roosevelt called him, "the Happy Warrior of the political battlefield." Smith won the nomination in 1928 and became the first Roman Catholic to make a run for the presidency. Vilified by the Ku Klux Klan and other anti–Catholic groups, describing him as the puppet of the Pope, the Democrats suffered massive defections to the Republicans in the South giving the election to Herbert Hoover.

Be simple in words, manners, and gestures. Amuse was well as instruct. If you can make a man laugh, you can make him think and make him like and believe in you.

1884 **Hideki Tojo:** Japanese military leader and statesman. Shortly after becoming Prime minister (1941–44), he initiated the Japanese attack on the U.S. military bases at Pearl Harbor, Hawaii. By 1944, he had assumed virtual control of all political and military decision-making. Later that year he was forced to resign following a number of military defeats. Arrested in 1945, he attempted suicide by shooting but survived to be tried and convicted of war crimes and hanged.

In the shadow of the prosperity of Europe and America, the colored people of East Asia and Africa have been sacrificed and forced into a state of semi-colonization.

1888 **Austin Osman Spare:** Draughtsman, philosopher and occult magician. Although an artist of considerable talent, he lived a secluded life, selling his unique work at low prices. His images of grotesque sexualized human figures and magical symbols became popular with avant-garde intellectuals. Became obsessed with sex magic and immersed himself in the worship of Iris and other Egyptian deities.

Great thoughts are against all doctrines of conformity.

1895 **Leslie Poles Hartley:** English author. Frequently compared to Henry James for his style and themes. Established a reputation for the macabre with short-stories such as *Night Fears*. Moved on to examinations of psychological relationships. Novels: *The Sixth Heaven*, *Eustace and Hilda*, and *The Go-Between*.

The past is foreign country; they do things differently there.

1928 **Bo Diddley:** Born **Otha Ellas Bates.** Influential African-American singer, songwriter and guitarist. "The Originator." Forever known for creating the "Bo Diddley beat," psychedelic sounds and one of the cornerstone rhythms of rock and roll. Many claim he was the one who put rock in rock and roll. Had most of his success on the R&B charts in the 1950s and early 60s. Hits included: "I'm a Man," "Road Runner," "Who Do You Love?" and "Diddley Wah Diddley."

Don't let your mouth write a check that your tail can't cash.

1935 **Omar Bongo:** Born **Albert Bernard Bongo,** he changed his name to **El Hadj Omar Bongo** when he converted to Islam in 1973. Gabon's President Leon Mba rewarded him for his faithfulness, by appointing Bongo his vice-president in 1967. He succeeded to the presidency that same year when his mentor died. Ruled over a one-party state for 16 years until elections were held, which he won, although observers generally regarded them rigged.

Globalization, far from putting an end to power diplomacy between States, has, on the contrary, intensified it.

1935 **Sandy Koufax:** Hall of Fame left-handed pitcher with the Brooklyn and L.A. Dodgers. Career attained its peak in the 1960s. Led NL in strikeouts four times, ERA, 5 straight years. Won 3 Cy Young Awards. MVP 1963. Helped the Dodgers win the 1965 World Series against the Minnesota Twins by pitching two shutouts. Had one perfect game (27 batters up, and 27 batters out) and three other no-hitters. Forced to retire at age 31 because of a chronic arthritic condition.

A guy who throws what he intended to throw, that's the definition of a good pitcher.

1965 **Heidi Fleiss:** Known as the "Hollywood Madam." Arrested at her Benedict Canyon Home, accused of running a high-priced call girl service, pandering, selling cocaine, conspiracy, money laundering and tax evasion. Sentenced to three years in prison, she served her time in a federal prison, which she described as a "lesbian hell." Revelations at her trial that she kept a little black book with all the names and dates of her celebrity clients sent a panic through Hollywood, but the book was never made public.

I don't regret what I did at all. It's consensual sex... These are men who are billionaires and these are women in their 20s. They are old enough to make adult decisions, adult choices.

1975 **Eldrick "Tiger" Woods:** American golfer, who at 30 became the youngest pro player to win 50 major PGA tournaments. A child prodigy of golf, from age 8 through 15 won the Optimist International Junior Golf Championship. While attending Stanford, became the first golfer to win three consecutive U.S. Amateur titles. Turned pro in August 1996 and immediately signed contracts worth millions with Nike and Titleist. Leading money winner and number 1 ranked player in the world several times.

I get to play golf for a living. What more can you ask for—getting paid for doing what you love.

1984 **LeBron James:** American basketball player. Not the first player to jump to the National Basketball

League after high school, but may prove to be the best. While at St. Vincent–St. Mary High School in Akron, Ohio, he was dubbed "The Chosen One" by Sports Illustrated." High School Player of the Year in both his junior and senior years. Drafted number one by the Cleveland Cavaliers, the 6–8 point guard was named Rookie-of-the-Year.

I don't need too much. Glamour and all that stuff doesn't excite me. I am just glad I have the game of basketball in my life.

OTHERS: 39 CE Roman Emperor **Titus**, 1552 English occultist **Simon Forman**, 1673 Ottoman Sultan **Ahmed III**, 1897 Italian author **Alfredo Bracchi**, 1899 Norwegian explorer **Helge Ingstad**, 1904 Russian composer **Dmitri Kabalevsky**, 1906 English director **Carol Reed**, 1913 Australian children's writer **Elyne Mitchell**, 1914 U.S. TV game show host **Bert Parks**, 1934 U.S. physicist **John Norris Bahcall**, 1934 U.S. singer **Del Shannon**, 1934 U.S. actor/dancer **Russ Tamblyn**, 1937 U.S. singer **Paul Stookey**, 1942 Russian dissident **Vladimir Bukovsky**, 1942 Slovenian historian **Janko Prunk**, 1946 U.S. singer **Patti Smith**, 1959 English comic actress **Tracey Ullman**

December 31

1320 **John Wycliffe:** English religious reformer. "The Morning Star of the Reformation." His attacks on the Church hierarchy, priestly power and the doctrine of transubstantiation are seen as precursors of the Reformation. Upheld the Bible as the sole guide for doctrine and questioned the scriptural basis for the papacy. Made the first English translation of the Bible, not only contributing to the religious development of the nation but exercised a formative influence upon the general growth of the English language.

Our clerics neither evangelize like the apostles, nor go to war like the secular lords, nor toil like laborers.

1491 **Jacques Cartier:** French navigator and explorer. Made three voyages of exploration to North America as an agent for King Francis I of France. The original intent was to search for the Northwest Passage to the Orient. Surveyed the coast of Canada and the St. Lawrence River as far as the site of present day Montreal. Provided the basis for French claims to the region. Speaking of the barren land of Newfoundland:

In all the north land I do not see a cartload of good earth. To be short, I am rather inclined to believe that this is the land God gave to Cain.

1869 **Henri Matisse:** French painter and sculptor. Bold use of brilliant non-naturalistic colors in works such as *Open Window Collioure*, made him the leader of the "Fauves" (wild beasts), a name given by a hostile critic. His large figure compositions, such as *The Dance*, heralded a new style based on simple reductive line, giving a rhythmic decorative pattern on a flat ground of vivid color. He observed: "Drawing is putting a line round an idea." Other paintings: *Woman with a Hat* and *The Red Studio*.

There are always flowers for those who want to see them.

1880 **George Catlett Marshall:** American soldier and statesman. Chief of Staff (1939–45). Became Secretary of State in 1947. Originated the "Marshall Aid Plan" for the postwar reconstruction of Europe. Passed by Congress in 1948 it invited European nations to outline their requirements for economy recovery in order that material and financial aid could be used most effectively. Between 1948 and 195, $13.5 billion was distributed. Marshall was awarded the Nobel Peace Prize in 1953.

Our policy is directed not against any country or doctrine but against hunger, poverty, desperation and chaos.

1884 **Elizabeth Arden:** Born **Florence Nightingale Graham.** Canadian-born American cosmetician and businesswoman. Opened her beauty salon on New York's Fifth Avenue in 1909. Effective advertising gave her brand a select and elegant image, contributing to her phenomenal business success. Ultimately owned more than 100 salons in America and Europe. Her range of cosmetics comprised more than 300 products.

Treat a horse like a woman and a woman like a horse. And they'll both win for you.

1908 **Simon Wiesenthal:** Austrian Jewish survivor of Nazi concentration camps. Dedicated his life to finding and prosecuting former Nazis. Enlisting the assistance of West Germany, Israel and other governments, tracked down some 1000 unprosecuted war criminals, most notably Adolf Eichmann, who was responsible for carrying out Adolf Hitler's final solution and for administering concentration camps in which 6 billion Jews perished. Brought back to Israel from Argentina, where he hid after the war, he was tried and executed. Wiesenthal opened the Jewish Documentation Center in Vienna, and continued to trace Nazi war criminals when other countries had ceased to pursue them.

Survival is a privilege which entails obligations. I am forever asking myself what I can do for those who have not survived... I think I am one of the last witnesses. And a last witness, before he leaves this world, has an obligation to speak out.... My work is a warning for the murderers of tomorrow.

1929 **Jeremy Bernstein:** American physicist, educator and writer. Known for the clarity of his writing for the lay reader on issues of modern physics. Books: *Albert Einstein: And the Frontiers of Physics*, *Bell Labs in the Information Age*, *Modern Physics*, *Oppenheimer: Portrait of an Enigma*, *Hitler's Uranium Club*, and *The Life It Brings*.

Never speak more clearly than you think.

1930 **Odetta:** African-American folksinger and musician, born **Odetta Holmes Gordon**. Training for a classical and operatic career when a visit to a San Francisco Bay coffee house featuring folk music wakened her interest. Known for her mellow style, striking contralto voice and African motifs. Repertoire includes gospel, blues, spirituals, and folk songs, such as "Take This Hammer," "Sometimes I Fell Like a Motherless Child" and "Blowin' in the Wind." Awarded the Presidential Medal of Arts in 1999.

Folk music straightened my spine and kinked up my hair. It has given me a sense of us as people.

1941 **Sarah Miles:** English actress. Made her screen debut in 1962 in the role of a nymphet student who seduces schoolmaster Laurence Olivier in *Term of Trial.* Went on to play other seductive and provocative roles. Oscar nominated for *Ryan's Daughter*. Other films: *The Servant, Lady Caroline Lamb* and *The Hireling.* Twice married to playwright-director Robert Bolt. Published three volumes of autobiography: *A Right Royal Bastard, Serves Me Right* and *Bolt from the Blue.*

There's a little bit of hooker in every woman. A little bit of hooker and a little bit of God.

1943 **John Denver:** Born **Henry John Deutschendorf, Jr.** American singer, songwriter, actor, environmentalist and humanitarian. Recorded some 300 songs, about half of which he wrote, filled with the love and appreciation of the natural world. Adopted the name "Denver" after his favorite city. *Poems, Prayers and Promises* was a breakthrough, mainly due to the song "Take Me Home Country Roads." His first top ten album was *Rocky Mountain High.* Had number one songs with "Sunshine on My Shoulders," "Annie's Song," and "Thank God I'm a Country Boy."

Perhaps love is like a resting place, a shelter from the storm. It exists to give you comfort. It is there to keep you warm. And in those times of trouble, when you are most alone, the memory of love will bring you home.

1945 **Diane von Fürstenberg:** Born **Diane Simone Michelle Halfin** in Brussels, Belgium. American fashion designer, known for her form hugging clothes. Her first husband was Austrian-Italian Prince Egon of Fürstenberg. Moved to New York, she began a business selling knit dresses. Her simple wrap dress, launched in 1972, symbolized female freedom for an entire generation. Her advice to women: "Go for what you want to do. Attitude is everything.

I design for the woman who loves being a woman.

1945 **Constance Elaine "Connie" Willis:** American science fiction writer. Won six Nebula, nine Locus Poll and eight Hugo Awards (more than any other sci-fi writer) and the John W. Campbell Memorial Award for her first novel, *Lincoln's Dream.* Her stories range from hilarious to deadly serious. Protagonists are generally strong-willed individuals. Other Books: *Doomsday Book, Uncharted Territory, To Say Nothing of the Dog* and *Inside Job.*

Writers are too neurotic to ever be happy.

OTHERS: 1514 Flemish anatomist **Andreas Vesalius**, 1668 Dutch humanist **Herman Boerhaave**, 1815 Union general **George Meade**, 1860 Governor of Egypt **Ismail Pasha**, 1864 U.S. astronomer **Robert G. Aitken**, 1870 U.S. baseball umpire **Tom Connally**, 1881 German painter **Max Pechstein**, 1894 Polish actress **Pola Negri**, 1903 Ukrainian violinist **Nathan Milstein**, 1905 English-born composer **Jule Styne**, 1928 French cartoonist **Siné**, 1934 Islamic scholar **Akram Awan**, 1937 Israeli biologist **Avram Hershko**, 1937 Welch actor **Anthony Hopkins**, 1943 British actor **Ben Kingsley**, 1947 Canadian musician **Burton Cummings**, 1948 U.S. Disco music singer **Donna Summer**, 1958 U.S. actress/dancer **Bebe Neuwirth**

Index of People

Individuals with capsule descriptions and a quotation are *italicized*